# Fodor's 98
# Caribbean

D0003243

**The complete guide, thoroughly up-to-date**

Packed with details that will make your trip

**The must-see sights, off and on the beaten path**

What to see, what to skip

**Mix-and-match vacation itineraries**

City strolls, countryside adventures

**Smart lodging and dining options**

Essential local do's and taboos

**Transportation tips, distances and directions**

Key contacts, savvy travel! tips

**When to go, what to pack**

Clear, accurate, easy-to-use maps

Fodor's Travel Publications, Inc.
New York • Toronto • London • Sydney • Auckland
www.fodors.com/

# Fodor's Caribbean

**EDITOR:** Caroline V. Haberfeld

**Editorial Contributors:** Pamela Acheson, Robert Andrews, Carol Bareuther, David Brown, Anto Howard, Christina Knight, Lynda Lohr, Karl Luntta, JoAnn Milivojevic, Kate Pennebaker, Melissa Rivers, Eileen Robinson-Smith, Heidi Sarna, Helayne Schiff, M. T. Schwartzman (Gold Guide editor), Jordan Simon, Dinah Spritzer, Simon Worrall, Jane E. Zarem

**Editorial Production:** Janet Foley

**Maps:** David Lindroth, *cartographer*; Robert Blake, *map editor*

**Design:** Fabrizio La Rocca, *creative director*; Guido Caroti, *associate art director*; Jolie Novak, *photo editor*

**Production/Manufacturing:** Mike Costa

**Cover Photograph:** Catherine Karnow/Woodfin Camp

## Copyright

## Special Sales

Fodor's Travel Publications are available at special discounts for bulk purchases for sales promotions or premiums. Special editions, including personalized covers, excerpts of existing guides, and corporate imprints, can be created in large quantities for special needs. For more information, contact your local bookseller or write to Special Markets, Fodor's Travel Publications, 201 East 50th Street, New York, NY 10022. Inquiries from Canada should be directed to your local Canadian bookseller or sent to Random House of Canada, Ltd., Marketing Department, 1265 Aerowood Drive, Mississauga, Ontario L4W 1B9. Inquiries from the United Kingdom should be sent to Fodor's Travel Publications, 20 Vauxhall Bridge Road, London SW1V 2SA, England.

PRINTED IN THE UNITED STATES OF AMERICA

10 9 8 7 6 5 4 3 2 1

# CONTENTS

## Maps and Plans

# ON THE ROAD WITH FODOR'S

**W**E'RE ALWAYS THRILLED to get letters from readers, especially one like this:

*It took us an hour to decide what book to buy and we now know we picked the best one. Your book was wonderful, easy to follow, very accurate, and good on pointing out eating places, informal as well as formal. When we saw other people using your book, we would look at each other and smile.*

Our editors and writers are deeply committed to making every Fodor's guide "the best one"—not only accurate but always charming, brimming with sound recommendations and solid ideas, right on the mark in describing restaurants and hotels, and full of fascinating facts that make you view what you've traveled to see in a rich new light.

## About Our Writers

Our success in achieving our goals—and in helping to make your trip the best of all possible vacations—is a credit to the hard work of our extraordinary writers.

**Pamela Acheson** spent 18 years in New York City as a publishing executive before heading south to divide her time between Florida and the Caribbean. She writes extensively about both areas and is a regular contributor to *Travel & Leisure, Caribbean Travel and Life, Florida Travel and Life, Fodor's Florida, Fodor's Caribbean,* and *Fodor's Virgin Islands.* She is the author of *The Best of the British Virgin Islands* and *The Best of St. Thomas* and is currently working on *The Best of the Bahamas* and several Florida guides.

St. Thomas–based writer and dietitian **Carol M. Bareuther** publishes two weekly columns on food, cooking, and nutrition in the *Virgin Islands Daily News* and serves as U.S. Virgin Islands stringer for the Reuters News Service International. She also writes about sports and travel for *Islands' Nautical Scene, Caribbean Week, Tropic Times,* and the *Virgin Islands Business Journal,* as well as other publications. She is the author of two books,

*Sports Fishing in the Virgin Islands* and *Virgin Islands Cooking.*

**Lynda Lohr** spent the last 13 years as a St. John resident, much of it swimming at her favorite Hawksnest Beach. She's a veteran mainland and U.S. Virgin Islands journalist who works regularly for local, regional, and national publications. She lives with her cat and her boyfriend in a tiny cottage overlooking Cruz Bay.

Before settling back home in Cape Cod, **Karl Luntta** spent a dozen years living and working in Africa, the South Pacific, and the Caribbean. Now a full-time travel writer, he is the author of *Jamaica Handbook, Caribbean Handbook,* and *Virgin Islands Handbook,* as well as *Caribbean: The Lesser Antilles.* He has contributed numerous articles and photographs to publications such as *Caribbean Travel and Life, Cape Cod Life,* and the *Boston Globe.* He has also published fiction and is a humor columnist with the *Cape Cod Times.*

**JoAnn Milivojevic** is a freelance writer and video producer based in Illinois, whose love affair with the Caribbean began 10 years ago while scuba diving in the Turks and Caicos Islands. She has produced video programs on the Cayman Islands and St. Kitts and Nevis; her articles on the Caribbean have appeared in publications nationwide. She travels regularly to the islands to "wine her waist" to Soca music, collect folktales, and dive the salty blue.

**Melissa Rivers** was married barefoot on a sugary beach in Montego Bay. If she had to plan a honeymoon there today, she'd be hard pressed to choose a place to stay. She also covered the Caymans, and as an avid snorkeler and diver, could not recommend the islands more highly. Melissa travels extensively and has also contributed to *Fodor's Mexico, Fodor's Canada, Fodor's USA, Fodor's Great American Learning Vacations,* and *Fodor's Great American Sports and Adventure Vacations.*

Hurricane Marilyn blew **Eileen Robinson-Smith** out of the Caribbean and returned her to her lakefront home in Charleston,

South Carolina. For the previous six years she lived in St. Thomas, St. Croix, St. John, and Tortola. As an editor with the *Virgin Islander,* she began her travels throughout the islands and added more Caribbean destinations to her repertoire while travel editor of the *Virgin Islands Journal.* She is known nationally for her food and travel writing. Back in Charleston, she now freelances for local, regional, and national publications.

**Jordan Simon** has visited nearly every speck of land in the Caribbean for Fodor's, *Caribbean Travel & Life, Modern Bride, Physicians Travel & Meeting Guide, Travel & Leisure,* and *Travelage.* He is the author of *Fodor's Colorado, Fodor's Branson,* and the *USA Today Ski Atlas,* among others.

Husband-and-wife team **Simon Worrall** and **Kate Pennebaker** have years of Caribbean experience between them. Kate Pennebaker first dove when she was dropped off the back of a boat in Dominica with a tank at the age of 10 by her explorer stepfather, Peter Gimbel. She has been going back to the islands, as a diver and photographer, ever since. Simon Worrall is a British-born journalist. His many credits include the *London Sunday Times Magazine, Esquire, Harper's and Queen, Men's Journal,* and *Geo.*

**Jane Zarem** is a freelance writer from Connecticut who travels frequently to the Caribbean. Among the score of islands she has explored, she finds it difficult to pick a favorite—she loves them all. She is a member of the New York Travel Writers' Association and the International Food, Wine & Travel Writers' Association, and has contributed to numerous Fodor's guides, among them *New England USA, Cape Cod, Bahamas,* and *Great American Sports and Adventure Vacations,* as well as *Caribbean.*

## New This Year

This year, Fodor's joins Rand McNally, the world's largest commercial mapmaker, to bring you a detailed color map of the Caribbean. Just detach it along the perforation and drop it in your tote bag.

On the Web, check out Fodor's site (http://www.fodors.com/) for information on major destinations around the world and travel-savvy interactive features. The Web site also lists the 80-plus radio stations nationwide that carry the Fodor's Travel Show, a live call-in program that airs every weekend. Tune in to hear guests discuss their wonderful adventures—or call in to get answers for your most pressing travel questions.

## How to Use This Book

### Organization

Up front is the **Gold Guide,** an easy-to-use section divided alphabetically by topic. Under each listing you'll find tips and information that will help you accomplish what you need to in the Caribbean. You'll also find addresses and telephone numbers of organizations and companies that offer destination-related services and detailed information and publications.

The first chapter in the guide, Destination: Caribbean, helps get you in the mood for your trip. New and Noteworthy cues you in on trends and happenings, What's Where gets you oriented, Pleasures and Pastimes describes the activities and sights that really make the Caribbean unique, an Island Finder chart helps you compare qualities of all the islands, Fodor's Choice showcases our top picks, and Festivals and Seasonal Events alerts you to special events you'll want to seek out.

The chapters in this book are listed alphabetically by island; each island's section covers lodging, dining, beaches, outdoor activities and sports, shopping, nightlife and the arts, exploring, and ends with a section called A to Z, which tells you how to get there and get around and gives you important local addresses and telephone numbers.

### Icons and Symbols

★   Our special recommendations
✕   Restaurant
⌂   Lodging establishment
⚠   Campgrounds
☺   Good for kids (rubber duckie)
☞   Sends you to another section of the guide for more information
⊠   Address
☎   Telephone number
☉   Opening and closing times
💰   Admission prices (those we give apply to adults; substantially reduced fees are almost always available for children, students, and senior citizens)

## Hotel Facilities

We always list the facilities that are available—but we don't specify whether they cost extra: When pricing accommodations, always ask what's included. In addition, assume that all rooms have private baths unless otherwise noted.

Throughout the Caribbean there are numerous meal plans offered: **European Plan** (EP, with no meals), **Full American Plan** (FAP, with all meals), **Modified American Plan** (MAP, with breakfast and dinner daily), **Continental Plan** (CP, with a Continental breakfast daily), or **All-inclusive** (all meals and most activities). At the end of each review, we have listed the meal plans the hotel offers.

A Full American Plan may be ideal for travelers on a budget who don't want to worry about additional expenses, but travelers who enjoy a different dining experience each night will prefer to book rooms on the European Plan. Since some hotels insist on the Modified American Plan, particularly during the high season, you might want to find out whether you can exchange dinner for lunch or for meals at neighboring hotels.

## Restaurant Reservations and Dress Codes

Reservations are always a good idea; we note only when they're essential or when they are not accepted. Book as far ahead as you can, and reconfirm when you get to town. Unless otherwise noted, the restaurants listed are open daily for lunch and dinner. We mention dress only when men are required to wear a jacket or a jacket and tie. Look for an overview of local habits in the Gold Guide and in the What to Wear sections of the dining introductions for each island.

## Credit Cards

The following abbreviations are used: **AE**, American Express; **D**, Discover; **DC**, Diners Club; **MC**, MasterCard; and **V**, Visa.

## Don't Forget to Write

You can use this book in the confidence that all prices and opening times are based on information supplied to us at press time; Fodor's cannot accept responsibility for any errors. Time inevitably brings changes, so always confirm information when it matters—especially if you're making a detour to visit a specific place. In addition, when making reservations be sure to mention if you have a disability or are traveling with children, if you prefer a private bath or a certain type of bed, or if you have specific dietary needs or other concerns.

Were the restaurants we recommended as described? Did our hotel picks exceed your expectations? Did you find a museum we recommended a waste of time? If you have complaints, we'll look into them and revise our entries when the facts warrant it. If you've discovered a special place that we haven't included, we'll pass the information along to our correspondents and have them check it out. So send us your feedback, positive *and* negative: email us at editors@fodors.com (specifying the name of the book on the subject line) or write the Caribbean editor at Fodor's, 201 East 50th Street, New York, New York 10022. Have a wonderful trip!

Karen Cure
*Editorial Director*

## The Caribbean

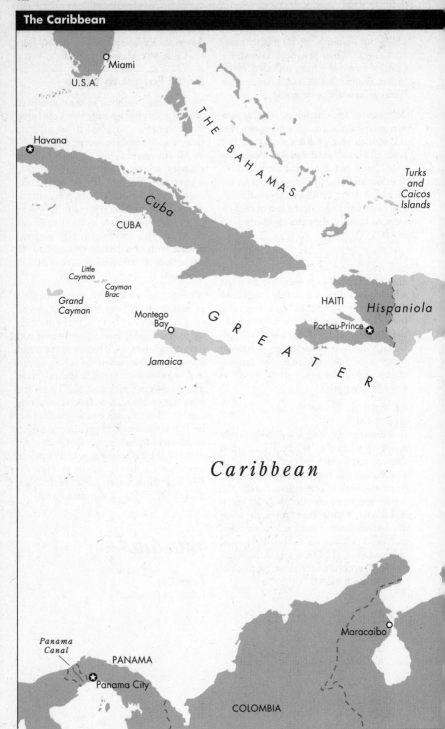

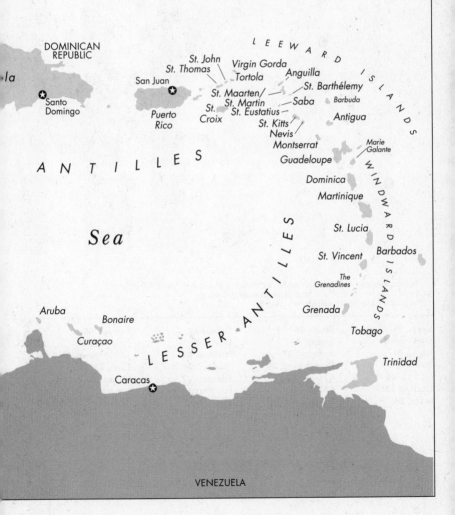

0       200 miles

0       300 km

N

ATLANTIC OCEAN

DOMINICAN
REPUBLIC

*la*

LEEWARD ISLANDS

St. John
St. Thomas     Virgin Gorda
                    Tortola        Anguilla
San Juan                          St. Barthélemy
                St. Maarten/      Saba        Barbuda
          St.   St. Martin   St. Eustatius
          Croix              St. Kitts        Antigua
Puerto                       Nevis
Rico                    Montserrat
Santo                                        Marie
Domingo                   Guadeloupe         Galante

A N T I L L E S                    Dominica
                                   Martinique

                                                    WINDWARD ISLANDS

*Sea*                           St. Lucia

                          St. Vincent        Barbados

                              The
                          Grenadines

Aruba                          Grenada
      Bonaire
   Curaçao                                   Tobago
                    L E S S E R   A N T I L L E S
          Caracas                            Trinidad

VENEZUELA

x

# World Time Zones

Numbers below vertical bands relate each zone to Greenwich Mean Time (0 hrs.).
Local times frequently differ from these general indications,
as indicated by light-face numbers on map.

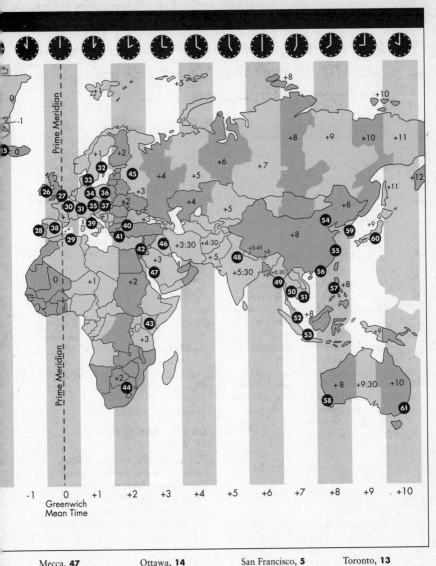

# SMART TRAVEL TIPS A TO Z

*Basic Information on Traveling in the Caribbean,
Savvy Tips to Make Your Trip a Breeze, and
Companies and Organizations to Contact*

**THE GOLD GUIDE / SMART TRAVEL TIPS**

## A

### AIR TRAVEL

#### MAJOR AIRLINE OR LOW-COST CARRIER?

Most people choose a flight based on price. Yet there are other issues to consider. Major airlines offer the greatest number of departures; smaller airlines—including regional, low-cost, and no-frill airlines—usually have a more limited number of flights daily. Major airlines have frequent-flyer partners, which allow you to credit mileage earned on one airline to your account with another. Low-cost airlines offer a definite price advantage and fewer restrictions, such as advance-purchase requirements. Safety-wise, low-cost carriers as a group have a good history, but **check the safety record before booking** any low-cost carrier; call the Federal Aviation Administration's Consumer Hotline (☞ Airline Complaints, *below*).

For information on airports and major airlines serving the Caribbean from the United States, *see* individual island chapters.

➤ SMALLER AIRLINES: **American Eagle** (☎ 800/433–7300) to most islands via San Juan. **Carnival Air Lines** (☎ 800/824–7386) to Dominican Republic, Nassau, Puerto Rico.

➤ FROM THE U.K.: **British Airways** (☎ 0345/222–111). **British West Indian Airways** (☎ 0181/570–5552). **Caledonian** (☎ 01293/567–100).

#### GET THE LOWEST FARE

The least-expensive airfares to the Caribbean are priced for round-trip travel. Major airlines usually require that you **book far in advance and stay at least seven days** and no more than 30 to get the lowest fares. Ask about "ultrasaver" fares, which are the cheapest; they must be booked 90 days in advance and are nonrefund-able. A little more expensive are "supersaver" fares, which require only a 30-day advance purchase. Remember that penalties for refunds or scheduling changes are stiffer for international tickets, usually about $150. International flights are also sensitive to the season: **plan to fly in the off season** for the cheapest fares. If your destination or home city has more than one gateway, **compare prices to and from different airports.** Also price flights scheduled for off-peak hours, which may be significantly less expensive.

To save money on flights from the United Kingdom and back, **look into an APEX or Super-PEX ticket.** APEX tickets must be booked in advance and have certain restrictions. Super-PEX tickets can be purchased at the airport on the day of departure—subject to availability.

#### DON'T STOP UNLESS YOU MUST

When you book, **look for nonstop flights** and **remember that "direct" flights stop at least once.** International flights on a country's flag carrier are almost always nonstop; U.S. airlines often fly direct. Try to **avoid connecting flights,** which require a change of plane. Two airlines may jointly operate a connecting flight, so ask if your airline operates every segment—you may find that your preferred carrier flies you only part of the way.

#### USE AN AGENT

Travel agents, especially those who specialize in finding the lowest fares, can be especially helpful when booking a plane ticket. When you're quoted a price, **ask your agent if the price is likely to get any lower.** Good agents know the seasonal fluctuations of airfares and can usually anticipate a sale or fare war. However, waiting can be risky: The fare could go *up* as seats become scarce, and you may wait so long that your preferred flight sells out. A wait-and-see strategy works best if your plans are flexible, but if you must arrive and depart on certain dates, don't delay.

## CHECK WITH CONSOLIDATORS

Consolidators buy tickets for scheduled flights at reduced rates from the airlines then sell them at prices that beat the best fare available directly from the airlines, usually without advance restrictions. Sometimes you can even get your money back if you need to return the ticket. Carefully read the fine print detailing penalties for changes and cancellations, and **confirm your consolidator reservation with the airline.**

➤ CONSOLIDATORS: **United States Air Consolidators Association** (✉ 925 L St., Suite 220, Sacramento, CA 95814, ☎ 916/441–4166, FAX 916/441–3520).

## CONSIDER A CHARTER

Charters usually have the lowest fares but are not dependable. Departures are infrequent and seldom on time, flights can be delayed for up to 48 hours or can be canceled for any reason up to 10 days before you're scheduled to leave. Itineraries and prices can change after you've booked your flight, so you must **be very careful to choose a legitimate charter carrier.** Don't commit to a charter operator that doesn't follow proper booking procedures. Be especially careful when buying a charter ticket. Read the fine print regarding refund policies. If you can't pay with a credit card, **make your check payable to a charter carrier's escrow account** (unless you're dealing with a travel agent, in which case his or her check should be made payable to the escrow account). The name of the bank should be in the charter contract.

## AVOID GETTING BUMPED

Airlines routinely overbook planes, knowing that not everyone with a ticket will show up, but sometimes everyone does. When that happens, airlines ask for volunteers to give up their seats. In return these volunteers usually get a certificate for a free flight and are rebooked on the next flight out. If there are not enough volunteers the airline must choose

who will be denied boarding. The first to get bumped are passengers who checked in late and those flying on discounted tickets, **so get to the gate and check in as early as possible,** especially during peak periods.

Always **bring a photo ID to the airport.** You may be asked to show it before you are allowed to check in.

## ENJOY THE FLIGHT

For better service, **fly smaller or regional carriers,** which often have higher passenger-satisfaction ratings. Sometimes you'll find leather seats, more legroom, and better food. However, be sure to **reconfirm your flights on interisland carriers.** Passengers are often subject to their whim: If there are no other passengers on your booked flight, you may be requested (actually, ordered) to take a more convenient departure for the airline, or your plane may make unscheduled stops to pick up more clients or cargo. There are usually weight restrictions; if you don't travel light, you could be subject to outrageous surcharges. It's all part of the excitement—and unpredictability—of Caribbean travel.

For more legroom, **request an emergency-aisle seat;** don't however, sit in the row in front of the emergency aisle or in front of a bulkhead, where seats may not recline.

If you don't like airline food, **ask for special meals when booking.** These can be vegetarian, low-cholesterol, or kosher, for example.

Some carriers have prohibited smoking throughout their systems; others allow smoking only on certain routes or even certain departures from that route, so **contact your carrier regarding its smoking policy.**

## COMPLAIN IF NECESSARY

If your baggage goes astray or your flight goes awry, complain right away. Most carriers require that you file a claim immediately.

➤ AIRLINE COMPLAINTS: U.S. Department of Transportation **Aviation Consumer Protection Division** (✉ C-75, Washington, DC 20590, ☎ 202/366–2220). **Federal Aviation Administration (FAA) Consumer Hotline** (☎ 800/322–7873).

SMART TRAVEL TIPS / THE GOLD GUIDE

## C

### CAMERAS, CAMCORDERS, & COMPUTERS

Always **keep your film, tape, or computer disks out of the sun.** Carry an extra supply of batteries, and **be prepared to turn on your camera, camcorder, or laptop** to prove to security personnel that the device is real. Always **ask for hand inspection of film,** which becomes clouded after successive exposure to airport x-ray machines, and **keep videotapes and computer disks away from metal detectors.**

➤ PHOTO HELP: Kodak Information Center (☎ 800/242–2424). *Kodak Guide to Shooting Great Travel Pictures,* available in bookstores or from Fodor's Travel Publications (☎ 800/533–6478); $16.50 plus $4 shipping.

### CUSTOMS

Before departing, **register your foreign-made camera or laptop with U.S. Customs** (☞ Customs & Duties, *below*). If your equipment is U.S.-made, call the consulate of the country you'll be visiting to find out whether the device should be registered with local customs upon arrival.

### CAR RENTAL

For information on car-rental agencies and costs in the Caribbean, *see* individual island chapters.

### CUT COSTS

To get the best deal, **book through a travel agent who is willing to shop around.**

Also **ask your travel agent about a company's customer-service record.** How has it responded to late plane arrivals and vehicle mishaps? Are there often lines at the rental counter, and, if you're traveling during a holiday period, does a confirmed reservation guarantee you a car?

Be sure to **look into wholesalers,** companies that do not own fleets but rent in bulk from those that do and often offer better rates than traditional car-rental operations. Prices are best during off-peak periods. Rentals booked through wholesalers must be paid for before you leave the United States.

➤ RENTAL WHOLESALERS: **Auto Europe** (☎ 207/842–2000 or 800/223–5555, FAX 800/235–6321). The **Kemwel Group** (☎ 914/835–5555 or 800/678–0678, FAX 914/835–5126).

### NEED INSURANCE?

When driving a rented car you are generally responsible for any damage to or loss of the vehicle. You also are liable for any property damage or personal injury that you may cause while driving. Before you rent, **see what coverage you already have** under the terms of your personal auto-insurance policy and credit cards.

### BEWARE SURCHARGES

Before you pick up a car in one city and leave it in another, **ask about drop-off charges or one-way service fees,** which can be substantial. Note, too, that some rental agencies charge extra if you return the car before the time specified on your contract. To avoid a hefty refueling fee, **fill the tank just before you turn in the car,** but be aware that gas stations near the rental outlet may overcharge.

### MEET THE REQUIREMENTS

For driver's license requirements, *see* individual island chapters.

### CHILDREN & TRAVEL

### CHILDREN IN THE CARIBBEAN

Caribbean islands and their resorts are increasingly sensitive to families' needs. Many now have children's programs. Baby food is easy to find, but outside major hotels you may not find such items as high chairs and cribs. When choosing a destination, **consider whether or not English is spoken widely;** the language barrier can frustrate children.

Be sure to plan ahead and **involve your youngsters** as you outline your trip. When packing, include things to keep them busy en route. On sightseeing days try to schedule activities of special interest to your children. If you are renting a car don't forget to **arrange for a car seat** when you reserve.

### LODGING

Children are welcome in all except the most exclusive resorts; many hotels allow children under 12 or 16 to stay free in their parents' room (be sure to **ask the cutoff age** when booking). In addition, several hotel chains have children's programs, and many hotels and resorts arrange for baby-sitting. Representative of the services and activities available are the complimentary "Just Us Kids" program for children ages 5–12 at Aruba's Sonesta Resorts at Seaport Village; the camp available for children ages 5–12 all summer, at Christmastime, and at Easter at Puerto Rico's Hyatt Regency Cerromar Beach and Hyatt Dorado Beach; and the activities program for kids 5–12 at Puerto Rico's El San Juan Hotel and Casino.

Jamaica's all-inclusive Boscobel Beach specializes in families and offers a small army of SuperNannies, a petting zoo, crafts classes, and a disco for teens. On St. Thomas in the U.S. Virgin Islands, the Stouffer Grand Beach Resort and Doubletree Sapphire Beach Resort and Marina have half- and full-day programs for children ages 4–12. Club Med's St. Lucia and Dominican Republic resorts offer Mini Club programs for children ages 2–11.

Also **consider apartment and villa rentals** (☞ Lodging, *below*). When you book, be sure to **ask about the availability of baby-sitters,** housekeepers, and medical facilities.

➤ BEST CHOICES: In Aruba, the Sonesta Resorts at Seaport Village (☎ 800/766–3782). In Puerto Rico, the **Hyatt Regency Cerromar Beach** and the **Hyatt Dorado Beach** (☎ 800/233–1234) and the **El San Juan Hotel and Casino** (☎ 800/468–2818). In Jamaica, **Boscobel Beach** (☎ 800/859–7873) In St. Thomas in the U.S. Virgin Islands, the **Stouffer Grand Beach Resort** (☎ 800/468–3571). In Nevis, **Four Seasons** (☎ 800/332–3442). In Barbados, **Almond Beach Village** (☎ 800/425–6663).

## FLYING

As a general rule, infants under two not occupying a seat fly at greatly reduced fares and occasionally for free. If your children are two or older **ask about children's airfares.**

In general the adult baggage allowance applies to children paying half or more of the adult fare. When booking, **ask**

**about carry-on allowances for those traveling with infants.** In general, for babies charged 10% of the adult fare you are allowed one carry-on bag and a collapsible stroller, which may have to be checked; you may be limited to less if the flight is full.

According to the FAA, it's a good idea to use safety seats aloft for children weighing less than 40 pounds. Airlines, however, can set their own policies: U.S. carriers allow FAA-approved models but usually require that you buy a ticket, even if your child would otherwise ride free, since the seats must be strapped into regular seats. Airline rules vary regarding their use, so it's important to **check your airline's policy about using safety seats during takeoff and landing.** Safety seats cannot obstruct any of the other passengers in the row, so get an appropriate seat assignment as early as possible.

When making your reservation, **request children's meals or a free-standing bassinet** if you need them; the latter are available only to those seated at the bulkhead, where there's enough legroom. Remember, however, that bulkhead seats may not have their own overhead bins, and there's no storage space in front of you—a major inconvenience.

## GROUP TRAVEL

If you're planning to take your kids on a tour, look for companies that specialize in family travel.

➤ FAMILY-FRIENDLY TOUR OPERATORS: **Families Welcome!** (✉ 92 N. Main St., Ashland, OR 97520, ☎ 541/482–6121 or 800/326–0724, 𝖥𝖠𝖷 541/482–0660). **Rascals in Paradise** (✉ 650 5th St., Suite 505, San Francisco, CA 94107, ☎ 415/978–9800 or 800/872–7225, 𝖥𝖠𝖷 415/442–0289).

CONSUMER PROTECTION

Whenever possible, **pay with a major credit card** so you can cancel payment if there's a problem, provided that you can supply documentation. This is a good practice whether you're buying travel arrangements before your trip or shopping at your destination.

If you're doing business with a particular company for the first time, **contact your local Better Business Bureau and the attorney general's** offices in your state and the company's home state, as well. Have any complaints been filed?

Finally, if you're buying a package or tour, always **consider travel insurance** that includes default coverage (☞ Insurance, *below*).

➤ LOCAL BBBS: **Council of Better Business Bureaus** (⌧ 4200 Wilson Blvd., Suite 800, Arlington, VA 22203, ☎ 703/276–0100, FAX 703/525–8277).

## CRUISING

Cruising the Caribbean is perhaps the most relaxed and convenient way to tour this beautiful part of the world: You get all of the amenities of a Stateside hotel and enough activities to guarantee fun, even on rainy days. Cruising through the islands is an entirely different experience from staying on one island.

Cruise ships usually call at several Caribbean ports on a single voyage but are at each port for only one night. Thus, although you may be exposed to several islands, you don't get much of a feel for any one of them.

As a vacation, a cruise offers total peace of mind. All important decisions are made long before boarding. The itinerary is set, and the total cost of your vacation is known almost to the penny. For details, see *Fodor's Worldwide Cruises and Ports of Call*; the Cruise Primer chapter is particularly helpful if you're cruising for the first time.

To get the best deal on a cruise, **consult a cruise-only travel agency.**

➤ ORGANIZATIONS: To find out which ships are sailing where and when they depart, contact the **Caribbean Tourism Organization** (⌧ 20 E. 46th St., 4th floor, New York, NY 10017, ☎ 212/682–0435). The **Cruise Lines International Association** (CLIA) publishes a useful pamphlet entitled "Cruising Answers to Your Questions"; to order a copy send a self-addressed business-size envelope with 52¢ postage to CLIA (⌧ 500 5th Ave., Suite 1407, New York, NY 10110).

➤ CRUISE LINES: **American Canadian Caribbean Line** (⌧ Box 368, Warren,

RI 02885, ☎ 401/247–0955 or 800/556–7450). **Carnival Cruise Lines** (⌧ Carnival Pl., 3655 N.W. 87th Ave., Miami, FL 33178, ☎ 305/599–2600). **Celebrity Cruises** (⌧ 5200 Blue Lagoon Dr., Miami, FL 33126, ☎ 800/437–3111). **Clipper Cruise Line** (⌧ 7711 Bonhomme Ave., St. Louis, MO 63105, ☎ 800/325–0010). **Club Med** (⌧ 40 W. 57th St., New York, NY 10019, ☎ 800/258–2633). **Commodore Cruise Line** (⌧ 800 Douglas Rd., Coral Gables, FL 33134, ☎ 305/529–3000). **Costa Cruise Lines** (⌧ World Trade Center, 80 S.W. 8th St., Miami, FL 33130, ☎ 800/462–6782). **Crystal Cruises** (⌧ 2121 Ave. of the Stars, Los Angeles, CA 90067, ☎ 800/446–6620). **Cunard Line** (⌧ 555 5th Ave., New York, NY 10017, ☎ 800/221–4770). **Dolphin/Majesty Cruise Lines** (⌧ 901 South American Way, Miami, FL 33132, ☎ 800/532–7788). **Holland America Line** (⌧ 300 Elliott Ave. W, Seattle, WA 98119, ☎ 800/426–0327). **Norwegian Cruise Line** (⌧ 95 Merrick Way, Coral Gables, FL 33134, ☎ 800/327–7030). **Premier Cruise Line** (⌧ Box 517, Cape Canaveral, FL 32920, ☎ 800/473–3262). **Princess Cruises** (⌧ 10100 Santa Monica Blvd., Los Angeles, CA 90067, ☎ 310/553–1770). **Radisson Seven Seas Cruises** (⌧ 600 Corporate Dr., Suite 410, Fort Lauderdale, FL 33334, ☎ 800/333–3333). **Renaissance Cruises** (⌧ 1800 Eller Dr., Suite 300, Box 350307, Fort Lauderdale, FL 33335, ☎ 800/525–2450). **Royal Caribbean Cruise Line** (⌧ 1050 Caribbean Way, Miami, FL 33132, ☎ 800/327–6700). **Royal Olympic Cruises** (⌧ 1 Rockefeller Plaza, Suite 315, New York, NY 10020, ☎ 800/872–6400). **Seabourn Cruise Line** (⌧ 55 Francisco St., San Francisco, CA 94133, ☎ 800/351–9595). **Seawind Cruise Line** (⌧ 1750 Coral Way, Miami, FL 33145, ☎ 800/258–8006). **Silversea Cruises** (⌧ 110 E. Broward Blvd., Fort Lauderdale, FL 33301, ☎ 305/522–4477 or 800/722–6655). **Special Expeditions** (⌧ 720 5th Ave., New York, NY 10019, ☎ 800/762–0003). **Star Clippers** (⌧ 4101 Salzedo Ave., Coral Gables, FL 33146, ☎ 800/442–0551). **Windjammer Barefoot Cruises** (⌧ 1759 Bay Rd., Miami Beach, FL 33139, ☎ 800/327–2602). **Windstar Cruises** (⌧ 300 Elliott Ave. W, Seattle, WA 98119, ☎ 800/258–7245).

When shopping, **keep receipts** for all of your purchases. Upon reentering the country, **be ready to show customs officials what you've bought.** If you feel a duty is incorrect, appeal the assessment. If you object to the way your clearance was handled, get the inspector's badge number. In either case, first ask to see a supervisor, then write to the port director at the address listed on your receipt. Send a copy of the receipt and other appropriate documentation. If you still don't get satisfaction you can take your case to customs headquarters in Washington.

## ON ARRIVAL

*See* individual island chapters for customs information.

## ENTERING THE U.S.

You may bring home $400 worth of foreign goods duty-free if you've been out of the country for at least 48 hours and haven't already used the $400 allowance or any part of it in the past 30 days. You may bring home $600 worth of foreign goods duty-free if you've been out of the country for at least 48 hours and haven't used the $600 allowance or any part of it in the past 30 days. This allowance, higher than the standard $400 exemption, applies to two dozen countries included in the Caribbean Basin Initiative (CBI). If you visit a CBI country and a non-CBI country, such as Martinique, you may still bring in $600 worth of goods duty-free, but no more than $400 may be from the non-CBI country. If you're returning from the U.S. Virgin Islands (USVI), the duty-free allowance is $1,200. If your travel included the USVI and another country—say, the Dominican Republic—the $1,200 allowance still applies, but at least $600 worth of goods must be from the USVI.

Travelers 21 and older may bring back 1 liter of alcohol duty-free. In addition, regardless of your age, you are allowed 200 cigarettes and 100 non-Cuban cigars. (At press time, a federal rule restricting tobacco access to persons 18 years and older did not apply to importation.) Antiques, which the U.S. Customs Service defines as objects more than 100 years old, enter duty-free, as do original works of art done entirely by hand, including paintings, drawings, and sculptures.

You may also send packages home duty-free: up to $200 worth of goods for personal use, with a limit of one parcel per addressee per day (and no alcohol or tobacco products or perfume worth more than $5); label the package PERSONAL USE, and attach a list of its contents and their retail value. Do not label the package UNSOLICITED GIFT, or your duty-free exemption will drop to $100. Mailed items do not affect your duty-free allowance on your return.

➤ INFORMATION: **U.S. Customs Service** (Inquiries, ⊠ Box 7407, Washington, DC 20044, ☎ 202/927–6724; complaints, ⊠ Commissioner's Office, 1301 Constitution Ave. NW, Washington, DC 20229; registration of equipment, ⊠ Resource Management, 1301 Constitution Ave. NW, Washington, DC 20229, ☎ 202/927–0540).

## ENTERING CANADA

If you've been out of Canada for at least seven days you may bring in C$500 worth of goods duty-free. If you've been away for fewer than seven days but more than 48 hours, the duty-free allowance drops to C$200; if your trip lasts 24–48 hours, the allowance is C$50. You may not pool allowances with family members. Goods claimed under the C$500 exemption may follow you by mail; those claimed under the lesser exemptions must accompany you.

Alcohol and tobacco products may be included in the seven-day and 48-hour exemptions but not in the 24-hour exemption. If you meet the age requirements of the province or territory through which you reenter Canada you may bring in, duty-free, 1.14 liters (40 imperial ounces) of wine or liquor *or* 24 12-ounce cans or bottles of beer or ale. If you are 16 or older you may bring in, duty-free, 200 cigarettes and 50 cigars; these items must accompany you.

You may send an unlimited number of gifts worth up to C$60 each duty-free to Canada. Label the package UNSOLICITED GIFT—VALUE UNDER $60. Alcohol and tobacco are excluded.

*THE GOLD GUIDE / SMART TRAVEL TIPS*

➤ INFORMATION: **Revenue Canada**
(✉ 2265 St. Laurent Blvd. S, Ottawa,
Ontario K1G 4K3, ☎ 613/993–
0534, 800/461–9999 in Canada).

### ENTERING THE U.K.

From countries outside the European
Union (EU), including those covered
in this book, you may import, duty-
free, 200 cigarettes or 50 cigars; 1
liter of spirits or 2 liters of fortified or
sparkling wine or liqueurs; 2 liters of
still table wine; 60 milliliters of perfume; 250 milliliters of toilet water;
plus £136 worth of other goods,
including gifts and souvenirs.

➤ INFORMATION: **HM Customs and
Excise** (✉ Dorset House, Stamford
St., London SE1 9NG, ☎ 0171/202–
4227).

## D
### DISABILITIES & ACCESSIBILITY

### ACCESS IN THE CARIBBEAN

In the Caribbean very few attractions
and sights are equipped with ramps,
elevators, or wheelchair-accessible
rest rooms. However, major new
properties are planning with the needs
of travelers with disabilities in mind.
Wherever possible in our lodging
listings, we indicate whether special
facilities are available.

### TIPS & HINTS

When discussing accessibility with an
operator or reservationist, **ask hard
questions.** Are there any stairs, inside
*or* out? Are there grab bars next to
the toilet *and* in the shower/tub? How
wide is the doorway to the room? To
the bathroom? For the most extensive
facilities meeting the latest legal
specifications, **opt for newer accommodations,** which are more likely to
have been designed with access in
mind. Older buildings or ships may
offer more limited facilities. Be sure to
**discuss your needs before booking.**

➤ COMPLAINTS: **Disability Rights
Section** (✉ U.S. Dept. of Justice, Box
66738, Washington, DC 20035-6738,
☎ 202/514–0301 or 800/514–0301,
FAX 202/307–1198, TTY 202/514–
0383 or 800/514–0383) for general
complaints. **Aviation Consumer
Protection Division** (☞ Air Travel,
*above*) for airline-related problems.
**Civil Rights Office** (✉ U.S. Dept. of
Transportation, Departmental Office

of Civil Rights, S-30, 400 7th St. SW,
Room 10215, Washington, DC
20590, ☎ 202/366–4648) for problems with surface transportation.

### LODGING

**Divi Hotels** (☎ 800/367–3484),
which has six properties in the
Caribbean, runs one of the best dive
programs for people with disabilities
at its resort in Bonaire.

### TRAVEL AGENCIES &
### TOUR OPERATORS

The Americans with Disabilities Act
requires that travel firms serve the
needs of all travelers. That said, you
should note that some agencies and
operators specialize in making travel
arrangements for individuals and
groups with disabilities.

➤ TRAVELERS WITH MOBILITY PROB-
LEMS: **Access Adventures** (✉ 206
Chestnut Ridge Rd., Rochester, NY
14624, ☎ 716/889–9096), run by a
former physical-rehabilitation coun-
selor. **Accessible Journeys** (✉ 35 W.
Sellers Ave., Ridley Park, PA 19078,
☎ 610/521–0339 or 800/846–4537,
FAX 610/521–6959), for escorted tours
exclusively for travelers with mobility
impairments. **CareVacations** (✉ 5019
49th Ave., Suite 102, Leduc, Alberta
T9E 6T5, ☎ 403/986–6404, 800/
648–1116 in Canada) has group
tours and is especially helpful with
cruise vacations. **Hinsdale Travel
Service** (✉ 201 E. Ogden Ave., Suite
100, Hinsdale, IL 60521, ☎ 630/
325–1335), a travel agency that
benefits from the advice of wheelchair
traveler Janice Perkins. **Tomorrow's
Level of Care** (✉ Box 470299,
Brooklyn, NY 11247, ☎ 718/756–
0794 or 800/932–2012), for nursing
services and medical equipment.
**Wheelchair Journeys** (✉ 16979
Redmond Way, Redmond, WA
98052, ☎ 206/885–2210 or 800/
313–4751), for general travel arrangements.

➤ TRAVELERS WITH DEVELOPMENTAL
DISABILITIES: **New Directions** (✉ 5276
Hollister Ave., Suite 207, Santa Bar-
bara, CA 93111, ☎ 805/967–2841,
FAX 805/964–7344).

### DISCOUNTS & DEALS

Be a smart shopper and **compare all
your options before making a choice.**
A plane ticket bought with a promo-

tional coupon may not be cheaper than the least expensive fare from a discount ticket agency. For high-price travel purchases, such as packages or tours, keep in mind that what you get is just as important as what you save. Just because something is cheap doesn't mean it's a bargain.

## LOOK IN YOUR WALLET

When you use your credit card to make travel purchases you may get free travel-accident insurance, collision-damage insurance, and medical or legal assistance, depending on the card and the bank that issued it. American Express, MasterCard, and Visa provide one or more of these services, so **get a copy of your credit card's travel-benefits policy.** If you are a member of the American Automobile Association (AAA) or an oil-company-sponsored road-assistance plan, always **ask hotel or car-rental reservationists about auto-club discounts.** Some clubs offer additional discounts on tours, cruises, or admission to attractions. And don't forget that auto-club membership entitles you to free maps and trip-planning services.

## DIAL FOR DOLLARS

To save money, **look into "1-800" discount reservations services,** which use their buying power to get a better price on hotels, airline tickets, even car rentals. When booking a room, always **call the hotel's local toll-free number** (if one is available) rather than the central reservations number—you'll often get a better price. Always ask about special packages or corporate rates.

When shopping for the best deal on hotels and car rentals **look for guaranteed exchange rates,** which protect you against a falling dollar. With your rate locked in you won't pay more even if the price goes up in the local currency.

➤ AIRLINE TICKETS: ☎ 800/FLY–4–LESS.

## SAVE ON COMBOS

Packages and guided tours can both save you money, but don't confuse the two. When you buy a package your travel remains independent, just as though you had planned and booked the trip yourself. Fly-drive packages, which combine airfare and car rental, are often a good deal.

## JOIN A CLUB?

Many companies sell discounts in the form of travel clubs and coupon books, but these cost money. You must use participating advertisers to get a deal, and only after you recoup the initial membership cost or book price do you begin to save. If you plan to use the club or coupons frequently you may save considerably. Before signing up, find out what discounts you get.

➤ DISCOUNT CLUBS: **Entertainment Travel Editions** (✉ Box 1068, Trumbull, CT 06611, ☎ 800/445–4137), $28–$53, depending on destination. **Great American Traveler** (✉ Box 27965, Salt Lake City, UT 84127, ☎ 800/548–2812) $49.95 per year. **Moment's Notice Discount Travel Club** (✉ 7301 New Utrecht Ave., Brooklyn, NY 11204, ☎ 718/234–6295), $25 per year, single or family. **Privilege Card International** (✉ 201 E. Commerce St., Suite 198, Youngstown, OH 44503, ☎ 330/746–5211 or 800/236–9732) $74.95 per year. **Sears's Mature Outlook** (✉ Box 9390, Des Moines, IA 50306, ☎ 800/336–6330) $14.95 per year. **Travelers Advantage** (✉ CUC Travel Service, 3033 S. Parker Rd., Suite 1000, Aurora, CO 80014, ☎ 800/548–1116 or 800/648–4037), $49 per year, single or family. **Worldwide Discount Travel Club** (✉ 1674 Meridian Ave., Miami Beach, FL 33139, ☎ 305/534–2082), $50 per year family, $40 single.

## DIVING

The Caribbean offers some of the best scuba diving in the world. For a list of training facilities where you can earn your diving certification card, write to **PADI** (✉ Professional Association of Diving Instructors, 1251 E. Dyer Rd., #100, Santa Ana, CA 92705). For more information, *see* Diving *in* Chapter 1.

## DRIVING

➤ AUTO CLUBS: In the United States, **American Automobile Association** (☎ 800/564–6222). In the United Kingdom, **Automobile Association** (**AA,** ☎ 0990/500–600), **Royal Automobile Club** (RAC, ☎ 0990/722–722 membership, 0345/121–345 insurance).

# E

## ELECTRICITY

The general rule in the Caribbean is 110 and 120 volts AC, and the outlets take the same two-prong plugs found in the United States, but there are exceptions, particularly on the French islands and those with a British heritage. Be sure to **check with your hotel** when making reservations. If you are traveling to an island that uses a foreign system, **bring a converter and an adapter.**

If your appliances are dual-voltage, you'll need only an adapter. Don't use 110-volt outlets, marked FOR SHAVERS ONLY, for high-wattage appliances such as blow-dryers. Most laptops operate equally well on 110 and 220 volts and so require only an adapter.

# F

## FURTHER READING

*Caribbean Style* (Crown Publishers) is a coffee-table book with magnificent photographs of the interiors and exteriors of homes and buildings in the Caribbean. Short stories—some dark, some full of laughs—about life in the southern Caribbean made *Easy in the Islands,* by Bob Schacochis, a National Book Award winner. Schacochis has an ear for local patois and an eye for the absurd. To familiarize yourself with the sights, smells, and sounds of the West Indies, pick up Jamaica Kincaid's *Annie John,* a richly textured coming-of-age novel about a girl growing up on Antigua. The short stories in *At the Bottom of the River,* also by Kincaid, depict island mysteries and manners. *Omeros* is Nobel Prize–winning Trinidadian poet Derek Walcott's imaginative Caribbean retelling of the *Odyssey.* Anthony C. Winkler's novels, *The Great Yacht Race, The Lunatic,* and *The Painted Canoe,* provide scathingly witty glimpses into Jamaica's class structure. Another notable chronicle of Caribbean life and customs is the provocative, imaginative novel *Wide Sargasso Sea,* by Jean Rhys. James Michener depicted the islands' diversity in his novel *Caribbean.* To probe island cultures more deeply, read V. S. Naipaul, particularly his *Guerrillas, The Loss of El Dorado* and *The Enigma of Arrival;* Eric William's

*From Columbus to Castro;* and Michael Paiewonsky's *Conquest of Eden.*

# G

## GAY & LESBIAN TRAVEL

➤ TOUR OPERATORS: **R.S.V.P. Travel Productions** (✉ 2800 University Ave. SE, Minneapolis, MN 55414, ☎ 612/379–4697 or 800/328–7787), for cruises and resort vacations for gays. **Olivia** (✉ 4400 Market St., Oakland, CA 94608, ☎ 510/655–0364 or 800/631–6277), for cruises and resort vacations for lesbians. **Atlantis Events** (✉ 9060 Santa Monica Blvd., Suite 310, West Hollywood, CA 90069, ☎ 310/281–5450 or 800/628–5268), for mixed gay and lesbian travel.

➤ GAY- AND LESBIAN-FRIENDLY TRAVEL AGENCIES: **Advance Damron** (✉ 1 Greenway Plaza, Suite 800, Houston, TX 77046, ☎ 713/682–2002 or 800/695–0880, FAX 713/888–1010). **Club Travel** (✉ 8739 Santa Monica Blvd., West Hollywood, CA 90069, ☎ 310/358–2200 or 800/429–8747, FAX 310/358–2222). **Islanders/Kennedy Travel** (✉ 183 W. 10th St., New York, NY 10014, ☎ 212/242–3222 or 800/988–1181, FAX 212/929–8530). **Now Voyager** (✉ 4406 18th St., San Francisco, CA 94114, ☎ 415/626–1169 or 800/255–6951, FAX 415/626–8626). **Yellowbrick Road** (✉ 1500 W. Balmoral Ave., Chicago, IL 60640, ☎ 773/561–1800 or 800/642–2488, FAX 773/561–4497). **Skylink Women's Travel** (✉ 3577 Moorland Ave., Santa Rosa, CA 95407, ☎ 707/585–8355 or 800/225–5759, FAX 707/584–5637), serving lesbian travelers.

# H

## HEALTH

There are few real hazards. The small lizards that seem to have overrun the islands are harmless, and poisonous snakes are hard to find, although you should exercise caution while bird-watching in Trinidad. The worst problem may well be the tiny sand flies known as no-see-ums, which tend to appear after a rain, near wet or swampy ground, and around sunset, and the mosquitos, which on some islands are particularly present from November to March. You may want to **bring along a good repellent.**

Sunburn or sunstroke can be serious. A long-sleeve shirt, a hat, and long pants or a beach wrap are essential on a boat, for midday at the beach, and whenever you go out sightseeing. **Use sunblock lotion** on nose, ears, and other sensitive areas, **limit your sun time** for the first few days, and be sure to **drink enough liquids.**

Since health standards vary from island to island, inquire about local conditions before you go. No special shots are required for most Caribbean destinations; where they are, we have made note of it.

## MEDICAL PLANS

No one plans to get sick while traveling, but it happens, so **consider signing up with a medical-assistance company.** Members get doctor referrals, emergency evacuation or repatriation, 24-hour telephone hot lines for medical consultation, cash for emergencies, and other personal and legal assistance. Coverage varies by plan, so **review the benefits carefully.**

➤ MEDICAL-ASSISTANCE COMPANIES: **International SOS Assistance** (✉ Box 11568, Philadelphia, PA 19116, ☎ 215/244–1500 or 800/523–8930; ✉ Box 466, pl. Bonaventure, Montréal, Québec H5A 1C1, ☎ 514/874–7674 or 800/363–0263; ✉ 7 Old Lodge Pl., St. Margarets, Twickenham TW1 1RQ, England, ☎ 0181/744–0033). **MEDEX Assistance Corporation** (✉ Box 5375, Timonium, MD 21094, ☎ 410/453–6300 or 800/537–2029). **Traveler's Emergency Network** (✉ 3100 Tower Blvd., Suite 1000B, Durham, NC 27707, ☎ 919/490–6055 or 800/275–4836, FAX 919/493–8262). **TravMed** (✉ Box 5375, Timonium, MD 21094, ☎ 410/453–6380 or 800/732–5309). **Worldwide Assistance Services** (✉ 1133 15th St. NW, Suite 400, Washington, DC 20005, ☎ 202/331–1609 or 800/821–2828, FAX 202/828–5896).

## DIVERS' ALERT

**Do not fly within 24 hours of scuba diving.**

## INSURANCE

Travel insurance is the best way to **protect yourself against financial loss.** The most useful policies are trip-cancellation-and-interruption, default, medical, and comprehensive insurance.

Without insurance you will lose all or most of your money if you cancel your trip, regardless of the reason. It's essential that you **buy trip-cancellation-and-interruption insurance,** particularly if your airline ticket, cruise, or package tour is nonrefundable and cannot be changed. When considering how much coverage you need, look for a policy that will cover the cost of your trip plus the nondiscounted price of a one-way airline ticket, should you need to return home early. Also **consider default or bankruptcy insurance,** which protects you against a supplier's failure to deliver.

Medicare generally does not cover health-care costs outside the United States, nor do many privately issued policies. If your own policy does not cover you outside the United States, **consider buying supplemental medical coverage.** Remember that travel health insurance is different from a medical-assistance plan (☞ Health, *above*).

Citizens of the United Kingdom can buy an annual travel-insurance policy valid for most vacations during the year in which it's purchased. If you are pregnant or have a preexisting medical condition, make sure you're covered.

If you have purchased an expensive vacation, particularly one that involves travel abroad, comprehensive insurance is a must. **Look for comprehensive policies that include trip-delay insurance,** which will protect you in the event that weather problems cause you to miss your flight, tour, or cruise. A few insurers sell waivers for preexisting medical conditions. Companies that offer both features include Access America, Carefree Travel, Travel Insured International, and Travel Guard (☞ *below*).

Always **buy travel insurance directly from the insurance company;** if you buy it from a travel agency or tour operator that goes out of business you probably will not be covered for the agency or operator's default—a major risk. Before you make any purchase, **review your existing health and home-owner's policies** to find out whether they cover expenses incurred while traveling.

➤ TRAVEL INSURERS: In the United States, **Access America** (✉ 6600 W. Broad St., Richmond, VA 23230, ☎ 804/285–3300 or 800/284–8300), **Carefree Travel Insurance** (✉ Box 9366, 100 Garden City Plaza, Garden City, NY 11530, ☎ 516/294–0220 or 800/323–3149), **Near Travel Services** (✉ Box 1339, Calumet City, IL 60409, ☎ 708/868–6700 or 800/654–6700), **Travel Guard International** (✉ 1145 Clark St., Stevens Point, WI 54481, ☎ 715/345–0505 or 800/826–1300), **Travel Insured International** (✉ Box 280568, East Hartford, CT 06128-0568, ☎ 860/528–7663 or 800/243–3174), **Travelex Insurance Services** (✉ 11717 Burt St., Suite 202, Omaha, NE 68154-1500, ☎ 402/445–8637 or 800/228–9792, FAX 800/867–9531), **Wallach & Company** (✉ 107 W. Federal St., Box 480, Middleburg, VA 20118, ☎ 540/687–3166 or 800/237–6615). In Canada, **Mutual of Omaha** (✉ Travel Division, 500 University Ave., Toronto, Ontario M5G 1V8, ☎ 416/598–4083, 800/268–8825 in Canada). In the United Kingdom, **Association of British Insurers** (✉ 51 Gresham St., London EC2V 7HQ, ☎ 0171/600–3333).

# L

## LODGING

Plan ahead and **reserve a room well before you travel to the Caribbean.** If you have reservations but expect to arrive later than 5 or 6 PM, tell the management in advance. Unless so advised, some places will not hold your reservations after 6 PM. Also, be sure to **find out what the quoted rate includes**—use of sports facilities and equipment, airport transfers, and the like—and whether the property operates on the European Plan (EP, with no meals), Continental Plan (CP, with Continental breakfast), Breakfast Plan (BP, with full breakfast), Modified American Plan (MAP, with two meals), or Full American Plan (FAP, with three meals), or is all-inclusive (including three meals, all facilities, and drinks unless otherwise noted). Be sure to **bring your deposit receipt** with you in case questions arise.

Decide whether you want a hotel on the leeward side of the island (with calm water, good for snorkeling) or the windward (with waves, good for surfing). Decide, too, whether you want to pay the extra price for a room overlooking the ocean or pool. Also **find out how close the property is to a beach**; at some hotels you can walk barefoot from your room onto the sand; others are across a road or a 10-minute drive away.

Nighttime entertainment is alfresco in the Caribbean, so if you go to sleep early or are a light sleeper, ask for a room away from the dance floor.

Air-conditioning is not a necessity on all islands, most of which are cooled by trade winds, but it can be a plus if you enjoy an afternoon snooze. Breezes are best in second-floor rooms, particularly corner rooms. If you like to sleep without air-conditioning, make sure that windows can be opened and have screens.

In this book, we categorize properties by price. Prices are intended as a guideline only. Larger hotels with more extensive facilities cost more, but the Caribbean is full of smaller places with charm, individuality, and prices that make up for their lack of activities—which are generally available on a pay-per-use basis everywhere.

## APARTMENT & VILLA RENTALS

If you want a home base that's roomy enough for a family and comes with cooking facilities, **consider a furnished rental.** These can save you money, however some rentals are luxury properties, economical only when your party is large. Home-exchange directories list rentals (often second homes owned by prospective house swappers), and some services search for a house or apartment for you (even a castle if that's your fancy) and handle the paperwork. Some send an illustrated catalog; others send photographs only of specific properties, sometimes at a charge. Up-front registration fees may apply.

➤ RENTAL AGENTS: **At Home Abroad** (✉ 405 E. 56th St., Suite 6H, New York, NY 10022, ☎ 212/421–9165, FAX 212/752–1591). **Europa-Let/Tropical Inn-Let** (✉ 92 N. Main St., Ashland, OR 97520, ☎ 541/482–

5806 or 800/462–4486, FAX 541/482–0660). **Property Rentals International** (✉ 1008 Mansfield Crossing Rd., Richmond, VA 23236, ☎ 804/378–6054 or 800/220–3332, FAX 804/379–2073). **Rental Directories International** (✉ 2044 Rittenhouse Sq., Philadelphia, PA 19103, ☎ 215/985–4001, FAX 215/985–0323). **Rent-a-Home International** (✉ 7200 34th Ave. NW, Seattle, WA 98117, ☎ 206/789–9377 or 800/488–7368, FAX 206/789–9379). **Vacation Home Rentals Worldwide** (✉ 235 Kensington Ave., Norwood, NJ 07648, ☎ 201/767–9393 or 800/633–3284, FAX 201/767–5510). **Villas and Apartments Abroad** (✉ 420 Madison Ave., Suite 1003, New York, NY 10017, ☎ 212/759–1025 or 800/433–3020, FAX 212/755–8316). **Villas International** (✉ 605 Market St., Suite 510, San Francisco, CA 94105, ☎ 415/281–0910 or 800/221–2260, FAX 415/281–0919). **Hideaways International** (✉ 767 Islington St., Portsmouth, NH 03801, ☎ 603/430–4433 or 800/843–4433, FAX 603/430–4444) is a travel club whose members arrange rentals among themselves; yearly membership is $99.

## HOME EXCHANGES

If you would like to exchange your home for someone else's, **join a home-exchange organization,** which will send you its updated listings of available exchanges for a year and will include your own listing in at least one of them. Making the arrangements is up to you.

➤ EXCHANGE CLUBS: **HomeLink International** (✉ Box 650, Key West, FL 33041, ☎ 305/294–7766 or 800/638–3841, FAX 305/294–1148) charges $83 per year.

## M
### MONEY

## ATMS

Before leaving home, **make sure that your credit cards have been programmed for ATM use in the Caribbean.** Note that Discover is accepted mostly in the United States. Local bank cards often do not work overseas or may access only your checking account; **ask your bank about a MasterCard/Cirrus or Visa debit card,** which works like a bank

card but can be used at any ATM displaying a MasterCard/Cirrus or Visa logo. These cards, too, may tap only your checking account; check with your bank about their policy.

➤ ATM LOCATIONS: **Cirrus** (☎ 800/424–7787). A list of **Plus** locations is available at your local bank.

## CURRENCY EXCHANGE

For the most favorable rates, **change money at banks.** Although fees charged for ATM transactions may be higher abroad than at home, Cirrus and Plus exchange rates are excellent, because they are based on wholesale rates offered only by major banks. You won't do as well at exchange booths in airports or rail and bus stations, in hotels, in restaurants, or in stores, although you may find their hours more convenient. To avoid lines at airport exchange booths, **get a small amount of local currency before you leave home.**

➤ EXCHANGE SERVICES: **International Currency Express** (☎ 888/842–0880 on the East Coast or 888/278–6628 on the West Coast for telephone orders). **Thomas Cook Currency Services** (☎ 800/287–7362 for telephone orders and retail locations).

## TRAVELER'S CHECKS

Traveler's checks are widely accepted throughout the Caribbean. If your checks are lost or stolen, they can usually be replaced within 24 hours. To ensure a speedy refund, buy your checks yourself (don't ask someone else to make the purchase). When making a claim for stolen or lost checks, the person who bought the checks should make the call.

## P
### PACKING FOR THE CARIBBEAN

Dress on the islands is light and casual. Bring loose-fitting clothes made of natural fabrics to see you through days of heat and humidity. Take a cover-up for the beaches, not only to protect you from the sun but also to wear to and from your hotel room. Bathing suits and immodest attire are frowned upon off the beach on many islands. A sun hat is advisable, but you don't have to pack one—inexpensive straw hats are available everywhere. For shopping and sightseeing, bring walking shorts, jeans, T-shirts, long-sleeve cotton shirts, slacks, and sundresses. You'll need a light sweater for protection from the trade winds, and at higher altitudes. Evenings are casual, but "casual" can range from really informal to casually elegant, depending on the establishment. A tie is rarely required, but jackets are sometimes de rigueur in fancier restaurants and casinos.

Bring an extra pair of eyeglasses or contact lenses in your carry-on luggage, and if you have a health problem, **pack enough medication** to last the entire trip or have your doctor write you a prescription using the drug's generic name, because brand names vary from country to country. It's important that you **don't put prescription drugs or valuables in luggage to be checked**: It might go astray. To avoid problems with customs officials, carry medications in the original packaging. Also, don't forget the addresses of offices that handle refunds of lost traveler's checks.

### LUGGAGE

In general, you are entitled to check two bags on flights within the United States and on international flights leaving the United States. A third piece may be brought on board, but it must fit easily under the seat in front of you or in the overhead compartment.

If you are flying between two foreign destinations, note that baggage allowances may be determined not by piece but by weight—generally 88 pounds (40 kilograms) in first class, 66 pounds (30 kilograms) in business class, and 44 pounds (20 kilograms) in economy. If your flight between two cities abroad *connects* with your transatlantic or transpacific flight, the piece method still applies.

Airline liability for baggage is limited to $1,250 per person on flights within the United States. On international flights it amounts to $9.07 per pound or $20 per kilogram for checked baggage (roughly $640 per 70-pound bag) and $400 per passenger for unchecked baggage. Insurance for losses exceeding these amounts can be bought from the airline at check-in for about $10 per $1,000 of coverage; note that this coverage excludes a rather extensive list of items, which is shown on your airline ticket.

Before departure, **itemize your bags' contents** and their worth, and label the bags with your name, address, and phone number. (If you use your home address, cover it so that potential thieves can't see it readily.) Inside each bag, **pack a copy of your itinerary.** At check-in, **make sure that each bag is correctly tagged** with the destination airport's three-letter code. If your bags arrive damaged or fail to arrive at all, file a written report with the airline before leaving the airport.

### PASSPORTS & VISAS

Once your travel plans are confirmed, **get a passport even if you don't need one to enter the country you're visiting**—it's always the best form of ID. It's also a good idea to **make photocopies of the data page**; leave one copy with someone at home and keep another with you, separated from your passport. If you lose your passport, promptly call the nearest embassy or consulate and the local police; having a copy of the data page can speed replacement.

*See* individual island chapters for specific requirements.

### U.S. CITIZENS

➤ INFORMATION: **Office of Passport Services** (☎ 202/647–0518).

### CANADIANS

➤ INFORMATION: **Passport Office** (☎ 819/994–3500 or 800/567–6868).

### U.K. CITIZENS

Some islands require passports; others do not but may require a British Visitor's Passport.

➤ INFORMATION: **London Passport Office** (☎ 0990/21010) for fees and documentation requirements and to request an emergency passport.

### S

### SENIOR-CITIZEN TRAVEL

To qualify for age-related discounts, **mention your senior-citizen status up front** when booking hotel reservations (not when checking out) and before you're seated in restaurants (not when paying the bill). Note that discounts may be limited to certain menus, days, or hours. When renting a car, **ask about promotional car-rental discounts,** which can be cheaper than senior-citizen rates.

➤ EDUCATIONAL TRAVEL PROGRAMS: **Elderhostel** (✉ 75 Federal St., 3rd floor, Boston, MA 02110, ☎ 617/426–7788).

### STUDENTS

The Caribbean is not as far out of a student's budget as you might expect. All but the toniest islands, such as St. Barthélemy, have camping facilities, inexpensive guest houses, or small no-frills hotels. You're most likely to meet students from other countries in the French and Dutch West Indies, where many go on holiday or sabbatical. Puerto Rico, Jamaica, Grenada, and Dominica, among others, have large resident international student populations at their universities.

To save money, **look into deals available through student-oriented travel agencies.** To qualify you'll need a bona fide student ID card. Members of international student groups are also eligible.

➤ STUDENT IDS AND SERVICES: **Council on International Educational Exchange** (✉ CIEE, 205 E. 42nd St., 14th floor, New York, NY 10017, ☎ 212/822–2600 or 888/268–6245, FAX 212/822–2699), for mail orders only, in the United States. **Travel Cuts** (✉ 187 College St., Toronto, Ontario M5T 1P7, ☎ 416/979–2406 or 800/667–2887) in Canada.

➤ HOSTELING: **Hostelling International—American Youth Hostels** (✉ 733 15th St. NW, Suite 840, Washington, DC 20005, ☎ 202/783–6161, FAX 202/783–6171). **Hostelling International—Canada** (✉ 400-205 Catherine St., Ottawa, Ontario K2P 1C3, ☎ 613/237–7884, FAX 613/237–7868). **Youth Hostel Association of England and Wales** (✉ Trevelyan House, 8 St. Stephen's Hill, St. Albans, Hertfordshire AL1 2DY, ☎ 01727/855215 or 01727/845047, FAX 01727/844126. Membership in the United States, $25; in Canada, C$26.75; in the United Kingdom, £9.30.

## T
### TELEPHONES

### CALLING HOME

Before you go, **find out the local access codes** for your destinations. AT&T, MCI, and Sprint long-distance services make calling home relatively convenient, but you may find the local access number blocked in many hotel rooms. First ask the hotel operator to connect you. If the hotel operator balks, ask for an international operator, or dial the international operator yourself. One way to improve your odds of getting connected to your long-distance carrier is to travel with more than one company's calling card (a hotel may block Sprint, for example, but not MCI). If all else fails, call your phone company collect in the United States or call from a pay phone in the hotel lobby.

➤ TO OBTAIN ACCESS CODES: **AT&T USADirect** (☎ 800/874–4000). **MCI Call USA** (☎ 800/444–4444). **Sprint Express** (☎ 800/793–1153).

### TOUR OPERATORS

Buying a prepackaged tour or independent vacation can make your trip to the Caribbean less expensive and more hassle-free. Because everything is prearranged you'll spend less time planning.

Operators that handle several hundred thousand travelers per year can use their purchasing power to give you a good price. Their high volume may also indicate financial stability. But some small companies provide more personalized service; because they tend to specialize, they may also be more knowledgeable about a given area.

### A GOOD DEAL?

The more your package or tour includes, the better you can predict the ultimate cost of your vacation. Make sure you know exactly what is covered, and **beware of hidden costs.** Are taxes, tips, and service charges included? Transfers and baggage handling? Entertainment and excursions? These can add up.

If the package or tour you are considering is priced lower than in your wildest dreams, **be skeptical.** Also, **make sure your travel agent knows** the accommodations and other services. Ask about the hotel's location, room size, beds, and whether it has a pool, room service, or programs for children, if you care about these. Has your agent been there in person or sent others you can contact?

## BUYER BEWARE

Each year consumers are stranded or lose their money when tour operators—even very large ones with excellent reputations—go out of business. So **check out the operator.** Find out how long the company has been in business, and ask several agents about its reputation. **Don't book unless the firm has a consumer-protection program.**

Members of the National Tour Association and United States Tour Operators Association are required to set aside funds to cover your payments and travel arrangements in case the company defaults. Nonmembers may carry insurance instead. Look for the details, and for the name of an underwriter with a solid reputation, in the operator's brochure. Note: When it comes to tour operators, **don't trust escrow accounts.** Although there are laws governing charter-flight operators, no governmental body prevents tour operators from raiding the till. For more information, *see* Consumer Protection, *above*.

➤ TOUR-OPERATOR RECOMMENDATIONS: **National Tour Association** (✉ NTA, 546 E. Main St., Lexington, KY 40508, ☎ 606/226–4444 or 800/755–8687). **United States Tour Operators Association** (✉ USTOA, 342 Madison Ave., Suite 1522, New York, NY 10173, ☎ 212/599–6599, FAX 212/599–6744).

## USING AN AGENT

Travel agents are excellent resources. When shopping for an agent, however, you should **collect brochures from several sources**; some agents' suggestions may be skewed by promotional relationships with tour and package firms that reward them for volume sales. If you have a special interest, **find an agent with expertise in that area** (☞ Travel Agencies, *below*). Don't rely solely on your agent, who may be unaware of small-niche operators. Note that some special-interest travel companies only

sell directly to the public and that some large operators only accept bookings made through travel agents.

## SINGLE TRAVELERS

Prices for packages and tours are usually quoted per person, based on two sharing a room. If traveling solo, you may be required to pay the full double-occupancy rate. Some operators eliminate this surcharge if you agree to be matched with a roommate of the same sex, even if one is not found by departure time.

## GROUP TOURS

Among companies that sell tours to the Caribbean, the following are nationally known, have a proven reputation, and offer plenty of options. The classifications used below represent different price categories, and you'll probably encounter these terms when talking to a travel agent or tour operator. The key difference is usually in accommodations, which run from budget to better, and better-yet to best.

➤ DELUXE: **Globus** (✉ 5301 S. Federal Circle, Littleton, CO 80123-2980, ☎ 303/797–2800 or 800/221–0090, FAX 303/347–2080).

## PACKAGES

Like group tours, independent vacation packages are available from major tour operators and airlines. The companies listed below offer vacation packages in a broad price range.

➤ AIR/HOTEL: **American Airlines Fly AAway Vacations** (☎ 800/321–2121). **Cayman Airtours** (☎ 800/247–2966). **Certified Vacations** (✉ 110 E. Broward Blvd., Fort Lauderdale, FL 33302, ☎ 954/522–1440 or 800/233–7260). **Continental Vacations** (☎ 800/634–5555). **Delta Dream Vacations** (☎ 800/872–7786, FAX 954/357–4687). **US Airways Vacations** (☎ 800/455–0123). Puerto Rico only: **TWA Getaway Vacations** (☎ 800/438–2929). **United Vacations** (☎ 800/328–6877).

➤ FROM THE U.K.: **Caribbean Connection** (✉ Concorde House, Forest St., Chester CH1 1QR, ☎ 01244/341–131). **Caribtours** (✉ 161 Fulham Rd., London SW3 6SN, ☎ 0171/581–3517). **Kuoni Travel** (✉ Kuoni House, Dorking, Surrey RH5

4AZ, ☎ 01306/742–222). **Hayes and Jarvis** (✉ Hayes House, 152 King St., London W6 0QU, ☎ 0181/748–5050).

## THEME TRIPS

➤ ADVENTURE: **American Wilderness Experience** (✉ 2820-A Wilderness Pl., Boulder, CO 80301-5454, ☎ 303/444–2622 or 800/444–0099, FAX 303/444–3999).

➤ GOLF: **Stine's Golftrips** (✉ Box 2314, Winter Haven, FL 33883-2314, ☎ 813/324–1300 or 800/428–1940, FAX 941/325–0384).

➤ LEARNING: **Earthwatch** (✉ Box 9104, 680 Mount Auburn St., Watertown, MA 02272, ☎ 617/926–8200 or 800/776–0188, FAX 617/926–8532) for research expeditions. **National Audobon Society** (✉ 700 Broadway, New York, NY 10003, ☎ 212/979–3066, FAX 212/353–0190). **Natural Habitat Adventures** (✉ 2945 Center Green Ct., Boulder, CO 80301, ☎ 303/449–3711 or 800/543–8917, FAX 303/449–3712). **Oceanic Society Expeditions** (✉ Fort Mason Center, Bldg. E, San Francisco, CA 94123-1394, ☎ 415/441–1106 or 800/326–7491, FAX 415/474–3395). **Smithsonian Study Tours and Seminars** (✉ 1100 Jefferson Dr. SW, Room 3045, MRC 702, Washington, DC 20560, ☎ 202/357–4700, FAX 202/633–9250).

➤ SAILING SCHOOLS: **Annapolis Sailing School** (✉ Box 3334, 601 6th St., Annapolis, MD 21403, ☎ 410/267–7205 or 800/638–9192). **Offshore Sailing School** (✉ 16731-110 McGregor Blvd., Fort Meyers, FL 33908, ☎ 941/454–1700 or 800/221–4326, FAX 941/454–1191).

➤ SPAS: **Spa-Finders** (✉ 91 5th Ave., #301, New York, NY 10003-3039, ☎ 212/924–6800 or 800/255–7727).

➤ SCUBA DIVING: **Rothschild Dive Safaris** (✉ 900 West End Ave., #1B, New York, NY 10025-3525, ☎ 800/359–0747, FAX 212/749–6172). **Tropical Adventures** (✉ 111 2nd Ave. N, Seattle, WA 98109, ☎ 206/441–3483 or 800/247–3483, FAX 206/441–5431). **See & Sea Travel** (✉ 50 Francisco St., #205, San Francisco, CA 94133, ☎ 415/434–3400 or 800/348–9778, FAX 415/434–3409).

➤ VILLA RENTALS: **Unusual Villas & Island Rentals** (✉ 101 Tempsford La., Penthouse 9, Richmond, VA 23226, ☎ FAX 804/288–2823). **Villas International** (✉ 605 Market St., San Francisco, CA 94105, ☎ 415/281–0910 or 800/221–2260, FAX 415/281–0919).

➤ YACHT CHARTERS: **Alden Yacht Charters** (✉ 1909 Alden Landing, Portsmouth, RI 02871, ☎ 401/683–1782 or 800/662–2628, FAX 401/683–3668). **Cat Ppalu Cruises** (✉ Box 661091, Miami, FL 33266, ☎ 305/888–1226 or 800/327–9600, FAX 305/884–4214). **Huntley Yacht Vacations** (✉ 210 Preston Rd., Wernersville, PA 19565, ☎ 610/678–2628 or 800/322–9224, FAX 610/670–1767). **Lynn Jachney Charters** (✉ Box 302, Marblehead, MA 01945, ☎ 617/639–0787 or 800/223–2050, FAX 617/639–0216). **The Moorings** (✉ 19345 U.S. Hwy. 19 N, 4th floor, Clearwater, FL 34624-3193, ☎ 813/530–5424 or 800/535–7289, FAX 813/530–9474). **Nicholson Yacht Charters** (✉ 78 Bolton St., Cambridge, MA 02140-3321, ☎ 617/661–0555 or 800/662–6066, FAX 617/661–0554). **Ocean Voyages** (✉ 1709 Bridgeway, Sausalito, CA 94965, ☎ 415/332–4681 or 800/299–4444, FAX 415/332–7460). **Russell Yacht Charters** (✉ 404 Hulls Hwy., #175, Southport, CT 06490, ☎ 203/255–2783 or 800/635–8895). **SailAway Yacht Charters** (✉ 15605 S.W. 92nd Ave., Miami, FL 33157-1972, ☎ 305/253–7245 or 800/724–5292, FAX 305/251–4408).

## TRAVEL AGENCIES

A good travel agent puts your needs first. **Look for an agency that specializes in your destination, has been in business at least five years, and emphasizes customer service.** If you're looking for an agency-organized package or tour, your best bet is to choose an agency that's a member of the National Tour Association or the United States Tour Operator's Association (☞ Tour Operators, *above*).

➤ LOCAL AGENT REFERRALS: Ameri-can Society of Travel Agents (✉ ASTA, 1101 King St., Suite 200, Alexandria, VA 22314, ☎ 703/739–2782, FAX 703/684–8319). **Alliance of Canadian Travel Associations** (✉ 1729 Bank St., Suite 201, Ottawa,

THE GOLD GUIDE / SMART TRAVEL TIPS

Ontario K1V 7Z5, ☎ 613/521–0474, FAX 613/521–0805). **Association of British Travel Agents** (⊠ 55–57 Newman St., London W1P 4AH, ☎ 0171/637–2444, FAX 0171/637–0713).

### TRAVEL GEAR

Travel catalogs specialize in useful items, such as compact alarm clocks and travel irons, that can **save space when packing.** They also offer dual-voltage appliances, currency converters, and foreign-language phrase books.

➤ MAIL-ORDER CATALOGS: **Magellan's** (☎ 800/962–4943, FAX 805/568–5406). **Orvis Travel** (☎ 800/541–3541, FAX 540/343–7053). **TravelSmith** (☎ 800/950–1600, FAX 800/950–1656).

## U
### U.S. GOVERNMENT

The U.S. government can be an excellent source of inexpensive travel information. When planning your trip, **find out what government materials are available.**

➤ ADVISORIES: **U.S. Department of State American Citizens Services Office** (⊠ Room 4811, Washington, DC 20520); enclose a self-addresses, stamped envelope. **Interactive hot line** (☎ 202/647–5225, FAX 202/647–3000). **Computer bulletin board** (☎ 202/647–9225).

➤ PAMPHLETS: **Consumer Information Center** (⊠ Consumer Information Catalogue, Pueblo, CO 81009, ☎ 719/948–3334) for a free catalog that includes travel titles.

## V
### VISITOR INFORMATION

Almost all islands have a U.S.–based tourist board, listed with its name and address in the A to Z section of each island chapter; they can be good sources of general information, up-to-date calendars of events, and listings of hotels, restaurants, sights, and shops. The Caribbean Tourism Organization is another resource, especially for information on the islands that have very limited representation in the United States. There is no all-Caribbean tourist organization in the United Kingdom, but check the phone book for individual island tourist offices.

➤ CARIBBEAN-WIDE INFORMATION: **Caribbean Tourism Organization** (⊠ 20 E. 46th St., New York, NY 10017-2452, ☎ 212/682–0435, FAX 212/697–4258; ⊠ Vigilant House, 120 Wilton Rd., London SW1V 1JZ, England, ☎ 0171/233–8382).

## W
### WHEN TO GO

The Caribbean high season has traditionally been winter, usually extending from December 15 to April 14. This is when northern weather is at its worst, not necessarily when Caribbean weather is at its best. In fact, winter is when the Caribbean is at its windiest. It's also the most fashionable, the most expensive, and the most popular time to visit, and most hotels are heavily booked. You have to make your reservations at least two or three months in advance for the very best places (and sometimes a year in advance for the most exclusive spots). Hotel prices drop 20%–50% for summer (after April 15); cruise prices also fall. Saving money isn't the only reason to visit the Caribbean during the off-season. Temperatures are only a few degrees warmer, and more and more hotels and restaurants are staying open year-round, so things aren't as dead-quiet as they used to be. September, October, and November are least crowded, but hotel facilities can be limited and some restaurants may be closed. Singles in search of partners should visit in high season or in summer, or choose a resort with a high year-round occupancy rate.

The flamboyant flowering trees are at their height in summer and so are most of the flowers and shrubs of the West Indies. The water is clearer for snorkeling, and smoother for sailing in the Virgin Islands and the Grenadines, in May, June, and July. Generally speaking, there's more planned entertainment in winter. The peak of local excitement on many islands, most notably Trinidad, St. Vincent, and the French West Indies, is Carnival.

### CLIMATE

The Caribbean climate is fairly constant. Average year-round temperature for the region is 78°F–85°F. The extremes of temperature are 65°F low, 95°F high, but as everyone knows, it's the humidity, not the heat, that makes you suffer, especially when the two go hand in hand. You can count on downtown shopping areas being hot at midday any time of the year, but air-conditioning provides some respite. Stay near beaches, where water and trade winds can keep you cool, and shop early or late in the day.

As part of the fall's rainy season, hurricanes occasionally sweep through the Caribbean. Check the news daily, and keep abreast of brewing tropical storms by reading Stateside papers if you can get them. The rainy season consists mostly of brief showers interspersed with sunshine. You can watch the clouds come over, feel the rain, and remain on your lounge chair for the sun to dry you off. A spell of overcast days is "unusual," as everyone will tell you.

High places can be cool, particularly when the Christmas winds hit Caribbean peaks (they come in late November and last through January). Since most Caribbean islands are mountainous (notable exceptions being the Caymans, Aruba, Bonaire, and Curaçao), the altitude always offers an escape from the latitude. Kingston (Jamaica), Port-of-Spain (Trinidad), and Fort-de-France (Martinique) swelter in summer; climb 1,000 ft or so and everything is fine.

➤ FORECASTS: **Weather Channel Connection** (☎ 900/932–8437), 95¢ per minute from a Touch-Tone phone.

# 1 Destination: Caribbean

# THE MANY FACES OF THE ISLANDS

F YOU HAVE SEEN ONE ISLAND you have by no means seen them all. Tiny 5-square-mi Saba has less in common with the vast 19,000-square-mi Dominican Republic than Butte, Montana, has with Biloxi, Mississippi. Butte and Biloxi, however different in terrain and traits, sit in the same country and the citizenry speak more or less the same language. Saba, which is Dutch, and the Dominican Republic, whose roots are in Spain, simply sit in the same sea.

The Caribbean has towering volcanic islands, such as Saba; islands with lush rain forests, such as Dominica and Guadeloupe; and some islands, notably Puerto Rico, that have both rain forests and deserts. Glittering discos, casinos, and dazzling nightlife can be found on such islands as Aruba and the Dominican Republic, and throughout the region there are isolated cays with only sand, sea, sun, lizards, and mosquitoes. Some islands, Puerto Rico and St. Kitts among them, have ancient forts to view, while Barbados, Puerto Rico, and the Caicos Islands have caverns and caves to explore. There are also places like Grand Turk, where the only notable sights to see are beneath the translucent sea.

Different though they are in many ways, the islands are stylistically similar. The style setter is the tropical climate. Year-round summertime temperatures and a plethora of beaches produce a pace that's known as "island time." Only the trade winds move swiftly. Operating on island time means, "I'll get to it when the spirit moves me."

Similarities are also attributable to the history of the region. The Arawaks paddled up from South America and populated the islands more than 1,000 years ago. In the early 14th century, the cannibalistic Caribs, who gave the area its name, arrived, probably from Brazil or Venezuela, then polished off the peaceful Arawaks and managed, for a time at least, to scare the living daylights out of the Europeans who sailed through in search of gold. (The original name of the Caribs was Galibi, a word the Spanish corrupted to *Canibal*—the origin of the word "cannibal.") Christopher Columbus made four voyages through the region between 1492 and 1504, christening the islands while dodging the Carib arrows. He landed on or sailed past all of the Greater Antilles and virtually all of the eastern Caribbean islands.

From the 16th century until the early 19th century, the Dutch, Danes, Swedes, English, French, Irish, and Spanish fought bitterly for control of the islands. Some islands have almost as many battle sites as sand flies. Having gained control of the islands and annihilated the Caribs, the Europeans established vast sugar plantations and brought in Africans to work the fields. With the abolition of slavery in the mid-19th century, Asians were imported as indentured laborers. Today, the Caribbean population is a rich gumbo of nationalities, including Americans and Canadians who have retired to and invested in the islands.

It must be remembered that the Caribbean, like the European continent, is made up of individual countries, each with customs, immigration officials, and, in some instances, political difficulties. Most of the islands have opted for independence; others retain their ties to the mother country. They are developing nations, and many have severe economic and unemployment problems.

Virtually all of the islands depend upon tourism. And, human nature being what it is, many islanders resent their dependency on tourist dollars. Like as not, the person who serves you has stood in a long line, vying with other anxious applicants for the few available jobs. After serving your meals and cleaning your luxurious room, he or she returns to a tiny shack knowing full well that in less than a week you will have shelled out more than an islander makes in a month.

Some visitors object to encountering resentment, when all they seek is a pleasant vacation and they've paid dearly for it. Some feel rather keenly that they'd always like hot water—or at least *some* water—when they turn on the shower; in even the most luxurious resorts there are times when things simply don't work, and that's a fact of Caribbean life. And other visitors simply have no patience with island time.

On the other hand, there are those who travel to the Caribbean year after year. Some return to the same hotel on the same beach on the same island, while the more adventurous try to sample as much as this smorgasbord has to offer.

# NEW AND NOTEWORTHY

A decade ago some Caribbean islands put more emphasis on tourism than others did. St. Maarten and the Virgin Islands actively sought tourists, while St. Lucia relied on its banana crop and Guadeloupe on its sugarcane for revenue. Now, however, the scramble for tourists and the dollars they bring is fast becoming the primary focus of all the Caribbean islands.

Although the competition for tourists hasn't led to lower prices—in fact, some governments have been increasing tourist taxes to pay for advertising—it has created more travel options. New hotels open all the time, old hotels are renovated, and ways to get to and from the islands are multiplying.

Airline service to and from the Caribbean is expanding. **American Airlines** now covers most of the islands with either direct flights from the mainland or with connecting flights through San Juan on its subsidiary, American Eagle. **ALM,** the Antillean airline, is also becoming a major carrier to many of the islands, with departures from Atlanta and Miami as well as interisland flights. Renovations of Trinidad's **Piarco Airport** have been completed, and Tobago has started direct air service from the United States via **BWIA** and **American Airlines.** Nevis's **Newcastle Airport** is receiving an $18 million overhaul, slated for completion in early 1998, to increase air traffic and make it accessible to jet service. Plans are also afoot to expand the runways and modernize the buildings at the **St. Kitts airport,** in hopes of attracting more airlines.

They are also investing $20 million in deepening its harbor and expanding its pier and marina. **Dominica's cruise-ship dock** is new, making the island it twice as accessible to travelers.

In the natural-disaster department, this year has been rather interesting. Traditionally, September through November is spent trying to dodge the continual **hurricanes** that swirl around the islands. The 1996–97 season hit mainly Puerto Rico, St. Thomas, and St. John and grazed a few others. Those that were spared used the opportunity to reconstruct some of the damage done from when they got hit the year before. Meanwhile, after centuries of lying dormant, Montserrat's **volcano** erupted, killing nine people, injuring others, and devastating a large part of the island. Emergency aid from Britain has been allocated and as of press time the island has not been evacuated.

But the islands persevere. In fact, in St. Thomas's Charlotte Amalie harbor, 50 acres of quiet, quaint **Water Island** transferred ownership from the Department of the Interior to the territorial government in December 1996. This makes Water Island the fourth largest and newest Virgin Island, behind siblings St. Croix, St. Thomas, and St. John. Re-establishment of a hotel is planned as are concessions for Honeymoon Beach. Water Island was the site of the U.S. Army's Fort Segarra back in the 1940s.

Chances are that you or someone you love has received a new area code recently. All over the world, as telecommunications booms, telephone companies have had to come up with creative ways of accommodating the ever-increasing need for **new telephone numbers.** It's even reached the islands of the Caribbean. This year a handful of islands, including Grenada, Jamaica, Anguilla, and Aruba, changed their area codes. For still other islands, new area codes will go into effect at various times throughout the life of this book. We give the original code because it's the most efficient way for you to connect with your party. As new codes become operational, for a certain period of time if you dial the old area code a recording will indicate the new number and then connect you. See Telephones and Mail in the A to Z section that ends each island's chapter for the latest information.

## Island Finder

| Island | Cost of Island | Number of rooms* | Nonstop flights | Cruise ship port | U.S. dollars accepted | Historic sites | Natural beauty | Lush | Arid | Mountainous | Rain forest | Beautiful beaches | Good roads | |
|---|---|---|---|---|---|---|---|---|---|---|---|---|---|---|
| Anguilla | $$$ | 978 | | | • | | | | • | | | • | | |
| Antigua & Barbuda | $$$$ | 3,317 | • | • | • | • | • | | • | | | • | • | |
| Aruba | $$ | 6,150 | • | • | • | | • | | • | | | • | • | |
| Barbados | $$ | 6,000 | • | • | • | • | • | | | | | • | • | |
| Bonaire | $$ | 803 | • | | • | | | | | | | | • | |
| British Virgin Islands | $$$ | 1,224 | | • | • | | • | • | | • | • | • | | |
| Cayman Islands | $$$$ | 3,453 | • | • | • | | | | • | | | • | • | |
| Curaçao | $$ | 2,200 | • | • | • | | | | | | | | • | |
| Dominica | $ | 757 | | | • | | • | • | | • | • | | | |
| Dominican Republic | $ | 28,000 | • | | | • | • | • | | • | • | | | |
| The Grenadines | $ | 500 | | | | | | | | • | | • | | |
| Grenada | $$$ | 1,652 | | • | • | • | • | • | | • | • | • | | |
| Guadeloupe | $$ | 7,798 | | • | | | • | • | | • | • | | • | |
| Jamaica | $$$ | 18,935 | • | • | • | | • | • | | • | | • | • | |
| Martinique | $$$ | 6,960 | • | • | | | • | • | | • | • | | • | |
| Montserrat | $$ | 710 | | • | • | | • | • | | • | | | | |
| Nevis | $$$ | 400 | | | • | • | • | • | | • | | • | | |
| Puerto Rico | $ | 10,363 | • | • | • | • | • | • | • | • | • | • | • | |
| Saba | $ | 96 | | • | | | • | | | • | | | • | |
| St. Barthélemy | $$$$ | 715 | | • | • | | • | | | • | | • | • | |
| St. Eustatius | $ | 95 | | • | | • | | | | • | • | | | |
| St. Kitts | $$ | 1,200 | | • | • | | • | • | | • | • | • | | |
| St. Lucia | $$ | 2,919 | • | • | • | • | • | • | | • | | | | |
| St. Martin/St. Maarten | $$$ | 5,638 | • | • | • | | | • | | • | | • | • | |
| St. Vincent | $$ | 730 | | • | • | • | • | • | | • | • | | | |
| Trinidad | $ | 1,462 | • | | | | | | | | • | | | |
| Tobago | $$ | 1,500 | • | | | | | | | • | • | • | | |
| Turks and Caicos | $$$ | 1,300 | • | | • | | | | • | | | • | | |
| **U.S. Virgin Islands:** | | | | | | | | | | | | | | |
| St. Croix | $$ | 1,104 | | • | • | • | • | • | | • | • | | • | |
| St. John | $$ | 713 | | • | • | • | • | • | | • | | • | • | |
| St. Thomas | $$ | 3,217 | • | • | • | | | | | • | | • | • | |

* Figures based on 1996 estimates

| Public transportation | Fine dining | Local cuisine | Shopping | Music | Casinos | Nightlife | Diving and Snorkeling | Sailing | Golfing | Hiking | Ecotourism | Villa rentals | All-inclusives | Campgrounds | Luxury resorts | Secluded getaway | Good for families | Romantic hideaway |
|---|---|---|---|---|---|---|---|---|---|---|---|---|---|---|---|---|---|---|
|  | ● | ● | ● | ● |  |  | ● |  |  |  |  | ● | ● |  | ● | ● |  | ● |
| ● | ● | ● | ● |  | ● | ● | ● | ● | ● |  |  |  | ● |  | ● |  | ● |  |
| ● | ● | ● | ● | ● | ● | ● | ● | ● | ● | ● |  |  | ● |  | ● |  | ● | ● |
| ● | ● | ● | ● | ● |  | ● | ● |  | ● | ● |  | ● | ● |  | ● |  | ● |  |
|  |  |  |  |  | ● |  | ● | ● |  | ● | ● |  |  |  | ● |  |  |  |
| ● | ● | ● | ● | ● |  | ● | ● | ● | ● | ● | ● | ● | ● |  | ● | ● | ● | ● |
|  | ● |  | ● |  |  | ● | ● |  | ● |  | ● | ● | ● |  | ● |  | ● |  |
| ● | ● | ● | ● |  | ● | ● | ● | ● |  | ● |  |  |  |  |  |  | ● |  |
| ● |  | ● |  |  |  |  | ● |  |  | ● | ● | ● |  |  |  | ● |  | ● |
| ● |  | ● |  |  | ● | ● | ● | ● | ● | ● |  | ● | ● |  | ● | ● |  | ● |
|  |  | ● |  |  |  |  | ● | ● |  | ● | ● | ● |  |  | ● | ● | ● | ● |
| ● | ● | ● | ● | ● |  | ● | ● | ● | ● | ● | ● |  | ● |  | ● | ● |  | ● |
| ● | ● | ● | ● | ● |  | ● | ● | ● | ● | ● | ● |  | ● | ● | ● |  |  |  |
| ● | ● | ● | ● | ● | ● | ● | ● | ● | ● | ● | ● | ● | ● |  | ● |  | ● | ● |
| ● | ● | ● |  |  |  | ● | ● | ● | ● | ● |  | ● |  | ● |  |  |  |  |
| ● | ● | ● |  |  |  | ● | ● | ● | ● | ● | ● |  |  |  |  |  | ● |  |
|  | ● |  |  | ● |  |  | ● |  |  |  |  |  |  |  | ● | ● |  | ● |
| ● | ● | ● | ● | ● | ● | ● | ● | ● | ● | ● | ● | ● | ● | ● | ● | ● | ● | ● |
|  |  | ● |  |  |  |  | ● |  |  | ● | ● | ● |  |  | ● | ● |  | ● |
|  | ● | ● | ● |  |  | ● | ● |  |  | ● |  | ● |  |  | ● | ● |  | ● |
|  |  | ● |  |  |  |  | ● |  |  | ● | ● |  |  |  |  | ● |  |  |
|  | ● | ● |  | ● |  | ● | ● | ● | ● | ● |  |  | ● |  | ● |  |  |  |
| ● | ● | ● | ● | ● |  | ● | ● | ● | ● | ● | ● | ● |  |  | ● |  | ● | ● |
| ● | ● | ● | ● |  |  | ● | ● | ● |  | ● |  | ● | ● |  | ● |  | ● | ● |
| ● |  | ● |  | ● |  | ● | ● | ● |  | ● | ● |  |  |  | ● |  | ● |  |
| ● |  | ● |  | ● |  | ● | ● |  | ● |  |  |  |  |  | ● |  | ● |  |
|  |  | ● |  | ● |  |  |  |  | ● |  |  |  |  |  |  | ● |  |  |
|  |  |  |  |  | ● |  | ● |  |  | ● | ● |  | ● |  | ● |  |  | ● |
|  |  |  |  |  |  |  |  |  |  |  |  |  |  |  |  |  |  |  |
|  | ● | ● | ● | ● |  | ● | ● | ● | ● | ● | ● | ● |  |  | ● |  | ● |  |
|  | ● | ● | ● |  |  | ● |  | ● |  | ● | ● | ● | ● | ● | ● | ● | ● | ● |
| ● | ● | ● | ● |  |  | ● | ● | ● | ● |  |  |  | ● | ● | ● |  | ● |  |

# WHAT'S WHERE

## Finding Your Own Place in the Sun

The Caribbean Sea, an area of more than a million square miles, stretches south of Florida down to the coast of Venezuela. In the northern Caribbean are the **Greater Antilles**—the islands closest to the United States—composed of Cuba, Jamaica, Haiti, the Dominican Republic, and Puerto Rico. (Haiti and Cuba are not included in this book.) The **Cayman Islands** lie south of Cuba. The **Lesser Antilles**—greater in number but smaller in size than the Greater Antilles—are divided into three groups: the **Leewards** and the **Windwards** in the eastern Caribbean, and the islands in the **southern Caribbean.** The eastern Caribbean islands, from the Virgin Islands in the north all the way south to Grenada, form an arc between the Atlantic Ocean and the Caribbean Sea. Islands in the Leeward chain in order of appearance are the U.S. and British Virgin Islands, Anguilla, St. Martin/St. Maarten, St. Barthélemy, Saba, St. Eustatius, St. Kitts, Nevis, Barbuda, Antigua, Montserrat, and Guadeloupe; the Windwards are composed of Dominica, Martinique, St. Lucia, St. Vincent and the Grenadines, and Grenada. Barbados is just east of this group. In the southern Caribbean, off the coast of Venezuela, Trinidad and Tobago are anchored in the east, while Aruba, Bonaire, and Curaçao (known as the ABC Islands) bathe in the western waters. The **Turks and Caicos Islands,** which lie in the Atlantic Ocean between Florida and the north coast of Hispaniola (Haiti and the Dominican Republic), are part of the Bahamas but are included in this book because of their proximity to and affinity with the Caribbean islands.

# PLEASURES AND PASTIMES

Here are some suggestions on where to go for some of the Caribbean's major pleasures. Consult the Island Finder chart on the following pages to help you choose your destination.

## Boating and Sailing

Whether you charter a yacht with crew or captain a boat yourself, the waters of the Caribbean are excellent for sailing, and the many secluded bays and inlets provide ideal spots to drop anchor and picnic or explore. The marinas on Tortola in the **British Virgin Islands,** at Secret Harbour in **Grenada,** throughout **St. Vincent and the Grenadines,** St. Thomas in the **U.S. Virgin Islands,** and Port la Royale and Oyster Pond in **St. Martin** are the starting points for some of the Caribbean's finest sailing. Yachtspeople also favor the waters around **Antigua** and put in regularly at Nelson's Dockyard, which hosts a colorful regatta in late April or early May.

## Casinos and Nightlife

You can flirt with Lady Luck until the wee small hours in the dazzling casinos of **Aruba,** Santo Domingo, **Dominican Republic;** San Juan, **Puerto Rico; St. Maarten;** and **Curaçao. Barbados** is loaded with lively night places, and San Juan's glittering floor shows are legendary. The merengue, born in the **Dominican Republic,** is exuberantly danced everywhere on the island, as is salsa on Puerto Rico. Both **Guadeloupe** and **Martinique** claim to have begun the beguine, and on both islands it is danced with great gusto, although the *zouk* (all-night revelry) is now the rage.

## Cuisine

The cuisine on **Martinique** and **Guadeloupe** is a marvelous marriage of Creole cooking and classic French dishes; you'll find much of the same on the other French islands of **St. Martin** and **St. Barts.** You'll also find a fine selection of French wines in the French West Indies. Anegada, in the **British West Indies,** is, arguably, where you'll find the best lobster in the Caribbean. And you must try flying fish, the national dish of **Barbados. Grenada,** the spice island, has an abundance of seafood and an incredible variety of fruits and vegetables. On **St. Lucia,** where countless banana plantations cover the mountainsides, you'll find the many varieties grown here prepared in dozens of ways—and as both fruit and vegetable.

## Diving

Jacques Cousteau named Pigeon Island, off the west coast of **Guadeloupe,** one of the 10 best dive sites in the world. The Wall off Grand Turk in the **Turks and Caicos**

**Islands** is a sheer drop of 7,000 ft and has long been known by scuba divers. The eruption of **Martinique**'s Mt. Pelée at 8 AM on May 8, 1902, resulted in the sinking of several ships. **St. Eustatius** boasts an undersea "supermarket" of ships, as well as entire 18th-century warehouses, somewhat the worse for wear, below the surface of Oranjestad Bay. The waters surrounding all three of the **Cayman Islands** are acclaimed by experts, who also make pilgrimages to **Bonaire**'s 86 spectacular sites. **Tortola** is famous in diving circles for the wreck of the RMS *Rhone*. **Tobago** has a great array of unspoiled coral reefs, and it's the only place in the Caribbean that divers can regularly sight huge manta rays. **Saba** has some of the best advanced diving with its Marine Park and deep dive sites.

POINTERS➤ While **scuba** (which stands for self-contained underwater breathing apparatus) looks and is surprisingly simple, *call your physician before your vacation and make sure that you have no condition that should prevent you from diving!* A full checkup is an excellent idea, especially if you're over 30. Since it can be dangerous to travel on a plane after diving, you should schedule both your diving courses and travel plans accordingly.

Learning to dive with a reputable instructor is also a must. In addition to training you how to resurface slowly enough, a qualified instructor can teach you to read "dive tables," the charts that calculate how long you can safely stay at certain depths.

Many resorts offer short courses consisting of two to three hours of instruction on land and time in a swimming pool or waist-deep water to get used to the mouthpiece and hose (known as the regulator) and the mask. A shallow 20-ft dive from a boat or beach, supervised by the instructor, follows.

Successful completion of this introductory course may prompt you to do further coursework to earn a certification card—often called a C-card—from one of the major accredited diving organizations: NAUI (National Association of Underwater Instructors), CMAS (Confederation Mondiale des Activités Subaquatiques, which translates into World Underwater Federation), NASE (National Association of Scuba Educators), or PADI (Professional Association of Diving Instructors). PADI offers a free list of training facilities (☞ Diving *in* the Gold Guide).

## Foreign Culture

AFRICAN➤ **Trinidad** moves with the rhythm of calypso and is the stomping ground of a flat-out, freewheeling Carnival that rivals the pre-Lenten celebrations in Rio and New Orleans. The Trinidadians, whose African heritage has been augmented by many Asian races, have built up one of the most prosperous commercial centers in the Caribbean. Haiti was once another option. (It's now politically volatile and is not covered in this book.)

BRITISH➤ **St. Kitts** is known as the Mother Colony of the West Indies; it was from here that British colonists were dispatched in the 17th century to settle Antigua, Barbuda, Tortola, and Montserrat. If you're a history buff, you won't want to miss Nelson's Dockyard at **Antigua**'s English Harbour or the hunkering fortress of Brimstone Hill on St. Kitts. Sports fans who understand the intricacies of cricket can watch matches between **Nevis** and St. Kitts teams. And the waters around Antigua and the **British Virgin Islands** are a mecca for serious sailors. **Barbados,** with its lovely trade winds, has cricket, horseracing at Garrison Savannah, and rugby. A British colony from 1627, the island gained independence in 1966.

DUTCH➤ **Saba, St. Eustatius, St. Maarten, Bonaire,** and **Curaçao** all fly the Dutch flag, but there the similarity ends. Saba is a tiny volcanic island known for its beauty, its friendly inhabitants, and its gingerbread-trimmed houses. Curaçao's colorful waterfront shops and restaurants are reminiscent of Amsterdam. Quiet St. Eustatius—affectionately called Statia—has well-preserved historical sites and is famed for being the first foreign nation to salute the new American flag in 1776. The main streets of Philipsburg, the capital of St. Maarten, are lined with colorful Dutch colonial buildings replete with fretwork and verandas. Bonaire is best known for its excellent scuba diving.

FRENCH➤ **Martinique, Guadeloupe, St. Martin,** and **St. Barthélemy** (often called St. Barts or St. Barths) compose the French West Indies. The language, the currency, the cuisine (the most imaginative in the Caribbean), the culture, and the style are très French. St. Barts is the quietest, Martinique the liveliest, St. Martin the friendliest, and Guadeloupe the lushest. And as an extra added attraction, you can wing over from Guadeloupe to see what life is like on the nearby islands of Les Saintes, Marie Galante, and La Désirade.

SPANISH➤ In the **Dominican Republic,** which occupies the eastern two-thirds of the island of Hispaniola, the language and culture are decidedly Spanish. The Colonial Zone of Santo Domingo is the site of the oldest city in the Western Hemisphere, and its restored buildings reflect the 15th-century Columbus period. One also gets a sense of the past in **Puerto Rico**'s Old San Juan, with its narrow cobblestone streets and filigreed iron balconies.

## Getting Away from It All

If you're looking to back out of the fast lane, you can park at a secluded, spartan mountain lodge on **Dominica,** one of the friendliest islands in the Caribbean. Or opt for the quiet grandeur of a renovated sugar plantation on **Nevis,** where you can feast in an elegant dining room or enjoy a barbecue on the beach. Tranquil **Anguilla,** with soft white beaches nudged by incredibly clear water, offers posh resorts as well as small, inexpensive, locally owned lodgings. From the low-key **Turks and Caicos Islands,** which lie in stunning blue-green waters, you can boat to more than a score of isolated cays to which even the term "low-key" would imply too fast a pace. **St. Kitts** is another peaceful green oasis, with lovely beaches and upscale, "great house" accommodations in the bargain. **St. Lucia** offers a plethora of places, from the simple to the simply elegant, for "liming" (we call it "hanging out"), the favorite local pastime. On tiny **Saba** there is little to do but tuck into a small guest house, admire the lush beauty of the island, and chat with the friendly Sabans. Nearby **St. Eustatius** is another friendly, laid-back island, as is **Montserrat. St. Vincent and the Grenadines** offer three tiny, private-island luxury resorts: Young Island, Palm Island, and Petit St. Vincent.

## Golf

According to those who have played it, the course at Casa de Campo in the **Dominican Republic** is one of the best in the Caribbean. The course at the Four Sea-

sons Resort on **Nevis** is also challenging (and breathtaking). Golfers on St. Thomas, **U.S. Virgin Islands,** play the spectacular Mahogany Run. There are superb courses in **Puerto Rico,** including four shared by the Hyatt Dorado Beach and the Hyatt Regency Cerromar Beach. **Jamaica** has 10 courses, including top-rated Tryall near Montego Bay, and the new Negril Hills Golf Club. Golf is second only to cricket in **Barbados**; the Royal Westmoreland Golf Club opened its first 18 holes for the 1996 season; another nine holes are under way. The **Cayman Islands** now have an 18-hole championship golf course, the Links at Safehaven, and **Aruba** has its first 18-hole course, Robert Trent Jones–designed Tierra del Sol.

## History

**Antigua**'s well-preserved Nelson's Dockyard is a must for history aficionados. The ancient colonial zones of both Santo Domingo, **Dominican Republic,** and Old San Juan, **Puerto Rico,** should also be high on your "history" list. The Historical Society in **St. Eustatius** (Statia) publishes an excellent walking tour. Brimstone Hill on **St. Kitts** is a well-maintained fortress with several museums full of military memorabilia. **Nevis** has many sugar mills restored as comfortable hotels. Port Royal, outside Kingston, **Jamaica,** was a pirates' stronghold until an earthquake shook things up in 1692. **Grenada** has historical sites that reflect its British and French background as well as the more recent turbulence of 1983.

## Luxury Resorts

A wealth of posh resorts awaits those who seek comfort in the lap of luxury. **Anguilla,** rapidly becoming one of the Caribbean's most popular destinations, has the dazzling Malliouhana and the Moroccan-style Cap Juluca. **Antigua's** elegant Curtain Bluff has a long list of well-heeled repeat guests. The Sandy Lane Hotel, on **Barbados**'s Gold Coast, hosts British Royals, heads of state, captains of industry, and others who can afford its top-of-the-line elegance and flawless service. The Four Seasons resort on **Nevis** combines European grace with state-of-the-art sports facilities and Caribbean casualness. On **Jamaica** there's the well-established Half Moon Club, Montego Bay. **Puerto Rico**'s El Conquistador Resort and Country Club, with five individual hotels, is a luxurious world unto itself. On French **St. Martin,** La Samanna draws the rich and not-so-famous. For the ultimate in luxurious privacy, the **British Virgin Islands** has exclusive Necker Island, a 74-acre private island with elegant accommodations. Intimate Le Toiny on **St. Barts** draws worldly personalities. And Caneel Bay Resort on **St. John, U.S. Virgin Islands,** has seven beaches and takes up 170 acres inside the Virgin Islands National Park boundaries.

## Music

Calypso was born in **Trinidad; Jamaica** is the home of reggae; the **Dominican Republic** gave the world the merengue; and both **Martinique** and **Guadeloupe** claim to be the cradle of the beguine. The music of **Barbados** ranges from the soca and calypso heard during the Crop-Over Festival (mid-July–early August) to the hottest jazz. **St. Lucia** is also proud of its annual Jazz Festival (held each May since 1992). Salsa reigns in **Puerto Rico.** Steel drums, limbo dancers, and jump-ups are ubiquitous in the Caribbean. Jump-up? Simple. You hear the music, jump up, and dance.

## Nature

**Dominica,** laced with rivers and streams, is a ruggedly beautiful island with arguably the lushest, most untamed vegetation in the Caribbean. **Puerto Rico**'s luxuriant 28,000-acre El Yunque is the only rain forest in the U.S. forestry system. Little **Saba** is awash with giant vegetation, and the island's Mt. Scenery is justly named. **Guadeloupe**'s 74,000-square-acre Natural Park boasts dramatic waterfalls, cool pools, and miles of hiking trails. Majestic Mt. Pelée, a not entirely dormant volcano, towers over **Martinique**'s rain forest; on **St. Eustatius,** adventurers can crawl down into a jungle cradled within a volcanic crater; and on **St. Lucia** you can drive right into a volcano.

## Snorkeling

Snorkeling requires no special skills, and most hotels that rent equipment have a staff member or, at the very least, a booklet offering instruction in snorkeling basics.

As with any water sport, it's never a good idea to snorkel alone, especially if you're out of shape. You don't have to be a great swimmer to snorkel, but occasionally currents come up that require stamina. The four dimensions as we know them seem altered underwater. Time seems to slow and stand still, so wear a water-resistant watch and let someone on land know when to expect you back.

Remember that taking souvenirs—shells, pieces of coral, interesting rocks—is forbidden. Many reefs are legally protected marine parks, where removal of living shells is prohibited because it upsets the ecology.

## Sunbathing

Just plain basking is one of the great pleasures of a Caribbean vacation, but before abandoning yourself to the tropics, you would be well advised to take precautions against the ravages of its equatorial sun. Be sure to use a sunscreen with a sun-protection factor, or SPF, of at least 15; if you're engaging in water sports, be sure the sunscreen is waterproof. At this latitude, the safest hours for sunbathing are 4–6 PM, but even then it is wise to limit exposure during your first few days to 15–20 minutes. Keep your system plied with fruit juices and water, and avoid coffee, tea, and alcohol, which hasten the dehydration process.

## Swimming

The calm, leeward Caribbean side of most islands has the safest and most popular beaches for swimming. There are no big waves, there is little undertow, and the salt water—which buoys the swimmer or snorkeler—makes staying afloat almost effortless.

The windward, or Atlantic, side of the islands, however, is a different story: Even strong, experienced swimmers should exercise caution here. The ocean waves are powerful and can be dangerous; unseen currents, strong undertows, and uneven, rocky bottoms may scuttle the novice. Some beaches post signs or flags daily to alert swimmers to water conditions. Pay attention to them! Where there are no flags, stick to wading and sunbathing.

Few beaches or pools in the Caribbean—even those at the best hotels—are protected by lifeguards, so you and your children swim at your own risk.

## Waterskiing

Some large hotels have their own water-skiing concessions, with special boats, equipment, and instructors. Many beaches (especially those in Barbados), however, are patrolled by private individuals who own boats and several sizes of skis; they will offer their services through a hotel or directly to vacationers or can be hailed like taxis. Ask your hotel staff or other guests about their experiences with these entrepreneurs. Be *sure* they provide life vests and at least two people in the boat: one to drive and one to watch the skier at all times.

## Windsurfing

Windsurfing is as strenuous as it is exciting, so it may not be the sport to try on your first day out, unless you're already in excellent shape. Always windsurf with someone else around who can go for help if necessary.

# FODOR'S CHOICE

## Beaches

★ **Shoal Bay, Anguilla.** This 2-mi, L-shape beach of talcum-powder-soft white sand may get crowded, but that's only because it's one of the prettiest in the Caribbean.

★ **Green Cay, British Virgin Islands.** Sail to this little piece of heaven, off the shore of Jost Van Dyke, and pretend you were shipwrecked (while you drink a rum punch). There's absolutely nothing here, just intensely blue water, a couple of palm trees, and soft white sand.

★ **Seven Mile Beach, Grand Cayman.** It's actually 5½ mi of powdery white sand, litter- and peddler-free, and headquarters for the island's water-sports concessions.

★ **Grande Anse Beach, Grenada.** Clear, gentle surf laps the gleaming sand of this 2-mi beach. To the north, you can see the narrow mouth of St. George's Harbour and the pastel houses, with their fish-scale tile rooftops, that climb the surrounding hillsides.

★ **Negril, Jamaica.** Although it's no longer untouched by development, this 7-mi stretch of sand is still a beachcomber's Eden. Nude-beach areas are found along sections where no hotel or resort has been built.

★ **Macaroni Beach, Mustique.** Surfy swimming (be careful!), powdery white sand, a few palm huts and picnic tables, and very few people are the draws here.

★ **Anse du Gouverneur, St. Barthélemy.** This beautiful, secluded spot offers good snorkeling and views of St. Kitts, Saba, and St. Eustatius.

## Diving/Snorkeling

★ **Reefs around Bonaire.** An enormous range of coral as well as parrotfish, surgeon fish, angelfish, eels, snappers, and grouper are just some of the creatures you may see in the Bonaire Marine Park. The park encompasses the entire coastline around Bonaire and Klein Bonaire and includes more than 80 dive sites.

★ **Wreck of the *Rhone*, British Virgin Islands.** A Royal Mail Ship sunk by a hurricane in 1867, and still well preserved, makes for magnificent diving.

★ **Stingray City, Cayman Islands.** These islands are a diver's paradise, and this is one of their most unique sites. Dozens of unusually tame stingrays swim and twist around divers in the shallow waters.

★ **Scotts Head, Dominica.** Dramatic underwater walls and sudden drops line the coast here.

★ **Saba's Marine Park.** Encircling the entire island, the marine park features submerged pinnacles of land (at about the 70-ft depth mark), where all kinds of sea creatures rendezvous.

★ **Turks and Caicos Island's reefs.** More than 200 square mi of reefs surround these islands.

## Hotels

★ **Cap Juluca, Anguilla.** This spectacular 179-acre resort wraps around the edge of Maunday's Bay and almost 2 mi of sugary white-sand beach. $$$$

★ **Curtain Bluff, Antigua.** The setting is breathtaking—high on a bluff between the wild Atlantic and calm Caribbean. The ambience is pure country-club elegance. $$$$

★ **Hyatt Regency Aruba Resort & Casino, Aruba.** With central public areas styled after a Spanish grandee's villa, this is the top-flight luxury resort on the island. $$$$

★ **Sandy Lane Hotel, Barbados.** Rooms are nothing short of spectacular, bathrooms are vast and luxurious, the beach is one of the best on the island, and the staff treats you like royalty. $$$$

★ **Biras Creek, Virgin Gorda, British Virgin Islands.** A former guest bought this resort and completely renovated it, from building a new kitchen to lining the beach with magnificent palm trees; it's now a spectacular hideaway. $$$$

★ **Spice Island Inn Beach Resort, Grenada.** The spacious suites, fabulous bathrooms, and private plunge pools or in-room whirlpools are great, but it's actually the location right on beautiful Grande Anse Beach that steals the show. $$$$

★ **Sans Souci Lido, Jamaica.** As if the decorative luxury of this pastel cliffside palace weren't enough, a free spa session is also offered. $$$$

★ **Habitation Lagrange, Martinique.** Experience the old-world charms of Martinique's plantation-house society at this beautiful 19th-century manor house. The restaurant also boasts one of the best chefs on the island. $$$$

★ **Four Seasons Resort, Nevis.** This model chain property strikes just the right balance between posh and casual; it also boasts a superb Robert Trent Jones II–designed championship golf course, a fine family program, and the sensuous Pinney's Beach at your doorstep. $$$$

★ **Horned Dorset Primavera, Puerto Rico.** The emphasis here is on privacy and relaxation. The pounding of the surf and the squawk of the resident parrot are the only sounds you'll here as you lounge on the beach. $$$$

★ **Caneel Bay Resort, St. John, U.S. Virgin Islands.** With seven beaches spread out over 170 acres, this open-air resort is a sun worshipers paradise. A fitness center, tennis, myriad water sports, and good restaurants make it hard for guests to stir from this luxury property. $$$$

★ **Golden Lemon, St. Kitts.** St. Kitts and its sister island are beloved by Caribbean aficionados for their impeccably restored plantation inns (and their often eccentric owners); Arthur Leaman, a former design editor of *House and Garden,* has fashioned a jewel with an equally eclec-

tic, international, and refined decor and clientele. $$$$

★ **Anse Chastanet Hotel, St. Lucia.** Rooms were designed to meld into the tropical mountainside, with louvered wooden walls open to stunning Piton and Caribbean vistas or to the deep, shady green of the forest. $$$–$$$$

★ **La Samanna, St. Martin.** This luxurious, secluded hotel overlooks the ravishing Baie Longue beach and offers accommodations that are perfect right down to their fresh flowers and potpourri. $$$$

★ **Ritz-Carlton, St. Thomas.** Built like a palatial Italian villa, there is elegance everywhere from the marbled-floor reception area to a pool that seems to flow right into the sea. $$$$

★ **Young Island Resort, St. Vincent.** On its own private island a stone's throw from shore, these luxury cottages are halfway between Swiss Family Robinson's tree house and the Ritz. $$$$

★ **Grace Bay Club, Providenciales, Turks and Caicos.** Enjoy the views from your suite of Grace Bay's stunning turquoise waters, and take advantage of the expertly pampering service. $$$

## Restaurants

★ **Malliouhana, Anguilla.** Sparkling crystal and fine china, exquisite service, and a spectacularly romantic, candlelit, open-air setting are the perfect match for this restaurant's exceptional haute French cuisine. $$$$

★ **Julian's, Antigua.** Everything about this cozy eatery is stylish, from the simple yet striking decor to the chef's sophisticated takes on traditional dishes. $$$

★ **Gasparito Restaurant, Aruba.** Tasty local cuisine is served in the refined gallery atmosphere of an authentic country house. $$

★ **Sandy Bay, Barbados.** Each morning a van is sent to scour the island for the freshest produce and seafood: The results—succulent grilled dolphinfish and lobster, lamb dressed with thyme and wild rosemary—are heavenly. $$$

★ **Hemingway's, Grand Cayman.** Enjoy the breezes on Seven Mile Beach while sipping a Seven Mile Meltdown (dark rum, peach schnapps, pineapple juice, and fresh coconut) and savoring grouper stuffed with sweet corn and crab. *$$–$$$*

★ **Château de Feuilles, Guadeloupe.** It's a bit of a trip, but velvety sea urchin pâté, kingfish fillet with vanilla, and pineapple flan are worth every mile. *$$$*

★ **Le Fromager, Martinique.** From its perch above St-Pierre, this beautiful restaurant offers views of the town's red roofs and the sea beyond, as well as delectable crayfish colombo, marinated octopus, and sole pecheur in a Creole sauce. *$$*

★ **Carl Gustaf, St. Barthélemy.** Sweeping views of Gustavia harbor and delectable classic French cuisine with an island accent are the draws here. *$$$$*

★ **Top Hat, St. Croix, U.S. Virgin Islands.** Both the wonderful Danish menu and the Danish owners are reminders of St. Croix's colonial past. Try the *frikadeller* (meatballs in a tangy sauce) and fried Camembert with lingonberries. *$$$$*

★ **Chez Martine, St. Martin.** Chef Thierry de Launay studied under Joël Robuchon; his fois gras claims a loyal following. *$$$$*

★ **Veni Mange, Trinidad.** Allyson Hennessey, a Cordon Bleu–trained chef with a local TV talk show, cooks up the best Creole lunches in town. *$$*

★ **Anacaona, Providenciales, Turks and Caicos.** This is a true gourmet dining experience, minus the attitude. Traditional French recipes are combined with Caribbean fruits, vegetables, and spices. *$$–$$$*

★ **Virgilio's, St. Thomas, U.S. Virgin Islands.** Come here for some of the best northern Italian cuisine in the islands, and don't leave without having a Virgilio's cappuccino, a chocolate-and-coffee drink so rich it's dessert. *$$$$*

# FESTIVALS AND SEASONAL EVENTS

Regardless of when Carnival season starts on each island, it always means days and nights of continuous partying. There's a celebration going on from January through August—it's just a matter of being on the right island.

The first Carnival of the season is also the longest. **Martinique**'s Carnival begins in early January and lasts through the first day of Lent, in mid-February. **Guadeloupe**'s Carnival starts a day later and also continues until Lent, finishing with a parade of floats and costumes on Mardi Gras (Fat Tuesday) and a huge bash on Ash Wednesday. **Curaçao**'s Carnival season lasts from late January to early February. All of these Carnivals feature music, dance, and a costumed parade.

February brings a flood of Carnival events, including those on **Bonaire, Dominica, Puerto Rico, St. Lucia, St. Martin** (the French side of the island), **St. Barthélemy, Carriacou,** and **Trinidad and Tobago,** all of which combine feasting, dancing, music, and parades. During Carnival on **Trinidad and Tobago,** adults and children alike are swept up in the excitement of Playing Mas'— the state of surrendering completely to the rapture of fantastic spectacle, parades, music, and dancing.

Spring brings the **Barbados, St. Thomas (U.S. Virgin Islands),** and **Saint Maarten** (Dutch side of the island) Carnivals in April and the **Cayman Islands'** Carnival, which begins on Grand Cayman in May. In July, the season reaches **Saba** and the **Dominican Republic,** whose popular 10-day Merengue Festival features entertainment from outdoor bands and orchestras and the best cuisine from local hotel chefs. In **St. John (U.S. Virgin Islands)** residents hold their version of Carnival with the July 4 celebration. **Anguilla,** the **British Virgin Islands,** and **Grenada** start Carnival in early August with street dancing, calypso competitions, the Carnival Queen Coronation, and sumptuous beach barbecues. The **Turks and Caicos** Islands finish the string of festivals during the last days of the month. **St. Croix (U.S. Virgin Islands)** holds its annual Christmas Festival in late December.

Many other festivals celebrate the islands' rich local cultures. Barbados's **Holetown Festival** commemorates the first settlement of Barbados, on February 17, 1627, with a week of fairs, street markets, and revelry. St. Barts chimes in with its own weeklong **gastronomic festival** in late April, which not only celebrates local cuisine but also spotlights different regional fare and the wines of France. The Historical and Cultural Foundations organize the **St. Martin Food Festival** in May. During the **Tobago Heritage Festival** in July, each village on Trinidad and Tobago mounts a different show or festivity. Beginning in July and continuing through August, Barbados celebrates the **Crop-Over Festival,** a monthlong cheer for the end of the sugarcane harvest. Calypsonians battle for the coveted Calypso Monarch award, and Bajan cooking abounds at the massive Bridgetown Market street fair. Grenada's **Rainbow City Festival,** with arts and crafts displays, a street fair, and a cultural show, takes place the first weekend of August in the island's second city, Grenville. On a Sunday in early August, Guadeloupe holds a **Fête des Cuisinières** and celebrates the masters of Creole cuisine with a five-hour banquet that is open to the public. The **Hatillo Festival of the Masks,** held in December in Puerto Rico, is a carnival featuring folk music and dancing, as well as parades in which islanders don brightly colored masks and costumes. Grenada's **Carriacou Parang Festival,** just before Christmas, is a two-day cultural celebration featuring Big Drum Dance; it's the only event outside Africa where this traditional dance is still performed.

Sports enthusiasts, tourists, and islanders enjoy the many regattas. Grenada's **New Year Fiesta Yacht Race** in late January is highlighted by the Around Grenada sailing contest. In mid-January, the **Barbados Windsurfing World Cup** takes place on the southeast coast of the island, one of the top three windsurfing locations in the world. Grenada's **Sailing Festival** in early

February combines yacht races, regattas, "a sail past parade," entertainment, and other events. Antigua's **Sailing Week** in April brings together more than 300 yachts from around the world. The Bequia **Easter Regatta** (St. Vincent and the Grenadines) takes place Easter weekend. The British Virgin Islands' **Spring Regatta,** the **Curaçao Regatta,** and the U.S. Virgin Islands' **International Rolex Cup Regatta** take place in April. Boat racing is the national sport in Anguilla, and the most important competitions take place on **Anguilla Day,** May 30. The British Virgin Islands host the **Hook In and Hold On Boardsailing Regatta** in June and July. In July, windsurfers from across the Caribbean gather at the **Caribbean Boardsailing Championships** in St. Thomas.

Martinique hosts the **Tour des Yoles Rondes** point-to-point yawl race in early August, the **Canouan Regatta** is held in the Grenadines, and the annual **Sailing Regatta** in Bonaire takes place in October. The St.

Croix Yacht Club holds the **Mumm's Cup Regatta** on Veteran's Day weekend in early November. The **Route du Rosé,** a transatlantic regatta of tall ships that set sail from St-Tropez in early November, is welcomed to St. Barts in December with a round of festivities. The **Thanksgiving Regatta** in St. John is a chance for local sailors to compete against each other, culminating in a celebration at Skinny Leg's Bar. St. Lucia is the end-point of the **Atlantic Rally for Cruisers,** an annual yacht race across the Atlantic, from the Canary Islands to Rodney Bay, during which a week of events and parties marks the occasion.

Throughout the summer months, there's marlin mania out on the North Drop, a 100-fathom drop-off located off the coast of the U.S. Virgin Islands. Anglers from around the world fish in the **July Open Tournament, American Yacht Harbor Billfish Tournament,** and **U.S.V.I. Open/Atlantic Blue Marlin Tournament** out of St. Thomas. St. Thomas is the home to

some 20 world sport fishing records.

Music lovers should also take note of several other annual events. In January, St. Barthélemy is host to an international collection of soloists and musicians as part of the **Annual St. Barts Music Festival.** The **Barbados Caribbean Jazz Festival** in Bridgetown features performances of original compositions and traditional jazz for three days in mid-January. The **St. Lucia Jazz Festival,** in May, attracts enthusiasts to four days of performances by legendary performers at a number of outdoor venues. At the end of June, the **Aruba Jazz and Latin Music Festival** is held in Oranjestad, offering well-known entertainers performing Latin, pop, jazz, and salsa music at Mansur Stadium. And the **August Reggae Sunsplash International Music Festival** is getting hotter every year, as the best, brightest, and newest of the reggae stars gather to perform in open-air concerts in Montego Bay on Jamaica.

# 2 Anguilla

*Anguilla is a scrubby-looking island, but it is ringed with some of the most beautiful beaches in the Caribbean. Elegant, one-of-a-kind resorts are tucked along its shores and fine dining is the norm, but there are also casual little inns and beach bars you can belly up to in bare feet.*

Updated by
Pamela
Acheson

**B**EACH LOVERS BECOME GIDDY when they first spot Anguilla (rhymes with vanilla) from the air and see the blindingly white sand and lustrous blue and aquamarine waters that rim this scrubby piece of land. The island's star attractions are its dozens and dozens of gorgeous, soft-sand beaches. An inspirational setting for sunbathers, the island also possesses exceptionally clear waters and coral reefs just offshore, which mean good snorkeling can be found almost everywhere. If you don't like the sand, you won't find a lot to do here. There are no glittering casinos or nightclubs and no duty-free shops stuffed with irresistible buys (although you're only about 30 watery minutes away from the bustle of St. Martin/St. Maarten's resorts and casinos). Peace, quiet, and pampering account for the island's popularity among travelers searching for a Caribbean getaway. Times are slowly changing, however, and there are now six traffic lights on the island instead of the solitary signal of years past.

This dry, limestone isle is the most northerly of the Leeward Islands, lying between the Caribbean Sea and the Atlantic Ocean. It stretches, from northeast to southwest, about 16 mi and is only 3 mi across at its widest point. The highest spot is 213 ft above sea level, and there are neither streams nor rivers, only saline ponds used for salt production. The island's name, a reflection of its shape, is most likely a derivative of *anguille,* which means "eel" in French.

In 1631 the Dutch built a fort here, but no one has been able to locate its site. English settlers from St. Kitts colonized the island in 1650, and, except for a brief period of independence with St. Kitts–Nevis in the 1960s, Anguilla has remained a British colony ever since.

From the early 1800s various island units and federations were formed and disbanded, with Anguilla all the while simmering over its subordinate status and enforced union with St. Kitts. Anguillans twice petitioned for direct rule from Britain and twice were ignored. In 1967, when St. Kitts, Nevis, and Anguilla became an associated state, the mouse roared, kicked St. Kitts policemen off the island, held a self-rule referendum, and for two years conducted its own affairs. A British "peace-keeping force" then parachuted down to the island, squelching Anguilla's designs for autonomy but helping a team of royal engineers stationed there to improve the port and build roads and schools. Today Anguilla elects a House of Assembly and its own leader to handle internal affairs, while a British governor is responsible for public service, the police, and judiciary and external affairs.

The territory of Anguilla includes a few islets or cays, such as Scrub Island to the east, Dog Island, Prickly Pear Cays, Sandy Island, and Sombrero Island. The island's population numbers about 8,000, predominantly of African descent but also including descendants of Europeans, especially Irish. Historically, because the limestone land was hardly fit for agriculture, attempts at enslavement and colonization never lasted long; consequently, Anguilla doesn't bear the scars of slavery found on so many other Caribbean islands. Because the island couldn't be farmed successfully (although cotton was produced here for a while), Anguillans became experts at making a living from the sea and are known for their boatbuilding and fishing skills. Tourism is the growth industry of the island's stable economy, but the government is determined to keep expansion at a slow and cautious pace to protect the island's natural resources and beauty. New hotels—scattered throughout Anguilla—are being kept small, select, and casino-free. The island has cho-

Lodging

## Lodging

Anguilla has a wide range of accommodations. There are grand and
sumptuous resorts, apartments and villas from the deluxe to the simple, and small, cozy, locally owned guest houses. Because Anguilla has
so many beautiful and uncrowded beaches, it is not necessary (the way
it is on some other islands) for beach lovers to choose a particular property because of its beach. If calling to reserve a room in a resort, inquire about special packages and the various meal plans available.

| CATEGORY | COST* |
|---|---|
| $$$$ | over $400 |
| $$$ | $275–$400 |
| $$ | $150–$275 |
| $ | under $150 |

*All prices are for a standard double room, excluding 8% tax and 10% service
charge.*

### Hotels

**$$$$** ★ **Cap Juluca.** This spectacular 179-acre resort wraps around the edge
of Maunday's Bay, encompassing almost 2 mi of sugary white-sand
beach. Within its sparkling white, Moorish-style, two-story villas are
some of the most luxurious and oversize accommodations in the
Caribbean. Rooms are elegantly but comfortably decorated, with Moroccan fabrics, Brazilian hardwood, and built-in plumply cushioned
seating areas. The immense bathrooms vary in design, but many have
two-person soaking tubs and look out to private sun porches or gardens. Chatterton's, the hotel's casual Mediterranean-style grill, overlooks the water and is open for lunch and dinner. Dinner is also served
at the elegant adjoining restaurant, Eclipse at Pimms (☞ Dining,
*below*). A new, romantic wedding gazebo surrounded by gardens is a
lovely spot to tie the knot. ⊠ *Box 240, Maunday's Bay,* ☎ *809/497–*
*6666 or 800/235–3505,* FAX *809/497–6617. 98 units, 7 private villas.*
*3 restaurants, bar, room service, pool, golf privileges, 3 tennis courts,*
*croquet, fitness center, windsurfing, boating, shop, library, laundry ser-*
*vice. AE, V. CP, MAP.*

**$$$$** ★ **Malliouhana.** This ultrasophisticated resort, Anguilla's classiest,
with a remarkable 70% rate of repeat guests, sits on 25 lush tropical
acres on a promontory that juts out between two exquisite beaches.
The lobby entrance, boutique, restaurants, and bar are in a grand, multi-
tiered, open-air building with tile floors and beautifully maintained mahogany walls. Accommodations are sleekly decorated, with white
walls and tile floors, rattan furniture, and Haitian prints; marble bathrooms have oversize tubs. The restaurant is the most elegant on the
island. Also, children will like the small beachfront playground. A new
villa with three suites and its own private pool is great for family get-
togethers. ⊠ *Box 173, Meads Bay,* ☎ *809/497–6111 or 800/372–1323,*
FAX *809/497–6011. 20 doubles, 15 junior suites, 15 1-bedroom suites,*
*4 2-bedroom suites, 1 3-bedroom villa. Restaurant, bar, 3 pools, beauty*
*salon, massage, 4 tennis courts, exercise room, windsurfing, shops, play-*
*ground. No credit cards. EP, MAP.*

**$$$** ★ **Cinnamon Reef Beach Club.** Low-key luxury sets the tone at this small,
appealing resort. Most of the whitewashed, split-level villas are nes-
tled among the palm trees along the narrow beach, while five are
tucked on a bluff. Each casually decorated villa has a living room, raised
bedroom, dressing room, sunken shower, and patio, along with little
extras such as a hammock, built-in hair dryer, and minibar. This is a

## Anguilla

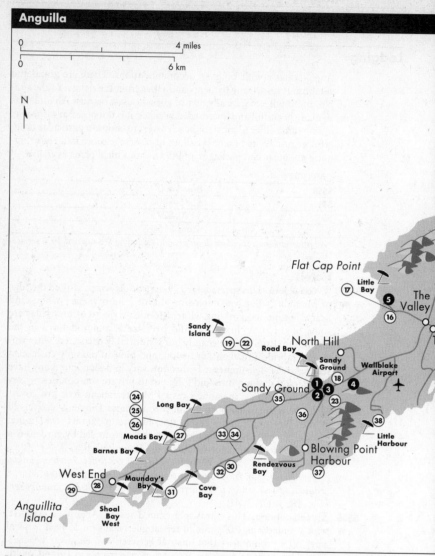

**Exploring**
Amerindian Mini-Museum, **8**
Bethel Methodist Church, **4**
Crocus Hill Prison, **5**
Heritage Collection, **9**
Island Harbour, **7**
Old Factory, **2**

Sandy Ground, **1**
Wallblake House, **3**
Warden's Place, **6**

**Dining**
Aquarium, **35**
Arlo's, **23**
Blanchard's, **24**
Cafe at Cove Castles, **29**
Casablanca, **30**
Eclipse at Pimms, **31**
Ferryboat Inn, **37**

La Fontana, **12**
Hibernia, **10**
Johnno's, **20**
Koal Keel, **15**
Lucy's Harbour View Restaurant, **36**
Malliouhana, **26**
Old House, **18**
Palm Court, **38**

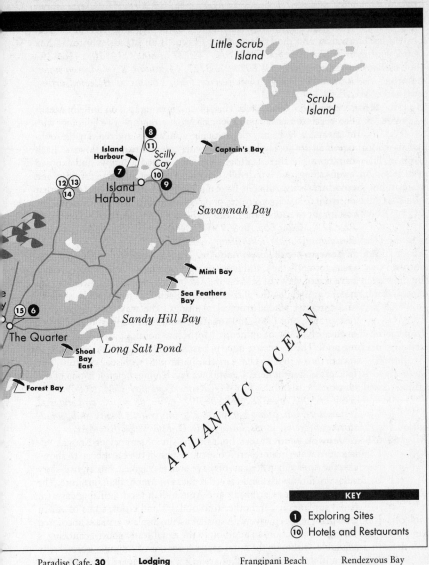

*Little Scrub Island*

*Scrub Island*

**8**

**11** *Scilly Cay*

**Island Harbour**

☂ **Captain's Bay**

**7**

**10**

**9**

**12 13**

**14**

Island Harbour

*Savannah Bay*

☂ **Mimi Bay**

☂ **Sea Feathers Bay**

*Sandy Hill Bay*

**15 6**

The Quarter

☂ **Shoal Bay East**

*Long Salt Pond*

☂ **Forest Bay**

*ATLANTIC OCEAN*

**KEY**

**❶** Exploring Sites

**⑩** Hotels and Restaurants

Paradise Cafe, **30**
Le Petit Patissier, **15**
Pizzazz, **28**
Riviera Bar & Restaurant, **19**
Roy's, **16**
Zara's, **14**

**Lodging**
Arawak Beach Resort, **11**
Cap Juluca, **31**
Cinnamon Reef Beach Club, **38**
Ferryboat Inn, **37**
Fountain Beach, **12**

Frangipani Beach Club, **27**
Inter-Island Hotel, **17**
Malliouhana, **26**
Mariners Cliffside Beach Resort, **21**
Pineapple Beach Club, **33**

Rendezvous Bay Hotel, **34**
Shoal Bay Villas, **13**
La Sirena, **25**
Sonesta Beach Resort Anguilla, **32**
Syd-an's, **22**

friendly place with a gracious staff and lots of repeat guests. The restaurant chefs have won a number of the Anguilla Chefs of the Year awards, and the Friday-night barbecue is an island favorite. ⊠ *Box 141, Little Harbour,* ☏ *809/497–2727 or 800/223–1108; 416/485–8724 in Canada;* FAX *809/497–3727. 14 studios, 8 1-bedroom suites. Restaurant, lounge, room service, pool, 2 tennis courts, windsurfing. AE, MC, V. EP, MAP.*

$$$ ★ 🏨 **Frangipani Beach Club.** This splashy, inviting spot on brilliant Meads Bay beach consists of pink, Spanish Mediterranean–style buildings with archways, stone balustrades, wrought-iron railings, and red-clay-tile roofs. Grounds are lushly landscaped with colorful tropical flowers. Each one-, two-, or three-bedroom suite has arched windows and exposed beam ceilings and is tastefully decorated with blond rattan furniture and colorful fabrics. All units have marble-tiled bathrooms and doors that open out to spacious terraces or balconies; many have full kitchens. The restaurant overlooks the ocean and has a French-influenced menu. ⊠ *Box 328, Meads Bay,* ☏ *809/497–6442 or 800/892–4564. 24 units. Restaurant, 2 bars, windsurfing. AE. EP.*

$$$ 🏨 **Sonesta Beach Resort Anguilla.** This pink-and-green Moorish fantasia, formerly the Casablanca, is right on the beach, and many rooms have grand views of St. Martin. Although by far the gaudiest-looking hotel on Anguilla, the glitz of the architecture is tempered by the lush and carefully tended tropical plantings. The way to reception, the restaurants, and the 1,200-square-ft pool is through a long, domed, open-air hallway of authentic Moroccan mosaics past a long reflecting pool. The rooms are done in pastel green-and-pink prints and Moroccan throw rugs and have marble bathrooms with spacious tubs. The fancier restaurant here, Casablanca (☞ *Dining, below*), is one of the best on the island. ⊠ *Box 444, Rendezvous Bay West,* ☏ *809/497–6999 or 800/766–3782,* FAX *809/497–6899. 88 rooms and suites. 2 restaurants, bar, piano bar, pool, 2 tennis courts, health club, windsurfing, bicycles, shops, library. AE, D, MC, V. EP, BP, MAP.*

$$–$$$ 🏨 **Arawak Beach Resort.** Built on the site of an ancient Arawak village, this waterfront resort is one of the first in the Caribbean to showcase the Amerindian heritage of the region. Hexagonal, breezy, two-story villas are fitted with hand-carved replicas of Amerindian furniture. The restaurant serves Caribbean and Amerindian food, utilizing cassava, papaya, plantains, and other traditional island crops, some of which grow right in the courtyard. A small museum displays artifacts uncovered during construction. In addition to the usual water sports, canoeing is available. Although the hotel beach is not one of Anguilla's best, Scilly Cay and its beautiful beaches are just a minute away by launch. This is a no-smoking property, and alcoholic beverages are not served, although you may bring your own. ⊠ *Box 98, Island Harbour,* ☏ *809/497–4888,* FAX *809/497–4898. 13 rooms, 3 junior suites, 1 luxury suite. Restaurant, pool, water sports, shop. AE. EP.*

$$–$$$ ★ 🏨 **Fountain Beach.** The family who owns this tiny, delightful property along beautiful Shoal Bay is of Italian descent, and the family's heritage is evident in the resort's Mediterranean-style white stucco buildings. Each unit comes with a fully equipped kitchen, a large bathroom with an open sunken shower, and a view of the sea. Furnishings are rattan and colorfully painted wicker, and Haitian art decorates the walls. Despite the long bumpy road to the hotel, guests from all over the island head to La Fontana (☞ *Dining, below*), the hotel's Italian restaurant, for dinner. ⊠ *Box 474, Shoal Bay,* ☏ FAX *809/497–3491. 10 1-bedroom suites, 2 junior suites. Restaurant, 2 pools, 2 tennis courts. AE, MC, V. EP, MAP. Closed Sept.*

$$–$$$ 🏨 **Mariners Cliffside Beach Resort.** This popular and very casual resort has recently undergone a major redo. All rooms have been com-

pletely remodeled and now have bright Caribbean fabrics. It's set at the far end of the beach at Sandy Ground, Anguilla's busiest stretch of sand, and is just a short stroll from a number of beach bars and restaurants. Accommodations vary considerably in size and price range, from deluxe two-bedroom, two-bath cottages with full kitchens to small rooms with twin beds, minibars, and shower baths. Charter the resort's Boston whaler for picnics, snorkeling, and fishing trips. Local musicians perform at the new restaurant, Carnivals, decorated with colorful carnival costumes and paintings depicting life on the island. ⊠ *Box 139, Sandy Ground,* ☏ *809/497–2671 or 800/223–0079,* FAX *809/497–2901. 32 1-bedroom suites, 35 studios. 2 restaurants, 2 bars, pool, hot tub, tennis court, water sports, shop, laundry service. AE, MC, V. EP, MAP, FAP, All-inclusive (drinks not included).*

**$$–$$$** 🏨 **Pineapple Beach Club.** Rooms here are in white West Indian–style bungalows strung along the edge of Rendezvous Bay, one of Anguilla's longest beaches. From a chaise on your charming veranda, the view of the ocean is framed by vine-covered trellises and gingerbread trim. Most bungalows have five rooms, and each room has mahogany furnishings, hand-embroidered linens, a huge tile shower, and ceiling fans. The restaurant features both Continental and Caribbean cuisine. ⊠ *Box 157, Rendezvous Bay,* ☏ *809/497–6061 or 800/223–0079,* FAX *809/497–6019. 27 rooms. Restaurant, fans, pool, exercise room, windsurfing, fishing, shop. AE, MC, V. EP, All-inclusive.*

**$$–$$$** 🏨 **Shoal Bay Villas.** This small condominium hotel is tucked in a grove of palm trees on 2 mi of splendid sand. Units are brightly decorated in pink and blue, with painted rattan furniture; all but the poolside doubles have fully equipped kitchens. There's no air-conditioning, but all rooms have ceiling fans. The Reefside Beach Bar is an informal open-air restaurant open for breakfast, lunch, and dinner. All water sports can be arranged, and meal and room packages can be tailored to fit your needs. Children are not allowed during the winter. ⊠ *Box 81, Shoal Bay,* ☏ *809/497–2051 or 800/722–7045; 212/535–9530 in NY; 416/283–2621 in Canada;* FAX *809/497–3631. 2 studios, 2 2-bedroom units, 7 1-bedroom units, 2 doubles. Restaurant, bar, pool. AE, MC, V. EP, BP, MAP.*

**$$** 🏨 **La Sirena.** You'll find one of the island's best values at this person-
★ able, well-run hotel set among tropical greenery overlooking Meads Bay. La Sirena doesn't have the chic elegance of Malliouhana, but it lets you stay just down the beach for about a third of the cost. Choose one of the five spacious villas or one of the 20 guest rooms. Buildings are white stucco with red tile roofs and lots of balconies and terraces. The interior decor is typical Caribbean—rattan furniture and pastel-print fabrics. Rooms are cooled by ceiling fans. The restaurant, which serves a variety of French and Caribbean cuisine, is on the second floor and open to the sea breezes. ⊠ *Box 200, Meads Bay,* ☏ *809/497–6827 or 800/331–9358; 212/251–1800 in NY;* FAX *809/497–6829. 20 rooms, 3 2-bedroom villas, 2 3-bedroom villas. Restaurant, bar, 2 pools, snorkeling, car rental. AE, MC, V. EP, MAP.*

**$–$$** 🏨 **Rendezvous Bay Hotel.** Opened in 1972, Anguilla's first resort sits amid 60 acres of coconut groves on the fine white sand of Rendezvous Bay, just a mile from the ferry dock. Owner Jeremiah Gumb has turned the lounge into a showcase for his elaborate electric train set, complete with tunnels and multiple tracks. The original guest rooms are about 100 yards from the beach and are quite spare (although they have recently been repainted), with one double and one single bed, a private shower bath, Haitian art on the walls, and ceiling fans (no air-conditioning). Much newer two-story villas along the shore contain spacious, air-conditioned one-bedroom suites with refrigerators or kitchenettes. These are decorated with natural wicker and pastel prints and can be joined to form larger suites. There's a wide sand beach and also a rocky stretch of coast that is great for snorkeling. ✉ *Box 31, Rendezvous Bay,* ☎ *809/497–6549; 908/738–0246 or 800/274–4893 in the U.S.; 800/468–0023 in Canada;* ℻ *809/497–6026. 20 rooms, 24 1-bedroom villa suites. Restaurant, lounge, 2 tennis courts, windsurfing, recreation room. AE, MC, V. EP, MAP.*

$  🍴 **Ferryboat Inn.** The spacious apartments at this small family-run complex are a bargain. Each is simply decorated with white or pastel fabrics and has a full kitchen, dining area, cable TV, and ceiling fans. It's on a small beach and just a short walk from the ferry dock. The two-bedroom beach house is air-conditioned. All rooms and the open-air restaurant look out across the water toward hilly, more-populated St. Martin, which is gorgeous at night with its host of sparkling lights. ✉ *Box 189, Blowing Point,* ☎ *809/497–6613,* ℻ *809/497–3309. 6 1- and 2-bedroom apartments, 1 beach house. Restaurant, bar, windsurfing. AE, MC, V. EP.*

$  🍴 **Inter-Island Hotel.** Rooms and two small one-bedroom apartments at this modest establishment are simply furnished with wicker and rattan. There is no air-conditioning, but some rooms have a breezy open balcony. Most rooms have refrigerators, and all have cramped shower bathrooms that define the term "water closet." The homey restaurant serves hearty breakfasts and offers heaping servings at its West Indian dinners. The nearest beach is a two-minute drive away. ✉ *Box 194, The Valley,* ☎ *809/497–6259 or 800/223–9815; 800/468–0023 in Canada;* ℻ *809/497–5381. 12 rooms, 2 1-bedroom apartments. Restaurant, bar, transportation to beach. AE, D, MC, V. EP.*

$  🍴 **Syd-an's.** These very basic efficiencies are a true bargain. Each has a kitchenette and shower bath and is comfortably furnished. Road Bay, with all its bustling activity, is just across the street. ✉ *Sandy Ground,* ☎ *809/497–3180,* ℻ *809/497–2332. 6 studios. Kitchenettes, shop. AE, MC, V. EP.*

### Villas and Condominiums

The tourist office has a complete listing of vacation rentals. You can also contact **Sunshine Villas** (✉ Box 142, Blowing Point, ☎ 809/497–6149, ℻ 809/497–6021), the **Anguilla Connection** (✉ Island Harbour, ☎ 809/497–4403, ℻ 809/497–4402), or **Select Villas of Anguilla** (✉ Box 256, George Hill, ☎ 809/497–5810, ℻ 809/497–5811), all of which offer one- to three-bedroom houses for rent. Apartments for rent on the island are plentiful. The following are a selection.

$$$$  🍴 **Cove Castles Villa Resort.** All of these glistening white, futuristic sculp-
★  tures are actually luxuriously comfortable, very elegant and very private apartments. Each is decorated with custom-made wicker furniture, raw silk cushions, and hand-embroidered sheets. Balconies are wide and secluded, the kitchens are state-of-the-art, and the property is on one of Anguilla's prettiest beaches. The new "supervilla" here is super-luxurious, with a grand atrium entrance, a contemporary kitchen, and a 75-ft veranda looking out to the ocean. ✉ *Box 248, Shoal Bay West,* ☎ *809/497–6801 or 800/348–4716; 800/468–0023 in Canada;* ℻ *809/497–6051. 4 3-bedroom villas, 8 2-bedroom villas, 1 4-bedroom villa. Restaurant, tennis court, shop. AE, MC, V.*

$$$  🍴 **Paradise Cove.** Two-story buildings rimmed with balconies and patios and set amid beautiful tropical landscaping house this group of luxury apartments. The units are spacious and charming and overlook a courtyard with two Jacuzzis and a large pool. It is a very short walk to quiet Cove Beach. One- and two-bedroom units are furnished in rattan and wicker with colorful tropical-print fabrics. All have fully equipped kitchens and private laundry facilities. Maid service and private cooks are available. ✉ *Box 135, Cove Beach,* ☎ *809/497–2259*

or 800/553–4939, FAX 809/497–2149. *14 units. Restaurant, bar, pool, shop, playground, laundry service. AE, MC, V.*

$$$  ⊞ **Sea Grape Beach Club.** The attractive white stucco and red-tile-roof buildings of this complex on Meads Bay contain luxurious 2,000-square-ft, two-bedroom condominiums. A blue-trimmed arched doorway in each unit leads to an airy common room, where enormous windows offer spectacular views of the beach. Each condo has three bathrooms, king-size beds, huge closets, and a very private deck. ⊠ *Box 65, The Valley,* ☎ 809/497–6433 or 809/497–6541, FAX 809/497–6410. *6 condos. Restaurant, bar, water sports. AE, MC, V.*

$$  ⊞ **Allamanda Beach Club.** Enjoy a view of the ocean from your balcony at this casual resort. One-bedroom suites and studios fill the three-story white stucco buildings just off the beach. Views are better from the higher floors. All units have tile floors, full kitchens, and tropical-print decor. The new restaurant, Zara's (☞ *Dining, below*), is a popular draw. ⊠ *Box 662, Upper Shoal Bay Beach,* ☎ 809/497–5217, FAX 809/497–5216. *16 units. Pool. MC, V.*

$$  ⊞ **Blue Waters.** These glistening white, Moorish-style buildings sit at
★  one end of a spectacular ½-mi-long beach and are within walking distance of several excellent restaurants. Sunny one- and two-bedroom units are appealingly decorated with pastel fabrics and have white tile floors, separate dining areas, full kitchens, and comfortable balconies or terraces. ⊠ *Box 69, Shoal Bay West,* ☎ 809/497–6292, FAX 809/497–3309. *9 apartments. AE, MC, V.*

$$  ⊞ **Easy Corner Villas.** These modest one-, two-, and three-bedroom apartments are adequately furnished and have well-equipped kitchens with microwaves. Only three of the units have air-conditioning. Number 10 is a deluxe two-bedroom villa. The location, on a bluff overlooking Road Bay, means you have to walk five minutes to the beach, but the price is right. ⊠ *Box 65, South Hill,* ☎ 809/497–6433 or 809/497–6541, FAX 809/497–6410. *10 units. AE, MC, V.*

$$  ⊞ **Rainbow Reef.** Three seaside acres provide a dramatically beautiful setting for this tiny group of villas. Each self-contained unit has two bedrooms, a fully equipped kitchen, a spacious dining and living area, and a large gallery overlooking the sea. A gazebo with beach furniture and barbecue facilities is perched right above the beach. ⊠ *Box 130, Sea Feather Bay,* ☎ 809/497–2817 or 708/325–2299. *4 villas. No credit cards.*

$$  ⊞ **Skiffles Villas.** These self-catering villas, perched on a hill overlooking
★  Road Bay, are usually booked a year in advance. The one-, two-, and three-bedroom apartments have fully equipped kitchens, floor-to-ceiling windows, and pleasant porches. ⊠ *Box 82, Lower South Hill,* ☎ 809/497–6619, 219/642–4855, or 219/642–4445; FAX 809/495–6110. *5 units. Pool. No credit cards.*

# Dining

For such a small island, Anguilla has an extraordinary number of excellent restaurants that range from truly elegant establishments to down-home seaside shacks. Most restaurants are open to the breezes, and many have terraces where you can dine under the stars. Even very expensive restaurants can be in simple (although usually very well decorated) open-air structures. Call ahead—in the winter to make a reservation, and in the late summer and fall to confirm if the place you've chosen is open. Restaurants not affiliated with a hotel often tack on an additional 5% to the service charge if you pay by credit card.

## What to Wear

During the day, casual clothes are widely accepted: Shorts will probably be fine, although many establishments don't allow cover-ups over bathing suits. In the evening, shorts are acceptable at the extremely casual eateries; but elsewhere, sundresses or nice casual pants for women and pants for men are appropriate. Some hotel restaurants expect a degree of formality and may have a jacket requirement in high season; ask when you make your reservation.

| CATEGORY | COST* |
|---|---|
| $$$$ | over $45 |
| $$$ | $35–$45 |
| $$ | $25–$35 |
| $ | under $25 |

*per person for a three-course meal, excluding drinks and 8% sales tax

## West End

$$$$  ✕ **Cafe at Cove Castles.** Elegant, intimate dinners are served here amid a garden overlooking beautiful Shoal Bay. Each season a new menu of consistently excellent dishes combines the best of Caribbean and French cooking. Past favorites include West Indian chicken stew, lobster medallions with ginger sauce, roasted vegetable lasagna, balsamic-marinated tuna with sautéed spinach, veal chops in truffle cream sauce, and fresh pasta with julienned vegetables. There are only seven tables here, and resort guests have priority, so call for reservations well in advance. ⊠ *Shoal Bay West,* ☎ *809/497–6801. Reservations essential. AE. Closed Sept.–Nov. No lunch.*

$$$$  ✕ **Eclipse at Pimms.** Belgian restaurateur Bernard Erpicum, owner of the trendy celebrity hot spot Eclipse in Los Angeles, took this restaurant over at the end of 1996. "Cuisine of the Sun" is the theme of the California-inspired menu, and selections include roasted local wahoo with an almond-orange crust and flash-grilled ahi tuna with tropical salsa. Risottos, pastas, and sashimi are also available. The setting is right at the water's edge on a half-moon bay and open to the soft tropical evening breezes. ⊠ *Cap Juluca, Maunday's Bay,* ☎ *809/497–6666. Reservations essential. AE, MC, V.*

$$$$  ✕ **Malliouhana.** Sparkling crystal and fine china, exquisite service,
★ and a spectacularly romantic, candlelit, open-air setting are the perfect match for this restaurant's exceptional haute French cuisine. Consulting chef Michel Rostang, renowned for his Paris boîte, and chef Alain Laurent create a new menu each season. Past choices have included conch chowder with fennel, grilled snapper with pumpkin, lobster medallions with seasoned polenta, and chicken breasts from Bresse stuffed with asparagus. Don't pass up desserts here, which have included a roast pear in Sauternes with walnut brioche and cinnamon ice cream. The wine cellar contains nearly 25,000 bottles. ⊠ *Meads Bay,* ☎ *809/497–6111. Reservations essential. AE, MC, V. Closed Sept.–Oct.*

$$$  ✕ **Blanchard's.** At restaurateurs Bob and Melinda Blanchard's popu-
★ lar waterfront spot, with floor-to-ceiling doors that fold back to let in the breezes, you can dine on elements of Cajun, Caribbean, and Asian cooking. The green chili corn cakes, wild mushroom ragout, and Indonesian beef satay make good starters and can be followed by swordfish stuffed with leeks and fontina cheese or red snapper brushed with a balsamic mango glaze. Fish is the house specialty, but you can also order Black Angus hand-cut steaks, free-range chicken, or one of the daily pasta specials. Desserts are tempting, especially the cappuccino brownies and a remarkable gingerbread box filled with warm bananas and cinnamon cream. There is also a 2,000-bottle wine cellar and a selection of fine Armagnacs and cognacs. ⊠ *Meads Bay,* ☎ *809/497–6100. Reservations essential. AE, MC, V. Closed Sun. No lunch.*

**$$$** ✕ **Paradise Cafe.** Seductive aromas from the kitchen and the tinkling of wind chimes waft through this informal, breezy beachfront restaurant overlooking Shoal Bay. The chef draws from a wealth of cuisines— French, Italian, Cajun, Mediterranean, and Asian—in the preparation of seafood, chicken, and beef. Among the standouts are West Indian bouillabaisse, pan-seared grouper in a toasted almond and peanut crust, and rockfish fillet flash-fried in peanut oil and served with a sake and tamarind sauce. Hamburgers, salads, soups, and individual pizzas round out the more simple lunch menu. ⊠ *Shoal Bay West,* ☎ *809/497–6010. AE, MC, V. Closed Mon.*

**$$** ✕ **Pizzazz.** Two Cape Cod restaurateurs originally opened this appealing spot on busy Sandy Ground and found immediate popularity. They've picked up and moved shop and now have a spot on trendy West End. The menu is better than ever and features a variety of veal, seafood, chicken, and pasta dishes, including fresh mussels and clams, osso buco, and lobster fra diavolo. The olive bread comes straight from their oven and is delicious. ⊠ *West End,* ☎ *809/497–2386. MC, V. No lunch.*

## Sandy Ground, South Hill, and Rendezvous Bay

**$$$$** ✕ **Casablanca.** Multiarched ceilings covered with pastel Moroccan mosaics, and nighttime views of the lights of St. Martin twinkling across the water, lend a dramatic air to this favored dining spot. Veal chop with a ragout of vegetables, roast Cornish hen with mashed sweet potatoes, and filet mignon with an onion and marsala compote are a few of the entrées found on the eclectic menu, which combines Caribbean and South American flavors. The mascarpone pumpkin cheesecake may sound a bit unorthodox, but it's the hit of the dessert list. ⊠ *Rendezvous Bay,* ☎ *809/497–6999. AE, MC, V.*

**$$$** ✕ **Riviera Bar & Restaurant.** The door opened here in 1980, and the Riviera has been popular ever since. The chef has created an unusual menu of French, Creole, and Asian specialties—French cheeses, homemade pâté, sushi, sashimi, oysters sautéed in soy sauce and sake, and conch in a spicy Creole sauce are typical offerings. The grilled lobster and fish soup à la Provençale are highly recommended. Crowds head here Saturday evenings for special paella or couscous dinners. The beachside setting is relaxed and informal, and there's a very happy happy hour from 6 to 7 daily. Live bands play here frequently in season. ⊠ *Sandy Ground,* ☎ *809/497–2833. AE, V.*

**$$** ✕ **Ferryboat Inn.** This charming waterside restaurant is just a short walk
★ from the ferry dock at Blowing Point. Tables are open to the breezes, and the nighttime view of St. Martin's glimmering lights lends a romantic atmosphere. The French onion and black-bean soups, grilled lobster, lobster thermidor (the house specialty), and *entrecôte du vin au poivre* (a house version of steak au poivre with a red wine sauce) are all delicious. There are also veal and chicken dishes, hamburgers, and omelets. ⊠ *Cul de Sac Rd., Blowing Point,* ☎ *809/497–6613. AE, MC, V. No lunch Sun.*

**$$** ✕ **Lucy's Harbour View Restaurant.** A swinging gate forms the entrance to this terrace restaurant. Sweeping sea views and Lucy's delicious whole red snapper are the specialties here; curried and Creole dishes, such as conch and goat, are also favored selections. Be sure to try the sautéed potatoes (but be very cautious with the tableside hot sauce). A reggae band plays on Wednesday and Friday nights. ⊠ *South Hill,* ☎ *809/497– 6253. No credit cards. Closed Sun.*

**$–$$** ✕ **Arlo's.** This popular Italian restaurant, on a hilltop overlooking the
★ sea, is under new ownership and now includes an expansive dining terrace. It still serves the best pizza on the island, but the menu has gotten a bit fancier. If you don't want pizza as a main course, share one as an appetizer, then choose from a list of entrées that includes farfalle

with salmon in a dill sauce, chicken stuffed with mushrooms and peppers in a lobster sauce, spaghetti Bolognese, and lasagna. There's always a nightly appetizer and entrée special. ⊠ *South Hill,* ☎ *809/497–6810. MC, V. Closed Sun. and Sept.–Oct. No lunch.*

$  ✕ **Aquarium.** An upstairs terrace, the Aquarium is all gussied up with gingerbread trim, bright blue walls, and red tablecloths. For lunch, there are sandwiches and burgers. Stewed lobster, curried chicken, barbecued chicken, and mutton stew are offered at night. This is a popular spot with locals. ⊠ *South Hill,* ☎ *809/497–2720. No credit cards. Closed Tues. and Sun.*

$  ✕ **Johnno's.** Performances by the island band Dumpa and the AnVibes make this *the* place to be on Sunday afternoons, but the grilled or barbecued lobster, kingfish, snapper (all of which Johnno catches himself), and chicken are good any time. This is a classic Caribbean beach bar, attracting a funky eclectic mix, from locals to movie stars. ⊠ *Sandy Ground,* ☎ *809/497–2728. No credit cards.*

## The Valley and George Hill

$$$  ✕ **Koal Keel.** This restaurant, in a restored 18th-century great house
★   that was once part of a sugar and cotton plantation, provides a nice contrast to the island's ubiquitous beachfront eateries. In the entranceway sits an antique mahogany bed, and the dining room is furnished with period furniture. The original handwrought stone walls are broken by window-size open spaces, creating a cool, breezy atmosphere. A replica of the house's original rock oven is used to bake fresh breads and to roast chickens and racks of lamb. The cuisine here is "Euro-Carib," and Chef Smoke makes abundant use of local ingredients like fresh fish, mangoes, and coconut. Try the Island Pea Soup, a smooth blend of pigeon peas and Caribbean sweet potatoes, then move on to the succulent goatfish with snow peas and ginger, the lobster ravioli, or the smoked grouper on a bed of leeks. The chocolate fondant is worth saving room for. More than 20,000 bottles of wine are stored in the wine cellar here. ⊠ *The Valley,* ☎ *809/497–2930. Reservations essential. AE, MC, V. Closed Sept.–mid-Oct.*

$$$  ✕ **Palm Court.** This stylish eatery in the Cinnamon Reef Beach Club
★   is a long palm-lined corridor with red terra-cotta tile floors, Haitian furniture, a beautiful mural of the many varieties of local fish, and huge, arched picture windows fronting the Caribbean. Frenchman Didier Rochat and Anguillan Vernon Hughes collaborate in the creation of an exciting nouvelle Caribbean menu. Char-grilled tuna with cinnamon tomato raisin sauce, queenfish roasted in phyllo and served with saffron cappellini, and swordfish steak in passion-fruit salsa are house specialties. The mango puffs in caramel sauce are justly famous. ⊠ *Cinnamon Beach Club, Little Harbour,* ☎ *809/497–2727. AE, MC, V. Closed mid-Sept.–mid-Oct.*

$–$$  ✕ **Old House.** Guests enjoy the relaxing atmosphere and the local cui-
★   sine at this lovely restaurant on a hill near the airport. Tables are covered with white-and-green tablecloths and are decorated with fresh flowers, even at breakfast, when regulars know to order the island fruit pancakes. For lunch or dinner try the conch simmered in lime juice and wine, curried local lamb with pigeon peas and rice, or Anguillan pot fish cooked in a sauce of limes, garlic, and tomatoes. ⊠ *George Hill,* ☎ *809/497–2228. MC, V.*

$  ✕ **Le Petit Patissier.** Freshly brewed teas, espresso, and cappuccino plus just-baked pastries, breads, and cakes are served from morning to night indoors or on the small balcony of this café above the well-known restaurant Koal Keel (☞ *above*). ⊠ *The Valley,* ☎ *809/497–2930. AE, MC, V. Closed Sept.–mid-Oct.*

$ ✕ **Roy's.** The dainty pink-and-white-covered deck belies the rowdy reputation of Roy and Mandy Bosson's pub, an Anguillan mainstay with some of the island's best buys. The menu's most popular items are Roy's fish-and-chips, cold English beer, pork fricassee, and a wonderful chocolate rum cake. Sunday's lunch special is roast beef and Yorkshire pudding. A faithful clientele gathers in the lively bar. ✉ *Crocus Bay,* ☎ *809/497–2470. MC, V. Closed Mon. No lunch Sat.*

### East End

$$$ ✕ **Hibernia.** One of the island's most creative menus is served in this delightful wood-beamed cottage restaurant. Unorthodox yet delectable culinary pairings—inspired by the chef's travels from France to the Far East—include duck breast with grilled almonds and passion-fruit sauce, fricassee of lobster in mustard cinnamon sauce, spicy lobster soufflé, and breast of chicken cooked with honey and mild chilies. There is also an unusual Thai-inspired bouillabaisse of assorted local seafood. For dessert, try the talked-about prunes in Armagnac chocolate sauce with homemade chestnut ice cream. ✉ *Island Harbour,* ☎ *809/497–4290. AE, MC, V. Closed Mon.*

$$–$$$ ✕ **Zara's.** Award-winning island chef Shamash presides at this cozy new restaurant at the Allamanda Beach Club, where the cuisine is a mix of Italian and Caribbean. Try the lobster pasta in a white wine sauce, the garlic-crusted snapper, or the very popular seafood platter, which has a bit of everything from conch to calamari. Grilled chicken, steaks, and veal are also available. ✉ *Upper Shoal Bay,* ☎ *809/497–3229. No credit cards.*

$$ ✕ **La Fontana.** Northern Italian dishes at this small restaurant have spicy island touches, thanks to the Rastafarian chef. Possibilities include fettuccine *al limone* (with a sauce of black olives, lemon, Parmesan, and butter), pasta with lobster and fresh herbs, and a daily Rasta pasta special, such as linguine with tomatoes and shrimp. Also on the menu are grilled duck, steak, fish, and chicken, as well as a fantastic lobster dish cooked with black olives, capers, and tomatoes. ✉ *Fountain Beach Hotel, Shoal Bay,* ☎ *809/497–3492. AE, MC, V. Closed Wed. and Sept.*

# Beaches

Renowned for their beauty, the dazzling white-sand beaches here are the best reason to come to Anguilla, and each one is different. You'll find long beaches that are great for walking, deserted beaches, and beaches lined with bars and restaurants, accompanied by surf ranging from wild to supercalm.

### Northeast Coast

**Captain's Bay** rewards you with peaceful isolation for making the grueling, four-wheel-drive-only trip along the inhospitable dirt road that leads to the northeastern end of the island toward Junk's Hole. The surf here slaps the sands with a vengeance, and the undertow is quite strong—wading is the safest water sport.

The mostly calm waters of **Island Harbour** are surrounded by a long, slender beach. For centuries Anguillans have put out from these sands in colorful, handmade fishing boats to seek the day's catch. There are several beach bars and restaurants, and this is the departure point for the three-minute boat ride to **Scilly Cay.** From this boat, you can get snorkeling equipment, but at times the waters are too rough to see much. A beach bar on Scilly Cay serves drinks and grilled seafood.

### Northwest Coast

**Barnes Bay** is a superb spot for windsurfing and snorkeling. In high season this beach can get a bit crowded with day-trippers from St. Martin.

At **Little Bay,** sheer cliffs embroidered with agave and creeping vines rise up behind a small gray-sand beach, usually accessible only by water (it's a favored spot for snorkeling and night dives). Virtually assured of total privacy, the hale and hearty can also clamber down the cliffs by rope to explore the caves and surrounding reef.

The clear blue waters of **Road Bay** beach are usually dotted with yachts. The Mariners Cliffside Beach Resort, several restaurants, a water-sports center, and lots of windsurfing and waterskiing activity make this area (often referred to as Sandy Ground) an active and commercial one. It's a typical Caribbean scene daily as fishermen set out in their boats and goats ramble the littoral at will. The snorkeling is not very good here, but the bay does specialize in glorious sunset vistas.

From a distance, **Sandy Island,** nestled in coral reefs about 2 mi offshore from Road Bay, appears to be no more than a tiny speck of sand and a few spindly palm trees. It has the look of a classic deserted island, but it's got the modern-day comforts of a beach boutique, beach bar, and restaurant. Use of snorkeling gear and underwater cameras is free. A ferry heads there every hour from Sandy Ground.

## Southeast Coast

**Mimi Bay** is a difficult-to-reach, isolated, ½-mi-long beach east of Sea Feathers Bay. The trip is worth it. When the surf is not too rough, the barrier reef makes for great snorkeling.

Not far from Sea Feathers Bay is **Sandy Hill,** a base for fishermen. Here you can buy fish and lobster right off the boats and snorkel in the warm waters. Don't plan to sunbathe—the beach is quite narrow here.

Unfortunately, it's no longer a secret that **Shoal Bay East**—Shoal Bay, via Shoal Bay Road—is one of the prettiest beaches in the Caribbean. But this 2-mi L-shape beach of talcum-powder-soft white sand is definitely still worth a visit. There are beach chairs, umbrellas, and a backdrop of sea-grape and coconut trees, and for seafood and tropical drinks there's Trader Vic's, Uncle Ernie, and the Round Rock. Souvenir shops for T-shirts, suntan lotion, and the like abound. There's good snorkeling in the offshore coral reefs, and the water-sports center here can arrange diving, sailing, and fishing trips.

## Southwest Coast

The good news and the bad news about **Cove Bay** is the same—it's virtually deserted. There are no restaurants or bars, just calm waters, coconut trees, and soft sand that stretches down to Maunday's Bay.

One of the most popular beaches, wide, mile-long **Maunday's Bay** is known for good swimming and snorkeling; you can rent water-sports gear at Tropical Watersports (☞ Water Sports, *below*). Try Eclipse at Pimms (☞ Dining, *above*), at Cap Juluca, for fine food and drink.

**Rendezvous Bay** is 1½ mi of pearl-white sand. Here the water is calm, and there's a great view of St. Martin. The Anguilla Great House Beach Resort's open-air beach bar is handy for snacks and frosty island drinks.

Adjacent to Maunday's Bay is **Shoal Bay West,** a dazzling beach with several striking villa complexes, including the sculpturelike Cove Castles. Stop for lunch at the Paradise Cafe (☞ Dining, *above*) and ask someone there to point out the best snorkeling spots. Beachcombers may find lovely conch shells here.

# Outdoor Activities and Sports

## Cycling
There are plenty of flat stretches, making wheeling pretty easy.

Bikes can be rented from **Multiscenic Tours** (☎ 809/497–5810), which offers mountain bikes at George Hill and the Blowing Point Ferry Terminal.

## Deep-Sea Fishing
Albacore, dolphin, and kingfish are among the sea creatures angled after off Anguilla's shores. Trips can be arranged through **Sandy Island Deep Sea Fishing** in Sandy Ground (☎ 809/497–6395), or you can head to Sandy Ground and see which of the many locals who provide trips are available. Fishing tackle, diving gear, and other sports equipment are available at the **Tackle Box Sports Center** (⌧ The Valley, ☎ 809/497–2896).

## Diving
Seven sunken wrecks and a long barrier reef offer excellent diving opportunities. The **Dive Shop** (☎ 809/497–2020) is a full-service dive operator with a PADI 5-Star Training Center.

## Horseback Riding
Ride English or Western at **El Rancho–Del Blues** (☎ 809/497–6164). Two rides are scheduled daily, and both end with an afternoon swim at one of Anguilla's many fine beaches.

## Sea Excursions
Picnic, swimming, and diving excursions to Prickly Pear, Sandy Island, and Scilly Cay are available through **Sandy Island Enterprises** (☎ 809/497–6395). **Anguilla Sails Ltd.** (☎ 809/497–2253) offers day sails, sunset sails, and moonlight cruises. *Chocolat* (☎ 809/497–3394) is a 35-ft catamaran that is available for private charter and also has scheduled day, sunset, and evening excursions to various nearby cays. **BING!** (☎ 809/497–6395) specializes in day, evening, and overnight trips for two to four people in a 37-ft sailboat.

## Tennis
Peter Burwash International, highly respected for its tennis programs, manages the tennis program at the **Malliouhana** (☎ 809/497–6111), which has four Laykold hard courts. **Cap Juluca** (☎ 809/497–6666) has three hard courts managed by Peter Burwash International. Two Deco Turf tournament courts are at **Cinnamon Reef Beach Club** (☎ 809/497–2727). You'll find two tennis courts at the **Fountain Beach and Tennis Club** (☎ 809/497–6395). **Rendezvous Bay** (☎ 809/497–6549) has two tennis courts. There's a single tennis court at **Cove Castles** (☎ 809/497–6801). The **Mariners Cliffside Beach Resort** (☎ 809/497–2671) has one tennis court.

## Water Sports
The major resorts offer complimentary Windsurfers, paddleboats, and water skis to their guests. If your hotel has no water-sports facilities, you can get in gear at the **Dive Shop** (☎ 809/497–2020). The Dive Shop also has PADI instructors, short resort courses, and more than a dozen dive sites; also, **Sundancer**, its 30-ft powerboat, is available for charters. **Tropical Watersports** (☎ 809/497–6666) rents Sunfish and Hobie Cats. Sailboats and speedboats can be rented at **Sandy Island Enterprises** (☎ 809/497–6395).

# Shopping

Shopping tips can be found in the informative free publications *Anguilla Life* and *What We Do in Anguilla*, but you have to be a truly dedicated shopper to peel yourself off the beach and poke around in Anguilla's few shops. For a better selection, catch the ferry to Marigot on St. Martin and spend the day in chic boutiques showcasing the latest in Italian and French fashion. For local arts and crafts, many artists will hold open studios in addition to showing their work in the shops listed below; the tourist office can provide brochures.

## Good Buys

### CLOTHES

**Azemmour Boutique** (⊠ Cap Juluca, Maunday's Bay, ☎ 809/497–6666) specializes in European swimwear and also carries cover-ups, sandals, and beach bags, in addition to fine jewelry.

**Beach Stuff** (⊠ Back St., South Hill, ☎ 809/497–6814), in its brightly painted building, attracts the younger crowd with bathing suits and cover-ups, sunglasses, T-shirts, and other sportswear.

**Boutique at Malliouhana** (⊠ Meads Bay, ☎ 809/497–6111) is the most upscale shop on Anguilla, selling such designer specialties as jewelry by Oro De Sol, La Perla swimwear, Go Silk resort wear, and Robert LaRoche sunglasses.

**Caribbean Fancy** (⊠ George Hill Rd., ☎ 809/497–3133) features Ta-Tee's line of cool, crinkle-cotton resort wear and also sells books, coffees and spices, and gift items.

**Caribbean Style** (⊠ Rendezvous Bay, ☎ 809/497–6717) has a small but eclectic collection of everything from sandals to jewelry to furniture.

**Java Wraps** (⊠ George Hill Rd., ☎ 809/497–5497), a small outpost of the Caribbean chain, carries superb batik clothing for the whole family.

**La Romana** (⊠ Meads Bay, ☎ 809/497–6181), a miniversion of the well-known international specialty boutique, is the place to go for swimwear, Fendi fashions, and fine luggage.

**La Sirena Boutique** (⊠ Meads Bay, ☎ 809/467–6827) is bursting with colorful dresses, slacks, belts, and other accessories.

**Objets D'Art Collectibles** (⊠ Warden's Place, The Valley, ☎ 809/497–2787) is a gallery that also sells "wearable art," sandals, jewelry, and fabrics.

**Oluwakemi's Afrocentric Boutique** (⊠ Lansome Rd., The Valley, ☎ 809/497–5411) sells books, sandals, umbrellas, jewelry, T-shirts, hats, and a variety of other garments. You can also choose from an array of fabrics and have virtually any item of apparel custom-made.

**Sunshine Shop** (⊠ South Hill, ☎ 809/497–6964) stocks cotton pareos, silk-screen items, cotton resort wear, and hand-painted Haitian wood items.

**Valley Gap** (⊠ Shoal Bay Beach, ☎ 809/497–2754) sells a selection of local crafts, plus T-shirts and swimwear.

**Vanhelle Boutique** (⊠ Sandy Ground, ☎ 809/497–2965) is a little shop with an appealing selection of gift items, as well as Brazilian swimsuits for men and women.

**Whispers** (⊠ Cap Juluca, ☎ 809/497–6666) carries Caribbean handcrafts and stylish resort wear for men and women.

FOOD TO GO

If you plan to picnic (on the beach or in your room), try the **Fat Cat Gourmet** (✉ George Hill, ☎ 809/497–2307) for escargots to go, as well as take-out quiche, soups, chili, chicken, and conch dishes.

**Amy's Bakery** (✉ Blowing Point, ☎ 809/497–6775) turns out home-made pies, cakes, tarts, cookies, and breads.

LOCAL ARTS AND CRAFTS

**Alicea's Place** (✉ The Quarter, ☎ 809/497–3540), a small boutique, sells locally made ceramics and pottery and lifelike wooden flowers from Bali.

**Anguilla Arts and Crafts Center** (✉ The Valley, ☎ 809/497–2200) carries a wide selection of island crafts.

**Cheddie's Carving Shop** (✉ The Cove, ☎ 809/497–6027) showcases Cheddie's own fanciful creatures crafted out of wonderfully textured woods, including mahogany, walnut, and driftwood. Even the whimsically carved desk and balustrade in his studio testify to his vivid imagination.

**Devonish Cotton Gin Art Gallery** (✉ The Valley, ☎ 809/497–2949) purveys the wood, stone, and clay creations of Courtney Devonish, an internationally known potter and sculptor, as well as works by other prominent local artists.

**Michéle R. Lavalette Art Studio** (✉ North Hill, ☎ 809/497–5668) displays original oils, pastels, and watercolors.

**Mother Weme** (✉ The Valley, ☎ 809/497–4504) is an internationally known artist who paints charming montages of Anguillan and general Caribbean life, incorporating homes, churches, marketplaces, and people. Call for an appointment.

**New World Gallery** (✉ The Valley, ☎ 809/407–5950) has frequent exhibits of local art and sells artwork, jewelry, textiles, and antiquities.

**Scruples Gift Shop** (✉ Social Security Bldg., The Island, ☎ 809/497–2800) offers simple gift items, such as shells, handmade baskets, wood dolls, hand-crocheted mats, lace tablecloths, and bedspreads.

# Nightlife

Most of the major hotels feature some kind of live entertainment almost nightly in season. A Calypso combo plays most nights at **Cinnamon Reef Beach Club** (✉ Little Harbour, ☎ 809/497–2727). The **Dune Preserve** (✉ Rendezvous Bay, no phone) is the home of Bankie Banx, Anguilla's most popular recording star, who performs here weeknights. During high season, **Eclipse at Pimms** and **Chatterton's** (✉ Cap Juluca, ☎ 809/497–6666) have live music at dinner. Things are pretty loose and lively at **Johnno's** beach bar (☎ 809/497–2728) in Sandy Ground, which has live music and alfresco dancing Wednesday and Saturday nights as well as Sunday afternoons, when it feels as if the entire island population is in attendance. **Rafe's** (✉ South Hill, ☎ 809/497–3914) is the spot to go for late-night—sometimes even all-night—food, music, and dance. For soft dance music after a meal, go to **Lucy's Palm Palm** (☎ 809/497–2253) at Sandy Ground; there is usually a live band on Tuesday and Friday evenings. **Uncle Ernie's** (✉ Shoal Bay, no phone) often has music, and a lively crowd heads here almost every night. At **Smitty's** (✉ Island Harbour, ☎ 809/497–4300) the crowd swings all day and well into the night. There's live music nightly in season at the **Malliouhana** (✉ Meads Bay, ☎ 809/497–6111) during cocktail hours. The **Mayoumba Folkloric Theater,** a group made up of the best performers in the Anguilla Choral Circle, performs song-and-dance skits depicting Antillean and Caribbean culture with African drums and a string band. They appear every Thursday night at **La Sirena** (⊠ Meads Bay, ☎ 809/497–6827).

Local groups include Keith Gumbs and the Mellow Tones, Spraka, Megaforce, Joe and the Invaders, Dumpa and the AnVibes, and Sleepy and the All-Stars, a string-and-scratch band. Steel Vibrations, a pan band, often entertains at barbecues and West Indian evenings.

## Exploring Anguilla

Exploring on Anguilla is mostly about checking out the spectacular beaches and classy resorts. There are only a few roads on the island, and none of them are marked, so it's fairly easy to get lost your first time out. Having a map, and checking it frequently against passing landmarks, is essential. If you didn't get a map at the airport, the ferry dock, or your hotel, head to the tourist office in the Valley (☞ Visitor Information *in* Anguilla A to Z, *below*).

*Numbers in the margin correspond to points of interest on the Anguilla map.*

SIGHTS TO SEE

**❽ Amerindian Mini-Museum.** A small display of objects used by the Arawak Indians that inhabited Anguilla centuries ago is showcased here. There is also a 4- by 8-ft oil painting suggesting what Big Springs, a nearby Amerindian ceremonial ground, might have looked like when Amerindians lived there. ⊠ *Arawak Beach Resort, Island Harbour,* ☎ *809/497–4888.* ☞ *Free.* ☉ *Mon.–Sat. 9–4:30.*

**❹ Bethel Methodist Church.** An excellent example of skillful island stonework can be found in the walls of this charming little building, not far from Sandy Ground, at South Hill. It also has some colorful stained-glass windows. ⊠ *South Hill, no phone.*

**❺ Crocus Hill Prison.** On the highest point in Anguilla—213 ft above sea level—the historical prison is pretty much in ruin, but the view is outstanding. ⊠ *Valley Rd. at Crocus Hill.*

**❾ Heritage Collection.** Anguillan artifacts, old photographs, and records trace the island's history from the days of the Arawaks to the present at this new museum. Ancient pottery shards and stone tools along with photographs of the island in the early 20th century are quite interesting. ⊠ *East End at Pond Ground,* ☎ *809/497–4440.* ☞ *Free.* ☉ *Mon.–Sat. 10–4:30.*

**❼ Island Harbour.** Anguillans have been fishing for centuries in the brightly painted, simple, handcrafted fishing boats that line the shore of the harbor. It's hard to believe, but skillful pilots take these little boats out to sea as far as 50 or 60 mi. Late afternoon is the best time to see the day's catch—piles of lobsters and wriggling local fish. ⊠ *Island Harbour, at northwest end of island, facing Island Harbour Bay.*

**❷ Old Factory.** For many years the cotton that was grown on Anguilla and imported to England was ginned in the beautiful historic building that is now the home of the **Devonish Cotton Gin Art Gallery.** Much of the original ginning machinery is intact and on display here. ⊠ *The Valley,* ☎ *809/497–2949.* ☞ *Free.* ☉ *Daily 10–4.*

**❶ Sandy Ground.** This is by far the most active and most developed of the island's beaches, and almost everyone who comes to Anguilla stops by here at least one afternoon or evening. Little open-air bars and restaurants line the shore, and there are several little boutiques, a dive shop,

and a small commercial pier. This is where you catch the ferry for tiny
**Sandy Island**, just 2 mi offshore.

❸ **Wallblake House.** On Wallblake Road, just north of the roundabout,
is a plantation house built in 1787 by Will Blake (Wallblake is probably a corruption of his name). High living, invasions by the French
in 1796, and legends of murders pervade the atmosphere here. Now
owned and actively used by the Catholic Church, the estate has spacious rooms, with ceilings edged with handsome carving. On the
grounds are an ancient vaulted stone cistern and an outbuilding called
the Bakery (which wasn't used for making bread at all but for baking
turkeys and hams). Call Father John (☎ 809/497–2405) to make an
appointment to tour the plantation. ⊠ *The Valley.*

❻ **Warden's Place.** This former sugar-plantation great house, built in the
1790s, is one of the two oldest buildings on Anguilla. Now the location of the Koal Keel restaurant (☞ Dining, *above*), for many years it
served as the residence of the chief administrator of the island, who
also doubled as the only medical practitioner. The building is a fine
example of island stonework. ⊠ *The Valley.*

# Anguilla A to Z

## Arriving and Departing

### BY BOAT

Two firms run ferryboats frequently between Anguilla and St. Martin.
Boats leave from Blowing Point on Anguilla every half hour from 7:30
to 5 and from Marigot on St. Martin every half hour from 8 to 5:30.
There are also evening ferries that leave from Blowing Point at 6 and
9:15 and from Marigot at 7 and 10:45. You pay a $2 departure tax be-
fore boarding and the $9 one-way fare ($11 evenings) on board. Don't
buy a round-trip ticket, because it restricts you to the boat on which it
is purchased. On very windy days the 20-minute trip can be bouncy, and
if you suffer from motion sickness, you may want medication. An information booth outside the customs shed in Blowing Point is usually
open daily from 8:30 to 5, but sometimes the attendant wanders off.

### BY PLANE

**American Airlines** (☎ 809/497–3131 or 800/433–7300) is the major
airline with nonstop flights from the continental United States to its
hub in San Juan, from which the airline's **American Eagle** flies three
times daily (twice daily off-season) to Anguilla. **Windward Islands
Airways** (Winair; ☎ 809/775–0183) wings in daily from St. Thomas
and at least three times a day from St. Maarten's Juliana Airport. **LIAT**
(☎ 809/465–2286) comes in from Antigua, Nevis, St. Kitts, St. Maarten, and St. Thomas. **Air Anguilla** (☎ 809/497–2643) offers several
flights daily from St. Maarten, the U.S. Virgin Islands, and the British
Virgin Islands and provides air-taxi service on request from neighboring islands. **Tyden Air** (☎ 809/497–2719) has scheduled flights four
times a week to both St. Thomas and St. Kitts from Anguilla and offers charter day trips to many neighboring islands.

### FROM THE AIRPORT

At **Wallblake Airport** you'll find taxis lined up to meet the planes. A
trip from the airport to Sandy Ground will cost about $8, to West End
resorts between $14 and $20.

### FROM THE DOCKS

Taxis are always waiting to pick passengers up at the Blowing Point
landing. It costs $12 to get to the Malliouhana hotel, $15 to the Cap
Juluca hotel, and $17 to the most distant hotels.

## Currency

Legal tender here is the Eastern Caribbean dollar (E.C.), but U.S. dollars are widely accepted. (You'll often get change in E.C. dollars.) The E.C. dollar is fairly stable relative to the U.S. dollar, hovering between EC$2.60 and $2.70 to the U.S. dollar. Credit cards are not always accepted, and it's hard to predict where you'll need cash. Some resorts will only settle in cash; a few will also accept personal checks. Be sure to carry lots of small bills; change for a $20 bill is often difficult to obtain. Note: Prices quoted are in U.S. dollars unless indicated otherwise.

## Emergencies

**Police** and **fire:** ☎ 911; 809/497–2333 for nonemergencies. **Hospital:** There is a 24-hour emergency room at the **Princess Alexandra Hospital** (✉ Stoney Ground, ☎ 809/497–2551). **Ambulance:** ☎ 809/497–2551. **Pharmacies:** The **Government Pharmacy** (✉ The Valley, ☎ 809/497–2551), in Princess Alexandra Hospital, is open daily from 8:30–8:30; the **Paramount Pharmacy** (✉ Waterswamp, ☎ 809/497–2366) is open Monday–Saturday 8:30–8:30 and has a 24-hour emergency service.

## Getting Around

CAR RENTALS

This is your best bet for maximum mobility if you're comfortable driving on the left and don't mind some jostling. Anguilla's roads are generally paved (in a manner of speaking), but those that are not can be incredibly rutted, even those leading to a fancy hotel. Observe the 30 mph speed limit, and watch out for the four-legged creatures—goats, sheep, and cows—that amble across the road. To rent a car you'll need a valid driver's license and a local license, which can be obtained for $6 at any of the car-rental agencies. **Avis** (☎ 809/497–6221 or 800/331–1212) rents sedans and four-wheel-drive vehicles. **Budget** (☎ 809/497–2217 or 800/472–3325) has many four-wheel and sedans to choose from. **Connors (National)** (☎ 809/497–6433 or 800/328–4567) rents four-wheel-drive vehicles and air-conditioned sedans. Head to **Island Car Rental** (☎ 809/497–2723) for car rentals, including four-wheel vehicles. Count on $35 to $45 per day's rental, plus insurance. Motorcycles and scooters are available for about $30 per day from **R & M Cycle** (☎ 809/497–2430).

TAXIS

Taxi rates are regulated by the government, and there are fixed fares from point to point. Fares, which are government regulated, should be listed in brochures the drivers carry. Posted rates are for one or two people; each additional passenger adds $3 to the total. Tipping is welcome.

## Guided Tours

A round-the-island tour by taxi will take about 2½ hours and will cost $40 for one or two people, $5 for each additional passenger. **Bennie's Tours** (✉ Blowing Point, ☎ 809/497–2788) and **Malliouhana Travel and Tours** (✉ The Valley, ☎ 809/497–2431) put together personalized package tours of the island.

## Language

English, with a strong West Indian lilt, is spoken here.

## Opening and Closing Times

Banks are open Monday–Thursday 8–3 and Friday 8–5. Shopping hours vary. No two shops seem to have the same hours, but many are certainly open between 10 and 4. Call the shop, ask at the tourist office for opening and closing times, or adopt the island way of doing things: If it's not open when you stop by, stop by again.

## Passports and Visas

U.S. and Canadian citizens need proof of identity. A passport is preferred (even one that has expired within the last five years). Also acceptable is a photo ID, such as a driver's license, *along with* a birth certificate (with raised seal), voter registration card, or naturalization papers. All visitors must also have a return or ongoing ticket. Visitor's passes are valid for stays of up to three months. British citizens must have a passport.

## Precautions

The manchineel tree, which resembles an apple tree, shades many beaches. The tree bears poisonous fruit, and the sap from the tree causes painful blisters. Avoid sitting beneath the tree, because even dew or raindrops falling from the leaves can blister your skin.

Be *sure* to take along insect repellent—mosquitoes can be pesky in the late afternoon.

Anguilla is a quiet, relatively safe island, but there's no point in tempting fate by leaving your valuables unattended in your hotel room, on the beach, or in your car.

## Taxes and Service Charges

The government imposes an 8% tax on accommodations. The departure tax is $10 at the airport, $2 if you leave by boat. A 10% service charge is added to all hotel bills and most restaurant bills. If you're not certain about the restaurant service charge, ask. If you are particularly pleased with the service, you can certainly leave a little extra. Tip taxi drivers 10% of the fare.

## Telephones and Mail

To call Anguilla from the United States, dial area code 264 + 497 + the local four-digit number. (The area code was recently changed from 809.) International direct dial is available on the island. To make a local call on the island, just dial the four-digit number. **Cable & Wireless** (✉ Wallblake Rd., ☎ 809/497–3100) is open weekdays 8–6, Saturday 9–1, Sunday 10–2 and sells Caribbean Phone Cards ($5, $10, $20 denominations) for use in specially marked phone booths. The card can be used for local calls and calls to other islands. You can also use the card to call the United States and, in this case, bill the call to MasterCard or Visa. Inside the departure lounge at the Blowing Point ferry and at the airport, there is an AT&T USADirect access telephone for collect or credit-card calls to the United States.

Airmail letters to the United States cost EC60¢; postcards, EC25¢.

## Visitor Information

In the United Kingdom, contact the **Anguilla Tourist Office** (✉ 3 Epirus Rd., London SW6 7UJ, ☎ 0171/937–7725).

On Anguilla, the **Anguilla Tourist Office** (✉ Social Security Bldg., The Valley, ☎ 809/497–2759 or 800/553–4939, ℻ 809/497–2710) is open weekdays 8–noon and 1–4.

# 3 Antigua

*One could spend an entire year exploring Antigua's 366 beaches, all of them public—some absolutely deserted and others lined with resorts offering sailing, diving, windsurfing, and snorkeling. Antigua has hotels to please travelers of all kinds, from those seeking refined elegance, to those in search of beachfront merriment or quiet snoozing, to those charmed by beautifully restored historic inns.*

Updated by
Jordan Simon

**A**NTIGUA (AN-*TEE*-GA), the largest of the British Leeward Islands (108 square mi), has a strong sense of national identity and a rich historic inheritance. Its cricketers, like the legendary Viv Richards (arguably the greatest batsman the game has ever seen), are famous throughout the Caribbean. Its people are known for their sharp commercial spirit (a typically revealing—and disarming—sign reads DIANE'S BOUTIQUE AND CAR PARTS); their wit; and, unfortunately at the government level, their corruption.

Lord Horatio Nelson headquartered his fleet in Antigua during colonial times, and English Harbour, in the southeast of the island, is steeped in that era's history. At its center, Nelson's Dockyard, now a national park, is Antigua's answer to Williamsburg, Virginia—a carefully restored gem of British Georgian architecture. Accommodations here are generally in smaller, inn-type hotels. For Anglophiles and history buffs, English Harbour and the surrounding villages and sight will be immensely rewarding.

Those in search of beaches, nightlife, shopping, and restaurants will want to head to the northwestern end of the island, where resorts and hotels are scattered from Five Islands Harbour, south of St. John, to Dickenson Bay and points north.

One of the least-developed parts of the island is in the southwest, in the shadow of Antigua's highest mountain, Boggy Peak. Fry's Bay and Darkwood Beach hold long, unspoiled scimitars of sand.

The original inhabitants of Antigua were a people called the Siboney. They lived here as early as 4,000 years ago and disappeared mysteriously, leaving the island unpopulated for about 1,000 years. When Columbus arrived in 1493, the Arawaks had set up housekeeping. The English took up residence in 1632. After 30-odd years of bloody battles involving the Caribs, the Dutch, the French, and the English, the French ceded the island to the English in 1667. Unlike many other Caribbean islands, which spent centuries being reflagged by various nations, Antigua remained under English control until achieving full independence, with its sister island Barbuda (26 mi to the north), on November 1, 1981.

The combined population of the two islands is about 70,000, only 1,200 of whom live on Barbuda. Tourism is the main industry here—new condominiums and the renovation and expansion of the major hotels are among the results of a recent building boom—and the government is seeking to broaden its monetary resources by reintroducing agriculture and manufacturing into the economy.

## Lodging

Scattered along Antigua's sandy beaches and tropical hillsides are resorts of all kinds—exclusive, elegant hideaways; romantic restored inns; casual, go-barefoot-everywhere places; and all-inclusive hot spots for couples. Choose accommodations near St. John's—anywhere between Dickenson Bay and Five Islands Harbour—if you want to be close to the action. English Harbour, though far from St. John's, has the best inns and several excellent restaurants, and it is the hangout for the yachting crowd. The resorts scattered elsewhere on the island cater more to guests who want to stay put or are seeking seclusion. Many properties sustained some damage during the 1995 hurricanes, but most have been renovated, including the exclusive Galley Bay, a longtime favorite of the Caribbean jetset. Even the famed thatched-hut double bungalows of the Gauguin Village have been rebuilt, and despite the addition of 24 deluxe beachfront rooms, the Galley Bay retains an intimate feel. A more moderate yet popular property, the all-condo Banana Cove is also doubling in size as units are converted into standard hotel rooms, with expanded facilities including a new restaurant, pool, and tennis court. Renamed Mango Bay, it should have opened its doors by mid-1997. The price categories below reflect the room cost during high season.

| CATEGORY | COST* |
|---|---|
| $$$$ | over $375 |
| $$$ | $275–$375 |
| $$ | $150–$275 |
| $ | under $150 |

*All prices are for a standard double room, excluding 8½% tax and 10% service charge.*

$$$$   ⊠ **Curtain Bluff.** Howard Hulford built this resort more than 30 years
★   ago, and he's still very active in its management. You're likely to see him puttering around his beloved gardens or tasting a new wine for his legendary cellar of 20,000 bottles. The resort is named for its spectacular setting on a bluff bordered on one side by the wild Atlantic Ocean and on the other by the calm Caribbean. Standard rooms with wicker furnishings and terraces or balconies are in two-story beachfront buildings facing the Caribbean. Suites zigzag up the bluff on the Atlantic side and are some of the finest accommodations on Antigua—huge split-level apartments with two balconies, a large living room, and, up a flight of steps, a spacious bedroom. Swiss chef Reudi Portmann has ruled the kitchen of the greenery-filled open-air restaurant since the resort opened. Jacket and tie are required for dinner of classic Continental cuisine, except on Wednesday and Sunday. Resort extras include complimentary deep-sea fishing and PADI dive resort course. Curtain Bluff's exceptional service and country-club ambience appeal to a more mature crowd, along with occasional honeymooners and families. ⊠ *Box 288, St. John's,* ☎ *268/462–8400; 212/289–8888 in NY;* FAX *268/462–8409. 61 rooms and suites. 2 restaurants, lounge, in-room safes, putting green, 4 tennis courts, croquet, exercise room, squash, water sports. AE. FAP. Closed mid-May–mid-Oct.*

$$$$   ⊠ **K Club.** "K" stands for Krizia, the famed Italian designer; her dra-
★   matic style and touch animate every nook and cranny of this superdeluxe Barbuda hideaway, a member of the Leading Hotels of the World. The public spaces gleam with white tiles and columns, natural wicker furnishings with oversize cushions, and striking cloth-and-bronze sculptures. All rooms and cottages open onto the champagne-color beach. The decor is chic and cool: white wicker and tile livened by turquoise and mint fabrics, wonderful wooden chairs whimsically carved with pineapples, speckled ceramic lamps, bamboo mats, towering fruit sculptures, showers submerged in vegetation, and amusing paintings. Each unit has its own kitchenette on a private veranda. The cuisine here is an innovative fusion of Tuscan grilling and Caribbean ingredients. Rates of $1,100 per couple and up may seem steep, but privacy and discretion are assured. No children under 12 are allowed. ⊠ *Coco Point, Barbuda,* ☎ *268/460–0300,* FAX *268/460–0305. 39 units. Restaurant, bar, grill, pool, hot tub, 9-hole golf course, 2 tennis courts, snorkeling, windsurfing, waterskiing, fishing, recreation room. AE, MC, V. MAP, FAP.*

$$$$   ⊠ **St. James's Club.** This out-of-the-way hotel is on the 100-acre spit of land that helps form Mamora Bay. Rooms and one-bedroom suites in the main buildings at the water's edge on the tip of the peninsula

are painted in pastel colors; some have romantic canopy beds. You enter past the "villa village," a tight cluster of two-bedroom units atop the hills that spill down toward the main hotel. Although also well decorated, these villas include views of your neighbor's roof. You can dine at the three restaurants in the main building: the Rainbow Garden, an elegant spot for a seafood dinner; the more casual, alfresco Docksider Cafe for island cuisine; or the Poolside Reef Deck, a breakfast and lunch spot. Overall, the St. James tends to live off its *renommé* (it is affiliated with other like-named properties in London and Paris) rather than what it delivers. After all, the resort started life as a Holiday Inn, and it shows. The casino is a hoot, filled with brass and tacky red-fringed lamp shades that a bordello might reject. And service is shockingly indifferent. That said, the beaches and extensive sports facilities—and such amenities as a hotel helicopter that can be chartered for sightseeing— make this a fine, if overpriced, full-service resort. ⊠ *Box 63, St. John's,* ☎ *268/460–5000 or 800/274–0008,* ℻ *268/460–3015. 178 units. 3 restaurants, 5 bars, room service, 3 pools, beauty salon, hot tub, massage, golf privileges, 7 tennis courts, croquet, exercise room, horseback riding, scuba diving, dive shop, marina, snorkeling, windsurfing, boating, waterskiing, shops, casino, nightclub, playground. AE, MC, V. EP, MAP.*

**$$$–$$$$** ⌂ **Pineapple Beach Club.** A broad stone walk leads directly from the reception area to the beach of this bustling, all-inclusive resort. All rooms are on or very near the beach, but some have only partial ocean or garden views. Rooms have redwood louvered windows, terra-cotta floors, and vivid Caribbean colors. There are no phones or TVs, but fax and phone service is available at the front desk. The new public spaces are impressive: open, flowing, in stone and tile, with wicker furnishings, handsome local paintings, and enormous potted plants. The main restaurant and the Pelican grill serve well-above-average cuisine, a savvy blend of Caribbean and Continental dishes; of the two, the Pelican offers a more intimate ambience. The Outhouse Bar is a classic Caribbean hangout, perched atop a hill with sweeping views and seemingly held together by business cards, license plates, and driftwood. With a full array of water sports, nightly entertainment, and an electronic casino, Pineapple Beach is an activity-oriented place, but it quiets down soon after midnight. ⊠ *Box 54, St. John's,* ☎ *268/463–2006 or 800/345–0356,* ℻ *268/465–2452. 125 rooms. 2 restaurants, bar, pool, 4 tennis courts, croquet, horseshoes, volleyball, kayaking, water sports. AE, MC, V. All-inclusive.*

**$$$** ⌂ **Hawksbill Beach Hotel.** Thirty-seven acres of the bucolic Five Islands peninsula, including five beaches (you can bathe in the buff at one) of fine tan sand, make up the grounds of this sprawling resort. The main building, the reception area, and the dining room rest on a small bluff that commands a sweeping view of the sea and Montserrat beyond, set off by the restored ruins of a sugar mill in the foreground. Gingerbread-trimmed West Indian–style cottages surrounded by grass lawns and facing the sea hold deluxe accommodations with wicker furnishings, tile floors, and floral pastels. Less expensive rooms are in garden-view cottages, most of which have restricted beach views and are the same size as the pricier beachfront units. Bedrooms, even in the deluxe category, are small, but guests here spend most of their time outside. There is no air-conditioning, TV, or phone. The classiest accommodations are in the three-bedroom West Indian Great House, an old, colonial-style building with king-size beds, tile floors, wicker furniture, and kitchenettes. Fourteen secluded deluxe beachfront rooms, elevated on a minibluff that promises the finest vistas of all, were added in 1997. Men are requested not to wear short sleeves into the dining room after 7 PM. And though children are more welcome than they used to be

**40**

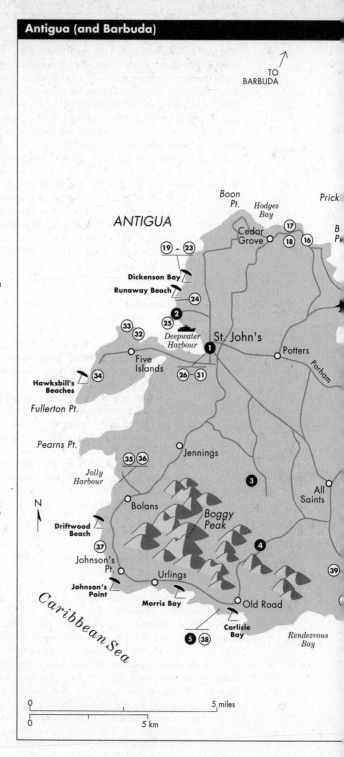

Antigua (and Barbuda)

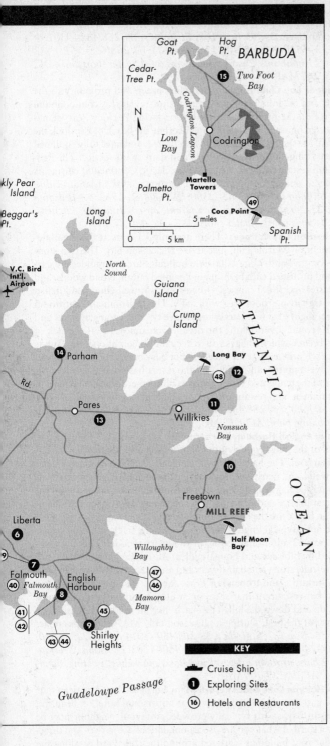

Lord Nelson Beach
Hotel, **16**
Pineapple Beach
Club, **48**
Rex Blue Heron, **37**
Rex Halcyon Cove
Beach Resort, **23**
Royal Antiguan
Resort, **33**
St. James's Club, **46**
Sandals, **20**
Siboney Beach
Club, **22**
Yepton Beach
Resort, **32**

("screamers" not included), Hawksbill is more a place for young couples and singles. Breakfast and the use of most water-sports facilities are complimentary. ⊠ *Box 108, St. John's,* ☎ *268/462–0301 or 800/223–6510; 416/622–8813 in Canada;* FAX *268/462–1515. 113 rooms. 2 restaurants, 2 bars, pool, tennis court, water sports. AE, DC, MC, V. BP, MAP.*

$$$ 🖫 **Hodges Bay Club.** A great snorkeling beach and proximity to the airport and St. John's are good reasons to stay at this condominium property on the prestigious north shore, facing Prickley Pear Island. Connected one- and two-bedroom villas line the beach or overlook the pool. All are spacious, comfortably decorated, and have fully equipped kitchens, king-size beds, balconies, and daily maid service. The Pelican Club restaurant here, which serves classic Continental cuisine, is considered one of the best hotel dining rooms on the island. ⊠ *Box 1237, St. John's,* ☎ *268/462–2300;* FAX *268/462–1962. 4 1-bedroom villas, 22 2-bedroom villas. Restaurant, air-conditioning, kitchens, pool, 2 tennis courts, water sports. AE, DC, MC, V. EP.*

$$–$$$ 🖫 **Dickenson Bay Cottages.** There are only 13 units at this small development on Marble Hill, just above Dickenson Bay. The two-story black- or gray-and-white villa-style buildings are surrounded by gardens and furnished with high-quality painted rattan, blond woods, and soft pastel and floral fabrics. Downstairs is a well-equipped kitchen and a large living room area with a TV. The bedroom and bathroom are up a flight of stairs. Larger units have two bedrooms upstairs and a large veranda overlooking the ocean. One annoyance is the lack of a cross breeze, which obliges you to keep the air conditioner on. Guests have beach privileges at the excellent but busy beach at Halcyon Cove, just a five-minute walk away, and the resort has an arrangement for the use of the tennis and water-sports facilities there at a 20% discount. Entertainment and restaurants are available at nearby resorts. ⊠ *Box 1379, St. John's,* ☎ *268/462–4940,* FAX *268/462–4941. 13 rooms. Air-conditioning, pool. AE, DC, MC, V. EP.*

$$–$$$ 🖫 **Inn at English Harbour.** The reception area, bar and dining room, and six of the guest rooms of this inn sit atop a hill with views of English Harbour. The bar, with its green leather chairs, wooden floors, stone walls, and maritime prints, is one of the most pleasant on the island, and the flagstone-terrace dining room offers an unparalleled romantic ambience and dependable Continental fare. Off to the side of the main house are the hilltop rooms, in individual, cottage-style units nestled among typical English gardens. Down the steep hill, right on the beach, are 22 additional rooms in two-story wooden buildings surrounded by hibiscus and bougainvillea. All rooms have phones, wall safes, refrigerators, and hair dryers and are attractively furnished with rattan furniture and tropical or floral fabrics. Also on the beach is a second bar-restaurant that stays open until 6 PM. A shuttle bus runs guests up and down the hill. The beach, like all those in English Harbour, is not the best. During high season only MAP bookings are accepted. ⊠ *Box 187, St. John's,* ☎ *268/460–1014 or 800/223–6510;* ☎ *800/424–5500 in Canada;* FAX *268/460–1603. 28 rooms. 2 restaurants, 2 bars, in-room safes, refrigerators, snorkeling, boating, windsurfing. AE, MC, V. EP, MAP.*

$$–$$$ 🖫 **Rex Halcyon Cove Beach Resort.** Many European and American tour groups patronize this large, somewhat impersonal hotel on beautiful Dickenson Bay, so it's typically crowded and your neighbor may be paying a third of what you are. Accommodations are in two- and three-story flat-roof buildings scattered around the courtyard or along the beach. They have white tile floors and are decorated with blond wood and mint fabrics. All have a private balcony or patio, but only higher-grade accommodations have a full bath, a TV, and a refrigerator. A

water-sports center on the busy beach offers excursions on a glass-bottom boat and waterskiing, in addition to the usual activities. The Warri Pier restaurant, set on stilts over the ocean, serves fine seafood and grilled items all day long. While you're on the walkway that connects it to the beach, be sure to look into the water—it's filled with schools of colorful fish. ✉ *Box 251, St. John's,* ☎ *268/462–0256,* FAX *268/462–0271. 194 rooms, 16 1-bedroom suites. 2 restaurants, 4 bars, ice cream parlor, air-conditioning, pool, beauty salon, 4 tennis courts, water sports, shops, car rental. AE, D, DC, MC, V. EP, MAP.*

$$–$$$ 🏨 **Royal Antiguan Resort.** This nine-story high-rise hotel, possibly the island's ugliest, is set on the waterside a few miles south of St. John's. The hotel caters to groups and conventions and is by far the most "stateside-like" hotel on Antigua; though sterile, it's perfect "entry-level" Caribbean, with all the amenities and facilities of a moderate American chain. Rooms and suites have minibars and TVs; higher categories have VCRs and marble vanities. Among the facilities here are a huge ballroom used for meetings and cocktail parties, a shopping arcade, and a 5,500-square-ft casino with blackjack, roulette, craps, baccarat, and 130 slot machines, all played by Atlantic City rules. An ongoing several-million-dollar renovation has brightened the hotel's interior, and the grounds and facade have also received a much-needed face-lift—royal blue awnings now shade the terraces, sewage is no longer dumped into the now-crystalline lagoon, the tennis courts have been resurfaced, and the gardens are immaculately tended. Fancier shops now line the arcade, and the cuisine, a sophisticated fusion of island ingredients and nouvelle preparations, has been greatly improved. ✉ *Deep Bay, St. John's,* ☎ *268/462–3733 or 800/228–9898,* FAX *268/462–3732. 300 rooms. 3 restaurants, 4 bars, air-conditioning, minibars, pool, golf privileges, 5 tennis courts, dive shop, snorkeling, windsurfing, boating, waterskiing, fishing, casino, shop. AE, D, MC, V. EP, MAP, All-inclusive.*

$$–$$$ 🏨 **Sandals.** Pool competitions, beach volleyball, aerobics sessions, ★ and evening social events are but a few of the activities at this couples-only resort. The schedule of events is organized by a "play maker," who will cajole (but not force) you to join in the fun, but you can still enjoy this place if you just want to read and relax. Everything, from the tennis coaching to the pedal boats, the scuba diving to the swim-up pool-bars, discos, and meals, is included in the price. For a little extra, you can even get married in front of a miniature waterfall. Rooms facing the beach or a garden and rondavels facing the beach are spacious. All units have coffeemakers, TVs, patios, and hair dryers. Many have four-poster or frilly beds, and all are light and fresh in pastels and/or bright floral fabrics. The four restaurants prepare Continental, Italian, Japanese, and southwestern-steak-house fare. Public areas are handsome, especially the beachfront restaurant, with its yellow-and-white awnings and ceiling painted like an azure sky dusted with clouds. The open-air reception area, with stone arches, stained glass, and marble floors, opens onto a courtyard with painted tile stairways and an unimpeded view to the sea. ✉ *Box 147, St. John's,* ☎ *268/462–0267 or 800/726–3257 in the U.S.;* FAX *268/462–4135. 191 rooms and suites. 4 restaurants, 4 bars, air-conditioning, in-room safes, 5 pools, 5 hot tubs, spa, 2 tennis courts, exercise room, scuba diving, snorkeling, windsurfing, boating, waterskiing, shop, nightclub. AE. All-inclusive.*

$$–$$$ 🏨 **Siboney Beach Club.** When Tony Johnson arrived in Antigua in the ★ late '50s, he planned to stay just a few weeks. Instead, he ended up building or refurbishing some of the island's finest resorts and eventually opened his own small gem set in an exquisite tropical garden on Dickenson Bay. Each suite has a small bedroom, a cleverly designed Pullman kitchen, a modestly furnished living room, and a plant-filled

patio or balcony that looks out to tropical greenery. Their decor varies slightly, but all rooms feature rattan and rich tropical fabrics; most units are air-conditioned. Room 9 is for those who revel in sea views, but the soothing sound of the surf permeates even those with partial views. A few yards away is an excellent, although often busy, calm-water beach and the Coconut Grove (☞ Dining, *below*), where guests can enjoy great breakfasts and lunches as well as candlelight dinners at the water's edge. The staff is exceptionally friendly, and Tony is always available to offer advice and good cheer. ⊠ *Box 222, St. John's,* ☎ *268/462–0806 or 800/533–0234,* FAX *268/462–3356. 12 suites. Restaurant, bar, pool. AE, MC, V. EP, MAP.*

**$$** ⊞ **Colonna Beach Hotel.** The architecture at this promising property is an appealing blend of Caribbean and Mediterranean: Red-tile and stucco buildings with terra-cotta floors surround a faux sugar mill. The most magnificent touch is the 700-square-meter free-form pool, said to be the largest in the Lesser Antilles. Units, all with TVs, hair dryers, and patios or balconies, run the gamut from standard hotel rooms to two- and three-bedroom villas (some of which were poorly designed and don't catch a cross breeze). The fresh interiors have immaculate tile floors, wicker and rattan furnishings, and imported Italian fabrics with designs that range from bold stripes to soft seashell colors. The public spaces look a tad dilapidated, but the rooms are well maintained and even so-called garden-view units have at least a partial sea view. The junior suites, a good value, have two patios and a sofa bed for the kids. Two artificial "eyebrow" beaches (which do lead to a charming island gazebo) are among this resort's drawbacks, along with the constant threat of bankruptcy (this place has seen its share of financial troubles). But the staff is generally engaging and helpful, the location between the airport and St. John's is central, and the two restaurants (one or the other of which is often closed) serve fine Italian food. ⊠ *Box 591, St. John's,* ☎ *268/462–6263,* FAX *268/462–6430. 117 units. 2 restaurants, 3 bars, air-conditioning, in-room safes, minibars, pool, water sports, casino. AE, D, MC, V. EP, MAP.*

**$$** ⊞ **Copper and Lumber Store Hotel.** Overlooking the marina at English Harbour, this former supply store for Nelson's Caribbean fleet and fine example of Georgian British architecture has been beautifully transformed into a gracious inn. Warm brick, hardwood floors, timbered ceilings, and burgundy-leather armchairs and sofas lend the property an old-world charm unique in the West Indies. Antique washstands, secretaries, four-poster canopy beds, and other Georgian furnishings decorate the suites; additional touches in many include wrought-iron chandeliers, old sailing prints, mahogany steamer trunks, brass sinks, and faux gas lamps. All suites have showers, and though they lack air-conditioning, ceiling fans create nice breezes. Unfortunately, many rooms have become frayed around the edges and could use a face-lift. A ferry service shuttles guests to a beach on the other side of English Harbour. Be warned that the hotel sits inside a national park and visitors stream through the area during the day. ⊠ *Box 184, St. John's,* ☎ *268/460–1058 or 800/275–0877; 800/463–0877 in Canada;* FAX *268/460–1529. 14 suites. Restaurant, pub. AE, MC, V. EP, MAP.*

**$$** ⊞ **Yepton Beach Resort.** This Swiss-designed, full-service, all-suites resort is set on Hog John Bay on the Five Islands peninsula, not far from St. John's. The Mediterranean-style white-stucco buildings are situated so that accommodations have views on one side of the resort's attractive beach and on the other side of a lagoon dotted with pelicans and egrets. Two-room suites hold a bedroom and a large living room with a kitchenette, and studios have a Murphy bed and a kitchenette. The units are carefully maintained, though typically bland in dark rattan and glass furnishings, with pastel fabrics and island prints. Many different packages are available. ⊠ *Box 1427, St. John's,* ☏ *268/462–2520 or 800/361–4621,* FAX *268/462–3240. 38 units. Restaurant, air-conditioning, kitchenettes, pool, 2 tennis courts, water sports. AE, MC, V. EP, MAP, All-inclusive.*

$ ⊡ **Admiral's Inn.** This lovingly restored 18th-century Georgian inn is ★ the centerpiece of the magnificent Nelson's Dockyard complex. Once the engineers' office and warehouse (its bricks were originally used as ballast for British ships), the Admiral's Inn reverberates with history. The best rooms, upstairs in the main building, have the original timbered ceilings, complete with iron braces, hardwood floors, and massive whitewashed brick walls. Straw floor mats from Dominica and views through wispy Australian pines to the sunny harbor beyond complete the effect. The rooms in the garden annex are smaller and somewhat airless. The Loft, which used to be the dockyard's joinery, has two big bedrooms, an enormous kitchen, and a magnificent view from the timbered living room onto the busy harbor. Be aware that this inn sits smack in the middle of a bustling daytime tourist attraction, although there's a complimentary beach shuttle and use of water sports at Falmouth Beach Apartments. ⊠ *Box 713, St. John's,* ☏ *268/460–1027, 800/223–5695, or 800/223–9815;* FAX *268/460–1534. 14 rooms, 1 2-bedroom apartment. Restaurant, pub. AE, MC, V. EP, MAP.*

$ ⊡ **Catamaran Hotel.** This plantation-style house, with apricot, white, and black trim and a wraparound veranda supported by classical-style pediments, sits on a Falmouth Harbour beach lined with palm and almond trees. The best rooms are the eight first-floor suites, with four-poster beds, full baths, kitchenettes, and private balconies. None of the rooms have air-conditioning, a TV, or a telephone. Yet for those who want a low-key, low-priced, tranquil resort, this property 2 mi from English Harbour offers excellent value. ⊠ *Box 958, Falmouth,* ☏ *268/460–1036,* FAX *268/460–1506. 16 rooms. Restaurant, bar, kitchenettes, marina, shops. AE, MC, V. EP.*

$ ⊡ **Falmouth Beach Apartments.** The best accommodations at this sister hotel to the Admiral's Inn (☞ *above*) are in a colonial-style house on the property's small, palm-lined beach. These quiet, simple units are basically one large room—a bedroom–living-room–kitchenette combination—and a bathroom with a shower. All open onto a wraparound veranda with views of the water and the hilly peninsula opposite. Units have no air-conditioning (those upstairs catch the breezes better), and no telephones or TVs. Accommodations in four modern buildings perched on the hillside have separate kitchens, bedrooms with twin beds, and bathrooms with showers. Old maps or striking artworks jazz up the standard rattan-and-beige-tile decor. All apartments have daily maid service. The sheltered beach is perfect for toddlers and small children who are learning to swim. ⊠ *Box 713, Falmouth Harbour,* ☏ *268/460–1094 or 800/223–5695,* FAX *268/460–1534. 28 rooms. Water sports. AE, MC, V. EP.*

$ ⊡ **Jolly Harbour Beach Resort Marina and Golf Club.** As its name suggests, this is more a vacation-home compound than a mere resort. Although the main activity area strives to re-create a Mediterranean village with red-tile roofs and pale-mustard arches and columns, the 500-acre development generally lacks style. That said, its simple villas—cookie-cutter duplex units that seem straight from the Sunbelt—are perhaps the best bargain on Antigua. All look out onto the beach or marina and have kitchens, ceiling fans (only 20 units currently have air-conditioning), two bedrooms, and full baths. The units are individually decorated, but most favor wicker furnishings, off-white tile floors, and pastel colors. Jolly Harbour is ideal for families on a budget or those who want everything at their fingertips: Guests not only have the use of the facilities here but also those of a sister resort, the

hideous, all-inclusive Club Antigua next door. The golf course is scheduled for an expansion from 9 to 18 holes in mid-1998. ⊠ *Box 1793,
Jolly Harbour,* ☎ *268/462–6166,* FAX *268/462–6167. 502 villas (approximately 220 in rental pool at any given time). 4 restaurants, 2 bars,
pool, 9-hole golf course, 4 tennis courts, squash, marina, water sports,
shops. AE, MC, V. EP.*

$ 🏨 **Lord Nelson Beach Hotel.** If you don't mind a bit of chipped paint
and organized chaos, you'll love this funky, laid-back resort run for
decades by the Fuller family until new management took over after the
1995 hurricanes. The best rooms are in a two-story, apricot-color
building looking directly onto the property's horseshoe-shape beach.
Each unit is a hodgepodge of design elements: One room has beautiful tile floors and an ornately carved bed from Dominica that is so high
you almost need to be a pole-vaulter to get into it, and several others
have four-poster beds, antique armoires, and vivid local still lifes.
Guests eat in the timbered dining room, draped with fishnets and
dominated by a replica of the boat in which Captain Bligh was cast
off from the *Bounty*; expect hearty dishes such as stuffed pork chops,
wahoo, and snapper. Because the resort is fairly isolated (5 mi from
St. John's), figure an extra EC$25 into your budget for cab fare to
any meal you have elsewhere. An extensive collection of windsurfing boards, easy access to the water, and a dedicated pro have made
the Lord Nelson a mecca for windsurfers. ⊠ *Box 155, St. John's,*
☎ *268/462–3094,* FAX *268/462–0751. 16 rooms. Restaurant, bar,
dive shop, windsurfing. AE, MC, V. EP, MAP, FAP. Closed Sept.*

$ 🏨 **Rex Blue Heron.** When Rex Hotels purchased this faded little re-
sort on one of the island's loveliest beaches, management gave it a complete overhaul. The seemingly endless tiled reception area, filled with
potted plants, polished-wood rafters, and oversize rattan furnishings
with brilliantly hued cushions, is perhaps its most imposing aspect. Everything else is on a smaller scale, from the cozy pool to even cozier
rooms. Don't be misled by the mousy faux stucco buildings. Each room
has hardwood or gleaming white tile floors, powder-blue and tropical-print fabrics, stylish ceramic lamps, a patio or a terrace, and a hair
dryer. All but the standard ones have air-conditioning, satellite TV, and
dazzling ocean views. It's almost impossible to get a reservation, since
discerning European tour operators keep it booked throughout the year.
The low prices, intimacy, and seclusion lure a young, hip clientele.
⊠ *Box 1715, Johnson's Point,* ☎ *268/462–8564 or 800/255–5859,*
FAX *268/462–8005. 40 rooms. Restaurant, bar, pool, water sports,
shop. AE, D, MC, V. EP, MAP.*

# Dining

Antigua's restaurants prepare a range of cuisines, and you can find excellent food whether you feel like dressing up or dressing down. There
are elegant Continental and French restaurants, casual waterfront
bistros, and beach bars you can enter barefoot. It's impossible not to
find fresh seafood on the menu, and virtually every chef incorporates
local ingredients and elements of West Indian and Creole cuisine. Alas,
the food is often overcooked, even in the tonier establishments.

Most menus list prices in E.C. dollars, but you should make sure
which currency you're dealing with. It's also a good idea to ask if credit
cards are accepted. Prices below are in U.S. dollars. Dinner reservations are needed during high season.

## What to Wear

Perhaps because of the island's British heritage, Antiguans tend to
dress more formally for dinner than is the custom on many of the other

Caribbean islands. A few places, which will be noted, require a jacket. Wraps and shorts (no beach attire) are de rigueur for lunch, except at local hangouts.

| CATEGORY | COST* |
|---|---|
| $$$$ | over $50 |
| $$$ | $35–$50 |
| $$ | $20–$35 |
| $ | under $20 |

*per person for a three-course meal, excluding drinks, service, and 7% sales tax

$$$ ✕ **Alberto's.** Set above Willoughby Bay on Antigua's southeast side,
★ this superior Italian restaurant is a bit out of the way but popular nevertheless. The ebullient owner, Alberto, taught his culinary secrets to his English wife, Vanessa, and the two turn out delicious seafood prepared with an Italian accent. Try fresh island lobster (perhaps grilled with basil and garlic); cockles Alberto; the chef's creation of the evening (you're in luck if it's baked grouper in pine-nut crust or snapper *marechiaro,* in a tomato, olive, and caper sauce); or more traditional dishes such as eggplant parmigiana, osso buco, or linguine with clams. The ravioli in creamy walnut sauce and breadfruit in garlic parsley butter are sheer heaven. Tables line a balcony open to the breezes and hung with bougainvillea, and painted china graces the walls (check out the octopuses and squids on the plates by the bar). ✉ *Willoughby Bay,* ☎ *268/460–3007 or via VHF 68. Reservations essential. AE, D, MC, V. Closed Mon. and July–Oct. No lunch.*

$$$ ✕ **Coconut Grove.** Coconut palms grow up through the roof of this
★ open-air thatched restaurant, candles flicker gently in lanterns illuminating colorful local artwork, and waves lap the white-coral sand a few feet away. For a romantic evening, head here when there's a full moon and reserve Table 1, closest to the water and under the stars. The menu always includes freshly grilled local lobster and choices of other fresh seafood, plus lamb, steak, and such island-tinged fare as fish tacos, jerk chicken with banana guava ketchup, and addictive coconut shrimp. After an uneven period, the service and the kitchen now complement the unparalleled setting. ✉ *Siboney Beach Club, Dickenson Bay,* ☎ *268/462–1538. MC, V.*

$$$ ✕ **Colombo's.** This open-air restaurant on a small bay in English Harbour has views of palm trees, historic cannons, and the water in the distance. Various pennants draped around the bar attest that this is a big yachtie hangout. The extensive menu is condensed during the off-season, but you can still order such creative dishes as grouper carpaccio, *gamberoni Antigua* (shrimp flambéed in rum in ginger sauce), lobster in basil sauce, and veal with wild mushrooms. At lunchtime there are also light salads, hamburgers, and sandwiches. On Wednesday nights a reggae band entertains. ✉ *Galleon Beach Club, English Harbour,* ☎ *268/460–1452. AE, MC, V.*

$$$ ✕ **Julian's.** You enter this restaurant—Antigua's finest—through a
★ lovely historic courtyard. The reception area strikes an immediate note of elegance, with vibrant islandscapes contrasting with stark white walls and wood beams. The intimate dining room (only eight tables) has olive straw-and-rattan chairs, lime-green shutters, and black-and-white napery. Chef and co-owner Julian Waterer brilliantly counterpoints flavors and colors: Even something as straightforward as lentil soup is perfectly textured. Other choices on the rotating menu might include blackened Brie with grapefruit, asparagus, and honey; wild mushroom, leek, and feta strudel in onion compote; crab and red snapper terrine with ginger lime sauce; or peppered veal sweetbreads pan-seared with bacon over field greens in a cider vinaigrette. You can order

some excellent wines by the glass off the well-considered list. ⊠ *Corn Alley and Church La., St. John's,* ☎ *268/462–4766. AE, D, MC, V. Closed Mon. No lunch Sun.*

**$$$**   ✕ **Le Bistro.** This Antiguan institution, run by husband-and-wife team Raffaele and Phillippa Esposito, is remarkably consistent in every aspect, starting with a casually elegant decor, which favors accents of peach and pistachio that are perfectly color-coordinated with the napery, brick tile work, jade chairs, and even the painted sheet-metal lighting fixtures. Trellises cannily divide the large space into intimate sections, with tables staggered just the right distance apart. The chefs, who all hail from France, delight in blending their regional fare with indigenous ingredients. You might start with fresh seafood roulade in calypso dill sauce or shrimp stuffed with seafood mousse laced with saffron sauce. Sterling entrées include a perfect roast duck in mango sauce and an unimpeachable rack of lamb. As for dessert, Le Bistro's version of Death by Chocolate is a lingering, exquisite torture to the taste buds. ⊠ *Hodges Bay,* ☎ *268/462–3881. Reservations essential. AE, MC, V. Closed Mon. No lunch.*

**$$–$$$**   ✕ **Lobster Pot.** A fishing boat sits in the center of this beachfront
★ restaurant's flagstone dining room, and sea breezes sweep in through the open gallery. The owners restored the restaurant impeccably after Hurricane Marilyn's devastation (1995), enlarging and opening up the space but preserving its romantic ambience. The best seats are right on the water. The long (seven pages!) and diverse menu is a mix of fresh seafood, pasta, and Creole- and Caribbean-style dishes. Starters include the lobster and pineapple phyllo with tamari and chili dips, and the grilled baby eggplant stuffed with cheese and herbs. Follow these with coconut-milk curry shrimp; baked breast of chicken stuffed with goat cheese, broccoli, and sun-dried tomatoes; herb-encrusted swordfish in tomato sauce; or succulent lobster. For dessert try the apple crepes in honey-and-island-spice sauce. The wine list is well considered and very fairly priced, with most selections in the $20 range. ⊠ *Runaway Bay,* ☎ *268/462–2856. D, MC, V.*

**$$–$$$**   ✕ **Wardroom Restaurant.** An atmosphere of Olde England pervades this restaurant on the ground floor of the beautifully restored Copper and Lumber Store. The dining room, with massive brick walls and stained wood beams, opens out to a courtyard hung with bougainvillea and to views of the floodlit battlements of English Harbour. The menu is international, mixing dishes such as West African peanut soup with lobster in puff pastry, a good selection of local fish dishes, and even lamb cutlets. ⊠ *Nelson's Dockyard,* ☎ *268/460–1058. AE, DC, MC, V. Closed Wed. No lunch.*

**$$**   ✕ **Admiral's Inn.** Known as the Ad to yachtspeople around the world,
★ this historic English Harbour inn is a must for Anglophiles and mariners. At the bar inside, you can sit and soak up the centuries under dark, timbered wood (the bar top even has the names of sailors from Nelson's fleet carved into it), but most guests tend to sit on the terrace under shady Australian gums to enjoy the views of the harbor complex and Clarence House opposite. Specialties include curried conch, fresh snapper with equally fresh limes, and lobster thermidor. The pumpkin soup is not to be missed. ⊠ *Nelson's Dockyard,* ☎ *268/460–1027. Reservations essential. AE, MC, V.*

**$$**   ✕ **Al Porto.** This unassuming Jolly Harbour spot, with a dark, cramped interior with unusual, almost disturbingly hallucinogenic paintings and a sunny but simple terrace overlooking the marina, is an unexpected surprise. It looks like the kind of place where pasta would be overcooked and flailing in canned tomato sauce. Instead, you'll receive dazzling antipasti (yummy eggplant parmigiana), creative pizzas (try the seafood), and lovingly prepared northern Italian fare. Specials might be fresh mahimahi *livornese* (onions, tomatoes, garlic, olives), chicken *valdostana* (grilled with mushrooms, tomatoes, onions), or tagliatelle with cèpes. Indeed, you're in for a treat if the owners have just returned from visiting their aunt in Parma: they "smuggle" back genuine Parma ham, sharp Pecorino, and delectable porcinis. ✉ *Jolly Harbour,* ☎ 268/462–6166. AE, MC, V.

**$$** ✗ **Commissioner's Grill.** The gaudy exterior—in raspberry, mango, blueberry, and lavender—of this 19th-century tamarind warehouse seems edible itself. The interior is more restrained, with white tile floors, powder-blue chairs, floral tablecloths, and nice local touches like bronze wind chimes, Antiguan pottery, conch shells, and historic maps. The day's specials, scrawled on a blackboard, might include whelks in garlic butter, snapper in lobster sauce, marinated conch, or shrimp Creole. Fresh local seafood is the obvious choice, although beef and poultry are also reliable. ✉ *Commissioner Alley and Redcliffe St., St. John's,* ☎ 268/462–1883. AE, DC, MC, V.

**$$** ✗ **Home.** When Carl Thomas returned to his native Antigua after years in New York, he decided to open a restaurant in his boyhood home, a '50s bungalow in a quiet suburb of St. John's. He completely refurbished the original house, knocked down walls to create one large space, and planted an herb and vegetable garden. Modern, unfinished pine furniture and polished wood floors give the place an airy atmosphere. Unusual ceramic candlesticks adorn the tables, and walls are hung with African and Caribbean art. The menu, which Carl dubs "Caribbean haute cuisine," is ambitious for Antigua. Unfortunately, the quality is quite uneven. Carl could use a stronger hand with his seasonings. Grouper in herb sauce and other simpler offerings are more successful than such intriguing dishes as molasses pepper steak. Don't miss the smoked fish, a house specialty, and bread pudding with whiskey sauce. ✉ *Gambles Terr., St. John's,* ☎ 268/461–7651. AE, MC, V. Closed Sun. No lunch weekdays.

**$$** ✗ **Redcliffe Tavern.** Every item on the tavern's part northern Italian, part Continental, part Creole menu is wonderfully fresh. The dinner menu includes delicious pastas, marinated grilled chicken, fresh local lobster, spicy Creole crab puffs, and a smoked salmon and shellfish terrine in lime mousseline. The lunch menu also lists salads, sandwiches, and hamburgers. The dining room is on the second floor of a restored colonial warehouse set amid the courtyards of Redcliffe Quay. Brick and stone walls are decorated with antique water-pumping equipment still bearing the original English maker's crests. Salvaged from all over the island, the old machines, with their flywheels and pistons, have been imaginatively integrated into the restaurant's structure—one supports the buffet bar. You can also dine on the treetop-level terrace. ✉ *Redcliffe Quay, St. John's,* ☎ 268/461–4557. AE, MC, V.

**$$** ✗ **Shirley Heights Lookout.** This restaurant is set in an 18th-century fortification high on a bluff, with a breathtaking view of English Harbour below. The first-floor pub opens onto the lookout point. Upstairs, there's a cozy, windowed dining room with hardwood floors and beamed ceilings. Pub offerings include burgers, sandwiches, and barbecue, while upstairs you can order the likes of pumpkin soup and lobster in lime sauce. If you like to be at the center of things, come here Sunday around 3 PM or Thursday around 3:30, when locals, yachters, and visitors troop up the hill for the barbecue. Livened by steel-band and reggae music, it lasts well into the evening. ✉ *Shirley Heights,* ☎ 268/463–1785. Reservations essential in season in dining room. AE, MC, V.

**$–$$** ✗ **Calypso.** The St. John's professional set frequents this cheerful outdoor spot. At lunchtime it is packed with smartly dressed lawyers and government functionaries smoking cigars and chatting over traditional

Caribbean food. Tables are arranged under green umbrellas on a sunny trellised patio dominated by the remains of a brick kiln. Specials change every day, but you can usually count on stewed lamb, grilled lobster, and baked chicken served with rice, dumplings, and fungi, a pastalike vegetable dish made of cornmeal and okra. ✉ *Redcliffe St., St. John's,* ☎ *268/462–1965. AE, MC, V. Closed Sun. No dinner Sat.–Thurs.*

**$–$$**  ✕ **Russell's.** Vivacious owner Russell Hodge had the brilliant idea of restoring a part of Fort St. James, with its gorgeous views of the bay and headlands, and converting it into an open-air restaurant. Potted plants and faux-Victorian gas lamps lend a romantic aura to the cool stone-and-wood terrace. The menu—delectable local specialties with an emphasis on seafood—is listed on a blackboard. You might start with conch fritters or whelks in garlic butter, then try an excellent snapper Creole. Live jazz is a lure Sunday nights. Russell's sister Valerie owns the estimable Shirley Heights Lookout (☞ *above*), and sister Patsy operates the delightful Pumpkin Runner, a fast-food van dispensing savory local dishes every night in St. John's. The Hodges might well be Antigua's first family of food. ✉ *Fort James,* ☎ *268/462–5479. AE, DC.*

**$**  ✕ **Big Banana-Pizzas on the Quay.** This tiny, often crowded spot is
★ tucked into one side of a restored warehouse with broad plank floors and stonework archways. It serves some of the best pizza on the island, topped with traditional and not-so-traditional items. You can also enjoy tasty specials like conch salad. It's a busy lunch and dinner spot, and there is live entertainment some evenings. ✉ *Redcliffe Quay, St. John's,* ☎ *268/462–2621. AE, MC, V.*

## Beaches

All of Antigua's beaches are public, and many are dotted with resorts that provide water-sports-equipment rentals and a place to grab a cool drink. Sunbathing topless or in the buff is strictly illegal except on one of the small beaches at Hawksbill Beach Club. Beware that on the one or two days a week that cruise ships dock in St. John's (check with your hotel for specific dates), buses drop off loads of cruise-ship passengers on virtually all the west-coast beaches. Choose this day to tour the island by car, visit one of the more remote east-end beaches, or take a day trip to Barbuda.

### Antigua

**Carlisle Bay** has a large coconut grove and two long, snow-white beaches over which the estimable Curtain Bluff resort sits. Standing on the bluff of this peninsula, you can see the almost-blinding blue waters of the Atlantic Ocean drifting into the Caribbean Sea. **Dickenson Bay** has a lengthy stretch of powder-soft white sand and exceptionally calm water. Here you'll find small and large hotels, supercasual beach bars, and beachfront restaurants. Water-sports equipment can be rented at the Halcyon Cove. **Driftwood Beach** is a delightful taupe ribbon on the southwest coast that's anchored by a lively beach bar, which serves terrific local food, including fresh lobster, for lunch. **Five Islands Peninsula** has four secluded beaches (including one for bathing in the buff) of fine tan sand and coral reefs for snorkeling. The Hawksbill Beach Hotel is here. **Half Moon Bay,** a ¾-mi crescent of sand, is a prime area for snorkeling and windsurfing. On the Atlantic side of the island, the water can be quite rough at times. **Johnson's Point** is a deliciously deserted beach of bleached white sand on the southwest coast. **Long Bay,** on the far eastern coast, has coral reefs in water so shallow that you can actually walk out to them. Along the beach are the Long Bay Hotel and the rambling Pineapple Beach Club. **Pigeon Point,** near English Harbour, is a fine white-sand beach with calm water. Several restaurants and bars are nearby. **Runaway Beach** is home to the Barrymore Beach Hotel and the Runaway Beach Hotel, so its stretch of white sand can get crowded. Refresh yourself with hot dogs and beer at the Barrymore's Satay Hut.

## Barbuda

**Coco Point** on Barbuda is an uncrowded 8-mi stretch of white sand. Barbuda, encircled by reefs and shipwrecks, is great for scuba diving.

# Outdoor Activities and Sports

Almost all the resort hotels can provide fins and masks, Windsurfers, Sunfish, catamarans, and other water-related gear (☞ Lodging, *above*).

## Bicycling

Try **Sun Cycles** (⊠ Nelson Dr., Hodges Bay, ☎ 268/461–0324) for short- or long-term leases.

## Boating

**Halcyon Cove Watersports** (⊠ Dickenson Bay, ☎ 268/462–0256) offers waterskiing and other water rides and rents small boats. **Nicholson Yacht Charters** (☎ 800/662–6066) are real professionals. A long-established island family, they can charter you anything from a 20-ft ketch to a giant schooner. **Sea Sports** (⊠ Dickenson Bay, ☎ 268/462–3355) rents Jet Skis and Sunfish and offers parasailing and waterskiing trips. The atmosphere here can be hectic.

## Deep-Sea Fishing

The waters surrounding Antigua teem with game fish like marlin, wahoo, and tuna. *Nimrod* (☎ 268/463–8744) is a 50-ft cruiser whose captain, Terry Bowen, is extremely knowledgeable. Sunset cruises and island circumnavigations are also offered. The 45-ft Hatteras Sport-fisherman *Obsession* (☎ 268/462–2824) has top-of-the-line equipment, including an international standard fighting chair, outriggers, and handcrafted rods.

## Fitness Center

**Benair Fitness Club** (⊠ Country Club Rd., Hodges Bay, ☎ 268/462–1540) has fitness equipment, a Jacuzzi, aerobics classes, and a juice bar. **Fitness Shack** (⊠ Dickenson Bay, ☎ 268/462–5223) has extensive fitness equipment and aerobics classes. **Lotus Health Centre** (⊠ Dickenson Bay, ☎ 268/462–2231) offers spa treatments, including Swedish massage, foot reflexology, and various kinds of facials.

## Golf

**Cedar Valley Golf Club** (⊠ Friar's Hill, northeast of St. John's, ☎ 268/462–0161) has an 18-hole course.

## Horseback Riding

**Spring Hill Riding Stables** (⊠ Falmouth, ☎ 268/460–1333) offers trail rides on the beach or through the bush.

## Sailing

**Antigua School of Sailing** (⊠ St. John's, ☎ 268/462–2026) offers short resort courses.

## Scuba Diving

With all the wrecks and reefs, there are lots of undersea sights to explore. **Dive Antigua** (☎ 268/462–3483) offers certification courses and day and night dives from Rex Halcyon Cove. **Dockyard Divers** (☎ 268/464–8591, FAX 268/460–1179) is in the English Harbour area. Owned by British ex–merchant seaman Captain A. G. Fincham, it's one of the oldest-established outfits on the island and offers diving and snorkeling trips, PADI courses, and dive packages with accommodations.

## Sea Excursions

*Jolly Roger* (☎ 268/462–2064) cruises, on a true-to-life replica of a pirate ship, come complete with "pirate" crew, limbo dancing, plank walking, and other pranks. **Kokomo Cats** (☎ 268/462–7245) runs several different cruises, including one to deserted beaches, one to English Harbour, and one to sunset-gazing spots. *Paradise I* (☎ 268/462–4158), a 45-ft Beneteau yacht, offers both lunch or sunset cruises. The glass-bottom **Shorty's** (☎ 268/462–6326) offers various snorkeling trips to Bird Island, as well as sunset cruises and lobster picnics. Board the glass-bottom *Splish Splash* (☎ 268/462–3483) for two-hour snorkeling trips to Paradise Reef (landlubbers get almost as good a view from the boat). *Titi I* (☎ 268/460–1452), a 34-ft motorboat powered with twin 300 Evinrudes, will take you to nearby islets, remote beaches, or out for specially tailored snorkeling trips. The boat is based in Falmouth Harbour, but its operators will pick you up almost anywhere. **Wadadli Cats** (☎ 268/462–4792) operates various cruises, including a circumnavigation of the island, on its three sleek catamarans.

## Spectator Sports

For information about sports events, contact **Antigua Sports and Games** (☎ 268/462–1925).

CRICKET

Practically the only thing most Americans know about this game is that there's something called a sticky wicket. Here, as in Britain and all the West Indies, the game is a national passion. Youngsters play on makeshift pitches, which apparently are comparable to sandlots, and international matches are fought out in the stadium on Independence Avenue in St. John's.

## Tennis

The **Temo Sports Complex** (✉ Falmouth Bay, ☎ 268/463–1781) has two floodlit tennis courts, three glass-backed squash courts, showers, a sports shop, and snack bars. Many of the larger resorts have their own tennis courts. The **St. James's Club** (☎ 268/460–5000) has seven (five lighted for night play); **Sandals** (☎ 268/462–0267), two; **Rex Halcyon Cove Beach Resort** (☎ 268/462–0256), four (lighted); and Curtain Bluff (☎ 268/462–8400), four Har-Tru and a grass court. Guests have top priority. For nonguests, court fees are about $30 an hour.

## Waterskiing

**Halcyon Cove Watersports** (☎ 268/462–0256) and **Sea Sports** (☎ 268/462–3355), both at Dickenson Bay, will take you waterskiing.

## Windsurfing

Most major hotels offer windsurfing equipment. **Halcyon Cove Watersports** (☎ 268/462–0256) offers rentals and instruction. **Windsurfing Antigua** (✉ Lord Nelson Beach Hotel, ☎ 268/462–3094 or 268/462–9463), run by expert Patrick Scales, is the spot for serious board sailors.

# Shopping

Antigua's duty-free shops are at Heritage Quay; they're the reason so many cruise ships call here. Bargains can be found on perfumes, liqueurs and liquor (including, of course, Antiguan rum), jewelry, china, and crystal. As for local items, look for straw hats, baskets, batik, pottery, and hand-printed cotton clothing.

## Shopping Areas

**Redcliffe Quay,** on the waterfront at the south edge of St. John's, is by far the most appealing shopping area. Here several restaurants and more than 30 boutiques, many with one-of-a-kind items, are set around landscaped courtyards shaded by colorful trees. **Heritage Quay,** also in St. John's, has 35 shops—including many that are duty-free—that cater primarily to the cruise-ship crowd that docks almost at its doorstep. Outlets here include Benetton, the Body Shop, Polo, Gucci, and Oshkosh B'Gosh. The main tourist shops in St. John's are along **St. Mary's, High,** and **Long streets.**

## Good Buys

### BOOKS AND MAGAZINES

**Flower Basket** (⊠ Nevis St., ☎ 268/462–0411) is not only a flower shop, but also has the latest U.S. magazines, newspapers, and bestselling paperback books. Nevis Street seems to end, but keep going, it's a few steps along. **Map Shop** (⊠ St. Mary's St., ☎ 268/462–3993) has a "must" buy for those interested in Antiguan life: the paperback *To Shoot Hard Labour: The Life and Times of Samuel Smith, an Antiguan Workingman.* Also check out any of the books of Jamaica Kincaid, whose works on her native Antigua have won international, albeit controversial, acclaim.

### CHINA AND CRYSTAL

**Little Switzerland** (⊠ Heritage Quay, ☎ 268/462–3108) houses pricey buys in a luxurious, and air-conditioned, setting. **Norma's Duty-Free Shop** (⊠ Heritage Quay Shopping Center and the Halcyon Cove, ☎ 268/462–0172) offers the usual range of delicate sets, from Lladro to Limoges. **Specialty Shoppe** (⊠ St. Mary's St., ☎ 268/462–1198) has wares that make impressive presents.

### CIGARS, LIQUOR, AND LIQUEURS

**Cigar Shop** (⊠ Heritage Quay, ☎ 890/462–2677) sells Cuban cigars, but remember that it's illegal to bring them back to the United States. **Manuel Diaz Liquor Store** (⊠ Long and Market Sts., ☎ 268/462–0440) has a wide selection of Caribbean rums and liqueurs. The **Warehouse** (⊠ St. Mary's St., ☎ 268/462–0495) offers bargains on imported wines and liquor.

### CLOTHING AND FABRICS

**Base** (⊠ Redcliffe Quay, ☎ 268/460–2500) is the brainchild of English designer Steven Giles, whose striped or hip monochrome cotton-and-Lycra resortwear remains all the rage on the island. **CoCo Shop** (⊠ St. Mary's St., ☎ 268/462–1128) is a favorite source for Sea Island cotton designs, Daks clothing, and Liberty of London fabrics, along with the shop's own designs for the country-club set. **Galley Boutiques** (⊠ Main shop in English Harbour, ☎ 268/460–1525; ⊠ St. James's Club, ☎ 268/460–1333) is where Janie Easton sells her original designs at reasonable prices. **Jacaranda** (⊠ Redcliffe Quay, ☎ 268/462–1888) sells batiks, sarongs, and swimwear. **Noreen Phillips** (⊠ Redcliffe Quay, ☎ 268/462–3127) creates glitzy appliquéd and beaded evening wear inspired by the colors of the sea and sunset. **A Thousand Flowers** (⊠ Redcliffe Quay, ☎ 268/462–4264) carries resort wear made of comfortable silks, linens, and batiks from all over the world and has many unusual items. The flowing hand-dyed sundresses, blouses, T-shirts, shorts, and scarves of the famed **Caribelle Batik** (⊠ St. Mary's St., ☎ 268/462–2972) duplicate the festive colors of a Caribbean Carnival.

### JEWELRY

**Colombian Emeralds** (⊠ Heritage Quay, ☎ 268/462–2086) is the largest retailer of Colombian emeralds in the world. The **Goldsmitty**

(⊠ Redcliffe Quay, ☎ 268/462–4601) is Hans Smit, an expert goldsmith who turns gold, black coral, and precious and semiprecious stones into one-of-a-kind works of art. (Beware that environmental groups discourage tourists from purchasing corals that are designated as endangered species, because the reefs are often harvested carelessly.)

**Norma's Duty-Free Shop** (⊠ Heritage Quay Shopping Center and the Halcyon Cove, ☎ 268/462–0172) has jewelry bargains.

LOCAL ART AND CRAFTS

**Craft Originals Studio** (⊠ Coast Rd., ☎ 268/463–2519) is where Trinidadian Natalie White sells her sculptured cushions and wall hangings, all hand-painted on silk and signed. **Decibels** (⊠ Redcliffe Quay, ☎ 268/462–3955) offers a United Nations of craftwork, from Creole houses to Mexican raku pottery. **Handicraft Centre** (⊠ High and Thames Sts., St. John's, ☎ 268/462–0639) specializes in island products—straw bags, mahogany warri boards, pottery, and hand-painted T-shirts and sundresses. **Harmony Hall** (⊠ At Brown's Bay Mill, near Freetown, ☎ 268/460–4120) is the Antiguan sister to the original Jamaica location. In addition to "Annabella Boxes," books, and cards, there are pottery and ceramic pieces, carved wooden fantasy birds, and an ever-changing roster of exhibits. **Island Arts Galleries** (⊠ Alton Pl., Sandy La., behind Hodges Bay Club, ☎ 268/461–3332; ⊠ Heritage Quay, ☎ 268/462–2787; ⊠ St. James's Club, ☎ 268/460–5000), run by artist-filmmaker Nick Maley and his wife, Gloria, is a melting pot for Caribbean artists, with prices ranging from $10 to $15,000. **Mimosa** (⊠ Heritage Quay, ☎ 268/462–2923) sells hand-painted wind chimes and porcelain clowns in island dress. **Seahorse Studios** (⊠ At Cobbs Cross, en route to English Harbour, ☎ 268/463–1417), opened by John and Katie Shears, presents the works of good artists in a bucolic setting.

You can see original slave shackles in the overgrown courtyard of **Coates Cottage** (⊠ Lower Nevis St., ☎ 268/462–3636), a peeling, 18th-century gingerbread that holds superb local artworks and crafts; an added bonus is that artists and artisans often utilize the space as a temporary studio. **Kate Designs** (⊠ Redcliffe Quay, ☎ 268/460–5971) imports acclaimed artist Kate Spencer's distinctive work from neighboring St. Kitts: lovely hand-painted silk scarves and sarongs, as well as vividly colored place mats, paintings, prints, even note cards.

PERFUME

**CoCo Shop** (⊠ St. Mary's St., ☎ 268/462–1128) stocks exotic island fragrances. **Little Switzerland** (⊠ Heritage Quay, ☎ 268/462–3108) has an extensive selection of European scents for men and women. **La Parfumerie** (⊠ Heritage Quay, ☎ 268/462–2601) imports high-priced scents. **Scent Shop** (⊠ High St., ☎ 268/462–0303) in downtown St. John's offers scent-sational buys in perfumes and cosmetics.

# Nightlife

Most of Antigua's evening entertainment centers on the resort hotels, which present calypso singers, steel bands, limbo dancers, and folkloric groups on a regular basis. Check with the Department of Tourism for up-to-date information.

The **Bay House** (⊠ Tradewinds Hotel, Marble Hill, ☎ 268/462–1223) is in a small hilltop hotel perpetually booked by British Airways flight attendants, who have made the bar a lively, gossipy hangout—and perhaps the closest thing Antigua has to a stylish singles bar. There is live piano music (often drowned out by boisterous singing). Don't come for the overpriced food, which runs from clichéd to creative, but for the company, who lounge at the bar or by the adjacent pool as if this were your hip, rich uncle's country estate. **Big Banana** (⊠ Redcliffe Quay, ☎ 268/462–2621) presents live dance bands well into the night on Tuesday and Thursday.

**Colombo's** (⊠ Galleon Beach Club, English Harbour, ☎ 268/460–1452) is the place to be on Wednesday night for live reggae. The down-home **Crazy Horse Saloon** (⊠ Redcliffe Quay, ☎ 268/462–7936) corrals tourists and locals for everything from pool tournaments to Mexican and country-and-western bands to happy-hour specials like two-for-one margaritas or all-you-can-eat wings. The **Jolly Roger** (⊠ Dickenson Bay, ☎ 268/462–2064) lures a boisterous group for its four-hour Saturday-night cruises. Sail under the stars for a barbecue with an open bar, and dance to live island music.

The **Lemon Tree** (⊠ Long and Church Sts., St. John's, ☎ 268/461–1969) restaurant swings every night but Sunday in season until at least 11 PM, with everything from acoustic to jazz to reggae accompanying the equally eclectic international fare. **Millers by the Sea** (⊠ Runaway Beach, ☎ 268/462–9414 ) draws a crowd that spills over onto the beach for its ever-popular happy hour and live nightly entertainment. This is the place to come and dance on the beach way into the night (or to mingle with cruise-ship passengers on heavy-traffic days). **Russell's** (⊠ Fort James, ☎ 268/462–5479) presents live jazz combos on Sunday nights. **Shirley Heights Lookout** (⊠ Shirley Heights, ☎ 268/463–1785) hosts Sunday-afternoon barbecues that continue into the night with music and dancing. It's the place to be Sunday afternoons and Thursday evenings, when local residents, visitors, and the yachting crowd gather for boisterous fun and the latest gossip.

## Casinos
There are four major casinos on Antigua, as well as several holes-in-the-wall that feature mainly one-armed bandits. Hours vary depending on the season and whether or not cruise ships are in, so it's best to inquire upon your arrival to the island. The "world's largest slot machine" as well as gaming tables are at the **King's Casino** (⊠ Heritage Quay, ☎ 268/462–1727). The **St. James's Club** (⊠ Mamora Bay, ☎ 268/463–1113) has a rather flamboyant casino with a European ambience. The casino at the **Royal Antiguan Resort** (⊠ Deep Bay, ☎ 268/462–3733) is a model of those in Atlantic City, New Jersey.

## Discos
**Ribbit** (⊠ Donovans, Green Bay, ☎ 268/462–7996) attracts a lively mix of locals and tourists who dance the night away (no shorts allowed). It's open Wednesday–Saturday from 10:30 PM. The **Web** (⊠ Old Parham Rd., St. John's, ☎ 268/462–3186) and **Grasshopper** (⊠ Airport Rd., no phone) attract a somewhat rowdier, more heavily local crowd.

# Exploring Antigua

Before you start, study your map for a minute or two. Road names are not posted, so you will need to have a sense of where you are heading if you hope to find it. The easiest way to get to anything is to see if a popular restaurant is near it, since easy-to-spot signs leading the way to restaurants are posted all over the island. (You'll see tons of them nailed to a post at every crossroad.) If you start to feel lost along the way, don't hesitate to ask anyone you see for directions. Bear in mind that locals generally give directions in terms of landmarks that may not seem much like landmarks to you (turn left at the yellow house, or right at the big tree). All major hotels provide free maps and island brochures. If you happen to be in St. John's, stop in at the Tourist Bureau, at the corner of Long and Thames streets. It's a good idea to wear a swimsuit under your clothes while you're sightseeing—one of the sights to strike your fancy may be a secluded beach. Be sure to bring your camera along. There are some picture-perfect spots around the island.

*Numbers in the margin correspond to points of interest on the Antigua (and Barbuda) map.*

SIGHTS TO SEE

**⑬ Betty's Hope.** Just outside the village of Pares, a marked dirt road leads to the village of Betty's Hope, Antigua's first sugar plantation, founded in 1650. You can tour the twin windmills and view exhibits on the island's sugar era. The village isn't much now, but the private trust overseeing its restoration has ambitious plans.

**❺ Curtain Bluff.** At the tip of a tiny outcropping of land, between Carlisle Bay and Morris Bay, Curtain Bluff offers dramatic views of the color contrasts where waters of the Atlantic Ocean meet those of the Caribbean Sea. From here, the main road skirts the southwest coast, dancing in and out of hardwood trees and offering tantalizing glimpses of lovely beaches and spectacular views. The road then veers away from the water and goes through the villages of Bolans and Jennings.

**⑫ Devil's Bridge.** This natural formation, sculpted by the crashing breakers of the Atlantic at Indian Creek, is a national park. Blowholes have been carved by the hissing, spitting surf. They may be hard to spot at first, but just wait until a wave bursts through!

**❽ English Harbour.** The most famous of Antigua's attractions lies on the coast, just south of Falmouth. In 1671 the governor of the Leeward Islands wrote to the Council for Foreign Plantations in London, pointing out the advantages of this landlocked harbor. By 1704 English Harbour was in regular use as a garrisoned station.

In 1784, 26-year-old Horatio Nelson sailed in on HMS *Boreas* to serve as captain and second-in-command of the Leeward Island Station. Under his command was the captain of HMS *Pegasus,* Prince William Henry, Duke of Clarence, who was to ascend the throne of England as William IV. The prince was Nelson's close friend and acted as best man when Nelson married the young widow Fannie Nisbet on Nevis in 1787.

When the Royal Navy abandoned the station at English Harbour in 1889, it fell into a state of decay. The Society of the Friends of English Harbour began restoring it in 1951, and on Dockyard Day, November 14, 1961, **Nelson's Dockyard** was opened with much fanfare.

The dockyard is reminiscent, albeit on a much smaller scale, of Williamsburg, Virginia. Within the compound there are crafts shops, hotels, and restaurants. It is a hub for oceangoing yachts and serves as headquarters for the annual Sailing Week Regatta. A community of mariners keeps the area active in season. Beach lovers tend to stay elsewhere on the island, but visitors who enjoy history and who are part of (or like being around) the nautical scene often choose one of the nearby hotels. If you'd like to get a look at the area from the water, board the *Horatio Nelson* for a 20-minute guided cruise (☞ Guided Tours *in* Antigua A to Z, *below*).

The **Admiral's House Museum** displays ship models, a model of English Harbour, silver trophies, maps, prints, and Nelson's very own telescope and tea caddy. ⊠ *English Harbour,* ☎ *268/463–1053 or 268/463–1379.* 🎟 *$2.* ☺ *Daily 8–6.*

On a ridge overlooking the dockyard is **Clarence House** (☎ 268/463–1026), built in 1787 and once the home of the duke of Clarence. Princess Margaret and Lord Snowdon spent part of their honeymoon here in 1960, and Queen Elizabeth and Prince Philip have dined here. It is now used by the governor-general as a country home; visits are possible when he is not in residence. The place is decorated pretty much as it was in the 18th century and is definitely worth a visit.

NEED A BREAK?   Cool off with the yachting crowd on the terrace of the **Admiral's Inn** (✉ English Harbour, ☎ 268/460–1027), where the deeply tanned crews can keep an eye on their multimillion-dollar babies offshore—and on each other. The people-watching is first-rate, and so are the banana daiquiris (with or without Antiguan rum).

**❼ Falmouth.** This town sits on a lovely bay backed by former sugar plantations and sugar mills. **St. Paul's Church** was rebuilt on the site of a church once used by troops during the Nelson period.

**❹ Fig Tree Drive.** This road takes you through the rain forest, which is rich in mangoes, pineapples, and banana trees (*fig* is the Antiguan word for banana). The rain-forest area is the hilliest part of the island—**Boggy Peak**, to the west, is the highest point, rising to 1,319 ft.

**❻ Fort George.** East of **Liberta**, one of the first settlements founded by freed slaves, on Monk's Hill, this fort was built from 1689 to 1720. It wouldn't be of much help to anybody these days, but among the ruins you can make out the sites for its 32 cannons, its water cisterns, the base of the old flagstaff, and some of the original buildings.

**❷ Fort James.** Named after King James II, this fort was constructed between 1704 and 1739 as a lookout point for the city and St. John's Harbour. The ramparts overlooking the small islands in the bay are in ruins, but 10 cannons still point out to sea.

**❿ Harmony Hall.** Northeast of Freetown (follow the signs) is this interesting art gallery. A sister to the Jamaican gallery near Ocho Rios, Jamaica, Harmony Hall is built on the foundation of a 17th-century sugar-plantation great house. Artists Graham Davis and Peter and Annabella Proudlock, who founded the Jamaican gallery, teamed up with local entrepreneur Geoffrey Pidduck to create an Antiguan art gallery specializing in high-quality West Indian art. A large gallery is used for one-man shows, and another exhibition hall displays watercolors. A small bar and an outside restaurant under the trees are open in season. ✉ *Brown's Mill Bay,* ☎ *268/463–2057.* ⊙ *Daily 10–6.*

**⓫ Indian Town.** Archaeological digs at this national park have revealed evidence of Carib occupation. This is one of the prettier parts of the island.

**❸ Megaliths of Greencastle Hill.** It's an arduous but rewarding climb to these eerie rock slabs. Some say the megaliths were set up by humans for the worship of the sun and moon; others believe they are nothing more than unusual geological formations.

**⓮ Parham.** This tiny village is a splendid, sleepy example of a traditional colonial settlement. **St. Peter's Church,** built in 1840 by Thomas Weekes, an English architect, is an octagonal Italianate building whose facade was once richly decorated with stucco, though it suffered considerable damage during the earthquake of 1843.

**❶ St. John's.** Antigua's capital, home to some 40,000 people (approximately half the island's population), lies at sea level at the inland end of a sheltered bay on the northwest coast of the island. The city has seen better days, but it is undergoing a face-lift, and there are some notable historic sights, pleasant shopping areas, and good restaurants. Although much of the city looks shabby, it is definitely worth a visit. Most of the gift stores and restaurants are near the waterfront. Up the hill is Antigua's downtown, with stores carrying major appliances, plumbing supplies, and other goods unlikely to be of interest to tourists.

Signs at the **Museum of Antigua and Barbuda** say PLEASE TOUCH, encouraging citizens and visitors to explore Antigua's past. Try your hand at the educational video games. Exhibits interpret the history of the nation from its geological birth to its political independence in 1981. There are fossil and coral remains from some 34 million years ago, a life-size replica of an Arawak house, models of a sugar plantation and a wattle-and-daub house, and a minishop with handicrafts, books, historical prints, and paintings. The colonial building that houses the museum is the former courthouse, which dates from 1750. ⊠ *Church and Market Sts.,* ☎ *268/462–1469.* ☜ *Free.* ☉ *Weekdays 8:30–4, Sat. 10–1.*

At the south gate of the **Anglican Cathedral of St. John the Divine,** there are figures of St. John the Baptist and St. John the Divine said to have been taken from one of Napoléon's ships and brought to Antigua. The original church was built in 1681, replaced by a stone building in 1745, and destroyed by an earthquake in 1843. The present building dates from 1845. With an eye to future earthquakes, the parishioners had the interior completely encased in pitch pine, hoping to forestall heavy damage. The church was elevated to the status of cathedral in 1848. ⊠ *Between Long and Newgate Sts.,* ☎ *268/461–0082.*

Shopaholics head directly for **Heritage Quay,** a continually expanding multimillion-dollar shopping complex. Two-story buildings showcase stores specializing in duty-free goods, sportswear, T-shirts, imports from down-island (paintings, T-shirts, straw baskets), and local crafts, plus several restaurants and a casino. Cruise-ship passengers disembark here from the 500-ft-long pier. ⊠ *High and Thames Sts.*

**Redcliffe Quay,** set at the water's edge just south of Heritage Quay, is the most appealing part of St. John's. Attractively restored buildings in a riot of cotton-candy colors house shops, restaurants, and boutiques and are linked by courtyards and landscaped walkways. This is the shopping area favored by residents and return guests. There are no duty-free shops, but there are many other interesting choices. There are also cafés where you can sit and ponder the scene of two centuries ago, when slaves were held here prior to being sold.

NEED A      At **Hemingway's** (⊠ Jardine Court, ☎ 268/462–2763), a historic clap-
BREAK?      board house painted the same hues—coral, aqua, lime—as the potent tropical concoctions it serves, in the center of St. John's, you can sit on the upstairs veranda and drink papaya and mango juice or have breakfast and watch the bustling life of the streets below.

At the far south end of town, where Market Street forks into Valley Road and All Saints Road, a whole lot of haggling goes on every Friday and Saturday, when locals jam the public **marketplace** to buy and sell fruits, vegetables, fish, and spices. Be sure to ask before you aim a camera; expect the subject of your shot to ask for a tip. This is shopping the old-time Caribbean way, a jambalaya of sights, sounds, and smells.

**❾ Shirley Heights.** This bluff affords a spectacular view of English Harbour. The heights are named for Sir Thomas Shirley, the governor who fortified the harbor in 1787. Not far from Shirley Heights is the **Dows Hill Interpretation Centre,** where observation platforms provide still more sensational vistas of the whole English Harbour area. There's a multimedia presentation on the island's history and culture, from the days of the Amerindians to the present. *For information, call National Parks Authority at 268/460–1053.* ✉ *EC$15.* ⊙ *Daily 9–5.*

## Barbuda

**⑮ Barbuda.** Twenty-six mi north of Antigua is Barbuda—a flat, 62-square-mi coral atoll with 17 mi of pinkish white-sand beaches. Almost all the island's 1,200 people live in **Codrington.** Barbuda's 8-mi **Coco Point Beach** lures beachcombers, and the island is ringed by wrecks and reef, making it a great draw for divers and snorkelers. Ornithologists and bird lovers come here, too. The **Bird Sanctuary,** a wide mangrove-filled lagoon, is home to an estimated 170 species of birds, including frigate birds with 8-ft wingspans.

The sole historic ruin here is **Martello Tower,** which is believed to have been a lighthouse built by the Spaniards before the English occupied the island. LIAT (☞ Arriving and Departing *in* Antigua A to Z, *below*) has regularly scheduled daily flights from Antigua to Barbuda (with departure times just right for day-trippers); air and boat charters are also available (contact the Department of Tourism). Those wishing to overnight here can choose from two superluxury resorts and several guest houses.

# Antigua A to Z

## Arriving and Departing

BY PLANE

**American Airlines** (☎ 268/462–0950 or 800/433–7300) has daily direct service from New York and Miami, as well as several flights from San Juan that connect with flights from more than 100 U.S. cities. **Air Canada** (☎ 268/462–1147 or 800/776–3000) has nonstop service from Toronto. **Air France** (☎ 268/462–1763 or 800/237–2747) has nonstop service from Paris. **British Airways** (☎ 268/462–3219 or 800/247–9297) has nonstop service from London. **BWIA** (☎ 268/462–3101 or 800/327–7401) has nonstop service from New York, Miami, and Toronto. **Continental** (☎ 268/462–5353 or 800/231–0856) offers service from several North American cities. **LIAT** (☎ 268/462–0701) has daily flights from Antigua to Barbuda, as well as to and from many other Caribbean islands. **Lufthansa** (☎ 800/645–3880) has nonstop service from Frankfurt.

**V. C. Bird International Airport** is a major hub for traffic between Caribbean islands; it is always busy with tiny planes taking off and landing.

FROM THE AIRPORT

Taxis meet every flight, and drivers will offer to guide you around the island. The taxis are unmetered, but rates are posted at the airport and drivers are required to carry a rate card with them. The fixed rate from the airport to St. John's is US$12 (although drivers have been known to *quote* E.C. dollars) and from the airport to English Harbour, $21.

## Currency

Local currency is the Eastern Caribbean dollar (EC$), which is tied to the U.S. dollar and fluctuates only slightly. At hotels, the rate is EC$2.60 to US$1; at banks, it's about EC$2.70. American dollars are readily accepted, although you will usually receive change in E.C. dollars. Be sure you understand which currency is being used, since most places quote prices in E.C. dollars. Most hotels, restaurants, and duty-free

shops take major credit cards, and all accept traveler's checks. It's a
good idea to inquire at the tourist office or your hotel about the current credit-card policy. Note: Prices quoted are in U.S. dollars unless
indicated otherwise.

## Emergencies
**Ambulance:** ☎ 268/462–0251. **Fire:** ☎ 268/462–0044. **Police:**
☎ 268/462–0125. **Holberton Hospital** (✉ Hospital Rd., St. John's,
☎ 268/462–0251, 268/462–0252, or 268/462–0253) has a 24-hour
emergency room. Medical and other supplies are available at **City
Pharmacy** (✉ St. Mary's St., St. John's, ☎ 268/462–1363) and **Health
Pharmacy** (✉ Redcliffe St., St. John's, ☎ 268/462–1255).

## Getting Around
### BUSES
You'll see two bus stations in St. John's, near the Botanical Gardens
and near Central Market, but don't expect to see many buses. Bus schedules here epitomize what is called "island time," which is to say they
roll when the spirit (infrequently) moves them.

### CAR RENTALS
To rent a car, you'll need a valid driver's license and a temporary permit ($12), which is available through the rental agent. Rentals aver-
age about $50 per day in season, with unlimited mileage. You'll
probably get a better daily rate if you rent for several days. Most agencies rent automatic, stick-shift, and right- and left-hand-drive vehicles,
as well as four-wheel-drive vehicles ($55 per day). Although these
four-wheel drives will get you more places and are refreshingly open,
beware that the roads are full of potholes, and a day in such a vehicle
can leave you feeling as if you've been through a paint-mixing machine!
Remember to drive on the left (pay particular attention getting in and
out of rotaries and making turns), and know that virtually all roads
are unmarked. Fortunately, you will not have to deal with the incredibly steep curves that are on so many other Caribbean islands.

Among the agencies are **Budget** (✉ St. John's, ☎ 268/462–3009 or
800/472–3325), **National** (✉ St. John's, ☎ 268/462–2113 or 800/328–
4567), **Thrifty** (✉ Airport, ☎ 268/462–0976), **Hertz** (✉ St. John's, also
Jolly Harbour, ☎ 268/462–4114), **Dollar** (✉ St. John's, ☎ 268/462–
0362), and **Avis** (✉ Airport or St. James's Club, ☎ 268/462–2840).
You can also rent Honda scooters for $30 per day ($40 daily by the
week) at **Shipwreck** (✉ English Harbour, ☎ 268/460–2711).

### TAXIS
If you're uncomfortable about driving on the left or are prone to
getting lost, a taxi is your best bet, although fares mount up quickly.
Taxis are unmetered, but rates are fixed from here to there, and drivers are required to carry a rate card at all times. They'll even take you
from the St. John's area to English Harbour and wait for a "reasonable" amount of time (about a half hour) while you look around, for
about $40.

## Guided Tours
Virtually all taxi drivers double as guides, and you can arrange an island tour with one for about $20 an hour. Every major hotel has a cab-
bie on call and may be able to negotiate a discount, particularly
off-season.

**Alexander, Parrish Ltd.** (✉ St. John's, ☎ 268/462–0387) specializes
in island tours and can also arrange overnight stays. **Antours** (✉ St.
John's, ☎ 268/462–4788) gives half- and full-day tours of the island.
Antours is also the American Express representative on the island.

**Bryson's Travel** (⊠ St. John's, ☎ 268/462–0223) fashions personalized tours of the island, as well as cruises and deep-sea-fishing trips. **Estate Safari Adventure** (☎ 268/462–4713) operates tours to the "wilds" of Antigua's interior, where there are few marked trails and roads are rough. You'll see deserted plantation houses, rain-forest trails, and ruined sugar mills and forts. The luxuriant tropical forest around the island's highest point, Boggy Peak, is especially worth seeing. The cost of the tour (about $60 per person) includes lunch and snorkeling at a secluded beach. **Horatio Nelson** (⊠ Dockyard Divers, ☎ 268/464–8591) provides a good view of English Harbour from the water; hop on board for the 20-minute guided cruise. The tour costs $6 per person, and the boat leaves every half hour from 9 to 5 daily. **Tropikelly** (☎ 268/461–0383) offers an off-road adventure in a four-wheel drive, allowing participants to appreciate the island's topography. Hiking is involved, though it's not strenuous. The tour visits the island's plantation houses, forts, and rain forests.

## Language
Antigua's official language is English.

## Opening and Closing Times
Although some stores still follow the tradition of closing for lunch, most shops, especially in season, are open Monday–Friday 9–5 and Saturday 8–noon or 8–3. Hours vary from bank to bank, but generally they are open Monday–Thursday 8–2 and Friday 8–4.

## Passports and Visas
U.S. and Canadian citizens need proof of identity. A valid passport is most desirable, but a birth certificate is acceptable provided it has a raised or embossed seal and has been issued by a county or state (not a hospital) and provided that you also have some type of photo identification, such as a driver's license. A driver's license by itself is not sufficient. British citizens need a passport. All visitors must present a return or ongoing ticket.

## Precautions
Some beaches are shaded by manchineel trees, whose leaves and applelike fruit are poisonous to touch. Most of the trees are posted with warning signs and should be avoided; even raindrops falling from them can cause painful blisters. If you should come in contact with one, rinse the affected area and contact a doctor.

Throughout the Caribbean, incidents of petty theft are increasing. Leave your valuables in the hotel safe-deposit box; don't leave them unattended in your room or on the beach. Also, the streets of St. John's are fairly deserted at night, so it's not a good idea to wander out alone.

## Taxes and Service Charges
Hotels collect a 7% government room tax and usually add a 10% service charge to your bill. In restaurants, a 10% service charge is usually added to your bill (sometimes 7% tax as well), and it is customary to leave another 5% if you are pleased with the service. Taxi drivers expect a 10% tip. The departure tax is $10.

## Telephones and Mail
To call Antigua from the United States, dial 1, then area code 268, then the local seven-digit number. Few hotels have direct-dial telephones, but connections are easily made through the switchboard. The Caribbean Phone Card, available in $5, $10, and $20 amounts, can be used for local and long-distance calls and for access to AT&T USA Direct lines. There are now quite a few phones that accept the phone cards, and they work much better than the regular pay phones. You can purchase

the card from most hotels or from a post office. Some phone-card booths can now access Sprint and MCI. In addition, there are several Boatphones scattered throughout the island at major tourist sights; simply pick up the receiver and the operator will take your credit-card number (any major card) and assign you a PIN (personal identification number). Calls using your PIN are then charged to that credit card.

To place a call to the United States, dial 1, the appropriate area code, and the seven-digit number, or use the phone card or one of the AT&T USA Direct phones, which are available at several locations, including the airport departure lounge, the cruise terminal at St. John's, and the English Harbour Marina. To place an interisland call, dial the local seven-digit number.

In an emergency, you can make calls from **Cable & Wireless (WI) Ltd.** (⊠ 42–44 St. Mary's St., St. John's, ☎ 268/462–9840; ⊠ Nelson's Dockyard, English Harbour, ☎ 268/463–1517).

Airmail letters to North America cost EC90¢; postcards, EC45¢. The post office is at the foot of High Street in St. John's.

## Visitor Information

Before you go, contact the **Antigua and Barbuda Tourist Offices** in the United States (⊠ 610 5th Ave., Suite 311, New York, NY 10020, ☎ 212/541–4117; ⊠ 25 S.E. 2nd Ave., Suite 300, Miami, FL 33131, ☎ 305/381–6762; a new toll-free information number [☎ 888/268–4227] has live operators standing by weekdays 9–5), in Canada (⊠ 60 St. Clair Ave. E, Suite 304, Toronto, Ontario M4T 1N5, ☎ 416/961–3085), and in the United Kingdom (⊠ Antigua House, 15 Thayer St., London W1M 5LD, ☎ 0171/486–7073).

Once on Antigua, visit the **Antigua and Barbuda Department of Tourism** (⊠ Thames and Long Sts., St. John's, ☎ 268/462–0480), open Monday–Thursday 8–4:30, Friday 8–3. There is also a tourist-information desk at the airport, just beyond the immigration checkpoint. The tourist office gives limited information. You may have more success with the **Antigua Hotels Association** (⊠ Long St., St. John's, ☎ 268/462–3703), which also provides assistance.

# 4 Aruba

*Balmy sunshine, silky sand, aquamarine waters, natural scenic wonders, outstanding dining, duty-free shopping, and an array of nightly entertainment . . . Aruba's got it in spades. It's also unusual in its range of choices, from world-class oceanfront resorts equipped with gourmet restaurants and high-dollar casinos to intimate neighborhood motels and diners not far off the beach.*

Updated by
Melissa Rivers

IMAGINE ARUBA AS ONE BIG *LOVE BOAT* CRUISE. Most of its 29 hotels sit side by side down one major strip along the southwestern shore, with restaurants, exotic boutiques, fiery floor shows, and glitzy casinos right on their premises. Nearly every night there are organized theme parties, treasure hunts, beachside barbecues, and fish fries with steel bands and limbo or Carnival dancers. Surround all this with warm blue-green waters that afford clear visibility up to 100 ft, and you've got the perfect sun destination for travelers seeking entertainment and activities.

The "A" in the ABC Islands, Aruba is small—only 19½ mi long and 6 mi across at its widest point. Once a member of the Netherlands Antilles, Aruba became an independent entity within the Netherlands in 1986, with its own royally appointed governor, a democratic government, and a 21-member elected Parliament. With education, housing, and health care financed by an economy based on tourism, the island's population of 84,500 recognizes visitors as valued guests. The national anthem proclaims, "The greatness of our people is their great cordiality," and this is no exaggeration. Waiters serve you with smiles, English is spoken everywhere, and hotel hospitality directors appear delighted to serve your special needs. Direct air service from the United States makes Aruba an excellent choice for even a short vacation.

The island's distinctive beauty lies in its countryside—an almost extraterrestrial landscape full of rocky deserts, divi-divi trees, cactus jungles alive with the chittering of wild parakeets, secluded coves, and aquamarine vistas with crashing waves. With its low humidity and average temperature of 82°F, Aruba has the climate of a paradise. Sun, cooling trade winds, friendly and courteous service, modern and efficient amenities, golf and tennis clubs, modern casinos, glorious beaches, duty-free shopping, and some of the best cuisine in the Caribbean (the island swept the Caribbean Culinary Competition in late 1996) are Aruba's strong suit and help fill its more than 7,000 hotel rooms.

## Lodging

Hotels are fairly expensive in Aruba. To save money, take advantage of the many airline and hotel packages, which are plentiful and considerably less expensive than the one-night rate. Or go during low season (summer), when rates are discounted up to 40%.

Most of the hotels are west of Oranjestad along L. G. Smith and J. E. Irausquin boulevards and are miniresort complexes, with—get ready—their own drugstores, boutiques, fitness centers, beauty parlors, casinos, restaurants, gourmet delis, water-sports centers, and car-rental and travel desks. Meeting rooms, room service, laundry and dry cleaning services, in-room safe and minibar or refrigerator, and babysitting are standard amenities at all but the smallest properties, and daily activities (beach bingo or volleyball, aquacise or aerobics, craft classes, even Papiamento lessons, and separate supervised activities for children) are usually part of the package. Children often get free accommodation in their parents' room; check with the property for age qualifications. Hotel restaurants and clubs are open to all guests on the island, so you can visit other properties no matter where you're staying. Most hotels, unless specified, do not include meals in their room rates.

| CATEGORY | COST* |
|----------|-------|
| $$$$ | over $300 |
| $$$ | $225–$300 |
| $$ | $150–$225 |
| $ | under $150 |

*All prices are for a standard double room during high season, excluding 6% government tax and 11% service charge.*

$$$$   🏨 **Americana Aruba Beach Resort & Casino.** Teeming activity surrounds the clover-leaf-shape pool with a waterfall and two whirlpool tubs at the heart of this large resort. The buzz is indicative of the atmosphere in general: A social director is always cajoling you to participate in everything from beer-drinking contests to bikini shows. The property recently underwent a $3.5 million face-lift, and rooms are now done in richer shades of purple, green, and yellow and furnished in light rattan. Still, this one is just not as luxurious as others in its price range. White-tiled bathrooms are a bit tight, and balconies are no more than narrow step-outs. However, it remains popular with American and Canadian tour groups. ⊠ *J. E. Irausquin Blvd. 83, Palm Beach,* ☏ *297/8–24500 or 800/447–7462,* FAX *297/8–23191. 419 rooms. 2 restaurants, 4 bars, pool, 2 outdoor hot tubs, 2 tennis courts, exercise room, Ping-Pong, volleyball, beach, water sports, casino. AE, D, DC, MC, V. EP, All-inclusive.*

$$$$   🏨 **Aruba Marriott Resort and Stellaris Casino.** Aruba's newest (1995)— and most expensive—luxury high-rise resort opened on the far end of Palm Beach close to the Tierra del Sol golf course. You'll hear the sound of water everywhere, whether it's the trickling of streams and waterfalls in the elegant marble lobby and around the tropically landscaped free-form pool or the beating of the surf. The rooms are spacious and attractively appointed (crisp, clean forest-green-on-white decor softened by floral bedspreads and pastel watercolor paintings), and all have an ocean view and a balcony. The hotel's pricey gourmet restaurant, Tuscanny's, has developed a strong reputation in a short amount of time. ⊠ *L. G. Smith Blvd. 101, Palm Beach,* ☏ *297/8–69000 or 800/223–6388,* FAX *297/8–60649. 413 rooms, 18 suites. 3 restaurants, 5 bars, café, no-smoking floors, pool, indoor and outdoor hot tubs, massage, saunas, spa, 3 tennis courts, aerobics, health club, horseshoes, volleyball, water sports, scuba diving, shops, casino, concierge. AE, D, DC, MC, V. EP, MAP, FAP, All-inclusive.*

$$$$   🏨 **Hyatt Regency Aruba Resort & Casino.** This $57 million resort, a
★   favorite among Aruba's luxury properties, looks like a Spanish grandee's palace, with Art Deco–style flourishes and a multilevel pool with waterfalls, a two-story water slide, and a lagoon stocked with tropical fish and black swans. Rooms, done in gemstone color schemes and dark mahogany furnishings, have tiny step-out balconies and a lot of little extras. Four excellent restaurants are on the premises, among them Olé and Ruinas del Mar. Their design is exquisite: stone and marble "ruins" surrounded by moats, waterfalls, and splashing fountains. It is a truly romantic resort with lush grounds perfect for an evening stroll—a top choice for honeymooners. ⊠ *J. E. Irausquin Blvd. 85, Palm Beach,* ☏ *297/8–61234 or 800/233–1234,* FAX *297/8–61682. 342 rooms, 18 suites. 4 restaurants, 5 bars, snack bar, no-smoking floor, room service, pool, beauty salon, 2 outdoor hot tubs, massage, sauna, steam rooms, 2 tennis courts, health club, volleyball, beach, dive shop, dock, water sports, fishing, shops, casino, playground. AE, DC, MC, V. EP, MAP.*

$$$–$$$$   🏨 **Sonesta Resorts at Seaport Village.** For those who enjoy being in
★   the thick of things, this sprawling property downtown is surrounded by shops, restaurants, and casinos galore. The resort includes two hotels: the newer one with roomy suites set near a small man-made beach, and the original high-rise with compact but attractive rooms

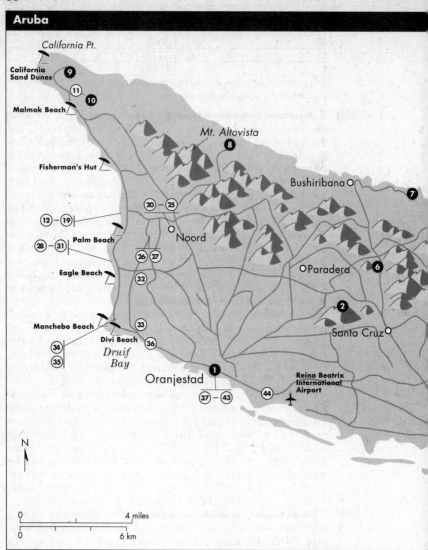

**Exploring**

Alto Vista Chapel, **8**

California Lighthouse, **9**

Frenchman's Pass, **3**

Guadirikiri Fontein Caves, **5**

Hooiberg (Haystack Hill), **2**

Malmok, **10**

Natural Bridge, **7**

Oranjestad, **1**

Rock Formations (Ayo and Casibari), **6**

San Nicolas, **4**

**Dining**

Benihana, **33**

Boonoonoonoos, **38**

Brisas del Mar, **45**

Buccaneer Restaurant, **20**

Charlie's Restaurant & Bar, **46**

Chez Mathilde, **39**

Frankie's Prime Grill, **43**

Gasparito Restaurant and Art Gallery, **21**

Kowloon, **40**

Old Cunucu House, **15**

Old Mill, **26**

The Paddock, **42**

La Paloma, **22**

Papiamento, **23**

Le Petit Café, **41**

Valentino's, **24**

Ventanas del Mar, **11**

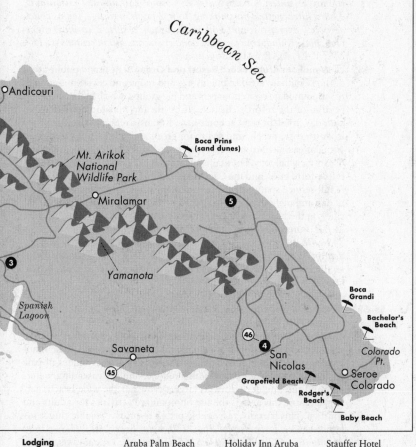

**KEY**

❶ Exploring Sites

⑪ Hotels and Restaurants

Caribbean Sea

ᵒAndicouri

Boca Prins
(sand dunes)

*Mt. Arikok
National
Wildlife Park*

ᵒMiralamar

❺

*Yamanota*

❸

*Spanish
Lagoon*

Boca
Grandi

Bachelor's
Beach

㊻

❹

San
Nicolas

*Colorado
Pt.*

Savaneta

㊺

Grapefield Beach

ᵒSeroe
Colorado

Rodger's
Beach

Baby Beach

**Lodging**

Americana Aruba
Beach Resort &
Casino, **16**

Amsterdam
Manor Beach
Resort, **28**

Aruba Blue Village
Suites, **32**

Aruba Marriott
Resort & Stellaris
Casino, **12**

Aruba Palm Beach
Hotel & Casino, **18**

Bucuti Beach
Resort, **31**

Bushiri Beach
Resort, **36**

La Cabana All Suite
Beach Resort &
Casino, **29**

Coconut Inn, **25**

Divi Aruba Beach
Resort, **34**

Holiday Inn Aruba
Beach Resort &
Casino, **13**

Hyatt Regency Aruba
Resort & Casino, **14**

Mill Resort, **27**

Radisson Aruba
Caribbean Resort &
Casino, **17**

Sonesta Resorts at
Seaport Village, **37**

Stauffer Hotel
Aruba, **30**

Tamarijn Aruba, **35**

Vistalmar, **44**

Wyndham Aruba
Beach Resort and
Casino, **19**

above the Seaport Mall (pick the quieter garden-view rooms here). In the resort lobby, which connects to the mall, parrots fly free in the tropical garden atrium and guests board motor skiffs headed for the resort's 40-acre private island—perfect for day trips. The gourmet restaurant, L'Escale, is one of Aruba's most creative—and expensive. This lively property is a top choice for singles and offers plenty for families, too. ⊠ *L. G. Smith Blvd. 9, Oranjestad,* ☎ *297/8–36000 or 800/766–3782,* FAX *297/8–34389. Sonesta Resort & Casino: 285 rooms, 15 suites; Sonesta Suites & Casino: 250 suites. 4 restaurants, 4 bars, kitchenettes, no-smoking floor, 2 pools, massage, tennis court, aerobics, exercise room, volleyball, beach, shops, 2 casinos, nightclub, playground, coin laundry, concierge, convention center. AE, DC, MC, V. EP, MAP, FAP, All-inclusive.*

**$$$** 🏨 **Wyndham Aruba Beach Resort and Casino.** The grand public areas of the Wyndham are dazzling in size and scope and cavernous enough to accommodate conventioneers and big groups, which make up a good portion of the resort's clientele. If bustle and nonstop activity make your day, you'll be right at home here. Rooms, average in size, are pretty in dusty rose, peach, and sea-foam green and thoughtfully equipped with coffeemaker, iron and ironing board, refrigerator, hair dryer, and ocean-view balcony. Fountains splash playfully into the 8,000-square-ft free-form pool, and the Casablanca Casino has Rick's Place in mind. A full-service spa, with all the muds and rubs, an extensive program of day and night activities for the kids, and a Red Sail water-sports facility on the beach are pluses. There is a fee for use of the health club. ⊠ *J. E. Irausquin Blvd. 77, Palm Beach,* ☎ *297/8–64466 or 800/996–3426,* FAX *297/8–68217. 378 rooms, 66 suites. 4 restaurants, 4 bars, deli, pool, wading pool, beauty salon, massage, sauna, steam room, tennis court, health club, Ping-Pong, shuffleboard, volleyball, beach, dive shop, water sports, shops, casino, playground, concierge, convention center. AE, DC, MC, V. EP, CP, MAP, FAP.*

**$$–$$$** 🏨 **Holiday Inn Aruba Beach Resort & Casino.** This is one of the larger properties on Palm Beach, but its size is cleverly camouflaged. Three buildings of seven stories each are set apart from each other along a sugary, palm-dotted beach. Rooms, redone during resort-wide renovations in 1996, are clean, spacious, and attractive in shades of pale green and rose. The pool was also redone, and it's cascading waterfalls and sunning deck draw as large a crowd as the wide beach, perhaps because this area is the site of organized activities for adults and children. This friendly, reasonably priced resort is a reliable choice for families. ⊠ *J. E. Irausquin Blvd. 230, Palm Beach,* ☎ *297/8–63600 or 800/465–4329,* FAX *297/8–65165. 600 rooms. 3 restaurants, 3 bars, no-smoking rooms, refrigerators, pool, massage, 6 tennis courts, boccie, exercise room, Ping-Pong, beach, dock, dive shop, water sports, shops, casino, concierge. AE, DC, MC, V. EP, MAP, FAP.*

**$$–$$$** 🏨 **Mill Resort.** Two-story red-roof buildings flank the open-air common areas of this small condominium hotel. Request one of the rooms renovated in 1996; they are far more attractive and modern, with a pastel tropical decor. The junior suites have a king-size bed, a sitting area, and a kitchenette. Studios have a full kitchen but only a queen-size convertible sofa bed, a tiny bathroom, and no balcony. This moderately priced resort is popular with couples seeking a quiet getaway and with families with small children. To the relief of many guests, there is no casino and no organized evening activities; action can be found at the nearby large resorts, and the beach is only a five-minute walk away (though there is a beach shuttle). At press time, there was talk of adding another 200 rooms and taking over management of the neighboring Old Mill restaurant (☞ Dining, *below*). ⊠ *J. E. Irausquin Blvd. 330, Noord,* ☎ *297/8–67700,* FAX *297/8–67271. 200 rooms. Bar,* *grill, grocery, kitchenette, pool, wading pool, saunas, 2 tennis courts, exercise room, coin laundry. AE, DC, MC, V. EP.*

**$$–$$$** ⊞ **Radisson Aruba Caribbean Resort & Casino.** Called La Grande Dame of the Caribbean, this resort was the first high-rise on the island. Liz Taylor used to stay here when she was married to Eddie Fisher, so the outgoing staff is used to filling special needs. The broad beach dotted by shade huts is the site of many of the resort's organized activities. A comprehensive renewal has brought flowers, artwork, and a generally festive air to the lobby. Of the sunny air-conditioned rooms with balconies, 65% have a full-ocean view. Larger TVs, bamboo furniture, and tropical-print bedspreads and curtains are among the welcome recent additions. ⊠ *J. E. Irausquin Blvd. 81, Palm Beach,* ☎ *297/8–66555 or 800/333–3333,* ℻ *297/8–63260. 353 rooms, 19 suites. 3 restaurants, 4 bars, café, ice cream parlor, no-smoking rooms, pool, 4 tennis courts, basketball, boccie, exercise room, shuffleboard, volleyball, beach, dive shop, water sports, shops, casino, library, playground. AE, D, DC, MC, V. EP, MAP, FAP.*

**$$** ⊞ **Bucuti Beach Resort.** The intimate, European-style Bucuti Beach is a
★ refreshingly peaceful antidote to the impersonal feel of some larger, bustling resorts. From the moment you are seated and handed a refreshing cool towel in the new lobby, it's clear that the gracious staff has an understanding of the art of hospitality. Hacienda-style buildings house enormous rooms with bright floral decor, sparkling tile floors, and terrace or balcony with ocean view. The resort has an enviable beach location, on the widest, most secluded section of Eagle Beach. The breezy oceanfront Pirate's Nest restaurant, which looks like a beached galleon, is known islandwide for its excellent theme dinners. ⊠ *J. E. Irausquin Blvd. 55-B, Eagle Beach,* ☎ *297/8–36141 or 800/528–1234,* ℻ *297/8–25272. 63 rooms. Restaurant, bar, pool, exercise room, volleyball, beach, bicycles, shop. AE, D, DC, MC, V. CP, MAP.*

**$$** ⊞ **Divi Aruba Beach Resort.** The motto at this popular Mediterranean-style low rise remains "barefoot elegance," which means you can streak through the lobby in your bikini. The main section of the resort has standard guest rooms, beachfront lanai rooms, and casitas (garden bungalows) that look out onto individual courtyards and for the most part are only steps away from the beach. The guest rooms are on the island's water system, which means the water is cooled and heated by Mother Nature—just another reason to wish for warm weather. Remodeled bathrooms, white tile floors, updated light wood furniture, and fresh paint have helped tremendously. There is a daily activities program and theme dinners each night; the Red Parrot restaurant offers romantic beachside dining. ⊠ *L. G. Smith Blvd. 93, Divi Beach, Oranjestad,* ☎ *297/8– 23300 or 800/554–2008,* ℻ *297/8–31940. 203 rooms. 2 restaurants, 2 bars, refrigerators, 2 pools, outdoor hot tub, tennis court, shuffleboard, volleyball, beach, dive shop, water sports, mountain bikes, shops. AE, D, DC, MC, V. EP, MAP, FAP, All-inclusive.*

**$$** ⊞ **La Cabana All Suite Beach Resort & Casino.** At the top end of Eagle Beach, across the busy road from the sand, is Aruba's largest time-sharing complex. The original four-story building faces the beach and forms a horseshoe around a huge free-form pool complex with a water slide, poolside bar, outdoor café, and water-sports center. One-third of the rooms have a full sea view. All the oddly configured but comfortable rooms—studio suites or one-bedroom suites—come with a fully equipped kitchenette, a small balcony, and a whirlpool bath for two. Pricier suites and villas are separated from the main building by a parking lot, making them more secluded and quieter. Shuttle buses run guests over to the upscale casino, where the hotel has a theme restaurant and the Tropicana showroom. ⊠ *J. E. Irausquin Blvd. 250, Eagle Beach,* ☎ *297/8–39000 or 800/835–7193; 212/251–1710 in NY;* ℻ *297/8–*

*37208. 803 suites. 4 restaurants, 3 bars, ice cream parlor, grocery, 3 pools, 3 outdoor hot tubs, massage, sauna, aerobics, basketball, health club, racquetball, shuffleboard, squash, volleyball, beach, dive shop, water sports, shops, casino, theater, playground, coin laundry, chapel. AE, DC, MC, V. EP, MAP, FAP, All-inclusive.*

**$–$$** ⊞ **Amsterdam Manor Beach Resort.** This attractive, gabled, mustard-color hotel looks like part of a Dutch colonial village. Rooms are furnished either in Dutch modern or provincial style and range from smallish studios with a balcony and whirlpool bathtub to deluxe two-bedroom suites with peaked ceilings, whirlpool bathtub and shower, and full kitchen. It's a cozy enclave surrounding a lovely pool with waterfall marred only slightly by the noise of traffic from J. E. Irausquin Boulevard. At least glorious Eagle Beach is just across the street. Complimentary diving lessons are available twice each week and there aren't many other planned activities, so the property stays fairly peaceful. ✉ *J. E. Irausquin Blvd. 252, Eagle Beach,* ☎ *297/8–71492 or 800/766–6016,* FAX *297/8–71463. 72 units. Restaurant, bar, pool, snorkeling, playground, coin laundry. AE, MC, V. EP.*

**$–$$** ⊞ **Aruba Palm Beach Hotel & Casino.** Dotting the drive leading up to this pink, eight-story Moorish palazzo are pink-swaddled palm trees. Around the other side is a large, well-manicured tropical garden good for sunning, with a pair of vociferous parrots guarding the entrance. The oversize guest rooms are cheerfully decorated in plaids and tropical prints; each has a large walk-in closet and a postage-stamp balcony that overlooks the ocean, the pool, or the gardens. An organized activities program keeps things hopping here. For a peaceful meal, eat alfresco in the rock-garden setting of the Seawatch Restaurant. For live music, try the Players Club lounge. A limbo and steel-band show is scheduled one night a week. ✉ *J. E. Irausquin Blvd. 79, Palm Beach,* ☎ *297/8–63900 or 800/345–2782,* FAX *297/8–61941. 186 rooms. 2 restaurants, 2 bars, deli, room service, pool, wading pool, 2 tennis courts, volleyball, beach, dive shop, water sports, shops, casino. AE, D, DC, MC, V. EP, MAP.*

**$** ⊞ **Aruba Blue Village Suites.** If a plumper wallet is more important to you than a beachfront location, this comfortable enclave tucked away from the hotel strip in a residential area is the answer. The single-story apartments form an open-ended rectangle around one of two pools (where the barbecues are held once a week); each basic but tidy apartment has a full kitchen, sparse Dutch-style furnishings, and air-conditioned bedrooms. Studios are a fine budget option for a family of four, and there's a playground and pool area for the little ones. It's 1½ mi to Eagle Beach, but there's shuttle service a few times a day. If you want to go sightseeing or shopping, though, you'll need a car. ✉ *Cunucu Abao 37, Oranjestad,* ☎ *297/8–78618 or 800/338–3108,* FAX *297/8–70081. 56 studios, 1- and 2-bedroom suites. 2 pools, sauna, exercise room, Ping-Pong, playground. AE, DC, MC, V. EP.*

**$** ⊞ **Bushiri Beach Resort.** Two long, low buildings—built around three hot tubs surrounded by lush foliage and situated on a wide expanse of beach—make up Aruba's first all-inclusive resort. These buildings are old and nondescript, and although the rooms were renovated, they remain fairly plain. But the Bushiri is a hotel-training school, a factor that shines in the enthusiastic staff. Where this resort shines is in its full daily activities program for adults and supervised program for kids. Island tours and casino trips, three meals a day, a poolside barbecue, and a midnight buffet, as well as all beverages, are part of the package—considering all that's included, it's quite a bargain. ✉ *L. G. Smith Blvd. 35, Oranjestad,* ☎ *297/8–25216, 800/462–6867, or 800/462–6868;* FAX *297/8–26789. 150 rooms, 4 suites. Restaurant, 2 bars, grill, refrigerators, pool, wading pool, beauty salon, 3 outdoor* *hot tubs, 2 tennis courts, exercise room, Ping-Pong, beach, water sports, boating, fishing, airport shuttle. AE, DC, MC, V. All-inclusive.*

**$** ⊡ **Coconut Inn.** It's best to have a car if you're staying at this budget hotel, a five-minute drive inland from hotel row on Palm Beach. Request one of the "deluxe studios" in the two-story white building and accept no substitute (the rest of the rooms are old, musty, and dark). These new rooms have a microwave and refrigerator; strong, quiet air-conditioners; white tile floors and bathrooms; modern furnishings; and small balcony or patio overlooking the rectangular pool. Continental breakfast, included in the $80-a-night tariff, is served in the informal restaurant next to the pool. The public bus stops nearby. ⊠ *Angelo Rojer, Noord 31, Noord,* ☎ *297/8–66288,* 𝔽𝔸𝕏 *297/8–65433. 24 rooms. Restaurant, pool, coin laundry. MC, V. CP.*

**$** ⊡ **Stauffer Hotel Aruba.** The four-story Stauffer Hotel offers the best value in accommodations in the high-rise resort zone. Built in 1994 on busy J. E. Irausquin Boulevard across from Palm Beach and the facilities of the Aruba Palm Beach Resort (available for use by the Stauffer guests), there are no grand sea views or sparkling pool here, but $100 per night buys a snug, modern motel-style room in a prime location. There's also a bus stop nearby, so a rental car isn't necessary unless you want to explore the island on your own. ⊠ *J. E. Irausquin Blvd. 370, Palm Beach,* ☎ *297/8–60855,* 𝔽𝔸𝕏 *297/8–60856. 100 rooms. Water sports, shop. AE, D, DC, MC, V. EP.*

**$** ⊡ **Tamarijn Aruba.** A series of low-rise buildings stretches along the property of this all-inclusive resort on Bravo Beach. The spacious oceanfront rooms have a casual feel, with woven fiber mats on dark tile floors, light rattan and wood furnishings, and patios or balconies. The package here covers meals and snacks, all beverages, nightly entertainment (including theme nights), tickets to the Bon Bini Festival, a sunset cruise, and an array of activities including mountain biking, snorkeling, sailing, and windsurfing (lessons are included as well). It's a low-key, active place catering primarily to couples and families looking for a bargain. The only price you'll pay is that service here could stand some improvement. ⊠ *J. E. Irausquin Blvd. 41, Bravo Beach,* ☎ *297/8–24150 or 800/554–2008,* 𝔽𝔸𝕏 *297/8–31940. 236 rooms. 3 restaurants, 4 bars, snack bar, 2 pools, barbershop, 2 tennis courts, Ping-Pong, shuffleboard, volleyball, beach, water sports, fishing, mountain bikes, shops. AE, D, DC, MC, V. All-inclusive.*

**$** ⊡ **Vistalmar.** There's no beach here, but the sea is just across the street, along with a swimming pier. Simply furnished air-conditioned one-bedroom apartments have a full kitchen, living room–dining room, and broad sunporch. The friendly owners provide snorkel gear and stock the refrigerator with fixings for breakfast. The drawback to this small complex is its distance from town, but a rental car is included in the rate. ⊠ *A. O. Yarzagaray, Bucutiweg 28, Noord,* ☎ *297/8–28579,* 𝔽𝔸𝕏 *297/8–22200. 8 rooms. Coin laundry. No credit cards. CP.*

# Dining

Aruba grabbed the gold at the 1996 Caribbean Culinary Competition, so while you can definitely get something at a fast-food joint, you can also expect to enjoy many outstanding meals during your visit. Most resorts here offer better-than-average hotel dining and several meal plans. But before you purchase a Full American Plan (FAP), which includes breakfast, lunch, and dinner, try one of the numerous excellent and reasonably priced restaurants. Restaurants serve a variety of cuisines, although most menus are specifically designed to please American palates—you can get fresh surf and New York turf almost anywhere. It's worth experimenting with Aruban specialties—*pan bati* is a mildly sweet beaten bread that resembles a pancake, and *keshi yena* is a marvelous baked concoction of gouda cheese stuffed with spices and meat or seafood in a rich brown sauce.

On Sunday, it may be difficult to find a restaurant outside of the hotels that's open for lunch, and many restaurants are closed for dinner on Sunday or Monday night. Good hotel options, though, are the extensive buffet at the Holiday Inn or the wonderful champagne brunch at the Hyatt. Reservations are essential for dinner during high season.

## What to Wear

Even the finest restaurants require at the most only a jacket for men and a sundress for women. The air-conditioning does get cold, so don't go bare-armed. And anytime you plan to eat in the open air, remember to douse yourself from head to toe first with insect repellent—the mosquitoes can get unruly.

| CATEGORY | COST* |
|----------|-------|
| $$$ | over $30 |
| $$ | $20–$30 |
| $ | under $20 |

*per person for a three-course meal, excluding drinks, 10%–15% service charge, and tax*

$$$ ✕ **Chez Mathilde.** This elegant restaurant occupies one of the last surviving 19th-century houses in Aruba. Ask to sit in the swooningly romantic Pavilion Room, which has an eclectic mix of turn-of-the-century Italian and French decor, ivy-covered walls, and curtained nooks and crannies for privacy. Then sit back and enjoy the high culinary standards of the French-style menu, which is constantly being re-created by the Dutch chef. Feast on artfully presented baked escargots with herbs and garlic, bouillabaisse with garlic croutons and cream and Cognac to taste, grilled Canadian salmon with a delicate balsamic dressing, or filet mignon in signature pepper sauce prepared table-side. The chef has a deft touch with sauces. Then, too, there's crêpes suzette and a chocolate gâteau to tempt the taste buds. ⊠ *Havenstraat 23, Oranjestad,* ☎ *297/8–34968. Reservations essential. AE, DC, MC, V. No lunch Sun.*

$$$ ✕ **Papiamento.** Longtime restaurateurs Lenie and Eduardo Ellis decided Aruba needed a bistro that was cozy yet elegant, intimate, and always romantic. So they converted their 130-year-old home into just such a spot. Guests can feast sumptuously indoors surrounded by antiques, or outdoors in a patio garden decorated with enormous ceramics (designed by Lenie) and filled with ficus and palm trees adorned with lights. The chef utilizes flavors from both Continental and Caribbean cuisines to produce favorites that include seafood and meat dishes. Try the Dover sole, the Caribbean lobster, shrimp and red snapper cooked table-side on a hot marble stone, or the "claypot" for two—a medley of seafoods prepared in a sealed clay pot. ⊠ *Washington 61, Noord,* ☎ *297/8–64544. Reservations essential. AE, MC, V. Closed Mon. No lunch.*

$$$ ✕ **Valentino's.** The airy two-level dining room is invitingly dressed in sparkling white and shades of mint green. The tables are placed comfortably far apart, and the service is attentive without being overbearing. The Italian menu has knockouts such as the Caribbean lobster on a bed of linguine with marinara sauce. A festive atmosphere makes the restaurant popular with celebrating Arubans. You'll find their gaiety infectious. All this atmosphere makes it so that the restaurant is usually booked up days in advance. ⊠ *Caribbean Palm Village, Noord 43E,* ☎ *297/8–62700. Reservations essential. AE, DC, MC, V. Closed Sun. No lunch.*

**$$   ✕ Benihana.** Japanese cuisine is fairly new on the dining scene in Aruba, and newest of them is this American-based hibachi-grill chain restaurant, conveniently located in the hotel zone. The chefs put on a flashy show of twirling knives as they slice and dice steak, chicken, shrimp, and vegetables at one of 14 cooking tables. Rice, soup, salad, grilled vegetables, and green-tea ice cream (or sherbet) come with the meal. There's also a sushi bar. A Japanese singer croons for guests on weekends. ⊠ *Sasakiweg z/n, Oranjestad,* ☎ *297/8–26788. AE, MC, V.*

**$$   ✕ Buccaneer Restaurant.** Imagine you're in a sunken ship—fishnets and turtle shells hang from the ceiling, and through the portholes you see live sharks, barracudas, and groupers swimming by. That's the Buccaneer, a virtual underwater grotto snug in an old stone building flanked by heavy black chains. Add to that a fantastic 5,000-gallon saltwater aquarium, plus 12 more porthole-size tanks. The surf-and-turf cuisine is prepared by the chef-owners with European élan. Order the fresh catch of the day or more exotic fare, such as shrimps with Pernod or smoked pork cutlets with sausage, sauerkraut, and potatoes. Go early (around 5:45 PM) to get a booth next to the aquariums. ⊠ *Gasparito 11-C, Noord,* ☎ *297/8–66172. AE, MC, V. Closed Sun. No lunch.*

**$$   ✕ Frankie's Prime Grill.** In the splashy new Royal Plaza Mall, Frankie's
**★** (owned by the same family who operates the successful Le Petite Café [☞ *below*]) specializes in Argentinian prime beef and grilled seafood. Diners can eat on the palm-filled wraparound terrace or in the more refined, air-conditioned interior of this favorite spot. Prime *churrasco* (a thick slab of beef prepared Argentinian-style) and *scampi los barquitos* (jumbo shrimp sautéed in butter and garlic) are the most popular items. Start with the garlicky escargots, seafood crepe, or Caesar salad (big enough for two), and try to leave room for *tres lechi* (a cool Cuban cake made with three different types of milk). ⊠ *Royal Plaza 135, Oranjestad,* ☎ *297/8–38471 or 297/8–38473. AE, DC, MC, V.*

**$$   ✕ Gasparito Restaurant and Art Gallery.** As the name states, this
**★** charming restaurant also serves as a gallery showcasing the works of local artists on softly lit white walls. It's set in an authentic *cunucu* (country house) in Noord not far from the hotel strip. The Aruban specialties—pan bati, keshi yena, fish croquettes, conch stew, stewed chicken, Creole-style fish fillet—are also works of art, so it comes as no surprise that Gasparito's chefs walk away with top awards in Caribbean culinary competitions. Service is discreet and very accommodating (they'll stay open if guests come for a late dinner). ⊠ *Gasparito 3, Noord,* ☎ *297/8–67044. AE, D, MC, V. Closed Sun. No lunch.*

**$$   ✕ Old Mill** (De Olde Molen). A gift from the queen of Holland, this real Dutch mill was shipped brick by brick to Aruba in 1920 and reassembled here. For starters, try the seafood crepe Neptune, flamed with Pernod. Also excellent are the beef stroganoff, Wiener schnitzel, grilled jumbo shrimp, and the Dutch fries—crunchy little nuggets of potato. There are two dinner seatings, at 6:30 and 9. At press time, there was talk of the restaurant's being taken over by the Mill Resort; but with luck, the menu and the focus on quality food will remain the same. ⊠ *J. E. Irausquin Blvd. 330, Noord,* ☎ *297/8–62060. Reservations essential. AE, DC, MC, V. Closed Sun. No lunch.*

**$$   ✕ Ventanas del Mar.** The name means windows on the sea, which couldn't be more appropriate considering the setting above the Tierra del Sol Golf Course at the western tip of the island. This quietly elegant restaurant features floor-to-ceiling windows that look out across the back nine holes and the rolling sand dunes to the sea. Sandwiches, salads, conch fritters, nachos, and quesadillas fill the midday menu; at night the focus is on seafood (roasted red snapper, crab cakes, grilled garlic shrimp, panfried oysters) and meat (prime rib, veal chop in rosemary demi-glace, herbed half chicken). ✉ *Tierra del Sol Golf Course, Malmokweg,* ☎ *297/8–67800. AE, MC, V.*

**$–$$** ✗ **Boonoonoonoos.** The name—say it just as it looks!—means "extraordinary," a bit of hyperbole for this Austrian-owned Caribbean bistro in the heart of Oranjestad, but in the fiercely competitive Aruban restaurant business, you gotta have a gimmick. The specialty here is Pan-Caribbean cuisine. The decor is simple, but the tasty food, served with hearty portions of peas, rice, and plantains, makes up for the lack of tablecloths, china, and crystal. The roast chicken Barbados is sweet and tangy, marinated in a piña colada sauce. The Jamaican jerk ribs (a 300-year-old recipe) are tiny but spicy, and the satin-smooth hot pumpkin soup drizzled with cheese and served in a pumpkin shell may as well be dessert. Avoid the place when it's crowded, since the service and the quality of the food deteriorate. ✉ *Wilhelminastraat 18A, Oranjestad,* ☎ *297/8–31888. AE, MC, V. No lunch Sun.*

**$–$$** ✗ **Brisas del Mar.** This friendly 16-table place overlooking the sea makes
★     you feel as if you're dining in an Aruban home. Old family recipes use traditional indigenous ingredients like the aromatic *yerbiholé* leaf and the sizzling Mme. Jeanette pepper. Try the smashing steamy fish soup (which would do a Marseillais proud), *keri keri* (shredded fish kissed with annatto seed), or some of the best pan bati on the island. Fresh catch of the day cooked Aruban-style (panfried and covered in a tangy Creole sauce, or panfried in garlic butter on request) has drawn a crowd here for more than 20 years. It's so good, it justifies the taxi ride needed to reach it—10 mi east of Oranjestad in the town of Savaneta. ✉ *Savaneta 222A, Savaneta,* ☎ *297/8–47718. AE, MC, V. No lunch Mon.*

**$–$$** ✗ **Old Cunucu House.** On a small estate in a residential neighborhood three minutes from the high-rise hotels, this 75-year-old white stucco home with slanting roofs, wood beams, and a terra-cotta courtyard filled with bougainvillea has been converted to a laid-back seafood-and-international restaurant. Dine on red snapper (or whatever fish happens to be fresh that day), almond-fried shrimp with lobster sauce, Cornish hen, New York sirloin, or beef fondue à deux. An Aruban trio sings and plays background music every Friday, and on Saturday evening a mariachi band serenades the patrons. ✉ *Palm Beach 150, Noord,* ☎ *297/8–61666. AE, MC, V. Closed Sun. No lunch.*

**$** ✗ **Charlie's Restaurant & Bar.** Now an institution, Charlie's has been
★     a San Nicolas hangout for more than 50 years. During the oil-refinery days, it was a hopping bar for all kinds of rough-and-scruffs. Now tourists flock here to gawk at the decor: License plates, hard hats, baseball pennants, intimate apparel, and credit cards cover and crowd every inch of the walls and ceiling. House specialties are Argentinian tenderloin and "shrimps—jumbo and dumbo" (dumb because they were caught). You'll have to peel the shell off the shrimp scampi, but needing to wash up afterward gives you a reason to go check out the incredible "decor" in the rest room. And don't leave before trying Charlie's special "honeymoon sauce" (so called because it's really hot). ✉ *Zeppenfeldstraat 56, San Nicolas,* ☎ *297/8–45086. No credit cards. Closed Sun.*

**$** ✗ **Kowloon.** In addition to many Chinese provinces, Indonesia is also represented on the menu here. Try the *bami goreng,* a noodle-based dish with shreds of shrimp, pork, vegetables, and an Indonesian blend of herbs and spices. Saté, curried dishes, and steak prepared in a variety of ways are also available. The modern Asian decor blends easily with the island's palms and sands. ✉ *Emmastraat 11, Oranjestad,* ☎ *297/8–24950. AE, MC, V.*

**$ ✕ La Paloma.** "The Dove" is a no-frills, low-key Italian eatery tightly packed with tables that are typically overflowing with patrons. Top seller on the international and Italian menu is veal Paisano (layered veal, mozzarella, ricotta, and spinach, baked to bubbling). Caesar salad and minestrone soup are house specialties. Drop by for the family atmosphere, simple food, and reasonable prices. ⊠ *Noord 39, Noord,* ☎ *297/8– 62770. AE, MC, V. Closed Tues. No lunch.*

**$ ✕ Le Petit Café.** The motto here is "Romancing the Stone"—referring to tasty cuisine cooked on hot stones. Alfresco dining in the bustling square lets diners keep an eye on things, but fumes from nearby traffic tend to spoil the meal. Jumbo shrimp, sandwiches, ice cream, and fresh fruit dishes are light choices. A second edition of this popular café has opened in the American Hotel. ⊠ *Emmastraat 1, Oranjestad,* ☎ *297/8– 26577;* ⊠ *American Hotel, J. E. Irausquin Blvd. 83,* ☎ *297/8–64368. AE, DC, MC, V. No lunch Sun.*

**$ ✕ The Paddock.** This typical Dutch *eet-café* (a café serving full meals) is a casual open-air terrace on the downtown waterfront overlooking the pier and whichever cruise ships happen to be in port. French bread with Brie, fried eggs, bami goreng, saté, and fresh seafood salads are among the lunch and dinner offerings here. All-you-can-eat spareribs ($10) are the focus on Wednesdays. There's no automatic service charge in the bill, so remember to tip the jean-clad wait staff. ⊠ *L. G. Smith Blvd. 13, Oranjestad,* ☎ *297/8–32334. MC, V.*

# Beaches

Beaches in Aruba are legendary in the Caribbean: white sand, turquoise waters, and virtually no garbage, for everyone takes the "no littering" sign—NO TIRA SUSHI—very seriously, especially with an AFl500 fine. The influx of tourists in the past decade, however, has crowded the major beaches, which back up to the hotels along the southwestern strip. These beaches are public, and you can make the two-hour hike from the Holiday Inn to the Bushiri Beach Hotel free of charge and without ever leaving sand. If you go strolling during the day, make sure you are well protected from the sun—it scorches fast, and the trade winds can make it feel deceptively cooler. Luckily, there's at least one covered bar (and often an ice cream stand) at virtually every hotel you pass. If you take the stroll at night, you can hotel-hop for dinner, dancing, gambling, and late-night entertainment. On the northern side of the island, heavy trade winds make the waters too choppy for swimming, but the vistas are great and the terrain is wonderfully suited to sunbathing and geological explorations.

**Baby Beach.** On the island's eastern tip, this semicircular beach borders a bay that is as placid as a wading pool and only 4–5 ft deep—perfect for tots and terrible swimmers. Thatched shaded areas are good for cooling off. You may occasionally find topless sunbathers here.

**Boca Grandi.** Just west of Bachelor's Beach, on the northwest coast (near the Seagrape Grove and the Aruba Golf Club), Boca Grandi is excellent for wave jumping and windsurfing. Strong swimming skills are a must here.

**Boca Prins.** Near the Fontein Cave and Blue Lagoon, this beach is about as large as a Brazilian bikini, but with two rocky cliffs and tumultuously crashing waves, it's as romantic as you get in Aruba. This is not a swimming beach, however. Boca Prins is famous for its backdrop of enormous vanilla sand dunes. You'll need a four-wheel drive to make the trek here. Bring a picnic lunch, a beach blanket, and sturdy sneakers.

**Eagle Beach.** Across the highway from what is quickly becoming known as Time-Share Lane is Eagle Beach on the southern coast. Not long ago, it was a nearly deserted stretch of pristine sands dotted with the occasional thatched picnic hut. Now that the time-share resorts are completed, this beach is one of the more hopping on the island.

**Fisherman's Hut.** Next to the Holiday Inn, this beach is a windsurfer's haven. Take a picnic lunch (tables are available) and watch the elegant purple, aqua, and orange sails struggle in the wind.

**Grapefield Beach.** To the north of San Nicolas, this gorgeous beach is perfect for advanced windsurfing.

**Malmok Beach.** On the northwestern shore, this lackluster beach, also known as Boca Catalina, borders shallow waters that stretch out 300 yards from shore, making it perfect for beginners learning to windsurf. Right off the coast here is a favorite haunt for divers—the wreck of the German ship *Antilla,* scuttled in 1940.

**Manchebo Beach** (formerly Punta Brabo Beach). In front of the Manchebo Beach Resort, this impressively wide stretch of white powder is where officials turn a blind eye to topless sunbathers.

**Palm Beach.** Once called one of the 10 best beaches in the world by the *Miami Herald,* this is the stretch behind the Americana Aruba, Aruba Hilton Hotel and Casino, Aruba Palm Beach, and Holiday Inn hotels. It's the center of Aruban tourism, offering the best in swimming, sailing, and fishing. During high season, however, it's a sardine can.

**Rodger's Beach.** Next to Baby Beach on the eastern tip of the island, this is a beautiful curving stretch of sand only slightly marred by the view of the oil refinery at the far side of the bay.

## Outdoor Activities and Sports

### Bowling

The **Eagle Bowling Palace** (⌧ Pos Abou, ☎ 297/8–35038) has 12 lanes, a cocktail lounge, and a snack bar; it's open 10 AM to 2 AM. Games run $5.75–$11.20, depending on the time of play.

### Deep-Sea Fishing

With catches including barracuda, kingfish, bonito, and black and yellow tuna, deep-sea fishing is great sport on Aruba. Many charter boats are available for a half- or full-day sail. **De Palm Tours** (☎ 297/8–24400 or 800/766–6016, FAX 297/8–23012) can arrange trips for up to six people, in a variety of boat sizes and styles. Half-day tours, including all equipment, soft drinks, and boxed lunch, are around $250 for up to four people; full-day tours run about $500. **Pelican Tours** (☎ 297/8–31228 or 297/8–24739) and **Red Sail Sports** (☎ 297/8–61603) also arrange deep-sea-fishing charters.

### Golf

An 18-hole par-71 golf course, **Tierra del Sol** (⌧ Malmokweg, ☎ 297/8–67800), opened in 1995 on the northwest coast near the California Lighthouse. Designed by Robert Trent Jones, Jr., the par-71, 6,811-yard championship course combines Aruba's native beauty, such as the flora, cacti, and rock formations, with the lush greens of the world's best courses. The $120 greens fee includes a golf cart. Club rentals are $25–$45. Half-day "No Embarrassment" golf clinics, a bargain at $40, include lunch in the clubhouse. The charming Ventanas del Mar restaurant (☞ Dining, *above*) in the clubhouse is worth a visit in its own right.

**Aruba Golf Club** (⌧ Golfweg 82, near San Nicolas, ☎ 297/8–42006) has a nine-hole course with 20 sand and five water traps, roaming goats, and lots of cacti. There are 11 AstroTurf greens, making 18-hole tournaments a possibility. The clubhouse contains a bar and men's and women's locker rooms. The course's official U.S. Golf Association rating is 67; greens fees are $7.50 for 9 holes, $10 for 18 holes. Caddies and club rentals are available.

Two elevated 18-hole minigolf courses surrounded by a moat are available at **Joe Mendez Adventure Golf** (⊠ Sasakiweg, ☎ 297/8–76625). There are also paddleboats and bumper boats, a bar, and a snack stand. A round of minigolf is $6.50 per 18 holes. It's open from noon until 11:30 PM.

### Hiking

There are no marked trails through the **Arikok National Wildlife Park,** but that doesn't mean you can't blaze your own. Watch for snakes in this arid landscape, and carry water with you. Wild donkeys, goats, rabbits, parakeets, and a plethora of lizards (even the occasional iguana) will be your companions. The park is crowned by 577-ft Mt. Arikok, so climbing is also a possibility.

**De Palm Tours** (⊠ L. G. Smith Blvd. 142, ☎ 297/8–24400 or 800/766–6016, FAX 297/8–23012) offers a guided three-hour trip to remote sites of unusual natural beauty accessible only on foot. The fee is $25 per person, including refreshments and transportation; a minimum of four people is required.

### Horseback Riding

There are three ranches offering riding on the island, some taking you on jaunts along the beach, others on longer trail rides through countryside flanked by cacti, divi-divi trees, and aloe vera plants. **De Palm Tours** (⊠ L. G. Smith Blvd. 142, ☎ 297/8–24400 or 800/766–6016, FAX 297/8–23012) books them all with advance reservations; rates run about $20 for an hour-long countryside tour, $35 for a two-hour beach tour. Remember to wear a hat and take lots of suntan lotion.

### Land Sailing

Carts with a Windsurfer-type sail are rented at **Aruba SailCart** (⊠ Bushiri 23, ☎ 297/8–35133) at $15 (single seater) and $20 (double seater) for 30 minutes of speeding back and forth across a dirt field. Anyone can learn to drive the cart in just a few minutes. Rentals are available from 9 AM to sunset; food and drinks are served until 10 PM.

### Parasailing

Motorboats from Eagle and Palm beaches tow people up and over the water for about 15 minutes ($40 for a single seater, $70 for a tandem).

### Snorkeling and Scuba Diving

With visibility up to 90 ft, Aruban waters are excellent for snorkeling in shallow waters, and scuba divers will discover exotic marine life and coral. Certified divers can go wall diving or reef diving—or explore wrecks sunk during World War II. The *Antilla* shipwreck—a German freighter sunk off the northwest coast of Aruba near Palm Beach—is a favorite spot with divers and snorkelers.

Prices are generally comparable among the better snorkel and scuba-diving operators on the island. Expect snorkel gear to rent for about $15 per day, snorkel trips to cost around $25. Scuba rates are not much more at around $30 for a one-tank reef or wreck dive, $45 for a two-tank dive, $35 for a night dive. Resort courses (introduction to scuba diving) average $70, complete open-water certification around $300.

Among the top operators in Aruba are **Aruba Pro Dive** (⊠ Ponton 88, ☎ 297/8–25520), **Charlie's S.E.A. Scuba** (⊠ San Nichlas, ☎ 297/8–

45086), **Scuba Aruba** (Seaport Mall, ☎ 297/8–34142), and **Mermaid Sports Divers** (✉ Manchebo Beach Resort, ☎ 297/8–35546). **De Palm Tours** (✉ L. G. Smith Blvd. 142, ☎ 297/8–24400 or 800/766–6016, FAX 297/8–23012) offers daily snorkeling and scuba-diving trips. However, its rates ($30–$45) are the most expensive on the island. **Pelican Watersports** (✉ Holiday Inn Beach Resort, ☎ 297/8–63600) offers snorkeling and scuba diving, as well as scuba instruction and certification. It also offers wreck and night dives at reasonable rates. **Red Sail Sports** (✉ L. G. Smith Blvd. 83, ☎ 297/8–61603) offers scuba packages, resort courses, PADI-certification courses, night diving, and underwater camera rental.

### Tennis

Aruba's winds add a certain challenge to the best of swings, but world-class tennis has just arrived, at the **Aruba Racquet Club** (☎ 297/8–60215). The $1.4 million club was designed by Stan Smith Design International and is near the Aruba Marriott. There are eight tennis courts (six lighted), as well as a swimming pool, an aerobics center, and a restaurant on the grounds. Court fees are $10 per hour.

### Windsurfing

**Pelican Watersports** (✉ Holiday Inn Beach Resort, ☎ 297/8–63600) rents equipment and offers instruction with a certified Mistral instructor. Stock and custom boards rent for $40 per two hours, $60 per day. Pelican offers lessons three times a day; call for a schedule.

**Red Sail Sports** (✉ L. G. Smith Blvd. 83, ☎ 297/8–61603) offers two-hour beginner lessons for $45 ($60 for two people). It also rents Fanatic boards and regular windsurfing boards by the hour, day, and week.

Windsurfing instruction and board rental are also available through **Sailboard Vacation** (✉ L. G. Smith Blvd. 462, ☎ 297/8–61072), **Roger's Windsurf Place** (✉ L. G. Smith Blvd. 472, ☎ 297/8–61918), and **De Palm Tours** (✉ L. G. Smith Blvd. 142, ☎ 297/8–24400 or 800/766–6016, FAX 297/8–23012). Complete vacation packages for windsurfers are also provided through all of the above operators.

## Shopping

Caya G. F. Betico Croes—Aruba's chief shopping street—makes for a pleasant diversion from the beach and casino life. *Duty-free* is a magic word here. Major credit cards are welcome virtually everywhere, U.S. dollars are accepted almost as often as local currency, and traveler's checks can be cashed with proof of identity. Shopping malls have arrived in Aruba, so when you finish walking the main street, stop in at a mall to browse through the chic boutiques.

Aruba's souvenir and crafts stores are full of Dutch porcelains and figurines, as befits the island's Netherlands heritage. Dutch cheese is a good buy (you are allowed to bring up to 1 pound of hard cheese through U.S. customs), as are hand-embroidered linens and any products made from the native aloe vera plant—sunburn cream, face masks, and skin refreshers. Since there is no sales tax, the price you see on the tag is the price you pay. Don't try to bargain. Arubans consider it rude to haggle, despite what you may hear to the contrary.

### Specialty Shops

At **Artesania Aruba** (✉ L. G. Smith Blvd. 178, ☎ 297/8–37494) you'll find charming Aruban home-crafted pottery, silk-screened T-shirts and wall hangings, and folklore objects. There's a kiosk in the shopping district on Betico Croes as well. The **Artistic Boutique** (✉ Caya G. F. Betico Croes 25, ☎ 297/8–23142; ✉ Aruba Hilton, ☎ 297/8–

New on the dancing scene are the round **Cobalt Club** (Royal Plaza Mall, L. G. Smith Blvd. 172, Oranjestad, ☎ 297/8–38381) atop the Royal Plaza Mall downtown, where merengue, salsa, soca, and other Latin and Caribbean tunes and indoor and outdoor bars keep the party moving. Also new is **City One** (✉ Italiastraat 42, ☎ 297/8–33888), the island's largest disco, with a cavernous dance floor, two bars, and big-screen TVs that flash music videos and recent release films.

## Specialty Theme Nights

One of the unique things about Aruba's nightlife is the number of specialty theme nights offered by the hotels: At last count there were more than 30. Each "party" features a buffet dinner and entertainment, followed by dancing. Best bets are **Aruban Folkloric** on Friday at the Manchebo Beach Hotel, **Pirates Night** on Sunday at the Bucuti Beach Resort, **Brazilian Jungle Night** on Saturday at the Bushiri Beach Resort, and **Caribbean Carnival Royale** on Monday at the Costa Linda. The top show groups tend to rotate among the resorts, so there's bound to be something going on every night of the week. For a complete list, contact the Aruba Tourism Authority (☎ 297/8–60242).

An Aruban must is the **Bon Bini Festival,** held every Tuesday evening from 6:30 to 8:30 PM in the outdoor courtyard of the Fort Zoutman Museum. *Bon Bini* is Papiamento for "welcome," and this tourist event is the Aruba Institute of Culture and Education's way of introducing you to all things Aruban. Stroll by the stands of Aruban foods, drinks, and crafts or watch Aruban entertainers perform Antillean music and folkloric dancing. It's a fun event and a good way to meet other tourists. Look for the clock tower. ✉ *Oranjestraat,* ☎ *297/8–22185.* 🎟 *$3.*

## Theater

**Tropicana** (✉ J. E. Irausquin Blvd. 250, ☎ 297/8–69806), La Cabana All Suite's cabaret theater and nightclub, features first-class Las Vegas–style reviews and a special comedy series every weekend. The **Wyndham Aruba** (✉ J. E. Irausquin Blvd. 77, ☎ 297/8–64466) showcases an entertaining Cuban review from 8 to 10 PM Tuesday through Saturday in its theater.

**Twinklebone's House of Roast Beef** (✉ Noord 124, ☎ 297/8–26780) does serve succulent prime rib and the like. But it's best known for the fun, impromptu cabaret of Carnival music put on by the staff every night but Sunday. Some customers find it hokey; others eat it up.

# Exploring Aruba

Oranjestad, the capital of Aruba, is good for shopping by day and dining by night, but the "real Aruba"—what's left of a wild, untamed beauty—can be found only in the countryside. Rent a car, take a sightseeing tour, or hire a cab for $25 an hour (for up to four people). The main highways are well paved, but on the windward side of the island some roads are still a mixture of compacted dirt and stones. Although a car is fine, a four-wheel drive will allow you to explore the unpaved interior. Traffic is sparse, and you can't get lost. If you do lose your way, just follow the divi-divi trees (because of the direction of the trade winds, the trees are bent toward the leeward side of the island, where all the hotels are). Signs leading to sights of interest are often small and hand-lettered, so watch closely (though this is slowly changing as the government puts up official road signs).

Few beaches outside the hotel strip have refreshment stands, so take your own food and drink. And one more caution: Note that there are *no* public bathrooms—anywhere—once you leave Oranjestad, except in the infrequent restaurant.

*Numbers in the margin correspond to points of interest on the Aruba map.*

**8** **Alto Vista Chapel.** Alone near the northwest corner of the island sits the scenic little Alto Vista Chapel. The wind whistles through the simple mustard-color walls, eerie boulders, and looming cacti. Along the side of the road back to civilization are miniature crosses painted with depictions of the Stations of the Cross and hand-lettered signs exhorting PRAY FOR US, SINNERS, and the like—a primitive yet powerful evocation of faith. To get there, follow the rough, winding dirt road that loops around the northern tip of the island, or from the hotel strip take Palm Beach Road through three intersections and watch for the asphalt road to the left just past the Alto Vista Rum Shop.

**9** **California Lighthouse.** At the far northern end of the island stands the closed lighthouse. It is surrounded by huge boulders that look like extraterrestrial monsters; in this stark landscape, you'll feel as though you've just landed on the moon. There is a placard explaining the history of the lighthouse and the wreck of the German ship the *California* (just off the tip of the island here) next to the trattoria.

**5** **Caves.** Anyone looking for geological exotica should head for the northern coast, driving northwest from San Nicolas. Stop at the two old Indian caves **Guadirikiri** and **Fontein.** Both were used by the native Indians centuries ago (notice the fire mark in the ceiling above); sadly, the cave walls are marred by modern graffiti. You may enter the caves, but there are no guides available, and bats are known to make appearances (not to worry—they won't bother you). Wear sneakers and take a flashlight or rent one ($10) from the soda vendor who has set up shop here. Just before the Fontein and Guadirikiri caves lies the **Tunnel of Love** (also known as Huiliba), a heart-shape tunnel containing naturally sculpted rocks that look just like the Madonna, Abe Lincoln, even a jaguar. The climb through the tunnel is strenuous and should not be attempted by anyone not in good physical condition. It's definitely not recommended for elderly people or young children. Remember, admission is free to all three caves—don't be deterred by the occasionally pushy vendors.

**3** **Frenchman's Pass.** A bit of history can be found along this dark, luscious stretch of road arbored by overhanging trees and bordered by towering cacti. Local legend claims that the French and native Indians warred here during the 17th century for control of the island. To get there, drive east on L. G. Smith Boulevard past a shimmering vista of blue-green sea toward San Nicolas, on what is known as the sunrise side of the island. Turn left where you see the drive-in theater (a popular hangout for Arubans), drive to the first intersection, turn right, and follow the curve to the right. Gold was discovered on Aruba in 1824, and nearby you'll find the massive cement-and-limestone ruins of the **Balashi Gold Smelter Ruins** (take the dirt road veering to the right)—a lovely place to picnic and listen to the parakeets. A magnificent gnarled divi-divi tree guards the entrance.

**2** **Hooiberg.** Translated to mean Haystack Hill, this 541-ft peak is inland just past the airport. If you have the energy, climb the 562 steps up to the top for an impressive view of the city. To get there from Oranjestad, turn onto Caya C. F. Croes (shown on island maps as 7A) toward Santa Cruz; the peak will be on your right.

**10** **Malmok.** On the drive to the northern tip of the island you'll pass through Malmok, where Aruba's wealthiest families reside. Jutting above the water not far off Malmok Beach, one of the finest spots for shelling, snorkeling, and windsurfing, are parts of the wreck of the German ship *Antilla*, scuttled here in 1940.

**❼ Natural Bridge.** This bridge, at the midway mark on the windward coast, was sculpted out of coral rock by centuries of raging wind and sea. To get to it, follow the main road inland (Hospitalstraat) and then signs that lead the way. Just before you reach the Natural Bridge you'll pass the massive and intriguing stone ruins of the **Bushiribana Gold Smelter**, which resembles a crumbling fortress, and a section of surf-pounded coastline called Boca Mahose. Near the natural bridge is a café overlooking the water and a souvenir shop stuffed with trinkets, T-shirts, and postcards for reasonable prices.

**❶ Oranjestad.** Aruba's charming Dutch capital is best explored on foot. There are many shopping malls with boutiques and shops. The palm-lined thoroughfare in the center of town runs between pastel-painted buildings, old and new, of typical Dutch design.

At the **Archaeology Museum** you'll find two rooms chockablock with fascinating Indian artifacts, farm and domestic utensils, and skeletons. Across the street you'll see the handsome Protestant church. ⊠ *Zoutmanstraat 1,* ☎ *297/8–28979.* 🎟 *Free.* ☉ *Weekdays 8–noon and 1–4.*

One of the island's oldest buildings, **Fort Zoutman** was built in 1796 and used as a major fortress in the skirmishes between British and Curaçao troops. The Willem III Tower, named for the Dutch monarch of that time, was added in 1868. The fort's Historical Museum displays centuries' worth of Aruban relics and artifacts in an 18th-century Aruban house. ⊠ *Zoutmanstraat z/n,* ☎ *297/8–26099.* 🎟 *$1.15.* ☉ *Weekdays 9–noon and 1:30–4:30.*

Tiny **Numismatic Museum,** next to St. Francis Roman Catholic Church, displays coins and paper money from more than 100 countries. ⊠ *Zuidstraat 7,* ☎ *297/8–28831.* 🎟 *Free.* ☉ *Weekdays 7:30–noon and 1–4:30.*

**❻ Rock Formations.** The massive boulders at **Ayo** and **Casibari** are said to be a mystery since they don't match the geological makeup of the island. Whether they're a mystery or not, you can climb to the top for fine views of Aruba's arid countryside or snapshots of brown or blue lizards as you hike among the towering cactus surrounding the formations. Climbing is not recommended for children or older visitors—there are no handrails on the way up and you must climb through tunnels and on narrow steps and ledges to reach the top. At Ayo you'll find ancient pictographs in a small cave (the entrance is protected by iron bars so that the artifacts are protected from vandalism). Access to Casibari is via the Tanki Highway 4A and to Ayo is via Highway 6A; watch carefully for the turnoff signs near the center of the island on the way to the windward side.

**❹ San Nicolas.** During the heyday of the Exxon refineries, Aruba's oldest village was a bustling port; now it's dedicated to tourism, with the main-street promenade full of interesting kiosks. The **China Clipper Bar** on Main Street used to be a famous "red-light" bar frequented by sailors docked in port. Another institution is **Charlie's Bar,** a San Nicolas hangout for more than 50 years (☞ *Dining, above*). Stop in for a drink and advice on what to do on this section of the island. The entire San Nicolas district is undergoing a massive revitalization project that will introduce parks, a cultural center, a central market, and an arts promenade, but it's hard to say what will be completed by 1998.

# Aruba A to Z

## Arriving and Departing

BY PLANE

Aruba is 2½ hours away from Miami and four hours from New York. Flights leave daily to Aruba from New York area airports and Miami International Airport with easy connections from most American cities. **Air Aruba** (☎ 297/8–23151 or 800/862–7822), the island's official airline, flies nonstop to Aruba daily from Miami and Newark. Twice-weekly service has begun from Baltimore. **American Airlines** (☎ 297/8–22006 or 800/433–7300) offers daily nonstop service from both Miami and New York. **ALM** (☎ 297/8–23546 or 800/327–7230), the major airline of the Dutch Caribbean islands, flies six days a week nonstop from Miami and twice weekly from Fort Lauderdale to Aruba. Air Aruba and ALM also have connecting flights to Caracas, Bonaire, Curaçao, and St. Maarten as well as other Caribbean islands. ALM also offers a "Visit Caribbean Pass" for interisland travel. From Toronto and Montréal, you can fly to Aruba on American Airlines via San Juan. American also has connecting flights from several U.S. cities via San Juan.

## Currency

Arubans happily accept U.S. dollars virtually everywhere, so there's no real need to exchange money, except for necessary pocket change (for soda machines or pay phones). The currency used, however, is the Aruban florin (AFl), which at press time exchanged to the U.S. dollar at AFl1.77 for cash, AFl1.79 for traveler's checks, and to the Canadian dollar at AFl1.51. The Dutch Antillean florin (used in Bonaire and Curaçao) is not accepted in Aruba. If you need fast cash, you'll find international ATMs that accept international cards at the major malls, Caribbean Mercantile Bank, and Amro Bank. Major credit cards and traveler's checks are widely accepted (with ID). Prices quoted here are in U.S. dollars unless otherwise noted.

## Emergencies

**Police:** ☎ 11000. **Hospital:** ✉ Horacio Oduber, ☎ 74300. **Pharmacy:** ✉ Botica del Pueblo, ☎ 22154. **Ambulance** and **Fire:** ☎ 115. All hotels have house doctors on call 24 hours a day. Call the front desk.

## Getting Around

Remember, the island's winding roads are poorly marked, if at all (though this is slowly changing as the government installs new road signs and more clearly mark sights of interest). The major tourist attractions are fairly easy to find; others you'll happen upon only by sheer luck (or with an Aruban friend).

BICYCLES, MOPEDS, AND MOTORCYCLES

Rates vary according to the make of the vehicle; expect to pay around $20 for an 80CC to $40 for a 250CC. For Yamaha scooters, contact **George's Cycle Center** (✉ L. G. Smith Blvd. 136D, ☎ 297/8–25975). Other moped, scooter, and motorcycle rental companies are **Ron's Motorcycle Rental** (✉ Bakval 17A, ☎ 297/8–62090), **Nelson Motorcycle Rental** (✉ Gasparito 10A, ☎ 297/8–66801), **New York Cycles and Scooters** (✉ Noord 76, ☎ 297/8–63885), and **Semver Cycle Rental** (✉ Noord 22, ☎ 297/8–66851). **Pablito's Bike Rental** (✉ L. G. Smith Blvd. 234, ☎ 297/8–78655) rents mountain bikes for $10 per day.

BUSES

Buses run hourly trips between the beach hotels and Oranjestad. One-way fare is $1, and exact change is preferred. Buses also run down the coast from Oranjestad to San Nicolas for the same fare. Contact the Aruba Tourism Authority (☎ 297/8–21019) for a bus schedule, or inquire at the front desk of your hotel.

## CAR RENTALS

You'll need a valid U.S. or Canadian driver's license to rent a car, and you must be able to meet the minimum age requirements of each rental service, implemented for insurance reasons. **Budget Rent-a-Car** (☎ 800/472–3325) rents to drivers between 25 and 65, **Avis** (☎ 800/331–1212) rents to drivers between 23 and 70, and **Hertz** (☎ 800/654–3131) rents to drivers older than 21. A deposit of $500 (or a signed credit-card slip) is required. Rental rates are between $50 and $65 per day. Insurance is available starting at $10 per day, and all companies offer unlimited mileage. Local car-rental companies generally have lower rates. Make reservations before visiting the island, and opt for a four-wheel-drive vehicle if you plan to explore the island's natural sights.

Local addresses and phone numbers for the rental agencies are **Avis** (⊠ Kolibristraat 14, ☎ 297/8–28787; ⊠ Airport, ☎ 297/8–25496), **Budget Rent-a-Car** (⊠ Kolibristraat 1, ☎ 297/8–2860), **Hertz, De Palm Car Rental** (⊠ L. G. Smith Blvd. 142, Box 656, ☎ 297/8–24545; ⊠ Airport, ☎ 297/8–24886), **Dollar Rent-a-Car** (⊠ Grendeaweg 15, ☎ 297/8–22783; ⊠ Airport, ☎ 297/8–25651; ⊠ Manchebo, ☎ 297/8–26696), **National** (⊠ Tanki Leendert 170, ☎ 297/8–21967; ⊠ Airport, ☎ 297/8–25451), **Thrifty** (⊠ Balashi 65, ☎ 297/8–55300; ⊠ Airport, ☎ 297/8–35335), and **Hedwina Car Rental** (⊠ Bubali 93A, ☎ 297/8–76442; ⊠ Airport, ☎ 297/8–30880).

## TAXIS

There is a dispatch office at the airport (☎ 297/8–22116); you can also flag down taxis on the street. Since taxis do not have meters, rates are fixed and should be confirmed before your ride begins. Add $1 to the fare after midnight and on holidays. All Aruba's taxi drivers have participated in the government's Tourism Awareness Programs and have received their Tourism Guide Certificate. An hour's tour of the island by taxi will run you about $25, for a maximum of four people per car. A taxi from the airport to most hotels will run $12–$17.

## Guided Tours

### BOAT CRUISES

If you try a cruise around the island, know that trimarans give a much smoother ride than monohull boats on choppy waters stirred up by the trade winds. Sucking on lemon or lime candy may help a queasy stomach; avoid going with an empty stomach. The most popular and reputable sailing cruises are offered by **De Palm Tours** (☎ 297/8–24400 or 800/766–6016, FAX 297/8–23012), **Mi Dushi** (☎ 297/8–28919), **Red Sail Sports** (☎ 297/8–24500), **Pelican Watersports** (☎ 297/8–31228), **Pirate Cruises** (☎ 297/8–24554), and **Wave Dancer** (☎ 297/8–25520).

Moonlight cruises offer stunning views and cost about $25 per person. (Be prepared to sail with a lot of sappy honeymooners.) There are also a variety of snorkeling, dinner and dancing, and sunset party cruises to choose from, priced from $25 to $60 per person. Contact **Red Sail Sports** (☎ 297/8–24500), **Pelican Watersports** (☎ 297/8–31228), or **De Palm Tours** (☎ 297/8–24400 or 800/766–6016, FAX 297/8–23012). One favorite is the four-hour snorkel, sail, open-bar, and lunch cruise aboard the *Mi Dushi,* a beautifully restored 1925 Swedish sailboat. This two-masted wooden vessel is captained by Mario Maduro and a fun crew who act as lifeguards, snorkel instructors, bartenders, galley staff, deckhands, and storytellers. Two stops are made for snorkeling; save your energy for the second one at the wreck of the *Antilla.* Cost is $45.

### ORIENTATION TOURS

Aruba's highlights can be seen in a day. Although most highways are in excellent condition, signs and directions are haphazard, making a guided tour your best option for exploring if you have only a short time. **De Palm Tours** (✉ L. G. Smith Blvd. 142, ☎ 297/8–24400 or 800/766–6016, 𝔽𝔸𝕏 297/8–23012) has a near monopoly on the Aruban sightseeing business; reservations may be made through its general office or at hotel tour-desk branches. The basic 3½-hour tour hits the high spots of the island, including Santa Anna Church, Casibari Rock Formation, the Natural Bridge, and the Gold Smelter Ruins. Wear tennis or hiking shoes (there'll be optional climbing) and note that the air-conditioned bus can get cold. The tour, which begins at 9:30 AM, picks you up in your lobby and costs $20 per person. There's also a fun full-day Jeep Adventure tour ($55 per person) that hits some popular spots that are difficult to find on your own. Take a bandanna to cover your mouth, as the ride on rocky dirt roads can get quite dusty. De Palm also offers full-day tours of Caracas, Venezuela ($240, passport required), and Curaçao ($200). Prices include round-trip airfare, transfers, sightseeing, and lunch; there is also free time for shopping. **Aruba Friendly Tours** (✉ Cumana 20, Oranjestad, ☎ 297/8–23230, 𝔽𝔸𝕏 297/8–33074) also offers tours of Aruba's main sights.

SPECIAL-INTEREST TOURS

For a tour of prehistoric Indian cultures, volcanic formations, and natural wildlife, contact archaeologist Egbert Boerstra of **Marlin Booster Tracking, Inc.,** at Charlie's Bar (☎ 297/8–41513). The fee for a four-hour tour is $50 per person, including a cold picnic lunch and beverages. Tours can be given in English, Dutch, German, Spanish, and French.

Hikers will enjoy a guided three-hour trip to remote sites of unusual natural beauty accessible only on foot. The fee is $25 per person, including refreshments and transportation; a minimum of four people is required. Contact **De Palm Tours** (☎ 297/8–24400 or 800/766–6016, 𝔽𝔸𝕏 297/8–23012).

You can now explore an underwater reef teeming with marine life without getting wet. **Atlantis Submarines** (✉ Seaport Village Marina, ☎ 297/8–36090) operates a 65-ft, air-conditioned sub that takes 46 passengers 95–150 ft below the surface along Aruba's Barcadera Reef. The two-hour trip (including boat transfer to the submarine platform and 50-minute plunge) costs $70 for adults, $29 for children 4–16. If you are not a scuba diver, the hour in the submarine is the next best thing to being down among the fish and coral. Another option is the **Seaworld Explorer** (☎ 297/8–62807), a semisubmersible that allows passengers to sit and view Aruba's marine habitat from 5 ft below the surface. Cost is $33 for the 1½-hour tour.

**Colibri Helicopters** (☎ 297/8–931832) offers a 20-minute Island Adventure tour that treats guests to a bird's-eye view of California Lighthouse, the sand dunes, the Gold Smelter Ruins, the Natural Bridge, Oranjestad, and visiting cruise ships. Cost is $98 per person. A shorter 10-minute flight zooms over the beaches of the island and a sunken WWII freighter for $49 per person.

Romantic **horse-drawn-carriage rides** through the city streets of Oranjestad run $30 for a 30-minute tour; hours of operation are 7–11 PM and rides depart from the clock tower at the Royal Plaza Mall.

## Language

Everyone on the island speaks English, but the official language is Dutch.

## Opening and Closing Times

Shops are generally open between 8 AM and noon and 2 PM and 6 PM, Monday through Saturday. Some stores stay open through the lunch hour, noon–2 PM, and many open when cruise ships are in port on Sundays and holidays. Nighttime shopping at the Alhambra Bazaar runs 5 PM–midnight. Bank hours are weekdays from 8 to noon and 1:30 to 4. The Aruba Bank at the airport is open on Saturday from 9 to 4 and on Sunday from 9 to 1.

## Passports and Visas

U.S. and Canadian residents need only show proof of identity—a valid passport, birth certificate, naturalization certificate, green card, valid nonquota immigration visa, or a valid voter registration card. All other nationalities must submit a valid passport.

## Precautions

It's a relatively safe island, but common-sense rules still apply. Don't leave things in a rental car, and lock the car when you leave it. Leave valuables in your hotel safe, and don't leave bags unattended in the airport, on the beach, or on tour transports. Arubans are very friendly, so you needn't be afraid to stop and ask anyone for directions.

International traffic signs and Dutch-style traffic signals (with an extra light for turning lane) can be misleading for some American drivers, so use extreme caution, especially at intersections, until you grasp the rules of the road.

Mosquitoes can be bothersome during the rainy season (November through March), so pack some repellent. The strong trade winds are a relief in the subtropical climate, but don't hang your bathing suit on a balcony—it will probably blow away. Help Arubans conserve water and energy: Turn off air-conditioning when you leave your room, and keep your faucets turned off.

## Taxes and Service Charges

Hotels collect a 6% government tax and usually add an 11% service charge to room bills. You will sometimes see a $3-per-day energy surcharge tacked on to the hotel bill. Restaurants usually add a 10%–15% service charge to your bill. The departure tax is $20. An ABB tax (a value added tax) was initiated in mid-1996, and you'll pay it in all but the duty-free shops.

## Telephones and Mail

To dial direct to Aruba from the United States, dial 011–297–8, followed by the number in Aruba (the area code was recently changed from 809). Local and international calls in Aruba can be made via hotel operators or from the Government Long Distance Telephone, Telegraph, and Radio Office, SETAR, in the post office building in Oranjestad. When dialing locally in Aruba, simply dial the five-digit number. To reach the United States, dial 001, then the area code and number. Local calls from a pay phone cost AFl.25.

Telegrams and telexes can be sent through SETAR, at the Post Office Building in Oranjestad or via your hotel. There is also a SETAR office in the new Royal Plaza Mall and in front of the Hyatt Regency hotel, adjacent to the hotel's parking lot (☎ 297/8–67138).

You can send an airmail letter from Aruba to the United States and Canada for AFl1.40; a postcard for AFl.60, to Europe AFl1.50 and AFl.70.

## Visitor Information

Contact the **Aruba Tourism Authority** at ☎ 800/862–7822 or at one of the following offices (✉ One Financial Plaza, Suite 136, Fort Lauderdale, FL 33394, ☎ 954/767–2720, FAX 954/767–0432; ✉ 199 14th St. NE, Suite 2008, Atlanta, GA 30309-3688, ☎ 404/892–7822, FAX 404/873–2913; ✉ 1000 Harbor Blvd., Ground Level, Weehawken, NJ 07087, ☎ 201/330–0800, FAX 201/330–8757; ✉ 12707 North Freeway, Suite 138, Houston, TX 77060-1234, ☎ 713/872–7822, FAX 713/872–7872; ⊠ 86 Bloor St. W, Suite 204, Toronto, Ontario, M5S 1M5, ☎ 416/975–1950 or 800/268–3042). In Aruba, the **Aruba Tourism Authority** (⊠ L. G. Smith Blvd. 172, Eagle Beach, Aruba, ☎ 297/8–23777, FAX 297/8–34702) has free brochures and information officers who are ready to answer any questions.

# 5  Barbados

*The most British of all the Caribbean islands, here cricket and high tea are as common as calypso and rum. Exclusive West Coast retreats have long been the playground of the rich; the lively South Coast is where you'll find the action. Barbados is classy, busy, and fun.*

**B**ARBADOS HAS A LIFE OF ITS OWN that continues after the tourists have packed up their sun oils and returned home. The government is stable, business operations are sophisticated, and unemployment is relatively low, so the difference between haves and have-nots is less marked—or at least less visible—than on some islands. The 260,000 Bajans (Barbadians) are a warm, friendly, and hospitable people. They are genuinely proud of their country and welcome visitors as privileged guests.

Updated by
Jane E. Zarem

Barbados sits at the most easterly point of all the Caribbean islands, partially in the Atlantic Ocean and partially in the Caribbean Sea. It is 21 mi long, 14 mi wide, and relatively flat, although the highest point, Mt. Hillaby, has an elevation of 1,115 ft. Most people live between Speightstown, on the northwest coast, and Oistins, in the south, the urban area surrounding Bridgetown, the capital. Others reside in tiny hamlets scattered around the island.

Beaches along the tranquil West Coast—in the lee of the northwest trade winds—are backed by first-class resorts. Additional hotels stretch along the beaches on the South Coast, where Americans (couples more often than singles) tend to congregate. British and Canadian visitors often favor the posh hotels in the parish of St. James. As on the other islands in the Caribbean, the beaches of Barbados are open to the public; all are lovely, with white sand, and many are secluded.

Toward the northeast are rolling hills and valleys covered by impenetrable acres of sugarcane. The Atlantic surf pounds against gigantic boulders along the rugged east coast, where the Bajans themselves have vacation homes. Elsewhere on the island, crisscrossed by almost 900 mi of good roads, are small villages, historic plantation houses, stalactite-studded caves, a wildlife preserve, and the Andromeda Gardens, one of the most attractive small tropical gardens in the world.

No one is sure whether the name Los Barbados ("the bearded ones") refers to the beardlike root that hangs from the island's fig trees, to the bearded natives who greeted the Portuguese "discoverer" of the island in 1536, or to any other theory surrounding the appellation. The name Los Barbados was being used almost a century later when the British landed—by accident—in what is now Holetown, in the parish of St. James. They colonized the island in 1627, and British rule remained uninterrupted until the island achieved independence in 1966.

Barbados retains a very British atmosphere. Afternoon tea is a ritual at numerous hotels. Cricket, the national sport, is also the national passion—Barbados produces some of the world's top players. Polo, "the sport of kings," is played all winter. The British tradition of dressing for dinner is firmly entrenched, yet the island's atmosphere is hardly stuffy. This is still the Caribbean, after all.

## Lodging

The southern and western shores of Barbados are lined with hotels and resorts of every size and price, offering accommodations ranging from private villas and elegant hotels to modest but comfortable rooms in simple inns. Apartment and home rentals and time-share condominiums have become widely available and are growing increasingly popular among visitors to the island. Most of the hotels run on the EP meal plan but also offer CP or MAP, and a few are all-inclusive.

The location of your hotel is important. Hotels to the north of Bridgetown, in the West Coast parishes of St. Peter, St. James, and St.

Michael, tend to be self-contained resorts with stretches of empty road between them that discourage strolling to a neighborhood bar or restaurant. Along the South Coast, in Christ Church, many of the hotels cluster near or along the busy strip known as St. Lawrence Gap, where dozens of small restaurants, bars, and nightclubs are close by. Hotels listed here are grouped by parish.

| CATEGORY | COST* |
|---|---|
| $$$$ | over $350 |
| $$$ | $250–$350 |
| $$ | $150–$250 |
| $ | under $150 |

*All prices are for a standard double room, excluding 7½% government tax and 10% service charge.

## St. James

**$$$$**  🏨 **Coral Reef Club.** Guests here spend their days relaxing on the white-sand beach or around the pool, taking time out for the hotel's superb afternoon tea. The public areas ramble along the beach and face the Caribbean Sea, and small coral-stone cottages are scattered over the surrounding 12 flower-filled acres. (The cottages farthest from the beach are a bit of a hike to the main house.) The rooms are spacious, each with air-conditioning and ceiling fans, a small patio, and fresh flowers. The restaurant, under the direction of Bajan chef Graham Licorish, is noted for its inventive cuisine, which combines local cooking with European flair. Most guests are on a MAP. Another convenience is the free shuttle into Bridgetown. ⊠ *Porters,* ☎ *246/422–2372,* FAX *246/422–1776. 68 rooms. Restaurant, air-conditioning, fans, pool, beach, snorkeling, windsurfing, waterskiing. AE, MC, V. EP, MAP.*

**$$$$**  🏨 **Glitter Bay.** In the 1930s, Sir Edward Cunard, of the English shipping family, bought this estate, built a Great House and a beach house that resembled his palazzo in Venice. Cunard's parties in honor of visiting aristocrats and celebrities gave Glitter Bay an early reputation for grandeur and style. Today, newer buildings angled back from the beach contain 70 one- to three-bedroom suites, some with full kitchens; the beach house is now five garden suites. Manicured gardens separate the reception area and a large, comfortable tea lounge from an alfresco dining room (where evening entertainment is held), the pool, and a half mile of beach. Glitter Bay is more casual and family-oriented than its next-door sister property, the Royal Pavilion (☞ *below*), but the resorts share facilities, including complimentary water sports, and dining privileges. ⊠ *Porters,* ☎ *246/422–4111,* FAX *246/422–3940. 70 rooms. Restaurant, air-conditioning, pool, golf privileges, 2 tennis courts, beach, water sports. AE, DC, MC, V. EP, MAP.*

**$$$$**  🏨 **Royal Pavilion.** Of the 75 rooms here, 72 are oceanfront suites; the
★  remaining three are nestled in a garden villa. The ground-floor rooms allow guests simply to step through sliding doors, cross their private patio, and walk onto the sand. Second- and third-floor rooms have the advantage of an elevated view of the sea. Breakfast and lunch are served alfresco along the edge of the beach. Afternoon tea and dinner are in the Palm Terrace (☞ Dining, *below*). The Royal Pavilion attracts sophisticated guests who want serenity (bringing children under the age of 12 is discouraged during the winter months). Recreational facilities and dining privileges are shared with the adjoining and more informal sister hotel, Glitter Bay (☞ *above*). ⊠ *Porters,* ☎ *246/422–4444,* FAX *246/422–3940. 75 rooms. 2 restaurants, 2 bars, air-conditioning, pool, beauty salon, golf privileges, 2 tennis courts, beach, water sports. AE, DC, MC, V. EP.*

**92**

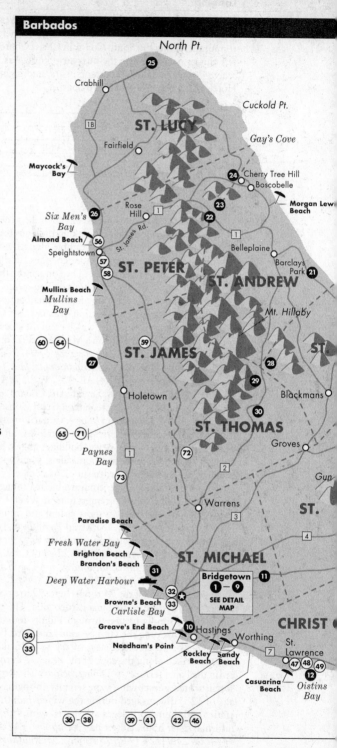

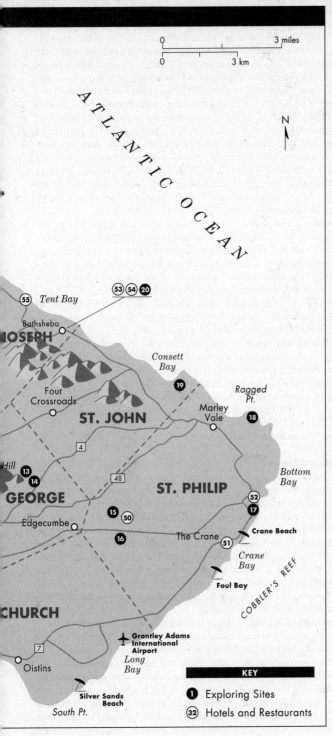

Sandy Bay
Restaurant, **67**
Sunbury Plantation
House, **50**
Waterfront Cafe, **32**
Witch Doctor, **43**

**Lodging**
Accra Beach Hotel &
Resort, **38**
Almond Beach
Club, **68**
Almond Beach
Village, **56**
Atlantis Hotel, **53**
Barbados Hilton, **35**
Casuarina Beach
Club, **46**
Club Rockley
Barbados, **37**
Cobblers Cove
Hotel, **57**
Coconut Creek
Club, **66**
Coral Reef Club, **60**
Crane Beach Hotel, **51**
Discovery Bay
Hotel, **64**
Divi Southwinds Beach
Resort, **44**
Edgewater Inn, **54**
Glitter Bay, **61**
Grand Barbados
Beach Resort, **33**
Little Bay Hotel, **42**
Oasis Hotel, **40**
Royal Pavilion, **62**
Sam Lord's Castle, **52**
Sandridge, **58**
Sandy Beach Island
Resort, **39**
Sandy Lane Hotel, **67**
Southern Palms, **45**
Treasure Beach, **69**
Windsurf Village
Barbados, **49**

**$$$$**  ⊞ **Sandy Lane Hotel.** This prestigious hotel has set a standard for el-
★  egance and style since 1961. On one of the best beaches in Barbados,
with acres of well-tended grounds, Sandy Lane is one of the most impressive hotels in the Caribbean. The white coral structure, with marble throughout has a grand staircase leading to the best beach on the
West Coast. The scene, the style, and the atmosphere are reminiscent
of *The Great Gatsby.* All rooms overlook the sea and have private balconies for eating breakfast and watching magnificent sunsets. Rooms
are nothing short of spectacular; bathrooms are vast and luxurious.
Afternoon tea, fine dining, and personalized service all add to the
charm. You'll be treated like royalty—in fact, royalty does stay here.
Plan to dress up, particularly in season—no jeans or shorts after 7 PM.
⊠ *Hwy. 1,* ☎ *246/432–1311,* ℻ *246/432–2954. 90 rooms, 30 suites.
3 restaurants, 5 bars, air-conditioning, pool, beauty salon, 18-hole golf
course, 5 tennis courts, health club, beach, water sports, baby-
sitting, children's programs. AE, DC, MC, V. EP, MAP.*

**$$$**  ⊞ **Coconut Creek Club.** The atmosphere is casual at this luxury cot-
tage colony, set on handsomely landscaped grounds with a small pri-
vate beach and a bar pavilion for entertainment and dancing. From a
low bluff, the hotel overlooks the ocean, and steps lead down to two
secluded coves. Some rooms have ocean views; others overlook the gar-
den or pool. Televisions are available on request for a small fee. ⊠ *Reser-
vations: Box 249, Bridgetown; Hwy. 1,* ☎ *246/432–0803,* ℻
*246/432–0272. 53 rooms. Bar, dining room, air-conditioning, pool,
beach, water sports, baby-sitting. AE, DC, MC, V. EP, MAP.*

**$$$**  ⊞ **Discovery Bay Hotel.** In historic Holetown, site of the British "dis-
covery" and settlement of the island, this quiet hotel—with a grand,
white-columned, plantation-style entrance—is surrounded by 4½ acres
of tropical gardens and bordered by a broad strand of Caribbean
beach. Deluxe rooms have ocean views; others open onto a central lawn
and pool area. A shuttle to Bridgetown is available to guests on weekdays. ⊠ *Hwy. 1, Holetown,* ☎ *246/432–1301,* ℻ *246/432–2553. 87
rooms. Restaurant, air-conditioning, pool, Ping-Pong, beach, shop. AE,
D, DC, MC, V. EP.*

**$$$**  ⊞ **Treasure Beach.** Most of the one-bedroom suites of this compact
resort create a horseshoe around a small garden and pool, other suites
have sea views, but all are just steps from the beach. Suites are spa-
cious, with kitchenettes and sitting rooms that open onto large patios
or verandas with louvered, full-length shutters for privacy. The restau-
rant's reputation for gourmet dining and fine service attracts an out-
side clientele as well as hotel guests. The atmosphere here is quiet and
pleasant. Guests, particularly British vacationers, often stay two or three
weeks, giving the hotel an almost residential quality. ⊠ *Paynes Bay,*
☎ *246/432–1346,* ℻ *246/432–1094. 24 1-bedroom suites, 1 2-bed-
room penthouse suite. Restaurant, air-conditioning, pool, beach, water
sports. AE, DC, MC, V. EP, MAP.*

**$$–$$$**  ⊞ **Almond Beach Club.** In this hotel, everything is included in the price
of the room—all you want to eat and drink (including wine and liquor),
water sports, boat trips, tennis, a Bajan beach picnic, shopping excursions
to Bridgetown, departure transportation to the airport, and service and
taxes. Accommodations are in one-bedroom suites with balconies,
two-bedroom duplex suites, and individual poolside or garden-view
rooms. The food is excellent, from the breakfast buffet and four-course
lunch to the afternoon tea and pastries and the intimate, candlelit ser-
vice at dinner. If your stay is seven days or more, you can choose the
dine-around program—dinner or lunch at area restaurants with round-
trip transportation included. The exchange program with Almond
Beach Village (☞ *below*) includes golf privileges; shuttle service is
provided. The Almond Beach Club doesn't have the enforced-activity,

"whistle-blowing" atmosphere of some other all-inclusives. ⊠ *Vauxhall,* ☎ *246/432–7840 or 800/425–6663,* 🗚 *246/432–2115. 161 rooms. 2 restaurants, 4 bars, air-conditioning, 3 pools, sauna, tennis court, squash, beach, water sports, shop. AE, MC, V. All-inclusive.*

### St. Peter

**$$$$**
★
🏨 **Cobblers Cove Hotel.** This all-suite resort, 12 mi up the West Coast from Bridgetown, combines comfort and informal elegance in an English-style country house. The pink-and-white building and the tropical gardens are bordered on three sides by stone walls, giving the property a self-contained ambience. This fine retreat overlooking the sea and small beach is the only member of the Relais & Châteaux organization in Barbados. There's an excellent gourmet restaurant and a club-like lounge-library, and the bar becomes the evening gathering spot. For all-out luxury, stay in the new Colleton Suite or the Camelot Suite. Guests enjoy special rates and guaranteed tee times at the nearby Royal Westmoreland Golf Course. No children under 12 are allowed from late January to late March. ⊠ *Hwy. 1,* ☎ *246/422–2291 or 800/890–6060,* 🗚 *246/422–1460. 40 suites. Restaurant, bar, snack bar, air-conditioning, pool, tennis, water sports, baby-sitting. AE, MC, V. CP, MAP.*

**$$$**
★
🏨 **Almond Beach Village.** The sister hotel to the Almond Beach Club (☞ *above*) in St. James, this is a spacious 30-acre resort on a mile of beachfront, with an executive, three-par golf course (clubs provided), nine pools, a full range of land and water sports, and other guest activities (shopping excursions to Bridgetown, island tours, a Bajan picnic off-property, a Caribbean cooking school, and a dine-around program). A shuttle between the Village and the Club allows guests to use both resorts' facilities. Guest rooms, in seven low-rise buildings, are spacious, comfortable, and attractively decorated. A family section has junior and one-bedroom suites, a nursery, a play area, a wading pool, and a supervised Kid's Klub. An historic sugar mill on the property is a lovely spot for wedding ceremonies. The restaurants serve Continental, Italian, and native cuisine. All meals (including beverages), activities, and departure transfers are included in the rates. ⊠ *Hwy. 1,* ☎ *246/422–4900 or 800/425–6663,* 🗚 *246/422–1581. 288 rooms. 4 restaurants, 5 bars, air-conditioning, 9 pools, wading pool, 9-hole golf course, 5 tennis courts, exercise room, squash, beach, water sports, shop, dance club. AE, MC, V. All-inclusive.*

**$$**
🏨 **Sandridge.** Six new waterfront suites and a new dining room with lounge have been added to this fashionable beachfront property near Speightstown. Guest rooms have been restyled in bright colors with tropical furnishings; some rooms have kitchenettes. Ground-floor accommodations have wide doors and ramps, allowing easy access for guests with disabilities. A supervised children's program makes this property particularly attractive to families. The resort's second pool has been remodeled to include a dramatic waterfall and deck of coral stone. ⊠ *Road View,* ☎ *246/422–2361,* 🗚 *246/422–1965. 58 rooms. 2 restaurants, 2 bars, air-conditioning, 2 pools, beach, water sports, baby-sitting. AE, DC, MC, V. EP.*

### St. Michael

**$$–$$$**
🏨 **Barbados Hilton.** This large resort, just five minutes from Bridgetown, bustles with activity from the people who come to attend seminars and conferences. An atrium lobby greets you when you arrive, and there's a 1,000-ft-wide man-made beach with full water sports and lots of shops to keep you busy. All rooms and suites have balconies. ⊠ *Needham's Point,* ☎ *246/426–0200,* 🗚 *246/436–8946. 184 rooms. Restaurant, 2 bars, lobby lounge, air-conditioning, pool, 4 tennis courts, health club, beach. AE, DC, MC, V. EP.*

$$ ■ **Grand Barbados Beach Resort.** A mile south of Bridgetown on Carlisle Bay, this convenient hotel has comfortable rooms and suites. The white-sand beach is lapped by a surprisingly clear sea despite the oil refinery nearby. The Aquatic Club executive floor has rooms whose rates include a Continental breakfast and secretarial services. Nightly live music, a dance floor, and a 260-ft-long pier that's perfect for romantic walks add to the enjoyment of a stay here. ⊠ *Box 639, Bridgetown,* ☎ *246/426–4000,* FAX *246/429–2400. 133 rooms. 2 restaurants, air-conditioning, pool, barbershop, beauty salon, hot tub, sauna, tennis court, exercise room, beach, shops. AE, DC, MC, V. EP.*

## Christ Church

$$ ■ **Accra Beach Hotel & Resort.** Totally renovated in 1996, the four-story Accra reopened with beautifully appointed rooms and suites, each with a balcony facing the sandy white beach. Rooms are attractively decorated in soft pastel colors. Six duplex penthouse suites have sitting rooms downstairs and a spacious bedroom and huge bath with whirlpool upstairs. Between the hotel and its beach are a large double pool, snack bar, and poolside bar for drinks. In the evening, after sumptuous dining in the Sirocco restaurant, take a turn on a dance floor that's open to the stars. Children under 12 stay free in their parents' room. ⊠ *Box 73W, Rockley,* ☎ *246/435–8920,* FAX *246/435–6794. 122 rooms. 3 restaurants, 2 bars, air-conditioning, pool, beauty salon, squash, beach, shops, meeting room. AE, DC, MC, V. EP, MAP.*

$$ ■ **Casuarina Beach Club.** This luxury apartment hotel consists of five clusters of Spanish-style buildings in 7½ acres of gardens. The hotel takes its name from the casuarina pines that surround it. The quiet setting provides a dramatic contrast to that of other South Coast resorts. The bar and restaurant are on the beach—900 ft of pink sand. A reception area includes small lounges where you can get a dose of TV (there aren't any in the bedrooms). Rooms have kitchenettes and large balconies. Scuba diving, golf, and other activities can be arranged. The Casuarina Beach is popular with those who prefer self-catering holidays in a secluded setting yet want to be close to nightlife and shopping. ⊠ *St. Lawrence Gap,* ☎ *246/428–3600 or 800/223–9815,* FAX *246/428–1970. 134 rooms. Restaurant, bar, air-conditioning, pool, 2 tennis courts, squash, beach, shop. AE, DC, MC, V. EP.*

$$ ■ **Club Rockley Barbados.** Some of these time-share condominiums have been transformed into an all-inclusive resort with one- and two-bedroom accommodations with balcony or patio. The remaining time-share condominiums are set apart from the hotel facility. On 65 acres near (but not on) one of the most popular beach areas in Barbados, the resort offers an extensive list of guest amenities and an excellent location for golfers and tennis players. ⊠ *Golf Club Rd., Hastings,* ☎ *246/435–7880,* FAX *246/435–8015. 288 rooms. 2 restaurants, 3 bars, air-conditioning, 7 pools, beauty salon, 9-hole golf course, 5 tennis courts, squash, shops. AE, DC, MC, V. All-inclusive.*

$$ ■ **Divi Southwinds Beach Resort.** In this resort, on 20 lush acres, the toss-up is whether to take one of the one-bedroom suites, with a balcony and kitchenette overlooking the gardens and pool, or one of the smaller and older-looking rooms, just steps from the sandy white beach. Though all the rooms are pleasant, the buildings themselves are rather plain. Guests come here for action, and that includes making full use of the scuba and water-sports facilities. ⊠ *St. Lawrence Gap,* ☎ *246/428–7181 or 800/367–3484,* FAX *246/428–4674. 166 rooms. 2 restaurants, air-conditioning, 3 pools, putting green, 2 tennis courts, beach, water sports, shops. AE, MC, V. EP, MAP.*

$$ ■ **Sandy Beach Island Resort.** On a wide, sparkling white beach, this comfortable hotel has a popular poolside bar and the Beachfront

Restaurant, which serves a West Indian buffet Tuesday and Saturday nights. The accommodations have been reconfigured and upgraded to include large one-bedroom suites, the restaurant has been enlarged, and a boardwalk gazebo, roof garden, and spectacular free-form pool have been added to the grounds. Scuba-diving certification, deep-sea fishing, harbor cruises, and catamaran sailing can be arranged. It's also a convenient walk to St. Lawrence Gap for restaurants and entertainment. ✉ *Worthing,* ☎ *246/435–8000,* FAX *246/435–8053. 89 units. Restaurant, bar, air-conditioning, pool, beach. AE, DC, MC, V. EP.*

$$ 🏨 **Southern Palms.** A plantation-style hotel on a 1,000-ft stretch of pink sand near the Dover Convention Center, this is a convenient businessperson's hotel and a good choice for active guests wanting to be near the Gap's shops and restaurants. You may choose from standard bedrooms, deluxe oceanfront suites with kitchenettes, and a four-bedroom penthouse. Each wing of the hotel has its own small pool. ✉ *St. Lawrence Gap,* ☎ *246/428–7171,* FAX *246/428–7175. 93 rooms. 2 restaurants, bar, air-conditioning, 2 pools, miniature golf, tennis court, beach, water sports, shop, convention center. AE, DC, MC, V. EP.*

$ 🏨 **Little Bay Hotel.** This small hotel is a find for anyone who wants to go easy on the wallet and yet sleep to the sounds of the sea. Each room has a private balcony, bedroom, small lounge, and kitchenette. Ceiling fans will keep you cool, but there are no TVs in the rooms—you can catch up on the news and watch sports in the small lounge next to the popular restaurant, Southern Accents. ✉ *St. Lawrence Gap,* ☎ *246/435–7246,* FAX *246/435–8574. 10 rooms. Restaurant, bar, lounge, beach. AE, MC, V. EP.*

$ 🏨 **Oasis Hotel.** The Oasis (formerly the Sichris Hotel) is a real find. More attractive inside than it appears from the road, it's a comfortable and convenient self-contained hotel. Just minutes from the city, the one-bedroom suites all have kitchenettes and private balconies or patios. It's a walk of two or three minutes to the beach. ✉ *Worthing,* ☎ *246/435–7930,* FAX *246/435–8232. 24 rooms. Restaurant, bar, air-conditioning, pool. AE, DC, MC, V. EP.*

$ 🏨 **Windsurf Village Barbados.** A small hotel that began as a gathering place for windsurfing enthusiasts, Windsurf Village Barbados (formerly Benston Windsurfing Club Hotel) is now a complete school and center for the sport, with plans to expand the facility even more. The rooms are spacious and sparsely furnished to accommodate the active and young crowd who choose this bare-bones hotel right on the beach. The bar and restaurant overlook the water. All sports can be arranged, but windsurfing (learning, practicing, and perfecting it) is king. ✉ *Maxwell Main Rd.,* ☎ *246/428–9095,* FAX *246/428–2872. 18 rooms. Restaurant, bar, beach, windsurfing. AE, MC, V. EP.*

## St. Philip

$$$ 🏨 **Crane Beach Hotel.** This remote hilltop property on a cliff overlooking the dramatic Atlantic coast remains one of the special places of Barbados. The Crane Beach has suites and one-bedrooms. Rooms are decorated with four-poster beds and antique furniture; rates vary depending on the view. Corner suite 1 is one of the nicest rooms, with its two walls of windows and patio terrace. The Roman-style pool with columns separates the main house from the dining room. To reach the beach, you walk down some 200 steps onto a beautiful stretch of sand thumped by waves that are good for both bodysurfing and swimming. ✉ *Crane Bay,* ☎ *246/423–6220,* FAX *246/423–5343. 18 rooms. Restaurant, bar, 2 pools, 4 tennis courts, beach. AE, DC, MC, V. EP, MAP.*

$$ 🏨 **Sam Lord's Castle.** Set on the Atlantic coast about 14 mi east of Bridgetown, Sam Lord's Castle is not a castle with moat and towers but a great house surrounded by 72 acres of grounds, gardens, and beach.

The seven rooms in the main house have canopied beds; downstairs, the public rooms have furniture by Sheraton, Hepplewhite, and Chippendale—for admiring, not for sitting. Additional guest rooms in surrounding cottages have conventional hotel furnishings. The beach is a mile long, the Wanderer Restaurant offers Continental cuisine, and there are even a few slot machines, as befits a pirate's lair. A special tennis package includes unlimited court time, airport transfers, and a Thursday Shipwreck party. ⊠ *Long Bay,* ☎ *246/423–7350,* FAX *246/423–5918. 234 rooms. 3 restaurants, air-conditioning, 3 pools, 7 tennis courts, beach. AE, D, DC, MC, V. EP, MAP.*

### St. Joseph

$  🏨 **Atlantis Hotel.** The Atlantis provides a warm, pleasant atmosphere in a quiet area of the majestically rocky Atlantic coast, where the views out to the open sea are mesmerizing. The hotel is modest, yet the congeniality and the Bajan food more than make up for that. There's a beachfront, but Bathsheba beach is right next door and a safer place to swim and surf. ⊠ *Bathsheba,* ☎ *246/433–9445. 8 rooms. Restaurant, bar, beach. AE. EP.*

$  🏨 **Edgewater Inn.** If you enjoy peace and quiet and want a room with
★ a view, this is the place. The inn is perched on a cliff overlooking the pounding surf and unusual rock formations at Bathsheba Beach. Bounded by Joe's River, a national park, and a 9-mi strip of sand, the property also backs up to an 85-acre rain forest. Yoga classes, nature walks, and guided hikes are available to guests. All rooms have an ocean view and handmade mahogany furniture. In fact, doors, moldings, and dining-room furniture are also fashioned from hand-hewn local mahogany. A shuttle will meet your plane or take you shopping, snorkeling, or pub crawling. But overall, you must be content with watching the birds and butterflies, taking a hike, or surfing Soup Bowl most of the time. ⊠ *Bathsheba, St. Joseph,* ☎ *246/433–9900,* FAX *246/433–9902. 20 rooms. Restaurant, bar, pool, beach. AE, MC, V. CP.*

### Villas and Condominiums

Villas, private homes, and condos are available for rent south of Bridgetown in the Hastings-Worthing area, along the coast of St. James, and in St. Peter. As an example, two- to three-bedroom condos near the beach start at $800–$1,000 per week in the summer months—double that in winter. Most include maid service, and a cook can be arranged through the owner or manager. Rentals are also available through Barbados realtors; among them are **Alleyne, Aguilar & Altman** (⊠ Rosebank, St. James, ☎ 246/432–0840), **Bajan Services** (⊠ St. Peter, ☎ 246/422–2618), and **Ronald Stoute & Sons Ltd.** (⊠ St. Philip, ☎ 246/423–6800). The **Barbados Tourism Authority** (☎ 246/427–2623, FAX 246/426–4080) has a listing of apartments and rates. In the United States, contact **At Home Abroad** (☎ 212/421–9165) or Jan Pizzi at **Villa Vacations** (☎ 617/593–8885 or 800/800–5576).

## Dining

The better hotels and restaurants of Barbados have employed chefs trained in New York and Europe to attract and keep their sophisticated clientele. Gourmet dining here usually involves fresh seafood, beef, or veal with finely blended sauces.

West Indian cuisine offers an entirely different dining experience. The African heritage brings to the table rice, peas, beans, and okra, the staples that make a perfect base for slowly cooked meat and fish dishes. Many side dishes are cooked in oil (the pumpkin fritters can be addictive). And be cautious at first with the West Indian condiments; like the sun, they are hotter than you think.

Some local specialties:

**Buljol** is a cold salad of marinated, raw codfish, tomatoes, onions, sweet peppers, and celery.

**Callaloo** soup is made from okra, crabmeat, the spinachlike vegetable that gives the dish its name, and seasonings.

**Christophines** and **eddoes** are tasty, potato-like vegetables often served with curried shrimp, chicken, or goat.

**Conkies** are a mixture of cornmeal and coconut, pumpkin, raisins, sweet potatoes, and spices served wrapped in a banana leaf.

**Cou-cou** is a mix of cornmeal and okra with a spicy Creole sauce made from tomatoes, onions, and sweet peppers; it is often served with steamed flying fish.

**Pepper-pot stew,** a hearty mix of oxtail, beef chunks, and "any other meat you may have," simmered overnight, is flavored with *cassareep,* an ancient preservative and seasoning that gives the stew its dark, rich color.

Most menus include dolphinfish, kingfish, snapper, and flying fish prepared every way imaginable. Flying fish is a Bajan delicacy—so popular it has become a national symbol. Shellfish abounds; on the other hand, so does steak. For breakfast and dessert you'll find mangoes, soursop, papaya (pawpaw) and, in season, softball-size "mammy apples," a sweet, thick-skinned fruit with giant seeds.

Among the liquid refreshments of Barbados, there are, in addition to the local and omnipresent Banks beer and Mount Gay rum, **falernum** (a liqueur concocted of rum, sugar, lime juice, and almond essence) and **mauby** (a nonalcoholic drink made by boiling bitter bark and spices, straining the mixture, and sweetening it).

## What to Wear

Barbados's British heritage and large resident population keep the dress code rather conservative and, on occasion, more formal than it is on neighboring islands. This can mean a jacket and tie for gentlemen and a cocktail dress for ladies in some restaurants. Other places are more casual, although you'll find jeans, shorts, and beach attire frowned upon at dinnertime.

| CATEGORY | COST* |
|---|---|
| **$$$** | over $40 |
| **$$** | $25–$40 |
| **$** | under $25 |

*per person for a three-course meal, excluding drinks and 10% service charge

**$$$** ✕ **Bagatelle Great House.** The restored plantation house (circa 1645) that houses one of the oldest restaurants in Barbados is designated a "house of architectural and historical interest" by the Barbados National Trust. French and Caribbean cuisine is served for a light lunch or elegant dinner. Inside the castlelike walls, the ambience is romantic and very much like a private Colonial home. For more intimate dining, the garden terrace offers tables for two. Upstairs is a gallery of Caribbean art, a craft showroom, and a gift shop. ⊠ *Hwy. 2A, St. Thomas,* ☎ *246/421–6767. Reservations essential. AE, MC, V.*

**$$$** ✕ **Carambola.** Dramatic lighting and a cliffside setting overlooking the
★ Caribbean make this alfresco restaurant in St. James one of the most romantic on the island. It also serves some of the best food. The menu is a mix of Asian and classic French cuisine with a Caribbean touch.

Start with a spicy, Caribbean-style crab tart, served with hollandaise sauce on a bed of sweet pepper coulis. For an entrée, try fillet of king-fish broiled with ginger, coriander, and spring onions, or sliced duck breast with a wild mushroom fumet served with stuffed tomatoes and *gratin dauphinoise* (potatoes au gratin). When you think you can't eat another bite, the *citron gâteau* (lime mousse on a bed of lemon coulis) is a wonderfully light finish. ⊠ *Derricks, St. James,* ☎ *246/432–0832. Reservations essential. AE, MC, V. Closed Sun. No lunch.*

**$$$**   ✕ **Christophenes.** This elegant restaurant in the Royal Westmoreland Club House offers a lovely atmosphere and fine cuisine. The menu is diverse, if only because it is the inspiration of two chefs—one French, one Barbadian. Enjoy a truly gourmet experience at dinner, or enjoy a lighter repast at lunch. Early-bird golfers may grab a bite of break-fast before or after their 18 holes. ⊠ *St. James,* ☎ *246/422–4653. Reservations essential. AE, MC, V.*

**$$$**   ✕ **The Cliff.** Chef Paul Owens and manager Manuel Ward have cre-
★        ated one of the finest dining establishments in Barbados. Imaginative art accents the candlelit dining room, and every table has a view of the sea. The artistic mood extends to the innovative menu, which offers selections of excellent cuts of meat and fresh fish, creatively presented and accompanied by the freshest vegetables and greens you'll find anywhere. Don't skip dessert, which falls in the "sinful" category. ⊠ *Derricks, St. James,* ☎ *246/432–1922. AE, DC, MC, V. No lunch.*

**$$$**   ✕ **La Maison.** This restaurant, in a colonial-style mansion, Balmore
★        House, exudes elegance with its English country furnishings and pan-eled bar opening onto a beachfront dining terrace. The mood is set for the terrific gourmet cuisine. A French chef, from the Loire Valley, cre-ates seafood specials, including a flying-fish parfait appetizer. Passion-fruit ice cream is a dessert special. ⊠ *Holetown, St. James,* ☎ *246/432–1156. AE, DC, MC, V. Closed Mon.*

**$$$**   ✕ **Palm Terrace.** The Palm's French executive chef and his team apply their talents to an international à la carte menu that combines Barba-dian produce with top-quality imports. The result is modern European creations, such as mille-feuille of home-smoked chicken with tomato, chives, and carrots in a light mustard cream sauce. Fresh mint accents New Zealand rack of lamb, and panfried crab becomes a stuffing for the breast of chicken entrée. Each evening there is a roast from the carvery. Widely spaced tables, comfortable chairs, and palms swaying under floor-to-ceiling arches creates a formal yet relaxed ambience as you dine facing the Caribbean Sea. ⊠ *Royal Pavilion Hotel, Porters, St. James,* ☎ *246/422–4444. AE, DC, MC, V. Closed Sun. No lunch.*

**$$$**   ✕ **Sandy Bay Restaurant.** The renowned Sandy Lane Hotel is the per-
★        fect place for an elegant meal overlooking one of the best beaches on the island. Munich-born chef Hans Schweitzer, formerly of the Mid-summer House in Cambridge, England, has modernized the cuisine by introducing *art culinair* to this historic resort. Dishes on the table d'hôte menu are mostly light fare, elegantly dressed with silky sauces, and accented with fresh vegetables. Grilled dolphinfish, lobster and shrimp tempura, and lamb with honey, thyme, and wild rosemary are among the entrées. Friday night, there's an international buffet. To se-cure the best produce, a van scours the island every morning for the freshest vegetables and fish. Desserts are French, creamy, and delicious. Be sure to dress for the occasion. ⊠ *Sandy Lane Hotel and Golf Club, St. James,* ☎ *246/432–1311. Reservations essential. AE, MC, V.*

**$$**    ✕ **Brown Sugar.** A special-occasion atmosphere prevails at Brown Sugar, set in a restored West Indian wooden house across from the Grand Barbados Beach Resort outside Bridgetown. Dozens of ferns and hang-ing plants decorate the breezy multilevel restaurant. An extensive and authentic West Indian lunch buffet (noon to 2:30)—from cou-cou to pepper-pot stew—is popular with local businesspeople. Dinner entrées include charbroiled ginger beef, Creole orange chicken, and homemade desserts, such as angel-food chocolate mousse cake, passion-fruit or nutmeg ice cream, and lime cheesecake. ⊠ *Aquatic Gap, Bay St., St. Michael,* ☎ *246/426–7684. AE, DC, MC, V. No lunch Sat.*

**$$** ✕ **Fathoms.** Veteran restaurateurs Stephen and Sandra Toppin open Fathoms beach restaurant seven days a week for lunch and dinner. Its 22 well-dressed tables are scattered from the inside dining rooms to the patio's ocean edge. Dinner may bring a grilled lobster, local rabbit, jumbo baked shrimp, or cashew-crusted kingfish. In the evenings, you can also grab a drink, a bite to eat, and a game of pool at Canyons, the upstairs bar. Fathoms is casual by day, candlelit by night. ⊠ *Paynes Bay, St. James,* ☎ *246/432–2568. AE, MC, V.*

**$$** ✕ **Ile de France.** French owners Martine (from Lyon) and Michel (the
★ chef, from Toulouse) Gramaglia have turned the pool and garden areas of the Windsor Hotel into an island "in" spot. White latticework opens to the night sounds, soft French music plays, and a single, perfect hibiscus dresses each table. Among the classic French selections, the menu features delicately flavored Caribbean seafood and fabulous desserts—tarte Tatin, crème brûlée, and their original banana terrine. If you yearn for classic French cuisine, this is the place to be. ⊠ *Windsor Hotel, South Coast Main Rd., Hastings, Christ Church,* ☎ *246/435–6869. Reservations essential. MC, V. Closed Mon. No lunch.*

**$$** ✕ **Josef's.** Swede Nils Ryman successfully created a menu from the unusual combination of Caribbean and Scandinavian fare. That, of course, means great fresh fish and seafood, including local lobster from the island's rocky east coast, and toast Skagen, made from diced shrimp blended with mayonnaise and fresh dill. Stroll around the garden before moving to the alfresco dining room downstairs or to the simply decorated room upstairs for a table that looks out over the sea. ⊠ *Waverly House, St. Lawrence Gap, Christ Church,* ☎ *246/435–6541. AE, MC, V.*

**$$** ✕ **Pisces.** Fish is the way to go at this excellent waterfront restaurant
★ in lively St. Lawrence Gap. Flying fish, dolphinfish, crab, kingfish, shrimp, prawns, and lobster are prepared any way from charbroiled to sautéed. There are also some chicken and beef dishes. Other specialties include conch fritters, tropical gazpacho, and seafood terrine with a mango sauce. The homemade rum raisin ice cream is a top choice for dessert. Enjoy your meal in a contemporary setting filled with hanging tropical plants and twinkling white lights that reflect on the water. ⊠ *St. Lawrence Gap, Christ Church,* ☎ *246/435–6564. AE, DC, MC, V. No lunch.*

**$$** ✕ **Plantation Restaurant and Garden Theater.** The Bajan buffet and entertainment on Wednesday and Friday are big attractions here (☞ Nightlife and the Arts, *below*). The Plantation is in a renovated Barbadian residence surrounded by spacious grounds above the Southwinds Resort. Barbadian cuisine is served either indoors or on the terrace. ⊠ *St. Lawrence Rd., Christ Church,* ☎ *246/428–5048. AE, MC, V. No lunch.*

**$$** ✕ **Rose and Crown.** A variety of fresh seafood is served in this casual eatery, but it's the local lobster that's high on diners' lists. Indoors is a paneled bar; outdoors are tables on a wraparound porch. ⊠ *Prospect, St. James,* ☎ *246/425–1074. AE, MC, V. Closed Sat. No lunch.*

**$$** ✕ **Witch Doctor.** The interior of Witch Doctor is decorated with pseudo-African art, which gives a lighthearted, carefree atmosphere to this casual hangout across the street from the sea. The sensible menu includes traditional Barbadian dishes, such as steamed flying fish with rice and vegetables, as well as American fare and seafood. ⊠ *St. Lawrence Gap, Christ Church,* ☎ *246/435–6581. MC, V. No lunch.*

$  ✕ **Atlantis Hotel.** The seemingly endless luncheon buffet and magnificent ocean view make this restaurant a real find. Under the direction of owner-chef Enid Maxwell, the staff serves up an enormous Bajan buffet daily, with pumpkin fritters, spinach cake, pickled breadfruit, fried flying fish, roast chicken, pepper-pot stew, and West Indian–style okra and eggplant. Homemade coconut pie tops the dessert list. All that for $12.50 per person, except for Sundays, when a few dishes are added to the groaning board and the price becomes $17.50. ⊠ *Atlantis Hotel, Bathsheba, St. Joseph,* ☎ *246/433–9445. AE.*

$  ✕ **Bonito Beach Bar & Restaurant.** When you tour the rugged east coast, plan to arrive in Bathsheba at lunchtime and stop at Mrs. Enid Worrell's Bonito Beach Bar for wholesome West Indian home cooking. The view of the Atlantic coast from the second-floor dining room of this otherwise plain restaurant is magnificent. Lunch might be a choice of fried fish, baked chicken, or beef stew, accompanied by local vegetables and salads fresh from the family garden. If your timing is right, Mrs. Worrell may have homemade cheesecake for dessert. Be sure to try the fresh fruit punch—with or without rum. The Bajan luncheon buffet, on Wednesdays and Sundays from 1 to 3, is popular. ⊠ *Coast Rd., Bathsheba, St. Joseph,* ☎ *246/433–9034. No credit cards.*

$  ✕ **David's Place.** Come here for first-rate food in a first-rate location—a black-and-white Bajan cottage overlooking St. Lawrence Bay. Waves slap against the pilings of the open-air deck, providing a rhythmic accompaniment to your authentic Barbadian meal. The specialties—local flying fish, pepper-pot stew, curried shrimp—and other entrées, including a vegetarian platter, come with homemade cheese bread. Dessert might be banana pudding, carrot cake with rum sauce, or a cakelike dessert called cassava pone. ⊠ *St. Lawrence Main Rd., Worthing, Christ Church,* ☎ *246/435–9755. AE, MC, V. Closed Mon.*

$  ✕ **Edgewater Inn.** You'll step into truly natural surroundings here, a perfect luncheon stop when touring the East Coast. The inn is surrounded by an 85-acre rain forest, a national park, and a river. It overlooks 9 mi of beach, including Barbados's famed Soup Bowl. The dining room is furnished with tables and chairs hand-carved from local mahogany. Meanwhile, you can enjoy light fare of sandwiches, salads, and French-bread pizzas or a traditional Bajan feast and dessert buffet. Dinners are also served, but mostly it's inn guests who partake. ⊠ *Bathsheba, St. Joseph,* ☎ *246/433–9900. AE, MC, V.*

$  ✕ **Sunbury Plantation House.** In the Courtyard Restaurant, on a patio
★   surrounded by beautiful gardens, luncheon is served to visitors as part of the house tour (if you wish). The Bajan buffet includes chicken and fish, salads, rice and peas, and steamed local vegetables. Trifle, pastries, and ice cream are dessert choices. Sandwiches and other à la carte items are available, too. A special mood is created in the evening, when small groups dine in the plantation-house dining room. ⊠ *St. Philip,* ☎ *246/423–6270. Reservations essential. AE, MC, V.*

$  ✕ **Waterfront Cafe.** Facing the busy harbor in Bridgetown, this friendly bistro is the perfect place to enjoy a drink, snack, or meal. Locals and tourists gather at outdoor café tables for sandwiches, salads, fish, pasta, pepper-pot stew, and tasty Bajan snacks. The panfried flying-fish sandwich is especially popular. In the evening, from the brick and mirrored interior, you can gaze through the arched windows while you savor '90s-style Creole cuisine, enjoy the cool trade winds, listen to the live music, and let time pass. ⊠ *The Careenage, Bridgetown, St. Michael,* ☎ *246/427–0093. AE, DC, MC, V. Closed Sun.*

# Beaches

Barbados beaches are all open to the public. Although nonguests may not always have immediate access to hotel beaches, you can walk onto almost any beach from an adjacent one. Beaches on the West Coast have gentle Caribbean surf and are shaded by leafy mahogany trees. South-coast beaches, dotted with tall palms, have medium-to-high surf; the waves get bigger the farther southeast you go. On east-coast beaches, the Atlantic Ocean surf can be rough with a strong undertow, so swimming and surfing are risky there.

## West Coast Beaches

The West Coast has the stunning coves and white-sand beaches that are dear to postcard publishers—plus calm, clear water for snorkeling, scuba diving, and swimming. West Coast beaches continue almost unbroken from Almond Beach Village in the north down to Bridgetown. Elegant private homes and luxury hotels take up most of the beachfront property in this area, which is why this stretch of sandy shoreline is called Barbados's Gold Coast.

Although West Coast beaches are seldom crowded, they are not the place to find isolation. Owners of private boats stroll by, offering waterskiing, parasailing, and snorkel cruises. There are no concession stands, but hotels welcome nonguests for terrace lunches (wear a cover-up). Picnic items and necessities can be bought at the Sunset Crest shopping center in Holetown. The afternoon clouds and sunsets are breathtaking from any of the West Coast beaches.

**Brighton Beach,** just north of Bridgetown, is not far from the port. It's a large beach, with a beach bar; and being close to town, it's a favorite for locals.

**Mullins Beach,** south of Speightstown at Mullins Bay, is a good place for a swim and is safe for snorkeling. There's easy parking on the main road, and when you want a break from the sun, Mullins Beach Bar has snacks and drinks.

**Paynes Bay,** south of Holetown, is the site of a number of luxury hotels. It's a very pretty area, with plenty of beach to go around. Parking areas and access are available opposite the Coach House Pub. Grab a bite to eat at Bomba's Beach Bar.

## South Coast Beaches

South Coast beaches are much busier than those on the West Coast and generally draw a younger, more active crowd. The quality of the beach itself is consistently good; the reef-protected waters are safe for swimming and snorkeling.

**Accra Beach,** in Rockley, is very popular. There are lots of people, lots of activity, food and drink nearby, and rental equipment for snorkeling and other water sports. There's a car park at the beach.

The cove at **Bottom Bay,** north of Sam Lord's Castle, is lovely. Follow the steps down the cliff to a strip of white sand lined by coconut palms and faced by an aquamarine sea. There's even a cave to explore. It's out of the way and not near restaurants, so bring a picnic lunch.

**Casuarina Beach,** at the Casuarina Beach Club in the St. Lawrence Gap area, is a beach with lots of breeze and a fair amount of surf. Public access is from Maxwell Coast Road.

Where the South Coast meets the Atlantic side of the island, the waves roll in bigger and faster. **Crane Beach** has for years been a popular swimming beach, and the waves are a favorite with bodysurfers. This can be rough water, so exercise caution.

**Foul Bay** is ruggedly attractive and lives up to its name only for sailboats; for swimmers and alfresco lunches (pack your own picnic), it's perfect.

**Greaves End Beach,** south of Bridgetown at Aquatic Gap, between the Grand Barbados Beach Resort and the Barbados Hilton in St. Michael, is a good spot for swimming.

**Needham's Point,** with its lighthouse, is one of Barbados's best beaches. It's crowded with local people on weekends and holidays.

In Worthing, next to the Sandy Beach Island Resort, **Sandy Beach** has shallow, calm waters and a picturesque lagoon. It's an ideal location for families, with beach activities on weekends. There's parking on the main road and plenty of places nearby to buy food or drink.

**Silver Sands Beach,** close to the southern-most point of the island, has a beautiful expanse of white sand beach, with a stiff breeze that appeals to windsurfers.

## East Coast Beaches

With long stretches of open beach and crashing ocean waves, rocky cliffs, and verdant hills, the windward side of Barbados won't disappoint anyone who seeks dramatic views. But be cautioned: Swimming at East Coast beaches is treacherous and *not* recommended. The waves are high, the bottom tends to be rocky, and the currents are unpredictable. Limit yourself to enjoying the view and watching the surfers—who have been at it since they were kids.

Miles of beach follow the wild coast at **Bathsheba** and **Cattlewash,** where the pounding surf of the Atlantic is mesmerizing. This is where Barbadians keep second homes and spend holidays. Swimming in these waters can be extremely dangerous even for strong swimmers. Bring a picnic or have lunch at one of the local restaurants with a view.

A worthwhile, little-visited beach for those who don't mind trekking about a mile off the beaten path, **Morgan Lewis Beach** is east of Morgan Lewis Mill, the oldest intact windmill on the island. Turn east on the small road that goes to the town of Boscobelle (between Cherry Tree Hill and Morgan Lewis Mill); but instead of going to town, take the even less-traveled road (unmarked on most maps; you will have to ask for directions) that goes down the cliff to the beach. What awaits is more than 2 mi of unspoiled, uninhabited white sand and sweeping views of the Atlantic coastline. You may see a few Barbadians swimming, sunning, or fishing, but for the most part you'll have privacy.

# Outdoor Activities and Sports

## Fishing

**Blue Jay Charters** (☎ 246/422–2098) has a 45-ft, fully equipped fishing boat, with a crew that knows the waters where blue marlin, sailfish, barracuda, and kingfish play.

## Golfing

Barbadians love golf, and golfers love Barbados. Greens fees range from $12.50 for nine holes at Belair to $145 for 18 holes at Royal Westmoreland Golf Club.

**Almond Beach Village** (☎ 246/422–4900), on the northwest corner of the island, has a nine-hole executive course for guest use only; clubs are provided. The **Belair Par-3** (☎ 246/423–4653) course is on the rugged East Coast, near Sam Lord's Castle. **Club Rockley Barbados** (☎ 246/435–7873), on the South Coast, has a challenging nine-hole course. The **Royal Westmoreland Golf Club** (☎ 246/422–4653) has a world-class Robert Trent Jones Jr. 18-hole course that meanders through the 500-acre Westmoreland Sugar Estate, past million-dollar villas, and overlooks the scenic West Coast. Nine additional holes are under way. To play here, you must stay at a hotel with access privileges. The prestigious **Sandy Lane Club** (☎ 246/432–1145) has a challenging 18-hole championship course. The dramatic seventh hole is famous for both its elevated tee and its incredible view.

## Hiking

Hilly but not mountainous, the interior of Barbados is ideal for hiking. The **Barbados National Trust** (✉ No. 2, 10th Ave., Belleville, St. Michael, ☎ 246/436–9033) sponsors free 5-mi walks year-round on Sunday, from 6 AM to about 9:30 AM and from 3:30 PM to 5:30 PM, as well as special moonlight hikes when the heavens permit. Newspapers announce the time and meeting place (or you can call the Trust).

## Horseback Riding

The **Caribbean International Riding Center** (✉ Auburn, St. Joseph, ☎ 246/433–1453 or 246/420–1246) offers one-hour rides through nearby gullies for $27.50 and a special ride through the countryside to Villa Nova Great House, including lunch and a tour of the house, for $187.50; transportation to and from your hotel is included. On the West Coast, **Brighton Stables** (✉ Black Rock, St. Michael, ☎ 246/425–9381) offers one-hour rides along beaches and palm groves for $27.50, including transportation.

## Parasailing

Parasailing is available, wind conditions permitting, on the beaches of St. James and Christ Church. **Skyrider Parasail** (☎ 246/420–6362) operates from Bay Street in Bridgetown, but the boat does pickups all along the West Coast. Just flag down the speedboat, though the operator may find you first. Rates are $45 per flight—and they even take credit cards (MasterCard and Visa). Children and the physically challenged present no problem.

## Sailing Excursions

Party boats depart from the Careenage or Bridgetown Harbour area. For around $55, lunchtime snorkeling and cocktail-hour sunset catamaran cruises are available on **Limbo Lady** (☎ 246/420–5418) and on **Irish Mist, Spirit of Barbados, Tiami II,** and **Tropical Dreamer** (☎ 246/427–7245). **Secret Love** (☎ 246/432–1972), a 41-ft Morgan sailboat, offers daily lunchtime or evening snorkel cruises.

The red-sailed **Jolly Roger** "pirate" party ship makes lunch-and-rum cruises along the West Coast for $52 (✉ Fun Cruises, ☎ 246/436–6424).

A motor vessel rather than a sailboat, the 100-ft M/V **Harbour Master** has four decks, fun and games, food and drink, and an adventurous spirit. It can land on beaches to access many hotels; you can view the briny deep from its on-board 34-seat semisubmersible. It leaves Bridgetown for four- and five-hour cruises along the West Coast, stopping in Holetown and at beaches along the way. ☎ *246/430–0900.* 🖃 *$50.* ☼ *Tues. and Thurs.–Sat.*

## Scuba Diving

**Dive sites** are concentrated along the West Coast, between Bridgetown and Maycocks Bay, St. Lucy. Certified divers can explore reefs, wrecks, and the walls of "blue holes," the huge circular depressions in the ocean floor. Underwater visibility is generally 80–90 ft. Not to be missed is the *Stavronikita,* a 356-ft Greek freighter that was deliberately sunk at about 135 ft; hundreds of butterfly fish hang out around its mast, and the thin rays of sunlight that filter down through the water make exploring the huge ship a wonderfully eerie experience. Virtually every part of the ship is accessible. A one-tank dive runs about $40–$45; two-tank, $50–$55.

Many dive shops provide **instruction** in scuba diving—a three-hour beginner's "resort" course (about $75) or a weeklong certification course (about $350), followed by a shallow dive—usually on Dottin's Reef, off Holetown.

Barbados has a **decompression chamber,** based at the Barbados Defence Force Dive Accident Unit (⊠ St. Ann's Fort, St. Michael, ☎ 246/436–6185), available to divers on a 24-hour basis.

**Dive Boat Safari** (⊠ Barbados Hilton, St. Michael, ☎ 246/427–4350) offers full diving and instruction services. The **Dive Shop, Ltd.** (⊠ Aquatic Gap, near Grand Barbados Beach Resort, St. Michael, ☎ 246/426–9947) has one- and two-tank dive trips, or you can purchase a six-dive package. **Exploresub Barbados** (⊠ St. Lawrence Gap, Christ Church, ☎ 246/435–6542) is a PADI five-star training facility that offers a full range of daily dives. **Hightide** (⊠ Sandy Lane Hotel, St. James, ☎ 246/432–0931) offers one- and two-tank dives, night reef/wreck/drift dives, the full range of PADI instruction, and free transportation.

## Snorkeling

Gear for **snorkeling** can be rented for a small charge from nearly every hotel. Snorkelers can usually accompany dive trips for about $20 for a two-hour trip (☞ Scuba Diving, *above*).

## Squash

**Accra Beach Hotel and Resort** (⊠ Rockley, Christ Church, ☎ 246/435–8920) and **Almond Beach Village** (⊠ St. Peter, ☎ 246/422–4900) offer squash to guests. At **Club Rockley Barbados** (⊠ Rockley, Christ Church, ☎ 246/435–7880) nonguests can reserve courts for $10 per hour. At the **Barbados Squash Club** (⊠ Marine House, Christ Church, ☎ 246/427–7913), courts can be reserved at the rate of $9 for 45 minutes.

## Submarining

Minisubmarine voyages are enormously popular with families and those who enjoy watching fish without getting wet. The great-for-kids, 48-passenger *Atlantis III* turns the Caribbean into a giant aquarium. The 45-minute trip aboard the Canadian-built, 50-ft submarine takes you to wrecks and reefs as deep as 150 ft below the surface for a look at what even sport divers rarely see. The nighttime dives, using high-power searchlights, are spectacular. Classical music plays while an oceanography specialist informs during both day and night dives, either of which last about 90 minutes. ⊠ *Bridgetown Harbour, Spring Garden Hwy.,* ☎ 246/436–8929. ☞ $70.

Children will love the *Atlantis SEATREC* (Sea Tracking and Reef Exploration Craft), which allows passengers to "snorkel without getting wet!" The 46-passenger vessel has large viewing windows 6 ft below the surface where you can stay dry and still view the underwater marine life on a near-shore reef. ⊠ *Bridgetown Harbour, Spring Garden Hwy.,* ☎ 246/436–8929. ☞ $29.50.

## Surfing

The best **surfing** is available on the East Coast, and most wave riders congregate at the Soup Bowl, near Bathsheba. An annual international surfing competition is held on Barbados every September, when the surf is at its peak.

## Tennis

Most hotels have tennis courts that can be reserved day and night. Be sure to pack your whites, as appropriate dress is expected on the court. Public courts are available with no fee and no reservations at **Folkestone Park** (✉ Holetown, ☎ 246/422–2314) and at the **National Tennis Centre** (✉ Sir Garfield Sobers Sports Complex, Wildey, St. Michael, ☎ 246/437–6010) for $12 per hour with reservations.

## Waterskiing

Waterskiing is offered through **Blue Reef Watersports** at the Royal Pavilion Hotel, St. James (☎ 246/422–4444). **Private speedboat owners** troll for business along the waterfront in St. James and Christ Church, but keep in mind that with these independent operators, you water-ski at your own risk.

## Windsurfing

The best places to windsurf are at **Club Mistral**, Silver Sands Hotel, Maxwell (☎ 246/428–7277), **Silver Rock Windsurfing Club**, Silver Rock Hotel, Silver Sands Beach (☎ 246/428–2866), and **Windsurf Village Barbados**, Maxwell (☎ 246/428–9095), all on the southeast coast of the island, where the Barbados Windsurfing Championships are held mid-January. Barbados ranks as one of the best locations in the world for windsurfing—part of the World Cup Windsurfing Circuit.

Windsurfing boards and equipment are often guest amenities at the larger hotels and can be rented by nonguests. The **Windsurf Village Barbados** (✉ Maxwell Main Rd., Christ Church, ☎ 246/428–9095) caters specifically to windsurfing aficionados.

## Spectator Sports

### CRICKET

The island is mad for cricket, and you can sample a match at almost any time of year. Although the season is from May through late December, test matches are usually played from January through April. The newspapers give the details of time and place. Tickets to **cricket matches at Kensington Oval** range from $5 to $25.

### HORSE RACING

Horse racing takes place on alternate Saturdays, from January to March and May to December, at the **Garrison Savannah** in Christ Church, about 3 mi south of Bridgetown. ✉ *Christ Church*, ☎ *246/426–3980.* ✑ *$5.* ⊙ *1:30 on race days.*

### POLO

Polo matches are held at the **Polo Club** in Holders Hill, St. James (☎ 246/432–1802 or 246/421–6852), on Wednesdays and Saturdays from September to March for about $2.50. Hang around the club room after the match. That's where the lies, the legends, and the invitations happen.

### RUGBY

The rough-and-tumble game of rugby is played at the Garrison Savannah, and touring teams are always welcome; schedules are available from the **Barbados Rugby Club.** Contact Victor Roach (☎ 246/435–6543).

### SOCCER

The "football," or soccer, season runs from January through June at National Stadium. For game information contact the **Barbados Football Association** (✉ Box 1362, Belleville, St. Michael, ☎ 246/228–1707 or 246/228–0149).

# Shopping

Traditionally, **Broad Street** and its side streets in Bridgetown have been
the center for shopping. Stores are known for their high-quality merchandise, good service, and excellent value. Hours are generally weekdays 9–5 and Saturday 8–1. Branches of the largest Broad Street
fashion and department stores are at the Cruise Ship Terminal, at the
airport, and in large hotels. There are two **Chattel House Village** complexes (⊠ St. Lawrence Gap; Holetown), each a cluster of brightly colored shops where you can buy local products, rums and liqueurs,
hand-designed clothing, beachwear, and souvenirs. At the **Cruise Ship
Terminal** shopping mall, cruise-ship passengers can buy both duty-free
goods and Barbadian-made merchandise at dozens of shops, boutiques, and vendor carts and stalls. **DaCostas Mall** (⊠ Broad St.,
Bridgetown) has 35 shops that sell everything from Piaget to postcards.
The **Quayside Shopping Center** (⊠ Rockley, Christ Church, ☎ 246/428–
2474) is small but has a group of exclusive shops.

## Antiques

Barbadian and British antiques and fine memorabilia are the stock of
**Greenwich House Antiques** (⊠ Greenwich Village, Trents Hill, St.
James, ☎ 246/432–1169). It's a whole plantation house full of antique
Barbadian mahogany furniture, crystal, silver, china, and pictures and
is open daily from 10:30 AM to 6 PM.

**Antiquaria** (⊠ Spring Garden Hwy., St. Michael's Row, Bridgetown,
☎ 246/426–0635), a pink Victorian house next to the Anglican cathedral, sells antique silver, brassware, mahogany furniture, and maps and
engravings of Barbados. A branch is in Holetown, St. James (☎
246/432–2647), opposite Sandpiper Inn. They're both open every day
but Sunday.

## Boutiques

**Coconut Junction & Lazy Days** (⊠ Quayside Shopping Center, Rockley, ☎ 246/435–8115), actually two shops in one, have top-quality
beachwear, beach accessories, and beach equipment—including surf and
boogie boards.

Carol Cadogan's **Cotton Days Designs** (⊠ Ramsgate Cottage, Lower
Bay St., ☎ 246/427–7191) is a very upscale shop that sets the international pace with all-cotton collage creations that have been declared
"wearable art." These are fantasy designs, with prices that begin
around $250. Fortunately, she takes credit cards.

Another shop worth a visit is **Origins—Colours of the Caribbean** (⊠
The Careenage, ☎ 246/436–8522), where original hand-painted and
batik clothing, imported cottons, linens and silks for day and evening,
and handmade jewelry and accessories are the order of the day. The
hand-painted T-shirt dresses, priced at about $100, are fabulous.

**Signatures** (⊠ Broad St., Bridgetown, ☎ 246/431–5577) specializes
in cosmetics, fragrances, and skin care. On the first floor, the Beauty
Spa offers facials, massages, and consultations.

At **Sunny Shoes Inc.** (⊠ Cave Shepherd, Broad St., ☎ 246/431–2121)
concessionaire DeCourcey Clarke will make a pair of women's strap
sandals while you wait—in any color(s) you wish—for $26–$30.

## Duty-Free Luxury Goods

Bridgetown's **Broad Street stores** offer duty-free values on luxury goods,
such as fine bone china, crystal, cameras, porcelain, leather, stereo and
video equipment, jewelry, perfume, and clothing. Prices for many items
are often 30%–50% less than those back home. In order to purchase

items duty-free, visitors must produce ongoing travel tickets and a passport at the time of purchase—or you can have your purchases delivered free to the airport or harbor for pickup. Duty-free alcohol and tobacco products *must* be delivered to you at the airport or harbor.

**Cave Shepherd** (☎ 246/431–2121), the island's only true department store, offers a wide selection of tax-free luxury goods at five locations, including Broad Street, the airport, and the Cruise Ship Terminal.

**Correia's** (✉ Prince William Henry St., ☎ 246/429–5985), just off Broad Street, sells gold, diamond, and gemstone jewelry and watches—at 30% less than U.S. retail—under the watchful eye of Maurice and Marcelle Correia, certified gemologists.

**De Lima's** (✉ 20 Broad St., ☎ 246/426–4644) is the centerpiece of its own small mall and stocks high-quality imports. Among the specialty shops here are several jewelry stores and a few crafts stores.

**Harrison's** is a large specialty retailer with 11 locations on the island, including two large stores on Broad Street. Luxury name-brand goods from the fashion corners of the world are available at duty-free prices.

**Louis Bayley** is one of the fine shops at DaCosta's Mall, on Broad Street (☎ 246/430–4842), and has six other locations. You'll find perfume, jewelry and fine watches, cameras and audio equipment, Swarovski and Waterford crystal, and Wedgwood china at duty-free prices.

**The Royal Shop** (✉ 32–34 Broad St., ☎ 246/429–7072) carries fine watches and jewelry fashioned in Italian gold, Caribbean silver, diamonds, and other gemstones.

## Handicrafts

Island handicrafts are everywhere: woven mats and place mats, dresses, dolls, handbags, shell jewelry, wooden carvings, and local artwork.

**Best 'n the Bunch** (✉ St. Lawrence Gap, ☎ 246/428–2474) is in a brightly painted building at the Chattel House Village. Look here for jewelry designed and crafted by Bajan David Trottman.

The **Best of Barbados** shops (✉ Mall 34, Broad St., Bridgetown, ☎ 246/436–1416, and 11 other locations) offer the highest-quality artwork and crafts, both "native style" and modern designs. A local artist, Jill Walker, sells her watercolors and prints here.

**Earthworks** (✉ Edgehill Heights, No. 2, St. Thomas, ☎ 246/425–0223) is a family-owned and -operated pottery where you can purchase anything from a complete dinner service to a one-of-a-kind clay art piece.

**Pelican Village** (✉ Harbour Rd., between Cheapside Market and Bridgetown Harbour, ☎ 246/426–4391) offers bargains from local craftspeople. In a cluster of open-air, conical shops, you can watch as goods are crafted. Locally made handbags and leather goods, coconut-shell accessories, mahogany items, and grass rugs and mats are good buys.

For arts from Barbados and elsewhere in the Caribbean, visit the **Verandah Art Gallery** (✉ Broad St., Bridgetown, ☎ 246/426–2605).

At **Women's Self Help** (✉ Broad St., next to Nelson's Statue, ☎ 246/426–2570), you can find homemade embroidery and crochet work, shell art, baskets, children's clothes, jams and jellies, and candy.

# Nightlife and the Arts

## Nightlife

When the sun goes down, the musicians come out and folks go limin' in Barbados (anything from hanging out to a chat-up or jump-up). Competitions among reggae groups, steel bands, and calypso singers are major events, and tickets can be hard to come by—but give it a try.

Most of the large resorts have weekend shows for visitors, and there is a selection of dinner shows. The dinner show at the **Sherbourne Centre,** Barbados's convention center, is called "1627 and All That." It has a 17th-century Barbados theme and is performed by the energetic dancers of the Barbados Dance Theater. ⊠ *Two Mile Hill, east of Bridgetown, St. Michael,* ☎ *246/431–7600.* ⊴ *$50 for dinner, show, and open bar; $25 show only.*

Island residents have their own favorite nightspots. The most popular one is still **After Dark** (⊠ St. Lawrence Gap, Christ Church, ☎ 246/435–6547), with the longest bar on the island, a jazz-club annex, and an outdoor area where headliners appear live.

For the adventurous party-lover, a late-night (after 11) excursion to **Baxter Road,** "the street that never sleeps," is de rigueur for midnight Bajan street snacks, local rum, great gossip, and good storytelling. Enid & Livy's and Collins are just two of the long-standing favorite haunts.

**Club Xanadu** is a mid-December–April cabaret. David McCarty, who danced on Broadway and with the New York City Ballet, has joined forces with chanteuse Jean Emerson; on Thursday and Friday nights along with local strutters, they put on the hottest show in town. Dinner—served in the upstairs flower-decked dining room—and show cost $44; cabaret admission only, approximately $12.50. ⊠ *Ocean View Hotel, Hastings,* ☎ *246/427–7821. Reservations essential.*

Stop in for an evening of mellow jazz at **Cobbler's Cove.** ⊠ *Hwy. 1, St. Peter,* ☎ *246/422–2291.*

**Harbour Lights,** in a typical old Barbadian home, has a beachfront location. It claims to be the "home of the party animal" and, most any night, features dancing under the stars to live reggae and soca music. ⊠ *Marine Villa, Bay St., Bridgetown, St. Michael,* ☎ *246/436–7225.*

On Wednesday and Friday evenings at **Plantation Restaurant and Garden Theater,** the "Barbados Tropical Spectacular" calypso cabaret show features dancing, fire-eating, limbo, steel-band music, and the award-winning sounds of Spice & Company. The cost for a Barbadian cuisine dinner, unlimited drinks, transportation, and the show is $52.50; for the show and drinks only, you pay $25. ⊠ *St. Lawrence Rd., Christ Church,* ☎ *246/428–5048. AE, MC, V.*

For a more refined evening, enjoy dancing to a steel band or a string quartet at Sandy Lane Hotel's **Starlight Terrace.** ⊠ *Hwy. 1, St. Peter,* ☎ *246/432–1311.*

### BARS AND INNS

Barbados supports the rum industry in more than 1,600 "rum shops," simple bars where people (mostly men) congregate to discuss the world's ills, and in more sophisticated inns, where you'll find world-class rum drinks made with the island's renowned Mount Gay and Cockspur rums. **Bert's Bar** at the Abbeville Hotel (⊠ Rockley, Christ Church, ☎ 246/435–7924) serves the best daiquiris in town . . . any town. **The Boatyard** (⊠ Bay St., Bridgetown, ☎ 246/436–2622) stays open until the wee hours and is popular with both locals and visitors. **Bubba's Sports Bar** (⊠ Rockley Main Rd., Christ Church, ☎ 246/435–6217) has two satellite dishes, a 10-ft video screen, and 12 additional TVs where you can watch live sports action while sipping a Banks or enjoying a Bubba burger, or both. **Coach House** (⊠ Paynes Bay, St. James, ☎ 246/432–1163) is the only West Coast nightspot with live entertainment Tuesday through Saturday nights. Also try **Ship Inn** (⊠ St. Lawrence Gap, Christ Church, ☎ 246/435–6961), a friendly pub with live bands, and **Waterfront Cafe** (⊠ The Careenage, Bridgetown, ☎ 246/427–0093) for sophisticated jazz and dancing.

## The Arts

**Barbados Art Council.** The gallery shows drawings, paintings, and other art, with a new show about every two weeks. ⊠ *2 Pelican Village, Harbour Rd., Bridgetown,* ☎ 246/426–4385. ☞ *Free.* ☉ *Weekdays 10–5, Sat. 9–1.*

**Barbados Gallery of Art** (⊠ The Garrison, Bush Hill, St. Michael, ☎ 246/228–0149) opened in this location in 1996 with a permanent collection of 20th-century Barbadian and Caribbean fine art. Changing exhibitions are also on view.

The **Natural Cultural Foundation Gallery** (⊠ Queen's Park, Bridgetown, ☎ 246/427–2345), the island's largest gallery, is managed by the National Culture Foundation and presents monthlong exhibits.

A selection of private art galleries offers Bajan and West Indian art at collectible prices. The **Studio Art Gallery** (⊠ Fairchild St., Bridgetown, ☎ 246/427–5463) exhibits local work (particularly that of Rachael Altman) and will frame purchases.

# Exploring Barbados

The island is divided into 11 parishes. The terrain and vegetation change dramatically as you wander from parish to parish. So do the pace and ambience of each area. Bridgetown is a busy and sophisticated city. Gold Coast resorts and private homes ooze luxury, whereas the small villages and plantations scattered throughout the rest of central Barbados mark the island's history. The remote East Coast, with its cliffs and heavy surf, has been designed by the Atlantic Ocean. The northeast is called Scotland, because that's what it looks like. And along the lively South Coast, there's an energy that continues day and night.

The Barbados National Trust, headquartered at 10th Avenue, Belleville, St. Michael (☎ 246/426–2421), has designed the **Heritage Passport,** a 50% discounted admission to Barbados's most popular attractions and historic sites. A Full Passport includes 16 sites and costs $35; a Mini-Passport includes five sites and costs $18. Children under 12 are admitted free if accompanied by a Passport holder (maximum two children per passport). Passports may be purchased at hotels, Trust headquarters, or at the sites.

## Bridgetown

**❶ Bridgetown** is a bustling city and a major Caribbean duty-free port. The principal thoroughfare is Broad Street, which leads west from Trafalgar Square. The busy capital is complete with rush hours and traffic congestion. Sightseeing will take only an hour or so, and the shopping area is compact.

SIGHTS TO SEE
*Numbers in the margin correspond to points of interest on the Bridgetown map.*

❾ **Barbados Museum.** This intriguing museum, in the former Military Prison, has artifacts from Arawak days (around 400 BC) and mementos of military history and everyday life in the 19th century. You'll see cane-harvesting implements, lace wedding dresses, ancient (and frightening) dentistry instruments, and slave sale accounts kept in a spidery copperplate handwriting. Wildlife and natural history exhibits, a gift shop, and a good café are also here. ⊠ *Hwy. 7, Garrison Savannah,* ☎ *246/427–0201.* ⊡ *Bds$10.* ⊙ *Mon.–Sat. 9–5, Sun. 2–6.*

**8** **The Careenage.** The finger of sea that made early Bridgetown a natural harbor and a gathering place is where working schooners were careened (turned on their sides) to be scraped of barnacles and repainted. Today the Careenage serves mainly as a berth for pleasure yachts and charter boats. The two bridges over the Careenage are the Chamberlain Bridge and the Charles O'Neal Bridge.

**5** **Harry Bayley Observatory.** Built in 1963, this is the headquarters of the Barbados Astronomical Society. The observatory, equipped with a 14-inch reflector telescope, is rather unique in the Caribbean. ⊠ *Off Hwy. 6, Clapham,* ☎ *246/426–1317 or 246/422–2394.* ⊡ *$4.* ⊙ *Fri. 8:30 AM–11:30 PM.*

**2** **Jewish Synagogue.** This is the oldest synagogue in the Western Hemisphere. The original building, dating from 1654, was destroyed in a hurricane. It was rebuilt in 1833 and has recently been restored. ⊠ *Synagogue La.,* ☎ *246/426–5792.* ⊙ *Weekdays 9–4.*

**6** **Parliament Buildings.** Built around 1870, these buildings, adjacent to Trafalgar Square, house the third oldest Parliament of the British Commonwealth. A series of stained-glass windows depicting British monarchs from James I to Queen Victoria adorn these Victorian government buildings. Like so many smaller buildings in Bridgetown, they stand beside a growing number of modern offices.

**3** **Queen's Park.** Northeast of Bridgetown, Queen's Park has one of the largest trees in Barbados, an immense baobab more than 10 centuries old. The historic Queen's Park House, former home of the commander of the British troops, has been converted into a theater, with an exhibition room on the lower floor and a restaurant. ⊙ *Daily 9–5.*

**4** **St. Michael's Cathedral.** Although no one has proved it conclusively, George Washington, on his only visit outside the United States, is said to have worshiped at St. Michael's Cathedral, east of Trafalgar Square. The structure was built between 1784 and 1786 and survived the 1831 hurricane that devastated much of Barbados.

**7** **Trafalgar Square.** In the center of town, across from the Parliament Buildings and the Careenage, its monument to Lord Horatio Nelson predates Nelson's Column in London's Trafalgar Square by 27 years.

## The West Coast

Speightstown and Holetown are the island's other major towns (after Bridgetown, the capital). Holetown is the center of the Gold Coast resort area and the place where Captain John Powell landed in 1625 and claimed the island in the name of King James. The port city of Speightstown is more characteristically West Indian with its 19th-century architecture (many of the buildings have been restored or are undergoing work) and quaint shops and restaurants. The natural history of Barbados is also represented in the central parishes by fascinating caves, a mile-long gully, and beautiful tropical vegetation.

*Numbers in the margin correspond to points of interest on the Barbados map.*

SIGHTS TO SEE

**11** **Emancipation Memorial.** This larger-than-life statue of a slave—with raised hands, evoking both contempt and victory, and broken chains hanging from each wrist—is commonly referred to as the "Bussa Statue." Bussa was the man who, in the early part of the 19th century, led the first slave rebellion in Barbados. The statue's location at the

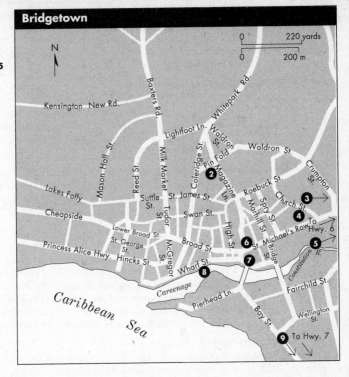

**Bridgetown**

St. Barnabas Roundabout (intersection of the ABC Highway and Highway 5, St. Michael), overlooking a broad expanse of cane field, makes the monument all the more moving.

**28** **Flower Forest.** Enjoy meandering through 8 acres of fragrant flowering bushes, canna and ginger lilies, puffball trees, and more than a hundred other species of flora in a tranquil setting. From this area, you can also have a beautiful view of Mt. Hillaby. ⊠ *Richmond Plantation, Hwy. 2, St. Joseph,* ☎ *246/433–8152.* 🎟 *$6.* ⊙ *Daily 9–5.*

**27** **Folkestone Marine Park & Visitor Centre.** On land and off there's a lot to enjoy here: A museum illuminates some of the island's marine life; and for some firsthand viewing, there's an underwater snorkeling trail around Dottin's Reef (glass-bottom boats are available for nonswimmers). A dredge barge sunk in shallow water is home to myriad fish, and it and the reef are popular with scuba divers. Also keep your eyes out for huge sea fans, soft coral, and the occasional giant turtle. ⊠ *Holetown, St. James,* ☎ *246/422–2314.* 🎟 *50¢. Closed Mon.*

**13** **Francia Plantation House.** Owned and occupied by descendants of the original owner, the house built in 1913 in a style that blends European and Caribbean influences. You can tour the house and gardens. ⊠ *St. George,* ☎ *246/429-0474.* 🎟 *$1.50.* ⊙ *Weekdays 10–4.*

**14** **Gun Hill Signal Station.** The view from Gun Hill is so pretty it seems almost unreal. Shades of green and gold cover the fields all the way to the horizon, the picturesque gun tower is surrounded by brilliant flowers, and the white limestone lion behind the garrison is a famous landmark. Military invalids were once sent here to convalesce. ⊠ *St. George,* ☎ *246/429-1358.* 🎟 *$4.* ⊙ *Mon.–Sat. 9–5.*

**30** **Harrison's Cave.** This pale-gold limestone cavern, complete with stalactites, stalagmites, subterranean streams, and a 40-ft waterfall, is an unusual find in the Caribbean. The one-hour tours are made by electric tram (hard hats are provided, but all that may fall on you is a little dripping water) and fill up fast, so you may want to reserve a spot ahead of time. ⊠ *Hwy. 2, St. Thomas,* ☎ *246/438–6640.* 🎟 *$7.50.* ⊙ *Daily 9–6; last tour at 4.*

**㉛ Mount Gay Rum Visitors Centre.** Take a 45-minute tour to learn the colorful story behind the world's oldest rum and about the rum-making process. The tour concludes with a tasting, and rum can be purchased at the gift shop. You can stay on for lunch if you wish. The center is just five minutes north of the port and downtown Bridgetown. ⊠ *Spring Garden Hwy.,* ☎ *246/425–8757.* 🎟 *$5.* ⊙ *Weekdays 9–4.*

**㉙ Welchman Hall Gully.** Part of the National Trust in St. Thomas, here's another chance to commune with nature. Acres of labeled flowers and trees stretch along in a mile-long natural gully, with the occasional green monkey showing itself and great peace and quiet. ⊠ *St. Thomas,* ☎ *246/438–6671.* 🎟 *$5.* ⊙ *Daily 9–5.*

## The East Coast

The Atlantic Ocean crashes dramatically against the East Coast of Barbados, where, over eons, the waves have eroded the shoreline into caves, arches, cliffs, and sea rocks that look like giant mushrooms. Narrow roads weave among the ridges, and small villages cling to hillsides that slide into the sea. Local people come to the coastal areas called Bathsheba and Cattlewash to spend weekends and holidays.

SIGHTS TO SEE

**★ ⑳ Andromeda Gardens.** A fascinating collection of unusual and beautiful plant specimens from around the world are cultivated in 6 acres of gardens nestled among streams, ponds, and rocky outcroppings in the cliffs overlooking the sea above the Bathsheba coastline. The gardens were created in 1954 with flowering plants collected by the late horticulturist Iris Bannochie. They are now administered by the Barbados National Trust. The Hibiscus Café serves snacks and drinks, and there's a Best of Barbados gift shop on the property. ⊠ *Bathsheba, St. Joseph,* ☎ *246/433–9384.* 🎟 *$5.* ⊙ *Daily 9–5.*

**㉕ Animal Flower Cave.** Small sea anemones, or sea worms, resemble jewellike flowers when they open their tiny tentacles. They live in small pools—some large enough to swim in—in a cave at the northern tip of Barbados. The view from inside the cavern as waves break just outside is magnificent. ⊠ *North Point, St. Lucy,* ☎ *246/439–8797.* 🎟 *$1.50.* ⊙ *Daily 9–4.*

**㉑ Barclays Park.** Just north of Bathsheba, this park was given to the people of Barbados by Barclays Bank. It offers a gorgeous view of the ocean, plus picnic facilities. At the nearby **Chalky Mount Potteries,** you'll find potters making and selling their wares.

**⑲ Codrington Theological College.** The coral-stone buildings and serenely beautiful grounds of Codrington College, an Anglican seminary founded in 1745, stand on a cliff overlooking Consett Bay. Visitors are welcome to tour the buildings and grounds, including a well-laid-out nature trail. Keep in mind, though, that this is a theological college and beachwear is not appropriate. ⊠ *St. John,* ☎ *246/433–1274.* 🎟 *$2.50.* ⊙ *Daily 10–4.*

**⑯ Rum Factory and Heritage Park.** A long entrance through the cane fields brings you to the first rum distillery to be built in Barbados in this century. Opened in late 1996 on a 350-year-old molasses and sugar plantation, the spotless, high-tech distillery produces ESA Field white rum and its premium Alleyne Arthur varieties. Adjacent is the 7-acre Heritage Park, which showcases Bajan skills and talents in its Art Foundry and Cane Pit Amphitheatre, along with an array of shops and carts filled exclusively with local products, crafts, and foods. ⊠ *Foursquare Plantation, St. Philip,* ☎ *246/423–6669.* ⚏ *$12.* ☉ *Sun.–Thurs. 9–5, Fri.–Sat. 9–9.*

**⓯ Sunbury Plantation House & Museum.** Lovingly rebuilt after a 1995 fire destroyed everything but the 2½-ft-thick flint-and-stone walls of this 300-year-old plantation house, Sunbury is once again an elegant representation of life on a Barbadian sugar estate in the 18th and 19th centuries. Period furniture has been donated to lend an air of authenticity. Plan to come for lunch (☞ Dining, *above*). ⊠ *St. Philip,* ☎ *246/423–6270.* ⚏ *$5 tour only; $12.50 with buffet lunch.* ☉ *Daily 10–5.*

## Northern Barbados

The northern reaches of the island, St. Peter and St. Lucy parishes, provide a range of terrain. Between the tiny fishing towns along the northwestern coast and the sweeping views out to the Atlantic Ocean on the northeastern coast are forest and farm, moor and mountain. Most guides include this loop on a daylong island tour—it's a beautiful drive.

SIGHTS TO SEE

**☝ ㉓ Barbados Wildlife Reserve.** The reserve is home to herons, land turtles, a kangaroo, screeching peacocks, innumerable green monkeys, geese, brilliantly colored parrots, and a friendly otter. The fauna are not in cages, so step carefully and keep your hands to yourself. The preserve has been much improved in recent years with the addition of a giant walk-in aviary and natural-history exhibits. Terrific photo opportunities are everywhere. ⊠ *Farley Hill, St. Peter,* ☎ *246/422–8826.* ⚏ *$10.* ☉ *Daily 10–5.*

**㉒ Farley Hill.** At this national park in northern St. Peter, across the road from the Barbados Wildlife Reserve, the imposing ruins of a once-magnificent plantation great house are surrounded by gardens, lawns, an avenue of towering royal palms, and gigantic mahogany, whitewood, and casuarina trees. Partially rebuilt for the filming of *Island in the Sun,* the 1957 film starring Harry Belafonte and Dorothy Dandridge, the structure was later destroyed by fire. Behind the estate, there's a sweeping view of the part of Barbados called Scotland for its rugged landscape. ⊠ *St. Peter.* ⚏ *$1.50 per car; walkers free.* ☉ *Daily 8:30–6.*

**㉔ St. Nicholas Abbey.** This property was named for a former owner, a prominent farmer with no religious connection to St. Nicholas. It is the oldest (circa 1650) great house in Barbados and is worth visiting for its stone-and-wood architecture—one of only three original Jacobean-style houses still standing in the Western Hemisphere. It has Dutch gables, finials of coral stone, and an herb garden in a medieval design. Fascinating home movies by the present owner's father record Bajan town and plantation life in the 1930s. ⊠ *Near Cherry Tree Hill, St. Lucy,* ☎ *246/422–8725.* ⚏ *$2.50.* ☉ *Weekdays 10–3:30.*

**㉖ Six Men's Bay.** On the northwest coast, on Highway 1 beyond Speightstown, a winding road takes you through tiny fishing and boatbuilding villages in what is truly picture-postcard Barbados—a far cry from the tourist areas.

## The South Coast

The heavily traveled south coast of Christ Church is much more built up than the St. James Parish coast in the west. Here you'll find St. Lawrence Gap, with its condos, high-rise hotels, beach parks, many places to eat and shop, and the traffic (including public transportation) that serves them.

Many chattel houses, the property of tenant farmers and typically Barbadian in style, are farther to the southwest. These ever-expandable houses were built to be dismantled and moved when necessary.

SIGHTS TO SEE

⑩ **George Washington House.** In 1751, long before the American Revolution, George Washington brought his brother Lawrence to Barbados to recover from tuberculosis. At this house at the top of Bush Hill, in the historic Garrison area south of Bridgetown, the brothers spent seven weeks, during which time poor George contracted smallpox.

⑫ **Oistins.** The major town along the South Coast of Barbados, Oistins is a fishing area where boats leave before dawn each morning and return to the waterfront fish market with their catches. The annual Oistins Fish Festival, held at the end of March, is a weekend of celebration, boat racing, arts and crafts, dancing, and singing.

⑱ **Ragged Point Lighthouse.** Appropriately named, this is where the sun first shines on Barbados and its dramatic Atlantic seascape. You can see the entire east coast from the lighthouse—particularly fascinating on a stormy day.

⑰ **Sam Lord's Castle.** The Regency house built by the buccaneer Sam Lord is considered by many to be the finest mansion in Barbados. Built in 1820 and now part of a resort (☞ Lodging, *above*), the opulent estate features double verandas on all sides and magnificent plaster ceilings created by Charles Rutter, who crafted the ceilings in England's Windsor Castle. Most of the rooms are furnished with the fine mahogany furniture and gilt mirrors Sam Lord is reputed to have acquired from passing ships that he lured onto treacherous reefs by hanging lanterns in palm trees to simulate harbor lights. ⊠ *Long Bay, St. Philip,* ☎ *246/423–7350.* ⊠ *$5; hotel guests free.* ☉ *Daily 10–4.*

# Barbados A to Z

## Arriving and Departing

### BY BOAT

Bridgetown's Deep Water Harbour is on the northwest side of Carlisle Bay. Barbados is a popular cruise port—half the annual visitors to the island are cruise passengers. Up to eight cruise ships can dock at one time at the snazzy **Cruise Ship Terminal.** Passengers can browse in 19 duty-free shops and 13 local retail stores in the terminal's attractive shopping arcade; a dozen vendors display their handcrafts in colorful reproductions of chattel houses just outside the building. Downtown Bridgetown is a ½-mi walk from the pier; a taxi costs about $3 each way.

### BY PLANE

**American Airlines** (☎ 246/428–4170 or 800/433–7300) and **BWIA** (☎ 246/426–2111 or 800/538–2942) both have nonstop flights between New York and Grantley Adams International Airport in Barbados and direct flights between Miami and Barbados. American serves Barbados from other U.S. cities with connecting flights through San Juan. **Air Jamaica** (☎ 800/523–5585) has daily nonstop service from New York. From Canada, **Air Canada** (☎ 246/428–5077 or 800/776–3000) flies nonstop from Toronto. From London, **British Airways** (☎ 800/247–9297) has nonstop service and BWIA connects through Trinidad.

Inter-island service is scheduled on **LIAT** (☎ 246/495–1187), **Air Martinique** (☎ 246/431–0540), and **BWIA; Air St. Vincent/Air Mustique** (☎ 246/428–1638) links Barbados with St. Vincent and the Grenadines.

FROM THE AIRPORT

**Airport taxis** are not metered. A large sign at the airport announces the fixed rate to each hotel or parish, stated in both Barbados and U.S. dollars (about $28 to Speightstown, $20 to West Coast hotels, $10–$13 to South Coast ones). The Adams-Barrow-Cummins (ABC) Highway bypasses Bridgetown, which saves time getting to the West Coast.

## Currency

The **Barbados dollar** (Bds$1) is tied to the U.S. dollar at the rate of Bds$2 to US$1. Both currencies are accepted island-wide. Prices quoted throughout this chapter are in U.S. dollars unless noted otherwise.

## Emergencies

**Emergency and Police:** ☎ 112. **Ambulance:** ☎ 115. **Fire:** ☎ 113. **Hospitals:** Queen Elizabeth Hospital, ⊠ Martindales Rd., St. Michael, ☎ 246/436–6450; Bayview Hospital (private), ⊠ St. Paul's Ave., Bayville, St. Michael, ☎ 246/436–5446. **Scuba-diving accidents:** Divers' Alert Network (DAN), ☎ 246/684–8111 or 246/684–2948. **24-hour decompression chamber:** ⊠ Coast Guard Defence Force, St. Ann's Fort, Garrison, St. Michael, ☎ 246/436–6185.

## Getting Around

BUSES

**Buses and maxitaxis** provide a great opportunity to experience local color, and your fellow passengers will be eager to share their knowledge. Blue buses with a yellow stripe are public, yellow buses with a blue stripe are private, and private maxitaxis may be any color. ZR vans, white with a burgundy stripe, are also private. All travel constantly along Highway 1 (St. James Road) and Highway 7 (South Coast Main Road) and are inexpensive (Bds$1.50 for any destination; exact change required on public buses, appreciated on private ones), plentiful, reliable, and usually packed. Bus stops are marked by small signs on roadside poles that say TO CITY or OUT OF CITY, meaning the direction relative to Bridgetown. Flag down the bus with your hand, even if you're standing at the stop; they don't always stop automatically.

CAR RENTALS

It's a pleasure to explore Barbados by car. Take time to study a map—although small signs tacked to trees and poles at intersections in the island's interior point the way to most attractions. The remote roads are in good repair, yet few are well lighted at night—and night falls quickly at about 6 PM. Even in full daylight, the tall sugarcane fields lining the road in interior sections can make visibility difficult. Use caution: Pedestrians often walk in the roads. And remember: Drive on the left, and be especially careful negotiating roundabouts (traffic circles).

To rent a car you must have an international driver's license or **Barbados driving permit,** obtainable at the airport, police stations, and major car-rental firms for $5 if you have a valid driver's license.

Nearly 30 offices rent **cars** or **minimokes** (open-air vehicles) for $75–$85 a day (or about $275 a week), usually with a three- or four-day minimum; rental cars with air-conditioning are $85–$90 a day, or approximately $275–$285 a week. The fee generally includes insurance and a local driver's license. All rental companies provide pickup and delivery service, offer unlimited mileage, and accept major credit cards.

**Gas** costs nearly $4 a gallon. The **speed limit,** in keeping with the pace of life, is 37 mph in the country, 21 mph in town.

Among the car-rental firms are **Dear's Garage** (⊠ Christ Church, ☎ 246/429–9277 or 246/427–7853), **National** (⊠ Bush Hall, St. Michael, ☎ 246/426–0603), **P&S Car Rentals** (⊠ St. Michael, ☎ 246/424–2052),

Sunny Isle (⊠ Worthing, ☎ 246/435−7979), and **Sunset Crest Rentals**
(⊠ St. James, ☎ 246/432−1482).

Scooters rent for about $31 a day for two-seaters, with a $100 refundable
deposit. Bicycles rent for about $10 a day, or $50 per week, with a $50
refundable deposit. Both are for rent at **FunSeekers** (⊠ Main Rd., Rockley, Christ Church, ☎ 246/435−8206).

**Taxis** operate at a fixed hourly rate of Bds$35 for up to three passen-
gers. For short trips, the rate per mile (or part thereof) should not exceed Bds$3. Settle the rate before you start off, and agree on whether
it's in U.S. or Barbados dollars. Most drivers will gladly narrate a tour.

## Guided Tours

Barbados has a lot to see. A half- or full-day bus or taxi tour is a good
way to get your bearings and can be arranged by your hotel. The price
varies according to the number of attractions included; an average full-
day tour (five–six hours) costs about $30–$50 per person and generally includes lunch and admissions.

**Bajan Helicopters** (⊠ Bridgetown Heliport, ☎ 246/431−0069) offers
an eagle's-eye view of Barbados. Price per person ranges from $65 for
a 20- to 25-minute "Discover Barbados" tour to $115 for a 30- to 35-
minute full "Island Tour".

Every Wednesday afternoon from mid-January through mid-April, the
**Barbados National Trust** (☎ 246/436−9033 or 246/426−2421) offers
a bus tour of historical great houses and modern private homes open
for public viewing. The cost is $17.50 per person, which includes ad-
missions to the houses and transportation to and from your hotel.

**Highland Outdoor Tours** (⊠ Canefield, St. Thomas, ☎ 246/438−8069)
specializes in adventure trips to the island's seldom-seen natural wonders. Visitors have the option of half-day or full-day horseback treks
(including a bareback ride in the surf), scenic hiking expeditions, and
tractor-drawn jitney rides through some of Barbados's great plantations. Prices range from $25 per person for a short, two-hour planta-
tion tour by open jitney to $100 per person for the 7-mi Horseback
Trek. A 5-mi Scenic Safari Hike is $70. All tours include refreshments
and transportation to and from your hotel.

**Mystic Mountain Bike Tours** (⊠ Prospect, St. James, ☎ 246/424−4730)
takes riders of all abilities on half- and full-day guided mountain-bike
excursions. Bikes and equipment, hotel transfers, lunch and refreshments, and a support vehicle are provided. Prices begin at $47.50.

**L. E. Williams Tour Co.** (☎ 246/427−1043) offers an 80-mi island tour
for about $50. A bus picks you up between 8:30 and 9:30 AM and takes
you through Bridgetown, the St. James beach area, past the Animal
Flower Cave, Farley Hill, Cherry Tree Hill, Morgan Lewis Mill, the
East Coast, St. John's Church, Sam Lord's Castle, and Oistin's fishing
village, and to the parish of St. Michael, with drinks along the way
and a West Indian lunch at the Atlantis Hotel in Bathsheba.

Sally Shearn operates **VIP Tour Services** (⊠ Hillcrest Villa, Upton, St.
Michael, ☎ 246/429−4617) and personalizes tours to suit your taste.
Bajan-born Ms. Shearn knows her island well and provides a swim at
her favorite beach. She picks up her clients in an air-conditioned Mer-
cedes-Benz and charges $30 per hour for four people, with a minimum
of five hours.

## Language

English is spoken everywhere. Some words spoken in the Bajan dialect have an almost Irish lilt.

## Opening and Closing Times

Bridgetown stores are open weekdays 9–5, Saturday 8–1. Out-of-town locations may stay open later. Some supermarkets are open daily 8–6 or later. Banks are open Monday–Thursday 8–3, Friday 8–5; at the airport, the Barbados National Bank is open from 8 AM until the last plane leaves or arrives, seven days a week (including holidays).

## Passports and Visas

To enter Barbados, U.S. and Canadian citizens need proof of citizenship and a return or ongoing ticket. Acceptable proof of citizenship is a valid passport or an original birth certificate and a photo ID; a voter registration card or baptismal certificate is not acceptable. British citizens need a valid passport.

## Precautions

Take normal precautions: Don't tempt people by leaving valuables unattended on the beach or in plain sight in your room, and don't pick up hitchhikers.

Insects aren't much of a problem on Barbados, but if you plan to hike or spend time on secluded beaches, it's wise to use insect repellent.

The little green apples that fall from the large branches of the manchineel tree may look tempting, but they are poisonous to eat and toxic to the touch. Even taking shelter under the tree when it rains can give you blisters. Most manchineels are identified with signs. If you do come in contact with one, go to the nearest hotel and have someone there phone for a physician.

The water on the island is plentiful and safe to drink in both hotels and restaurants. It is naturally filtered through 1,000 ft of pervious coral.

## Taxes and Service Charges

At the airport you must pay a departure tax of Bds$25 (about US$12.50) in either currency before leaving Barbados; there is no charge for children 12 and under. A 7½% government tax is added to hotel bills; a 10% service charge is added to hotel bills and to most restaurant checks. Any additional tip recognizes extraordinary service. When no service charge is added, tip maids $1 per room per day, waiters 10%–15%, taxi drivers 10%. Airport porters and bellboys expect US$50¢–$1 per bag.

## Telephones and Mail

The area code for Barbados is 246. Except for emergency numbers (☞ Emergencies, *above*) all phone numbers have seven digits and begin with 22, 23, 42, or 43.

An airmail letter from Barbados to the United States or Canada costs Bds90¢ per half ounce; an airmail postcard costs Bs65¢. Letters to the United Kingdom are Bds$1.10; postcards are Bds70¢. The main post office, in Cheapside, Bridgetown, is open weekdays 7:30–5; branches in each parish are open weekdays 8–3:15.

## Visitor Information

For information before you go, contact the **Barbados Tourism Authority. In the United States:** ⊠ 800 2nd Ave., 2nd floor, New York, NY 10017, ☎ 212/986–6516 or 800/221–9831, FAX 212/573–9850; ⊠ 2442 Hinge St., Troy, MI 48083, ☎ 810/740–7835, FAX 810/740–9434; ⊠ 3440 Wilshire Blvd., Suite 1215, Los Angeles, CA 90010, ☎ 213/380–2198, FAX 213/384–2763. **In Canada:** ⊠ 5160 Yonge St., Suite

1800, N. York, Ontario M2N–6L9, ☎ 416/512–6569 or 800/268–9122, ℻ 416/512–6581. **In the United Kingdom:** ✉ 263 Tottenham Court Rd., London W1P 0LA, ☎ 0171/636–9448, ℻ 0171/637–1496.

In Barbados, the **Barbados Tourism Authority** is on Harbour Road in Bridgetown (☎ 246/427–2623, ℻ 246/426–4080). Hours are 8:30–4:30 weekdays. Information booths, staffed by Tourism Authority representatives, are located at Grantley Adams International Airport (☎ 246/428–0937) and at Bridgetown's Cruise Ship Terminal (☎ 246/426–1718).

# 6 Bonaire

*Bonaire, long catering to divers drawn to the incredibly beautiful reefs in a marine system protected since 1979, is expanding its horizons. Now snorkelers, hikers, bikers, kayakers, and nature enthusiasts will find facilities and tours aimed specifically at their needs and interests. And there are also new luxury resorts on the island offering pampering, fine dining, and solitude for vacationers in search of rest and revitalization. Thankfully, the island is evolving into more than simply a dive destination, and visitors can now discover as much beauty above the waterline as below.*

Updated by
Melissa Rivers

**I**F ARUBA IS FOR THE HIGHEST ROLLERS, Bonaire is for the deepest divers—not to exclude the snorkelers, of course. Divers come to Bonaire as pilgrims to their holy land. Here, diving is learned, photographed, and perfected. Even the license plate says "A Diver's Paradise." The luxuriant reefs that encircle Bonaire have remained free of exploitation. The government, way back in 1979, when green was just becoming a color to be dealt with, designated all surrounding waters as a marine park and threw in a ban on spearfishing and coral collecting. The underwater park includes, roughly, the entire coastline, from the high-water tidemark to a depth of 200 ft, all protected by strict laws. Because the Bonairians desperately want to keep their paradise intact, any diver with a reckless streak is firmly requested to go elsewhere. Thanks to their foresight and strict diving regulations (including required warm-up dives with a local instructor), the world can enjoy Bonaire's underwater bounty.

Bonaire, on land, is a stark desert island, perfect for the individualist who is turned off by the overcommercialized high life of the other Antillean islands. The island boasts a spectacular array of exotic wildlife—from fish to fowl to flowers—that will keep nature watchers awestruck for days. It's the kind of place where you'll want to rent a four-wheel drive and go dashing off madly in search of flamingos, iguanas, or even the yellow-winged parrot named the Bonairian lora.

This little (112 square mi) island is for nature lovers and sports enthusiasts rather than gamblers, shopping maniacs, or lounge lizards. The island itself may be lacking in "resort splendor," but what lies off its shores keeps divers enthralled, and its unhurried pace pleases all in search of uninterrupted relaxation. With fewer than 14,000 inhabitants, the island has the feeling of a small community with a gentle pace. As the locals say, folks simply come here to dive, eat, dive, sleep, and dive. But, they also come to kayak, mountain bike, hike, snorkel, and simply soak in the sunshine and natural beauty of the island.

## Lodging

Hotels on Bonaire, with the exception of Harbour Village and Plaza Resort Bonaire, cater primarily to avid divers who spend their days underwater and come up for air only for evening festivities. Hence, hotel facilities tend to be modest, with clean but unadorned rooms, small swimming pools, a restaurant, and perhaps a bar. Services are often limited to laundry, baby-sitting, car rental, and travel services; unless noted below, room service is not typically available. Groomed sandy beaches are not a requisite for a hotel, but an efficient dive shop is. Many resort accommodations have fully equipped kitchens and in-room safes. Although the larger hotels offer a variety of meal plans, most are on the European Plan. As a general rule, hotel restaurants are more expensive than restaurants in town. There are, however, all-inclusive packages available at an extra per-day charge at many properties. Divers can take advantage of very good prices by comparing the packages offered by the hotels. Ask the tourist office (☞ *below*) for a listing.

The **Bonaire Government Tourist Office** (☎ 800/826–6247) can help you find suitable guest houses and smaller rental apartments. Rental apartments are also available through **T.L.C. Inns of Bonaire** (☎ 599/7–5516; 800/748–8733 in the U.S.; FAX 599/7–5517), **Bonaire Sunset Villas** (☎ 800/223–9815, FAX 599/7–8118), **Sunset Oceanfront Apartments** (☎ 800/223–9815, FAX 599/7–8865), **Club Laman Caribe** (☎ 599/7–

6840, FAX 599/7–7741), and **Black Durgon Inn Properties** (☎ 599/7–5736; 800/526–2370 in the U.S.; FAX 599/6–8846).

| CATEGORY | COST* |
|---|---|
| $$$$ | over $225 |
| $$$ | $150–$225 |
| $$ | $100–$150 |
| $ | under $100 |

*All prices are for a standard double room in high season, excluding a $6.50-per-person, per-night, government room tax, 6% VAT, and 10%–15% service charge.*

**$$$$** ★ **Harbour Village Beach Resort.** This upscale resort on a lovely palm tree–lined beach has it all, for divers and nondivers. Wide walkways bordered by lush foliage and blooming tropical flowers separate nine low-rise, Mediterranean-style buildings, with Moorish arches and red barrel-tile roofs. Pleasant rooms and suites are done in dusty rose and aqua with white tile floors and natural wood furniture and have French doors leading to a terrace or patio. A full-service European spa and fitness center offers every body treatment and an array of physical activities. There's also a water-sports center with dive shop, a tennis program, and a nine-hole golf course that was poised to open in 1998. It's so well run that even seekers of the quiet life will be satisfied. ⊠ *Kaya Gobernador Debrot, Box 312,* ☎ *599/7–7500 or 800/424–0004,* FAX *599/7–7507. 64 rooms, 8 oceanfront suites, 70 condominium units. 5 restaurants, 3 bars, café, refrigerators, room service, pool, outdoor hot tub, sauna, steam room, 4 tennis courts, aerobics, health club, beach, dive shop, marina, water sports, water taxi, bicycles, shopping arcade, library. AE, DC, MC, V. EP, MAP, FAP.*

**$$$$** **Plaza Resort Bonaire.** The opening of this new resort adjacent to the airport (there are no early-morning or late-night flights, so don't worry about sleeping soundly) brought a second luxury option to Bonaire. This flagship property of the Dutch Van der Valk hotel chain features lush tropical grounds winding around a man-made lagoon, a gorgeous stretch of beach, loads of resort amenities, an activities program, and the largest guest rooms available on the island. Terra-cotta tile floors, green rattan furnishings, and pastel floral bedspreads carry the tropical theme through. Bathrooms are enormous and equipped with deep bathtub, double sinks, and bidet. It's a large property, so take along your walking shoes. ⊠ *J. A. Abraham Blvd. 80,* ☎ *599/7–2500; 800/766-6016 for U.S. representative;* FAX *599/7-7133. 224 suites, 1- and 2-bedroom villas. 3 restaurants, 4 bars, café, refrigerators, room service, pool, wading pool, beauty salon, 4 tennis courts, aerobics, beach, marina, dive shop, water sports, bicycles, shops, casino. AE, DC, MC, V. EP, MAP, FAP.*

**$$$$** **Port Bonaire Resort.** Opened adjacent to the airport in late 1994, Port Bonaire is a group of luxury apartments and penthouses with patios or balconies that look out on the ocean (although there's no beach). The overall design, with tile roofs and pastel exteriors, is called Dutch Mediterranean. Families will find the fully equipped kitchens handy; they even have microwaves, dishwashers, and clothes-washing machines. Daily maid service is a welcome convenience. There are no facilities to speak of on the property, but guests can use those at the new sister Bonaire Plaza Resort next door (you'll need a rental car to get to the sister resort and into town). ⊠ *c/o Plaza Resort Bonaire, J. A. Abraham Blvd. 80,* ☎ *599/7–2500; 800/766-6016 for U.S. representative;* FAX *599/7–7133. 26 units. Pool. AE, DC, MC, V. EP.*

**$$$** ★ **Captain Don's Habitat.** Once a sort of extended home of Captain Don Stewart, the island's wildest sharp-shooting personality, Habitat can no longer pass itself off as a mere guest house for divers. Stewart's Curaçaoan

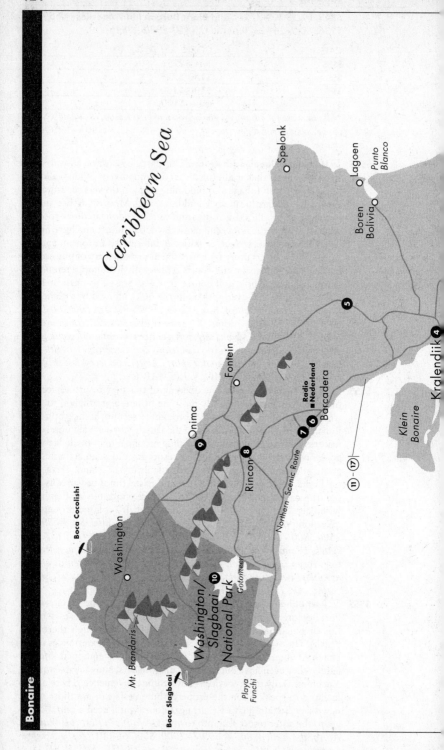

*Caribbean Sea*

Spelonk

Lagoen
*Punto
Blanco*

Boren
Bolivia

**5**

**Kralendijk 4**

Fontein

*Klein
Bonaire*

Onima
**9**

**Radio
Nederland**
**6** Barcadera

**7**

Rincon **8**

*Northern Scenic Route*

⑪ – ⑰

**Boca Cocolishi**

Washington

**10**

*Cotomeer*

*Washington/
Slagbaai
National Park*

*Mt. Brandaris*

**Boca Slagbaai**

*Playa
Funchi*

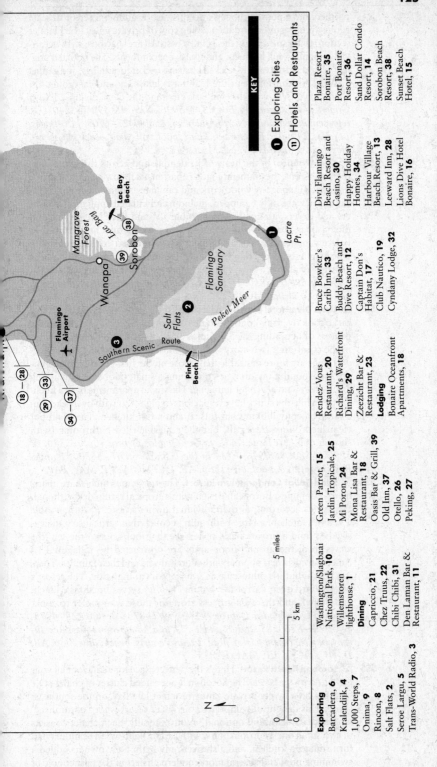

**KEY**

1 Exploring Sites

11 Hotels and Restaurants

Plaza Resort Bonaire, **35**
Port Bonaire Resort, **36**
Sand Dollar Condo Resort, **14**
Sorobon Beach Resort, **38**
Sunset Beach Hotel, **15**

Divi Flamingo Beach Resort and Casino, **30**
Happy Holiday Homes, **34**
Harbour Village Beach Resort, **13**
Leeward Inn, **28**
Lions Dive Hotel Bonaire, **16**

Bruce Bowker's Carib Inn, **33**
Buddy Beach and Dive Resort, **12**
Captain Don's Habitat, **17**
Club Nautico, **19**
Cyndany Lodge, **32**

Rendez-Vous Restaurant, **20**
Richard's Waterfront Dining, **29**
Zeezicht Bar & Restaurant, **23**

**Lodging**
Bonaire Oceanfront Apartments, **18**

Green Parrot, **15**
Jardin Tropicale, **25**
Mi Poron, **24**
Mona Lisa Bar & Restaurant, **18**
Oasis Bar & Grill, **39**
Old Inn, **37**
Otello, **26**
Peking, **27**

Washington/Slagbaai National Park, **10**
Willemstoren lighthouse, **1**

**Dining**
Capriccio, **21**
Chez Truus, **22**
Chibi Chibi, **31**
Den Laman Bar & Restaurant, **11**

**Exploring**
Barcadera, **6**
Kralendijk, **4**
1,000 Steps, **7**
Onima, **9**
Rincon, **8**
Salt Flats, **2**
Seroe Largu, **5**
Trans-World Radio, **3**

partners have poured money into this resort, adding a set of upscale rooms (junior suites) and then a long row of private villas (the Hamlet section) that rank among the island's best: All are spacious, with ocean-view verandas, full kitchens, and stylish appointments. The updated original 11 cottages have fully stocked kitchens, wicker furnishings, and garden views. The atmosphere at the Habitat is laid-back and easygoing (no rooms have TVs), with the emphasis on round-the-clock diving. ⊠ *Kaya Gobernador Debrot 103, Box 88,* ☎ *599/7–8290,* FAX *599/7–8240. U.S. representative: Habitat North American,* ☎ *800/327–6709. 11 cottages, 11 villas, 24 suites. Restaurant, 2 bars, pool, volleyball, beach, dive shop, bicycles. AE, D, MC, V. EP, MAP, FAP.*

$$$   🏨 **Club Nautico.** In the heart of Kralendijk and across the street from the waterfront, these amenity-laden apartments follow a nautical theme in the rich mahogany woodwork and cabinetry trimmed with brass fittings. They are fully equipped, including all kitchen appliances, washers and dryers, air-conditioning, cable TV, and have large living and dining areas, spacious bathrooms with deep soaker tubs, and a furnished balcony or terrace. A complimentary water taxi to Klein Bonaire whisks guests to pristine beaches in minutes and there are also boat charters available. ⊠ *Kaya Jan N.E. Craane 24, Kralendijk,* ☎ *599/7–5800,* FAX *599/7–5850. 15 1- and 2-bedroom apartments. Restaurant, bar, pool, marina. MC, V. EP.*

$$$   🏨 **Lions Dive Hotel Bonaire.** The successful Lions Dive group from Curaçao took over this condominium resort in mid-1996. Then began the process of upgrading the 31 studios and one- and two-bedroom suites in the coral-pink two-story buildings. For privacy, rooms on the second floor are more desirable than those on the first because the rooms are set around a quadrangle containing a small pool and sunbathing area—there's no beach for lounging. The studio apartments have a kitchenette, while the suites have a spacious living room with overhead fan, a large balcony looking out to sea, and a full kitchen. The plain but clean bedrooms are small, but their marble-tiled bathrooms (with shower only) are large. ⊠ *Kaya Gobernador Debrot 90, Box 380,* ☎ *599/7–5580; 888/546–6734 in the U.S.;* FAX *599/7–5680. 31 units. Restaurant, bar, pool, dive shop. AE, DC, MC, V. CP, MAP, FAP.*

$$$   🏨 **Sand Dollar Condominium Resort.** These spacious time-share apartments combine a European design with a tropical rattan decor, though this varies according to the individual owner's taste. Each has cable TV, a full kitchen, a large bathroom, a couch that turns into a queen-size bed, and a private patio or terrace that looks out to the sea (the views from the ground-floor units are obstructed by foliage). This American enclave is popular with serious divers and their families. There is a beach, but it's minuscule and disappears at high tide. The resort's waterfront Green Parrot (☞ Dining, *below*) serves breakfast, lunch, and dinner, and there's a grocery store for those who prefer to cook. ⊠ *Kaya Gobernador Debrot 79,* ☎ *599/7–8738 or 800/228–4773,* FAX *599/7–8760. 85 studios and 1-, 2-, and 3-bedroom units. Restaurant, bar, ice cream parlor, pool, 2 tennis courts, beach, dive shop. AE, D, DC, MC, V. EP, MAP, FAP.*

$$$   🏨 **Sorobon Beach Resort.** Here's the perfect place for acting out all your *Swept Away* fantasies. The Sorobon is a secluded cluster of chalet-style cottages on a lovely private sandy beach at Lac Bay, on the southeast shore. This delightfully unpretentious small resort is for "naturalists" who take its "clothing-optional" motto literally. Each chalet consists of two small one-bedroom units, with simple light-wood Scandinavian furnishings, a kitchen, and a shower-only bath. New owners added a swimming pool and several more modern chalets in the past couple of years, and expansion projects continue through 1998. In keeping with the get-away-from-it-all concept, there's no air-conditioning, TV, tele-

phone, or radio in the rooms. A daily shuttle will take you to town. ✉ *Box 14, Lac Bay,* ☎ *599/7–8080 or 800/828–9356,* FAX *599/7–5363. 30 rooms in 15 2-bedroom chalets. Restaurant, bar, fans, in-room safes, kitchenettes, beach, snorkeling, boating, library, laundry service, airport shuttle. AE, MC, V. EP.*

**$$–$$$** ⌧ **Divi Flamingo Beach Resort and Casino.** This plantation-style resort consists of a hotel and the Club Flamingo studio apartments, which have the newest and nicest rooms. It's the oldest hotel on the island— a former internment camp for German POWs during World War II, and even those rooms that have been "renovated" still cry out for new furnishings and another coat of fresh paint. However, its dive facility and upbeat activities programs still draw a fair share of repeat guests. The dive operation even has specially trained masters who teach scuba diving to individuals with disabilities and dive with them. ✉ *J. A. Abraham Blvd. 40,* ☎ *599/7–8285; 800/367–3484 for U.S. representative;* FAX *599/7–8238. 105 rooms, 40 time-share units. 2 restaurants, 2 bars, 2 pools, outdoor hot tub, tennis court, beach, 2 dive shops, casino. AE, D, MC, V. EP, MAP, All-inclusive.*

**$$** ⌧ **Bonaire Oceanfront Apartments.** These simply furnished one- and two-bedroom apartments overlook the sea at this small complex with pool, conveniently located just a three-minute walk from central Kralendijk. All of the apartments have cable TV, air-conditioned bedrooms, patio or balcony, and small, fully equipped kitchens. ✉ *Kaya Grandi, Kralendijk,* ☎ *599/7–4000 or 800/748–8733,* FAX *599/7–2211. 12 units. In-room safes, pool. MC, V. EP.*

**$$** ⌧ **Sunset Beach Hotel.** This 12-acre resort encompasses one of the island's better hotel beaches (though all rooms are set back from the beach, and even the best have only a garden view). There's also a water-sports concession and a thatched-roof seaside restaurant where the popular Bonairian Theme Night takes place on Saturday nights. Request one of the renovated rooms, which were gutted in 1996, replacing old wooden floors, funky colored furniture, and plumbing fixtures with tidy white tile floors, rattan furnishings, tropical-print curtains and bedspreads, and all new plumbing. ✉ *Kaya Gobernador Debrot 75, Box 333,* ☎ *599/7–8448 or 800/344–4439,* FAX *599/7–8118. 142 rooms, 3 1-bedroom suites. 2 restaurants, in-room safes, refrigerators, pool, 3 outdoor hot tubs, 2 tennis courts, Ping-Pong, shuffleboard, volleyball, beach, dive shop, water sports, dry cleaning and laundry service, travel services, car rental. AE, D, DC, MC, V. EP, FAP, MAP.*

**$–$$** ⌧ **Bruce Bowker's Carib Inn.** American diver Bruce Bowker started his
★ small diving lodge out of a private home, continually adding on to and refurbishing the air-conditioned inn, about a mile from the airport. Rattan furnishings, cable TVs, completely renovated kitchens, and a family-style atmosphere have turned his homey hostelry into one of the island's best bets, albeit one that gets booked far in advance by repeat guests. Bowker knows everybody by name and loves to fill special requests. Novice divers will enjoy Bowker's small scuba classes (one or two people); PADI (Professional Association of Diving Instructors) certification is available. The beach is just a sliver but is fine for shore entries. ✉ *Box 68,* ☎ *599/7–8819,* FAX *599/7–5295. 10 units. Refrigerators, pool, beach, dive shop. AE, MC, V. EP.*

**$–$$** ⌧ **Buddy Beach and Dive Resort.** Very reasonable rates and cozy, well-equipped accommodations keep guests coming back to enjoy this growing complex on the beach. The original 10 apartments, given a face-lift and air-conditioning in 1995, are small but clean, with a kitchenette, tile floors, twin beds, a sleep sofa, and a shower-only bathroom. Those facing northwest have million-dollar views of the ocean beyond the streams that wind through the resort's central garden. There are also four three-story buildings with studios, one-, two-, and three-bedroom apartments to choose from. ⊠ *Kaya Gobernador Debrot, Box 231,* ☎ *599/7–5080 or 800/786–3483,* FAX *599/7–8647. 40 studio and 1- to 3-bedroom condominium units. Restaurant, 2 pools, beach, dive shop. AE, D, MC, V. EP.*

$  🏠 **Cyndany Lodge.** If a plump wallet is more important to you than fancy beachfront accommodations, consider Cyndany Lodge, a small complex of basic motel-style rooms in a quiet residential area within walking distance of the beach and dive shop at the Divi Flamingo Beach Resort and Casino (☞ *above*). The tiled rooms are basic but clean and air-conditioned and outfitted with a refrigerator and wet bar. Inexpensive breakfast and lunch items are available at the small, open-air café in the courtyard. ⊠ *Kaya Inglatera 12,* ☎ *599/7–5516 or 800/748–8733,* FAX *599/7–5517. 12 rooms. Café. AE, MC, V. EP.*

$  🏠 **Happy Holiday Homes.** In a quiet residential area not far from the airport, this small complex of bungalows is an ideal budget option. The homey accommodations are spic-and-span clean and have a barbecue and deck furniture on the sun terrace or garden patio, fully equipped kitchen, living-dining area, air-conditioned bedrooms, and cable TV, all for under $100 per night. The friendly owners, Louise and Val Villanueva, go all out for their guests, from grocery shopping to arranging car rental or diving and windsurfing packages. ⊠ *Punt Vierkant 9,* ☎ *599/7–8405,* FAX *599/7–8605. 12 1- and 2-bedroom bungalows. In-room safes, laundry facilities, airport shuttle. MC, V. EP.*

$  🏠 **Leeward Inn.** American owners Don and Ditta Balstra have restored this 80-year-old guest house and modernized its six rooms. Those who eschew luxury in favor of basic amenities and budget rates come for the friendly service and the inexpensive meals at the on-site Harthouse Café. The pastel-painted rooms have light tile floors, twin beds, mix-and-match furniture, and modern bathrooms (shower only, except for one room). Television, refrigerator, and air-conditioning have been added to a few rooms (ceiling fans and breezes keep things cool in other rooms). The location, just three blocks from Kralendijk, is a block from the sea and a 10-minute walk to the Divi Flamingo beach. ⊠ *Kaya Grandi 60, Kralendijk,* ☎ *599/7–5516 or 800/748–8733,* FAX *599/7–5517. 5 rooms, 1 suite. Restaurant. AE, MC, V. EP.*

# Dining

With the steady increase in the number of restaurants on the island over the last several years, your dining options are more varied than ever. Menus cover anything from French, Continental, Mexican, Indonesian, and Chinese to Italian fare, and in just about every restaurant you'll have a fresh seafood choice brought in from the surrounding waters. In season, try the snapper, wahoo, or dorado (a mild white fish). Meat lovers will appreciate the Argentinian beef popping up on menus around the island, while vegetarians will be pleased with dishes prepared from the fresh fruits and vegetables shipped in from Venezuela. The other good news is that dining on Bonaire is far less expensive than on neighboring islands. Thankfully, other than a sandwich shop and a pizza parlor, fast-food joints have not yet hit the island.

## What to Wear

Dress on the island is casual but conservative. Most restaurants don't allow beachwear; even casual poolside restaurants prefer a sarong or cover-up.

| CATEGORY | COST* |
|---|---|
| $$$ | over $25 |
| $$ | $15–$25 |
| $ | under $15 |

*per person for a three-course meal, excluding drinks, 6% VAT, and 10%–15% service charge*

**$$$** ✕ **Chez Truus.** From this relaxed, café-style terrace, you can watch the people strolling the quiet waterfront across the street. You can have a drink at the bar while waiting for your meal, or even take in a game of billiards. There's an à la carte menu, imaginatively blending Caribbean influences with Continental standards such as dorado fillet with Brie in a light mustard sauce. A separate bar menu features smaller portions and lighter fare, including *sate*. Save room for Chez Truus's signature chocolate mousse, served chilled. Look for the landmark red British phone booth that sits outside the door. ✉ *Kaya C. E. B. Hellmund 5,* ☎ *599/7–8617. AE, MC, V. Closed Mon. No lunch.*

**$$$** ✕ **Jardin Tropicale.** The only elevator on the island whisks diners to
★ this rooftop restaurant. It's a quiet, romantic spot, with ivy and dichondra vining above windows framing views of the twinkling town lights below; it's also enclosed and air-conditioned, so come to relax over a leisurely meal. The menu is French, built around seasonal produce, seafood, and meat. Salad with chicken, mango, and coconut or Dutch smoked salmon and marlin are good starters. Follow up with fillet of sole with soufflé of lobster or filet mignon with red wine and heavy cream sauces. If you can't make up your mind, opt for the three-course, prix-fixe special menu. It wouldn't be a French restaurant without sinful desserts, so go all out and order the Grand Dessert (a sampler platter with a bit of everything). ✉ *La Terraza Shopping Center, Kaya Grandi,* ☎ *599/7–5718. MC, V. Closed Mon. No lunch.*

**$$–$$$** ✕ **Capriccio.** Classic Italian finally made its way to Bonaire with the
★ opening of this wonderful Italian-run eatery. The pastas are handmade daily, and there's a true climate-controlled wine cellar. You'll have a choice of casual à la carte dining on the terrace or a romantic, candlelit dinner in the tonier, air-conditioned dining room. If your appetite is hearty, go for the six-course, prix-fixe "tour of the menu." Otherwise, sure bets are the smoked fish appetizer, prosciutto with hearts-of-palm salad, pumpkin ravioli with sage and Parmesan, gnocchi al pesto, lamb with mustard sauce, and (surprisingly) turkey breast in sweet-and-sour sauce with stewed cabbage. Pizza, calzone, and other standards are, of course, available. ✉ *Kaya Isla Riba 1,* ☎ *599/7–7230. AE, MC, V. Closed Tues. No lunch Sun.*

**$$–$$$** ✕ **Mona Lisa Bar & Restaurant.** Here you'll find Continental fare, along with a few authentic Dutch and Indonesian dishes. The most popular plate is the pork tenderloin drizzled with peanut sauce. Somehow, Mona Lisa has become renowned for fresh vegetables. This is also a late-night hangout for local schmoozing and light snacks or fresh catch of the day, served until about 2 AM in the colorful bar adorned with various baseball-style caps. The intimate dining room, presided over by a copy of the famous painting of the smiling lady, is decorated with brick-and-iron grillwork, lace curtains, and whirring ceiling fans. ✉ *15 Kaya Grandi,* ☎ *599/7–8718. AE, MC, V. Closed weekends.*

**$$** ✕ **Chibi Chibi.** The Chibi Chibi, in an unusual, open-air, beach-facing wooden structure, is praised for its menu of local, American, and Continental fare. Try the fettuccine Flamingo (this is one of the Divi Flamingo Resort's restaurants) or the *keshi yena* (baked Gouda stuffed with meat or seafood and spices). Fish is also a specialty. ✉ *Divi Flamingo Beach Resort and Casino, J. A. Abraham Blvd. 40,* ☎ *599/7–8285. AE, D, MC, V. No lunch.*

$$    ✕ **Den Laman Bar & Restaurant.** A 6,000-square-ft aquarium provides the backdrop to this casual, nautically decorated restaurant. Eat indoors next to the glass-enclosed "ocean show" (request a table in advance) or outdoors on the noisier patio overlooking the sea. Pick a fresh Caribbean lobster from the tank or order red snapper Creole, a hands-down winner. Homemade cheesecake is a draw, as is the live entertainment each Saturday night. ⊠ *Kaya Gobernador Debrot 77,* ☎ *599/7–8955. AE, MC, V. Closed Tues. No lunch.*

$$    ✕ **Old Inn.** Potted plants surround the wicker chairs of this friendly restaurant across the street from the Plaza Resort Bonaire (☞ Lodging, *above*). The food is equally eclectic: French, barbecue, or Indonesian. Try the snails in garlic sauce, the *nasi goreng* (fried rice), or the pork medallions in mushroom sauce. ⊠ *J. A. Abraham Blvd., Kralendijk,* ☎ *599/7–6666. MC, V. No lunch.*

$$    ✕ **Otello.** This unpretentious Italian restaurant resides in an orange octagonal building a block off the main street downtown. The exterior belies the charming Mediterranean decor and romantic candlelit tables inside. Tagliatelle with creamy Parmesan and ground meat sauce is the signature pasta. There's also lobster or meat lasagna, shrimp in balsamic vinegar, and filet mignon with green peppers. An array of wines, cappuccino, and espresso helps round out the meal. ⊠ *Kaya Prinses Marie 4,* ☎ *599/7–4449. MC, V. Closed Mon.*

$$    ✕ **Rendez-Vous Restaurant.** The terrace of this café, draped with a canopy of electric stars, is the perfect place to watch the world of Bonaire go by as you fill up on warm, freshly baked French bread with garlic butter, hearty homemade soups, seafood, steaks, and vegetarian specialties. The Dutch pea soup, sautéed veggies baked in puff pastry, and sautéed squid, shrimp, or conch are the favorites. All-you-can-eat pork ribs draw a crowd on Wednesday. ⊠ *3 Kaya L. D. Gerharts,* ☎ *599/7–8454. AE, MC, V. Closed Sun.*

$$    ✕ **Richard's Waterfront Dining.** Animated and congenial owner Richard
★    Beady's alfresco eatery on the water is casually romantic and has become the most recommended restaurant on the island—a reputation that's well deserved. Richard, originally from Boston, sets the tone by personally checking on every table. The fresh daily menu is listed on large blackboards, and the food is consistently excellent, catering to American palates with flavorful, not spicy, preparations. Among the best dishes are conch *alajillo* (fillet of conch with garlic and butter), shrimp primavera, and grilled wahoo. Filet mignon béarnaise satisfies those seeking something other than creatures from the deep. ⊠ *60 J. A. Abraham Blvd.,* ☎ *599/7–5263. MC, V. Closed Mon. No lunch.*

$–$$    ✕ **Green Parrot.** This family-run restaurant, on the dock of the Sand Dollar Condominium Resort, serves the biggest hamburgers and the best strawberry margaritas on the island. Char-grilled steaks, Creole fish, and barbecued chicken and ribs go perfectly with the crispy onion loaf. Transplanted Englishman Kirk Gosden, who manages the place, has added theme dinner nights; Monday dine on Italian, Saturday come for the barbecue buffet. This is where you'll find both the American expatriates and tourists hanging out. ⊠ *Sand Dollar Condominium Resort, Kaya Gobernador Debrot 79,* ☎ *599/7–5454. AE, MC, V.*

$–$$    ✕ **Zeezicht Bar & Restaurant.** Zeezicht (pronounced *zay-zeekt* and meaning sea view) is one of the better restaurants in town open for three meals a day. At breakfast and lunch you'll get basic American fare with an Antillean touch, such as a fish omelet. Dinner is either on the terrace overlooking the harbor or in the homey, rough-hewn main room. Locals are dedicated to this hangout, especially for the seviche, conch sandwiches, and the Zeezicht special soup with conch, fish, shrimp, and oysters. ⊠ *Kaya Corsow 10, across from Karel's Beach Bar,* ☎ *599/7–8434. AE, MC, V.*

$ ✕ **Mi Poron.** Set in the breezy courtyard of a traditional Bonarian home, Mi Poron serves up the true flavor of the island, from stewed conch or goat to fried fish. As you pass through the house to the courtyard, take a moment to look at the decor and furnishings typical of Bonairian homes in the not-so-distant past. Mi Poron is a delicious step back in time. ⊠ *Kaya Caracas 1,* ☎ *599/7–5199. MC, V. Closed Mon. No lunch Sun.*

$ ✕ **Oasis Bar & Grill.** Near the far southern end of the island, the Oasis presents a harmonious blend of terra-cotta tile floors and comfortable rattan furnishings surrounding a half-moon bar. There's also an area for alfresco dining on the brick terrace. Caesar and Greek salad, popcorn shrimp, steak strips, burgers, and a variety of chicken preparations fill out the grill menu. This casual eatery is a favorite of those headed to Lac Bay for windsurfing. ⊠ *Kaminda Sorobon 64, Lac Bay,* ☎ *599/7–8198. AE, MC, V. Closed Mon.*

$ ✕ **Peking.** Of the half dozen Chinese restaurants on the island, locals prefer Peking. The air-conditioned dining room is not fancy: it's packed with round dining tables topped by lazy Susans, but you'll be glad they're there to give you easy access to the huge servings of delicious food. Chicken in black bean sauce, egg rolls, fried rice dishes, and other Cantonese standards are available, as are steaks, local seafood, and Indonesian dishes such as *nasi goreng*. Take-out is also an option. ⊠ *Kaya Korona,* ☎ *599/7–7170. AE, DC, MC, V. Closed Wed.*

# Beaches

Beaches in Bonaire are not the island's strong point. Don't come expecting Aruba-length stretches of glorious white sand. The island's beaches are smaller, and though the water is indeed blue (several shades of it, in fact), the sand is not always white. You can have your pick of beaches in Bonaire according to color: pink, black, or white. The best hotel beaches are found at Harbour Village, Sunset Beach, and Sorobon (the only clothing-optional beach on the island, reserved for the exclusive use of hotel guests).

Hermit crabs can be found along the shore at **Boca Cocolishi,** a black-sand beach in Washington/Slagbaai National Park on the northeast coast. This beach gives new meaning to the term "windswept": Cooling breezes whip the water into a frenzy as the color of the sea changes from midnight blue to aquamarine. The water is too rough for anything more than wading; however, the spot is perfect for an intimate picnic *à deux*. To get there, take the Northern Scenic Route to the park, and then ask for directions at the gate.

Inside Washington/Slagbaai Park is **Boca Slagbaai,** a beach of coral fossils and rocks with interesting coral gardens that are good for snorkeling just offshore. Bring scuba boots or canvas sandals to walk into the water, because the coral "beach" is rough on bare feet. The gentle surf makes it an ideal place for picnicking or swimming, especially for children. The exquisite ocher-and-russet building here houses a restaurant serving fine lunches Thursday through Sunday.

**Lac Bay Beach,** adjacent to the Sorobon Resort Beach, is *the* spot for windsurfing on Bonaire. There's a restaurant-bar at the far end near the bay entrance, and a couple of windsurfing-equipment rental outfits along the beach.

As the name suggests, the sand at **Pink Beach** has a pinkish tint that takes on a magical shimmer in the late-afternoon sun. The water is suitable for swimming, snorkeling, and scuba diving. Take the Southern Scenic Route on the western side of the island, past the Trans-World

Radio station, close to the slave huts. A favorite hangout for Bonairians on the weekend, it is virtually deserted during the week.

**Playa Funchi,** a Washington Park beach, is notable for the lagoon on one side, where flamingos nest, and the superb snorkeling on the other, where iridescent green parrot fish swim right up to shore.

## Outdoor Activities and Sports

### Deep-Sea Fishing
Captain Cornelis of **Big Game Sportfishing** (☎ 599/7–6500, FAX 599/7–5517) offers deep-sea charters for those in search of wahoo, marlin, tuna, swordfish, and sailfish. His rates, which cover bait, tackle, and refreshments, average $350 for a half day, $500 for a full day for up to four people. **Piscatur Charters** (☎ 599/7–8774) offers light-tackle angler reef fishing for jacks, barracudas, and snappers from a 15-ft skiff. Rates are $200 for a half day, $300 for a full day. The 42-ft sportfisherman *Piscatur* is available for charter at $350 for a half day, $500 for a full day, and carries up to six passengers. Bone fishing runs $200 for a half day.

### Horseback Riding
Hour-long trail rides at the 166-acre **Kunuku Warahama Ranch** (☎ 599/7–607324) take riders through groves of cactus where iguanas, wild goats, donkeys, and flamingos reside. Reserve one of the gentle pinto and palaminos a day in advance, and try to go earlier in the morning, when it's a bit cooler. There's an alfresco restaurant, a golf driving range, and two playgrounds for the kids to help fill the warmer afternoon hours.

### Mountain Biking
Twenty-one speed mountain bikes are the perfect way to explore the more than 180 mi of unpaved roads (in addition to the many paved roads) on Bonaire. Rentals (which include trail maps, water bottles, helmet, lock, repair, and first aid kits) and half-day and full-day guided excursions ($40 and $65 respectively, in addition to bike rental) are available from **Cycle Bonaire** (✉ Kaya L. D. Gerharts 11D, ☎ 599/7–7558).

### Scuba Diving
Bonaire has some of the best reef diving this side of Australia's Great Barrier Reef. In fact, the island is unique primarily for its incredible dive sites: It takes only 5–25 minutes to reach your site, the current is usually mild, and although some reefs have very sudden, steep drops, most begin just offshore and slope gently downward at a 45° angle. General visibility runs 60 to 100 ft, except during surges in October and November. An enormous range of coral can be seen, from knobby-brain and giant-brain coral to elkhorn, staghorn, mountainous star, gorgonian, and black coral. You're also likely to encounter schools of parrot fish, surgeonfish, angelfish, eels, snapper, and grouper. Beach diving is excellent just about everywhere on the leeward side of the island, so night diving is highly popular. There are dive sites here suitable for every skill level, from beginner to deep open-water to advanced wreck divers.

The well-policed Bonaire Marine Park, which encompasses the entire coastline around Bonaire and Klein Bonaire, remains an underwater wonder because visitors take the rules here seriously. Do not even think about (1) spearfishing; (2) dropping anchor; or (3) touching, stepping on, or collecting coral. Divers must pay an admission charge of $10, for which they receive a colored plastic tag (to be attached to an item of scuba gear) entitling them to one calendar year of unlimited diving in the marine park. The fees are used to maintain the underwater park. Tags are available at all scuba facilities and from the

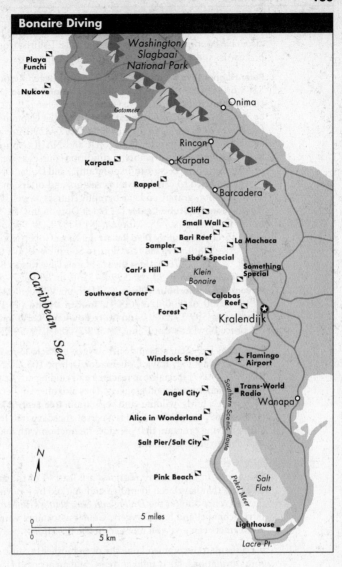

## Bonaire Diving

- Playa Funchi
- Nukove
- Washington/ Slagbaai National Park
- Gotomeer
- Onima
- Rincon
- Karpata
- Karpata
- Barcadera
- Rappel
- Cliff
- Small Wall
- Bari Reef
- La Machaca
- Sampler
- Ebo's Special
- Carl's Hill
- Klein Bonaire
- Something Special
- Southwest Corner
- Calabas Reef
- Forest
- Kralendijk
- Caribbean Sea
- Windsock Steep
- Flamingo Airport
- Angel City
- Trans-World Radio
- Wanapa
- Alice in Wonderland
- Salt Pier/Salt City
- N
- Pink Beach
- Pekel Meer
- Salt Flats
- Southern Scenic Route
- 5 miles
- 0
- 0   5 km
- Lighthouse
- Lacre Pt.

marine park headquarters in the Barcadera (☎ 599/7–8444). Check-out dives—diving first with a master before going out on your own—are required on the island and can be arranged through any dive shop. All dive operations on Bonaire now offer free buoyancy-control, advanced buoyancy-control, and photographic buoyancy-control classes. Check with any dive shop for the schedule.

There is a hyperbaric decompression chamber next to the hospital in Kralendijk (☎ 599/7–8187 or 599/7–8900 for emergencies).

### DIVE OPERATIONS

Bonaire hotels frequently offer dive packages, which include accommodations, boat trips, shore diving, air, and use of tanks. Ask the Bonaire tourist office for a brochure describing the various packages. Organized tours are not necessary on Bonaire, as many dive sites are easily accessible from shore and clearly marked by yellow stones on the roadside. Most hotels have dive centers: The competition for quality and variety is fierce. Before making a room reservation, inquire about specific dive/room packages that are available. Many of the dive shops also have boutiques where you can purchase T-shirts, tropical jewelry, postcards, and color slides showing underwater views.

**Peter Hughes Dive Bonaire** (⊠ Divi Flamingo Beach Resort, ☎ 599/7–8285 or 800/367–3484), **Sand Dollar Dive and Photo** (⊠ Sand Dollar Condominium Resort, Kaya Gobernador Debrot 79, ☎ 599/7–5252 or 800/288–4773), and **Habitat Dive Center** (⊠ Captain Don's Habitat, Kaya Gobernador Debrot 103, ☎ 599/7–8290) are all PADI dive facilities qualified to offer both PADI and NAUI (National Association of Underwater Instructors) certification courses as well as IDD (the primary European certification program). Sand Dollar Dive and Photo is also qualified to certify dive instructors and offers an array of underwater photography and videography courses as well. Other centers include **Bonaire Scuba Center** (⊠ Black Durgon Inn, ☎ 599/7–5736; in the U.S., ⊠ Box 775, Morgan, NJ 08879, ☎ 908/566–8866 or 800/526–2370), **Buddy Dive Resort** (⊠ Kaya Gobernador Debrot 85, ☎ 599/7–5080), **Dive Inn** (⊠ Close to South Pier, Kaya C. E. B. Hellmund, ☎ 599/7–8761), **Lions Dive** (⊠ Lions Dive Resort Bonaire, Kaya Gobernador Debrot 90, ☎ 599/7–5580 or 800/327–5425), **Great Adventures at Harbour Village** (⊠ Harbour Village Beach Resort, ☎ 599/7–7500 or 800/424–0004), **Toucan Diving** (⊠ Plaza Resort Bonaire, ☎ 599/7–2500), and **Bruce Bowker's Carib Inn Dive Center** (⊠ Bruce Bowker's Carib Inn, ☎ 599/7–8819, FAX 599/7–5295).

Americans Jerry Schnabel and Suzi Swygert of **Photo Tours N.V.** (⊠ Captain Don's Habitat, Kaya Gobernador Debrot 103, ☎ 599/7–5390, FAX 599/7–4089) specialize in teaching and guiding novice through professional underwater photographers. They also offer land-excursion tours of Bonaire's birds, wildlife, and vegetation. **Dee Scarr's Touch the Sea** (⊠ Box 369, ☎ 599/7–8529) is a personalized (two to four people at a time) diving program that provides interaction with marine life; it is available to certified divers.

DIVE SITES

The *Guide to the Bonaire Marine Park* lists 44 of the more than 80 dive sites that have been identified and marked by moorings. Another fine reference book is the *Diving and Snorkeling Guide to Bonaire* by Jerry Schnabel and Suzi Swygert. Guides associated with the various dive centers can give you more complete directions.

It's difficult to recommend one site over another because all have lush coral formations, fairly mild currents, and an array of fascinating marine life. The following are a few popular sites to whet your appetite; these and selected other sites are pinpointed on our Bonaire Diving map.

Take the trail down to the shore adjacent to the Trans-World Radio station; dive in and swim south to **Angel City,** one of the shallowest and most popular sites in a two-reef complex that includes Alice in Wonderland. The boulder-size green-and-tan coral heads are home to black margates, Spanish hogfish, gray snappers, and large purple tube sponges.

Go to the free slide show on Tuesday at the Sand Dollar Condominium Resort to catch a glimpse of the elkhorn and fire coral, queen angelfish, and other wonders of **Bari Reef,** just off the resort's pier.

**Calabas Reef,** off the Divi Flamingo Beach Resort, is the island's busiest dive site. All divers using the hotel's facilities make their warm-up dive here, where they can inspect the wreck sunk for just this purpose. The site is replete with Christmas-tree worms, sponges, and fire coral adhering to the ship's hull. Fish life is frenzied, with the occasional octopus putting in an appearance.

You'll need to catch a boat to reach **Forest,** a dive site off the coast of Klein Bonaire, so named for the abundant black-coral forest found there. This site gets a lot of fish action, including a resident spotted eel that lives in a cave.

**Rappel** is one of the most spectacular dives, near the Karpata Ecological Center. The shore is a sheer cliff, and the lush coral growth is home to an unusual variety of marine life, including occasional orange sea horses, squid, spiny lobsters, and spotted trunkfish.

**Small Wall** is one of Bonaire's three complete vertical wall dives. Located off the Black Durgon Inn, it is one of the island's most popular night-diving spots. Access is made by boat (Black Durgon guests can access it from shore). The 60-ft wall is frequented by squid, turtles, tarpon, and barracudas and has dense hard and soft coral formations; it also allows for excellent snorkeling.

**Something Special,** just south of the entrance of the marina, is famous for its garden eels, which wave about from the relatively shallow sand terrace looking like long grass in a breeze.

**Windsock Steep,** in front of the small beach opposite the airport runway, is an excellent shore dive ranging from 20 to 80 ft and a popular place for snorkeling close to town. The current is moderate, the elkhorn coral profuse; you may also see angelfish and rays here.

## Sea Kayaking

Sea kayaking has taken off in a big way in Bonaire, especially among divers and snorkelers, who use the kayak to reach new and different dive sites and simply tow the craft along during their dive. Nondivers use kayaks to explore the flora and fauna of the island's rich mangroves (use plenty of insect repellent before touring a mangrove). Guided trips and kayak rentals are available from **Sand Dollar Dive and Photo** (☎ 599/7–5252).

## Snorkeling

Don't consider snorkeling the cowardly diver's sport; in Bonaire the experience can be anything but elementary because the surface water tends to be choppy due to the trade winds. For only $6–$11 per day, you can rent a mask, fins, and snorkel at any hotel with a water-sports center (☞ Lodging, *above*). The better spots for snorkeling are on the leeward side of the island, where you have shore access to the reefs, and along the west side of Klein Bonaire, where the reef is better developed.

Bonaire, in conjunction with *Skin Diver Magazine,* developed the world's first **Guided Snorkeling Program** in 1996. The highly educational and entertaining program begins with a slide show presenting a variety of topics, from a beginner's look at reef fish, coral, and sponges to advanced fish identification, mangroves, and night snorkeling. Participants also preview the site they will visit with a certified snorkel guide. There are 12 sites, providing something suitable for all skill levels. Guided snorkeling can be arranged through most resort dive shops (☞ Lodging, *above*); the cost is $25 (discounts available for more than one session) and includes slide presentations, transportation to the site, snorkel gear, and a guided tour of the site.

## Swimming

Beaches good for swimming can be found anywhere along the western coast of the island. Excellent sites are **Pink Beach** and **Boca Cai.**

The best resort beaches are found at **Harbour Village Beach Resort, Sunset Beach Hotel,** and **Divi Flamingo Beach Resort and Casino.** Or take the **Seacow Water Taxi** (☎ 599/9–607126; $10 round-trip, minimum 2 passengers) from the Club Nautico Pier in Kralendijk to **Klein Bonaire,** an islet where you can spend the day playing king of the dune. Except for a few forgotten sneakers, there is absolutely *nothing* on Klein Bonaire, so remember to take some food, drink, and suntan lotion along. And don't miss the boat back home.

### Tennis

Tennis is available for free to the guests at the **Plaza Resort Bonaire, Sunset Beach Hotel, Divi Flamingo Beach Resort,** and the **Sand Dollar Condominium Resort** (☞ Lodging, *above*). Plan to play in the early morning or evening hours to avoid the worst of the day's heat.

### Waterskiing

**Club Nautico** (☎ 599/7–5800) and **Great Adventures at Harbor Village** (☎ 599/7–7500) can make arrangements for you to water-ski—from lessons on how to stay above the water to showing off for your friends. The cost is around $20 for 15 minutes of skiing.

### Windsurfing

Lac Bay, a protected cove on the east coast, is ideal for windsurfing. Novices will find it especially comforting since there's no way to be blown out to sea. **Windsurfing Bonaire,** known locally as Jibe City (☎ FAX 599/7–5363; ☎ 800/748–8733 for a U.S. representative), offers courses for beginning to advanced board sailors. Lessons cost $20; board rentals start at $20 an hour, $40 for a half day. There are regular pickups at all the hotels at 9 AM and 1 PM; ask your hotel to make arrangements. The **Bonaire Windsurfing Place** (☎ 599/7–2740 or 800/225–0102), commonly referred to as the Place, set up shop on Sorobon Beach in 1996. They rent the latest Mistral and Naish equipment for $35–$60 per hour. A two-hour lesson priced at $35 includes equipment rental; the three-day-lesson package is a real bargain at $150.

## Shopping

You can get to know all the shops in Bonaire in a matter of a few hours, but sometimes there's no better way to enjoy some time out of the sun and sea than to go shopping, particularly if your companion is a dive fanatic and you're not. Almost all the shops are on the Kaya Grandi or on adjacent streets and in tiny malls. There are several snazzy boutiques worth a browse. One word of caution: Buy as many flamingo T-shirts as you want, but don't take home items made of goatskin or tortoiseshell; they are not allowed into the United States.

### Cigars, Havana Style

Cigar smokers will find friends at **Little Holland** (✉ Harborside Mall, ☎ 599/7–5670) as they breathe in the smoky splendor of Havana cigars. Montecristo, H. Upmann, Romeo & Juliet, and Cohiba are in residence. Far from being banished to the porch, cigar smokers will be welcomed into a special acclimatized Cedar Cigar Room.

### Clothing

**Benetton** (✉ Kaya Grandi 19, ☎ 599/7–5107) has added Bonaire to its list of franchises in the Caribbean and makes the claim that prices here are 30% less than in New York. Colorful cotton resort wear is available at **Bye-Bye Bonaire** (✉ Harbourside Mall, ☎ 599/7–7578). **Best Buddies** (✉ Kaya Grandi 32, ☎ 599/7–7570) stocks a selection of Indonesian batik shirts and pareos, bathing suits, cover-ups, and Bonaire T-shirts.

## Perfume and Cosmetics

**Sparky's** (✉ Harborside Mall, ☎ 599/7–5288) sells name-brand, duty-free perfumes and makeup from Lancôme, Clinique, Estée Lauder, Chanel, Nina Ricci, and Ralph Lauren, to name a few.

## Souvenirs and Crafts

The **Bonaire Art Gallery** (✉ Kaya L. D. Gerharts 10, ☎ 599/7–7120) showcases the works (paintings, etchings, and jewelry) of local artists. **Donzie** (✉ Kaya Bonaire adjacent to Zeezicht Bar and Restaurant, ☎ 599/7–7642) offers unique jewelry created from island odds and ends (shiny beads, sun-bleached bones, and sea-polished colored glass) as well as local art, second-hand clothing, and antiques. Island tunes are available at **Mundo Musical** (✉ Kaya Grandi 13, ☎ 599/7–8174). **Littman Gifts** (✉ Kaya Grandi 35, ☎ 599/7–8091) is the place for batik cloth by the yard, European costume jewelry, T-shirts, framed underwater pictures, wooden divers, and glass flamingos. **Caribbean Arts and Crafts** (✉ Kaya Grandi 38A, ☎ 599/7–5051) offers unique Mexican onyx, papier-mâché clowns, woven wall tapestries, painted wooden fish and parrots, straw bags, and handblown glass vases. **Things Bonaire** (✉ Kaya Grandi 38C, ☎ 599/7–8423) offers T-shirts, shorts, colorful earrings, batik dresses, souvenirs, and guidebooks. A government-funded crafts center, **Fundashon Arte Industri Bonairiano** (✉ J. A. Abraham Blvd., Kralendijk, catercorner to post office, no phone) sells locally made necklaces of black coral, hand-painted shirts and dresses, and the "fresh craft of the day."

# Nightlife and the Arts

## Nightlife

Most divers are exhausted after they finish their third, fourth, or fifth dive of the day, which probably explains why there are so few discos in Bonaire. **Fantasy Disco** (✉ Kaya L. D. Gerharts 11, ☎ 599/7–6345) is the island's main dance spot. It's spacious, features big-screen TVs and taped merengue, jazz, rock, reggae, and occasional live performances. Lady's Night on Wednesday is very popular.

The popular bar **Karel's** (✉ Kaya J.N.E. Craane 12, ☎ 599/7–8434), on the waterfront across from the Zeezicht Bar and Restaurant, sits on stilts above the sea and is *the* place for mingling with islanders, dive pros, and tourists, especially Friday and Saturday nights, when there's live island and pop music.

The **Bonaire Twin Cinema** (✉ Kaya Prinses Marie, Kralendijk, ☎ 599/7–2400) opened in downtown Kralendijk in 1996. There are four to six showings a day of recent-release movies (primarily American hits, but occasionally there are films from Europe and Latin America). Tickets are $Naf10.

Happy hours are very popular on the island, especially at **Captain Don's Habitat** (✉ Kaya Gobernador Debrot 103, ☎ 599/7–8290) on Thursday night. The **Plaza Resort Bonaire** (✉ J. A. Abraham Blvd. 80, ☎ 599/7–2500) has its happy hour on Friday night. The music is live, and the drink specials keep coming.

For years the island had only one casino, the **Divi Flamingo Beach Casino** (☎ 599/7–8285), which opens at 8 PM and is closed Sunday. A newer and fancier casino opened at the **Plaza Resort Bonaire** (☎ 599/7–2500) in late 1995. At press time, the **Harbour Village Beach Resort** talked of opening a small but fancy casino sometime in 1998.

## The Arts

Slide shows of underwater and above-water scenes keep both divers and nondivers fascinated in the evenings. Dee Scarr, a dive guide, presents the fascinating "Touch the Sea" show Monday night at 8:45, from the beginning of November to the end of June, at **Captain Don's Habitat** (☎ 599/7–8290). Check with the Habitat for other shows (Bonaire Above and Below, Sea Turtles, Adventures of Captain Don, etc.) throughout the week. **Sunset Beach Hotel** (☎ 599/7–8448) offers slide shows on identifying sea critters Tuesday night at 8:45 and on the island's flora and fauna Thursday night at 8:15. Flora and fauna of the Caribbean are the focus of the slide show presented by naturalist Jerry Ligon Thursday night at 8:15 at the **Sand Dollar Condominium Resort** (☎ 599/7–8738).

Top performers on the island, including guitarist **Cai-Cai Cecelia,** the **Kunuku Band,** and **Duo Flamingo,** migrate among the island's top resorts to entertain throughout the week. Don't miss the Bonairian folklore nights, with live island music and dancing along with typical local foods, Tuesday night at 8 at **Captain Don's Habitat** (☎ 599/7–8290) and the **Sunset Beach Hotel** (☎ 599/7–8448) on Saturday at 7:30.

Check out the list of "Bonaire's Weekly Happenings" at the tourist information office or inquire at the front desk of your hotel for times and locations of activities.

# Exploring Bonaire

Two routes, north and south from Kralendijk, the island's small capital, are possible on the 24-mi-long island; either one will take from a few hours to a full day, depending upon whether you stop to snorkel, swim, dive, or lounge.

*Numbers in the margin correspond to points of interest on the Bonaire map.*

## Kralendijk

❹ Bonaire's capital city of **Kralendijk** (population 2,500) is five minutes from the airport and a short walk from Bruce Bowker's Carib Inn and the Divi Flamingo Beach Resort. There's really not much to explore here, but there are a few sights worth noting in this small, very tidy city.

Kralendijk has one main drag, J. A. Abraham Boulevard, which turns into **Kaya Grandi** in the center of town. Along it are most of the island's major stores, boutiques, restaurants, duty-free shops, and jewelry stores.

Across Kaya Grandi, opposite the Littman jewelry store, is Kaya L. D. Gerharts, with several small supermarkets, the ALM office, a handful of snack shops, and some of the better restaurants. Walk down the narrow waterfront avenue called Kaya C. E. B. Hellmund, which leads straight to the **North and South piers.** In the center of town, the Harbourside Mall has numerous chic boutiques. Along this route you will see **Fort Oranje,** with cannons pointing to the sea. From December through April, cruise ships dock in the harbor once or twice a week. The elegant white structure that looks like a tiny Greek temple is the **Fish Market;** local fishermen no longer bring their catch here to sell (they sell out of their homes these days), but you'll find plenty of fresh vegetables and fruits.

## South Bonaire

The trail south from Kralendijk is chock-full of icons—both natural and man-made—that tell the minisaga of Bonaire. Rent a four-wheel drive (a car will do, but during the rainy months the roads can become muddy, making traction difficult) and head south along the Southern Scenic Route. The roads wind through otherworldly desert terrain, full of organ-pipe cacti and spiny-trunk mangroves—huge stumps of salt-water trees that rise out of the marshes like witches. Watch for long-haired goats and lizards of all sizes.

SIGHTS TO SEE

**❷ Salt Flats.** When touring the southern section of the island, you can't miss the salt flats, voluptuous white drifts that look something like huge mounds of vanilla ice cream. Harvested once a year, the "ponds" are owned by the Akzo Nobel Salt Company, which has reactivated the 19th-century salt industry with great success. (One reason for that success is that the ocean on this part of the island is higher than the land—which makes irrigation a snap.) Keep a lookout for the three 30-ft obelisks—white, blue, and red—that were used to guide the trade boats coming to pick up the salt. Look also in the distance across the pans to the abandoned solar salt works that is now a designated **flamingo sanctuary.** With the naked eye, you might be able to make out a pink-orange haze just on the horizon; with binoculars you will see a sea of bobbing pink bodies. The sanctuary is completely protected, and no entrance is allowed (flamingos are extremely sensitive to disturbances of any kind), but if luck is on your side, somewhere along the far southern route you'll find some flamingos close enough to the road to hear and see more clearly.

**Slave Huts.** The gritty history of the salt industry is revealed in Rode Pan, the site of two groups of tiny slave huts. The white grouping is on the right side of the road opposite the Akzo Nobel Salt Works; the second grouping, called the red slave huts (though they appear yellow), stretches across the road a bit farther on toward the southern tip of the island. During the 19th century, the salt workers, imported slaves from Africa, worked the fields by day, then crawled into these huts at night to sleep. Each Friday afternoon, they walked seven hours to Rincon to weekend with their families, returning each Sunday to the salt pans. In recent years, the government has restored the huts to their original simplicity. Only very small people will be able to go inside, but take a walk around and poke your head in for a look.

**❸ Trans-World Radio.** The first landmark you'll come to on the Southern Scenic Route is an unexpected symbol of modernism—the towering 500-ft antennas of one of the most powerful stations in Christian broadcasting. From here, evangelical programs and gospel music are transmitted daily in five languages to all of North, South, and Central America, as well as the entire Caribbean.

**❶ Willemstoren Lighthouse.** At the southern tip of the island, Bonaire's first lighthouse was built in 1837 and is now automated (but closed to visitors). Take some time to explore the beach and notice how the waves, driven by the trade winds, play a crashing symphony against the rocks. Locals make a habit of stopping here to collect pieces of driftwood in spectacular shapes and to build fanciful pyramids from found objects washed ashore.

## North Bonaire

The Northern Scenic Route takes you right into the heart of Bonaire's natural wonders—desert gardens of towering cacti (*kadushi,* used to prepare soup, and the thornier *yatu,* used to build cactus fencing), tiny coastal coves, dramatically shaped coral grottoes, and plenty of fantastic panoramas. The road also weaves through spectacular eroded pink-and-black limestone walls and eerie rock formations with fanciful names like the Devil's Mouth and Iguana Head (you'll need a vivid imagination and sharp eye to recognize them).

A snappy excursion with the requisite photo stops will take about 2½ hours, but if you pack your swimsuit and a hefty picnic basket (forget about finding a Burger King), you could spend the entire day exploring this northern sector, including a few hours snorkeling in Washington/Slagbaai Park. Head out from Kralendijk on the Kaya Gobernador N. Debrot until it turns into the Northern Scenic Route. Note that once you pass the Radio Nederland radio towers, you cannot turn back to Kralendijk. The narrow road becomes one-way until you get to Landhuis Karpata, and you will have to follow the cross-island road to Rincon and return via the main road through the center of the island.

SIGHTS TO SEE

**❻ Barcadera.** Once used to trap goats, this cave is one of the oldest in Bonaire; there's even a tunnel that looks intriguingly spooky. It's the first sight along the northern route; watch closely for a yellow marker on your left before you reach the towering Radio Nederland antennas. Pull off across from the entrance to the Bonaire Caribbean Club, and you'll discover some stone steps that lead down into a cave full of stalactites and vegetation.

**Goto Meer.** This saltwater lagoon near the northern end of the island is a popular **flamingo hangout.** Bonaire is one of the few places in the world where pink flamingos nest. The spindly legged creatures—affectionately called "pink clouds"—at first look like swizzle sticks. But they're magnificent birds to observe—and there are about 15,000 of them in Bonaire. The best time to catch them at home is January through June, when they tend to their gray-plumed young. For the best view of these shy birds, take the newly paved access road running alongside the lagoon through the jungle of cacti to the parking and observation area on the rise overlooking the lagoon and Washington/Slagbaai Park beyond.

**Landhuis Karpata.** This mustard-color building was the landhouse of an aloe plantation over a hundred years ago. Notice the rounded outdoor oven where aloe was boiled down before exporting the juice. At press time, the Bonairian government was considering making Karpata a rest stop and drink stand, since there is nothing of the sort in this section of the island. We can only hope!

**❼ 1,000 Steps.** Once you've passed the Radio Nederland towers on the main road headed to the north end of the island, watch closely for a short yellow marker on the opposite side of the road to locate 1,000 Steps, a limestone staircase carved right out of the cliff. If you take the trek down them, you'll discover a lovely coral beach and protected cove where you can snorkel and scuba dive. Actually, you'll climb only 67 steps, but it feels like 1,000 when you walk up them carrying your scuba gear.

**❾ Onima.** Small signposts direct the way to the **Indian inscriptions** found on a 3-ft limestone ledge that juts out like a partially formed cave entrance. Look up to see the red-stained designs and symbols inscribed on the limestone, said to have been the handiwork of the Arawak Indians when they inhabited the island centuries ago. The pictographs were recently dated—they're at least 500 years old—and new descriptive placards were being erected at press time. To reach Onima, pass through Rincon on the road that heads back to Kralendijk, but take the left-hand turn before Fontein.

**❽ Rincon.** The original Spanish settlement on the island, Rincon became home to the slaves brought from Africa to work on the plantations and salt fields. Superstition and voodoo lore still have a powerful impact here, more so than in Kralendijk, where the townspeople work hard at suppressing the old ways. Rincon is now a well-kept cluster of pastel cottages and century-old buildings that constitute Bonaire's oldest village. Watch your driving here—both goats and dogs often sit right in the middle of the main drag. There are a couple of local eateries, but the real temptation is **Prisca's Ice Cream** (☎ 599/7–6334), to be found at her house on Kaya Komkomber (watch for the hand-lettered road sign).

**❺ Seroe Largu.** Just off the main road, this spot, at 394 ft, is one of the highest on the island. A winding path leads to a magnificent daytime view of Kralendijk's rooftops and the island of Klein Bonaire; at night, the twinkling city lights below make this a romantic stop. The road was recently paved, making the drive much easier.

**❿ Washington/Slagbaai National Park.** Once a plantation producing divi-divi trees (whose pods were used for tanning animal skins), aloe (used for medicinal lotions), charcoal, and goats, the park is now a model of conservation, designed to maintain fauna, flora, and geological treasures in their natural state. The 13,500-acre tropical desert terrain can easily be toured by the dirt roads. As befits a wilderness sanctuary, the well-marked, rugged roads force you to drive slowly enough to appreciate the animal life and the terrain. A four-wheel drive is a must. (Think twice about coming here if it rained the day before—the mud you may encounter will be more than inconvenient.) If you are planning to hike, bring a picnic lunch, camera, sunscreen, and plenty of water. There are two different routes: The long one, 22 mi (about 2½ hours), is marked by yellow arrows; the short one, 15 mi (about 1½ hours), is marked by green arrows. Goats and donkeys may dart across the road, and if you keep your eyes peeled, you may catch sight of large iguanas, camouflaged in the shrubbery.

Bird-watchers are really in their element here. Right inside the park's gate, flamingos roost on the salt pad known as **Salina Mathijs,** and exotic parakeets dot the foot of **Mt. Brandaris,** Bonaire's highest peak, at 784 ft. Some 130 species of colorful birds fly in and out of the shrubbery in the park. Keep your eyes open and your binoculars at hand. (For choice beach sites in the park, *see* Beaches, *above*.) Swimming, snorkeling, and scuba diving are permitted, but visitors are requested not to frighten the animals or remove anything from the grounds. There is absolutely no hunting, fishing, or camping allowed. A useful guidebook to the park is available at the entrance for about $6. ☎ 599/7–8444. ☎ $5. ☉ *Daily 8–5, but you must enter before 3.*

# Bonaire A to Z

## Arriving and Departing

BY PLANE

**ALM** (☎ 599/7–7400 or 800/327–7230) and **Air Aruba** (☎ 599/7–8300 or 800/882–7822) will get you to Bonaire. ALM has two nonstop flights a week from Miami, daily flights via Curaçao from Miami, and two flights a week from Atlanta tied in with United. ALM flies to Aruba, Curaçao, Jamaica, and St. Maarten, as well as other Caribbean islands, using Curaçao as its Caribbean hub. It also offers a Visit Caribbean Pass, which allows easy interisland travel. Air Aruba flies three days a week from Newark and daily from Miami to Aruba with connecting service to Bonaire. **United Airlines** (☎ 800/241–6522) offers connecting service with **Antillean Air** (☎ 599/7–8500 or 800/327–7230) from Miami twice a week.

FROM THE AIRPORT

Bonaire's Flamingo Airport is tiny, but you'll appreciate its welcoming ambience. The customs check is perfunctory if you are arriving from another Dutch isle; otherwise you will have to show proof of citizenship, plus a return or ongoing ticket. Rental cars and taxis are available at the airport, but try to arrange the pickup through your hotel. A taxi will run between $8 and $12 (for up to four people) to most hotels.

## Currency

The great thing about Bonaire is that you don't need to convert your American dollars into the local currency, the NAf guilder. U.S. currency and traveler's checks are accepted everywhere, and the difference in exchange rates is negligible. Banks accept U.S. dollar banknotes at the official rate of NAf1.78 to the U.S. dollar, traveler's checks at NAf1.80. The rate of exchange at shops and hotels ranges from NAf1.75 to NAf1.80. The guilder is divided into 100 cents. Note: Prices quoted here are in U.S. dollars unless indicated otherwise.

## Emergencies

**Police** and **Fire:** For emergency assistance call ☎ 599/7–80004. **Ambulance:** ☎ 599/7–8900. **Hospital: St. Franciscus Hospital,** Kralendijk (☎ 599/7–8900); there is a hyperbaric chamber for diving emergencies. **Pharmacies: Botika Bonaire** (☎ 599/7–8905) or **Botika Korona** (☎ 599/7–7552).

## Getting Around

You can zip about the island in a car or a four-wheel drive. Scooters and bicycles are less practical but can be fun, too. Just remember that there are miles of unpaved road (though several leading to sights of interest on the northern end of the island were paved in late 1995); the roller-coaster hills at the national park require a strong stomach; and during the rainy season, mud—called Bonairian snow—can be difficult to navigate. All traffic stays to the right, and, delightfully, there is yet to be a single traffic light. Signs or green arrows are usually posted to leading attractions; if you stick to the paved roads and marked turnoffs, you won't get lost.

BICYCLES

**Bonaire Bicycle & Motorbike Rental** (☎ 599/7–8226), **Hot Shot Rentals** (☎ 599/7–7166), and **Harbour Village Beach Resort** (☎ 599/7–7500) rent regular, hybrid, and Dutch touring bikes. For mountain bikes, try **Captain Don's Habitat** (☎ 599/7–8290 or 599/7–8913) or **Cycle Bonaire** (☎ 599/7–7558). Rates average around $15–$20 per day, and a credit-card or cash deposit is usually required.

CAR RENTALS

**Budget** (☎ 599/7–7424) rents cars, Suzuki minivans, and four-wheel drives at its six locations, but reservations can be made only at the head office. Pickups are at the airport (☎ 599/7–8315) and at several hotels. It's always a good idea to make advance reservations (☎ 800/472–3325 in the U.S., FAX 599/7–8865). Prices range from $35 a day for a Suzuki minivan to $60 a day for an automatic, air-conditioned four-door sedan. Other agencies are **Avis** (☎ 599/7–5795, FAX 599/7–5793), **Dollar Rent-a-Car** (☎ 599/7–8888, ☎ 599/7–5588 at the airport; FAX 599/7–7788), **Sunray** (☎ FAX 599/7–4888), **Avanti Rentals** (☎ 599/7–5661), **Netty's Car Rental** (☎ 599/7–5120), **Rich Car Rental** (☎ 599/7–5388, FAX 599/7–4421), and **AB Car Rental** (☎ 599/7–8980 or 599/7–5410, FAX 599/7–5034). There is a government tax of $3.50 per day per car rental.

SCOOTERS

Scooters are available from **Bonaire Bicycle & Motorbike Rental** (☎ 599/7–8226), **Avanti Scooters** (☎ 599/7–5661), and **Hot Shot Rentals** (☎ 599/7–7166). Single seaters cost around $26 per day or $130 per week, while double seaters run $32 per day or $175 per week.

TAXIS

Taxis are unmetered; they have fixed rates controlled by the government. A trip from the airport to your hotel will cost between $10 and $15 for up to four passengers. A taxi from most hotels into town costs between $5 and $8. Fares increase from 7 PM to midnight by 25% and from midnight to 6 AM by 50%. Taxi drivers are usually knowledgeable enough about the island to conduct half-day tours; they charge about $30 for up to four passengers for half-day northern- or southern-route tours. Call **Taxi Central Dispatch** (☎ 599/7–8100 or dial 10), or inquire at your hotel.

## Guided Tours

If you don't like to drive, **Bonaire Sightseeing Tours** (☎ 599/7–8778, FAX 599/7–4890) will chauffeur you around the island on various tours, among them a two-hour Northern Island Tour ($16), which visits the 1,000 Steps; Goto Lake; Rincon, the oldest settlement on the island, and Indian inscriptions at Onima; and a two-hour Southern Island Tour ($16), which covers Akzo Nobel Salt Company, a modern salt-manufacturing facility where flamingos gather; Lac Bay; and the oldest lighthouse on the island. A half-day city-and-country tour ($22) visits sights in both the north and south. **Baranka Tours** (☎ 599/7–2200, FAX 599/7–2211) offers similar tours at slightly less cost. **Ayubi's Tours** (☎ 599/7–5338) also offers several half- and full-day island tours. **Bonaire Nature Tours** (☎ 599/7–7714) offers full-day natural-history tours of Bonaire's Washington/Slagbaai National Park ($50, entrance fee and guided snorkeling included), 13,500 acres of majestic scenery, wildlife, unspoiled beaches, and tropical flora. Half-day cave and swamp tours are also available.

BOAT TOURS AND CRUISES

The Siamese sailing junk *Samur* (☎ 599/7–5433), the 56-ft privateer's ketch *Mistress* (☎ 599/7–8330), the sailing yacht *Lady Curzon* (☎ 599/7–2050), the 56-ft ketch *Sea Witch* (☎ 599/7–5433), and the trimaran *Woodwind* (☎ 599/7–8285) offer a variety of cruises for snorkeling, picnicking, and watching the sunset. Prices range from $25 to $50 per person. A private day's cruise on the sailboat *Oscarina* (☎ 599/7–8290 or 599/7–8988) is $350 for a party of four. A three-day Curaçao cruise aboard the *Sea Witch* runs $250 per person. The *Samur* features a seven-course Thai dinner cruise once each week; even at $90 per head, it always sells out well in advance. For those who prefer to skipper their own vessel, charter sailboats are available from **Club Nautico** (☎ 599/7–5800). Glass-bottom-boat trips are offered on the *Bonaire Dream* (☎ 599/7–8239 or 599/7–4514). The 1½-hour trip costs $23 and leaves twice daily, except Sunday, from the Harbour Village Marina.

## Language

The official language is Dutch, but few speak it, and even then only on official occasions. The street language is Papiamento, a mixture of Spanish, Portuguese, Dutch, English, African, and French—full of colorful Bonairian idioms that even Curaçaoans sometimes don't get. You'll light up your waiter's eyes, though, if you can remember to say *Masha danki* (thank you). English is spoken by most people working at the hotels, restaurants, and tourist shops, but a Spanish phrase book may come in handy.

## Opening and Closing Times

Stores in the Kralendijk area are generally open Monday through Saturday 8–noon and 2–6 PM. On Sundays and holidays, and when cruise ships arrive, most shops open for a few extra hours. Most restaurants are open for lunch and dinner, but few not affiliated with hotels are open for breakfast. Banks stay open from 8 to 4 Monday through Friday.

## Passports and Visas

U.S. and Canadian citizens need offer only proof of identity, so a passport, notarized birth certificate, or voter registration card will suffice. British subjects may carry a British Visitor's Passport, available from any post office; all other visitors must carry an official passport. In addition, any visitor who steps onto the island must have a return or ongoing ticket and is advised to confirm that reservation 48 hours before departure.

## Precautions

Because of violent trade winds pounding against the rocks, the windward (eastern) side of Bonaire is much too rough for diving. The *Guide to the Bonaire Marine Park* (available at dive shops around the island) specifies the level of diving skill required for 44 sites, knows what it's talking about. No matter how beautiful a beach may look, heed all warning signs regarding the rough undertow.

During Bonaire's "rainy season" (November–April), the mosquitos can be fierce. Smart, happy people douse themselves, including their arms, legs, and face, with repellent and also spray their hotel room before going to bed. Open-air restaurants usually have a can of repellent handy.

Get an orientation on what stings underwater and what doesn't. As the island's joke goes, you won't appreciate Bonaire until you've stepped on a long-spined urchin, but by then, you won't appreciate the joke.

Bonaire has a reputation for being one of the friendliest and safest island in the Caribbean, but lately, even residents are locking their car doors. Don't leave your camera in an open car, and leave your money, credit cards, jewelry, and other valuables in your hotel's safety-deposit box.

## Taxes and Service Charges

Hotels charge a room tax of $6.50 per person, per night, and many hotels (not all) add a 10%–15% maid service charge to your bill. Most restaurants add a 10%–12% service charge to your bill. VAT (Value Added Tax) of 6% went into effect in mid-1996, so tack that on to dining and lodging costs. There's no sales tax on purchases in Bonaire. Departure tax when going to Curaçao is $5.75. For all other destinations it's $10.

## Telephones and Mail

It's difficult for visitors to Bonaire to get involved in dramatic, heart-wrenching phone conversations or *any* phone discussions requiring a degree of privacy: Only about one-third of the major hotels have phones in their rooms, so calls must be made from hotel front desks or from the central telephone-company office in Kralendijk. Telephone connections have improved, but static is still common. To call Bonaire from the United States, dial 011–599–7 + the local four-digit number. When making interisland calls, dial the local four-digit number. Local phone calls cost NAf25¢.

At press time, airmail postage rates to the United States and Canada were NAf1.75 for letters and NAf90¢ for postcards; to Britain, Naf2.50 for letters and NAf1.25 for postcards.

## Visitor Information

Contact the **Bonaire Government Tourist Office** (✉ 10 Rockefeller Plaza, Suite 900, New York, NY 10020, ☎ 212/956–5911 or 800/826–6247, FAX 212/956–5913) for advice and information on planning your trip. Ask about diving packages, either including accommodations or not. In Bonaire, stop by the **Bonaire Tourist Board** (✉ Kaya Simon Bolivar 12, ☎ 599/7–8322 or 599/7–8649, FAX 599/7–8408) office for a map and list of weekly events.

# 7 The British Virgin Islands

*Tortola, Virgin Gorda, and Outlying Islands*

*The British Virgin Islands are a spectacularly beautiful cluster of mountainous islands, and although they are now regularly visited by cruise ships, they retain their quiet, laid-back, and friendly atmosphere.*

Updated by
Pamela
Acheson

**T**HE BRITISH VIRGIN ISLANDS consist of about 50 islands, islets, and cays that are serene, seductive, and spectacularly beautiful. Although at some points they lie only a mile or so from the U.S. Virgin Islands, the B.V.I. have managed to retain their quiet, friendly, and very laid-back character. It's true that the last five years have seen a huge increase in the number of automobiles and the construction of a cruise-ship dock, but for the most part the B.V.I. remain happily free of the runaway development that has detracted from the charm of so many other West Indian islands.

The pleasures to be found here are of the understated sort—sailing around the multitude of tiny, nearby islands; diving to the wreck of the RMS *Rhone*, sunk off Salt Island by a nasty hurricane in 1867; snorkeling in one of hundreds of wonderful spots; walking empty beaches; seeing some spectacular views from the island's peaks; and settling down on some breeze-swept terrace to admire the sunset.

One reason the B.V.I. have retained this sense of blissful simplicity is their strict building codes. No building can rise higher than the surrounding palms—two stories is the limit. The lack of direct air flights from the mainland United States also helps the British islands retain the endearing qualities of yesteryear's Caribbean. One first has to get to Puerto Rico, 60 mi to the west, or to nearby St. Thomas in the United States Virgin Islands and catch a small plane to the little airports on Beef Island/Tortola and Virgin Gorda. Many of the travelers who return year after year prefer arriving by water, either aboard their own ketches and yawls or on one of the convenient ferryboats that cross the turquoise waters between St. Thomas and Tortola. The B.V.I. government has approved a major expansion of the Beef Island/Tortola airport, which is scheduled for completion in 2003, so those seeking the simplicity of the B.V.I. might want to head here soon.

Tortola, about 10 square mi, is the largest of the islands, and Virgin Gorda, with 8 square mi, ranks second. The islands scattered around them include Jost Van Dyke, Great Camanoe, Norman, Beef Peter, Salt, Cooper, Ginger, Dead Chest, and Anegada, among others. Tortola is the most populated of the B.V.I. and has the largest number of hotels, restaurants, and shops. Virgin Gorda offers a limited number of restaurants and shops and resorts on the island are mostly self-contained. Jost Van Dyke has become a major charter boat anchorage, and although little bars now line the beach at Great Harbour, there are few places to stay overnight on the island. The other islands are either uninhabited or have a single hotel or resort, but many, like Peter Island, offer excellent anchorages and their bays and harbors are extremely popular with overnighting boaters.

Sailing has always been a popular activity in the B.V.I. The first arrivals here were a romantic seafaring tribe, the Siboney Indians. Christopher Columbus was the first European to visit, in 1493. Impressed by the number of islands dotting the horizon, he named them *Las Once Mil Virgines* (The 11,000 Virgins) in honor of the 11,000 virgin companions of Saint Ursula, martyred in the 4th century.

In the ensuing years, the Spaniards passed through these waters fruitlessly seeking gold. Then came the pirates, who found the islands' hidden coves and treacherous reefs an ideal base from which to prey on passing galleons crammed with Mexican and Peruvian gold, silver, and spices. The most notorious of these predatory men were Blackbeard Teach, Bluebeard, Captain Kidd, and Sir Francis Drake, who lent his name to the channel that sweeps through the two main clusters of the B.V.I.

In the 17th century, these colorful cutthroats were replaced by the Dutch, who, in turn, were soon sent packing by the British. It was the British who established a plantation economy and for the next 150 years developed the sugar industry. African slaves were brought in to work the cane fields while the plantation-owning families reaped the benefits. When slavery was abolished in 1838, the plantation economy quickly faltered, and the majority of the white population returned to Europe.

The islands dozed, a forgotten corner of the British empire, until the early 1960s. In 1966 a new constitution, granting greater autonomy to the islands, was approved. Although the governor is still appointed by the queen of England, his limited powers concentrate on external affairs and local security. Other matters are administered by the legislative council, consisting of representatives from nine island districts. General elections are held every four years. The arrangement seems to suit the British Virgin Islanders just fine: The mood is serene, with none of the occasional political turmoil found on other islands.

In the 1960s Laurance Rockefeller and American expatriate Charlie Cary brought the beginnings of tourism to the B.V.I. In 1965 Rockefeller set about creating the Little Dix resort on Virgin Gorda. A few years later, Cary and his wife, Ginny, established the Moorings marina complex on Tortola, and sailing in the area burgeoned. For a long time, tourism accounted for most of the B.V.I.'s income, but now offshore banking is the number one industry. However, the majority of jobs are still tourism-related. British Virgin Islanders love their unspoiled tropical home and are determined to maintain its easygoing charms, for both themselves and the travelers who are their guests.

# TORTOLA

## Lodging

The number of rooms available in the B.V.I. is small compared with that at other destinations in the Caribbean; what is available is also often in great demand, and the prices are not low. The top-of-the-line resorts here are among the most expensive in the Caribbean and are sometimes difficult to book even off-season. Even the more moderately priced hotels command top dollar during the season; off-season, however, they are legitimate bargains at about half the price. In addition, many of the hotels offer rates that include all three meals.

| CATEGORY | COST* |
|----------|-------|
| $$$$ | over $300 |
| $$$ | $200–$300 |
| $$ | $100–$200 |
| $ | under $100 |

*All prices are for a standard double room in high season, excluding 7% hotel tax and 10% service charge.

$$$–$$$$  ⊞ **Long Bay Beach Resort.** This is Tortola's finest hotel. The mile-long
★   arc of white sand from which this resort gets its name graces the front of many a B.V.I. postcard. A wide variety of accommodations includes 32 deluxe beachfront rooms, with two queen-size beds or one king-size four-poster bed, marble-top wet bars, and showers with Italian tiles. There are also smaller beach cabanas, 10 cozy, tropical hideaways set on stilts right at the water's edge. Hillside choices include small but adequate rooms, studios with a comfortable seating area, and roomy

one- and two-bedroom villas; all have balconies with lovely views. The Beach restaurant has a charming upper-level deck and offers all-day dining. The Garden restaurant serves gourmet dinners in a romantic, candlelit setting. There's a new fitness center, and Peter Burwash runs the tennis program. ⊠ *Box 433, Road Town,* ☎ *284/495–4252 or 800/729–9599,* FAX *284/495–4677. 62 rooms, 20 villas. 2 restaurants, 2 bars, pool, putting green, 2 tennis courts, beach, shop, meeting room. AE, MC, V. EP, MAP.*

$$$–$$$$ 🏨 **Sugar Mill Hotel.** The owners of this small, out-of-the-way hotel, Jeff and Jinx Morgan, opened it more than two decades ago after becoming well-established travel and food writers. The reception area, bar, and well-known Sugar Mill Restaurant are in the ruins of a centuries-old sugar mill and are decorated with bright Haitian artwork. Rather plain guest houses are scattered on the hillside; the rooms are furnished in soft pastels and rattan and have ceiling fans. Some have air-conditioning. (Light sleepers should request an air-conditioned room to block out the roosters, who start crowing long before dawn.) There's a small circular swimming pool set into the hillside and a tiny beach where lunch is served on a shady terrace. ⊠ *Box 425, Road Town,* ☎ *284/495–4355,* FAX *284/495–4696. 20 rooms. 2 restaurants, 2 bars, fans, pool, beach, snorkeling. AE, MC, V. EP, MAP.*

$$–$$$$ 🏨 **Moorings-Mariner Inn.** Headquarters for the Moorings Charter operation and popular with yachting folk who find its full-service facilities convenient and the companionship of fellow "boaties" congenial, this is also a good choice for those who want to be within easy walking distance of town. The atmosphere is a combination of laid-back and lively, and the rooms, including four suites, are large and comfortable. Rooms have peach tile floors and bright, tropical-print bedspreads and curtains; all also have a small kitchenette and a balcony. Most rooms face the water, except for eight, which overlook the pool or the tennis court. ⊠ *Box 139, Road Town,* ☎ *284/494–2331,* FAX *284/494–2226. 40 rooms. Restaurant, bar, kitchenettes, pool, tennis court, volleyball, dive shop, shop. AE, MC, V. EP.*

$$–$$$$ 🏨 **Prospect Reef Resort.** This brightly painted sprawling resort overlooks Sir Francis Drake Channel. There are 11 types of units, ranging from simple rooms to rooms with kitchenettes to two-story, two-bedroom units with private interior courtyards. All have a balcony or patio and face either the water or the hotel's gardens. There are 7 acres of neatly manicured grounds with creative rock paths and a network of lagoons. In addition to a large swimming pool and diving pool, Prospect Reef has a saltwater pool sectioned off from the sea with large rocks and a narrow, artificial beach. The resort has its own harbor, where sailboats are available for day trips or longer excursions. A special camp for kids is available. ⊠ *Box 104, Road Town,* ☎ *284/494–3311,* FAX *284/494–5595. 130 rooms. 2 restaurants, 2 bars, snack bar, 3 pools, wading pool, beauty salon, putting green, 6 tennis courts, beach, dive shop, snorkeling, shops, convention center. AE, MC, V. EP.*

$$–$$$$ 🏨 ★ **Treasure Isle Hotel.** Bright shades of lemon, violet, and mango pink cover the exterior of this pretty hillside property, which overlooks the harbor. The proximity of Road Town and several marinas makes this hotel a handy base. The air-conditioned rooms are spacious and accented with fabrics printed with Matisse-like patterns. Open to the breezes and the heady aroma of tropical flowers, the Spy Glass Bar with its comfortable lounge is the perfect place to relax and look out at a stunning view of the harbor and islands in the distance. There is daily transportation to Cane Garden Bay. ⊠ *Box 68, Road Town,* ☎ *284/494–2501,* FAX *284/494–2507. 40 rooms. Restaurant, 2 bars, air-conditioning, pool, scuba diving, boating. AE, MC, V. EP.*

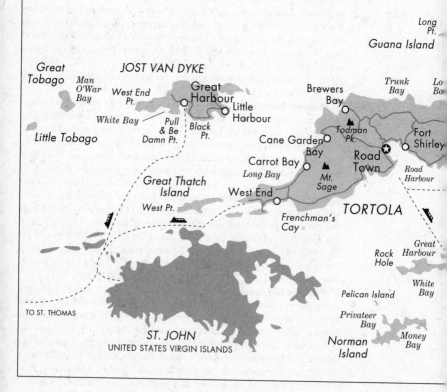

*ATLANTIC*

Long
Pt.
*Guana Island*

*Great
Tobago*    Man
O'War
Bay    West End
Pt.    JOST VAN DYKE    Great
Harbour    Little
Harbour    Brewers
Bay    *Trunk
Bay*    Lo
Ba

*White Bay*    Pull
& Be
Damn Pt.    Black
Pt.    Cane Garden
Bay    *Todman
Pk.*    Fort
Shirley

*Little Tobago*    Carrot Bay    Road
Town    *Road
Harbour*

*Long Bay*    Mt.
Sage

Great Thatch
Island    West End    TORTOLA

West Pt.    Frenchman's
Cay

*Great
Harbour*

Rock
Hole

*White
Bay*

Pelican Island

TO ST. THOMAS    *Privateer
Bay*

ST. JOHN    Norman
Island    *Money
Bay*
UNITED STATES VIRGIN ISLANDS

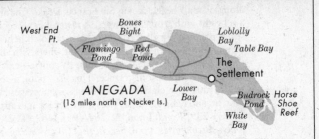

West End Pt.

Bones Bight

Loblolly Bay

Table Bay

Flamingo Pond

Red Pond

The Settlement

ANEGADA
(15 miles north of Necker Is.)

Lower Bay

Budrock Pond

Horse Shoe Reef

White Bay

O C E A N

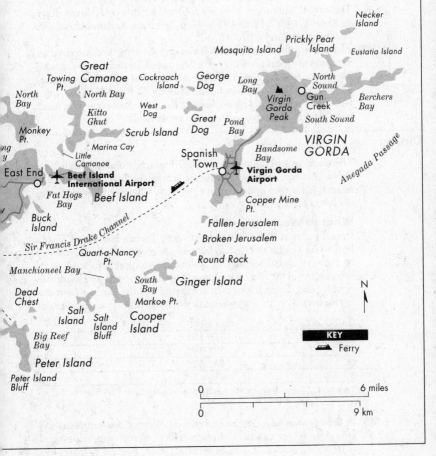

Necker Island

Prickly Pear Island

Mosquito Island

Eustatia Island

Great Camanoe

Towing Pt.

Cockroach Island

George Dog

Long Bay

North Sound

North Bay

North Bay

Kitto Ghut

West Dog

Virgin Gorda Peak

Gun Creek

Berchers Bay

Monkey Pt.

Scrub Island

Great Dog

Pond Bay

South Sound

VIRGIN GORDA

Marina Cay

Little Camanoe

Spanish Town

Handsome Bay

East End

Beef Island International Airport

Virgin Gorda Airport

Anegada Passage

Fat Hogs Bay

Beef Island

Copper Mine Pt.

Buck Island

Fallen Jerusalem

Sir Francis Drake Channel

Quart-a-Nancy Pt.

Broken Jerusalem

Manchioneel Bay

Round Rock

N

Dead Chest

South Bay

Ginger Island

Salt Island

Markoe Pt.

Cooper Island

Big Reef Bay

Salt Island Bluff

KEY

Peter Island

Ferry

Peter Island Bluff

0       6 miles

0       9 km

**$$–$$$$**  ⊞ **The Villas at Fort Recovery Estates.** The appealing one- to four-bed-
★   room bungalows here are built around the remnants of a Dutch fort,
along a small beach facing Sir Francis Drake Channel. The grounds
are bright with tropical flowers. A tasteful new second story features
seven penthouse villas. All units have patios, kitchens, and excellent
views. Although there's no restaurant, there is a dinner menu, and
three-course meals—delivered course by course—can be served in your
living room or on your terrace. There's a pool, a recently expanded
beach, plus yoga classes, exercise classes, massages, VCRs and videos
for rent, and baby-sitting services. Fitness packages are available as well.
⊠ *Box 239, Road Town,* ☎ *284/495–4467,* ℻ *284/495–4036. 17
units. Kitchenettes, pool, beach, shop, baby-sitting. AE, MC, V. EP.*

**$$–$$$**  ⊞ **Sebastian's on the Beach.** The best accommodations here are the
eight small rooms that open right onto the beach. They're airy and
white, simply decorated with floral-print curtains and bedspreads,
have either terraces or balconies, and great ocean views. There is no
air-conditioning, but ceiling fans and louvered windows keep the rooms
cool, and you are lulled to sleep by the sound of the ocean. Bathrooms
have only stall showers. The 18 rooms that don't face the beach are
very basic, lack views, and can be noisy. Some of these rooms are a
cross the street and are quite a bit cheaper than the beachfront rooms.
The casual restaurant here is excellent. ⊠ *Box 441, Road Town,*
☎ *284/495–4212,* ℻ *284/495–4466. 26 rooms. Restaurant, bar, fans,
beach, snorkeling, shop. AE. EP.*

**$**  ⌂ **Brewer's Bay Campground.** If you care to camp, both prepared and
bare sites are located on Brewer's Bay, one of Tortola's prime snorkel-
ing spots. Check out the ruins of the distillery that gave the bay its name.
There are public bathrooms but no showers. ⊠ *Box 185, Road Town,*
☎ *284/494–3463. 10 prepared and 18 bare sites. Restaurant, bar, beach,
windsurfing, shop, baby-sitting. No credit cards.*

# Dining

There's no lack of dining options on Tortola. Seafood is plentiful, and
although other fresh ingredients are scarce, the island's chefs are an
adaptable lot who apply creative genius to whatever the weekly sup-
ply boat delivers.

## What to Wear

Casual but neat is the way to go on both Tortola and Virgin Gorda.
Beachwear is a bit too casual, but nice shorts are fine during the day.
At the very casual restaurants, shorts are acceptable to wear in the
evening, but at the nicer restaurants long pants for men and sundresses
or chic resort wear for women are considered the norm. Resort din-
ing rooms may require a jacket; ask when you make your reservations.

| CATEGORY | COST* |
|---|---|
| **$$$$** | over $35 |
| **$$$** | $25–$35 |
| **$$** | $15–$25 |
| **$** | under $15 |

*per person for a three-course meal, excluding drinks and service; there is no
sales tax in the B.V.I.*

**$$$**  ✕ **Brandywine Bay.** For the best romantic dining, don't miss this hill-
★   side gem, where candlelit alfresco tables have a sweeping view of
neighboring islands. Italian owner-chef Davide Pugliese prepares food
the Tuscan way—grilled with lots of fresh herbs. The remarkable
menu, which hostess Cele Pugliese describes tableside, can include
homemade mozzarella, foie gras, grilled local wahoo, and grilled veal
chops with ricotta and sun-dried tomatoes. Roast duck, a specialty, is

served with an exotic sauce such as berry, mango, orange and ginger, or passion fruit. The lemon tart and the tiramisu are irresistible. There's also an excellent wine list. ⊠ *Sir Francis Drake Hwy., east of Road Town,* ☎ *284/495–2301. AE, MC, V. Closed Sun. No lunch.*

$$$  ✕ **Skyworld.** The longtime owner-chef of the well-known Upstairs
★  restaurant recently took over this mountaintop aerie and brought his superb menu with him. The sunset views here are breathtaking; watch the western horizon go ablaze with color, and then settle back in the casually elegant dining room to feast on some delectable cuisine. The superbly cooked filet mignon with peaches and an outstanding port wine sauce is truly exceptional. Other house specialties include a delicious lobster au gratin appetizer, grilled local fish, roast duck, and key lime pie. This is also a special place for lunch. Not only are the sandwiches on home-baked bread delicious, but the restaurant and the observation tower above offer the B.V.I.'s highest—and absolutely most spectacular—360-degree view of numerous islands and cays. Even St. Croix (40 mi away) and Anegada (20 mi away) can be seen on a clear day. ⊠ *Ridge Rd.,* ☎ *284/494–3567. AE, MC, V.*

$$$  ✕ **Sugar Mill Restaurant.** The candles gleam and the background music is pleasingly mellow in this well-known restaurant. The lovely stone dining room is built in the ruins of a centuries-old sugar mill. The copper cauldron that is now a bubbling fountain was once used for the mill's rum production. Well-prepared selections on the à la carte menu include pasta and vegetarian entrées. Oysters Caribe or wild mushroom bisque are good choices for starters. House favorite entrées include the Jamaican jerked pork roast with pineapple chipotle sauce, spicy Caribbean sausage with Creole sauce, mahogany glazed duck, and fresh local fish with herb butter. Although the setting is romantic, service here can be a bit on the speedy side. ⊠ *Apple Bay,* ☎ *284/495–4355. AE, MC, V. No lunch.*

$$–$$$  ✕ **Lime 'n' Mango.** A long open-air veranda is the romantic setting for this popular restaurant at the Treasure Isle Hotel. The menu features both local specialties and, surprisingly, authentic Mexican cuisine. Try the conch fritters, saltfish cakes, or Jamaican calamari for an appetizer. The fajitas (chicken, beef, or vegetarian), without a doubt the best Mexican entrée, arrive sizzling in a hot iron fry pan along with a basket of wraps. The coconut shrimp is also popular, and the Anegada lobster is always fresh. ⊠ *Treasure Isle Hotel, Road Town,* ☎ *284/494–2501. AE, MC, V.*

$$  ✕ **The Apple.** This small, inviting restaurant is in a West Indian house. Soft candlelight creates a relaxed atmosphere as diners sample fish steamed in lime butter, conch or whelk in garlic sauce, and other local seafood dishes. There is a traditional West Indian barbecue and buffet every Sunday evening from 7 to 9, and coconut chips and conch fritters are served at happy hour, from 5 to 7 on weekdays. The excellent lunch menu includes sandwiches, meat and vegetarian lasagna, lobster quiche, seafood crepes, and stuffed croissants. ⊠ *Little Apple Bay,* ☎ *284/495–4437. AE, MC, V.*

$$  ✕ **C and F Restaurant.** Just outside Road Town, on a side street past the Moorings, is one of the island's most popular restaurants. Crowds head here for the best barbecue in town (chicken, fish, and ribs), fresh local fish prepared any way you wish, and excellent curries. Sometimes you have to wait for a table, but it is worth it. ⊠ *Purcell Estate,* ☎ *284/494–4941. Reservations not accepted. AE, MC, V. No lunch.*

$$  ✕ **The Fishtrap.** Dine alfresco at this restaurant, which serves grilled local fish, steaks, and chicken plus Mexican and Asian selections. Friday and Saturday there's a barbecue with a terrific salad bar; prime rib is the special on Sunday. The lunch menu includes burgers and sal-

ads. ✉ *Columbus Centre, Wickham's Cay, Road Town,* ☎ *284/494–2636. AE, MC, V. No lunch Sun.*

**$$**   ✕ **Spaghetti Junction.** This funky spot is a hit with the boating crowd. Penne with a spicy tomato sauce, spinach-mushroom lasagna, and capellini with shellfish are house specialties here, but the menu also includes more traditional Italian fare (veal or chicken parmigiana, pastas, etc.). Sun-dried tomatoes in the Caesar salad are a nice twist. Check out the gorilla in the rest room. ✉ *Waterfront Dr., Road Town,* ☎ *284/494–4880. No credit cards. Closed Sept. No lunch.*

**$–$$** ✕ **Capriccio di Mare.** The owners of the well-known Brandywine Bay
★ restaurant (☞ *above*) also run this authentic Italian café. People stop by in the morning for an espresso and a fresh pastry and all day long for a cappuccino or a tiramisu, delicious toast Italiano (grilled ham and Swiss-cheese sandwiches), fresh salads, perfectly cooked linguine or penne with a variety of sauces, or crispy-crust tomato-and-mozzarella pizza topped with hot Italian sausage or fresh grilled eggplant. Try the Mango Bellini, a mango and Italian sparkling-wine mixture that's a variation on the famous Bellini Cocktail served by Harry's Bar in Venice. ✉ *Waterfront Dr., Road Town,* ☎ *284/494–5369. Reservations not accepted. No credit cards. Closed Sun.*

**$–$$** ✕ **Fort Wine Gourmet.** Tables are positioned to provide views through the French doors of this charming spot, which doubles as a gourmet deli. It's open all day and is a great place for an espresso or a cappuccino, a fresh pastry, or a tasty salad or sandwich. ✉ *Main St., Road Town,* ☎ *284/494–3036. Reservations not accepted. AE, MC, V.*

**$–$$** ✕ **Virgin Queen.** The sailing and rugby crowd and locals gather here to play darts, drink beer, and eat Queen's Pizza (some say it's the best pizza in the Caribbean) or some of the excellent West Indian and English fare. The delicious menu includes saltfish, barbecued ribs with beans and rice, bangers and mash (sausages and mashed potatoes), shepherd's pie, and chili. ✉ *Fleming St., Road Town,* ☎ *284/494–2310. Reservations not accepted. No credit cards. Closed Sun.*

# Beaches

Beaches in the B.V.I. are less developed than, say, on St. Thomas or St. Croix. You'll also find fewer people. Try to get out on a boat at least one day during your stay, whether a dive-snorkeling boat or a day-trip sailing vessel. It's sometimes the best way to get to the most virgin Virgin beaches on the less-populated islands (some have no road access).

Tortola's north side has a number of postcard-perfect, palm-fringed white-sand beaches that curl luxuriantly around turquoise bays and coves. Nearly all are accessible by car (preferably with four-wheel drive), albeit down bumpy roads that corkscrew precipitously. Facilities range from none to several beach bars with rest rooms.

**Apple Bay,** which includes **Little Apple Bay** and **Cappoon's Bay,** is the spot to go if you want to surf; good waves are never a sure thing, but January and February are usually high times here. The beach itself is pretty narrow. Sebastian's, the very appealing hotel here, caters especially to those in search of the perfect wave. ✉ *North Shore Rd.*

**Brewers Bay** is good for snorkeling. There's a campground here, but in the summer you'll find almost nobody around. The beach and its old sugar mill and rum-distillery ruins are just north of Cane Garden Bay (up and over a steep hill), just past Luck Hill. ✉ *Brewers Bay Rd. W or Brewers Bay Rd. E.*

**Cane Garden Bay** rivals St. Thomas's Magens Bay in beauty but is Tortola's most popular beach (it's the closest beach to Road Town) and one of the B.V.I.'s best-known anchorages. It's a grand beach for jogging if you can resist staying out of that translucent water. You can rent sailboards and such, and for noshing or sipping you can go to Stanley's Welcome Bar, Rhymer's, the Wedding, Myett's, or Quito's Gazebo, where local recording star Quito Rhymer sings island ballads four nights a week. For true romance, nothing beats stargazing from the bow of a boat, listening to Quito's love songs drift across the bay. ⊠ *Cane Garden Bay Rd.*

**Elizabeth Beach** is a wide beach lined with palm trees and is accessible by walking down a private road. The undertow can be severe here during the winter. ⊠ *Ridge Rd.*

**Josiah's Bay** is a favorite place to hang-10. The beach is wide and very often deserted and is a nice place to come for a quiet picnic, although in winter the undertow can be strong. ⊠ *Ridge Rd.*

**Long Bay (East)**'s scenery on Beef Island draws superlatives and is visited only by a knowledgeable few. There's a view of Little Camanoe and Great Camanoe islands, and if you walk around the bend to the right, you can see little Marina Cay and Scrub Island. Long Bay is also a good spot for interesting seashell finds. Take the Queen Elizabeth II Bridge to Beef Island and watch for a small dirt turnoff on the left before the airport. Follow the road that curves along the east side of the dried-up marsh flat—don't drive directly across the flat. ⊠ *Beef Island Rd.*

**Long Bay (West)** is a stunning mile-long stretch of white sand, and the road that leads to it offers panoramic views of the bay (bring your camera). Long Bay Beach Resort sits along part of it, but the whole beach is open to the public. The water is not as calm as that at Cane Garden or Brewer's Bay, but it is still very swimmable. ⊠ *Long Bay Rd.*

**Smuggler's Cove** is on Lower Belmont Bay. After bouncing your way to this beautiful beach, you'll really feel as if you've found a hidden paradise (although don't expect to be alone on weekends). Have a beer or a toasted cheese sandwich, the only items on the menu, at the *extremely* casual snack bar. There is a fine view of the island of Jost Van Dyke, and the snorkeling is good. ⊠ *Belmont Rd.*

**Trunk Bay** is directly north of Road Town, midway between Cane Garden Bay and Beef Island. About the only thing you'll find moving here is the surf. You'll have to hike down a *ghut* (gully) from the high Ridge Road. ⊠ *Ridge Rd.*

# Outdoor Activities and Sports

## Horseback Riding

Equestrians should get in touch with **Shadow Stables** (⊠ Ridge Rd., ☎ 284/494–2262), which offers small group rides down to the beaches or up in the hills. The **Ellis Thomas Riding School** (⊠ Sea Cows Bay, ☎ 284/494–4442) teaches riding but also has trips into Tortola's hills and along the beaches.

## Sailboarding

One of the best spots for sailboarding is at Trellis Bay on Beef Island. **Boardsailing B.V.I.** (⊠ Trellis Bay, Beef Island, ☎ 284/495–2447) has rentals, private lessons, and group rates.

## Sailing and Boating

The B.V.I. offer some of the finest sailing waters in the world, with hundreds of boats available for charter—with or without crew—as well as numerous opportunities for day sails.

The **Moorings** (✉ 1305 U.S. 19 S, Suite 402, Clearwater, FL 34624, ☎ 800/535–7289), based in Road Town, is the largest operator in the Caribbean and offers sailboats in a wide range of sizes, with or without crew. **Virgin Island Sailing** (✉ Box 146, Road Town, Tortola, B.V.I., ☎ 800/382–9666), a top brokerage house, is who to contact for help in chartering a boat and crew for an extended trip.

### Scuba Diving and Snorkeling

Good snorkeling can be found almost anywhere, and there are numerous diving sites. **Baskin-in-the-Sun** (✉ Box 108, Road Harbour, ☎ 284/494–2858 or 800/233–7938) rents equipment and offers instruction, snorkeling excursions, and day and night dives.

**Underwater Safaris Ltd.** (✉ Box 139, Road Town, ☎ 284/494–3235 or 800/537–7032), which rents snorkeling and diving equipment, has day and night dives seven days a week and many levels of instruction.

### Sportfishing

A number of companies can transport and outfit you for fishing. On Tortola try **Miss Robbie Charter Fishing** (✉ Fort Burt Marina, ☎ 284/494–3193).

### Tennis

Several resorts on Tortola have tennis courts for guests' use. For a fee, nonguests may use courts at **Prospect Reef** (✉ Road Town, ☎ 284/494–3311).

## Shopping

The British Virgins are not known as a shopping haven, but there are interesting finds, particularly artwork. Don't be put off by an informal shop entrance. Some of the best purchases in the B.V.I. lie behind a shop-worn door.

### Shopping Districts

Most of the shops on Tortola are clustered on and off Road Town's **Main Street** and at **Wickham's Cay** shopping area, adjacent to the marina. There is also an ever-growing group of art, jewelry, clothing, and souvenir stores at **Soper's Hole** on Tortola's West End.

### Specialty Stores

ART AND ANTIQUES

**Caribbean Fine Arts Ltd.** (✉ Main St., Road Town, ☎ 284/494–4240) is a small shop with a wide range of Caribbean art, including original watercolors, oils, and acrylics, as well as signed prints, limited-edition serigraphs, and turn-of-the-century sepia photographs. **Collector's Corner** (✉ Columbus Centre, Wickham's Cay, ☎ 284/494–3550) carries antique maps, watercolors by local artists, gold and silver jewelry, coral, and larimar, a pale blue Caribbean gemstone. **Islands Treasures** (✉ Soper's Hole Marina, ☎ 284/495–4787) is the place to find watercolors, paintings, pottery, sculpture, model ships, coffee-table books on the Caribbean, and prints of Caribbean maps and scenes. **Sunny Caribbee Art Gallery** (✉ Main St., Road Town, ☎ 284/494–2178) has one of the largest displays in the Caribbean of paintings, prints, and watercolors by artists from virtually all of the Caribbean islands.

CLOTHING

**Arawak** (✉ On the dock at Nanny Cay, ☎ 284/494–5240) carries gifts, sportswear, and resort wear for men and women, accessories, and children's clothing. **Domino** (✉ Main St., Road Town, ☎ 284/494–5879) features a colorful array of comfortable, light cotton clothing (some from Indonesia) as well as island jewelry and gift items. **Sea Urchin** (✉ Columbus Centre, Road Town, ☎ 284/494–2044; ✉ Waterfront

Dr., Road Town, ☎ 284/494–6234; ⊠ Soper's Hole Marina, ☎ 284/ 495–4850) has a great selection of island-living designs: print shirts and shorts, slinky swimsuits, sandals, and T-shirts, plus books and maps of the B.V.I. **Violet's** (⊠ Wickham's Cay I, ☎ 284/494–6398) stocks beautiful silk lingerie and a small line of designer dresses.

### FOOD AND DRINK

**Ample Hamper** (⊠ Village Cay Marina, Wickham's Cay, ☎ 284/494– 2494; ⊠ Soper's Hole Marina, ☎ 284/495–4684) sells cheeses, wines, fresh fruits, and canned goods from the United Kingdom and the United States. It will provision yachts and rental villas. **Fort Wine Gourmet** (⊠ Main St., Road Town, ☎ 284/494–3036), a café-cum-store, carries a remarkably sophisticated selection of gourmet items and fine wines, including Petrossian caviars and Hediard goods from France. **Gourmet Galley** (⊠ Wickham's Cay II, Road Town, ☎ 284/494– 6999) stocks a fine selection of wines, cheeses, and fresh fruits and vegetables and provides full provisioning for yachtspeople and villa renters.

### GIFTS

**Buccaneer's Bounty** (⊠ Main St., Road Town, ☎ 284/494–7510) is a brand-new gift shop that carries a delightful assortment of greeting cards, nautical and tropical artwork, books on seashells, and books on the islands. J. R. O'Neal, Ltd. (⊠ Main St., Road Town, ☎ 284/494– 2292) carries fine crystal, Royal Worcester china, a wonderful selection of hand-painted Italian dishes, hand-blown Mexican glassware, ceramic housewares from Spain, and woven rugs and tablecloths from India. **Pink Pineapple** (⊠ Prospect Reef Resort, ☎ 284/494–3311) has a remarkable array of gift items, from wearable artwork and hand-painted jewelry to watercolors and batik fabric. **Pusser's Company Store** (⊠ Main St. and Waterfront Rd., Road Town, ☎ 284/494–2467; ⊠ Soper's Hole Marina, ☎ 284/495–4603) draws crowds with its selection of nautical memorabilia, an entire line of clothes and gift items bearing the Pusser's logo, and handsome decorator bottles of Pusser's rum. **Sunny Caribbee Herb and Spice Company** (⊠ Main St., Road Town, ☎ 284/494–2178), in a brightly painted West Indian house, packages its own herbs, teas, coffees, herb vinegars, hot sauces, natural soaps, skin and suntan lotions, Caribbean art, and hand-painted decorative accessories. A small branch of this store is located at the Skyworld restaurant (☞ Dining, *above*). **Turtle Dove Boutique** (⊠ Flemming St., Road Town, ☎ 284/494–3611) is among the best in the B.V.I. for French perfume, international swimwear, and silk dresses, as well as gifts and accessories for the home.

### JEWELRY

**Felix Gold and Silver Ltd.** (⊠ Main St., Road Town, ☎ 284/494–2406) may not be much to look at from the outside, but inside jewelers handcraft exceptionally fine jewelry. Choose from island or other themes, or have something custom made; in some cases, the shop will make it for you within 72 hours. **Samarkand** (⊠ Main St., Road Town, ☎ 284/494–6415) specializes in handmade gold and silver pendants, earrings, bracelets, and pins, many with an island theme, plus genuine Spanish pieces of eight.

### TEXTILES

**Caribbean Handprints** (⊠ Main St., Road Town, ☎ 284/494–3717) creates silk-screened fabrics, sold by the yard or fashioned into dresses, shirts, pants, bathrobes, beach cover-ups, and beach bags.

**Zenaida** (⊠ Frenchman's Cay, ☎ 284/495–4867) displays the fabric finds of Argentinean Vivian Jenik Helm, who travels through South America, Africa, and India in search of batiks, hand-painted and hand-blocked fabrics, and interesting weaves. You can choose from her fabulous pareus and wall hangings, unusual bags, belts, sarongs, scarves, and ethnic jewelry.

## Nightlife

Tortola has a number of watering holes, many of which are especially popular with yachties. Check the weekly *Limin' Times* for current schedules of entertainment.

**Bomba's Shack** (⊠ Apple Bay, ☎ 284/495–4148) draws crowds to hear live bands on Sunday, Wednesday, and every full moon. **Jolly Rodger** (⊠ West End, ☎ 284/495–4559) has live music Friday and Saturday. **Pusser's Landing** (⊠ Soper's Hole, ☎ 284/494–4554) hosts live bands from Thursday through Sunday. **Quito's Gazebo** (⊠ Cane Garden Bay, ☎ 284/495–4837) is where B.V.I. recording star Quito Rhymer sings his own island ballads Sunday, Tuesday, and Thursday nights starting at 8:30. Friday and Saturday, Quito and the band the Edge pump out a variety of tunes. **Sebastian's** (⊠ Apple Bay, ☎ 284/495–4214) often has live music on Saturday and Sunday. **Stanley's Welcome Bar** (⊠ Cane Garden Bay, ☎ 284/495–4520) gets rowdy when crews stop by to party.

## Exploring Tortola

The drives on Tortola are dramatic, with dizzying roller-coaster dips and climbs and glorious views. Leave plenty of time to negotiate the hilly roads and drink in the irresistible vistas at nearly every hairpin turn. Distractions are the real danger here, from the glittering mosaic of azure sea, white skies, and emerald islets to the ambling cattle and grazing goats roadside.

*Numbers in the margin correspond to points of interest on the Tortola map.*

SIGHTS TO SEE

**❻ Belmont Point.** This sugar-loaf promontory has been described as a giant, green gumdrop. It's at the west end of **Long Bay**, a mile-long stretch of white sand, home to the appealing Long Bay Beach Resort. The large island visible in the distance is Jost Van Dyke.

**❼ Bomba's Surfside Shack.** One of the Caribbean's most famous bars, on the north shore of Tortola, Bomba's is worth a look even if you generally skip bars. The shack is festooned with everything from license plates to crepe-paper leis to colorful graffiti. It's hard to believe that this ramshackle place is one of the liveliest nightspots on Tortola and home of the famous Bomba Shack "Full Moon" party. Every full moon, bands play here all night long and people flock here from all over Tortola and from other islands. ⊠ *North Coast Rd.,* ☎ *284/495–4148.* ☉ *Daily 11–11 or later.*

**❾ Cane Garden Bay.** Crystalline water and a silky stretch of sand make this one of Tortola's most popular getaways. Its existence is no secret, however, and it can get crowded, especially when cruise ships are in Road Harbour.

**❷ Fort Burt.** The most intact historic ruin on Tortola, Fort Burt was built by the Dutch in the early 17th century to safeguard Road Harbour. It sits on a hill on the western edge of town and is now the site of a small hotel and restaurant. The foundations and magazine remain, and the structure offers a commanding view of Road Town. ⊠ *Waterfront Dr., no phone.* 🎫 *Free.* ☉ *Daily dawn–dusk.*

**4 Fort Recovery.** The unrestored ruins of this 17th-century Dutch fort sit amid a profusion of tropical greenery on the grounds of the Villas at Fort Recovery Estates. There are no guided tours, but the public is welcome to stop by. ⊠ *Waterfront Dr.,* ☎ *284/485–4467.* 🖼 *Free.*

**5 Frenchman's Cay.** On this little island connected by a causeway to Tortola's West End, there's a marina and a captivating complex of pastel-hued West Indian–style buildings with shady second-floor balconies, colonnaded arcades, shuttered windows, and gingerbread trim that showcase art galleries, shops, and restaurants. **Pusser's Landing** is a lively place where you can grab a cold drink (many are made with Pusser's famous rum) and a sandwich and watch the boats come and go from the harbor.

**8 North Shore Shell Museum.** On Tortola's north shore, this casual museum has a very informal exhibit of shells, unusually shaped driftwood, fish traps, and traditional wooden boats. ⊠ *North Shore Rd., no phone.* 🖼 *Free.* ☉ *Daily dawn–dusk.*

**11 Queen Elizabeth II Bridge.** You'll have to pay a toll (50¢ for passenger cars, $1 for vans and trucks) to cross this narrow bridge connecting Tortola and **Beef Island**. It's worth it if only for the sight of the toll taker extending a tin can attached to the end of a board through your car window to collect the fee.

**1 Road Town.** The laid-back capital of the British Virgin Islands is on the south coast of Tortola and looks out over Road Harbour. **Main Street** and the **waterfront** have shops and traditional pastel-painted West Indian buildings with high-pitched, corrugated tin roofs; bright shutters; and delicate fretwork trim.

**Sir Olva Georges Square,** across from the ferry dock and customs office, is open to the harbor on its eastern side, and a handful of Tortolans can generally be found enjoying the breeze that sweeps in from the water. The General Post Office is at the opposite end of the square. The hands of the clock atop this building permanently pointed at 10 minutes to 5 until last year, when they mysteriously started pointing at 5 minutes to 12, rather appropriate in this drowsy town, where time does seem to be standing still.

**Wickham's Cay** provides broad views of the wide harbor, home of countless sailing vessels and yachts and a base of the well-known yacht-chartering enterprise the Moorings. Along with banks, a post office, and stores and boutiques, there's also a **B.V.I. Tourist Board** office here that can provide sightseeing brochures and the latest information on everything from taxi rates to ferry-boat schedules. ⊠ *Wickham's Cay I,* ☎ *284/494–3134.* ☉ *Weekdays 9–5.*

The 2.8-acre **J. R. O'Neal Botanic Gardens** showcases lush gardens of tropical plant life. There are sections devoted to prickly cacti and succulents, fern and orchid hothouses, medicinal herb gardens, and plants and trees indigenous to the seashore. ⊠ *Station Ave.,* ☎ *284/494–4557.* 🖼 *Free.* ☉ *Mon.–Sat. 8–4, Sun. noon–5.*

**3 Sage Mountain National Park.** At 1,716 ft, Tortola's Sage Mountain is the highest peak in the B.V.I. The best unobstructed views up here are from the top. From the parking area, a trail leads in a loop not only to the peak itself but also to the island's small rain forest, sometimes shrouded in mist. Most of the island's forest was cut down over the centuries to clear land for sugarcane, cotton, and other crops, as well as pastureland and timber. But in 1964 this park was established to preserve the remaining rain forest. You'll see mahogany trees, white cedars, mountain guavas, elephant-ear vines, mamey trees, and giant

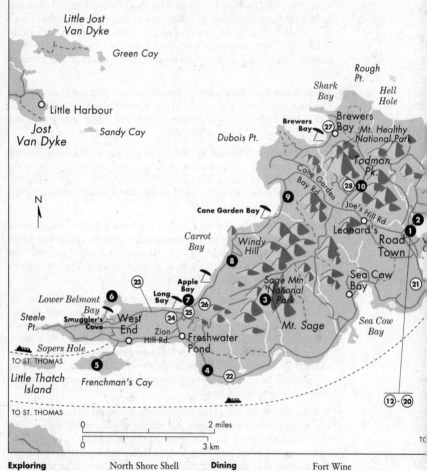

ATLANTIC OCEAN

Little Jost Van Dyke

Green Cay

Rough Pt.

Shark Bay

Hell Hole

Jost Van Dyke

Little Harbour

Sandy Cay

Brewers Bay

Brewers Bay 27

Mt. Healthy National Park

Dubois Pt.

Todman Pk.

Cane Garden Bay Rd.

28 10

Joe's Hill Rd.

9

Leonard's

2

1

Road Town

Cane Garden Bay

Carrot Bay

Windy Hill

8

Sea Cow Bay

N

Sage Mtn. National Park

3

21

23

Apple Bay

Lower Belmont Bay

6

Long Bay

7

26

25

Steele Pt.

Smuggler's Cove

West End

24

Mt. Sage

Sea Cow Bay

Sopers Hole

TO ST. THOMAS

Zion Hill Rd.

Freshwater Pond

5

Little Thatch Island

Frenchman's Cay

4

22

TO ST. THOMAS

| 0 | | 2 miles |
| 0 | | 3 km |

12 – 20

**Exploring**
Belmont Point, **6**
Bomba's Surfside Shack, **7**
Cane Garden Bay, **9**
Fort Burt, **2**
Fort Recovery, **4**
Frenchman's Cay, **5**

North Shore Shell Museum, **8**
Queen Elizabeth II Bridge, **11**
Road Town, **1**
Sage Mountain National Park, **3**
Skyworld, **10**

**Dining**
The Apple, **25**
Brandywine Bay, **29**
C and F Restaurant, **15**
Capriccio di Mare, **17**
The Fishtrap, **18**

Fort Wine Gourmet, **16**
Lime 'n' Mango, **19**
Skyworld, **28**
Spaghetti Junction, **20**
Sugar Mill Restaurant, **26**
Virgin Queen, **14**

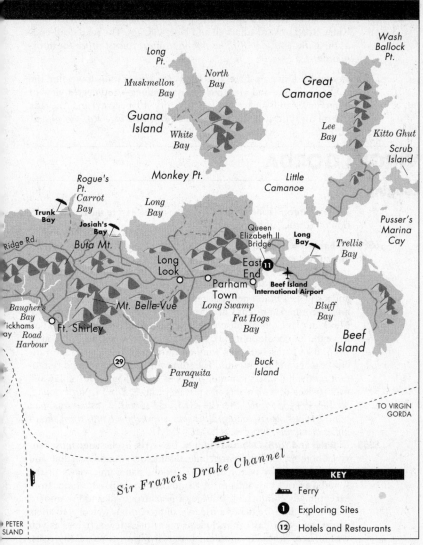

Long
Pt.

Wash
Ballock
Pt.

*Muskmellon
Bay*

*North
Bay*

**Great
Camanoe**

**Guana
Island**

*White
Bay*

*Lee
Bay*

*Kitto Ghut*

*Scrub
Island*

*Monkey Pt.*

*Little
Camanoe*

*Rogue's
Pt.
Carrot
Bay*

*Pusser's
Marina
Cay*

**Trunk
Bay**

*Long
Bay*

Queen
Elizabeth II
Bridge

**Long
Bay**

*Trellis
Bay*

**Josiah's
Bay**

*Ridge Rd.*

**Buta Mt.**

**Long
Look**

**East
End** ❶❶

**Parham
Town**

**Beef Island
International Airport**

*Baugher's
Bay*

**Mt. Belle-Vue**

*Long Swamp*

*Fat Hogs
Bay*

*Bluff
Bay*

ickhams
ay *Road
Harbour*

◯ **Ft. Shirley**

**Beef
Island**

㉙

*Paraquita
Bay*

*Buck
Island*

TO VIRGIN
GORDA

*Sir Francis Drake Channel*

⬛ PETER
SLAND

| KEY | |
|---|---|
| 🛳 | Ferry |
| ❶ | Exploring Sites |
| ⑫ | Hotels and Restaurants |

**Lodging**

Brewer's Bay
Campground, **27**

Long Bay Beach
Resort, **23**

Moorings-Mariner
Inn, **12**

Prospect Reef
Resort, **21**

Sebastian's on the
Beach, **24**

Sugar Mill Hotel, **26**

Treasure Isle
Hotel, **13**

The Villas at Fort
Recovery Estates, **22**

bulletwoods, and such birds as mountain doves and thrushes. Take a taxi from Road Town or drive up Joe's Hill Road and make a left onto Ridge Road toward Chalwell and Doty villages. The road dead-ends at the park. ⊠ *Ridge Rd., no phone (contact tourist office for information).* ⊠ *Free.*

**⑩ Skyworld.** Drive up here and climb the observation tower for the B.V.I.'s highest—and absolutely most stunning—360-degree view of numerous islands and cays. Even St. Croix (40 mi away) and Anegada (20 mi away) can be seen on a clear day. ⊠ *Ridge Rd., no phone.* ⊠ *Free.*

# VIRGIN GORDA

## Lodging

For price information on hotels, *see* the price chart *in* the Lodging section of Tortola, *above.*

**$$$$** 🏨 **Biras Creek Hotel.** A longtime guest purchased Biras Creek in 1995
**★** and turned it into one of the classiest resorts in the B.V.I. The general manager, Jamie Holmes, brings years of Caribbean hotel experience to this secluded, 150-acre hideaway. Virtually everything was redone, and it still feels brand-new. Each unit has a bedroom and a living-room area decorated in bright Caribbean colors and fabrics. The floors are Mexican tile. Units are discreetly hidden among the trees, and if you leave the air-conditioning off, the sound of the waves will lull you to sleep. Bike paths and trails winding through woods lead to the various beaches and restaurants. The stonework open-air bar and restaurant on the hill offers stunning views of North Sound. A "Sailaway" package includes two nights on a private yacht. ⊠ *Box 54, North Sound,* ☎ *284/494–3555,* 🖷 *284/494–3557. 34 rooms. 2 restaurants, bar, pool, 2 tennis courts, hiking, 2 beaches, snorkeling, windsurfing, boating, waterskiing, bicycles. AE, MC, V. FAP.*

**$$$$** 🏨 **Bitter End Yacht Club and Marina.** This is the liveliest and most convivial hotel in the B.V.I. Stretching along North Sound coastline and accessible only by boat, the BEYC enjoys panoramic views of the sound, Leverick Bay, and nearby islands. Accommodations range from exceptionally comfortable hillside or beachfront villas to live-aboard yachts. The BEYC extends a friendly, unpretentious welcome to all its guests, and your day can include as many or as few activities as you wish. There are daily snorkeling and diving trips to nearby reefs, cruises, windsurfing lessons, lessons at the Nick Trotter Sailing School, and excursions to nearby attractions. Regarded as offering the best sailing instruction in the Caribbean, the school helps both seasoned salts and beginners sharpen their nautical skills. When the sun goes down, the festivities continue at the Clubhouse, an open-air restaurant overlooking the sound. ⊠ *Box 46, North Sound,* ☎ *284/494—2746,* 🖷 *284/494–3557. 100 rooms. 2 restaurants, bar, pool, beach, marina. AE, MC, V. FAP.*

**$$$$** 🏨 **Little Dix Bay.** Relaxed elegance is the hallmark of this longtime fa-
**★** vorite, which for 30 years has remained one of the outstanding resorts in the Caribbean. It's tucked among the mangroves, along the edge of a sandy beach. The hexagonal rooms have stone and wood walls and are decorated in Caribbean prints. The spacious open-air library has daily stateside newspapers if you want to stay in touch. Lawns are beautifully manicured; the reef-protected beach is long and silken; and the candlelight dining in an open peak-roof pavilion is a memorable experience. Tennis, sailing, snorkeling, waterskiing, and bicycling are included in the rate. Popular with honeymooners, and older couples who

have been coming back for years, Little Dix is a quiet place favored by couples. The accommodations are superb, the service thoughtful and attentive, and the setting unforgettable. ⊠ *Box 70,* ☎ *284/495–5555,* FAX *284/495–5661. 102 rooms. 3 restaurants, 2 bars, 7 tennis courts, beach, snorkeling, windsurfing, boating, waterskiing, marina, bicycles, shop. AE, MC, V. EP, MAP, FAP.*

$$–$$$$ 🏨 **Guavaberry Spring Bay Vacation Homes.** These unusual hexagonal cottages are perched on stilts. You'll feel as if you're in a tree house, amid the swaying branches and chirping birds. One- and two-bedroom units are situated on a hill, a short walk from a tamarind-shaded beach and not far from the mammoth boulders and cool basins of the famed Baths. ⊠ *Box 20, Virgin Gorda,* ☎ *284/495–5227,* FAX *284/495–7367. 21 units. Beach, shop. No credit cards. EP.*

$$–$$$$ 🏨 **Olde Yard Inn.** Owners Charlie Williams and Carol Kaufman have
★ cultivated a refreshingly unique atmosphere at this quiet retreat just outside Spanish Town. Classical music plays in the bar; books line the walls of the octagonal library cottage. French-accented cuisine is lovingly prepared and served with style in the high-ceiling dining rooms. The lunch restaurant overlooks the pool and features fresh salads, excellent chili, and hamburgers and sandwiches. Guest rooms are cozy and simply furnished. Arrangements can be made for day sails and scuba-diving excursions. There's a large pool and a health club where you can work out, take exercise classes, and receive massages. The inn is not on the beach, but free transportation is provided. In the warmer months you may want to request an air-conditioned room; the hotel's location means trade winds are less noticeable here. ⊠ *Box 26, Spanish Town,* ☎ *284/495–5544,* FAX *284/495–5986. 14 rooms. Restaurant, bar, pool, croquet, library. AE, MC, V.*

$$–$$$ 🏨 **Leverick Bay Hotel.** The 16 hillside rooms of this small hotel are decorated in pastels and hung with original artwork. All rooms have refrigerators, balconies, and lovely views of North Sound. Four two-bedroom condos are also available. A Spanish colonial–style main building houses a restaurant operated by Pusser's of Tortola. ⊠ *Box 63,* ☎ *284/495–7421,* FAX *284/495–7367. 16 rooms. Restaurant, bar, pool, beauty salon, beach, dive shop, snorkeling, shops, coin laundry. AE, D, MC, V. EP.*

# Dining

For price information on restaurants, *see* the price chart in the Dining section of Tortola, *above.*

$$$ ✕ **Biras Creek.** This hilltop restaurant, with its signature turret roof,
★ is one of the most stunning settings for a meal in all of the B.V.I. Broad stairs lead to an open-air lounge and restaurant with beautiful views of North Sound. The gourmet menu changes daily but includes four or five choices each for appetizer, entrée, and dessert. Grilled local wahoo with ginger and carrot sauce, lobster with spicy Caribbean sauce, and roast duck with plum sauce are some of the enticing entrées offered. Delightful desserts include key lime pie, a warm treacle tart, and hot brownies with chocolate sauce. ⊠ *North Sound,* ☎ *284/494–3555. Reservations essential. AE, MC, V.*

$$$ ✕ **Drake's Anchorage.** You come by boat (provided free) to this serene and romantic candlelit spot right at the water's edge. Dine on lobster dorado (encrusted with bananas and bread crumbs), rack of lamb, or steak au poivre and velvety chocolate mousse. ⊠ *North Sound,* ☎ *284/494–2252. Reservations essential. AE, MC, V.*

$$$ ✕ **Little Dix Bay.** For an elegant evening out, you can't do better than
★ this: The candlelight in the main open-air pavilion is enchanting, the menu sophisticated, the service attentive. The dinner menu changes daily,

but there is always a fine selection of superbly prepared seafood, meat, and vegetarian entrées from which to choose. The lunch buffet here is one of the best in the Caribbean. ⊠ *Spanish Town,* ☎ *284/495–5555, ext. 174. AE, MC, V.*

**$$$**  ✕ **Olde Yard Inn.** Dinner here is a civilized and charming affair. The
★  intimate dining room is suffused with gentle classical melodies and the scent of herbs. A cedar roof covers the breezy, open-air room decorated with old-style Caribbean charm. The French-accented cuisine includes lamb chops with mango chutney, chicken breast in a rum cream sauce, garlic shrimp, grilled local fish and lobster, and steaks. For great chili, burgers, or salads at lunch, stop by the poolside **Sip and Dip Grill.** ⊠ *The Valley, north of marina,* ☎ *284/495–5544. AE, MC, V.*

**$$–$$$**  ✕ **Giorgio's Italian Restaurant.** Gaze out at the stars and listen to the water lap against the shore while dining on penne arrabbiata, veal scaloppini, filet mignon with mushrooms, or fresh local fish. Pizzas and sandwiches are the fare at lunch at this pleasant, casual establishment, which is right on the water. ⊠ *Mangoe Bay, 10 mins north of Yacht Harbour,* ☎ *284/495–5684. MC, V.*

**$$**  ✕ **Bath and Turtle.** You can really sit back and relax at this informal
★  patio tavern with its friendly staff. Choose from the simple menu's burgers, well-stuffed sandwiches, pizzas, pasta dishes, and daily specials. Live entertainment is presented on Wednesday and Sunday nights. ⊠ *Virgin Gorda Yacht Harbour,* ☎ *284/495–5239. MC, V.*

**$–$$**  ✕ **Crab Hole.** Callaloo soup, saltfish, stewed goat, rice and peas, green bananas, curried chicken roti, and other West Indian specialties are the draw at this homey hangout. ⊠ *The Valley,* ☎ *284/495–5307. No credit cards.*

**$**  ✕ **Mad Dog's.** Piña coladas are the specialty at this breezy bar outside of the Baths. The all-day menu includes BLTs, hot dogs, and burgers. ⊠ *The Valley,* ☎ *284/495–5830. Reservations not accepted. MC, V.*

## Beaches

The best beaches are most easily reached by water, although they are accessible on foot, usually after a moderately strenuous hike of 10 to 15 minutes.

Anybody going to Virgin Gorda must experience swimming or snorkeling among its **unique boulder formations.** But why go to **the Baths,** which is usually crowded, when you can catch some rays just north at **Spring Bay** beach, which is a gem, and, a little farther north, at the **Crawl?** Both are easily reached from the Baths on foot via Lee Road, or by swimming. ⊠ *Lee Rd.*

From Biras Creek or Bitter End on the north shore, you can walk to **Bercher's Beach** and along the windswept coast. ⊠ *No road, but paths from both resorts.*

Footpaths from Bitter End and foot and bike paths from Biras Creek lead to **Deep Bay,** a calm, well-protected swimming beach. ⊠ *No road, but paths from both resorts.*

Mosquito Island's **Hay Point Beach** is a broad band of white sand accessible only by boat or by path from the dock at Drake's Anchorage resort.

**Leverick Bay** is a small, busy beach-cum-marina that fronts a resort restaurant and pool. Don't come here to be alone, but do come if you want a lively little place and a break from the island's noble quiet. The view of Prickly Pear Island is an added plus, and there's a dive facility right here to motor you out to beautiful Eustatia Reef just across North Sound. ⊠ *Leverick Bay Rd.*

It's worth going out to **Long Bay** (near Virgin Gorda's northern tip, past the Diamond Beach Club) for the snorkeling (Little Dix Bay resort has outings here). The drive takes about a half hour after the turnoff from North Sound Road, and a dirt road makes up part of the route. ⊠ *Plum Tree Bay Rd.*

For a wonderfully private beach close to Spanish Town, try **Savannah Bay.** It may not always be completely deserted, but it's a lovely long stretch of white sand. ⊠ *North Sound Rd.*

Prickly Pear Island has a calm swimming beach at **Vixen Point Beach.**

# Outdoor Activities and Sports

## Sailboarding
**Nick Trotter Sailing School** (⊠ Bitter End Yacht Club, North Sound, ☎ 284/494–2746) has beginner and advanced courses.

## Scuba Diving and Snorkeling
For snorkelers, perhaps the most popular spot in the B.V.I. is at the famed Baths on Virgin Gorda. Dive and snorkel sites can be found near the North Sound area of Virgin Gorda. Contact **Dive BVI** (⊠ Virgin Gorda Yacht Harbour, ☎ 284/495–5513 or 800/848–7078).

## Sportfishing
On Virgin Gorda contact **Captain Dale** (☎ 284/495–5225), who operates the 38-ft Bertram *Classic* out of Biras Creek.

## Tennis
The **Biras Creek Hotel** (⊠ North Sound, ☎ 284/494–3555) has two lighted Astroturf courts. Courts and lessons are available to guests, and to nonguests for a fee. There is a pro here.

# Shopping

## Shopping Districts
On Virgin Gorda there is a cluster of shops at the bustling Yacht Harbour in Spanish Town and also boutiques located within the individual hotel complexes. Several of the best are at **Little Dix Bay, Bitter End Yacht Club, Biras Creek,** and **Olde Yard Inn.** There is also a small collection of shops at Leverick Bay.

## Specialty Stores

### CLOTHING
**Next Wave** (⊠ Virgin Gorda Yacht Harbour, ☎ 284/495–5623) has bathing suits, T-shirts, and tote bags. **Pelican's Pouch Boutique** (⊠ Virgin Gorda Yacht Harbour, ☎ 284/495–5599) has a large selection of swimsuits plus cover-ups, beach hats, T-shirts, and accessories.

### FOOD AND DRINK
**Bitter End's Emporium** (⊠ Bitter End Yacht Club, North Sound, ☎ 284/494–2745) is a great place to stop for such edible treats as local fruits, bakery goods, and cheeses. **Virgin Island Bakery** (⊠ Virgin Gorda Yacht Harbour, no phone) is the place to stop for freshly baked loaves, rolls, muffins, and cookies, and sandwiches and sodas to go. You get a whiff of the fresh breads before you even get in the door.

### GIFTS
**Palm Tree Gallery** (⊠ Leverick Bay, ☎ 284/495–7421) has an excellent selection of books about the B.V.I., good maps, handcrafted jewelry, and local artwork. **Pusser's Company Store** (⊠ Leverick Bay, ☎ 284/495–7369) sells its famous rum, as well as various sundries with the Pusser's logo. **Thee Artistic Gallery** (⊠ Virgin Gorda Yacht

Harbour, ☎ 284/495–5761) features Caribbean jewelry, 14kt gold nautical jewelry, maps, collectible coins, and some crystal.

LOCAL CRAFTS

**Tropical Gift Collections** (⊠ Top of the Baths Shops, ☎ 284/495–5374) sells locally made spices, hats, handbags, and pottery. **Virgin Gorda Craft Shop** (⊠ Virgin Gorda Yacht Harbour, ☎ 284/495–5137) displays the work of local artists. Choose among West Indian jewelry and crafts styled in straw, shells, and other local materials, or pick up clothing and paintings by Caribbean artists.

# Nightlife

Consult the *Limin' Times,* which is published weekly, for current schedules.

**Bath and Turtle** (⊠ Virgin Gorda Yacht Harbour, ☎ 284/495–5239) hosts local bands Wednesday and Sunday evenings. **Chez Bamboo** (⊠ Across from Virgin Gorda Yacht Harbour, ☎ 284/495–5752) is the place to go for jazz Thursday and Saturday nights. **Pirate's Grill** on Saba Rock (☎ 284/495–9638) has a nightly jam session. Bring your own instrument or use one of theirs.

# Exploring Virgin Gorda

For great views of nearby islands and of Virgin Gorda's own eccentric shape, just drive or take a taxi on North Sound Road, which runs across Virgin Gorda's hilly center. You'll notice nary a dwelling nor sign of mundane civilization up here, only a green mountain slope on your left (if you're driving north) and a spectacular view down to South Sound on the right. From here, too, you can also look back and get a wonderful sense of Virgin Gorda's stringy, crooked shape: Back there, looking flat and almost like a separate island, is the Valley. Because of this shape, Virgin Gorda is one of those places where you can get a bird's-eye (or map's-eye) view of things from right inside your car.

*Numbers in the margin correspond to points of interest on the Virgin Gorda map.*

SIGHTS TO SEE

**❸ The Baths.** It's well worth your time to visit Virgin Gorda's most celebrated sight. Giant boulders, brought to the surface eons ago by a vast volcanic eruption, are scattered about the beach and in the water. Some are almost as large as small houses and form remarkable grottoes. Climb between these rocks to swim in the many pools. Early morning and late afternoon are the best times to visit, since the Baths and the beach here are usually crowded with cruise-ship passengers and day-trippers visiting from Tortola. (If it's privacy you crave, follow the shore north for a few hundred yards to reach several quieter bays—**Spring,** the **Crawl, Little Trunk,** and **Valley Trunk**—or head south along the trail to **Devil's Bay.** These beaches have the same giant boulders as those found at the Baths.) It's a 35-yard walk from the parking lot to the beach. ⊠ *Lee Rd., no phone.* 🎫 *Free.*

**❹ Copper Mine Point.** Here you'll see a tall stone shaft silhouetted against the sky and a small stone structure overlooking the sea. These are the ruins of a copper mine established here 400 years ago and worked first by the Spanish, then by English miners until the early 20th century. This is one of the few places in the B.V.I. where you won't see islands along the horizon. ⊠ *Copper Mine Rd., no phone.* 🎫 *Free.*

**❻ Leverick Bay.** A resort, a tiny beach, a marina, a restaurant, a cluster of shops, and some luxurious hillside villas are here. This is also where a launch picks up passengers for Drake's Anchorage, a resort on nearby **Mosquito Island.** You can view the island from the top of one of the narrow hillside roads; the hunk of land straight ahead is **Prickly Pear,** which has been named a national park to protect it from development.

**➋ Little Fort National Park.** A 36-acre wildlife sanctuary and the ruins of an old fort can be found here. Piles of giant boulders similar to those found at **the Baths** are scattered throughout the park. ⊠ *Spanish Town Rd., no phone.* 🎫 *Free.*

**➊ Spanish Town.** Virgin Gorda's main settlement, on the island's southern wing, is a peaceful village so tiny that it barely qualifies as a town at all. Also known as the Valley, Spanish Town is home to a marina, a small cluster of shops, and a couple of car-rental agencies. Just north of town is the ferry slip. At the **Virgin Gorda Yacht Harbour** you can stroll along the dock front or do a little browsing in the shops there.

**➎ Virgin Gorda Peak National Park.** A small sign on North Sound Road marks the trail up to the 265-acre park and the island's 1,359-ft summit. Sometimes the sign is missing, so keep your eyes open for a set of stairs that disappears into the trees. It's about a 15-minute hike up to a small clearing, where you can climb a ladder to the observation tower's platform. If you're keen for some woodsy exercise or just want to stretch your legs, go for it. Unfortunately, the view at the top is somewhat tree-obstructed. ⊠ *North Sound Rd., no phone.* 🎫 *Free.*

# OUTLYING ISLANDS

## Lodging

For price information on hotels, *see* the price chart *in* the Lodging section of Tortola, *above.*

### Anegada

**$$$–$$$$** 🏨 **Anegada Reef Hotel.** This is the only hotel on the island, and it has just 16 motel-like rooms. People come here for peace rather than luxury. There's a narrow strip of beach at the hotel, but beach lovers will want to spend their days on the beautiful deserted beaches on the other side of the island. Snorkeling and diving are as good on Anegada as anywhere else in the islands. Bonefishing in the flats is a favorite activity, and deep-sea-fishing trips can be arranged. If you favor true laid-back living and absolutely no schedules, this is the spot for you. ⊠ *Anegada,* ☎ *284/495–8002,* 🖷 *284/495–9362. 16 rooms. Restaurant, bar, beach, dive shop, snorkeling, shop. MC, V. FAP.*

### Cooper Island

**$$$$** 🏨 **Cooper Island Beach Club.** Two West Indian–style cottages house 12 no-frills units with a living area, a small but complete kitchen, and a balcony. This is a wonderful place to lead a somewhat back-to-basics existence: The only water available is rain collected in a cistern, and because of the limited amount of electricity, you won't be able to use a hair dryer, an iron, or any other electric appliance. There is ample opportunity to mingle, however, at the bar, which fills nightly with a new group of boaters. ⊠ *Box 859, Road Town, Tortola,* ☎ *413/659–2602, or 800/542–4624. 12 rooms. Restaurant, beach, dive shop. MC, V.*

### Guana Island

**$$$$** 🏨 **Guana Island Club.** Fifteen extremely comfortable guest rooms, each with its own living room area, are spread among seven houses scattered along the top of a hillside on this totally private island. The units are simply decorated in Caribbean style, with rattan furniture and

Mountain Pt.

Hay Po

Long Bay

George Dog

Cockroach Island

Great Dog

West Dog

5

Mango Bay (13)

*Sir Francis Drake Channel*

Little Dix Bay

Savannah Bay

Colison Pt.

(12)

(11)

Handsome Bay

TO TORTOLA

St. Thomas Bay

Spanish Town

(9)

(10)

Virgin Gorda Airport

Fort Pt.

(2)(1)

Valley Trunk Bay

Little Trunk Bay

The Crawl

Spring Bay

(8)

(3)(7)

(4)

Copper Mine Bay

Copper Mine Pt.

Crook's Bay

Stoney Bay

Fallen Jerusalem

**Exploring**
The Baths, **3**
Copper Mine Point, **4**
Leverick Bay, **6**
Little Fort National Park, **2**
Spanish Town, **1**
Virgin Gorda Peak National Park, **5**

**Dining**
Bath and Turtle, **9**
Biras Creek, **15**
Crab Hole, **10**
Drake's Anchorage, **14**
Gíorgio's Italian Restaurant, **13**
Little Dix Bay, **12**

Mad Dog's, **7**
Olde Yard Inn, **11**

**Lodging**
Biras Creek Hotel, **16**
Bitter End Yacht Club and Marina, **17**
Guavaberry Spring Bay Vacation Homes, **8**
Leverick Bay Hotel, **15**

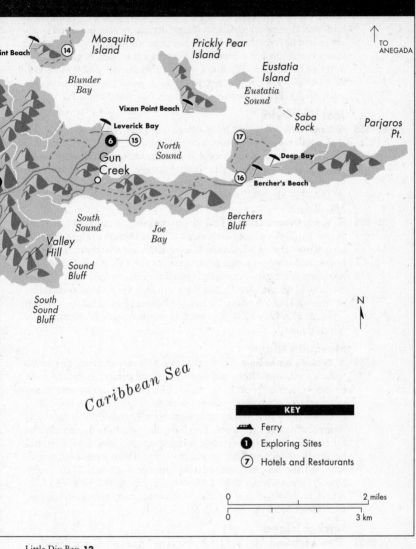

Little Dix Bay, **12**
Olde Yard Inn, **11**

ceiling fans, and each has a porch. The island's many trails make it a favorite spot for hikers, there are great beaches to walk to, and it's a bird-watching paradise. Guests mingle during cocktail hour, and meals are served at several large tables, but there are some tables for two if you prefer to dine as a couple. The restaurant is open to guests of the hotel only. ⊠ *Box 32, Road Town, Tortola,* ☎ *284/494–2354,* FAX *914/967–8048. 15 rooms. Restaurant, fans, 2 tennis courts, croquet, hiking, beach, snorkeling, boating. No credit cards. FAP.*

## Jost Van Dyke

$$–$$$   🏨 **Sandcastle.** This tiny, four-cottage hideaway (with a staff of eight) is on a half mile of white beach on remote White Bay. There's nothing to do here—except maybe snooze in a hammock, read, gaze, walk, swim, rest, and savor sophisticated cuisine by candlelight. Arrangements can be made for diving, sailing, and sportfishing trips. ⊠ *White Bay,* ☎ *284/775–5262,* FAX *284/775–5262. 4 cottages. Restaurant, bar, beach. MC, V. FAP.*

$$–$$$   🏨 **Sandy Ground Estates.** Tucked into the foliage along the edge of one of Jost Van Dyke's East End beaches is this collection of eight privately owned one- and two-bedroom houses. Each one is architecturally different, and interiors range from spartan to stylish. Kitchens are fully equipped and can be prestocked (you'll want to do this, since supplies are limited on the island), and there are four very casual restaurants within walking distance. ⊠ *Sandy Ground, East End of Jost Van Dyke,* ☎ *284/495–3391. 8 1- and 2-bedroom houses. Kitchens, beach. No credit cards. EP.*

## Mosquito Island

$$$$   🏨 **Drake's Anchorage.** Set on the edge of its own island, this small,
★   secluded getaway offers true privacy and the pampering of the more elegant resorts without the formality. Changing for dinner here means switching from a bathing suit to comfortable cottons. The three West Indian–style, waterfront bungalows contain 10 comfortably furnished rooms, including two suites. There are also two fully equipped villas for rent. There are hiking trails, water-sports facilities, four delightful beaches with hammocks here and there, and a highly regarded restaurant—a truly peaceful, rejuvenating experience. ⊠ *Box 2510, North Sound, Virgin Gorda,* ☎ FAX *284/494–2254 or* ☎ *800/624–6651. 10 rooms in 3 bungalows, 2 villas. Restaurant, bar, hiking, 4 beaches, snorkeling, boating, shop. AE, MC, V. FAP.*

## Necker Island

$$$$   🏨 **Necker Island.** You and 19 of your closest friends can rent this whole island. In fact, that's the only way you can stay at this ultraexpensive, ultrachic getaway of the likes of Princess Di and Oprah Winfrey. There are five beaches, many walks, a tennis court, and a luxurious villa with 20 spacious guest rooms. ⊠ *Necker Island,* ☎ *284/494–2757. Villa. Tennis court, 5 beaches, boating. AE, MC, V. FAP.*

## Peter Island

$$$$   🏨 **Peter Island Resort and Yacht Harbour.** This luxury resort includes an elegant and a casual restaurant, five beaches, a stunning freshwater pool, tennis courts, and a Peter Burwash tennis program. It also has a complete water-sports program, a 20-station fitness trail that meanders through palm trees, and 10 mi of walking trails. The most desirable rooms are in quadriplex cottages that are tucked among beds of radiant tropical flowers at the edge of the beach. They are spacious and comfortably furnished (although the fabrics are on the dark side) and have excellent views. The pool-, garden-, and ocean-view rooms are a bit run down and could use some refurbishment. Those seeking seclusion should be aware that the resort's beaches are on bays that

are popular anchorages, and the restaurants, beaches, and hiking trails can be somewhat hectic with day-trippers and the charter-boat crowd. For the last several years, there has been a constant turnover of resident managers, and service here is somewhat inconsistent. The hotel will be closed for major renovations from June 1997 to December 1, 1997. ⊠ *Box 211, Road Town, Tortola,* ☎ *284/494–2000 or 800/346–4451,* FAX *284/495–2500. 50 rooms, 2 villas. 2 restaurants, 2 bars, pool, 4 tennis courts, exercise room, 5 beaches, dive shop, windsurfing, boating, mountain bikes, helipad. AE, MC, V. EP, MAP, FAP.*

### Pusser's Marina Cay

**$$** ⌂ **Pusser's Marina Cay Hotel.** Pusser's Marina Cay is home to Pusser's Restaurant, Pusser's Store, and this hotel. Six units are available—four rooms and two suites. Rooms are on the small side but are comfortably furnished and perched above the water's edge. The islet is quite small, and there's not much to do but relax. It's a great place to lie on the beach, get some sun, and snorkel. But if you want to explore, you can easily get to Tortola or Virgin Gorda. There's free (and frequent) ferry service to the dock on Beef Island. ⊠ *Pusser's Marina Cay,* ☎ *284/494–2174. 6 units. Restaurant, beach. AE, MC, V. EP.*

## Beaches

Jost Van Dyke's **Great Harbour Beach** is calm and lined with little restaurants.

A popular spot for day-trippers from St. Thomas is Jost Van Dyke's **White Bay Beach,** a tidy stretch of white sand.

**Marina Cay Beach** on Marina Cay is tiny but calm, and there is good snorkeling just offshore.

Palm-fringed **Dead Man's Bay,** on Peter Island, called one of the world's 10 most romantic beaches, is just a short hike from the dock. Both ends of the beach provide good snorkeling, and you'll find a bar and restaurant for lunch.

If you feel like taking a hike on Peter Island instead of heading down to Dead Man's Bay, follow the road up, and when it levels off bear right and head down to the other side of the island and secluded **White Bay.**

Mosquito Island's **Long Beach** usually has calm water, with some good snorkeling at the far end.

Mosquito Island's tiny **Honeymoon Beach** is reachable only by hiking along a rocky path.

Cooper Island's **Manchioneel Bay Beach** isn't much of a beach, but there is terrific snorkeling just offshore.

Farther off, and reachable by plane as well as by boat, is beach-ringed, reef-laced Anegada. The best beach here is **Loblolly Bay Beach** on the western side of the island.

## Outdoor Activities and Sports

### Scuba Diving and Snorkeling

The famed wreck of the RMS *Rhone,* off Salt Island, is reason enough to dive during your B.V.I. stay. Dive and snorkel sites also abound near the smaller islands of Norman, Peter, Cooper, Ginger, the Dogs, and Jost Van Dyke, and in the wreck-strewn waters off Anegada. A branch of **Dive BVI** (⊠ Virgin Gorda Yacht Harbour, ☎ 284/495–5513 or 800/848–7078) is located on Peter Island.

# Shopping

### Gifts

**Pusser's Company Store** (✉ Marina Cay, ☎ 284/494–2174), on a Pusser's-dominated islet, stocks its own brand of rum, plus a line of clothes and other items bearing the company's logo.

# Nightlife

### Jost Van Dyke

One of the busiest nocturnal spots in the B.V.I. is little Jost Van Dyke. Check out **Club Paradise** (☎ 284/495–9267) for live music on weekends. **Foxy's Tamarind** (☎ 284/495–9258) is where you can find the famous Foxy, who plays calypso most afternoons. Local bands play music several nights a week. Reuben sings at **Sandcastle's Soggy Dollar Bar** (☎ 284/495–9888).

# Exploring Outlying Islands

Just across the channel from Road Town on Tortola is **Peter Island,** an 1,800-acre island known for its exclusive resort. **Jost Van Dyke,** the sizable island north of Tortola's western tip, is a good choice for travelers in search of isolation and good hiking trails; it has a small hotel, a cluster of rental villas, and two campgrounds, but only two small settlements, few cars, and limited electricity. Guests of the resort on **Guana Island** also enjoy the nature trails and wildlife sanctuary on this private island just above the eastern tip of Tortola. **Pusser's Marina Cay** is a snug 6-acre islet near Great Camanoe, just north of Beef Island, east of Tortola, with a Pusser's store, restaurant, and hotel. **Cooper Island** is a green, hilly island on the south side of Sir Francis Drake Channel. It has a restaurant and a 12-room hotel and has long been a popular anchorage. **Necker** is a private island just north of Virgin Gorda with accommodations for 20 that can only be rented as a block. **Anegada,** about 16 mi north of Virgin Gorda's North Sound, is a flat mass of coral 11 mi long and 3 mi wide with a population of only about 160 and a single hotel. Visitors are chiefly scuba divers, snorkelers, lovers of deserted beaches, and fishermen, some of whom come for the bonefishing here. (For more information on these islands, *see* Lodging, *above.*)

# THE BRITISH VIRGIN ISLANDS A TO Z

## Arriving and Departing

### BY BOAT

Various ferries connect St. Thomas, U.S.V.I., with Tortola and Virgin Gorda. **Inter-Island Boat Services' *Sundance II*** (☎ 284/776–6597) connects St. John and West End on Tortola daily. **Native Son, Inc.** (☎ 284/495–4617) operates three ferries—***Native Son, Oriole,*** and ***Voyager Eagle***—and offers service between St. Thomas and Tortola (West End and Road Town) daily. **Smiths Ferry Services** (☎ 284/494–4430 or 284/494–2355) carries passengers between downtown St. Thomas and Road Town and West End on Monday through Saturday and offers daily service between Red Hook on St. Thomas and Tortola's West End. **Speedy's Ferries** (☎ 284/495–5240) runs between Virgin Gorda, Tortola, and St. Thomas on Tuesdays, Thursdays, and Saturdays.

### BY PLANE

No nonstop service is available from the United States to the B.V.I.; connections are usually made through San Juan, Puerto Rico, or St.

Thomas, U.S.V.I. Airlines serving both San Juan and St. Thomas include **American** (☎ 800/433–7300), **Continental** (☎ 800/231–0856), and **Delta** (☎ 800/241–4141). **American Eagle** (☎ 800/433–7300) flies from San Juan to Tortola. **Air St. Thomas** (☎ 284/495–5935) flies between St. Thomas and Virgin Gorda. Regularly scheduled service between the B.V.I. and most other Caribbean islands is provided by **Leeward Islands Air Transport (LIAT)** (☎ 284/495–1187). Many Caribbean islands can also be reached via **Gorda Aero Service** (☎ 284/495–2271), a charter service.

## Currency
British though they are, the B.V.I. have the U.S. dollar as the standard currency.

## Emergencies
**Police:** ☎ 999. **Medical emergency:** ☎ 999. **Hospital:** On Tortola there is **Peebles Hospital** in Road Town (☎ 284/494–3497). On Virgin Gorda, there is a clinic in Spanish Town, or the Valley (☎ 284/495–5337). There is also a clinic on Virgin Gorda at North Sound (☎ 284/495–7310).

**Pharmacies:** If you need a pharmacy in Road Town try **J. R. O'Neal Drug Store** (☎ 284/494–2292). **Lagoon Plaza Drug Store** (☎ 284/494–2498) is a full-service pharmacy in Road Town.

## Further Reading
Vernon Pickering's *Concise History of the British Virgin Islands* is a wordy but worthy guide to the events and personalities that shaped the region. Look for copies of *A Place Like This: Hugh Benjamin's Peter Island,* a charming, eloquent, and very personal tale by Hugh Benjamin, a Kittitian who has spent the past 20 years living in the British Virgin Islands.

For linguists, *What a Pistarckle!,* by Lito Valls, gives the origins of the many expressions you'll be hearing, and historians will enjoy *Eyewitness Accounts of Slavery in the Danish West Indies* by Isidor Paiewonsky. *Conquest of Eden,* by Michael Paiewonsky, includes excerpts from the logs of Christopher Columbus and journals of noblemen and is beautifully illustrated with woodcuts. For sailors, Simon Scott has written a *Cruising Guide to the Virgin Islands.* If you happen to be traveling with children, be sure to pick up a copy of *Visiting the Virgin Islands with the Kids,* by Richard B. Myers.

On the B.V.I., the *Island Sun* and the *BVI Beacon* are the best local papers for everything from entertainment listings to local gossip. The *Welcome Tourist Guide,* which is published every other month, is comprehensive and available free at airports and larger hotels.

## Getting Around
BOATS

**Speedy's Fantasy** (☎ 284/495–5240) runs between Road Town, Tortola, and Spanish Town, Virgin Gorda, daily. **Smith's Ferry** (☎ 284/494–4430) makes daily runs between Road Town, Tortola, and Spanish Town, Virgin Gorda. Running daily between Virgin Gorda's North Sound (Bitter End Yacht Club) and Beef Island, Tortola, are **North Sound Express** (☎ 284/494–2746) boats. The **Peter Island Ferry** (☎ 284/495–2000) runs daily between Peter Island's private dock on Tortola just east of Road Town and Peter Island. **Jost Van Dyke Ferry Service** (☎ 284/495–2997) makes the run between Jost Van Dyke and Tortola's West End several times a day via the *When* ferry.

BUSES

For information about rates and schedules on Tortola, call **Scato's Bus Service** (☎ 284/494–2365).

CAR RENTALS

Driving on Tortola and Virgin Gorda is not for the timid. Roller-coaster roads with breathtaking ascents and descents and tight turns that give new meaning to the term "hairpin curves" are the norm. It's a challenge well worth trying, however; the ever-changing views of land, sea, and neighboring islands are among the most spectacular in the Caribbean. Most people will strongly recommend renting a four-wheel-drive vehicle. Driving is on the left side of the road. It's easy to become accustomed to it if you drive slowly, think before you make a turn, and pay attention when driving in and out of the occasional traffic circle, locally called a "roundabout." Speed limits are 30–40 mph outside town and 10–15 mph in residential areas. A valid B.V.I. driver's license is required and can be obtained for $10 at car-rental agencies. You must be at least 25 and have a valid driver's license from another country to get one.

**Avis** (☎ 284/494–3322) rents four-wheel-drive vehicles and cars in Road Town, Tortola. **Budget** (☎ 284/494–2639 in Wickham's Cay I, ☎ 284/494–5150 in Wickham's Cay II), which rents both cars and four-wheel-drive vehicles, has two offices in Road Town, Tortola. **Hertz** (☎ 284/495–4405) rents four-wheel drives and cars at its office at West End.

**Mahogany Rentals** (☎ 284/495–5469) provides taxi service all over the island of Virgin Gorda. **Andy's Taxi and Jeep Rental** (☎ 284/495–5252 or 284/495–5353) offers taxi service from one end of the island to the other.

TAXIS

Your hotel staff will be happy to summon a taxi for you. On Tortola, there are B.V.I. Taxi Association stands in Road Town near the ferry dock (☎ 284/494–2875) and Wickham's Cay I (☎ 284/494–2322); there's one on Beef Island at the airport (☎ 284/495–2378). You can also usually find a taxi at the Soper's Hole ferry dock, West End, where ferries from St. Thomas arrive. On Virgin Gorda, Mahogany and Andy's (☞ *above*) also provide taxi service.

## Guided Tours

If you'd like to do some chauffeured sightseeing on Tortola (there's a three-person minimum), get in touch with the **B.V.I. Taxi Association** (☎ 284/494–2875, 284/494–2322, or 284/495–2378). **Style's Taxi Service** (☎ 284/494–2260 during the day; 284/494–3341 at night) offers tours around the island and boat tours. **Travel Plan Tours** (☎ 284/494–2872) can arrange island tours, boat tours, and yacht charters. **Scato's Bus Service** (☎ 284/494–2365), in Road Town, provides public transportation, special tours with group rates, and beach outings. Guided tours on Virgin Gorda can be arranged through **Andy's Taxi and Jeep Rental** (☎ 284/495–5252). **Mahogany Rentals and Island Tours** (☎ 284/495–5469) has guided island tours.

## Language

British English, with a West Indian inflection, is the language spoken.

## Opening and Closing Times

Stores are generally open from 9 to 5 Monday through Saturday. Bank hours are Monday through Thursday 9–2:30 and Friday 9–2:30 and 4:30–6.

## Passports and Visas

Upon entering the B.V.I., U.S. and Canadian citizens are required to present some proof of citizenship. A valid passport is best, but an expired passport *plus* either a birth certificate, voter-registration card, or driver's license with photo ID is acceptable.

## Precautions

Although there are generally no perils from drinking the water in these islands, it is a good idea to ask if the water is potable when you check into your hotel.

Animals in the B.V.I. are not dangerous, but they can be road hazards. Give goats, sheep, horses, and cows the right of way.

Mosquitoes are not usually a problem in these breeze-blessed isles, but it is always a good idea to bring some repellent along. Beware, however, of the little insects called no-see-ums. They're for real and are especially pesky at twilight near the water. So if you're going for an evening stroll on the beach, apply some type of repellent liberally. No-see-um bites itch worse than mosquito bites and take a lot longer to go away. Prevention is the best cure, but witch hazel (or a dab of gin or vodka) offers *some* relief if they get you.

## Taxes and Service Charges

Hotels collect a 7% accommodations tax, which they will add to your bill along with a 10% service charge. Restaurants may put a similar service charge on the bill, or they may leave it up to you. It is customary to tip 15%, so if 10% is added and you liked the service, then consider leaving an additional 5%. For those leaving the B.V.I. by air, the departure tax is $10; by sea it is $5.

## Telephones and Mail

The area code for the B.V.I. is now 284 (changed in October 1997 from 809). To call anywhere in the B.V.I. once you've arrived, dial only the last five digits: Instead of dialing 494–1234, just dial 4–1234. A local call from a public pay phone costs 25¢. Coin-operated pay phones are frequently on the blink, but phones that use the **Caribbean Phone Card,** available in $5, $10, and $20 denominations, are a handy alternative. The cards are sold at most major hotels and many stores and can be used in special Phone Card telephones. You can call anywhere in the world with them (although rates to the U.S. are cheaper if you use AT&T). For credit-card or collect long-distance calls to the United States, look for special USADirect phones that are linked to an AT&T operator, or dial 111 from a pay phone and charge the call to your MasterCard or Visa. USADirect and pay phones can be found at most hotels and in towns.

There are post offices in Road Town on Tortola and in Spanish Town on Virgin Gorda. Postage for a first-class letter to the United States is 35¢ and for a postcard 20¢. (It might be noted that postal efficiency is not first class in the B.V.I.) For a small fee, **Rush It** in Road Town (☎ 284/494–4421) or Spanish Town (☎ 284/495–5821) offers most U.S. mail and UPS services via St. Thomas the next day.

## Visitor Information

Before you go, contact the **British Virgin Islands Tourist Board** (✉ 370 Lexington Ave., Suite 313, New York, NY 10017, ☎ 212/696–0400 or 800/835–8530) or the **British Virgin Islands Information Office** (✉ 1804 Union St., San Francisco, CA 94123, ☎ 415/775–0344 or 800/232–7770). British travelers can write or visit the **BVI Information Office** (✉ 110 St. Martin's La., London WC2N 4DY, ☎ 0171/2404259).

On Tortola there is a **B.V.I. Tourist Board Office** (✉ Box 134, Road Town, Tortola, ☎ 284/494–3134) at the center of Road Town near the ferry dock, just south of Wickham's Cay I. For all kinds of useful information about these islands, including rates and phone numbers, get a free copy of the *Welcome Tourist Guide,* available at hotels and many restaurants and stores.

# 8 Cayman Islands

The Caymans, a trio of islands that are rather flat and arid, have some of the best scuba diving in the Caribbean. Grand Cayman is almost city-like: here you can scuba, shop, fine dine, windsurf, jet ski, golf, dance, and more. The other two "sisters" are far more laid-back with Little Cayman catering almost exclusively to scuba divers.

Updated by
JoAnn
Milivojevic

**T**HE VENERABLE OLD *SATURDAY EVENING POST* dubbed
them "the islands that time forgot." No longer: The
Cayman Islands, a British Crown colony that includes Grand Cayman, Cayman Brac, and Little Cayman, are now one
of the Caribbean's hottest destinations, world-renowned for two offshore activities: banking and scuba diving. The former pays dividends
in the manicured capital of George Town, bulging as it does with some
554 offshore banks. The latter is on vivid display in the translucent
waters and the colorful variety of marine life protected by the government, which has created a marine parks system in all three islands.

Why do metropolis-weary visitors trek 480 mi south of Miami, filling
the hotels and condominiums that line famed Seven Mile Beach, even
during the slow summer season? Their dollars certainly go further in
other Caribbean destinations, for in Grand Cayman—which positively
reeks of suburban prosperity (residents joke that the national flower
is the satellite dish)—the U.S. dollar is worth 80 Cayman cents, and
the cost of living is 20% higher than in the United States.

Effective advertising accounts for some visitors, but the secret is word-
of-mouth testimonials. The Cayman Islanders—the population is
around 31,000, almost all of it residents of Grand Cayman—are
renowned for the courteous and civil manners befitting their British
heritage. Visitors won't find hasslers or panhandlers or any need to
look apprehensively over their shoulder on dark evenings, for the
colony enjoys a very low crime rate. Add to that permanent political
and economic stability, and you have a fairly rosy picture.

Columbus is said to have sighted the islands in 1503, but he didn't stop
off to explore. He did note that the surrounding sea was alive with turtles, so the islands were named Las Tortugas. The name was later
changed to Cayman.

The islands stayed largely uninhabited until the late 1600s, when
Britain took over the Cayman Islands and Jamaica from Spain under
the Treaty of Madrid. Cayman attracted a mixed bag of English,
Dutch, Spanish, and French settlers, pirates, refugees from the Spanish Inquisition, shipwrecked sailors, and deserters from Oliver Cromwell's
army in Jamaica. Today's Caymanians are the descendants of those nationalities.

The caves and coves of the islands—still fascinating to explore—were
a perfect hideout for pirates like Blackbeard and Sir Henry Morgan,
who plundered Spanish galleons hauling riches from the New World
of South America to Spain. Many a ship also fell afoul of the reefs surrounding the islands, often with the help of the Caymanians, who lured
the vessels to shore with beacon fires. Some of the old pioneer homes
on the islands were made from the remains of those galleons.

The legend of the Wreck of the Ten Sails was to have a lasting effect
on the Caymanians. In 1794 a convoy of 10 Jamaican ships bound for
England foundered on the reefs, but the islanders managed to rescue
everyone. Royalty was purportedly aboard, and a grateful George III
decreed that Caymanians should forever be exempt from conscription
and never have to pay taxes; however, research completed in 1994 shows
this tale to be purely fictional.

The Cayman Islands are still a British colony. A governor appoints three
official members to the Legislative Assembly and has to accept the advice of the Executive Council in all matters except foreign affairs, defense, internal security, and civil-service appointments.

# GRAND CAYMAN

## Lodging

The success of the Cayman Islands as a resort destination means you should book ahead for holidays. Most lodgings require a seven- or 14-day minimum stay at Christmastime. During the summer season, it's possible to find lodging even on short notice. If you stay in a condominium, you can book on a daily basis and stay any length of time. While about a third of the visitors come for the diving, a growing number are young honeymooners. There are few accommodations in the economy range, so guests must be prepared for resort prices.

Most of the larger hotels along Seven Mile Beach don't offer meal plans. The smaller properties that are more remote from the restaurants usually offer MAP or FAP (to estimate rates for hotels offering MAP or FAP, add about $40 per person per day to the average price ranges below). More than half the Caymans' rooms are rental condos and villas; all are equipped with fully stocked kitchens, telephones, satellite television, air-conditioning, living and dining areas, and patios and are individually decorated (most following a pastel tropical scheme). **Cayman Islands Reservation Service** (☎ 800/327–8777) can describe and book most condominiums and villas on the islands.

| CATEGORY | COST* |
|----------|-------|
| $$$$ | over $260 |
| $$$ | $200–$260 |
| $$ | $145–$200 |
| $ | under $145 |

*All prices are for a standard double room in winter, excluding 6% tax and 10% service charge.*

### Hotels

$$$$  ★  🏨 **Hyatt Regency Grand Cayman.** Painted sky blue and white and set amid gorgeous grounds, the Hyatt is adjacent to the Britannia Golf Course. The rooms, moderate in size, have a marble entranceway, oversize bathtub, French doors, and a veranda. Regency Club accommodations include its own concierge, complimentary Continental breakfast, and early-evening hors d'oeuvres and cocktails. At Camp Hyatt, kids 3–12 can participate in a supervised activities program for a cost of around $50 a child per day. Though it's by far the poshest lodging in the Cayman Islands, rates are comparably outrageous, especially for the so-called deluxe rooms, which differ only in they have a golf-course or courtyard view. ⊠ *Box 1698, Grand Cayman,* ☎ *345/949–1234 or 800/233–1234,* 🗚 *345/949–8528. 225 rooms, 10 suites; 44 rooms in Regency Club; 35 1-, 2-, 3-, and 4-bedroom villas. 3 restaurants, 4 bars, air-conditioning, minibars, 4 pools, beauty salon, hot tub, massage, golf course, 4 tennis courts, croquet, dive shop, marina, water sports, shops, car rental, conference rooms. AE, D, DC, MC, V. EP, BP, MAP.*

$$$$  🏨 **Spanish Bay Reef.** Grand Cayman's only all-inclusive resort is by far the most secluded of any property along the west shore. Pale pink two-story stucco units are surrounded by flowering trees and bushes on their own small sandy beach. An outdoor dining-bar area around the pool and overlooking the ocean has tables under a semicircular white-latticed arcade. There's also a spacious, coral-stone indoor bar and dining area. Simple but comfortable guest rooms, with bright Caribbean print bedspreads and curtains, are connected by boardwalks. The resort is on the northwest tip of the island, several miles past Seven Mile Beach in West Bay. Spanish Bay Reef itself is a deep drop-off, which means superior diving and snorkeling; instruction in both is offered.

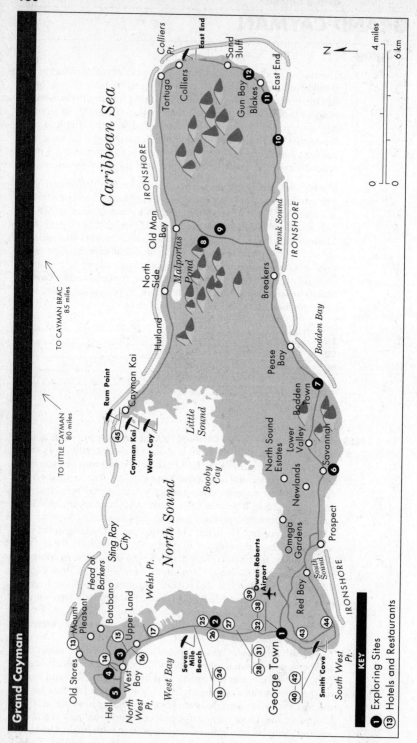

# Grand Cayman

Caribbean Sea

TO LITTLE CAYMAN
80 miles

TO CAYMAN BRAC
85 miles

IRONSHORE

North Sound

Little Sound

Booby Cay

Malportas Pond

IRONSHORE

Frank Sound

IRONSHORE

East End

Sand Bluff

East End

Colliers Pt.

Colliers

Tortuga

Gun Bay

Blakes

Old Man Bay

North Side

Hutland

Breakers

Bodden Bay

Pease Bay

Bodden Town

Savannah

Lower Valley

Newlands

North Sound Estates

Prospect

Omega Gardens

Red Bay

South Sound

Rum Point

Cayman Kai

Water Cay

Sting Ray City

Head of Barkers

Mount Pleasant

Batabano

Upper Land

Welsh Pt.

West Bay

North West Pt.

Old Stores

Hell

Seven Mile Beach

Owen Roberts Airport

George Town

Smith Cove

South West Pt.

## KEY

1  Exploring Sites

13  Hotels and Restaurants

4 miles

6 km

N

## Cayman Brac and Little Cayman

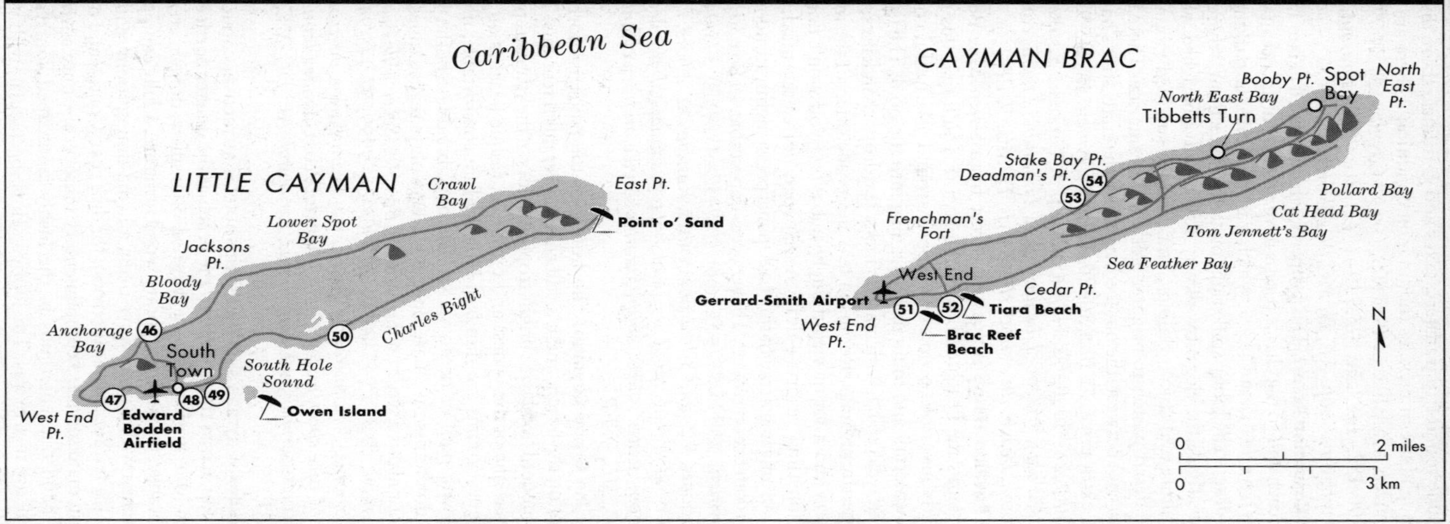

Caribbean Sea
LITTLE CAYMAN
CAYMAN BRAC
Crawl Bay
East Pt.
Point o' Sand
Lower Spot Bay
Jacksons Pt.
Bloody Bay
Anchorage Bay
South Town
West End Pt.
Edward Bodden Airfield
South Hole Sound
Owen Island
Charles Bight
Frenchman's Fort
Stake Bay Pt.
Deadman's Pt.
North East Bay
Booby Pt.
Spot Bay
North East Pt.
Tibbetts Turn
Pollard Bay
Cat Head Bay
Tom Jennett's Bay
Sea Feather Bay
Cedar Pt.
West End
Gerrard-Smith Airport
West End Pt.
Tiara Beach
Brac Reef Beach
N
0
2 miles
0
3 km


**Exploring**
Blow Holes, **10**
Bodden Town, **7**
Cayman Island Turtle Farm, **4**
Cayman Maritime Treasure Museum, **2**
East End, **11**
George Town, **1**
Hell, **5**
Mastic Trail, **8**
Old Homestead, **3**
Pedro's Castle, **6**
Queen Elizabeth II Botanic Park, **9**
Queen's View, **12**

**Dining**
Almond Tree, **32**
Billy's Place, **33**
Breadfruit Tree Garden, **38**
Chef Tell's Grand Old House, **42**
Cracked Conch, **14**
Crow's Nest, **44**
Garden Loggia, **27**
Golden Pagoda, **28**
Hemingway's, **26**
Hog Sty Bay Cafe, **35**
Lantana's, **23**
Lillian's, **39**
Lobster Pot, **34**
Ottmar's, **25**
The Wharf, **30**
White Hall Bay, **36**

**Lodging**
Adam's Guest House, **43**
The Beachcomber, **19**
Brac Reef, **51**
Caribbean Brac, **53**
Caribbean Club, **23**
Discovery Point, **15**
Divi Tiara, **52**
Eldemire's Guest House, **41**
Grand Pavilion, **24**
Grapetree/Cocoplum, **31**
Holiday Inn, **18**
Hyatt Regency, **20**
Indies Suites, **17**
Little Cayman Beach Resort, **50**
Paradise Villas, **48**
Pirates Point, **47**
Radisson Resort, **29**
Retreat at Rum Point, **45**
Sam McCoy's, **46**
Sleep Inn, **37**
Southern Cross, **49**
Spanish Bay Reef, **13**
Sunset House, **40**
Victoria House, **16**
Villas of the Galleon, **21**
Walton's Mango Manor, **54**
Westin Casuarina, **22**

Rates include round-trip transfers, taxes and gratuities, shore diving, boat dives, and use of bicycles (not in mint condition). There are also fishing charters available. ⊠ *Box 903, Grand Cayman,* ☎ *345/949– 3765 or 800/482–3483,* FAX *345/949–1842. 50 units. Restaurant, bar, pool, hot tub, dive shop. AE, D, MC, V. All-inclusive.*

$$$$    🏨 **Westin Casuarina Resort.** This property, which opened in late 1995, is on the beach and so the choice rooms have at least partial ocean view (standards have an "island" view, which translates into the parking lot and main drag). The lobby spills right on to the waterfront, where tall royal palms shade the elegant walkway. Rooms have bleached white-wood furniture and stucco ceilings, and decor of subdued mountain colors and desert pastels to brighter jade and ultramarine. There isn't much difference between the one-bedroom and the suite, so it's hardly worth the extra price. ⊠ *Box 30620, Grand Cayman,* ☎ *345/945– 3800 or 800/228–3000,* FAX *345/949–5825. 351 rooms, 5 suites. 2 restaurants, 2 bars, grill, pool, beauty salon, 2 hot tubs, 2 tennis courts, exercise room, beach, dive shop, shops. AE, D, MC, V. EP.*

$$$–$$$$    🏨 **Grand Pavilion Hotel.** Across the street from Seven Mile Beach
★    (where it shares the beach club with the Hyatt), you'll find this intimate, quietly luxurious property wrapped around a beautiful courtyard with waterfall and fountains cascading into the pool. The lobby is august but welcoming, with marble floors, teardrops chandeliers, and plush leather furnishings. Rooms in teal and peach offer all the modern comforts and a lot of well-thought-out extras you won't find at the other bustling resorts—daily newspaper, coffee/tea machine, bathrobes, an amazing array of toiletries, pants press, nightly turndown, even an in-room fax on request. The service is impeccable. ⊠ *Box 30117, Grand Cayman,* ☎ *345/947–5656 or 800/437–4824,* FAX *345/947– 5353. 88 rooms, 5 2- and 3-bedroom suites. Restaurant, 2 bars, café, lounge, air-conditioning, minibars, pool, hot tub, sauna, golf privileges, exercise room, water sports, shop, laundry service and dry cleaning. AE, D, DC, MC, V. EP.*

$$$–$$$$    🏨 **Holiday Inn Grand Cayman.** This hotel was the pioneer resort establishment on the beach, and it's still cheerful yet unpretentious. The sprawling modern hotel with bright tropical colors in the spacious public rooms has one of the widest and most picturesque beaches on the strip. The guest rooms are standard Holiday Inn: comfortable, if not luxurious, with pool or ocean views. The huge breakfast buffet is a value, and don't miss the "Barefoot Man," who plays reggae tunes on the piano four nights a week on the patio. ⊠ *Box 904, Seven Mile Beach, Grand Cayman,* ☎ *345/947–4444 or 800/421–9999,* FAX *345/947– 4213. 215 rooms. 3 restaurants, 2 bars, ice cream parlor, air-conditioning, pool, dive shop, water sports, nightclub, coin laundry, laundry service, business services, meeting rooms, car rental. AE, DC, MC, V. EP, BP, MAP.*

$$$    🏨 **Indies Suites.** Cayman's only all-suite hotel is attractive, comfort-
★    able, and right across the road from the beach at the quieter north end of the Seven Mile stretch. One- or two-bedroom suites, done in cream and burnt orange, have contemporary wood furniture, a fully equipped modern kitchen with a microwave oven, a living-dining room (with a sleeper sofa), a terrace, and a storeroom for dive gear. Continental buffet breakfast, maid service, a complimentary sunset cruise once a week, and a live band that entertains in the lushly landscaped courtyard twice a week are nice extras. The lobby itself is spectacular, with vintage 1930s Fords on display. ⊠ *Box 2070 GT, Seven Mile Beach, Grand Cayman,* ☎ *345/947–5025 or 800/654–3130,* FAX *345/947–5024. 38 suites. Bar, snack bar, grocery, air-conditioning, pool, hot tub, dive shop, snorkeling, water sports, coin laundry. AE, MC, V. CP.*

$$$  ⊞ **Radisson Resort Grand Cayman.** This five-story luxury property is
★   on Seven Mile Beach, just 1 mi from George Town. Designed in colonial style with arched doorways, the hotel's airy pale yellow and marble lobby opens onto a plant-filled courtyard. Families like the large adjoining rooms done in bright tropical colors; all have balconies facing either the ocean or a garden court. There's a beach bar near the pool, a dive shop offering every possible water sport, a full-service spa, and a snorkeling reef just 50 ft offshore. As it has the largest conference center on the island, it's predictably popular for convention and incentive travel. ⊠ *Box 30371, Seven Mile Beach, Grand Cayman,* ☎ *345/949–0088 or 800/333–3333,* ℻ *345/949–0288. 315 rooms, 4 suites. Restaurant, bar, snack bar, air-conditioning, pool, beauty salon, hot tub, spa, beach, dive shop, water sports, shops, laundry service and dry cleaning, meeting rooms, car rental. AE, D, DC, MC, V. EP.*

$$  ⊞ **Sleep Inn.** This two-story Choice Hotels affiliate is a quick stroll
★   from Seven Mile Beach, close to the airport, and just a mile from George Town's shops, making it excellent value. Air-conditioned rooms are motel-modern, with peaches-and-cream pastels and modern wood furnishings. The Dive Inn dive shop is here, as are tours and car and motorcycle rentals. ⊠ *Box 30111, Grand Cayman,* ☎ *345/949–9111,* ℻ *345/949–6699. 124 rooms. Bar, grill, air-conditioning, pool, hot tub, dive shop, water sports, shop, laundry service and dry cleaning, meeting room, car rental. AE, D, MC, V. EP.*

$–$$  ⊞ **Sunset House.** Low-key and laid-back describe this resort with sparse, motel-style rooms on the ironshore south of George Town, 4 mi from Seven Mile Beach. A congenial staff, popular bar, and seafood restaurant are pluses, but it's the diving and dive packages that attract most guests. Full dive services include free waterside lockers, two- and three-tank dives at the better reefs around the island, and Cathy Church's U/W Photo Center. It's a five-minute walk to a sandy beach, 10 minutes to George Town. ⊠ *Box 479, S. Church St., Grand Cayman,* ☎ *345/949–7111 or 800/854–4767,* ℻ *345/949–7101. 59 rooms. Restaurant, bar, air-conditioning, 2 pools, hot tub, dive shop. AE, D, DC, MC, V. EP, BP, MAP.*

## Condominiums and Villas

**Cayman Islands Department of Tourism** provides a complete list of condominiums and small rental apartments in the $$ range. Many of these are multibedroom units that become affordable when shared by two or more couples. Rates are higher during the winter season, and there may be a three- or seven-night minimum. The following complexes bear a marked similarity to one another: All are equipped with fully stocked kitchens, telephones, satellite television, air-conditioning, living and dining areas, and patios, and are individually decorated (most following a pastel tropical scheme). Differences arise in property amenities and proximity to town. All are well maintained and directly on the beach, though you will need a car for grocery shopping. **Cayman Islands Reservation Service** (⊠ 6100 Blue Lagoon Dr., Suite 150, Miami, FL 33126, ☎ 800/327–8777), **Cayman Villas** (⊠ Box 681, Grand Cayman, ☎ 345/947–4144 or 800/235–5888, ℻ 345/949–7471), **and Hospitality World Ltd.** (⊠ Box 30123, Grand Cayman, ☎ 345/949–3458 or 800/232–1034, ℻ 345/949–7054) can also make reservations.

$$$$  ⊞ **The Beachcomber.** Set in the middle of Seven Mile Beach, each of the simply furnished apartments in this older condo community has a view of the ocean from a private, screened patio. There is a grocery store just across the street and countless shopping and dining outlets within walking distance, so once you're here, you don't really need a car. The Beachcomber reef is just offshore for snorkeling, and palapas on the beach provide shade when the sun gets a bit too warm. ⊠ *Box*

*1799, Seven Mile Beach, Grand Cayman,* ☎ *345/947–4470 or 800/327–8777,* FAX *345/947–5019. 23 units. Grills, air-conditioning, pool, beach, coin laundry. AE, MC, V.*

$$$$ 🏨 **Caribbean Club.** Eighteen one- and two-bedroom villas (six on the beach) make up this quiet island condominium getaway. Although secluded, these units are not quite on a par with the truly deluxe properties on the island; however, they recently received newly tiled baths, fresh paint jobs, and wicker furniture. There is maid service. Children under age 11 are not allowed in the winter season. ⊠ *Box 30499, Seven Mile Beach, Grand Cayman,* ☎ *345/947–4099 or 800/327–8777,* FAX *345/947–4443. 18 villas. Restaurant, bar, air-conditioning, tennis court, beach, coin laundry, laundry service and dry cleaning. AE, MC, V. EP, MAP.*

$$$$ 🏨 **Discovery Point Club.** At the quiet, far north end of Seven Mile Beach in West Bay, 6 mi from George Town, this complex offers a lovely beach with peace and seclusion and is within walking distance of great snorkeling in the protected waters of Cemetery Reef. Tennis courts, a hot tub, and a pool for relaxation are part of the appeal here. Kids 12 and under stay free during the off-season (April–December). ⊠ *Box 439, West Bay, Grand Cayman,* ☎ *345/947–4724 or 800/327–8777,* FAX *345/947–5051. 45 units. Grills, pool, hot tub, 2 tennis courts, beach, coin laundry. AE, MC, V.*

$$$$ 🏨 **Victoria House.** The one-, two-, and three-bedroom units in this simple building have white walls and tile floors and are decorated with muted Caribbean prints and rattan furniture. You may choose from a range of activities including tennis and water sports. The Victoria is 3 mi north of town on a quiet stretch of Seven Mile Beach; if you're an early riser, you may catch a glimpse of giant sea turtles on the sand. ⊠ *Box 30571, Seven Mile Beach (near West Bay), Grand Cayman,* ☎ *345/947–4233,* FAX *345/947–5328. 25 units. Air-conditioning, tennis, scuba diving, beach, snorkeling, coin laundry. AE, MC, V.*

$$$$ 🏨 **Villas of the Galleon.** The exteriors of these deluxe stucco cottages look somewhat shabby, but the units themselves are attractive and beautifully maintained. Each duplex one- or two-bedroom unit has full kitchen, terrace, enormous closets (a big plus for families), and individual decor, such as eggshell tile floors, pastel finishes, and rattan furnishings. The location couldn't be better: perched on the widest section of Seven Mile Beach, just across from the Jack Nicklaus–designed Links Golf Club. ⊠ *Box 1797, Seven Mile Beach, Grand Cayman,* ☎ *345/947–4433,* FAX *345/947–4705. 74 units. Grills, air-conditioning, beach, coin laundry. AE, MC, V.*

$$$–$$$$ 🏨 **Grapetree/Cocoplum.** A half mile from George Town on Seven Mile Beach, these sister condos are adjacent to one another. Grapetree's two-bedroom, two-bath units are carpeted, with traditional wicker furnishings and a beige and brown decor. Cocoplum's units are similar, with Caribbean pastel prints, and its grounds have more plants and trees. ⊠ *Box 1802, Seven Mile Beach, Grand Cayman,* ☎ *345/949–5640 or 800/635–4824,* FAX *345/949–0150. 51 units. Air-conditioning, 2 pools, tennis court, beach. AE, MC, V.*

$$$–$$$$ 🏨 **Retreat at Rum Point.** The Retreat has its own narrow beach with casuarina trees, far from the madding crowd on the north-central tip of Grand Cayman, 27 mi from town. Up to six people can rent a two-bedroom villa here. Two or three people are comfortable in the one-bedroom units. The decor in these privately owned condos vary, but most have a tropical decor featuring heavy wicker furniture, and all are spacious and include a washer and dryer. There are dive facilities nearby, where you can take advantage of superb offshore diving, including the famed North Wall. You'll be stranded without a car; it's a 35-minute drive to George Town or the airport. ⊠ *Box 46, North Side,*

*Grand Cayman,* ☎ *345/947–9135,* FAX *345/947–9058. 23 units. Restaurant, bar, air-conditioning, pool, sauna, tennis court, exercise room, racquetball. MC, V.*

### Guest Houses and B&Bs

They may be some distance from the beach and short on style and facilities, but these lodgings offer rock-bottom prices (all fall well below our $ category), a friendly atmosphere, and your best shot at getting to know the locals. Rooms are clean and simple, often with cooking facilities, and most have private bathrooms. Many establishments have outdoor grills and picnic tables for guest use. A rental car is recommended. These establishments do not accept personal checks or credit cards but do take reservations through the **Cayman Islands Reservation Service** (☎ 800/327–8777).

**Adam's Guest House** (⊠ Box 312, on Melnac Ave. near Seaview Hotel, Grand Cayman, ☎ 345/949–2512, ☎ FAX 345/949–0919), 1 mi south of George Town and 4 mi from the beach, has five rooms, all with kitchenette. **Eldemire's Guest House** (⊠ Box 482, on South Church St., Grand Cayman, ☎ 345/949–5387, FAX 345/949–6987), Grand Cayman's first guest house, has seven rooms and is a 15-minute drive to Seven Mile Beach, but less than a mile south of pretty Smith Cove Bay.

## Dining

Grand Cayman's restaurants satisfy every palate and pocketbook. Gourmet Continental cuisine is available to the high rollers, and ethnic food can be had at moderate prices. West Indian fare in dining spots serving locals is the best in taste and value.

Seafood, not surprisingly, appears on most restaurant menus. Fish—including grouper, snapper, dolphin, tuna, wahoo, and marlin—is served either simply (baked, broiled, steamed) or Cayman-style (with peppers, onions, and tomatoes). Conch, the meat of a large pink mollusk, is ubiquitous in stews and chowders and as fritters or panfried ("cracked"). Caribbean lobster is available but is often quite expensive, and other shellfish are in short supply in local waters. The only traditional culinary treat of the islands is turtle soup, stew, or steak, but fewer restaurants carry them these days.

All the restaurants reviewed are on Grand Cayman because there are few to none on the sister islands (visitors eat at the resorts and guest houses). Dining out here can be expensive, so replenish your billfold, because some places do not accept plastic. Many restaurants add a 10%–15% service charge to the bill, so check before leaving a tip.

### What to Wear

Smart casual wear (slacks and sundresses) is acceptable throughout the Caymans for dinner in all but a few places. The nicer resorts and more expensive restaurants may require a jacket, especially in high season; ask when making reservations. Shorts are usually acceptable during the day, but unless you're going to an ultracasual beach bar, beachwear (bathing suits, cover-ups, tank tops, etc.) is a no-no. Most restaurants have an alfresco dining section, and if you plan to dine under the stars, ask for bug spray they provide—the mosquitoes are fierce after sunset.

| CATEGORY | COST* |
| --- | --- |
| $$$ | over $30 |
| $$ | $20–$30 |
| $ | under $20 |

*per person, excluding drinks and service charge*

**$$$**   ✕ **Chef Tell's Grand Old House.** TV celebrity chef Tell Erhardt's menu features Continental entrées and a few local specialties. Among the spicier appetizer choices is fried coconut shrimp with mustard apricot sauce. On the milder side are entrées such as lobster "The Chef's Way," dipped in egg batter and sautéed with shallots, mushrooms, and white wine, and coffee-lacquered duck with fresh pear chutney. The ocean-side gazebos, surrounded by palms and cooled by ceiling fans, are the liveliest and best spots for dining. The excellent service adds to this gracious dining experience. ⊠ *S. Church St.,* ☎ *345/949–9333. Reservations essential for dinner. DC, MC, V. Closed Sun. No lunch Sat.*

**$$$**   ✕ **Garden Loggia Cafe.** The Hyatt's indoor-outdoor café opens onto the most beautifully landscaped garden courtyard on the island. The Caribbean decor includes pastel colors, ceiling fans, and marble-top tables. The restaurant, serving Italian and Oriental cuisine, opens for dinner only during high season (mid-December–May). It's the weekly Sunday champagne brunch, featuring everything from fresh seafood to waffles and custom-made omelets, that draws a crowd. Reserve a seat as early as possible to avoid disappointment. ⊠ *Hyatt Regency Grand Cayman, West Bay Rd.,* ☎ *345/949–1234. Reservations essential. AE, D, DC, MC, V.*

**$$$**   ✕ **Ottmar's.** This quietly elegant restaurant is styled after a West In-
  ★     dian great house. Jade carpeting, peach walls, linen, a trickling fountain, mahogany furniture, and glass chandeliers create an attractive setting for the excellent service. Favorites on the international menu include bouillabaisse, chicken breast Oscar (topped with crab, asparagus, and hollandaise), and French pepper steak (flamed in cognac and doused with green peppercorn sauce and crème fraîche). ⊠ *Clarion Grand Pavilion, West Bay Rd.,* ☎ *345/941–5879 or 345/947–5882. Reservations essential. AE, D, DC, MC, V. No lunch.*

**$$$**   ✕ **The Wharf.** Stylishly decorated in blue and white, the Wharf looks onto a veranda and the nearby sea. On the surf-and-turf menu are conch fritters, home-smoked salmon, "Seafood a L'aneth" (lobster and scallops in dill sauce), veal scallopini, and steak fillet béarnaise; anything on the fresh daily menu is recommended. Live Paraguayan music entertains diners. The Ports of Call bar is a perfect spot from which to watch the sun set, and tarpon feeding off the deck is a nightly (9 PM) spectacle here. ⊠ *West Bay Rd.,* ☎ *345/949–2231. AE, D, MC, V. No lunch weekends.*

**$$–$$$**  ✕ **Hemingway's.** Sea views and breezes attract diners to this classy open-
  ★     air restaurant on Seven Mile Beach. In the evening (except Sunday), candlelight and a guitarist complete the romantic atmosphere. Nouvelle Caribbean and seafood dishes include pumpkin-coated mahimahi with mango juice, macadamia-crusted pork loin, and grouper stuffed with crab and sweet corn in a jerk cream sauce. Portions are large, and service is superb. For a tropical drink, try the Seven Mile Meltdown, with dark rum, peach schnapps, pineapple juice, and fresh coconut. ⊠ *West Bay Rd. across from Hyatt,* ☎ *345/947–5700. AE, D, DC, MC, V.*

**$$–$$$**  ✕ **Lantana's.** Alfred Schrock, longtime chef at the Wharf Restaurant,
  ★     now creates excellent American-Caribbean lunches and dinners here. Enjoy lobster quesadillas, homemade lamb sausage, or blackened king salmon over cilantro linguine with banana fritters and cranberry relish. If you come for nothing else, *don't* miss the incredible roasted garlic soup and the apple pie. The decor of the bi-level restaurant—potted plants, teak furniture, painted wooden fish—places you in the perfectly serene island state of mind. ⊠ *Caribbean Club, West Bay Rd.,* ☎ *345/947–5595. AE, D, MC, V. No lunch weekends.*

**$$–$$$**  ✕ **Lobster Pot.** The second-floor terrace of this cozy restaurant overlooks the bay downtown, so the sunsets are an extra attraction. The menu includes both Continental dishes and such Caribbean specialties as conch chowder, seafood curry, shrimp Diane, and, of course, lobster. This place is popular, and the constant turnover creates a rather frenzied atmosphere. If you can't make it for dinner, drop by the pub and have a frozen banana daiquiri. ⊠ *N. Church St.,* ☎ *345/949–2736. AE, D, MC, V.*

**$$** ✕ **Crow's Nest.** This secluded seafood restaurant, about a 15-minute drive south of George Town, is located in a rustic West Indian Creole cottage set amid overgrown foliage and flowering shrubs right on the beach (diners often go snorkeling after lunch). For the best breezes you should sit on the enclosed terrace, which is draped in fishnets. The shark du jour, herb-crusted dolphin with lobster sauce, swordfish with jerk mayo, and shrimp and conch dishes are excellent, as is the chocolate fudge rum cake. ⊠ *South Sound Rd.,* ☎ *345/949–9366. AE, MC, V. No lunch Sun.*

**$$** ✕ **Golden Pagoda.** Hakka-style cooking (similar to using a hibachi) is featured at this well-known Chinese restaurant. Among its specialties are moo goo gai pan, butterfly shrimp, and chicken in black-bean sauce. Take-out (takie-outie, they call it) is now available, as are showy Japanese teppanyaki dinners (minimum two persons) Tuesday through Saturday night. ⊠ *West Bay Rd.,* ☎ *345/949–5475. Reservations essential for Japanese dinner. AE, MC, V. No lunch weekends.*

**$$** ✕ **White Hall Bay.** This popular local hangout occupies a charming traditional Caymanian waterfront home, hung with gourds, straw bags, and marvelous black-and-white photos of old-timers. The food is equally traditional, from sultry turtle and pepper-pot stews (both seeming to have bubbled for years) to luscious yam cake and coconut cream pie. ⊠ *N. Church St.,* ☎ *345/949–8670. AE, D, MC, V.*

**$–$$** ✕ **Cracked Conch by the Sea.** The new location of this old island fa-
★ vorite provides patio diners with a panoramic view of the sea. Specialties of this popular seafood restaurant, the originator of cracked (tenderized and panfried) conch, include conch fritters, conch chowder, spicy Cayman-style snapper, turtle steak, and other seafood offerings. The Sunday buffet is divine with a array of island-style curries and jerk meats; don't miss the cassava cake, a thick, sweet spongy desert. ⊠ *West Bay Rd. near Turtle Bay Farm,* ☎ *345/947–5217. MC, V.*

**$–$$** ✕ **Hog Sty Bay Cafe.** Lots of socializing goes on in the casual atmosphere of this English-style café on the harbor in George Town. A simple menu of sandwiches, hamburgers, and Caribbean dishes will satisfy you for lunch and dinner. This is the classic Caribbean hangout, with hand-painted wooden fish hanging everywhere, an invigorating mix of zany residents, and curious tourists. Many believe the conch fritters served here are the best in town. Come to watch the sun set from the seaside patio or to enjoy the weekday happy hour. ⊠ *N. Church St.,* ☎ *345/949–6163. AE, MC, V.*

**$** ✕ **Almond Tree.** If you're looking for authentic island atmosphere in modern Grand Cayman, this eatery combines architecture from the South Seas isle of Yap with bones, skulls, and bric-a-brac from Africa, South America, and the Pacific. Good-value seafood entrées include turtle steak and fresh grouper, with "All-U-Can-Eat" entrées for CI$12 on Wednesday and Friday. ⊠ *N. Church St.,* ☎ *345/949–2893. AE, MC, V. Closed Sun.*

**$** ✕ **Billy's Place.** Billy's, the yellow-and-blue diner in the Kirk Supermarket parking lot, surprises in many ways. In addition to hearty servings of jerk chicken, pork, goat, shrimp, conch, fish, lobster, and burgers, you can order Indian *pakoras* (vegetable fritters), tandoori chicken or shrimp, and several curried selections. Service tends to be abrupt, but the crowds don't seem to mind. ⊠ *N. Church St.,* ☎ *345/949–0470. AE, D, MC, V. Closed Sun.*

$ ✕ **Breadfruit Tree Garden.** Tucked away in a secluded spot, this jewel is a local's favorite where the price is certainly right. The jerk chicken rivals any on the island. Also on the menu are curry chicken and stewed pork, oxtail, rice and beans, and homemade soups; drinks include breadfruit, mango, passion fruit, and carrot juice. The interior has a slightly kitschy look with silk roses, white porch swings, straw hats, empty birdcages, and fake ivy crawling along the ceiling. It's open until the wee hours, which makes this a good midnight munchie stop. ⊠ *Eastern Ave., George Town,* ☎ *345/945–2124. No credit cards.*

$ ✕ **Lillian's.** Island and Spanish dishes are the specialties at this diner, which is always filled with locals during lunchtime. Daily specials include barbecue ribs, meat loaf, and fish rundown, a stew made with fish plantain, cassava, sweet potato, and breadfruit in a white sauce (squirt a bit of lime on it and it's perfection). Lillian occasionally makes "Fish Tea," which is really a soup and is said to be an aphrodisiac. ⊠ *Christian Plaza, near airport, on North Sound Rd.,* ☎ *345/949–2178. Closed Sun. No dinner. No credit cards.*

## Beaches

You may read or hear about the "dozens of beaches" of these islands, but that's more exaggeration than reality. Grand Cayman's west coast, the most developed area of the entire colony, is where you'll find its famous **Seven Mile Beach** (actually 5½ mi long) and its expanses of powdery white sand. The beach is litter-free and sans peddlers, so you can relax in an unspoiled, hassle-free (if somewhat crowded) atmosphere. This is also Grand Cayman's busiest vacation center, and most of the island's accommodations, restaurants, and shopping centers are on this strip. You'll find headquarters for the island's aquatic activities in various places along the strip (☞ Outdoor Activities and Sports, *below*).

Grand Cayman has several smaller beaches that may more correctly be called coves, including **Smith Cove,** off South Church Street, south of the Grand Old House—a popular bathing spot with residents on weekends.

The best shore-entry snorkeling locations are off the ironshore south of George Town, at **Eden Rock** (☎ 345/949–7243) and **Parrot's Landing** (☎ 345/949–7884); north of town, at the reef just off the **West Bay Cemetery** on Grand Cayman's west coast; and in the reef-protected shallows of the island's north and south coasts, where coral and fish life are much more varied and abundant.

The best windsurfing is just off the beaches in **East End,** at Colliers, by Morritt's Tortuga Club. The beach can be lovely if it's kept clean of seaweed tossed ashore by trade winds, but the windsurfing is the real draw here. Seldom discovered by visitors unless they're staying here are the beautiful beach areas of **Cayman Kai** (which was undergoing some development at press time), **Rum Point,** and, even more isolated and unspoiled, **Water Cay.** These are favored hideaways for residents and popular Sunday picnic spots.

## Outdoor Activities and Sports

### Deep-Sea Fishing

If you enjoy action fishing, Cayman waters have plenty to offer—blue and white marlin, yellowfin tuna, sailfish, dolphin, and wahoo. Bonefish and tarpon are also plentiful off Little Cayman. Some 25 boats are available for charter, offering fishing options that include deep-sea, reef, bone, tarpon, light-tackle, and fly-fishing. Grand Cayman charter operators to contact are **Charter Boat Headquarters** (☎ 345/947–

4340), **Crosby Ebanks** (☎ 345/947–4049), **Island Girl** (☎ 345/947–3029), and **Bayside Watersports** (☎ 345/949–3200).

## Diving and Snorkeling

To call the Cayman Islands a scuba diver's paradise is not overstating the case. Jacques Cousteau named Bloody Bay (off Little Cayman) one of the world's top dives, and the famed Cayman Wall, off Grand Cayman, ranks up there as well. Pristine water (often exceeding 100-ft visibility), breathtaking coral formations, and plentiful and exotic marine life await divers. A host of top-notch dive operations offer a variety of services, instruction, and equipment. A Grand Cayman must-see for adventurous souls is **Stingray City,** which has been called the best 12-ft dive (or snorkel) in the world. Here are dozens of unusually tame stingrays who, accustomed to being fed first by fishermen and now by divers, suction squid off divers' outstretched palms and gracefully swim and twist around the divers in the shallow waters.

Divers are required to be certified and possess a "C" card or take a short resort or full certification course. A certification course, including classroom, pool, and boat sessions as well as checkout dives, takes four to six days and costs $350–$400. A short resort course usually lasts a day and costs about $80–$100. It introduces the novice to the sport and teaches the rudimentary skills needed to make a shallow, instructor-monitored dive.

All dive operations on Cayman are more than competent; among them are **Aquanauts** (☎ 345/945–1990 or 800/357–2212), **Bob Soto's** (☎ 345/947-4631 or 800/262–7686), **Don Foster's** (☎ 345/949–5679 or 800/833–4837), **Eden Rock** (☎ 345/949–7243), **Parrot's Landing** (☎ 345/949–7884 or 800/448–0428), **Red Sail Sports** (☎ 345/949–8745 or 800/255–6425), and **Sunset Divers** (☎ 345/949–7111 or 800/854–4767). **Turtle Reef Divers** (☎ 345/949–1700) is among the first to offer Nitrox dives/certification (a diver's bottom time is extended). Their location next to the Turtle Farm is excellent for shore dives and is off the beaten path of other dive operators. The brand-new dive gear is another plus. Request full information on all operators from the Department of Tourism (☞ Visitor Information *in* Cayman Islands A to Z, *below*). A single-tank dive averages $45; a two-tank dive, about $55. Snorkel-equipment rental runs from $5 to $15 a day.

Most operations can rent all diving gear, including equipment for underwater photography; Bob Soto's, Don Foster's, and Cathy Church's U/W Photo Center (in Sunset House [☞ Lodging, *above*]) have facilities for film processing and underwater photo courses.

One-week live-aboard dive cruises are available aboard the 110-ft *Cayman Aggressor III* (☎ 800/348–2628) and the luxury yacht *Little Cayman Diver II* (☎ 800/458–2722).

## Fitness

Most hotels and resorts offer fitness facilities. **World Gym** (✉ West Bay Rd., across from Cinema, ☎ 345/949–5132) has machines, weights, a sauna, a whirlpool, daily aerobics classes, and personal trainers on staff. Daily membership is $10; weekly, $25.

## Golf

The **Grand Cayman–Britannia** golf course (☎ 345/949–8020), next to the Hyatt Regency, was designed by Jack Nicklaus. The course is really three in one—a nine-hole par-70 regulation course, an 18-hole par-57 executive course, and a Cayman course (played with a Cayman ball that goes about half the distance of a regulation ball). Greens fees range from $40 to $80. Golf carts ($15–$25) are mandatory.

Windier, and therefore more challenging, is the **Links at Safe Haven**
(☎ 345/949–5988), Cayman's first 18-hole championship golf course,
set amid a virtual botanical garden of indigenous trees, plants, and flowering shrubs. The Roy Case–designed par-71, 6,519-yard course also
has an aqua driving range (the distance markers and balls float), a two-
story clubhouse, locker rooms, a pro shop, a patio bar with live jazz
happy hours on weekends, and a fine restaurant serving Continental
and Caribbean cuisine daily for lunch and dinner. Greens fees run to
$60. Golf carts ($15–$20 per person) are mandatory.

## Hiking

Nature trails abound on all three islands (on the sister islands, it's best
to ask locals for directions—you'll probably be standing right next to
the start of a trail without realizing it). Guided nature walks are available at the National Trust's Mastic Trail on Grand Cayman (✉ Off
Frank Sound Rd., ☎ 345/949–1996), a rugged 2-mi slash through pristine woodlands, mangrove swamps, and ancient rock formations.
Tours are by appointment, daily 10–3, and cost $30 per person.

## Tennis

Most hotels and condo complexes have tennis courts for guests.

## Water Sports

Water skis, Windsurfers, Hobie Cats, and Jet Skis are available at
many of the aquatic shops along Seven Mile Beach (☞ Diving and
Snorkeling, *above*). **Sailboards Caribbean** (☎ 345/949–1068) offers
windsurfing rentals, lessons for beginners, and a full gamut of courses
through high-wind advanced levels. **Cayman Windsurf** (☎ 345/947–
7492) offers windsurfing lessons and rentals at the East End of the island at Morritt's Tortuga Club and on North Sound by Safe Haven.

# Shopping

Grand Cayman has two money-saving attributes—duty-free merchandise and the absence of a sales tax. Prices on imported merchandise—English china, Swiss watches, French perfumes, and Japanese
cameras and electronic goods—are often lower than elsewhere, but not
always. To make sure you get a bargain, come prepared with a price
list of items you are thinking of buying and comparison shop. The main
shopping areas are **Elizabethan Square, Cardinal Avenue,** and the chic
**Kirk Freeport Plaza,** known for its fine jewelry, plus duty-free china,
crystal, Gucci items, perfumes, and fine cosmetics. Unusual jewelry can
also be found, ranging from authentic sunken treasure and ancient coins
made into necklaces and pins to relatively inexpensive rings and earrings made from semiprecious stones, coral, and seashells. **Tortuga Rum
Company's** (☎ 345/949–7701, 345/949–7866, or 345/949–7867)
scrumptious rum cake (sealed fresh until opened) is sweet and moist
and makes a great souvenir.

## Arts and Crafts

Debbie van der Bol runs an arts-and-crafts shop called **Pure Art**
(☎ 345/949–9133) on South Church Street and at the Hyatt Regency
(☎ 345/947–5633). She sells watercolors, wood carvings, and lacework
by local artists, as well as her own sketches and cards. Original prints,
paintings, and sculpture with a tropical theme are found at **Island Art
Gallery** (☎ 345/949–9861) in the Anchorage Shopping Center in George
Town. The **Kennedy Gallery** (☎ 345/949–8077), in West Shore Center
and on Fort Street in George Town, features primarily limited-edition
pastel watercolors of typical Cayman scenes by Robert E. Kennedy.

The **Heritage Crafts Shop** (☎ 345/949–7093), near the harbor in
George Town, sells local crafts and gifts. The **West Shore Shopping Cen-**

ter, on Seven Mile Beach near the Radisson, offers good-quality island art, beachwear, and more. The **Queen's Court Shopping Center,** on Seven Mile Beach close to town, offers an array of souvenirs, crafts, and gifts. **Calico Jack's** (⊠ West Bay Rd., George Town, ☎ 345/949–4373) is a good source for local T-shirts, casual resort wear, and dive gear (truly self-contained, it also operates a dive shop and pub).

### Black Coral

Black coral products are exquisite and a popular choice. However, environmental groups discourage tourists from purchasing any coral that is designated as endangered species, because the reefs are not always harvested carefully. If you feel differently, there are a number of local craftsmen who create original designs and finish their own work. The coral creations of **Bernard Passman** (⊠ Fort St., George Town, ☎ 345/949–0123) won the approval of the English royal family. Beautiful coral pieces are also found at **Richard's Fine Jewelry** (⊠ Harbour Dr., George Town, ☎ 345/949–7156), where designers Richard and Rafaela Barile attract their fair share of celebrities. **Carey Cayman Coral** (⊠ South Sound Rd., no phone) is a workshop run by Carey Hurlstone. Carey, a gentle bear of a man covered with tattoos, professes he was a biker with the Hell's Angels before coming home to Cayman to work as a craftsman. He makes black coral jewelry and figurines and carves glass. Carey's workmanship is superb, and his prices are quite reasonable for the quality.

## Nightlife

Each of the island hot spots attracts a different clientele. The **Holiday Inn** (☎ 345/947–4444) offers something for everyone: **Coconuts** (☎ 345/947–5757), the hotel's original comedy club, features young American stand-up comedians who entertain every Wednesday through Sunday. Crowds also gather poolside, where the island-famous "Barefoot Man" sings and plays the piano four nights a week. Dancing is spontaneous and welcome, and it's a great spot to people-watch.

**Long John Silver's Nightclub** (☎ 345/949–7777), at the Treasure Island Resort, is a spacious, tiered club that is usually filled to capacity when the island's top bands play there. **Sharkey's** (⊠ Falls Shopping Center, Seven Mile Beach, ☎ 345/947–5366) is a popular disco and bar filled with rock-and-roll paraphernalia of the 1950s. Latest to hit the hot-spot list is the **Planet** (☎ 345/949–7169), featuring nightly drink specials, live entertainment, and theme nights; the youngish crowd can get pretty rowdy, and brawls aren't exactly out of the ordinary here.

Locals and visitors frequent the **Cracked Conch** (⊠ West Bay Rd., near Turtle Farm, ☎ 345/947–5217) for karaoke, classic dive films, and a great happy hour with hors d'oeuvres Tuesday–Friday evenings.

For current entertainment, look at the freebie magazine *What's Hot* or check the Friday edition of the *Caymanian Compass* for listings of music, movies, theater, and other entertainment possibilities.

## Exploring Grand Cayman

There are three main sightseeing areas on Grand Cayman. The first, the historic capital of George Town, is easily explored on foot and conveniently perched on one side of Seven Mile Beach. The West End is noted for its quixotic jumble of affluent colonial neighborhoods and rather tawdry tourist attractions. The less developed East End contains natural attractions, from blowholes to botanical gardens, as well as the remains of the original settlements. Figure a whole day to explore the lengthy island—including a stop at a beach for a picnic or swim.

*Numbers in the margin correspond to points of interest on the Grand Cayman map.*

## George Town

**❶ George Town.** Begin exploring the capital by strolling along the waterfront, Harbour Drive. The circular gazebo is where visitors from the cruise ships disembark. Diagonally across the street is the **Elmslie Memorial United Church,** named after Scotsman James Elmslie, the first Presbyterian missionary to serve in the Caymans. The church was the first concrete block building built in the Cayman Islands. Its vaulted ceiling, wood arches, and sedate nave reflect the quietly religious nature of island residents. Along your rambles, you'll come across **Fort Street,** a main shopping street where you'll also notice the small clock tower dedicated to Britain's King George V and the huge fig tree manicured into an umbrella shape. Here, too, is a statue (unveiled in 1994) of national hero James Bodden, the father of Cayman tourism. Across the street is the **Cayman Islands Legislative Assembly Building,** next door to the 1919 **Peace Memorial Building.**

On Edward Street, you'll find the charming **library,** built in 1939; it has English novels, current newspapers from the United States, and a small reference section. It's worth a visit just for the old-world atmosphere and a look at the shields depicting Britain's prominent institutions of learning that decorate the ceiling beams. Across the street is the **courthouse.** Down the next block is the financial district, where banks from all over the world have offices.

Straight ahead is the **General Post Office,** also built in 1939, with its strands of decorative colored lights and some 2,000 private mailboxes on the outside. (Mail is not delivered on the island.) Behind the post office is **Elizabethan Square,** a shopping and office complex on Shedden Road that houses various food, clothing, and souvenir establishments. The courtyard, with benches around a pleasant garden and fountain, is a good place to rest your feet.

Built in 1833, the **Cayman Islands National Museum** was used as a courthouse, a jail (now the gift shop), a post office, and a dance hall before being reopened in 1990 as a museum. It is small but fascinating, with excellent displays and videos illustrating the history of Cayman plant, animal, human, and geological life. Pick up a walking-tour map of George Town at the museum gift shop before leaving. ⊠ *Harbour Dr.,* ☎ *345/949–8368.* 🎫 *$5.* ☉ *Weekdays 9–5, Sat. 10–4.*

NEED A BREAK?

Follow your nose north on Harbour Drive, which becomes North Church Street, to the **Wholesome Bakery and Café** (☎ 345/949-7588), which adds the homey smell of baking bread to the sea breezes off George Town Harbour. Stop in here for the delectable meat patties, generous slices of pie, and coconut or rum raisin ice cream.

**❷ Cayman Maritime Treasure Museum.** Just outside of George Town is this "treasure." Dioramas here show how Caymanians became seafarers, boatbuilders, and turtle breeders. An animated figure of Blackbeard the pirate spins salty tales about the pirates and buccaneers who "worked" the Caribbean. Since the museum is owned by a professional treasure-salvaging firm, it's not surprising that there are a lot of artifacts from shipwrecks. ⊠ *West Bay Rd., near Hyatt Regency,* ☎ *345/947–5033.* 🎫 *$5.* ☉ *Mon.–Sat. 9–5.*

## Around the Island

To see the rest of the island, rent a car or scooter, or take a guided tour (☞ Cayman Islands A to Z, *below*). A full-day guided tour (sufficient to see the major sights) is comparable in cost to a single day of car rental. The flat road that circles the island is in good condition, with clear signs. Venturing away from the Seven Mile Beach strip, you'll encounter the more down-home character of the island.

WEST END

**④ Cayman Island Turtle Farm.** Started in West Bay in 1968, this is the most popular attraction on the island today, with some 200,000 visitors a year. There are turtles of all ages, from Ping Pong–ball-size eggs to day-old hatchlings to huge 600-pounders that can live to be 100 years old. The Turtle Farm was set up both as a conservation and a commercial enterprise; it releases about 5% of its stock back out to sea every year, harvests turtles for local restaurants, and exports the by-products. (Note: U.S. citizens cannot take home any turtle products because of a U.S. regulation banning their import.) In the adjoining café, you can sample turtle soup or turtle sandwiches while looking over an exhibit about turtles. ⊠ *West Bay Rd.,* ☎ *345/949–3893.* 🎫 *$5.* ⊙ *Daily 8:30–5.*

**⑤ Hell.** This tiny village is little more than a patch of incredibly jagged rock formations called ironshore. The big attraction here is a small post office, which sells stamps and postmarks cards from Hell (a postcard of bikini-clad beauties emblazoned "When Hell freezes over" tells you what to expect), and lots of T-shirt and souvenir shops. Almost unbelievably, a nearby nightclub, called the Club Inferno, is run by the Mc-Doom family.

**③ Old Homestead.** Formerly known as the West Bay Pink House, this is probably the most photographed home in Grand Cayman. The picturesque pink-and-white Caymanian cottage was built in 1912 of wattle and daub around an ironwood frame, and tours, led by cheery Mac Bothwell, who grew up in the house, present a nostalgic and touching look at life in Grand Cayman before the tourism and banking boom. ⊠ *West Bay Rd.,* ☎ *345/949–7639.* 🎫 *$5.* ⊙ *Mon.–Sat. 8–5.*

EAST END

**⑩ Blow Holes.** These make the ultimate photo opportunity as crashing waves force water into caverns and send geysers shooting up through the ironshore (calcified coral ledge).

**⑦ Bodden Town.** In the island's original capitol you'll find an old cemetery on the shore side of the road. Graves with A-frame structures are said to contain the remains of pirates, but, in fact, they may be those of early settlers. There are also the ruins of a fort and a wall erected by slaves in the 19th century for defense. A curio shop serves as the entrance to what's called the **Pirate's Caves,** partially underground natural formations that are more hokey (decked out with fake treasure chests and mannequins in pirate garb) than spooky.

**⑪ East End.** The claim to fame of this area—besides being the island's first recorded settlement—is that it's home to renowned local musician Fiddle Man, a.k.a. Radley Gourzong, who occasionally performs his distinctive form of music (akin to Louisiana's backwater zydeco) here with his band, the Happy Boys.

**⑧ Mastic Trail.** In the 1800s, this woodland trail was often used as a shortcut to and from the North Side. The low-lying area was full off hardwood trees, including mahogany, West Indian cedar, and the mastic that early settlers used to build their homes. Along the trail, you'll see an abundance of trees, birds, and plants unique to this old-growth forest. It's on National Trust territory and you can call to book a guide. ⊠ *Frank Sound Rd.,* ☎ *345/949–0121.*

❻ **Pedro's Castle.** Built in 1780, this modest burgher's home hardly qualifies for palatial status but lays claim to being the oldest structure on the island. Legends linked to the structure abound, but what is known is that the building was struck by lightning in 1877 and left in ruins until bought by a restaurateur in the 1960s. Gutted once again by fire in 1970, the building was purchased by the government in 1991 for restoration as a historic landmark. As yet there has not been too much progress and there's not much to see but scaffolding. ⊠ *East End, South Sound Rd., Savannah, no phone.* 🖼 *Free.*

NEED A
BREAK?

The large and airy **Lighthouse at Breakers Restaurant** (⊠ Breakers, ☎ 345/947–2047) has booth seating around spectacular waterfront windows and offers seafood and Italian cuisine.

❾ **Queen Elizabeth II Botanic Park.** This 60-acre wilderness preserve showcases the variety of habitats and plants native to the islands. Interpretive signs identify the flora along the walking trail. Halfway along the trail is a walled compound housing the rare blue iguana found only in remote sections of the Caymans. You will also see native orchids and, if you're lucky, the brilliant green Cayman parrot. ⊠ *Frank Sound Rd.,* ☎ 345/947–9462. 🖼 *$3.* ☉ *Daily 7:30–5:30.*

⓬ **Queen's View.** This functions as both a lookout point and a monument dedicated by Queen Elizabeth in 1994 to commemorate the legendary **Wreck of the Ten Sails,** which took place just offshore.

# CAYMAN BRAC

Brac, the Gaelic word for "bluff," aptly identifies this island's most distinctive feature, a rugged limestone cliff that runs down the center of the island's 12-mi length and soars to 140 ft at its eastern end. Lying 89 mi northeast of Grand Cayman, Brac is accessible via Cayman Airways and Island Air. Only 1,200 people live on the island, in communities such as Watering Place and Spot Bay. It's easy to strike up a chat with the friendly residents; in fact, you'll often have to be the one to end the conversation if you expect to do anything else that day. Crime is practically unheard of—they hold court for a single day about once every three months.

## Lodging

The rates for most hotels on Cayman Brac and Little Cayman include meals, and in some cases drinks and diving as well, making them a better value than their prices reveal at first glance. (In general, the food is far better at Little Cayman properties than at the Brac hotels.) Much cozier and more intimate than their Grand Cayman counterparts, hoteliers treat guests like family; indeed, many divers create whimsical artwork fashioned from driftwood, dead coral, and artifacts they pick up underwater to splash the hotel dining rooms and bars with color and originality.

### Hotels

$$–$$$$   🏨 **Brac Reef Beach Resort.** This resort lures divers and vacationers who come to savor the special ambience of this tiny island. Unfortunately, none of the rooms have a water view, as the building is set back from the shore. Ground floor rooms have patios, and half of the second floor has private balconies. The pool, pretty beach, snorkeling, guest bicycles, dive shop, and two-story covered dock (whose gazebo is glorious on a star-filled night, when you can see brilliantly hued fish darting about) are additional reasons to stay here. The modest all-inclusive pack-

age rates include three buffet meals daily, all drinks, airport transfers, and taxes and service charges. There's even an all-inclusive dive package. ✉ Box 56, Cayman Brac, ☎ 345/948–7323 or 800/327–3835; 813/323–8727 in FL; FAX 345/948–7207. 40 rooms. Restaurant, bar, air-conditioning, pool, hot tub, tennis court, dive shop, bicycles. AE, D, MC, V. EP, MAP, FAP, All-inclusive.

**$$–$$$** 🏨 **Divi Tiara Beach Resort.** At this resort renowned for its top-quality diving facility, the rooms are getting a bit worn but have tile floors, bright tropical prints, rattan furniture, louvered windows, balconies, and ocean views (from most rooms; standards have neither view nor TV). The more expensive rooms have whirlpool bathtubs. A shuttle takes guests across the island to a great snorkeling spot. Kids 16 and under stay free in their parents' room. ✉ Box 238, Cayman Brac, ☎ 345/948–1553; 919/419–3484 or 800/801–5550 in the U.S.; FAX 345/948–7316 or 919/419–2075 in the U.S. 70 rooms. Restaurant, bar, pool, tennis court, volleyball, dive shop, snorkeling, water sports, fishing, shop. AE, MC, V. EP, MAP, FAP, All-inclusive.

**$** 🏨 **Walton's Mango Manor.** This lovely, two-story, old West Indian home
**★** has five rooms with private baths. Beautiful antiques are peppered throughout the house, including the stairway handrail, which is a relic from an old ship. The nearby ironshore beach is perfect to walk along at sunrise. The proprietors can arrange for any number of activities from game fishing to scuba diving and will be delighted to fill you in on Brac history. As only breakfast is included, you'll want to have a car so you can get out for other meals and explore the island. Those who long for peace and quiet in a tranquil setting will adore this place. ✉ Box 56, Stake Bay, Cayman Brac, ☎ FAX 345/948–0518. 5 rooms. Air-conditioning, fans. AE, MC, V. CP.

### Condominiums and Villas

**$$** 🏨 **Caribbean Brac Beach Village.** This small condo complex built in 1992
**★** enjoys the same pretty beach as the other resorts, but for the money you get a two-bedroom, 2½-bath fully furnished apartment right on the sand. Kids 11 and under stay free with their parents, making this a family money saver. Beige walls and rattan furniture, white tile floors, and pastel floral prints give the units a bright, airy look. With advance notice, the management company will stock your kitchen with groceries and arrange for dive packages, rental cars, and maid service (each at minimal additional cost). ✉ Box 4, Stake Bay, Cayman Brac, ☎ 345/948–2265 or 800/791–7911, FAX 345/948–2206. 16 rooms. Restaurant, bar, air-conditioning, pool, coin laundry. MC, V. EP.

## Beaches

The accommodations on the **southwest coast** have fine small beaches, better for sunning than for snorkeling because of the abundance of turtle grass in the water. Excellent snorkeling can be found immediately offshore of the now-defunct **Buccaneer's Inn** on the north coast, where an old Russian warship was sunk as an artificial reef. It's a bit of a swim, but the seas aren't choppy and visitors regularly snorkel to it.

## Outdoor Activities and Sports

### Diving and Snorkeling

**Brac Aquatics** (☎ 345/949–1429 or 800/544–2722) and **Divi Tiara** (☎ 345/948–1553 or 800/367–3484) offer scuba and snorkeling.

## Exploring Cayman Brac

Cayman Brac is a spelunker's paradise: You can explore the island's large caves (namely **Peter's, Great, Bat,** and **Rebeka's**) some of which are still used for hurricane protection. Wear sneakers for exploring, not flip-flops; some of the paths to the caves are steep and rocky.

In addition to displaying the implements used in the daily lives of Bracers in the 1920s and 1930s, the two-room **Cayman Brac Museum** (⊠ Old Government Administration Bldg., Stake Bay, ☎ 345/948–2622) showcases a few oddities, such as a 4,000-year-old Viking ax. The variety of Brac flora includes unusual orchids, mangoes, papaya, agave, and cacti. The museum is open weekdays 9–noon and 1–4 and Saturday 9–noon. The endangered Cayman Brac parrot is most easily spotted in the **Parrot Preserve** on Major Donald Drive (also known as Lighthouse Road); this 6-mi dirt road also leads to ironshore cliffs that offer the best panoramic view of North East Point and the open ocean. Parts of the island are unpopulated, so you can explore truly isolated areas both inland and along the shore. Two hotels catering to divers and a rental condo complex are on the southwest coast. Swimming is possible, but unlike at Seven Mile Beach, the bottom is rocky and clogged with turtle grass.D/r

# LITTLE CAYMAN

Only 7 mi away from Cayman Brac is Little Cayman Island, which has a population of about 100 on its 12 square mi. This is a true hideaway: few phones, fewer shops, no nightlife—just spectacular diving, great fishing, and laid-back camaraderie. Visitor accommodations are mostly in small lodges.

## Lodging

### Hotels

**$$–$$$**  🏨 **Little Cayman Beach Resort.** Considerably less rustic than those of
  ★  other Little Cayman resorts, the air-conditioned rooms in this two-story property have modern furnishings in jewel-tone tropical colors. Only Rooms 115, 116, 215, and 216 have a water view—and you don't pay extra. The elegant (for Little Cayman) dining room overlooking the bar area seats 50 for family-style buffet meals. Double hammocks are slung under beach palapas. The resort offers diving and fishing packages and also caters to bird-watchers and soft-adventure eco-tourists. Paddleboats, sailboats, kayaks, a complete dive operation, tennis, and free bicycles provided for exploring the island keep guests busy. All-inclusive packages are available for both divers and nondivers and include three meals daily, all alcoholic and soft drinks, airport transfers, taxes, and gratuities. ⊠ *Blossom Village, Little Cayman,* ☎ *345/948–1033 or 800/327–3835,* ℻ *345/948–1045. 32 rooms. Restaurant, bar, pool, hot tub, tennis court, dive shop, fishing, bicycles, shop. AE, D, MC, V. EP, MAP, FAP, All-inclusive.*

**$$–$$$**  🏨 **Pirates Point Resort.** The guest-house feel of this comfortably infor-
  ★  mal resort generates almost instant camaraderie among the guests, and many come back year after year. The charming, individually decorated rooms have tiled floors, white rattan and wicker furnishings, ceiling fans, and louvered windows. But Pirates Point is most notable for its flamboyant owner, Texan Gladys Howard, whose warm down-home welcome belies her upscale meals (she trained at Cordon Bleu with Julia Child, James Beard, and Jacques Pepin). "Relaxing" rates (for nondivers) include the mouthwatering meals and wine; all-inclusive rates include meals, alcoholic beverages, two daily boat dives, fishing, and picnics on uninhabited Owen Island. ⊠ *Little Cayman,* ☎ *345/948–1010 or 800/654–7537,* ℻ *345/948–1011. 10 rooms. Restaurant, bar, dive shop, fishing, bicycles, airport shuttle. MC, V. FAP, All-inclusive.*

$$–$$$   🏨 **Southern Cross Club.** This, the first property on Little Cayman, is under
★   new ownership and has been completely renovated. The rooms, in cottages spread along a pretty beach, have a simple pastel decor with wicker furniture, ceiling fans, air-conditioning, and painted cement floors. All have fabulous views of the sparkling turquoise sea. Diving and fishing (deep-sea, light-tackle, bottom, and bonefishing) are the draw here. The scuba shop offers Nitrox diving. Service and meals are impeccable. ✉ *Box 44, Little Cayman,* ☎ *345/948–1099 or 800/899–2582; 317/636–9501 in the U.S.;* FAX *317/636–9503. 10 rooms. Restaurant, bar, dive shop, snorkeling, fishing, bicycles, airport shuttle. AE, MC, V. FAP.*

$$   🏨 **Sam McCoy's Diving and Fishing Lodge.** Be prepared for an ultra-
★   casual experience: This is an ordinary family house with very simple but cheerful bedrooms and baths in royal and powder blues. There's no bar or restaurant per se; guests just eat at a few tables by the beach barbecue outdoors or with Sam and his family in the thatched dining room, draped with fishing nets, diving artifacts, and guests' artwork. Fans like it for its owner's infectious good nature, the superb diving and snorkeling just offshore, and the family atmosphere. "Relaxing" rates (for nondivers) include three meals a day and airport transfers; all-inclusive rates also include beach and boat diving. Sam's son, Chip, is the most experienced local fishing guide on the island; his bonefishing trips are around $20 an hour. ✉ *Little Cayman,* ☎ *800/626–0496,* ☎ FAX *345/948–0026. 6 rooms. Air-conditioning, fans, pool. No credit cards. FAP, All-inclusive.*

### Condominiums and Villas

$–$$   🏨 **Paradise Villas.** If you're looking for cozy, one-bedroom self-catering units, all with kitchens, air-conditioning, and terrace opening onto the beach, look no further. The 12 units here are sunny, breezy, and simply but immaculately appointed with rattan and muted abstract fabrics. ✉ *Little Cayman,* ☎ *345/948–0004. 12 units. Pool, dive shop. AE.*

# Beaches

The beaches **Point o' Sand,** on the eastern tip, and **Owen Island,** off the south coast, are isolated patches of powder that are great for sunbathing and worth every effort to reach by car, bike, or boat.

# Outdoor Activities and Sports

### Deep-Sea Fishing

**Sam McCoy's Fishing & Diving** (☎ 345/949–2891 or 800/626–0496) and **Southern Cross Club** (☎ 800/899–2582) offer deep-sea fishing. June is dubbed Million Dollar Month; registered anglers can win cash and vacation prizes by landing record-breaking catches. Five tournaments are held, each with its own rules, records, and entrance fees. For information and applications, write to the Million Dollar Month Committee (✉ Box 878 GT, Grand Cayman, Cayman Islands, B.W.I.).

### Diving and Snorkeling

Contact **Paradise Divers** (☎ 345/948–0004 or 800/450–2084), **Reef Divers** (☎ 345/948–1033), **Sam McCoy's Fishing & Diving** (☎ 345/949–2891 or 800/626–0496), or the **Southern Cross Club** (☎ 800/899–2582). Each hotel also has its own instructors.

# Exploring Little Cayman

In addition to enjoying privacy, the real attractions of Little Cayman are diving in spectacular **Bloody Bay,** off the north coast, and fishing, which includes angling for tarpon and bonefish. You can also go birding at the **Governor Gore Bird Sanctuary,** established in 1994 and home to 5,000 pairs of red-footed boobies (the largest colony in the Western Hemisphere) and 1,000 magnificent frigate birds. Nature abounds, from the eerie waterscape of **Tarpon Pond,** where silvery tarpon pirouette in the sun amid a maze of gnarled, knobby mangrove trees to bird preserves where red-footed boobies, black frigates, and snowy egrets compete for lunch in dramatic dive-bombing battles.

And if Little Cayman ever gets too busy, there is one final retreat—**Owen Island,** which is just 200 yards offshore. Accessible by rowboat, it is in the middle of a blue lagoon and has a sandy beach. Take your own picnic if you plan to spend the day.

# CAYMAN ISLANDS A TO Z

## Arriving and Departing

BY PLANE

**Cayman Airways** (☎ 800/422–9626) flies nonstop to Grand Cayman from Miami two or three times daily, from Tampa four times a week, from Orlando three times a week, and from Houston and Atlanta three times a week. **American Airlines** (☎ 800/433–7300) has daily nonstop flights from both Miami and Raleigh/Durham, North Carolina. **Northwest** (☎ 800/447–4747) has regularly scheduled nonstop flights from Miami. **US Airways** (☎ 800/428–4322) flies daily nonstop from Tampa and three times a week from Pittsburgh and Charlotte, North Carolina. **American Trans Air** (☎ 800/225–2995) is a charter service offering direct weekly flights from Indianapolis and Cincinnati. **Cayman Airtours** (☎ 800/247–2966) offers package deals. Air service from Grand Cayman to Cayman Brac and Little Cayman is offered via Cayman Airways and **Island Air** (☎ 345/949–5152 or 800/922–9606). Flights land at Owen Roberts Airport, Gerrard-Smith Airport, or Edward Bodden Airfield. **Airport Information:** For flight information, call 345/949–5252.

Upon arrival, some hotels offer free pickup at the airport. Taxi service and car rentals are also available.

## Currency

Although the American dollar is accepted everywhere, you'll save money if you go to the bank and exchange U.S. dollars for Cayman Island (CI) dollars, worth about US$1.20 at press time. The Cayman dollar is divided into a hundred cents with coins of 1¢, 5¢, 10¢, and 25¢ and notes of $1, $5, $10, $25, $50, and $100. There is no $20 bill. Prices are often quoted in Cayman dollars, so it's best to ask. All prices quoted here are in U.S. dollars unless otherwise noted.

## Emergencies

**Police and Hospitals:** ☎ 911. **Ambulance:** ☎ 555. **Pharmacy:** Island Pharmacy (☎ 345/949–8987) in West Shore Centre on Seven Mile Beach. **Divers' Recompression Chamber:** ☎ 345/949–4234 or 555.

## Getting Around

If your accommodations are along Seven Mile Beach, you can walk or bike to the shopping centers, restaurants, and entertainment spots along West Bay Road. George Town is small enough to see on foot. If you're touring Grand Cayman by car, there's a well-maintained road that circles the island; it's hard to get lost. If you want to see the sights or simply get away from the resort, you'll need a rental car or moped on Little Cayman and Cayman Brac; your hotel can make the arrangements for you. Otherwise, airport transfers are included in most resort rates, and many resorts offer bicycles for local sightseeing.

BICYCLES AND SCOOTERS

When renting a motor scooter or bicycle, don't forget that you need sunblock and that driving is on the left. Bicycles ($10–$15 a day) and scooters ($25–$30 a day) can be rented from **Bicycles Cayman** (☎ 345/949–5572), **Cayman Cycle** (☎ 345/947–4021), and **Soto Scooters** (☎ 345/947–4363).

CAR RENTALS

Grand Cayman is relatively flat and fairly easy to negotiate if you're careful of the traffic. To rent a car, bring your current driver's license and the car-rental firm will issue you a temporary permit ($5). Most firms have a range of models available, from compacts to Jeeps to minibuses. Rates range from $35 to $55 a day. The major agencies have offices in a plaza across from the airport terminal, where you can pick up and drop off vehicles. Just remember, driving is on the left.

Car-rental companies are **Ace Hertz** (☎ 345/949–2280 or 800/654–3131), **Budget** (☎ 345/949–5605 or 800/472–3325), **Cico Avis** (☎ 345/949–2468 or 800/331–1212), **Coconut** (☎ 345/949–4377 or 800/262–6687), **Economy** (☎ 345/949–9550), **Soto's 4X4** (☎ 345/945–2424), and **Thrifty** (☎ 345/949–6640 or 800/367–2277).

TAXIS

Taxis offer island-wide service. Fares are determined by an elaborate rate structure set by the government, and although it may seem pricey for a short ride (fare from Seven Mile Beach for four people to the airport ranges from $10 to $15), cabbies rarely try to rip off tourists. Ask to see the chart if you want to double-check the quoted fare. **A.A. Transportation** (☎ 345/949–7222), **Cayman Cab Team** (☎ 345/947–1173), and **Holiday Inn Taxi Stand** (☎ 345/947–4491) offer 24-hour service.

## Guided Tours

Money-saving packages (everything from honeymoon trips to air-hotel deals) are offered through hotels and through **TourScan, Inc.** (☎ 800/962–2080 or 203/655–3451) and **Cayman Airtours** (☎ 800/247–2966).

AIR TOURS

**Cayman Helicopter Tours** (☎ 345/949–4400) operates a six-passenger, air-conditioned helicopter that makes quick work of taking in the geographical features of Grand Cayman. The waters around the island are so clear that you can see shipwrecks, stingrays, and shallow reefs from the air. Fares start at around $150 per person. **Seaborne Flightseeing Adventures** (☎ 345/949–6029) offers a 25-minute narrated "flightseeing" tour for $56 per person.

LAND TOURS

Guided day tours of the island can be arranged with **A.A. Transportation Services** (☎ 345/949–7222; ask for Burton Ebanks), **Majestic Tours** (☎ 345/949–7773), **Reids Premier Tours** (☎ 345/949–6531), **Rudy's Travellers Transport** (☎ 345/949–3208), and **Tropicana Tours** (☎ 345/949–0944). Half-day tours average $30–$50 a person and generally include a visit to the Turtle Farm and Hell in West Bay, drives along Seven Mile Beach and through George Town, and time for shopping downtown. In addition to those stops, full-day tours, which average $55–$75 per person and include lunch, also visit Bodden Town to see pirate caves and graves and the East End to see blowholes on the ironshore and the site of the famous "Wreck of the Ten Sails."

WATER TOURS

The most impressive sights are underwater. Don't miss a trip on **Atlantis Submarine** (☎ 345/949–7700), which takes 48 passengers, a driver, and a guide down along the Cayman Wall to depths of up to

100 ft for close-up views of the abundant, colorful marine life. This $2.8 million submarine has entertained hundreds of thousands of passengers, has all sorts of safety features, including a constantly circling surface-monitor boat, and is air-conditioned. Through its large windows, you can see huge barrel sponges, corals in extraterrestrial-like configurations, strange eels, and schools of beautiful and beastly fish. Night dives are quite dramatic, because the artificial lights of the ship make the colors more vivid than they are in daytime excursions. Costs range from around $60 to $80 per person for trips from an hour to an hour and a half in length. The company also operates private trips on a research submersible that reaches depths of 800 ft. In the **Seaworld Explorer** (☎ 345/949–8534), passengers sit before windows in the hull of the boat just 5 ft below the surface, observing divers who swim around with food, attracting fish to the craft. The cost of this hour-long trip is $29.

Guided snorkeling trips, available through **Charter Boat Headquarters** (☎ 345/947–4340), **Captain Eugene's Watersports** (☎ 345/949–3099), and **Kirk Sea Tours** (☎ 345/949–6986), usually include stops at Stingray City Sandbar, Coral Garden, and Conch Bed, the top snorkel sites. Full-day trips include lunch prepared on the boat or onshore and cost under $40 per person; half-day trips average $25. Glass-bottom-boat trips also cost around $25 and are available through **Aqua Delights** (☎ 345/947–4786), **Cayman Mermaid** (☎ 345/949–8100), and **Kirk Sea Tours** (☎ 345/949–6986).

Sunset sails, dinner cruises, and other theme (dance, booze, pirate, etc.) cruises are available aboard the **Jolly Roger** (☎ 345/949–8534), a replica of a 17th-century Spanish galleon; **Blackbeard's Nancy** (☎ 345/949–8988), a 1912 topsail schooner; and the **Spirit of Ppalu** (☎ 345/949–1234), a 65-ft glass-bottom catamaran. Party cruises typically run $20–$50 per person.

## Language
English is spoken everywhere; local publications are also in English.

## Opening and Closing Times
Banking hours are generally Monday–Thursday 9–2:30 and Friday 9–1 and 2:30–4:30. Shops are open weekdays 9–5, and on Saturday in George Town from 10 to 2; in outer shopping plazas, they are open from 10 to 5. Shops are usually closed Sunday except in hotels.

## Passports and Visas
American and Canadian citizens do not have to carry passports, but they must show some proof of citizenship, such as a birth certificate or voter registration card, plus a return ticket. British and Commonwealth subjects do not need a visa but must carry a passport. Visitors to the islands cannot be employed without a work permit.

## Precautions
Locals zealously conserve fresh water, so don't waste a precious commodity. Caymanians also strictly observe and enforce laws that prohibit collecting or disturbing endangered animal, marine, and plant life and historical artifacts found throughout the islands and surrounding marine parks; simply put, take only pictures and don't stand on reefs.

Penalties for drug and firearms importation and possession of controlled substances include large fines and prison terms.

Theft is not widespread, but be smart: Lock up your room and car and secure valuables as you would at home. Outdoors, marauding blackbirds called ching chings have been known to carry off jewelry if it is left out in the open.

Poisonous plants on the island include the maiden plum, the lady hair, and the manchineel tree. If in doubt, don't touch. The leaves and applelike fruit of the manchineel are poisonous to touch and should be avoided; even raindrops falling from them can cause painful blisters.

## Taxes and Service Charges

Hotels collect a 10% government tax and add a 10% service charge to your bill. Many restaurants add a 10%–15% service charge. At press time, the departure tax was CI$8 (US$10).

## Telephones and Mail

For international dialing to Cayman, the area code is 345 (recently changed from 809). To call outside, dial 0 + 1 + area code and number. You can call anywhere, anytime, through the cable and wireless system and local operators. To make local calls, dial the seven-digit number. To place credit-card calls, dial 110. AT&T USADirect (☎ 800/872–2881) and MCI Direct (☎ 800/624–1000) can be used from any public phone and most hotels.

Beautiful stamps are available at the main post office in downtown George Town and at the philatelic office in West Shore Plaza. Both are open weekdays from 8:30 to 3:30 and Saturday from 8:30 to 11:30. Sending a postcard to the United States, Canada, the Caribbean, or Central America costs CI20¢. An airmail letter is CI30¢ per half ounce. To Europe and South America, the rates are CI25¢ for a postcard and CI40¢ per half ounce for airmail letters.

## Visitor Information

For the latest information on activities and lodging, write or call any of the offices of the **Cayman Islands Department of Tourism:** ✉ 6100 Blue Lagoon Dr., 6100 Waterford Bldg., Suite 150, Miami, FL 33126-2085, ☎ 305/266–2300; ✉ 2 Memorial City Plaza, 820 Gessner, Suite 170, Houston, TX 77024, ☎ 713/461–1317; ✉ 420 Lexington Ave., Suite 2733, New York, NY 10170, ☎ 212/682–5582; ✉ 9525 W. Bryn Mawr Ave., Suite 160, Rosemont, IL 60018, ☎ 708/678–6446; ✉ 3440 Wilshire Blvd., Suite 1202, Los Angeles, CA 90010, ☎ 213/738–1968; ✉ 234 Eglinton Ave. E, Suite 306, Toronto, Ontario M4P 1K5, ☎ 416/485–1550; ✉ Trevor House, 100 Brompton Rd., Knightsbridge, London SW3 1EX, ☎ 0171/581–9960.

The main office of the **Department of Tourism** is in the Pavilion, (✉ Cricket Sq. and Elgin Ave., ☎ 345/949–0623). Information booths are at the airport (☎ 345/949–2635); in the George Town Craft Market, on Cardinal Avenue, open when cruise ships are in port (☎ 345/949–8342); and in the kiosk at the cruise-ship dock in George Town (no phone). There is also an island-wide tourist hot line (☎ 345/949–8989). You can also contact the **Tourist Information and Activities Service** (☎ 345/949–6598, FAX 345/947–6222) day or night for complete tourist information and free assistance in booking island transportation, tours, charters, cruises, and other activities.

# 9 Curaçao

Curaçao, the largest island of the Netherland Antilles, is also the most staunchly Dutch, from architecture, cuisine, and language (Dutch is spoken more often than Papiamento, the language common to all the Netherland Antilles) to the waves of blond tourists arriving daily from Amsterdam. Pastel-painted historical buildings housing boutiques and small restaurants draw the attention in Willemstad, the capital city, while towering cacti and mustard-color landhouses catch the eye throughout the countryside.

Updated by
Melissa Rivers

**C**URAÇAO IS AN ISLAND FOR EXPLORERS. Its charming Dutch capital, underwater park, Seaquarium, floating market, and dozens of little cove beaches give it a taste of everything, and it is apt to please most tastes. Thirty-five miles north of Venezuela and 42 mi east of Aruba, Curaçao, at 38 mi long and 2–7½ mi wide, is the largest island in the Netherlands Antilles. The sun smiles down on the island, but it's never stiflingly hot: The gentle trade winds are always refreshing. Water sports attract enthusiasts from all over the world, and some of the best reef diving is here. Though the island claims 38 beaches, it doesn't have long stretches of silky sand; rather, beaches are rocky stretches of washed-up coral that eventually breaks down into smooth white or pink sand. The island is dominated by an arid countryside, rocky coves, and a sprawling capital built around a natural harbor. Until recently, the economy was based not on tourism but on oil refining and catering to offshore corporations seeking tax hedges. Although tourism has become a major economic force in the past decade, with millions of dollars invested in restoring old colonial landmarks and modernizing hotels, Curaçao's atmosphere remains comparatively low-key—offering an appealing alternative to the commercialism of many other islands.

As seen from the Otrabanda of Willemstad by the first-time visitor, Curaçao's "face" will be a surprise—spiffy rows of pastel-colored town houses that look transplanted from Holland. Although the gabled roofs and red tiles show a Dutch influence, the gay colors of the facades are peculiar to Curaçao. It is said that a popular governor suffered from migraines, a condition irritated by the color white, so all the houses were painted in colors. Government funding has allowed for a tremendous boost in restoration of these houses, so you'll notice bright new coats of paint. The dollhouse look of the landhouses or *landhuizen* (plantation houses) makes a cheerful contrast to the stark cacti and the austere shrubbery that dot the countryside.

The history books still cannot agree on who discovered Curaçao—one school of thought believes it was Alonzo de Ojeda, while another says it was Amerigo Vespucci—but they agree that it was around 1499. The first Spanish settlers arrived in 1527. In 1634 the Dutch came via the Netherlands West India Company. They promptly shipped off the Spaniards and the few remaining Indians—survivors of the battles for ownership of the island, famine, and disease—to Venezuela. Eight years later, Peter Stuyvesant began his rule as governor, which lasted until he left for New York around 1645. Twelve Jewish families arrived from Amsterdam in 1651, and by 1732 there was a synagogue; the present structure is the oldest synagogue still in use in the Western Hemisphere. Over the years, the city built massive fortresses to defend against French and British invasions—many of those ramparts now house unusual restaurants and hotels. The Dutch claim to Curaçao was finally recognized in 1815 by the Treaty of Paris. In 1954 Curaçao became an autonomous part of the Kingdom of the Netherlands, with a governor appointed by the queen, an elected parliament, and an island council.

Today Curaçao's population is derived from more than 50 nationalities in an exuberant mix of Latin, European, and African roots and a Babel of tongues, resulting in superb restaurants and an active cultural scene. The island, like its Dutch settlers, is known for its religious tolerance, and tourists are warmly welcomed.

# Curaçao

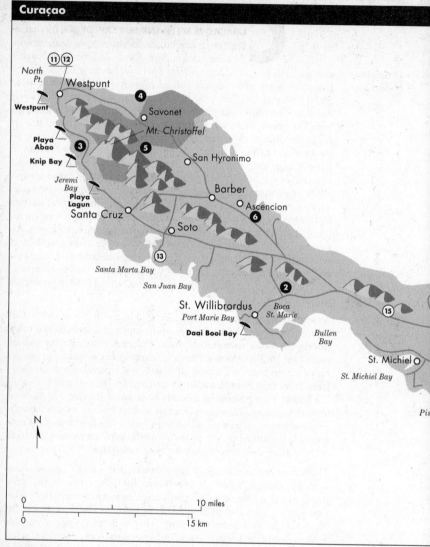

North Pt.

(11)(12)

Westpunt

**Westpunt**

**4**

Savonet

**Playa Abao**

**3**

Mt. Christoffel

**Knip Bay**

**5**

San Hyronimo

Jeremi Bay

**Playa Lagun**

Barber

Santa Cruz

Ascencion

**6**

Soto

**13**

Santa Marta Bay

San Juan Bay

**2**

St. Willibrordus

Boca St. Marie

**15**

Port Marie Bay

**Daai Booi Bay**

Bullen Bay

St. Michiel

St. Michiel Bay

Pis

N

| 0 | | 10 miles |
| 0 | | 15 km |

**Exploring**
Boca Tabla, **4**
Christoffel Park, **5**
Country House
Museum, **6**
Curaçao
Seaquarium, **10**

Curaçao Underwater
Marine Park, **9**
Hato Caves, **7**
Landhuis
Brievengat, **8**
Landhuis Jan Kok, **2**
Landhuis Knip, **3**
Willemstad, **1**

**Dining**
Bistro Le
Clochard, **19**
Cactus Club, **34**
Café du Port, **26**
Dee Taveerne, **35**
Emerald
Steakhouse, **17**

Fort Nassau
Restaurant, **32**
Fort
Waakzaamheid, **22**
Golden Star
Restaurant, **31**
Jaanchi's Restaurant, **11**
L'Orangerie, **28**

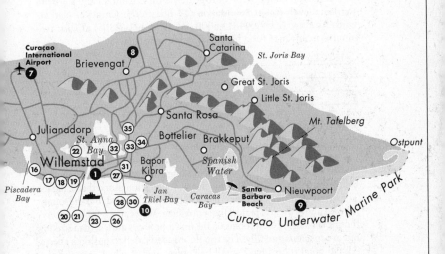

# Lodging

Curaçao offers an array of accommodations, from large beachfront resorts spread along the island's southern coast to budget and business-class hotels in downtown Willemstad, where business travelers and shopping fanatics have easy access to the city center. Beach hotels on the southwestern end of the island tend to be small, secluded, and peaceful but are a 30- to 45-minute drive from town. Those beach hotels just east and west of Willemstad proper tend to be large-scale, bustling luxury resorts. Most hotels provide either beach or shopping shuttles, baby-sitting, laundry service, car rental, and business and travel services. The larger hotels provide activity programs (both for adults and for children) and offer free or discounted accommodations for children staying in their parents' room. They also either include a Continental breakfast or offer a large buffet breakfast. Full American Plans are not popular because of the abundance of good restaurants.

Rentals are popular with European visitors. Contact the **Curaçao Tourism Development Foundation** (✉ Box 3266, Curaçao, Netherlands Antilles, ☎ 5999/461–6000, FAX 5999/461–2305) at least two months in advance for a list of available properties.

| CATEGORY | COST* |
|---|---|
| $$$ | over $225 |
| $$ | $150–$225 |
| $ | under $150 |

*All prices are for a standard double room, including 7% government tax and 12% service charge.*

$$$   🏨 **Curaçao Caribbean Hotel and Casino.** This five-story complex near the Trade Center is self-contained, with one of the best-organized activities programs on the island, including rum-swizzle parties, volleyball, T-shirt painting, Papiamento lessons, walking tours, and theme nights. The lovely champagne-color coves can become crowded, but the lounging area above them is perfect for sunbathing. Water sports include everything imaginable. Guest rooms on the first four floors are less than striking but are spacious and tidy. The top floor is dedicated to business guests. All the hotel rooms have small balconies, half of which face the sea. ✉ Box 2133, Piscadera Bay, Willemstad, ☎ 5999/462–5000 or 800/344–1212, FAX 5999/462–5846. 181 rooms, 15 suites. 3 restaurants, 2 bars, coffee shop, room service, pool, 2 tennis courts, exercise room, shuffleboard, volleyball, beach, dive shop, marina, water sports, shops, casino, concierge floor. AE, D, DC, MC, V. EP, MAP.

$$$   🏨 **Kadushi Cliffs.** If you've brought the family for a week or more, you might want to rent a condo at Kadushi Cliffs, in the peaceful, lush western part of the island. The modern two-bedroom villas here are all attractively furnished and have fully equipped, modern kitchens. A pool and a restaurant are the only real facilities (there's a tiny beach), but this keeps the noise and traffic level down. Regulars return year after year for the solitude and seclusion. You'll need a rental car to see anything else of the island or go to Willemstad for dining and shopping. ✉ Westpunt, ☎ 5999/864–0200 or 800/448–8355, FAX 5999/864–0282. 12 villas. Restaurant, bar, in-room safes, kitchens, refrigerators, in-room VCRs, pool, tennis court, volleyball, beach, playground. AE, DC, MC, V. EP.

$$$   🏨 **Princess Beach Resort and Casino.** You can't beat the location of this Holiday Inn Crowne Plaza property: You're on one of the most beautiful beaches in Curaçao and right in front of the Underwater Marine Park. Guest rooms are spacious, if somewhat worn and musty smelling (except for those in the newer high-rise tower), with fine ocean or garden views. The pathway to the rooms is through lush, tropical grounds.

This is a high-energy place, with lively happy hours, popular theme buffet dinners, and a slew of sports activities and nightly entertainment. It is also one of the few hotels on the island to offer designated no-smoking rooms. ⊠ *Martin Luther King Blvd. 8,* ☎ *5999/736–7888 or 800/327–3286,* FAX *5999/461–4131. 332 rooms, 8 suites. 3 restaurants, 4 bars, in-room safes, no-smoking rooms, room service, 2 pools, exercise room, volleyball, beach, dive shop, dock, water sports, shops, casino. AE, DC, MC, V. EP, CP, MAP, FAP.*

$$$ 🏨 **Sonesta Beach Hotel & Casino.** Curaçao's most luxurious resort is
★ a sprawling, burnished-ocher low rise, built to blend in with the surrounding Dutch colonial–style architecture. The impressive approach leads you through lushly landscaped grounds brimming with oleander, hibiscus, and gently swaying palms; the beach is gorgeous. The tasteful accommodations have a muted tropical pastel color scheme and either a terrace or a balcony. Striking contemporary art adorns the walls. Price is determined solely by view, though all rooms have at least a partial ocean vista. There's also an array of daily activities and nightly entertainment. ⊠ *Box 6003, Piscadera Bay,* ☎ *5999/736–8800 or 800/766–3782,* FAX *5999/462–7502. 212 rooms, 32 suites. 3 restaurants, 2 bars, minibars, no-smoking rooms, room service, pool, wading pool, 2 outdoor hot tubs, massage, saunas, steam rooms, 2 tennis courts, aerobics, health club, volleyball, water sports, dive shop, shops, casino, concierge. AE, D, DC, MC, V. EP, MAP, FAP.*

$$ 🏨 **Habitat Curaçao.** The island's newest option is a casual dive resort 12 mi west of Willemstad on the beach at Rif St. Marie. It's a sprawling property with clusters of ocher-colored, red-roofed buildings surrounded by tropical foliage and connected by stairways and winding paths. The air-conditioned rooms, referred to as junior suites because of the spacious, furnished terrace or balcony attached to each, take their bright colors and decor from the coral reef just offshore. Each has a fully equipped kitchenette and roomy bathroom with shower, but no TV or phone. The raised pool next to the ocean affords grand vistas, and the top-notch dive facilities offer 24-hour diving. ⊠ *Coral Estates, Rif St. Marie,* ☎ *5999/864–8800 or 800/327–6709,* FAX *5999/864–8464. 56 suites, 20 2-bedroom cottages. Restaurant, bar, pool, beach, dive shop, dock, shops, meeting room. AE, DC, MC, V. EP, CP.*

$$ 🏨 **Holiday Beach Hotel and Casino.** This former Holiday Inn is a four-story, U-shape, aquamarine-colored building surrounding a pool. Rooms, which desperately need a face-lift, have a beige, emerald, and rose color scheme, with bleached wood and rattan furniture. The lobby is spacious to permit the assembly of tour groups, and one of the island's largest casinos, Casino Royale, is off the lobby. The crescent beach is quite large for Curaçao and dotted with palm trees. Although this is an older property, it's a fair choice for value on a budget. ⊠ *Box 2178, Otrabanda, Pater Euwensweg, Willemstad,* ☎ *5999/462–5400 or 800/223–9815,* FAX *5999/462–4397. 200 rooms. 2 restaurants, 2 bars, refrigerators on request, room service, pool, 2 tennis courts, Ping-Pong, shuffleboard, volleyball, beach, water sports, dive shop, casino, video games, playground. AE, DC, MC, V. EP.*

$$ 🏨 **Lions Dive Hotel Curaçao.** This yellow-and-blue caravansary is a hop, skip, and plunge away from the Seaquarium, on a quarter mile of private beach. Most of the guests are dive enthusiasts satisfied by the top-notch scuba center and the young staff, who are eager to please. Rooms are airy, modern, and light-filled, with tile floors and large bathrooms (showers only). French doors lead out to a spacious balcony or terrace, and every room has a view of the sea. The Sunday-night happy hour is especially festive, with a merengue band playing poolside. By midnight, however, the only sound to be heard is the whir of your room's air conditioner. Dive packages are offered with Underwater Curaçao.

✉ *Bapor Kibra, Curaçao,* ☎ *5999/461–8100 or 888/546–6734,* FAX *5999/461–8200. 72 rooms. Restaurant, bar, in-room safes, pool, exercise room, beach, dive shop, dock, water sports. AE, DC, MC, V. EP.*

**$–$$**  ⊞ **Avila Beach Hotel.** The royal family of Holland and its ministers stay
★     at this 200-year-old mansion overlooking the ocean for three good reasons: the privacy, the personalized service, and the peacefulness. There is a room here for everyone, from the budget-priced, basic rooms in the original house to larger, more modern rooms in the moderately priced La Belle Alliance section to the luxurious rooms in the Blues Wing, built in late 1996 on a rocky peninsula stretching out to sea. The restaurant has a unique outdoor dining area shaded by an enormous tree. A terrace with Adirondack chairs (referred to on the island as Avila chairs) overlooks the two crescent beaches and the pier bar where live jazz takes center stage Thursday and Saturday evenings. Many consider this quiet, family-owned-and-operated hotel the best buy on the island. ✉ *Box 791, Penstraat 130134, Willemstad,* ☎ *5999/461–4377 or 800/448–8355,* FAX *5999/461–1493. 107 rooms, 8 suites. 2 restaurants, 2 bars, kitchenettes, refrigerators, tennis court, beach, conference center. AE, DC, MC, V. EP, MAP.*

**$**  ⊞ **Coral Cliff Resort and Beach Club.** Seclusion and rustic simplicity are everything here. Set on a pretty half-moon beach a 45-minute ride west of Willemstad, the resort, which seems to be perpetually under construction, is popular with Dutch tourists. Deluxe rooms are comfortable and attractive, with motel-modern furnishings, shower-only bathrooms, and small balconies. Romantics opt for the junior suites with whirlpool tub on the balcony. A pool with swim-up bar, a wading pool, and eight villas suitable for families were added in 1997; further expansion calls for 21 more rooms to be completed in 1998. A shuttle runs guests into town for shopping; otherwise, you'll need a car for sightseeing and dining off-property. ✉ *Box 3782, Santa Marta Bay,* ☎ *5999/864–2666 or 800/223–9815,* FAX *5999/864–1781. 62 units. Restaurant, bar, pool, miniature golf, tennis court, Ping-Pong, beach, dive shop, dock, billiards, casino, playground, coin laundry, meeting room. AE, D, DC, MC, V. EP, BP, MAP, FAP.*

**$**  ⊞ **Landhaus Daniel.** Dating back to 1630, this plantation house was never a part of a farm but served as an inn for travelers going east or west on the island. The property, near the narrow center of the island, has a restaurant, a pool, and a dive center. Rooms are tiny but clean, with basic furnishings. All have private bathrooms with showers; only two are air-conditioned (the rest have ceiling fans), but the trade winds usually take care of any excessive heat at night. This is a fine budget option and has the fun atmosphere of a youth hostel with its billiards, darts, and TV room. ✉ *Wegnaar Westpunt,* ☎ *5999/864–8400. 10 rooms. Restaurant, bar, pool, dive shop. AE, MC, V. EP, MAP.*

**$**  ⊞ **Otrabanda Hotel & Casino.** Built in 1990, this little city hotel—a superior value—is across the harbor from downtown Willemstad, in the historic Otrabanda section. Standard rooms are cramped but appealing, with terrific harbor views, rattan furnishings, refrigerators on request, and paintings of country scenes. The most attractive and roomiest are those tucked under the peaked roof. A swimming pool and large sun terrace were added in late 1996. ✉ *Breedestraat, Otrabanda,* ☎ *5999/462–7400,* FAX *5999/462–7299. 42 rooms, 3 suites. Restaurant, bar, coffee shop, snack bar, pool, casino. AE, MC, V. CP.*

**$**  ⊞ **Porto Paseo Hotel and Casino.** This charming property on the Otra-
★     banda side of the harbor recalls a typical landhouse, with tropical gardens, lamp-lit flagstone courtyard, rock walls, and mustard-color bungalow-style buildings with red-tile roofs. At its center is the hotel, a restored 17th-century building. It's a remarkably peaceful, private place amid the city's bustle. Squawking white cockatoos preside over the en-

trance to an open-air bar splashed with murals depicting island life and overlooking Santa Anna Bay. The unadorned but pleasant rooms, all with showers, shimmer in silver, mauve, and ecru. ⊠ *De Rouvilleweg 47, Willemstad*, ☎ *5999/462–7878 or 800/287–2226*, ⨳ *5999/462–7969. 45 rooms, 4 suites. Restaurant, bar, kitchenettes, pool, casino. AE, DC, MC, V. EP, CP.*

$ 🏨 **Van Der Valk Plaza Hotel and Casino.** "Please don't touch the passing ships" is the slogan at the island's first high-rise hotel and the only hotel in the world with marine-collision insurance. The ships do come close, since the structure is built right into the massive walls of a 17th-century fort at the entrance of Willemstad's harbor. You give up beachfront (you have beach privileges at Seaquarium and there's a beach shuttle) for walking access to the city's center. Consequently, it's a business traveler's oasis, but there are loads of activities to satisfy vacationers, too. The lobby is marble, with handsomely upholstered furniture and a winding lagoon and waterfall. Aging decor and worn furnishings in the guest rooms are a letdown in comparison, but renovations are scheduled. ⊠ *Box 229, Plaza Piar, Willemstad*, ☎ *5999/461–2500 or 800/447–7462*, ⨳ *5999/461–6543. 236 rooms, 18 suites. 2 restaurants, 3 bars, snack bar, in-room safes, room service, pool, exercise room, dive shop, casino, business services, meeting rooms. AE, DC, MC, V. CP.*

# Dining

Dine under the boughs of magnificent old trees, in the romantic gloom of wine cellars in renovated landhouses, or on the ramparts of 18th-century forts. Curaçaoans partake of some of the best Indonesian food in the Caribbean, and you'll also find fine French, Swiss, Dutch, and Swedish fare.

## What to Wear

Dress in restaurants is almost always casual (though beachwear is generally not acceptable). Some of the resort dining rooms and nicer restaurants require that men wear jackets, especially in high season; ask when you make reservations. Do take a wrap or a light sweater with you—most restaurants keep air conditioners at full blast.

| CATEGORY | COST* |
|---|---|
| $$$$ | over $40 |
| $$$ | $30–$40 |
| $$ | $15–$30 |
| $ | under $15 |

*per person for a three-course meal, excluding drinks and service charge*

$$$$ ✕ **Dee Taveerne.** From the intricate detail of its antiques and brick-
★ work to its impressive Continental menu, this restaurant is the most elegant, romantic spot on the island. You'll dine in the whitewashed wine cellar of a magnificent renovated octagonal country estate, built in the 1800s by an exiled Venezuelan revolutionary. The best appetizer is the salmon carpaccio with laurel bay dressing en brioche. The entrées are rich and decadent: velvety lobster bisque finished with Armagnac, sautéed goose liver in plum sauce, smoked eel with horseradish. Finish with the unforgettable broiled pears, topped with vanilla ice cream and drenched with Curaçao chocolate liqueur. ⊠ *Landhuis Groot Davelaar, on Silena, near Promenade Shopping Center*, ☎ *5999/737–0669. AE, D, DC, MC, V. Closed Sun.*

$$$$ ✕ **L'Orangerie.** A romantic setting and gourmet Continental cuisine await you at this pricey restaurant at the Princess Beach Resort (☞ *Lodging, above*). Favorites from the seasonal à la carte menu include the chateaubriand and the lobster—but don't make your selection until you

hear the daily specials. The prix-fixe option is a bit of a savings. ⊠ *Princess Beach Resort, Martin Luther King Blvd. 8,* ☎ *5999/465–5955. AE, DC, MC, V. Closed Mon. No lunch.*

**$$$–$$$$** ✕ **Bistro Le Clochard.** This romantic gem is built into the 18th-century Rif Fort—an oasis of arched entryways, exposed brickwork, wood beams, and lace curtains. Cocktails and hors d'oeuvres are served on the Waterside Terrace, with its view of the floating bridge and harbor. The French and Swiss dishes are consistently well prepared, though pricey. Try the fresh-fish platters or the veal in mushroom sauce. Savor the fondue and let yourself get carried away by the unusual setting; save room for the chocolate mousse. Avoid weekends, when an inexplicably corny duo plays, but you might enjoy the complimentary snacks of Friday's 5-to-7 Hungry Hour. ⊠ *On the Otrabanda, Rif Fort,* ☎ *5999/462–5666. AE, DC, MC, V. Closed Sun. No lunch Sat.*

**$$$** ✕ **Emerald Steakhouse.** Set in the Sonesta Beach Hotel, Emerald is probably the best steak house on the island and is certainly one of the most sophisticated settings. Candlelit tables, rich wood paneling, and a pianist playing through the meal make this a good choice for a special dinner. Start with Caesar salad à deux, prepared tableside. The beef dishes, featuring thick USDA prime cuts, are grilled and sauced to taste; there's also a vegetarian offering and some seafood on the menu. ⊠ *Piscadera Bay,* ☎ *5999/736–8800. AE, D, DC, MC, V. No lunch.*

**$$$** ✕ **Fort Nassau Restaurant.** This is *the* place to view twinkling Curaçao at night. High on a hilltop overlooking Willemstad, the restaurant is built into an 18th-century fort with a 360-degree view. Go for a drink in the breezy Battery Terrace bar or dine in air-conditioned comfort in front of the huge bay windows. The menu is diverse, from rabbit, duck, pigeon, and beef preparations to lightly broiled fish (ask the waiter what's fresh). Stay away from the enticing yet overly complex stabs at innovative cuisine: The simple selections are best here. Dinner seatings are at 7 and 9 PM. ⊠ *Schottengatweg 82, near Juliana Bridge,* ☎ *5999/461–3450. Reservations essential. AE, D, DC, MC, V. No lunch weekends.*

**$$$** ✕ **La Pergola.** Built into the stuccoed walls of the Waterfort Arches, with huge picture windows fronting the rambunctious sea and a pretty pink-and-white arbor wound with bunches of grapes, La Pergola offers creative variations on Italian standards. Try the smoked salmon drizzled with olive oil and studded with cloves or the grouper siciliana with capers, olives, anchovies, tomatoes, and garlic. Pizza reigns supreme (13 choices) on the terrace menu. ⊠ *Waterfort Arches, Willemstad,* ☎ *5999/461–3482. AE, DC, MC, V. No lunch Sun.*

**$$–$$$** ✕ **Pirates.** A friendly and efficient wait staff delivers dish after dish of superb seafood, including oyster soup, seviche, paella, and conch. The sea bass Creole-style is delicious, as is the red snapper in almond sauce. The decor is nautical (if somewhat hokey), with an anchor, a watch tower, and, of course, a mermaid. ⊠ *Curaçao Caribbean Hotel,* ☎ *5999/462–8500. AE, DC, MC, V.*

**$$** ✕ **Fort Waakzaamheid Tavern.** High on a hill overlooking Willemstad and the harbor, this fort was captured by Captain Bligh of HMS *Bounty* two centuries ago. Now it is controlled by an Irishman, Tom Farrel, who operates an open-air restaurant and bar in the evening. The atmosphere is informal, and the food is primarily barbecued seafood and steaks decorated with your own makings from a salad bar. You will be equally well greeted if you go just for cocktails and snacks—and the sunsets are magnificent. ⊠ *Off main highway on Otrabanda side of suspension bridge, Seru Domi, Willemstad,* ☎ *5999/462–3633. AE, D, MC, V. Closed Tues. No lunch.*

**$$** ✕ **Mambo Beach.** On the west end of Seaquarium Beach (and we do mean *on* the beach), Mambo Beach is a hip, open-air bar and grill spread over the sand that serves surprisingly good food for breakfast, lunch, and dinner. Baguettes dominate the lunch menu, while steaks, fresh seafood, and pasta fill the dinner menu. The half-order bowl of pasta is large enough to feed two, especially if you start with cold cucumber soup, seafood salad, or calamari. This is a fantastic place to watch the setting sun, but don't forget your insect repellent and apply it liberally. ✉ *Seaquarium Beach,* ☎ *5999/461–8999. AE, MC, V.*

$$ ✕ **Rijsttafel Indonesia Restaurant.** An antique rickshaw guarding the
★ entrance sets the mood in this tranquil spot. No steaks or chops served here, just exotic delicacies that make up the traditional Indonesian banquet called rijsttafel, where some 16 to 25 dishes are set buffet-style around you. Smaller appetites should opt for the *nasi rames,* a miniversion with only eight dishes. Vegetarians will be pleased that a 16-course vegetable rijsttafel is also available. An à la carte menu includes fried noodles, fresh jumbo shrimp in garlic, and combination meat-and-fish platters. The walls are hung with beautiful Indonesian puppets ($25–$40) that make stunning gifts. ✉ *Mercurriusstraat 13–15, Salina,* ☎ *5999/461–2606. AE, DC, MC, V. No lunch Sun.*

$$ ✕ **Seaview.** This casual terrace eatery is nestled snugly in the corner of the Waterfort Arches, where the surf pounds against the rocks—you expect the sea to drench you at any minute. Try the tender pepper fillet or the tangy *salpicon de mariscos,* a version of seviche that includes everything from octopus to shrimp vinaigrette. The chef also creates such specialties as green-and-white asparagus en brioche. It's a great place to watch the pyrotechnics of the sun at dusk. ✉ *Waterfort Arches, Willemstad,* ☎ *5999/461–6688. AE, DC, MC, V. No lunch Sun.*

$ ✕ **Cactus Club.** A veritable grove of aloe and cacti greets you in the courtyard of this Caribbean version of Bennigan's. The inside is surprisingly subdued: faux Tiffany lamps, hanging plants, whirring ceiling fans. Food is cheap and filling, including fettuccine Alfredo, fajitas, buffalo wings, Cajun snapper, and burgers. It's predictably popular with both locals and homesick Americans. ✉ *Van Staverenweg 6,* ☎ *5999/737–1600. DC, MC, V.*

$ ✕ **Café du Port.** This alfresco harborfront café serves a variety of baguette sandwiches—the salmon salad and pâté are good choices—and cold drinks, from shakes and sodas to fancier alcohol-infused libations. Egg dishes and ham and Dutch cheese are available for breakfast. It's a scenic little spot to cool off with a drink when those feet get tired of walking; the view of the floating bridge is splendid. ✉ *Handelskade 13, Punda,* ☎ *5999/465–0670. AE, MC, V.*

$ ✕ **Golden Star Restaurant.** This place looks and feels more like a friendly roadside diner, but the native food here is among the best in town. Owner Marie Burke turns out such Antillean specialties as *bestia chiki* (goat stew), shrimp Creole, and delicately seasoned grilled conch, with generous heaps of rice, fried plantains, and avocado. Steaks and chops can be had for the asking. ✉ *Socratestraat 2,* ☎ *5999/461–8828. AE, DC, MC, V. Closed Tues.*

$ ✕ **Jaanchi's Restaurant.** Tour buses stop regularly at this open-air
★ restaurant for lunches of mouthwatering Curaçaoan dishes. The main-course specialty is a hefty platter of fresh-caught fish, conch, or shrimp with potatoes or *funchi* (corn bread) and vegetables on the side. You can also try stewed goat here. Curaçaoans joke that Jaanchi's "iguana soup is so strong it could resurrect the dead"—truth is, it tastes just like chicken soup, only better. But Jaanchi Jr. says, if you want iguana, you should order in advance "because we have to go out and catch them." He's not kidding. He usually closes at 6:30 PM but will stay open later if you call ahead to reserve a spot. ✉ *Westpunt 15,* ☎ *5999/864–0126. AE, DC, MC, V.*

# Beaches

Curaçao has some 38 beaches, but unfortunately some are rocky and litter-strewn. The best way to find "your" beach is to rent a Jeep, motor scooter, or heavy-treaded car. Ask your hotel to pack a picnic basket and go exploring. Curaçao doesn't have Aruba's long stretches of sand; instead, you'll discover the joy of inlets: tiny bay openings to the sea marked by craggy cliffs, exotic trees, and scads of interesting pebbles. Imagine a beach that's just big enough for two. Beware of thorns and keep an eye out for flying fish. They propel their tails through the water until they reach a speed of 44 mph, then spread their fins and soar.

Hotels with the best beaches include the Sonesta Beach Hotel (impressively long); the Princess Beach (impressively sensuous); and the Lions Dive Beach Resort on the Seaquarium Beach (impressive for its amenities). No matter where you're staying, beach-hopping to other hotels can be fun. Nonguests are supposed to pay the hotels a beach fee, but often there is no one to collect.

**Daai Booi Bay** is a sandy shore dotted with thatched shelters. The road to this public beach (follow signs from the church of St. Willibrordus) is a small paved highway flanked by thick lush trees and huge organ-pipe cacti. The beach is curved, with shrubbery rooted into the side of the rocky cliffs—a great place for swimming. **Knip Bay** has two parts: Big (Groot) Knip and Little (Kleine) Knip. Only Little Knip is shaded with trees, but these are manchineels, so steer clear of them. Also beware of cutting your feet on beer-bottle caps. Both beaches have alluring white sand, but only Big Knip has changing facilities. Big Knip also has several tiki huts for shade and calm turquoise waters that are perfect for swimming and lounging. The protected cove, flanked by sheer cliffs, is usually a blast on Sunday, when there is occasionally live music. To get there, take the road to the Knip Landhouse, then turn right. Signs will direct you. **Playa Abao,** northwest of Knip Bay, has crystal-clear turquoise water and a small beach. Sunday afternoons are crowded and festive. There's a snack bar and public toilets. **Westpunt,** on the northwest tip of the island, is shady in the morning. It doesn't have much sand, but you can sit on a shaded rock ledge. On Sunday, watch the divers jump from the high cliff. The bay view is worth the trip. **Playa Lagun,** southeast of Playa Forti, is dotted with powder-blue camping huts and caught between towering gunmetal gray cliffs. Cognoscenti know this is one of the best places to snorkel—you may even go nose to nose with the resident giant squid. You'll pay a fee ($2.25 per person) to enter **Seaquarium's Beach,** but the array of amenities (rest rooms, showers, boutiques, water-sports center, snack bar, restaurant with beach bar, thatched shelters and palm trees for shade, security patrols, even a calling station to call or fax home) on this 500-meter man-made beach and calm waters protected by a carefully placed breakwater are well worth it. **Santa Barbara,** a popular family beach on the eastern tip, is reached by driving through one of Curaçao's toniest neighborhoods, Spanish Water, where gleaming white yachts replace humble fishing fleets. The beach has changing facilities and a snack bar but charges a small admission fee, usually around $2.25 per person. Around the bend, **Caracas Bay** is a popular dive site, with a sunken ship so close to the surface that snorkelers can view it clearly.

# Outdoor Activities and Sports

## Fitness Centers

**Body Beach** (✉ Lions Dive Hotel, ☎ 5999/465–7969) is open to nonguests for a fee. It schedules exercise classes and is equipped with the latest fitness equipment. **Sundance Health & Fitness Center** (✉

John F. Kennedy Blvd. at Rif Recreation Area, ☎ 5999/462–7740) has all the gentle luxuries, including Turkish bath, sauna, whirlpool, massage, and beauty treatments. A professional medical staff is on hand.

## Golf

**Curaçao Golf and Squash Club** (⊠ Wilhelmenalaan, ☎ 5999/737–3590) welcomes visitors daily 8–8 in high season. The nine-hole course offers a challenge because of the stiff trade winds and the sand greens. Greens fees are $20. Two squash courts are open daily 8–6.

## Horseback Riding

**Ashari's Ranch** (⊠ Groot Piscadera Kaya A23, ☎ 5999/869–0315) is the only stable to offer romps to the beach. It costs $30 for a 1½ hour ride. Trail rides are available at **Christoffel Park** (☎ 5999/864–0363), with prices ranging from $25 to $70 depending on the trail and length of time selected. Make reservations well in advance for a park tour on these gentle, smooth-gaited "paseo" horses.

## Jogging

**Rif Recreation Area,** locally known as the *corredor,* stretches from the water plant at Mundo Nobo to the Sonesta Beach Hotel. It consists of more than a mile of palm-lined beachfront, a wading pond, and a jogging track with an artificial surface, as well as a big playground. There is good security and street lighting along the entire length of the beachfront.

## Sailing

**Sail Curaçao** (⊠ Yachtclub Asiento, Spanish Water, ☎ 5999/767–6003) offers day sails, sailing instruction, snorkeling trips, and windsurfing. **Top Watersports Curaçao** (⊠ Seaquarium Beach, ☎ 5999/461–7343) rents sail boards for windsurfing.

## Tennis

Most hotels (including Sonesta Beach, Curaçao Caribbean, Princess Beach, and Holiday Beach) offer well-paved courts, illuminated for day and night games. These courts are usually occupied by guests of the hotels. Your best bet if you're not staying at one of these properties is the **Santa Catherina Sports Complex** (☎ 5999/767–7028), where court time costs $20 an hour.

## Water Sports

Curaçao has facilities for all kinds of water sports, thanks to the government-sponsored **Curaçao Underwater Marine Park** (☎ 5999/864–2424), which includes almost a third of the island's southern diving waters. Scuba divers and snorkelers can enjoy more than 12½ mi of protected reefs and shores, with normal visibility from 60 to 80 ft (up to 150 ft on good days). With water temperatures ranging from 75° to 82°F, wet suits are generally unnecessary. No coral collecting, spearfishing, or littering is allowed. An exciting wreck to explore is the SS *Oranje Nassau*, which ran aground more than 90 years ago and now hosts hundreds of exotic fish and unusually shaped coral.

Most hotels either offer their own program of water sports or will be happy to make arrangements for you. An introductory scuba resort course usually runs about $60–$75.

**Coral Cliff Diving** (☎ 5999/864–2822) offers an open-water certification course ($330) and a full schedule of dive and snorkeling trips to Curaçao's southwest coast. It also rents pedal boats, Hobie Cats, and underwater cameras. **Habitat Curaçao**'s (☎ 5999/864–8800) new dive center offers a full array of training, from a two-day, three-dive introductory course ($100) to underwater video ($165) and photography courses ($275–$400). **Peter Hughes Divers** (☎ 5999/465–8991), at the Princess Beach Resort, rents equipment (including underwater camera) and conducts diving and snorkeling trips. Two-tank boat dives run $55, while three days of unlimited shore diving costs $33. Also available is a cabin cruiser for half- or full-day deep-sea fishing excursions. **Seascape** (☎ 5999/462–5000 or 5999/462–5905), at the Curaçao Caribbean Hotel and Casino, specializes in snorkeling and scuba-diving trips to reefs and underwater wrecks in every type of water vehicle—from pedal boats, kayaks, and water scooters to water skis and Windsurfers. A six-dive package costs $165 and includes unlimited beach diving plus one boat dive per day and one night dive. Snorkeling gear costs about $10 a day to rent. Deep-sea fishing for a maximum of four people can also be arranged; it costs $350 for a half day, $560 for a full day. **Underwater Curaçao** (☎ 5999/461–8100) offers complete vacation-dive packages in conjunction with the Lions Dive Hotel & Marina. Its fully stocked dive shop, between the Lions Dive Hotel and the Curaçao Seaquarium, rents and sells equipment. Personal instruction and group lessons are conducted on state-of-the-art dive boats. One dive will run you $35; dive-only packages, such as a seven-day unlimited shore dive option priced at $145, are available. **Top Watersports Curaçao** (☎ 5999/461–7343) on Seaquarium Beach rents water scooters ($45–$60), canoes ($6–$8), snorkel gear ($12), and floating mats ($3).

## Spectator Sports

**Centro Deportivo Curaçao** (✉ Bonamweg 49, ☎ 5999/737–6620), a modern and comfortable stadium about 10 minutes from town, holds soccer matches and baseball games from March through October. It's open daily 9:30–12:30 and 1–6.

# Shopping

Curaçao has long enjoyed the reputation of having some of the best shops in the Caribbean, with classier displays and a better variety than on many islands, but don't expect posh Madison Avenue boutiques. With a few exceptions (such as at Benetton, which recently moved into the Caribbean with a vengeance), the quality of women's fashions here lies along the lines of sales racks. Many shops are closed on Monday and virtually all lock up by 6 PM the remainder of the week. If you're looking for bargains on Swiss watches, cosmetics, cameras, crystal, perfumes, Nike or Reebok sneakers, or electronic equipment, do some comparison shopping back home and come armed with a list of prices. Willemstad is no longer a free port: there's now a tax and consequently prices are higher.

## Shopping Areas

Most of the shops are concentrated in Willemstad's Punda within about a six-block area. The main shopping streets are Heerenstraat, Breedestraat, and Madurostraat. Heerenstraat and Gomezplein are pedestrian malls, closed to traffic, and their roadbeds have been raised to sidewalk level and covered with pink inlaid tiles.

## Good Buys

**Bamali** (✉ Breedestraat 2, ☎ 5999/461–2258) sells Indonesian batik clothing, leather bags, and charming handicrafts. **Boolchand's** (✉ Heerenstraat 4B, ☎ 5999/461–2262) handles an interesting variety of merchandise behind a facade of red-and-white-checked tiles. Stock up here on French perfumes, British cashmere sweaters, Italian silk ties, Dutch dolls, Swiss watches, and Japanese cameras. **Julius L. Penha & Sons** (✉ Heerenstraat 1, ☎ 5999/461–2266), in front of the Pontoon Bridge, sells French perfumes, Hummel figurines, linen from Madeira, delftware, and handbags from Argentina, Italy, and Spain. The store also has an extensive cosmetics counter. **Little Switzerland** (✉ Breedestraat

# Shopping 15

44, ☎ 5999/461–2111) is the place for duty-free shopping; you'll find perfumes, jewelry, watches, crystal, china, and leather goods at significant savings. **Sparky's** (✉ Braastraat 23, ☎ 5999/461–7462) carries all the major brands of cosmetics and perfume.

## CLOTHING

**Benetton** (✉ Madurostraat 4, ☎ 5999/461–4619, and other locations) has winter stock in July and summer stock in December; all of it is 20% off the retail price. **Boutique Aquarius** (✉ Breedestraat 9, ☎ 5999/461–2618) sells Fendi merchandise for 25% less than in the United States. Fendi fanatics can stock up on belts, shoes, pocketbooks, wallets, and even watches. **Boutique Liska** (✉ Schottegatweg Oost 191-A, ☎ 5999/461–3111) draws local residents shopping for smart women's fashions. **Clog Dance** (✉ De Rouvilleweg 9B, ☎ 5999/462–3280) is where to go if you long for Dutch clogs, cheeses, tulips, delftware, Dutch fashions, or chocolate. **Crazy Look** (✉ Madurostraat 32, ☎ 5999/461–1440) has French, Italian, and Dutch fashions with a hip European look, as well as trendy sweatshirts and baggy pants. For the latest European shoes to go with a funky new outfit, visit **Cinderella** (✉ Haaranstraat 4, ☎ 5999/461–5000).

## DELICACIES

**Toko Zuikertuintje** (✉ Zuikertuintjeweg, ☎ 5999/737–0188), a supermarket built on the original 17th-century Zuikertuintje Landhuis, is where most of the local elite shop for all sorts of European and Dutch delicacies. Shopping here for a picnic is a treat in itself.

## JEWELRY AND WATCHES

**Gandelman** (✉ Breedestraat 35, ☎ 5999/461–1854; ✉ Sonesta Beach Hotel, ☎ 5999/462–8386) has watches by Cartier and Piaget, leather goods by Prima Classe, and Baccarat and Daum crystal. **La Zahav N.V.** (✉ Curaçao International Airport, ☎ 5999/868–9594) is one of the best places to buy gold jewelry—with or without diamonds, rubies, and emeralds—at true discount prices. The shop is in the airport transit hall, just at the top of the staircase.

## LINENS

**New Amsterdam** (✉ Gomezplein 14, ☎ 5999/461–2469) is the place to price hand-embroidered tablecloths, napkins, and pillowcases. Tablecloths begin at $35, double bedspreads at $100.

## LOCAL CRAFTS

**Arawak Craft Factory** (✉ Cruise Terminal, Otrabanda, ☎ 5999/462–7249) has a factory showroom of native-made crafts. You can purchase a variety of tiles, plates, pots, and tiny replicas of landhouses. **Black Koral** (✉ Princess Beach Hotel, ☎ 5999/465–2122) is owned by Dutch-born artisan Bert Knubben, one of Curaçao's true characters. For the past 30 years, he's been designing and sculpting the most exciting black-coral jewelry in the Caribbean—and he even dives for the coral himself, with special permission from the government. Dolphin pendants and twiglike earrings finished in 14-karat gold are excellent buys. Call before you drop by. **Fundason Obra di Man** (✉ Bargestraat 57, Punda, ☎ 5999/461–2413) stocks native crafts and curios. Particularly impressive are the posters of Curaçao's architecture. **Kas di Arte Kursou** (✉ Breedestraat 126, Otrabanda, ☎ 5999/864–2516) carries a variety of handmade souvenirs. **Gallery 86** (✉ Trompstraat, Punda, ☎ 5999/461–3417) features the works of local artists and occasionally those of South Americans and Africans. **Landhuis Groot Santa Martha** (✉ Santa Martha, ☎ 5999/864–1559) is where artisans with disabilities fashion handicrafts of varying types.

# Nightlife

Friday is the big night out, with rollicking happy hours—most with live music—at several hotels, most notably the Holiday Beach and Avila Beach (☞ Lodging, *above*). The once-a-month open house at Landhuis Brievengat (☞ Exploring, *below*) is a great way to meet interesting locals—it usually offers a folkloric show, snacks, and local handicrafts. Every Friday night the landhouse holds a big party with two bands. Check with the tourist board for the schedule of folkloric shows at various hotels. The Sonesta Beach, Van Der Valk Plaza, Curaçao Caribbean, Holiday Beach, Otrabanda, and Princess Beach hotels all have casinos that are open daily 1 PM–4 AM.

### BARS

**Blues** (⊠ Avila Beach Hotel, Penstraat 130, ☎ 5999/461–4377) focuses on live jazz Thursday and Saturday. The bar is at the end of the pier; magnificent sunset views are guaranteed. A well-lit indoor-outdoor bar, **Rum Runners** (⊠ Otrabanda Waterfront, De Rouvilleweg 9, ☎ 5999/462–3038) serves up tapas in a casual atmosphere that's reminiscent of a college fraternity hall. At press time, a second location of this popular club had just opened at Habitat Curaçao (☎ 5999/864–8800). **Mambo Beach** (☎ 5999/461–8999), an open-air bar on Seaquarium Beach, draws a hip, young crowd; beach volleyball and a live bands are often featured during happy hour on Sunday. **Keizershof,** a complex of renovated heritage buildings at the corner of Otrabanda's Hoogstraat and Rouvilleweg, has it all, with two restaurants and a café in addition to dancing under the stars at **Keizershof Terrace** (☎ 5999/462–3493) and sing-alongs at **Pianobar Kalimba** (☎ 5999/462–3583).

### DISCOS

The Salina district is the spot for clubbing: You'll find everything from merengue to house. **Club Safari** (⊠ Lindbergweg, Salina, ☎ 5999/465–5433) attracts the more mature crowd seeking late-night pleasures, with a line on Saturday night that stretches down the block. **Façade** (⊠ Lindbergweg 32, Salina, ☎ 5999/461–4640) is a hip Curaçao dance spot and a great place to meet locals who favor the Latin flare of the music here. It's dark and cool, with huge bamboo chairs for lounging. The disco floor, complete with flashing lights, is often shared by a variety of intense live bands. The **Jail Club** (⊠ Keukenplein, ☎ 5999/465–8610) comes complete with a warden, caged or chained dancers, graffiti lit by black light, and, on the mellower second floor, individual "cells" for private rendezvous.

# Exploring Curaçao

Willemstad, the capital in the southern half of the island, is cut in two by Santa Anna Bay. There are three ways to make the crossing from one side to the other: (1) drive or take a taxi over the Juliana Bridge, (2) traverse the Queen Emma Pontoon Bridge on foot, or (3) ride the free ferry, which runs when the Pontoon bridge is open for passing ships. All the major hotels outside of town offer free shuttle service to town once or twice daily. Shuttles coming from the Otrabanda side leave you at Rif Fort. From there it's a short walk north to the foot of the Pontoon Bridge. Shuttles coming from the Punda side leave you near the main entrance to Fort Amsterdam.

The Weg Maar Santa Cruz road through the village of Soto winds to the northwest tip of the island through landscape that Georgia O'Keeffe might have painted—towering cacti, flamboyant dried shrubbery, and aluminum-roof houses. Throughout this *cunucu,* or countryside, you'll see native fishermen hauling in their nets, women pounding cornmeal, and an occasional donkey blocking traffic. Land-houses, large plantation houses from centuries past, dot the country-side, though most are closed to the public. Their facades, however, can often be glimpsed from the highway. To explore the eastern side of the island, take the coastal road—Martin Luther King Boulevard—from Willemstad about 2 mi to Bapor Kibra. Here you'll find the Seaquar-ium and the Underwater Park.

*Numbers in the margin correspond to points of interest on the Curaçao map.*

SIGHTS TO SEE

**④ Boca Tabla.** At Boca Tabla, the sea has carved a magnificent grotto. Safely tucked in the back, you can watch and listen to the waves crash-ing ferociously against the rocks. ✉ *Westpunt Hwy., just past village of Soto.*

**★ ⑤ Christoffel Park.** This fantastic 4,450-acre garden and wildlife preserve centers on the towering Mt. Christoffel. The park consists of three for-mer plantations with individual trails that take about 1 to 1½ hours each to traverse. You may drive your own car (if it has heavy-treaded wheels) or rent a four-wheel drive with an accompanying guide (NAf150 for up to five passengers). Start out early (by 10 AM the park starts to feel like a sauna), and if you're going solo, first study the *Excursion Guide to Christoffel Park* sold at the front desk of the elegant, if dilapidated, Land-huis Savonet (the plantation house turned Natural History Museum); it outlines the various routes and identifies the flora and fauna found here. There is a 20-mi network of roads, and no matter what route you take, you'll be treated to views of hilly fields full of prickly-pear cacti, divi-divi trees, bushy-haired palms, and exotic flowers that bloom unpredictably after November showers. There are also caves—the strong at heart will revel in the rustling of bat wings and the sight of scuttling scorpion spi-ders (not poisonous)—and ancient Indian drawings.

As you drive through the park, keep a lookout for tiny deer, goats, and small wildlife that might suddenly dart in front of your car. The whip snakes and minute silver snakes you may encounter are not poisonous. White-tail hawks may be seen on the green route, white orchids and crownlike passionflowers on the yellow route. Climbing the 1,239-ft Mt. Christoffel on foot is an exhilarating experience and a definite chal-lenge to anyone who hasn't grown up scaling the Alps. The park's guide-book claims the round-trip will take you one hour, and Curaçaoan adolescent boys do make a sport of racing up and down, but it's really more like two (sweaty) hours from the base of the mountain for a rea-sonably fit person who's not an expert hiker. And the last few feet are deadly. The view from the peak, however, *is* thrilling—a panorama of the island, including Santa Marta Bay and the tabletop mountain of St. Hironimus. On a clear day, you can even see the mountain ranges of Venezuela, Bonaire, and Aruba. ✉ *Savonet,* ☎ *5999/864–0363.* ⛁ *Park and museum $9, museum only $3.* ☉ *Mon.–Sat. 8–4, Sun. 6–3; last admittance 1 hr before closing.*

**⑥ Country House Museum.** This thatched-roof cottage is a living museum demonstrating country life as it was in the 19th century. It's filled with antique furniture, farm implements, and clothing typical of colonial life on the island. Out back is a minifarm with vegetable garden, penned donkeys, and caged parrots, eagles, and iguana. Look closely at the fence—it's made of living cacti. There's also a snack bar. A fes-tival featuring live music and local crafts takes place here on the first Sunday of each month. ✉ *Dokterstuin 27,* ☎ *5999/864–2742.* ⛁ *$1.50.* ☉ *Tues.–Fri. 9–4, weekends 9–5.*

🖑 ⑩   **Curaçao Seaquarium.** The Seaquarium is *the* place to see the island's underwater treasures without getting your feet wet. It's the world's only public aquarium where sea creatures are raised and cultivated totally by natural methods. Where else can you hand-feed a shark (or watch a diver do it)? The **Animal Encounters** section consists of a broad, 12-ft-deep open-water enclosure that brings you face to face with a variety of jaws. Snorkelers and divers are welcome to swim freely with stingrays, tarpon, groupers, and such. Diving instruction and equipment are part of the package; it's a thrilling introduction to the sport in a controlled environment, and, in fact, up to 75% of participants have never tried diving before. The highlight for most is the variety of sharks in one section of the enclosure, safely divided off by mesh fencing and thick Plexiglas; divers and snorkelers can feed the sharks by hand in perfect safety through holes in the Plexiglas. If shark feeding isn't your cup of tea, there is an underwater observatory where you can watch. The cost is $55 for divers, $30 for snorkelers, which includes admission to the Seaquarium, training in snorkeling and scuba diving, use of equipment, and food for the fish, turtles, and sharks. Reservations for Animal Encounters must be made 24 hours in advance.

You can spend several hours mesmerized by the 46 freshwater tanks full of more than 400 varieties of exotic fish and vegetation found in the waters around Curaçao, including sharks, lobsters, turtles, corals, and sponges. Look out for the more than 5-ft-long mascot, Herbie the lugubrious jewfish. One outdoor enclosure houses a sea lion and a sea bear (yes, they're different, like a horse and a mule). There's a snack bar and restaurant on the grounds in case you get hungry. There are also glass-bottom-boat tours, fun feeding shows, and a viewing platform overlooking the wreck of the steamship SS *Oranje Nassau,* which sank in 1906 and now sits in 10 ft of water. A nearby 495-yard man-made beach is well suited to novice swimmers and children, and bathroom and shower facilities are available. A souvenir shop sells some of the best postcards and coral jewelry on the island. ✉ *Bapor Kibra,* ☎ *5999/461–6666,* 🅵🅰🆇 *5999/461–3671.* 🎫 *$13.25.* ☉ *Daily 8:30–6.*

⑨   **Curaçao Underwater Marine Park.** About 12½ mi of untouched coral reefs have been granted the status of national park. Mooring buoys placed at the most interesting dive sites on the reef provide safe anchoring and prevent damage to the reef. Several sunken ships lie awaiting visitors in the deep. The park stretches along the south shore from the Princess Beach Hotel in Willemstad to the eastern tip of the island. ✉ *Off southeast shore,* ☎ *5999/461–8131.*

⑦   **Hato Caves.** Hour-long guided tours wind down into various chambers to the water pools, voodoo chamber, wishing well, fruit bats' sleeping quarters, and Curaçao Falls, where a stream of silver joins with a stream of gold (they're colored by lights) and is guarded by a limestone "dragon" perched nearby. Hidden lights illuminate the limestone formations and gravel walkways. This is one of the better Caribbean caves open to the public, but keep in mind that there are 49 steep steps to reach the entrance, and the cave itself is dank and hot (though they've put electric fans in some areas to provide relief). ✉ *Head northwest toward airport, take right onto Gosieweg, follow loop right onto Schottegatweg, take another right onto Jan Norduynweg, a final right onto Rooseveltweg, and follow signs,* ☎ *5999/868–0379.* 🎫 *$6.25.* ☉ *Daily 10–5.*

⑧   **Landhuis Brievengat.** This mustard-colored plantation house is a fine example of the island's past. You can see the original kitchen still intact, the 18-inch-thick walls, fine antiques, and the watch towers once used for lovers' trysts. The restaurant, open only on Wednesday and Friday, serves a fine rijstaffel. Friday night a party is held on the wide wraparound terrace, with two bands and plenty to drink ($6 cover charge). On the last Sunday of the month (6–7:30 PM), this estate holds an open house with crafts demonstrations and folkloric shows. ⊠ *10-min drive northeast of Willemstad, near Centro Deportivo sports stadium,* ☎ *5999/737–8344.* ⊡ *$1.* ☺ *Mon.–Sat. 9:15–12:15 and 3–6.*

**❷ Landhuis Jan Kok.** For a splendid view, and some unusual island tales of ghosts, visit this mid-17th-century plantation house overlooking the salt pans. Since the hours are irregular, be sure to call ahead to arrange a tour of this reputedly haunted house, or stop by on Sunday mornings, when the proprietor occasionally opens the small restaurant behind her home and serves delicious Dutch pancakes. ⊠ *Weg Naar San Willibrordus,* ☎ *5999/864–8087.* ⊡ *$3.* ☺ *Weekdays 11 AM–8 PM, but call ahead to arrange tour.*

**❸ Landhuis Knip.** In terms of the number of slaves held, this was the largest plantation on the island in its prime. It therefore comes as no surprise that the slave revolt took place here in 1795. The renovated plantation house near the western tip of the island is filled with period furnishings, clothing, and other household goods. You can also walk around the extensive stables and barns used in the operation of this maize plantation. ⊠ *Weg Naar Santa Cruz,* ☎ *5999/864–0244.* ⊡ *$2; free Sun.* ☺ *Sun.–Fri. 9–noon and 2–4.*

## Willemstad

**❶** What does **Willemstad,** the capital of Curaçao, have in common with New York City? Broadway, for one. Here it's called Breedestraat, but the origin is the same. Dutch settlers came here in the 1630s, the same period when they sailed through the Narrows to Manhattan, bringing with them original red-tile roofs, first used on the trade ships as ballast and later incorporated into the architecture of Willemstad.

Willemstad is a favorite cruise stop for two reasons: The shopping is considered among the best in the Caribbean, and a quick tour of most of the downtown sights can be managed within a six-block radius. Santa Anna Bay slices the city down the middle: On one side is the Punda, and on the other is the Otrabanda (literally, the "other side"). Think of the Punda as the side for tourists, crammed with shops, restaurants, monuments, and markets. Otrabanda is less touristy, with lots of narrow, winding streets full of private homes notable for their picturesque gables and Dutch-influenced designs.

SIGHTS TO SEE

**Curaçao Museum.** Housed in a century-old former plantation house, this small museum is filled with artifacts, paintings, and antique furnishings that trace the island's history. This is also the venue for art exhibitions that visit the island. ⊠ *Leeuwenhoekstraat,* ☎ *5999/462–3873.* ⊡ *$2.25.* ☺ *Weekdays 9–noon and 2–5, Sun. 10–4.*

**Floating Market.** Each morning dozens of Venezuelan schooners laden with tropical fruits and vegetables arrive at this bustling market on the Punda side of the city. Fresh mangoes, papayas, and exotic vegetables vie for space with freshly caught fish and herbs and spices. It's probably too much to ask a tourist to arrive by 6:30 AM, when the buying is best, but there's plenty of action to see throughout the afternoon. Any produce bought here, however, should be thoroughly washed before eating. Note: At press time the floating market was temporarily located across Waaigat Channel while the city renovated the dock area. ⊠ *Sha Caprileskade.*

**Fort Amsterdam.** Step through the archway and enter another century. The entire structure dates from the 1700s, when it was the center of the city and the most important fort on the island. Now it houses the governor's residence, the Fort Church, the ministry, and other government offices. Outside the entrance a series of majestic gnarled *wayaka* trees are fancifully carved with a dragon, a giant squid, and a mermaid—the work of noted local artist Mac Alberto, who can be seen strolling the streets impeccably garbed in blinding white suits, a courtly boutonniere in his lapel. ⊠ *Foot of Queen Emma Bridge.*

**Mikveh Israel-Emanuel Synagogue.** This synagogue was dedicated in 1732 by the Jewish community that came from Amsterdam in 1651 to establish a new congregation. Jews from Portugal and Brazil, fleeing persecution, soon joined them, and by the early 1700s more than 2,000 Jews were in residence. This temple, the oldest still in use in the Western Hemisphere, is one of the most important sights in Curaçao and draws 20,000 visitors a year. Enter through the Spanish-tiled courtyard around the corner from Columbusstraat on Hanchi Di Snoa, and ask the front office to direct you to the guide on duty. A unique feature is the brilliant white sand covering the synagogue floor, a remembrance of Moses leading his people through the desert and of the Diaspora. The Hebrew letters on the four pillars signify the names of the Four Mothers of Israel: Sarah, Rebecca, Rachel, and Leah. The fascinating **Jewish Cultural Museum** (☎ 5999/461–1633) in the back displays Jewish antiques (including a set of circumcision instruments) and artifacts from Jewish families collected from all over the world. The gift shop has excellent postcards and commemorative medallions. English and Hebrew services are held Friday at 6:30 PM and Saturday at 10 AM. Men who attend should wear a jacket and tie. ⊠ *Hanchi Di Snoa 29,* ☎ *5999/461–1067.* ⊡ *Small donation expected in synagogue; Jewish Cultural Museum $2.* ☉ *Weekdays 9–11:45 and 2:30–5 (closing time depends on schedule of services).*

**Old Market (Marche).** Behind the post office is where you'll find local women preparing hearty Antillean lunches at the Old Market. For $4–$6 you can enjoy such Curaçaoan specialties as *funchi* (corn bread), *keshi yena* (Gouda cheese stuffed with meat), goat stew, fried fish, peas and rice, and fried plantains. ⊠ *De Ruyterkade.*

**Plaza Piar.** This plaza, next to Fort Amsterdam, was dedicated to Manuel Piar, a native Curaçaoan who fought for the independence of Venezuela under the liberator Simon Bolívar. On one side of the plaza is the **Waterfort,** a bastion dating from 1634. The original cannons are still positioned in the battlements. The foundation, however, now forms the walls of the Van Der Valk Plaza Hotel.

**Queen Emma Bridge.** This bridge is affectionately called the Swinging Old Lady by the natives. If you're standing on the Otrabanda side, take a few moments to scan Curaçao's multicolored "face" on the other side of Santa Anna Bay. If you wait long enough, the bridge will swing open (at least 30 times a day) to let the seagoing ships pass through. The original bridge, built in 1888, was the brainchild of the American consul Leonard Burlington Smith, who made a mint off the tolls he charged for the bridge. Initially, the charge was 2¢ per person for those wearing shoes, free to those crossing barefoot. Today it's free to everyone.

**Queen Juliana Bridge.** This 1,625-ft-long bridge, to the north of the Queen Emma Bridge, was completed in 1974 and stands 200 ft above water—a great vantage point for photos of the city. It's the bridge you drive over to cross to the other side of the city, and although the route is time-consuming (and more expensive if you're going by taxi), the view is worth it. At every hour of the day, the sun casts a different tint over the city, creating an ever-changing panorama; the nighttime view, rivaling Rio's, is breathtaking.

**Scharloo.** The Wilhelmina Drawbridge connects Punda with the once-flourishing district of Scharloo, where the early Jewish merchants first built stately homes. The end of the district closest to Kleine Werf is now a red-light district and is pretty run down, but the rest of the area is well worth a visit. The architecture along Scharlooweg (much of it dating from the 17th century) is intriguing, and, happily, many of the structures that had become dilapidated have been meticulously renovated.

## Curaçao A to Z

### Arriving and Departing

BY PLANE

**American Airlines** (☎ 5999/869–5707 or 800/433–7300) flies direct daily from Miami. **ALM** (☎ 5999/869–5533 or 800/327–7230), Curaçao's national airline, maintains frequent service from Miami and Atlanta. For Atlanta departures, ALM has connecting services (through-fares) to most U.S. gateways with Delta. ALM also offers a Visit Caribbean Pass, allowing easy interisland travel. **Air Aruba** (☎ 5999/868–3777 or 800/882–7822) has daily direct flights to Curaçao (flights make brief stops in Aruba) from both Miami and Newark airports. Air Aruba also has regularly scheduled service to Curaçao from Baltimore, and to Aruba and Bonaire. **Guayana Air** (☎ 5999/461–3033 or 5999/869–5533) now offers nonstop service from New York. **KLM** (☎ 5999/465–2747) flies direct from Amsterdam. **E Liner Airways** (☎ 5999/868–5099 or 5999/560–4773) has interisland service, including sightseeing and beach tours of Aruba and Bonaire.

### Currency

U.S. dollars—in cash or traveler's checks—are accepted nearly everywhere, so there's no need to worry about exchanging money. However, you may need small change for pay phones, cigarettes, or soda machines. The currency in the Netherlands Antilles is the guilder, or florin, as it is also called, indicated by an fl or Naf on price tags. The U.S. dollar is considered very stable; the official rate of exchange at press time was NAf1.77 to the U.S. $1. Note: Prices quoted here are in U.S. dollars unless indicated otherwise.

### Emergencies

**Police** or **fire:** ☎ 114. **Hospitals:** For medical emergencies, call **St. Elisabeth's Hospital** (☎ 5999/462–4900 or 5999/462–5100) or an ambulance (☎ 112). The hospital is equipped with a hyperbaric chamber. **Pharmacies: Botica Popular** (✉ Madurostraat 15, ☎ 5999/461–1269), or ask your hotel for the nearest one. After normal business hours, dial 2222 to see which pharmacy has the night rotation.

### Getting Around

CAR RENTALS

You can rent a car from **Budget** (☎ 5999/868–3466 or 800/472–3325), **Avis** (☎ 5999/461–1255 or 800/331–1212), **Dollar** (☎ 5999/461–3144), or **National Car Rental** (☎ 5999/868–3489 or 800/328–4567) at the airport or have one delivered free to your hotel. Rates typically range from about $60 a day for a Toyota Tercel to about $75 for a four-door sedan or four-wheel drive; add 6% tax and required $10 daily insurance. If you're planning to do country driving or rough it through Christoffel Park, a four-wheel drive is best. All you'll need is a valid U.S. or Canadian driver's license.

TAXIS

Taxi drivers have an official tariff chart, with fares from the airport vicinity to Willemstad and the nearby beach hotels running about $10–$15, $30–$40 to hotels in the west end of the island. Taxis tend to be moderately priced, but since there are no meters, you should confirm the fare with the driver before departure. There is an additional 25% surcharge after 11 PM. Taxis are readily available at hotels; in other cases, call Central Dispatch at ☎ 5999/869–0747.

## Guided Tours

A guided tour can save you time and energy, though it is easy to cover the island yourself in a rented car. Most hotels have tour desks where arrangements can be made with reputable tour operators.

**Casper Tours** (☎ 5999/465–3010) has very personal, amiable service. For around $25 per person, you'll be escorted around the island in an air-conditioned van, with stops at the Juliana Bridge, the salt lakes, Knip Bay for a swim, the grotto at Boca Tabla, and Jaanchi's Restaurant—famous for its native cuisine—for lunch (not included). **Curven Tours** (☎ 5999/737–9806) offers island tours and special packages to Venezuela. **Shorex** (☎ 5999/462–8833) books a variety of entertaining island tours, including the Willemstad Trolley Train Tour ($15), which passes all the major downtown sights in an hour, and Eastern Highlights, a five-hour tour that visits Curaçao Ostrich Farm, Fort Nassau, an herb garden, and Landhuis Jan Thiel ($27). **Taber Tours** (☎ 5999/737–6637) offers a three-hour East Tour ($13) that includes visits to the Curaçao Liqueur Factory at Landhuis Chobolobo, the Curaçao Museum, and the Bloempot shopping center. An array of countryside tours and day trips to Aruba ($175) and Bonaire ($145) are also available. For personalized history and nature tours, contact **Dornasol Tours** (☎ 5999/868–2735); half-day tours run $25 and full-day tours are $40 per person.

BOAT TOURS

**Seaworld Explorer** (☎ 5999/462–8833), a semisubmersible, runs hour-long tours of the island's beautiful coral reefs ($30). Many sailboats and motorboats offer comparably priced sunset cruises ($30), snorkel trips ($25), and day-long snorkel and picnic trips to Klein Curaçao ($50), the "clothes optional" island between Curaçao and Bonaire. Top choices among the many boats are the 90-ft, turbo-driven *Waterworld* (☎ 5999/465–6042), the twin-masted sailboat *Vira Cocha* (☎ 5999/560–0292), the 120-ft Dutch sailing ketch *Insulinde* (☎ 5999/560–1340), and the 90-ft schooner *Bounty* (☎ 5999/560–1887).

## Language

Dutch is the official language, but the vernacular is Papiamento—a mixture of Dutch, African, French, Portuguese, Spanish, and English. Developed during the 18th century by Africans, Papiamento evolved in Curaçao as the mode of communication between landowners and their slaves. These days, however, English as well as Spanish—and, of course, Dutch—are studied by schoolchildren. Anyone involved with tourism—shopkeepers, restaurateurs, and museum guides—speaks English.

## Opening and Closing Times

Most shops are open Monday–Saturday 8–noon and 2–6. Banks are open weekdays 8–3:30 or 8–11:30 and 1:30–4.

## Passports and Visas

U.S. and Canadian citizens traveling to Curaçao need only proof of citizenship and a valid photo ID. A voter's registration card or a notarized birth certificate (not a photocopy) will suffice—a driver's license will *not*. British citizens must produce a passport. All visitors must show an ongoing or return ticket.

## Precautions

Mosquitoes definitely exist on Curaçao, at least during the rainy season. The bad news is the rainy season falls between November and April, coinciding with the tourist high season. To be safe, keep perfume to a minimum, be prepared to use insect repellent before dining alfresco, and spray your hotel room at night—especially if you've opened a window.

If you plan to go into the water, beware of long-spined sea urchins, which can be painful if you come in contact with them.

Do not eat any of the little green applelike fruits (they even smell like apples) of the manchineel tree: They're poisonous. In fact, steer clear of the trees altogether; raindrops or dewdrops dripping off the leaves can blister your skin. If contact does occur, rinse the affected area with water and, in extreme cases, get medical attention. Usually, the burning sensation won't last longer than two hours.

Crime is on the increase in Curaçao, so common-sense rules apply. Lock rental cars, use the theft deterrent device if provided by the rental firm, and do not leave valuables in the car. Use the in-room safe or leave valuables at the front desk of your hotel, and never leave bags unattended at the airport, on tours, or on the beach.

## Taxes and Service Charges

Hotels collect a 7% government tax and add a 12% service charge to the bill; restaurants add 10%–15%. Most shops and restaurants also tack on 6% ABB tax (a new value-added tax aimed specifically at tourists). The airport international departure tax is NAf122.50 (about $13), while interisland departure tax is NAf10 (about $5.65).

## Telephones and Mail

Phone service through the hotel operators in Curaçao is slow, but direct-dial service, both on-island and to the United States, is fast and clear. Hotel operators will put the call through for you, but if you make a collect call, do check immediately that the hotel does not charge you as well. To call Curaçao direct from the United States, dial 011–5999 plus the number in Curaçao. To place a local call on the island, dial the seven-digit local number. An airmail letter to the United States, Canada, or the United Kingdom costs NAf2.25, a postcard NAf1.25.

## Visitor Information

Contact the **Curaçao Tourist Board** (✉ 475 Park Ave. S, Suite 2000, New York, NY 10016, ☎ 212/683–7660 or 800/270–3350, FAX 212/683–9337; ✉ 330 Biscayne Blvd., Suite 808, Miami, FL 33132, ☎ 305/374–5811 or 800/445–8266, FAX 305/374–6741 for information).

In Curaçao, the **Curaçao Tourism Development Foundation** has two offices on the island where multilingual guides are ready to answer questions. You can also pick up maps, brochures, and a copy of *Curaçao Holiday*. The main office is in Willemstad at Pietermaai No. 19 (☎ 5999/461–6000); the other is at the airport (☎ 5999/868–6789).

# 10 Dominica

*If you want to take a temporary leave of absence from the rat race, this is the place to do it. Hike in the rain forest, scuba dive, explore volcanic lakes, whale-watch . . . this isn't called the Nature Island for nothing.*

**T**HE NATIONAL MOTTO emblazoned on the coat of arms of the Commonwealth of Dominica reads "*Après Bondi, c'est la terre.*" It is a French-Creole phrase meaning "After God, it is the land." On this unspoiled isle, the land is indeed the main attraction: It turns and twists, towers to mountain crests, then tumbles to falls and valleys. The weather is equally dramatic: Torrential rain, dazzling sunshine and, above all, rainbows, are likely to greet you in the course of a single day.

Updated by
Kate
Pennebaker
and Simon
Worrall

They say that if Christopher Columbus were to come back today, Dominica (pronounced dom-in-*ee*-ka) would be the only island in the Caribbean that he would recognize. Much of the interior is still covered by a luxuriant rain forest and remains inaccessible by road: a wild place straight out of Conan Doyle's *Lost World*. The Smithsonian has called Dominica a giant plant laboratory, unchanged for 10,000 years. The rugged northwest of the island is home to the last survivors of the region's original inhabitants, the Caribs. Folklore and superstition have also survived. In the villages of the green interior, you'll still find people who believe in *souqouyans* and *loups-garous,* diabolical spirits that can purportedly fly. *Obeah,* a system of magic originating in Africa, still has numerous practitioners.

Wedged between two rich French islands, Guadeloupe to the north and Martinique to the south, Dominica has always been something of an anomaly. Its most famous sons have been daughters: Jean Rhys, the novelist, and Dame Eugenia Charles, "Iron Lady" of the Caribbean—the only woman to have headed a government in this part of the world. Its official language is English, its family and place-names French, its religion predominantly Catholic. Driving is on the left. It is only 29 mi long and 16 mi wide, has a population less than that of Huntington, Long Island, but is an independent commonwealth with a seat at the United Nations. Unusual for the Caribbean, its economy is still based on agriculture. Bananas, not tourist dollars, are the largest money-earner.

Nature has always been Dominica's greatest enemy. It had too many mountains to make the cultivation of sugar profitable. It had too many rivers to make an effective road network viable. It rained too much. Throughout its history, Dominica has also been sorely tried by hurricanes: by David in 1979, by Hugo in 1989, and by Marilyn in 1995. But today nature is also Dominica's greatest asset. There may not be casinos or swim-up bars, but if you want to take a temporary leave of absence from the 20th century to hike in the rain forest, scuba dive, or explore volcanic lakes, this is the place to do it. Dominica has only just begun to discover its vast potential. Mountain lodges are being built. Life is being breathed back into old plantation houses. If realized, the Waitikubuli Trail, a proposed hiking trail that will traverse the island from north to south, will be the most spectacular of its kind in the Caribbean. The people are as friendly and polite as ever. It is how the Caribbean used to be. It is a village where everyone knows everyone, traffic moves at 30 mph, and people still have that rarest of commodities, time: time to chat on a street corner or laze over a long lunch. Within days of arriving, even the most frantic workaholic will have slowed to island pace.

## Lodging

If you're looking for swim-up bars and casinos, you've picked the wrong island. If you want small, family-run hotels, stick around. Prices are low, and staffs are extremely friendly and down-to-earth. The only beachfront hotels are in the Portsmouth area, the one exception being Castaways on Mero Beach. Roseau's seaside facilities have splendid Caribbean views but are beachless. The most interesting accommodations are found at the mountain lodges, nature retreats, and refurbished plantation houses that are springing up all over the island.

Most hotels offer a MAP plan; considering the uniformity of Dominica's restaurants and the difficulty of getting around, this option makes sense. Dominican hoteliers seldom differentiate between high and low season—though a few have caught on.

| CATEGORY | COST* |
|---|---|
| $$$ | over $100 |
| $$ | $65–$100 |
| $ | under $65 |

*All prices are for a standard double room, excluding 5% tax, 3% sales tax, and 10%–15% service charge.*

## Hotels

**$$$** **Fort Young Hotel.** Once the island's main military installation, Fort
★ Young is now Roseau's top downtown hotel. The fort was built in the late 1700s, and decorative features from that era, like the cannons at the entrance, flagstone floors, and massive walls, convey a sense of history. The cliffside setting offers dramatic views and keeps you away from the mosquitoes. It's worth paying extra for a room facing the ocean. Rooms have small balconies, air-conditioning, ceiling fans, shower baths, cable TV, and modern furnishings. The Marquis de Bouille restaurant (☞ Dining, *below*) is one of the best on the island. ⊠ *Box 519, Roseau,* ☎ *809/448–5000,* FAX *809/448–5006. 73 rooms. Restaurant, bar, air-conditioning, fans, pool, dance club. AE, MC, V. EP, MAP, FAP.*

**$$$** **Garraway Hotel.** The owner proudly compares Dominica's first international, standard business hotel to a Ramada or Marriott. It's an apt comparison, though the Garraway, which is in downtown Roseau by the waterfront, is unusually tasteful and elegant for a business hotel. Local paintings and vetiver mats add a distinctive touch to the decor of the public spaces. Rooms are large and decorated mainly in soft seashell colors like sea foam, coral, and powder blue; all have direct-dial phones and cable TV. Suites have sitting rooms of varying sizes and sofa beds. The higher floors survey a colorful jumble of rooftops that seems straight from a Chagall canvas. The restaurant specializes in creative Creole cuisine, and the downstairs bar has a great view of the ocean. ⊠ *Bay Front, Box 789, Roseau,* ☎ *809/449–8800,* FAX *809/449–8807. 20 rooms, 11 suites. Restaurant, bar, air-conditioning, hot tub, meeting room. AE, DC, MC, V. EP.*

**$$$** **Lauro Club.** The murmur of the sea and the sound of the crickets
★ are all you are likely to hear at this charming, small cliff-top resort started by a Swiss couple from Neuchatel. The villas, named after Caribbean dances like the quadrille and limbo, are well built, with solar panels on the roofs and plenty of space between you and your neighbors. Each has a large sitting area with a trundle bed, a bedroom with a double bed, and a well-equipped kitchenette set on a spacious, hardwood veranda. Six have direct sea views; the other four are up the hill a bit but still catch a glimpse of the water. There is a small swimming pool, but much more interesting is the wooden stairway that corkscrews down the cliff to a place where you can swim among giant, volcanic boulders. As the Club is in Salisbury, between Roseau and Portsmouth (and about 13 mi from each), you'll probably need to rent a car. ⊠ *Grand Savanne, Salisbury, Box 483,* ☎ *809/449–6602,* FAX *809/449–6603. 10 units. Restaurant, bar, kitchenettes, pool, beach. AE, MC, V. EP, MAP.*

$$$    ⊞ **Petit Coulibri Guest Cottages.** You need a four-wheel-drive vehicle
★    to reach this aerie, perched high above the village of Soufrière on an
extremely bumpy road. But once there, you won't want to come down.
For a start, you have Dominica's most spectacular view: in one direc-
tion, across the blue water to Martinique; in the other, to the jungly
slopes of Morne Fou (Mad Mountain). Owners Loye and Barney
Barnard (she's from Savannah, he's a Yankee from the Berkshires) have
created Dominica's top lodging, perhaps one of the top in the Caribbean.
They designed the three individual stone-and-wood duplex cottages (the
loft bedrooms have pillow-level views of the sea) then decorated them
tastefully with stained-glass windows, local crafts and watercolors, maple
beds swathed in mosquito netting, and ceramic-and-straw lamps.
Hardwoods were generally used, and there are interesting design de-
tails, like the knotted branch used as a newel post. Only the plywood
ceilings lower the tone. Each cottage has two bedrooms, a kitchenette,
and a huge balcony. Travelers on a budget might consider the two stu-
dio rooms. They are smaller, with views into foliage, not sea, and have
smaller verandas, but they are still very pleasant spaces. The whole com-
plex is an ecotourist's delight: Everything is solar-powered or run on
batteries, water comes from cisterns, trees grow through the living room.
The rugged surrounding mountains offer numerous hikes, and the
Marine Reserve at Scott's Head, Dominica's premier dive site, is a stone's
throw away. ⊠ *Petit Coulibri Estate near Soufrière, Box 331, Roseau,*
☎ ℻ *809/446–3150. 3 cottages, 2 studios. Dining room, kitchenettes,
pool. AE, MC, V. EP.*

$$$    ⊞ **Red Rock Haven.** These stylish self-contained cottages perched
★    above the Atlantic are the perfect place to get away from it all. All have
terrace and ocean view and are charmingly furnished with local crafts
and designer linens. Well-stocked bookshelves are a wonderful bonus
(you're encouraged to make a contribution when you leave). The
beach, arguably the prettiest on the island, is within walking distance,
but you'll need a car to reach everything else. ⊠ *Pointe Baptiste, Calibishie; mailing address: Box 71, Roseau,* ☎ *809/448–2181,* ℻
*809/448–5787. 3 cottages. Bar, pool, sauna, shop. AE, MC, V. EP.*

$$–$$$    ⊞ **Anchorage Hotel.** The dilapidated squash court and spluttering dive
boat say it all. Years of wear and tear, combined with the demands of
the owners' numerous other business interests, have taken their toll on
this hotel. Make sure you reserve one of the renovated rooms, which
have clay-tile floors and madras fabrics, in the two-story galleried section. Despite recent refurbishment, other units remain rather dark and
lifeless. ⊠ *Box 34, Roseau,* ☎ *809/448–2638,* ℻ *809/448–5680. 32
rooms. Restaurant, bar, pool, squash. AE, D, MC, V. EP, MAP, FAP.*

$$–$$$    ⊞ **Castaways Beach Hotel.** A young crowd, most of them divers (dive
packages are offered), flocks to this beachfront hotel in Mero, 11 mi
north of Roseau. Daytime activity centers on its mile-long beach. In
the evening, the focus is on the restaurant and terrace, which are attractive, although the food leaves something to be desired. The festive
Sunday brunch with live music packs them in. Rooms are spacious,
with balconies overlooking the beach, but are rather dingy. Some have
air-conditioning and cable TV. Though the tennis court is in poor condition, guests are charged extra to use it. ⊠ *Box 5, Roseau,* ☎ *809/449–
6244 or 800/322–2222,* ℻ *809/449–6246. 27 rooms. Restaurant, 2
bars, tennis court, beach, scuba diving, water sports. AE, MC, V.
Closed early Sept.–mid-Oct. EP, MAP.*

$$–$$$    ⊞ **Evergreen Hotel.** The newer annex at this small hotel, 2 mi from
downtown Roseau, may be somewhat lacking in authentic island
charm, but make sure you request a room here. It includes six bright,
modern, air-conditioned rooms with bright print fabrics, rattan furnishings, cable TV, large shower baths, and balconies with lovely sea

Dominica

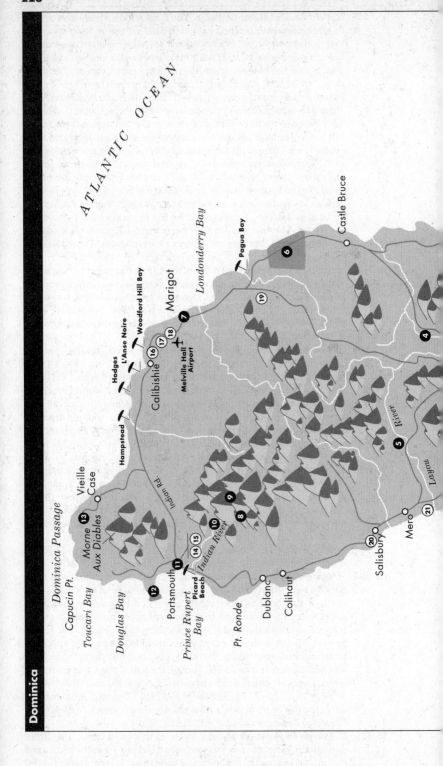

ATLANTIC OCEAN

Castle Bruce

Pagua Bay

6

Londonderry Bay

Marigot

19

7

Woodford Hill Bay

L'Anse Noire

18

17

16

Melville Hall Airport

Calibishie

Hodges

4

5

River

Hampstead

Layou

9

Union Rd.

Vieille Case

Morne Aux Diables

Dominica Passage

13

Capucin Pt.

Toucari Bay

Douglas Bay

8

10

15

14

11

12

Portsmouth

Prince Rupert Bay

Picard Beach

Indian River

21

Mero

20

Salisbury

Dublanc

Colihaut

Pt. Ronde

229

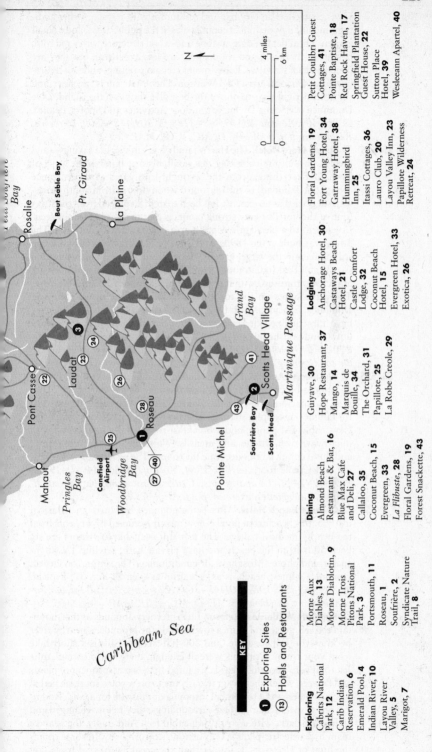

Caribbean Sea

*Pringles Bay*

*Woodbridge Bay*

Mahaut

Pont Casse

Canefield Airport

Laudat

Roseau

Pointe Michel

Pt. Giraud

Rosalie

La Plaine

*Bout Sable Bay*

*Grand Bay*

Scotts Head Village

*Soufrière Bay*

Scotts Head

Martinique Passage

**KEY**

🛈 Exploring Sites

⑬ Hotels and Restaurants

**Exploring**
Cabrits National Park, **12**
Carib Indian Reservation, **6**
Emerald Pool, **4**
Indian River, **10**
Layou River Valley, **5**
Marigot, **7**
Morne Aux Diables, **13**
Morne Diablotin, **9**
Morne Trois Pitons National Park, **3**
Portsmouth, **11**
Roseau, **1**
Soufrière, **2**
Syndicate Nature Trail, **8**

**Dining**
Almond Beach Restaurant & Bar, **16**
Blue Max Cafe and Deli, **27**
Callaloo, **35**
Coconut Beach, **15**
Evergreen, **33**
*La Flibuste*, **28**
Floral Gardens, **19**
Forest Snackette, **43**
Guiyave, **30**
Hope Restaurant, **37**
Mango, **14**
Marquis de Bouille, **34**
The Orchard, **31**
Papillote, **25**
La Robe Creole, **29**

**Lodging**
Anchorage Hotel, **30**
Castaways Beach Hotel, **21**
Castle Comfort Lodge, **32**
Coconut Beach Hotel, **15**
Evergreen Hotel, **33**
Exotica, **26**
Floral Gardens, **19**
Fort Young Hotel, **34**
Garraway Hotel, **38**
Hummingbird Inn, **25**
Itassi Cottages, **36**
Lauro Club, **20**
Layou Valley Inn, **23**
Papillote Wilderness Retreat, **24**
Petit Coulibri Guest Cottages, **41**
Pointe Baptiste, **18**
Red Rock Haven, **17**
Springfield Plantation Guest House, **22**
Sutton Place Hotel, **39**
Wesleeann Apartel, **40**

0 ——— 4 miles
0 ——— 6 km

N

views, as well as an airy bar and restaurant with terrace. Other additions include a pool, Italian ceramic tiles in the public areas, and a small garden. The older building, a stone-and-wood structure with a red roof, has more character, and rooms here are less expensive, but they are plain and lack sea views. Public rooms contain paintings and wood carvings by noted local artist Carl Winston. The restaurant is excellent, and the hotel is right next to one of the best dive shops on the island, Dive Dominica (☞ Scuba Diving *in* Outdoor Activities and Sports, *below*). ✉ Box 309, Roseau, ☎ 809/448–3288, FAX 809/448–6800. 16 rooms. Restaurant, bar, pool. AE, D, MC, V. CP, MAP.

$$–$$$ ★ 🏨 **Sutton Place Hotel.** The Harris family has sunk its life savings—and then some—into refurbishing this small, historic hotel in the heart of Roseau. Everything, from the wrought-iron gates at the entrance (bought in Trinidad) to the tauroniro wood floors (from South America), suggests that no expense has been spared. Steps lead from the street (one of the hotel's many strong points is that there is a 24-hour security guard) to a pleasant reception area decorated with antiques. The house was built in the 1890s, and some of the original stonework can still be seen in the large, ground-floor restaurant, which serves good Creole and East Indian food. Standard rooms on the second floor are attractively furnished with fabrics and fittings imported from New York. The three suites on the top floor are some of the nicest rooms in Dominica: Spacious, with two queen beds or a four-poster bed, they have fully equipped kitchenettes, antique furnishings, teak louvered windows, and polished wood floors. ✉ 25 Old St., Roseau, ☎ 809/448–8700, FAX 809/448–3045. 5 rooms, 3 suites. Restaurant, bar, air-conditioning, fans. AE, D, MC, V. CP, MAP.

$$–$$$ 🏨 **Wesleeann Apartel.** From the outside, this hotel looks like a French apartment block plunked down on the edge of the Caribbean. That said, the spacious one-, two-, and three-bedroom apartments are ideal for families or couples sharing. Apartments have a balcony with a sea view, cable TV, phone, and a breakfast room, and a kitchenette with microwave oven, fridge, and utensils. White tile floors, white rattan, and floral chintz fabrics decorate the rooms. The restaurant serves Italian and Creole food. ✉ Box 1764, Roseau, ☎ 809/449–0419, FAX 809/449–2473. 12 apartments, 1 suite. Restaurant, bar, air-conditioning, kitchenettes, exercise room. AE, MC, V.

$$ 🏨 **Coconut Beach Hotel.** After being pounded by Hurricane Marilyn in 1995, this beachfront hotel is now mostly occupied by students from the nearby medical college. The few still available to visitors are set back 50 ft from the beach and have private bath, satellite TV, kitchenette, and phone. Most have air-conditioning. The setting, on Picard, Dominica's finest beach, is as delightful as ever. ✉ Box 37, Roseau, ☎ 809/445–5393, FAX 809/445–5693. 22 rooms. Restaurant, bar, air-conditioning, kitchenettes. AE, D, MC, V. EP, MAP.

$ ★ 🏨 **Papillote Wilderness Retreat.** Lush greenery abounds at this mountain retreat, geese and guinea fowl ramble the grounds, a nearby river beckons you to take a dip, and 200-ft Trafalgar Falls is a short hike from your room. As if this weren't enough, there's also owner Anne Jean-Baptiste's botanical garden: a mind-boggling assortment of plants and flowers, which she may graciously use to brew you a soothing herbal infusion—bergamot to combat insomnia or *l'oiselles* for a cold. Rooms are not as spectacular as their surroundings; they're low-ceilinged and somewhat dark, with a rustic, log-cabin feel. And, sadly, the island's main hydroelectric plant is only a stone's throw away. In some rooms the hum of electricity is louder than the croaking of tree frogs. Yet Papillote remains a special place, imbued with the energy and commitment of its owner and staffed by some of the friendliest personnel on the island. The terrace-style restaurant, which has fine views of the surrounding mountains, serves good, moderately priced meals. ⊠ *Box 67, Roseau,* ☎ *809/448–2287,* 𝔽𝔸𝕏 *809/448–2286. 10 rooms. Restaurant, bar, shop. AE, DC, MC, V. EP, MAP.*

## Guest Houses and Lodges

$$$
★ **Exotica.** Fae and Atherton Martin, a prominent local couple (he is a former Minister of Agriculture and the current president of the Dominica Conservation Association), created this small, exceptionally peaceful resort in 1995. Getting here is an adventure in itself. You corkscrew up the mountainside through vegetation that grows lusher with every turn, until you reach a property covered in flowers and fruit trees, perched 1,600 ft above the ocean. The villas are handsome buildings of treated wood and stone, with red galvanized roofs fitted with solar panels. The interiors, with their American-style furnishings, pitched ceilings, and tile floors, are bright and cheerful. Each unit contains a bedroom with two (extra-long) double beds, a large living room with trundle bed, a kitchenette, bathroom, phone, and TV. If you don't want to cook, the Sugar Apple café offers delicious Creole food cooked by Fae, using produce from the organic garden. A nearby river (a 20-minute walk away) is a good spot for swimming. Nature lovers will enjoy the many birds to be spotted around the property, the more than 50 varieties of flowers and 30 types of fruit trees, as well as the great hikes on nearby Morne Anglais. The views of the ocean in the distance are breathtaking. If you're really lucky, you might even see a whale spouting, right from your veranda. ⊠ *Box 109, Roseau,* ☎ *809/448–8839,* 𝔽𝔸𝕏 *809/448–8829. 8 villas. Restaurant, kitchenettes. AE, MC, V.*

$$$
★ **Pointe Baptiste.** Alec Waugh wrote a book here. Noel Coward was a visitor. Princess Margaret stayed during her honeymoon. And it's easy to see why. This weathered plantation house exudes old-world charm. The setting, above a beautiful beach, is divine; the antiques-filled interior, patrician. There are three rooms in the main house, which also contains a superb library. A whitewashed cottage straight out of a Ralph Lauren catalog contains an additional room. That said, this is not a place for the smart set: It's an old house, with antiquated fittings, and guests are expected to "do" for themselves (though a local cook can be provided by arrangement). As the main house can be rented only in its entirety, and you will need a car to do anything, a stay here is not for all pocketbooks, either. For those wanting something more affordable, the family also runs D'Auchamps Apartments, an attractive property on the other side of the island, near Trafalgar Falls. ⊠ *c/o Mrs. Geraldine Edwards, Calibishie Village,* ☎ *809/445–7322,* 𝔽𝔸𝕏 *809/445–8343. 3 rooms, 1 cottage. No credit cards.*

$$
★ **Castle Comfort Lodge.** This excellent dive lodge, run by enthusiastic locals Derek and Ginette Perryman, wins a loyal following for its first-rate dive shop and excellent-value dive packages. Rooms are in two buildings: one directly on the sea, the other at the back of the property. Each room has white rattan furnishings, fish-pattern fabrics, and a veranda. The back rooms are smaller but make up for it by offering cable TV and phone. As a bonus, the home-cooked meals, eaten on a large, airy terrace, are bountiful and delicious. The Perrymans can also arrange inland adventures and nature walks. Their MAP package, which includes five days of diving and a night dive, is one of the best deals on Dominica. ⊠ *Box 63, Roseau,* ☎ *809/448–2188,* 𝔽𝔸𝕏 *809/448–6088. 15 rooms. Restaurant, dive shop. AE, MC, V. MAP.*

$$
★ **Hummingbird Inn.** The ambience of this simple hilltop retreat, just a short drive from Roseau and Canefield Airport, is created by owner Jean James Finucane, an American-educated Dominican with an endearing smile and a passion for hummingbirds. Two hillside bunga-

lows with outstanding Caribbean views hold 10 rooms. Interiors are simple—white walls, terra-cotta-tile floors, and peaked wooden ceilings. Varnished wooden hurricane windows can be left open all night to let in fresh breezes and the sounds of tree frogs and the ocean a few hundred yards below. There's no air-conditioning, TV, or phones. Instead, there are tropical fixtures like ceiling fans, handmade quilts, hammocks slung strategically on the wraparound terraces, and tables fashioned out of gommier and red cedar wood. One large suite also has a stately, mahogany four-poster bed and kitchen. Jean is an expert on Creole cooking, and the Hummingbird's cook is perhaps the best of any guest house on Dominica. ⊠ *Box 20, Roseau,* ☎ FAX *809/449–1042. 9 rooms, 1 suite. Restaurant, bar, fans. AE, MC, V. EP, MAP.*

**$–$$**    🏨 **Floral Gardens.** It's a surprise to find a Swiss chalet–style hotel, complete with latticed windows and flower boxes, on the edge of a rainforest reserve; owner O. J. Seraphin, a former prime minister and full-time human dynamo, is probably the only person who could carry it off. The hotel has grown bit by bit over the years, something that is reflected in the higgledy-piggledy layout and variable quality of the rooms. The oldest rooms are in the main building; although they are decorated with island crafts and homey fabrics, they have a slightly claustrophobic feel. Larger units are across the road and overlook the Layou River. An additional 12 rooms—including three suites—were added in 1995. The restaurant here (☞ Dining, *below*) is one of the best on the island, and the hotel's location is convenient for river bathing, hiking, and relaxing on the beaches of the northeast coast. Hurricane Marilyn did considerable damage in 1995, but this merely gave the irrepressible O. J. an excuse to undertake further renovations and expansions. He's already added a waterfall pool and botanical garden. At press time, he was overseeing the building of a minimall, comprising six boutiques, each one showcasing a different island craft or product. ⊠ *Concord,* ☎ *809/445–7636,* FAX *809/445–7636. 18 rooms. Restaurant, shop. AE, MC, V. EP, MAP.*

**$–$$**    🏨 **Itassi Cottages.** Run by the same family that owns the excellent Sut-
★    ton Place Hotel (☞ *above*), these three self-contained cottages pretty well live up to the promise in the brochure: ". . . for discerning travelers who are not necessarily loaded." They can each house two to six people and are much homier than most other island lodgings, with a mix of antiques, straw mats, beautiful handmade floral bedspreads, calabash lamps, and wraparound porches with hammocks and sweeping views of Roseau, Scotts Head, and the Caribbean. Ideal for long-term stays, each cottage has a kitchen, ceiling fans, and cable TV, and there is a shared laundry facility. Grounds are beautifully landscaped and include a tennis court. ⊠ *Box 319, Roseau,* ☎ *809/448–4313,* FAX *809/448–3045. 3 cottages. Fans, kitchens, tennis court, laundry service. AE, MC, V.*

**$–$$**    🏨 **Layou Valley Inn.** Tamara Holmes and her late husband built this tropical-style country inn, nestled in the foothills of the national park. She's an extremely chatty Russian whom some guests may find rather overpowering. She once translated for NASA, has a story about everything, and whips up excellent French and Creole food. The rooms are simple and clean, and the sunken lounge (an oasis of hand-hewn mosaics, stone floors, exquisite wood carvings, and hanging plants) and glass-fronted dining area are comfortable, attractive places where guests mingle. There is excellent swimming in nearby rivers. Unfortunately, the place is showing signs of wear and tear, and, according to latest reports, is up for sale. The surroundings of lush rain forest and the peaks of the Morne Trois Pitons are as superb as ever. ⊠ *Box 196, Roseau,* ☎ *809/449–6203,* FAX *809/448–5212. 5 rooms. Restaurant, bar. AE, MC, V. EP, MAP.*

**$–$$** ⚇ **Springfield Plantation Guest House.** This 19th-century plantation house, built on a lush, 200-acre property, feels like something out of Jean Rhys's *Wide Sargasso Sea*. It's a bit gloomy and run-down, but full of character. The wood-paneled dining room displays antique furniture, a piano, hat stands, and pictures of clipper ships, and a portrait of King George V hangs on the wall. Most of the rooms are upstairs in the main house; Room 16, which has a four-poster bed and antique furniture, is especially imposing. The other rooms are split between a guest cottage and a long, wooden building across the court-yard. The ancient ovens and refrigerators in some of the rooms sug-gest that time has, indeed, stood still here. The property also serves as the Centre for Environmental Protection, so the restaurant serves Creole food, much of it prepared with organic vegetables grown on the estate. There are nature trails and good swimming in nearby rivers. ⊠ *Box 456, Roseau,* ☎ *809/449–1401,* ☏ *809/449–2160. 15 rooms. Restaurant, bar. AE, MC, V. EP, CP, MAP, FAP.*

# Dining

Dominica may be only a few miles from Martinique and Guadeloupe, the culinary capitals of the Caribbean, but don't expect gourmet din-ing or excellent wines here. Look, instead, for Creole fare utilizing the cornucopia of fresh vegetables that grow in the fertile Dominican soil. There are sweet green plantains, *kushkush* yams, breadfruit, and dasheen (a tuber similar to the potato called taro elsewhere)—these and other staples are known as ground provisions. You'll find fresh fish on virtually every menu (often cooked in *sancouche*) and occasionally moun-tain "chicken"—a euphemism for a large frog called *crapaud*. Two rare delicacies for the intrepid diner are *manicou* (a small opossum) and the tender, gamey *agouti* (a large, indigenous rodent)—both are best smoked or stewed. The favorite local drink is rum, or gin, mixed with coconut milk.

## What to Wear

Dominica is far from the chic fashion world. Clothes here are practi-cal and traditional—for dinner it's shirt and trousers for men and modest dresses for women. During the day, nice shorts are acceptable at most places, but beach attire is frowned upon.

| CATEGORY | COST* |
|---|---|
| **$$$** | over $35 |
| **$$** | $15–$35 |
| **$** | under $15 |

*per person for a three-course meal, excluding drinks, service charge, and 3% tax*

**$$$** ✕ **La Robe Creole.** This is the best restaurant in Roseau, housed in a
★ pretty building near the cathedral. Take your pick from an eclectic à la carte menu. Callaloo and crab soup, made with dasheen and coconut, is a specialty. Other tasty options include lobster and conch crepes, char-coal-grilled fish and meats, barbecued chicken, and a selection of sal-ads. The dining room is a cozy place, with wood rafters, ladder-back chairs, and colorful madras tablecloths. The downstairs take-out annex, the Mouse Hole, is an inexpensive place to stock up for your picnic. The restaurant also makes its own delicious mango chutney, which can be bought in local shops. ⊠ *3 Victoria St., Roseau,* ☎ *809/448–2896. AE. Closed Sun.*

**$$** ✕ **Evergreen.** Enjoy a relaxing meal on a large airy terrace overlook-ing the sea. It's decorated with bright tropical prints, crystal teardrop chandeliers, and a striking art deco–style bar in stark gray, black, and white. Delicious dinners include a choice of soup and salad; the entrées of chicken, fish, and beef are served with local fruits and vegetables, such as kushkush and plantains. Homemade desserts include fresh fruit, cake, and ice cream. ⊠ *Evergreen Hotel, Roseau,* ☎ *809/448–3288. AE, MC, V.*

**$$**  ✕ **Floral Gardens.** You may feel as if you're dining in a private home
★   at this warm, welcoming restaurant, particularly if owner O. J. Seraphim is around. Wood paneling, rough-hewn timber beams, and vetiver mats create a rustic atmosphere. Tables are laid out in an L-shape in the main building, and there are more tables in a gallery-style building across the road, overlooking the river. The food is delectable; sample local specialties, such as crapaud, agouti, or crayfish caught by the local Carib Indians, whose reservation adjoins the property. There are also vegetarian dishes. ⊠ *Floral Gardens Hotel, Concord,* ☎ *809/445–7636. AE, MC, V.*

**$$**  ✕ **Guiyave.** This popular lunchtime restaurant in the center of Roseau is actually two businesses in one. Downstairs is a pastry shop, where owner Hermina Astaphan makes chicken patties, spicy *rotis* (Caribbean burritos), and a scrumptious selection of pies, tarts, and cakes. These can also be ordered at the upstairs restaurant (run by her son), along with more elaborate fare, such as mountain chicken, steamed fish, and chicken in a sweet-and-sour sauce. You may dine in the green-and-white wood-paneled dining room, which has a bar at one end, or on the sunny balcony perched above Roseau's colorful streets—the perfect spot to indulge in one of the fresh-squeezed tropical juices. ⊠ *15 Cork St., Roseau,* ☎ *809/448–2930. AE, MC, V. No dinner.*

**$$**  ✕ **La Flibuste.** The name is French for "pirate," and the buccaneer theme has been incorporated in both the food and the decor. Prints of galleons line the stairs, and photos and movie posters of swashbucklers adorn the walls. Dishes have names like "Captain Bligh" (chicken breast), "Long John Silver's" (a grilled brochette of chicken), and "the Galleon" (grilled lamb chops). A small bar at the back offers a modest selection of cocktails and wines. There is live music on Sundays. ⊠ *27 Great Marlborough St., Roseau,* ☎ *809/448–0501. D, MC, V. Closed Mon. No lunch weekends.*

**$$**  ✕ **Mango.** Locals frequent this unassuming restaurant, with its vases overflowing with fresh flowers and beautiful mural depicting the Indian River. Diners enjoy both the comparatively refined ambience and Peter Pascal's solid home cooking. The *lambi* (conch) is tender as can be, the goat *colombo* (curry) has quite a kick, and the mountain chicken is succulent. This is one of the few places where you can find breego, a tiny flavorful conch. ⊠ *Bay St., Portsmouth,* ☎ *809/445–3099. No credit cards.*

**$$**  ✕ **Marquis de Bouille.** The upscale, attractive, candlelit dining room
★   at the historic Fort Young Hotel, with its stone walls and wood-rafter ceiling, is one of the better restaurants on the island. The Indian chef adds a touch of his homeland cuisine to Continental and Dominican dishes (the special may be mountain chicken tandoori). The menu also includes callaloo and pumpkin soup, grilled lobster, and blue marlin in a lime sauce. ⊠ *Fort Young Hotel, Roseau,* ☎ *809/448–5000. AE, MC, V.*

**$$**  ✕ **The Orchard.** A spacious, unadorned dining room opens onto a pleasant, covered courtyard, surrounded by latticework. Chef Joan Cools-Lartique whips up Creole-style coconut shrimp, lobster, black pudding, mountain chicken, callaloo soup with crabmeat, and other island delicacies, as well as an assortment of sandwiches, for the changing menu. ⊠ *31 King George V St., Roseau,* ☎ *809/448–3051. AE, D, MC, V.*

**$$**  ✕ **Papillote.** Anne Jean-Baptiste's stone-and-tile restaurant boasts
★   botanical gardens right outside, a bubbling hot-spring pool (just the spot to savor a lethal rum punch before or after dinner) and is just as

popular with birds and butterflies—and tour groups—as ever. Try the bracing callaloo soup, dasheen puffs, chicken rain forest (marinated with papaya and wrapped in banana leaves), and, if they're on the menu, the succulent *bouk* (tiny, delicate river shrimp). ⊠ *Papillote Wilderness Retreat, Trafalgar Falls Rd., Box 2287, Roseau,* ☎ *809/448–2287. AE, D, MC, V.*

**$–$$** ✗ **Almond Beach Restaurant & Bar.** If you're visiting one of the island's northeast beaches, stop here for a lunch of callaloo soup, lobster, or octopus. Select from tantalizing fruit juices, including guava, passion fruit, and soursop, or one of the spice rums. Try the *pweve* (patois for pepper) or *lapsenth*, a violet-scented pick-me-up and digestive. The genial owners, Mr. and Mrs. Joseph, are experts on local culture and custom and sometimes arrange a traditional belé dance or jing-ping (a type of folk music) concert on busy weekends. ⊠ *Calibishi,* ☎ *809/445–7783. AE, D, MC, V.*

**$–$$** ✗ **Callaloo Restaurant.** Mrs. Marge Peters is the vivacious hostess of this small, informal eatery. She takes pride in age-old cooking traditions and uses only the freshest local produce. (What she does with breadfruit alone—roasted slabs, puffs, creamy velouté, juice, pie— could fill a cookbook.) Changing lunch and dinner specials might include pepper-pot soup, curried conch, or the signature crab callaloo, fragrant with cumin, coconut cream, lime, clove, and garlic. Most everything here is homemade, including juices (try the sea moss— "puts lead in your pencil") and ice cream (the soursop is marvelous). ⊠ *63 King George V St., Roseau,* ☎ *809/448–3386. No credit cards.*

**$** ✗ **Blue Max Cafe and Deli.** No prizes for guessing the former profession of Mourad Zarkha, the owner of this popular Roseau café. The onetime pilot has filled the walls with photos of fighter planes and airline posters. Marble-topped tables, a small bar, and ceiling fans complete the decor. On the menu is Dominica's best selection of American-style sandwiches (roast beef and pastrami are favorites), plus a few local specialties such as flying-fish. For those who are on a self-catering holiday, the deli offers cold cuts and cheeses imported from the States. ⊠ *16 Hanover St., Roseau,* ☎ *809/449–8907. MC, V. Closed Sun.*

**$** ✗ **Coconut Beach.** This casual beachfront restaurant is popular with visiting yacht owners, expatriate medical students from the nearby school, and anyone interested in an afternoon on a stretch of white-sand beach. Fresh tropical drinks and local seafood dishes are the specialty here; sandwiches and rotis are also served. The mahimahi is delicious. ⊠ *Coconut Beach Hotel (☞ Lodging, above),* ☎ *809/445–5393. AE, D, MC, V.*

**$** ✗ **Forest Snackette.** If you've been diving in Sourfrière, you won't want to miss this place. Set in the remains of the island's finest lime orchards, with views of the lush, surrounding mountains and distant sea, it manages to be far more pleasant than the simple, open-sided concrete building with its galvanized roof at first suggests. The decor includes smart green tables and striped director's chairs. Breakfasts of eggs and bacon and fried plantains and hearty lunches of kingfish, tuna, and mahimahi, served with vegetables from the restaurant's own garden, are some of the dishes on offer. ⊠ *Soufrière,* ☎ *809/448–7105. Reservations essential. No credit cards.*

**$** ✗ **Hope Restaurant.** You don't come here for the ambience—you come for genuine Creole cooking at rock-bottom prices. Mountain chicken and agouti are served with generous sides of provisions, for barely half the price charged at fancier restaurants. Hope provides local flavor in every sense of the phrase: It's filled with old men playing dominoes and cabbies whose runs have just ended (they always know a good deal). It's open every day for breakfast, lunch, and dinner. ⊠ *15 Steber St., Roseau,* ☎ *809/448–2019. No credit cards.*

# Beaches

If you want to hang out on sugar-white beaches there are plenty of better places to do it than Dominica. You'll mostly find dark-sand beaches, evidence of the island's volcanic origins. What's pleasant about swimming off rocky beaches is that the water is deeper and bluer, and far more interesting for snorkeling. The best sand beaches are around Portsmouth or in the northeast of the island.

### Northeast Coast

**Pagua Bay,** a quiet, secluded beach of dark sand, is on the Atlantic and is best suited to strong swimmers. **Woodford Hill Bay, Hampstead, L'Anse Noir,** and **Hodges** are some of the most beautiful beaches on the island and are excellent for snorkeling and scuba diving, though all this wind-tossed beauty can be dangerous to swimmers, since there are strong underwater currents as well as whipped-cream waves. From these beaches you can see the French island of Marie Galante in the distance.

### Northwest Coast

**Picard Beach,** on the northwest coast, is the island's best beach. Great for windsurfing and snorkeling, it's a 2-mi stretch of brown sand fringed with coconut trees. The Picard Beach Cottage Resort and Coconut Beach Hotel are along this beach.

### Southeast Coast

In the southeast, near La Plaine, **Bout Sable Bay** is not much good for swimming, but the surroundings are stirringly elemental: Towering red cliffs challenge the rollicking Atlantic.

### Southwest Coast

The beaches south of Roseau are not great, but the snorkeling and scuba diving are excellent because of the dramatic underwater walls and sudden drops. At **Scotts Head** and **Soufrière Bay,** you will find some of the finest snorkeling and scuba diving in the world. At one spot, volcanic vents puff steam into the sea; the experience has been described as "swimming in champagne."

## Outdoor Activities and Sports

### Boating

Motorboat and sailing trips can be arranged through **Dominica Tours** (☎ 809/448–2638) and the **Castaways Beach Hotel** (☎ 809/449–6245).

### Hiking

Dominica is rightly renowned for its superb hiking. Majestic mountains, clear rivers, and lush, green vegetation all combine to make rambling about a great pleasure. The island is, in fact, crisscrossed by ancient footpaths, some created by the "Nègres Marron," escaped slaves (including some Carib Indians) who established camps in the mountains. There are now ambitious plans to incorporate these old trails into the Waitikibuli Trail, which would traverse the island from north to south and be one of the Caribbean's finest eco-tourist amenities. Existing trails range from easy-going to arduous. For the former, all you'll need are sturdy, rubber-soled shoes and an adventurous spirit. For both, bring insect repellent.

For the hike to **Boiling Lake** or the climb up **Morne Diablotin** you will need hiking boots, a guide, and water. Guides will charge about $30–$35 per person and can be contacted through the Dominica Tourist Office or the Forestry Division (☎ 809/448–2401 or 809/448–2638).

## River Swimming

With 365 rivers—one for every day of the year—it's not surprising that river swimming is one of the most popular pastimes on Dominica. All the rivers are clean, but the best one for swimming and inner-tubing is the **Layou River.** In some places, you can sunbathe and picnic on its banks.

## Scuba Diving

"Amazing! Incredible! Fantastic!" These are some of the words people use when they surface after a dive in Dominica. Voted one of the top 10 dive destinations in the world by *Skin Diver* magazine, Dominica is a paradise for divers and snorkelers alike. The diving is especially good in the southeast of the island, around Soufrière Bay, the site of a submerged volcanic crater. The area has recently been designated a Marine Reserve, with stringent regulations in force to prevent the degradation of the ecosystem. Within half a mile of the shore, the water drops almost vertically to 800 ft and then 1,500 ft. Visibility frequently extends to 100 ft. There are not so many large fish as on some other islands (they are not fed here), but marine life is abundant. Shoals of several thousand boga fish, Creole wrasse, or blue cromis are not uncommon, and you might even see a spotted moray eel or a honeycomb cowfish. Crinoids (rare elsewhere) are also abundant, as are giant barrel sponges. The opportunities for underwater photography, particularly macrophotography, are unparalleled. The going rate is about $60–$65 for a two-tank dive or $80–$90 for a resort course with two open-water dives.

**Castaways Beach Hotel** (☎ 809/449–6245 or 800/934–3483), 11 mi north of Roseau, has diving at its water-sports center. But it's a long way from the finest sites. **Dive Dominica** (✉ Castle Comfort, ☎ 809/448–2188 or 800/544–7631, FAX 809/448–6088) has three boats and is one of the longest-established dive shops on the island. Owners Derek and Ginette Perryman are NAUI-approved instructors. They also offer PADI and SSI courses, snorkeling and resort dives for beginners. For the advanced set, there are dives on drop-offs, walls, and pinnacles—by day or night. Their MAP package is great value. **Dominica Dive Resorts, Waitukubuli** (✉ Anchorage Hotel, ☎ 809/448–2638; ✉ Portsmouth Beach Hotel, ☎ 809/445–5142) are run by PADI-certified owners and offer both resort courses and full certification. **Nature Island Dive** (✉ Soufrière, ☎ 809/449–8181) is an excellent operation run by three enthusiastic couples who share four nationalities (Canadian, British, American, and Dominican) among them. Right on the doorstep of the best diving sites, they have two dive boats, with a capacity for 10 per boat, and offer full PADI courses and PADI-approved resort courses.

## Snorkeling

Major island operators rent equipment: **Anchorage Hotel** (☎ 809/448–2638), **Castaways Beach Hotel** (☎ 809/449–6245), **Coconut Beach Hotel** (☎ 809/445–5393), **Picard Beach Cottage Resort** (☎ 809/445–5131), and **Sunshine Village** (☎ 809/445–5066).

## Whale-Watching

There are few sights more thrilling than seeing a pod of five sperm whales one hundred yards ahead of your boat flipping their massive tails up into the air just before they deep-dive. Humpback whales, false killer whales, and orcas are also occasionally seen, but it is the large numbers of sperm whales (they calve in Dominica's 3,000-ft-deep waters) that are the stars of the show. Two operations currently run afternoon tours: **Anchorage Hotel** (☎ 809/448–2638) and **Dive Dominica** (☎ 809/448–2188). Of the two, Dive Dominica offers the best deal—the boat has a viewing platform and the skipper, Derek Perryman, is a genial, knowledgeable guide.

### Windsurfing

Contact **Anchorage Hotel** (☎ 809/448–2638), **Castaways Beach Hotel** (☎ 809/449–6245), or **Picard Beach Cottage Resort** (☎ 809/445–5131).

## Shopping

### Gift Ideas

The distinctive handicrafts of the Carib Indians include traditional baskets made of dyed *larouma* reeds and waterproofed with tightly woven *balizier* leaves. These crafts are sold at the reservation as well as in Roseau's shops. Dominica is also noted for its spices (especially saffron), hot peppers, bay rum, and coconut-oil soap; its vetiver-grass mats are sold all over the world. Cafe Dominique, the local equivalent of Jamaican Blue Mountain coffee, is an excellent buy. Dominican rum is stronger, and rougher, than French brands—try Macoucherie. Proof that the old ways live on in Dominica can be found in the number of herbal doctors setting up shop in the streets of Roseau. One stimulating memento of your visit is rum steeped with Bois Bandé (scientific name Richeria Grandis), a tree whose bark is reputed to have aphrodisiacal properties. You can find it at Tropicrafts (☞ *below*) and in the supermarkets (try **Whitchurch** on Kennedy Ave. or Dominica's newest supermarket, **Brizee's,** in Canefield). One of the best places for gifts is the **old market,** just behind the museum, in Roseau. Slaves were once sold here, but today it is the scene of happier trading: crafts, T-shirts, spices, and batik are all on sale in open-air booths set up on the cobblestones.

**Balisier** (✉ 35 Great George St., no phone) is the spot for charming sunbonnets, carnival dolls, island jewelry, and hand-painted T-shirts.

**Caribana Handcrafts** (✉ 31 Cork St., Roseau, ☎ 809/448–2761) sells ceramics, wood carvings, and baskets.

**Dominica Pottery** (✉ Bayfront St. and Kennedy Ave., Roseau, no phone) is run by a local priest, whose products are fashioned with various local clays and glazes.

**Fadelle's** (✉ 28 Kennedy Ave., Roseau, ☎ 809/448–2686) sells straw and woodwork, as well as soaps, sauces, and perfumes.

**Just Us Originals** (✉ 8 Castle St., Roseau, ☎ 809/448–6602) is the brainchild of Toronto-born Betty Alleyn. At her stand in the old marketplace in Roseau, she sells dolphin-shape earrings made from the pod of the sand-box tree, colorful polymer clay ornaments, refrigerator magnets, and hair barrettes, as well as driftwood sculptures featuring Dominican folklore.

**NDFD Small Business Mini Mall** (✉ 9 Great Marlborough St., Roseau, ☎ 809/448–0412) was opened with the help of the government, which actively encourages local artisans. Among the more notable booths are **Caribbean Perfumes,** fragrant with teas, scents, and potpourri, and the **Blow Kalbass Healing Center,** which sells natural products touted to cure everything from acne to rheumatism.

**Papillote Wilderness Retreat** (✉ Roseau, ☎ 809/448–2287) has a gift shop with an excellent selection of wood carvings from Haiti.

**Rainforest Shop** (✉ 17 Old St., Roseau, ☎ 809/448–8834) sells everything from toucan-shape toothbrush holders to doorstops decorated with hand-painted volcanoes. The goods come from all over the Caribbean as well as Central and South America. All are brightly colored and hand-painted. One dollar from every sale goes toward protecting the rain forest.

**Tropicrafts** (✉ 41 Queen Mary St., Roseau, ☎ 809/448–2747; ✉ Bay St., Portsmouth, ☎ 809/445–5956) has a back room where you can watch the local ladies weaving. Here you'll find wood carvings, rum, hot sauces, and local perfumes, in addition to traditional Carib baskets, hats, and woven mats.

## Nightlife

When the moon comes up, the Dominicans go out to party, especially in February during Carnival. The Fortress Disco, at the Fort Young Hotel, is popular. So, too, are the steel bands and calypso groups that play at most of the larger hotels—the Castaways, Anchorage, Garraway, and Reigate Hall. Music to be heard elsewhere includes reggae, ska, calypso, and jing ping, a type of folk music featuring the accordion, the *quage* (a kind of washboard instrument), drums, and a boom boom (a percussive instrument).

**Carib 2000** (✉ Johnson's Ave., Roseau, ☎ 809/448–1677) serves seafood and cocktails to an upscale crowd. On Friday and Saturday nights there are live steel bands and jazz.

**Club Coconuts** (✉ 3 mi north of Roseau, ☎ 809/449–1489), at Rockaway Beach, has live ska, reggae, and R&B.

**Shipwreck** (✉ In Canefield industrial area, ☎ 809/449–1059) has live reggae and taped music on weekends and a Sunday bash that starts at noon and continues into the night.

**Warehouse** (✉ Outside Roseau toward airport, ☎ 809/449–1303) is *the* disco for locals on Dominica, especially on weekends.

**Wykie's La Tropical** (✉ 51 Old St., Roseau, ☎ 809/448–8015) is a classic Caribbean hole-in-the-wall and gathering spot for the island's movers and shakers, especially during Friday's happy hour, when they nibble on stewed chicken or black pudding, then stay on for a local calypso band or some jing ping.

## Exploring Dominica

Despite the small size of this almond-shape island, it can take a couple of hours to get between many of the island's popular destinations; roads are in poor shape and travel is relatively slow. The amount of time you spend hiking, mountain climbing, bird-watching, or just enjoying the scenery will determine how much you can see during one round-the-island trip. It takes about four days of solid trekking to take in the whole of Dominica. The highways ringing most of the island's perimeter have been upgraded in recent years; but more remote destinations remain somewhat inaccessible, and it's wise to hire a car and driver or to take an escorted tour (☞ Guided Tours *in* Dominica A to Z, *below*).

*Numbers in the margin correspond to points of interest on the Dominica map.*

SIGHTS TO SEE

**⑫ Cabrits National Park.** Just north of the town of Portsmouth, this 250-acre park is, along with Brimstone Hill in St. Kitts, Shirley Heights in Antigua, and Fort Charlotte in St. Vincent, one of the most significant historic sites in the Caribbean. The heart of the park is the **Fort Shirley** military complex. Built by the British between 1770 and 1815, it once comprised 50 major structures, including batteries, powder magazines, and storehouses, as well as barracks and officers quarters to house 500 men. With the help of the Royal Navy (who send sailors ashore to work on the site each time a ship is in port) and local volunteers, historian Lennox Honychurch has restored the fort. There is also a small museum that highlights the natural and historic aspects of the park. The cruise-ship facility offers a cooperative crafts shop, a continuously screened film about Fort Shirley, and occasional live dance or music performances. The herbaceous swamps nearby are an important site for several species of rare plants, including the white mangrove.

**6** **Carib Indian Reservation.** A fierce warrior race who sprinkled newborn male babies with their fathers' blood, the Caribs were, for centuries, the implacable enemies of the colonists. For this they were hunted down and exterminated. Finally, in 1903, they were granted these 3,700 acres of land, and their chief was allowed to call himself "king" and endowed with an annual allowance of 6 sterling. Don't expect a lot in the way of ancient culture and costume. The folks who gave the Caribbean its name live pretty much like other West Indians, as fishermen and farmers. Despite this, they have maintained their traditional skills of wood carving and basket weaving. The exquisitely made baskets can be found at numerous roadside stands. Considering the high quality of the work, the prices are ridiculously low, so to bargain would be offensive. A point of interest on the reservation is **L'Escalier Tête Chien** ("Dog's Head Staircase")—a hardened lava flow that juts down to the ocean. The Atlantic here is particularly fierce and roily, the shore marked with countless coves and inlets; according to Carib legend, nearby Londonderry Islets metamorphose at night into grand canoes to take the spirits of the dead out to sea. Look for the altar at the reservation's Roman Catholic church at Salibia; it was once a canoe. The Caribs still build their own canoes—long, elegant crafts scooped from the trunk of a single gommier tree. If you are lucky, you can watch this being done on the beach at **Castle Bruce**, a few miles to the south of the reservation.

NEED A BREAK?
Stop for lunch or a cold drink at the **Carib Territory Guesthouse** (☎ 809/445-7256), owned by Caribs Charles and Margaret Williams. They offer half- or full-day walks through the territory. For those who want to stay overnight, there are eight basic rooms. A good selection of Carib crafts is sold here.

**4** **Emerald Pool.** It's only a 20-minute walk down a trail to this swirling, fern-bedecked basin into which a 50-ft waterfall splashes. Lookout points along the way provide sweeping views of the windward (Atlantic) coast and the forested interior.

**10** **Indian River.** Portsmouth is the place to embark for a canoe or rowboat ride up this lazy, tropical river, which snakes through lush rain forest thick with mangrove trees and exotic bird life. The guides here are notoriously overeager (they will try to get you into a powerboat, which will scare off all the birds), so choose carefully or ask your hotel to recommend someone. If you don't want to do the canoe ride, take the road along the Indian River valley northeast to the Atlantic, considered by many to be one of the prettiest roads of the island. Twisting through embankments of red clay festooned with ferns, coconut trees, and bananas, you pass villages with French names like Dos D'Ane and Paix Bouche, which proudly announce their populations (300 is a megalopolis) as you enter them and where brightly painted shanties vie with the flowers for color.

**5** **Layou River Valley.** This is perhaps Dominica's most spectacular spot. Situated at the bottom of a deep gorge, with lush terraces of bananas, cacao, citrus fruits, and coconuts, the river is the island's longest and largest, with quiet pools, beaches, waterfalls, and rapids. It's a great place for a full day's swimming and shooting the rapids, or just sunning and picnicking. The remains of Hillsborough Estate, once a rum-producing plantation, are also here.

**⑦ Marigot.** The largest settlement on the east coast (population 5,000) is not a particular point of interest, but it is a good jumping-off point to explore the northeast coast, with its steep cliffs, dramatic reefs, and rivers swirling down through forests of mangroves and fields of coconut. The nearby beaches of Woodford Hill Bay, Hampstead, L'Anse Noir, and Hodges are excellent for snorkeling and scuba diving.

**⑱ Morne Aux Diables.** In the far north of Dominica is this peak, which soars 2,826 ft above sea level and slopes down to Toucari Bay and Douglas Bay on the west coast, where you'll find long stretches of dark-sand beach.

**⑨ Morne Diablotin.** At 4,747 ft, it is the island's highest summit. It takes its name from a bird, known in English as the black-capped petrel, which was prized by hunters in the 18th-century. There aren't many left today, but Dominica is still a birder's paradise: 135 species live or migrate here, including bananaquits, exotic flycatchers, and fluorescent hummingbirds. Morne Diablotin, in the northern forest reserve, is a good place to see them, though the hike to the top is not one that you should attempt alone. You'll need a good guide (☞ Hiking, *above*), sturdy shoes, a warm sweater, and firm resolve.

**③ Morne Trois Pitons National Park.** Dedicated as a national park in 1975, this 17,000-acre swath of lush, mountainous land in the south-central interior of the island is the crown jewel of the "Nature Island." Named after one of the highest (4,600 ft.) mountains on the island, it contains bubbling volcanoes, majestic waterfalls, and cool mountain lakes. For naturalists, there are four different types of vegetation zones to browse through. Ferns grow 30 ft tall and wild orchids sprout from trees. Sunlight leaks through green canopies, and a gentle mist rises over the jungle floor. A system of trails has been developed in the park, but a shortage of funds, excessive rainfall, and the profusion of vegetation all make them hard to maintain. Access to the park is possible from most points of the compass, though the easiest approach is via the small, mountaintop village of Laudat, 7 mi from Roseau.

About 5 mi out of Roseau, the Wotton Waven Road branches off toward **Sulphur Springs,** where you'll see the belching, sputtering, and gurgling release of hot springs along a river and nearby field—evidence of the area's restless volcanic activity. At the base of Morne Micotrin, you'll find two crater lakes: The first, at 2,500 ft, is **Freshwater Lake,** which was believed to be haunted by a vindictive mermaid and a monstrous serpent with a gemlike carbuncle on its forehead. Farther on is **Boeri Lake,** fringed with greenery and with purple hyacinths floating on its surface. But the undisputed highlight of the park is **Boiling Lake.** The world's second-largest boiling lake, it is a cauldron of gurgling gray-blue water, 70 yards wide, of unknown depth, with water temperatures from 180°F to 197°F. It is believed that the lake is not a volcanic crater but a flooded fumarole—a crack through which gases escape from the molten lava below. The hike up to the lake is challenging, and you will be slipping and sliding the whole way up. You should go only with a guide (☞ Hiking, *above*) and will have to leave at about 8 AM for this all-day, 7-mi (round-trip) trek. Guides keep small groups of hikers (usually six to eight maximum) under a watchful eye at all times. You will return exhausted, covered with mud, nicks, and scrapes, but glowing with satisfaction that you've seen one of the wonders of the world. On your way to the lake, you'll pass through the **Valley of Desolation**, a sight that definitely lives up to its name. Harsh sulphuric fumes have destroyed virtually all the vegetation in what was once a lush forested area. Stay on the trail to avoid breaking through the crust that covers the hot lava below, unless you want to make your own journey to the center of the earth.

Also in the National Park are the island's three highest waterfalls: Sari Sari, Middleham, and the spectacular Trafalgar Falls. All three falls are more than 150 ft high. If you're in decent shape and possess agility and balance, it's worth hiking up the riverbed to the cool pools at the bases of the twin **Trafalgar Falls**. The taller of the two is where hot, orange-colored sulfuric and ferric waters mix with the crash of cold river water; taking a dip is an exhilarating experience.

⑪ **Portsmouth.** The past of this rather drab town is more illustrious than its present. It was once intended to be the capital of Dominica, thanks to its superb natural harbor on **Prince Rupert Bay**. In its heyday, as many as 400 ships docked here at one time. In 1782 it was also the site of one of the most decisive naval engagements between the French and the English, the Battle of Les Saintes. The English won that one, but lost the much tougher fight against the mosquitoes breeding in the nearby swamps. As a result, Roseau, not Portsmouth, is today the capital. Maritime traditions are continued here by the yachting set, and there are more than 2 mi of good, sandy beaches fringed with coconut trees and a few small hotels. Unfortunately, the effects of Hurricane Marilyn in 1995 are still evident.

❶ **Roseau.** With a population of only 20,000, Roseau (pronounced rose-*oh*) must be one of the smallest capital cities in the world. In 45 minutes, you have walked it all, and you are more likely to see goats and chickens than statues and fountains. But if you give it a chance, you will make friends with this slow-moving Caribbean town, with its unusual wood-and-stone houses, brightly painted shutters and roofs, and bustling marketplace. The locals are some of the friendliest people in the Caribbean, with none of the attitude you find in islands like St. Thomas or Antigua. Indeed, they are so helpful that, even before you have a chance to ask them directions, they will be shepherding you through the streets. New developments at **Bayfront** have brightened up the waterfront. The old court house now houses the excellent new **Dominica Museum**, labor of love of local writer and historian Lennox Honychurch. The **Fort Young Hotel**, built as a British fort in the 18th century, is also worth a visit. The state house, public library, and Anglican cathedral are all nearby.

NEED A
BREAK?

**Cocorico** (⊠ 58 King George St., Roseau, no phone), the brainchild of a young couple from Lille, is a bit of France in downtown Roseau. In a pretty Creole dwelling, which they have decorated in blue and white, you can drink espresso and eat *baguettes au jambon* or beef *a la française*. There is also a modest selection of French produce, including chocolate from Martinique and (of all things) tripes from Brittany.

The 40-acre **Botanical Gardens**, founded in 1891 as an annex of Kew Gardens, in London, is a pleasant place to stroll about and watch cricket games. There is an extensive collection of tropical plants and trees. The **national park office** is also here. It can provide tour guides and a wealth of printed information. ⊠ *National Park Office,* ☎ *809/ 448–2401, ext. 417.* ⊙ *Mon. 8–1 and 2–5, Tues.–Fri. 8–1 and 2–4. Dominica Museum, no phone.* ⊠ *$1.* ⊙ *Weekdays 9–5, Sat. 9–1.*

NEED A
BREAK?

Sit in the garden of the late Jean Rhys, the Dominican-born novelist who wrote *Wide Sargasso Sea*. The garden has been turned into an informal garden eatery, the **World of Food** (✉ Queen Mary St. and Field's La., ☎ 809/448–6125). If you've never read Rhys's books, stop off at **Paperbacks** (✉ 6 Cork St., ☎ 809/448–2370).

**②** **Soufrière.** This lazy, sunbaked village at the southernmost tip of the island was first settled by French lumbermen in the 17th century. The Frenchness of Soufrière (the name comes from the nearby sulfur springs) can still be felt in the Roman Catholic church. Built of volcanic stone, with red and blue trim, it is the prettiest on the island. Today, Soufrière is, literally, the jumping-off point for some of the finest diving and snorkeling in the Caribbean (☞ Outdoor Activities and Sports, *above*). From Scotts Head, a narrow peninsula that encircles the bay, there are wonderful views of Martinique.

**⑧** **Syndicate Nature Trail.** The road at the bend near Dublanc that leads to the Syndicate Estate also leads to the 200-acre site of **Project Sisserou.** This protected site, which includes the Syndicate Nature Trail, has been set aside with the help of some 6,000 schoolchildren, each of whom donated 25¢ for the land where the endangered Sisserou parrot (found only in Dominica) flies free. At last estimate, there were only about 60 of these shy and beautiful birds, covered in rich green feathers with a mauve front.

# Dominica A to Z

## Arriving and Departing

### BY FERRY

**Atlantika** (✉ c/o Trois Pitons Travel, ☎ 809/448–6977) runs jet catamarans from Guadeloupe to Martinique, with stops at Les Saintes and Dominica, on Wednesday, Friday, Saturday, and Sunday. **Express des Isles** (✉ c/o Whitchurch Shipping & Tours, ☎ 809/448–2181) has scheduled service Monday, Wednesday, Friday, and Saturday from Guadeloupe in the north to Martinique in the south, with stops at Les Saintes and Dominica. The crossing, in a jet catamaran, takes approximately 90 minutes and offers superb views of the other islands.

### BY PLANE

**American Eagle** (☎ 800/433–7300) flies every day from San Juan. **LIAT** (☎ 809/462–0700) connects with flights from the United States on Antigua, Barbados, Guadeloupe, Martinique, St. Lucia, St. Maarten, and San Juan. **Air Guadeloupe** (☎ 809/448–2181) flies from Pointe-à-Pitre. The newest service, **Cardinal Airlines** (☎ 809/449–0600), connects from both Antigua, Barbados, and St. Maarten.

### FROM THE AIRPORT

**Canefield Airport** (about 3 mi north of Roseau) handles only small aircraft and daytime flights; landing here can be a hair-raising experience for those uneasy about flying. Cab fare is about $8 to Roseau. **Melville Hall Airport,** on the northeast coast, handles larger planes; although interesting, the 90-minute drive through the island's rain forest to Roseau is bumpy, exhausting, and costs about $50 by private taxi or $17 per person by co-op cab.

## Currency

The official currency is the Eastern Caribbean dollar (EC$). Figure about EC$2.60 to the US$1. U.S. dollars are readily accepted, but you'll usually get change in EC dollars. Major credit cards are widely accepted, as are traveler's checks. Prices quoted here are in U.S. dollars unless indicated otherwise.

## Emergencies

**Police, fire, and ambulance:** ☎ 999. **Hospital: Princess Margaret Hospital** (⊠ Federation Dr., Goodwill, ☎ 809/448–2231 or 809/448–2233). **Pharmacy: Jolly's Pharmacy** (⊠ 12 King George V St., Roseau, ☎ 809/448–3388).

## Getting Around

CAR RENTALS

If it doesn't bother you to drive on the left on potholed mountainous roads with hairpin curves, rent a car and strike out on your own. Daily car-rental rates begin at $35 (weekly about $190), plus collision damage insurance at $6 a day and personal accident insurance at $2 a day, and you'll have to put down a deposit and purchase a visitor's driving permit for EC$20. You can rent a car from **Avis** (⊠ 4 High St., Roseau, ☎ 809/448–2481), **Wide Range Car Rentals** (⊠ 79 Bath Rd., Roseau, ☎ 809/448–2198), **Valley Rent-a-Car** (⊠ Goodwill Rd., Roseau, ☎ 809/448–3233), or **Anselm's Car Rental** (⊠ 3 Great Marlborough St., Roseau, ☎ 809/448–2730). **Budget Rent-a-Car** (⊠ Canefield Industrial Estate, ☎ 809/449–2080) offers daily rates, three-day specials, and weekly and monthly rates.

TAXIS

Taxis are available at the airports and in Roseau. The rates are fixed by the government, but prices can usually be negotiated. **Mally's Tour & Taxi Service** (☎ 809/448–3114) and **Julius John's** (☎ 809/449–1968) are two of the better operators.

Taxi drivers are also happy to offer their services as guides at the cost of $18 an hour, per car of four, with tip extra. It's a good idea to get a recommendation from your hotel manager or the Dominica Division of Tourism (☞ Visitor Information, *below*) before selecting a guide and driver.

VANS

This is a cheap, though not always dependable, means of transportation. Minivans cruise the island and, like taxis, will stop when hailed. You can also catch a minivan in Roseau by the bridges crossing the Roseau River.

## Guided Tours

**Dominica Tours** (☎ 809/448–2638) conducts a wide variety of hiking and photo safari tours in sturdy four-wheel-drive vehicles. Prices range from $15 to $100 per person, depending upon the length of the trip and whether picnics and rum punches are included. The real pros, however, are **Ken's Hinterland Adventure Tours** (☎ 809/448–4850, FAX 809/448–8486). Ken's provides vans with knowledgeable guides (ask for Sonia Lander; she's the best on the island) and can design expeditions to fit your needs. The botanical and ornithological tours are excellent. One of the most exciting tours is a hike down the dramatic Layou River gorge. Four-wheel-drive vans equipped with air-conditioning and two-way radios ensure that you will get in, and out, of the green interior safely and comfortably. Ken's also offers sea kayaking, a wonderful opportunity to explore the scalloped coast. Tours cost from $25 to $50 per person.

## Language

The official language is English, but most Dominicans also speak a French-Creole patois.

## Opening and Closing Times

Business hours are weekdays 8–1 and 2–4, Saturday 8–1. Banks are open Monday–Thursday 8–3, Friday 8–5.

## Passports and Visas

U.S. and Canadian citizens must present a driver's license or passport and a return or ongoing ticket. British citizens must show a passport.

## Precautions

Bring insect repellent. If you are susceptible to motion sickness, be sure to bring along some medication, as the roads twist and turn dramatically and the local drivers barrel down them at dizzying speeds. If you plan on hiking even the simplest trail, bring along extra clothing and hiking boots or athletic sneakers to change into; trails are very rugged and often very muddy. Note: Unlike on neighboring Martinique and Guadeloupe, topless bathing is not in vogue on Dominica. A note in the government tourist guide also states that swimsuits may not be worn in the street.

## Taxes and Service Charges

Hotels collect a 5% government tax, restaurants a 3% tax. The departure tax is US$12 or EC$30. All hotels and restaurants add a 10% service charge to your bill. Tipping is welcomed.

## Telephones, Electricity, and Mail

To call Dominica from the United States, dial area code 809 and the local access code, 44, followed by the five-digit local number. On the island, you need to dial only the five-digit number. The island has efficient direct-dial international service. All pay phones are equipped for local and overseas dialing. Dominica's area code is scheduled to change to 767.

Electric voltage is 220/240 AC, 50 cycles. American appliances require an adapter.

First-class (airmail) letters to the United States and Canada cost EC95¢; postcards cost EC50¢.

## Visitor Information

Before you go, contact the **Dominican Tourist Office** (✉ 10 E. 21st St., Suite 600, New York, NY 10010, ☎ 212/475–7542, FAX 212/460–8287). In the United Kingdom, contact the **Dominica Tourist Office** (✉ 1 Collingham Gardens, London SW5 0HW, ☎ 0171/835–1937 or 0171/370–5194).

Once on Dominica, contact the main office of the **Division of Tourism** (✉ National Development Corp., Valley Rd., Box 293, Roseau, ☎ 809/448–2045). The tourist desk at the **post office** (✉ Bay St., no phone) is open weekdays 8–4, Saturday 9–1. The office at **Canefield Airport** (☎ 809/449–1242) is open weekdays 7 AM–6 PM. The office at **Melville Hall Airport** (☎ 809/445–7051) is open weekdays 7 AM–6 PM.

# 11 Dominican Republic

*The unspoiled scenery of the Dominican Republic will take your breath away, and so can the Merengue—the wonderful, sexy dance that Dominicans celebrate 365 days a year. The latin culture of Puerto Rico is shared here, and the warmth you'll find on 1,000 miles of beaches can only be matched by the residents' hospitality.*

Updated by
Eileen
Robinson Smith

**S**PRAWLING OVER TWO-THIRDS OF THE ISLAND of Hispaniola, which it shares with Haiti, the Dominican Republic is a delightful country with the kind of magic that Mexico is famous for. Its people are among the most likable in the entire Caribbean: Friendly and hospitable by nature, they will do their level best to assure you have a memorable vacation if you return their courtesy. It also happens to be one of the least expensive Caribbean destinations.

Santo Domingo, its capital, is the oldest continuously inhabited city in this half of the globe, and visitors have difficulty tearing themselves away from the city's 16th-century Colonial Zone. Sunseekers head for the beach resorts of Puerto Plata, Barahona, Samaná, Bavaro, Punta Cana, and La Romana. The highest peak in the West Indies is here: Pico Duarte (10,370 ft) lures serious hikers to the central mountain range. Ancient sunken galleons and coral reefs divert divers and snorkelers. A strong recommendation is to couple a stay in the capital with a short beach-resort vacation.

Columbus happened upon this island on December 5, 1492, and on Christmas Eve his ship, the *Santa María*, was wrecked on the Atlantic shore. He named it La Isla Española ("the Spanish island"), established a small colony, and sailed back to Spain on the *Pinta*. Santo Domingo, which is on the south coast, was founded in 1496 by Columbus's brother, Bartholomew Columbus, and Nicolás de Ovando and during the first half of the 16th century became the bustling hub of Spanish commerce and culture in the New World. The Spanish colonials intermarried first with the Taino Indians and later the African slaves, and today nearly everyone is a shade of brown and Spanish speaking.

Hispaniola (a derivation of *La Isla Española*) has had an unusually chaotic history, replete with bloody revolutions, military coups, yellow-fever epidemics, invasions, and bankruptcy. In the 17th century, the western third of the island was ceded to France. A slave revolt in 1804 resulted in the establishment there of the first black republic, Haiti. Dominicans and Haitians battled for control of the island on and off throughout the 19th century. The Dominicans declared themselves independent from Haiti in 1844 and from Spain in 1865. The country was, however, bankrupt by the turn of the century. The United States helped to administer the island's finances, and eventually U.S. Marines occupied the country from 1916 to 1924, until a new Dominican constitution was signed. Rafael Trujillo ruled the Dominican Republic with an iron fist from 1930 until his assassination in 1961. A short-lived democracy was overthrown soon thereafter, followed by another occupation by the U.S. Marines in 1965. The country has been relatively stable since the early 1970s, and administrations have been staunch supporters of the United States.

American influence looms large in Dominican life. Many Dominicans have relatives living in the United States, and many speak at least rudimentary English. Still, it is a vibrantly Latin country, and the Latino flavor contrasts sharply with the culture of the British, French, and Dutch islands.

Dominican towns and cities are generally not quaint, neat, or particularly pretty. Poverty is everywhere, but the country is also alive and chaotic, sometimes frenzied, sometimes laid-back. Like most other Latinos, Dominicans love a party, and Santo Domingo hosts a Carnival in late February. The *renowned Festival del Merengue* is held in late July and early August; all one has to do is listen to the fast-paced merengue, one of the country's most famous exports, to feel the energy, dynamism, and vitality of the Dominicans. In October the Puerta Plata Festival transforms the Amber Coast into one giant fiesta. Celebrating is rampant throughout the Christmas holidays, culminating with Three Kings Day on the sixth of January.

In recent years, tourism has played an increasingly important role on the island, and the government, under the new president, Lionel Fernandez Reyna, is making it an even higher priority. The country's tourist zones are incredibly varied and include extravagant Casa de Campo (where many rich Santo Domingans have villas), the package-tour hotels of Playa Dorada, Santo Domingo's exquisite Colonial Zone, Jarabacoa in its gorgeous mountain setting, and the world-weary beauty of Barahona and the Samaná peninsula.

## Lodging

Your options here vary from rustic country inns to some of the world's newest and poshest resorts. An ambitious development plan continues, especially on the north coast. The Dominican Republic has the largest hotel inventory (30,000 rooms and growing) in the Caribbean. Puerto Plata alone has 9,800 rooms and hosts 300,000 tourists a year. The fierce competition translates into some of the best hotel buys in the Caribbean. Be sure to inquire about special packages when you call to reserve; arranging your hotel through a tour operator will cost considerably less, especially if airfare and transfers are included in the package price. Rooms are air-conditioned unless otherwise noted.

Hotels in Santo Domingo base their tariffs on the EP and maintain the same room rates throughout the year. In contrast, resorts have high winter and low summer rates, with the low rate reducing the room prices by as much as 50%. All-inclusive properties are concentrated along the north coast. More and more hotels are turning all-inclusive, but those that haven't offer EP or MAP. Our prices, in U.S. dollars, are based on a double room during the high season. For meal plans, add $20–$30 per person to the room-only rate listed below; for all-inclusive, add $40–$45 per person.

| CATEGORY | COST* |
|---|---|
| $$$$ | over $175 |
| $$$ | $125–$175 |
| $$ | $75–$125 |
| $ | under $75 |

*All prices are for a standard double room, excluding 10% service charge and 13% tax.*

### Boca Chica/Juan Dolio

$$–$$$ **Renaissance Capella Beach Resort.** This deluxe resort, opened in 1994,
★ is striving to become the top southern-coast destination, with the exception, of course, of Casa de Campo. Set on 17½ acres punctuated with park benches and manicured bushes, the resort is built on the same scale as a grand hotel in southern Spain. The exterior is a pale yellow stucco with white latticework and columns, coral stonework, and a red-tile peaked roof. Other buildings are a hodgepodge of architectural styles, from Victorian (with white colonnaded porticoes) to Moorish. Rooms have hibiscus-patterned fabrics, botanical prints of tropical flowers, and either a terrace or balcony. Chambermaids wear colorful Dominican costumes, and the concierges speak four languages. Two of the restaurants are in the open air with thatched roofs. At 10 each evening, a show featuring dance, music, or both takes place in the Pescador restaurant. If you are seeking something a cut above most other

Dominican resorts, the vast array of amenities and facilities is bound to please. ⊠ *Villas Del Mar, Box 4750, Santo Domingo,* ☎ *809/526–1080 or 800/468–3571,* ℻ *809/526–1088. 261 rooms, 22 suites. 3 restaurants, 3 bars, 2 pools, massage, sauna, 2 tennis courts, health club, dive shop, water sports, boating, shops, dance club, recreation room. AE, D, MC, V. EP, MAP.*

**$$** 🏨 **Hamaca Beach Hotel.** One of the best of the genre, this large, all-
**★** inclusive resort is a half hour east of Santo Domingo and just a few minutes from Las Américas Airport. The impressive reception area has terra-cotta floors, wicker furnishings, and huge floral arrangements. Spacious guest rooms are furnished in painted rattan and dark woods. Floral linens coordinate with pale green tile floors. There's a lovely cham-pagne-color beach, with two huge thatch-roofed bars. Extra touches, such as a fruit and juice bar and free mopeds, contribute to the high occupancy. There is a lot of casino action here, and the disco, open to locals on the weekends, shuts down at 7 AM. ⊠ *Boca Chica Beach,* ☎ *809/523–4611 or 800/945–0792,* ℻ *809/566–2436. 465 rooms. 4 restaurants, 3 bars, grill, 2 tennis courts, archery, horseback riding, scuba diving, snorkeling, windsurfing, boating. AE, MC, V. All-inclusive.*

## The Amber Coast

**$$$** 🏨 **Paradise Beach Resort and Club.** Of the 14 hotels in the Playa Do-
**★** rada complex, this hotel stands out on two counts: It is one of the few that front the beach and it has a unique design. Its cluster of low-rise buildings with white-tile roofs and latticed balconies and windows follows winding paths through palms, birds-of-paradise, and hibiscus from the reception area down to the beach. Rooms are decorated in a carefully chosen palette of pastel greens and blues. Standard rooms have one double or two twin beds; some of the one-bedroom apart-ments have kitchens. In the center of the resort is a free-form pool, with a water channel that winds its way from the pool to the beach. Two of the resort's three restaurants (not the gourmet Italia) are open-air and on the beach. ⊠ *Box 337, Playa Dorada,* ☎ *809/586–3663 or 800/752–9236,* ℻ *809/320–4858. 436 rooms, 174 suites. 3 restau-rants, 3 bars, 18-hole golf course, 2 tennis courts, horseback riding, water sports, bicycles, shops, dance club. AE, DC, MC, V. All-inclusive.*

**$$–$$$** 🏨 **Flamenco Beach Resort, Villas Doradas,** and **Playa Dorada Beach Resort.** Guests can use the facilities at all three of these hotels, which are lined up one after the other on the mile-long white-sand beach. They're all known for their high occupancy, high energy, lively night life, and variety of social and sports programs, but the similarities end there. Rooms at the older Playa Dorada are dowdy and sadly in need of refurbishment, as are the public spaces and furnishings. Villas Do-radas is a step up. Rooms are attractive and hung with abstract paint-ings; all have cable TV and a safe. The Chinese restaurant here is surprisingly good, as is the newer Brazilian restaurant down at the beach. The newer Flamenco is definitely the best of the trio. The glorious pub-lic spaces include cobblestone and Andalusian brick floors. The main free-form pool (with swim-up bar) is designed to resemble a lake, complete with waterfall and lapping waves. Oversize rooms and suites have tasteful rattan furnishings, terra-cotta floors, bright floral upholstery, minibar, cable TV, and a balcony or terrace. Club Miguel Angel is a hotel within a hotel offering premium concierge service. The only thing missing at the Flamenco is an ocean view. *Flamenco:* ⊠ *Playa Dorada, Puerto Plata,* ☎ *809/320–5084,* ℻ *809/320–6319. 582 units. 6 restaurants, 3 bars, 2 pools, 2 tennis courts, water sports, shops. Villas Doradas:* ⊠ *Box 1370, Puerto Plata,* ☎ *809/320–3000,*

# Dominican Republic

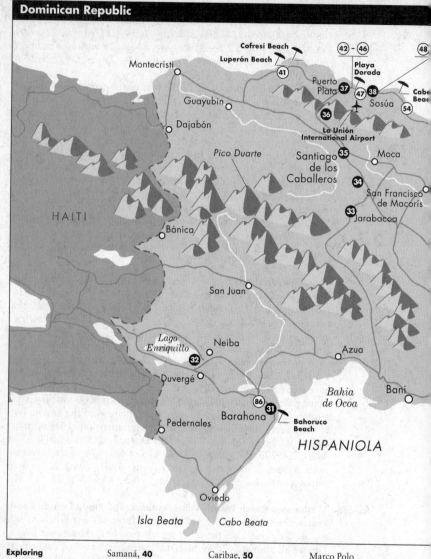

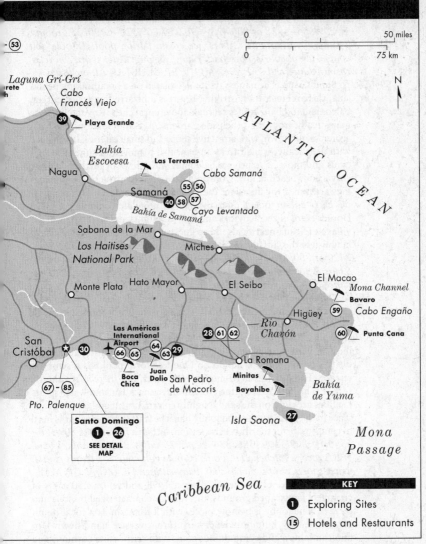

Laguna Grí-Grí

Cabo
Francés Viejo

**39** ▲ **Playa Grande**

*Bahía
Escocesa*

Nagua

**Las Terrenas**

*Cabo Samaná*

Samaná **55 56**

**40 58 57**

*Bahía de Samaná* *Cayo Levantado*

Sabana de la Mar

*Los Haitises
National Park*

Miches

Monte Plata

Hato Mayor

El Seibo

El Macao

*Mona Channel*

**Bavaro**

Higüey **59** *Cabo Engaño*

*Río
Charón*

**60** ▲ **Punta Cana**

San
Cristóbal **30**

**Las Américas
International
Airport**
**66 65**

**64**

**28 61 62**

**63 29**

**Boca
Chica**

**Juan
Dolio** San Pedro
de Macorís

La Romana

**Minitas**

**Bayahibe**

*Bahía
de Yuma*

**67 – 85**

*Pto. Palenque*

**Santo Domingo**

**1 – 26**

**SEE DETAIL
MAP**

*Isla Saona* **27**

*Mona
Passage*

*Caribbean Sea*

**ATLANTIC OCEAN**

0 — 50 miles
0 — 75 km

N

**KEY**

**1** Exploring Sites

**15** Hotels and Restaurants

**Lodging**

Bavaro Beach
Resort, **59**

Cabarete Beach
Hotel, **54**

Caribbean Village
Club and Resort, **46**

Casa Bonita, **86**

Casa de Campo, **62**

Cayo Levantado, **57**

Club Marina, **51**

Flamenco Beach
Resort, Villas Doradas,
and Playa Dorada
Beach Resort, **47**

Gran Hotel Lina
and Casino, **69**

Grand Ventana, **42**

Hamaca Beach
Hotel, **66**

Hotel Cofresi, **41**

Hotel El Embajador
and Casino, **77**

Hotel Gran Bahía, **56**

Hotel Hispaniola, **84**

Hotel Palacio, **85**

Hotel Santo
Domingo, **67**

Inter-Continental
Hotel V
Centenario, **79**

Jaragua Renaissance
Resort and Casino, **76**

Marco Polo Club, **52**

Paradise Beach
Resort and Club, **44**

Puerto Plata Beach
Resort and Casino, **45**

Punta Cana Beach
Resort, **60**

Renaissance Capella
Beach Resort, **63**

Sand Castle, **49**

Santo Domingo
Hilton Hotel and
Casino, **68**

Victoria Resort, **43**

Villa Serena, **55**

FAX *809/320–4790. 207 rooms. 5 restaurants, 2 bars, pool, 3 tennis courts, water sports, car rental. Playa Dorada:* ⊠ *Box 272, Puerto Plata,* ☎ *809/586–3988 or 800/423–6902,* FAX *809/320–1190. 252 rooms, 1 suite. 4 restaurants, 2 bars, ice cream parlor, pool, 18-hole golf course, tennis courts, horseback riding, jogging, water sports, bicycles, casino, dance club. AE, DC, MC, V. EP, MAP, FAP, All-inclusive.*

$$–$$$   ▣ **Sand Castle.** The name says it all. Isolated on a breathtaking penin-
★      sula, this architecturally striking resort is a bizarre fantasy of curves, balconies, and balustrades set high above coral cliffs. Royal palms rise majestically from the beachside gardens. Accommodations are built around a minitown, with attractive shops and small eateries, landscaped with artistically pruned trees and shrubs. Rooms and suites are spacious and most have private balconies with views of the bay and the curvaceous beach below. Done in muted pastels, attractive wall hangings are a nice touch, as are the stained-glass windows. Hourly shuttles carry guests some 8 mi to the densely populated complex of Playa Dorado. Organized activities and the restaurants and attractions of the village of Sosua nearby also keep guests busy, but many prefer just to languish at the cliffside pool. ⊠ *Puerto Chiquito, Sosua,* ☎ *809/571– 2420 or 800/446–5963,* FAX *809/571–2000. 240 units. 3 restaurants, 5 bars, 2 pools, horseback riding, water sports, dive shop, bicycles, shops, dance club, convention center. AE, MC, V. EP, MAP.*

$$      ▣ **Caribbean Village Club and Resort.** Rooms in the newer Royale building have kitchenettes and cable TV and are simply decorated in peach tones. The older Tropicale is a series of small houses with connecting skywalks. Rooms here are more like miniapartments, perfect for families, all with terrace or balcony, kitchenette, small sitting area, marble floors, and light pastel decor. One free-form pool has a swim-up terrace. The beach is a 10-minute hike away, but there's free shuttle service. The hotel's La Tortuga restaurant, a snack bar, and water-sports facilities are right on the sand. Nightly entertainment and dancing take place in the patio lounge and lobby bar. The staff genuinely works hard to compensate for the off-beach location. ⊠ *Playa Dorada,* ☎ *809/586– 5350,* FAX *809/320–5386. 336 rooms, 26 suites. 3 restaurants, 3 bars, grill, grocery, kitchenettes, pool, 18-hole golf course, 2 tennis courts, water sports, shops, dance club, baby-sitting. AE, MC, V. CP, MAP.*

$$      ▣ **Grand Ventana.** Opened in August 1996 and set on 250 acres of creatively landscaped grounds, this hotel is characterized by style and pizzazz. The lobby is a show piece, with a fountain as a focal point, surrounded by Filipino-wicker furniture, oversize hand-hewn Dominican tables, and commodious sofas with crisp white cushions and striped pillows. The resort's main buffet dining room is divided into three open-air sections in neo-Victorian gazebos of green and rose hues. On the bougainvillea-filled terrace above, weddings are staged. Accommodations are in two handsome buildings with canopied entrances, ocher stucco facades, and red-tile roofs. Most rooms have sea views somewhat obstructed by palms, tall sea-grape bushes, and the picket fence that helps privatize the most tranquil beach on the strip. At dinner, let the moonlit waves mesmerize as you sample fried squid, fish soup with Pernod and dumplings, curried red snapper, and grilled lobster. ⊠ *Box 22, Playa Dorada, Puerto Plata,* ☎ *809/412–2525,* FAX *809/412–2526. 303 rooms, 31 suites. 3 restaurants, 3 bars, grocery, 2 pools, beauty salon, sauna, 2 tennis courts, exercise room, water sports, bicycles, shops, dance club, recreation room, convention center, car rental. AE, DC, MC, V. EP, MAP, FAP, All-inclusive.*

$$      ▣ **Marco Polo Club.** In an enclosed property with tree gardens and a lagoon, this Victorian-style complex has three-story luxury apartments with kitchens, ceramic tile floors, quality rattan furnishings with green floral-print fabric, tile baths with Jacuzzis, and balconies with French

doors that open to the sea. Prices are for up to four persons and include a full breakfast. Holland International sometimes takes all of the rooms for its package tours, so reserve well in advance. Fifty waterfront rooms are under construction for completion in mid-1998. ⊠ *Marco Polo Club, Concordia Hotels, Sosua,* ☎ *809/571–3128,* ℻ *809/571–3233. 8 apartments. 2 restaurants, bar, 2 pools, beach, dance club. AE, MC, V.*

**$$** 🏨 **Puerto Plata Beach Resort and Casino.** More of a village than a resort, Puerto Plata's 7 acres take in cobblestone pathways, colorful gardens, and suites in 23 porticoed two- and three-story buildings. Accommodations have terra-cotta floors and a primarily mint and jade decor, with cable TV, mini-refrigerator, and balcony or terrace. An activities center sets up water-sports clinics, arranges horseback rides, and so forth. The resort also caters to the little ones, with children's games and such. La Lechuza is the glitzy disco. Ylang-Ylang, named after the evening flower that blooms here, is a highly rated gourmet restaurant and catering service. The Neptune restaurant across the road on the beach is good for seafood. This resort is just outside of town and a ways from Playa Dorada, which will be a plus for some. ⊠ *Box 600, Av. Malecón, Puerto Plata,* ☎ *809/586–4243 or 800/223–9815,* ℻ *809/586–4377. 216 units. 4 restaurants, bar, pool, outdoor hot tub, 4 tennis courts, water sports, casino, nightclub. AE, MC, V. MAP, All-inclusive.*

**$$** 🏨 **Victoria Resort.** A delightful new addition to Playa Dorado, Victoria Resort is a study in pastels and gingerbread fretwork. It has an open ★ and airy design, wicker furniture on marble tiles in the reception area, and bizarre carnival masks against mint green walls. Deluxe accommodations are housed in a two-story building set apart for peace and quiet. Spacious, with expensive plantation-style wicker furniture and tile floors, each has either a balcony or terrace. The Grande Club House looks onto a flower-filled lake, a pool, and hot tub adorned with white columns and market umbrellas. There's also a view of the Isabel de Torres Mountain. The alfresco café where the buffets are laid out has food that is far better than the usual, both Dominican and international. At night guests adjourn to the Lotus Club on the second floor, which has a piano bar and a wraparound terrace. ⊠ *Box 22, Puerto Plata,* ☎ *809/320–1200,* ℻ *809/320–4862. 124 rooms, 66 junior and master suites. 3 restaurants, tennis court, horseback riding, water sports, nightclub. AE, DC, MC, V. All-inclusive.*

**$–$$** 🏨 **Cabarete Beach Hotel.** This delightful small hotel is set right on a ★ tantalizing curve of golden sand ideal for windsurfing and swimming (the surrounding reef protects it from fierce breakers). Deluxe rooms—recommended—are those with full ocean view and air-conditioning. Standards (some with air-conditioning) are slightly smaller and noisier. All rooms are decorated with bright framed prints, blond woods, and rocking chairs. The lovely terrace restaurant is known for its bountiful breakfast buffets of luscious homemade breads, muffins, and pastries. The Tropical Bar—a riot of painted gourds and coconuts, colorful murals, and thatching—prides itself on its eight fresh fruit juices daily and more than 50 exotic libations. The BIC Windsurf Center is right next door. The staff is unfailingly helpful and courteous. ⊠ *Cabarete,* ☎ *809/571–0755,* ℻ *809/571–0831. 24 rooms. Restaurant, bar, shop. AE, MC, V. EP, MAP.*

**$–$$** 🏨 **Hotel Cofresi.** Rooms here are rather basic and somewhat cramped, but the staff is courteous and the setting is breathtaking. The resort is built on Atlantic reefs and the sea spritzes its waters into the peaceful man-made lagoon and pools along the beach. Most rooms have cable TV, hair dryer, safe, and kitchenette. There are jogging and exercise trails, paddleboats for the lagoon, scuba-diving clinics, and evening entertainment, including a disco. The restaurants specialize in flavorful Dominican fare. ⊠ *Box 327, Costambar,* ☎ *809/586–2898,* ℻ *809/586–8064. 237 rooms, 5 suites. 2 restaurants, 2 bars, 3 pools (1 saltwater), tennis court, horseback riding, water sports, boating, bicycles, dance club, recreation room. AE, MC, V. All-inclusive.*

$ 🏨 **Club Marina.** This charming beige stucco and red-tile hotel is owned by the beachfront Casa Marina resort, and although you're paying only half as much as guests there, you get the use of all its facilities. Eduardo de Lora, a master stained-glass craftsman, designed the Club, and everything displays his creative touch: The pool is landscaped with rocks, giving it a natural grotto feel, and spiral staircases are embedded with shards of glass (there are no exposed edges). The rooms themselves are plain but impeccably neat, with a well-worn integrity. The blue-and-white tiles, lilac bedspreads, and closets painted jade green brighten them up. All units have cable TV, private bath, and a small balcony. The beach is a five-minute walk. ⊠ *Alejo Martínez St., Sosua,* ☎ *809/571–3939. 50 rooms. Restaurant, pool. AE, MC, V. MAP.*

## Barahona

$$ 🏨 **Casa Bonita.** In the scenic southwest, this gentrified country inn is a charming alternative to the high-rise hotels and heavily trafficked all-inclusive properties. Julio and Virginia Schiffino expanded their home and added 12 criolla-style cottages with roofs of thatched cana, rough-hewn walls, and simple furnishings. Six have air-conditioning. The assembly of casitas faces the sea or the verdant rain forest of the Sierra de Bahoruco and two mountain rivers. The open-air gallery, adjacent sitting areas, and restaurant overlook the pool area and are tastefully decorated with comfortable sofas and scads of colorful throw pillows. Your meals will include such criolla specialties as *sancucho* (thick meat stew) and *arroz con pollo* (rice with chicken). By 1998, the owners' nearby deluxe Barhoruco Beach Resort should be fully operational. ⊠ *Barahona,* ☎ *809/696–0215,* ℻ *809/223–0548. Restaurant, bar, pool. AE, V. MAP.*

## La Romana

$$$$ 🏨 **Casa de Campo.** "House in the Country" is an interesting appellation for this deluxe resort, which sprawls over 7,000 acres and accommodates some 3,000 guests. Indeed, many wealthy Dominicans have luxurious second homes here. The complex includes 350 casitas (double rooms) and 150 one-, two-, and three-bedroom villas with fully equipped kitchens. For many, the main attractions are the two 18-hole golf courses: One of them, called Teeth of the Dog, has seven holes that skirt the sea and is rated the best in the Caribbean. Casa de Campo is also a sportsperson's paradise, with 13 tennis courts, horseback riding, polo, archery, trapshooting, and every imaginable water sport. Minibuses provide free transportation around the resort, but you can also rent electric golf carts, scooters, and bicycles (villa renters are provided with golf carts). An excellent children's program (including "kid's night out," when children spend the evening at a center with games, videos, and supervision) is great for families. Oscar de la Renta helped design much of the resort, owns a villa, and has a boutique in Altos de Chavón, the re-created medieval, Mediterranean village and art colony on the property. Some rooms and villas are decorated in Laura Ashley style, others with bolder, more abstract touches. The resort is—in a word—awesome. The advantage of staying here is that the resort has its own airport. American Airlines flies in daily from Miami, and American Eagle flies in twice a day from San Juan. The disadvantage is that there are few attractions in the vicinity of the hotel other than the hotel's own campus—not that most guests mind. ⊠ *Box 140, La*

*Romana,* ☎ *809/523–3333 or 800/877–3643,* 𝕱𝕬𝕏 *809/523–8548. 350 rooms, 150 2- to 4-bedroom villas. 9 restaurants, 8 bars, 13 pools, hot tub, sauna, 2 18-hole golf courses, 13 tennis courts, archery, exercise room, horseback riding, marina, shops. AE, DC, MC, V. EP, MAP.*

## Punta Cana

**$$$**  🖭 **Bavaro Beach Resort.** This huge, sprawling, four-star luxury resort,
**★**  actually a complex of five low-rise hotels, is situated on the glorious 20-mi stretch of Punta Cana beach. Each room has a private balcony or terrace, cable TV, and refrigerator. The biggest rooms are at the Bavaro Beach Hotel, with hemp and wood furnishings and bright-striped upholstery. The Bavaro Gardens is decorated in vivid primary colors. The Bavaro Casino Hotel has several duplex suites ideal for families. All of the accommodations at the Bavaro Golf Hotel are suites with kitchenettes—a real money saver if you're willing to cook. The Bavaro Palace is the most refined and subdued, with such touches as marble vanities. A social director coordinates a wide variety of daily activities, and there is nightly entertainment at each hotel. The resort has an aloof air about it, but this has more to do with the clientele than the staff, which is very friendly. Most important, the beach is fabulous and among the best in the Dominican Republic. ✉ *Higüey,* ☎ *809/682–2162 or 800/858–0606,* 𝕱𝕬𝕏 *809/682–2169. 1,359 rooms. 9 restaurants, 14 bars, 7 pools, beauty salon, 18-hole golf course, 6 tennis courts, archery, horseback riding, water sports, bicycles, shops, casino, 2 dance clubs, nightclub. AE, MC, V. MAP, FAP.*

**$$$**  🖭 **Punta Cana Beach Resort.** Several pretty coral-and-aquamarine
**★**  buildings dot the lush grounds of this rambling resort. The handsome lobby sets a civilized tone with Dominican crafts, birdcages, and lots of plants. Rooms are spare but pleasant, primarily in jade, coral, and cream, with wicker furnishings. Opt for one of the 54 deluxe rooms, all with balconies, which were recently added in the new Cocotal building. The ½-mi private beach is gorgeous, and there are nature walks on a marked and guided eco-trail into the mahogany forest, where you can take a dip in several natural freshwater pools. There are lots of activities here, too, including nightly musical entertainment by the friendly staff, headed by a long-term G.M., Antonio Bayarri, who adds that touch of class. Classy and romantic is the gourmet room with a piano man on the baby grand. A 36-hole golf course and a 450-room hotel are scheduled to open in 1998. ✉ *Punta Cana Beach (mailing address: Box 1083, Santo Domingo),* ☎ *809/221–2262 or 800/972–2139,* 𝕱𝕬𝕏 *809/687–8745. 395 units. 5 restaurants, 3 bars, grocery, pool, beauty parlor, 4 tennis courts, water sports, shop, dance club, babysitting, children's programs, playground. AE, DC, MC, V. MAP.*

## Samaná

**$$–$$$**  🖭 **Hotel Gran Bahía.** Overdevelopment has not yet reached the pretty
**★**  water's edge where this small, all-inclusive resort is housed in what was formerly priced out as a top-star hotel. The modern colonial Victorian has graceful verandas and balconies looking out over the pool and the sea beyond; you can see schools of whales frolicking offshore during the winter. The superb views make breakfast on your private balcony a treat. Guest rooms are exceptional—extra-large, with cheerful floral prints, tiled floors, and pastel watercolor paintings. The grand yet welcoming reception area and three-story white colonnaded atrium surround a spectacular fountain flanked with numerous cozy nooks for cocktails or reading. Dining alfresco is pleasant, or alternatively you can try the pastel-pretty gourmet room. Musicians at the pool area, which looks like a town square in Mexico, serenade with Spanish ballads. ✉ *Box 2024, Santo Domingo,* ☎ *809/538–3111 or 800/372–1323,* 𝕱𝕬𝕏 *809/538–2764. 110 rooms. 2 restaurants, bar, pool, beauty*

*salon, golf privileges, 2 tennis courts, archery, exercise room. AE, MC, V. All-inclusive.*

**$$** ⊞ **Cayo Levantado.** This tranquil hotel is tucked into the lush greenery of the tiny island national park just off the Samaná coast. The exquisite fringe of pearly white beach is overrun weekends with day-trippers, and if you've traveled all the way to this remote outpost for a party atmosphere, you won't mind the makeshift stalls hawking T-shirts, paintings, beer, a massage, and delicious grilled items. There's another, smaller beach on the other side of the island for the romantically inclined, and farther down is where the lunchtime buffet is served—a heavy, almost Germanic meal with lots of stews, meat and potatoes, and few salads. The rooms, either in the main building or in bungalows, are simple, large, and appealing, with writing desks, wicker furnishings, bright pastel fabrics, and satellite TV and telephones. Alas, as they were all built in the '70s by the government, only two rooms and one cottage have sea views, and the food must improve. ⊠ *Cayo Levantado,* ☎ *809/538–3141,* FAX *809/538–2998. 44 rooms. 2 restaurants, bar, pool, snorkeling, boating, fishing, shop. AE, MC, V. All-inclusive.*

**$$** ⊞ **Villa Serena.** Tucked away in a remote corner of the island in un-
★ spoiled Samaná, this little-known, 11-room hotel is a gem. Located down the beach from the tiny fishing village of Las Galeras, it is at the end of the long road from Puerto Plata, a three-hour scenic drive. Croatian expatriates Natasha Despotovic and Kresimir Zovko have created an intimate place where each of the rooms is individually decorated to provide different moods. All have lanais overlooking the Bahía de Rincón. Some rooms have air-conditioning; those that don't have ceiling fans. The restaurant serves the best food on the peninsula, and a large veranda provides an excellent spot for a cocktail. Two of Samaná's prettiest and most deserted beaches, Playa Colorado and Playa de Rincón, are easily reached by water taxi, horseback, or hike from the hotel. The hotel has a private beach in front, as well as a small, free-form pool. ⊠ *Apartado Postal 51–1, Las Galeras, Samaná,* ☎ *809/696–0065,* FAX *809/538–2545. 11 rooms. Restaurant, bar, pool, horseback riding, bicycles, scuba diving, snorkeling. AE, MC, V. MAP.*

## Santo Domingo

**$$$–$$$$** ⊞ **Jaragua Renaissance Resort and Casino.** Fourteen acres of gar-
★ dens, waterfalls, and fountains surround this pink, ultramodern complex, which is more like a Las Vegas hotel. Top-name entertainers are booked into the 800-seat La Fiesta Showroom, master chefs from four countries tend to the cuisine, great massages are available at affordable prices in the spa, and the casino covers 20,000 square ft. Spacious rooms have three phones, 21-channel satellite TV, minibar, and hair dryer. Each floor has a different decor, one in peach and burgundy, another apricot and mint. Penthouse suites have their own hot tubs. Rates are based on view (garden, pool, or ocean). Twelve cabanas surround the Olympic-size free-form pool—an oasis in the middle of this bustling, chaotic city. The courteous and professional staff makes you feel welcome. ⊠ *Av. George Washington 367, Santo Domingo,* ☎ *809/221–2222 or 800/468–3571,* FAX *809/686–0528. 300 rooms and suites. 5 restaurants, 4 bars, minibars, pool, hot tubs, saunas, spa, golf privileges, 4 tennis courts, casino, dance club. AE, MC, V. EP, MAP, FAP.*

**$$$** ⊞ **Inter-Continental Hotel V Centenario.** Santo Domingo's newest five-
★ star hotel on the Malecón is the choice of well-heeled business travelers. Marble floors and pillars give the reception area a crisp, fresh feel. The rooms are a refreshing change, furnished in attractive earth tones, Dominican handicrafts, and burnished rattans. Each has a mini-

refrigerator, cable TV, and an electronic safe. You can try your luck at the casino or take time out to relax in the lounge with its subdued lighting and enticing easy chairs. The cellar tapas bar has become a favorite after-work hangout for locals. A casual coffee shop looks out over the Caribbean; the pool, with its new, striped outdoor furnishings, shares a sea-view terrace with a bar and an alfresco seafood restaurant. ✉ *Av. George Washington 218, Santo Domingo,* ☎ *809/221–0000,* FAX *809/221–2020. 200 rooms, 26 suites. 3 restaurants, 2 bars, in-room safes, refrigerators, pool, sauna, tennis court, exercise room, squash, shops, casino, free parking. AE, MC, V. EP, MAP, FAP.*

$$$ 🏨 **Santo Domingo Hilton Hotel and Casino.** After 20 years as a Sheraton hotel, the 11-story property just down from the Jaragua reopened in the summer of 1997 as a Hilton. The hotel, which enjoys strong commercial business from the United States, is still owned by Oscar Lama, a leading Dominican businessman. Before the hotel raised the Hilton flag, all guest rooms were treated to new furniture, bedspreads, carpets, bathroom floors—the works. The renovation of all public spaces, restaurants, bars, lobby, grand ballroom, pool, and gym, was in process at press time. The restaurants have always enjoyed a solid reputation. In the center of the Malecón action, at the casino, the usual drinks and cigarettes are on the house, and hostesses dish out a rich, flavorful soup to gamblers to keep up their strength. ✉ *Box 1493, Santo Domingo,* ☎ *809/686–6666 or 800/325–3535,* FAX *809/687–8150. 242 rooms, 16 suites. 3 restaurants, 3 bars, minibars, no-smoking rooms, pool, beauty salon, 2 tennis courts, health club, shops, casino, dance club, travel services. AE, DC, MC, V. EP, MAP, FAP.*

$$–$$$ 🏨 **Hotel Hispaniola.** Catering to a younger, fun crowd and lots of Italians, the hotel's Spanish-style lobby connects to an active casino filled with striking paintings, stained glass, and towering floral arrangements. Next is La Pizetta, one of the city's finest Italian gourmet rooms, festive in the colors of the Italian flag. Refurbished guest rooms are spacious and furnished mostly in chintz, wicker, and handcrafted Dominican pine. All have balconies, phones, and cable TV. The gracious staff deserves very high marks. Guests here have privileges at the Hotel Santo Domingo (☞ *below*) across the street. ✉ *Avs. Independencia and Abraham Lincoln, Box 2112, Santo Domingo,* ☎ *809/221–7111 or 800/877–3643,* FAX *809/535–4050. 165 rooms. 2 restaurants, bar, minibars, pool, casino, dance club, conference rooms. AE, MC, V. EP, MAP, FAP.*

$$–$$$ 🏨 **Hotel Santo Domingo.** Surrounded by walled gardens with 14 del-
★    icately manicured acres overlooking the Caribbean, this hotel is favored by businesspeople and diplomats. Many VIPs check into the Excel Club for extra perks. Dominican-born Oscar de la Renta helped design the interiors of the guest rooms, which have balconies. The elegant Alcázar restaurant, in de la Renta's romantic Moorish dining room, is open only on a limited basis. The regular merengue combo at dimly lit Las Palmas makes it a local favorite for music and dancing, but it is loud, especially considering the staid, gentile surroundings. It is the Marrakesh Café & Bar that has a loyal, sophisticated, and fun crowd, which makes it come alive during the week. The Casablanca-style decor complements the lobby with its red-enameled pagoda chairs and potted palms. Arched doors with mahogany louvers open to two courtyards that hold most facilities. A trellised arcade lined with potted plants leads to a delightful pool surrounded by greenery. ✉ *Avs. Independencia and Abraham Lincoln, Box 2112, Santo Domingo,* ☎ *809/221–7111 or 800/877–3643,* FAX *809/535–4050. 220 rooms. 3 restaurants, 2 bars, pool, beauty salon, sauna, 3 tennis courts, conference rooms, helipad. AE, MC, V. EP, MAP, FAP.*

$$  🏨 **Gran Hotel Lina and Casino.** The whitewashed, modern cinder-block structure of this hotel gives little hint of its stylish, exquisite interior, which gleams with marble floors, mirrored brass colonnades, and striking modern artwork. The rather plain rooms, mostly in dusky rose, are air-conditioned with double beds, mini-refrigerators, huge marble baths, and cable TVs and exude a staid, secure ambience. In the rear courtyard, the large, laned pool is complemented by a children's pool, whirlpool, and sauna set amid lovely palm-studded grounds, plus a gym and tennis court. The hotel staff is helpful and well trained to international standards by the owners, the Spanish Barcelo chain. ⊠ *Box 1915, Santo Domingo,* ☎ *809/563–5000 or 800/858–0606,* 𝔽𝔸𝕏 *809/686–5521. 214 rooms, 4 suites. Restaurant, coffee shop, piano bar, 2 pools, sauna, 2 tennis courts, health club, casino, nightclub. AE, DC, MC, V. EP, MAP, FAP.*

$$  🏨 **Hotel El Embajador and Casino.** At the grand front entrance, a bevy of multinational flags waves a welcome to this white, high-rise hotel. Although not as spectacular as it was in its prime, the newly refurbished lobby area with its Chippendale furniture and crystal chandeliers is still imposing, certainly by Dominican standards. Although the furnishings in the standard rooms, a variation of French provincial, are similar to those in the executive concierge floor, that level offers more perks and is the choice of business travelers with liberal expense accounts. The pool is open to the public and is a popular weekend gathering place for resident foreigners. The Jardin de Jade serves marvelous Chinese food, and the casino is also popular. While not on the Malécon, it's in a residential neighborhood close by and is quiet and safe. ⊠ *Av. Sarasota 65, Santo Domingo,* ☎ *809/221–2131 or 800/457–0067,* 𝔽𝔸𝕏 *809/532–4494. 304 rooms, 12 suites. 2 restaurants, 2 bars, minibars, pool, 4 tennis courts, shops, casino. AE, DC, MC, V. EP, MAP.*

$  **Hotel Palacio.** In the heart of the Colonial Zone, on Duarte Street, is this recently renovated, 18th-century former residence of ex-president Buenaventura Baez. It looks like a museum: Antique lights illuminate the bar, and the public spaces are enhanced with Spanish colonial antiques, reproductions, and enough artwork to give it a gallery effect. Six rooms have just been added and all have kitchenettes. They are tastefully decorated and retain a dignified charm. The sunroof is equipped with a gym and bubbling Jacuzzi, and there is a Spanish patio bar, but no restaurant. Businesspeople gravitate to this hotel, not only because it is unique and one of the least expensive, but also for its secretarial services—even Internet and professional guides. ⊠ *106 Calle Duarte, Zona Colonial,* ☎ *809/682–4730,* 𝔽𝔸𝕏 *809/687–5535. 16 rooms, 2 suites. Bar, in-room safes, minibars, hot tub, exercise room. AE, MC, V.*

## Dining

Most restaurants begin serving dinner around 6 PM, but the locals don't generally turn up until 9 or 10. There are Italian, Spanish, French, Chinese, and Japanese restaurants, and others serving traditional island fare. Dominicans have a love affair with Italian food, which is documented by the number of successful Italian restaurants listed below. Regrettably, many local restaurants in heavily touristed areas like the Amber Coast are closing, victims of the all-inclusive craze. Hotel restaurants uniformly range from fair to good; consult lodging listings for additional recommendations. Some favorite local dishes you should sample are paella, *sancocho* (a thick stew usually made with five different meats and served with rice and avocado slices), *arroz con pollo* (rice with chicken), *plátanos* (plantains) in all their tasty varieties, and *tortilla de jamón* (spicy ham omelet). Many meals are finished with *majarete,* a tasty cornmeal custard. Presidente, Bohemia, and Quisqueya are the local beers, Barceló (the *Anejo* or aged Barcelo is as smooth as cognac), Bermúdez, and Brugal the local rums. Wine is on the expensive side because it has to be imported. It also doesn't travel well, as it often gets exposed to tropical heat. Chilean wines are the exception to this and are what most resorts use for their house wine. Generally the reds are quite pleasing, the whites not necessarily so.

## What to Wear

In resort areas, shorts and beach wraps are acceptable at lunch; for dinner, especially at gourmet restaurants, long pants, skirts, and collared shirts are the norm. Dress tends to be more formal in Santo Domingo, both at lunch and dinner, with long pants required for men and dresses suggested for women. Ties are not required anywhere.

| CATEGORY | COST* |
| --- | --- |
| $$$ | over $30 |
| $$ | $20–$30 |
| $ | under $20 |

*per person for a three-course meal, excluding drinks, 10% service charge, and 13% sales tax*

## Boca Chica

**$-$$** ✕ **Neptuno's Club.** This breezy seaside eatery is little more than a shack perched above the water, seemingly held together by the barnacles of marine memorabilia. For the choicest table, reserve the one at the far end of the dock. Stay with the simple preparations of the fresh fish, like grilled sea bass and grouper; the lobster is always good. Sautéed squid comes sizzling to the table in a fry pan. True gourmet this isn't, but the lively crowd and gin-clear waters make it memorable. ⊠ *Boca Chica Beach,* ☎ *809/523–4703. MC, V. Closed Mon.*

## La Romana

**$$$** ✕ **Casa del Rio.** Look out over the virtual jungle on the banks of the
★ Rio Chavón while you dine in the ultraromantic, candlelit stone cellar of a 16th-century-style castle. The elegant decor is a mere backdrop for the imaginative creations put forth by chef Philippe Mongereau. One of the originators of neo-Caribbean cuisine, he couples classical French methodology with indigenous ingredients and culinary preparation. Signature dishes include lobster tail glazed with vanilla vinaigrette, and baked suckling pig wrapped in Chinese cabbage leaves with a honey and Thai curry sauce. Mongereau believes that vegetarians are not provided with enough choices during their travels and expands his menu to feature new items for them. ⊠ *Altos de Chavón,* ☎ *809/523–3333, ext. 2345. Reservations essential. Jacket required. AE, DC, MC, V. No lunch.*

## The Amber Coast

**$$-$$$** ✕ **La Puntilla de Piergiorgio.** Atop a cliff with a steep ocean drop, this haute Italian restaurant bills itself as "therapy to happiness" and it just might be. You're pampered by caring waiters, as you sit overlooking the precipice on wrough-iron chairs at round tables with pink and white linen. Cascades of pink bougainvillea rustle around you in the cooling sea breeze. The food is exceptional: You might start with escargot, then select from gnocci with a tomato-basil cream sauce, shrimp-laced fettucine, or a simple grilled lobster. Crepes Suzette is an elegant dessert. There are tall trees, mature gardens, and a covered bandstand and gazebo where live bands play and folklorico ballet is performed. Free transportation from area hotels brings you to the restaurant in festive, decorated horse-drawn wagons. ⊠ *Calle La Puntilla #1, El Batey, Sosua,* ☎ *809/571–2215. FAX 809/571–2786. AE, DC, MC, V.*

$$–$$$   ✕ **Marco Polo Club.** This seaside luxury apartment complex has two
fine restaurants (☞ *above*). *Ristorant Sabatini* is housed in an original Victorian open-air building with wooden decks that hang over the
sea. Potted palms and overhead fans add to the sultry, tropical ambience. One can find dishes from all parts of Italy, although Tuscany specialties are featured. Choose from the antipasto buffet, and then go to
a pasta like tortellini sabatini with fresh seafood in a cream sauce. When
reserving a waterfront table ask for number four, on the corner under
a three-sided gazebo. *L'Etoile d'Or* is an intimate, gourmet room enclosed by antique distressed-pine walls and pine and glass doors. Great
options include goat-cheese salad with apples, snapper in coconut
milk, and Chateaubriand with Roquefort and shallot sauces. ⊠ *Marco
Polo Club, Sosua,* ☎ *809/571–3128. AE, MC, V.*

$–$$   ✕ **Caribae.** Aquariums teeming with all kinds of sea creatures deco-
rate the dining room of this warm, unassuming spot. You can choose
your own lobster, shrimp, and oysters for the barbecue. Costs are
low, because the restaurant has its own shrimp farm and grows its own
100% organic vegetables. ⊠ *Camino Libre 70, Sosua,* ☎ *809/571–
3138. MC, V.*

$   ✕ **Guajiro's Caribbean Cafe.** Visit this casual Sosua eatery for some
of the best inventive local cuisine in the area. Try the green plantain
soup or *yuca* (an island tuber) in *mojo* (a lime, garlic, and olive oil marinade) to start, then *pollo à la merengue* (sweet and spicy coriander
chicken) or *filetillo saltado* (catch of the day, usually in *sofrito,* a savory sauce of garlic and green pepper rouged with tomato). For a filling meal, order the Cubano sandwich, bursting with roast pork, ham,
cheese, and pickles. Thatching, nautical paraphernalia dangling from
the rafters, rough-hewn wood tables and chairs, and traditional hats,
shirts, and machetes on the walls give the place a rustic country feel.
Latin jazz nights are scheduled regularly and draw a rollicking crowd.
⊠ *Calle Pedro Clisande, El Batey, Sosua,* ☎ *809/571–2161. Reservations not accepted. AE, MC, V.*

## Juan Dolio

$$–$$$   ✕ **L'Ecrevisse.** The intimate gourmet room of Talenquera Beach Re-
sort, L'Ecrevisse is one of the country's only strongholds of delicious,
innovative Caribbean cuisine. It is among the few restaurants in the
world to have earned two annual Awards of Excellence from *Wine Spectator* magazine for its wine list with some 475 selections. Select a California Conumdrum from Caymus, a 1986 Chevalier-Montrachet or
even a 1982 Mouton-Rothschild to complement your meal. Among
the excellent appetizers is the cold lobster with avocado and calypso
sauces. Mango sorbet with guavaberry sauce clears the palate for entrées like the fillet Sir Francis Drake—a perfect tenderloin wrapped
in filo leaves with a tangy tamarind sauce or a sea bass with shrimp,
fine herbs, and island fruits. Finish with a soufflé and one of the great
dessert wines of the world. Decor is formal and romantic, and service
is white glove, but overall the atmosphere is relaxed. ⊠ *Talanquera
Country & Beach Resort, Juan Dolio Beach,* ☎ *809/526–1510,*
FAX *809/541–1292. AE, DC, MC, V.*

## Samaná

$$   ✕ **Café de France.** Local aficionados swear the beef here is among the
best in the Dominican Republic—try the fillet in mushroom or pep-
percorn sauce. Seafood here is also dependable: One standout is shrimp
(or grouper) in garlic-coconut sauce. The small bistro is on the waterfront
and is simply decorated, with white stucco walls and red tablecloths.
An even more casual annex serves knockout pizzas. ⊠ *Malécon,
Samaná, no phone. MC, V.*

$$ ✕ **Villa Serena.** At the very end of the long road from Puerto Plata is
★ this lovely small hotel and restaurant. Located on the beach and the
Bahía del Rincón at the tiny village of Las Galeras, the restaurant is in
an open-air pavilion facing the trade winds. Specialties include fresh
fish caught by local fishermen and delicious homemade desserts. ✉ *Las
Galeras, Samaná,* ☏ *809/696–0065. MC, V.*

## Santo Domingo

$$$ ✕ **Pappalapasta.** Delicious Italian food and a location around the cor-
★ ner from the Presidential Palace make this eatery popular with politi-
cians, diplomats, and the businesspeople seeking their favor. A series
of intimate dining rooms are handsomely decorated with rattan and
polished hardwood furnishings, abstract artwork, richly colored Tiffany-
style lamps, and cut-glass windows. Start with a classic selection of antipasto—carpaccio, eggplant Parmesan, and tuna with capers. Pumpkin
ravioli in almond-amaretto butter and gnocchi al pesto are standouts
in the pasta selection. You may also opt for the sublime sea bass *à la
meunière* (breaded and topped with butter, parsley, and lemon juice)
or snapper *chiaro di mare* (with olives, capers, garlic, tomato, and peppers). The service, although attentive, is surprisingly leisurely; maybe
they're waiting discreetly for your deal to be consummated. ✉ *Dr. Baez
23,* ☏ *809/689–4849. Jacket required. AE, MC, V. Closed Mon.*

$$$ ✕ **Vesuvio.** Capital-city denizens flock to this superb Italian restaurant
★ and institution, where everything on the lengthy menu is either freshly
caught, homemade, or homegrown. Vesuvio has spent 40 years as the
best in its business, yet refuses to rest on its laurels. Part of the restau-
rant's appeal is the lively ambience created by well-heeled Dominican
families relishing their meal. Start with antipasti—kingfish carpaccio
dancing in zesty capers, onions, and basil-infused olive oil or *calamares
al vino blanco* (squid in white-wine sauce)—then segue into *scaloppina
al tarragon* (veal with tarragon). The pièce de résistance is the dessert
cart. (**Vesuvio II** is at ✉ Av. Tiradentes 17, ☏ 809/562–6060.) ✉ *Av.
George Washington 521,* ☏ *809/221–3333. Reservations not ac-
cepted. Jacket required. AE, DC, MC, V.*

$$–$$$ ✕ **La Briciola.** The owners of this upscale Milan restaurant did an ex-
emplary job of modernizing the interiors of these adjoining, 16th-
century colonial buildings while preserving their architectural integrity.
The arch-ceiling, stone-and-brick main dining room and more casual
piano bar overlook an interior courtyard whose trees are romantically
illuminated at night. A vocalist serenades. Cerise upholstery, mahogany
furnishings, wooden chandeliers, and Italian tile work create a warm
atmosphere. Excellent fresh pastas include velvety *gnocchi fume* (with
Scamorze cheese, ham, and cream). Meat dishes take a backseat to the
deftly prepared seafood, such as grouper al limone, but the lamb osso
buco is popular. Have the paternal owner, Franco Ricobono, help you
select from the extensive, all-Italian wine list. His son Alexandro can
help choose a *grappa* to complement the delicious tiramisu. ✉ *Calle
Arzobispo Merino 152-A at Padre Bellini,* ☏ *809/688–5055. Jacket
required. AE, DC, MC, V. Closed Sun.*

$$–$$$ ✕ **Lina.** Lina was the personal chef of Trujillo, and she taught her secret
★ recipes to the chefs of this stylish contemporary restaurant, still a favorite
of Santo Domingo movers and shakers. Brass columns, mirrored ceil-
ing, planters, Villeroy & Boch china, and a pianist tickling the ivories
set the elegant tone. The extensive menu favors Continental and haute
Dominican dishes. Paella is the best-known specialty, but other offer-
ings include filet mignon Roquefort, red snapper in coconut or almond
cheese sauce, and a casserole of mixed seafood flavored with Pernod. ✉
*Gran Hotel Lina, Av. Máximo Gómez at Av. 27 de Febrero,* ☏ *809/686–
5000. Reservations essential. Jacket required. AE, DC, MC, V.*

$$-$$$    ✕ **Spaghettissimo.** A relatively new star in the dining galaxy, it is one that deserves the word-of-mouth fame it is enjoying. Owner Frederic Gollong is a character and has genuine hospitality, dry wit, and European charm. The canopied entrance leads first to the bar and then to the antipasto bar and modern dining room with white napery. From the complementary tomato and basil *bruschetta* to delicacies like the meringue confection aptly named "The Cloud," the quality and freshness of the food are apparent. Savor Frederic's own smooth foie gras and the roasted red and yellow peppers in olive oil. For a pasta course, try a penne with artichokes, meaty mushrooms, and sun-dried tomatoes with olive oil. ✉ *13 Paseo de Los Locubres,* ☎ *809/565–3708 or 809/547–2650. AE, DC, MC, V.*

$$    ✕ **Don Pepe.** This may sound like a Mexican fast-food joint, but it was once the home of one of Santo Domingo's old families, the Guerreros. This fine Spanish restaurant with its pink stucco arched interiors still looks like an elegant residence. Demi-pillars, chandeliers, and European tiles add to the effect. The owner, Pepe (real name Jose Maria Diez), serves traditional Spanish fare, using high-quality ingredients. Soups are particularly flavorful, such as *sopa de ajo* (garlic soup) and black bean. For tapas (appetizers), order the octopus Gallega style. Poultry and game, like the rabbit in wine sauce, are good choices, as are the paella and *los mariscos* (shellfish). Finish with flan and a *teja,* a thin, dark cookie the shape of a roof tile. ✉ *Calle Santiago at Av. Pasteur,* ☎ *809/689–7612. AE, DC, MC, V.*

$$    ✕ **Fonda de la Atarazana.** Dinner and dancing on the brick patio of a 17th-century building in the Colonial Zone make for a very romantic evening. It is known more for its atmosphere than its food. ✉ *La Atarazana 5,* ☎ *809/689–2900. AE, MC, V.*

$$    ✕ **Mesón de la Cava.** The capital's most unusual restaurant (and a tourist trap) is more than 50 ft below ground in a natural cave complete with stalagmites and stalactites. You must descend a circular staircase, ducking rock protrusions, to dine on Continental standards like prime fillet with Dijon flambé, and tournedos Roquefort. Seafood preparations tend to be more adventurous, such as red snapper poached in white wine and served with coconut sauce, but the food takes a backseat to the spectacular setting. There is loud live music and dancing nightly until 1 AM, although sometimes you may wish a majestic silence to fall over the cathedralesque grotto. ✉ *Av. Mirador del Sur,* ☎ *809/533–2818. Reservations essential. Jacket required. AE, DC, MC, V.*

$$    ✕ **Restaurant Sully.** Sully (pronounced *sue*-lee) is the name of the owners of this Spanish-Dominican restaurant, run with great family pride. Patrons have confidence in the quality of the food and, notably, the freshness of the seafood: It's the big draw here, and tourists will take a 15-minute cab ride from the Malécon to sample it. Food is served steaming hot, from the Spanish bouillabaisse to mussels in a pureed marinara sauce. Several variations of paella are offered, from the traditional *Valenciana* to the more daring *Negra,* black from the ink of the squid. Lobster has 10 different preparations, with the *langosta en salsa verde* and the lobster in brandy sauce most popular. ✉ *19 Av. Charles Sumner, at Calle Las Caobas,* ☎ *809/682–2169,* ℻ *809/566–6405. AE, DC, MC, V.*

$    ✕ **El Conuco.** Conuco means countryside—and it's hard to believe that
★    this open-air thatched hut, alive with hanging plants, hibiscus, and frangipani and decorated with basketry, sombreros, license plates, and graffiti, is smack in the center of Santo Domingo. This is a superb place to sample typical Dominican cuisine, from *la bandera* (white rice, kidney beans, and stewed beef duplicating the colors of the flag) to a magnificent, delicately flaky *bacalao de la comai* (cod in white cream sauce with garlic and onions). The ambience is always celebratory; waiters

occasionally take to makeshift drum sets to accompany the merengue tapes. ⊠ *152 Casimiro de Moya,* ☎ *809/221–3231. MC, V.*

$ ✕ **La Bahía.** The catch of the day is always tops at this unpretentious spot. Try the kingfish in coconut sauce. The conch, which appears in a variety of dishes, is also good. For starters, try the *sopa palúdica,* a thick soup made with fish, shrimp, and lobster and served with tangy garlic bread. The decor strikes a nautical note, with fishing nets and seashells. ⊠ *Av. George Washington 1,* ☎ *809/682–4022. Reservations not accepted. AE, MC, V.*

$ ✕ **Ludovino's** and **Joaquin's.** Shacks and stands serving cheap eats for people on the run are a Dominican tradition, as much a part of the culture and landscape as the Colonial Zone. Two such shacks have become legends in Santo Domingo; both are in working-class districts outside the normal tourist loop. El Palacio de los Yaniqueques (everyone calls it Ludovino's after the nutty owner) is famed for its johnny-cakes—fried dough stuffed with everything from chicken to seafood. You pay the cashier when you order and get a free thimbleful of strong, sweet coffee while you wait for your food. Joaquin's serves up the best pork sandwich—laden with onions, tomatoes, pickles, and seasonings—in the Western world. The price for a filling meal? Two bucks at either. *Ludovino's:* ⊠ *19 Summer Wells, no phone. Joaquin's:* ⊠ *Av. Abraham Lincoln and Max Henríquex Ureña St., no phone.*

## Beaches

The Dominican Republic has more than 1,000 mi of beaches, including the Caribbean's longest strip of white sand—Punta Cana/Bavaro. Many beaches are accessible to the public and may tempt you to stop for a swim. Be careful: Some have dangerously strong currents.

**Boca Chica** is the beach closest to Santo Domingo (2 mi east of Las Américas Airport, 21 mi from the capital), and it's crowded with city folks on weekends. This beach was once a virtual four-lane highway of fine white sand. "Progress" has since cluttered it with plastic beach tables, chaise longues, pizza stands, and beach cottages for rent. But the sand is still fine, and you can walk far out into clear blue water, which is protected by natural coral reefs that help keep the big fish at bay. **Cabarete Beach,** on the north coast, has ideal wind and surf conditions that have made it an integral part of the international windsurfing circuit. **Juan Dolio** is a narrow beach of fine white sand about 20 minutes east of Boca Chica (☞ *above*). The Metro Hotel and Marina, the all-inclusive Decameron, Renaissance Capella, Talenquera Resort, and Punta Garza Beach Club are on this beach. **Luperón Beach,** about an hour west of Puerto Plata, is a wide white-sand beach fit for snorkeling, windsurfing, and scuba diving. The Luperón Beach Resort is handy for rentals and refreshments. **Playa Grande,** on the north coast, is a long stretch of powdery sand that is slated for development. The Playa Grande Hotel has already disturbed the solitude. With this exception, the entire northeast coast seems like one unbroken golden stretch, unmaintained and littered with kelp, driftwood, and the occasional beer bottle. If you don't mind the lack of facilities and upkeep, you have your pick of deserted beaches. **Puerto Plata,** still developing on the north Amber Coast, is about to outdo San Juan's famed Condado strip—especially the Playa Dorada area. The beaches are of soft beige or white sand, with lots of reefs for snorkeling. The Atlantic waters are great for windsurfing, waterskiing, and fishing expeditions. **Punta Cana,** the gem of the Caribbean, is a 20-mi strand of pearl-white sand shaded by trees and coconut palms. Located on the easternmost coast, it is the home of several top resorts. **La Romana** is the home of the 7,000-acre Casa de Campo resort, so you're not likely to find any private place in the sun here. The area is home to miniature **Minitas Beach** and lagoon, and the long, white-sand, palm-lined crescent of **Bayahibe Beach,** which is accessible only by boat. **Sosua** has a lovely beach where calm waters gently lap at long stretches of soft white sand. Unfortunately the backdrop here is a string of tents, with hawkers pushing cheap souvenirs. You can, however, get snacks and rent water-sports equipment from the vendors. **Las Terrenas,** on the north coast of the Samaná peninsula, looks like something from *Robinson Crusoe*: Tall palms list toward the sea, away from the mountains; the beach is narrow but sandy; and best of all, there is nothing man-made in sight—just vivid blues, greens, and yellows. Two adjacent hotels are right on the beach at nearby Punta Bonita.

## Outdoor Activities and Sports

Although there is hardly a shortage of outdoor activities here, the resorts have virtually cornered the market on sports, including every conceivable water sport. In some cases, facilities may be available only to guests. You can check with the tourist office for more details. Listed below is a mere smattering of the island's athletic options.

### Bicycling

Pedaling is easy on pancake-flat beaches, but there are also steep hills in the Dominican Republic. Bikes are available at **Dorado Naco** (⊠ Dorado Beach, ☎ 809/320–2019), **Jack Tar Village** (⊠ Puerto Plata, ☎ 809/586–3800), **Hotel Cofresi** (⊠ Puerto Plata, ☎ 809/586–2898), and **Villas Doradas** (⊠ Playa Dorada, Puerto Plata, ☎ 809/320–3000).

### Boating

Hobie Cats and pedal boats are available at **Heavens** (⊠ Playa Dorada, ☎ 809/586–5250). Check also at **Casa de Campo** (⊠ La Romana, ☎ 809/523–3333) and **Club Med** (⊠ Punta Cana, ☎ 809/567–5228).

### Deep-Sea Fishing

Marlin and wahoo are among the fish that folks angle for here. Arrangements can be made through **Casa de Campo** (⊠ La Romana, ☎ 809/523–3333) or **Actividas Acuaticás** (⊠ Playa Dorada, ☎ 809/586–3988). Fishing is best between January and June.

### Golf

**Casa de Campo** has two 18-hole Pete Dye courses that are open to the public and a third for the private use of villa owners. The **Bávaro Beach** resort complex shares an 18-hole course. The **Playa Dorada** hotels have their own 18-hole Robert Trent Jones–designed course; there is also a nine-hole course nearby at the **Costambar** complex. Guests in Santo Domingo hotels are usually allowed to use the 18-hole course at the **Santo Domingo Country Club** on weekdays—*after* members have teed off. There is a nine-hole course outside of town, at Lomas Lindas. A new Pete Dye course is at the **Metro Country Club,** east of Santo Domingo on the road to La Romana.

### Hiking

At 10,370 ft, **Pico Duarte** is the highest peak in the West Indies and a favorite for serious mountain climbers. Hire a guide in La Ciénaga, one hour and 8½ mi west of Jarabacoa, if you are prepared and equipped for an arduous 12-mi, two-day climb; you can also rent a mule there. The National Park Service (☎ 809/472–4204) can assist you with obtaining a guide.

### Horseback Riding

**Casa de Campo** (⊠ La Romana, ☎ 809/523–3333) has a dude ranch on its premises, saddled with 2,000 horses. You can even arrange for polo lessons (it's a major stop on the international circuit). In Puerto Plata, **Gran Chaparral** (☎ 809/320–4250) offers beach rides.

## Sailing

Sailboats are available at **Club Med** (Punta Cana) and **Casa de Campo** (La Romana).

## Scuba Diving

Ancient sunken galleons, undersea gardens, and offshore reefs are the lures here. For equipment and trips, contact **Dominican Adventures Dive Center** (⊠ Santo Domingo, ☎ 809/472–1718). Most resorts have dive shops on the premises or can arrange trips for you. Be sure to ask when making reservations.

## Spectator Sports

### BASEBALL

Baseball is the national pastime and passion. Major leaguers hone their skills in the Professional Winter League, which plays from late October through January. Call **Liga de Béisbol** (☎ 809/567–6371) for details on the five teams and their schedule of play. You can also consult newspaper listings, or your hotel can reserve tickets. You may not reach an English-speaking representative at Liga de Béisbol.

### HORSE RACING

There are races year-round at the **Hipódromo V Centenario.** ⊠ *Av. Las Américas, Santo Domingo,* ☎ *809/687–6060.* 🎫 *Free.* 🕙 *Daily 8 AM–2:45 PM.*

### POLO

The ponies pound down the field at **Sierra Prieta** (Santo Domingo) and at **Casa de Campo** (La Romana). The season runs from October through May. For information about polo games, call 809/565–6880.

## Tennis

There must be a million nets laced around the island, and most of them can be found at the large resorts.

## Windsurfing

Between June and October, **Cabarete Beach** offers what many consider to be optimal windsurfing conditions: wind speeds at 20–25 knots and 3- to 15-ft waves. The Professional Boardsurfers Association has included Cabarete Beach in its international windsurfing slalom competition. The novice is also welcome to learn and train on modified boards stabilized by flotation devices. **Carib BIC Center** (⊠ Cabarete Beach, ☎ 809/571–0640, FAX 809/571–0649) offers accommodations, equipment, and professional coaching and instruction.

# Shopping

The hot ticket in the Dominican Republic is amber jewelry. This island has the world's largest deposits of amber, and the prices here for the translucent, semiprecious stones, which range in color from pale lemon to dark brown, are unmatched. The most valuable stones are those in which tiny insects or small leaves are embedded. (Don't knock it till you've seen it.) When buying amber, beware of fakes, which are especially prevalent with street vendors. Visit a reputable dealer or store and ask how you can tell the difference between real amber and imitations.

The Dominican Republic is the homeland of designer Oscar de la Renta, and you may want to stop at some of the chic shops that carry his creations. In the crafts department, hand-carved wood rocking chairs are big sellers, and they are sold unassembled and boxed for easy transport. La Vega is famous for its *diablos cojuelos* (devil masks) and Santiago for its cigars, which rival the best Havanas. Look also for the delicate, ceramic lime figurines that symbolize the Dominican culture.

Bargaining is both a game and a social activity in the Dominican Republic, especially with street vendors and at the stalls in El Mercado Modelo. Vendors are disappointed and perplexed if you don't haggle. They also tend to be tenacious, so unless you really have an eye on buying, don't even stop to look.

## Shopping Districts

**El Mercado Modelo** in Santo Domingo is a covered market in the Colonial Zone bordering Calle Mella with a dizzying selection of Dominican crafts. The restored buildings of **La Atarazana** (⊠ Across from Alcázar in the Colonial Zone) are filled with shops, art galleries, restaurants, and bars. One of the main shopping streets in the Colonial Zone is **Calle El Conde,** which has been transformed into an exclusively pedestrian thoroughfare. **El Conde Gift Shop** (⊠ Calle El Conde 153, Santo Domingo, ☎ 809/682–5909) is the spot for exquisite mahogany carvings. Some of the best shops on **Calle Duarte,** a main shopping street in the Colonial Zone, are north of the Colonial Zone, between Calle Mella and Avenida de Las Américas. **Plaza Criolla** (⊠ Av. 27 de Febrero at Av. Anacaona) is filled with shops that sell everything from scents to nonsense.

Two major commercial malls in Santo Domingo are **Unicentro** (⊠ 406 Av. Abraham Lincoln) and **Plaza Central** (⊠ Avs. Bolívar and 27 de Febrero), which include such top boutiques as **Jenny Polanco, Nicole B,** and **Benetton,** which has a coffeehouse on its second level with rotating exhibits by up-and-coming young artists.

In Puerto Plata, the seven showrooms of the **Tourist Bazaar** (⊠ Calle Duarte 61) are in a wonderful old galleried mansion with a patio bar. Another cluster of shops is at the **Plaza Shopping Center** (⊠ Calle Duarte at Av. 30 de Marzo). A popular shopping street for jewelry and local souvenirs is **Calle Beller.**

In **Altos de Chavón,** art galleries and shops are grouped around the main square.

## Good Buys

AMBER

**Ambar Tres** (⊠ La Atarazana 3, Colonial Zone, Santo Domingo, ☎ 809/688–0474) carries a wide selection of the Dominican product.

DOMINICAN ART

In Santo Domingo, the **Arawak Gallery** (⊠ Av. Pasteur 104, ☎ 809/685–1661) specializes in pre-Columbian artifacts and contemporary pottery and paintings. **Galería de Arte Nader** (⊠ Hotel Nicolás Nader, Colonial Zone, ☎ 809/687–6674) showcases top Dominican artists in a variety of media. **Novo Atarazana** (⊠ Atarazana 21, ☎ 809/685–0582) has an assortment of local artwork.

In Puerta Plata, the **Collector's Corner Gallery and Gift Shop** (⊠ Plaza Shopping Center, Calle Duarte at Av. 30 de Marzo, no phone) offers a wide range of souvenirs, including amber.

In Santiago, try **Artesanía Lime** (⊠ Autopista Duarte, Km 2½, Santiago, ☎ 809/582–3754) for mahogany carvings as well as Carnival masks.

Check out the Dominican fashions at **Jenny Polanco's** boutiques in the Santo Domingo Hilton, formally the Sheraton (☎ 809/686–6666, ext. 2270), Plaza Central (☎ 809/541–5929), and the Paradise Beach Resort and Club in Playa Dorada (☎ 809/586–3663, ext. 314).

DUTY FREE
Duty-free shops selling liquors, cameras, and the like are at the **Centro de los Héroes** (⊠ Av. George Washington), the **Hotel El Embajador**, (☞ Lodging, *above*) and **Las Américas Airport.**

# Nightlife

Get a copy of the magazine *Vacation Guide* and the newspaper *Touring*, both of which are available free at the tourist office and at hotels, to find out what's happening around the island. Also look in the *Santo Domingo News* and the *Puerto Plata News* for listings of events. The monthly *Dominican Fiesta* also provides up-to-date information.

## Cafés

**Café Atlántico** (⊠ Av. J.A. Aybar 152, at Abraham Lincoln, ☎ 809/565–1841) is responsible for bringing happy hour and Tex-Mex cooking to the Dominican Republic. (Its sister restaurants of the same name are hot spots in Washington, DC, and Miami Beach.) Usually young, very lively, and very friendly, the late-afternoon yuppie crowd comes for the music, the food, the exotic drinks, and the energetic atmosphere. Mondays interestingly, and Fridays, are the best nights. **Museo del Jamón** (⊠ La Atarazana 9, ☎ 809/688–9644) is a casual boîte (with displays on curing ham, hence the name) that is popular Thursday and Sunday evenings after 10 for its folkloric dance shows, with the brilliantly lit Alcazar as a thrilling backdrop.

## Casinos

Gambling is a leisure activity that is offered, but it is a sideline rather than the raison d'être as in, say, Las Vegas. Most of the casinos are concentrated in the larger hotels of Santo Domingo, but there are others here and there, and all offer blackjack, craps, and roulette. Casinos are open daily 3 PM–4 AM. You must be 18 to enter, and jackets are required. In Santo Domingo, the most popular casinos are in the **Embajador** (⊠ Av. Sarasota, ☎ 809/533–2131), the **Gran Hotel Lina** (⊠ Av. Máximo Gómez, ☎ 809/563–5000), the **Hispaniola** (⊠ Av. Independencia, ☎ 809/221–7111), and the **Jaragua** (⊠ Av. Independencia, ☎ 809/686–2222).

## Clubs and Discos

You'll soon discover that there is no such thing as last call in the Dominican Republic. Customers usually decide when closing time will be.

**La Aurora** (⊠ Av. Hermanos Deligne, ☎ 809/685–6590) is where the capitaleños go when all the partying is over. This lush after-hours supper club is set in a rustic garden. Savor typical dishes, even sancocho, at 4 in the morning. Here you'll see not only party goers but also the musicians who entertained them. It's a spot of preference for Santo Domingo's hottest band, 4:40. **Bachata Rosa** (⊠ Colonial Zone, 9 La Atarazana, ☎ 809/688–0969 or 809/682–7726), named after a popular song by the Dominican merengue megastar Juan Luis Guerra (he is part-owner), is the "in" disco for capitaleños. There's live music on many nights. **Disco Free** (☎ Av. Ortega y Gaset, ☎ 809/565–8100) is Santo Domingo's gay club. The music is a mix of merengue, salsa, and New York house. Tables and a balcony surround the dance floor. It's open Thursday to Sunday. **Guácara Taína** (⊠ 655 Rómulo Betancourt Ave., ☎ 809/530–2666), a cultural center–disco set in a cave, hosts folkloric dances during the early evening and transforms into one of the city's hottest nightspots later on. The world's only disco grotto, it boasts two dance floors, three bars, and lots of nooks and crannies. **Las Palmas** (⊠ Hotel Santo Domingo, Avs. Independencia and Abraham Lincoln, ☎ 809/221–7111) has a happy hour from 6 to 8 PM.

Happy hours are joyous indeed at Santo Domingo's top hotels, thanks to two-for-one drinks and energetic bands. This one's a favorite of residents for its performances by local merengue bands. **Pyramide** (⊠ Corner of Avs. Pedro Clisante and Dr. Rosen, Sosua, no phone), in the heart of El Batey, is a disco with the best sound and lights in town. **Tops** (⊠ Plaza Hotel, Av. Tiradentes, ☎ 809/541–6226), the most appealing dance club in Puerto Plata, is on the 12th floor of the Plaza Hotel and has a great view. The multilevel, mirrored, and metal space also hosts a variety of special events, from lingerie fashion shows to the latest bands.

Nearly every hotel in Puerto Plata has a disco and frequent live entertainment. **Crazy Moon** (⊠ Paradise Beach Resort and Club, ☎ 809/320–3663) is a lively disco where Latin music is mixed with American and Euro dance tunes. **Andromeda** (⊠ Heavens, ☎ 809/586–5250) is a dance club and video bar that gets going late (after 1 AM).

# Exploring the Dominican Republic

## Santo Domingo

Spanish civilization in the New World began in the 12-block area of Santo Domingo called the Colonial Zone. This historical area is now a bustling, noisy district with narrow cobbled streets, shops, restaurants, and residents. It is easy to imagine this old city as it was when the likes of Columbus, Cortés, Ponce de León, and pirates sailed in and out and colonists were settling themselves in the New World. Tourist brochures boast that "history comes alive here"—a surprisingly truthful statement.

A quick taxi tour of the old section takes about an hour, but if you're interested in history, you'll want to spend a day or two exploring the many old "firsts," and you'll want to do it in the most comfortable shoes you own. Wearing shorts, miniskirts, and halter tops in churches is considered inappropriate. Men in Santo Domingo never wear shorts. (Note: Hours and admission charges are erratic).

Parque Independencia separates the old city from the new. Avenidas 30 de Marzo, Bolívar, and Independencia traverse the park and mingle with avenues named for George Washington, John F. Kennedy, and Abraham Lincoln. Modern Santo Domingo is a sprawling, noisy city with a population of close to 2 million.

*Numbers in the margin correspond to points of interest on the Santo Domingo map.*

SIGHTS TO SEE

**㉕ Acuario Nacional.** The largest aquarium in the Caribbean has an impressive collection of tropical fish and dolphins, though its construction was a controversial public expenditure. ⊠ *In Sans Souci district on Av. de las Américas*, ☎ 809/592–1509. ⊡ *Free.* ☉ *Weekdays 8–5, Sat. 8–4, Sun. 9–12:30.*

**Agua Splash Caribe.** This aquapark across from the aquarium (☞ *above*) features the usual water slides, "river rapids," and wave pools. A schedule of spectacular water revues is planned for the evenings. ⊠ *Av. España*, ☎ 809/591–5927. ⊡ *RD$50 Tues.–Fri., RD$80 weekends.* ☉ *Tues.–Sun. 10–7.*

**❺ Alcázar de Colón.** The castle of Don Diego Colón, built in 1514, was painstakingly reconstructed and restored in 1957. Forty-inch-thick coral limestone walls were patched and shored with blocks from the original quarry. The Renaissance structure, with its balustrade and double row of arches, has strong Moorish, Gothic, and Isabelline influ-

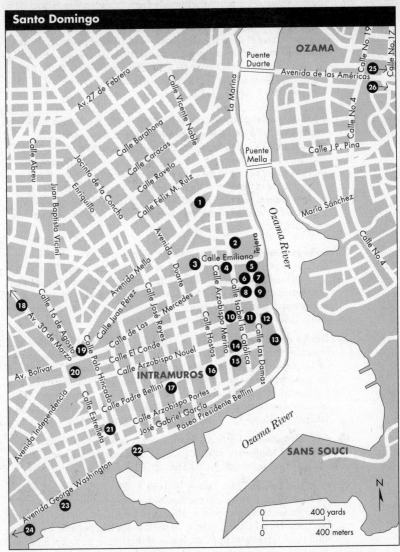

# Santo Domingo

ences. There are 22 rooms, furnished in a style to which the viceroy of the island would have been accustomed—right down to the dishes and the viceregal shaving mug. Many of the period paintings, statues, tapestries, and furnishings were donated by the University of Madrid. ✉ *On Plaza de España (just off Calle Emiliano Tejera at the foot of Calle Las Damas),* ☎ *809/687–5361.* 🎫 *RD$10.* ☉ *Mon. and Wed.–Fri. 9–5, Sat. 9–4, Sun. 9–1.*

NEED A BREAK? If you wind up near La Atarazana by midday, join the Reserve Bank and Telecom staff at the **Café Montesinos** (✉ Calle La Atarazana 23, ☎ 809/689–0580) for a typical Dominican noonday meal. For RD$90 you can try fish or beef in a succulent Creole sauce, a tasty bean soup with plantains, or one of the other hearty dishes on the menu. If you happen to be in the area in the late afternoon, stop in for a pizza and a drink at **Drake's Pub** (✉ Calle La Atarazana 25, ☎ 809/687–8089). There's a fine view of the Alcázar from here, and the place fills up with congenial locals and foreigners.

**⓫ Calle Las Damas.** The New World's oldest street, the "Street of the Ladies" was named after the elegant ladies of the court who, in the Spanish tradition, promenaded in the evening. Here you'll see a sundial dating from 1753 and the **Casa de los Jesuitas,** which houses a fine research library for colonial history as well as the Institute for Hispanic Culture. 🎫 *Free.* ☉ *Weekdays 8–4:30.*

**❼ Capilla de los Remedios.** The Chapel of Our Lady of Remedies was originally built in the 17th century as a private chapel for the family of Francisco de Dávila. Early colonists also worshiped here before the completion of the cathedral. Its architectural details, particularly the lateral arches, are evocative of the Castilian Romanesque style. ✉ *Calle Las Damas, at the foot of Calle de Las Mercedes, no phone.* 🎫 *Free.* ☉ *Mon.–Sat. 9–6; Sun. masses begin at 6 AM.*

**⓬ Casa de Bastidas.** There is a lovely inner courtyard here with tropical plants and temporary exhibit galleries. ✉ *Calle Las Damas, just off Calle El Conde, no phone.* 🎫 *Free.* ☉ *Tues.–Sun. 9–5.*

**❹ Casa del Cordón.** This house, built in 1503, is the Western Hemisphere's oldest surviving stone house. It's recognizable by the sash of the Franciscan order carved in stone over the arched entrance. Columbus's son Diego Colón, viceroy of the colony, and his wife lived here until the Alcázar was finished. It was in this house, too, that Sir Francis Drake was paid a ransom to prevent him from totally destroying the city. ✉ *Corner of Calle Emiliano Tejera and Calle Isabel la Católica, no phone.* 🎫 *Free.* ☉ *Weekdays 8:30–4:30.*

**⓯ Casa de Tostado.** The house was built in the first decade of the 16th century and was the residence of writer Don Francisco Tostado. Its twin Gothic windows are the only ones that are still in existence in the New World. It now houses the **Museo de la Familia Dominicana** (Museum of the Dominican Family), which features exhibits on the wellheeled Dominican family in the 19th century. ✉ *Calle Padre Bellini, near Calle Arzobispo Meriño,* ☎ *809/689–5057.* 🎫 *RD$10.* ☉ *Thurs.–Tues. 9–2.*

**⓮ Catedral Santa María la Menor.** The coral limestone facade of the first cathedral in the New World towers over the south side of the Parque Colón (☞ *below*). Spanish workmen began building the cathedral in 1514 but left off construction to search for gold in Mexico. The church was finally finished in 1540. Its facade is composed of architectural elements from the late Gothic to the plateresque style. Inside, the high altar is made of beaten silver, and in the treasury there is a magnificent collection of gold and silver. Some of its 14 lateral chapels serve as mausoleums for noted Dominicans, including Archbishop Meriño, who was once president of the Dominican Republic. Of interest is the Chapel of Our Lady of Antigua, which was reconsecrated by John Paul II in 1984. In the nave are four Baroque columns, carved to resemble royal palms, which for more than four centuries guarded the magnificent bronze and marble sarcophagus containing (say Dominican historians) the remains of Christopher Columbus, whose last wish was to be buried in Santo Domingo. The sarcophagus was most recently moved to the Columbus Memorial Lighthouse—only the latest in the Great Navigator's posthumous journeys. ⊠ *Calle Arzobispo Meriño,* ☎ *809/689–1920.* ▨ *Free.* ☉ *Mon.–Sat. 9–4; Sun. masses begin at* 6 AM.

**⑲ Concepción Fortress.** Within the old city walls, this fortress was the northwest defense post of the colony. ⊠ *Calle Palo Hincado at Calle Isidro Duarte, no phone.* ▨ *Free.* ☉ *Tues.–Sun. 9–6.*

**㊀ ㉖ El Faro a Colón** (Columbus Memorial Lighthouse). This striking—if not exactly architecturally significant—lighthouse monument and museum dedicated to the Great Navigator is shaped like a pyramid cross (although from ground level it looks like a giant concrete casket). The lighthouse complex was completed in 1992, its inauguration coinciding with the 500th anniversary of Christopher Columbus's landing on the island. Along with its showpiece laser-powered lighthouse, the complex holds the tomb of Columbus (moved there after 400 years in the Catedral Santa María la Menor; ☞ *above*) and six museums featuring exhibits related to Columbus and early exploration of the New World. One museum focuses on the long, rocky, and often controversial history of the lighthouse memorial itself and another on the Great Navigator's posthumous peregrinations (Cuba, Spain, and the Dominican Republic have all laid claim to—and hosted—his remains, which even today are a subject of controversy). ⊠ *Av. España,* ☎ *809/591–1492.* ▨ *RD$10.* ☉ *Tues.–Sun. 10–5.*

**⑨ Hostal Palacio Nicolás de Ovando.** This was once the residence of Nicolás de Ovando, one of the principal organizers of the colonial city. It was transformed into a hotel, which has since closed. ⊠ *Calle Las Damas 44,* ☎ *809/687–3101.*

**⑯ Iglesia y Convento Dominico.** This graceful building with the rose window is the Dominican Church and Convent, founded in 1510. In 1538 Pope Paul III visited here and was so impressed with the lectures on theology that he granted the church and convent the title of university, making it the oldest institution of higher learning in the New World. ⊠ *Calle Padre Bellini and Av. Duarte,* ☎ *809/682–3780.* ▨ *Free.* ☉ *Tues.–Sun. 9–6.*

**⑱ Jardín Botánico Nacional Dr. Rafael M. Moscoso.** The Dr. Rafael M. Moscoso National Botanical Garden, the largest garden in the Caribbean, is north of town in the Arroyo Hondo district. Its 445 acres include a Japanese garden, a great ravine, a glen, a gorgeous display of orchids, and an enormous floral clock. You can tour the gardens by train, boat, or horse-drawn carriage. ⊠ *Av. República de Colombia at Av. de los Proceres,* ☎ *809/687–6211.* ▨ *RD$10.* ☉ *Tues.–Sun. 9–5.*

**㊀** In the 320-acre **Parque Zoológico Nacional** (National Zoological Park), not far from the botanical gardens, animals roam free in natural habitats. There is an African plain, a children's zoo, and what the zoo claims is the world's largest birdcage. ⊠ *Av. Máximo Gómez at Av. de los Proceres,* ☎ *809/562–2080.* ▨ *RD$5.* ☉ *Tues.–Sun. 9–6.*

**2  La Atarazana.** The Royal Mooring Docks was once the colonial commercial district, where naval supplies were stored. There are eight restored buildings, the oldest of which dates from 1507. It now houses crafts shops, restaurants, and art galleries. ⊠ *Calle La Atarazana.*

**17  La Iglesia de Regina Angelorum.** The Church of Regina Angelorum dates from 1537. The church was damaged during the Haitian regime, from 1822 to 1844, but you can still appreciate its Baroque dome, Gothic arches, and traceries. ⊠ *Corner of Calle Padre Bellini and Calle José Reyes,* ☎ *809/682–2783.* ☜ *Free.* ☉ *Mon.–Sat. 9–6.*

**23  Malecón.** Avenida George Washington, which is lined with tall palms and Las Vegas–style tourist hotels, breezes along the Caribbean Sea. The Parque Litoral de Sur, better known as the Malecón, borders the avenue from the colonial city to the Hotel Santo Domingo, a distance of about 3 mi. The seaside park, with its cafés and places to relax, is a popular spot, but beware of pickpockets.

**22  Montesina.** One of the first things you'll see as you approach the Colonial Zone is this statue, only slightly smaller than the Colossus of Rhodes, staring out over the Caribbean Sea. Montesina was the Spanish priest who came to the Dominican Republic in the 16th century to appeal for human rights for Indians.

**6  Museo de las Casas Reales.** The Museum of the Royal Houses has collections displayed in two early 16th-century palaces that have been altered many times over the years. Exhibits cover everything from antique coins to replicas of the *Niña,* the *Pinta,* and the *Santa María.* There are statue and cartography galleries, coats of armor and coats of arms, coaches and a royal court room, gilded furnishings, and Indian artifacts. The first room of the former Governor's Residence has a wall-size map marking the routes sailed by Columbus's ships on expeditions beginning in 1492. ⊠ *Calle Las Damas at Calle de Las Mercedes,* ☎ *809/682–4202.* ☜ *RD$10.* ☉ *Tues.–Sat. 9–4:45, Sun. 10–1.*

**8  National Pantheon.** The building, which dates from 1714, was once a Jesuit monastery and later a theater. Trujillo had it restored in 1955 with an eye toward being buried there. (He is buried instead at Père Lachaise in Paris.) An allegorical mural of his assassination is painted on the ceiling above the altar, where an eternal flame burns. The impressive chandelier was a gift from Spain's Generalissimo Franco. ⊠ *Calle Las Damas, near corner of Calle de Las Mercedes, no phone.* ☜ *Free.* ☉ *Mon.–Sat. 10–5.*

**10  Parque Colón.** The huge statue of Columbus here dates from 1897 and is the work of French sculptor Gilbert. On the west side of the square is the **old town hall** and, on the east, the **Palacio de Borgella,** residence of the governor during the Haitian occupation of 1822–44 and presently the seat of the Permanent Dominican Commission for the **Fifth Centennial of the Discovery and Evangelization of the Americas.** Gallery spaces house architectural and archaeological exhibits pertaining to the fifth centennial.

**20  Parque Independencia.** Independence Park, on the far western border of the Colonial Zone, is a big city park dominated by the marble and concrete **Altar de la Patria.** The impressive mausoleum was built in 1976 to honor the founding fathers of the country (Duarte, Sánchez, and Mella).

**24  Plaza de la Cultura.** Landscaped lawns, modern sculptures, and sleek buildings make up the Plaza de la Cultura. Among the buildings are the **National Theater** (☎ 809/687–3191), which stages performances in Spanish; the **National Library** (☎ 809/688–4086), in which the written word is Spanish; and museums and art galleries, whose notations are also in Spanish. The **Museum of Dominican Man** (☎ 809/687–3623) traces the migrations of Indians from South America through the Caribbean islands. The **Museum of Natural History** (☎ 809/689–0106) examines the flora and fauna of the island. In the **Gallery of Modern Art** (☎ 809/682–8260), the works of 20th-century Dominican and foreign artists are displayed. ✉ *Museums RD$10 each.* ⊙ *Tues.–Sat. 10–5.*

㉑ **Puerta de la Misericordia.** The "Gate of Mercy" is part of the old wall of Santo Domingo. It was here on the plaza, on February 27, 1844, that Ramón Mata Mella, one of the country's founding fathers, fired the shot that began the struggle for independence from Haiti. ✉ *Calle Palo Hincado at Calle Arzobispo Portes.*

❸ **San Francisco Monastery.** Constructed between 1512 and 1544, the monastery contained the church, chapel, and convent of the Franciscan order. Sir Francis Drake's demolition squad significantly damaged the building in 1586, and in 1673 an earthquake nearly finished the job, but when it's floodlit at night, the majestic ruins are indeed dramatic. ✉ *Calle Hostos at Calle Emiliano.*

❶ **Santa Bárbara Church.** This combination church and fortress, the only one of its kind in Santo Domingo, was completed in 1562. ✉ *Av. Mella, between Calle Isabel la Católica and Calle Arzobispo Meriño, no phone.* ✉ *Free.* ⊙ *Weekdays 8–noon; Sun. masses begin at 6 AM.*

⓭ **Torre del Homenaje.** You won't have any trouble spotting the Tower of Homage in the Fort Ozama. The fort sprawls two blocks south of the Casa de Bastidas, with a brooding crenellated tower that still guards the Ozama River. Built in 1503 to protect the eastern border of the city, the sinister tower was the last home of many a condemned prisoner. ✉ *Paseo Presidente Bellini, overlooking Río Ozama, no phone.* ✉ *RD$10.* ⊙ *Tues.–Sun. 8–7.*

## The East Coast

Las Américas Highway (built by the dictator Trujillo as a place for his son to race his sports cars) runs east along the coast from Santo Domingo to La Romana—about a two-hour drive. All along the highway are small resort-hotel complexes where you can find refreshments or stay overnight.

East of La Romana are Punta Cana and Bavaro, glorious beaches on the sunrise side of the island. Along the way is Higüey, an undistinguished collection of ramshackle buildings notable only for its controversial church and shrine (someone apparently had a vision of the Virgin Mary), consecrated by Pope John Paul II in 1984, which resembles a pinched, concrete McDonald's arch.

*Numbers in the margin correspond to points of interest on the Dominican Republic map.*

SIGHTS TO SEE

㉘ **Altos de Chavón.** Cattle and sugarcane used to be the two big mainstays around La Romana. That was before Gulf & Western created (and subsequently sold) the Casa de Campo resort, which is a very big business, indeed, and Altos de Chavón, a re-creation of a 16th-century Mediterranean village and art colony on the resort grounds. It sits on a bluff overlooking the Río Chavón, about 3 mi east of the main facility of Casa de Campo. You can drive there easily enough, or you can take one of the free shuttle buses. There are cobblestone streets lined with lanterns, wrought-iron balconies and wooden shutters, and courtyards swathed with bougainvillea. More than a museum piece, this village is a place where artists live, work, and play. There is an art school, affiliated with New York's Parsons School of Design; a disco; an archaeological museum; five restaurants; and a 5,000-seat outdoor amphitheater where Frank Sinatra and Julio Iglesias have entertained. The focal point of the village is **Iglesia St. Stanislaus,** which is named after the patron saint of Poland in tribute to the Polish pope John Paul II, who visited the Dominican Republic in 1979 and left some of the ashes of St. Stanislaus behind.

**Boca Chica Beach.** About 20 minutes east of Santo Domingo, this beach is popular because of its proximity to the capital; it's absolutely mobbed on weekends.

**㉗ Isla Saona.** Just off the east coast of Hispaniola lies this island, now a national park inhabited by sea turtles, pigeons, and other wildlife. Caves on the island were once used by Indians. The beaches are beautiful, and legend has it that Columbus once strayed ashore here.

**㉚ Parque de los Tres Ojos.** About 1½ mi outside the capital is the Park of the Three Eyes. The "eyes" are cool blue pools peering out of deep limestone caves, and it's actually a four-eyed park. If you've a mind to, you can look into the eyes more closely by climbing down into the caves.

**㉙ San Pedro de Macorís.** The national sport and the national drink are both well represented in this city, an hour or so east of Santo Domingo. Some of the country's best *béisbol* games are played in **Tetelo Vargas Stadium.** Many major-league players in the States have roots here. The grander homes in the area most likely belong to Dominican baseball stars like George Bell. The **Macorís Rum distillery** is on the eastern edge of the city. Outside town is **Juan Dolio,** a beach and resort area popular with *capitaleños* and German tourists.

## The Southwest

**㉛ Barahona.** The latest area to be developed in the Dominican Republic is still wild and pristine. Here mountains carpeted with emerald rain forests and laced with silvery streams slope down into sugary white stretches of sand. One can bathe in the cascades of icy mountain rivers or in hot thermal springs surrounded by dense foliage, llanai vines, and fruit trees. Barahona is a tropical Garden of Eden. Be tempted to come while you and yours can still have it all to yourself.

**㉜ Lago Enriquillo.** The largest lake in the Antilles is near the Haitian border. The salt lake is also the lowest point in the Antilles: 114 ft below sea level. It encircles wild, arid, and thorny islands that serve as sanctuary to such exotic birds and reptiles as the flamingo, the iguana, and the caiman—the indigenous crocodile.

## The Cibao Valley

The heavily trafficked road north from Santo Domingo, known as the Autopista Duarte (slated to be opened as a four-lane divided highway in 1998), cuts through the lush banana plantations, rice and tobacco fields, and royal poinciana trees of the Cibao Valley. All along the road there are stands where, for a few centavos, you can buy ripe pineapples, mangoes, avocados, chicharrones (either fried pork rinds or chicken pieces), and fresh fruit drinks.

**㉝ Jarabacoa.** Nature lovers should consider a trip to Jarabacoa, in the mountainous region known rather wistfully as the Dominican Alps. There is little to do in the town itself but eat and rest up for excursions on foot, horseback, or by motorbike taxi to the surrounding waterfalls and forests—quite incongruous in such a tropical country. Accommodations in the area are rustic but comfortable. Recommended are **Alpes Dominicanos** (☎ 809/581–1462), which offers both hotel rooms with kitchenettes and individual self-service cottages, and the hacienda-style motel **Pinar Dorado** (☎ 809/574–2820).

**㉞ La Vega Vieja.** In the heart of the Cibao is La Vega. Founded in 1495 by Columbus, it is the site of one of the oldest settlements in the New World. The inquisitive will find the tour of the ruins of the original settlement, the Old La Vega, a rewarding experience. About 3 mi north of La Vega is **Santo Cerro** (Holy Mount), site of a miraculous apparition of the Virgin and therefore many local pilgrimages. The **Convent of La Merced** is there, and the views of the Cibao Valley are breathtaking. The new town boasts a remarkable church of its own, **Concepcíon de la Vega**, constructed in 1992 to commemorate the 500th anniversary of the discovery (and evangelization) of America. The unusual modern Gothic style—all curvaceous concrete columns, arches, and buttresses—is striking indeed.

La Vega is also celebrated for its Carnival, featuring the haunting, disturbing devil masks. These papier-mâché creations are incredibly intricate, fanciful gargoyle demons painted in surreal colors with spiked horns and real cow's teeth contributing eerie authenticity. The skill is usually passed down for generations; several artisans work in dark, cramped studios throughout the area. The studio closest to downtown is that of José Luis Gomez. Ask any local (tip 10–20 pesos) to guide you to his atelier (no phone). José speaks no English but will show you the stages of mask development. He sells the masks, which make extraordinary wall hangings, for US$50–$60, a great buy considering the craftsmanship.

**㉟ Santiago de los Caballeros.** The second city of the Dominican Republic, where many past presidents were born, sits about 90 mi northwest of Santo Domingo. It is an industrial center with a charming provincial ambience. A massive monument honoring the restoration of the republic guards the entrance to the city. Traditional yet progressive, Santiago is relatively new to the tourist scene but, time allowing, set aside a day or two to explore this city, which dates back to the 1500s. Architecturally diverse, there are colonial-style buildings with wrought-iron details and tiled porticos, plus many homes reflecting a Victorian influence with the requisite gingerbread latticework and fanciful colors. Santiago is a center for processing tobacco leaf. You can gain an appreciation of the art and skill of Dominican (similar to Cuban) cigar making with a colorful tour of **E. Leon Jiménez Tabacalera** (☎ 809/563–1111 or 809/535–5555). The best hotel in town is the **Gran Almirante** (☎ 809/580–1992).

## The Amber Coast

The Autopista Duarte ultimately leads (in three to four hours from Santo Domingo) to the Amber Coast, so called because of its large, rich, and unique deposits of amber. The coastal area around Puerto Plata is a region of splashy resorts and megadevelopments like Costambar and Playa Dorada. The north coast boasts more than 70 mi of beaches, with condominiums and villas going up fast. The farther east from Puerto Plata and Sosua you get, the prettier and less spoiled the scenery becomes. The Autopista runs past Cabarete, a neat little village that's a popular windsurfing haunt, and Playa Grande. The powdery white-sand beach remains miraculously undisturbed and unspoiled by development.

SIGHTS TO SEE

**㊳ Laguna Grí-Grí.** This swampland, smack out of the Louisiana bayou country, has the added attraction of a cool blue grotto that almost outdoes the Blue Grotto of Capri. Laguna Grí-Grí is only about 90 minutes west of Puerto Plata, in Río San Juan (ask your hotel concierge for directions off the Autopista).

**36** **Mt. Isabel de Torres.** Southwest of Puerto Plata, this mountain soars 2,600 ft above sea level. On the mountain there is a botanical garden, a huge statue of Christ, and a spectacular view. You can take a cable car to the top (although it is occasionally out of service). The cable was first laid in 1754, but rest assured that it's been replaced since then. Lines can be long, and once on top of the mountain, you will wonder if it was worth the time. Don't eat at the restaurant—the food is awful. ⊠ *Follow signs from the Autopista, no phone.* ⊟ *RD$20 round-trip.* ⊙ *Cable car operates Tues. and Thurs.–Sun. 8–6.*

**37** **Puerto Plata.** Although now quiet and almost sleepy, this was a dynamic city in its heyday. You can get a feeling for this past in the magnificent Victorian **Glorieta** (Gazebo) in the central **Parque Independencia.** Next to the park, the **Catedral de San Felipe** recalls a simpler, colonial past. On Puerto Plata's own Malecón, the **Fortaleza de San Felipe** protected the city from many a pirate attack and was later used as a political prison. The fort is most dramatic at night.

Puerto Plata is also the home of the **Museum of Dominican Amber,** a lovely galleried mansion and one of several tenants in the Tourist Bazaar. The museum displays and sells the Dominican Republic's national stone. Semiprecious, translucent amber is actually fossilized pine resin that dates back about 50 million years, give or take a few millennia. The north coast of the Dominican Republic has the largest deposits of amber in the world (the only other deposits are found in Germany and the former USSR). ⊠ *Calle Duarte 61,* ☎ *809/586–2848.* ⊟ *RD$15.* ⊙ *Mon.–Sat. 9–5.*

**40** **Samaná.** Back in 1824, a sailing vessel called the *Turtle Dove,* carrying several hundred escaped American slaves from the Freeman Sisters' underground railway, was blown ashore in Samaná. The escapees settled and prospered, and today their descendants number several thousand. The churches here are Protestant; the worshipers live in villages called Bethesda, Northeast, and Philadelphia; and the language spoken is an odd 19th-century form of English—although you're more likely to hear Spanish.

The wealth of marine life in the surrounding waters is beginning to attract more specialty tourists. Sportfishing at Samaná is considered to be among the best in the world. In addition, about 3,000 humpback whales winter off the coast of Samaná from December to March. Major whale-watching expeditions like those out of Massachusetts are being organized and should boost the region's economy without scaring away the world's largest mammals.

Samaná makes a fine base for exploring the area's natural splendors. Most hotels on the peninsula arrange tours to **Los Haitises National Park,** a remote, unspoiled rain forest with limestone knolls, crystal lakes, mangrove swamps teeming with aquatic birds, and caves stippled with Taino petroglyphs. **Las Terrenas,** a remote stretch of beautiful, nearly deserted beaches on the north coast of the Samaná peninsula, is barely known to North American tourists, although French Canadians and Europeans, especially Germans, have begun making the long trek to this latter-day hippie haven, which also attracts surfers and windsurfers. There are several modest seafood restaurants (the best is **Boca Fina,** no phone), a dusty main street in the town of Las Terrenas, a small airfield, the comparatively grand all-inclusive **El Portillo Beach Club** (☎ 809/688–5785), and several congenial hotels right on the beach at Punta Bonita. If you're seeking tranquillity and are happy just hanging out drinking beer and soaking up the sun, this is the place for you. The road from Samaná, even though it is longer and not paved, is a lot less strenuous than the route over the hills from Sanchez.

**38**   **Sosua.** This small community was settled during World War II by 600 Austrian and German Jews. After the war, many of them returned to Europe or went to the United States, and most of those who remained married Dominicans. Only a few Jewish families reside in the community today, and there is only one small one-room synagogue. The flavor of the town is decidedly Spanish. (Note: The roads off the Autopista are horribly punctured with potholes and ruts. The city has been laying down water mains, and road repair may happen sometime before the end of the century.)

Sosua has become one of the most frequently visited tourist destinations in the country, favored by French Canadians and Europeans. Hotels and condos are going up at breakneck speed. It actually consists of two communities, **El Batey**, the modern hotel development, and **Los Charamicos**, the old quarter, separated by a cove and one of the island's prettiest beaches. The sand is soft and white; the water, crystal clear and calm. The walkway above the beach is packed with tents filled with souvenirs, pizzas, and even clothing for sale—a jarring note in this otherwise idyllic setting.

NEED A BREAK?     **P.J.'s International Pub Café** (✉ Calle Pedro Clisante, no phone), in the center of Sosua, is a shack seemingly glued together by old license plates, business cards, beer posters, and yellowing calendars. Fifteen pesos will buy you a pint of draft. The ambience, courtesy of colorful expatriates and scruffy young Europeans, is free.

# Dominican Republic A to Z

## Arriving and Departing

### BY PLANE

The Dominican Republic has two major international airports: **Las Américas International Airport,** about 20 mi outside Santo Domingo, and **La Unión International Airport,** about 15 mi east of Puerto Plata on the north coast. **American Airlines** (☎ 800/433–7300) has the most extensive service to the Dominican Republic. It flies nonstop from New York and Miami to Santo Domingo, Puerto Plata, and La Romana and offers connections to both Santo Domingo and Puerto Plata from San Juan, Puerto Rico. **American Eagle** (☎ 809/542–5151 or 800/433–7300) has a daily flight to Santo Domingo, two flights a day from San Juan to La Romana, and several flights weekly to Punta Cana. **Continental** (☎ 800/231–0856) flies nonstop from Newark to Puerto Plata and Santo Domingo. **TWA** (☎ 800/221–2000) flies nonstop to Santo Domingo from New York's Kennedy Airport. Minneapolis-based **TransGlobal Tours** (☎ 800/338–2160) offers weekly charters during the winter season from the Twin Cities to Puerto Plata.

Several regional carriers serve neighboring islands. **ALM** (☎ 800/327–7230) connects Santo Domingo to St. Maarten and Curaçao. There is also limited domestic service available from Herrera Airport in Santo Domingo to other airfields in La Romana, Samaná, and Santiago. The Barahona International Airport has the capabilities of handling large jet aircraft. For now, mostly charters and private planes fly in.

The remodeled and enlarged Las Américas (Santo Domingo) and La Unión (Puerto Plata) facilities are sophisticated by Latin American standards, and they're busy. Anticipate long lines and allow 1½ to two hours for checking in for an international flight. Do confirm your flight two days in advance. Try to travel with carry-on luggage, and keep a sharp eye on it and on any baggage coming off the carousels, particularly if it is black, because everyone else's will be, too. If you fly out of a U.S. airport such as Miami, where a shrink-wrap service is offered, avail yourself of it. Plastic-wrap your bag like meat in a supermarket and no one is likely to tamper with it. Be prepared for a daunting experience as you leave customs. There will be a frenzy of waiting friends, relatives, drivers, and *buscones* (porters) along with a din of excitement.

FROM THE AIRPORT

Taxis are available at the airport, and the 25-minute ride into Santo Domingo averages RD$250 (about US$21). Taxi fares from the Puerto Plata airport average RD$200. Some order has been imposed outside the airport—taxis line up and, for the most part, charge the official established rates. If you have arranged for a hotel transfer, which is a good idea, a representative should be waiting for you in the immigration hall.

## Currency

The coin of the realm is the Dominican peso, which is divided into 100 centavos. It is written RD$ and fluctuates relative to the U.S. dollar. At press time, RD$13.75 was equivalent to US$1. Always make certain you know in which currency any transaction is taking place. Do yourself a favor and carry a pocket calculator unless you can easily divide 14 into hundreds of pesos. Although all transactions are required by law to be in pesos, there is a growing black market for hard currency; be wary of offers to exchange U.S. dollars at a rate more favorable than the official one. It used to be illegal to exchange greenbacks with black marketers on the street, who offer a tempting rate. It is no longer; however, they count out money so fast that by the time you do a recount, "they're outta there." Prices quoted here are in U.S. dollars unless noted otherwise.

## Emergencies

**Police:** In Santo Domingo, ☎ 711; 586–2804 in Puerto Plata; 571–2233 in Sosua. However, do not expect too much from the police, aside from a bit of a hassle and some paperwork that they will consider the end of the matter. In general, the police will favor a Dominican over a foreigner in a car accident.

**Hospitals:** Santo Domingo emergency rooms that are open 24 hours are **Centro Médico Universidad Central del Este** (UCE) (✉ Av. Máximo Gómez 68, ☎ 809/221–0171), **Clínica Abreu** (✉ Calle Beller 42, ☎ 809/688–4411), and **Clínica Gómez Patino** (✉ Av. Independencia 701, ☎ 809/685–9131). In Puerto Plata, you can go to **Clínica Dr. Brugal** (✉ Calle José del Carmen Ariza 15, ☎ 809/586–2519). In Sosua, try the **Centro Médico Sosua** (✉ Av. Martinez, ☎ 809/571–3949). Most major hotels have a doctor on call who will come to your room with a little black bag, for about $45, which is considerably more than if you were to drag your ailing body to a clinic.

**Pharmacies:** Pharmacies that are open 24 hours a day are, in Santo Domingo, **San Judas Tadeo** (✉ Av. Independencia 57, ☎ 809/689–664); in Puerto Plata, **Farmacia Deleyte** (✉ Av. John F. Kennedy 89, ☎ 809/5862583). Many of the pharmacies in the city will deliver to your hotel.

## Getting Around

BUSES

Traditionally, *públicos* are small blue-and-white or blue-and-red cars that run regular routes, stopping to let passengers on and off. But now everyone is getting into the act. Anyone who owns a car can operate it as a *público* and after 5 PM many do, considering it as their second job. The fare is RD$2. Competing with the públicos are the *conchos* or *colectivos* (privately owned buses), whose drivers coast around the major thoroughfares, leaning out of the window or jumping out to try to persuade passengers to climb aboard. It's a colorful, if cramped, way to get around town. The fare is about RD$1. Privately owned, air-conditioned buses make regular runs to Santiago, Puerto Plata, and other destinations. You should make reservations by calling **Metro Buses** (⊠ Av. Winston Churchill; in Santo Domingo, call 809/566–7126; 809/586–6062 in Puerto Plata; 809/587–4711 in Santiago) or **Caribe Tours** (⊠ Av. 27 de Febrero at Leopoldo Navarro, ☎ 809/221–4422). One-way bus fare from Santo Domingo to Puerto Plata is RD$80 (about US$6), and it takes four long hours. Caribe shows bilingual movies, and this line is favored by the locals; buses are often filled to capacity, especially on weekends, when there are lots of small children.

Frequent service to the town of La Romana is provided by **Express Bus.** Buses depart from Revelos Street in front of Enriquillo Park, every hour on the hour, starting at 5 AM through to 9 PM, with exactly the same schedule from Romana. The office of this bus line is now closed and consequently there is no phone. However, there is a ticket-taker who will take your 40 pesos (US$2.90). Travel time is one hour and 40 minutes, and if luck is with you, you will get the larger bus, which will show an American movie.

*Voladoras* (fliers) are vans that run from Puerto Plata's Central Park to Sosua and Cabarete a couple of times each hour for RD$10. They don't run on a reliable schedule and are not always labeled with their destination.

### CAR RENTALS

You'll need a valid driver's license from your own country and a major credit card and/or cash deposit. Cars can be rented at the airports and at many hotels. Among the known names are **Avis** (☎ 809/535–7191), **Budget** (☎ 809/562–6812), **Hertz** (☎ 809/221–5333), and **National** (☎ 809/562–1444). Rates average US$70 and up per day, depending upon the make and size of the car. Some local outfits, like **Nelly Rent-a-Car** (☎ 809/544–1800; 800/526–6684 in the U.S.) and **McBeal** (☎ 809/688–6518), give decidedly better rates, starting at around $43 a day for their smallest compact in Santo Domingo but about $53 in the tourist area of Puerto Plata. Driving is on the right. Many Dominicans drive recklessly, often taking their half of the road out of the middle, but they will flash their headlights to warn against highway patrols. The first-time visitor to the island may marvel how some cars are still on the road at all!

It is strongly suggested that—with the exception of driving within the major cities—you do not drive at night. If for some unavoidable reason you must, especially on the narrow, unlighted mountain roads, exercise extreme caution. Many local cars are without headlights or taillights. Bicyclists do not have any lights, cows and goats wander onto the pavement, and there is always pedestrian traffic on the sides of the road. Traffic and directional signs are less than adequate, and unseen potholes (some 5- to 6-ft wide and more than 1 ft deep) can easily break a car's axle. The road between Santo Domingo and Santiago, the major commercial highway in the country, has thankfully been expanded into a four-lane divided highway. Beware of the road between Santiago and Puerto Plata—it can feel like maneuvering on a lunar landscape. Surprisingly, many of the more scenic secondary roads are in good shape. Be sure to talk to someone at your hotel before embarking on a driving tour. Keep in mind that gas stations are few and far between in some of the remote regions. Finally, the 80-km-per-hour (50-mi-per-hour) speed limit is strictly enforced. If you drive anywhere outside the city limits of Santo Domingo, there is more than a good chance you will be pulled over for speeding, even if you weren't. You will be expected to pay a bribe of about RD$40 (about US$3). Pay it, smile, and gripe later. The hassles encountered if you don't are just not worth it. The police count on these payoffs to augment their meager incomes (low-level public servants make very little here, less than a domestic, around US$100 a month, so it is told ).

MOTORBIKE TAXIS

Known as *motoconchos*, these bikes are a popular and inexpensive way to get around such tourist areas as Puerto Plata, Sosua, and Jarabacoa. Bikes can be flagged down both on the road and in town; rates vary from RD$3 to RD$20 per person, depending upon distance. Be careful: No helmets are provided, and the Domingans drive like maniacs!

PLANE

Incredibly, there is no local scheduled airline service between Santo Domingo and Puerto Plata, Samaná, or Punta Cana. If you lack the time to travel overland, you can charter a small plane for trips around the island and to neighboring countries, and for surprisingly inexpensive rates. Contact Jimmy or Irene Butler at **Air Taxi** (⊠ Núñez de Cáceres 2, Santo Domingo, ☎ 809/227–8333 or 809/567–1555).

TAXIS

Taxis, which are government regulated, line up outside hotels and restaurants. The taxis are unmetered, and the minimum fare within Santo Domingo is about RD$50 (US$4), but you can bargain for less if you order a taxi away from the major hotels. Some taxis are not allowed to pick up from hotels and so hang out on the street in front. On the average, they are a $1 cheaper per ride. Hiring a taxi by the hour and with any number of stops is RD$125 (US$10) per hour with a minimum of two hours. Be sure to establish the time that you start; drivers like to advance the time a little. Always carry small denominations, like 5-, 10-, and 20-peso notes, because it is rare when a driver will either have or admit to having any change. Taxis can also drive you to destinations outside the city. Rates are posted in hotels and at the airport. Sample fares are RD$1,000 (US$80) to La Romana and RD$1,900 (US$150) to Puerto Plata. If you're negotiating, the going rate is RD$5 per kilometer. Round-trips are considerably less than twice the one-way fare. Call **El Conde Taxi** (☎ 809/563–6131) or **Tecni-Taxi** (☎ 809/567–2010 in Santo Domingo, 809/320–7621 in Puerto Plata).

In a separate category are radio taxis, which are convenient if you'd like to schedule a pickup—and a wise choice if you don't speak Spanish. The fare is negotiated over the phone when you make the appointment. The most reliable company is **Apolo Taxi** (☎ 809/541–9595). The standard charge is RD$100 per hour during the day, RD$120 at night, no minimum, with as many stops as you like. These figures may rise, since gas prices have escalated 28%. Gas is now $1.89 a gallon and $2.32 for high test. Many people protested when these hikes were inaugurated, and who wouldn't; Americans wouldn't sit still for it, and many Dominicans make only $5 a day.

Avoid unmarked street taxis, particularly in Santo Domingo—they're a little risky, and there have been incidents of robberies.

You could go in high-Dominican style and hire a limo and a driver, even if it's just for a special night. Call the **Limousine Connection**

(☎ 809/540–5304 or 809/567–3435), where rates run around $49 per hour.

## Guided Tours

**Apolo Tours** (☎ 809/586–5329) offers a full-day tour of Playa Grande and tours to Santiago (including a casino tour) and Sosua. It will also arrange transfers between your hotel and the airport, day sightseeing tours, and custom and small-group tours along the north coast, which include stops along the way for swimming and an overnight stay at Samaná. **Cafemba Tours** (☎ 809/586–2177) runs various tours of the Cibao Valley and the Amber Coast, including Puerto Plata, Sosua, and Río San Juan. **Caribbean Jeep Safaris** (☎ 809/571–1924) is an English-speaking outfit that runs Jeep tours in the mountains behind Puerto Plata and Sosua, ending up at the Cabarete Adventure Park, where you can swim in an underground pool and explore caves with Taino rock paintings. Buffet lunch and unlimited drinks are included in the RD$600 price. **Ecoturisa** (☎ 809/221–4104) arranges ecological tours and cultural and scientific expeditions, many of them tailored to the clients' needs. **Iguana Mamma, Mountain Bike and Hiking** offers adventure tours with an ecological conscience, with 20% of the profits being donated to both the local environment and education. Phone 800/571–0908 for an ecologically correct good time. **Winchester Tours** (☎ 800/391–2473) hails from New England and specializes in wildlife and bird-watching tours to Barahona, for groups of 6–10 nature lovers. Fred Sladen, president, also acts as tour leader. Having lived in the Caribbean for 15 years, he is a recognized authority on neo-tropical birds and ecosystems, as well as a very personable host. He, too, donates to conservation organizations in the D.R. **Prieto Tours** (☎ 809/685–0102) operates Gray Line of the Dominican Republic. It offers half-day bus tours of Santo Domingo, nightclub tours, beach tours, tours to Cibao Valley and the Amber Coast, and a variety of other tours. **Turinter** (☎ 809/685–4020) tours include dinner and a show or casino visit, a full-day tour of Samaná, and specialty tours (museum, shopping, fishing).

## Language

Before you travel to the Dominican Republic, you should know at least a smattering of Spanish. Guides at major tourist attractions and front-desk personnel in the major hotels speak a fascinating form of English, though they sometimes have trouble understanding tourists. Traffic signs and restaurant menus, except at popular tourist establishments, are in Spanish. Using smiles and gestures will help, and you can manage with just English, but you will be given all of the extra courtesies if you try to speak the language of the people.

## Opening and Closing Times

Regular office and shop hours are weekdays 8–12:30 and 2:30–5, Saturday 8–noon. Government offices are open weekdays 7:30–2:30. Banking hours are weekdays 8:30–4:30.

## Passports and Visas

U.S. and Canadian citizens must have either a valid passport or proof of citizenship, such as an original (not photocopied) birth certificate, and a tourist card. Legal residents of the United States must have an alien registration card (green card), a valid passport, and a tourist card. British citizens need only a valid passport; no entry visa is required. The requisite tourist card costs $10, and you should be sure to purchase it at the airline counter when you check in and then fill it out on the plane. You can purchase the card on arrival at the airport, but you may encounter long lines. Be advised that only U.S. cash (not traveler's checks) is acceptable. Keep the bottom half of the card in a safe place, because you'll need to present it to immigration authorities when you leave. All foreign visitors must pay a $10 departure tax, as well. Both it and the tourist card must be paid for in U.S. dollars, so allow for it.

## Precautions

This is one island where people do drink from the tap, especially in the better hotels and resorts, unlike in nearby Haiti, for example, where it isn't even a consideration. However, even many local residents take their water from a bottle, both at home and in restaurants, and that is the safe way to go. In Santo Domingo, as in any other big city, be conscious of your wallet or pocketbook, especially around the Malecón (waterfront boulevard), where pickpockets have been caught in the past. Any robberies can usually be attributed to the great disparity between the rich and the poor. You will see, mainly at night, men in civies with shoulder rifles standing guard outside businesses or homes. Do not be unnerved by it. It is the Dominican equivalent of a Pinkerton or security guard. In general, the island is very safe, and you do not hear of violent crime against tourists. If you elect to rent a car, and it is a big decision, be sure to have some kind of stress-reducing techniques available. Getting behind the wheel here makes the streets of Rome or Paris seem like peaceful, country lanes. Buy amber only from reputable shops. The attractively priced piece offered by the street vendor is more than likely plastic.

## Taxes and Service Charges

Hotels and restaurants add a service charge (10% in hotels and in restaurants) and now there is a 13% government tax. If you see an abbreviation on a bill that looks like a service charge and the waiter tells you that it is not a tip but rather tax, know that it is both and he is trying to get a double gratuity. As in the states, if you found the service to your liking, which is most often the case, do tip that extra 5%–10%. It is customary to leave a dollar per day for the hotel maid. Taxi drivers expect a 10% tip especially when they have had to lift luggage or to wait. Skycaps and hotel porters expect at least RD$5 per bag.

## Telephones and Mail

To call the Dominican Republic from the United States, dial area code 809 and the local number. Connections are clear and easy to make. Remember that English is not widely spoken. Fortunately, service from the Dominican Republic is very good. There is direct-dial service to the United States; just dial 1, followed by the area code and number.

Airmail postage to North America for a letter or postcard costs RD$2, to Europe RD$4, and may take up to three weeks to reach the destination. Or you can pay almost US$1.45 to buy a pale green stamp for "fast mail" in a gift shop (post offices are not easily found); supposedly it will take a card only three days to get to the States.

## Visitor Information

Before you go, contact the **Dominican Republic Tourist Office** (⌧ 1501 Broadway, Suite 410, New York, NY 10036, ☎ 212/575–4966 or 888/374–6361, ℻ 212/575–5448; ⌧ 2355 Salzedo Ave., Suite 307, Coral Gables, FL 33134, ☎ 305/444–4592 or 888/358–9594; ⌧ 1464 Crescent St., Montréal, Québec, Canada H3A 2B6, ☎ 514/933–6126). Contact a U.S. office if you would like material sent to you before your trip. Be prepared to wait at least two weeks to get requested material sent to you. If you are in a rush, let them know.

In the Dominican Republic, the **Secretary of Tourism** (⌧ Officinas Guberbamentales Bldg. D, ☎ 809/221–4660, ℻ 809/682–3806) is in Santo Domingo in a complex of government offices at the corner of Avenida

Mexico and Avenida 30 de Marzo. Unless you are seeking sistance, it is not worth making the trek here for the limited offered to tourists. Another source of information is the **Dominican To Information Center** (☎ 800/752–1151) in Santo Domingo. In 1998, tourism officials promise, there will be information kiosks set up along the Malécon and other tourist areas. The **tourist office** (⊠ Playa Long Beach, ☎ 809/586–3676) is in Puerto Plata and is open weekdays 9–2:30.

# Grenada

*Grenada's sweetly naive spirit and eye-popping natural beauty juxtapose with top facilities and sensible development. St. George's is one of the most charming capital cities in the Caribbean; Grand Anse, one of the finest beaches. A trek to the rain forest, with its thundering waterfalls and lush vegetation, is a must.*

**G**RENADA, A JEWEL OF AN ISLAND only 21 mi long and 12 mi wide, is bordered by 45 beaches and countless secluded coves, crisscrossed by nature trails, and filled with spice plantations, tropical forests, and select hotels that cling to hillsides and overlook the sea.

Updated by
Jane E. Zarem

If the Irish hadn't beaten them to the name, Grenadians might very well have called their land the Emerald Isle, for the lush rain forests and the thick vegetation on the hillsides give it a great, green beauty that few places in the world can match. In the eastern Caribbean 12 degrees north of the equator, Grenada is the most southerly of the Windward Islands. The nation of Grenada really consists of three inhabited islands: Grenada is the largest, with 120 square mi and a population of about 96,000 people; Carriacou, 16 mi north of Grenada, has 13 square mi and a population of about 5,000; and Petit Martinique, 5 mi northeast of Carriacou, has just 486 acres and a population of 700. Although Carriacou and Petit Martinique are popular for day trips or fishing and snorkeling excursions, most of the tourist activity is on Grenada. This is also where you'll find the nation's capital, St. George's, and it's eponymous harbor—the largest and busiest on Grenada.

Known as the Isle of Spice, Grenada is a major producer of nutmeg, cinnamon, mace, cocoa, and other common spices. The pleasant aroma of spices fills the air: at the markets where they're sold from large burlap bags, in restaurants where chefs believe in using them liberally, and in pubs where nutmeg is sprinkled liberally on rum punches.

Grenada was sighted by Columbus in 1498. Although he never set foot on the island, he gave it the name Concepción. Throughout the 17th century, it was the scene of bloody battles between the indigenous Carib Indians and the French. The Caribs finally lost to the French in 1651, committing mass suicide by leaping off a cliff rather than submitting to their captors. The French, however, lost the island to the British in 1762, thus beginning the seesaw of power between the two nations that became a familiar tale on many of the Windward Islands.

In 1967 Grenada became part of the British Commonwealth. Seven years later, it was granted total independence. The New Jewel Movement (NJM) seized power in 1979, formed the People's Revolutionary Government, and named as prime minister Maurice Bishop, who established controversial ties with Cuba. Bishop's prime ministry lasted until 1983, when a coup d'état led to his execution, along with that of many of his supporters. NJM Deputy Prime Minister Bernard Coard and Army Commander Hudson Austin then took over the government. U.S. troops invaded the island on October 25, 1983, and evacuated the American students who were attending St. George's University Medical School. Coard and Austin were arrested, and resistance to the invasion was quickly quelled.

Herbert A. Blaize was elected prime minister in December 1984. With many millions of dollars in U.S. and Canadian aid, his government began reorganizing Grenada's economy to focus on agriculture, light manufacturing, and tourism. The country rebuilt roads and installed a direct-dial telephone system. Grenada's modern Point Salines International Airport, which opened in 1984, enabled jets to land and allowed night landings. It still has one of the longest runways in the Caribbean.

The election in June 1995 of the New National Party, under the leadership of Dr. Keith Mitchell, continues the peaceful progress of this island nation. Grenada's popularity as a vacation destination increases

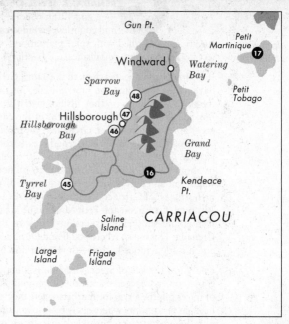

## Grenada (and Carriacou)

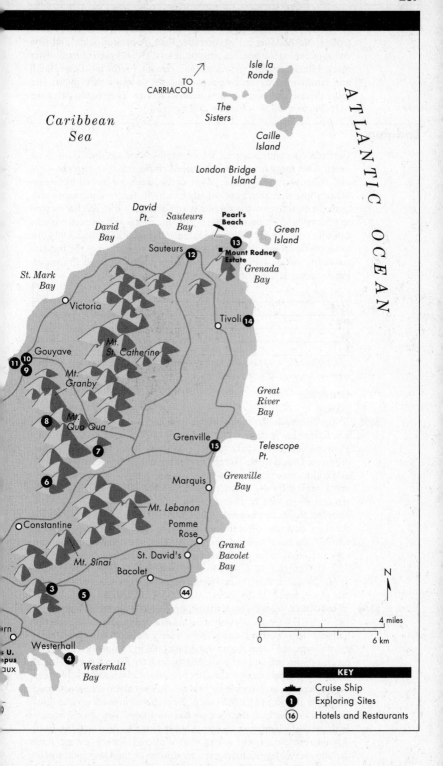

Isle la
Ronde

TO
CARRIACOU

The
Sisters

Caille
Island

*Caribbean
Sea*

London Bridge
Island

*ATLANTIC OCEAN*

David
Pt.

*Sauteurs
Bay*

**Pearl's
Beach**

Green
Island

David
Bay

Sauteurs

**13**

■ **Mount Rodney
Estate**

**12**

*Grenada
Bay*

St. Mark
Bay

○ Victoria

Mt.
St. Catherine

Tivoli ● **14**

Gouyave

**11 10**
**9**

Mt.
Granby

*Great
River
Bay*

**8**

Mt.
Qua Qua

**7**

Grenville
**15**

*Telescope
Pt.*

**6**

Marquis

*Grenville
Bay*

○ Constantine

Mt. Lebanon

Pomme
Rose

Mt. Sinai

St. David's ○

Bacolet

*Grand
Bacolet
Bay*

**3**

**5**

**(44)**

N

rn

s U.
pus
aux

Westerhall

**4**

*Westerhall
Bay*

| 0 | | | 4 miles |
|---|---|---|---|
| 0 | | | 6 km |

| KEY | |
|---|---|
| ⚓ | Cruise Ship |
| ● | Exploring Sites |
| (16) | Hotels and Restaurants |

each year as more and more travelers seek new and exotic sunny destinations. Any expansion of the tourism industry is carefully controlled. No building can stand taller than a coconut palm, and new construction on the beaches must be at least 165 ft from the high-water mark. Hotels, resorts, and restaurants remain, for the most part, small and family-owned, run by people who get to know their guests and pride themselves on giving personalized service. They're typical of the islanders as a whole—friendly and hospitable.

## Lodging

Grenada's accommodations are primarily on or around Grand Anse Beach. They range from simply furnished kitchenette apartments to suites of Caribbean-style elegance. Many of the hotels are owned by Grenadians; those that aren't are usually run by British or American expatriates who thrive on the simplicity of Grenadian life. The hotels tend to be small and intimate, with friendly managers and owners. Visitors can often opt for BP, CP, or MAP, depending on the season. Only one hotel on the island is all-inclusive. The plans specified in the individual listings below apply year-round unless otherwise noted. Prices during the summer are discounted by up to 40%.

| CATEGORY | COST* |
|---|---|
| $$$$ | over $225 |
| $$$ | $175–$225 |
| $$ | $125–$175 |
| $ | under $125 |

*All prices are for a standard double room in high season, excluding 8% government tax and 10% service charge.

### Grenada

HOTELS

$$$$ 🏨 **The Calabash.** Rooms in this all-suite hotel on the peninsula L'Anse aux Epines are scattered over 8 acres of tropical gardens overlooking a curved beach and yacht harbor on Prickly Bay and just a few minutes from Grand Anse. Twenty-two of the suites have whirlpool baths, and eight suites each have a private pool. All have a veranda, where breakfast is delivered. L'Anse aux Epines juts out of the island's southern coast just east of Point Salines International Airport, so early-morning flights can bounce you out of bed if the wind is blowing in the right direction—but it's not annoying enough to ruin a vacation. Cicely's, the hotel's award-winning restaurant (☞ Dining, *below*), enjoys a reputation for good West Indian food and fine service. ⊠ *Box 382, St. George's,* ☎ *473/444–4234 or 800/528–5835,* 𝖥𝖠𝖷 *473/444– 5050. 30 suites. Restaurant, bar, air-conditioning, pool, tennis, exercise room, beach, water sports. AE, MC, V. BP, MAP.*

$$$$ 🏨 **LaSOURCE.** Minutes from the airport (but away from the flight path), LaSOURCE is Grenada's only all-inclusive resort. The grand reception hall leads to a courtyard around which are arranged the Oasis spa-treatment rooms, the Great Room restaurant (and its colonnaded dining terrace), a piano bar, and the pool. Bedrooms have Persian rugs on Italian marble floors, Jamaican mahogany furniture and woodwork, high ceilings, balconies, and marble bathrooms. Rooms are in four-story buildings, and all rooms face the beach. Be prepared to walk up and down lots of stairs, because there are no elevators here. You can experiment with the chef's light spa cuisine or choose richer menu selections. In addition to the usual resort sports, yoga is offered—or try fencing. Rates include *everything*, including spa treatments at the Oasis, and tipping is banned. ⊠ *Pink Gin Beach, Box 852, St. George's,* ☎ *473/444–2556 or 800/544–2883,* 𝖥𝖠𝖷 *473/444–2561. 100 rooms. 2 restaurants, piano*

*bar, air-conditioning, pool, beauty salon, hot tub, sauna, spa, 9-hole golf course, 2 tennis courts, aerobics, archery, Ping-Pong, volleyball, 2 beaches, scuba diving, snorkeling, sailing, windsurfing, waterskiing, cabaret. AE, MC, V. All-inclusive.*

**$$$$** 🏨 **Mahogany Run.** Just over the hill from Grand Anse Beach, this colony of Mediterranean-style buildings slopes down to Morne Rouge Beach. Sixteen deluxe suites are stacked on six levels. Each one (some air-conditioned) has a living room, kitchen, bedroom, and luxurious bath. All have either a covered veranda or patio, with dramatic views of the bay. Guests can walk down to Morne Rouge Beach or take the free water shuttle to Dr. Groom's Beach Club, where there's water sports, beach volleyball, and a café that serves local cuisine. Rates include airport transfers, housekeeping, and breakfast cooked and served in your suite. Children under 12 are not allowed. ⊠ *Morne Rouge, Box 730, St. George's,* ☎ *473/444–3171,* ℻ *473/444–3172. 16 suites. Restaurant, bar, air-conditioning, beach. AE, MC, V. EP, BP, CP.*

**$$$$** 🏨 **Mariposa Beach Resort.** Like its adjacent sister property, Mahogany Run (☞ *above*), Mariposa's rooms are piled atop one another to resemble a hillside Mediterranean village by the sea. Each room, which can accommodate two people, has a water view, a covered veranda or garden, and a bathroom with Italian tiles. It's a short walk downhill to Morne Rouge Beach or a water taxi ride to the beach club. The restaurant specializes in seafood and Continental dishes. ⊠ *Morne Rouge, Box 730, St. George's,* ☎ *473/444–3171,* ℻ *473/444–3172. 32 rooms. Restaurant, bar, air-conditioning, beach. AE, MC, V. MAP.*

**$$$$** 🏨 **Spice Island Beach Resort.** You won't find a better location in ★ Grenada than this stylish resort. Some guest suites are, literally, right on Grand Anse Beach—when you step out of your room, your feet are in the sand. Other suites have terraces overlooking the garden, sea, and sunset. The luxurious accommodations are spacious, brightly decorated in the colors of sand and coral, with vast mirrored closets. Some suites have private plunge pools, others have spa Jacuzzis that could submerge a family of four. Four Royal Private Pool Suites, each a spacious 1,473 square ft, are the ultimate luxury. It's like having your own beach house, with a 16- by 20-ft pool, a garden, a sundeck, and a private fitness area with exercise bike and sauna. Guests may dine on Continental and West Indian cuisine at Spice's terrace dining room or at Blue Horizon's La Belle Creole (☞ *Dining, below*). No children under five are allowed in winter, and no children under 12 in pool suites year-round. ⊠ *Box 6, Grand Anse, St. George's,* ☎ *473/444–4258 or 800/223–9815,* ℻ *473/444–4807. 56 suites. Restaurant, bar, air-conditioning, fans, minibars, golf privileges, tennis court, exercise room, beach, water sports, bicycles, shop, cabaret. AE, D, DC, MC, V. CP, MAP.*

**$$$** 🏨 **Coyaba Beach Resort.** Coyaba means "heaven" in the Arawak In- ★ dian language. Right on Grand Anse Beach—certainly a heavenly spot—Coyaba is comfortable and offers guests terrific value. A loyal clientele returns again and again, giving Coyaba a consistently high occupancy rate. Guests enjoy playing tennis and volleyball, relaxing at the pool with a swim-up bar, and dining in a bamboo-walled restaurant or terrace. Rooms, decorated with natural wood and Arawak-inspired folk art, are in several peachy-pink two-story buildings, which surround 5½ acres of beautifully landscaped lawns and gardens; the beach is just beyond the gardens. Most rooms have a water view. There's entertainment at night. ⊠ *Box 336, Grand Anse, St. George's,* ☎ *473/444–4129 or 800/223–9815,* ℻ *473/444–4808. 70 rooms. Restaurant, 2 bars, air-conditioning, pool, tennis court, beach, water sports, shop. AE, D, DC, MC, V. EP, BP, CP, MAP, FAP.*

**$$$** 🏨 **Grenada Renaissance Resort.** The location (across from the Grand Anse Shopping Center) is convenient, the 20 acres of grounds are lush and beautiful, the rooms are comfortable, and the amenities include an on-site car-rental agent and a tour desk. Ceilings in the guest rooms are low, however, and the rooms less spacious than those at competing resorts. Still, all rooms have king-size or twin beds and satellite TV, and the hotel faces Grand Anse Beach. ⊠ *Box 441, Grand Anse, St. George's,* ☎ *473/444–4371,* 📠 *473/444–4800. 184 doubles, 2 luxury suites. 2 restaurants, air-conditioning, pool, barbershop, beauty salon, 2 tennis courts, health club, scuba diving, beach, water sports, shops, business services. AE, DC, MC, V. EP, MAP.*

**$$$** 🏨 **Rex Grenadian.** This massive resort near the airport is popular with European tour groups. The snazziest rooms and suites are adjacent to the central building, a white, faux-Palladian palace with lofty ceilings, vast arched windows, trellised walkways, and tiled terraces. Other rooms are in eight two-story cliffside buildings with either a garden or ocean view. All rooms have balconies and king or twin beds and are decorated in robin's-egg blue and taupe, with rattan furniture. Basic garden-view rooms have a ceiling fan and shower. For an extra $25 you can have air-conditioning, tub, and hair dryer. A separate pool area, with a terrace restaurant and bar, overlooks one of two beaches. All kinds of activities are available—water sports, rainy-day programs (bingo, local dialect classes, dance lessons), evening shows, happy hours. ⊠ *Point Salines, Box 893, St. George's,* ☎ *473/444–3333 or 800/255–5859,* 📠 *473/444–1111. 212 rooms. 8 restaurants, bar, café, piano bar, pool, sauna, 2 tennis courts, health club, 2 beaches, scuba diving, snorkeling, windsurfing, boating, waterskiing, cabaret, business services. AE, D, DC, MC, V. EP, MAP.*

**$$$** 🏨 **Secret Harbour Resort.** On a cliff overlooking Mount Hartman Bay, away from the throng on the south coast, this luxurious resort attracts the yachting crowd. Moorings Club Mariner Watersports Centre, on site, has a fleet of small sailboats and yachts available for day or long-term charter. The resort has 20 private suites, each beautifully decorated with two antique four-poster full-size beds and an Italian-tile bath. Water-sports equipment, including Windsurfers, Sunfish, and sailboats, is complimentary to guests. No children under 12 are accepted. ⊠ *L'Anse aux Epines, Box 11, St. George's,* ☎ *473/444–4439,* 📠 *473/444–4819. 20 suites. 2 restaurants, bar, pool, air-conditioning, tennis court, beach, windsurfing, boating. AE, D, DC, MC, V. EP, MAP.*

**$$**
★ 🏨 **Blue Horizons Cottage Hotel.** Spice Island Beach Resort's (☞ *above*) sister hotel is an especially good value. Each comfortable cottage has a kitchenette, private terrace, TV, phone, and hair dryer. Deluxe suites have separate sitting/dining rooms and king-size or two double beds; superior studios have dining alcoves and king-size beds. Handsome mahogany furniture is set off by white walls and cool, tile floors. Palms stud the large, sunny lawn around the swimming pool, and Grand Anse Beach is a short walk down the hill. Guests may eat at Blue Horizon's La Belle Creole or at Spice Island (☞ *Dining, below*). Complimentary water sports, tennis, and fitness facilities (at Spice Island) and the pool (at Blue Horizons) are available to guests of either hotel. ⊠ *Box 41, Grand Anse, St. George's,* ☎ *473/444–4316 or 473/444–4592, 800/223–9815 in the U.S.;* 📠 *473/444–2815. 26 deluxe suites, 6 superior studios. Restaurant, 2 bars, air-conditioning, kitchenettes, pool. AE, MC, V. EP, CP, MAP.*

**$–$$** 🏨 **Flamboyant Hotel and Cottages.** The rooms and suites of this Grenadian-owned hotel/self-catering resort have one of the island's best views, sweeping over the entire Grand Anse Bay to St. George's. All are simply furnished, with a balcony that faces the beautiful view. One-bedroom suites and two-bedroom cottages each have a kitchen and lounge, making this an especially good deal for families. Be prepared to climb stairs: The rooms are built into a rather steep hill, and the stairway to Grand Anse Beach is at least 100 steps. But don't worry: Halfway down you can stop for a dip in the freshwater pool, grab a bite at the Beachside Terrace restaurant (West Indian and Continental cuisine), or pull up a chair at the cabana bar. ⊠ *Box 214, St. George's,* ☎ *473/444–4247, * FAX *473/444–1234. 17 rooms, 20 suites, 2 cottages. Restaurant, bar, air-conditioning, minibars, pool, beach, snorkeling, cabaret. AE, D, MC, V. EP, BP, MAP.*

**$–$$** 🏨 **True Blue Inn.** Although the "blue" in the inn's name derives from the area's origin as an indigo plantation, it could just as easily reflect the beautiful color of Prickly Bay, which the inn overlooks. Spacious one-bedroom apartment units are perched cliffside, among the trees, each with a private veranda overlooking the sea. Two-bedroom cottages are nestled in private seaside gardens. Both the apartments and the cottages have large, fully equipped kitchens, ceiling fans, and cable TV. Sunsets are spectacular from Indigo's, the inn's deck restaurant. Light meals, barbecues, and cocktails are served dockside at the Landing, where boaters frequently come for dinner, tying up at the private dock. It's a five-minute drive to Grand Anse Beach, but you can swim in the bay. ⊠ *Box 308, St. George's (Old Mill Ave., True Blue),* ☎ *473/444–2000 or 800/742–4276, * FAX *473/444–1247. 10 units. 2 restaurants, bar, air-conditioning, fans, pool, scuba diving, boating, laundry service. AE, MC, V. EP.*

**$** 🏨 **La Sagesse Nature Center.** This secluded getaway is on a lovely bay 10 mi east of Point Salines International Airport. The grounds include a salt-pond bird sanctuary, thick mangroves, and several hiking trails. The main guest house has two high-ceilinged suites with kitchenettes. There is also a two-bedroom beach cottage, with a wraparound veranda, and two budget-priced rooms behind the restaurant. All rooms have private baths, screened-in patios, and ceiling fans—and are just 30 ft from the beach. The only TV is in the bar. Plan on renting a car if you stay this far out, although Mike Meranski, the cheerful American owner, will run guests into town for grocery supplies and shopping. ⊠ *Box 44, St. David's,* ☎ *473/444–6458 or 800/322–1753,* FAX *473/444–6458. 6 rooms. Restaurant, bar, beach. MC, V. EP.*

### APARTMENT HOTELS

These fully equipped units often represent a great budget alternative, especially for families. Contact the tourist office for additional listings.

**$$$** 🏨 **Twelve Degrees North.** Eight top-of-the-line (and most expensive) one- and two-bedroom apartments come with private beach, pool, tennis, and maid service (which includes cooking and doing your laundry). Sunfish and ocean kayaks are available for guest use; fishing, scuba diving, and day sails can be arranged. A minimum stay of one week is required during high season, and children under 15 are not allowed. ⊠ *Box 241, L'Anse aux Epines, St. George's,* ☎ *473/444–4580 or 800/322–1753,* FAX *473/444–4580. 8 apartments. Pool, tennis court, beach, snorkeling, boating. AE, V. EP.*

**$** 🏨 **Wave Crest Holiday Apartments.** Owner-manager Joyce DaBreo runs a tight ship. She and her husband take great pains to keep all 20 sunny one- and two-bedroom self-catering apartments spotless and well maintained. Each unit has a telephone and cable TV. Restaurants, Grand Anse shopping center, and the beach are only a five-minute walk away. ⊠ *Box 278, St. George's,* ☎ *473/444–4116,* FAX *473/444–4847. 14 1-bedroom apartments, 6 2-bedroom apartments. Air-conditioning, baby-sitting. AE, D, MC, V.*

VILLA AND PRIVATE-HOME RENTALS

Several local agencies handle rentals of villas and private homes: The most reliable is **Villas of Grenada** (⊠ Box 218, St. George's, ☎ 473/440–1896, ℻ 473/444–4529). In-season rates range from about $600 a week for a two-bedroom home with a pool to about $3,500 for a six-bedroom home on the beach.

### Carriacou

$$ 🏨 **Caribbee Inn.** This is a lovely, small, country house high on a promontory overlooking the sea—perfect for a honeymoon. The panoramic views are magnificent, particularly at sunset. Hillside suites are themed (Colonial, South American, West Indian) and have four-poster beds and Italian tile flooring. One suite has a step-up shower with views of the bay; another has its own beach. Breakfast and dinner are served in the dining room—and don't be surprised if a low-flying macaw joins you. The inn is somewhat isolated but offers great opportunities for nature walks. There's an airport courtesy car, but you may want to rent a car to get around. ⊠ *Prospect,* ☎ *473/443–7380,* ℻ *473/443–8142. 7 rooms, 3 suites. Bar, dining room, beach, snorkeling, library. AE, MC, V. EP, MAP.*

$ 🏨 **Silver Beach Resort.** Stretches of pristine beach surround this suite hotel. All suites have one bedroom, private patios, and ocean views (but no TVs); some units are self-catering. The scuba facilities here are the biggest in the Grenadines. Certification courses are available for beginners and experienced divers. Spearfishing excursions can also be arranged. The open-air restaurant by the water is the best place on the island for a hearty, early-morning breakfast. ⊠ *Silver Beach,* ☎ *473/443–7337,* ℻ *473/443–7165. 16 suites. Restaurant, scuba diving, snorkeling, windsurfing, shop. AE, MC, V. EP, CP, MAP.*

## Dining

Unlike many other Caribbean islands, which have a scarcity of fresh produce and must rely on imports, Grenada has everything from cabbages and tomatoes to bananas, mangoes, papaya (called pawpaw), plantains, melons, callaloo (similar to spinach), breadfruit, oranges, tangerines, limes, christophines (similar to squash), and avocados—the list is endless. And all the dishes are enhanced by the wide range of spices grown here. Be sure to try one of the exotic ice creams made from guava or nutmeg.

Fresh seafood of all kinds, including lobster and oysters, is also plentiful. Conch, known here as *lambi,* is popular and appears on menus in some form, often curried or as a stew. Almost all Grenadian restaurants serve seafood and at least some native dishes.

Rum punches are served everywhere, but no two places make them exactly alike—except that nutmeg is always grated on top. Carib, the local beer, is also very popular and quite good.

### What to Wear

Dining in Grenada is a casual experience. Collared shirts and long pants for gentlemen and casual sundresses for ladies are apropos; even the fanciest restaurants don't require gentlemen to wear a jacket.

| CATEGORY | COST* |
|---|---|
| **$$$** | over $40 |
| **$$** | $20–$40 |
| **$** | under $20 |

*per person for a three-course meal, excluding drinks, service, and 8% government tax

GRENADA

**$$$** ✕ **Canboulay.** Trinidadians Erik and Gina-Lee Johnson put Canboulay
★ on the map with their exciting reconfigurations of local cuisine. The
menu changes often, but regular items include crab crepes with a puree
of callaloo, breadfruit vichyssoise, African *bobotie* (spiced, raisin-stud-
ded ground beef topped with a baked custard), five-star versions of *roti*
(curried meat, potatoes, and beans wrapped in a giant tortilla), and
nutmeg ice cream. The frozen chocolate-mocha cheesecake has bro-
ken hearts, and anything the Johnsons do with shrimp—coconut-beer-
batter-it, or peanut-sauce-it—is memorable. Thursday is Jazz Night.
Canboulay is high on a hill overlooking Grand Anse, and the dining
room's shutters open to hilltop breezes and a grand view that's espe-
cially nice at lunchtime. ✉ *Morne Rouge, St. George's,* ☎ *473/444–
4401. Reservations essential. AE, D, MC, V. Closed Sun. No lunch Sat.*

**$$$** ✕ **Cicely's.** The open-air restaurant at the Calabash hotel, named for
award-winning chef Cicely Roberts, is small and pretty, surrounded
by palms and tropical flowers. The prix-fixe dinner is a good deal; past
menus have included fillet of kingfish with roast potatoes and fried plantains and chicken with ginger and chive sauce. Cheese and English-style
biscuits with coffee, tea, or cocoa top off your meal. There's nightly
cabaret and piano entertainment. ✉ *L'Anse aux Epines,* ☎ *473/444–
4234. AE, MC, V.*

**$$$** ✕ **La Belle Creole.** Creative West Indian cuisine and a wraparound view
★ of Grand Anse are the claims to fame of this romantic hillside restau-
rant. The lunch and fixed-price dinner menus are always changing, but
reappearing favorites include appetizers of Grenadian caviar (roe of
the white sea urchin), soursop mousse, and lobster-egg flan as well as
entrées of baked stuffed rainbow runner, lobster à la Creole, and
callaloo quiche. On Sunday, a local band plays at the lunchtime pool-
side barbecue. The graciousness of the staff is bound to impress even
the most jaded traveler. ✉ *Blue Horizons Cottage Hotel, Grand Anse,
St. George's,* ☎ *473/444–4316. Reservations essential for nonhotel
guests. AE, MC, V.*

**$$$** ✕ **Le Bistro.** A touch of Paris in Grenada is the idea here. Located at
Ross Point, close to St. George's, the restaurant has beautiful views of
sparkling lights of both the harbor and Grand Anse. The fine French
cuisine will make your mouth water: The à la carte menu might include fillet of fish with finely minced *herbes de provence* or roast duck
with Port wine sauce. A special *menu dégustation,* allowing you to sample the chef's specialties, is priced at $40. Le Bistro has only 40 seats,
so it's smart to book a day or so in advance in high season. ✉ *Ross
Point,* ☎ *473/444–0191. AE, MC, V. Closed Sun.*

**$$$** ✕ **Spice Island Beach Resort.** Diners tend to dress for the five-course,
★ fixed-price evening meal at this open-air, hotel dining room (reserva-
tions for nonhotel guests are limited). The ivy-hung terrace is separated
from Grand Anse Beach by the narrowest of paths. Roast beef or
calves' liver are as likely to appear on the menu as local fare, of which
the unlikely sounding grapefruit consommé is a sublime example. A
dessert table loaded with pineapple pie, nutmeg ice cream, chocolate
truffle torte, and the like. Wednesday is Grenadian Night, when crab
back, sea egg, roast suckling pig, and all the trimmings are on the table,
followed by dancing under the stars. Fridays feature an equally festive
barbecue and steel-band music. ✉ *Grand Anse,* ☎ *473/444–4258 or
473/444–4423. Reservations essential. AE, D, MC, V.*

**$$** ✕ **The Boatyard.** Embassy personnel and expatriates fill this lively
restaurant, in the middle of a marina. Burgers, fish-and-chips, and deep-
fried shrimp are served at lunchtime. At dinner you may order club
steaks, lobster, and different types of meat and seafood brochettes. In

season there's a steel band on Saturday nights. ⊠ *Spice Island Marina, L'Anse aux Epines,* ☎ *473/444–4662. MC, V. Closed Mon.*

**$$**    ✕ **Coconut Beach, the French Creole Restaurant.** Take local seafood, add butter, wine, and Grenadian herbs, and you have excellent French Creole cuisine. Throw in a beautiful setting at the northern end of Grand Anse Beach, and this West Indian cottage becomes a delightful spot for lunch or dinner. Lobster is a specialty and may be wrapped in a crepe, dipped in garlic butter, or added to spaghetti. In season, there's a beach barbecue with live music each Wednesday, Friday, and Sunday night. It's open daily from 10 AM to 10 PM, and free transportation can be arranged. ⊠ *Grand Anse Beach,* ☎ *473/444–4644. AE, MC, V.*

**$$**    ✕ **Joe's Steak House.** Need a break from West Indian cuisine and want an all-American steak? Just a five-minute walk from the Grand Anse hotels, you'll find charcoal-broiled USDA-certified steaks done to your liking, as well as ribs, lobster, chicken, fish, and more. Kids can pick from their own menu. Joe's is open from 5 to 11 PM and can get crowded. ⊠ *Le Marquis Complex, Grand Anse,* ☎ *473/444–4020 or 473/444–4379. AE, MC, V. Closed Mon.*

**$$**    ✕ **The Nutmeg.** Fresh seafood, homemade West Indian dishes, great hamburgers, and the view of the harbor are reasons that local residents and visitors like the Nutmeg. You can watch the harbor traffic through the large open windows as you eat. Try the great callaloo soup, curried lambi, lobster, or shrimp, or just stop by for a drink and a roti. ⊠ *The Carenage, St. George's,* ☎ *473/440–2539. AE, D, MC, V.*

**$$**    ✕ **Red Crab.** This pub is a favorite meeting and eating spot for local and expats, especially on Saturday nights. The curried lambi and shrimp crepes keep the regulars coming back. Seafood, particularly lobster, and steak are the staples of the menu; hot garlic bread comes with all orders. You can eat inside or under the trees and stars. There's live music Monday and Friday in season. ⊠ *L'Anse aux Epines (near the Calabash),* ☎ *473/444–4424. AE, MC, V. Closed Sun.*

**$$**    ✕ **Rudolf's.** This informal pub offers fine West Indian fare, as well as fish-and-chips, sandwiches, and burgers. Skip the attempts at haute cuisine "Viennoise" or "Parisienne," and enjoy the crab back, lambi, and delectable nutmeg ice cream. This is *the* place for eavesdropping on local gossip. Even for Grenada, the rum punches are lethal. It's open from 10 AM to midnight for lunch and dinner. ⊠ *The Carenage, St. George's,* ☎ *473/440–2241. MC, V. Closed Sun.*

**$$**    ✕ **Tabanca at Journey's End.** Alfresco dining on a terrace at the edge of the sea, with spectacular views of the Grand Anse waterfront and St. George's Harbour, is the lure for those wanting a touch of romance with their terrific seafood dinner. The fillet of kingfish topped with a poached egg wins raves, as does the fresh broiled grouper. Carib beer is on tap, and the special rum punch hits the spot. ⊠ *Grand Anse Beach,* ☎ *473/444–1300. AE, D, DC, MC, V. Closed Tues. No lunch.*

**$**    ✕ **Cot Bam.** An acronym for "Club on the Beach at Morne Rouge," Cot Bam is actually on Grand Anse Beach, next to the Coyaba Beach Resort and within walking distance of all the Grand Anse hotels. The casual atmosphere of this bar-restaurant-nightclub, with its tin roof and tile floor is open for breakfast, lunch, and dinner. Stroll from the beach onto the outdoor terrace for a Carib beer and a chicken roti with coleslaw. Or come in the evening for the special lambi curry or other native dishes served inside and eat, dance, or chat the night away. ⊠ *Grand Anse,* ☎ *473/444–2050. AE.*

**$**    ✕ **La Boulangerie.** This French bakery and coffee shop, convenient to the Grand Anse hotels, is a great place for breakfast or a light meal. You can order a French croissant, baguette, *pain au chocolat,* and other special breads and pastries. It also serves espresso, juices, sandwiches, and roasted chicken. It's open from 8 AM to 8 PM daily except Sunday, when it closes at 2 PM. ⊠ *Le Marquis Shopping Complex, Grand Anse,* ☎ *473/444–1131. AE, MC, V.*

$ ✕ **La Sagesse.** A perfect spot to soothe the most frazzled of souls, this open-air restaurant and beach bar is on a secluded cove 20 minutes from Grand Anse. You can combine your meal with a swim or hike. Select from sandwiches, salads, or lobster for lunch. Lambi, smoked marlin, dolphinfish, fillet of grouper, and tuna steak are joined on the dinner menu by a daily vegetarian special. Transportation to and from your hotel is provided. ⊠ *La Sagesse Nature Center, St. David's,* ☎ *473/444–6458. AE, MC, V.*

$ ✕ **Mama's.** Mama's has been a fixture for years. Following the tradition of their late mother, one of Mama's daughters will set generous helpings of local specialties before you—roast turtle, lobster salad, callaloo soup, christophine salad, or fried plantain, as well as such exotica as *tatou* (armadillo), *manicou* (opossum), and sea urchin. There is no menu: Up to 25 native dishes are served family style at a fixed EC$45 per person. You will not leave hungry. ⊠ *Lagoon Rd., St. George's,* ☎ *473/440–1459. Reservations essential. No credit cards.*

CARRIACOU

$ ✕ **Callaloo Restaurant & Bar.** Right on Main Street, this quaint second-floor restaurant has extraordinary views of Sandy Island and Hillsborough Bay. Be sure to sample the callaloo soup. Excellent seafood dishes, including lobster thermidor, are reasonably priced. ⊠ *Hillsborough,* ☎ *473/443–8004. AE, MC, V. Closed Sept.*

$ ✕ **Scraper's.** Good things are happening at Tyrrel Bay. Scraper's serves up lobster, conch, and fresh catches, along with a simple spirit and decor seasoned with occasional calypsonian serenades (owner Steven Gay "Scraper" is a pro). Order a rum punch and exercise your right to do nothing. ⊠ *Tyrrel Bay,* ☎ *473/443–7403. AE, D, MC, V.*

# Beaches

Grenada has some 80 mi of coastline, 65 bays, and 45 white-sand beaches—many in secluded little coves—and all are public. Most beaches are on the Caribbean, south of St. George's in the Grand Anse and L'Anse aux Epines areas, where the majority of the hotels are also clustered. Virtually every hotel, apartment complex, and residential area has easy access to a beach or tiny cove.

**Grand Anse Beach,** about a 10-minute ride from St. George's, is the loveliest and most popular beach on Grenada. It's a gleaming, 2-mi semicircle of sand lapped by clear, gentle surf. Brilliant rainbows frequently spill a spectrum of color into the aquamarine sea or the high green mountains that frame St. George's Harbour to the north. Mature sea-grape trees provide shady areas to escape the midday sun. Vendors selling spices, palm hats and baskets, hair-braiding services, T-shirts, and coral jewelry punctuate a day on this beach. **La Sagesse Beach,** at La Sagesse Nature Center on Grenada's southern coast, is a lovely, quiet refuge with a strip of powdery white sand. Plan a full day with nature walks and a delicious lunch at the small inn adjacent to the beach. **Morne Rouge Beach** is on the Caribbean, about 1 mi south of Grand Anse Bay and 3 mi south of St. George's Harbour. The beach forms a half-mile-long crescent and has a gentle surf that is excellent for swimming. A small café serves light meals during the day. In the evening, there's a disco, Fantazia 2001 (☞ Nightlife, *below*). **Pink Gin Beach** is at Point Salines, near the airport. Besides Grenada's two mega-resorts, Rex Grenadian and LaSOURCE, you'll also find the Aquarium Beach Club with open-air dining, bar, events, snorkeling on an offshore reef, and kayak rentals. Consider spending time here before an afternoon flight. **Pearl's Beach,** north of Grenville on the island's Atlantic coast, has miles of light gray sand fringed with palm trees. The beach is usually deserted, and the surf can be high. Near the beach is Grenada's old (pre-1983) airport runway.

## Outdoor Activities and Sports

### Bicycling

Level ground is rare in Grenada, but that doesn't stop the aerobically primed. What's more, 15-speed mountain bikes are available for a much more reasonable rate than are four-wheel-drive vehicles. You can rent bikes at **Ride Grenada** (⊠ L'Anse aux Epines, ☎ 473/444–1157). Caution: Roads are narrow and winding, and sharing lanes with fast-moving vehicles can be hazardous.

### Fishing

Deep-sea fishing around Grenada is excellent, with marlin, sailfish, yellowfin tuna, and dolphinfish topping the list of good catches. The annual **Spice Island Game Fishing Tournament** is held in late January. Half-day and full-day sportfishing excursions on *Xiphias Seeker,* a 35-ft Bertram Sport Fisherman, are available through **Evans Chartering Services** (☎ 473/444–4422 or 473/444–4217).

### Golf

**Grenada Golf and Country Club** (☎ 473/444–4128), near Grand Anse, has a nine-hole course and is open to visitors. Greens fees are EC$7. Your hotel can make arrangements for you.

### Hiking

Mountain trails wind through **Grand Etang National Park and Forest Preserve** (☎ 473/440–6160), and if you're lucky, you may get a glimpse of a monkey or some exotic birds on your hike. There are trails for all levels, from a self-guiding nature trail around Crater Lake to the most demanding one that leads up to Mount Qua Qua (2,300 ft).

At 4 PM on alternate Saturdays throughout the year, **Hash House Harriers** (☎ 473/440–3343) welcomes not-so-serious runners and walkers for exercise and fun in the countryside.

### Sailing

As the "Gateway to the Grenadines," Grenada attracts significant numbers of seasoned yachters and day sailers to its waters. **Moorings' Club Mariner Watersports Center** (☎ 473/444–4439 or 473/444–4549), at the Secret Harbour Hotel on the southeast shore, has half- and full-day charter yachts and a range of Shore 'n' Sail programs, developed by America's Cup racer Steve Colgate, for beginning and experienced sailors. **Seabreeze Yacht Charters** (☎ 473/444–4924; 800/387–3998 from the U.S.) at the Spice Island Marine Centre rents sailing or power yachts, with or without crew. **Starwind Enterprise** (☎ 473/440–3678 or 473/440–2508) offers day, half-day, and sunset sailing trips along Grenada's southwest coast.

### Scuba Diving and Snorkeling

Diving in this area is excellent, with visibility up to 200 ft. Hundreds of varieties of fish and more than 40 species of coral await underwater explorers. The best snorkeling is around small islands off Carriacou's coastline. A superb spot for diving is the site of what is sometimes dubbed the *Titanic* of the Caribbean. The *Bianca C,* a 600-ft cruise ship that caught fire and sank in 1961, settled in waters more than 100 ft deep and is now home to giant turtles, spotted eagle rays with 15-ft wingspans, and a 350-pound grouper that lives in the ship's smokestack.

**Dive Grenada** (⊠ Cot Bam on Grand Anse Beach and the Calabash Hotel at L'Anse aux Epines, ☎ 473/444–1092, FAX 473/440–6699) offers scuba and snorkeling trips to reefs and shipwrecks, including night dives and special excursions to the *Bianca C*. PADI-certified diving instruction, ranging from a resort course for novices to a dive-master program, is available. **Grand Anse Aquatics, Ltd.** (⌂ Coyaba Beach Resort on Grand Anse Beach, ☎ 473/444–4129) offers scuba and snorkeling trips and diving instruction, including resort courses for novices. Single dives are $45; *Bianca C* dives, $60; snorkeling trips, $20. **SCUBA World** (⌂ Rex Grenadian Resort in Point Salines, ☎ 473/444–3333, ext. 584; ⌂ Grenada Renaissance Resort on Grand Anse Beach, ☎ 473/444–4371, ext. 638; ⌂ Secret Harbour Resort, ☎ 473/444–4504) offers professional instruction to beginners and advanced divers alike, has a complete inventory of modern equipment, and runs daily excursions to the best dive sites on Grenada. **Carriacou Silver Diving** (⌂ Main St., Hillsborough, Carriacou, ☎ 473/443–7882) is a fully equipped, PADI-certified dive center. Dive trips, including night dives, visit Carriacou's virgin reefs, spectacular underwater walls, and mysterious caves. **Tanki's Watersport Paradise, Ltd.** (⌂ Paradise Beach, Carriacou, ☎ 473/443–8406) offers scuba diving at more than 20 sites, including trips to Sandy Island—a beautiful white-sand atoll, with an extensive reef system, just off shore. Night dives can be arranged.

## Tennis

Several hotels have tennis courts that are free to their guests: **Calabash** (☎ 473/444–4234), **Secret Harbour** (☎ 473/444–4548), **Coyaba Beach Resort** (☎ 473/444–4129), **Spice Island Beach Resort** (☎ 473/444–4258), **Grenada Renaissance** (☎ 473/444–4371), **Coral Cove** (☎ 473/444–4217), **LaSOURCE** (☎ 473/444–2556), **Rex Grenadian** (☎ 473/444–3333), and **Twelve Degrees North** (☎ 473/444–4580). Visitors who are not staying at one of these hotels may play on public courts in Grand Anse or opt for a day pass at LaSOURCE.

## Triathlon

Each January, triathletes from around the world compete in Grenada's annual **International Triathlon.** The two-day competition starts and finishes at Grand Anse Beach. Participants compete in a 1½-km swim, a 25-km cycling race, and a 5-km run on the first day. A three-person relay takes place on the second day. Teams must include at least one female and have a combined age of at least 100 years.

# Shopping

The best souvenirs of Grenada are little spice baskets filled with cinnamon, nutmeg, mace, bay leaf, vanilla, turmeric, and ginger. You can buy them for as little as $2 in practically every shop, at the market, or from vendors who stroll the beach in Grand Anse. Beach vendors also sell fabric dolls, T-shirts, coral jewelry, seashells, and hats and baskets handwoven from green palm fronds.

## Good Buys

ST. GEORGE'S

**Arawak Islands** (⌂ Upper Belmont Rd., ☎ 473/444–3577) produces exotic island perfumes, colognes, body oils, soaps, herbal teas, and potpourris—all packaged for gift-giving. Their workshop is on site. No credit cards are accepted. **Art Fabrik** (⌂ Young St., ☎ 473/440–0568) is a batik studio, where you can watch artisans paint fabric with hot wax. The dyeing room is on the first floor; as likely as not, you'll see lengths of batik hanging out to dry in the courtyard. You can buy batik by the yard ($22–$27, depending on the width) or fashioned into dresses, shirts, shorts, hats, scarves, and more. **Gifts Remembered** (⌂ Cross St., ☎ 473/440–2482; ⌂ Coyaba Beach Resort, ☎ 473/444–4129) is crammed with wonderful, inexpensive stuff, including brightly painted ceramic boats and buses laden with fruit and smiling islanders, T-shirts, spices, sundries, and hand-painted masks made from calabash halves. **Marketing & National Importing Board** (⊠ Young St., ☎ 473/440–1791) stocks fruits and vegetables, spices, hot sauces, molasses, nutmeg, and other local products. **Spice Island Perfumes** (⊠ On the Carenage, ☎ 473/440–2006) is a treasure trove of local fragrances, body oils, and natural extracts of spices and herbs. Best of all are its tiny wooden pots of solid perfume, including bitter orange, jasmine, or spice for around $8. **Tikal** (⊠ Young St., ☎ 473/440–2310), a long-established boutique, is well known for its exquisite baskets, artwork, jewelry, carvings, batik items, and fashions, both locally made and imported from Africa and Latin America. **Turbo Charge Records & Tapes** (⊠ St. John's St., ☎ 473/440–0586) is where to go for the latest reggae, calypso, soca, and steel-band music. **White Cane Industries** (⊠ At far end of Carenage, ☎ 473/444–2014) stocks bargain baskets, hats, and spectacularly colored rag rugs, all handwoven locally by blind craftspeople. Credit cards are not accepted. **Yellow Poui Art Gallery** (⊠ At intersection of Cross St. and the Esplanade, ☎ 473/440–3001) displays artwork from Grenada, Jamaica, Trinidad, and Guyana and canvases by expatriate European artists.

The **open-air market** (⊠ Market Sq., no phone) is open weekday mornings, but Saturday morning is the best—and busiest—time to go. Vendors sell fruits and vegetables from their own gardens, coconut water, and spices—a feast for the eyes as well as for the stomach. You'll also find clothing, leather sandals, and handcrafted items for sale.

### GRAND ANSE

**Gift Shop** (⊠ Grand Anse Shopping Centre, ☎ 473/444–4408) is an outlet for imported luxury items such as watches, leather goods, fine jewelry, crystal, and china, at duty-free prices. **Imagine** (⊠ Grand Anse Shopping Centre, ☎ 473/444–4028) specializes in island handicrafts, including fashions, ceramics, and batik fabrics. **United Artists Art Gallery** (⊠ Le Marquis Complex, ☎ 473/444–5022) displays a unique collection of top-quality artwork. You'll find wood and stone carvings, painted masks, paintings, furniture, and other objets d'art created by artists from Grenada, Carriacou, and Petit Martinique.

### CARRIACOU

In L'Esterre on Carriacou, hand-painted signs announce "This way to the great artist," **Canute Calliste.** If you get lost, one of his many grandchildren will lead the way. Works by Calliste, colorful watercolors of island scenes, are also available at the Carriacou Museum.

# Nightlife

## Grenada

Grenada's nightlife is centered mainly on the resort hotels. During winter, Spice Island Beach Resort, the Calabash, Coyaba, Rex Grenadian, and the Grenada Renaissance have steel band or other entertainment several nights of each week (☞ Lodging, *above*). Your hotel or the tourist information office will have information about where various bands are performing on a given night.

**Beachside Terrace** (⊠ Flamboyant Hotel, Grand Anse, ☎ 473/444–4247) is casual and unpretentious and draws an international set for crab racing on Monday nights, a live steel band on Wednesdays, and a beach barbecue with calypso music on Friday evenings. **Boatyard** (⊠ L'Anse aux Epines, ☎ 473/444–4662), at the Marina, is the place to be on Friday night from 11 PM till sunup, when international discs are spun by a smooth-talkin' local DJ. **Cot Bam** (⊠ Grand Anse Beach, ☎ 473/444–2050) hits the spot for visitors who want something simple, lively, and friendly for little money. Dancing, dining, and socializing take place nightly. The place is open until 3 AM on Friday and Saturday. **Fantazia 2001** (✉ Gem Apartments premises, Morne Rouge, ☎ 473/444–4224 or 473/444–1189) is a popular disco on the beach, where soca and reggae are played, along with international favorites, from 9:30 PM until the wee hours. Wednesday is Golden Oldies Night. It's dark and loud and fun, with a mix of locals and tourists. There is a small cover charge (EC$5) on Friday and Saturday nights. **Rhum Runner** (✉ On Carenage, St. George's, ☎ 473/440–2198), a 60-ft twin-deck catamaran, leaves from the fire station jetty at 7:30 PM each Friday and Saturday night for a moonlit cruise in the waters around St. George's and Grand Anse, returning about midnight. Tickets are EC$20, and reservations are recommended. **Rhum Runner II**, a 72-ft sister ship, operates sunset dinner cruises on Wednesday evening from 6 to 9 PM for $40 per person. **Le Sucrier** (✉ Sugar Mill, Grand Anse, ☎ 800/444–1068) is open on Wednesday, Thursday, Friday, and Saturday from 9 PM to 3 AM and attracts a young crowd with comedy and a disco on Thursday and "oldies" night on Wednesday.

### Carriacou

**Hillsborough Bar** (☎ 473/443–7932) is a small, white, flat-topped structure on the main street of the island's seat of government, a town populated by no more than about 600 citizens, including owner Edward Primus. Brave the twin otter (small airplane) to Carriacou, and then buy yourself a drink—the rum flows freely.

## Exploring Grenada

It may be hard to pull yourself away from the beach to see the rest of this lovely island, but a day or so of exploring is worth the effort. St. George's is a picturesque capital city, with a busy harbor, interesting shops, and several historic sites. A trip into the countryside and a visit to a spice plantation and a nutmeg processing plant will help you see what makes Grenada tick. Along the scenic coast road, you're likely to come across a group of strapping young fishermen in a tug-of-war with the sea, pulling in an enormous fishing net; it's an all-day job, and a share of the catch is the reward. Passing through tiny villages, you'll receive waves from locals perched on the verandas of colorful cottages, and see women carrying baskets of laundry on their heads. A guide can take more adventurous sightseers hiking into the thick of the rain forest or for a swim under a waterfall in lush, Eden-like surroundings. Touring Grenada is a treat for the senses—the scenery is eye-popping, and the scent of nutmeg fills the air.

Carriacou, Petit Martinique, and a handful of uninhabited specks that are included in the nation of Grenada are north of Grenada island and part of the Grenadines, an archipelago of 32 tiny islands and cays. You can fly into Carriacou's Lauriston Airport from Grenada or come by sea. Schooners leave from St. George's Harbour twice a week, ferrying cargo and passengers on a 4½-hour voyage. *Osprey Express,* a semi-hovercraft, makes the overseas voyage to Carriacou and Petit Martinique every day except Wednesday, taking just 1½ hours each way. The per-person fare is EC$40 one-way, EC$75 round-trip.

*Numbers in the margin correspond to points of interest on the Grenada (and Carriacou) map.*

SIGHTS TO SEE

**❻ Annandale Falls and Visitors' Centre.** A mountain stream cascades 50 ft into a pool surrounded by exotic tropical flora, such as liana vines and elephant ears. This is a good spot for swimming and picnicking.

✉ *Main interior road, 15 mins east of St. George's,* ☎ *473/440–2452.*
🕐 *Daily 9–5.*

**➌ Bay Gardens.** Just outside St. George's is a private horticultural paradise
where 450 species of flowers and plants that grow on the island are cultivated in patterns mimicking their growth in the wild. Eight acres of
paths are open to visitors. Bay Gardens is in the suburb of St. Paul's, a
short drive into the countryside from town. ✉ *St. Paul's.* 💲 *$1.* 🕐 *Daily
during daylight hrs.*

**⓬ Carib's Leap.** At Sauteurs (the French word for leapers), at the northernmost tip of the island, Carib's Leap (also called Leapers Hill) is the
100-ft cliff from which Carib Indians flung themselves in 1651, pre-
ferring to die rather than submit to the French invaders.

**⓰ Carriacou.** This little island (13 square mi) packs a lot of punch—rum
punch, that is. With more than a hundred rum shops and only one gas
station, Carriacou will bring the fastest metabolism down to a quiet
purr. This island hideaway exudes the kind of ebullient spirit and
goodwill that you want to find in a Caribbean retreat. Come here if
you want peace. Don't bother if you want luxurious amenities or if
you would suffer coldly a parrot on your breakfast table!

Hillsborough is Carriacou's main town. Rolling hills cut a wide swath
through the island's center, from Gun Point, in the north, to Tyrrel Bay,
in the south. The small town of Windward, on the east coast, is traditionally a boatbuilding community. Originally built for interisland
commerce, the boats are now built for fishing and pleasure sailing. Passing through town, you'll likely encounter several half-built hulls on the
roadside. If you're lucky, your visit may coincide with the launching
of a new boat, traditionally a time of great celebration.

In February, fun-lovers are drawn to Carriacou for **Carnival** festivities,
a four-day event with parades, music, and frivolity. In August, the **Carriacou Regatta**—the largest sailing event in the Grenadines—attracts
yachts and sailboats from throughout the Caribbean for three days of
races between Grenada and Carriacou. Festivities include cultural activities and Big Drum dance performances—a harvest dance performed,
outside of Africa, only on Carriacou.

Carriacou's colonial past parallels Grenada's, although Carriacou's tiny
size has restricted its political role to a minor part in the area's history.
The only museum in the eastern Caribbean that is owned by the people, not the government, is the **Carriacou Museum** (✉ Paterson St.,
Hillsborough), behind Gramma's Bakery. Housed in an old cotton gin-
nery, it has displays of unearthed Amerindian, European, and African
artifacts and a gift shop loaded with locally made items. The museum
is open daily 9:30–4; admission is $2.

**Sandy Island,** just off the west coast of the island opposite Silver Beach
Resort, is a gorgeous spot of sand punctuated by a stand of palm trees.
For a few dollars, a local fellow with a motorboat will transport you
back and forth. Bring your snorkeling gear.

**➑ Concord Falls.** The coast road north from St. George's winds past soaring mountains and valleys covered with palms, bamboo, banana and
breadfruit trees, and tropical flowers. Off the road, about 8 mi north
of St. George's, are the Concord Falls, with a small visitor center, a
viewing platform, and a changing room for donning a bathing suit. During the dry months (January to May), when the currents aren't too strong,
you can take a dip under the cascades of the lower falls. If you're up
to it, hike 2 mi through tropical forest to a second, spectacular waterfall, which thunders down over huge boulders and creates a small

pool (no swimming permitted at the upper falls). The path is clear, but it's smart to use a guide. ⌧ *Coast Rd.* ☞ *$1 for changing room.*

**❾ Dougaldston Estate.** Just south of Gouyave, this estate has a spice factory where you can see cocoa, nutmeg, mace, cloves, cinnamon, and other spices laid out on giant racks to dry in the sun. One of the workers will be glad to explain the process. You can purchase a bag of cinnamon bark, cloves, bay leaves, mace, or nutmeg for about $2 each. ⌧ *Gouyave, no phone.* ☞ *$1.* ☉ *Weekdays 9–4.*

**⓫ Fisherman's Museum.** On the outskirts of Gouyave in a place called Mabouya, Anthony Joseph operates a small museum dedicated to the island's fishermen. The collections, assembled over the past 20 years, touch on fishing equipment, the resources of the sea, the forest's impact, the life of the beach, and the social life of the fishermen. Mr. Joseph is your tour guide, and his narrative is enchanting. ⌧ *Western Main Rd., Gouyave, no phone.* ☞ *75¢.* ☉ *Daily 9–4.*

**❷ Grand Anse.** Most of the island's hotels and nightlife are in Grand Anse or the adjacent community of L'Anse aux Epines, which means Prickly Bay. There's a public entrance to Grand Anse Beach at Camerhogne Park, adjacent to Coyaba Beach Hotel and just a few steps from the main road. St. George's University Medical School, which for years had an enviable location directly on the beach, has consolidated its facility in True Blue, a nearby residential area, overlooking a picturesque cove. In earlier times, the True Blue area was an indigo plantation.

A short walk from the resorts of Grand Anse is the **Grand Anse Shopping Centre,** which includes a supermarket–liquor store, clothing store, bank, fast-food restaurant, and several small gift shops with good-quality souvenirs and such luxury items as English china and Swedish crystal. The **Marquis Complex,** across the street, has restaurants, shops, an art gallery, and tourist services (☞ Shopping, *above*).

**☝ ❼ Grand Etang National Park.** In the middle of lush, mountainous Grenada is a bird sanctuary and forest reserve, with miles of hiking trails and streams for fishing. Visit the informative Grand Etang Forest Center to view displays on the local flora and fauna. A forest manager is on hand to answer questions. Crater Lake, in the crater of an extinct volcano, is a 30-acre glasslike expanse of cobalt blue water. ⌧ *Main interior road, between Grenville and St. George's,* ☎ *473/440–6160.* ☞ *$1.* ☉ *Daily 8:30–4.*

**⓯ Grenville.** The island's second-largest city is reminiscent of a French market town. Saturday is market day, and the town fills with people doing their weekly shopping. Schooners set sail from Grenville for the outer islands. The local spice-processing factory, Grenville Cooperative Nutmeg Association (☎ 473/442–7241), is open to the public.

**☝ ❺ Laura Herb and Spice Garden.** The 6½-acre sight is part of an old plantation in the village of Laura, in St. David's, just 6 mi east of Grand Anse. It belongs to the Minor Spices Cooperative and is funded by the European Union. Visitors see and learn about medicinal spices and herbs, including cocoa, clove, nutmeg, pimiento, cinnamon, turmeric, and tonka beans (vanilla). A 45-minute tour of the spice-processing plant includes explanations of the medicinal benefits of the various products. ⌧ *Laura,* ☎ *473/443–2604.* ☞ *$2.* ☉ *Weekdays 8–4.*

**⓭ Levera National Park and Bird Sanctuary.** This portion of Grenada's protected parkland encompasses 450 acres at the northeastern tip of the island, where the Caribbean Sea meets the Atlantic Ocean. Facilities include a visitor center, changing rooms, a small amphitheater, and a gift shop. The thick mangroves provide food and protection for nesting seabirds and seldom-seen tropical parrots. Some fine Arawak ruins and petroglyphs can be seen, as well. The first islet of the Grenadines is visible in the distance.

☝ ❿ **Nutmeg Processing Cooperative.** Gouyave is the center of Grenada's nutmeg industry. A tour of the Nutmeg Processing Cooperative in the center of town makes a fragrant and fascinating half hour. Workers in the three-story plant, which turns out 3 million pounds of Grenada's most famous export per year, sort nutmegs by hand and pack them in burlap bags for shipping worldwide. ✉ *Gouyave,* ☎ *473/444–8337.* 🎫 *$1.* 🕐 *Weekdays 10–1 and 2–4.*

⓱ **Petit Martinique.** Five miles northeast of Carriacou is Petit Martinique, the smallest of Grenada's inhabited islands. Like Carriacou and Grenada, Petit Martinique was settled by the French. Most visitors to Petit Martinique come on fishing trips; the island does not really have tourist facilities.

⓮ **River Antoine Rum Distillery.** At this local operation, kept open primarily as a museum, rum is produced by the same methods used since the distillery opened in the mid-1700s. The result is a potent overproof rum that will knock your socks off. ✉ *River Antoine Estate, St. Patrick's,* ☎ *473/442–7109.* 🎫 *$1.* 🕐 *Guided tours daily 9–4.*

❶ **St. George's.** Grenada's capital city and major port is one of the most picturesque and authentic West Indian towns in the Caribbean. Pastel-painted buildings with orange-tile roofs cling to the curving shore along horseshoe-shape **St. George's Harbour.** Small, rainbow-hued houses rise up from the waterfront and disappear into steep green hills. On weekends, a windjammer is likely to be anchored in the harbor, giving the entire scene a 19th-century appearance.

**The Carenage,** the road and walkway around St. George's Harbour, is the capital's main thoroughfare. Warehouses, small shops, and restaurants face the water. At the southern side of the Carenage, near the Grenada Board of Tourism office, is the pier where cruise ships dock. **Young Street,** a main shopping street, starts at the northern side of the Carenage, rises steeply uphill, then descends sharply to the marketplace.

The **Grenada National Museum** (✉ Young and Monckton Sts., ☎ 473/440–3725), a couple of blocks off the Carenage, is set in the foundation of an old French army barracks and prison built in 1704. The small museum has exhibits of news items, photos, and proclamations regarding the intervention, along with memorabilia depicting various other periods in Grenada's history—replicas of posters advertising the sale of "slaves . . . of good character," the young Josephine Bonaparte's marble bathtub, 18th-century rum-making equipment, seashells and artifacts, and a Miss World 1970 portrait. The museum is open weekdays 9–4:30 and Saturday 10–1:30; admission is $1.

On the bay side of St. George's, facing the sea and separated from the harbor by the Sendall Tunnel, the **Esplanade** is the location of the open-air meat and fish markets. At high tide, waves sometimes crash against the seawall. This area is also the terminus of the minibus route.

Don't miss picturesque **Market Square,** a block from the Esplanade at Granby Street. It's open weekday mornings but really comes alive Saturday from 8 AM to noon. Vendors sell baskets, spices, brooms, clothing, knickknacks, coconut water, and fresh produce, including tropical fruit you can eat on the spot. Market Square is also where parades and political rallies take place—and the beginning of the minibus routes to outer areas of the island.

St. George's has several fine old churches that are worth visiting. **St. Andrew's Presbyterian Church,** built in 1830, is at the intersection of Halifax and Church streets. Also known as Scots' Kirk, it was built with the help of the Freemasons. **St. George's Anglican Church,** on Gore Street, was built in 1826. It's a beautiful stone and pink stucco building filled with statues and plaques depicting Grenada in the 18th and 19th centuries. **St. George's Methodist Church,** on Green Street near Tyrrel Street, was built in 1820 and is the oldest original church in the city. The tower of **St. George's Roman Catholic Church** dates from 1818, but the current church building was built in 1884.

On Church Street, **York House,** built around 1800, is home to Grenada's Houses of Parliament and Supreme Court. It and the neighboring Registry building, built in 1780, are fine examples of early Georgian architecture.

**Marryshow House** (⊠ Tyrrel St., near Bain Alley, ☎ 473/440–2451), built in 1917, combines Victorian and West Indian architecture. It's home to the Marryshow Folk Theatre, Grenada's first cultural center. Plays, West Indian dance and music, and poetry readings are presented here on occasion. The house is open weekdays 8:30–4:30 and Saturday 9–1; admission is free.

**Fort George** is high on the hill at the southern tip of Church Street. The fort, which rises above the entrance to the harbor, was built by the French in 1705 to defend the harbor. No shots were ever fired until October 1983, when Prime Minister Bishop and some of his followers were assassinated in the courtyard. The fort now houses police headquarters but is open to the public daily during daylight hours; admission is free. The 360-degree view from here is spectacular.

On Richmond Hill, high above St. George's and the harbor, historic **Fort Frederick** provides a magnificent view. The fort was completed in 1791; it was the headquarters of the People's Revolutionary Government during the infamous intervention of 1983. Today, visitors can get a bird's-eye view of the prison, on top of an adjacent hill, where the perpetrators of that event are still incarcerated.

In St. Paul's, five minutes outside St. George's, **de la Grenade Industries** (⊠ Box 788, St. George's, ☎ 473/440–3241) is a local spice-processing plant that began in 1960 as a small cottage industry and today manufacturers award-winning products made from nutmeg and other homegrown fruits and spices: syrups, jams and jellies, and liqueur. Visitors are welcome to watch the process—each day it may be a different product—and purchase gift items from the retail operation on site. The plant is open weekdays 8–5 and Saturday 9–12:30; admission is free.

❹ **Westerhall.** This residential area about 5 mi southeast of St. George's is known for its beautiful villas, gardens, and panoramic views. A great deal of pricey development is happening here: European and North American retirees and local businesspeople are building elegant homes with striking views of the sea.

# Grenada A to Z

## Arriving and Departing

### BY PLANE

**American Airlines** (☎ 800/433–7300 or 473/444–2222) has daily flights into Grenada's Point Salines International Airport from major U.S. and Canadian cities via its San Juan hub. **BWIA** (☎ 800/327–7401, 800/538–2942 in Miami, or 473/444–4134) flies direct from New York and Miami. **Air Canada** (☎ 800/776–3000) flies from Toronto via Barbados. **British Airways** (☎ 800/247–9297 or 473/440–2796) flies from London twice a week.

**LIAT** (Leeward Islands Air Transport, ☎ 473/440–2796 or 473/440–2796), **Region Air** (☎ 473/444–1117), **Airlines of Carriacou** (☎ 473/444–3549 or 473/444–1479), and **HelenAir** (☎ 473/444–4101, ext. 2090) each have scheduled service between Grenada and Carriacou's Lauriston Airport. Recent renovations to Carriacou's airport included expanding the runway and adding lights for night landings.

FROM THE AIRPORT

No bus service is available between the Point Salines airport and hotels, but taxis are readily available. Fares to St. George's and the hotels of Grand Anse and L'Anse aux Epines are $10–$12. Rides taken between 6 PM and 6 AM incur a $2.50 surcharge. From Carriacou's Lauriston Airport to Hillsborough, the fare is $2.50.

## Currency

Grenada uses the Eastern Caribbean (EC) dollar. At press time, the exchange rate was fixed at EC$2.67 to US$1. Money can be exchanged at any bank or hotel, but U.S. currency and traveler's checks are widely accepted. Although prices are usually quoted in EC dollars, be sure to ask which currency is referred to when you make purchases and business transactions. Hotels are not permitted to give foreign currency in change or on departure. Most hotels, major restaurants, and shops accept credit cards.

## Emergencies

**Police and fire:** ☎ 911. **Ambulance:** In St. George's, Grand Anse, and L'Anse aux Epines, ☎ 434. In St. Andrew's, ☎ 724. **Hospitals:** St. George's Hospital (☎ 473/440–2051); St. Andrew's Hospital, Mirabeau (on the east coast) (☎ 473/442–7251); Carriacou Hospital (☎ 473/443–7400). **Pharmacies:** Gitten's (✉ Halifax St., St. George's, ☎ 473/440–2165 or 473/440–2340 after hrs) is open weekdays and Saturday 9–8, Sunday and public holidays 9–noon. Gitten's Drugmart (✉ Main Rd., Grand Anse, ☎ 473/444–4954 or 473/440–2340 after hrs) is open weekdays and Saturday 9–8, Sunday and public holidays 9–noon. Parris' Pharmacy Ltd. (✉ Victoria St., Grenville, ☎ 473/442–7330), on the windward side of the island, is open Monday–Wednesday and Friday 9–4:30, Thursday 9–1, and Saturday 9–7.

## Getting Around

BUSES

Privately owned 15-passenger minivans ply the winding road between St. George's and Grand Anse. Hail one anywhere along the way, pay EC$1, and hold on to your hat. They pass by frequently from about 6 AM to 8 PM daily except Sundays and holidays. You can get anywhere on the island via these minivans for EC$1–EC$5 per person—a bargain by any standard—but be prepared for packed vehicles, unpredictable schedules, loud music, and some hair-raising maneuvers.

CARS

Roads are mountainous and winding once you get beyond the Grand Anse area, and driving is on the left. To rent a car, you will need a valid driver's license with which you may obtain a local permit from the traffic department (at the fire station on the Carenage) or some car-rental firms at a cost of EC$30. Rental cars (including four-wheel-drive vehicles) cost $45–$60 a day or $220–$285 a week with unlimited mileage. Gas costs about $2.60 per gallon. Your hotel can arrange a rental for you.

**David's** (☎ 473/444–3399 or 473/444–3038, FAX 473/444–4404) maintains four offices: Point Salines International Airport, Grenada Renaissance Resort, Rex Grenadian Hotel, and the Limes in Grand Anse. **Dollar Rent-a-Car** (☎ 473/444–4786, FAX 473/444–4788) is at Point Salines Airport. **Avis** (☎ 473/440–3936 or 473/440–2624; 473/444–4563 after hours; FAX 473/440–4110) is at Spice Island Rental on Paddock and Lagoon roads in St. George's. In the True Blue area, call **McIntyre Bros. Ltd.** (☎ 473/444–3944; 473/443–5319 after hrs; FAX 473/444–2899). In Carriacou, **Barba's Auto Rentals** (☎ 473/443–7454, FAX 473/443–8137) will meet you at the airport.

TAXIS

Taxis are plentiful and rates are set by the government. The trip between Grand Anse and St. George's costs about EC$20. An EC$10 surcharge is added to all fares for rides taken between 6 PM and 6 AM. Taxis are often waiting for fares at hotels, at the cruise-passenger welcome center, and on the Carenage.

**Water taxis** are available at the Carenage, and it's a lovely perspective on a warm day. For about EC$1.50, you can be hand-rowed from one side of the Carenage to the other; for EC$5, a motorized water taxi will deliver you to your Grand Anse–area hotel.

## Guided Tours

On at least one day of your stay in Grenada, be sure to get off the beach and out into the countryside to experience the magnificent scenery that nature has bestowed on this island. Guided tours regularly take individuals or small groups on sightseeing excursions in and around St. George's, to Grand Etang National Park, to spice plantations in Gouyave, on hikes in the rain forest, and on day trips to Carriacou.

For a special treat, take part in Grenada's **People-to-People Program.** With a little advance notice, you can meet local people with similar interests and foster an intercultural friendship—play a round of golf, attend a church service, have lunch, or simply sightsee with your island host. For details, contact Edyth Leonard at New Trends Tours (✉ Box 797, St. George's, ☎ 473/444–1236, FAX 473/444–4836).

TOUR OPERATORS

**Amerindian Tours** (☎ 473/440–9686) offers innovative tours of Grenada's waterfalls, spice plantations, old forts, and historic sites. **Arnold's Tours** (☎ 473/440–0531 or 473/440–2213, FAX 473/440–4118) offers several land, sea, and "Lan-Sea" combination tours. Prices range from $25 for an island tour, hiking trip, or sunset cruise to $140 for an all-day cruise to Carriacou. Dennis Henry of **Henry's Safari Tours** (☎ 473/444–5313, FAX 473/444–4847) knows Grenada like the back of his hand. He offers adventurous hikes and four-wheel-drive-vehicle safaris, or you can design your own tour. Depending on the size of the group, a full-day island tour, including lunch, costs $40–$55 per person; a six-hour hike to Concord Falls is $30–$45 per person. **Spiceland Tours** (☎ 473/440–5180) offers several five- and seven-hour island tours, from an "Urban/Suburban" tour of St. George's and the South Coast to an "Emerald Forest Tour" highlighting Grenada's natural beauty. Other reputable operators that offer similar guided tours are **Sunshine Tours** (☎ 473/444–4296), **Sunsation Tours** (☎ 473/444–1594), and **Caribbean Horizons** (☎ 473/444–1555).

## Language

English is the official language of Grenada.

## Opening and Closing Times

Stores are generally open 8 AM–4 or 4:30 PM weekdays, 8 AM–1 PM on Saturday. Most are closed Sunday, although tourist shops usually open if a cruise ship is in port. Banks in St. George's are open Monday–

Thursday 8 AM–1:30 or 2 PM, Friday 8 AM–5 PM. The main post office, on Lagoon Road in St. George's, is open 8 AM–3:30 PM weekdays.
Each town or village has a post office branch.

## Passports and Visas

Passports are not required of U.S., Canadian, or British citizens, provided visitors have two proofs of citizenship (one with photo) and a
return air ticket. A passport, even an expired one, is the best proof of
citizenship. A driver's license with photo *and* an original birth certificate or voter registration card will also suffice.

## Precautions

Secure your valuables in the hotel safe. Avoid walking alone late at night
in the Grand Anse/L'Anse aux Epines hotel districts; it's dark enough to
bump into things, maybe even into one of the cows that graze silently
by the roadside in Grand Anse. Mosquitoes adore tourists, especially after
heavy rains; and on the beach, tiny sand flies begin to bite after 4 PM;
bring repellent. Water from hotel taps is perfectly safe to drink.

## Taxes and Service Charges

Hotels and restaurants add an 8% government tax. Many hotels and
restaurants add an additional 10% service charge to your bill. If not,
a 10% gratuity should be added for a job well done.

The departure tax is EC$35 (US$13.50) for adults and EC$17.50
(US$6.75) for children ages 5–11, payable in either currency. Children
under five are exempt. A surcharge of EC$10 (US$4) is levied when
departing Carriacou.

## Telephones and Mail

Grenada has a fully digital telecommunications service and can be di-
aled directly from the United States and Canada. The area code is 473,
which was changed on October 31, 1997. If you are calling before this
date, continue to use the old 809 area code. From Grenada, direct-dial
calls can placed worldwide from pay phones, card phones, and most
hotel room phones.

Airmail rates for letters to the United States and Canada are EC75¢
for a half-ounce letter and EC35¢ for a postcard.

## Visitor Information

The **Grenada Board of Tourism** (☎ 473/440–2001 or 473/440–2279,
FAX 473/440–6637), located on the south side of the Carenage, in St.
George's, distributes maps, brochures, and information on accom-
modations, tours, and other services. You'll want to pick up a copy of
*Greeting,* the official publication of the Board of Tourism and the
Grenada Hotel Association. It's available free in most hotels.

For information before leaving home, contact the **Grenada Board of
Tourism** in the United States (✉ 820 2nd Ave., Suite 900D, New York,
NY 10017, ☎ 212/687–9554 or 800/927–9554, FAX 212/573–9731);
in Canada (✉ 439 University Ave., Suite 820, Toronto, Ontario M5G
1Y8, ☎ 416/595–1339, FAX 416/595–8278); or in the United Kingdom
(✉ 1 Collingham Gardens, Earl's Court, London SW5 0HW, ☎ 0171/
370–5164 or 0171/370–5165, FAX 0171/370–7040).

Hotel reservations may be made at any of the hotels that are members
of the **Grenada Hotel Association** by calling 800/223–9815 in the
United States or Canada, 212/545–8469 in New York State, or fax-
ing them at 473/444–4847.

# 13 Guadeloupe

*Not just one island, Guadeloupe is an archipelago, with dramatically different kinds of landscape, a rich history, and all the things that the French connection brings: delicious food, excellent wine, grumpy waiters, topless sunbathing, and helter-skelter driving. Allez-y!*

Updated by
Kate
Pennebaker
and Simon
Worrall

**I**T'S A STEAMY HOT SATURDAY in August. There may be a tropical depression brewing somewhere to the west—it's that time of year. But the mood in Pointe-à-Pitre, Guadeloupe's commercial center, is anything but depressing. Amid music and laughter, women adorned with gold jewelry and dressed in clothes made of the traditional madras and foulard parade through the streets. Balanced on their heads are huge baskets decorated with miniature kitchen utensils and filled with mangoes, papayas, breadfruits, christophines, and other island edibles. The procession wends its way to the Cathédrale de St-Pierre et St-Paul, where a high mass is celebrated. A five-hour feast with music, song, and dance will follow.

The Fête des Cuisinières (Cooks' Festival) takes place annually in honor of St. Laurent, patron saint of cooks. The parading *cuisinières* are the island's women chefs, an honored group. This festival gives you a tempting glimpse of one of Guadeloupe's stellar attractions—its more than 200 restaurants that serve some of the best food in the Caribbean.

Guadeloupe looks like a giant butterfly resting on the sea between Antigua and Dominica. Its wings—Basse-Terre and Grande-Terre—are the two largest islands in the 659-square-mi Guadeloupe archipelago. The Rivière Salée, a 4-mi seawater channel flowing between the Caribbean and the Atlantic, forms the "spine" of the butterfly. Smaller, flatter Grande-Terre (218 square mi) is dry, flat, and sandy. It was once sugarcane country but today survives on intensively developed tourism. It has the best beaches, restaurants, casinos, resorts, and clubs. Basse-Terre ("low land") is wild, wet, and mountainous. It used to lag behind Grande-Terre, but in recent years it has begun to find its own distinct identity as the place for adventure tourism: hiking, whale-watching, diving, or deep-sea fishing. Its lush, precipitous west coast is as beautiful as any other place in the Caribbean. On Les Saintes, La Désirade, Marie-Galante, and the other islands of the archipelago, you will find places that have remained largely untouched by the world.

Guadeloupe was annexed by France in 1674. During the French Revolution, battles broke out between royalists and revolutionaries on the island. In 1794 Britain responded to the call from Guadeloupe royalists to come to their aid, and that same year France dispatched Victor Hugues to sort things out. (In virtually every town and village you'll run across a "Victor Hugues" street, boulevard, or park.) After his troops banished the British, Hugues issued a decree abolishing slavery and guillotined recalcitrant planters. The ones who managed to keep their heads fled to Louisiana or hid in the hills of Grande-Terre, where their descendants now live. Hugues—"the Robespierre of the Isles"—was soon relieved of his command, slavery was reestablished by Napoléon, and the French and English continued to battle over the island. The 1815 Treaty of Paris restored Guadeloupe to France, and in 1848, due largely to the efforts of Alsatian Victor Schoelcher, slavery was abolished. The island has been a *département* of France since 1946, and in 1974 it was elevated to a *région,* administered by a prefect appointed from Paris. With Martinique, St. Barts, and St. Martin, it forms part of what is known as *les Antilles Françaises,* or French West Indies.

An old saying of the French Caribbean refers to *"Les Grands Seigneurs de la Martinique et les Bons Gens de la Guadeloupe"* (the lords of Martinique and the bourgeoisie of Guadeloupe). And though there are few aristocrats left on Martinique these days, the saying still holds some truth in Guadeloupe. Look about you in the restaurants or at the beach, and you will see the faces of middle-class France. They come here to swim and sunbathe, scuba dive or hike. Most come on package tours. But sugar, not tourism, is still Guadeloupe's primary source of income. Currently, only about 10% of the workforce is employed in the tourism industry. At harvest time in January, the fields teem with workers cutting cane and the roads are clogged with trucks taking the harvest to distilleries.

Everything about Guadeloupe—from the *franglais* (*le topless, le weekend, le snack-bar*) to the zippy little cars and ubiquitous "vendeuses de plage" (girls who model bathing suits on *le beach* and do a striptease show in the process)—is French. And whether in hotel corridors or on the beach, at breakfast or on a dive boat, cigarette smoke is as much a part of the ambience as the tropical breeze. The prices are Parisian. Unlike on St. Martin and St. Barts there are stiff taxes on most goods. To really feel at home here, some *français* is indispensable. Even then, you will sometimes receive a bewildered response, as the Guadeloupeans' Creole patois greatly affects their pronunciation.

# Lodging

Guadeloupe doesn't have the selection of elegant, tasteful hotels found on Martinique, but you can opt for a splashy hotel with a full complement of resort activities or head for a small inn called a Relais Creole. If French is not your forte, you'll fare better in the large hotels. Gosier and Bas-du-Fort have been the main venues for resort hotels, but the areas around Ste-Anne and St-François also have their fair share of resorts. There are also small hotels on Iles des Saintes and Marie-Galante. More, and better, hotels are also opening on Basse-Terre. Most hotels include buffet breakfast in their rates. Prices decline 25%–40% in the off-season.

For information about villas, apartments, and private rooms in modest houses, contact **Gîtes de France** (☎ 590/91–64–33). For additional information about apartment-style accommodations, contact the **ANTRE Association** (☎ 590/88–53–09).

| CATEGORY | COST* |
|---|---|
| $$$$ | over $300 |
| $$$ | $225–$300 |
| $$ | $150–$225 |
| $ | under $150 |

*All prices are for a standard double room, excluding* taxe de séjour, *which varies from hotel to hotel, and 10%–15% service charge.*

## Guadeloupe

$$$$ ★ 🏨 **La Cocoteraie.** You get the most luxury the island has to offer here, and you pay for it—between $300 and $600 a night. This very private annex to Le Méridien (☞ *below*) consists of 50 suites housed in smart, blue and white colonial-style buildings. Twenty are directly on the beach, the rest have views of either the marina or the extravagantly large pool, fringed by blue-and-white Chinese vases. Each has a large living room, veranda, one small bathroom, and a spacious bathroom with hexagonal tub that looks out onto the water and a separate shower. The decor is a handsome blend of bright pastels, mahogany furnishings, and madras upholstery. The Robert Trent Jones–designed golf course is just across the road, and you also have full use of the facilities of Le Méridien. Under the energetic leadership of the on-site manager, Fidel Montana, the resort is focusing more and more on the American market. The staff all speak English, and the restaurant's international cuisine caters to the lighter tastes popular in the United States. ⊠ *Ave. de l'Europe, St-François 97118,* ☎ *590/88–79–81 or 800/543–4300,* FAX *590/88–78–33. 50 suites.*

**310**

# Guadeloupe

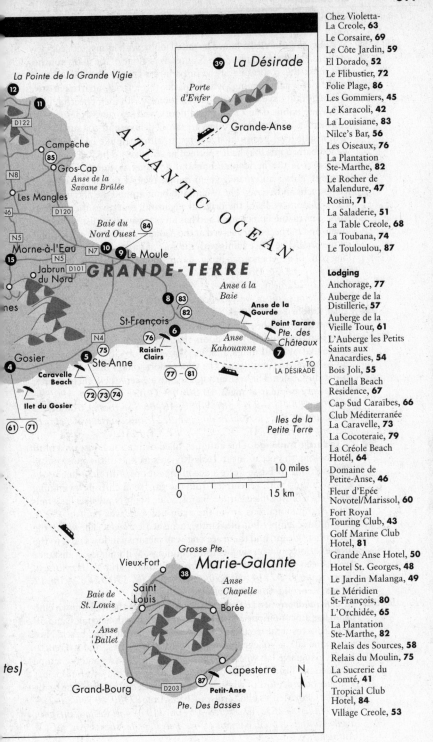

Chez Violetta-La Creole, **63**
Le Corsaire, **69**
Le Côte Jardin, **59**
El Dorado, **52**
Le Flibustier, **72**
Folie Plage, **86**
Les Gommiers, **45**
Le Karacoli, **42**
La Louisiane, **83**
Nilce's Bar, **56**
Les Oiseaux, **76**
La Plantation Ste-Marthe, **82**
Le Rocher de Malendure, **47**
Rosini, **71**
La Saladerie, **51**
La Table Creole, **68**
La Toubana, **74**
Le Touloulou, **87**

**Lodging**
Anchorage, **77**
Auberge de la Distillerie, **57**
Auberge de la Vieille Tour, **61**
L'Auberge les Petits Saints aux Anacardies, **54**
Bois Joli, **55**
Canella Beach Residence, **67**
Cap Sud Caraïbes, **66**
Club Méditerranée La Caravelle, **73**
La Cocoteraie, **79**
La Créole Beach Hotel, **64**
Domaine de Petite-Anse, **46**
Fleur d'Epée Novotel/Marissol, **60**
Fort Royal Touring Club, **43**
Golf Marine Club Hotel, **81**
Grande Anse Hotel, **50**
Hotel St. Georges, **48**
Le Jardin Malanga, **49**
Le Méridien St-François, **80**
L'Orchidée, **65**
La Plantation Ste-Marthe, **82**
Relais des Sources, **58**
Relais du Moulin, **75**
La Sucrerie du Comté, **41**
Tropical Club Hotel, **84**
Village Creole, **53**

*Restaurant, in-room safes, minibars, pool, 2 tennis courts, exercise room, beach. AE, DC, MC, V. CP, MAP.*

**$$$-$$$$** ★ ⌂ **Auberge de la Vieille Tour.** The raised lobby, with its magnificent view of the sea and the islands of Les Saintes, is just one of the many touches that make this resort one of the finest in the French Antilles. Another is the clever landscaping, which masks three large, apartment-style buildings that have the lowest-priced rooms. With their cheerful, blue-and-white nautical decor and tiled floors, and sea views, these are an excellent value. The finest rooms are the 32 deluxe, cliff-top suites, each with a split-level bedroom–living room with a trundle bed and glass-walled bathrooms that have spectacular sea views. The social focus of the resort is the handsome bar and gourmet restaurant. Monday evenings, guests and management mingle over *'ti punch* (pronounced tee poonch) and accras. The restaurant, built around the massive, 200-year-old stone walls of the original sugar mill that gives the resort its name, serves fine French food and has an extensive wine list. Breakfast, lunch, and barbecues are served at the Ajoupa, an open-sided building, by the pool. The place hums with the sort of quiet efficiency that only long years of experience can bring. As on most of Guadeloupe, the beach is rather *petit.* ✉ *Montauban, Gosier 97190,* ☎ *590/84–23–23 or 800/322–2223,* FAX *590/84–33–43. 160 rooms. 3 restaurants, bar, pool, 2 tennis courts, beach, shops. AE, DC, MC, V. BP, MAP.*

**$$$** ⌂ **La Créole Beach Hotel.** Ten acres of tropical greenery and two beaches are the lush setting for this comfortable hotel. Rooms are spacious and have sliding glass doors that open onto a balcony. Decor is dominated by vivid jungle fabrics. Mazelike corridors and pathways can be somewhat confusing. The water-sports center offers excursions to Ilet du Gosier. The restaurant, Le Zawag, serves excellent lobster and is very popular at night. ✉ *Box 19, Gosier 97190,* ☎ *590/90–46–46 or 800/755–9313,* FAX *590/90–46–66. 156 rooms, 6 duplexes. 2 restaurants, bar, air-conditioning, pool, 2 tennis courts, water sports, boating, car rental. AE, DC, MC, V. EP, CP, MAP.*

**$$$** ★ ⌂ **Le Jardin Malanga.** This antiques-filled plantation house on a bluff overlooking the ocean, near Trois-Rivières, is one of the most pleasant additions to Basse-Terre's accommodations. Alfresco lunches of grilled dorado with vegetables from the garden, a cliffside swimming pool, and a flower-filled garden are just some of the many delights available. Accommodations are in the main house (it was built in 1927), and in three simply but pleasantly furnished cottages. The white tile bathrooms gleam, and there are one-way picture windows next to the tubs that look out on the lush surroundings. Within a short distance are the eco-wonders of Basse-Terre's national park. ✉ *Hermitage, Trois-Rivières 97114,* ☎ *590/92–67–57,* FAX *590/92–67–58. 12 rooms. Air-conditioning, pool. AE, MC, V. CP.*

**$$-$$$** ⌂ **Club Méditerranée La Caravelle.** This version of the well-known club chain has air-conditioned twin-bed rooms, some with balconies, and 50 secluded acres at the western end of a magnificent white-sand beach. Nice extras include a volleyball court, calisthenics classes, and a French-English language lab where you can take French classes and use a tape recorder and headphones to practice. The property draws a fun-loving, younger crowd, most of whom are from France, and serves as the home port for Club Med's sailing cruises. ✉ *Ste-Anne 97180,* ☎ *590/88–21–00 or 800/258–2633,* FAX *590/88–06–06. 310 rooms. Restaurant, pub, air-conditioning, pool, 6 tennis courts, beach, water sports. AE, MC, V. All-inclusive.*

**$$-$$$** ⌂ **Fleur d'Epée Novotel/Marissol.** "If you can't beat them, join them" could be the motto for the merger of these two hotels on a cove in Bas-du-Fort. Once competitors, they have joined forces under the banner of the giant Groupe Accord. Tour groups from France are still the primary clientele, and when both hotels are full, the narrow strip of sand they share can get rather crowded. Rooms at the Fleur d'Epée are rather cramped, but the powder-blue fabrics and white tiles give them a pleasant, fresh look. All rooms have a terrace, most with views of the sea. ⊠ *Bas-du-Fort 97190,* ☎ *590/90–40–00,* ℻ *590/90–99–07. 400 rooms. 4 restaurants, bar, air-conditioning, minibars, pool, water sports. AE, D, DC, MC, V. CP, MAP.*

**$$–$$$** 🏨 **La Plantation Ste-Marthe.** You are a few miles inland from the coast
★ here, among gently rolling hills and fields, but the 7 acres of grounds are lovely, the ocean can be seen from some guest rooms, and there is shuttle service to the beach. If the place has one drawback, it is that it lacks atmosphere. Though bits of machinery from the old sugar refinery have been cleverly incorporated into the grounds, this is a designer version of a plantation house. But it is sumptuous. The august, almost baroque reception area has columns of pale blue and mango; vast murals; a winding, polished-wood double staircase; and black-and-white patterned marble floors. The rooms are in four three-story Creole-style buildings, with spacious terraces that overlook the large pool. They are large and elegant. Twenty-four duplex suites have loft-style bedrooms looking down upon a salon. Throughout the hotel, furniture is a unique modern adaptation of French period pieces that incorporate cane work. Mahogany beds and aquamarine and coral tile work contribute to the refined aura. The restaurant, one of the best on the island, is by the large free-form pool, designed to resemble a lake. ⊠ *St-François 97118,* ☎ *590/93–11–11 or 800/333–1970,* ℻ *590/88–72–47. 96 rooms, 24 duplexes. Restaurant, bar, air-conditioning, in-room safes, minibars, pool, meeting rooms. AE, MC, V. EP, MAP.*

**$$–$$$** 🏨 **Le Méridien St-François.** You couldn't pack more activity into one vacation than is offered by this hotel. The 150-acre resort puts out its own *A to Z Leisure Guide* and broadcasts from Télé Méridien to let you know what's going on. The activities director organizes everything from boccie to book lending. The beach hut is a busy place even off-season (partly because the Air France crews use the hotel). Standard rooms are modest, and wear and tear has taken its toll, but all have small balconies, about half of which face the sea. Odd-numbered rooms have the best views. Decor is standard to the Méridien chain, right down to the mint-and-orange fabrics and boxy configuration. This one at least sports a few individual touches, such as flowerpots on the balconies. ⊠ *St-François 97118,* ☎ *590/88–51–00 or 800/543–4300,* ℻ *590/88–40–71. 267 rooms, 10 suites. 2 restaurants, 2 bars, air-conditioning, pool, spa, 2 tennis courts, water sports, shops, dance club, car rental. AE, D, MC, V. CP, MAP.*

**$$** 🏨 **Anchorage.** The 27 acres of this resort are spread along the coast a few miles from St-François. Rooms are either in Creole-style buildings or in 34 villas that climb the rise behind them. All rooms have terra-cotta floors, rich russet-patterned bedspreads, ceramic lamps, and original touches like antique radios. The formal restaurant offers à la carte dining, but most evenings, guests attend the theme buffet dinner at the Blanc Mangé restaurant, where performers entertain on the large piazza. Across the piazza is an open-sided disco. The complex is so large that the trek to the man-made beach at one end can prompt you to use the car. It may not have the best beach on the island, but it does have the largest swimming pool. ⊠ *Anse des Rochers, St-François 97118,* ☎ *590/93–90–00,* ℻ *590/93–91–00. 356 rooms. 2 restaurants, grocery, snack bar, pool, 2 tennis courts, archery, shop, dance club, meeting rooms, car rental. MC, V. EP, MAP.*

**$$** 🏨 **Canella Beach Residence.** In this resort built to resemble a Creole village, you have a choice of single-level and duplex studios and junior and duplex suites. Each has its own terrace or balcony and a small kitchenette. Ask for a room on the top floor for the best views. Decor is a pleasant departure from pastels, with earth tones complementing the white tile floors and rattan furnishings. Unlike the other Pointe de la Verdure hotels, the Canella Beach enjoys its own semiprivate cove. Water sports are free, and there is a beach bar for refreshments. Set back from the beach are the swimming pool and tennis courts. Another plus is the Verandah restaurant, where you can dine indoors in air-conditioning or enjoy the sea breezes outdoors. The menu includes Creole and French dishes. ⊠ *Pointe de la Verdure, Gosier 97190,* ☎ *590/90–44–00 or 800/223–9815; 212/251–1800 in NY;* ℻ *590/90–44–44. 146 rooms. Restaurant, pool, 4 tennis courts, snorkeling, windsurfing, boating, waterskiing, fishing. AE, DC, MC, V. EP, MAP.*

$$ 🏨 **Cap Sud Caraïbes.** This is a tiny Relais Creole on a country road between Gosier and Ste-Anne, just a five-minute walk from a quiet beach. The staff does its best to make you feel at home. Each individually decorated room has a balcony and either a shower or an enormous bath. It's homey and simple, but it's a good value for the money. ⊠ *Gosier 97190,* ☎ *590/85–96–02,* ℻ *590/85–80–39. 12 rooms. Bar, air-conditioning, pool, snorkeling, dry cleaning, laundry service, airport shuttle. MC, V. CP.*

$$ 🏨 **Fort Royal Touring Club.** This is one of the better hotels on Basse-Terre, though it caters to a lower-end, package-clientele. The modern white structure overlooks two pristine beaches. Spacious rooms all have a terrace or balcony with sea views, tile floors, handsome wicker and rattan furnishings, and mahogany beds. The hotel offers tours into the national park and plenty of activities, most of them beach-related. ⊠ *Pointe du Petit Bas-Vent, Deshaies 97126,* ☎ *590/25–50–00,* ℻ *590/25–50–01. 120 rooms, including 78 bungalows. Restaurant, bar, air-conditioning, 2 pools, miniature golf, 4 tennis courts, 2 beaches, dive shop, water sports. AE, MC, V. EP, CP, MAP.*

$$ 🏨 **Golf Marine Club Hotel.** Near the town's newer shops and restaurants, this small hotel offers a more moderately priced alternative to Le Méridien. But the hotel's name overpromises: It is not a club, the municipal golf course is across the street, and it has neither marina nor beach— the nearest public beach is two blocks away. The rooms each have a balcony, but those facing the street tend to be noisy. A third of the rooms are called mezzanine suites and have loft bedrooms and a roll-out couch in the lounge. On the patio terrace is a relaxed, informal restaurant. ⊠ *Ave. de l'Europe, B.P. 204, St-François 97118,* ☎ *590/88–60–60,* ℻ *590/88–68–98. 74 rooms, including 29 duplexes and 15 bungalows. Restaurant, pool, 2 tennis courts. AE, MC, V. CP, MAP.*

$$ 🏨 **Hotel St. Georges.** With its large, serpentine-shape pool and ultrahip bar, this new hotel was financed by the local chamber of commerce and opened in January 1997. The rooms are in three three-story buildings, which look like a Richard Rogers version of a Creole house. They are large and decorated with teak and rattan reproduction furniture and bright fabrics. All have spacious bathrooms and a small veranda. Although the hotel's position on a hill above the village of St-Claude is splendid, the architects surprisingly turned the views from the verandas inward, to the pool, and not to the mountains and ocean. ⊠ *Rue Gratien Parize, 97120 St-Claude,* ☎ *590/80–10–10,* ℻ *590/80–30–50. 38 rooms, 2 suites. Restaurant, bar, air-conditioning, pool, exercise room, squash, billiards, shop. D, MC, V. EP, CP, MAP.*

$$ 🏨 **L'Orchidée.** In the center of Gosier, this hotel is perfect for the businessperson who does not need resort facilities or a beach. Its spotless studios have dark-wood furnishings, teal fabrics, sparkling white tile floors, and balconies. On the ground floor a small shop serves morning coffee. Owner-manager Madame Karine Chenaf speaks English and can help you arrange your day. You also get free membership at the

local recreation center with pool. ✉ *32 blvd. Général de Gaulle, Gosier 97190,* ☎ *590/84–54–20,* FAX *590/84–54–90. 18 studios. Dining room, air-conditioning, kitchenettes, shop. MC, V. EP.*

**$$** 🏨 **Relais du Moulin.** A restored windmill serves as the reception room for this Relais Creole tucked in Châteaubrun, near Ste-Anne. A spiral staircase leads up to a TV-reading room, from which there is a splendid view. Accommodations are in bungalows. Rooms are immaculate but claustrophobic, somehow managing to pack in twin beds, small terraces, and kitchenettes. The restaurant overlooks the restored windmill. Try the house specialty: grouper and lobster served with Creole sauce or stuffed with fresh homemade pâté. A *menu dégustation* for 220F offers seven courses and is a good way to sample Creole cooking. The beach is a 10-minute hike away. ✉ *Châteaubrun, Ste-Anne 97180,* ☎ *590/88–23–96 or 800/223–9815,* FAX *590/88–03–92. 40 rooms. Restaurant, bar, air-conditioning, kitchenettes, pool, tennis court, archery, bicycles. AE, DC, MC, V. CP, MAP.*

**$$** 🏨 **Tropical Club Hotel.** Great windsurfing and swimming at the golden sand beach are big draws for this hotel on the northeastern coast of Grande-Terre. Set back from the beach is an almond-shape pool, adjacent to an open-sided dining room that serves French and Creole fare. The guest rooms are in three buildings on a rise. Each room has a double bed and two bunk beds, which are in an entrance annex—ideal for children (those under 21 stay free). Every room has a private balcony, a small kitchenette, and a view of the sea. The best views are from the top (third) floor rooms. There are three tennis courts nearby. ✉ *Le Moule, 97160,* ☎ *590/93–97–97,* FAX *590/93–97–00. 72 rooms. Restaurant, bar, air-conditioning, fans, kitchenettes, pool, boccie, exercise room, beach, windsurfing, shop. AE, MC, V. CP, MAP.*

**$–$$** 🏨 **Relais des Sources.** This newly opened Relais Creole is one of the better inns on Basse-Terre. The hotel is set in the foothills of Grosse Montagne, only a few hundred yards from the Ravine Chaude thermal baths, in a typically Guadeloupean landscape of sugarcane fields and sleepy villages. There are five (rather dark) rooms in the main building and 10 bungalows dotted about the shady property. The bungalows come with kitchenette, phone, and TV. The (extremely young) staff will take care of your every need—from baby-sitting to airport transfers. On the downside, you might mistake the swimming pool for a birdbath, and the nearest beach is 9 mi away. ✉ *Lamentin 91729,* ☎ *590/25–31–04,* FAX *590/25–30–63. 5 rooms, 10 bungalows. Restaurant, bar, air-conditioning, pool, shop. AE, MC, V. CP, MAP.*

**$** 🏨 **Auberge de la Distillerie.** This is one of the best Relais Creole on the
★ island: a homey country inn ideal for those who want to be close to the national park. The 12 rooms in the 19th-century house are individually decorated, with wicker furnishings, tile floors, wood beams, ceramic lamps, and local artwork. Each has a terrace; some have a refrigerator. The slightly larger bungalows have larger terraces. There's also a rustic wood chalet that sleeps two to four people. The restaurant, noted for its delectable Creole cuisine, is built around the partially enclosed pool. Boat trips on the Lézarde River can be arranged; you can also swim in the river. ✉ *Vernou 97170, D23, Petit-Bourg,* ☎ *590/94–25–91 or 800/322–2223,* FAX *590/94–11–91. 14 rooms. Restaurant, bar, patisserie, air-conditioning, pool. AE, MC, V. CP, MAP.*

**$** 🏨 **Domaine de Petite-Anse.** The ocher, red-roofed buildings of this resort spill down lushly landscaped hills overlooking the ocean. You're near a beach and close to the national park. Accommodations are either in hotel rooms or bungalows decorated with dark rattan and bright floral fabrics. Rooms are simple and small but well equipped. Be sure to request one with a balcony and sea view (they're the same price). Bungalows have a terrace, full bath, and kitchenette. This is one of Guadeloupe's premier spots for an active vacation and very popular with young French couples and families. The resort is noted for its dive shop and nature tours. The staff, although friendly, speaks limited English. ⊠ *Plage de Petite-Anse, Monchy, Bouillante 97125,* ☎ *590/98–78–78 or 800/322–2223,* ℻ *590/98–80–28. 135 rooms, 40 bungalows. Restaurant, bar, air-conditioning, in-room safes, refrigerators, pool, archery, volleyball, dive shop, water sports, boating, shop. AE, DC, MC, V. EP.*

$ ☷ **Grande-Anse Hotel.** Less than a mile from a black-sand beach and offering spectacular mountain views, this Relais Creole is a good choice for nature lovers. It's also near the ferry to Les Saintes. Bungalows have small balconies. The heavy polished wood furnishings should achieve antique status in a few years. Water sports and nature hikes can be arranged. ⊠ *Trois-Rivières 97114,* ☎ *590/92–90–47,* ℻ *590/92–93–69. 16 bungalows. Restaurant, bar, air-conditioning, refrigerators, pool. MC, V. CP, MAP.*

$ ☷ **La Sucrerie du Comté.** The ruins and rusting equipment (including a locomotive) of a 19th-century sugar factory litter the lawns and gardens here like hulking abstract sculptures. In fact, it is the historically significant grounds, along with the attractive public areas, that are the main attraction of this resort. The interiors of the fine restaurant and bar recreate plantation living, with wood beams, stone walls, and towering floral arrangements. Twenty-six bungalows duplicate the gingerbread architecture of the turn of the century, with small but pretty rooms. The nearest beach is a 10-minute stroll through a tangle of greenery. ⊠ *Comté de Lohéac, Ste-Rose 97115,* ☎ *590/28–60–17,* ℻ *590/28–65–63. 50 rooms. Restaurant, bar, air-conditioning, pool, tennis court. AE, DC, MC, V. CP, MAP.*

## Iles des Saintes

$–$$ ☷ **Village Creole.** Baths by Courrèges, dishwashers, freezers, and satel-
★ lite TV are among the amenities in this apartment hotel. Units are decorated simply but chicly, with unvarnished rattan and framed posters. Ghyslain Laps, the English-speaking owner and would-be chef, will help you whip up meals in the kitchen. If you'd prefer not to cook, he can provide you with a cook and housekeeper for an extra charge. A sailboat is available for excursions to Marie-Galante and Dominica. The small beach is too rough for swimming. ⊠ *Pte. Coquelet 97137, Terre-de-Haut,* ☎ *590/99–53–83,* ℻ *590/99–55–55. 22 duplexes. Beach, water sports, convention center, airport shuttle. MC, V. EP.*

$ ☷ **Bois Joli.** A beautiful setting, right on the bay, is the attraction here. Most of the rooms, either in the inn or one of the bungalows, are air-conditioned but rather drab. The restaurant serves wonderful clams in Creole sauce on a terrace that overlooks the sea. Water sports can be arranged, and the Anse Crawen nudist beach is a five-minute walk away. Pets are allowed. ⊠ *Terre-de-Haut 97137,* ☎ *590/99–50–38 or 800/223–9815,* ℻ *590/99–55–05. 21 rooms, 8 bungalows. Restaurant, bar, air-conditioning, pool, airport shuttle. MC, V. CP, MAP.*

$ ☷ **L'Auberge les Petits Saints aux Anacardies.** This is one of the most
★ distinctive properties in the archipelago. Ten rooms are tucked into this inn, trimmed with trellises and topped by dormers. Each room has twin beds and casement windows that open to a splendid view of gardens, hills, and the bay. Some also have sea views (Room 2's is extraordinary), and most have a private bath. A glorious clutter greets you in the reception area, which is crammed with antiques and objets d'art culled from owners Jean-Paul Coles' and Didier Spindler's world travels. Furnishings are a similarly odd assortment of antiques. There's a one-bedroom bungalow next to the main house. The restaurant is one of the best on the island. The hotel's private boat makes excursions around the islands. ⊠ *La Savane 97137, Terre-de-Haut,* ☎ *590/99–*

*50–99,* FAX *590/99–54–51. 10 rooms, 9 with private interior bath. Restaurant, bar, air-conditioning, pool, sauna. MC, V. CP, MAP.*

## Dining

Guadeloupe does not have the epicurean restaurants you find in St. Barts or St. Martin, but there is fine Creole food featuring the island's abundant seafood and vegetables, such as christophines and plantains. Favorite appetizers are *accras* (codfish fritters), *boudin* (highly seasoned pork sausage), and *crabes farcis* (stuffed land crabs). *Blaff* is a spicy fish stew. Lobster and *lambi* (conch) are widely available, as is *souchy*, a Tahitian version of sushi. The island boasts more than 700 restaurants, including those serving classic French, Italian, African, Indian, Vietnamese, and South American fare. But they are not cheap. Even the simplest Creole fare costs $20–$25. For a good meal you can expect to pay $50–$70 per person. The local libation of choice is the *'ti punch*—a heady concoction of rum, lime juice, and sugarcane syrup. The innocent-sounding little punch packs a powerful wallop.

### What to Wear

Dining is casual at lunch, but beach attire is a no-no. Except at the more laid-back marina and beach eateries, dinner is slightly more formal. Long pants, collared shirts, and skirts or dresses are appreciated, although not required.

| CATEGORY | COST* |
|---|---|
| $$$ | over $40 |
| $$ | $25–$40 |
| $ | under $25 |

*per person for a three-course meal, excluding drinks*

### Grande-Terre

$$$ ✕ **Auberge de la Vieille Tour.** This restaurant was extensively re-
★ designed in 1995. Guests now sit at tables grouped around the historic, whitewashed sugar mill, and there is a new, conservatory-style extension, with views up into lighted trees. Lionel Péan's cuisine is as good as ever. It's hard to choose from the changing menu, with entrées such as smoked swordfish with a two-pepper mousse and blinis, noisettes of lamb in honey and lime, and sea bream kissed with passion-fruit vinegar. You may want to opt for the *menu dégustation* for a representative sampling of Péan's work. There is an extensive (and expensive) wine list. A band plays cool jazz Wednesday–Saturday evenings. ✉ *Gosier,* ☎ *590/84–23–23. AE, DC, MC, V.*

$$$ ✕ **Auberge de St-François.** Claude Simon's country home is set in an orchard, and his tables are set with Royal Doulton china and fine crystal. Dining is indoors or on one of the flower-filled patios, with a superb view of Marie-Galante and Pointe des Châteaux. The house specialty is crayfish prepared in several ways (the unusual fricassee with bacon and scallops is a standout). The brochette of smoked shark with a pepper sauce and the conch dishes are also good. A *menu touriste* (180F) of three courses, each with a choice of three dishes, is an affordable alternative to the à la carte offerings. Monsieur Simon has a superior cellar of vintage wine and champagne to complement his cuisine. ✉ *St-François,* ☎ *590/88–51–71. MC, V. Closed Sun.–Mon.*

$$$ ✕ **Château de Feuilles.** This restaurant is worth a special trip. You will
★ savor no finer luncheon than one served by Martine and Jean-Pierre Dubost in this relaxed, stylish country setting. While waiting for your meal you can take a dip in the pool or stroll around the 2-acre farm. For an aperitif, about 20 different punch concoctions are made with different juices and flavors: Sample all if you dare. The changing menu may include goose *rillettes* (pâté), velvety sea urchin pâté, kingfish fil-

let with vanilla, swordfish with sorrel, or the deep-sea fish *capitan* grilled with lime and green pepper. For dessert, try the pineapple flan. The estate is 9 mi from Le Moule on the Campêche road, between Gros-Cap and Campêche. ⊠ *Campêche,* ☎ *590/22–30–30. MC, V. Closed Mon. No dinner (except for groups of 10 or more by reservation).*

$$$   ✕ **Chez Deux Gros.** The name is a play on one of France's most famous restaurants, Chez Trois Gros; though the food is not quite of that standard, you will eat extremely well. Culinary specialties include shrimp ravioli in saffron butter, marinated raw fish à la Gauguin, and salmon in a honey-and-vanilla sauce. The restaurant is built on a steep, plant-hung incline, with tables set in tiled alcoves and terraces. Sadly, what was once a small country road is now the main drag to Gosier and Ste-Anne; it's loud and passes just below the restaurant. Make sure you ask for a table in the antiques-filled room at the back. ⊠ *Gosier,* ☎ *590/84–16–20. MC, V. No lunch.*

$$$   ✕ **La Louisiane.** The owner, chef Daniel Hogon, who hails from the Carl-
★     ton in Cannes, prepares such traditional favorites as duck-liver confit with raspberry vinaigrette or smoked fish as starters, then crayfish flambé, fillet of beef in green pepper sauce, or roast rack of lamb. For dessert, try the charlotte of exotic fruits. The Menu Creole at 120F is a fine buy. The dozen tables of this small restaurant are on a terrace decorated with paintings and flower-filled hanging pots. The restaurant is on the road to Ste-Marthe, about 2 mi from St-François, and Monsieur Hogon will send a car for you upon request. You'll receive far better service if you speak adequate French. ⊠ *St-François,* ☎ *590/88–44–34. MC, V. Closed Mon.*

$$$   ✕ **La Plantation Ste-Marthe.** Housed in the ritziest resort on the island
★     (☞ Lodging, *above*), this restaurant serves exceptionally good French food. For starters, try the *salade auchoise,* a green salad with duck, or the *carpaccio de filet de boeuf,* thin slices of raw beef with aromatic herbs. Then move on to a bouillabaisse Creole or noisettes of lamb with thyme. The three-chocolate mousse for dessert is a killer. The wine list is extensive. ⊠ *St-François,* ☎ *590/93–11–11. AE, MC, V.*

$$$   ✕ **Le Côte Jardin.** The marina between Bas-du-Fort and Pointe-à-Pitre is a lively evening venue with a dozen restaurants, bar lounges, and shops around the quay. You can take your pick from pizzas to hamburgers, but for something more formal, try the creative cuisine at Le Côte Jardin. The plant-filled restaurant has white lace curtains, wicker peacock chairs, and coral and white napery. A menu of haute French Creole lists dishes that range from basic lamb Provençale and baked red snapper to more exotic *escargots de la mer* with garlic butter. Unfortunately, the staff has a tendency to behave like prima donnas. ⊠ *La Marina,* ☎ *590/90–91–28. AE, MC, V.*

$$–$$$ ✕ **La Toubana.** Perched on top of a cliff, this airy, open-sided restaurant is *the* place to go for lobster. Choose your own from the large *vivier* (tank) and then retire to the veranda with a 'ti punch to enjoy the spectacular view of the ocean. There is a basic lobster menu for 165F. For more exotic creations, expect to pay 295F. If you want to stay, the hotel on the same property has a cluster of simple but pleasant bungalows. There is also a swimming pool, and a small, private beach at the bottom of the cliff. A steel band plays in the evening. ⊠ *Durivage, Ste-Anne,* ☎ *590/88–25–57 or 800/322–2223. AE, MC, V.*

$$–$$$ ✕ **Le Bananier.** "Nouvelle cuisine Creole" is the specialty at this well-established Gosier restaurant, in other words, creatively prepared dishes using local produce. Try the stuffed rockfish or the poultry supreme with conch. The dining room, with its beamed ceiling and lush plants, is a cheery space, and chef Jean Clarus is one of the most experienced on the island. A wide selection of wines is available. ⊠ *Montauban, Gosier,* ☎ *590/84–34–85. MC, V.*

**$$–$$$** ✕ **Le Flibustier.** The word is French for buccaneer, and this rustic hill-top farmhouse plays on the theme for all it's worth. Waiters dress like extras from *Hook*. Roasting sides of meat are the backdrop for lots of piratical carrying-on. It's particularly lively after 8 PM, when staffers from the neighboring Club Med come in to hold court, smoke up a storm, and serenade attractive guests with ribald ditties. You can order a complete dinner—mixed salad, grilled lobster, coconut ice cream, petit punch, and half a pitcher of wine—or à la carte off the blackboard menu. ⊠ *La Colline, Fonds Thézan (between Ste-Anne and St-Felix),* ☎ 590/ 88–23–36. *No credit cards. Closed Mon. No lunch Sun.*

**$$–$$$** ✕ **Les Oiseaux.** The delights of this restaurant begin with its setting, ★ a stucco-and-stone house nestled amid a tangle of gardens overlooking the sea. Owner-chefs Claudette and Arthur Rolle have developed a menu of such dishes as *entrecôte Roquefort* (shark steak with coconut) and *marmite de Robinson* (a stew of dorado, kingfish, tuna, shrimp, and local vegetables). Ask Claudette to show you her book of local remedies. If your French is *very* good she might even prepare a special infusion for your particular complaint. Even if it isn't, be sure to sample a homemade *digestif* (after-dinner liqueur). Honeymoon couples will probably choose the *rhum d'amour.* ⊠ *Anse des Rochers,* ☎ 590/88–56–92. *Reservations essential. AE, MC, V. Closed Oct. No lunch Mon.–Wed.*

**$$–$$$** ✕ **Rosini.** This well-established restaurant in Bas-du-Fort offers some of the best Italian food on the island. Be sure to ask for a table on the upper level; the downstairs section is rather drab and impersonal. A specialty here is the homemade ravioli (try the mixed ravioli, which includes artichoke, salmon, and shrimp). Most of the other Italian classics, like osso buco or saltimbeca, are also on offer. Some of the more complex dishes, like the homemade gnocchi, have to be ordered 24 hours in advance. ⊠ *La Porte des Caraïbes, Gosier 97190,* ☎ 590/90-87– 81. *AE, D, MC, V.*

**$–$$** ✕ **Chez Violetta–La Creole.** The late Violetta Chaville established this restaurant's à la carte Creole menu when she was head of Guadeloupe's association of cuisinières (female chefs). Her brother has carried on her cooking traditions, dishing up specials such as red snapper in Belle Doudou sauce, a Creole mix of onions, tomatoes, peppers, and spices. The food, although still good, has been eclipsed by other island kitchens, but the restaurant remains a stop on many tourist itineraries and is popular with American visitors. ⊠ *Eastern outskirts of Gosier Village,* ☎ 590/84– 10–34. *AE, MC, V.*

**$–$$** ✕ **La Table Creole.** Carmélite Jeanne rules the kitchen of this little ter-★ race eatery, turning out dazzling Creole cuisine that is deceptively mild yet will heat you up like the noonday sun. Sea urchin gratin, succulent kingfish and snapper blaff, and goat *colombo* (curry) are among her memorable specialties. The menus at 80F and 100F are fabulous bargains. Fresh flowers are everywhere, and Madame Jeanne usually dresses colorfully to match. ⊠ *St-Félix,* ☎ 590/84–28–28. *MC, V. No dinner Sun.*

**$–$$** ✕ **Le Corsaire.** Le Corsaire rates highly among the restaurants on Gosier's main drag and the Route des Hôtels, vying with one another to offer the best-value menus. The waitstaff affects a piratical look with ponytails, earrings, and goatees. A *vivier* (lobster tank) and a flamboyant mural of a buccaneer and his ship dominate the decor. Maman, the cook, is a sweetie, singing out *"C'est bon?"* from the kitchen and nodding approvingly as you eat. For 99F you get a set menu, which might start with a conch tart or stuffed crab, then segue into beef brochette, octopus fricassee, or chicken *colombo* (curry). The King Creole menu at 120F nets you a large lobster. You can also order pizzas for 40F–52F. ⊠ *Rte. des Hôtels, Gosier,* ☎ 590/84–17–39. *AE, MC, V. No lunch Mon.*

$   ✕ **Folie Plage.** This lovely spot, north of Anse-Bertrand, is especially popular with families on weekends. Prudence Marcelin prepares reliable Creole food; superb court bouillon and imaginative curried dishes are among the specialties. There is a children's wading pool here. ⊠ *Anse Laborde,* ☎ *590/22–11–17. No credit cards.*

## Basse-Terre

$–$$   ✕ **Chez Clara.** Clara Laseur, who gave up a jazz-dancing career in Paris
★   to run her family's seaside restaurant with her mother, dishes out delicious Creole meals. Seating is on the inviting terrace of a gorgeous Creole house adorned with lacy gingerbread trim. Clara takes the orders (her English is excellent), and the place is often so crowded with her friends and fans that you may have to wait at the octagonal wooden bar before being seated. The food is worth the wait, however—check the daily specials listed on the blackboard, for example the succulent octopus or sublime ginger carambola sorbet. ⊠ *Ste-Rose,* ☎ *590/28– 72–99. MC, V. Closed Wed. and Oct. No dinner Sun.*

$–$$   ✕ **Le Karacoli.** With her flowing white dress and flamboyant style, Lu-
★   cienne Salcede, the owner of this pleasant seaside restaurant, looks as though she walked off the set of *Showboat.* The restaurant's entrance, along a rather scruffy lane by a campground, doesn't bode well, but this is one of the best restaurants on the spectacular west coast of Basse-Terre. There are two dining areas: inside, at dark, wood tables, or outside, on the terrace, where all you will hear are the splash of the waves and the rustling of coconut palms. The food is solid Creole fare: goat colombo, boudin, court bouillon. For dessert, try the banana flambé, heavily perfumed with rum, followed by a homemade *digestif* (after-dinner liqueur). By then, you'll be ready to stretch out on the chaise longues that Lucienne sets out just for that purpose. When you wake up, she'll even lend you a beach towel for a swim. ⊠ *La Grande-Anse, north of Deshaies,* ☎ *590/28–41–17. MC, V. No dinner.*

$–$$   ✕ **Le Rocher de Malendure.** You know the seafood is fresh here be-
★   cause the owner's husband, Francky, catches it himself. Tables are laid out on a series of airy, wooden verandas built up around the rock that gives the restaurant its name. The specialty is the *menu de la mer,* a pungent medley of *souchy* (the Tahitian version of sushi) and smoked fish. The dorado, swordfish, conch, and lobster from the restaurant's own *vivier* are all excellent. If you want to catch fish, as well as eat them, owner Ghiselaine Nouy will be happy to arrange a deep-sea fishing trip with Captain Francky. ⊠ *Bouillante,* ☎ *590/98–70–84. DC, MC. Closed 1st half of Sept. No dinner Sun.*

$   ✕ **Chez Jackye.** Jacqueline Cabrion serves Creole and African dishes in her cheerful, plant-filled seaside restaurant. Creole boudin is a house specialty, as are lobster (grilled, vinaigrette, or fricassee), fried crayfish, clam blaff, and goat in port sauce. There's also a wide selection of omelets, sandwiches, and salads. For dessert, try peach melba or banana flambé. The 120F menu will have you waddling out happily. ⊠ *Anse Guyonneau, rue de la Bataille, Pte. Noire,* ☎ *590/98–06–98. DC, MC, V. Closed Sun.*

$   ✕ **Les Gommiers.** A changing menu here may list crayfish soup, octopus fricassee, pork chops with banana, goat colombo, seafood paella, and grilled entrecôte. Banana splits and profiteroles are on the dessert list. For lunch, salade Niçoise and other light dishes are offered. Fixed menus at 70F and 100F are sensational values. Lovely peacock chairs grace the bar, and polished wood furnishings and potted plants fill the dining room. ⊠ *Rue Baudot, Pte. Noire,* ☎ *590/98–01–79. MC, V. No dinner Sun.–Tues.*

## Iles des Saintes, Terre-de-Haut

**$–$$** ✕ **El Dorado.** This is one of the best bets on Les Saintes. A plant-filled, Creole-style house with a double veranda, on Bourg's delightful main square, is the setting for tasty Creole fare. There is a three-course menu for 75F. The pizza, which is served only at night, is made on the premises, the beef for the barbecue steaks is imported from France, and there is a decent wine list. ⊠ *Bourg, Terre-de-Haut,* ☎ *590/99–54–31. MC. Closed Sun.*

**$–$$** ✕ **Nilce's Bar.** This piano bar and restaurant in a large, Creole-style house right on the waterfront, is *the* place for Terre-de-Haut's barefoot crowd. Owners Jacques and Odette Chan serve tapas, salads, and a wide selection of ice creams in the upstairs dining room. Downstairs, local musicians perform Brazilian, French, and Creole music. Dogs and children wander about—it's very casual and informal. The later it gets, the raunchier it gets, so come early. ⊠ *Bourg, Terre-de-Haut,* ☎ *590/99–56–80. MC, V. No lunch.*

**$–$$** ✕ **La Saladerie.** This delightful seaside terrace restaurant serves a so-
**★** phisticated mélange of Creole and Continental dishes. Begin with rillettes of smoked fish, *crabes farcis,* or a warm crepe filled with lobster, conch, octopus, and fish. Specialties include an assortment of smoked fish served cold and stuffed fish fillet served in a white-wine sauce. The wine list is pleasantly varied. This is the place for a light meal served with a great view. ⊠ *Anse Mirre,* ☎ *590/99–50–92. MC, V.*

**$–$$** ✕ **L'Auberge les Petits Saints aux Anacardies.** The restaurant of the island's prettiest inn is also open to nonguests. You sit out on an airy veranda overlooking the ocean. There is only one main dish per day; specialties include steak au poivre, grilled lobster, or smoked local fish. The wine list is excellent. ⊠ *La Savane,* ☎ *590/99–50–99. MC, V. Closed mid-Sept.–mid-Oct.*

## Marie-Galante

**$** ✕ **Le Touloulou.** The ultracasual Le Touloulou, on the curve of Petite-Anse beach, serves sumptuous seafood at down-to-earth prices. Chef Patrice Pillet's standouts include conch *feuilleté* (in puff pastry) with yams and the very local *bébélé* (tripe with breadfruit, plantains, and dumplings). There are set menus for 60F, 90F, and 140F. ⊠ *Petite-Anse,* ☎ *590/97–32–63. MC, V. Closed Mon. and mid-Sept.–mid-Oct.*

# Beaches

Guadeloupe's beaches are not spectacular. They are generally rather narrow (particularly since the hurricanes of 1995) and tend to be cluttered with cafés and impromptu parking lots in the sand. But they are all free and open to the public. For a small fee, hotels allow nonguests to use changing facilities, towels, and beach chairs. Some of the island's best beaches of soft white sand lie on the coast of Grande-Terre from Ste-Anne to Pointe des Châteaux. All along the western shore of Basse-Terre you'll see signposts to small beaches. The sand starts turning gray as you reach Pigeon Island; it becomes volcanic black as you work your way farther south. There are several nudist beaches (noted below), and topless bathing is commonplace. Note that the Atlantic waters on the northeast coast of Grande-Terre are too rough for swimming.

**Anse de la Gourde** is a beautiful stretch of sand that becomes very popular on weekends. It's between St-François and Pointe des Châteaux. **Caravelle Beach,** just outside the town of Ste-Anne, is one of the longest and prettiest stretches of beach on Grande-Terre, though there are rather dilapidated shacks and cafés scattered about the area. Protected by reefs, the beach makes a fine place for snorkeling. Club Med occupies one end of this beach. **La Grande-Anse,** just outside Deshaies, on the northwest coast of Basse-Terre, is a secluded beach of soft beige sand sheltered by palms. There's a large parking area but no facilities other than the Karacoli restaurant (☞ Dining, *above*). **Ilet du Gosier** is a little speck off the shore of Gosier where you can bathe in the buff. Take along a picnic for an all-day outing. The beach is closed on weekends. **Malendure** beach lies on the west coast of Basse-Terre, across from Pigeon Island. Jacques Cousteau called it one of the 10 best diving places in the world. Several scuba operations are based here (☞ Outdoor Activities and Sports, *below*). There are also glass-bottom-boat trips for those who prefer keeping their heads above water. **Petite-Anse,** on Marie-Galante, is a long gold-sand beach crowded with locals on weekends. During the week it's quiet, and there are no facilities other than the little seafood restaurant, Le Touloulou (☞ Dining, *above*). **Place Crawen,** Les Saintes's quiet, secluded beach for skinny-dipping, is a half mile of white sand on Terre-de-Haut. **Pointe Tarare** is a secluded strip of sand just before the tip of Pointe des Châteaux and is one of the most popular nudist beaches on Guadeloupe. There is a small bar-café in the parking area a four-minute walk away. **Les Pompierres,** a palm-fringed stretch of tawny sand, is a popular Les Saintes beach. **Souffleur,** on the west coast of Grande-Terre, north of Port-Louis, has brilliant flamboyant trees that bloom in the summer. There are no facilities on the beach, but you can buy the makings of a picnic from nearby shops.

## Outdoor Activities and Sports

### Bicycling

The French are mad about *le cyclisme,* so if you want to feel like a native, take to two wheels. Pedal fever hits the island in August every year, when hundreds of cyclists converge on the island for the 10-day Tour de Guadeloupe. You can rent bikes in Pointe-à-Pitre at **Vélon Tout Terrain** (☎ 590/97–85–40), which also offers mountain-bike tours in Basse-Terre and Marie-Galante. In St-François you can rent from **Espace VTT** (☎ 590/88–79–91).

### Boating

If you plan to sail these waters, you should be aware that the winds and currents of Guadeloupe tend to be strong. There are excellent, well-equipped marinas in Pointe-à-Pitre, Bas-du-Fort, Deshaies, St-François, and Gourbeyre. Bareboat or crewed yachts can be rented in Bas-du-Fort at **Dufour** (☎ 590/90–74–43), **Moorings** (☎ 590/90–81–81), **Star Voyages Antilles** (☎ 590/90–86–26), and **Stardust** (☎ 590/90–92–02). Most beachfront hotels rent Hobie Cats, Sunfish, pedal boats, motorboats, and water skis.

### Deep-Sea Fishing

Half- and full-day trips in search of bonito, dolphinfish, captain fish, barracuda, kingfish, marlin, and tuna can be arranged. The best skipper on the island is Captain Francky at **Le Rocher de Malendure** (⊠ Pigeon, Bouillante, ☎ 590/98–70–84). **Caraibe Peche** (⊠ Marina, Bas-du-Fort, ☎ 590/90–97–51) also does trips. Expect to pay about 3,500F for a half-day's boat charter and 4,500F for a full day.

### Fitness

**Gym Tropic** (⊠ Marissol hotel, Bas-du-Fort, ☎ 590/90–84–44) offers gym space for calisthenics and stretching, water exercise classes in the pool or the sea, yoga classes, and beauty care. **Viva Forme** (⊠ Bas-du-Fort, ☎ 590/90–98–74) has two squash courts as well as weights and machines for muscle toning.

## Flying

ULMs (Ultra Léger Motorisés) are popular with European tourists. The extremely lightweight seaplanes soar along the coast at approximately 100 ft. Go for a ride at **Holywind** (✉ Canella Beach Residence, Pointe de la Verdure, Gosier, ☎ 590/90–44–00) or **Le Meridien** (✉ St-François, ☎ 590/88–51–00). The cost is 170F for 10 minutes.

## Golf

**Golf Municipal St-François** (✉ St-François, ☎ 590/88–41–87) has an 18-hole Robert Trent Jones course, an English-speaking pro, a clubhouse, a pro shop, and electric carts for rental. The greens fee is 250F.

## Hiking

With hundreds of trails and countless rivers and waterfalls, Guadeloupe's **Parc National,** on Basse-Terre, is a paradise for those who don't want to just sit on the beach drinking piña coladas. Some of the trails should be attempted only with an experienced guide. All tend to be muddy, so wear a good pair of boots. Trips for up to 12 people are arranged by **Organisation des Guides de Montagne de la Caraïbe** (✉ Maison Forestière, Matouba, ☎ 590/94–29–11) or by the **Office de Tourisme de Basse-Terre** (☎ 590/82–24–83). A half day will cost about $80, a full day, $150. The acknowledged pros in the private sector are **Parfum d'Aventure** (✉ 1, Roche Blonval, St-François 97118, ☎ 590/88–47–62, 🖷 590/88–47–91), who offer everything from four-wheel-drive safaris to sea kayaking, hiking and white-water canoeing.

## Horseback Riding

Beach rides, picnics, and lessons are available through **Le Criolo** (✉ St-Felix, Gosier, ☎ 590/84–04–06). More exciting are the half- or full-day excursions offered by **La Manade** (✉ Saint-Claude, ☎ 590/81–52–21 ) on Basse-Terre. Trails lead through the rain forest, with spectacular views off the Soufrière. You can also fish for crayfish in the farm's ponds.

## Scuba Diving

Cousteau called the dive off Pigeon Island, on the west coast of Basse-Terre, one of the 10 best dives in the world. But when you compare it to other great sites, including neighboring Dominica, Cousteau's claim sounds more like French chauvinism than reality. The main diving area, at the Cousteau Underwater Park on Basse-Terre, offers routine dives to 60 ft. But the numerous glass-bottomed boats and day-trippers make the site feel like a crowded marine car-park. That said, the fish are spectacular. Guides and instructors here are certified under the French CMAS rather than PADI or NAUI. The atmosphere on the dive boats is not as friendly as on many islands (and everyone smokes!). Leading operations include **Caraïbes Plongées** (✉ Gosier, ☎ 509/90–44–90), **Chez Guy et Christian** (✉ Malendure, ☎ 590/98–82–43), **Les Heures Saines** (✉ Malendure, ☎ 590/98–86–63), which has its own hotel, and **Marine Anse Plongée** (✉ Bouillante, ☎ 590/98–78–78). On Isle des Saintes, the **Centre Nautique des Saintes** (✉ Plage de la Coline, Terre-de-Haut, ☎ 590/99–54–25) and **Espace Plongé Caraïbes** (✉ Bourg, ☎ 590/99–51–84) arrange dives.

## Snorkeling and Sea Excursions

Most hotels rent snorkeling gear and post information about excursions. The *King Papyrus* (✉ Marina Bas-du-Fort, ☎ 590/90–92–98) is a catamaran you can snorkel from that offers full-day outings replete with rum, dances, and games, as well as moonlight sails. **Nautilus Club** (✉ Plage de Malendure, ☎ 590/98–89–08) offers (rather crowded) glass-bottom-boat tours and snorkeling.

## Tennis

Courts are located at many hotels, including **Auberge de la Vieille Tour** (two courts), **Caravelle/Club Med** (six courts), **La Créole Beach** (two courts), **Golf Marine Club Hotel** (two courts), **Hamak** (one court), **Le Manganao** (four courts), **Le Méridien St-François** (two courts), and **Relais du Moulin** (one court). You can also play at the **Marina Club** (☎ 590/90–84–08) in Pointe-à-Pitre and at the **Tennis League of Guadeloupe** (☎ 590/90–90–97) at the Centre Lamby-Lambert Stadium in Gosier. Most are lighted for evening play.

## Windsurfing

Windsurfing is immensely popular here. Rentals and lessons are available at all beachfront hotels. Windsurfing buffs congregate at the **UCPA Hotel Club** (☎ 590/88–64–80) in St-François. You can also rent a *planche-à-voile* (Windsurfer)—try the **Callinago** (✉ Gosier, ☎ 590/84–25–25).

# Shopping

If shopping is your goal and you want to do it on a French island, head for Martinique—selection is better and you are more likely to be understood. But shopping can be fun in Pointe-à-Pitre at the street stalls around the harbor quay, in front of the tourist office, and at the two markets (the best is the **Marché de Frébault**). The main shopping streets are **rue Schoelcher, rue de Nozières,** and **rue Frébault,** the liveliest street in the city. Moreover, numerous small boutiques selling unique designs have opened in town. The more touristy shops are down at the **St-John Perse cruise terminal,** where an attractive mall is home to two dozen shops. Get an early start, because it gets very hot and sticky around midday. Bas-du-Fort's two shopping districts are the Mammouth Shopping Center and the Marina, where there are 20 or so boutiques and several restaurants. In St-François there are also several shops surrounding the marina. Many of the resorts have fashion boutiques. There are also a number of duty-free shops at Raizet Airport.

Many stores offer a 20% discount on luxury items purchased with traveler's checks or, in some cases, major credit cards. You can find good buys on anything French—perfumes, crystal, china, cosmetics, fashions, scarves. As for local handcrafted items, you'll see a lot of junk, but you can also find wood carvings, madras table linens, island dolls dressed in madras, finely woven straw baskets and hats, and salako hats made of split bamboo. Of course there's the favorite Guadeloupean souvenir—rum.

## Good Buys

### CHINA, CRYSTAL, AND SILVER

**Rosebleu** (✉ 5 rue Frébault, Pointe-à-Pitre, ☎ 590/82–93–43; also at airport) sells crystal and silver by top lines, including Christoffle.

### COSMETICS AND LINGERIE

**Soph't** (✉ 41, Immeuble Lesseps, Centre St-John Perse, Pointe-à-Pitre, ☎ 590/83–07–73) is the place to buy delicate, fanciful, and very French lingerie. **Vendome** (✉ 8–10 rue Frébault, Pointe-à-Pitre, ☎ 590/83–42–84) is Guadeloupe's exclusive purveyor of Stendhal and Germaine Monteil.

### LOCAL CRAFTS

**Tim Tim** (✉ Rue Jean Jaures, Pointe-á-Pitre, ☎ 590/83–48–71) is a nostalgia shop with elegant (and expensive) antiques ranging from Creole furniture to maps. **Boutique de la Plage** (✉ Blvd. Général de Gaulle, Gosier, ☎ 590/84–52–51) offers a mind-boggling jumble ranging from tacky tchotchke, like "fertility" sculptures, to sublime art naïf canvases for as little as $20. **La Case à Soie** (⊠ Ste-Anne, ☎ 590/88–11–31) creates flowing silk dresses and scarves in Caribbean colors. The **Centre Artisanat,** also in Ste-Anne offers a wide selection of local crafts. The **Centre d'Art Haitien** (⊠ 65 Montauban, Gosier, ☎ 590/84–32–60) is the place to buy imaginative art. **Brigitte Boesch,** a German-born painter who has exhibited all over the world, is now living in St-François (☎ 590/88–48–94) and is worth a visit. **Joel Nankin** (☎ 590/23–28–24), a Guadeloupean painter, specializes in masks and acrylic and sand paintings. On Basse-Terre, there is the **Centre de Broderie** (⊠ Vieux Fort, ☎ 590/92–04–14), which is renowned for its lacework. The Centre is built into the ruins of Fort L'Olive, and you can watch local ladies at work tatting intricate tablecloths, napkins, and place mats, according to traditions passed down over generations. This kind of stitchery is rare; unfortunately with the devaluation of the dollar, prices are *très cher*: $30 for a doily. If you're on the Isles des Saintes, head for **José Beaujour** (⊠ Terre-de-Bas, ☎ 590/99–80–20) for an authentic salako hat. **Mahogany Artisanat** (⊠ Bourg, Terre-de-Haut, ☎ 590/99–50–12) sells Yves Cohen's batik and hand-painted T-shirts in luminescent seashell shades. **Pascal Foy** (⊠ Rte. à Pompierres, ☎ 590/99–52–29) produces stunning homages to traditional Creole architecture: painted houses incorporating collage and *objets trouvés* that make marvelous wall hangings. Prices begin at $90.

PERFUMES

**L'Artisan Parfumeur** (⊠ Centre St., John Perse, Pointe-à-Pitre, ☎ 590/83–80–25) sells both top French and American brands and tropical scents. **Au Bonheur des Dames** (⊠ 49 rue Frébault, Pointe-à-Pitre, ☎ 590/82–00–30) offers an array of cosmetics and skin-care products, in addition to its perfumes. **Phoenicia** (⊠ Bas-du-Fort, Gosier, ☎ 590/90–85–56; ⊠ 8 rue Frébault, Pointe-à-Pitre, ☎ 590/83–50–36; ⊠ 121 bis rue Frébault, Pointe-à-Pitre, ☎ 590/82–25–75) sells various perfumes.

RUM AND TOBACCO

**Comptoir sous Douane** (⊠ Raizet Airport, ☎ 590/82–22–76) has a good selection of island rums and tobacco. **Delice Shop** (⊠ 45 rue Achille René-Boisneuf, Pointe-à-Pitre, ☎ 590/82–98–24) is the spot for island rums and items from France, from cheese to chocolate.

# Nightlife

Cole Porter notwithstanding, Guadeloupeans maintain that the beguine began here (the Martinicans make the same claim for their island). Discos come, discos go, and the current music craze is "zouk," but the beat of the beguine remains steady. Many of the resort hotels feature dinner dancing, as well as entertainment by steel bands and folkloric groups.

## Bars and Nightclubs

**Le Figuier Vert** (⊠ Mare Galliard, Gosier, ☎ 590/85–85–51) offers live jazz Friday and Saturday nights. **Le Jardin Brésilien** (⊠ Bas-du-Fort, ☎ 590/90–99–31), at the marina, has live music. So does **Jungle Café** (☎ 590/90–99–31). **Lele Bar** (⊠ Le Méridien, St-François, ☎ 590/88–51–00) draws locals and tourists alike. If you're on Les Saintes, check out **Café de la Marina** (☎ 590/99–53–78). Locals congregate here after the day-trippers leave; there's always someone playing the Santois version of a bagpipe. **Nilce's Bar** (⊠ Bourg, Terre-de-Haut, no phone), right at the pier in Bourg, is where sultry Brazilian chanteuse Nilce Laps holds sway nightly. This charming waterfront bistro is decorated with assorted authentic bistro antiques.

## Casinos

There are two casinos on the island. Both have American-style roulette, blackjack, and chemin de fer. Admission is $10. The legal age is 21, and you'll need a photo ID. Tie and jacket are not required, but "proper attire" means no shorts.

**Casino de Gosier** (⊠ Gosier, ☎ 590/84–18–33) has a bar and restaurant and is open Monday–Saturday 9 PM–dawn. Slot machines open at 10 AM. **Casino de St-François** (⊠ Marina, St-François, ☎ 590/88–41–31) has a snack bar and nightclub and is open Tuesday–Sunday 9 PM–3 AM.

## Discos

Night owls should note that carousing is not cheap. Most discos charge a cover of at least $8, which includes one drink (drinks cost about $5 each). **Caraïbes 2** (⊠ Carrefour de Blanchard, Bas-du-Fort, ☎ 590/90–97–16) features Brazilian dancing. In Gosier, try **New Land** (⊠ Rte. Riviera, ☎ 590/84–34–91) and **Zenith** (⊠ Rte. de la Riviera, ☎ 590/90–72–04). Outside Gosier, there is **Shiva 1** in Le Moule (☎ 590/23–53–59). On Basse-Terre, try **La Plantation** (⊠ Gourbeyre, ☎ 590/81–23–37) and **Chez Vaneau** (⊠ Mahaut, ☎ 590/98–25–72).

# Exploring Guadeloupe

There is a lot to see on Guadeloupe, and the island is one of the larger ones in the region. The capital, Pointe-à-Pitre, can be visited in half a day. To see each "wing" of the butterfly, you'll need to budget at least one day. Grande-Terre, which has better roads and is much easier to negotiate, has pretty villages all along its south coast; don't miss the spectacular Pointe des Châteaux. Rugged and mountainous Basse-Terre presents a challenge; getting about takes much longer. If time is a problem, head straight to the spectacular west coast; you could easily spend a day traveling its length, taking time to stop for a bit of sightseeing, lunch, and a swim. For the outlying islands, budget more time and more money, as you will probably have to fly there. Iles des Saintes, the most developed of them, is well worth an overnight stay.

*Numbers in the margin correspond to points of interest on the Guadeloupe map.*

## Grande-Terre

SIGHTS TO SEE

🔞 **Anse Bertrand.** The northernmost village in Guadeloupe lies 4 mi south of La Pointe de la Grande Vigie. It was the Caribs' last refuge and prosperous in the days of sugar. Most of the excitement these days takes place in the St-Jacques Hippodrome, where horse races and cockfights are held. The beach at nearby Anse Laborde is good for swimming.

② **Bas-du-Fort.** The main attraction here is the **Fort Fleur d'Epée**, an 18th-century fortress that hunkers on a hillside behind a deep moat. This was the scene of hard-fought battles between the French and the English in 1794. You can explore the well-preserved dungeons and battlements and, on a clear day, take in a sweeping view of Iles des Saintes and Marie-Galante.

🔟 **Edgar-Clerc Archaeological Museum.** This museum contains Amerindian artifacts from the personal collection of Edgar-Clerc, a well-known archaeologist and historian. There are several rooms with displays pertaining to the Carib and Arawak civilizations. ⊠ *La Rosette,* ☎ *590/23–57–57.* 🏛 *Free.* ☉ *Thurs.–Tues. 9–12:30 and 2–5.*

④ **Gosier.** This pretty village, with red-roofed villas perched above the sea, is reminiscent of a small town on the Côte d'Azur. People stroll about with baguettes under their arms or sit at sidewalk cafés reading *Le Monde* and drinking *planteurs*, the local rum punch. It is the island's major tourist center, with hotels and inns, nightclubs, shops, a casino, and a long stretch of sand.

**❸ Guadeloupe Aquarium.** This aquarium is one of the Caribbean's largest and ranked fourth in all of France. ✉ *Place Créole, off Rte. N4,* ☎ *590/90–92–38.* ✑ *35F.* ☉ *Daily 9–7.*

**⓬ La Pointe de la Grande Vigie.** This is the northernmost tip of the island. Park your car and walk along the paths that lead right out to the edge. There is a splendid view of Porte d'Enfer from here. On a clear day you can also see Antigua, 35 mi away.

**❾ Le Moule.** This port city of about 17,000 people was once the capital of Guadeloupe. It was bombarded by the British in 1794 and 1809 and by a hurricane in 1928. Canopies of flamboyants hang over narrow streets, where colorful vegetable and fish markets do a brisk business. The town hall, with graceful balustrades, and a small 19th-century neoclassical church are on the main square. Le Moule also has a beach protected by a reef, making it perfect for windsurfing.

**⓯ Morne-à-l'Eau.** This agricultural city of about 16,000 people is home to an amphitheater-shape cemetery, with black-and-white checkerboard tombs, elaborate epitaphs, and multicolored (plastic) flowers. It's the most spectacular cemetery on the island, and one of the finest in the French West Indies. On All Saints' Day it is the scene of a moving (and photogenic) candlelight service.

**❼ Pointe des Châteaux.** This is the Land's End of Guadeloupe, the easternmost point of the island where the Atlantic and the Caribbean are hurled together to crash against huge rocks, carving them into pyramid-like shapes. The jagged, majestic cliffs are reminiscent of the headlands of Brittany. The only human contribution to this elemental scene is a massive concrete cross. From this point there are spectacular views of the south and east coasts of Guadeloupe and the island of La Désirade. A St-John Perse poem, inscribed on a panoramic map, conjures the magic of the place. On weekends locals come in large numbers to walk their dogs, surf, or romance.

NEED A BREAK? **Paillote** (☎ 590/88–63–61) is a tiny roadside stand right on the *pointe* where you can get libations and light bites, such as lobster and fish grilled on a wood fire.

**⓫ Porte d'Enfer.** The Gate of Hell, 1½ mi north of Campêche, marks a dramatic point on the coast where two jagged cliffs are stormed by the wild Atlantic waters. One legend has it that a Madame Coco strolled out across the waves carrying a parasol and vanished without a trace.

**⓮ Port Louis.** This fishing village of about 7,000 is best known for the Souffleur beach. It was once one of the island's prettiest, but it has become a little shabby. Still, the sand is fringed by flamboyant trees, and though the beach is crowded on weekends, it's blissfully quiet during the week. There are also spectacular views of Basse-Terre.

**❺ Ste-Anne.** In the 18th century, this town, 8 mi east of Gosier, used to be a sugar-exporting center. Sand has replaced sugar as the town's most valuable asset. La Caravelle and the other soft white-sand beaches here are among the best in Guadeloupe. On a more spiritual note, Ste-Anne has a lovely cemetery with stark-white aboveground tombs.

**❻ St-François.** This town was once a simple little village primarily involved with fishing and harvesting tomatoes. The fish and tomatoes are still here, but so are some of the island's ritziest hotels. Avenue de l'Europe runs between the well-groomed 18-hole Robert Trent Jones municipal golf course and the man-made marina. On the marina side, a string of shops, hotels, and restaurants cater to tourists.

**8**   **Zévalos.** Four miles north of St-François is this handsome colonial mansion that was once the manor house of the island's largest sugar plantation.

## Pointe-à-Pitre

**1**   **Pointe-à-Pitre.** This city of some 100,000 people in the southwest of Grande-Terre is not the capital of Guadeloupe (that honor goes to the much smaller Basse-Terre), but it is the commercial and industrial hub of the island. It's bustling, noisy, and hot, a place of honking horns and traffic jams. The pulse is faster than in many other Caribbean capitals, though at night the streets are almost deserted.

Life has not been easy for Pointe-à-Pitre. The city has suffered severe damage over the years from earthquakes, fires, and hurricanes. The most recent damage was done by Hurricanes Frederick (1979), David (1980), and Hugo (1989). Standing on rue Frébault, you can see on one side the remaining French colonial structures and, on the other, the modern city. However, downtown is rejuvenating itself. Completion of the Centre St-John Perse has transformed old warehouses into a cruise-terminal complex that consists of a hotel (the Hotel St-John), three restaurants, space for 80 shops, and the headquarters for Guadeloupe's Port Authority.

The heart of the old city is **Place de la Victoire,** surrounded by wood buildings with balconies and shutters. Many sidewalk cafés have opened up on this revitalized square. At the southern edge, you can watch the busy harbor life. Place de la Victoire was named in honor of Victor Hugues's 1794 victory over the British. The sandbox trees in the park are said to have been planted by Hugues the day after the victory. During the French Revolution, Hugues ordered the guillotine to be set up in the square so that the public could witness the bloody end of 300 recalcitrant royalists. Today the palm-shaded park is a popular gathering place, with stalls selling everything from clothes to kitchen utensils, and gaggles of colorfully dressed women selling fruits and vegetables.

Even more colorful is the bustling **marketplace,** between rues St-John Perse, Frébault, Schoelcher, and Peynier. It is a cacophonous and colorful place where housewives bargain for papayas, breadfruits, christophines, tomatoes, and a bright assortment of other produce.

Anyone with an interest in French literature and culture won't want to miss the **Musée St-John Perse,** on rue Achille René-Boisneuf. It is dedicated to Guadeloupe's most famous son and one of the giants of world literature, Alexis Léger, better known as St-John Perse, winner of the Nobel Prize for Literature in 1960. Some of his finest poems are inspired by the history and landscape of his beloved Guadeloupe—above all, the sea. Before you go to the museum, look for his birthplace at No. 54 rue René-Boisneuf. The museum, housed in a restored colonial Steamboat Gothic house, contains a complete collection of his poetry, as well as some of his personal belongings. There are also works written about him and various mementos, documents, and photographs. ⊠ *Corner of rues Noizières and Achille René-Boisneuf,* ☎ *590/90–07–92.* ▦ *10F.* ☉ *Thurs.–Tues. 8:30–12:30 and 2:30–5:30.*

Guadeloupe's other famous son is celebrated at the **Musée Schoelcher,** at the corner of rues Schoelcher and Peynier. Victor Schoelcher, a high-minded abolitionist from Alsace, fought against slavery in the French

West Indies during the 19th century. The museum contains many of his personal effects, and exhibits trace his life and work. ⊠ *24 rue Peynier,* ☎ *590/82–08–04.* ⌷ *10F.* ☉ *Weekdays 8:30–11:30 and 2–5.*

For fans of French ecclesiastical architecture, there is the imposing **Cathédrale de St-Pierre et St-Paul,** on rue Alexandre Isaac. Built in 1807, it has been terribly battered by hurricanes and is now reinforced with iron pillars and ribs that look like leftovers from the Eiffel Tower. But the fine stained-glass windows and Creole-style upper balconies still make it worth a visit.

## Basse-Terre

Yellow butterflies—clouds of them—are the first thing you see when you arrive on Basse-Terre. Rugged, green, and mysterious, this half of Guadeloupe is mountain trails, lakes, waterfalls, and hot springs. It is the home of the Old Lady, as the Soufrière volcano is called locally, as well as of the capital, also called Basse-Terre. It has always played poor cousin to better-developed Grande-Terre, but in the era of eco-tourism that is changing fast. When it comes to natural beauty, Basse-Terre has it all. The northwest coast, between Bouillante and Grande-Anse, is especially magnificent. The road twists and turns up steep hills smothered in tropical vegetation, skirting deep blue bays before dropping down to colorful seaside towns. Constantly changing light, towering clouds, and frequent rainbows only add to the beauty. For hikers, the Parc National is crisscrossed by numerous trails, many of them following the old *traces,* routes that porters once took across the mountains.

SIGHTS TO SEE

③ **Allée du Manoir.** There's no trace of the manor house, but this magnificent tunnel of century-old royal palms, near the village of Capesterre, is still here. Soaring to as much as 100 ft, the palms have survived both hurricanes and the telephone company, which used to nail the telegraph wires into them.

③ **Basse-Terre.** Because Pointe-à-Pitre is so much bigger, few people suspect that this little town of 15,000 inhabitants is the capital and administrative center of Guadeloupe. But if you have any doubts, walk up the hill to the brand-new, state-of-the-art space **Théâtre Nationale,** where some of France's finest theater and opera companies perform. Paid for by Paris, it's a symbol of the new Basse-Terre. The town has had a lot to overcome. Founded in 1640, it has endured not only foreign attacks and hurricanes but sputtering threats from La Soufrière as well. The last major eruption was in the 16th century. The volcano seemed active enough to warrant the evacuation of more than 70,000 people in 1975.

A good place to start exploring the city is the imposing 17th-century **Fort Louis Delgrès.** There is also a small museum, which gives a good outline of Basse-Terre's history. The **Cathedral of Our Lady of Guadeloupe,** to the north across the Rivière aux Herbes, is also worth a short visit. On boulevard Felix Eboué you can see the impressive colonial buildings housing the government offices. Two main squares, both with gardens, **Jardin Pichon** and **Champ d'Arbaud,** give you a feel for how the city used to be. Not far away are the **botanical gardens.**

For shopping, walk down **rue Dr. Cabre,** with its brightly painted Creole houses and imposing church, Ste-Marie de Guadeloupe. The other main street is **rue St-François.** For a guided tour that is also fun for children, climb aboard *Pom, Pom* (☎ 590/81–24–83), a new miniature train that does a circuit of the major historic sites. It costs 40F for adults, 25F for children 5–12, and lasts 2½ hours.

Dining possibilities are thin on the ground in Basse-Terre, so head a few miles up the coast to **Le Caprice des Iles** in Bailiff (☎ 590/81-74-97) for lobster, *souchy*, or marlin tournedos on a veranda overlooking the sea. You can also have a swim.

**㉖ Bouillante.** The name, literally translated, means "boiling," and so it is no surprise that the main attraction here is the hot springs. At the Source de Thomas, a few minutes' walk up the old Thomas Road, you can loll around in a hot, smelly, natural bathing spa.

**㉒ Cascade aux Ecrevisses.** Part of the ☞ Parc National de la Guadeloupe, Crayfish Falls is one of the loveliest spots on the island. There is a marked trail (walk carefully—the rocks along the trail can be slippery) leading to the splendid waterfall dashing down into the Corossol River—a good place for a dip, though you probably won't have it to yourself. This is one of the most popular sights on the island.

**㉞ Chutes du Carbet.** Carbet Falls are the most spectacular waterfalls on Guadeloupe. Three of them, which drop from 65 ft, 360 ft, and 410 ft, can be reached by following a long, steep path from the village of Habituée. On the way up, you'll pass the **Grand Etang** (Great Pond), a volcanic lake surrounded by interesting plant life. For horror fans there is also the curiously named **Etang Zombi.**

After hiking around the falls, have a hearty lunch of Creole chicken, curried goat, or crayfish at **Chez Dollin-Le Crepuscule** (⌧ Habituée Village, ☎ 590/86-34-56). There's also a four-course menu.

**㉚ Etang As de Pique.** Reaching this lake, 2,454 ft above the town of Gourbeyre, is a challenge for hikers, but you can also drive to it in an hour via paved Palmetto Road. The 5-acre lake, formed by a lava flow, is named after its shape—French for "ace of spades."

**㉚ Les Mamelles.** Two mountains—Mamelle de Petit-Bourg at 2,350 ft and Mamelle de Pigeon at 2,500 ft—rise in the ☞ Parc National de la Guadeloupe. *Mamelle* means "breast," and when you see the mountains you'll understand why they are so named. Trails ranging from easy to arduous lace up into the surrounding mountains. There's a glorious view from the lookout point 1,969 ft up Mamelle de Pigeon. If you're a climber, you'll want to spend several hours exploring this area.

**㉘ Matouba.** This village was settled by East Indians whose descendants still practice ancient rites, including animal sacrifice. If you have an idle 10 hours or so, take off from Matouba for a 19-mi hike on a marked trail through the Monts Caraïbes to the east coast.

**㉝ Parc Archéologique des Roches Gravées.** Situated in the town of Trois-Rivières, this is the principal site in the Lesser Antilles containing rocks engraved and carved by the Arawaks. The park, which is set in a lovely botanical garden full of giant moss-covered boulders, stairways cut into the rock, and lush plants, is a haven of tranquillity. ⌧ Bord de la Mer, Trois-Rivières, ☎ 590/92-91-88. ▨ 4F. ◷ Daily 9–5.

**Parc National de la Guadeloupe.** This 74,100-acre park was recently elevated by UNESCO to the status of a recognized Biosphere Reserve, of which there are only 325 worldwide. For the eco-tourist, this is the place to come. Before going, pick up a *Guide to the National Park* from the tourist office, which rates the hiking trails according to difficulty. Note: The majority of mountain trails are in the southern half. The park is bisected by the **Route de la Traversée,** a 16-mi paved road lined with masses of thick tree ferns, shrubs, flowers, tall trees, and green plantains. It is the ideal point of entry to the park. Wear rubber-sole shoes and take along both swimsuit and sweater, and perhaps food for a picnic. Try to get an early start to remain ahead of the hordes of cruise-ship passengers who descend on La Traversée and the park for the day. ✉ *Administrative Headquarters, Basse-Terre,* ☎ *590/80–24–25.*

**㉑ Parc Tropical de Bras-David.** This part of the ☞ **Parc National de la Guadeloupe** is where you can park and explore various nature trails. The **Maison de la Forêt** has a variety of displays that describe (in French) the flora, fauna, and topography of the national park. It's open daily 9–5; admission is free. There are three marked botanical trails and picnic tables where you can enjoy an alfresco lunch.

**㉔ Petit-Bourg.** The highlight here is the Domaine de Valombreuse, a floral park not far from the town. Three hundred species of flowers, spice gardens, and numerous bird species make this a pleasant place for a stroll. There is also a restaurant in the gardens. ✉ *Petit-Bourg,* ☎ *590/95–50–50.* ▦ *38F.* ☉ *Daily 9–5.*

**㉕ Pigeon Island.** This tiny, rocky island, a few hundred yards off the coast of Malendure, is the site of the Jacques Cousteau Marine Reserve, the best scuba and snorkeling site on Guadeloupe (☞ Outdoor Activities and Sports, *above*). Les Heures Saines and Chez Guy, both on the attractive Malendure beach, conduct diving trips, and the glass-bottom *Aquarium* and *Nautilus* make daily trips to this spectacular site.

---

**NEED A BREAK?** There are several snack wagons at the Malendure beach, but the place to go is **Chez Toulouse** (no phone), a bar and café above the sand.

---

**⑱ Pointe-Noire.** This town has two small museums devoted to local products. **La Maison du Bois** offers a glimpse into the traditional use of wood on the island. Superbly crafted musical instruments and furnishings are on sale. Just across the road is **La Maison du Cacao,** a working cocoa plantation. Pointe-Noire is a good jumping-off point to explore the little-visited **northwest coast** of Basse-Terre. A magnificent coastal road skirts cliffs and tiny coves, dancing in and out of thick stands of mahogany and gommier trees and weaving through unspoiled fishing villages with boats and ramshackle houses as brightly colored as a child's finger painting. One of the most attractive villages is **Deshaies.** The northwest coast also encompasses the excellent beaches of Grande-Anse, Riflet, La Perle, and Ferry. *La Maison du Bois,* ☎ *590/98–17–09.* ▦ *5F.* ☉ *Tues.–Sun. 9:30–5:30. La Maison du Cacao,* ☎ *590/98–21–23.* ▦ *25F.* ☉ *Daily 9–5.*

**⑯ Ravine Chaude.** It's not Vichy, but this modest spa is a good place to soak after tackling the trails. It draws upon the area's healthful geothermal waters and caters almost entirely to locals, though efforts are being made to upgrade it for an international clientele. Massage, sauna, algae masks, and hydrotherapy are some of the available treatments. The surrounding landscape, in the foothills of Grosse Montagne, with its cane fields, country lanes, and colorful little villages, is very pleasant. ✉ *Lamentin,* ☎ *590/25–75–92.* ▦ *20F.* ☉ *Daily 8–8.*

**㉙ St-Claude.** This village lies on the western slopes of La Soufrière, with good views of "The Old Lady," as the volcano is called. You can get a closer look at it by driving up to the Savane à Mulets. From there leave your car and hike (with an experienced guide) the strenuous two-hour climb to the summit at 4,813 ft, the highest point in the Lesser Antilles. Here, sulfurous fumaroles and solidified lava flows make for an impressive scene. When you get back down, head for **La Maison du Volcan** (☎ 596/78–15–16), a museum that will tell you everything you need to know about volcanoes. The museum, open daily 9–5, is 15F.

⑰ **Ste-Rose.** As well as a sulfur bath, there are two good beaches, Amandiers and Clugny, and several interesting, small museums in Ste-Rose. **Le Domaine de Severin** is a historic rum distillery with a working paddle wheel; the restaurant in a restored colonial house is well known for its accras and colombos. The nearby **Musée du Rhum** is a bit of a tourist trap. It features the usual exhibits on the history of rum distillation and a collection of insects from the grotesque to the luminous, but at 40F a pop, it's overpriced. *Le Domaine de Severin,* ☎ *590/28–91–86.* 🎟 *Free.* 🕐 *Daily 8:30–12:30. Musée du Rhum, Bellevue,* ☎ *590/28–70–04.* 🎟 *40F.* 🕐 *Mon.–Sat. 9–1.*

㉓ **Vernou.** Many of the old mansions in this area remain in the hands of the original aristocratic families, the Bekés ("whites" in Creole), who can trace their lineage to before the French Revolution. Traipsing along a path that leads beyond the village through the lush forest, you'll come to the waterfall at **Saut de la Lézarde** (Lizard's Leap).

㉜ **Vieux Fort.** In 1980 40 local lace makers united to preserve—and display—the ancient tradition of lace making. At the **Centre de Broderie** (☞ Shopping, *above*) you can always see one of them at work. There are handkerchiefs, tablecloths, doilies, and even negligees for sale.

㉗ **Vieux-Habitants.** Several good beaches, a restored coffee plantation, and the oldest church on the island (1650) make this village well worth a stop.

⑲ **Zoological Park and Botanical Gardens.** Titi the Raccoon is the mascot of this privately owned zoo in the Parc National. The cramped cages are a sorrowful sight and the 25F entrance fee is a bit steep, but the views on the way there are stunning.

## Iles des Saintes

㊲ **Fort Napoléon.** Nobody ever fired a shot at or from this imposing fort, but it makes a fine museum. Galleries hold a collection of 250 modern paintings, heavily influenced by cubism and surrealism. But the thing to come for is the exhaustive exhibit on one of the greatest sea battles ever fought, the Battle of Les Saintes, when French admiral de Grasse proved no match for the firepower of the Royal Navy (history buffs may recall de Grasse from the American Revolution). You can also visit the well-preserved barracks and prison cells and admire the surrounding botanical gardens, which specialize in cacti of all sizes and descriptions. From the fort you can see Fort Josephine across the channel on the Ilet à Cabrit. ✉ *Bourg, no phone.* 🎟 *15F.* 🕐 *Daily 9–12:30.*

㊱ **Les Saintes.** The eight-island archipelago of Iles des Saintes, usually referred to as Les Saintes, dots the waters off the south coast of Guadeloupe. The islands are Terre-de-Haut, Terre-de-Bas, Ilet à Cabrit, Grand Ilet, La Redonde, La Coche, Le Pâté, and Les Augustins. Columbus discovered the islands on November 4, 1493, and christened them Los Santos in honor of All Saints' Day.

Only Terre-de-Haut and Terre-de-Bas are inhabited, with a combined population of 3,260. Many of les Saintois, as the islanders are called, are fair-haired, blue-eyed descendants of Breton and Norman sailors. Fishing is the main source of income for les Saintois, and the shores are lined with their boats and *filets bleus* (blue nets dotted with burnt-orange buoys). The fishermen wear hats called salakos, which look like inverted saucers or coolie hats. They are patterned after a hat said to have been brought here by a seafarer from China or Indonesia.

With 5 square mi and a population of about 1,500, **Terre-de-Haut** is the largest island and the most developed for tourism. Its "big city" is Bourg, which boasts one street and a few bistros, cafés, and shops.

Clutching the hillside are trim white houses with bright red or blue doors, balconies, and gingerbread frills.

Getting to Terre-de-Haut is an exhilarating affair, whether by land or sea. Air Guadeloupe has regular flights, and your whole life may flash before your eyes as you soar down to the tiny airstrip. However, the flight is mercifully brief, and you may prefer it to the choppy 35-minute ferry crossing from Trois-Rivières or the 60-minute ride from Pointe-à-Pitre. Ferries leave Trois-Rivières at about 8:30 AM (7:30 AM on Sunday) and return about 3 PM. From Pointe-à-Pitre the usual departure time is 8 AM, with return at 4 PM. The round-trip fare from either point is 160F. Check with the tourist office for up-to-date ferry schedules.

Terre-de-Haut's ragged coastline is scalloped with lovely coves and beaches, including the nudist beach at Anse Crawen. The beautiful bay, complete with sugarloaf, has been called a mini Rio. Although it makes a great day trip, you'll really get a feel for Les Saintes only if you stay over. There are three paved roads on the island, but don't even think about driving here—the roads are ghastly. Luckily, the island is so small you can get around by walking. It's a mere five-minute stroll from the airstrip and ferry dock to downtown Bourg.

For such a tiny place, Terre-de-Haut offers a variety of hotels and restaurants (☞ Dining *and* Lodging, *above*). There is also the **Centre Nautique des Saintes** (✉ Plage de la Coline, ☎ 590/99–54–25) and **Espace Plongé Caraïbes** (✉ Bourg, ☎ 590/99–51–84), should you wish to scuba dive off the islands.

## Marie-Galante

Columbus sighted this flat island on November 3, 1493, the day before he landed at Ste-Marie on Basse-Terre. He named it for his flagship, the *Maria Galanda,* and sailed on.

The ferry departs from Pointe-à-Pitre at 8 AM, 2 PM, and 5 PM with returns at 6 AM, 9 AM, and 3:45 PM. (Schedules often change, especially on the weekends, so check them at the tourist office or the harbor offices.) The round-trip costs 160F. You'll put in at Grand Bourg, the major city, with a population of about 8,000. A plane will land you 2 mi from Grand Bourg. If your French or phrase book is good enough, you can negotiate a price with the taxi drivers for touring the island.

**㉚ Marie-Galante.** Covering about 60 square mi, this is the largest of Guadeloupe's islands. It is dotted with ruined 19th-century sugar mills, and sugar is still one of its major products—the others are cotton and rum. One of the last refuges of the Caribs when they were driven from the mainland by the French, the island is now a favorite retreat of Guadeloupeans, who come on weekends to enjoy the beach at Petite-Anse.

You'll find dramatic coastal scenery, with soaring cliffs holding an angry ocean at bay, such as the Gueule Grand Gouffre (Mouth of the Giant Chasm) and Les Galeries (where millennia of erosion have sculpted a natural arcade), and enormous sun-dappled grottoes like Le Trou à Diable, whose underground river can be explored with a guide. Don't miss the **Château Murat** (☎ 590/97–03–79), a restored 17th-century sugar plantation and rum distillery that houses exhibits on the history of rum making and sugarcane production, as well as the admirable Ecomusée, whose displays celebrate local crafts and customs. The château is open daily 9:15–5; admission is 10F. And do visit the distilleries, especially **Père Labat,** whose rum is considered one of the finest in the Caribbean and whose atelier turns out lovely pottery.

There are several places near the ferry landing where you can get an inexpensive meal of seafood and Creole sauce. If you want to stay over, you can choose from Au Village de Ménard (5 bungalows, ☎ 590/97–77–02) in St-Louis, Auberge de l'Arbre à Pain (7 rooms, ☎ 590/97–73–69) in Grand Bourg, or Hotel Hajo (6 rooms, ☎ 590/97–32–76) in Capesterre. An entertainment complex in Grand Bourg called El Rancho has a 400-seat movie theater, a restaurant, terrace grill, snack bar, disco, and a few double rooms.

### La Désirade

**39**  **La Désirade.** According to legend, this is the "desired land" of Columbus's second voyage. He spotted it on November 3, 1493. The 8-square-mi island, 5 mi east of St-François, was for many years a leper colony. Most of today's 1,600 inhabitants are fishermen. The main settlement is Grande-Anse, where there is a pretty church and a 10-room hotel called L'Oasis (☎ 590/20–02–12). The restaurant is not fancy, but it serves excellent seafood.

There are good beaches here, notably Souffleur and Baie Mahault, and there's little to do but loll around on them. The island is virtually unspoiled by tourism and is likely to remain so in the foreseeable future.

Three or four minibuses meet the flights and ferries, and you can negotiate with one of them to get a tour. Ferries depart from St-François daily at 8 and 4. The return ferry departs daily at 3:30. However, be sure to check schedules.

## Guadeloupe A to Z

### Arriving and Departing

#### BY BOAT

Major cruise lines call regularly, docking at berths in downtown Pointe-à-Pitre about a block from the shopping district. **Trans Antilles Express** (☎ 590/83–12–45) and **Transport Maritime Brudey Frères** (☎ 590/90–04–48) provide ferry service to and from Marie-Galante and Les Saintes. The *Jetcat* and *Madras* ferries depart daily from the pier at Pointe-à-Pitre for Marie-Galante starting at 8 AM (check the schedule). The trip takes one hour, and the fare is 160F round-trip. For Les Saintes, Trans Antilles Express connects daily from Pointe-à-Pitre at 8 AM and from Terre-de-Haut at 4 PM. The trip takes 45 minutes and costs 160F round-trip. The *Socimade* (☎ 590/88–48–63) runs between La Désirade and St-François, departing daily at 8 AM and 4 PM. Return ferries depart daily at 3:30 PM. These schedules are subject to change and should be verified through your hotel or at the tourist office. The **Caribbean Express** (☎ 590/83–04–43) operates from Guadeloupe's Pointe-à-Pitre to Dominica and Martinique. The fare to Dominica is 450F, and the ride takes 2½ hours; the fare to Martinique is 450F and takes four hours. The ferry departs from Pointe-à-Pitre at 8 AM four days a week, but check the schedules because they frequently change.

#### BY PLANE

**American Airlines** (☎ 800/433–7300) is usually the most convenient, with year-round daily flights from more than 100 U.S. cities direct to San Juan and nonstop connections to Guadeloupe via American Eagle. **Air Canada** (☎ 800/776–3000) flies direct from Montréal and Toronto. **Air France** (☎ 800/237–2747) flies nonstop from Paris and Fort-de-France and has direct service from Miami and San Juan. **Air Guadeloupe** (☎ 590/82–28–35) flies daily from St. Martin/St. Maarten, St. Barts, Marie-Galante, La Désirade, and Les Saintes. **LIAT** (☎ 212/251–1717 or 590/82–00–84) flies from St. Croix, Antigua, and St. Maarten in the north and is your best bet from Dominica, Martinique, St. Lucia, Grenada, Barbados, and Trinidad.

FROM THE AIRPORT

You'll land at the brand-new Le Raizet International Airport, 2½ mi from Pointe-à-Pitre. Cabs line up outside. The metered fare is about 60F to Pointe-à-Pitre, 90F to Gosier, and 200F to St-François. Fares go up 40% on Sundays and holidays and from 9 PM to 7 AM nightly. For 5F, you can take a bus from the airport to downtown Pointe-à-Pitre.

## Currency

Legal tender is the French franc, equal to 100 centimes. At press time, the exchange rate was U.S.$1 to 5.65F, but currencies fluctuate daily. Some places accept U.S. dollars, but it's best to change your money into the local currency. Credit cards are accepted in most major hotels, restaurants, and shops, less so in smaller places and in the countryside. There are ATMs that accept Visa and MasterCard at the airport and at some banks (though they don't always work). Prices are quoted here in U.S. dollars unless otherwise noted.

## Emergencies

**Police:** In Pointe-à-Pitre (☎ 590/82–13–17), in Basse-Terre (☎ 590/81–11–55). **Fire:** In Pointe-à-Pitre (☎ 590/83–04–76), in Basse-Terre (☎ 590/81–19–22). **SOS ambulance:** ☎ 590/82–89–33 or **SAMU** (☎ 590/89–11–00). **Hospitals:** There is a 24-hour emergency room at the main hospital, **Centre Hôpitalier de Pointe-à-Pitre** (✉ Abymes, ☎ 590/89–10–10). There are 23 clinics and five hospitals located around the island. The tourist office or your hotel can assist you in locating an English-speaking doctor. **Pharmacies:** Pharmacies alternate in staying open around the clock. The tourist office or your hotel can help you locate the one that's on duty.

## Getting Around

BICYCLES

If you opt to tour the island by bike, you won't be alone. Biking is a major sport here (☞ Outdoor Activities and Sports, *above*).

BUSES

Modern public buses run from 5 AM to 6 PM. They stop along the road at bus stops and shelters marked ARRÊT-BUS, but you can also flag one down along the route.

CAR RENTALS

Your valid driver's license will suffice for up to 20 days, after which you'll need an international driver's permit. Guadeloupe has 1,225 mi of excellent roads (marked as in Europe), and driving around Grande-Terre is relatively easy. On Basse-Terre it will take more effort to navigate the hairpin bends on the mountains and around the eastern shore. Guadeloupeans are skillful drivers, but they do like to drive fast. Cars can be rented at **Avis** (☎ 590/82–33–47 or 800/331–1212), **Budget** (☎ 590/82–95–58 or 800/472–3325), **Hertz** (☎ 590/82–00–14 or 800/654–3131), **Thrifty** (☎ 590/91–42–17), and **Europcar** (☎ 590/21–13–52). Rental offices are at the airport as well as at the major resort areas. Car rentals cost a bit more on Guadeloupe than on the other islands: Count on about $60 a day for a small rental car. Note: Allow yourself an extra 30 minutes to drop off your car at the end of your stay—the rental return sites are still at the old airport, several miles away.

To rent RVs, contact **Antilles Locap Soleil** (☎ 590/90–95–72) or **Alligator Vacance** (☎ 590/26–72–71; 590/28–52–25 on Basse-Terre).

TAXIS

Taxis are metered and fairly pricey. During the day you'll pay about 60F from the airport to Pointe-à-Pitre, about 90F to Gosier, and about 200F to St-François. On Sundays, holidays, and between 9 PM and 7

AM, fares increase 40%. If your French is in working order, you can contact radio cabs at 590/82–00–00, 590/83–09–55, and 590/20–74–74. On Basse-Terre call 590/81–79–70.

VESPAS

Vespas (motorbikes) can be rented at **Vespa Sun** (many locations in Pointe-à-Pitre, ☎ 590/91–30–36) and **Equator Moto** (⊠ Gosier, ☎ 590/90–36–77). A scooter generally costs 200F per day, including insurance. You'll need to put down a 1,000F deposit.

## Guided Tours

Taxi tours have set fares to various points on the island. The tourist office or your hotel can arrange for an English-speaking taxi driver and even organize a small group for you to share the cost of the tour.

**Guides de Montagne de la Caraïbe,** O.G.M.C. (⊠ Maison Forestière, Matouba, ☎ 590/80–05–79), provides guides for hiking tours in the mountains. So, too, does the **Office du Tourisme** on Basse-Terre (☎ 590/81–24–83). A new, private venture, **Emeraude Guadeloupe** (☎ 590/81–98–28, FAX 590/81–98–12), offers everything from hikes up the volcano to botanical tours and visits to Creole homes. The guides are certified by the state, but you will probably need some French to understand them. For those who really want to challenge themselves, **Parfum d'Aventure** (⊠ Ste-Anne, ☎ 590/88–47–62) offers adventure excursions in Basse-Terre, including canyoning, canoeing on the Lézarde, sea kayaking, four-wheel driving, and hiking, from easy to grueling.

## Language

The official language is French. Everyone also speaks a Creole patois, which you won't be able to understand even if you're fluent in French. In the major hotels, most of the staff knows some English. However, communicating may be more difficult in the countryside. Some taxi drivers speak a little English. Arm yourself with a phrase book, a dictionary, patience, and a sense of humor.

## Opening and Closing Times

Banks are open weekdays 8–noon and 2–4. Crédit Agricole, Banque Populaire, and Société Générale de Banque aux Antilles have branches that are open Saturday. During the summer most banks are open 8–3. Banks close at noon the day before a legal holiday that falls during the week. As a rule, shops are open weekdays 8 or 8:30–noon and 2:30–6, but hours are flexible when cruise ships are in town.

## Passports and Visas

U.S. and Canadian citizens need only proof of citizenship. A passport is best (even one that expired up to five years ago). Other acceptable documents are a notarized birth certificate with a raised seal (not a photocopy) or a voter registration card accompanied by a government-authorized photo ID. A free temporary visa, good only for your stay in Guadeloupe, will be issued to you upon your arrival at the airport. British citizens need a valid passport, but no visa. In addition, all visitors must hold an ongoing or return ticket.

## Precautions

Put your valuables in the hotel safe. Don't leave them unattended in your room or on the beach. Keep an eye out for motorcyclists riding double, as they sometimes veer close to the sidewalk and snatch shoulder bags. It isn't a good idea to walk around Pointe-à-Pitre at night, because it's almost deserted after dark. If you rent a car, always lock it with luggage and valuables stashed out of sight.

Ask permission before taking a picture of an islander, and don't be surprised if the answer is a firm "No." Guadeloupeans are also deeply re-

ligious and traditional. Don't offend them by wearing short shorts or
swimwear off the beach.

## Taxes and Service Charges

The *taxe de séjour* varies from hotel to hotel but never exceeds $1.50
per person, per day. Most hotel prices include a 10%–15% service charge;
if not, it will be added to your bill.

Restaurants are legally required to include a 15% gratuity in the menu
price, and no additional gratuity is necessary. Tip skycaps and porters
about 5F. Many cab drivers own their own cabs and don't expect a
tip. You won't have any trouble ascertaining if a 10% tip is expected.

## Telephones and Mail

To call from the United States, dial 011–590, then the local number.
(To call person-to-person, dial 01–590.) It is not possible to place collect or credit-card calls to the United States from Guadeloupe. Coin-
operated phones are rare but can be found in restaurants and cafés. If
you need to make many calls outside of your hotel, purchase a Télécarte at the post office or other outlets marked TÉLÉCARTE EN VENTE
ICI. Télécartes look like credit cards and are used in special booths labeled TÉLÉCOM. Local and international calls made with the cards are
cheaper than operator-assisted calls.

To call the United States from Guadeloupe, dial 19 + 1 + the area code
and phone number. To dial locally in Guadeloupe, simply dial the six-
digit phone number.

Postcards to the United States cost 3.70F; letters up to 20 grams,
4.60F. Stamps can be purchased at the post office, *café-tabacs,* hotel
newsstands, and souvenir shops. Postcards and letters to the United
Kingdom cost 3.60F.

## Visitor Information

For information contact the **French West Indies Tourist Board** by call-
ing France-on-Call at 900/990–0040 (50¢ per minute 9 AM–7 PM). You
may write to the U.S. branches of the **French Government Tourist Of-
fice** (✉ 444 Madison Ave., New York, NY 10022; ✉ 9454 Wilshire
Blvd., Beverly Hills, CA 90212; ✉ 645 N. Michigan Ave., Chicago,
IL 60611) and write or call the branches in Canada and the United
Kingdom (✉ 1981 McGill College Ave., Suite 490, Montréal, Québec
H3A 2W9, ☎ 514/847–0211; ✉ 30 St. Patrick St., Suite 700, Toronto,
Ontario M5T 3A3, ☎ 416/593–6427; ✉ 178 Piccadilly, London
W1V 0AL, ☎ 0171/499–6911).

In Guadeloupe, the **Office Départemental du Tourism** has an office in Pointe-
à-Pitre (✉ 5 square de la Banque B.P. 1099, 97181 Cedex, ☎ 590/82–
09–30). The office is open weekdays 8–5, Saturday 8–noon. There is
also a tourist information booth at the airport and an Office du Tourisme
on Basse-Terre (☎ 590/81–24–83).

# 14 Jamaica

*Sun-drenched Jamaica is almost completely ringed by gorgeous white beaches. Come to be pampered at resorts, to sample fiery jerk chicken and a cool Red Stripe beer under a swaying palm, to listen to reggae music (the heartbeat of the island), and to get to know the locals who are accommodating, opinionated, and quick to smile.*

Updated by
Melissa Rivers

**T**HE THIRD-LARGEST ISLAND in the Caribbean (after Cuba and Puerto Rico), the English-speaking nation of Jamaica enjoys a considerable self-sufficiency based on tourism, agriculture, and mining. Its physical attractions include jungle mountaintops, clear waterfalls, and unforgettable beaches, yet the country's greatest resource may be the Jamaicans themselves. Although 95% of the population trace their bloodlines to Africa, their national origins lie in Great Britain, the Middle East, India, China, Germany, Portugal, South America, and many of the other islands in the Caribbean. Their cultural life is a wealthy one; the music, art, and cuisine of Jamaica are vibrant, with a spirit easy to sense but as hard to describe as the rhythms of reggae or a flourish of the streetwise patois.

In addition to its north-coast pleasure capitals—Montego Bay and Ocho Rios—Jamaica has a real capital in Kingston. For all its congestion and for all the disparity between city life and the bikinis and parasails to the north, Kingston is the true heart and head of the island. This is the place where politics, literature, music, and art wrestle for acceptance in the largest English-speaking city south of Miami, its actual population of nearly 1 million bolstered by the emotional membership of virtually all Jamaicans.

The first people known to have reached Jamaica were the Arawaks, Indians who paddled their canoes from the Orinoco region of South America about a thousand years after the death of Christ. Then, in 1494, Christopher Columbus stepped ashore at what is now called Discovery Bay. Having spent four centuries on the island, the Arawaks had little notion that his feet on their sand would mean their extinction within 50 years.

What is now St. Ann's Bay was established as New Seville in 1509 and served as the Spanish capital until the local government crossed the island to Santiago de la Vega (now Spanish Town). The Spaniards were never impressed with Jamaica; their searches found no precious metals, and they let the island fester in poverty for 161 years. When 5,000 British soldiers and sailors appeared in Kingston Harbor in 1655, the Spaniards did not put up a fight.

The arrival of the English, and the three centuries of rule that followed, provided Jamaica with the surprisingly genteel underpinnings of its present life—and the rousing pirate tradition fueled by rum that enlivened a long period of Caribbean history. The British buccaneer Henry Morgan counted Jamaica's governor as one of his closest friends and enjoyed the protection of His Majesty's government no matter what he chose to plunder. Port Royal, once said to be the "wickedest city of Christendom," grew up on a spit of land across from present-day Kingston precisely because it served so many interests. Morgan and his brigands were delighted to have such a haven, and the people of Jamaica profited by being able to buy pirate booty at terrific bargains.

Morgan enjoyed a prosperous life; he was knighted and made lieutenant governor of Jamaica before the age of 30, and, like every other good bureaucrat, he died in bed and was given a state funeral. Port Royal fared less well. On June 7, 1692, an earthquake tilted two-thirds of the city into the sea, the tidal wave that followed the last tremors washed away millions in pirate treasure, and Port Royal simply disappeared. In recent years divers have turned up some of the treasure, but most of it still lies in the depths, adding an exotic quality to the water sports pursued along Kingston's reefs.

The very British 18th century was a time of prosperity in Jamaica. This was the age of the sugar baron, who ruled his plantation great house and made the island the largest sugar-producing colony in the world. Because sugar fortunes were built on slave labor, however, production became less profitable when the Jamaican slave trade was abolished in 1807 and slavery was ended in 1838.

As was often the case in colonies, a national identity came to supplant allegiance to the British in the hearts and minds of Jamaicans. This new identity was given official recognition on August 6, 1962, when Jamaica became an independent nation with loose ties to the Commonwealth. The island today has a democratic form of government led by a prime minister and a cabinet of fellow ministers.

## Lodging

The island has a variety of destinations to choose from, each of which offers its own unique expression of the Jamaican experience.

**Kingston** is the most culturally active place in Jamaica. Some of the island's finest business hotels are here, and those high towers are filled with rooftop restaurants, English pubs, serious theater and pantomime, dance presentations, art museums and galleries, jazz clubs, upscale supper clubs, and disco dives.

**Mandeville,** 2,000 ft above the sea, is noted for its cool climate and proximity to secluded south-coast beaches. Most accommodations don't have air-conditioning (it's simply not needed) but are close to golf, tennis, horseback riding, and bird-watching areas.

**Montego Bay** has miles of hotels, villas, apartments, and duty-free shops. Although lacking much in the way of cultural stimuli, MoBay presents a comfortable island backdrop for the many conventions it hosts.

**Negril,** some 50 mi west of Montego Bay, was long a sleepy bohemian retreat. In the last decade the town has bloomed considerably and added a number of classy all-inclusive resorts (Beaches, Sandals Negril, Grand Lido, and Swept Away), with several more on the drawing board for the Bloody Bay (northeast of Negril Beach), which is now under development. Negril itself is only a small village, so there isn't much of historical significance to seek out. Then again, that's not what brings the sybaritic singles and couples here. The crowd is young, hip, and laid-back, here for the sun, the sand, and the sea.

**Ocho Rios,** on the northeast coast halfway between Port Antonio and Montego Bay, is hilly and lush, with rivers, riotous gardens, and a growing number of upscale resorts, many of which are all-inclusive. Ocho Rios's hotels and villas are all within short driving distance of a bustling crafts market, boutiques and duty-free shops, restaurants, and such scenic attractions as Dunn's River Falls, Fern Gully, Coyaba Gardens, and Prospect Plantation.

**Port Antonio,** described by poet Ella Wheeler Wilcox as "the most exquisite port on earth," is a seaside town nestled at the foot of verdant hills toward the east end of the north coast. The two best experiences to be had here are rafting the Rio Grande and stopping at the Trident, one of the island's classiest resorts. Today, Port Antonio enjoys the reputation of being Jamaica's most favored out-of-the-way resort.

**Runaway Bay,** the smallest of the resort areas, has a handful of modern hotels, a few new all-inclusive resorts, and an 18-hole golf course.

Jamaica was the birthplace of the Caribbean all-inclusive, the vacation concept that took the Club Med idea and gave it a lusty, excess-in-the-tropics spin. The all-inclusive resort has become the most popular vacation option in Jamaica, offering incredible values with rates from $145 to $350 per person per night. Rates include airport transfers; hotel accommodations; three meals a day plus snacks; all bar drinks, often including premium liquors; wine, beer, and soft drinks; a plethora of land and water sports, including golf, tennis, aerobics, basketball, boccie, croquet, horseshoes, lawn chess, Ping-Pong, shuffleboard, volleyball, scuba diving, and nonmotorized water sports (with instruction and equipment); an array of entertainment options (game rooms with billiards, darts, and/or slot machines; nightclubs; classes in local crafts, cooking, language, dance, and mixology; and a showroom or central theater with nightly entertainment); and all gratuities and taxes. The only surcharges are usually for such luxuries as massages, souvenirs, sightseeing tours, and weddings or vow-renewal ceremonies (though these are often included at any of the high-end all-inclusives). At times they may feel a bit like Pleasure Island, as all of your needs and most of your wants are taken care of. The all-inclusives have branched out, some of them courting families, others going after an upper crust that would not even have picked up a brochure a few years ago. Most require a three-night minimum stay.

If you're the exploring type who likes to get out and about, you may prefer an EP property. Many places offer MAP or FAP packages that include extras like airport transfers and sightseeing tours. Even if you don't want to be tied down to a meal plan, it pays to inquire, because the savings can be considerable. Rooms at most hotels come equipped with cable or satellite TV, air-conditioning, direct-dial phone, clock radio, and, in many cases, a safe. Larger properties usually have no-smoking rooms and rooms accessible to travelers with disabilities, as well room service, laundry service, meeting rooms and business services, boutiques and gift shops, a beauty parlor, a tour desk, and car rentals.

Resorts and hotels throughout the island have widely varying policies regarding children; some do not accept them, but those that do often allow up to two to stay free in their parents' room, even at several all-inclusive resorts. Others allow kids to stay free during the off-season, or offer discounted meal plans. Several all-inclusive resorts do not accept children under 16 or 18 years old. Baby-sitting is readily available at all properties that accept children. If you're planning to take the kids, ask lots of questions before booking a reservation, or have your travel agent search out the best deal for you.

Please note that the price categories listed below are based on winter rates. As a general rule, rates are reduced anywhere from 10% to 30% from April 30 to December 15. The **Jamaica Reservation Service** (☎ 800/526–2422 in the U.S. and Canada) can book resorts, hotels, villas, and guest houses throughout the country.

Welcome additions to Jamaica's lodging scene include **Breezes,** a new line of moderately priced all-inclusives introduced by SuperClubs (☎ 800/859–7873); the flagship Breezes took over Jamaica-Jamaica in Runaway Bay, and a second Breezes was constructed in 1995 on Doctors Cave Beach in MoBay. Not to be outdone by the competition, Sandals (☎ 800/726–3257) introduced the fancier, slightly more expensive **Beaches** all-inclusive resort, catering to singles, couples, and families; the very attractive flagship property on Negril Beach in Negril was just getting ready to open at press time. Another new family-oriented all inclusive set to join the ranks in 1998 is the upscale **Pebbles at Braco Village Resort** (☎ 800/654–1337) in Runaway Bay.

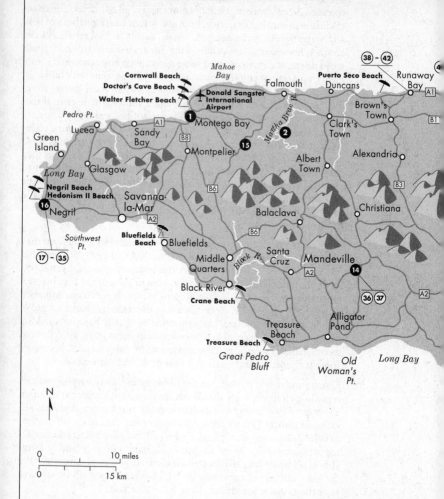

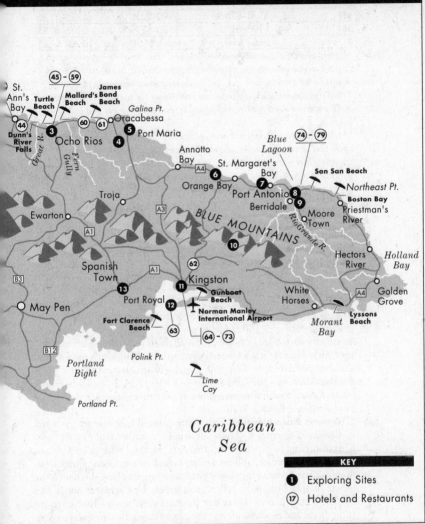

**KEY**

● Exploring Sites

⑰ Hotels and Restaurants

Breezes Runaway
Bay, **39**
Charela Inn, **23**
Ciboney, Ocho
Rios, **61**
Club Caribbean, **41**
Club Jamaica
Beach Resort, **52**
Coco La Palm, **34**
Comfort Suites, **55**
Couples, **53**
Crowne Plaza
Kingston, **68**
Devine Destiny, **19**

Dragon Bay, **76**
Enchanted
Garden, **46**
FDR, Franklyn D.
Resort, **42**
Goblin Hill, **75**
Grand Lido, **30**
H.E.A.R.T.
Country Club, **40**
Hedonism II, **29**
Hibiscus Lodge, **56**
High Hope Estate, **43**
Hotel Mocking
Bird Hill, **74**

Hotel Samsara, **33**
Jamaica Grande, **50**
Jamaica Inn, **51**
Jamaica Palace, **79**
Jamaica Pegasus, **73**
Mandeville Hotel, **37**
Morgan's Harbour
Hotel, Beach Club,
and Yacht Marina, **63**
Negril Cabins
Resort, **31**
Negril Gardens, **22**
Plantation Inn, **57**

Poinciana Beach
Resort, **27**
Point Village, **32**
Sandals Dunn's
River, **44**
Sandals Negril, **28**
Sans Souci Lido, **60**
Strawberry Hill, **62**
Swept Away, **25**
Terra Nova, **70**
Trident Villas
and Hotel, **78**
Wyndham New
Kingston, **66**

| CATEGORY | COST EP/BP* | COST MAP** | COST AI*** |
|---|---|---|---|
| $$$$ | over $245 | over $250 | over $275 |
| $$$ | $175–$245 | $190–$250 | $225–$275 |
| $$ | $105–$175 | $130–$190 | $175–$225 |
| $ | under $105 | under $130 | under $175 |

*EP prices are for a standard double room for two in winter, excluding 10% tax and any service charge. Many hotels either include breakfast in the tariff or offer a BP price, which includes breakfast as their minimum plan.

**MAP prices include daily breakfast and dinner for two in winter. Often MAP packages come with use of nonmotorized water sports and other benefits.

***All-inclusive (AI) winter prices are per person, double occupancy, and include tax, service, gratuities, all meals, drinks, facilities, lessons, and airport transfers. Motorized water sports and scuba are sometimes included; if it's important to you, ask.

## Kingston

$$$$  ⊞ **Strawberry Hill.** One of many island properties owned by Chris Black-
★    well, head of Island Records (the late Bob Marley's label), this Blue Mountains retreat 45 minutes north of Kingston offers refined luxury and absolute peace. Authors, musicians, and screenwriters come here for extended periods to relax, rejuvenate the creative juices, and work, encouraged by the remote, peaceful setting. The food is top notch, as are the staff and the accommodations—elegant Georgian-style villas appointed with mahogany furnishings and roomy balconies over-looking grand vistas. There's no air-conditioning here, simply because it's not needed at 3,100 ft above sea level. Sunday brunch, featuring an enormous Jamaican buffet, is an affair to remember, but reserve a spot early because it's a favored event among Kingston's movers and shakers. ⊠ *Irishtown, Box 590, Liguanea, St. Andrew,* ☎ *809/944–8400 or 800/688–7678,* ℻ *809/944–8404. 12 1-, 2-, and 3-bedroom villas. Restaurant, bar, refrigerators, room service, sauna, croquet, airport shuttle. AE, MC, V. BP.*

$$$  ⊞ **Crowne Plaza Kingston.** This ochre-colored high-rise sits on a hill in Constant Spring, a classy suburb 15 minutes from downtown Kingston. Sophisticated public areas are adorned with potted plants, overstuffed furniture, and intriguing Jamaican art. Decor varies from floor to floor; some of the amenity-laden rooms are blue-on-white, while others feature burgundy, yellow, and green color schemes and a mix of florals and plaids. There are business-class rooms that have in-room faxes and modems among their extra amenities. Request a room on the southwest side for grand sunset views, or time your dinner at Isabella's, the hotel's fine dining room, to catch the dwindling rays. ⊠ *211A Constant Spring Rd.,* ☎ *809/925–7676 or 800/618–6534,* ℻ *809/925–5757. 110 rooms, 40 suites. Restaurant, 2 bars, grill, in-room safes, kitchenettes, minibars, refrigerator, room service, pool, massage, sauna, tennis court, exercise room, jogging, squash, concierge. AE, DC, MC, V.*

$$$  ⊞ **Jamaica Pegasus.** The Jamaica Pegasus is one of three business-class hotels in the New Kingston area. The 17-story complex near down-town has an efficient and accommodating staff, old-world decor, and a newly renovated lobby. Other advantages here include an excellent business center, duty-free shops, and 24-hour room service. Guests on the business floors can check out complimentary cellular phones for use during their stay. At press time, only three floors (9–11) of rooms, all with balcony, coffee/tea setups, and voice mail, had received des-perately needed face-lifts. ⊠ *81 Knutsford Blvd., Box 333, Kingston,* ☎ *809/926–3690 or 800/225–5843,* ℻ *809/929–5855. 334 rooms, 16 suites. 2 restaurants, 2 bars, coffee shop, in-room safes, minibars,*

*pool, wading pool, beauty salon, 2 tennis courts, basketball, exercise room, jogging, playground, concierge. AE, DC, MC, V. EP, MAP.*

$$$ ⊞ **Wyndham New Kingston.** The high-rise Wyndham New Kingston is the best of Kingston's business hotels. The expansive marble lobby leads to attractive, well-appointed guest rooms. The concierge floors include complimentary cocktails, hors d'oeuvres, and Continental breakfast. Lots of extras include secured-access elevators, an American Airline's service desk, and in-room coffee/tea setup. Rates include admission to Jonkanoo, the hotel's hot nightclub (☞ Nightlife, *below*); there's also an art gallery. ⊠ *Box 112, Kingston,* ☎ *809/926–5430 or 800/526–2422,* FAX *809/929–7439. 284 rooms, 13 suites, 6 1- and 2-bedroom housekeeping units. 2 restaurants, 3 bars, in-room modem lines, in-room safes, pool, massage, sauna, 2 tennis courts, health club, shops, recreation room, concierge. AE, DC, MC, V. EP, MAP.*

$$ ⊞ **Morgan's Harbour Hotel, Beach Club, and Yacht Marina.** A favorite of the sail-into-Jamaica set, this small property has 22 acres of beachfront at the very entrance to the old pirate's town. Done in light tropical prints, the rooms are very basic, but many have a balcony and mini-refrigerator; the suites with loft bedrooms are the nicest. Ask for one in the newer wing. Because the hotel is so close to the airport, passengers on delayed or canceled flights are often bused here to wait. ⊠ *Port Royal, Kingston,* ☎ *809/967–8075 or 800/526–2422,* FAX *809/ 924–8562. 44 rooms, 6 suites. Restaurant, bar, refrigerators, room service, pool, volleyball, dive shop, water sports, fishing, billiards, dance club, airport shuttle. AE, MC, V. EP.*

$$ ⊞ **Terra Nova.** Set in the quieter part of New Kingston, 1 mi from the commercial district and within walking distance of Devon House, is the intimate Terra Nova hotel. Guest rooms are decked out in classical mahogany furniture and fine art. The El Dorado restaurant offers international cuisine and reasonably priced buffets. You'll also find formal high-tea service here on Thursdays. ⊠ *17 Waterloo Rd., Kingston 10,* ☎ *809/926–9334,* FAX *809/929–4933. 35 rooms. Restaurant, coffee shop, grill, lounge, in-room safes, no-smoking rooms, room service, pool. AE, DC, MC, V. EP.*

## Mandeville

$ ⊞ **Astra Country Inn & Restaurant.** Country is the key word in the name of this retreat, which is 2,000 ft up in the mountains. The low price reflects the nature of the very basic rooms here: They define spartan but are immaculately clean. There is no air-conditioning, but you shouldn't miss it this high in the mountains. The small restaurant is open from 7 AM to 9 PM and serves snacks in addition to breakfast, lunch, and dinner. The food is billed as "home cooking" and emphasizes fresh produce—lots of vegetables and fruit juices. The tariff here includes breakfast. ⊠ *Ward Ave., Box 60, Mandeville,* ☎ *809/962– 3265 or 800/526–2422,* FAX *809/962–1461. 20 rooms, 2 housekeeping suites. Restaurant, bar, kitchenettes, pool, sauna, laundry service. AE, MC, V. BP.*

$ ⊞ **Mandeville Hotel.** Tropical gardens wrap around the building, and flowers spill onto the terrace, where breakfast and lunch are served. Rooms are simple and breeze-cooled; suites have full kitchens. You'll need a car to get around town, go out for dinner, and get to the beach, which is an hour away. ⊠ *Box 78, Mandeville,* ☎ *809/962–2460 or 800/233–4582,* FAX *809/962–0700. 46 rooms, 17 1-, 2-, and 3-bedroom housekeeping suites. Restaurant, bar, coffee shop, kitchenettes, refrigerator, pool, golf privileges, baby-sitting, laundry service, meeting room, travel services. AE, MC, V. EP.*

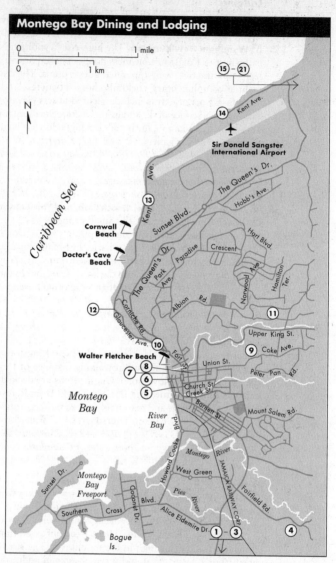

**Montego Bay Dining and Lodging**

## Montego Bay

**$$$$** ⭐ 🏨 **Round Hill Hotel and Villas.** The Hollywood set frequents this peaceful resort, 8 mi west of town on a hilly peninsula. Twenty-seven villas housing 74 suites are scattered over 98 acres, and there are 36 hotel rooms in Pineapple House, a two-story building overlooking the sea. Rooms are done in a refined Ralph Lauren style, with mahogany furnishings and terra-cotta floors. The villas are leased back to the resort by private owners and vary in decor, but jungle motifs are a favorite. All come with a personal maid and a cook to make your breakfast (for an extra charge), and several have private pools. The restaurant's good food and elegant presentation make feasting in the dining room, or better yet on the seaside terrace, a memorable treat. ⊠ *Box 64, Montego Bay,* ☎ *809/952–5150 or 800/237–3237,* 🖷 *809/952–2505. 36 rooms, 27 housekeeping villas. Restaurant, room service, pool, beauty salon, massage, 5 tennis courts, aerobics, exercise room, jogging, beach, water sports, shops, concierge, helipad. AE, DC, MC, V. EP, MAP, FAP, All-inclusive.*

**$$$$** 🏨 **Tryall Golf, Tennis, and Beach Club.** Part of a posh residential development 13 mi west of Montego Bay, Tryall clings to a hilltop overlooking a golf course and the Caribbean. Guests choose among numerous private villas dotting the 2,200-acre island plantation, each with its own pool, full staff (butler, cook, maid, and gardener), and golf cart. All accommodations are individually and plushly decorated. The fine dining room in the great house is elegant and serves Continental and Jamaican cuisine. A beautiful seaside golf course is one of this resort's more memorable features. It's also reputed to be one of the meanest courses in the world and as such hosts big-money tournaments. ✉ *Box 1206, Montego Bay,* ☎ *809/956–5660, 809/956–5667, or 800/742–0498;* 🖷 *809/956–5673. 57 villas. Restaurant, 2 bars, in-room safes, refrigerators, room service, pool, massage, driving range, 18-hole golf course, 9 tennis courts, jogging, beach, dive shop, water sports. AE, DC, MC, V. EP.*

**$$$–$$$$** 🏨 **Coyaba Beach Resort and Club.** Owners Joanne and Kevin Robert-
★ son live on the property, interacting with guests daily, giving this $10 million oceanfront retreat the feel of an intimate and inviting country inn. Coyaba is also very family friendly. The plantation-style great house, just east of Montego Bay, is a successful blend of modern amenities and old-world grace: Guest rooms are decorated with lovely colonial prints and hand-carved mahogany furniture, and sunshine from the tall windows pours over terra-cotta floors and potted plants. Baskets of spring water and freshly baked banana bread, weekly afternoon tea and evening cocktail parties, and tennis, scuba diving, and massage clinics are part of the package. ✉ *Mahoe Bay, Little River,* ☎ *809/953–9150 or 800/237–3237,* 🖷 *809/953–2244. 50 rooms. 2 restaurants, 3 bars, pool, outdoor hot tub, massage, tennis court, exercise room, volleyball, water sports, library, recreation room, playground. MC, V. EP, MAP, All-inclusive.*

**$$$–$$$$** 🏨 **Half Moon Golf, Tennis, and Beach Club.** For more than four decades
★ the 400-acre Half Moon Club resort has been a destination unto itself with a reputation for doing the little things right. Although it has mushroomed from 30 to more than 400 units, it has maintained its intimate, luxurious feel. The rooms, suites, and villas, whether in modern or Queen Anne style, are decorated in exquisite taste, with such flourishes as Oriental throw rugs and antique radios. Several villas—which come with a cook, butler, housekeeper, and rental car or golf cart—have private pools, and the mile-long stretch of beach is just steps away from every guest room. Recent additions to the property include an upscale shopping mall, 32 luxury villas with pools, a nature reserve, and a hospital. ✉ *Box 80, 7 mi east of Montego Bay,* ☎ *809/953–2211 or 800/227–3237,* 🖷 *809/953–2731. 407 rooms. 7 restaurants, 3 bars, 39 pools, outdoor hot tub, sauna, spa, 18-hole golf course, miniature golf, 13 tennis courts, aerobics, badminton, croquet, exercise room, horseback riding, Ping-Pong, squash, dive shop, water sports, bicycles, shops, theater, library, children's program (ages 3–10), playground, convention center, airport shuttle. AE, DC, MC, V. EP, MAP, FAP, All-inclusive.*

**$$$** 🏨 **Wyndham Rose Hall.** The veteran Wyndham Rose Hall, a self-contained resort built on the 400-acre Rose Hall Plantation, mixes recreation with a top-flight conference setup. A bustling business hotel popular with large groups, it has all the resort amenities: tennis courts, golf course, three interconnected pools, a nightclub, a water-sports center, and a shopping arcade. Rooms, renovated in 1997, feature tropical florals in shades of deep peach and are comfortable but somewhat sterile. A "Kid's Klub" with daily supervised activities for 5- to 12-year-olds is included in the rates. The waters off the thin crescent beach are good for sailing and snorkeling. ✉ *Box 999, Montego Bay,*

☎ 809/953–2650 or 800/996–3426, FAX 809/953–2617. *470 rooms, 19 suites. 4 restaurants, 3 bars, in-room safes, room service, massage, 3 pools, 6 tennis courts, golf course, aerobics, basketball, exercise room, volleyball, water sports, nightclub, playground, convention center. AE, DC, MC, V. EP, MAP, All-inclusive.*

$$$ ★ 🏨 **Sandals Montego Bay.** The largest private beach in Montego Bay is the spark that lights Sandals Montego Bay, one of the most popular couples resorts in the Caribbean. Its all-inclusive format and nonstop activities make it a bit like a cruise ship that remains in port, with rooms overlooking the bay. The revelers don't seem to mind the zooming planes (the airport is next door), and the atmosphere here remains one of a great, big fun party. Even the staff seem happy as they hum or sing their way through the workday. Rooms are basic but comfortable enough, and guests are seldom in them because there is so much to do. The Oleandor Restaurant is probably the best fine-dining outlet in the Sandals chain. ✉ *Box 100, Montego Bay,* ☎ *809/952–5510 or 800/726–3257,* FAX *809/952–0816. 243 rooms. 4 restaurants, 4 bars, snack bar, in-room safes, 2 pools, 3 outdoor hot tubs, saunas, 3 tennis courts, racquetball, beach, dive shop, water sports, library, concierge. 3-night minimum stay. AE, DC, MC, V. All-inclusive.*

$$$ 🏨 **Sandals Royal Jamaican.** Another all-inclusive resort for couples only, the Royal Jamaican is distinguished by Jamaican-style architecture arranged in a semicircle around attractive gardens. Although sportive and activities-laden, this property is a bit quieter and more genteel than the other Sandals and draws a nicely mixed international crowd. Standard rooms have lacquered furniture in light colors and mauve carpeting and bedspreads; bathrooms are small. The deluxe oceanfront rooms and suites are more elegant and inviting, with mahogany four-poster beds and floral-print fabrics. A colorful "dragon boat" carries guests across to Sandals's private island to dine at the Indonesian restaurant. ✉ *Box 167, Montego Bay,* ☎ *809/953–2231 or 800/726–3257,* FAX *809/953–2788. 190 rooms. 4 restaurants, 4 bars, in-room safes, 4 pools, beauty salon, 5 outdoor hot tubs, saunas, 3 tennis courts, aerobics, beach, dive shop, water sports, concierge. 3-night minimum stay. AE, DC, MC, V. All-inclusive.*

$$ 🏨 **Atrium at Ironshore.** Fifteen moderately priced, fully furnished apartments make up this small complex. Decor varies, but each of the charming units has pastel floral and plaid prints, cool white tile floors, beige rattan furniture, a patio or balcony, and a private housekeeper-cook on call. Large saltwater tanks full of tropical fish brighten the alfresco dining terrace near the waterfall-fed pool, and you'll often find lively games of darts or skittles under way in the English-style pub. A shopping mall with supermarket, cinema, and several boutiques is within walking distance, but you'll have to take a shuttle to the beach. ✉ *1084 Morgan Rd., Box 604,* ☎ *809/953–2605,* FAX *809/953–3683. 15 1½-, 2-, and 3-bedroom housekeeping suites. Restaurant, pub, kitchenettes, refrigerator, pool, coin laundry, meeting room. AE, DC, MC, V. EP.*

$–$$ 🏨 **Holiday Inn Sunspree Resort.** A $1.5 million renovation in 1996 did much to raise the level of this sprawling property to a family-oriented, all-inclusive resort, with activities day and night. Although the rooms, spread out in seven buildings, are cheerful enough, the hotel is big and noisy; those farthest from the pool and central dining and entertainment area are quietest. Room service is available for breakfast. The beach is just a palm-shaded sliver. ✉ *Box 480, Montego Bay,* ☎ *809/ 953–2485 or 800/352–0731,* FAX *809/953–2840. 496 rooms, 24 suites. 2 restaurants, 4 bars, 2 snack bars, in-room safes, no-smoking rooms, pool, 4 tennis courts, beach, dive shop, water sports, children's pro-*

gram (ages 3–17), playground, concierge, airport shuttle. AE, DC, MC, V. All-inclusive.

**$–$$** 🖫 **Sandals Inn.** If you're willing to do without a private beach (there's
★ a public one across the street), you can stay here for much less than at the other couples-only Sandals resorts. The inn is more intimate and far quieter than the other Sandals establishments; it's managed more as a small hotel than a large resort. The charming rooms are compact; most have balconies facing the pool. Dark carpet contrasts with white lacquered furniture and tropical-print fabrics. There's plenty to do here, and you can get in on the action at the other two MoBay Sandals by hopping aboard the free hourly shuttle. The in-town location makes the inn convenient to shopping and tours. ⊠ Box 412, Montego Bay, ☎ 809/952–4140 or 800/726–3257, FAX 809/952–6913. 52 rooms. 2 restaurants, 2 bars, in-room safes, pool, beauty salon, outdoor hot tub, tennis court, water sports, concierge, airport shuttle. 3-night minimum stay. AE, DC, MC, V. All-inclusive.

**$** 🖫 **Richmond Hill Inn.** The hilltop Richmond Hill Inn, a quaint, 200-year-old great house originally owned by the Dewars clan, enjoys spectacular views of the Caribbean and a great deal of peace, compared with MoBay's hustle. Decor tends toward the dainty and is a bit dated, with frilly lace curtains and doilies, lots of lavenders and mauves, and crushed-velvet furniture here and there. A free shuttle will take you to shopping and beaches, about 10–15 minutes away. ⊠ Union St., Box 362, Montego Bay, ☎ 809/952–3859 or 800/423–4095. 15 rooms, 4 suites. Bar, coffee shop, dining room, pool, laundry service. AE, MC, V. EP, MAP, FAP.

## Negril

**$$$$** 🖫 **Grand Lido.** The dramatic entrance of marble floors and columns, filled with Jamaican artwork, sets a tone of striking elegance at this SuperClubs all-inclusive property geared to the upper-income bracket. Well-appointed oceanfront and garden rooms are split-level and are some of the most spacious and stylish accommodations of the all-inclusives. For some, the pièce de résistance is a sunset cruise on the resort's 147-ft yacht, Zien, which was a wedding gift from Aristotle Onassis to Prince Rainier and Princess Grace of Monaco. Grand Lido attracts slightly more mature and settled couples and singles than does the usual Negril resort. The gourmet restaurant, Piacere, is one of Jamaica's best. ⊠ Box 88, Negril, ☎ 809/957–4010 or 800/859–7873, FAX 809/957–4317. 182 rooms, 18 suites. 3 restaurants, 9 bars, in-room safes, room service, 2 pools, 5 outdoor hot tubs, massage, 4 tennis courts, beaches, dive shop, water sports, library, concierge, laundry service, complimentary weddings. 3-night minimum stay. AE, DC, MC, V. All-inclusive.

**$$$–$$$$** 🖫 **Swept Away.** Fitness and health-conscious couples are the target market for this all-inclusive, which emphasizes sports and healthy cuisine. Twenty-six cottages containing 134 suites are spread along half a mile of drop-dead gorgeous beach. Each cottage has a private inner-garden atrium. The 10-acre sports complex across the road outclasses the competition by a long shot. The Feathers Continental Restaurant is open to nonguests. The compound's chefs concentrate on healthful dishes with lots of fish, white meat, fresh fruits, and vegetables. ⊠ Long Bay, Negril, ☎ 809/957–4040 or 800/545–7937, FAX 809/957–4060. 134 suites. 2 restaurants, 4 bars, in-room safes, pool, 2 outdoor hot tubs, massage, spa, 2 steam rooms and saunas, 10 tennis courts, aerobics, health club, jogging, racquetball, squash, dive shop, water sports, complimentary weddings. 3-night minimum stay. AE, DC, MC, V. All-inclusive.

**$$$** 🖫 **Hedonism II.** Here is the resort that introduced the Club Med–style all-inclusive to Jamaica years ago. Still wildly successful, Hedonism appeals mostly to single (60% of guests are), uninhibited vacationers who like a robust mix of physical activities. You can try everything from scuba diving to a trampoline clinic. Wood-trimmed public areas are filled with potted plants (and scantily clad guests). Handsome guest rooms have modern blond-wood furniture and mirrored ceilings above the king-size (or twin, depending on the set up requested) bed. There's no TV, but phones were added in 1997 renovations, as was a new nude pool and hot tub. Wooden floors in the hallways tend to echo traffic as the party atmosphere continues into the wee hours. If you come alone, expect to pay a hefty single supplement or get an assigned roommate. ⊠ Box 25, Negril, ☎ 809/957–5200 or 800/859–7873, FAX 809/957–5289. 280 rooms. 2 restaurants, 6 bars, 2 grills, in-room safes, 2 pools, 2 outdoor hot tubs, 6 tennis courts, squash, beaches, dive shop, water sports. AE, DC, MC, V. All-inclusive.

**$$$** 🏨 **Sandals Negril.** One of the best and longest stretches of Negril's 7-mi beach is a tempting reason to choose this Sandals resort. Couples looking for an upscale, sportive getaway and a casual atmosphere (you can wear dressy shorts to dinner) flock here. Water sports, including scuba diving, are emphasized; and the capable staff is happy both to teach neophytes and take out guests who are already certified. One pool is designated for scuba training. There's a nearby island, a huge swim-up pool bar, and a range of spacious accommodations. Both rooms and staff are sunny and appealing. ⊠ Box 10, Negril, ☎ 809/957–4216 or 800/726–3257, FAX 809/957–4338. 215 rooms. 4 restaurants, 4 bars, in-room safes, 3 pools, 2 outdoor hot tubs, saunas, 4 tennis courts, racquetball, squash, concierge. 3-night minimum stay. AE, DC, MC, V. All-inclusive.

**$$–$$$** 🏨 **Negril Cabins Resort.** These elevated timber cottages are nestled amid lush vegetation and towering royal palms. Rooms are open and airy, with floral bedspreads, gauzy curtains, natural wood floors, and high ceilings. Only "superior" rooms have air-conditioning; other rooms are cooled by ceiling fans and the breezes that come through the slatted windows. Televisions and bathtubs are also found only in the superior rooms (the other rooms have shower stalls); because these rooms are so popular, 50 more were added in 1996–97. The gleaming beach across the road is the site of a festive party once a week; for shopping, you can take the shuttle into town. A most convivial place, this property is popular with young Europeans. Reasonably priced dive packages are available, and kids under 16 stay free in their parents' room. ⊠ Norman Manley Blvd., Box 118, Negril, ☎ 809/957–5350 or 800/382–3444, FAX 809/957–5381. 100 rooms, 10 suites. 3 restaurants, 3 bars, in-room safes, room service, pool, outdoor hot tub, sauna, tennis court, exercise room, beach, dive shop, water sports, shop, recreation room, baby-sitting, playground. 3-night minimum stay. AE, MC, V. EP, MAP.

**$$** 🏨 **Charela Inn.** Each quiet, elegantly appointed room here has a pri-
★ vate balcony or a covered patio. The owners' French-Jamaican roots find daily expression in the kitchen, and there's an excellent selection of wines. The small beach here is part of the glorious 7-mi Negril crescent. The hotel's dining room, Café au Lait, focuses on local produce and seafood prepared with French-inspired sauces. ⊠ Box 33, Negril, Westmoreland, ☎ 809/957–4277 or 800/423–4095, FAX 809/957–4414. 39 rooms. Restaurant, bar, pool, beach, windsurfing, boating, laundry service. 5-night minimum stay. MC, V. EP, MAP.

**$$** 🏨 **Coco La Palm.** Constructed in 1995 and expanded in 1997, this quiet seaside hotel features oversize rooms (junior suites average 525 ft) in octagonal buildings set in a U shape around the pool. Amenities include mini-refrigerator, coffee/tea maker, air-conditioning and ceiling fan, and private patio or terrace overlooking the gardens (only seven rooms are beachfront and offer ocean views). Centered on Negril Beach, the sandy shoreline of Coco La Palm is dotted with palm trees. The beachside restaurant is open-air and casual. ⊠ *Norman Manley Blvd.,* ☎ *809/957–4227 or 800/896–0987,* FAX *809/957–3460. 41 rooms. Restaurant, bar, grill, pool, outdoor hot tub, beach, water sports. AE, DC, MC, V. EP, MAP.*

$$ ⊞ **Negril Gardens.** Towering palms and well-tended gardens surround the pink and white buildings of this hotel. Half of the rooms are beachside, half across the street overlooking the pool; all are attractive, with tile floors and rattan furniture in light colors (no telephones or televisions). Water sports are available at the beach. An ice cream parlor and jerk center (for takeout) were added in 1996. ⊠ *Box 58, Negril,* ☎ *809/957–4408 or 800/752–6824,* FAX *809/957–4374. 66 rooms. Restaurant, 2 bars, in-room safes, pool, tennis court, exercise room, water sports, bicycles, recreation room. AE, MC, V. EP, MAP, FAP, All-inclusive.*

$$ ⊞ **Poinciana Beach Resort.** The management here has created all-inclusive packages with families in mind. Advantages include a supervised children's program, baby-sitting (at an additional charge), a location across the street from Anancy Park, and one- and two-bedroom villas with kitchens. Rooms and suites have tile floors, and Jamaican prints adorn the walls. Adults have plenty of activities among the sports, casino-like slot machines, and nightly entertainment. One of Jamaica's prettiest palm-speckled sandy beaches awaits, along with a non-motorized water-sports center (scuba diving costs extra). ⊠ *Box 44, Negril,* ☎ *809/957–5100 or 800/468–6728,* FAX *954/749– 6794. 96 rooms, 12 suites, 18 villas. 3 restaurants, 2 bars, grill, 2 pools, beauty salon, massage, outdoor hot tub, 2 tennis courts, basketball, croquet, exercise room, shuffleboard, volleyball, beach, snorkeling, windsurfing, dance club, library, children's programs, playground, coin laundry. AE, MC, V. All-inclusive.*

$$ ⊞ **Point Village.** Built in 1992 as a condo-hotel, Point Village is now managed by Friends International Resorts as a moderately priced, family-friendly resort. One- and two-bedroom housekeeping suites with kitchens are a good choice for families not on the all-inclusive plan. Rooms have tile floors, basic furnishings, and individual decor (according to the unit owner's taste). Highly popular with tour groups, this sprawling property has two small crescent beaches (one clothing optional), rocky grottos to explore, fine snorkeling just offshore, and a petting zoo. ⊠ *Box 105, Negril,* ☎ *809/957–9170 or 800/752–6824,* FAX *809/957–5351. 177 rooms, including studios and 1-, 2-, and 3-bedroom housekeeping suites. Restaurants, 3 bars, 2 grills, grocery, freshand saltwater pools, outdoor hot tub, massage, tennis court, aerobics, exercise room, water sports, recreation room, children's programs, playground. AE, MC, V. EP, MAP, FAP, All-inclusive.*

$–$$ ⊞ **Devine Destiny.** Lush tropical forest surrounds this terra-cotta tile-roofed resort set 500 yards from the West End cliffs, well removed from the bustle and traffic of town. Spacious guest rooms have no telephones, radios, or televisions. Some rooms have kitchenettes and air-conditioning; be sure to state your preferences when making reservations. Most rooms overlook what the resort claims is the largest pool in Negril. Whether or not this is true matters little, for the free-form pool with graceful arched bridges, half-moon swim-up bar, and dining terrace is lovely. The beach is 20 minutes away on foot, but a daily shuttle makes it easily accessible. ⊠ *Summerset Rd., Box 117, West End, Negril,* ☎ FAX *809/957–9184. 44 rooms. 2 restaurants, bar, air-conditioning or fans, refrigerators, room service, pool, recreation room. AE, MC, V. EP.*

$   ⊞ **Hotel Samsara.** It's hard to beat the serenity and privacy found at Samsara, a cozy, budget-class hotel on the cliffs in Negril's West End. Tidy rooms with basic furnishings and balconies or patios are in the main hotel, in octagonal cottages, and unique "tower houses" (private thatched-roof rooms on pillars). Snorkeling and diving at the reef just offshore are highlights here. A shuttle carries guests to the beach at Legends, a sister property on Negril Beach. ⊠ *Box 23, Negril,* ☎ *809/957–4395,* ⦻ *809/957–4073. 50 rooms. 2 restaurants, sports bar, pool, outdoor hot tub, tennis court, Ping-Pong, dive shop, billiards, dance club. AE, MC, V. EP.*

## Ocho Rios

$$$$   ⊞ **Sans Souci Lido.** This pastel-pink cliffside fantasyland looks and feels
★   like a dream. Romantic oceanfront suites are equipped with oversize whirlpool tubs. Soothing, light colors are the base of the decor; blond wood furniture, cool tile floors, and sheer curtains are accented by pastel watercolors and Jamaican prints on the walls. A highlight is the pampering guests receive at Charlie's Spa in the form of a complimentary massage, body scrub, reflexology session, facial, manicure, and pedicure (book treatments as soon as you arrive, if not before). A stay here is a wonderfully luxurious experience and a hands-down favorite in Jamaica. ⊠ *Box 103, Ocho Rios,* ☎ *809/974–2353 or 800/859–7873,* ⦻ *809/974–2544. 13 rooms, 98 suites. 3 restaurants, 4 bars, grill, in-room safes, minibars, freshwater and mineral pools, hot tub, spa, 4 tennis courts, beach, library, laundry service, concierge, complimentary weddings. 3-night minimum stay. AE, DC, MC, V. All-inclusive.*

$$$–$$$$   ⊞ **Boscobel Beach.** This is a parent's dream of a Jamaican vacation,
★   an all-inclusive that makes families feel welcome. Everybody is kept busy all week for a single package price, and everyone leaves happy. The cheery day-care centers group children by age and offer an extensive array of entertaining and educational activities. Thoughtfully, there is an adults-only section of the resort (for when the kids want to get away— perhaps to the petting zoo). Bedspreads in bright sea-life motifs or soothing pastel florals spice up the white tile floors and creamy walls of the rooms and suites. ⊠ *Box 63, Ocho Rios,* ☎ *809/975–7330 or 800/859–7873,* ⦻ *809/975–7370. 103 rooms, 103 junior suites. 5 restaurants, 5 bars, in-room safes, refrigerators, 2 pools, wading pool, 2 outdoor hot tubs, massage, 4 tennis courts, beach, children's programs, nursery, playground, complimentary weddings. 2-night minimum stay. AE, DC, MC, V. All-inclusive.*

$$$–$$$$   ⊞ **Ciboney, Ocho Rios.** A Radisson Resort, this stately plantation property has 38 rooms in its great house and 264 spacious one-, two-, and three-bedroom villa suites on 45 lush hillside acres. It is operated as a luxury all-inclusive geared toward affluent adults, both singles and couples. Outstanding features are the European-style spa (guests receive complimentary massage, manicure, and pedicure) and four signature restaurants, including the Orchids restaurant, whose menu was developed by the Culinary Institute of America. Every villa has an attendant and a pool, giving guests the ultimate in privacy and pampering. A casual contemporary decor is found throughout—light-colored rattan, tile floors, and pastel fabrics. If there's a drawback here, it's how busy the place is and the fact that the private beach is a shuttle ride away. ⊠ *Box 728, Main St., Ocho Rios,* ☎ *809/974–1027 or 800/333–3333,* ⦻ *809/974–5838. 264 1-, 2-, and 3-bedroom suites, 38 rooms. 4 restaurants, 6 bars, in-room safes, kitchenettes, minibars, refrigerators, in-room VCRs, 2 pools, 1 indoor and 5 outdoor hot tubs, 2 saunas, spa, 2 steam rooms, 6 tennis courts, aerobics, basketball, croquet, squash, dive shop, water sports, dance club, concierge. AE, DC, MC, V. All-inclusive.*

**$$$–$$$$** 🏨 **High Hope Estate.** If you prefer a secluded location and personal attention to the frenetic activity of large beachfront resorts, High Hope is the answer. Families and groups can book the entire villa on an all-inclusive package, but rooms are also available on a bed-and-breakfast basis at this luxurious, 15th-century-style villa, set on 40 lush acres in the trade-wind-cooled hills of St. Ann's Bay, 7 mi west of Ocho Rios. The tranquillity here is undisturbed, the vista of 20 mi of Caribbean coastline superb. The estate features Italian marble floors, graceful arches, carved mahogany doors and trim, and sweeping verandas overlooking manicured lawns. The small staff provides attentive, warm service, and owner Dennis Rapaport is a charming host full of fascinating stories. There are no planned activities, no disco, no bustling beach (it's 10 minutes away by car); come to enjoy the peace, to explore the hibiscus- and orchid-dotted lawns, to listen to the twittering of tropical birds, and to watch the fireflies and falling stars. ✉ *Box 11, St. Ann's Bay,* ☎ *809/972–2277,* ᶠᴬˣ *809/972–1607. 6 rooms. Fans, pool, tennis court, library, laundry service. MC, V. EP, All-inclusive.*

**$$$–$$$$** 🏨 **Jamaica Inn.** A combination of class and quiet attracts a discerning crowd to this vintage property. There are weeks in season when every guest is on at least his or her second visit. Each room has its own veranda (larger than most hotel rooms) on the private cove's powdery champagne-color beach. The colonial decor is on the dark side, with Jamaican antique furniture, terrazzo floors, and walls hung with oil paintings. There are no TVs or radios. Jacket and tie are de rigueur after 7 PM during high season (December–April). ✉ *Box 1, Ocho Rios,* ☎ *809/974–2514 or 800/837–4670,* ᶠᴬˣ *809/974–2449. 44 rooms, 1 suite with private pool. Restaurant, 2 bars, room service, pool, croquet, exercise room, beach, snorkeling, boating, library, shop. AE, MC, V. MAP, FAP.*

**$$$–$$$$** 🏨 **Plantation Inn.** This hotel actually looks like a plantation—the Deep South variety à la *Gone with the Wind.* The whole place conjures up an existence as soft as a southern drawl. All the big, breezy rooms have big private balconies, and each has a dramatic view down to the sea. Corner rooms with mahogany half-canopied beds are the romantic choice. There's afternoon tea, and Jamaican cuisine is served at the popular restaurant, where dining and dancing by candlelight round out the romantic experience. ✉ *Box 2, Ocho Rios,* ☎ *809/974–5601 or 800/752–6824,* ᶠᴬˣ *809/974–5912. 59 rooms, 17 suites (including 2 villas). Restaurant, 2 bars, pool, massage, sauna, 2 tennis courts, croquet, exercise room, beach, water sports, library, children's programs (ages 5–12). AE, DC, MC, V. EP, MAP, All-inclusive.*

**$$$** 🏨 **Couples.** The emphasis at Couples is on romantic adventure for just
★ the two of you, and the all-inclusive concept eliminates the decision-making that can intrude on social pleasure. One-bedroom suites are designed for romance, with two-person hot tubs in the bathroom that peek through a window at the four-poster king-size bed. A new wing, with 40 rooms furnished in hand-carved mahogany, was added in late 1996. There's a lovely white beach for relaxation or water sports, and a private island where you can sunbathe in the buff. Couples has one of the highest occupancy rates of any resort on the island—and perhaps the most suggestive logo as well. There may be a correlation. ✉ *Tower Isle, St. Mary,* ☎ *809/975–4271 or 800/268–7537,* ᶠᴬˣ *809/975–4439. 201 rooms, 11 suites. 4 restaurants, 6 bars, in-room safes, room service, pool, 5 outdoor hot tubs, massage, sauna, 5 tennis courts, horseback riding, squash, complimentary weddings. 3-night minimum stay. AE, DC, MC, V. All-inclusive.*

**$$$** 🏨 **Sandals Dunn's River.** Twenty-five acres of manicured gardens surround
★ this luxury couples-only all-inclusive. The Continental-Italian masterpiece, set on a wide sugary beach, is the finest of Sandals's Ja-

maican resorts. The rooms are larger than at most other Sandals establishments and are decorated in light pink, blue, turquoise, and cream. Most have a balcony or patio overlooking the sea or the lush grounds. Oceanfront suites have four-poster beds. The resort draws a well-heeled crowd in their thirties and forties and prides itself on catering to every guest's every whim. ⊠ *Box 51, Ocho Rios,* ☎ *809/972–1610 or 800/726–3257,* ℻ *809/972–1611. 246 rooms, 10 suites. 4 restaurants, 7 bars, in-room safes, 2 pools, 3 outdoor hot tubs, saunas, steam rooms, putting green, 2 tennis courts, racquetball, concierge. 3-night minimum stay. AE, DC, MC, V. All-inclusive.*

**$$–$$$**    🏨 **Jamaica Grande.** This Ramada property, the largest conference hotel in Jamaica, attracts families, couples, singles (there are special singles activities, and no added singles supplement), and conference attendees. Even though it's a beachfront resort, the focal point is definitely the tiered and winding pool with waterfall, swaying bridge, and swim-up bar. Accommodations in the south building are a bit roomier, whereas those in the north have slightly better views. Kids are kept busy in the daily Club Mongoose activity program (included in the rates). The hotel's disco, Jamaic'N Me Crazy (☞ *Nightlife, below*), is *very* popular. ⊠ *Box 100, Ocho Rios,* ☎ *809/974–2201 or 800/228–9898,* ℻ *809/974–5378. 706 rooms, 14 suites. 5 restaurants, 9 bars, in-room safes, 3 pools, 2 outdoor hot tubs, massage, 4 tennis courts, children's programs (ages 2–12), nursery, playground, concierge, convention center. AE, DC, MC, V. EP, MAP, All-inclusive.*

**$**    🏨 **Club Jamaica Beach Resort.** This intimate all-inclusive has only 95
★    rooms, ensuring guests plenty of personal attention from the young, cheerful staff. The rooms are refreshing, with gleaming white tile floors, comfortable modern furnishings, and gem-tone color schemes; more than half look out on the ocean. Guests, identified by their plastic, hospital-style bracelets, tend to active middle-agers and can be seen participating in the resort's daily activities (including nonmotorized water sports on the public beach) and dancing the night away to live entertainment. The Ocho Rios craft market is adjacent to the resort. ⊠ *Box 342, Turtle Beach, Ocho Rios,* ☎ *809/974–6632 or 800/818–2964,* ℻ *809/974–6644. 95 rooms. Restaurant, 3 bars, in-room safes, pool, outdoor hot tub, beach, water sports. AE, DC, MC, V. All-inclusive.*

**$**    🏨 **Comfort Suites.** Families on a budget planning an extended stay might consider booking a suite at Comfort; the fully stocked kitchens here can help keep the dining bills down. This is also one of the few places you'll find designated no-smoking rooms (but be sure to specify no-smoking when making your reservation). Each unit, with typical white tile floors, rattan furniture, and tropical floral prints, is spacious and immaculately tidy. The two-bedroom suite has an open bathroom (it's divided from the main room by only a screen) with whirlpool tub in the lofted master bedroom. It's not on the beach (though it's close enough to walk, and a shuttle is provided), but suites in "A" block do have a partial ocean view. ⊠ *17 DaCosta Dr., Ocho Rios,* ☎ *809/974–8050 or 800/221–2222,* ℻ *809/974–8070. 60 1- and 2-bedroom suites. Restaurant, 2 bars, in-room safes, kitchenettes, refrigerators, no-smoking rooms, room service, outdoor hot tub, 2 tennis courts, airport shuttle. AE, DC, MC, V. EP, MAP, FAP.*

**$**    🏨 **Enchanted Garden.** Twenty stunning acres of gardens, filled with tropical plants and flowers and punctuated with a dramatic series of streams and waterfalls, certainly are enchanting. There is an aviary and a seaquarium where you can enjoy a delicatessen lunch or tea surrounded by tanks of fish and hanging orchids. The futuristic cream-color villas (some with private plunge pools) seem somewhat incongruous amid the natural splendor, but the rooms are comfort-

# In case you want to be welcomed there.

We're here to see that you're always welcomed at establishments everywhere. That's why millions of people carry the American Express® Card – for peace of mind, confidence, and security, around the world or just around the corner.

do more

Cards

# In case you're running low.

We're here to help with more than 118,000 Express Cash locations around the world. In order to enroll, just call American Express before you start your vacation.

do more

**Express Cash**

# And just in case.

We're here with American Express® Travelers Cheques and Cheques *for Two*.® They're the safest way to carry money on your vacation and the surest way to get a refund, practically anywhere, anytime.
Another way we help you...

do more ®

Travelers
Cheques

able, if somewhat small, and you're never far from the soothing sound of rushing water. Don't miss the guided garden tour, just one of dozens of activities here. There's a free shuttle to the beach, several minutes away. ⊠ *Box 284, Ocho Rios,* ☎ *809/974–5346 or 800/323–5655,* FAX *809/974–5823. 113 villa rooms and suites (some housekeeping units). 5 restaurants, 4 bars, 2 pools, outdoor hot tub, sauna, spa, Turkish bath, 2 tennis courts, croquet, beach, dive shop, water sports, library, airport shuttle. AE, DC, MC, V. All-inclusive.*

$ ⊡ **Hibiscus Lodge.** This gleaming white building with a blue awning sits amid beautifully manicured lawns laced with trellises, not too far from its tiny private beach. The impeccably neat, cozy rooms all have at least a partial sea view, terrace, and shower-bath but no phone. Air-conditioning and televisions were added in 1995. This Swiss- and Jamaican-run property may be Ocho Rios's best bargain, attracting a lot of repeat guests. There are two reefs just off the beach, so the snorkeling is great here. Breakfast is included in the room rate. ⊠ *Box 52, Ocho Rios,* ☎ *809/974–2676 or 800/526–2422,* FAX *809/974–1874. 26 rooms. Restaurant, bar, pool, outdoor hot tub, tennis court. AE, DC, MC, V. BP.*

## Port Antonio

$$$–$$$$ ⊡ **Trident Villas and Hotel.** If a single hotel had to be voted the most
★ likely for coverage by *Lifestyles of the Rich and Famous*, this would have to be it. Peacocks strut the manicured lawns, colonnaded walkways wind through whimsically sculpted topiary dotting the 14 acres, and the pool—buried in a rocky bit of land jutting out into crashing surf—is a memory unto itself. The luxurious Laura Ashley–style rooms, many with turrets, bay windows, and balconies or verandas, are awash in mahogany and local art; they do not have TVs or clocks. The truly gracious living and white-gloved dining will transport you back to the days of Empire. ⊠ *Box 119, Port Antonio,* ☎ *809/993–2602 or 800/428–4734,* FAX *809/993–2960. 8 rooms, 4 suites, 14 villas, 8 suites in castle. Restaurant, bar, in-room safes, minibars, pool, massage, 2 tennis courts, aerobics, croquet, beach, water sports, boating, library, concierge, helipad. AE, MC, V. BP, MAP.*

$$–$$$ ⊡ **Goblin Hill.** This lush 12-acre estate is set atop a hill overlooking San San Bay. Each attractively appointed villa comes with its own dramatic view, plus a housekeeper-cook to do the grocery shopping, cleaning, and cooking for you. The villas are not equipped with phones or TVs. The beach is a 10-minute walk away. Excellent villa and car-rental packages are available. ⊠ *Box 26, Port Antonio,* ☎ *809/925–8108 or 800/472–1148,* FAX *809/925–6248. 28 housekeeping villas. Bar, kitchenettes, pool, putting green, 2 tennis courts, beach, dive shop, snorkeling, windsurfing, boating, library, recreation room, playground. AE, MC, V. EP.*

$$ ⊡ **Dragon Bay.** Set on a scenic private cove (you may remember seeing it, and the beach bar, in Tom Cruise's movie *Cocktail*), Dragon Bay is an idyllic grouping of individually decorated villas surrounded by tropical gardens. Villa 35 has a private pool, a large living room, and two bedrooms with separate sitting rooms that have sofa beds. This place is very popular with German and Italian tour groups. ⊠ *Box 176, Port Antonio,* ☎ *809/993–8514 or 809/993–8751,* FAX *809/993–3284. 30 1-, 2-, and 3-bedroom villas. 2 restaurants, 2 bars, refrigerators, room service, pool, massage, 2 tennis courts, aerobics, exercise room, volleyball, beach, dive shop, water sports. AE, MC, V. EP, MAP, FAP, All-inclusive.*

$$ ⊡ **Hotel Mocking Bird Hill.** With dogs running around the hillside property and only 10 rooms overlooking the sea and the Blue Mountains, Mocking Bird Hill feels more like a cozy bed-and-breakfast than

a hotel. Owners Barbara Walker and Shireen Aga run an extremely environmentally sensitive operation: They've used bamboo instead of hardwood for furniture, solar panels to heat water, ceiling fans instead of ozone-depleting air-conditioning systems, local produce for meals in their Mille Fleurs dining terrace (which is open to the public as well), locally produced toiletries and stationery sets, and natural landscaping on their 7 acres. They also offer an array of eco-tour options in conjunction with other like-minded community members. The tasteful blue-on-white rooms do not have phones or televisions; most are designated no-smoking. ☒ *Box 254, Port Antonio,* ☎ *809/993–3370,* FAX *809/993–7133. 10 rooms. Restaurant, bar, in-room safes, nosmoking rooms, room service, pool, massage. AE, MC, V. EP, BP, MAP.*

$$  🏨 **Jamaica Palace.** Built to resemble a 17th-century Italian colonial mansion, this imposing and somewhat impersonal property rises in an expanse of white-pillared marble, with a black-and-white theme continued on the interior, including black lacquer and gilded oversize furniture. Each room has a semicircular bed on a concrete base, and original European objets d'art and Oriental rugs; some are more lavish than others. None are equipped with televisions, but they are available for rent. Although the hotel is not on the beach, there is a 114-ft swimming pool shaped like Jamaica. ☒ *Box 227, Port Antonio,* ☎ *809/ 993–2021 or 800/423–4095,* FAX *809/993–3459. 24 rooms, 56 suites. 3 restaurants, 2 bars, in-room safes, room service, pool, massage, helipad. AE, MC, V. EP, BP, MAP.*

$  🏨 **Bonnie View Plantation Hotel.** Accommodations here are spartan, mattresses are a tad lumpy, and the furnishings a bit frayed. But the hotel certainly lives up to its name: Guests come for the sublime views and air of tranquillity. The nicest rooms (more expensive) are those with private verandas. But you can open your window for a burst of invigorating mountain air or hang out in the restaurant and savor the unparalleled water panoramas. Beachcombers are forewarned: It's a 25-minute drive to the ocean. ☒ *Box 82, Port Antonio,* ☎ *809/993– 2752 or 800/423–4095,* FAX *809/993–2862. 20 rooms. Restaurant, pool. AE, MC, V. EP.*

## Runaway Bay

$$$–$$$$  🏨 **FDR, Franklyn D. Resort.** Jamaica's first all-suite, all-inclusive resort for families, this is the answer to parents' prayers. Upscale yet unpretentious, the pink buildings house spacious and well-thought-out one, two-, and three-bedroom villas and are grouped in a horseshoe around the swimming pool. Best of all, a "girl Friday" is assigned to each suite, filling the role of nanny, housekeeper, and (when desired) cook. She'll even baby-sit at night for a small charge. Most parents are so impressed that they wish they could take their girl Friday home with them when they leave. Children and teens are kept busy with daylong supervised activities and sports, although parents are free to join in, lounge around the pool, play golf, go scuba diving, or just enjoy uninterrupted time together. ☒ *Box 201, Runaway Bay, St. Ann's Bay,* ☎ *809/973–3067 or 800/654–1337,* FAX *809/973–3071. 76 suites. 3 restaurants, 4 bars, kitchens, pool, tennis court, beaches, children's programs (no age limit). AE, MC, V. All-inclusive.*

$$$  🏨 **Braco Village Resort.** Just west of Runaway Bay (a 15-minute drive),
★    this new, all-inclusive sister resort to FDR (☞ *above*) feels like a local version of Disney's Epcot Center, focusing on the cultural heritage, crafts, music, people, and food of Jamaica in a gingerbread and Georgian-style village. Boutiques, an art shop, and several restaurants including a jerk grill, a pastry shop, and a sidewalk café fan out from the pretty central fountain in the "town square." The meandering pool next to the white-sand beach is one of the largest in the country. Rooms, done

in bright tropical colors, are generously sized, and all but a few with garden views are steps from the 2,000-ft beach or have a great view of the ocean from the patio. It's an all-adult (age 16 and over) property, but a family phase, Pebbles at Braco Village, was just about to open at press time. ⊠ *Rio Bueno, Trelawny,* ☎ *809/954–0000 or 800/654–1337,* FAX *809/954–0020. 174 rooms, 6 suites. 4 restaurants, 3 bars, café, in-room safes, pool, 2 hot tubs, 9-hole golf course, 2 tennis courts, hiking, soccer, beaches, fishing, dance club, theater. AE, DC, MC, V. EP, MAP, FAP, All-inclusive.*

**$$** ★ **Breezes Runaway Bay.** Formerly known as Jamaica, Jamaica, this moderately priced SuperClubs all-inclusive emphasizes an active, sports-oriented vacation, from golf (at the nearby 18-hole course), tennis, and horseback riding to an array of water sports, including a Mistral windsurfing school. Expert instruction and top-rate equipment are part of the package. Extensively renovated rooms now have white tile floors, cozy love seats, televisions, carved wooden headboards in the shape of palm trees, and big marble bathrooms. Guests—often Germans, Italians, and Japanese—flock here for the psychedelically colored reef just off the beach, as well as the superb golf school. ⊠ *Box 58, Runaway Bay,* ☎ *809/973–2436 or 800/859–7873,* FAX *809/973–2352. 238 rooms, 4 suites. 2 restaurants, 4 bars, grill, in-room safes, pool, 3 outdoor hot tubs, 2 tennis courts, horseback riding, beaches, nightclub. 3-night minimum stay. AE, DC, MC, V. All-inclusive.*

**$** **Club Caribbean.** This all-inclusive markets itself to families on a budget. A series of typically Caribbean cottages, many with kitchenette, lines the long but narrow beach. The rooms are simple and clean, with rattan furnishings, and floral-print fabrics, but no telephone or TV. For more space, ask for one of the garden suites (with telephone and TV) added in late 1995. The place is very popular with European families. Swings provide seating in the gazebo bar, a popular hangout around sunset. ⊠ *Box 65, Runaway Bay,* ☎ *809/973–3507 or 800/223–9815,* FAX *809/973–3509. 134 rooms, 19 suites. Restaurant, 3 bars, in-room safes, pool, massage, 2 tennis courts, beaches, children's programs (ages 4–11), playground. AE, MC, V. EP, All-inclusive.*

**$** **H.E.A.R.T. Country Club.** It's a shame more visitors don't know about this place, perched above Runaway Bay and brimming with Jamaica's true character. While training young islanders interested in the tourism industry—H.E.A.R.T. stands for Human Employment and Resource Training—it also provides a quiet and pleasant stay for guests. The employees make an effort to please. Rooms were redecorated in 1995 and have either an ocean or pretty garden view. The tranquil restaurant serves delicious local and Continental specialties. An excellent beach is a 20-minute hike (uphill coming back) or a 5- to 10-minute drive away. ⊠ *Box 98, St. Ann's Bay,* ☎ *809/973–2671,* FAX *809/973–2693. 20 rooms. Restaurant, piano bar, massage. AE, MC, V. EP, MAP.*

# Dining

Sampling the island's cuisine introduces you to virtually everything the Caribbean represents. Every ethnic group that has made significant contributions on another island has made them in Jamaica, too, adding to a Jamaican stockpot that is as rich as its melting pot. So many Americans have discovered the Caribbean through restaurants owned by Jamaicans that the very names of the island's dishes have come to represent the region as a whole. Jamaican food represents a true cuisine, organized, interesting, and ultimately rewarding. It would be a terrible shame for anyone to travel to the heart of this complex culture without tasting several typically Jamaican dishes. Here are a few:

**Ackee and Saltfish.** Salted fish was once the best islanders could do between catches, so they invented this incredibly popular dish that joins saltfish (in Portuguese, *bacalao*) with ackee, a vegetable (introduced to the island by Captain Bligh of *Bounty* fame) that reminds most people of scrambled eggs.

**Curry Goat.** Young goat is cooked with spices and is more tender and has a gentler flavor than the lamb for which it was substituted by immigrants from India.

**Jerk Pork.** Created by the Arawaks and perfected by the Maroons, jerk pork is the ultimate island barbecue. The pork (the purist cooks the whole pig) is covered with a paste of hot peppers, pimento berries (also known as allspice), and other herbs and cooked slowly over a coal fire. Many think that the "best of the best" jerk comes from Boston Beach in Port Antonio.

**Patties.** These spicy meat pies elevate street food to new heights. Although they in fact originated in Haiti, Jamaicans excel at making patties and can give lessons to anybody.

**Pepper Pot.** The island's most famous soup—a peppery combination of salt pork, salt beef, okra, and the island green known as callaloo—is green, but at its best it tastes as though it ought to be red.

**Rice and Peas.** This traditional dish is known also as Coat of Arms and is similar to the *moros y christianos* of Spanish-speaking islands: white rice cooked with red beans, coconut milk, scallions, and seasoning.

Where restaurants are concerned, Kingston has the widest selection; its ethnic restaurants offer Italian, French, Cantonese, German, Thai, Indian, Korean, and Continental fare as well as Rasta natural foods. There are fine restaurants also in all the resort areas, and the list includes many that are in large hotels. Most of the restaurants outside the hotels in MoBay and Ocho Rios will provide complimentary transportation.

## What to Wear
Dress is casual chic (just plain casual at the local hangouts), except in Kingston and at the top resorts, some of which require semiformal wear in the evening during high season. People tend to dress up a little for dinner—just because they feel like it—so you may feel more comfortable in nice slacks or a sundress. Ask about the dress code when making your reservations.

| CATEGORY | COST* |
|---|---|
| $$$$ | over $40 |
| $$$ | $30–$40 |
| $$ | $20–$30 |
| $ | Under $20 |

*per person, excluding drinks, service, and tip*

## Kingston

$$$–$$$$  ✕ **Blue Mountain Inn.** The elegant Blue Mountain Inn is a 30-minute
★        taxi ride from New Kingston and worth every penny of the fare. On a former coffee plantation, the antiques-laden inn complements its English colonial atmosphere with Continental cuisine. All the classics of the beef and seafood repertoires are here, including chateaubriand béarnaise and lobster thermidor. ✉ *Gordon Town Rd.,* ☏ *809/927–1700 or 809/927–2606. Reservations essential. Jacket required. AE, MC, V. Closed Sun. No lunch.*

$$–$$$   ✕ **Palm Court.** Nestled on the mezzanine floor of the Wyndham New Kingston, the elegant Palm Court is open for lunch and dinner (lunch

is 11:30 AM–2:30 PM; dinner 6:30–10 PM). The menu is Continental; the rack of New Zealand lamb, sautéed snapper almondine, and grilled Chilean salmon are very tasty. ⊠ *Wyndham New Kingston,* ☎ *809/926–5430. AE, DC, MC, V. No lunch weekends.*

$$ ✗ **Ivor Guest House.** This elegant yet cozy restaurant set in an 1870s home in the hills above Kingston has an incredible view from 2,000 ft above sea level. Go for dinner, when the view is dramatically caught between the stars and the glittering brooch of Kingston's lights. International cuisine with Jamaican flare is served in prix-fixe four-course dinners that average $35 per person. Owner Hellen Aitken is an animated and cordial hostess. Afternoon tea here is a treat. There are three antiques-furnished guest rooms for those who want more time in this tranquil spot. ⊠ *Jack's Hill,* ☎ *809/977–0033 or 809/927–1460. Reservations essential. AE, MC, V. Closed Sept.*

$$ ✗ **Jade Garden.** On the third floor of the Sovereign Centre, the Jade Garden, with its shiny black lacquer chairs and views of the Blue Mountains, garners rave reviews for its Cantonese and Thai menu. Favorites include steamed fish in black-bean sauce, black mushrooms stuffed with shrimp, and shrimp with lychee. There is an inexpensive lunch buffet every Friday afternoon and dim sum on the last Sunday of each month. ⊠ *106 Hope Rd.,* ☎ *809/978–3476 or 809/978–3479. AE, MC, V.*

$$ ✗ **La Trattoria.** The old-world setting is as suitable for a business luncheon as for a romantic dinner for two. The northern Italian fare is classic—lasagna, manicotti, and spaghetti bolognaise are all on the menu—but a few interesting twists include linguine with jerk chicken in a cream sauce and the restaurant's signature dish, Pasta Carnival (pasta of the day tossed with cheese, local vegetables, olive oil, garlic, shrimp, and chicken). This Swiss-run restaurant is a delightful addition to Kingston's bountiful dining scene. ⊠ *29½ Munroe Rd.,* ☎ *809/977–1379. AE, MC, V. Closed Sun.*

$ ✗ **Hot Pot.** Jamaicans love the Hot Pot for breakfast, lunch, and dinner. Fricassee chicken is the specialty, along with other local dishes, such as mackerel run-down (salted mackerel cooked down with coconut milk and spices) and ackee and salted cod. The restaurant's fresh juices "in season" are the best—tamarind, sorrel, coconut water, soursop, and cucumber. ⊠ *2 Altamont Terr.,* ☎ *809/929–3906. Reservations not accepted. MC, V.*

$ ✗ **Peppers.** This casual outdoor bar with picnic tables is the in spot in Kingston. It's slow during weekday afternoons but frenetic all weekend—especially Friday nights. Sample the grilled lobster or jerk pork and chicken with the local Red Stripe beer, sit back and enjoy the local reggae band that plays. ⊠ *31 Upper Waterloo Rd.,* ☎ *809/925–2219. MC, V. Closed Sun.*

## Montego Bay

$$$–$$$$ ✗ **Georgian House.** A landmark restaurant in the heart of town, the Georgian House occupies a restored 18th-century building set in a shady garden courtyard. An extensive wine cellar complements the Continental and Jamaican cuisines, the best of which are the steaks and the dishes made with the local spiny lobster. Don't miss the gallery of Jamaican art. ⊠ *2 Orange St.,* ☎ *809/952–0632. Reservations essential. AE, DC, MC, V.*

$$$ ✗ **Julia's Italian Restaurant.** Couples flock to this romantic Italian restaurant set up in the hills overlooking the twinkling lights of MoBay. Diners choose from an à la carte or five-course fixed-price menu ($33–$45 per person, depending on the entrée) that includes homemade soups and pastas; entrées of fish, chicken, and veal; and scrumptious desserts. Don't expect the meal to equal the stupendous view, and you won't

be disappointed. ⊠ *Bogue Hill,* ☎ *809/952–1772 or 809/979–0744. Reservations essential. AE, MC, V.*

**$$$**  ✕ **Sugar Mill.** Seafood is served with flair at this terrace restaurant set
★  on the manicured grounds of the Half Moon Golf Course. Caribbean
specialties, steak, and lobster are usually offered in a pungent sauce
that blends Dijon mustard with Jamaica's own Pickapeppa sauce.
Otherwise, choices are the daily à la carte specials and anything flamed.
Live music and a well-stocked wine cellar round out the experience.
⊠ *Half Moon Golf Course,* ☎ *809/953–2228. Reservations essential
for dinner. AE, DC, MC, V.*

**$$–$$$**  ✕ **Day-O Plantation Restaurant.** Transport yourself back in time with
a fine meal served on the garden terrace of this Georgian-style plan-
tation house. Start with smoked marlin, then segue into seafood ragout,
broiled rock lobster with lemon butter, or beef fillet with béarnaise sauce,
and sweeten things up with one of the traditional Jamaican desserts
(rum pudding, sweet cakes, or fruit salad). ⊠ *Barnett Estate Planta-
tion, Fairfield,* ☎ *809/952–1825. AE, MC, V. Closed Mon.*

**$$–$$$**  ✕ **Norma at the Wharf House.** This sister property to creative chef and
entrepreneur Norma's successful Kingston restaurant has gathered
rave reviews as a supper club. The setting is a converted 300-year-old
stone sugar warehouse on the water, decorated in blue and white. In-
novative Jamaican cuisine ranges from Caribbean lobster steamed in
Red Stripe beer to jerk chicken with mangoes flambé. ⊠ *10 mins west
of MoBay in Reading,* ☎ *809/979–2745. Reservations essential for
dinner. MC, V. Closed May–Aug. No lunch Mon.–Wed.*

**$$**  ✕ **Pier 1.** Pier 1 writes the book daily on waterfront dining. After tropical drinks at the deck bar, you'll be ready to dig into the international
variations on fresh seafood, the best of which are the grilled lobster
and any preparation of island snapper. Several party cruises leave from
the marina here, and the restaurant is mobbed by locals who come to
dance on Friday night. ⊠ *Just off Howard Cooke Blvd.,* ☎ *809/952–
2452. AE, MC, V.*

**$$**  ✕ **Marguerites.** Another romantic choice in MoBay is Marguerites, a
pierside dining room specializing in seafood. Flambé is the operative
word here: Lobster, shrimp, fish, steak, and several desserts are pre-
pared in dancing flames as diners sip exotic cocktails. The Caesar
salad, prepared tableside, is a treat. ⊠ *Gloucester Ave.,* ☎ *809/952–
4777. Reservations essential. AE, DC, MC, V. No lunch.*

**$$**  ✕ **The Native.** This open-air stone terrace, shaded by a large poinciana
tree and overlooking Gloucester Avenue, specializes in Jamaican and
international dishes. To go native, start with smoked marlin, move on
to the Boonoonoonoos platter (a sampler of local dishes), and round
out with coconut pie or duckanoo (a sweet dumpling of cornmeal, coconut, and banana wrapped in a banana leaf and steamed). Caesar salad,
seafood linguine, and shrimp kabobs are fine alternatives. Live entertainment and candlelit tables make this a romantic choice for dinner
on weekends. A popular afternoon buffet on Sundays is more of a family affair. ⊠ *29 Gloucester Ave.,* ☎ *809/979–2769. Reservations essential for dinner. AE, MC, V.*

**$$**  ✕ **Town House.** Most of the rich and famous who have visited Jamaica
over the decades have eaten at the Town House. You will find specials
of the day and good versions of standard ideas (red snapper papillote
is the specialty, with lobster, cheese, and wine sauce), along with many
Jamaican favorites (curried chicken with breadfruit and ackee). The
18th-century Georgian house is adorned with original Jamaican and
Haitian art. There's alfresco dining on the stone patio. ⊠ *16 Church
St.,* ☎ *809/952–2660. Reservations essential for dinner. AE, DC,
MC, V. No lunch Sun.*

**$** ✕ **Le Chalet.** Don't let the French name fool you. This Denny's look-
★ alike, set in a nondescript shopping mall, serves heaping helpings of
some of the best Chinese and Jamaican food in MoBay. Tasty lobster
Cantonese costs only $15. ⊠ *32 Gloucester Ave.,* ☎ *809/952–5240.
AE, MC, V. No lunch Sun.*

## Negril

**$$** ✕ **Rick's Cafe.** Here it is, the local landmark complete with cliffs, cliff
divers, and powerful sunsets, all perfectly choreographed. Most folks
come for the drinks and the renowned sunset party, since the standard
pub menu is overpriced at this must-see tourist attraction. In the sun-
set ritual, the crowd toasts Mother Nature with rum drinks, shouts and
laughter, and ever-shifting meeting and greeting. When the sun slips
below the horizon, there are more shouts, more cheers, and more
rounds of rum. ⊠ *Lighthouse Rd.,* ☎ *809/957–0380. No credit cards.*

**$$** ✕ **Tan-ya's.** This alfresco restaurant overlooks the pool and hot tub
at Sea Splash Resort, an intimate, 15-suite property nestled amid palm
trees on lovely Negril Beach. Jamaican delicacies with an international
flavor are served for breakfast, lunch, and dinner. Try the excellent dev-
iled crab backs or the smoked marlin. ⊠ *Sea Splash Resort, Norman
Manley Blvd.,* ☎ *809/957–4041 or 800/245–2786. AE, DC, MC, V.*

**$–$$** ✕ **Margueritaville.** Here's another all-in-one entertainment option
★ where you can make a day of it in Negril. Set on a beautiful stretch of
Negril Beach, this new (1997) operation, sibling to the wildly popular Margueritaville in MoBay, is a sports bar, a disco, a beach club,
and a restaurant. There's an art gallery, a gift shop, a five-star PADI
dive shop, a Frisbee golf course, volleyball and basketball courts on
premises, and changing rooms for slipping out of your wet suit. Lobster is a house specialty; the all-you-can-eat lobster feast ($34.95 per
person) includes seafood chowder, garden salad, baked potato, vegetables, home-made bread, and all the rock lobster you can handle. Far
less expensive are the fish, chicken, and sandwich platters. There are
also more than 50 margaritas from which to choose. ⊠ *Norman Manley Blvd.,* ☎ *809/957–4467. AE, DC, MC, V.*

**$** ✕ **Cosmo's Seafood Restaurant and Bar.** Owner Cosmo Brown has made
★ this seaside open-air bistro a pleasant place to spend the afternoon—
and maybe stay on for dinner. The fresh fish is the main attraction,
and the conch soup, which is the house specialty, is a meal in itself.
There's also lobster (grilled or curried), fish-and-chips, and a catch-
of-the-morning. Customers often drop cover-ups to take a dip before
coffee and dessert and return later to lounge in chairs scattered under
almond and sea-grape trees. (There's an entrance fee for the beach alone,
but it's less than $1.) ⊠ *Norman Manley Blvd.,* ☎ *809/957–4330.
Reservations not accepted. AE, MC, V.*

**$** ✕ **Kuyaba on the Beach.** This charming thatched-roof eatery features
an international menu—including curried conch, kingfish steak, grilled
lamb with sautéed mushrooms, and an array of pasta dishes—and a
lively ambience, especially around the round bar. There's a crafts shop
on the premises, and chaise longues lining the beach, so come prepared
to spend some time, and don't forget a towel and bathing suit. ⊠ *Norman Manley Blvd.,* ☎ *809/957–4318. AE, MC, V.*

**$** ✕ **Sweet Spice.** This open-air mom-and-pop diner run by the Whytes
serves inexpensive, generous plates of conch steak, fried or curried
chicken, fresh-catch fish, oxtail in brown stew sauce, and other down-
home specialties. The fresh juices are quite satisfying. Drop by for breakfast, lunch, or dinner. ⊠ *1 White Hall Rd.,* ☎ *809/957–4621.
Reservations not accepted. MC, V.*

## Ocho Rios

**$$–$$$**  ✕ **Almond Tree.** One of the most popular restaurants in Ocho Rios,
★  the Almond Tree has a menu of Jamaican and Continental favorites:
pumpkin and pepper-pot soups, and many wonderful preparations of
fresh fish, veal piccata, and fondue. The swinging rope chairs of the
terrace bar and the tables perched above a lovely Caribbean cove are
great fun. ⊠ *83 Main St., Ocho Rios,* ☎ *809/974–2813. Reservations
essential for dinner. AE, DC, MC, V.*

**$$**  ✕ **The Ruins.** A 40-ft waterfall dominates the open-air Ruins restau-
rant, and in a sense it dominates the food as well. Surrender to local
preference and order the Lotus Lily Lobster, a stir-fry of the freshest
local shellfish, and then settle back and enjoy the tree-shaded deck and
the graceful footbridges that connect the dining patios. There's live en-
tertainment on weekends. ⊠ *DaCosta Dr., Ocho Rios,* ☎ *809/974–
2442. AE, MC, V.*

**$–$$**  ✕ **Evita's.** The setting here is a sensational 1860s gingerbread house
★  high on a hill overlooking Ocho Rios Bay. Large, open windows pro-
vide cooling mountain breezes and stunning views of city and sea. More
than 30 kinds of pasta are served here, ranging from lasagna Rasta-
fari (vegetarian) and fiery "jerk" spaghetti to rotelle *Colombo* (crabmeat with white sauce and noodles). There are also excellent fish
dishes—sautéed fillet of red snapper with orange sauce, scampi and
lobster in basil cream sauce, red snapper stuffed with crabmeat—and
several meat dishes, among them a tasty grilled sirloin with mushroom
sauce. Kids under 12 eat for half price, and light eaters will appreciate half-portion orders. ⊠ *Mantalent Inn, Eden Bower Rd.,* ☎ *809/974–
2333. AE, MC, V.*

**$–$$**  ✕ **Little Pub.** Alfresco dining in a village-square setting awaits at the
Little Pub on Main Street. It's a charming spot, but a bit too lively for
a romantic getaway; it has a bustling sports bar and energetic Caribbean
review featured several nights each week. Jamaican standards (jerk or
curried chicken, baked crab, sautéed snapper) accompany surf and turf,
lobster thermidor, pasta primavera, seafood stir-fry, crêpes Suzette, banana flambé, and other international dishes. Burgers and other standard pub fare are also available. ⊠ *59 Main St.,* ☎ *809/974–2324.
AE, MC, V.*

**$**  ✕ **The Healthy Way.** Set in the shopping center adjacent to the crafts
market, this health food store has a deli counter offering salads, soups,
steamed vegetable dishes, fresh fruit drinks, even tofu and veggie burgers. There are a few small tables to dine in-shop, but most patrons just
grab something to go. ⊠ *Ocean Village Shopping Center, Shop 54,*
☎ *809/974–9229. No credit cards. No dinner.*

**$**  ✕ **Ocho Rios Village Jerk Centre.** This blue-canopied, open-air eatery
★  is a good place to park yourself for frosty Red Stripe beer and fiery jerk
pork, chicken, or seafood. Milder barbecued meats, also sold by weight
(typically a quarter or half pound makes a good serving), also turn up
on the fresh daily chalkboard menu posted on the wall. It's lively at lunch,
especially when passengers from the nearby cruise ships swamp the place.
⊠ *DaCosta Dr.,* ☎ *809/974–2549. AE, MC, V.*

# Beaches

Jamaica has 200 mi of beaches, some of them still uncrowded. The
beaches listed below are public places (there is usually a small admission charge), and they are among the best Jamaica has to offer. In addition, nearly every resort has its own private beach, complete with
towels and water sports. Some of the larger resorts sell day passes to
nonguests. Generally, the farther west you travel, the lighter and finer
the sand.

## Discovery Bay

**Puerto Seco Beach** is frequented primarily by locals.

## Kingston Area

There are no good beaches in Kingston. Beachgoers can travel outside of the city, but the beaches there, as a rule, are not as beautiful as those in the resort areas.

**Fort Clarence,** a beach in the Hellshire Hills area southwest of the city, has changing facilities and entertainment. **Hellshire Beach,** in Bridgeport, about a 20- to 30-minute drive from Kingston, is the most popular stretch of sand. Here you'll find food and drink vendors, changing rooms, and plenty of (recorded) music. **Lime Cay** can be reached by boat (they can be hired from Morgan's Harbor Marina at Port Royal for a small fee). This island, just beyond Kingston Harbor, is perfect for picnicking, sunning, and swimming. **Lyssons Beach,** in Morant Bay, sometimes lures Kingstonians 32 mi east of the city to its lovely golden sand.

## Montego Bay

**Cornwall Beach** is lively, with lots of food and drink available, as well as a water-sports concession. **Doctor's Cave Beach** shows a tendency toward population explosion, attracting Jamaicans and tourists alike; at times it may resemble Fort Lauderdale at spring break. The 5-mi stretch of sugary sand has been spotlighted in so many travel articles and brochures over the years that it's no secret to anyone. On the bright side, Doctor's Cave is well fitted for all its admirers with changing rooms, colorful if overly insistent vendors, and a large selection of snacks. **Rose Hall Beach Club,** east of central MoBay near Rose Hall Great House, recently opened and is a secluded area (far less crowded than beaches in town) with changing rooms and showers, a water-sports center, volleyball and other beach games, and a beach bar and grill. **Walter Fletcher Beach,** near the center of town, offers protection from the surf on a windy day and therefore unusually fine swimming; the calm waters make it a good bet for children, too.

## Negril

**Negril Beach** was, not too long ago, a beachcomber's vision of Eden. Today much of the 7 mi of white sand is fronted by modern resorts, although the 2 mi of beach fronting Bloody Bay remain relatively untouched (however, the area was being developed at press time). The nude beach areas are found mostly along sections of the beach where no hotel or resort has been built, such as the area adjacent to Cosmo's (☞ Dining, *above*). A few resorts have built accommodations overlooking their nude beaches, thereby adding a new dimension to the traditional notion of "ocean view."

## Ocho Rios

**Turtle Beach,** stretching behind Jamaica Grande and Club Jamaica, is the busiest beach in Ocho Rios. This is where the islanders go to swim in Ocho Rios. **James Bond Beach,** east of Ocho Rios in the quaint village of Oracabessa, was opened in 1997 and is quickly becoming a favorite because of the live reggae performances often featured on the bandstand there.

## Port Antonio

**Boston Bay,** approximately 11 mi east of Port Antonio, beyond the Blue Lagoon, is a small, intimate beach. It's a good place to buy the famous peppery delicacy, jerk pork, available at any of the shacks spewing scented smoke along the beach. **San San Beach,** about 5 mi east of Port Antonio, has beautiful blue waters and is used mainly by area villa or hotel owners and their guests.

## South Coast

Those who seek beaches off the main tourist routes will want to explore Jamaica's unexploited south coast.

**Bluefields Beach,** near Savanna-La-Mar, south of Negril, is nearest to "civilization." **Crane Beach,** at Black River, has retained its natural beauty and has—so far—remained undiscovered by most tourists. **Treasure Beach** has to be the best that the south shore has to offer. Set by a quaint, quiet fishing village, the beach is undeveloped and is dotted with coves that are ideal for snorkeling.

# Outdoor Activities and Sports

The tourist board licenses all operators of recreational activities, which should ensure you of fair business practices as long as you deal with companies that display the decals.

## Fishing

Deep-sea fishing can be great around the island. Port Antonio gets the headlines with its annual Blue Marlin Tournament, and Montego Bay and Ocho Rios have devotees who talk of the sailfish, yellowfin tuna, wahoo, dolphinfish, and bonito. Licenses are not required. Boat charters can be arranged at your hotel.

## Golf

The best courses are found around Montego Bay at **Tryall** (☎ 809/956–5660), **Half Moon** (☎ 809/953–2731), **Rose Hall** (☎ 809/953–2650), and **Ironshore** (☎ 809/953–2800). Good courses are also found at **Caymanas** (☎ 809/997–8026) and **Constant Spring** (☎ 809/924–1610) in Kingston, at **SuperClubs Golf Club** (☎ 809/973–2561) and **Braco Village Resort** (☎ 809/954–0000) in Runaway Bay, and **Sandals Golf and Country Club** (☎ 809/975–0119) in Ocho Rios. A nine-hole course in the hills of Mandeville is called **Manchester Club** (☎ 809/962–2403). Great golf, rolling hills, and a "liquor mobile" go hand in hand at the **Negril Hills Golf Club** (☎ 809/957–4638) in Negril, which opened all 18 holes in 1995. **Prospect Plantation** (☎ 809/994–1058) in Ocho Rios and the **Anancy Family Fun and Nature Park** (☎ 809/957–4100) in Negril have 18-hole minigolf courses.

## Horseback Riding

Jamaica is fortunate to have the best equestrian facility in the Caribbean, **Chukka Cove** (☎ 809/972–2506 or 809/974–2239), near Ocho Rios. The resort, complete with stylishly outfitted villas, offers instruction in riding, polo, and jumping, as well as hour-long trail rides, three-hour beach rides, and six-hour rides to a recently restored great house. Weekends, in season, this is the place for hot polo action and equally hot social action. **Rocky Point Stables** (☎ 809/953–2286), just east of the Half Moon Club in Montego Bay; **Rhodes Hall Plantation Ltd.** (☎ 809/957–4258), between Green Island and Negril; and **Prospect Plantation** (☎ 809/994–1058), in Ocho Rios, also offer rides.

## Tennis

Many hotels have tennis facilities that are free to their guests, but some will allow nonguests to play for a fee. The sport is a highlight at **Coyaba Beach Resort** (☎ 809/953–9150), **Tryall** (☎ 809/956–5660), **Round Hill Hotel and Villas** (☎ 809/952–5150), **Sandals Montego Bay** (☎ 809/952–5510), and **Half Moon Golf Club** (☎ 809/953–2211) in Montego Bay; **Swept Away** (☎ 809/957–4040) in Negril; **Sandals Dunn's River** (☎ 809/972–1610), **Sans Souci Lido** (☎ 809/974–2353), and **Ciboney, Ocho Rios** (☎ 809/974–1027) in Ocho Rios; and **Breezes Runaway Bay** (☎ 809/973–2436) in Runaway Bay. In Kingston, the **Crowne Plaza** (☎ 809/925–7676), the **Jamaica Pegasus** (☎ 809/926–

3690), and the **Wyndham New Kingston** (☎ 809/926–5430) all have courts for guest use.

## Water Sports

The major areas for swimming, windsurfing, snorkeling, and scuba diving are Negril in the west and Port Antonio in the east. All the large resorts rent equipment for a deposit and/or a fee. Diving is perhaps the only option that requires training, because you need to show a C-card in order to participate. However, some dive operators on the island are qualified to certify you. Jamaica Tourist Board–licensed dive operators include **Resort Divers** (⊠ Montego Bay, ☎ 809/952–4285; ⊠ Ocho Rios, ☎ 809/974–5338; ⊠ Runaway Bay, ☎ 809/973–5750), **Reef Keeper Divers** (⊠ Negril, ☎ 809/957–4467), **Sundivers** (⊠ Negril, ☎ 809/957–4069), **Garfield Diving Station** (⊠ Ocho Rios, ☎ 809/974–5749), **Dolphin Divers** (⊠ Negril, ☎ 809/957–4944), **North Coast Marine** (⊠ Montego Bay, ☎ 809/953–2211), and **Sandals Beach Resort Watersports** (⊠ Montego Bay, ☎ 809/979–0104). All of these operators offer certification courses and dive trips. Most all-inclusive resorts offer free scuba diving to their guests. **Lady G'Diver** (⊠ San San Beach, Port Antonio, ☎ 809/993–9624) offers scuba diving, snorkeling, windsurfing, glass-bottom boating, and sailing; excursions start at $25 per person.

# Shopping

Shopping in Jamaica goes two ways: things Jamaican and things imported. The former are made with style and skill; the latter are duty-free luxury finds. Jamaican crafts take the form of resort wear, hand-loomed fabrics, silk screens, wood carvings, paintings, and other fine arts. Jamaican rum is a great take-home gift. So is Tia Maria, Jamaica's world-famous coffee liqueur. The same goes for the island's prized Blue Mountain and High Mountain coffees and its jams, jellies, and marmalades. Some bargains, if you shop around, include Swiss watches, Irish crystal, jewelry, cameras, and china. The top-selling French perfumes are also available alongside Jamaica's own fragrances.

## Shopping Areas

### KINGSTON

A shopping tour of the Kingston area should begin at Constant Spring Road or King Street. No matter where you begin, keep in mind that the trend these days is shopping malls, and in Jamaica they have caught on with a fever. The ever-growing roster includes Twin Gates Plaza, New Lane Plaza, the New Kingston Shopping Centre, Tropical Plaza, Manor Park Plaza, the Village, the Springs, and the newest (and some say nicest), Sovereign Shopping Centre.

A day at **Devon House** (⊠ 26 Hope Rd., Kingston, ☎ 809/929–6602) should be high on your shopping list. This is the place to find old and new Jamaica. The great house is now a museum with antiques and furniture reproductions and the Lady Nugent's Coffee Terrace outside. There are boutiques in what were once the house's stables: a branch of Things Jamaican, Jacaranda for leather finds, fine Battenburg lace at the Elaine Elegance, and some of the best tropical-fruit ice cream (mango, guava, pineapple, and passion fruit) at I-Scream.

### MONTEGO BAY AND OCHO RIOS

Although you should not rule out a visit to the "crafts market" on Market Street in MoBay, you should consider first how much you like being in the midst of pandemonium and haggling over prices and quality. The crafts markets in Ocho Rios are less hectic unless a cruise ship is in port, and the crafts markets in Port Antonio and Negril are good fun.

You'll find a plethora of T-shirts; straw hats, baskets, and place mats; carved wood statues; colorful Rasta berets; and cheap jewelry.

If you're looking to spend money, head for City Centre Plaza, Half Moon Village, Miranda Ridge Plaza, Montego Bay Shopping Center, St. James's Place, and Westgate Plaza in Montego Bay; in Ocho Rios, the shopping plazas are Pineapple Place, Ocean Village, the Taj Mahal, Coconut Grove, and Island Plaza. It's also a good idea to chat with salespeople, who can enlighten you about the newer boutiques and their whereabouts.

## Specialty Shops

ARTS AND CRAFTS

**Caribatik** (⊠ A–1, 2 mi east of Falmouth, ☎ 809/954–3314), the studio of the late Muriel Chandler, stocks silk batiks, by the yard or made into chic designs. Drawing on patterns in nature, Chandler translated the birds, seascapes, flora, and fauna into works of art. **Gallery of West Indian Art** (⊠ 1 Orange La., MoBay, ☎ 809/952–4547; ⊠ Round Hill, ☎ 809/952–5150) is the place to find Jamaican and Haitian paintings. A corner of the gallery is devoted to hand-turned pottery (some painted) and beautifully carved and painted birds and jungle animals. **Harmony Hall** (⊠ 8-min drive east on A–1 from Ocho Rios, ☎ 809/975–4222), a restored great house, is where Annabella Proudlock sells her unique wood Annabella Boxes. The covers feature reproductions of Jamaican paintings. Larger reproductions of paintings, lithographs, and signed prints of Jamaican scenes are also for sale, along with hand-carved wood combs—all magnificently displayed. Harmony Hall is also well known for its art shows by local artists. **Images Art Gallery** (⊠ Half Moon Club, ☎ 809/953–9043) showcases a fine collection of Jamaican art, from colorful works on canvas and paper to carefully hewn wooden sculptures. **Ital-Craft** (⊠ Shop 8, Upper Manor Park Shopping Plaza, 184C Spring Rd., Kingston, ☎ 809/931–0477) sells belts, bangles, and beads from its factory location. Although Ital-Craft's handmade treasures are sold in boutiques throughout Jamaica, we recommend a visit to the factory for the largest selection of the belts, made of spectacular shells, combined with leather, feathers, or fur. (The most ornate belts sell for about $75.) You'll also find some intriguing jewelry and purses here (many made from reptile skins). **Things Jamaican** (⊠ Devon House, 26 Hope Rd., Kingston, ☎ 809/929–6602; ⊠ 44 Fort St., MoBay, ☎ 809/952–5605) has two outlets and two airport stalls that display and sell some of the best native crafts made in Jamaica, with items that range from carved wood bowls and trays to reproductions of silver and brass period pieces.

BIKINIS

**Vaz Enterprises, LTD.** (⊠ 77 East St., Kingston, ☎ 809/922–9200), the manufacturing outlet of designer Sonia Vaz, sells teeny-weeny bikinis. They're also for sale at Sandals and other resorts.

JEWELRY

**L. A. Henriques** (⊠ Shop 12, Upper Manor Park Plaza, Kingston, ☎ 809/931–0613) sells high-quality jewelry made to order.

RECORDS

Reggae tapes by world-famous Jamaican artists, such as Bob Marley, Ziggy Marley, Peter Tosh, and Third World, can be found easily in U.S. or European record stores, but a pilgrimage to **Randy's Record Mart** (⊠ 17 N. Parade, Kingston, ☎ 809/922–4859) should be high on the reggae lover's list. Also worth checking are the **Record Plaza** (⊠ Tropical Plaza, Kingston, ☎ 809/926–7645), **Record City** (⊠ 14 King St., Port Antonio, ☎ 809/993–2836), **De Muzic Shop** (⊠ Island Plaza, Ocho

Rios, ☎ 809/974–9500), and **Top Ranking Records** (✉ Westgate Plaza, MoBay, ☎ 809/952–1216).

SANDALS
Cheap sandals are good buys in shopping centers throughout Jamaica. Although workmanship and leathers don't rival the craftsmanship of those found in Italy or Spain, neither do the prices (about $20 a pair). In Kingston, **Lee's Fifth Avenue Shoes** (✉ Tropical Plaza, ☎ 809/926–7486) is a good place to sandal-shop, as is **Jacaranda** (✉ Devon House, ☎ 809/929–6602), a leather store at Devon House. In Ocho Rios, the **Pretty Feet Shoe Shop** (✉ Ocean Village Shopping Centre, ☎ 809/974–5040) is a good bet. In Montego Bay, try **Westgate Plaza.**

## Gift Ideas

CIGARS
Fine Macanudo handmade cigars make great gifts and are easily carried. They can be bought on departure at Montego Bay airport (☎ 809/925–1082 for outlet information).

COFFEE
Blue Mountain coffee can be found at **John R. Wong's Supermarket** (✉ 1–5 Tobago Ave., Kingston, ☎ 809/926–4811). The **Sovereign Supermarket** (✉ Sovereign Center, 106 Hope Rd., ☎ 809/978–1254) has a wide selection of coffee and other goods. **Magic Kitchen Ltd.** (✉ Village Plaza, Shop 12, Kingston, ☎ 809/926–8894) sells the magic beans. If the stores are out of Blue Mountain, you may have to settle for High Mountain coffee, the natives' second-preferred brand.

## Rum

Jamaican-brewed rums and Tia Maria can be bought at either the Kingston or MoBay airports before your departure. As a general rule, only rum factories, such as Sangster's, are less expensive than the airport stores, and if you buy at the airport there's no toting of heavy, breakable bottles from your hotel.

# Nightlife

Jamaica—especially Kingston—supports a lively community of musicians. For starters there is reggae, popularized by the late Bob Marley and the Wailers and performed today by son Ziggy Marley, Jimmy Tosh (the late Peter Tosh's son), Gregory Isaacs, Third World, Jimmy Cliff, and many others. If your experience of Caribbean music has been limited to steel drums and Harry Belafonte, then the political, racial, and religious messages of reggae may set you on your ear; listen closely and you just might hear the heartbeat of the people. Those who already love reggae may want to plan a visit in mid-July to August for the Reggae Sunsplash. The four-night concert at the Bob Marley Performing Center (a field set up with a temporary stage), in the Freeport area of Montego Bay, showcases local talent and attracts such performers as Rick James, Gladys Knight and the Pips, Steel Pulse, Third World, and Ziggy Marley and the Melody Makers.

## Discos and Clubs

For the most part, the liveliest late-night happenings throughout Jamaica are in the major resort hotels. Some of the all-inclusives offer a dinner and disco pass from about $50.

KINGSTON
The most popular spots in Kingston are **Godfather's** (✉ 69 Knutsford Blvd., ☎ 809/929–5459), **Illusions** (✉ New Lane Plaza, ☎ 809/929–2125), **Jonkanoo** (✉ Wyndham New Kingston, ☎ 809/929–3390), and the trendy disco **Mirage** (✉ Sovereign Centre, ☎ 809/978–8557).

MONTEGO BAY

The hottest places in Montego Bay are **Sir Winston's Reggae Club** (✉ Kent Ave., ☎ 809/952–2084), **Walter's** (✉ 39 Gloucester Ave., ☎ 809/952–9391), **Hurricanes Disco** (✉ Breezes Montego Bay Resort, Gloucester Ave., ☎ 809/940–1150), and the **Rhythm Nightclub** (✉ Holiday Inn Sunspree Resort, ☎ 809/953–2485). After 10 PM on Friday nights, the crowd gathers at **Pier 1** (✉ Howard Cooke Blvd., ☎ 809/952–2452) opposite the straw market. Two very popular new sports bars, both on Gloucester Avenue, are the **Brewery** (☎ 809/940–2433) and **Margueritaville** (☎ 809/952–4777).

NEGRIL

Some of the best music will be found in Negril at **Alfred's** (☎ 809/957–4735), **De Buss** (☎ 809/957–4405), and at the hot, hot spot **Kaiser's Cafe** (☎ 809/957–4070), as well as the disco at **Hedonism II** (☎ 809/957–4200).

OCHO RIOS

The principal clubs in Ocho Rios are **Jamaic'N Me Crazy** (✉ Jamaica Grande, ☎ 809/974–2201), **Acropolis** (✉ 70 Main St., ☎ 809/974–2633), **Silks** (✉ Shaw Park Beach Hotel, ☎ 809/974–2552), and the **Little Pub** (✉ Main St., ☎ 809/974–2324), which produces Caribbean revues several nights each week.

PORT ANTONIO

In Port Antonio, if you have but one night to disco, do it at the **Roof Club** (✉ 11 West St., ☎ 809/993–3817). On weekends, from elevenish on, this is where it's all happening. An alternative for Port Antonio nightlife is the dance scene at **Shadows** (✉ 40 West St., ☎ 809/993–3823) or the live jazz performances on Saturday evenings at the **Blue Lagoon Restaurant** (✉ San San Beach, ☎ 809/993–8491).

# Exploring Jamaica

Jamaica can be both thrilling and extremely frustrating to tour, primarily due to the infrastructure of the country. Roads are, for the most part, full of potholes and, during the rainy season, can be entirely washed out (*always* check road conditions prior to heading out on your own to do any sightseeing). Primary roads that loop around and across the island are two lanes, signs are not prevalent, numbered addresses are seldom used outside of major townships, locals drive aggressively, and people and animals seem to have a particular talent for appearing out of nowhere before your vehicle. That said, Jamaica's natural scenery should not be missed. The solution? Stick to guided tours wherever possible—both to be safe and to avoid the virtually guaranteed frustration of navigating the island on your own.

*Numbers in the margin correspond to points of interest on the Jamaica map.*

SIGHTS TO SEE

⑩ **Blue Mountains.** Lush, with deep valleys and soaring peaks that climb into the clouds, the Blue Mountains rise to the north of Kingston. Admirers of Jamaica's wonderful coffee may wish to visit **Pine Grove**, a working coffee farm that doubles as an inn. It also has a restaurant that serves owner Marcia Thwaites's Jamaican cuisine. Another spot worth a visit is **Mavis Bank** and its Jablum coffee plant. Mavis Bank is delightfully primitive—especially considering the retail price of the beans it processes. A half-hour guided tour is available for $5; inquire when you arrive at the main office. Stop in World's End for a free tour of **Dr. Sangster's Rum Factory** (☎ 809/926–8888; call ahead), open weekdays 9–5. The small factory produces wonderful liqueurs flavored with local coffee beans, oranges, coconuts, and other Jamaican produce; samples are part of the tour.

On your way up (or back) from World's End, stop by Gloria Palomino's café-restaurant, the **Gap** (☎ 809/997–3032), open Tuesday–Sunday for breakfast and lunch. It's set 4,200 ft above sea level and is adjacent to several well-defined nature walking trails. Her gift shop sells the coveted Blue Mountain coffee.

Unless you are traveling with a local, do not rent a car and go to the Blue Mountains on your own, as the mountain roads wind and dip, hand-lettered signs blow away, and a tourist can easily get lost—not just for hours, but for days. Another way to see the Blue Mountains is by the downhill bicycle tour offered by **Blue Mountain Tours** (☞ Guided Tours *in* Jamaica A to Z, *below*).

**⓯ Cockpit Country.** Fifteen miles inland from Montego Bay is one of the most primitive areas in the West Indies, a terrain of pitfalls and potholes carved by nature in limestone. For nearly a century after 1655 it was known as the Land of Look Behind because British soldiers rode their horses back-to-back in pairs, looking out for the savage freedom fighters known as Maroons. Fugitive slaves who refused to surrender to the invading English, the Maroons eventually won a treaty of independence and continue to live apart from the rest of Jamaica in the Cockpit Country. The government leaves them alone, untaxed and virtually ungoverned by outside authorities.

**❻ Crystal Springs.** About 18 mi west of Port Antonio, Crystal Springs has more than 15,000 orchids, and hummingbirds dart among the blossoms, landing on visitors' outstretched hands. Hiking and camping are available here. ⊠ *Buff Bay,* ☎ *809/993–2609 or 809/996–1400.* 🖃 *J$100.* ⊙ *Daily 9–5.*

**❺ Firefly.** About 20 mi east of Ocho Rios in Port Maria, Firefly was once Sir Noël Coward's vacation residence and is now preserved in all its hilltop wonder by the Jamaican National Heritage Trust. Coward used to entertain jet-setters and royalty in the surprisingly spartan digs in an Eden-like setting. He wrote *High Spirits, Quadrille,* and other plays here. Coward's simple grave is on the grounds next to a small stage where his plays are occasionally performed. Recordings of Coward singing of mad dogs and Englishmen echo over the lawns. Guided tours include time in the photo gallery and a walk through the house and grounds, the viewing of a biographical video on Coward, and a drink in the gift shop. ⊠ *Port Maria,* ☎ *809/997–7201,* FAX *809/974–5830.* 🖃 *$10.* ⊙ *Mon.–Sat. 9–4.*

**❹ Golden Eye.** Between Oracabessa and Port Maria, east of Ocho Rios on the main coast road, Golden Eye was used in wintertime by Ian Fleming, the creator of James Bond, from 1946 until his death in 1964. Later Golden Eye served as home to reggae legend Bob Marley and to the founder of Island Records, Chris Blackwell. Today it can be seen only by those who can afford to rent it from the record company. It's an airy complex of deep-blue buildings, walls, and bookcases bursting with Bond memorabilia, and a private cove reached by stone steps that would have delighted 007.

**⓫ Kingston.** The reaction of most visitors to the capital city, on the southeast coast of Jamaica, is anything but love at first sight. In fact, only a small percentage of visitors to Jamaica see it at all. Kingston, for the tourist, may seem as remote from the resorts of Montego Bay as the loneliest peak in the Blue Mountains. Yet the islanders themselves can't seem to let it go. Everybody talks about Kingston, about their homes or relatives there, about their childhood memories. More than the sunny havens of the north coast, Kingston is a distillation of the true Jamaica. Parts of it may be dirty, crowded, often raucous, yet it is the ethnic cauldron that produces the cultural mix that is the nation's greatest natural resource. (Note, however, that when the sun sets even Kingstonians beat a quick path out of downtown Kingston, which is considered unsafe after dark.) Kingston is a cultural and commercial crossroads of international and local movers and shakers, art-show openings, theater (from Shakespeare to pantomime), and superb shopping. Here, too, the University of the West Indies explores Caribbean art and literature, as well as science. As one Jamaican put it, "You don't really know Jamaica until you know Kingston."

The first-time business or pleasure traveler may prefer to begin with New Kingston, which glistens with hotels, office towers, apartments, and boutiques. Newcomers may feel more comfortable settling in here and venturing forth from comfort they know will await their return.

Kingston's colonial past is very much alive away from the high-rises of the new city. **Devon House,** built in 1881 and bought and restored by the government in the 1960s, is filled with period furnishings. Shoppers will appreciate Devon House, for the firm Things Jamaican has converted portions of the space into some of the best crafts shops on the island. On the grounds you'll find one of the few mahogany trees to survive Kingston's ambitious but not always careful development. ⊠ *26 Hope Rd.,* ☎ *809/929–7029.* ✉ *J$110.* ☉ *Devon House Tues.–Sat. 9:30–5, shops Mon.–Sat. 10–6.*

Once you have accepted the fact that Kingston doesn't look like a travel poster—too much life goes on here for that—you may see your trip here for precisely what it is, the single best introduction to the people of Jamaica. Near the waterfront, the **Institute of Jamaica** is a natural history museum and library that traces the island's history from the days of the Arawaks to current events. The charts and almanacs here make fascinating browsing; one example, famed as the Shark Papers, is made up of damaging evidence tossed overboard by a guilty sea captain and later recovered from the belly of a shark. ⊠ *12 East St.,* ☎ *809/922–0620.* ✉ *Museum $2, library free.* ☉ *Mon.–Thurs. 9–5, Fri. 9–4.*

Jamaica's rich cultural life is evoked at the **National Gallery,** which was once at Devon House and can now be found at Kingston Mall near the reborn waterfront section. The artists represented here may not be household names in other nations, yet the paintings of such intuitive masters as John Dunkley, David Miller Sr., and David Miller Jr. reveal a sensitivity to the life around them that transcends academic training. Among other highlights from the 1920s through the 1980s are works by Edna Manley and Mallica Reynolds, better known as Kapo. Reggae fans touring the National Gallery will want to look for Christopher Gonzalez's controversial statue of Bob Marley. ⊠ *12 Ocean Blvd.,* ☎ *809/922–1561.* ✉ *Fees for special exhibits.* ☉ *Weekdays 11–4:30.*

Reggae fans will want to see the **Bob Marley Museum.** Painted in Rastafarian red, yellow, and green, this recording studio was built by Marley at the height of his career. The museum gives guided tours of the medicinal herb garden, the room where Marley was shot, his bedroom, and rooms wallpapered with magazine and newspaper articles chronicling his rise to stardom. The tour includes a 20-minute biographical film on his life; there's also a reference library if you want to learn more.

Certainly there is much here to help the outsider understand Marley, reggae, and Jamaica itself. The Ethiopian flag is a reminder that Rastas consider the late Ethiopian emperor Haile Selassie, a descendant of King Solomon and the Queen of Sheba, to be the Messiah. A striking mural by Jah Bobby, *The Journey of Superstar Bob Marley,* depicts the hero's life from its beginnings in a womb shaped like a coconut to enshrinement in the hearts of the Jamaican people. ⊠ *56 Hope Rd.,* ☏ *809/978–2991.* ▭ *J$180.* ⊙ *Mon.–Tues. and Thurs.–Fri. 9–5, Wed. and Sat. 12:30–6.*

NEED A BREAK? After touring the museum, stop to rest your feet and sip fresh fruit juice at the **Queen of Sheba** (no phone), an Ethiopian restaurant on the museum grounds. If you're hungry, you can sample local Jamaican dishes such as rice and peas or Ethiopian fare (strictly vegetarian) here as well.

There is also a fine **statue** of Bob Marley on Arthur Wint Drive across from the **National Stadium.**

Although no longer lovingly cared for, the **Royal Botanical Gardens at Hope** is a nice place to picnic or while away an afternoon. Donated to Jamaica by the Hope family following the abolition of slavery, the garden consists of 50 acres filled with tropical trees, plants, and flowers, most clearly labeled for those taking a self-guided tour. Free concerts are given here on the first Sunday of each month. ⊠ *Hope Rd.,* ☏ *809/927–1085.* ▭ *J$12.* ⊙ *Weekdays 10–5, weekends 10–5:30.*

Another good picnic spot is the **Rockfort Mineral Baths.** Named for the stone fort built above Kingston Harbour in 1694 by the British to guard against invasion, and for the natural mineral spring that emerged following a devastating earthquake in 1907, this complex was listed on the Jamaica National Heritage Trust after being restored by the Caribbean Cement Company. It draws Kingstonians who come to cool off in the invigorating spring water in the public swimming pool or to unwind tense muscles in private whirlpool tubs. You can also have a massage and visit the juice bar or the cafeteria before staking out your picnic spot on the landscaped grounds. ⊠ *Kingston (on A–1, just outside town),* ☏ *809/938–5055.* ▭ *Pool J$60; private baths start at J$380.* ⊙ *Weekdays 6:30–6, weekends 8–6.*

⑭ **Mandeville.** More than a quarter of a century after Jamaica achieved its independence from Great Britain, Mandeville seems like a hilly tribute to all that is genteel and admirable in the British character. At 2,000 ft above sea level, 70 mi southeast of Montego Bay, Mandeville is considerably cooler than the coastal area 25 mi to the south. Its vegetation is more lush, thanks to the mists that drift through the mountains. The people of Mandeville live their lives around a village green, a Georgian courthouse, tidy cottages and gardens, even a parish church. The entire scene could be set down in Devonshire, were it not for the occasional poinciana blossom or citrus grove.

Mandeville is omitted from most tourist itineraries even though its residents are increasingly interested in showing visitors around. It is still much less expensive than any of the coastal resorts, and its diversions include horseback riding, cycling, croquet, hiking, tennis, golf, birdwatching, and people-meeting.

The town itself is characterized by its orderliness. You may stay here several days, or a glimpse of the lifestyle may satisfy you and you'll scurry back to the steamy coast. **Manchester Club** (☏ 809/962–2403) features tennis, nine holes of golf, and well-manicured greens; Mrs. Stephenson conducts photographic tours of her **Gardens** (☏ 809/962–

2328), an arboretum filled with lovely orchids and fruit trees; and the natural **Bird Sanctuary at Marshall's Penn Great House** (☎ 809/963–8569) is visited by more than 25 species indigenous to Jamaica. Tours of this bird sanctuary are by appointment only and are led by owner Robert Sutton, one of Jamaica's leading ornithologists. Other sights worth visiting are **Lover's Leap,** where legend has it that two slave lovers leapt off the 1,700-ft-high cliff rather than be recaptured by their plantation owner, and the **High Mountain Coffee Plantation** (☎ 809/963–4211) in nearby Williamsfield, where free tours (by appointment only) show how coffee beans are turned into one of America's favorite morning drinks.

**❷ Martha Brae River.** One of the most popular excursions in Jamaica is rafting on this river. The gentle waterway takes its name from that of an Arawak Indian who killed herself because she refused to reveal the whereabouts of a local gold mine to the Spanish. According to legend, she finally agreed to take them there and, on reaching the river, used magic to change its course, drowning herself along with the greedy Spaniards. Her *duppy* (ghost) is said to guard the mine's entrance to this day. **Martha Brae River Rafting** (☞ Guided Tours *in* Jamaica A to Z, *below*) leads trips down the river. The ticket office, gift shops, a bar-restaurant, and swimming pool are at the top of the river. Bookings can be made through hotel tour desks.

**❶ Montego Bay.** The number and variety of its attractions make Montego Bay, on the island's north coast, the logical place to begin an exploration of Jamaica. Confronting the string of high-rise developments that crowd the water's edge, you may find it hard to believe that little of what is now Montego Bay (the locals call it MoBay) existed before the turn of the century. Today many explorations of Montego Bay are conducted from a reclining chair on Doctor's Cave Beach, with a table nearby to hold frothy drinks.

Led by a charming guide in period costume who recites poetry and sings songs of the period, the tour of the **Barnett Estates** is one of the best you'll find in Jamaica. The Kerr-Jarrett family has held the land here for 11 generations, and still grow coconut, mango, and sugarcane on 3,000 acres; you'll get samples during the plantation tour by horseback (one hour) which follows a tour of the great house. ⊠ *Granville Main Rd.,* ☎ *809/952–2382,* 🅕🅐🅧 *809/952–6342.* 🎫 *Great house tour $15; great house and plantation tour $45.* ⊙ *Great house 9:30–4:30; great house/plantation by horseback tours daily at 10 and 2.*

**Rose Hall Great House,** perhaps the greatest in the West Indies in the 1700s, enjoys its popularity less for its architecture than for the legend surrounding its second mistress, Annie Palmer, who was credited with murdering three husbands and a plantation overseer who was her lover. The story is told in two novels sold everywhere in Jamaica: *The White Witch of Rose Hall* and *Jamaica White.* There's a pub on site. ⊠ *East of Montego Bay, just across highway from Rose Hall resorts,* ☎ *809/953–2323.* 🎫 *$15.* ⊙ *Daily 9–6.*

**Greenwood Great House** has no spooky legend to titillate visitors, but it's much better than Rose Hall at evoking the atmosphere of life on a sugar plantation. The Barrett family, from which the English poet Elizabeth Barrett Browning was descended, once owned all the land from Rose Hall to Falmouth and built several great houses on it, including Greenwood. (The poet's father, Edward Moulton Barrett, "the Tyrant of Wimpole Street," was born at Cinnamon Hill, currently the private estate of country singer Johnny Cash.) Highlights of Greenwood include oil paintings of the Barretts, china made especially for the family by Wedgwood, a library filled with rare books printed as early as 1697, fine antique furniture, and a collection of exotic musical instruments. There's a pub on site as well. ⊠ *15 mi east of Montego Bay,* ☎ *809/953–1077.* 🎟 *$10.* ⊙ *Daily 9–6.*

**⑯ Negril.** Situated 55 mi southwest of Montego Bay on the winding coast road, Negril is no longer Jamaica's best-kept secret. In fact, it has begun to shed some of its bohemian, ramshackle atmosphere for the attractions and activities traditionally associated with Montego Bay. Applauding the sunset from Rick's Cafe may still be the highlight of a day in Negril, yet increasingly the hours before and after have come to be filled with conventional recreation.

One thing that has not changed around this west-coast center (whose only true claim to fame is a 7-mi beach) is the casual approach to life. As you wander from lunch in the sun to shopping in the sun to sports in the sun, you'll find that swimsuits are common attire. Want to dress for a special meal? Slip a caftan over your bathing suit.

Negril stretches along the coast south from the horseshoe-shape **Bloody Bay** (named during the period when it was a whale-processing center) along the calm waters of **Long Bay** to the Lighthouse section and the landmark **Rick's Cafe** (☎ 809/957–0380). Sunset at Rick's is a Negril tradition. Divers spiral downward off 50-ft-high cliffs into the deep green depths as the sun turns into a ball of fire and sets the clouds ablaze with color.

Even though you may be staying at one of the charming smaller inns in Negril, you may enjoy spending a day at **Hedonism II** (☞ Lodging, *above*), a kind of love poem to health, Mother Nature, and good (mostly clean) fun. The owners love to publicize the occasional nude volleyball game in the pool at 3 AM, but most of the pampered campers are in clothes and in bed well before that hour. And what if Hedonism II is not the den of iniquity it likes to appear to be? What it is, and what your day (10:30–5) pass ($50) gets you, is a taste of the spirit as well as the food and drink—and participation in water sports, tennis, squash, and other daily activities. Night passes ($35) cover dinner and entrance to the wild disco on the property. Reservations are a must.

Negril's newest attraction is the **Anancy Family Fun & Nature Park** (☎ 809/957–4100), just across the street from the family-oriented Poinciana Beach Resort. Named after the mischievous spider character in Jamaican folktales, the 3-acre site features an 18-hole miniature golf course, go-cart rides, a minitrain, a fishing pond, a nature trail, and three small museums (crafts, conservation, and heritage).

Around sunset, activity centers on **West End Road,** Negril's main (and only) thoroughfare, which comes to life in the evening with bustling bistros and ear-splitting discos. West End Road leads to the town's only building of historical significance, the **Lighthouse.** All anyone can tell you about it, however, is that it's been there for a while. Even historians find it hard to keep track of the days in Negril.

What is known of the island's history is that, in the 18th century, Negril was where the English ships assembled in convoys for the dangerous ocean crossing. Not only were there pirates in the neighborhood, but the infamous Calico Jack and his crew were captured right here, while they guzzled the local rum. All but two of them were hanged on the spot; Mary Read and Anne Bonney were pregnant at the time, and their execution was delayed.

**❸ Ocho Rios.** Perhaps more than anywhere else in Jamaica, Ocho Rios— 67 mi east of Montego Bay—presents a striking contrast of natural beauty and recreational development. The Jamaicans can fill the place by themselves, especially on a busy market day, when cars and buses from the countryside clog the heavily traveled coastal road that links Port Antonio with Montego Bay. Add a tour bus or three and the entire passenger list from a cruise ship, and you may find yourself mired in a considerable traffic jam.

Yet a visit to Ocho Rios is worthwhile, if only to enjoy its two chief attractions—Dunn's River Falls and Prospect Plantation. A few steps away from the main road in Ocho Rios are waiting some of the most charming inns and oceanfront restaurants in the Caribbean. Lying on the sand of what will seem to be your private cove or swinging gently in a hammock with a tropical drink in your hand, you'll soon forget the traffic that's only a brief stroll away.

The dispute continues as to the origin of the name Ocho Rios. Some claim it's Spanish for "eight rivers"; others maintain that the name is a corruption of *chorreras*, which describes a seemingly endless series of cascades that sparkle from the limestone rocks along this stretch of coast. For as long as anyone can remember, Jamaicans have favored Ocho Rios as their own escape from the heat and the crowds of Kingston.

**Dunn's River Falls** is an eye-catching sight: 600 ft of cold, clear mountain water splashing over a series of stone steps to the warm Caribbean. The best way to enjoy the falls is to climb the slippery steps. Don a swimsuit, take the hand of the person ahead of you, and trust that the chain of hands and bodies leads to an experienced guide. The leaders of the climbs are personable fellows who reel off bits of local lore while telling you where to step. ⊠ *Immediately off Main Rd. (A–1), between St. Ann's and Ocho Rios,* ☎ *809/974–2857.* ⌚ *$6.* ☉ *Daily 9–5.*

The **Prospect Plantation** tour is the best of several offerings that delve into the island's former agricultural lifestyle. It's not just for specialists; virtually everyone enjoys the beautiful views over the White River Gorge and the tour by jitney (a canopied open-air cart pulled by a tractor) through a plantation with exotic fruits and tropical trees planted over the years by such celebrities as Winston Churchill and Charlie Chaplin. Horseback riding over 900 acres is available as is minigolf, and there's a bar and gift shop on site, and rental villas for those who want more time to explore the extensive plantation. ⊠ *Hwy. A–1, just west of downtown Ocho Rios,* ☎ *809/994–1058.* ⌚ *$12.* ☉ *Daily 9–5; tours Mon.–Sat. at 10:30, 2, and 3:30, Sun. at 11, 1:30, and 3:30.*

The only major historic site in Ocho Rios is the **Old Fort,** built in 1777 as a defense against invaders from the sea. The original "defenders" spent much of their time sacking and plundering as far afield as St. Augustine, Florida, and sharing their bounty with the local plantation owners who financed their missions. Fifteen miles west is **Discovery Bay,** site of Columbus's landing, with a small museum of artifacts and Jamaican memorabilia.

Ocho Rios's newest attraction is the **Coyaba River Garden and Museum,** which features exhibits on Jamaica's many cultural influences (the national motto is "Out of Many, One People"). A guided 45-minute tour through the lush 3-acre gardens introduces you to the flora and fauna of the island. The museum covers the island's history from the time of the Arawak Indians up to the modern day. The complex includes a crafts and gift shop and a snack bar. ⊠ *Shaw Park Rd., Ocho Rios,* ☎ *809/974–6235.* ⌚ *$4.50.* ☉ *Daily 8–5.*

Other excursions of note are the one to Runaway Bay's Green Grotto Caves (and a boat ride on an underground lake); a ramble through the Shaw Park Botanical Gardens; a visit to Sun Valley, a working plantation with banana, coconut, and citrus trees; and a drive through Fern Gully, a natural canopy of vegetation filtered by sunlight (Jamaica has the world's largest number of fern species, more than 570).

**8** **Port Antonio.** Every visitor's presence in Port Antonio pays homage to the beginnings of Jamaican tourism. Early in the century the first tourists arrived here on the island's northeast coast, 133 mi east of Montego Bay, drawn by the exoticism of the island's banana trade and seeking a respite from the New York winters. The original posters of the shipping lines make Port Antonio appear as foreign as the moon, yet in time it became the tropical darling of a fast-moving crowd and counted Clara Bow, Bette Davis, Ginger Rogers, Rudyard Kipling, J. P. Morgan, and William Randolph Hearst among its admirers. Its most passionate devotee was the actor Errol Flynn, whose spirit still seems to haunt the docks, devouring raw dolphinfish and swigging gin at 10 AM.

Although the action has moved elsewhere, the area can still weave a spell. Robin Moore wrote *The French Connection* here, and Broadway's tall and talented Tommy Tune found inspiration for the musical *Nine* while being pampered at Trident.

For as long as anyone can remember, Port Antonio has been a center for some of the finest deep-sea fishing in the Caribbean. Dolphins (the delectable fish, not the lovable mammal) are the likely catch here, along with tuna, kingfish, and wahoo. In October the weeklong Blue Marlin Tournament attracts anglers from around the world. By the time enough beer has been consumed, it's a bit like the running of the bulls at Pamplona, except that fish stories carry the day.

A stroll through the town suggests a step into the past. **Queen Street,** in the residential Titchfield area, a couple of miles north of downtown Port Antonio, has several fine examples of Georgian architecture. **DeMontevin Lodge** (⊠ 21 Fort George St., on Titchfield Hill, ☎ 809/993–2604), owned by the Mullings family (the late Gladys Mullings was Errol Flynn's cook, and you can still get great food here), and the nearby **Musgrave Street** (the crafts market is here) are in the traditional sea-captain style that one finds along coasts as far away as New England.

The town's best-known landmark is **Folly,** on the way to Trident, a Roman-style villa in ruins on the eastern edge of East Harbor. The creation of a Connecticut millionaire in 1905, the manse was made almost entirely of concrete. Unfortunately, the cement was mixed with seawater, and it began to crumble as it dried. According to local lore, the millionaire's bride took one look at her shattered dream, burst into tears, and fled forever. Little more than the marble floor remains today. Note that Folly becomes something of a ganja hangout after sundown and should be avoided then.

A good way to spend a day in Port Antonio is swimming in the deep azure water of the **Blue Lagoon.** Although there's not much beach to speak of, there is a water-sports center, changing rooms, and a soothing mineral pool, off to one side under the shade of a tree. Yummy, inexpensive, Jamaican fare is served at a charming waterside terrace restaurant, where you'll find a live jazz band performing on Saturday nights. ⊠ *1 mi east of San San Beach,* ☎ *809/993–8491. Restaurant serves lunch only Mon.–Wed., dinner only Thurs.–Sun.*

A short drive east from Port Antonio deposits you at **Boston Bay,** which is popular with swimmers and has been enshrined by lovers of jerk pork.

The spicy barbecue was originated by the Arawaks and perfected by runaway slaves called the Maroons. Eating almost nothing but wild hog preserved over smoking coals enabled the Maroons to survive years of fierce guerrilla warfare with the English.

Some 6 mi northeast of Port Antonio in the village of Nonsuch are the **Athenry Gardens,** a 3-acre tropical wonderland, and the **Nonsuch Caves,** whose underground beauty has been made accessible by concrete walkways, railed stairways, and careful lighting. ⊠ *Athenry/Nonsuch,* ☎ *809/993–3740.* 🖼 *$5.* ⊙ *Daily 9–5.*

**⑫  Port Royal.** Just south of Kingston, Port Royal was called "the wickedest city in the world"—before an earthquake tumbled it into the sea in 1692. The spirits of Henry Morgan and other buccaneers add a great deal of energy to what remains. The proudest possession of St. Peter's Church, rebuilt in 1726 to replace Christ's Church, is a silver communion set said to have been donated by Morgan himself (who probably obtained it during a raid on Panama).

Port Royal is slated for a massive redevelopment project that will renovate existing sites of historical interest and introduce new museums, shops, restaurants, and perhaps even a cruise-ship pier. However, funding for these ambitious plans was not yet in place at press time.

A ferry from the square in downtown Kingston goes to Port Royal at least twice a day (though this may increase with proposed redevelopment of Port Royal), and the town is small enough to see on foot. If you drive out to Port Royal from Kingston, you'll pass several sights of interest, including remains of old forts virtually covered over by vegetation, an old naval cemetery (which has some intriguing headstones), and a bit farther on, a monument commemorating Jamaica's first coconut tree, planted in 1863 (there's no tree there now, just plenty of cactus and scrub brush).

You can no longer down rum in Port Royal's legendary 40 taverns (well, two small pubs still remain in operation), but you can explore the impressive remains of **Fort Charles,** once the area's major garrison. Built in 1662, this is the oldest surviving monument of British occupation of Jamaica. On the grounds is the small **Fort Charles Maritime Museum** and **Giddy House,** an old artillery storehouse that gained its name after being permanently tilted by the earthquake of 1907. Nearby, in the graveyard of **St. Peter Church,** is the tombstone of Lewis Galdy, who was swallowed up in the great earthquake of 1692, spewed into the sea, rescued, and lived another two decades in "Great Reputation." Nearby is the tomb of three small children, victims of the earthquake, recovered by archaeologists from Texas A&M University. ⊠ *Fort Charles, Port Royal,* ☎ *809/967–8059.* 🖼 *$4.* ⊙ *Daily 9:30–5; guided tours depart every ½ hr.*

NEED A BREAK? **Gloria's Rendezvous** (⊠ 5 Queen St., ☎ 809/967–8066), the brightly painted, ramshackle eatery across the street from the Port Royal Police Station, is wildly popular with Kingston locals escaping the sultry city heat on weekends. Delectable grilled fish and chicken are the draw; but come prepared to wait, because everything is prepared from scratch only after you place your order.

**❾  Rio Grande.** Rafting on the Rio Grande (yes, Jamaica has a Rio Grande, too) is a must. This is the granddaddy of the river-rafting attractions, an 8-mi-long swift green waterway from Berrydale to Rafter's Rest. Here the river flows into the Caribbean at St. Margaret's Bay. The trip of about three hours is made on bamboo rafts pushed along by a rafts-man who is likely to be a character. You can pack a picnic lunch and eat it on the raft or along the riverbank; wherever you lunch, a vendor of Red Stripe beer will appear at your elbow. A restaurant, bar, and souvenir shops are located at Rafter's Rest. The trip costs about $40 per two-person raft (☞ Guided Tours *in* Jamaica A to Z, *below*).

**❼ Somerset Falls.** Eight miles west of Port Antonio is Somerset Falls, a sun-dappled spot crawling with flowering vines. You can climb the 400 ft with some assistance from a concrete staircase. A brief raft ride takes you part of the way. ⊠ *Somerset Falls, no phone.* ▨ *J$35.* ☉ *Daily 10–5.*

**⓭ Spanish Town.** Located 12 mi west of Kingston on A–1, Spanish Town was the island's capital under Spanish rule. The town boasts the tiered Georgian **Antique Square**, the **Jamaican People's Museum of Crafts and Technology** (in the Old King's House stables), and **St. James**, the oldest cathedral in the Western Hemisphere. Spanish Town's original name was Santiago de la Vega, which the English corrupted to St. Jago de la Vega, both meaning St. James of the Plains. Contact the Jamaica National Heritage Trust (☎ 809/922–1287) for further information on this heritage town.

# Jamaica A to Z

## Arriving and Departing

BY PLANE

**Donald Sangster International Airport** (☎ 809/952–3124), in Montego Bay, is the most efficient point of entry for visitors destined for Montego Bay, Ocho Rios, Runaway Bay, and Negril. **Norman Manley International Airport** (☎ 809/924–8235), in Kingston, is best for visitors to the capital or Port Antonio.

**Air Jamaica Express** (☎ 809/952–5401 in Montego Bay, 809/923–8680 in Kingston), a new subsidiary of Air Jamaica, provides shuttle services on the island. Be sure to reconfirm your departing flight a full 72 hours in advance. **Air Jamaica** (☎ 809/952–4100 in Montego Bay, 809/922–4661 in Kingston, or 800/523–5585) provides the most frequent service from U.S. cities, including Los Angeles, San Francisco, New York, Philadelphia, Baltimore, Chicago, Atlanta, Ft. Lauderdale, Miami, and Orlando. **American Airlines** (☎ 809/952–5950 in Montego Bay, 809/924–8305 in Kingston, or 800/433–7300) flies nonstop daily from New York, Miami, and San Juan. **US Airways** (☎ 800/428–4322) flies in from Baltimore and Charlotte. **Continental** (☎ 809/952–4495 or 800/231–0856) flies in four times a week from Newark. **Northwest Airlines** (☎ 800/225–2525) has daily direct service to Montego Bay from Minneapolis and Tampa. Panamanian carrier **Copa** (☎ 809/926–1762) offers service between Miami and Kingston. **Cubana** (☎ 809/978–3410) flies in from Havana. **Air Canada** (☎ 809/952–8271 or 800/776–3000) offers daily service from Toronto, Halifax, Winnipeg, and Montreal in conjunction with Air Jamaica. **British Airways** (☎ 809/952–3771 in Montego Bay, 809/929–9020 in Kingston, or 800/247–9297) connects the island with London as does Air Jamaica.

## Currency

The Jamaican government abolished the fixed rate of exchange for the Jamaican dollar, allowing it to be traded publicly and subject to market fluctuations. At press time the Jamaican dollar was worth about J$34 to US$1. Currency can be exchanged at airport bank counters, exchange bureaus, or commercial banks. Prices quoted are in U.S. dollars unless otherwise noted.

## Emergencies

**Police and air-rescue:** ☎ 119. **Fire department and ambulance:** ☎ 110. **Hospitals: University Hospital** (✉ Mona, Kingston, ☎ 809/927–1620), **Cornwall Regional Hospital** (✉ Mt. Salem, Montego Bay, ☎ 809/952–5100), **Port Antonio General Hospital** (✉ Naylor's Hill, Port Antonio, ☎ 809/993–2646), and **St. Ann's Bay Hospital** (✉ St. Ann's Bay, ☎ 809/972–2272). **Pharmacies: Jamaica Pegasus hotel** (✉ 81 Knutsford Blvd., Kingston, ☎ 809/926–3690), **McKenzie's Drug Store** (✉ 16 Strand St., Montego Bay, ☎ 809/952–2467), and **Great House Pharmacy** (✉ Brown's Plaza, Ocho Rios, ☎ 809/974–2352).

## Getting Around

### BICYCLES, MOPEDS, AND MOTORCYCLES

The front desks of most major hotels can arrange the rental of bicycles, mopeds, and motorcycles. Daily rates run from about $45 for a moped to $70 for a Honda 550. Deposits of $100–$300 or more are required. However, we highly recommend that you *not* rent a moped or motorcycle. The strangeness of driving on the left, the less-than-cautious driving style that prevails on the island, the abundance of potholes, and the prevalence of vendors who will approach you at every traffic light are just a few reasons to skip cycles. If you want to venture out on your own, rent a car.

### BUSES

Buses are the mode of transportation Jamaicans use most, and consequently buses are *extremely* crowded and slow. They're also not air-conditioned and rather uncomfortable. Yet the service is fairly frequent between Kingston and Montego Bay and between other significant destinations. Schedule or route information is available at bus stops or from the bus driver.

The riotously painted **Soon Come Shuttles** in MoBay operate on two routes (central route downtown, $1; eastern route, which hits Rose Hall Great House and the hotels east of downtown, $2), providing inexpensive transit from the hotel zone to the shopping and dining in town. Red Stripe beer and reggae music keep passengers entertained en route. Schedules and stop locations are available at hotel information desks.

### CAR RENTALS

Traffic keeps to the left in Jamaica, and those who are unfamiliar with driving on the left will find that it takes some getting used to. Please note that driving in Jamaica is a chore and can be extremely frustrating (not the way to spend a vacation). You must constantly be on guard—for enormous potholes, people and animals darting out in the street, and aggressive drivers.

Jamaica has dozens of car-rental companies throughout the island. Because rentals can be difficult to arrange once you've arrived, you must make reservations and send a deposit before your trip. (Cars are scarce, and without either a confirmation number or a receipt you may have to walk.) You must be at least 21 years old to rent a car (at least 25 years old at several agencies), have a valid driver's license (from any country), and have a valid credit card. You may be required to post a security of several hundred dollars before taking possession of your car; ask about it when you make the reservation. Rates average $65–$120 a day. Best bets are **Avis** (☎ 800/331–1212 or 809/952–4543 in Montego Bay, 809/924–8013 in Kingston), **Budget** (☎ 809/952–3838 in Montego Bay, 809/924–8762 in Kingston), **Hertz** (☎ 800/654–3131 or 809/979–0438 in Montego Bay), and **National** (☎ 800/328–4567 or 809/979–0438 in Montego Bay, 809/929–7204 in

Kingston, 809/974–2266 in Ocho Rios). In Jamaica, try the branch offices in your resort area or try **Island Car Rentals** (☎ 809/952–5771 in Montego Bay, 809/926–5991 in Kingston), **United Car Rentals** (☎ 809/952–3077), or **Jamaica Car Rental** (☎ 809/952–5586 in Montego Bay, 809/924–8217 in Kingston).

TAXIS

Some but not all of Jamaica's taxis are metered. If you accept a driver's offer of his services as a tour guide, be sure to agree on a price before the vehicle is put into gear. All licensed taxis display red Public Passenger Vehicle (PPV) plates. Cabs can be summoned by telephone or flagged down on the street. Rates are per car, not per passenger, and 25% is added to the metered rate between midnight and 5 AM. Licensed minivans are also available and bear the red PPV plates. JUTA is the largest taxi franchise and has offices in all resort areas.

TRAINS

At press time, rail service between Kingston and Montego Bay was suspended.

## Guided Tours

Half-day tours are offered by a variety of operators in the important areas of Jamaica. The best great-house tours include Rose Hall, Greenwood, and Devon House. Plantations to tour are Prospect, Barnett Estates, and Sun Valley. The Appleton Estate Tour uses a bus to visit villages, plantations, and a rum distillery. The increasingly popular waterside folklore feasts are offered on the Dunn's, Great, and White rivers. The significant city tours are in Kingston, Montego Bay, and Ocho Rios.

AIR TOURS

**Helitours Jamaica Ltd.** (☎ 809/974–2265 or 809/974–1108) in Ocho Rios offers helicopter tours of Jamaica, ranging from 15 minutes to an hour at prices that vary accordingly ($65–$225).

LAND TOURS

**Blue Mountain Tours** (☎ 809/974–7705, FAX 809/974–0635) offers a daylong downhill bicycle tour of the mountains, which coasts 18 mi down from 5,060 ft through coffee plantations and rain forests. The cost is about $80 and includes lunch. **Maroon Attraction Tours Co.** (☎ 809/952–4546) leads full-day tours from Montego Bay to Maroon headquarters at Accompong, giving visitors a glimpse of the society of Maroons, descendants of fugitive slaves, who live in Cockpit Country. The cost is under $80 per person. **Touring Society of Jamaica** (☎ 809/975–7158 in Ocho Rios, 809/967–1792 in Kingston, or 809/944–8400; FAX 809/944-8408 in the Blue Mountains), operated by American Lynda Lee Burke, offers several eco-tours, from birding in the Blue Mountains to exploring the natural history of Cockpit Country. **Valley Hikes** (☎ FAX 809/993–3881) in Port Antonio offers guided hikes up the Rio Grande Valley or a combination hiking-rafting trip. Horseback tours of the area can also be arranged.

SEA TOURS

**Calico Sailing** (☎ 809/952–5860, FAX 809/979–0843) offers snorkeling trips and sunset cruises on the waters of Montego Bay; costs are $50 and $25, respectively. **An Evening on the Great River** (☎ 809/952–5047 or 809/952–5097) is a must for tour groups, yet fun nonetheless. The adventure includes a boat ride up the torch-lit river, a full Jamaican dinner, open bar, a native folklore show, and dancing to a reggae band. It costs around $60 per person with hotel pickup and return, less if you arrive via your own transport. Tours are offered Sunday through Thursday. **Martha Brae River Rafting** (☎ 809/952–0889) leads trips down the Martha Brae River, about 25 mi from most hotels in Montego Bay. The cost is just under $40 per raft (two per raft) for the 1½-hour river run. **Mountain Valley Rafting** (☎ 809/952–0527 or 809/952–6388) runs trips down the River Lethe, approximately 12 mi (about 50 minutes) southwest of Montego Bay. The trip is about $50 per raft (two per raft), lasting an hour or so, through unspoiled hillside country. Bookings can also be made through hotel tour desks. **Rio Grande Attractions Ltd.** (☎ 809/993–2778) guides raft trips down the Rio Grande (☞ Exploring, *above*). The cost is $40 per raft. **South Coast Safaris Ltd.** (☎ 809/965–2513) has guided boat excursions up the Black River for some 10 mi (round-trip), into the mangroves and marshlands to see the alligators, birds, and plant life, aboard the 25-passenger *Safari Queen* and 25-passenger *Safari Princess*. Cost is around $15. **Undersea Tours MoBay** (☎ 809/922–1287) offers you a good look at MoBay's marine sanctuary without getting wet by booking passage (around $40) on a semisubmersible craft.

TOUR OPERATORS

Quality tour operators include **Caribic Tours** (☎ 809/953–9895), **Glamour Tours** (☎ 809/979–8415), **Greenlight Tours** (☎ 809/952–2650), **Tourwise** (☎ 809/974–2323), and **SunHoliday Tours** (☎ 809/952–5629).

## Language

The official language of Jamaica is English. Islanders usually speak a patois among themselves, a lyrical mixture of pigeon English, Spanish, and various African languages.

## Opening and Closing Times

Normal business hours for stores are weekdays 8–4, Saturday 8–1. Banking hours are generally Monday–Thursday 9–2, Friday 9–noon and 2–5.

## Passports and Visas

Passports are not required of visitors from the United States or Canada, but every visitor must have proof of citizenship, such as a birth certificate or a voter registration card (a driver's license is not enough). British visitors need passports but not visas. Each visitor must possess a return or ongoing ticket. Declaration forms are distributed in flight to keep customs formalities to a minimum.

## Precautions

Do not let the beauty of Jamaica cause you to relax the caution and good sense you would use in your own hometown. Never leave money or other valuables in your hotel room; use the safe-deposit boxes that most establishments make available. Carry your funds in traveler's checks, not cash, and keep a record of the check numbers in a secure place. Never leave a rental car unlocked, and never leave valuables, even in a locked car. Finally, resist the call of the wild when it presents itself as a scruffy-looking native offering to show you the "real" Jamaica. Jamaica on the beaten path is wonderful enough; don't take chances by wandering far from it. And ignore efforts, however persistent, to sell you a ganja joint. Carry along some insect repellent and a strong sunscreen to avoid natural hazards.

## Taxes and Service Charges

Hotels collect a 10% government consumption tax on room occupancy. The departure tax is J$500. Most hotels and restaurants add a 10% service charge to your bill. If not, a 10% to 20% tip is appreciated.

## Telephones and Mail

As we went to press, the area code for Jamaica changed from 809 to 876. Direct telephone, telegraph, telefax, and telex services are available.

At press time, airmail postage from Jamaica to the United States or Canada was under J$10 for letters and postcards.

## Visitor Information

Before you go, contact the **Jamaica Tourist Board** (✉ 801 2nd Ave., 20th floor, New York, NY 10017, ☎ 212/856–9727 or 800/233–4582, FAX 212/856–9730; ✉ 500 N. Michigan Ave., Suite 1030, Chicago, IL 60611, ☎ 312/527–1296, FAX 312/527–1472; ✉ 1320 S. Dixie Hwy., Suite 1100, Coral Gables, FL 33146, ☎ 305/665–0557, FAX 305/666–7239; ✉ 3440 Wilshire Blvd., Suite 1207, Los Angeles, CA 90010, ☎ 213/384–1123, FAX 213/384–1780; ✉ 1 Eglinton Ave. E, Suite 616, Toronto, Ontario M4P 3A–1, ☎ 416/482–7850, FAX 416/482–1730; ✉ 1–2 Prince Consort Rd., London SW7 2BZ, ☎ 0171/224–0505, FAX 0171/224–0551).

In Jamaica, the main office of the **Jamaica Tourist Board** is in Kingston (✉ 2 St. Lucia Ave., New Kingston, Box 360, Kingston 5, ☎ 809/929–9200). There are also JTB desks at both Montego Bay and Kingston airports and offices in Black River (☎ 809/965–2074), Montego Bay (☎ 809/952–4425), Negril (☎ 809/957–4243), Ocho Rios (☎ 809/974–2570), and Port Antonio (☎ 809/993–3051).

If you'd like to delve into the heart of Jamaica rather than simply explore her sybaritic pleasures, the tourist board will arrange for you to spend a little time with a local host family through the **Meet the People** program. They'll try to match interests, vocations, ages, whatever, so you'll have some common ground. There's no fee involved (other than for activities you and your hosts might select); this is the best way to come to know the warmth and good companionship the island has to offer.

# 15 Martinique

*Gauguin loved it for its vibrant colors, tropical vegetation, and refined people. Add gourmet restaurants, wonderful beaches, and joie de vivre, and you have Martinique today.*

**T**HE ARAWAKS named Martinique *Madinina,* "Island of Flowers." Exotic wild orchids, frangipani, anthurium, jade vines, flamingo flowers, and hundreds of vivid varieties of hibiscus still grow on the island. But, these days, you are more likely to smell Chanel No. 5 and espresso than flowers. Martinique is a tropical suburb of Paris: a rich, highly developed island with a six-lane highway, the biggest shopping malls, and some of the finest restaurants in the Caribbean.

Updated by
Kate
Pennebaker
and Simon
Worrall

Everything about Martinique, from the snappy new airport to the beautiful, old plantation houses, has style. Even the women working at the rental-car agencies look as though they are dressed for an evening at the opera. It's no surprise, then, that the island, along with Barbados, has one of the highest standards of living in the Caribbean. In their dealings with foreigners, the Martinicans are courteous, polite, and self-assured, qualities anchored in the privileged position that the island has enjoyed historically.

As Jamaica was the key to the British-ruled islands, so Martinique was the administrative, social, and cultural center of the French Antilles. Guadeloupe was an island of merchants and shopkeepers. Martinique was a rich, aristocratic island, famous for its beautiful women and gracious living, which gave birth to an empress and saw the full flowering of plantation-house society with its servants and *soirées,* wine cellars and snobbery.

This 425-square-mi island, the largest of the Windward Islands, has landscapes as varied as its culture and history. In the south, where most of the development, and the best beaches, are located, there are rolling hills and sugarcane fields. In the north, look for lush, tropical vegetation; fields of bananas and pineapples; deep gorges; towering cliffs; and one of the Caribbean's most impressive volcanos, Mont Peléé.

Martinique was squabbled over by Britain and France until 1815, when the island was ceded by treaty to Paris. Today, the French connection means excellent food and wine, grumpy waiters, superb roads, terrible pop music, democracy, and culture. Martinique has one of the finest jazz festivals in the Caribbean. In Patrick Chamoiseau it has a world-class novelist. It also has some of the highest prices in the Caribbean. A holiday in Martinique is not cheap. And as on Guadeloupe, you'll need some French to feel truly at home, though the locals are more forthcoming in English here.

It is not *like* France. It *is* France. Most everything shuts down at midday and reopens sometime after 2:30. Franglais is universal (*Les softs* is what you should look for if you want a soda), topless bathing almost *de rigueur,* the driving frenetic, and poodles are everywhere (French, of course).

## Lodging

Martinique's accommodations range from tiny inns called Relais Creoles to splashy tourist resorts and luxurious plantation houses. The majority of hotels are clustered in Pointe du Bout and Anse-Mitan on the Trois-Ilets peninsula across the bay from Fort-de-France, Le Diamant, and Ste-Anne. As on Guadeloupe, the tendency in recent years has been for the big resorts to go down-market and attract a mass package-tour clientele. There are only four four-star properties on the island; only one of them, Habitation Lagrange, would get a four-star rating on any other island. Most hotels have the busy, slightly frenetic feel that the

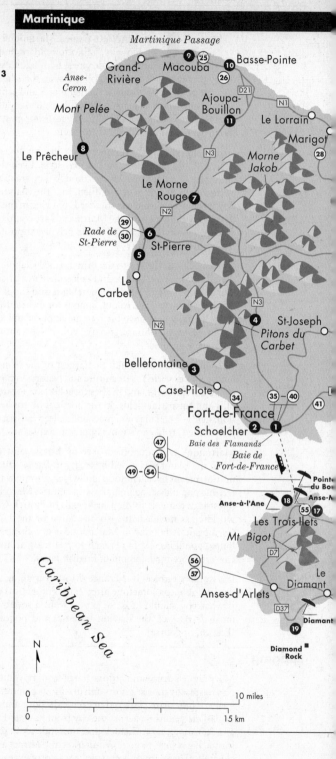

**KEY**

❶ Exploring Sites

㉕ Hotels and Restaurants

**Lodging**

Anse Caritan, **67**

Baie du Galion, **32**

Le Bakoua, **53**

La Batelière Hotel, **34**

Club Med/Buccaneer's Creek, **66**

Diamant Les Bains, **62**

Diamant-Novotel, **61**

Fregate Bleue, **45**

Habitation Lagrange, **27**

Impératrice, **39**

Lafayette, **40**

Leyritz Plantation, **26**

Manoir de Beauregard, **68**

Le Marine, **63**

Martinique Cottages, **43**

Le Méridien Trois-Ilets, **52**

Novotel Carayou, **54**

La Pagerie, **49**

Relais Caraïbes, **64**

Rivage Hotel, **50**

La Riviera, **44**

Saint Aubin, **33**

Valmenière, **41**

French seem to like. The major hotels usually include a large buffet breakfast of fresh fruit, croissants, baguettes, jam, and *café au lait*.

The **Villa Rental Service** (☎ 596/71–56–11, ℻ 596/63–11–64) can assist with rentals of homes, villas, and apartments. Most are in the south of the island near good beaches and can be rented on a weekly or monthly basis.

| CATEGORY | COST* |
| --- | --- |
| $$$$ | over $240 |
| $$$ | $150–$240 |
| $$ | $85–$150 |
| $ | under $85 |

*All prices are for a standard double room, excluding $1.50-per-person, per-night, tax and 10% service charge.*

### Basse-Pointe

$–$$
★
🏨 **Leyritz Plantation.** Sleeping on a former sugar plantation, in an antiques-furnished rooms of the manor house, cottages, or renovated slave cabin is certainly a novelty. Leyritz is isolated in the northern part of the island, on 16 acres of lush vegetation, with manicured lawns and stunning views of Mont Pelée. Nicest are the 10 cottage rooms, which have rough wood beams, mahogany four-poster beds, marble-top armoires, secretaries, and other antiques. The slightly larger former slave quarters have eaves, stone-and-stucco walls, more-contemporary furnishings, and madras linens. Ironically, it's the newer bungalows that are cramped and lacking individuality. Except for periodic invasions of cruise-ship passengers, it is very quiet here—a sharp contrast to the frenzied level of activity at the hotels in Pointe du Bout. You may not want to spend your entire vacation here, but it makes an interesting overnight stay while visiting the northern part of the island. There's free transportation to the beach, about 30 minutes away. ⊠ *Basse-Pointe 97218,* ☎ *596/78–53–92,* ℻ *596/78–92–44. 67 rooms. Restaurant, bar, air-conditioning, pool, tennis court. DC, MC. CP, MAP.*

### Fort-de-France

$$
🏨 **Impératrice.** The slightly musty rooms of the Impératrice are in a 1950s five-story building that overlooks La Savane park in the heart of the city. The front rooms are either the best or the worst, depending upon your sensibilities: They are noisy, but they overlook the city's activity. All rooms have a four-poster bed, TV, and private bath, and are decorated with bright Creole prints; 20 have balconies. Children under 8 stay free in the room with their parents, and children 8–15 stay at a 50% discount. The hotel also has a popular sidewalk café. ⊠ *Fort-de-France 97200,* ☎ *596/63–06–82 or 800/223–9815; 212/251–1800 in NY; 800/468–0023 in Canada;* ℻ *596/72–66–30. 24 rooms. Restaurant, bar, air-conditioning. AE, DC, MC, V. CP.*

$$
🏨 **Valmenière.** If you have to fly in, have a meeting, and fly out, this brand-new property, part of the Best Western group, is ideal. With its blue-tinted windows, high-tech elevator, and white tubular steel walkways, it would not be out of place in La Défense, Paris's business district. Perched on a hill between the airport and Fort-de-France, it is squeaky clean, efficient, and wired for work. The beds are king-size, and the imported French mattresses are a boon for anyone suffering from backache. The suites are large, with a separate entrance to the living room, abundant cupboard space, and a desk. Three *chambres de bureau* (business rooms) have beds that can fold away, turning the room into a flexible office space. The hotel offers a full range of business services, from fax machines to conference rooms and translation and secretarial assistance. There is also a good restaurant. For downtime, there is an exercise room in the basement as well as a pool and

# Pick up the phone.

# Pick up the miles.

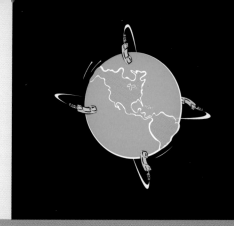

**Calling Card**

MCI

415 555 1234 2244
J.D. SMITH

WORLDPHONE

Use your MCI Card® to make an international call from virtually anywhere in the world and earn frequent flyer miles on one of seven major airlines.

Enroll in an MCI Airline Partner Program today. In the U.S., call **1-800-FLY-FREE.** Overseas, call MCI collect at **1-916-567-5151.**

1. To use your MCI Card, just dial the WorldPhone access number of the country you're calling from.
   (For a complete listing of codes, visit www.mci.com.)
2. Dial or give the operator your MCI Card number.
3. Dial or give the number you're calling.

| | |
|---|---|
| # American Samoa | 633-2MCI (633-2624) |
| # Antigua | #2 |
| (Available from public card phones only) | |
| # Argentina (CC) | 0800-5-1002 |
| # Aruba ÷ | 800-888-8 |
| # Bahamas | 1-800-888-8000 |
| # Barbados | 1-800-888-8000 |
| # Belize | 557 from hotels |
| | 815 from pay phones |
| # Bermuda ÷ | 1-800-888-8000 |
| # Bolivia ♦ | 0-800-2222 |
| # Brazil (CC) | 000-8012 |
| # British Virgin Islands ÷ | 1-800-888-8000 |
| # Cayman Islands | 1-800-888-8000 |
| # Chile (CC) | |
| To call using CTC ■ | 800-207-300 |
| To call using ENTEL ■ | 800-360-180 |
| # Colombia (CC) ♦ | 980-16-0001 |
| Columbia IIIC Access in Spanish | 980-16-1000 |
| # Costa Rica ♦ | 0800-012-2222 |
| # Dominica | 1-800-888-8000 |
| # Dominican Republic (CC) ÷ | 1-800-888-8000 |
| Dominican Republic IIIC Access in Spanish | 1121 |
| # Ecuador (CC) ÷ | 999-170 |
| El Salvador ♦ | 800-1767 |
| # Grenada ÷ | 1-800-888-8000 |
| Guatemala (CC) ♦ | 9999-189 |

| | |
|---|---|
| # Guyana | 177 |
| # Haiti (CC) ÷ | 193 |
| Haiti IIIC Access in French/Creole | 190 |
| Honduras ÷ | 122 |
| # Jamaica ÷ | 1-800-888-8000 |
| (From Special Hotels only) | 873 |
| # Mexico | |
| Avantel (CC) | 91-800-021-8000 |
| Telmex ▲ | 95-800-674-7000 |
| Mexico IIIC Access | 91-800-021-1000 |
| # Netherlands Antilles (CC) ÷ | 001-800-888-8000 |
| Nicaragua (CC) | 166 |
| (Outside of Managua, dial 02 first) | |
| Nicaragua IIIC Access in Spanish | ★2 from any public payphone |
| # Panama | 108 |
| Military Bases | 2810-108 |
| # Paraguay ÷ | 008-112-800 |
| # Peru | 0-800-500-10 |
| # Puerto Rico (CC) | 1-800-888-8000 |
| # St. Lucia ÷ | 1-800-888-8000 |
| # Trinidad & Tobago ÷ | 1-800-888-8000 |
| # Turks & Caicos ÷ | 1-800-888-8000 |
| # Uruguay | 000-412 |
| # U.S. Virgin Islands (CC) | 1-800-888-8000 |
| # Venezuela (CC) ÷ ♦ | 800-1114-0 |

Is this a great time, or what? :-)

# automation available from most locations. ÷ Limited availability. (CC) Country-to-country calling available to/from most international locations. ♦ Public phones may require deposit of coin or phone card for dial tone. ■ International communications carrier. ▲ When calling from public phones, use phones marked LADATEL. Limit one bonus program per MCI account. Terms and conditions apply. All airline program rules and conditions apply. ©1997 MCI Telecommunications Corporation. All rights reserved. Is this a great time or what? is a service mark of MCI.

sunroof on the top floor. Only the views—of an oil refinery, a landfill, and the island's main highway—remind you that the main purpose of the hotel is not leisure. ✉ *Ave. des Arawaks, Fort-de-France 97200,* ☎ *596/75–75–75,* FAX *596/75–69–70. 113 rooms, 7 suites. Restaurant, bar, pool, exercise room, business services. AE, DC, MC, V. CP.*

$ 🏨 **Lafayette.** If you want cheap lodgings in the heart of town, this is one of the few decent options. Owner Simone Broussillon is a mine of information and a great help. Rooms are rather dark and old-fashioned, with heavy wood furnishings, teal linens, and floral curtains. All have TV and phone. ✉ *5 rue de la Liberté, Fort-de-France 97200,* ☎ *596/73–80–50 or 800/223–9815,* FAX *596/60–97–75. 24 rooms. Bar. AE, DC, V. CP.*

## Lamentin

$ 🏨 **Martinique Cottages.** These garden bungalows set in the countryside have kitchenettes, terraces, cable TV, and phones. La Plantation restaurant is a gathering spot for gourmets. It specializes in *nouvelle cuisine Creole,* with such inventive delicacies as yellow banana and foie gras mille-feuille. The beaches are a 15-minute drive away. The cottages are difficult to find; take advantage of the property's airport transfers. ✉ *Lamentin 97232,* ☎ *596/50–16–09,* FAX *596/50–26–83. 8 rooms. Restaurant, kitchenettes. AE, MC, V. EP.*

## La Trinité

$$ 🏨 **Baie du Galion.** This new hotel, a member of the Best Western chain, is on the lovely, wild Presqu'île du Caravelle (Caravelle Peninsula). The medium-size rooms are furnished in a charming Creole style, with polished dark-wood furnishings and bright fabrics. All have TV, phone, and balcony; 50 also have kitchenette. Hiking is good in the adjacent nature reserve. The beach, though on the Atlantic, is relatively good for swimming, and the enormous pool is a focal point for guests. ✉ *Anse Tartane 97220,* ☎ *596/58–65–30 or 800/223–9815,* FAX *596/58–25–76. 146 rooms. Restaurant, bar, air-conditioning, in-room safes, refrigerators, pool, tennis court. AE, MC, V. BP, MAP.*

$$ 🏨 **Saint Aubin.** This restored coral-color colonial house, with pretty gables and intricate gingerbread trim, is in the countryside above the Atlantic coast. Each modern, if musty, room has wicker furnishings, TV, phone, and private bath. Those on the top floor are larger and ideal for families; five second-floor rooms open onto a shared balcony with sweeping views of the sea. This is a peaceful retreat, and only 3 mi from La Trinité, 2 mi from the Spoutourne sports center and the beaches on the Caravelle Peninsula. The inn's restaurant serves estimable Creole fare. Owner Guy Foret is an engaging host. ✉ *Box 52, La Trinité 97220,* ☎ *596/69–34–77 or 800/223–9815; 212/840–6636 in NY; 800/468–0023 in Canada;* FAX *596/69–41–14. 15 rooms. Restaurant, bar, air-conditioning, pool. AE, DC, MC, V. CP.*

## Le Diamant

$$$$ 🏨 **Diamant-Novotel.** This self-contained resort occupies half an island in an ideal windsurfing location. Just beyond the registration area, a footbridge spans a large pool on the way to the spacious guest rooms, each of which has a small balcony facing either the sea or the pool. Furnishings are cane and wicker painted pastel peach and green. The dining room is large and unromantic, set up to accommodate groups, but there is a pleasant terrace bar where a local band plays. A smaller, more formal restaurant is open during peak season. The four beaches on the 5-acre property are small. Children under 16 stay free with their parents. The staff speaks English and maintains a surprising level of enthusiasm and efficiency, given the hotel's size and the large number of tour groups. ✉ *Le Diamant 97223,* ☎ *596/76–42–42 or*

*800/322–2223,* FAX *596/76–22–87. 180 rooms. 2 restaurants, 3 bars, air-conditioning, pool, beauty salon, 2 tennis courts, 4 beaches, dive shop, water sports, shops, car rental. AE, DC, MC, V. CP, MAP.*

$$ **Diamant Les Bains.** For the last 30 years Hubert Andrieu and his
★ wife, Marie-Yvonne, have been doing everything they can to make people feel at home at this intimate, beachfront property. Andrieu, who trained locally and in Canada, is the chef, turning out fine, Creole dishes for the excellent, on-site restaurant. Marie-Yvonne manages the staff and the office. A few rooms are in the main house, above the restaurant, but most are in pretty, whitewashed chalets surrounded by flowers and palm trees. The tile floors, cheerfully painted furniture, and white ceilings, together with the light breeze that always plays off the ocean, gives them the feeling of an old-fashioned, seaside hotel. The beach is a few yards away, and there is a (small) pool in the center of the property. For those who just want to rest and relax, this quiet, pretty hotel is the perfect spot—although you will need to speak some French to feel truly at home. ⊠ *Le Diamant 97223,* ☎ *596/76–40–14 or 800/223–9815; 212/251–1800 in NY; 800/468–0023 in Canada;* FAX *596/76–27–00. 24 rooms. Restaurant, bar, air-conditioning, refrigerators, pool, water sports. MC, V. CP, MAP. Closed Sept.*

$$ **Le Marine.** Mini-apartments—one room with bed, kitchenette, and balcony—are in rows of pristine stucco buildings that progress down the hillside to the beach. The rooms are painted in mint, aqua, and periwinkle and decorated with bright abstract prints. The main building, which contains the restaurant, front desk, boutique, and flower shop, is 100 ft above the beach, and the pool is at the bottom of the hill, just above the beach. Guests can also use the water-sports equipment at Diamant-Novotel (☞ *above*) free of charge. The hotel caters to French families on tour packages, and the high turnover and large-group clientele contribute to the wear and tear on facilities, although management works hard at maintenance. ⊠ *Pointe de la Chery, Le Diamant 97233,* ☎ *596/76–46–00 or 800/221–4542,* FAX *596/76–25–99. 149 rooms. Restaurant, 2 bars, kitchenettes, 2 pools, 2 tennis courts, dive shop, fishing, shop. AE, DC, MC, V. CP, MAP.*

$$ **Relais Caraïbes.** Of all the hotels on Martinique, this one comes clos-
★ est to having the individuality and authenticity of a country inn, as well as good food and attractive accommodations. A note of immediate chic is struck in the thatched public rooms, awash in interior gardens, white wicker furnishings, and antiques ranging from bronze Indian elephants to African masks, culled from the world travels of owner Monsieur Senez. Twelve bungalows, decorated in a similar eclectic style, are spread over the manicured grounds with views of the sea and Diamond Rock. Each has a bedroom, a small salon with a sofa bed, a kitchenette, and a bathroom. There are also three standard rooms in the main house, which have unusual touches like hand-painted headboards. The pool is perched at the edge of a cliff that drops to the sea, and there's scuba instruction. The hotel is a mile off the main road, and you need a car to get around. The beach, however, is a short walk away. ⊠ *Pointe de la Chery, Le Diamant 97223,* ☎ *596/76–44–65 or 800/223–9815,* FAX *596/76–21–20. 15 rooms. Restaurant, bar, kitchenettes, pool, scuba diving, boating. AE, MC, V. CP, MAP.*

## Le François

$$$ **Fregate Bleue.** This is another of Martinique's distinctive inns. The
★ owner, Madame Yveline de Lucy de Fossarieu, left the management of Leyritz Plantation because she wanted the quiet life. In 1991 she opened the Fregate Bleue, an eight-room bed-and-breakfast. The hotel is a member of a French association called Les Relais du Silence, whose primary criterion is that the hotel be quiet. The house itself is capti-

vating, filled with light, plants, trompe l'oeil paintings, and hand-carved parrots. The rooms are delightful, their spaciousness accentuated by off-white furnishings, patterned carpets, and the occasional antique. Each also has a balcony, most of which overlook Les Ilets de l'Impératrice. All rooms have a small kitchenette and a modern bathroom with such niceties as bathrobes. Madame de Lucy serves *le petit déjeuner* (breakfast) on the upstairs veranda, and dinner, when requested. The nearest restaurants are a 10-minute drive away, and you must negotiate a rutted road to get to the highway. The Fregate Bleue's pool is small, but the beaches of Le François and Le Vauclin are five minutes away. ⊠ *Le François 97240 (5 mi south of Le François on Vauclin Rd.)*, ☎ *596/54–54–66 or 800/633–7411*, FAX *596/54–78–48. 7 rooms. Kitchenettes, pool. AE, MC, V. BP.*

**$** 🏨 **La Riviera.** Three pretty whitewashed buildings with red tile roofs overlook Le François Bay and do indeed look as if they were transported straight from St. Tropez. All rooms have a balcony opening onto breathtaking water views. Decor is contemporary and fresh, mostly in floral patterns. Owner-manager Marie-Anne Prian and her husband, Jacques, speak English and are most helpful. The restaurant serves marvelous Continental-tinged Creole cuisine; try the blaff of sea urchins or the omelet flamed with aged rum. A long private pier makes La Riviera popular with yachties. ⊠ *Rte. du Club Nautique, Le François 97240*, ☎ *596/54–68–54*, FAX *596/54–30–43. 14 rooms. Restaurant, bar, air-conditioning, minibars, boating. AE, MC, V. CP, MAP.*

## Les Trois-Ilets

**$$$$** 🏨 **Le Bakoua.** It's a sure sign that a hotel is going down-market when it sells rooms at reduced rates to airline crews: Le Bakoua is full of flight attendants and pilots from Corsair, a private French airline. Accommodations are in three hillside buildings and a fourth on the man-made white-sand beach. The decor is cushy-cum-rustic, with polished hardwood furnishings, frilly floral linens, and white tile floors. All rooms have a balcony or patio; bathroom with hand-painted tiles, marble vanity, and hair dryer; and the usual deluxe amenities. But at $275 a night (higher if you're on the beach), that's what you would expect. The beach is small and tends to get overrun with the ubiquitous *vendeuses de plage*, who try to sell you everything from skimpy bikinis to day-trips on a catamaran. The pool is above the beach, and the water flows over one side, giving the impression that the pool is part of the ocean. Entertainment consists of live music and shows nightly, including dancing, limbo, and Friday-night performances of Les Grands Ballets de la Martinique. ⊠ *Box 589, Fort-de-France 97200*, ☎ *596/66–02–02 or 800/221–4542; 0171/730–7144 in the U.K.;* FAX *596/66–00–41. 140 rooms, including 2 1-bedroom suites. 2 restaurants, bar, air-conditioning, minibars, pool, beauty salon, 2 tennis courts, beach, water sports, shop. AE, DC, MC, V. CP, MAP.*

**$$$$** 🏨 **Le Méridien Trois-Ilets.** There is a great deal of activity here, even in the low season, much of it revolving around the always-congested pool and man-made beach. Unfortunately, the hotel has aged. Despite sporadic redecorations, the boxy, oddly configured rooms, done in blond woods and floral fabrics, remain patchworked with repairs. They are air-conditioned and have wall-to-wall carpeting, built-in hair dryers and TVs. Some have balconies with a splendid view of the bay and of Fort-de-France. La Case Créole offers some of the better hotel dining on the island. The staff speaks excellent English, the atmosphere is the island's most convivial, and there's live entertainment nightly. ⊠ *Trois-Ilets 97229*, ☎ *596/66–00–00 or 800/543–4300; 212/245–2920 in NY;* FAX *596/66–00–74. 295 rooms, 2 luxury suites, 4 1-bedroom* suites. *2 restaurants, bar, air-conditioning, minibars, pool, 2 tennis courts, water sports, casino, car rental. AE, DC, MC, V. BP, MAP.*

**$$$**  ☎ **Novotel Carayou.** Part of the giant Accord group, this property has been extensively renovated and is now one of the snappier hotels on the island. The three-story, apartment-style buildings are not the most beautiful, but with their white, blue, and yellow trim they are cheerful and extremely clean. Each has white tile floors and blue fabrics, as well as spacious bathrooms. The main restaurant, where guests are served breakfast, is up a flight of steps on a terrace built over the water, with views of Fort-de-France. The Café Creole, at the somewhat cramped beach, also serves light meals. For those seeking a busy, action-packed vacation, the hotel offers a plethora of activities, from tennis (one rather poor court) to windsurfing, waterskiing, sailing, and paragliding, though not all of these are included in the base rate. Up to two children (under age 16) can stay free, and for 150F per day the Club Ti-Pirate will take them off your hands. The service here is somewhat languid, the clientele mostly package-tour groups from France. ⊠ *Trois-Ilets 97229,* ☎ *596/66–04–04 or 800/322–2223,* ₣ₐₓ *596/66–00–57. 200 rooms, 1 suite. Restaurant, bar, pool, tennis court, windsurfing, boating, waterskiing, shop. AE, MC, V. CP.*

**$$**  ☎ **La Pagerie.** La Pagerie looks as if it were plucked out of the Côte d'Azur and planted near the marina in Pointe du Bout. The hotel has small air-conditioned rooms and studios, all with bath and trim little balcony, and some with kitchenette. The decor is handsome throughout, with dark-wood furnishings, planters, and lace curtains, but in recent years the property has become slightly run down. Although the hotel has no beach or water-sports activities, it is within a short stroll of the resort hotels, restaurants, and activity. Lunch and dinner are served alfresco by the pool. The lively, cheerful atmosphere has made it a favorite evening watering hole of local expatriates and the sailing crowd. ⊠ *Pointe du Bout 97229,* ☎ *596/66–05–30; 800/221–4542 for U.S. reservations; 212/757–6500 in NY;* ₣ₐₓ *596/66–00–99. 98 rooms. Restaurant, bar, air-conditioning, pool. AE, MC, V. EP, MAP.*

**$**  ☎ **Rivage Hotel.** You get good value for your money at Maryelle and Jean Claude Riveti's small hotel. The place does have the air of a motor inn circa the Eisenhower years, but it's immaculately maintained, and the studios give you much more room than neighboring hotels at about a third of the cost. Each garden-view unit has a private bath and either a kitchenette (not always as clean as the rest of the property) or a mini-refrigerator. Breakfast and light meals are served in the friendly, informal snack bar. You should have no difficulty communicating: English, Spanish, and French are spoken. The beach is right across the road. ⊠ *Anse-Mitan 97229,* ☎ *596/66–00–53,* ₣ₐₓ *596/66–06–56. 17 rooms. Snack bar, air-conditioning, pool, beach, car rental. MC, V. EP.*

## Marigot

**$$$$**  ☎ **Habitation Lagrange.** It's worth flying to Martinique just to come
**★**      here. Nowhere else on the island do you feel the style and elegance of the old plantation-house society more than in this 19th-century manor house, set in a lush, fertile valley on the northeast coast. Everything— from the Staffordshire "Unicorn" tableware in the dining room to the antique shaving mirrors and Hermès toiletries in the bathrooms—is done with impeccable taste. When the sun goes down, you'll find yourself in one of the most romantic properties in the Caribbean. A huge entrance hall, hung with murals depicting Martinique's history, opens onto a bar and a small library where guests can browse or play solitaire or backgammon. Accommodations are in three different buildings. Rooms in the main building have four-poster beds, mahogany floors, beautiful linens, and tall French windows opening onto a wraparound

veranda. In the "Ecurie," which once served as the stables, are an additional three rooms. The original stone walls have been incorporated into the decor; parquet floors, huge windows, and canopy beds complete the picture. A pink-and-white, Creole-style building houses 12 rooms with gabled ceilings, furnished with mahogany armoires and wicker chaise longues and hung with chintz curtains. Superb gourmet food is served in the *ajouba*, a beautiful, wooden structure open to the night breeze. The wine list is one of the most extensive on the island. Giant ficus trees, a profusion of flowers, and a babbling brook make the grounds a delight to ramble around. ⊠ *Marigot 97225,* ☎ *596/53–60–60,* 𝖥𝖠𝖷 *596/53–50–58. 17 rooms, 1 suite. Dining room, bar, pool, tennis court, library. AE, DC, MC, V. BP, MAP. Closed Sept.–mid-Oct.*

## Schoelcher

$$$–$$$$
★ 🏨 **La Batelière Hotel.** On a flower-filled, 5-acre property north of Fort-de-France, this smart, resort hotel offers some of the island's largest rooms and by far its best tennis courts. It is extremely well run: Service is prompt, security intimidating (a veritable army of uniformed guards hovers about the main gate). Many rooms overlook the sea, and all have contemporary furniture, direct-dial phone, cable TV, radio, and private balcony or patio. The restaurant, where breakfast is served, is on an airy terrace with great views of the ocean. One level below that is the semicircular pool and pool bar. Below that, down a flight of steps, is a small beach sheltered from the waves by a breakwater. ⊠ *Schoelcher 97233,* ☎ *596/61–49–49 or 800/223–6510,* 𝖥𝖠𝖷 *596/61–62–29. 192 rooms, 5 duplexes, 2 suites. 2 restaurants, 2 bars, air-conditioning, pool, 6 tennis courts, water sports, shops, casino, dance club, meeting rooms. AE, DC, MC, V. CP, MAP.*

## Ste-Anne

$$$
🏨 **Anse Caritan.** This appealing property combines the amenities of a large hotel with the service and ambience of a more intimate one. It's nestled amid exquisite gardens fronting a ribbon of champagne-color sand. Management does its best to give the hotel an "island" feel. A large traditional fishing boat, or *gommier* sits next to the pool; and rooms, though nothing exceptional in soft colors like periwinkle, mauve, and gray, have unusual touches like hand-painted leaves and bamboo on the walls. Rooms have phones, safes, hair dryers, and a rough wood terrace or balcony, most with a sea view. The restaurant is known for its innovative Creole fare, and there's live music nightly. The staff is remarkably friendly and diligent. The Rasta gardener, for example, will pick herbs to soothe your sunburn, and the managers actually encourage guests' comments. ⊠ *Point des Salines, Ste-Anne 97227,* ☎ *596/76–74–12 or 800/322–2223,* 𝖥𝖠𝖷 *596/76–72–59. 96 rooms. Restaurant, bar, snack bar, air-conditioning, in-room safes, pool, water sports, dive shop, fishing, dance club. AE, MC, V. CP, MAP.*

$$$
★ 🏨 **Manoir de Beauregard.** Built in the early 18th century, this imposing plantation house was made into a hotel by the Saint-Cyr family in 1928. For more than 60 years it was one of the best small hotels in Martinique; then, tragically, in 1990, it was ravaged by fire. Now it has risen like the proverbial phoenix from the ashes. The main building, with its 2-ft-thick stone walls and mullioned windows, feels like a medieval abbey. Where the nave would be is a drawing room with bentwood rockers, chandeliers, and checkerboard marble floors. On either side of the drawing room are two "aisles" with sloping, beamed roofs; one serves as the bar, which leads out onto a sunny terrace and a small L-shape pool, while the other has been turned into a Creole dining room. The restaurant is across a small courtyard in a new, unattractive wooden building and serves such dishes as shrimp with green pepper sauce and other examples of *la nouvelle cuisine antillaise.*

Three bedrooms are upstairs in the main building. They have beamed ceilings, antique furniture, four-poster beds, and rich linens. Other rooms are in a modern annex at the other side of the property. Most are not very nice, but one is a gem: a circular tower room, with a four-poster bed, that was traditionally reserved for *les jeunes mariés* (honeymooners). All rooms have phones and TV. ⊠ *Chemin des Salines, Ste-Anne 97227,* ☎ *596/76–73–40,* FAX *596/76–93–24. 10 rooms. Restaurant, bar, air-conditioning, pool. AE, MC, V. CP.*

**$$–$$$** ⊞ **Club Med/Buccaneer's Creek.** Occupying 48 landscaped acres, Martinique's Club Med is an all-inclusive village with plazas, cafés, restaurants, a boutique, and a small marina. Air-conditioned pastel cottages contain twin beds and private shower bath. The only money you need spend here is for bar drinks, personal expenses, and excursions. There's a white-sand beach, a plethora of water sports, and plenty of nightlife. ⊠ *Pointe Marin 97180,* ☎ *596/76–72–72 or 800/258–2633; 212/750– 1670 in NY;* FAX *596/72–76–02. 300 rooms. 2 restaurants, 2 bars, air-conditioning, 7 tennis courts, fitness center, water sports, dance club, nightclub. AE, MC, V. All-inclusive (except drinks).*

# Dining

It used to be argued that Martinique had the best food in all the Caribbean, but many believe this top-ranking position has been lost to some of the other islands of the French West Indies—Guadeloupe, St. Barts, even St. Martin. Nevertheless, Martinique remains an island of restaurants serving classic French cuisine and Creole dishes, its wine cellars filled with fine French wines. Hotel restaurants are predictably good—consult the lodging listings for more recommendations—but some of the best restaurants are tucked away in the countryside, and therein lies a problem. The farther you venture from tourist hotels, the less likely you are to find English-speaking folk. But that shouldn't stop you from savoring the cuisine. The local Creole specialties are *colombo* (curry), *accras* (cod or vegetable fritters), *crabes farcis* (stuffed land crab), *écrevisses* (freshwater crayfish), *boudin* (Creole blood sausage), *lambi* (conch), *langouste* (clawless Caribbean lobster), *soudons* (sweet clams), *blaff* (fish or shellfish plunged into seasoned stock), and *oursin* (sea urchin). The favorite local libation is *'ti punch,* concocted of four parts white rum, one part sugarcane syrup (some people like a little more syrup), and a squeeze of lime.

Most restaurants offer a prix-fixe menu, often with several choices of entrées and wine. Finding a cheap, American-style bite at lunch is almost impossible. For additional savings, pick up a copy of the *Ti Gourmet* booklet at the tourist office and larger hotels; most of the restaurants listed offer a free drink or discount upon presentation.

## What to Wear

As in Guadeloupe, people dress for dinner in casual resort wear. Men don't wear jackets but do wear collared shirts. Women typically wear light cotton sundresses. Nice shorts are fine for lunch, but at dinnertime beach attire is too casual for most restaurants.

| CATEGORY | COST* |
|----------|-------|
| $$$ | over $50 |
| $$ | $30–$50 |
| $ | under $30 |

*per person for a three course meal, excluding drinks*

## Anse-d'Arlets

**$–$$** ✕ **Tamarin Plage Restaurant.** The lobster *vivier* (tank) in the middle of the room gives you a clue to the specialty here, but there are other recommendable offerings as well. Fish soup and Creole boudin are good starters; then consider court bouillon, crayfish fricassee, or octopus. The beachfront bar is a popular local hangout. ⊠ *Anse-d'Arlets,* ☎ *596/68–71–30. MC, V.*

$ ✕ **Bidjoul.** Many modest restaurants line the small side street that is actually Anse-d'Arlets's main drag. The street borders the water, and fishermen sail right up to the eateries with their latest catch. Bidjoul has a tiny dining room; opt for one of the tables set up under the canopy on the beach across the road. The salads (try the smoked salmon, or the *pêcheur,* with tuna, shrimp, crab, and rice) are huge, and the grilled fish as fresh as could be. So, too, is the fish at the neighboring restaurants, but the enthusiasm of Bidjoul's owner makes it stand out. It has become the popular gathering spot for watching the sun set into the Caribbean Sea. ⊠ *Anse-d'Arlets,* ☎ *596/68–65–28. Reservations not accepted. MC, V.*

## Basse-Pointe

$$–$$$ ✕ **Leyritz Plantation.** The pride of Martinique is *the* place all the cruise
★ passengers head to as soon as they disembark. The restored 18th-century plantation has exquisite stone walls, the ambience of a country inn, and a dramatic view of Mont Pelée. The menu is mostly Creole, featuring boudin, chicken with coconut, curried dishes, and steaks. ⊠ *Basse-Pointe,* ☎ *596/78–53–92. Reservations essential. MC, V.*

## Fort-de-France

$$$ ✕ **La Fontane.** Mango trees shade the wraparound veranda of this his-
★ toric, colonial-style house on the road to Balata, with distant views of Les Pitons de Carbet, a chain of volcanic hills, and Balata's wedding-cake cathedral. Inside you'll find Oriental rugs, fresh flowers, and a display of antiques that includes a handsome gramophone and a grandfather clock. Try *Le Bambou de la Fontane,* a salad of fish, tomato, corn, melon, and crayfish. Other options are cream soup with crab, lobster stewed with basil, *noisettes d'agneau* (medallions of lamb) with boletus mushrooms and mango, and the red snapper with lemon-lime sauce. For dessert, the *nuage de sorbet,* a medley of nine different homemade ice creams, is a treat. There is an excellent wine list, the espresso is not to be missed, and at 95F, the lunch menu is a bargain. ⊠ *Km 4, Rte. de Balata,* ☎ *596/64–28–70. Reservations essential. AE. Closed Sun.–Mon.*

$$ ✕ **Le Coq Hardi.** You'll need a road map to reach this bistro, which is at the bottom of a small one-way street. Once you are there, chef and patron Alphonse Sint-Ive, a genial butcher-turned-restaurateur, and ex-member of the French Foreign Legion, will help you choose your own steak and regale you with stories of his experiences in Vietnam. A specialty is the *coutancie* steak, a French version of Japanese Kobe steak. Cattle are fed exclusively on grain, plants, and beer, and the meat is flown in from Périgord. Tournedos Rossini (with artichoke hearts, foie gras, truffles, and Madeira sauce), *entrecôte bordelaise,* prime rib, and T-bone steaks are also on the menu. The decor (gruesome prints of cockfights) and red-blooded ambience make this an absolute no-no for animal lovers and vegetarians. ⊠ *Km 0.6, rue Martin Luther King,* ☎ *596/71–59–64. AE, MC, V. No lunch Wed. or Sat.*

$ ✕ **Le Marie Sainte.** Warm wood paneling, exposed beams, colorfully
★ tiled tables, and bright napery create a homey ambience in this wildly popular luncheon spot. It's worth waiting on the occasional line for the scrumptious *daube de poissons* (braised fish), crayfish, and banana beignets. ⊠ *160 rue Victor Hugo,* ☎ *596/70–00–30. AE, MC, V. Closed Sun. No dinner.*

$ ✕ **Le Second Soufflé.** This is heaven for vegetarians. The chef uses fresh
★ produce to make soufflés ranging from *aubergine* (eggplant) to *filet de*

*ti-nain* (small green bananas) with chocolate sauce. He also whips up such nonsoufflé items as eggplant ragout and okra quiche. The food echoes the famous Voltaire line painted on the wall: "Tu ne possèdes rien si tu ne digères pas bien" ("You have nothing if you don't have good digestion.") Even the decor pays tribute to the Martinican table, with colorful murals of fruits and vegetables. ⊠ *27 rue Blénac,* ☎ *596/ 63–44–11. No credit cards. Closed weekends.*

## Lamentin

**$$–$$$**     ✕ **Le Verger.** An orchard is the setting for this green-and-white coun-
★     try house not far from the airport. But you don't come for the locale— the food is the draw, and it's some of the very best on the island. Chef Bruno Hoang, who is also the owner's son, has years of experience in Paris under his belt, plus an insider's knowledge of local Creole traditions. He creates an oursin blaff that is justly renowned; to make it, you need 20 pounds of sea urchins (though it is only the eggs that are used); a rich broth of onion, spices, parsley, and white wine; and great patience. Pheasant, duck (try the perfect *magret* with green peppercorns), and other game are on the extensive menu. Classic French wines round out an excellent meal. Follow the signs for La Trinité; the entrance to the restaurant is on the right immediately after an Esso station. ⊠ *Pl. d'Armes,* ☎ *596/51–43–02. AE, DC, MC, V. Closed Sun.*

## Le Diamant

**$$$**     ✕ **Relais Caraïbes.** Parisian Jean Senez opened this individual bunga-
★     low colony *avec* restaurant and spends enough time in Paris to gather original objets d'art for decor and for sale. Lunch or dinner choices include spicy chicken Antilloise, a half lobster in two sauces, fish fillet in a basil sauce, and fricassee of country shrimp. The crisply decorated dining room, awash in fresh flowers, commands a clear view of Diamond Rock. ⊠ *Pointe de la Chery, Diamant,* ☎ *596/76–44–65. AE, MC, V. Closed Mon.*

**$$**     ✕ **L'Écrin Bleu.** The breathtaking views of the sea and St. Lucia would be reason enough to visit this terrace eatery, but you hardly need more incentive than is provided by the delectable and affordable seafood. Choose your own lobster or try the salmon tartare, sea bream in spiced beurre blanc, swordfish with saffron, or conch *en feuilleté* (in puff pastry). The gourmet menu (260F) includes crayfish in ginger or saffron sauce, half a grilled lobster, and John Dory in sweet pepper sauce. ⊠ *Rte. des Anse-d'Arlets,* ☎ *596/76–41–92. AE.*

**$–$$**     ✕ **Le Diam's.** With its brightly lit, open-sided dining room (the sea is only a few yards away), this is one of the most pleasant places to eat on Le Diamant's main street. Lemon-color walls, art naïf, and bright yellow tablecloths decorate the restaurant, which recently won first prize in a local gourmet competition. Judging by the mahimahi with sugarcane sauce, salmon in tarragon sauce, and spicy *gambas* (large prawns), it deserved to. For less demanding palates there are pizzas and pastas, as well as a good *menu enfant* (children's menu) for 40F. If you are staying in the Le Diamant area and don't have a car, they will even come fetch you and take you home—free. ⊠ *Pl. de l'Eglise,* ☎ *596/76– 23–28. AE, MC, V. Closed Tues. No lunch Wed.*

**$**     ✕ **Chez Christiane.** Don't be deceived by the seedy front bar (which
★     rocks during pool tournaments and free Friday rum tastings). The back dining room is delightful, with bamboo walls, fresh flowers, and local artist Roland Brival's imaginative paintings of local fauna (he adds texture with shards of green glass). The Creole cuisine is magnificent. The 70F menu might offer boudin, fried fish in caper sauce, and a *coupe glacée* (sundae). Other top choices are a smoky callaloo soup (here called *soupe verte aux crabes*), braised ray with ginger, and smoked chicken colombo. ⊠ *Rue Diamant,* ☎ *596/76–49–55. No credit cards.*

## Le François

$$$ ✕ **La Maison de l'Ilet Oscar.** To get to this Robinson Crusoe bistro under the palms you have to be fetched by fishing boat. The price of the boat trip is included in the two, fairly basic, seafood menus the restaurant offers. But it's the ambience that makes this place unusual. The Creole house was won by the present proprietor, who also owns Martinique's most upscale resort, Habitation Lagrange (☞ Lodging, *above*), in a poker game. Tables are laid out under palm trees at the water's edge. And before lunch, you will probably be taken to La Beignoir de Joséphine, a gorgeous, shallow pool with emerald-color water and white sand, where according to legend, Napoléon's ill-fated wife would swim. After your dip, you'll even get a glass of 'ti punch and some *accras* served to you as you stand in the water. ✉ *Le François 97240,* ☎ *596/53–60–60. Reservations essential. AE, MC, V.*

## Les Trois-Ilets

$$ ✕ **La Villa Creole.** The food at this fine bistro, now in its 17th year, is
★ superb; however, the real draw here is owner Guy Bruère-Dawson, a popular singer and guitarist who entertains during dinner. The setting is romantic, with tables laid out around two sides of a lush garden, and there is always an animated crowd. For starters, try the *salade de poisson cru mariné,* a Tahitian version of sushi, and for the main course, *Le Filet de St-Pierre et Z'Habitants,* a medley of local fish and crayfish. The café Creole, coffee laced with aged rum and chantilly, is delicious. ✉ *Anse-Mitan,* ☎ *596/66–05–53. Reservations essential. AE, DC, V. Closed Sun. No lunch Mon.*

$ ✕ **Au Poisson d'Or.** This typical Creole restaurant offers several excellent set menus. You might choose seafood callaloo, fried conch or sea urchin, or scallops sautéed in white wine. The decor is attractive: bamboo walls, straw thatching, madras napery, a veritable jungle of potted plants, and clever paintings of seafood. The only drawback is its position on the "wrong side" of the road, away from the beach. Choose a table in the front area of the terrace to benefit from any passing breezes. ✉ *Anse Mitan,* ☎ *596/66–01–80. Reservations not accepted. AE, MC. Closed Mon.*

$ ✕ **La Marina.** Beckoning red-and-white awnings and colorful murals give this breezy terrace a cheerful atmosphere. Views are of the yachts cruising in and out of their berths. Top choices include seafood risotto and lambi fricassee. Tasty pizzas and salads are the best budget options. ✉ *Pointe du Bout,* ☎ *596/66–02–32. AE, MC, V.*

$ ✕ **Les Passages du Vent.** This new bistro, housed in a pretty brick building on the main street of the village of Trois-Islets, opened in 1996. Inside, art naïf, shuttered windows, and a wooden ceiling and floors give the place a warm character. A terrace at the back offers an alfresco option. The menu is simple—grills, chicken, pizza, and seafood—but the young crowd that comes here is lively, and there is jazz and blues on Saturdays. ✉ *27 rue de l'Impératrice Joséphine, Trois-Islets,* ☎ *596/68–42–11. MC, V. Closed Mon.*

## Macouba

$–$$ ✕ **Pointe-Nord.** If you are driving around the northern end of the island, this new restaurant is one of the few watering holes in the area. Built among the ruins of the Perpigna rum distillery, with fine views of Dominica in the distance, it serves lunch seven days a week. Seafood is the specialty here; try the poached thazar, a local fish, marinated with red beans, onions, and tomatoes. It's busy on the weekend, so be sure you make a reservation. ✉ *Road to Grande-Rivière, Macouba,* ☎ *596/78–56–56. MC, V.*

## Morne-des-Esses

$$ ★ **✕ Le Colibri.** Jules Palladino, a large, gregarious man who clearly loves his food, is continuing a family culinary tradition with this little spot on the northeastern reaches of the island. Dishes—such as *tarte aux lambis,* a quiche made with conch paste, and *buisson d'écrevisses,* a pyramid of six giant freshwater crayfish decorated with flowers and accompanied by a tangy tomato sauce flavored with thyme, scallions, and tiny bits of crayfish—involve many hours of hard work in the kitchen. Some of the traditional Creole dishes, like stuffed pigeon and *cochon au lait* (suckling pig), are on offer here. There is an excellent wine list. The view, across the ocean, is spectacular. If you're lucky, you'll even get a rainbow. ⊠ *Morne-des-Esses,* ☎ *596/69–91–95. AE, MC, V. Closed Mon. off-season.*

## Ste-Anne

$$$ **✕ Aux Filets Bleus.** In addition to dining at this open-air eatery on the beach, you can go for a swim and dance to live music on top of the underground lobster tank. The cheerful decor takes its cue from the surrounding waters, rippling in various shades of blue from azure to teal. Be sure to check out the astonishing, angry mural outside the restaurant, all upraised fists and Picasso-esque profiles (à la *Guernica*). Fish soup, stuffed crab, and avocado vinaigrette are all good opening bids. In addition to an assortment of lobster entrées, there is grilled or steamed fish and octopus with red beans and rice. Prices are slightly above what you'd expect for basically straightforward cooking and beachfront ambience. ⊠ *Pointe Marin,* ☎ *596/76–73–42. AE, MC.*

$–$$ **✕ La Dunette.** Dinner at this restaurant, in the small Ste-Anne hotel of the same name, is served on a plant-hung terrace overlooking the sea. Wrought-iron chairs and tables and bright blue awnings add to the refreshing garden atmosphere. Your choices for lunch or dinner include fish soup, grilled fish or lobster, snapper stuffed with sea urchin, conch fricassee, and several colombos and tandooris. There is a piano bar in the evening, and waterskiing is offered after lunch for those who scoff at digestion. ⊠ *Ste-Anne,* ☎ *596/76–73–90. MC, V.*

$–$$ **✕ Poï et Virginie.** Facing the jetty in the center of Ste-Anne is this popular restaurant with bamboo walls, bright art naïf, ceiling fans, and colorful, fresh-cut flowers. It's had the honor of winning the *Clé d'Or Gault Millau* culinary award. The menu is extensive—from meats to fish—but the specialty is the lobster and crab salad. Other noteworthy dishes are lemon chicken in coconut milk, tuna with green peppers, and crayfish in saffron. Lunchtime is busy, especially on weekends; get here soon after noon if you want a table facing the bay, with views of St. Lucia in the distance. ⊠ *Rue de Bord de Mer, Ste-Anne,* ☎ *596/76–72–22. AE, DC, MC, V. Closed Mon. No lunch Tues.*

## Ste-Luce

$$ **✕ La Petite Auberge.** *Filet de poisson aux champignons* (fish cooked with mushrooms), conch flamed in aged rum, or *magret à la mangue* (duck breast with mango) are just some of the specialties here. Two *viviers,* one for lobster, the other for *Z'Habitants* (the local name for crayfish), ensure these options are fresh. The inn also has 12 guest rooms—all with rustic decor, air-conditioning, balcony, and mini-refrigerator—for an unbeatable 330F a night. ⊠ *Plage du Gros Raisins, Ste-Luce,* ☎ *596/62–59–70. AE, MC, V.*

## St-Pierre

$$ ★ **✕ Le Fromager.** This beautiful restaurant is perched high above St-Pierre, with smashing views of the town's red roofs and the sea beyond from the breezy terrace. Dining inside is also pleasant, thanks to the gleaming ecru tile floors, white wicker, polished hardwood furnishings, lace

tablecloths, old rum barrels, and potted plants. Superlative choices include crayfish colombo, marinated octopus, and duck fillet with pineapple. You may also opt for the 100F chef's choice menu, which might include avocado vinaigrette and sole sauce *pêcheur* (in a Creole sauce), as well as fruit or crème caramel. ⊠ *On road toward Fond St-Denis,* ☎ *596/78–19–07. AE, DC, MC, V.*

$ ✕ **La Factorérie.** The food is appealing and the views sweeping at this open-air restaurant alongside the ruins of the Eglise du Fort. Fresh vegetables from the nearby agricultural training school accompany grilled langouste, grilled chicken in a piquant Creole sauce, and the fresh catch of the day. This is a convenient spot to have lunch when visiting St-Pierre, but it is not worth a special trip. ⊠ *Quartier Fort, St-Pierre,* ☎ *596/78–12–53. Reservations essential. AE, MC, V.*

### Trinité

$$ ✕ **Le Vieux Galion.** This seaside restaurant plays up the nautical theme, with a huge aquarium and murals of old sailing ships complementing fantastic Atlantic views. The crashing surf serenades diners on the terrace. Owner Jean-Pierre Maur does wonders with seafood. Especially memorable are grouper rouged with peppers, Tahitian *poisson cru* (marinated raw fish), and conch *à l'armoricaine* (with tomato, garlic, crème fraîche, and cognac). ⊠ *Rte. du Tartane, Anse Bellune,* ☎ *596/58–20–58. AE, MC, V. Closed Wed.*

# Beaches

All of Martinique's beaches are open to the public, but hotels charge a fee for nonguests to use changing rooms and facilities. There are no official nudist beaches, but topless bathing is prevalent. Unless you're an expert swimmer, steer clear of the Atlantic waters, except in the area of Cap Chevalier and the Caravelle Peninsula. The soft, white-sand beaches are south of Fort-de-France; to the north the beaches are hard-packed gray volcanic sand. Some of the most pleasant beaches are around Ste-Anne and Ste-Luce.

**Anse-à-l'Ane** beach has picnic tables and a nearby shell museum. Cool off in the bar of the Le Calalou hotel. **Anse-Mitan** has golden sand and offers excellent snorkeling. Small, family-owned bistros are half hidden among palm trees nearby. **Anse-Trabaud** is on the Atlantic side, across the southern tip of the island from Ste-Anne. There is nothing here but white sand and the sea. **Diamant,** the island's longest beach (2½ mi), has a splendid view of Diamond Rock, but the waters are sometimes rough and the currents are strong. **Pointe du Bout** beaches are man-made and lined with luxury resorts, among them the Méridien and the Bakoua, but they tend to be rather small. **Pointe Marin** stretches north from Ste-Anne. A good windsurfing and waterskiing spot, it also has restaurants, campsites, sanitary facilities, and a 10F charge. Club Med occupies the northern edge. **Les Salines** is a 1½-mi cove of soft white sand lined with coconut palms. A short drive south of Ste-Anne, Les Salines is awash with families and children during holidays and on weekends but quiet and uncrowded during the week—even at the height of the winter season. This beach, especially the far end, is the most peaceful and beautiful.

# Outdoor Activities and Sports

### Bicycling

The **Parc Naturel Régional de la Martinique** (☎ 596/73–19–30) has designed biking itineraries off the beaten track. Mountain biking is popular in mainland France, and now it has reached Martinique. VTT (Vélo Tout Terrain) bikes specially designed with 18 speeds to handle all terrains may be rented from **V.T.Tilt** (⊠ Trois-Islets, ☎ 596/66–01–01). It also does some fun day tours, which include lunch.

## Boating

For boat rentals and yacht charters, check with **Stardust** (⊠ Port de Plaisance du Marin, ☎ 596/74–98–17; 909/678–2250 or 800/227–5317 in the U.S.), **Caraïbes Evasion** (⊠ Pointe du Bout marina, ☎ 596/66–02–85), **Moorings Antilles Françaises** (⊠ Port de Plaisance du Marin, ☎ 596/74–75–39), **Star Voyages** (⊠ Pointe du Bout marina, ☎ 596/68–16–75), and **Tropic Yachting** (⊠ Pointe du Bout marina, ☎ 596/66–03–85).

## Deep-Sea Fishing

Fish cruising these waters include tuna, barracuda, dolphinfish, kingfish, and bonito. For a day's outing on the 37-ft *Egg Harbor,* with gear and breakfast included, contact **Bathy's Club** (⊠ Méridien, ☎ 596/66–00–00). Charters of up to five days can be arranged on Captain Réné Alaric's 37-ft *Rayon Vert* (⊠ Auberge du Vare, Case-Pilote, ☎ 596/78–80–56). **Bleu Marine Evasion** (⊠ Le Diamant, ☎ 596/76–46–00) also offers excursions.

## Golf

At **Golf de l'Impératrice Joséphine** (⊠ Trois-Ilets, ☎ 596/68–32–81) there is a par-71, 18-hole Robert Trent Jones course with an English-speaking pro, fully equipped pro shop, a bar, and restaurant. A mile from the Pointe du Bout resort area and 18 mi from Fort-de-France, the club offers special greens fees for hotel guests and cruise-ship passengers. Normal greens fees are $40. An electric cart costs another $40.

## Hiking

Inexpensive guided excursions are organized year-round by the **Parc Naturel Régional de la Martinique** (⊠ 9 blvd. Général de Gaulle, Fort-de-France, ☎ 596/73–19–30).

## Horseback Riding

Excursions and lessons are available at the **Black Horse Ranch** (⊠ Near La Pagerie in Trois-Ilets, ☎ 596/68–37–80), **La Cavale** (⊠ Near Diamant on road to Novotel hotel, ☎ 596/76–20–23), **Ranch Jack** (⊠ Near Anse-d'Arlets, ☎ 596/68–37–69), and **Ranch Val d'Or** (⊠ Ste-Anne, ☎ 596/66–03–46).

## Sailing

Hobie Cats, Sunfish, and Sailfish can be rented by the hour from hotel beach shacks. Also check **Stardust** (⊠ Port de Plaisance du Marin, ☎ 596/74–98–17; 909/678–2250 or 800/227–5317 in the U.S.), **Soleil et Voile** (⊠ Le François, ☎ 596/66–09–14), **Club Nautique du Marin** (⊠ Le François, ☎ 596/74–92–48), and **Alphamar** (⊠ Trois-Ilets, ☎ 596/66–00–89).

## Scuba Diving

To explore the old shipwrecks, coral gardens, and other undersea sites, you must have a medical certificate and insurance papers. Among the island's dive operators are **Méridien Plongée** (⊠ Méridien, ☎ 596/66–00–00), **Plongée Passion** (⊠ Anses d'Arlets, ☎ 596/76–27–39), **Marine Hotel** (⊠ Le Diamant, ☎ 596/76–46–00), **Okeonos Club** (⊠ Le Diamant, ☎ 596/76–21–76), **Planete Bleue** (⊠ La Marina, Trois-Ilets, ☎ 596/66–08–79), and **Sub Diamond Rock** (⊠ Novotel, ☎ 596/76–42–42).

## Sea Excursions and Snorkeling

The glass-bottom boat *Seaquarium* (⊠ Trois-Islets, ☎ 596/66–05–50) and the semisubmersible *Aquascope* (⊠ Pointe du Bout marina, ☎ 596/68–36–09; ⊠ Ste-Anne, ☎ 596/74–87–41) conduct 45- to

60-minute excursions. For information on other sailing, swimming, snorkeling, and beach picnic trips, contact **Affaires Maritimes** (☎ 596/ 71–90–05).

### Sports Center
The **Anse-Spoutourne** (☎ 596/73–19–30), on the Caravelle Peninsula, is an open-air sports and leisure center offering sailing, tennis, and other activities.

### Tennis and Squash
In addition to its links, the **Golf de l'Impératrice Joséphine** (✉ Trois-Ilets, ☎ 596/68–32–81) has three lighted tennis courts. There are also two courts at **Le Bakoua** (☎ 596/66–02–02), six excellent courts at **La Batelière Hotel** (☎ 596/61–64–52), seven courts (six lighted) at **Club Med/Buccaneer's Creek** (☎ 596/76–74–52), two courts at **Diamant-Novotel** (☎ 596/76–42–42), one court at the **Leyritz Plantation** (☎ 596/78–53–92), and two courts at **Le Méridien Trois-Ilets** (☎ 596/66–00–00). Several other hotels have tennis courts that are available to nonguests when empty, including the **Primerêve Hotel** (☎ 596/69–40–40), **Anchorage Hotel** (☎ 596/76–92–32), and **Le Marine** (☎ 596/76–46–00). For additional information about tennis on the island, contact **La Ligue Régionale de Tennis** (✉ Petit Manoir, Lamentin, ☎ 596/51–08–00). An hour's court time averages 50F for nonguests. There are also three squash courts at the modern, aptly named **Squash Hotel** (✉ 3 blvd. de la Marine, ☎ 596/63–00–34), just outside Fort-de-France.

## Shopping

French fragrances and designer scarves, fine china and crystal, leather goods, and liquors and liqueurs are all good buys in Fort-de-France. Purchases are further sweetened by the 20% discount on luxury items when paid for by traveler's checks or certain major credit cards. Among local items, look for Creole gold jewelry, such as loop earrings, heavy bead necklaces, and slave bracelets; white and dark rum; and hand-crafted straw goods, pottery, and tapestries. In addition, U.S. customs allows you to bring some of the local flora into the country; ask when purchasing the flowers.

### Shopping Areas
The area around the cathedral in Fort-de-France has a number of small shops carrying luxury items. Of particular note are the shops on rue Victor Hugo, rue Moreau de Jones, rue Antoine Siger, and rue Lamartine. There's a Galleries Lafayette department store in downtown Fort-de-France, which sells everything from perfume to crockery. On the outskirts of Fort-de-France, shopping malls include Centre Commercial de Cluny, Centre Commercial de Dillon, Centre Commercial de Bellevue, and more than 100 boutiques at La Galleria in Le Lamentin.

### Good Buys
CHINA AND CRYSTAL
**Cadet Daniel** (✉ 72 rue Antoine Siger, Fort-de-France, ☎ 596/71–41–48) sells Lalique, Limoges, and Baccarat. **Roger Albert** (✉ 7 rue Victor Hugo, Fort-de-France, ☎ 596/71–71–71) carries crystal from all the major designers.

FLOWERS
**MacIntosh** (✉ 31 rue Victor Hugo, Fort-de-France, ☎ 596/70–09–50; ✉ Airport, ☎ 596/51–51–51) packages anthuriums, torch lilies, and lobster claws for shipment. **Les Petites Floralies** (✉ 75 rue Blénac, Fort-de-France, ☎ 596/71–66–16) has a wide selection of flowers and plants. Note: Some items may not clear U.S customs.

LOCAL HANDICRAFTS

Following the peeling roadside signs advertising *ateliers artisanales* (art studios) can yield unexpected treasures, many of them reasonably priced.

**Art et Nature** (⊠ Ste-Luce, ☎ 596/62–59–19) features Joel Gilbert's unique wood paintings, daubed with 20–30 shades of earth and sand. **Atelier Ceramique** (⊠ Just outside Le Diamant, ☎ 596/76–42–65) displays the crafts of owners and talented artists David and Jeannine England, who have lived in the Caribbean for more than a decade and are members of the small British expatriate community on the island. Whether or not you like their products—ceramics, paintings, and miscellaneous souvenirs—it's a rare chance to brush up on your English. **Galerie Arti-Bijoux** (⊠ 89 rue Victor Hugo, Fort-de-France, ☎ 596/63–10–62) has some unusual and excellent Haitian art—paintings, sculptures, ceramics, and intricate jewelry cases—at reasonable prices. **Centre des Métiers d'Art** (⊠ Rue Ernest Deproge, Fort-de-France, ☎ 596/70–25–01) exhibits authentic local arts and crafts. **L'Eclat de Verre** (⊠ Hwy. N4, outside Gros Morne, ☎ 596/58–34–03) specializes in all manner of glittering glasswork. **La Paille Caraibe** (⊠ Morne des Esses, 596/69–83–74) is where you can watch artisans at work at weaving straw baskets, mats, hats, and amphorae. **Artisanat & Poterie des Trois-Ilets** (⊠ Trois-Ilets, ☎ 596/68–18–01) allows you to watch the creation of pots, vases, and jars patterned after ancient Arawak and Carib traditions. **Victor Anicet** (⊠ Monésie, ☎ 596/68–25–42) fashions lovely ceramic masks and vases.

PERFUMES

**Airport minishops** sell the most popular scents at in-town prices, so there's no need to carry purchases around. **Roger Albert** (⊠ 7 rue Victor Hugo, Fort-de-France, ☎ 596/71–71–71) stocks such popular scents as Dior, Chanel, and Guerlain.

RUM

One of the best rums on the island is the Vieux Rhum from **JM distillery** (⊠ Macouba, ☎ 596/78–92–55). Rum can also be purchased at various other distilleries, including **Duquesnes** (⊠ Fort-de-France, ☎ 596/71–91–68), **St. James** (⊠ Ste-Marie, ☎ 596/69–30–02), **Clément** (⊠ Le François, ☎ 596/54–62–07), and **Trois Rivières** (⊠ Ste-Luce, ☎ 596/62–51–78).

# Nightlife and the Arts

The island is dotted with lively discos and nightclubs, but entertainment on Martinique is not confined to partying. Most leading hotels offer nightly entertainment in season, including the marvelous **Les Grand Ballets de Martinique,** one of the finest folkloric troupes in the Caribbean. In addition, many restaurants offer live combos, usually on weekends.

## Casinos

The **Casino Trois-Ilets** (⊠ Méridien, ☎ 596/66–00–30) is open from 9 PM to 3 AM Monday to Saturday. You must be at least 21 (with a picture ID) to enter, and there is a 70F admission charge (admission to slot-machine room is free). Try your hand at American and French roulette or blackjack.

## Discos

Your hotel or the tourist office can put you in touch with the current "in" places. It's also wise to check on opening and closing times and cover charges. For the most part, the discos draw a mixed crowd of locals and tourists, the young and the not-so-young. Some of the currently popular places are **L'Alibi** (⊠ Morne Tartenson, Fort-de-France, ☎ 596/63–45–15), **Le Manikou** (⊠ Zac de Rivière Roche, Fort-de-France, ☎ 596/50–96–99), **Le New Hippo** (⊠ 24 blvd. Allègre, Fort-de-France, ☎ 596/60–20–22), **Le Queen's** (⊠ La Batelière Hotel ☎ 596/61–49–49), and **Le Top** (⊠ Zone Artisanale, Trinité, ☎ 596/58–61–43).

## Jazz and Zouk

Currently the most popular music is zouk, which mixes Caribbean rhythm and an Occidental tempo with Creole words. Jacob Devarieux is the leading exponent of this style and is occasionally on the island. More likely, though, you will hear zouk music played by one of his followers at the hotels and clubs. Jazz musicians, like the music, tend to be informal and independent. They rarely hold regular gigs. The **Neptune** (⊠ Le Diamant, ☎ 596/76–25–47) is a hot spot for zouk. In season, you'll find one or two combos playing at clubs and hotels, but it is only at **Cocoloco** (⊠ Blvd. Alfassa, Fort-de-France, ☎ 596/63–63–77), next to the tourist office, that there are regular jazz sessions. For the last seven years Martinique has also hosted the Caribbean's premier **jazz festival.** It takes place in early December and, as well as showcasing the best of the islands, has attracted such top American performers as Branford Marsalis, Dizzy Gillespie, and Eddie Daniels.

## Other Music

**L'Amphore** (⊠ Behind Le Bakoua hotel, ☎ 596/66–03–09) is a late-night hangout with a popular piano bar. **Las Tapas** (⊠ 7 rue Garnier Pages, Fort-de-France, ☎ 596/63–71–23) presents flamenco or salsa and merengue bands. **La Villa Creole** (⊠ Anse-Mitan, ☎ 596/66–05–53) is a charming bistro whose owner, Guy Dawson, entertains nightly on the guitar—everything from Piaf to Sting, and some original ditties.

# Exploring Martinique

The north of the island will appeal to nature lovers, hikers, and mountain climbers. The drive from Fort-de-France to St-Pierre is impressive. The route across the island, via Morne Rouge, from the Caribbean to the Atlantic is spectacular. This is Martinique's wild side, a place of waterfalls, rain forest, and mountains. The highlight is Mont Pelée. The south is the more developed half of the island. This is where the resorts and restaurants are, as well as the casinos, shopping malls, and beaches.

*Numbers in the margin correspond to points of interest on the Martinique map.*

SIGHTS TO SEE

**⓫** **Ajoupa-Bouillon.** This flower-filled, 17th-century village in the midst of pineapple fields is the jumping-off point for two sights well worth visiting: the **Saut Babin,** a 40-ft-high waterfall, half an hour's walk from the village; and the **Gorges de la Falaise,** a river gorge where you can swim. **Les Ombrages** botanical gardens has marked trails through the rain forest. 🎫 *15F.* ☉ *Les Ombrages daily 8–4.*

**④** **Balata.** Two sights here are worth visiting: the **Balata Church,** an exact replica of Sacré-Coeur Basilica in Paris built in 1923 to commemorate those who died in World War I; and the **Jardin de Balata** (Balata Gardens). Jean-Philippe Thoze, a professional landscaper and devoted horticulturist, spent 20 years creating this collection of thousands of varieties of tropical flowers and plants. There are shaded benches where you can relax and take in the panoramic views of the mountains. ⊠ *Rte. de Balata,* ☎ *596/72–58–82.* 🎫 *30F.* ☉ *Daily 9–5.*

**⑩ Basse-Pointe.** Just south of this settlement on the Atlantic coast is a Hindu temple, one of the relics of the East Indians who settled in this area in the 19th century. The view of the eastern slope of Mont Pelée is lovely from here. But the highlight of Basse-Pointe is the estimable **Leyritz Plantation,** which has been a hotel for several years. When tour groups from the cruise ships are not swarming over the property, the rustic setting, complete with sugarcane factory and gardens, is delightful. Fans of the arcane can visit the plantation's **Musée de Poupées Végétales.** Where Rodin used marble, local artisan Will Fenton has used bananas, balisier (a tall grass), and other local plants to make dolls of famous French women—from Marie Antoinette to Madame Curie—all in extravagant period costumes. ⊠ *Musée de Poupées Végétales, Leyritz Plantation,* ☎ *596/78–53–92.* ⛶ *15F.* ☉ *Daily 9–5.*

**③ Bellefontaine.** This colorful fishing village has pastel houses on the hillsides and beautifully painted gommier canoes (fishing boats made from the gum tree) bobbing in the water. Look for the house built in the shape of a boat.

**⑬ Caravelle Peninsula.** Much of this peninsula, which thrusts 8 mi into the Atlantic Ocean, is under the auspices of the Regional Nature Reserve and offers places for trekking, swimming, and sailing. This is the home of **Anse-Spoutourne,** an open-air sports and leisure center operated by the nature reserve (☞ Outdoor Activities and Sports, *above*). Tartane has a popular beach with cool Atlantic breezes. The peninsula is also home to ☞ **Dubuc Castle.**

**⑲ Diamond Rock.** A mile offshore from the small, friendly village of Le Diamant is this volcanic mound. In 1804, during the squabbles over possession of the island between the French and the English, the latter commandeered the rock, armed it with cannons, christened it HMS *Diamond Rock,* and proceeded to use it as a warship. For almost a year and a half, the British held the rock, bombarding any French ships that came along. The French got wind of the fact that the British were getting cabin fever on their isolated ship-island and arranged a supply of barrels of rum for those on the rock. The French easily overpowered the inebriated sailors, ending one of the most curious engagements in naval history.

**NEED A BREAK?**    On the main drag of Le Diamant, with *les pieds dans l'eau* (its feet in the water), is **Pizza Pepe** (☎ 596/76–40–49). Here, you can order such creative pizzas as *océanique* (crab, onions, olives) and Ingrid (crème fraîche, salmon, olives). You can also get a plate of roast chicken or grilled shark.

**⑭ Dubuc Castle.** At the eastern tip of the ☞ **Caravelle Peninsula** are the ruins of this castle, once the home of the Dubuc de Rivery family, who owned the peninsula in the 18th century. According to legend, young Aimée Dubuc de Rivery was captured by Barbary pirates, sold to the Ottoman Empire, became a favorite of the sultan, and gave birth to Mahmud II.

**⑳ Forêt de Montravail.** A few miles north of ☞ **Ste-Luce,** this is one of the best places in the south of the island for a short hike through tropical forest. There is also an interesting group of Carib rock drawings.

**① Fort-de-France.** With its superb setting beneath the towering Pitons du Carbet on the Baie des Flamands, and its historic fort, Martinique's capital, home to about one-third of the island's 360,000 inhabitants, should be a grand place. It isn't. The most pleasant districts, like Bellevue and Schoelcher, are up on the hillside and require a car to get to.

The center of town is a warren of narrow streets (if you come by car you will find yourself sitting in endless gridlock). True, there are some good shops with Parisian wares (at Parisian prices) and lively street markets selling, among other things, human hair for wigs (starting price, 200F). But the heat, exhaust fumes, and litter tend to make exploring them a chore. At night, the city feels dark and gloomy, with little street life except for the extravagantly dressed *femmes de nuit* who openly parade the streets from 10 PM.

That said, there are interesting things to see here. The city's heart is **La Savane,** a 12½-acre landscaped park filled with tropical trees, fountains, and benches. It's a popular gathering place and the scene of promenades, parades, and impromptu soccer matches. Along the east side, there are numerous snack wagons selling everything from hot dogs and barbecued chicken to delicious fresh-squeezed juices. A statue of Pierre Belain d'Esnambuc, leader of the island's first settlers, is upstaged by Vital Dubray's flattering white Carrara marble statue of the empress Joséphine, Napoléon's first wife. Sculpted in a high-waisted Empire gown, Joséphine gazes toward Trois-Ilets across the bay, where in 1763 she was born Marie-Joseph Tascher de la Pagerie. The most imposing historic site is **Fort St-Louis,** which runs along the east side of La Savane. It is open Tuesday–Saturday 10–3 and is free. Near the harbor is a marketplace where local crafts and souvenirs are sold. Across from La Savane, you can catch the ferry *La Vedette* for the beaches at Anse-Mitan and Anse-à-l'Ane and for the 20-minute run across the bay to the resort hotels of Pointe du Bout. It's much faster than the journey round the bay by car and costs $5.

Rue de la Liberté runs along the west side of La Savane. At the corner of rue de la Liberté and rue Perrinon is the **Bibliothèque Schoelcher,** the wildly elaborate Byzantine-Egyptian-Romanesque–style public library. It was named after Victor Schoelcher, who led the fight to free the slaves in the French West Indies in the 19th century. The eye-popping structure was built for the 1889 Paris Exposition, after which it was dismantled, shipped to Martinique, and reassembled piece by ornate piece at its present location. ⊠ *Corner of rue de la Liberté and rue Perrinon,* ☎ *596/70–26–67.* ☉ *Mon., Tues., and Thurs. 8:30–12:30 and 2–6; Wed. and Fri. 8–1; Sat. 8:30–noon.*

At the southern end of rue de la Liberté is the **Musée Départementale de Martinique,** which contains exhibits on the pre-Columbian Arawak and Carib periods, including pottery, beads, and part of a skeleton that turned up during excavations in 1972. One exhibit examines the history of slavery; costumes, documents, furniture, and handicrafts from the island's colonial period are on display. ⊠ *9 rue de la Liberté,* ☎ *596/71–57–05.* ⊠ *15F.* ☉ *Weekdays 8:30–1 and 2:30–5, Sat. 9–noon.*

**Rue Victor Schoelcher** runs through the center of the capital's primary shopping district, a six-block area bounded by rue de la République, rue de la Liberté, rue de Victor Severe, and rue Victor Hugo. Stores feature Paris fashions (at Paris prices) and French perfume, china, crystal, and liqueurs, as well as local handicrafts. Also on rue Victor Schoelcher you'll find the Romanesque **St-Louis Cathedral,** the sixth to be built on the site (the others were destroyed by fire, hurricane, or earthquake). This one dates from 1878 and has lovely stained-glass windows. A number of Martinique's former governors are interred beneath the choir loft.

NEED A
BREAK?
**Couleur Café** (⊠ Corner of rue Victor Severe and rue Gallieni, ☎ 596/71–54–41) is a hip, open-sided hangout, with a bamboo ceiling, African tapestries, and roughly painted turquoise counter and chairs. It's

always jammed with gorgeous, impoverished young French people, who congregate to gossip, smoke, and scarf down fine salads, quiches, and *croque monsieurs* (open-faced ham and cheese sandwiches) every day from 10 AM to 2:30 PM.

The Galerie de Biologie et de Géologie at the **Parc Floral et Culturel,** in the northeastern corner of the city center, will acquaint you with the variety of exotic flora on this island. There's also an aquarium showing fish that can be found in these waters. The park contains the island's official cultural center, where there are sometimes free evening concerts. Wandering about the grounds, you'll run into musicians and artists, who may give you an impromptu lesson on playing the steel drum or working with driftwood. ⊠ *Pl. José-Marti, Sermac,* ☎ *596/71–66–25.* ☞ *Grounds free, aquarium 35F, Botanical and Geological Gallery 5F.* ☉ *Park daily dawn–10 PM; aquarium daily 9–7; gallery Tues.–Fri. 9:30–12:30 and 3:30–5:30, Sat. 9–1 and 3–5.*

The **Rivière Madame** meanders through the park and joins the bay at Pointe Simon. The river divides the downtown area from the ritzy residential district of Didier in the hills. Fronting the river, on avenue Paul Nardal, are the vibrantly noisy, messy, smelly vegetable and fish markets. One of the best shows in town occurs around 4 PM, when fishermen return with their catch, effortlessly tossing 100-pound bundles of rainbow-hued fish.

**⑯ Lamentin.** There is nothing pretty about Lamentin. The multibillion-franc airport, which opened in 1995, is the most notable landmark. The rest of the town is a sprawling industrial and commercial zone. There is one reason to stop here, though, and that is to gawk at the Caribbean's biggest, fanciest shopping malls: **Euromarché** and the brand-new **La Galleria,** a megamall housing 100 shops and boutiques where you can find everything from *pâté de foie gras* and Camembert to CDs and sunglasses.

**⑮ Le François.** A sizable city of some 16,000 inhabitants, this is the main city on the Atlantic coast. Sadly, the old wooden buildings are being replaced by concrete. But the classic West Indian cemetery, with its black-and-white tiles, is still here. The town's greatest attraction, however, is the **Habitation Clément.** This is Martinique's Williamsburg, complete with Creole ladies in traditional dresses dotted picturesquely around the grounds. Built with the wealth generated by its rum distillery, it is one of the finest plantation houses in the Caribbean. Lovingly preserved in its original 18th-century splendor, it offers a unique glimpse into the elegance and privilege of the old plantation-house society. French President Jacques Chirac visited. President Bush and François Mitterrand had a summit meeting here. Barbara Hendricks, the opera singer, loved it. The rum distillery is still operational and offers free tastings. The grounds contain a superb collection of historic trees. ⊠ *Habitation Clément,* ☎ *596/54–62–07.* ☉ *Daily 9–6.*

Le François is also noted for its snorkeling. Offshore are the privately owned **Les Ilets de l'Impératrice.** The islands received that name because, according to legend, this is where Empress Joséphine would come to bathe in shallow basins, known as *fond blancs* because of their white-sand bottoms. Group boat tours leave from the harbor ($30 per person includes lunch and drinks). You can also haggle with a fisherman to take you out for a while on his boat to indulge in the uniquely Martinican custom of standing waist-deep in warm water, sipping a 'ti punch, eating accras, and smoking. There is a fine bay 6 mi farther along the coast at **Le Robert,** though the town is somewhat lackluster.

Stop in at **Yva Chez Vava** (✉ Rte. 1 on eastern edge of Grand-Rivière, ☎ 596/55–72–72) for a rum punch and a lunch of seafood and Creole dishes, including an excellent fish soup and a tasty fricassee of crayfish.

**㉓  Le Marin.** The yachting capital of Martinique is also known for its colorful August carnival and its Jesuit church. Built in 1766, the church is one of the oldest on the island. One mile out of town, a small road leads to picturesque **Cap Chevalier.**

**❼  Le Morne Rouge.** This town, lying on the southern slopes of **Mont Pelée,** was destroyed by the volcano when it erupted in 1902. Today it's a popular resort spot and offers hikers some of the most spectacular mountain scenery on Martinique. This is the starting point for a climb up the 4,600-ft mountain. But don't try it without a guide unless you want to get buried alive under pumice stones. Instead, drive up to the **Refuge de l'Aileron.** From the parking lot it is a mile up a well-marked trail to the summit. Bring a sweatshirt, because it is often misty. From there, follow the **Route de la Trace** (Route N3), which winds south of Le Morne Rouge to St-Pierre. It used to be one of the main footpaths across the northern half of the island. It is steep and winding, but that didn't used to stop the *porteuses* of old: Balancing a tray, they would carry up to 100 pounds of provisions on their heads for the 15-hour trek to the Atlantic coast. Today, the Route de la Trace is one of the Caribbean's great drives.

**❽  Le Prêcheur.** This village, which is one of the prettiest on the island, was the childhood home of Françoise d'Aubigné, who later became the Marquise de Maintenon and the second wife of Louis XIV. At her request, the Sun King donated a handsome bronze bell to the village, which you can see hanging outside the church. **The Tomb of the Carib Indians,** on the way from St-Pierre, commemorates a sadder event. The site is actually a formation of limestone cliffs from which the last of the Caribs are said to have flung themselves to avoid capture by the Marquise's forebears.

**⓱  Les Trois-Ilets.** Named after the three rocky islands nearby, this lovely little village (population 3,000) has unusual brick and wood buildings roofed with antique tiles. It is known for its pottery, straw, and woodwork but above all as the birthplace of Napoléon's empress Joséphine. On the village square, where there is also a market and a fine *mairie* (town hall), you can visit the simple church where she was baptized Marie-Joseph Tascher de la Pagerie. The Martinicans have always been enormously proud of Joséphine, even though she reintroduced slavery on the island and most historians consider her to have been a rather shallow woman. A stone building that held the kitchen of the estate where she grew up is now home to the **Musée de la Pagerie.** (The main house blew down in the hurricane of 1766, when Joséphine was three.) It contains an assortment of memorabilia pertaining to Joséphine's life and rather unfortunate loves. She was married at 16 in an arranged marriage to Alexandre de Beauharnais. When he died, she married Napoléon, but he soon divorced her because she didn't produce any children. There are family portraits; documents, including a marriage certificate; a love letter written to her in 1796 by Napoléon; and various antique furnishings, including the bed she slept in as a child. ✉ *Trois-Ilets,* ☎ *596/68–38–34.* ⌑ *15F.* ☉ *Tues.–Sun. 9–5.*

The **Maison de la Canne** (at Pointe Vatable, as you leave town) will teach you everything you ever wanted to know about sugarcane. Exhibits take you through three centuries of sugarcane production, with displays of tools, scale models, engravings, and photographs. ✉ *Trois-Ilets,* ☎ *596/68–32–04.* ⌑ *15F.* ☉ *Tues.–Sun. 9–5:30.*

**㉔  Le Vauclin.** The return of the fishermen shortly before noon each day is the big event in this important fishing port on the Atlantic coast. There is also an 18th-century church here, the Chapel of the Holy Virgin. Nearby is the highest point in the south, **Mont Vauclin** (1,654 ft). A hike to the top will reward you with one of the best views on the island.

**❾  Macouba.** Named after the Carib word for fish, this village was a prosperous town in the 17th century, when tobacco made it rich. Today, its cliff-top location affords magnificent views of the sea, the mountains, and, on clear days, the neighboring island of Dominica. Macouba is home to the **JM distillery.** It produces the best *rhum vieux* (aged rum) on the island. A tour and samples are free. It is also the starting point for the island's most spectacular drive, the 6-mi route to Grand' Rivière on the northernmost point. This is Martinique at its greenest; groves of giant bamboo, cliffs hung with curtains of vines, and 7-ft tree ferns that seem to grow as you watch them. At the end of the road is **Grand' Rivière**, a sprawling fishing village at the foot of high cliffs which is, literally, the end of the road. On weekends, it's a bustling place with plenty of snack bars and cafés as well as colorfully painted boats pulled up on the beach. Hardy folk can trek 11 mi to the beach at Anse-Ceron on the northwest coast.

**❺  Musée Gauguin.** Martinique was a brief station in Paul Gauguin's wanderings but a decisive moment in the evolution of his art. He arrived from Panama in 1887 with friend and fellow painter Charles Laval and, having pawned his watch at the docks, rented a wooden shack on a hillside above this village. He stayed only seven months, before sickness and poverty drove him back to Paris, but the work he did here and on his return to France precipitated a change in his art. Indeed, he would later say that to understand him and his art one had to understand his Martinique period. Dazzled by the tropical colors and vegetation, Gauguin developed a style that directly anticipated his Tahitian paintings. This excellent museum is a labor of love on the part of local art historian Maiotte Dauphite and a group of other Martinicans. Though it has no originals (Gauguin's most famous Martinique painting, *Végétation Tropicale*, is in the Royal Scottish Museum in Edinburgh), the museum has an excellent set of reproductions. Indeed, this is the only place you can see all of Gauguin's Martinique work under one roof. There are also interesting exhibits of letters and documents relating to the painter, and an exhibition of local costumes. Another major artist also remembered here is the writer Lafcadio Hearn, who came to Martinique in the same year as Gauguin, on assignment for *Harper's* magazine. In his endearing book *Two Years in the West Indies,* he provides the most extensive description of the island before ☞ St-Pierre was buried in ash and lava. ✉ *Anse-Turin,* ☎ *596/78–22–66.* 🎫 *15F.* ☉ *Daily 9–5:30.*

**⑱  Pointe du Bout.** This area is filled with resort hotels, among them the Bakoua and the Méridien. The Pointe du Bout marina is a colorful spot where a whole slew of boats are tied up. The ferry to Fort-de-France leaves from here. More than anywhere else on Martinique, Pointe du Bout caters to the vacationer. A cluster of boutiques, ice cream parlors, and rental-car agencies forms the hub from which restaurants and hotels of varying caliber radiate. The beach at **Anse-Mitan** is one of the best on the island. At **Anse-à-l'Ane**, a little to the west of Pointe du Bout, there is a pretty white-sand beach complete with picnic tables. There are also numerous small restaurants and inexpensive guesthouse hotels here. Ten miles south is **Anse-d'Arlets,** a quiet backwater fishing village. You'll see fishermen's nets strung up on the beach to dry and pleasure boats on the water.

**❷ Schoelcher.** It's pronounced "shell-*cher*" and is home of the University of the French West Indies and Guyana. La Batelière Hotel (☞ Lodging, *above*), noted for its sports facilities, is also here.

**❻ St-Pierre.** The rise and fall of St-Pierre is one of the most remarkable stories in the Caribbean. Martinique's modern history began here when Belain d'Esnambuc, a French adventurer, cast anchor in 1635. He and his men settled and built a fort. By the turn of this century, St-Pierre was a flourishing city of 30,000. It was known as the Paris of the West Indies. There were cabarets, cafés, and a cathedral. Warehouses climbed the hills. As many as 30 ships at a time stood at anchor. By 1902, it was the most modern town in the Caribbean, with electricity, phones, and a tram. But in the spring of 1902, Mont Pelée began to rumble and spit out ash and steam. On May 2, it spewed out a river of lava that engulfed a factory, killing 25. City officials, however, ignored the warning, needing voters in town for an upcoming election. Shortly after 8 AM on May 8, 1902, two thunderous explosions rent the air. As it erupted, Mont Pelée split in half, belching forth a cloud of burning ash, poisonous gas, and lava that raced down the mountain at 250 mph. With temperatures of more than 3,600°F, St-Pierre was instantly vaporized. Thirty thousand people were killed in two minutes. The Paris of the West Indies had become its Pompeii. One man survived, though. Of all the inhabitants of St-Pierre, he was probably the last person anyone would have expected to live—and the last many would have wanted to. His name was Cyparis and he was a prisoner in the town's jail. Though he was scorched by the heat, the thick walls of his underground cell saved him. He was later pardoned and for some years afterward was a sideshow attraction at the Barnum & Bailey Circus.

For those interested in the eruption of 1902, the **Musée Vulcanologique** is a must. It was established in 1932 by American volcanologist Franck Perret. His collection includes photographs of the old town, documents, and a number of relics—some gruesome—excavated from the ruins, including molten glass, melted iron, and contorted clocks stopped at 8 AM. ⊠ *St-Pierre,* ☎ *596/78–15–16.* ◫ *15F.* ☉ *Daily 9–5.*

Today, St-Pierre is trying to reinvent itself. A snappy new Office du Tourisme is under construction; so, too, is a seafront promenade. Unfortunately, these projects have become bogged down in the complexities of European Union financing. But there are plenty of sidewalk cafés, some of which have live music, and you can also see the ruins of the island's first church (built in 1640), the theater, the toppled statues, and Cyparis's cell. The *Cyparis Express* is a small tourist train that runs through the city, hitting the important sights with a running narrative (in French). ⊠ *Departs from Pl. des Ruines du Figuier,* ☎ *596/55–50–92.* ◫ *30F.* ☉ *Runs every 45 mins, weekdays 9:30–1 and 2:30–5:30; call for exact times.*

**㉒ Ste-Anne.** A lovely white-sand beach and a Roman Catholic church are the highlights here. To the south is **Pointe des Salines,** the southernmost tip of the island and site of Martinique's best beach, **Les Salines,** 1½ mi of soft white sand. It's definitely *the* place for beach bums, and there is a lively scene here on weekends; *le topless* is almost de rigueur. Nearby is the **Petrified Forest,** known in French as the Savane des Petrifications. It's not a forest at all but a field of petrified boulders formed into the shape of logs.

**㉑ Ste-Luce.** With a sleepy main street that is deserted at midday and panoramic views across to the island of St. Lucia, this is one of the prettiest fishing villages on the island. Ste-Luce also has excellent beaches. To the east is **Pointe Figuier,** an excellent spot for scuba diving. On the way you will also find the **Ecomusée de Martinique,** despite its name more a historical than a natural museum. Holdings include artifacts from Arawak and Carib settlements through the plantation years. ⊠ *Anse Figuier,* ☎ *596/62–79–14.* ☑ *15F.* ☉ *Tues.–Sun. 9–5.*

NEED A
BREAK?

**Le Coup de Canon** (⊠ Place de la Vierge, Ste-Luce, ☎ 595/62–36–32) is a café with a stunning view of the water. Perched above the sea under two white awnings, it offers a simple chicken and seafood menu.

⑫ **Ste-Marie.** This town is home to about 20,000 Martinicans and is the commercial capital of the island's north. There is a lovely mid-19th-century church here, as well as the **Musée du Rhum,** operated by the St. James Rum Distillery. It is housed in a graceful galleried Creole house. Guided tours of the museum take in displays of the tools of the trade and include a visit to the distillery. And, yes, you may sample the product. ⊠ *Ste-Marie,* ☎ *596/69–30–02.* ☑ *Free.* ☉ *Weekdays 9–6, weekends 9–1.*

# Martinique A to Z

## Arriving and Departing

### BY FERRY

The **Express des Isles** (☎ 596/63–12–11) offers scheduled interisland service aboard a 128-ft, 227-passenger motorized catamaran, linking Martinique with Dominica, Guadeloupe, Les Saintes, and St. Lucia. For those who don't get seasick, it's an enormously pleasurable way to travel, with great views of the islands. Fares run approximately 25% below economy airfares. Sailings are not every day of the week for all destinations; check the schedule.

### BY PLANE

The most frequent flights from the United States are on **American Airlines** (☎ 800/433–7300), which has year-round daily service from more than 100 U.S. cities to San Juan. From there, the airline's American Eagle flies on to Martinique with a stop first at Guadeloupe. **Air France** (☎ 800/237–2747) flies direct from Miami and San Juan. **Air Canada** (☎ 800/776–3000) has service from Montréal and Toronto. **LIAT** (☎ 809/462–0700), with its extensive coverage of the Antilles, flies in from Antigua, St. Maarten, Guadeloupe, Dominica, St. Lucia, Barbados, Grenada, and Trinidad and Tobago. **Council Charter** (☎ 212/661–4546 or 800/765–6065) provides Saturday-to-Saturday flights out of New York's JFK and offers flight-lodging packages.

### FROM THE AIRPORT

You'll arrive at the new Lamentin International Airport, which is about a 15-minute taxi ride from Fort-de-France and about 40 minutes from the Trois-Ilets peninsula, the first of many resort areas on the southern beaches where most hotels are located.

## Currency

The currency used on Martinique is the French franc. At press time, the exchange rate was 5.65F to US$1. U.S. dollars are accepted in some hotels, but for convenience, it's better to convert your money into francs. Banks give a more favorable rate than hotels. A currency exchange service that also offers a favorable rate is **Change Caraibes,** in the arrivals building at Lamentin International Airport (☎ 596/51–57–91); it is open weekdays 7 AM–9 PM and Saturday 8:30–2. Another is in Fort-de-France (⊠ Rue Ernest Deproge, across from Tourist Office, ☎

596/60–28–40) and is open weekdays 7:30–6 and Saturday 8–12:30. Prices quoted here are in U.S. dollars unless indicated otherwise.

Major credit cards are accepted in hotels and restaurants in Fort-de-France and the Pointe du Bout areas; few establishments in the countryside accept them. There are ATMs at the airport and at branches of the Crédit Agricole bank, which are on the Cirrus system and also accept Visa and MasterCard. There is a 20% discount on luxury items paid for with traveler's checks or with certain credit cards.

## Emergencies
**Police:** ☎ 17. **Ambulance:** ☎ 70–36–48 or 71–59–48. **Fire:** ☎ 18. **Hospital:** There is a 24-hour emergency room at **Hôpital La Meynard** (✉ Châteauboeuf, just outside Fort-de-France, ☎ 596/55–20–00). **Pharmacies:** Pharmacies in Fort-de-France include **Pharmacie de la Paix** (✉ Corner rue Victor Schoelcher and rue Perrinon, ☎ 596/71–94–83) and **Pharmacie Cypria** (✉ Blvd. Général de Gaulle, ☎ 596/63–22–25).

## Getting Around
BICYCLES AND MOTORBIKES
Bikes, scooters, and motorbikes are all popular. They can be rented in Fort-de-France from **Funny** (☎ 596/63–33–05), **T. S. Location Sarl** (☎ 596/63–42–82), or **Loca Scoot** (☎ 596/63–55–84); in Ste-Anne at **Huet** (☎ 596/76–79–66); and in Ste-Luce at **Vespa Marquis** (☎ 596/60–02–84).

BUSES
Public buses are crowded and not recommended for the timid traveler. But eight-passenger minivans (license plates bear the letters TC) are an inexpensive—and fun—means of transportation. In Fort-de-France, the main terminal for the minivans is at Pointe Simon on the waterfront. There are frequent departures from early morning until 8 PM; fares range from $1 to $5.

CAR RENTALS
Unless you are at an all-inclusive resort, a car will be essential. With about 175 mi of well-paved and well-marked roads (albeit with international signs), Martinique is also a good place for driving. The Martinicans drive with aggressive abandon but are surprisingly courteous and will let you into the flow of traffic. Country roads are mountainous with hairpin curves. Watch out, too, for *dos d'anes* (literally, donkey backs), speed bumps that are extremely hard to spot—particularly at night—though if you hit one you'll know about it. Streets in Fort-de-France are narrow and choked with traffic during the day. If you want a detailed map, the *Carte Routière et Touristique* is available at bookstores. A full tank of gas will get you all the way around the island with gallons to spare.

A valid U.S driver's license is needed to rent a car for up to 20 days. After that, you'll need an International Driver's Permit. U.K. visitors can use their EU licenses. Rates are about $60 per day (unlimited mileage), but always question agents closely. If you book from the United States at least 48 hours in advance, you can qualify for a hefty discount. Among the many agencies are **Avis** (☎ 596/70–11–60 or 800/331–1212), **Budget** (☎ 596/63–69–00 or 800/472–3325), and **Hertz** (☎ 596/60–64–64 or 800/654–3131).

FERRIES
Weather permitting, *vedettes* (ferries) operate daily between Fort-de-France and the Marina Méridien in Pointe du Bout and between Fort-de-France and Anse-Mitan and Anse-à-l'Ane (all trips take about 25

minutes). The Quai d'Esnambuc is the arrival and departure point in Fort-de-France. At press time, the one-way fare was 30F.

TAXIS

Taxis are expensive. From the airport to Fort-de-France is about 100F; from the airport to Pointe du Bout, about 225F. A 40% surcharge is in effect between 8 PM and 6 AM and on Sunday. This means that if you arrive at Lamentin at night, depending on where your hotel is, it may be cheaper to rent a car from the airport and keep it for 24 hours than to take a one-way taxi to your hotel. To request a cab call ☎ 596/63–63–62 or 596/63–10–10.

## Guided Tours

For a personalized tour of the island, ask the tourist office to arrange a tour with an English-speaking taxi driver. There are set rates for tours to various points on the island, and if you share the ride with two or three other sightseers, the price will be whittled down.

**Madinina Tours** (⊠ 111–113 rue Ernest Deproge, Fort-de-France, ☎ 596/70–65–25) offers half- and full-day jaunts, with lunch included in the all-day outings. Boat tours are also available, as are air excursions to the Grenadines and St. Lucia. Madinina has tour desks in most of the major hotels. **Parc Naturel Régional de la Martinique** (⊠ 9 blvd. Général de Gaulle, Fort-de-France 97206, ☎ 596/73–19–30) organizes inexpensive guided hiking tours year-round. Descriptive folders are available at the tourist office.

## Language

Many Martinicans speak Creole, a mixture of Spanish and French. Try *sa ou fe* for hello. In major tourist areas you'll find someone who speaks English, but the courtesy of using a few French words, even if it is *Parlez-vous anglais?*, is appreciated. The people of Martinique are extremely courteous and will help you through your French. Even if you do speak fluent French, you may have a problem understanding the accent of the country people. Most menus are written in French, so a dictionary is helpful.

## Opening and Closing Times

Stores that cater to tourists are generally open weekdays 8:30–6, Saturday 8:30–1. Banking hours are weekdays 7:30–noon and 2:30–6.

## Passports and Visas

U.S. and Canadian citizens must have a passport (one that expired no more than five years ago is acceptable) or proof of citizenship, such as an original (not photocopied) birth certificate or a voter registration card accompanied by a government-authorized photo identification. British citizens are required to have a passport. In addition, all visitors must have a return or ongoing ticket.

## Precautions

Exercise the same safety precautions you would in any other big city. Don't leave jewelry or money unattended on the beach.

Beware of the *mancenillier* (manchineel) trees. These pretty trees with green fruits that look like apples are poisonous. Sap and even raindrops falling from the trees onto your skin can cause painful, scarring blisters. The trees have red warning signs posted by the Forestry Commission.

If you plan to ramble through the rain forest, be careful where you step. Fer-de-lances, and several other varieties of poisonous snake, exist on Martinique.

Except for the area around Cap Chevalier and the Tartane peninsula, the Atlantic waters are rough and should be avoided by all but expert swimmers.

## Taxes and Service Charges

A resort tax varies from hotel to hotel; the maximum is $1.50 per person per day. Rates quoted by hotels usually include a 10% service charge; some hotels add 10% to your bill. All restaurants include a 15% service charge in their menu prices.

## Telephones and Mail

To call Martinique station-to-station from the United States, dial 011 + 596 + the local six-digit number.

It is not possible to make collect calls from Martinique to the United States, but you can use a calling card. There are few coin telephone booths, and those are usually in hotels and restaurants. Most public telephones now use a Télécarte. Télécartes may be purchased from post offices, café-tabacs, and hotels.

To place an interisland call, dial the local six-digit number. To call the United States from Martinique, dial 19–1, area code, and the local number. For Great Britain, dial 19–44, area code (without the first zero), and the number.

Airmail letters to the United States cost 4.60F for up to 20 grams; postcards, 3.70F. For Great Britain, the costs are 4.40F and 3.60F, respectively. Stamps may be purchased from post offices, café-tabacs, and hotel newsstands.

## Visitor Information

For information contact the **French West Indies Tourist Board** (☎ 800/ 391–4909). You can also contact the **French Government Tourist Office, Martinique Promotion Bureau** (✉ 444 Madison Ave., New York, NY 10022, ☎ 800/391–4909; ✉ 9454 Wilshire Blvd., Beverly Hills, CA 90212, ☎ 310/271–2358; ✉ 676 N. Michigan Ave., Chicago, IL 60611, ☎ 312/751–7800; ✉ 1981 McGill College Ave., Suite 490, Montréal, Québec H3A 2W9, ☎ 514/844–8566; ✉ 1 Dundas St. W, Suite 2405, Toronto, Ontario M5G 1Z3, ☎ 416/593–4723 or 800/361– 9099; ✉ 178 Piccadilly, London W1V 0AL, ☎ 0181/124–4123).

On Martinique, the **Martinique Tourist Office** (✉ Blvd. Alfassa, ☎ 596/ 63–79–60) is open Monday–Thursday 8–5, Friday 7:30–5, Saturday 8–noon. The office's free maps and booklets, *Choubouloute* and *Martinique Info,* are useful. The Tourist Information Booth at Lamentin International Airport is open daily until the last flight has landed.

# 16 Montserrat

*Montserrat is a small, friendly island that tends to attract independent travelers who want a low-key, away-from-it-all vacation. If you want to pump iron, drink piña coladas, and boogie till dawn, you'll probably be bored. If you like seclusion, nature, and peace and quiet, you'll love it.*

**M**ONTSERRAT is one of the least-developed islands in the eastern Caribbean. The population is only about 11,000, and the scenery here is rugged and dramatic. Christopher Columbus sailed by the leeward coast of this Caribbean island in 1493, and, seeing the jagged mountains, he named it Montserrat, after the Santa Maria de Montserrate monastery near Barcelona, which is surrounded by similar terrain.

Updated by
Pamela
Acheson

The Carib Indians who inhabited the island then were still here in 1632, when dissident Irish Catholics fleeing persecution arrived from nearby St. Kitts. These new settlers found a green and luxuriant island whose topography strongly resembled that of their native Ireland, prompting Montserrat's nickname, the Emerald Isle of the Caribbean. Today the Irish influence is much diminished. Still, your passport is stamped with a shamrock upon arrival, the phone book is loaded with Irish places and surnames, and St. Patrick's Day is celebrated enthusiastically (albeit to commemorate a major 18th-century slave uprising).

Actually, the African influence is more pronounced, thanks to Montserrat's comparatively low profile. Newborns are still given "jumbie" nicknames to fool the evil spirits, and the related jumbie dances, designed to ward off or propitiate those spirits, are lusty and vibrant. The rollicking Carnival, two weeks of merrymaking held during the Christmas season, is a riot of color in traditional authentic costumes.

Although only 11 mi long and 7 mi wide, the island has three mountain ranges, and there are also dramatic waterfalls, dense rain forests, and fertile fields rich with mango, coconut, papaya, and banana trees. All this makes the island a hiker's heaven, and there are hundreds of trails, from easy beginner walks to arduous half-day trips that require a guide.

The highest point is Chance's Peak, which lies at the southern end of the island and rises to a height of 3,002 ft. Also in the southern hills is the volcano known as Galway's Soufrière. Incredibly, Montserrat has been under a volcano watch for some time. In 1995, after centuries of inactivity, the 3,000-ft volcano in Soufrière Hills shook itself back to life. But following some brief, intense activity, the volcano appeared to have settled back down. Then in 1996 British Geological Survey scientists working at the Montserrat Volcano Observatory noticed another considerable increase in volcanic activity, and until recently, there had been several small eruptions and the island was on various stages of volcanic alert.

As volcanic activity in the Soufrière Hills increased to substantially higher levels, the government, fearing a major eruption, eventually evacuated the entire southern third of the island, including the capital city of Plymouth. Instead of erupting, however, the volcano settled into a loose pattern of coughing a large plume of dust into the air every few months or so and then calming back down. Then, in mid-1997, the volcano erupted, killing nine people, injuring others, and doing substantial damage to the island. Emergency aid from Britain is being sent to help the island in its recovery.

Although many islanders have now been living in shelters for quite a while, they have adapted to the ongoing alert and extended evacuation with remarkable good humor and positive attitudes.

As far as the coverage of the island in this chapter is concerned, hotels, restaurants, and businesses closed due to the evacuation have been left in but are marked "TEMPORARILY CLOSED" since many of them intend to reopen when the evacuation order is lifted. The longer the evacuation lasts, of course, the less likely it is that every one of these establishments will be back in business. If you are considering a visit to the island, it would be wise to place a call directly to the Tourist Board in Montserrat (☞ Visitor Information, *below*) for the most current update on the state of the volcano.

## Lodging

The number of hotels on Montserrat is limited, with the two largest—the Vue Point and Montserrat Springs—the island's only real resorts. Small hotels that cater to businesspeople, guest houses, and a few bed-and-breakfasts are also available. Be aware that most hotels are "tropical-breeze-cooled": Only a few have rooms that are air-conditioned. Most of Montserrat's hotels operate on the Modified American Plan (MAP).

Alternatively, there are many villas of all sizes available for rent. Villas are not only affordable here; given their comforts and conveniences, many consider them preferable to the hotels. You can even request the properties where your favorite rock stars—from Sting to Elton John—have relaxed.

| CATEGORY | COST* |
|---|---|
| $$$ | over $145 |
| $$ | $75–$145 |
| $ | under $75 |

*All prices are for a standard double room in winter, excluding 7% tax and 10% service charge.

### Hotels

**$$$**   **Montserrat Springs Hotel and Villas.** TEMPORARILY CLOSED. Spacious rooms in this, the largest of the island's hotels, are in one wing
★ of the main building and in cottages scattered along the steep hillside sloping down to the beach. The bright and airy decor is primarily cream and white. Rooms have private balconies and cable TV; suites have separate living rooms and full kitchens. The beautiful outdoor pool, at 70 ft long, is one of the largest in the Caribbean. From the terrace surrounding it, you can take in sweeping views of the ocean in one direction and Chance's Peak in the other, the same great views that all the rooms have. At the beach bar you can luxuriate in a whirlpool filled with piping-hot mineral water direct from a soufrière. The restaurant serves good West Indian and Continental cuisine (☞ Dining, *below*). ⊠ Box 259, Plymouth, ☎ 809/491–2481 or 800/253–2134, ℻ 809/491–4070. 40 rooms, 6 suites. Restaurant, 2 bars, air-conditioning, room service, pool, 2 hot tubs, 2 tennis courts, exercise room, beach. AE, MC, V. EP, MAP.

**$$–$$$**   **Vue Pointe.** The moment you arrive here you feel as though both
★ the staff and the owners, Cedric and Carol Osborne, really care about your well-being. The gracious Monday-night cocktail parties that the Osbornes host at their house are a perfect example. The breeze-cooled

accommodations include 12 rooms in the main building and 28 hexagonal rondavels that spill down to the gray-sand beach on Old Road Bay. Each rondavel has a large bedroom, cable TV, and spacious bathroom, and most have great views of the ocean. In the main building a large lounge and bar overlook the pool; the Wednesday-night barbecue, with steel bands and other entertainment, is a well-attended event. In the adjacent sea-view restaurant (☞ Dining, *below*), you can have a candlelit dinner of local and international specialties (the chef is one of the most skilled on the island). A 150-seat conference center serves as a theater and disco. ⊠ *Box 65, Plymouth,* ☎ *809/491–5210 or 800/235–0709,* ℻ *809/491–4813. 12 rooms, 28 rondavels. Restaurant, bar, refrigerators, pool, 2 tennis courts, shuffleboard, windsurfing, fishing, recreation room, shop, conference center. AE, MC, V. EP, MAP.*

$$ 🏨 **Flora Fountain Hotel.** TEMPORARILY CLOSED. This is a hotel for people coming on business (only 35% of the clientele are tourists) or for those who appreciate an old, rambling hotel in the heart of town. The two-story structure is built around an enormous fountain that's sometimes lighted at night, with small tables scattered in the inner courtyard. There are 18 plainly decorated but adequate rooms, all with tile bath, and most with balconies. All rooms have phones but not all have TVs, so ask if it's important to you. The restaurant has a chef from Bombay who serves simple sandwiches and fine Indian dishes. Friday night's Indian buffet includes several meat and fish dishes; at least two kinds of rice, vegetable, and pork dishes with spices; *raita* (a yogurt sauce), and *samosa* (spicy meat patties). Children under 12 stay free when sharing the room with an adult. ⊠ *Box 373, Church Rd., Plymouth,* ☎ *809/491–6092,* ℻ *809/491–2568. 18 rooms. Restaurant, bar, air-conditioning. AE, D, MC, V. EP, CP, MAP.*

$–$$ 🏨 **Providence Estate House.** Perched on a bluff high above the ocean
★ with spectacular views of neighboring St. Kitts, Nevis, and Redonda is this two-unit bed-and-breakfast. The owners restored the former plantation house, a beautiful stone-and-wood building with a wraparound veranda, back to one of the finest examples of traditional Caribbean architecture on the island. The two guest rooms—one considerably larger than the other, both with cable TV—are on the ground floor and open directly onto the pool area. Both rooms have the original timbered ceilings and massive stone walls, which keep them cool in the summer, and are decorated with red quarry tiles and pastel fabrics. If there is any drawback, it is the location. The nearest restaurant is 3 mi away in Belham Valley, and the nearest beach is a hike down the hillside. But the owners are willing to make evening meals on request, and you can prepare your own meals in the kitchenette by the pool. A large breakfast of eggs, oatmeal, and fruits from the garden (in season) is included in the rate. ⊠ *Providence Estate House,* ☎ *809/491–6476,* ℻ *809/491–8476. 2 rooms. Kitchenette, pool. No credit cards. CP.*

$ 🏨 **Belham Valley Hotel.** On a hillside overlooking Belham Valley and the Belham Valley river, this hotel has a cottage and two apartments (a studio and a newer two-bedroom). All have a stereo, cable TV, a fully equipped kitchen, and a phone, though none are air-conditioned. It's the restaurant here that's the big draw, with its lovely views and great food (☞ Dining, *below*). The beach is an eight-minute walk away.

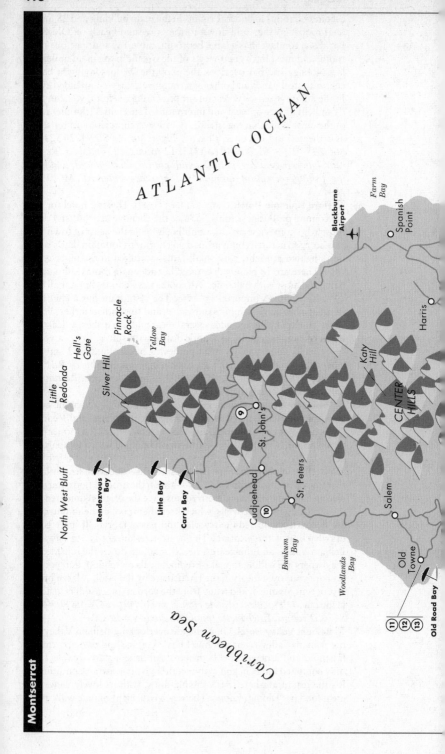

417

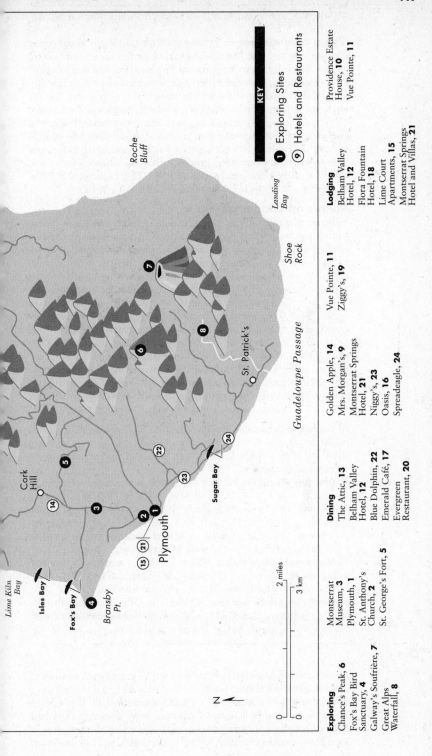

**KEY**

1 Exploring Sites

9 Hotels and Restaurants

Roche Bluff

Landing Bay

Shoe Rock

St. Patrick's

*Guadeloupe Passage*

Cork Hill

Lime Kiln Bay

Isles Bay

Fox's Bay

Bransby Pt.

Sugar Bay

Plymouth

0 — 2 miles
0 — 3 km

N

**Exploring**
Chance's Peak, **6**
Fox's Bay Bird
Sanctuary, **4**
Galway's Soufrière, **7**
Great Alps
Waterfall, **8**

Montserrat
Museum, **3**
Plymouth, **1**
St. Anthony's
Church, **2**
St. George's Fort, **5**

**Dining**
The Attic, **13**
Belham Valley
Hotel, **12**
Blue Dolphin, **22**
Emerald Café, **17**
Evergreen
Restaurant, **20**

Golden Apple, **14**
Mrs. Morgan's, **9**
Montserrat Springs
Hotel, **21**
Niggy's, **23**
Oasis, **16**
Spreadeagle, **24**

Vue Pointe, **11**
Ziggy's, **19**

**Lodging**
Belham Valley
Hotel, **12**
Flora Fountain
Hotel, **18**
Lime Court
Apartments, **15**
Montserrat Springs
Hotel and Villas, **21**

Providence Estate
House, **10**
Vue Pointe, **11**

⊠ *Box 409, Plymouth,* ☎ *809/491–5553. 3 units. Restaurant. AE, MC. EP.*

**$** 🏠 **Lime Court Apartments.** TEMPORARILY CLOSED. Right in the center of town, opposite the Parliament building, is this slightly run-down, large, white colonial-style apartment building. The downstairs apartments tend to be dark and airless and, with the sound of the generator and the puttering of the refrigerators, not very peaceful. But the large, well-equipped, two-bedroom, two-bath "penthouse," up a flight of steps at the top of the building, has a fine view from its balcony of the town's red rooftops and the sea beyond. It can sleep two couples and is reasonable at $45 per night. All apartments have kitchenettes with a stove and microwave, private bathrooms (showers only), and cable TV; there's also maid service. ⊠ *Box 250, Parliament St., Plymouth,* ☎ *809/491–3656. 8 apartments. AE, MC, V. EP.*

## Villas and Condominiums

Villas are plentiful on Montserrat, and there's a great range to choose from if you want a do-it-yourself vacation on the island. All the villa developments are on the west coast of the island, within 20 minutes of Plymouth by car. The majority are in the districts of Old Towne, Olveston, and Woodlands. The last is particularly noteworthy for its magnificent views of the ocean and its steep hillsides covered in lush vegetation. Prices are high for just two people (a one-bedroom is around $1,000 per week) but become more reasonable when the cost can be split among more people. Two-bedroom villas with a pool range from $1,000 to $2,400 per week; three-bedroom villas from $1,500 to $2,500; and four-bedroom villas from $2,500 to $3,000. There are villas of all sizes that are the ultimate in luxury and exceed even these prices. Off-season rates are as much as 50% lower (and usually negotiable), and some excellent bargains can be picked up by summer travelers. All villas come with maid service.

🏠 **Caribbean Connection Plus** (☎ 203/261–8603, FAX 203/261–8295) is a Stateside reservation service for about 50 one- to four-bedroom villas and some condos. It also has an on-island representative to ensure that all goes well.

🏠 **Isles Bay Plantation** (⊠ Box 64, Offices temporarily relocated to Belham, ☎ 809/491–5248, FAX 809/491–5016; ☎ FAX 0171/482–1071 in London), known locally as the Beverly Hills of Montserrat, has the crème de la crème of Montserrat's villas. Each house is set on approximately ½ acre of tropical landscaped gardens, has its own 40-ft pool, and is only a 10-minute walk from the beach.

🏠 **Montserrat Enterprises Ltd.** (⊠ Box 58, Offices temporarily relocated to Belham, ☎ 809/491–2431 [ask for Mr. Edwards], FAX 809/491–4660) has 22 villas in Old Towne, Woodlands, and Isles Bay.

🏠 **Neville Bradshaw Agencies** (⊠ Box 270, Offices temporarily relocated to Belham , ☎ 809/491–5270, FAX 809/491–5069) has a wide range of villas, mostly in Old Towne and Isles Bay.

# Dining

Despite its size, Montserrat offers a variety of dining options to fit all budgets. Most of the more inexpensive eateries are found in small cafés, some of which look like the proverbial hole-in-the-wall. Don't be deceived, as most offer delicious Caribbean home cooking. The island also has a lively assortment of rum shops—the Caribbean version of local bars—packed with islanders on Friday nights; you can join in and get a drink and a simple meal.

Montserrat's national dish is goatwater stew, made with goat meat and vegetables and similar to Irish stew. Goat meat is strong but tasty. Mountain "chicken" (actually enormous frogs) is also a great favorite. Yams, breadfruit, christophines (a kind of squash), limes, mangoes, papayas, and a variety of seafood are served in most restaurants. Home-brewed ginger beer, one of the finest traditional drinks of the West Indies, is widely available.

## What to Wear

In general, neat casual clothing is the norm at lunch and dinner. Beach attire is too casual. Although jackets are not required, shorts and jeans are not acceptable at the fancier restaurants for dinner.

| CATEGORY | COST* |
| --- | --- |
| $$$ | over $30 |
| $$ | $20–$30 |
| $ | under $20 |

*per person, excluding drinks and service*

**$$$** ✕ **Montserrat Springs Hotel.** TEMPORARILY CLOSED. The split-level cathedral-ceiling dining room, enclosed on three sides, faces a large pool and a sundeck, beyond which you can see the ocean. A menu of West Indian and Continental cuisine includes an excellent goatwater stew, local snapper with a Creole sauce, grilled tenderloin steak, and an excellent Spanish omelet. The Friday barbecue and Sunday buffet brunch are extremely popular, and reservations are a must. ✉ *Richmond Hill, Plymouth,* ☎ *809/491–2481. AE, MC, V.*

**$$$** ✕ **Vue Pointe.** Candlelit dining in the hillside hotel's restaurant over-
★ looking the sea makes for a very romantic evening. There is a nightly five-course table d'hôte menu, or you can order à la carte. West Indian–style mountain "chicken," kingfish, beef Wellington, and red snapper with Creole sauce are favorites. For dessert, it's hard to choose between the lime pie and the guava cheesecake. The Wednesday-night barbecue, accompanied by music from a steel band, is a popular island event. ✉ *Old Towne,* ☎ *809/491–5210. AE, MC, V.*

**$$–$$$** ✕ **Belham Valley Hotel.** Considered by many to be the best restaurant
★ on the island, this former private home offers intimate, elegant dining. The best tables are on the open-air terrace; hung with ferns and croton plants, it looks down over picturesque Belham Valley and the lights of Isle Bay Hill. The sound of tree frogs and the ocean waves mingles with the recorded music of Stan Getz, Astrud Gilberto, and other jazz greats. Hibiscus tumbles over stone walls and sprouts from table vases. Start with conch fritters or liver pâté, and progress to Seafood Delight (sautéed lobster, red snapper, and sea scallops in a vermouth sauce) or stuffed red snapper. Scrumptious desserts are mango or lime mousse, lemon cake, and a tropical fruit sundae with a ginger sauce. At lunchtime, the offerings are lighter: omelets, salads, and sandwiches. A Chinese menu is offered for lunch and dinner on Thursdays. The wine list is extensive. ✉ *Old Towne,* ☎ *809/491–5553. Reservations essential. AE, MC, V. No lunch weekends.*

**$$** ✕ **The Attic.** This popular lunch spot offers light meals in a casual and inviting atmosphere. Stop by for a spicy roti, a curry with chunks of potatoes and goat, beef, or chicken, wrapped in flat bread. It also comes vegetarian style. Quesadillas are another house specialty. ✉ *Old Towne,* ☎ *809/491–2008. No credit cards. No breakfast or dinner.*

**$$** ✕ **Emerald Café.** Ten white tables shaded by blue umbrellas both inside and on the terrace are perfect for a relaxing meal. Burgers, sandwiches, salads, and grilled chicken and fish are served at lunchtime. For dinner you can order tournedos sautéed in spicy butter, broiled or sautéed Caribbean lobster, T-bone steak, mountain chicken diablo, and giant swordfish steaks. The Island Coconut Pie and other homemade pastries are superb. There's also an ample list of liqueurs and wines, a full bar, and entertainment on weekends. ⊠ *Wapping,* ☎ *809/491–3821. MC. No lunch Sun.*

**\$\$** ✕ **Oasis.** TEMPORARILY CLOSED. A 200-year-old stone house is the setting for this charming restaurant. You can dine indoors in the intimate bar and lounge, but most choose the outdoor patio, which looks out onto colorful tropical flowers. Calypso mountain chicken, jumbo shrimp Provençale, red snapper with lime butter, and grilled sirloin steak are house specialties. Owners Eric and Mandy Finnamore are also well known for their British-style fish-and-chips. ⊠ *Wapping, Plymouth,* ☎ *809/491–2328. No credit cards. Closed Wed.*

**\$** ✕ **Blue Dolphin.** TEMPORARILY CLOSED. This is the place to come for su-
★ perb mountain chicken served with fresh local vegetables, the house specialty. The inside here may be short on ambience—the chairs are Naugahyde, and the menu is scrawled on a blackboard without prices or descriptions—but the seductive aromas wafting from the kitchen announce that the Blue Dolphin serves some of the best food on the island, including luscious pumpkin fritters and mouthwatering lobster. This eatery, set on a hill, also has a fabulous view of the town and sea. ⊠ *Amersham,* ☎ *809/491–3263. No credit cards.*

**\$** ✕ **Evergreen Restaurant.** TEMPORARILY CLOSED. This casual spot in downtown Plymouth is a good choice for local chicken, pizzas, and hamburgers. There are daily specials and fresh pastries. ⊠ *Plymouth,* ☎ *809/491–3514. No credit cards.*

**\$** ✕ **Golden Apple.** In this large, galleried stone building, you'll be served huge plates of good, local cooking. The restaurant's specialty is goat-water stew, cooked on weekends only, outside over an open fire. Souse, *pelau* (chicken-and-rice curry), stewed or curried conch, and mountain chicken are also excellent. Tables covered with cheerful red-and-white-checked tablecloths add to the relaxed atmosphere. There's also a grocery store attached. ⊠ *Cork Hill,* ☎ *809/491–2187. No credit cards.*

**\$** ✕ **Mrs. Morgan's.** Friday and Saturday are goatwater stew days at Mrs. Morgan's, and from 11:30 onward you can join the carloads of locals who make the trek up here to the north of the island to eat their fill. Order yourself a hearty bowl of the stew, which costs only EC\$8 (US\$3.50), and plunk yourself down at one of the four picnic tables in the simple, unadorned room. The stew is just the way it should be—with the flesh falling off the bone, brimming with dumplings and innards. If that doesn't sound appetizing, try the souse, baked chicken, or any of the other down-home specialties. ⊠ *Airport Rd., St. John's,* ☎ *809/491–5419. No credit cards.*

**\$** ✕ **Niggy's.** TEMPORARILY CLOSED. In his previous life, the owner was a British character actor in Hollywood. That was before he decided to trade the smell of greasepaint and the roar of the crowd for a place behind the bar in this extremely popular restaurant (the British governor eats here regularly). The setting is a simple clapboard cottage with yellow bella flowers trailing over the gate, and the food, served at picnic-style benches under a trellis of flowering plants, is excellent and a good value. Try the grilled steaks and chops, shrimp scampi, or one of the pasta specials. Inside at the bar, you'll be regaled with tales of Hollywood, and the whole place feels like a set for a Caribbean remake of *Casablanca.* There's entertainment weekends, and for those who want to stay over, there are two simple but clean rooms in the back. The property is a 10-minute drive from the center of Plymouth. ⊠ *Kinsale,* ☎ *809/491–7489. No credit cards. No lunch.*

**\$** ✕ **Spreadeagle.** TEMPORARILY CLOSED. This is a tiny place that you'll be glad you found if you visit Galway's Soufrière or Great Alps Falls. Peter "Bobb," the owner, keeps beer on ice and serves all sorts of beverages and light snacks. ✉ *German's Bay,* ☎ *809/491–7503. No credit cards.*

**$** ✗ **Ziggy's.** John and Marcia Punter's simply decorated restaurant is
**★** extremely popular and almost always full. This remains one of the best
bistros on the island. The owners create magical cuisine out of all the
fruits, vegetables, and spices that grow on Montserrat, including ginger, nutmeg, yams, plantain, christophine, and coconuts. Despite the
crowds, this restaurant has retained its "one seating per evening" policy. ✉ *Belham Valley,* ☎ *809/491–8282. No credit cards. Closed Sun.*

# Beaches

The sand on many of the beaches here often surprises visitors because
of its color. Sand on the south coast is of volcanic origin; usually referred to as black, it's actually light to dark gray. On the northwest
coast, the sand is beige or white. The calm beaches are on the western
side of the island, and some of them are most comfortably reached by
boat. The eastern, or Atlantic, coast is rockier, more windswept, and
less fertile. Steep cliffs make most of the beaches on that side of the island inaccessible.

## Northwest Coast

The generally calm waters are good for swimming at **Carr's Bay,** a gray-
sand beach.

Tucked between two hills is **Little Bay,** with a secluded, light-gray
beach. Nearby reefs offer excellent diving, but heavy swells are sometimes present. Although you can drive to this beach, some prefer to
take a sailboat.

**Rendezvous Bay,** Montserrat's only white-sand beach is a long, secluded
area good for swimming and walking. It is accessible by boat or by a
45-minute hike over a hill.

## Southwest Coast

Picnic tables, changing rooms, and outside showers dress up **Fox's Bay,**
just outside of Plymouth. It's a gray-sand beach, and there are numerous
reefs just offshore. A bird sanctuary is nearby.

**Isles Bay,** several miles north of Plymouth, offers walkers a long expanse of gray sand and a view of the island's only golf course.

**Old Road Bay,** a long stretch of gray sand several miles north of Plymouth, has a beach bar, dive shop, and water sports. This is a calm
swimming beach with excellent snorkeling.

**Sugar Bay,** to the south of Plymouth, is a beach of fine gray volcanic
sand. The Yacht Club overlooks this beach.

# Outdoor Activities and Sports

## Boating

**Vue Pointe** hotel (☎ 809/491–5210) offers sailing and snorkeling excursions to Rendezvous Bay, Little Bay, and Carr's Bay. The cost is $25
per person and includes a sandwich lunch and snorkeling equipment.

## Golf

The **Montserrat Golf Course** (☎ 809/491–5220), in the picturesque Belham Valley, is "slope rated" 116 by the USGA (in other words, it's incredibly hilly) and must be one of the few golf courses in the world
that can list gopher holes and iguanas among its hazards. The course
plays as a true 18-hole golf course, with 11 greens and 18 tees. Four
fairways run along the ocean. The rest are up hill and down dale. Watch
out for the iguanas—they collect golf balls.

## Hiking

Three mountain ranges, rain forests, and volcanic sulphur springs provide numerous hiking opportunities. There are many trails; guides are suggested for the longer and more difficult ones. To hire a knowledgeable guide, contact Cecil Cassell at the **Montserrat Tour Guides Association** (☎ 809/491–3160), call the department of tourism, or ask at your hotel. Be sure to wear sturdy rubber-soled shoes.

## Mountain Biking

At **Island Bikes** (⊠ Harney St., Plymouth, ☎ 809/491–5552, FAX 809/491–5552), Butch Miller and Susan Goldin, the bustling, can-do Americans who run the outfit, are self-confessed biking junkies and know the island like the backs of their own saddles. Rentals are $25 a day, $140 a week. The couple also conduct guided tours that include refreshments and a sag wagon for the faint of heart, offer van tours that drop four to 12 people off at a designated area (such as the top of Windy Hill), and can arrange bed-and-bike package tours. They sponsor two international cycle races each year and run the Island Bikes Mountain Bike Training Center, which offers off-road practice areas, downhill slalom areas, and numerous steep descent and ascent trails.

## Sailing, Snorkeling, and Scuba Diving

Snorkeling equipment is provided on the day cruises to the white-sand coves on the west coast; boats usually have an open bar. Arrangements can be made through the **Vue Pointe** hotel (☎ 809/491–5210).

**Sea Wolf Diving School** (☎ 809/491–7807) in Plymouth offers one- or two-tank dives, night dives, and instruction from PADI-certified instructors. Costs are about $40 for a one-tank dive and $60 for a two-tank dive.

**Danny Water Sports** (☎ 809/491–5645), operating out of the Vue Pointe hotel, rents snorkel equipment and Windsurfers and also offers fishing, Sunfish sailing, and waterskiing.

## Spectator Sports

Cricket is the national passion. Cricket and soccer matches are held from February through June in Sturge Park. Shamrock Car Park is the venue for netball and basketball games. Contact the tourist board (☎ 809/491–2230) for schedules.

## Tennis

There are lighted tennis courts at the **Vue Pointe** hotel (☎ 809/491–5210), the **Montserrat Springs Hotel** (☎ 809/491–2481), which is temporarily closed, and the **Montserrat Golf Club** (☎ 809/491–5220).

## Windsurfing

Contact **Danny Water Sports** (☎ 809/491–5645) to rent boards (about $10 for 45 minutes).

# Shopping

Montserrat's sea-island cotton is famous for its high quality, but, unfortunately, there is only a limited amount and it is not cheap. There are good buys on hand-turned pottery, straw goods, hand-screened prints, ceramic jewelry, and jewelry made from shells and coral. Montserratian stamps can be purchased at the post office or at the Philatelic Bureau, just across the bridge in Wapping. Two lip-smacking local food products are Cassell's hot sauce, available at most supermarkets, and Perk's Punch, an effervescent rum-based concoction manufactured by **J. W. R. Perkins, Inc.** (☎ 809/491–2596).

## Good Buys

CLOTHES

The **Jus' Looking** (TEMPORARILY CLOSED. ⊠ George St., Plymouth, ☏ 809/491–4076; ⊠ Airport, ☏ 809/491–4040) boutique features "sculpted," hand-painted pillows from Antigua; painted and lacquered boxes from the Dutch West Indies; Sunny Caribbee's jams, jellies, and packaged spices from the British Virgin Islands (including an Arawak love potion and a hangover cure); special teas; and Caribelle Batik's line of richly colored fabrics, shirts, skirts, pants, and dresses. The shop also has an excellent selection of local poetry and history books.

**Montserrat Shirts** (TEMPORARILY CLOSED. ⊠ Parliament St., ☏ 809/491–2892) has a good selection of men's tropical cotton shirts, plus T-shirts and sandals for the whole family. They will custom screen T-shirts.

**Etcetera** (TEMPORARILY CLOSED. ⊠ John St., ☏ 809/491–3299) is a little shop carrying colorful, lightweight cotton batik dresses, plus hats, beachwear, and a small but fine selection of local crafts. (If you're lucky, you may see someone making a hat of coconut palm fronds.)

The **Montserrat Sea Island Cotton Co.** (TEMPORARILY CLOSED. ⊠ Corner of George and Strand Sts., Plymouth, ☏ 809/491–7009), long famous for its cotton creations, has dresses, shirts, and other clothing items plus table linens, much of it made from local sea-island cotton.

CRAFTS

The **Tapestries of Montserrat** (TEMPORARILY CLOSED. ⊠ Parliament St., ☏ 809/491–2520), on the second floor of the John Bull Shop, offers a floor-to-ceiling display of hand-tufted creations—from wall hangings and pillow covers to tote bags and rugs—all with fanciful yarn adornments of flowers, carnival figures, animals, and birds. Owners Gerald and Charlie Handley will even help you create your own design for a small additional fee.

At **Carol's Corner** (⊠ Vue Pointe hotel, ☏ 809/491–5210), Carol Osborne sells everything related to Montserrat—stamps, copper bookmarks, paintings, the *Montserrat Cookbook,* Frane Lessac's books of prose, as well as a full line of swimwear and resort wear.

Drop by **Dutcher's Studio** (⊠ Olveston, ☏ 809/491–5253) to see hand-cut, hand-painted objects made from glass, ceramics, and old bottles, and some very appealing ceramic jewelry. If Paula Dutcher is there, ask about the morning iguana feeding at her house. Anywhere from five to 50 reptiles converge on her lawn, sunning themselves and eating hibiscus from your hand.

**Island House** (TEMPORARILY CLOSED. ⊠ John St., ☏ 809/491–3938) stocks a fine collection of Haitian art, Caribbean prints, and clay pottery.

**Sunset Gallery** (⊠ Parliament St., ☏ 809/491–5552) carries an excellent selection of local watercolors, prints, sculptures, and crafts.

# Nightlife

The hotels offer regularly scheduled barbecues and steel bands, and the small restaurants feature live entertainment in the form of calypso, reggae, rock, rhythm and blues, and soul.

**Niggy's** (⊠ Kinsale, ☏ 809/491–7489) usually has a vocalist and live jazz on Friday and Saturday nights. The **Yacht Club** (⊠ Wapping, ☏ 809/491–2237) has live island music on Friday nights. The **Plantation Club** (⊠ Wapping, upstairs over the Oasis, ☏ 809/491–2892) is a lively late-night place with taped rhythm and blues, soul, and soca. The **Inn on Sugar Bay** (⊠ Sugar Bay, ☎ 809/491–5067) has local bands entertaining most evenings. **La Cave** (TEMPORARILY CLOSED. ⊠ Evergreen Dr., Plymouth, no phone), featuring West Indian–style disco and Caribbean and international music, is popular among the young locals. **Nepcoden** (⊠ Weekes, no phone), with its ultraviolet lights, peace signs, and black walls, is a throwback to the '60s. In this cellar restaurant you can eat rotis or chicken for $6. **Colors** (⊠ Fox's Bay, no phone) is one of the island's most popular nightclubs, with live bands and lots of dancing on weekends.

## Exploring Montserrat

*Numbers in the margin correspond to points of interest on the Montserrat map.*

SIGHTS TO SEE

**Bamboo Forest.** The most likely place to spot the Montserrat national bird, *iaterus oberi,* or Montserrat oriole, found nowhere else on earth, is in the Bamboo Forest, a large tract of semi–rain forest inhabited by birds, frogs, and plants. It is home to many of the 100 species of birds that visit Montserrat. You will also see bromeliads, tulip and breadfruit trees, and a plethora of other tropical plants. Because no roads lead into the area and there are no marked paths, you are advised to go with a guide. The most knowledgeable guide is **Joseph Peters**, who will take you on a two- to three-hour tour and fill you in on the wildlife and botany. He can be reached at his home (☎ 809/491–6850) or via the Department of Tourism in Plymouth. You can also call the **Department of Agriculture** (☎ 809/491–2546). ⊠ *South Soufrière Hills.*

❻ **Chance's Peak.** TEMPORARILY CLOSED. The island's highest point pokes up 3,002 ft through the rain forests. The climb to the top is arduous, but there are now 2,000 makeshift stairs (thanks to Cable & Wireless, who added the wooden stairs after a hurricane to ease access to their mountaintop radio tower). If you do make it to the top, what little breath you may have left will be taken away by the view, *if* the clouds have parted. (Go early in the morning, when the clouds are least likely to be there.) ⊠ *Soufrière Hills via Old Fort Rd.*

❹ **Fox's Bay Bird Sanctuary.** Green herons, yellow crowned night herons, rare blue herons, coots, egrets, mangrove cuckoos, and kingfishers plus many lizards and iguanas call this 15-acre mangrove swamp home. The marked trail through the sanctuary begins right near Fox's Bay beach. ⊠ *Grove Rd.*

**Galway's Plantation.** TEMPORARILY CLOSED. Montserrat's most intact historical site is the 1,300-acre plantation built in the late 17th century by the prosperous Irishmen John and Henry Blake, who came to Montserrat from Galway. It has been earmarked as an important archaeological site by the Smithsonian. Amateur archaeologists come here annually in the summer, and the sugar boiling house and parts of both a wind-driven and cattle-driven sugar mill have been partially restored. ⊠ *Old Fort Rd.*

❼ **Galway's Soufrière.** TEMPORARILY CLOSED. The most spectacular scene on Montserrat is probably a 13-acre area of boiling hot springs and fumaroles of gurgling, bubbling (and quite smelly) molten sulfur. Getting here involves both driving on a rugged road and going on a fairly strenuous half-hour hike, and many people hire guides, arranged through the Montserrat Tour Guide Association (☞ Guided Tours, *below*). Everyone's heard the phrase "so hot you could fry an egg on it." Here your guide will almost certainly fry an egg to demonstrate the intense heat of the rocks. ⊠ *Soufrière Hills via Old Fort Rd.*

**⑧ Great Alps Waterfall.** TEMPORARILY CLOSED. Montserrat's White River creates dramatic falls as it plunges 70 ft down a rocky mountain wall and splashes into a shallow pool at the Great Alps Waterfall. It's a moderately strenuous 30- to 45-minute hike through thick rain forests to get there; for a refreshing break, just step in the pool and let the waters cascade right over you. ✉ *Old Fort Rd. at St. Patrick's Village.*

**❸ Montserrat Museum.** TEMPORARILY CLOSED. A restored sugar mill on Richmond Hill just north of town is a showcase for Montserrat history. Here you will find the museum, with its excellent collection of maps, historical records, artifacts (including some Arawak and Carib items), and all sorts of memorabilia pertaining to the island's growth and development. ✉ *Richmond Hill,* ☎ *809/491–5443.* 🎟 *Free (donations accepted).* ☉ *Sun. and Wed. 2:30–5 (call to confirm hrs).*

**❶ Plymouth.** TEMPORARILY CLOSED. The island's biggest town is neat and clean, its narrow streets lined with trim Georgian structures built mostly of stones that came from Dorset as ballast on old sailing vessels. On the south side, a bridge over Fort Ghaut ("gut," or ravine) leads to Wapping, where most of the restaurants are located.

It's hard not to notice the residence of the governor of Montserrat, **Government House,** which is a frilly Victorian house, painted green with white trim and decorated with a shamrock. It dates from the 18th century and is set amid extraordinarily lovely gardens. Although the public is not allowed inside, everyone is welcome to walk through the beautiful landscaping surrounding the building. ✉ *Peebles St., no phone.* 🎟 *Free.* ☉ *Mon.–Tues. and Thurs.–Fri. 10–noon.*

Great piles of local vegetables and fruits and vendors in brightly colored outfits mark the **Plymouth Market,** where islanders bring their produce on Friday and Saturday mornings. ✉ *Parliament St.* ☉ *Fri.–Sat. 7–noon.*

**❷ St. Anthony's Church.** TEMPORARILY CLOSED. Just north of town, this majestic structure built of gray stone is one of the prettiest churches on Montserrat. It was consecrated sometime between 1623 and 1666 and was rebuilt in 1730 following one of the many clashes between the French and the English in the area. Two silver chalices displayed in the church were donated by freed slaves after their emancipation in 1834. ✉ *Hwy. 2.*

**❺ St. George's Fort.** The fort itself is overgrown and in ruin, but the great view of Plymouth from the hilltop is well worth the trip. You can hike or drive. ✉ *Hwy 4.*

# Montserrat A to Z

## Arriving and Departing

BY PLANE

Although Antigua is not the only gateway, it's the best way to reach Montserrat. **BWIA** (☎ 800/538–2942) flies nonstop on Wednesday and Friday (plus Sundays in season) to Antigua from New York and on Monday, Wednesday, Thursday, and Friday from Miami; it also has regularly scheduled nonstop service from Toronto, Canada, and Heathrow Airport, London. **American Airlines** (☎ 800/433–7300) has connecting service from a number of U.S. cities through San Juan, Puerto Rico. **Air Canada** (☎ 800/776–3000) offers service from Toronto; **British Airways** (☎ 0181/897–4000 in Britain; ☎ 800/247–9297 in the U.S.) from Gatwick Airport, London; and **Lufthansa** (☎ 800/645–3880 in the U.S.) flies in from Frankfurt via Puerto Rico.

From Antigua's V. C. Bird International Airport, you can make your connections with **LIAT** (☎ 809/491–2533 or 800/253–5011) or **Montserrat Airways** (☎ 809/491–5342 or 809/491–6494) for the 15-minute flight to Montserrat.

You will land on the 3,400-ft runway at Blackburne Airport, on the Atlantic coast, about 11 mi from Plymouth.

FROM THE AIRPORT

Taxis meet every flight; the government-regulated fare from the airport to Plymouth is EC$29 (US$11).

## Currency
The official currency is the Eastern Caribbean dollar (EC$), often called beewee. At press time, the exchange rate was EC$2.67 to US$1. U.S. dollars are readily accepted, but you'll often receive change in beewees. Note: Prices quoted here are in U.S. dollars unless noted otherwise.

## Emergencies
**Police:** ☎ 999 or 809/491–2555. **Hospital:** There is a 24-hour emergency room at **Glendon Hospital** (✉ Plymouth, ☎ 809/491–2552). **Pharmacies: Lee's Pharmacy** (✉ Temporarily relocated to Belham; Evergreen Dr., Plymouth, ☎ 809/491–3274) and **Daniel's Pharmacy** (TEMPORARILY CLOSED. ✉ George St., Plymouth, ☎ 809/491–2908).

## Getting Around
CAR RENTALS

The island has more than 115 mi of paved (but potholed) roads. Unless you're uncomfortable about driving on the left, you won't have any trouble exploring. You'll need a valid driver's license, plus a Montserrat license, available at the airport or the Treasury Department on Strand Street in Plymouth weekdays 8:30–2:30. The fee is EC$30 (US$12). Rental cars cost about $35–$40 per day. The smaller companies, whose prices are generally 10%–25% cheaper, will negotiate, particularly off-season. **Jefferson's Car Rental** (✉ Dagenham, ☎ 809/ 491–2126) is a local rental company. Other agencies are **Reliable** (TEMPORARILY CLOSED. ✉ Plymouth, ☎ 809/491–6990), and **Ethelyne's Car Rental** (TEMPORARILY CLOSED. ✉ Plymouth, ☎ 809/491–2855).

MOUNTAIN BIKES

Montserrat is great mountain-bike country, with trails rated among the 50 best in the world. It's small, with relatively traffic-free roads and lots of challenging hills to try out all those gears. Potholes will present a constant challenge, as will the heat and steep gradients. Even so, biking is a great way to get around this island, where the majority of facilities, shops, and accommodations are concentrated in a small area on the west coast (☞ Outdoor Activities and Sports, *above*).

TAXIS

Taxis, private vehicles, or the M11 (a play on the local registration numbers, meaning your own two legs) are the main means of transport on the island. Taxis are always available at the airport, the main hotels, and the taxi stand in Plymouth (TEMPORARILY CLOSED. ☎ 809/491–2261; try the Vue Pointe hotel, ☎ 809/491–5210). The Tourist Board publishes a list of taxi fares to most destinations. Be sure to agree with your driver on the fare in advance and know whether you have agreed to pay in E.C. or U.S. dollars.

## Guided Tours
Guides are recommended when you are heading to Mount Chance, Galway's Soufrière, and the Great Alps Falls. Prices for two people range from $10 to $30. Guides and tours can be arranged by calling Cecil

Cassell, president of the **Montserrat Tour Guide Association** (☎ 809/491–3160, FAX 809/491–2052). Or you can call **John Ryner** (☎ 809/491–2190) and the aptly named **Be-Beep Taylor** (☎ 809/491–3787). Prices (fixed by the Department of Tourism) are EC$30 per hour (US$12) or EC$130–$150 (US$50–$58) for a five-hour day tour. Refreshments are extra. For further information, contact the Tourist Board.

## Language
It's English with more of a lilt than a brogue. You'll also hear a patois that's spoken on most of the islands.

## Opening and Closing Times
Most shops are open Monday to Saturday 8–noon and 1–4, and a good number close at noon on Wednesday. Banking hours vary slightly from bank to bank but are generally, at the minimum, Monday–Thursday 8–3 and Friday 3–5.

## Passports and Visas
U.S., Canadian, and British citizens only need proof of citizenship, such as a passport, a notarized birth certificate, or a voter registration card plus a photo ID, such as a driver's license. A driver's license by itself is *not* sufficient. All visitors must hold an ongoing or return ticket.

## Precautions
Ask for permission before taking pictures. Some residents may be reluctant photographic subjects, and they will appreciate your courtesy.

Most Montserratians frown at the sight of skimpily dressed tourists; do not risk offending them by strolling around town in short shorts and swimsuits (which are not acceptable even with a cover-up).

## Taxes and Service Charges
Hotels collect a 7% government tax and add a 10% service charge. Most restaurants add a 10%–15% service charge. If restaurants do not add the service charge, it's customary to leave a 10% or 15% tip. Taxi drivers should be given a 10% tip. The departure tax is EC$25 (about US$9).

## Telephones and Mail
To call Montserrat from the United States, dial area code 664 (recently changed from 809) and access code 491 plus the local four-digit number. International direct dial is available on the island; both local and long-distance calls come through clearly. To call locally on the island, you need to dial the seven-digit number, the first three digits of which are always 491.

Airmail letters and postcards to the United States and Canada cost EC$1.15 each. Montserrat is one of several Caribbean islands whose stamps are of interest to collectors. You can buy them at the main post office in Plymouth, open Monday, Tuesday, Thursday, and Friday 8:15–3:55 and Wednesday and Saturday 8:15–11:25 AM.

## Visitor Information
You can get information about Montserrat through the **Caribbean Tourism Organization** (✉ 20 E. 46th St., New York, NY 10017, ☎ 212/682–0435).

On Montserrat, the **Montserrat Tourist Board** (✉ Church Rd., Plymouth, ☎ 809/491–2230) is open weekdays 8–noon and 1–4.

# 17 Puerto Rico

*Puerto Rico, with its long beaches, green rain forests, towering mountains, and vibrant cultures, offers something for everyone. From the flashy casinos and exquisite restaurants of San Juan to the history and shopping opportunities of Old San Juan to the small inns and seaside resorts of the countryside, the island begs to be explored. With easy access from North America and Europe, and with the island's modern roads and uncomplicated logistics, now, more than ever, is the time to go.*

Updated by
Karl Luntta

EW CITIES IN THE CARIBBEAN are as steeped in Spanish tradition as Puerto Rico's Old San Juan. Originally built as a fortress enclave, the old city has myriad attractions, including restored 16th-century buildings, museums, art galleries, bookstores, and 200-year-old houses with balustraded balconies of filigreed wrought iron overlooking narrow cobblestone streets. This Spanish tradition also spills over into the island's countryside, from its festivals celebrated in honor of various patron saints in the little towns to the *paradores,* inexpensive but accommodating inns whose concept originated in Spain.

Puerto Rico is ringed with hundreds of beaches offering every imaginable water sport and acres of golf courses and tennis courts. It has, in San Juan's sophisticated Condado and Isla Verde areas, glittering hotels; flashy, Las Vegas–style shows; casinos; and frenetic discos. It has the ambience of the Old World in the seven-square-block area of the old city and in its quiet colonial towns. Out in the countryside lie its natural attractions, including the extraordinary, 28,000-acre Caribbean National Forest, more familiarly known as the El Yunque rain forest, with 100-ft-high trees (more than 240 species of them) and dramatic mountain ranges. You can hike through forest reserves laced with trails, go spelunking in vast caves, and explore coffee plantations and sugar mills. Having seen every sight on the island, you can then do further exploring on the outlying islands of Culebra, Vieques, Icacos, and Mona, where aquatic activities, such as snorkeling and scuba diving, prevail.

Puerto Rico, 110 mi long and 35 mi wide, was populated by several tribes of Indians when Columbus landed on the island on his second voyage in 1493. In 1508 Juan Ponce de León, the frustrated seeker of the Fountain of Youth, established a settlement on the island and became its first governor, and in 1521, he founded Old San Juan. For three centuries, the French, Dutch, and English tried unsuccessfully to wrest the island from Spain. In 1897 Spain granted the island dominion status. In 1899, as a result of the Spanish American War, Spain ceded the island to the United States, and in 1917, Puerto Ricans became U.S. citizens. In 1952 Puerto Rico became a semiautonomous commonwealth territory of the United States. There have been several referendums over the years where the island's political status has been put to a vote. The choices for Puerto Ricans have been independence, full statehood, or remaining a commonwealth. While strong opinions have been voiced on all sides, the vote has yet to produce statehood or independence.

Hurricanes have always been the bane of Caribbean islands, and 1996 proved to be a hard year for Puerto Rico. In September of that year, Hurricane Hortense ripped through the island as well as parts of the nearby Dominican Republic, creating mud slides that killed 15 and caused millions in damage. The island quickly recovered and nearly all hotels and roads reopened. Lasting damage was confined to some roads, trails, and information centers of the El Yunque rain forest, which expected full recovery by the 1997–98 season.

If you're a U.S. citizen, you need neither passport nor visa when you land at the bustling Luis Muñoz Marín International Airport, outside San Juan. You don't have to clear customs, and you don't have to explain yourself to an immigration official. Though the official language is Spanish, English is widely spoken, particularly by those in the tourism industry.

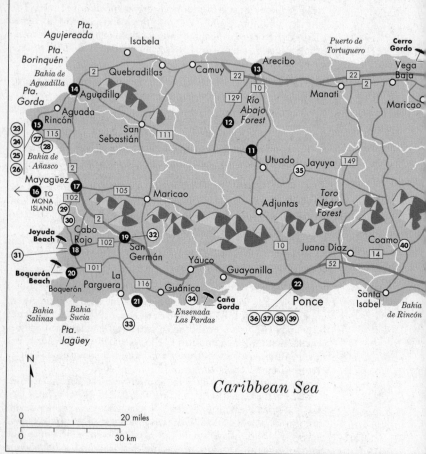

Caribbean Sea

N

0 ____ 20 miles
0 ____ 30 km

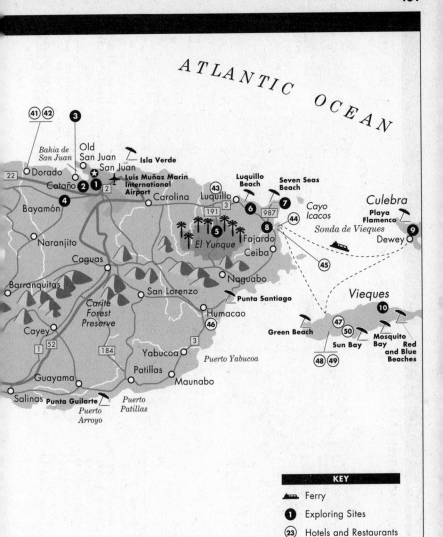

ATLANTIC OCEAN

Bahia de San Juan

41 42

3

Dorado

Cataño

Bayamón

Naranjito

Caguas

Barranquitas

Old San Juan

San Juan

Isla Verde

Luis Muñoz Marín International Airport

Carolina

Luquillo

El Yunque

5

Fajardo

Ceiba

Naguabo

San Lorenzo

Carite Forest Preserve

Cayey

Humacao

46

Luquillo Beach

6

Seven Seas Beach

7

Cayo Icacos

Sonda de Vieques

44

8

45

Culebra

Playa Flamenco

Dewey

9

Vieques

10

Green Beach

Sun Bay

47

50

Mosquito Bay

Red and Blue Beaches

48 49

Yabucoa

Patillas

Maunabo

Puerto Yabucoa

Guayama

Salinas

Punta Guilarte

Puerto Arroyo

Puerto Patillas

Punta Santiago

### KEY

🚢 Ferry

① Exploring Sites

㉓ Hotels and Restaurants

Lazy Parrot, **25**
Lupita's, **36**
Pastrami Palace, **24**
Restaurant El Ancla, **38**

**Lodging**
Casa del Francés, **50**
Copamarina Beach Resort, **34**

Crow's Nest, **47**
El Conquistador Resort and Country Club, **44**
Hacienda Tamarindo, **49**
Horned Dorset Primavera, **27**
Hotel Meliá, **39**
Hyatt Dorado Beach, **42**

Hyatt Regency Cerromar Beach, **41**
Inn on the Blue Horizon, **48**
Lemontree Waterfront Cottages, **28**
Palmas del Mar, **46**
Parador Baños de Coamo, **40**
Parador Boquemar, **31**

Parador Hacienda Gripiñas, **35**
Parador Oasis, **32**
Parador Villa Parguera, **33**
Ponce Hilton and Casino, **37**
Westin Rio Mar Beach Resort and Country Club, **43**

**432**

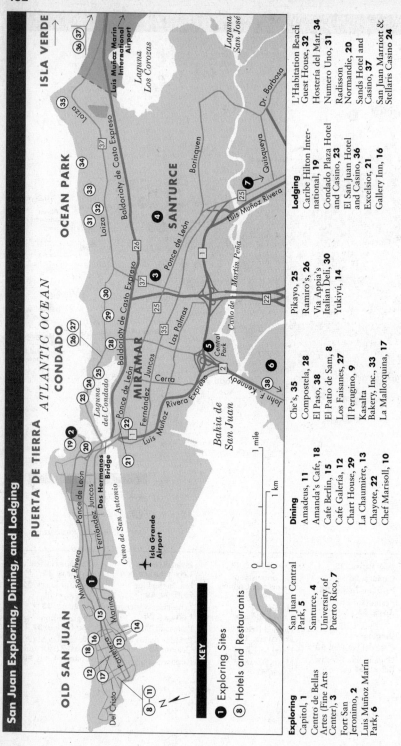

# San Juan Exploring, Dining, and Lodging

OLD SAN JUAN

PUERTA DE TIERRA

CONDADO

OCEAN PARK

ISLA VERDE

SANTURCE

MIRAMAR

ATLANTIC OCEAN

Bahía de San Juan

Laguna Los Corozas

Laguna San José

KEY

- ① Exploring Sites
- ⑧ Hotels and Restaurants

**Exploring**
Capitol, 1
Centro de Bellas Artes (Fine Arts Center), 3
Fort San Jerónimo, 2
Luis Muñoz Marín Park, 6
San Juan Central Park, 5
Santurce, 4
University of Puerto Rico, 7

**Dining**
Amadeus, 11
Amanda's Cafe, 18
Cafe Berlin, 15
Cafe Galeria, 12
Chart House, 29
La Chaumière, 13
Chayote, 22
Chef Marisoll, 10
Che's, 35
Compostela, 28
El Paso, 8
El Patio de Sam, 8
Los Faisanes, 27
Il Perugino, 9
Kasalta Bakery, Inc., 33
La Mallorquina, 17
Pikayo, 25
Ramiro's, 26
Via Appia's Italian Deli, 30
Yukiyú, 14

**Lodging**
Caribe Hilton International, 19
Condado Plaza Hotel and Casino, 23
El San Juan Hotel and Casino, 36
Excelsior, 21
Gallery Inn, 16
L'Habitation Beach Guest House, 32
Hostería del Mar, 34
Numero Uno, 31
Radisson Normandie, 20
Sands Hotel and Casino, 37
San Juan Marriott & Stellaris Casino, 24

# Lodging

Accommodations on Puerto Rico come in all shapes and sizes. Self-contained luxury resorts cover hundreds of acres. San Juan's high-rise beachfront hotels likewise cater to the cruise-ship and casino crowd; several target the business traveler. Outside of San Juan, the government-sponsored paradores are lodgings modeled after Spain's successful parador system. Some are rural inns, some offer motel-style (no-frill) apartments, and some are large hotels. They are required to meet certain standards, such as proximity to a sightseeing attraction or beach. Most have a small restaurant that serves local cuisine. Parador prices range from $50 to $125 for a double room. Reservations for all paradores can be made by writing Box 4435, Old San Juan Station, San Juan 00902, or by calling 800/443–0266 in the United States, 787/721–2884 in San Juan, or 800/981–7575 elsewhere in Puerto Rico. They are a phenomenal bargain but tend to get noisy and raucous on weekends, when families descend from the cities for a minivacation.

Most hotels in Puerto Rico operate on the European Plan (EP). In some larger hotels, however, packages are available that include several or all meals, while others offer all-inclusive deals. Also, beware when booking hotels outside of San Juan that rates most often do not include airport transfers. Be sure to ask if the hotel offers transportation, what the cost is, and if advance arrangements are necessary.

| CATEGORY | COST* |
| --- | --- |
| $$$$ | over $225 |
| $$$ | $150–$225 |
| $$ | $75–$150 |
| $ | under $75 |

*All prices are for a standard double room, excluding 7% tax (9% for hotels with casinos) and 10%–15% service charge.*

## Old San Juan

**$$–$$$** ★ 🏨 **Gallery Inn.** Owners Jan D'Esopo and Manuco Gandia restored this rambling, classically Spanish house, one of the oldest private residences in the area, and turned it into an inn. It's full of quirky details—winding, uneven stairs; private balconies; a music room with a Steinway grand piano; lots of public rooms, areas, and decks to hide out with a book; and small interior gardens. The rooms are individually decorated and have telephones but no televisions; most are air-conditioned. Views from the rooftop deck are some of the best in the old city—a panorama of the El Morro and San Cristóbal forts and the Atlantic. Galería San Juan, a small gallery and working studio, features various pieces by Jan D'Esopo, Bruno Lucchesi, and Teresa Spinner—sculpture and silk-screen prints fill nearly every nook and cranny of the inn. There is no restaurant, but meals can be cooked and served in the small dining room for groups upon request. The inn has no sign in front, so tell your taxi driver it's on the corner of Calles Norzagaray and San Justo. ✉ *204–206 Calle Norzagaray, Old San Juan 00901,* ☎ *787/722–1808,* FAX *787/724–7360. 16 rooms and suites. Bar. AE, MC, V. CP.*

## San Juan

**$$$$** ★ 🏨 **Caribe Hilton International.** Built in 1949, this property occupies 17 acres on Puerta de Tierra. Rooms have been modernized and refurbished over the years and have a crisp, pastel decor and balconies with ocean or lagoon views; the higher the floor, the better the view. Executive levels provide services such as private check-in and checkout, complimentary evening cocktails, and complimentary Continental breakfast for business travelers. The spacious atrium lobby—a hub of activity—is decorated with beige marble, waterfalls, and lavish tropical plants.

Restaurants include Batey del Pescador for seafood and Peacock Paradise for Chinese cuisine. The hotel has San Juan's only private beach, complete with the Islita bar and grill and a boardwalk at its edge. Guests interested in water sports are shuttled to the beach at Isla Verde. ✉ *Box 1872, San Juan 00902,* ☎ *787/721–0303 or 800/468–8585,* FAX *787/724–6992. 672 rooms and suites. 5 restaurants, air-conditioning, 2 pools, 6 tennis courts, exercise room, racquetball, squash, beach, casino, business services. AE, D, DC, MC, V. EP, CP, MAP.*

$$$$ 🏨 **Condado Plaza Hotel and Casino.** The Atlantic and the Condado Lagoon border this property. Two wings, appropriately named Ocean and Lagoon, are connected by an enclosed, elevated walkway over Avenida Ashford. Standard rooms have walk-in closets and separate dressing areas. There is a variety of suites, including spa suites with oversize Jacuzzis, and a fully equipped business center. The Plaza Club floor has 24-hour concierge service and a private lounge, and guests there receive complimentary Continental breakfast, afternoon hors d'oeuvres, and evening coffee. The Ocean wing sits on a small strip of public beach called La Playita la Condado, and there are two pools. Kids can find plenty to do at their own activity center, Camp Taino. Dining options include Tony Roma's (a branch of the American chain) and an informal restaurant poolside. ✉ *999 Av. Ashford, San Juan 00902,* ☎ *787/721–1000 or 800/468–8588,* FAX *787/722–7955. 589 rooms and suites. 7 restaurants, 3 bars, air-conditioning, 3 pools (1 saltwater), 2 hot tubs, 2 tennis courts, health club, beach, water sports, casino, business services. AE, D, DC, MC, V. EP, CP, MAP.*

$$$$ ★ 🏨 **El San Juan Hotel and Casino.** An immense, dripping chandelier illuminates the hand-carved mahogany paneling, Italian rose marble, and French tapestries in the huge, newly renovated lobby of this 12-acre resort on the Isla Verde beach. You'll be hard pressed to decide if you want a suite in the main tower, with whirlpool bath and wet bar; a garden lanai room with private patio and whirlpool bath; or a casita, with a sunken Roman bath. All rooms have CD player, three phones, modem jack, TV with VCR (some rooms feature a TV in the bathroom), minibar, and walk-in closets with an iron and board. Dark rattan furnishings are complemented by rich carpets and tropical-print spreads and drapes. This luxurious hotel attracts a moneyed mix of international business and leisure travelers. Don't miss the informal rooftop Margarita Bar; watching the sunset from here is a splendid end to a day of sightseeing. Or, relax at the lobby's Cigar Bar and sample some of Puerto Rico's finest cigars, selected from one of 56 humidors. ✉ *Av. Isla Verde, Box 2872, San Juan 00902,* ☎ *787/791–1000 or 800/468–2818,* FAX *787/791–0390. 389 rooms. 7 restaurants, 8 bars, air-conditioning, minibars, no-smoking rooms, in-room VCRs, 2 pools, wading pool, 3 hot tubs, 3 tennis courts, health club, beach, water sports, shops, casino, business services. AE, DC, MC, V. EP, MAP.*

$$$$ ★ 🏨 **San Juan Marriott and Stellaris Casino.** The red neon sign atop this San Juan hotel is a beacon to its excellent Condado location. The hotel opened in January 1995 and has been a keystone to the revival of tourism in the Condado. Rooms have soothing pastel carpeting, flowered spreads, attractive tropical artwork on the walls, and balconies overlooking the ocean, the pool, or both. Restaurants include Tuscany, for northern Italian cuisine, and the more casual La Vista, open 24 hours and popular for dining alfresco. On weekends, there's live entertainment in the enormous lobby, which, combined with the persistent ringing of slot machines from the adjoining casino, makes the area quite noisy (rooms are soundproof). Gorgeous Condado beach is right outside, as is a large pool area. The hotel's spa-gym is the best of any resort in Puerto Rico. ✉ *1309 Av. Ashford, San Juan 00907,* ☎ *787/722–7000 or 800/228–9290,* FAX *787/722–6800. 525 rooms,*

*13 suites. 3 restaurants, 2 lounges, air-conditioning, no-smoking rooms, beauty salon, hot tub, sauna, 2 tennis courts, health club, water sports, children's programs, business services, meeting rooms. AE, D, DC, MC, V. EP, MAP, FAP.*

**$$$$** ★ 🏨 **Sands Hotel and Casino.** One of Puerto Rico's largest casinos glitters just off the lobby, stunning artwork from around the world graces the public rooms, and a huge free-form pool lies between the hotel and its beach. Rooms, with tiny balconies (ask for one with an ocean view), have basic tropical decor, with a green, peach, and white color scheme and white rattan furniture. The exclusive Plaza Club section is that rare executive level worth the added expense, offering garden suites, a masseuse, a small gym, and other enticements. The Sands Tuscano restaurant offers live entertainment, including female impersonators in a "Legends Live" show, featuring Elvis, Liza, Betty Boop, and more. The Ruth's Chris Steak House, part of the national chain, serves some of the best steaks in town. ⊠ *187 Isla Verde Rd., Box 6676, Santurce, San Juan 00914,* ☎ *787/791–6100 or 800/544–3008,* 📠 *787/791–8525. 412 rooms. 4 restaurants, 2 lounges, air-conditioning, pool, beach, water sports, casino, recreation room, concierge, business center. AE, D, DC, MC, V. EP.*

**$$$** ★ 🏨 **Radisson Normandie.** This oceanfront, Art Deco hotel is a national landmark. It was built in 1939, in the shape of the fabled ocean liner of the same name. The pillars and molding throughout have been hand painted to restore the hotel to its original Deco splendor. Rooms have minibars, cable TV, coffeemakers, and hair dryers; some have sunrooms. Additional frills and pampering can be found at the seventh-floor executive club, where you receive complimentary Continental breakfast and evening hors d'oeuvres. You can make reservations to use the tennis courts at the Hilton next door. ⊠ *Corner of Av. Muñoz Rivera and Av. Rosales, Puerta Tierra, Box 50059, San Juan 00902,* ☎ *787/729–2929 or 800/333–3333,* 📠 *787/729–3083. 177 rooms. 2 restaurants, lounge, air-conditioning, pool, wading pool, health club, jogging, dive shop, snorkeling, water sports, boating, business services. AE, D, DC, MC, V. EP, MAP.*

**$$** 🏨 **Excelsior.** Across the Condado Lagoon in Miramar (a 15-minute walk or a two-minute shuttle to the beach), the Excelsior is off the beaten path in a commercial area of the city and is popular with business travelers. Room decor here is standard hotel fare, but the rates are a good value. Each room has a phone, fridge, cable TV, and a private bath with a hair dryer; some have kitchenettes. Fine carpets adorn the corridors, and sculptures decorate the glass-laden lobby. Augusto's, one of the hotel's restaurants, is highly respected for its international cuisine. Complimentary coffee, newspaper, and shoe shine are offered each morning. ⊠ *801 Av. Ponce de León, San Juan 00907,* ☎ *787/721–7400 or 800/289–4274,* 📠 *787/723–0068. 140 rooms. 2 restaurants, bar, air-conditioning, refrigerators, pool, exercise room, free parking. AE, D, DC, MC, V. EP.*

**$$** 🏨 **Hostería del Mar.** Right on the beach in Ocean Park, a residential neighborhood, this small, white inn–guest house is a wonderful alternative to the hustle and bustle of the Condado or Old San Juan—you have to go down to the beach and look west to see the high-rises of the Condado looming in the distance. Rooms here are attractive and simple, with tropical prints and rattan furniture, and many have ocean views. Four apartments have kitchenettes with microwaves and two-burner stoves. The staff is courteous and helpful. A vegetarian-oriented restaurant is on the ground floor facing the trade winds and offers fabulous views of the wide beach in front. ⊠ *1 Calle Tapia, Ocean Park, San Juan 00911,* ☎ *787/727–3302,* 📠 *787/268–0772. 8 rooms, 4 apartments, 1 minisuite. Restaurant, air-conditioning, beach. AE, DC, MC, V. EP.*

$$ ★ ⛱ **Numero Uno.** Several years ago, former New Yorkers Ester and Chris Laube bought this three-story, red-roofed guest house on the beach, spruced it up, and turned it into a very pleasant and comfortable accommodation. It's set in a quiet residential neighborhood, right in the middle of the nicest beach in San Juan. The simple but clean and recently renovated rooms offer double, queen-, or king-size beds, and most are air-conditioned or have ceiling fans. Three rooms have ocean views. A walled-in patio provides privacy for sunning or hanging out by the small pool, the bar, and restaurant, Pamela's. On the other side of the wall, a wide, sandy beach beckons: Beach chairs and towels are provided to guests. ✉ *1 Calle Santa Ana, Ocean Park, San Juan 00911,* ☎ *787/726–5010,* ℻ *787/727–5482. 12 rooms. Restaurant, bar, pool, beach. AE, MC, V. CP.*

$–$$ ⛱ **L'Habitation Beach Guest House.** On the beach in Ocean Park is this gay-oriented guest house with a definite French atmosphere. Owner Alain Tasca is from Paris by way of Guadeloupe and Key West. He has established a very relaxed ambience in this casual, nine-room accommodation. Rooms are well-sized, simple, and comfortable. Chambermaid Natasha sees to it that everything is kept clean and in its place and will chase after offenders who don't wash sand off their feet before entering the house. A bar and snack bar sit in a corner of a palm-shaded, sandy patio between the guest house and the beach. Rooms 8 and 9 are the largest rooms and have ocean views. Beach chairs and towels are provided: Pick one before you have one of Alain's margaritas—they'll knock your sandals off. ✉ *1957 Calle Italia, Ocean Park, San Juan 00911,* ☎ *787/727–2499,* ℻ *787/727–2599. 9 rooms. Bar, snack bar, air-conditioning, beach. AE, D, MC, V. CP.*

## Out on the Island

### CABO ROJO

$–$$ ⛱ **Parador Boquemar.** You can walk to the Boquerón public beach (one of the island's best) from this small parador at the end of Route 101. Rooms are comfortable, each decorated in the island uniform of tropical prints and rattan. Ask for a third-floor room with a balcony overlooking the water. La Cascada, a *mesón gastronómico* (☞ Dining, *below*), is well known for its superior traditional Puerto Rican cuisine. On weekends the lounge is filled with live music. At press time, the parador was adding 20 new rooms. ✉ *Box 133, Boquerón 00622,* ☎ *787/851–2158 or 800/443–0266,* ℻ *787/851–7600. 63 rooms. Restaurant, lounge, air-conditioning, minibars, refrigerators, pool. AE, D, DC, MC, V. EP.*

### COAMO

$ ⛱ **Parador Baños de Coamo.** On Route 546, Km 1, northeast of Ponce, this mountain inn is at the hot sulfur springs that are said to be the Fountain of Youth of Ponce de León's dreams. Rooms open onto latticed wooden verandas and have a pleasing blend of contemporary and period furnishings. The parador can make arrangements for you to ride Puerto Rico's glorious, unique breed of show horse called *paso fino.* ✉ *Box 540, Coamo 00769,* ☎ *787/825–2186 or 800/443–0266,* ℻ *787/825–4739. 48 rooms. Restaurant, lounge, air-conditioning, pool. AE, DC, MC, V. EP.*

### DORADO

$$$$ ⛱ **Hyatt Dorado Beach.** The ambience is a bit more subdued at this resort than at its sister, the Cerromar Beach (☞ *below*), and guests can take advantage of the facilities there. A variety of elegant accommodations are in low-rise buildings scattered over 1,000 lavishly landscaped acres—among the most beautiful in the Caribbean. Most rooms have private patios or balconies, and all have polished terra-cotta floors and

marble baths. Upper-level rooms in the Oceanview Houses have a view of the two half-moon beaches. ⊠ *Rte. 693, Km 10.8, Dorado 00646,* ☎ *787/796–1234 or 800/233–1234,* ℻ *787/796–2022. 298 rooms. 3 restaurants, 2 lounges, air-conditioning, 2 pools, wading pool, spa, 2 18-hole golf courses, 7 tennis courts, health club, hiking, jogging, water sports, bicycles, casino. AE, DC, MC, V. EP, MAP.*

**$$$$** ⊡ **Hyatt Regency Cerromar Beach.** One of the best sports-oriented resorts in the Caribbean, the family-oriented Cerromar has two Robert Trent Jones golf courses, 14 tennis courts, a spa and health club, jogging and biking trails, a 900-ft river pool, a Jacuzzi in a man-made cavern, a swim-up bar, and a three-story-high water slide. It's 22 mi west of San Juan, right on the Atlantic. The modern seven-story hotel is done up in tropical style. Rooms have tile floors, marble baths, and a king-size or two double beds. You'll find quieter rooms on the west side, away from the pool activity. Guests at the Cerromar and its sister facility, the Hyatt Dorado Beach (☞ *above*) a mile down the road, have access to the facilities of both resorts, and colorful red trolleys make frequent runs between the two. Sushi Wong's serves delicious pan-Asian cuisine, and Medici's is a sophisticated northern Italian eatery. ⊠ *Rte. 693, Km 11.8, Dorado 00646,* ☎ *787/796–1234 or 800/233–1234,* ℻ *787/796–4647. 506 rooms. 4 restaurants, 3 bars, air-conditioning, pool, spa, 2 18-hole golf courses, 14 tennis courts, health club, hiking, jogging, bicycles, casino, dance club. AE, DC, MC, V. EP, MAP.*

FAJARDO

**$$$$** ⊡ **Westin Rio Mar Beach Resort and Country Club.** This extensive resort,
**★** opened in 1996, is built on the grounds of a former Club Ríomar beach and country club. Set on 481 acres, the nouveau Spanish-Moorish resort, has red-tile roofs and a massive lobby with ocher floor tiles, ornate stairways, potted plants, and shimmering chandeliers. The rooms and suites are uniformly new and spacious and feature lots of dark-grained wood and floral patterns, in-room video games, and a balcony; the suites also have large desks. Don't get Suite 5099 or 5101—the balconies overlook the hotel's central air-conditioning ducts. The resort sits on two 18-hole golf courses, and it's kid-friendly as well. In addition to the beach, kids have their own activities centers indoors and out, and a large pool with a winding slide. The resort is about an hour from San Juan, and El Yunque is just minutes away. ⊠ *6000 Rio Mar Blvd., Río Grande 00745,* ☎ *787/888–6000 or 800/474–6627,* ℻ *787/888–6600. 528 rooms, 72 suites. 11 restaurants, bar, lounge, air-conditioning, in-room safes, minibars, no-smoking rooms, 2 pools, beauty salon, spa, 13 tennis courts, health club, beach, water sports, shops, casino, children's programs, recreation room, meeting rooms, car rental. AE, D, DC, MC, V. EP.*

GUÁNICA

**$$$** ⊡ **Copamarina Beach Resort.** Sprawling across 18 acres between the
**★** sea and the Guánica Dry Forest is this quiet, landscaped resort. The pool is the centerpiece of the property, surrounded by the open-air reception area, manicured lawns, the outdoor Las Palmas Cafe, the elegant Ballena restaurant and bar, and the building wings. The bay bottom on this section of beach is covered in seaweed, but secluded beaches with clear water can be found a few minutes' drive down the road. The spotless rooms have small terraces with water views and one queen-size or two double beds. Try the red snapper in the La Ballena dining room, and stop in the Las Palmas bar for the bartender's straight-up margarita. There are scuba-diving packages available, or you can arrange a snorkeling excursion to Gilligan's Island (about $3), an offshore key. ⊠ *Rte. 333, Km 6.5, Caña Gorda, Box 805, Guánica 00653,* ☎ *787/821–0505 or 800/468–4553,* ℻ *787/821–0070. 70 rooms. 2 restaurants, 2 bars, air-conditioning, 2 pools, hot tub, 2 ten-*

*nis courts, volleyball, bicycles, shop, recreation room, meeting rooms. AE, D, DC, MC, V. EP.*

$$$-$$$$ ☒ **Palmas del Mar.** This luxurious resort community is on 2,750 acres of a former coconut plantation on the sheltered southeast coast (about an hour's drive from San Juan). Two hotels, the 23-suite Palmas Inn and 102-room Wyndham Hotel, are the centerpieces of the complex. In the rustic yet elegant Wyndham, rooms are airy and spacious. The Palmas Inn suites, all with stunning sea or garden views, evoke luxurious Mediterranean villas, with pastel-pink connecting walkways, cobblestone plazas, and fountains adorned with hand-painted tile work. ☒ *Box 2020, Rte. 906, Humacao 00792,* ☎ *787/852–6000 or 800/468–3331,* FAX *787/852–6330. 102 rooms; 140 villas; 23 1-, 2-, and 3-bedroom suites. 10 restaurants, air-conditioning, pool, 18-hole golf course, 20 tennis courts, exercise room, horseback riding, beach, dive shop, marina, water sports, boating, fishing, bicycles, casino. AE, DC, MC, V. EP, MAP.*

$ ☒ **Parador Hacienda Gripiñas.** Don't stay here if you're looking for a
★ beach vacation: The sea is more than 30 mi away. This white hacienda is for those looking for a romantic mountain hideaway. Polished wood and beam ceilings warm the interior. Large, airy rooms are decorated with native crafts. Relaxation beckons at every turn: Rocking chairs nod in the spacious lounge, hammocks swing on the porch, and splendid gardens invite a leisurely stroll. Your morning coffee is grown on the adjacent working plantation, and its aroma seems to fill the grounds, as does the chirp of the ubiquitous coquis (tree frogs). ☒ *Rte. 527, Km 2.5, Box 387, Jayuya 00664,* ☎ *787/828–1717 or 800/443–0266,* FAX *787/721– 4698. 19 rooms. Restaurant, lounge, pool, hiking. AE. EP.*

$$ ☒ **Parador Villa Parguera.** This parador is a stylish hotel on Phos-
★ phorescent Bay. Large, colorfully decorated rooms all have a balcony or terrace. A spacious dining room, overlooking the small swimming pool and the bay beyond, serves excellent native and international dishes. Children under 10 stay free in their parents' room. Ask about honeymoon packages. ☒ *Rte. 304, Box 273, Lajas 00667,* ☎ *787/899–3975 or 800/443–0266,* FAX *787/899–6040. 62 rooms. Restaurant, lounge, air-conditioning, saltwater pool, dance club. AE, D, DC, MC, V. EP.*

$$$$ ☒ **El Conquistador Resort and Country Club.** This massive complex is
★ a world unto itself, divided into five self-contained hotels. It's perched dramatically atop a 300-ft bluff overlooking the Caribbean, the Atlantic, and the El Yunque rain forest. The architecture is a harmonious blend of Moorish and Spanish colonial: cobblestone streets, white stucco and terra-cotta buildings, open-air plazas with soaring arches and tinkling fountains, tiled benches, and gas lamps. Plants and colorful caged parrots decorate many of the open spaces. One of the five hotels, Las Olas, is actually built into the cliff face. Each room has a seating area with couch, glass-top coffee table, desk, chairs, and entertainment center. Enormous bathrooms have sunken tub, long marble countertop, makeup mirror, and walk-in closet. Nice extras include dimmer switches on bedside lamps, well-stocked minibars, CD players, and VCRs. The hotel's beach is the offshore Palomino Island, which you reach via shuttle boat. The pampering begins at LMM International Airport: The resort is one of the few on the island to provide deluxe motor-coach transfers. The ride is a little over an hour. ☒ *1000 Av. El Conquistador, Box 70001, Fajardo 00738,* ☎ *787/863–1000*

or 800/468–5228, FAX 787/863–6500. *918 rooms and suites. 11 restaurants, 3 bars, lounge, air-conditioning, minibars, in-room VCRs, 6 pools, spa, golf course, 7 tennis courts, health club, marina, water sports, shops, casino, nightclub, children's program, business services, convention center, car rental. AE, D, DC, MC, V. EP.*

## PONCE

**$$–$$$$** 🏨 **Ponce Hilton and Casino.** By far the biggest resort on the south coast, this cream-and-turquoise hotel, nestled amid 80 acres of landscaped gardens, caters to a corporate clientele. Completely self-contained, it offers three restaurants (La Hacienda's antiques mimic an old coffee plantation; the romantic and elegant La Cava has a working wine cellar and can be reserved for a private dinner; the informal La Terraza serves breakfast and lunch buffets as well as lighter dinner fare), access to a public beach, casino, shopping arcade, pool, and a disco with pool tables and live music on weekends. Although the lobby has all the warmth of an airline terminal, the large guest rooms are attractive enough; decorated in sky blue, teal, and peach, with modern rattan; and have balconies. A drawback is the hotel's location—a 10-minute cab ride from town. ⊠ *Rte. 14, 1150 Av. Caribe, Box 7419, Ponce 00732,* ☎ *787/259–7676 or 800/445–8667,* FAX *787/259–7674. 156 rooms, 8 suites. 3 restaurants, 5 bars, in-room safes, minibars, pool, beauty salon, hot tub, driving range, 4 tennis courts, basketball, exercise room, Ping-Pong, volleyball, beach, shops, casino, dance club, baby-sitting, business services, meeting rooms. AE, D, DC, MC, V. EP.*

**$–$$** 🏨 **Hotel Meliá.** Set in the heart of Ponce and facing the Parque de Bombas and the Ponce Cathedral, this family-owned hotel provides a wonderful, low-key base for exploring the marvelous turn-of-the-century architecture, museums, and landmarks of downtown Ponce. The lobby has an old-world feel, with high ceilings, blue- and beige-tiled floors, and well-worn but charming decor. (Note the antique telephone exchange desk by the restaurant door.) Rooms have standard, if somewhat dated, decor. Six of the rooms have balconies that overlook the park. Breakfast is served on the rooftop terrace, which offers pretty views of the city and mountains. A welcome addition is Mark's, the hotel restaurant recently opened by Mark French, former executive chef at the Ponce Hilton. The restaurant serves an eclectic menu, from teriyaki tuna to corn-crusted snapper to Long Island duck breast. ⊠ *2 Calle Cristina, Box 1431, Ponce 00733,* ☎ *787/842–0260,* FAX *787/841–3602. 80 rooms. Restaurant, bar, air-conditioning. AE, MC, V. CP.*

## RINCÓN

**$$$$** 🏨 **Horned Dorset Primavera.** The Spanish colonial–style resort is
★ tucked away amid lush landscaping overlooking the sea. The only sounds that you're likely to hear as you lounge on the long, secluded, narrow beach are the crash of the surf and an occasional squawk from Pompidou, the enormous parrot in the lounge. Suites have private balconies and are exquisitely furnished with antiques, including handsome mahogany four-poster beds, dressers, and nightstands. Casa Escondido, opened in 1995, has eight rooms—some have their own plunge pool and hot tub—and is designed as a turn-of-the-century Puerto Rican hacienda, with tile or wood floors, stately mahogany furnishings, private terraces, and black marble baths. There are no radios, televisions, or telephones in any of the resort's rooms. Children under 12 are not permitted. ⊠ *Rte. 429, Km 3, Box 1132, Rincón 00743,* ☎ *787/823–4030 or 787/823–4050,* FAX *787/823–5580. 30 rooms. Restaurant, lounge, air-conditioning, fans, pool, beach, library. AE, MC, V. EP.*

**$$** 🏨 **Lemontree Waterfront Cottages.** These sparkling, large apartments
★ sit right on the beach, with staircases from their decks to the sand. There are four units, each with a fully equipped kitchen, TV, and large deck

with mahogany-topped wet bar and gas grill. The owner-managers, Mary
Jeanne and Paul Hellings, have put their personal touches on the apartments. Paul creates all the detailed woodwork, and Mary Jeanne designs the interiors. The bright tropical decor includes local artwork on
the walls. There is one three-bedroom unit with two baths, one two-
bedroom unit, and two one-bedroom units. The one-bedroom units
have wooden cathedral ceilings and picture windows. There's weekly
maid service (linens are provided) and phones available by request. The
beach is small, but larger ones are close by. It's a 10-minute drive to
downtown Rincón. ⊠ *Rte. 429, Box 200, Rincón 00677,* ☎ *787/823–
6452,* ℻ *787/823–5821. 4 units. Kitchens, air-conditioning, beach,
laundry service. AE, MC, V.*

### SAN GERMÁN

$   ⊞ **Parador Oasis.** The Oasis, not far from the town's two plazas, was
★   a family mansion 200 years ago; the lobby retains a taste of the house's
history with peppermint-pink walls and white-wicker furniture. The
older rooms are convenient—right off the lobby—but show their age.
The newer rooms in the rear lack character but are functional, clean,
and a little roomier. ⊠ *72 Calle Luna, Box 144, San Germán 00683,*
☎ *787/892–1100 or 800/443–0266,* ℻ *787/892–1175. 52 rooms.
Restaurant, lounge, air-conditioning, pool, hot tub, sauna, exercise room.
AE, D, DC, MC, V. EP.*

### VIEQUES

$$$   ⊞ **Inn on the Blue Horizon.** Known for its restaurant, Cafe Blu, and its
★   octagonal Blu bar, this small hotel sits on 20 windswept acres fronting
the Caribbean. There are five rooms, but at press time, owners and for-
mer New Yorkers James Weis and Billy Knight had plans to add four
more. Some rooms have air-conditioning, and some have fans. Furnished
with antiques, the rooms are sumptuous and lovely, as is the patio-lounge
area. ⊠ *Rte. 996, Box 1556, Vieques 00765,* ☎ *787/741–3318. 5 rooms.
Restaurant, bar, pool. AE, MC, V. CP.*

$$–$$$   ⊞ **Casa del Francés.** Self-professed curmudgeon Irving Greenblatt, a for-
★   mer Bostonian, runs this atmospheric if somewhat run-down guest
house in a restored French sugar-plantation great house. Rooms are rather
plain but enormous, with vaulted 17-ft ceilings. The food is good, the
pool inviting, the guests an eclectic mix, and Irving a true character who
will regale you with horror stories of running a Caribbean hotel. The
sightseeing boat for the phosphorescent bay leaves from here. ⊠ *Box
458, Vieques 00765,* ☎ *787/741–3751,* ℻ *787/741–2330. 18 rooms.
Restaurant, bar, fans, pool, snorkeling. AE, MC, V. EP, MAP (compulsory
in season).*

$$–$$$   ⊞ **Hacienda Tamarindo.** Set on a windswept hill with sweeping views
★   of the Caribbean, the new Hacienda Tamarindo is the nicest place to
stay on Vieques. Owners Burr and Linda Vail left Vermont to build
this extraordinary small hotel—with a huge tamarind tree right in the
middle. The rooms are all individually decorated but share excellent
craftsmanship, like mahogany louvered doors, terra-cotta tiled floors,
and custom-tiled baths. Some of the rooms have private terraces, and
half of the rooms have air-conditioning, while the rest face the trade
winds. All are furnished with an eclectic mix of art and antiques
shipped from Vermont. A full American breakfast is served on the sec-
ond-floor terrace. Guests can walk down the hill to the Inn on the Blue
Horizon (☞ *above*) for dinner. Box lunches are available on request.
Children under 12 are not permitted. ⊠ *Rte. 996, Box 1569, Vieques
00765,* ☎ *787/741–8525,* ℻ *787/741–3215. 16 rooms. Bar, pool.
AE, MC, V. CP.*

$$ ★ ⬚ **Crow's Nest.** Owner Liz O'Dell has made her simple but comfortable inn a very satisfying place to stay. A southerner by way of Massachusetts, Liz is a wealth of information and hospitality. She will arrange for you to do just about anything that's available on the island. Her 13-room lodging, set on 5 hilltop acres with pretty ocean views, is a great value. All rooms have kitchenettes, and most are air-conditioned. Liz provides beach chairs and coolers for guests—a thoughtful touch. There is a lounge with TV/VCR, and one of the island's best restaurants, also called the Crow's Nest, is on the premises. ⊠ *Rte. 201, Km 1.6, Box 1521, Vieques 00765,* ☎ *787/741–0033,* ☏ *787/741–1294. 13 rooms. Restaurant, bar, kitchenettes, pool, car rental. AE, MC, V. EP.*

### Villa and Apartment Rentals

Villa and condominium or apartment rentals are becoming increasingly popular in Puerto Rico, particularly outside San Juan. If you are traveling with several people, these are often a very affordable option. Call the tourist information office in the area where you are interested in staying, or try the options listed below.

If you're part of a large group or you'd like to investigate off-season rates at higher-end properties in the Isla Verde area of San Juan, contact **Condo World** (⊠ 26645 W. Twelve Mile Rd., Southfield, MI 48034, ☎ 800/521–2980). For rentals out on the island, try **Island West Properties** (⊠ Rte. 413, Km 1.3, Box 700, Rincón 00677, ☎ 787/823–2323, ☏ 787/823–3254). It has weekly and monthly vacation rentals that fall into the $ to $$ range. For rentals on Vieques, the person to talk to is Jane Sabin at **Connections** (⊠ Box 358, Vieques 00765, ☎ 787/741–0023 or 800/772–3050). Or try **Acacia Apartments** (⊠ 236 Calle Acacia, Esperanza, Vieques 00765, ☎ 787/741–1856).

# Dining

The restaurant scene on the island has gotten a lot of attention lately for its innovativeness—not surprisingly because the quality of restaurants is among the best in the Caribbean. In San Juan you'll find everything from Italian to Thai, as well as superb local eateries serving *comidas criollas* (traditional Caribbean-Creole meals). Many of San Juan's best restaurants, such as Pikayo, Chayote, and Augusto's, are in small, lesser-known hotels. If you're staying in the capital, by all means venture out and sample the wealth of options available. *Mesónes gastronómicos* are restaurants designated as such by the government for preserving island culinary traditions and maintaining high standards. There are more than 40 of these restaurants island-wide. Wherever you go, it is *always* a good idea to make reservations in the busy season, from mid-November through April.

Puerto Rican cooking emphasizes local vegetables: Plantains are cooked a hundred different ways—*tostones* (fried green), *amarillos* (baked ripe), and chips. Rice and beans with tostones or amarillos are basic accompaniments to every dish. Locals cook white rice with *habichuelas* (red beans), *achiote* (annatto seeds), or saffron; brown rice with *gandules* (pigeon peas); and *morro* (black rice) with *frijoles negros* (black beans). Garbanzos and white beans are served in many daily specials. A wide assortment of yams is served baked, fried, stuffed, boiled, mashed, and whole. *Sofrito*—a garlic, onion, sweet pepper, coriander, oregano, and tomato puree—is used as a base for practically everything.

Beef, chicken, pork, and seafood are all rubbed with *adobo,* a garlic-oregano marinade, before cooking. *Arroz con pollo* (chicken with rice), *sancocho* (beef and tuber soup), *asopao* (a soupy rice with chicken or seafood), and *encebollado* (steak smothered in onions) are all typical plates.

Fritters, also popular, are served in snack places along the highways as well as at cocktail parties. You may find *empanadillas* (stuffed fried turnovers), *surrullitos* (cheese-stuffed corn sticks), *alcapurias* (stuffed green banana croquettes), and *bacalaitos* (codfish fritters).

Local *pan de agua* is an excellent French loaf bread, best hot out of the oven. It is also good toasted and should be tried in the *Cubano* sandwich (roast pork, ham, Swiss cheese, pickles, and mustard).

Local desserts include flans, puddings, and fruit pastes served with native white cheese. Homegrown mangoes and papayas are sweet, and *pan de azucar* (sugar bread) pineapples make the best juice on the market. Fresh *parcha* (passion fruit), *guarapo* (sugarcane), and *guanabana* (a fruit similar to papaya) juice are also sold cold from trucks along the highway. Puerto Rican coffee is excellent served espresso-black or generously cut *con leche* (with hot milk).

To sample local cuisine, consult the listing of *mesónes gastronómicos* in the *Qué Pasa* guide. These are more than 40 restaurants island-wide cited by the government for preserving island culinary traditions and maintaining high standards.

The best frozen piña coladas are served at the Caribe Hilton and the Hyatt Dorado Beach, although local legend has it that the birthplace of the piña colada is the Gran Hotel El Convento. Rum can be mixed with cola (known as a *cuba libre*), soda, tonic, juices, water, served on the rocks, or even up. Puerto Rican rums range from light white mixers to dark, aged sipping liqueurs. Look for Bacardi, Don Q, Ron Rico, Palo Viejo, and Barrilito.

## What to Wear

The dress code for restaurants in Puerto Rico varies greatly. The price category of a restaurant is usually a good indicator of its formality. For less expensive places, anything but beachwear is generally fine. Ritzier hotel dining rooms and expensive eateries will expect collared shirts for men and chic attire for women, although jacket and tie requirements are rare. However, Puerto Ricans enjoy dressing up for dinner, so chances are you'll never feel overdressed.

| CATEGORY | COST* |
|----------|-------|
| $$$$ | over $45 |
| $$$ | $30–$45 |
| $$ | $15–$30 |
| $ | under $15 |

*per person for a three-course meal, excluding drinks and service*

## Old San Juan

$$$$ ✕ **Chef Marisoll.** Set off a Venetianesque courtyard surrounded by ornate balconies (you can dine inside or out), this dark-wooded, high-ceilinged restaurant serves gourmet international cuisine. Start with a small duck Caesar salad or a cream of exotic wild mushroom soup. Then feast on a beef tenderloin or a fillet of salmon. For dessert, try chef Marisoll's specialty, a crème caramel. ⊠ *202 Calle Cristo,* ☎ *787/725–7454. AE, D, MC, V. Closed Mon. No lunch Sun.*

$$$$ ✕ **Il Perugino.** The best Italian restaurant in Old San Juan, this small
★ and intimate eatery set in a 200-year-old building stresses attentive service and delicious Italian cuisine. Classic carpaccios, scallops with porcini mushrooms and other exotic salads; homemade pastas like black fettuccine with crayfish and baby eels; hearty main courses such as rack of lamb with red wine sauce and aromatic herbs; and desserts like a killer tiramisu make this a must for serious gourmets. A choice from

the excellent wine cellar, housed in the former cistern, completes the experience. ⊠ *105 Calle Cristo,* ☎ *787/722–5481. AE, MC, V.*

**\$\$\$–\$\$\$\$** ✕ **La Chaumière.** Reminiscent of an inn in the French provinces, this intimate two-story restaurant with black-and-white tiled floors, heavy wood beams, and floral curtains serves onion soup, oysters Rockefeller, rack of lamb, scallops Provençale, and veal Oscar (layered with lobster and asparagus in béarnaise sauce) in addition to daily specials. The restaurant, under the same management since 1969, is one of the older French eateries on the island and one of the better ones. All that experience makes the service quite smooth. ⊠ *367 Calle Tetuan,* ☎ *787/722–3330. AE, DC, MC, V. Closed Sun. No lunch.*

**\$\$–\$\$\$** ✕ **Amadeus.** In an atmosphere of gentrified Old San Juan, a trendy,
★ pretty crowd enjoys the nouvelle Caribbean menu at this charming restaurant. The front dining room is attractive—whitewashed walls, dark wood, white tablecloths, ceiling fan—but go through the outside passage to the back dining room where printed cloths, candles, and exposed brick create an even more romantic dining. The roster of appetizers includes buffalo wings and plantain mousse with shrimp. Chicken breast stuffed with sun-dried tomatoes, cheese ravioli with a goat-cheese-and-walnut sauce, and Cajun-grilled mahimahi are a few of the delectable entrées. ⊠ *106 Calle San Sebastián,* ☎ *787/722–8635. AE, MC, V. Closed Mon.*

**\$\$–\$\$\$** ✕ **Cafe Galería.** This stylish, airy restaurant, with marble floors, white walls, and dark wood accents, is centered on a skylit atrium. Chef Figueroa prepares Italian and international cuisine, including fresh pastas and sauces (you mix and match), risottos, and seafood dishes as well as delicious local desserts like flan, *arroz con dulce* (rice pudding), and kiwi tart. ⊠ *205 Calle San Justo,* ☎ *787/725–0478. AE, MC, V. Closed Sun.*

**\$\$–\$\$\$** ✕ **La Mallorquina.** The food here is basic Puerto Rican and Spanish fare, such as asopao and paella, but the atmosphere is what recommends this spot. Said to date from 1848, this is the oldest restaurant in Puerto Rico, with pale pink walls and whirring ceiling fans, and a nattily attired wait staff that is friendly. ⊠ *207 Calle San Justo,* ☎ *787/722–3261. AE, MC, V. Closed Sun.*

**\$\$–\$\$\$** ✕ **Yukiyú.** The only Japanese restaurant in Old San Juan manages to
★ serve some of the best Japanese food in Puerto Rico under the supervision of chef Igarashi. Those craving a sushi bar should beeline for this establishment, as sushi is a specialty, along with teppan yaki. ⊠ *311 Recinto Sur,* ☎ *787/721–0653. AE, D, MC, V. No breakfast.*

**\$\$** ✕ **Amanda's Cafe.** This airy café, across from San Cristóbal on the north side of the city, offers seating inside or out with a view of the Atlantic and the old city wall. The cuisine is Mexican, French, and Caribbean, and the nachos, refreshing fruit frappés, and margaritas are the best in town. ⊠ *424 Calle Norzagaray,* ☎ *787/722–0187. AE, MC, V.*

**\$–\$\$** ✕ **El Patio de Sam.** A warm dark-wood and faux-brick interior and a wide selection of beers make Sam's a popular late-night gathering place. The menu is mostly steaks and seafood, with a few native dishes like asopao mixed in. Try the Samuel's Special pizza—mozzarella, tomato sauce, beef, pepperoni, and black olives: It feeds two or three. The dessert flans melt in your mouth. Live entertainment is offered every evening except Sunday. ⊠ *102 Calle San Sebastián,* ☎ *787/723–1149. AE, D, DC, MC, V.*

**\$** ✕ **Cafe Berlin.** This casual café, bakery, and delicatessen has outdoor
★ seating overlooking the Plaza Colón. Tasty vegetarian fare prevails—try one of the creative salads—but nonvegetarian dishes are also available. The Cafe's pastries, desserts, fresh juices, and Puerto Rican coffees are the perfect elixir to a day of touring Old San Juan. ⊠ *407 Calle San Francisco,* ☎ *787/722–5205. AE, MC, V. Closed Mon.–Tues.*

## San Juan

**$$$$** ✕ **Compostela.** Contemporary Spanish food and a serious 9,000-bot-
★ tle wine cellar are what draw the local dining elite to Compostela. The
restaurant, with its dark-wood interior and many plants, is honored yearly
in local competitions for specialties such as mushroom pâté and Port
*pastelillo* (meat-filled pastries), grouper fillet with scallops in salsa
verde, rack of lamb, duck with kiwi sauce, and paella. ✉ *106 Av. Condado, Santurce,* ☎ *787/724–6088. AE, DC, MC, V. Closed Sun.*

**$$$$** ✕ **Pikayo.** Chef Wilo Benet is one of the darlings in the foodie firma-
★ ment, thanks to his artful fusion of classic French, Caribbean Creole,
and California nouvelle cuisine with definite Puerto Rican flair. The beautifully presented dishes, which change regularly, are a feast for the eye
as well as the palate. Your meal might consist of tostones stuffed with
oven-dried tomatoes, followed by *monfongo* (spiced, mashed green
plantains topped with saffron shrimp) or a hearty land-crab stew. More
traditional and equally delicious dishes are also available. The decor is
smartly contemporary, with lots of black-and-white accents and comfortable banquettes, and the service is very attentive. ✉ *Tanama Princess
Hotel, 1 Calle Joffre, Condado,* ☎ *787/721–6194. AE, MC, V. Closed
Sun. No lunch Sat.*

**$$$$** ✕ **Ramiro's.** Step into a soft sea-green dining room for some imagi-
★ native Castillian cuisine. Chef-owner Jesus Ramiro is known for his
artistic presentation: flower-shape peppers filled with fish mousse, a
mix of seafood caught under a vegetable net, roast duckling with sugarcane honey, and, if you can stand more, a kiwi dessert sculpted to
resemble twin palms. ✉ *1106 Av. Magdalena, Condado,* ☎ *787/721–
9049. AE, DC, MC, V. No lunch Sat.*

**$$$–$$$$** ✕ **Chayote.** Slightly off the beaten path, this elegant and chic eatery
★ of earthen tones and contemporary Puerto Rican art is an "in" spot
to eat among the San Juan cognoscenti. The chef fuses haute interna-
tional cuisine with tropical panache. Appetizers include *sopa del día*
(soup of the day) made with local produce like yuca and yams, chay-
ote stuffed with prosciutto, and corn tamales with shrimp in coconut
sauce. Half of the entrées on the menu are seafood dishes, including
the excellent pan-seared tuna with Asian ginger sauce. The ginger flan
and the almond floating island in rum custard sauce are musts for dessert.
✉ *Hotel Olimpo Court, 603 Av. Miramar, Miramar,* ☎ *787/722–9385.
AE, MC, V. Closed Sun.*

**$$$–$$$$** ✕ **Los Faisanes.** This Continental stunner is one of San Juan's most dis-
★ tinguished eateries. Mahogany doorways, faux-Tiffany lamps, crisp
white and ecru napery, and Bernadaud china set a refined tone, carried
through by the equally elegant cuisine. Feast on roast duck with guava
and cinnamon, veal chops with scallion and mushroom sauce, and won-
derfully light soufflés. ✉ *1108 Av. Magdalena, Condado,* ☎ *787/725–
2801. AE, MC, V.*

**$$$** ✕ **Chart House.** It's no secret that the graceful veranda of this restored
Ashford mansion across from the Marriott is a perfect spot for cock-
tails, and a lively crowd gathers here in the evening. The upstairs open-
air dining rooms are splashed with bright marine-theme artwork.
The menu includes prime rib, steak, shrimp teriyaki, Hawaiian chicken,
and the signature dessert: mud pie. ✉ *1214 Av. Ashford, Condado,*
☎ *787/728–0110. AE, D, DC, MC, V. No lunch.*

**$$** ✕ **Che's.** Juicy *churrasco* (barbecued steaks), lemon chicken, and
grilled sweetbreads are specialties at this casual Argentinean restau-
rant. The hamburgers are huge, and the French fries are fresh. The
Chilean and Argentinean wine list is also decent. ✉ *35 Calle Caoba,
Punta Las Marias,* ☎ *787/726–7202. AE, D, DC, MC, V.*

**$ ✕ El Paso.** This family-run restaurant serves genuine Creole food seasoned for a local following. Specialties include asopao, pork chops, and breaded *empanadas* (meat pastries). There's always tripe on Saturday and arroz con pollo on Sunday. ⊠ *405 Av. De Diego, Puerto Nuevo,* ☎ *787/781–3399. AE, DC, MC, V.*

**$ ✕ Kasalta Bakery, Inc.** Make your selection from rows of display
★ cases offering a seemingly endless array of tempting treats. Walk up to the counter and order from an assortment of sandwiches (try the Cubano), meltingly tender octopus salad, savory *caldo gallego* (a soup jammed with fresh vegetables, sausage, and potatoes), cold drinks, strong café con leche, and luscious pastries. ⊠ *1966 Calle McLeary, Ocean Park,* ☎ *787/727–7340. AE, MC, V.*

**$ ✕ Via Appia's Italian Deli.** The only true sidewalk café in the Condado, this eatery serves pizzas, sandwiches, cold beer, and pitchers of sangria. It is a good place to people-watch, although the staff is somewhat grumpy. ⊠ *1350 Av. Ashford, Condado,* ☎ *787/725–8711. AE, MC, V.*

## Out on the Island

CABO ROJO

**$$ ✕ La Casona de Serafín.** This informal, ocean-side bistro specializes in steaks, seafood, and Puerto Rican *criolla* (Creole) dishes. The indoor dining room has bleached walls, mahogany furniture, and subdued red napkins. Try the tostones, asopao, and surrullitos, and follow up with the pumpkin-custard dessert. The somewhat dilapidated palm-fringed patio sits right on the beach, so you can listen to the waves lap the shore. ⊠ *Hwy. 102, Km 9, Playa Joyuda,* ☎ *787/851–0066. AE, MC, V.*

**$–$$ ✕ El Bohio.** A local favorite, this informal restaurant 15 minutes south of Mayagüez serves steak and a variety of seafood—all cooked just about any way you want it. You can dine on the large, enclosed wooden deck that juts out over the sea or in the dining room inside. ⊠ *Hwy. 102, Km 13.9, Playa Joyuda,* ☎ *787/851–2755. AE, DC, MC, V.*

FAJARDO

**$–$$ ✕ Anchor's Inn.** Under the direction of raffish owner Joe Cruz, this
★ *mesón gastronómico* is a perfect example that good things come in simple packages. The fisherman pull their boats into the nearby Fajardo Harbor, with flotillas of brightly colored yachts, and must head straight for the restaurant with their catch, for the seafood is as fresh and succulent as it gets. It shows up in such Puerto Rican dishes as surrullitos, asopao, and lobster *mofongo* (green plantains stuffed with seafood). There are 13 guest rooms upstairs. ⊠ *Rte. 987, Km 2.4,* ☎ *787/863–7200. AE, MC, V. Closed Tues.*

PONCE

**$$ ✕ Restaurant El Ancla.** The seafood and Puerto Rican specialties of this *mesón gastronómico* are served with tostones, *papas fritas* (French fries), and garlic bread. The menu ranges from lobster and shrimp to chicken, beef, and asopao. The salmon fillet with capers is one of the most popular dishes, and the piña coladas, with or without rum, and the flan are especially good. ⊠ *Av. Hostos Final 9, Playa-Ponce,* ☎ *787/840–2450. AE, D, DC, MC, V.*

**$ ✕ Lupita's.** A fine mariachi band patrols the mezzanine and courtyard of this festive Mexican restaurant Thursday through Sunday nights. The handsome arched dining room has an Aztec decor, with ponchos and serapes hung on the walls for added color. The food—Mexican-American standards like nachos, tacos, and chicken mole—is quite good, the margaritas and shooters even better, and the ambience festive. ⊠ *Calle Isabel 60,* ☎ *787/848–8808. AE, MC, V.*

RINCÓN

**$$$–$$$$**  ✕ **Horned Dorset Primavera.** Tucked away on the west coast of the is-
★  land in the posh hotel of the same name, this is the finest food you'll
encounter outside of San Juan. Owners Harold Davies and Kingsley Wrat-
ten take their dining room very seriously. Although tropical accents ap-
pear here and there, the cuisine is heavily Cordon Bleu–influenced:
Filet mignon in a mushroom sauce, braised lamb in red wine, and
grilled fish du jour are de rigueur here. A five-course, prix-fixe menu is
available for $48 per person. ✉ *Rte. 429, Km 3, Box 1132,* ☎ *787/823–
4030 or 787/823–4050. AE, MC, V.*

**$$**  ✕ **Black Eagle.** The inconsistent quality of the food here hasn't dimmed
its status as a Rincón dining landmark. It's on the water's edge, and you
dine on the veranda, listening to the lapping waves. The steak-and-
seafood menu lists breaded conch fritters, a fresh fish of the day, lobster,
and imported prime meats. ✉ *Rte. 413, Km 1, Ensenada,* ☎ *787/823–
3510. AE, DC, MC, V.*

**$$**  ✕ **El Molino del Quijote Restaurante.** Amid beautifully landscaped
gardens just off the beach, this festive, colorful restaurant with tile-topped
tables and local artwork serves Spanish and Puerto Rican cuisine. Try
the *bolas de pescado* (fish balls) appetizer and one of the paellas as an
entrée, or combine several appetizers for a meal. The sangria is terrific.
Two one-bedroom cabanas are available to rent. ✉ *Rte. 429, Km 3.3,*
☎ *787/823–4010. AE, MC, V. Closed Mon.–Thurs.*

**$–$$**  ✕ **Lazy Parrot.** Highly regarded by locals in Rincón for its fresh
mahimahi, filet mignon, and homemade desserts, this little restaurant
is also an art gallery and guest house. Perched in the hills, with mountain and ocean views, this is great place to kick back and listen to the
ever-present sound of the coquis. ✉ *Rte. 413, Km 4.1, Barrio Puntas,*
☎ *787/823–5654. AE, D, MC, V. Closed Mon. in winter and weekdays in summer.*

**$**  ✕ **Pastrami Palace.** A favorite ex-pat hangout, this friendly, small
restaurant and lunch counter in downtown Rincón serves American
basics from omelets, pancakes, and sandwiches to homemade pies, ice
cream, and excellent coffee. The colorful decor includes local artwork,
and there's a small library for lunchtime reading. An outdoor café is
called (groan) the Garden of Eatin. ✉ *Calle Parque,* ☎ *787/823–0102.
No credit cards. No dinner.*

## Beaches

By law, all of Puerto Rico's beaches are open to the public (except for
the Caribe Hilton's man-made beach in San Juan). The government
runs 13 *balnearios* (public beaches), which have dressing rooms, lifeguards, parking, and in some cases picnic tables, playgrounds, and camping facilities. Admission is free, parking $2. Most balnearios are open
9–5 daily in summer and Tuesday through Sunday the rest of the year.
Listed below are some major balnearios. You can also contact the Department of Recreation and Sports (☎ 787/722–1551 or 787/724–
2500).

**Boquerón Beach,** on the southwest coast, is a broad beach of hard-packed
sand fringed with coconut palms. It has picnic tables, cabin rentals,
bike rentals, basketball court, minimarket, scuba diving, and snorkeling. **Isla Verde,** a white-sand beach bordered by huge resort hotels, has
picnic tables and good snorkeling, with equipment rentals nearby. Set
near San Juan, it's a lively beach popular with city folk. **Luquillo Beach**
is crescent-shaped and comes complete with coconut palms, picnic tables, and tent sites. Coral reefs protect its crystal-clear lagoon from the
Atlantic waters, making it ideal for swimming. It's one of the largest
and best-known beaches on the island, and it gets crowded on week-

ends. **Ocean Park,** a residential neighborhood just east of the Condado, is home to the prettiest beach in San Juan. Here you'll find a mile-long, wide stretch of fine golden sand and often choppy but very swimmable waters. Very popular on weekends with local college students, this is also one of the cities' two beaches popular among gays (the other is in front of the Atlantic Beach Hotel). **Playa Flamenco,** one of the most beautiful beaches in the Caribbean, is on the north shore of Culebra. The 3-mi-long crescent has shade trees, picnic tables, and rest rooms and is popular on weekends with day-trippers from Fajardo. During the winter, storms in the North Atlantic often create great waves for bodysurfing. **Playa Soni,** on the eastern end of Culebra, is a wide strand of sparkling white sand on a protected bay with calm waters. Views of the islets of Culebrita, Cayo Norte, and St. Thomas are stunning. As there are no facilities and little shade, bring lots of water and an umbrella. **Seven Seas Beach,** an elongated beach of hard-packed sand east of Luquillo at Las Croabas, is always popular with bathers. It has picnic tables and tent and trailer sites; snorkeling, scuba diving, and boat rentals are nearby. **Sun Bay,** a white-sand beach on the island of Vieques, has shade trees, picnic tables, and tent sites and offers snorkeling and scuba diving. Boat rentals are nearby.

# Outdoor Activities and Sports

## Bicycling

The broad beach at Boquerón makes for easy wheeling. You can rent bikes at **Boquerón Balnearios** (⊠ Rte. 101, Boquerón, Dept. of Recreation and Sports, ☎ 787/722–1551 or 787/722–1771). In the Dorado area on the north coast, bikes can be rented at the **Hyatt Regency Cerromar Beach** (☎ 787/796–1234) or the **Hyatt Dorado Beach** (☎ 787/796–1234). Bikes are for rent at many of the hotels out on the island, including the **Ponce Hilton** (☎ 787/259–7676), **Westin Rio Mar,** ☎ 787/888–6000, ext. 3484), and the **Copamarina Beach Resort** (☎ 787/821–0505).

## Boating

Virtually all the resort hotels on San Juan's Condado and Isla Verda strips rent paddleboats, Sunfish, Windsurfers, kayaks, and the like. Contact **Condado Plaza Hotel Watersports Center** (☎ 787/721–1000, ext. 1361), the **El San Juan Hotel Watersports Center** (☎ 787/791–1000), or the **Caribe Hilton** (☎ 787/721–0303). Outside of San Juan, your hotel will be able either to provide rentals or recommend rental outfitters. **Iguana Water Sports** (⊠ Westin Rio Mar, ☎ 787/888–6000) has a particularly good selection.

## Fishing

Half-day, full-day, split charters, and big- and small-game fishing can be arranged through **Benitez Deep-Sea Fishing** (⊠ Club Náutico de San Juan, Miramar, ☎ 787/723–2292), **Castillo Watersports** (⊠ ESJ Towers, Isla Verde, ☎ 787/791–6195 or 787/726–5752), and **Caribe Aquatic Adventures** (⊠ Radisson Normandie, ☎ 787/724–1882, ext. 240). Out on the island, try **Tropical Fishing Charters** (⊠ El Conquistador, Fajardo, ☎ 787/863–1000 or 787/789–5564), **Dorado Marine Center** (⊠ 271 Méndez Vigo, ☎ 787/796–4645), and **Parguera Fishing Charters** (⊠ Lajas, ☎ 787/899–4698 or 787/382–4698).

## Fitness

While most hotels and resorts have some semblance of a gym for the buff-body crazed, three gyms in San Juan stand out for their superb equipment: **Le Spa Fitness Center** (⊠ San Juan Marriott, ☎ 787/722–7000), **Muscle Factory** (⊠ 1302 Av. Ashford, ☎ 787/721–0717), and **Fitness City** (⊠ 1959 Calle Loiza, Suite 401, Ocean Park, ☎ 787/268–

7773). Out on the island, the Westin Rio Mar also has a **Le Spa Fitness Center** (✉ Rte. 968, Río Grande, ☎ 787/888–6000, ext. 6285).

## Golf

There are four beautiful Robert Trent Jones–designed 18-hole courses shared by the **Hyatt Dorado Beach** and the **Hyatt Regency Cerromar Beach** hotels (✉ Dorado, ☎ 787/796–1234, ext. 3238 or 3016). You'll also find 18-hole courses at the **Palmas del Mar Resort** (✉ Humacao, ☎ 787/852–6000), the **Berwind Country Club** (✉ Río Grande, ☎ 787/876–3056), **Westin Rio Mar** (✉ Río Grande, ☎ 787/888–6000), and **Punta Borinquén** (✉ Aguadilla, ☎ 787/890–2987). The **Bahia Beach Plantation** (✉ Río Grande, ☎ 787/256–5600) is one of Puerto Rico's newer courses. There are two nine-hole courses out on the island, one at the **Club Deportivo del Oeste** (✉ Cabo Rojo, ☎ 787/851–8880), and one at the **Aguirre Golf Club** (✉ Aguirre, ☎ 787/853–4052). The **Ponce Hilton** (✉ Ponce, ☎ 787/259–7676) has a driving range. Be sure to call ahead when you plan to play; public hours at these courses vary, and you should schedule a tee time. As well, several hotel courses allow only guests, or give preference to guests.

## Hiking

Dozens of trails lace **El Yunque** (information: ✉ El Portal Tropical Forest Center, Rte. 191, ☎ 787/888–1810 or 787/888–1880). At press time, several trails and ranger stations at El Yunque were closed due to mud slides and other damage caused by Hurricane Hortense. You can also hit the trails in **Río Abajo Forest** (south of Arecibo) and **Toro Negro Forest** (east of Adjuntas). Each reserve has a ranger station.

## Horseback Riding

Puerto Rico's famous and unique *paso fino* horses, with their distinct gait, are often used for riding. Beach trail rides can be arranged at **Palmas del Mar Equestrian Center** (✉ Palmas del Mar, Humacao, ☎ 787/852–6000). **Hacienda Carabalí** (✉ Rte. 992, Km 4, Luquillo, ☎ 787/889–5820 or 787/889–4859) offers beach riding and rain-forest trail rides.

## Sailing

Sailing instruction is offered by **Palmas Sailing Center** (✉ Palmas del Mar, Humacao, ☎ 787/852–6000, ext. 10310) and most of the large resort hotels. Trips are offered by **Caribe Aquatic Adventures** (✉ Radisson Normandie, ☎ 787/729–2929, ext. 240) and **Castillo Watersports** (✉ ESJ Towers, Isla Verde, ☎ 787/791–6195 or 787/725–7970). Day trips start at $55. Rentals for small sailboats, Sunfish, and other boats are available at many hotels around the island.

## Snorkeling and Scuba Diving

There is excellent diving off Puerto Rico's coast. Some outfits offer package deals combining accommodations with daily diving trips. Escorted half-day dives range from $45 to $90 for one- and two-tank dives, including all equipment. Packages, which include lunch and other extras, start at $60. Night dives are often available at close to double the price. Snorkeling excursions, which include equipment rental and sometimes lunch, start at $25. Snorkel equipment rents at beaches for about $5.

Caution: Coral-reef waters and mangrove areas can be dangerous to novices. Unless you're an expert or have an experienced guide, avoid unsupervised areas and stick to the water-sports centers of major hotels.

Snorkeling and scuba-diving instruction and equipment rentals are available at **Boquerón Dive Shop** (✉ Main St., Boquerón, ☎ 787/851–2155); **Caribbean School of Aquatics** (✉ Taft No. 1, Suite 10F, San Juan, ☎ 787/728–6606); **Caribe Aquatic Adventures** (✉ Radisson Normandie, ☎ 787/729–2929, ext. 240); **Coral Head Divers** (✉ Palmas del Mar, Humacao, ☎ 787/852–6000 or 800/468–3331); **Dive Copamarina** (✉ Copamarina Beach Resort, Rte. 333, Guánica, ☎ 787/821–6009), where hotel-dive packages are available; **Island Queen** (✉ Rincón, ☎ 787/823–6301); **Parguera Divers Training Center** (✉ La Parguera, ☎ 787/899–4171); and **Viking Puerto Rico** (✉ Rincón, ☎ 787/823–7010).

## Spectator Sports

BASEBALL

The island's season runs October–February. Many major-league ballplayers in the United States got their start in Puerto Rico's baseball league, and some return in the off-season to hone their skills. Stadiums are in San Juan, Santurce, Ponce, Caguas, Arecibo, and Mayagüez; the teams also play once or twice in Aguadilla. Contact the tourist office for details or call **Professional Baseball of Puerto Rico** (☎ 787/765–6285).

HORSE RACING

Thoroughbred races are run year-round at **El Comandante Racetrack,** about 20 minutes east of San Juan. On race days—Wednesday, Friday, and Sunday—the dining rooms open at 12:30 PM. ✉ *Rte. 3, Km 15.3, Canóvanas,* ☎ *787/724–6060.* ☉ *Wed., Fri., and Sun. 12:30–6.*

## Surfing

The best surfing beaches are along the Atlantic coastline from Borinquén Point south to Rincón, where there are several surf shops, including **West Coast Surf Shop** (✉ 2 E. Muñoz Rivera St., ☎ 787/823–3935). Surfing is best from November through April. Aviones and La Concha beaches in San Juan and Casa de Pesca in Arecibo are summer surfing spots and have nearby surf shops.

## Tennis

If you'd like to use the courts at a property where you are not a guest, call in advance for information about reservations and fees. There are 17 lighted courts at **San Juan Central Park** (✉ Calle Cerra exit on Rte. 2, ☎ 787/722–1646); six lighted courts at the **Caribe Hilton International** (✉ Puerta de Tierra, ☎ 787/721–0303, ext. 1730); eight courts, four lighted, at **Carib Inn** (✉ Isla Verde, ☎ 787/791–3535, ext. 6); and two lighted courts at the **Condado Plaza Hotel** (✉ Condado, ☎ 787/721–1000, ext. 1775). Out on the island, there are 14 courts, two lighted, at **Hyatt Regency Cerromar Beach** (✉ Dorado, ☎ 787/796–1234, ext. 3040); seven courts, two lighted, at the **Hyatt Dorado Beach** (✉ Dorado, ☎ 787/796–1234, ext. 3220); 20 courts, four lighted, at **Palmas del Mar** (✉ Humacao, ☎ 787/852–6000, ext. 51); 13 lighted courts at the **Westin Rio Mar** (✉ Río Grande, ☎ 787/888–6000); four lighted courts at the **Ponce Hilton** (✉ Ponce, ☎ 787/259–7676); and four lighted courts at **Punta Borinquén** (✉ Aguadilla, ☎ 787/891–8778).

## Windsurfing

Many resort hotels rent Windsurfers to their guests, including the **El San Juan,** the **El Conquistador, Palmas del Mar,** the **Hyatts,** and the **Condado Plaza.** If your hotel doesn't provide them, they can probably help you make arrangements with a local outfitter.

# Shopping

San Juan is not a free port, and you won't find bargains on electronics and perfumes. You can, however, find excellent prices on china, crystal, fashions, and jewelry.

Shopping for local Caribbean crafts can be great fun. You'll run across a lot of tacky things you can live without, but you can also find some treasures, and in many cases you'll be able to watch the artisans at work. (For guidance, contact the Puerto Rico Tourism Company's Artisan Center, ☎ 787/721–2400, ext. 2201, or the Fomento Crafts Project, ☎ 787/758–4747, ext. 2291.)

Popular souvenirs and gifts include *santos* (small, hand-carved figures of saints or religious scenes), hand-rolled cigars, handmade *mundillo* lace from Aguadilla, Carnival masks (papier-mâché from Ponce and fierce *veijigantes* made from coconut husks in Loíza, an African-American enclave near San Juan), and fancy men's shirts called *guayaberas*. Also, some folks swear that Puerto Rican rum is the best in the world.

## Shopping Districts

**Old San Juan** is full of shops, especially on Cristo, Fortaleza, and San Francisco streets. **Plaza Las Américas,** south of San Juan, is the largest shopping mall in the Caribbean, with 200 shops, restaurants, and movie theaters. Other malls out on the island include the **Carolina Mall** near San Juan, **Plaza del Caribe** in Ponce, **Plaza del Carmen** in Caguas, and the **Mayagüez Mall.**

## Good Buys

### CLOTHING

You can get discounts on Hathaway shirts and Christian Dior clothing at **Hathaway Factory Outlet** (✉ 203 Calle Cristo, Old San Juan, ☎ 787/723–8946). Discounts on Ralph Lauren apparel are found at the **Polo/Ralph Lauren Factory Store** (✉ 201 Calle Cristo, Old San Juan, ☎ 787/722–2136). The **London Fog Factory Outlet** (✉ 156 Calle Cristo, Old San Juan, ☎ 787/722–4334) offers reductions on men's, women's, and children's raincoats. People line up to enter **Marshall's** (✉ Plaza de Armas, Old San Juan, ☎ 787/722–0874) for basic clothing and department store items. Try the **Bikini Factory** (✉ 3 Palmar Norte, Isla Verde, ☎ 787/726–0016) for stylish men's and women's swimwear.

### JEWELRY

There is gold, gold, and more gold at **Reinhold** (✉ 201 Calle Cristo, Old San Juan, ☎ 787/725–6878). For brand-name watches visit the **Watch and Gem Palace** (✉ 204 Calle San José, Old San Juan, ☎ 787/722–2136).

### LOCAL CRAFTS

For one-of-a-kind buys, head for **Puerto Rican Arts & Crafts** (✉ 204 Calle Fortaleza, Old San Juan, ☎ 787/725–5596). You should pay a visit to the **artisan markets** in Sixto Escobar Park (✉ Puerta de Tierra, ☎ 787/722–0369) and Luis Muñoz Marín Park (✉ Next to Las Américas Expressway west on Piñero Ave., Hato Rey, ☎ 787/763–0568). The **Haitian Gallery** (✉ 367 Calle Fortaleza, Old San Juan, ☎ 787/725–0986) carries Puerto Rican crafts and a selection of folksy, often inexpensive paintings from around the Caribbean. In Ponce, consult the **Casa Paoli Center of Folkloric Investigations** (✉ 14 Calle Mayor, ☎ 787/840–4115).

### PAINTINGS AND SCULPTURES

**Corinne Timsit International Galleries** (✉ 104 Calle San Jose, Old San Juan, ☎ 787/724–1039) features work by contemporary Latin American painters. **DMR Gallery** (✉ 204 Calle Luna, Old San Juan, ☎ 787/722–4181) features handmade furniture by artist Nick Quijano. **Galería Botello** (✉ 208 Calle Cristo, Old San Juan, ☎ 787/723–2879; ✉ Plaza Las Américas, ☎ 787/754–7430) exhibits and sells antique santos (religious sculptures). **Galería Gotay** (✉ 212 Calle San Francisco, Old San Juan, ☎ 787/722–5726) carries contemporary art in various media. Another gallery worth visiting is the **Galería San Juan** (✉ Gallery Inn, 204–206 Calle Norzagaray, Old San Juan, ☎ 787/722–1808), especially to view the sculptures of bronze artist Jan D'Esopo.

# Nightlife and the Arts

*Qué Pasa,* the official visitor's guide, has current listings of events in San Juan and out on the island. Also, pick up a copy of the *San Juan Star, Quick City Guide,* or *Sunspots,* and check with the local tourist offices and the concierge at your hotel to find out what's doing.

## Nightlife

Fridays and Saturdays are big nights in San Juan, so dress to party. Bars are usually always casual; however, if you try to go out in jeans, sneakers, and a T-shirt, you will probably be refused entry at most nightclubs or discos (except the gay ones), unless you look like a model.

### BARS

Calle San Sebastián in Old San Juan is lined with trendy bars and restaurants; if you're in the mood for barhopping, head in that direction—it's pretty crazy on weekend nights.

**Blue Dolphin** (⊠ 2 Calle Amapola, Isla Verde, ☎ 787/791–3083) is a hangout where you can rub elbows with some offbeat locals and enjoy stunning sunset happy hours. While strolling along the Isla Verde beach, just look for the neon blue dolphin on the roof—you can't miss it. **El Patio de Sam** (⊠ 102 Calle San Sebastián, Old San Juan, ☎ 787/723–1149) is an Old San Juan institution whose expatriate clientele claims it serves the best burgers on the island. The dining room is awash in potted plants and strategically placed canopies that create the illusion of dining on an outdoor patio. **Hard Rock Cafe** (⊠ 253 Recinto Sur, Old San Juan, ☎ 787/724–7625), almost as common as McDonald's these days, is in Old San Juan.

### CASINOS

By law, all casinos are in hotels, primarily in San Juan. The government keeps a close eye on them. Dress for the larger casinos tends to be on the more formal side, and the atmosphere is refined. The law permits casinos to operate noon–4 AM, but individual casinos set their own hours.

Casinos are in the following San Juan hotels (☞ Lodging, *above*): **Condado Plaza Hotel, Caribe Hilton, Sands, El San Juan, Holiday Inn Crowne Plaza** (⊠ Rte. 187, Isla Verde), and **Radisson Ambassador** (⊠ 1369 Ashford Ave., Condado). Elsewhere on the island, there are casinos at the **Hyatt Regency Cerromar** and **Hyatt Dorado Beach** hotels, and at **Palmas del Mar,** the **Ponce Hilton,** the **El Conquistador,** and the **Westin Rio Mar.**

### DISCOS

Out on the island nightlife is hard to come by, but there are discos in the **Ponce Hilton.**

**Amadeus** (⊠ El San Juan Hotel, Isla Verde, ☎ 787/791–1000) is a flashy disco in Isla Verde that attracts a well-dressed local crowd who come here to impress their dates and shake it. **Club Ibiza** (⊠ La Concha Hotel, ☎ 787/721–6090) is the hot spot on Fridays, with an interesting, mixed crowd. **Egypt** (⊠ Robert Todd Ave., San Juan, ☎ 787/725–4664 or 787/725–4675), the former Peggy Sue, is a new hot spot. **Krash** (⊠ 1257 Av. Ponce de León, Santurce, ☎ 787/722–1390) plays the best dance music on the island; gay crowds flock here. **Lazers** (⊠ 251 Calle Cruz, ☎ 787/721–4479), with multilevels and a landscaped roof deck overlooking San Juan, attracts different crowds on different nights; Thursdays and Sundays are gay nights.

### NIGHTCLUBS

The Sands Hotel's **Players Lounge** brings in such big names as Joan Rivers, Jay Leno, and Rita Moreno. Try El San Juan's **El Chico** to dance to Latin music in a western-saloon setting. The Condado Plaza Hotel's

**La Fiesta Lounge** sizzles with steamy Latin shows. The **Casino Lounge** offers live jazz Wednesday through Saturday. The El Centro Convention Center offers the festive **Olé Latino** Latin revue (☎ 787/722–8433). **Houlihan's** (✉ Av. Ashford, Condado, ☎ 787/723–8600) is a restaurant with an upstairs nightclub popular among the local party crowd. On weekends there is always a line of revelers on the sidewalk waiting to get in.

## The Arts

**LeLoLai** is a year-round festival that celebrates Puerto Rico's Indian, Spanish, and African heritage. Performances take place each week, moving from hotel to hotel, showcasing the island's music, folklore, and culture. Because it is sponsored by the Puerto Rico Tourism Company and major San Juan hotels, passes to the festivities are included in some packages offered by participating hotels. You can also purchase tickets to a weekly series of events for $10. Contact the El Centro Convention Center (☎ 787/723–3135; 787/791–1014 on weekends; 787/722–1513 for reservations). **La Tasca del Callejon** (✉ Calle Fortaleza 317, ☎ 787/721–1689) is renowned for its tapas bar and the cabaret show (usually including flamenco guitar) performed by its engaging, talented staff.

# Exploring Puerto Rico

*Numbers in the margin correspond to points of interest on the Old San Juan Exploring map.*

## Old San Juan

Old San Juan, the original city founded in 1521, contains authentic and carefully preserved examples of 16th- and 17th-century Spanish colonial architecture, some of the best in the New World. More than 400 buildings have been beautifully restored in a continuing effort to preserve the city. Graceful wrought-iron balconies, decorated with lush green hanging plants, extend over narrow streets paved with *adequines* (blue-gray stones originally used as ballast for Spanish ships). The old city is partially enclosed by the old walls, dating from 1633, that once completely surrounded it. Designated a U.S. National Historic Zone in 1950, Old San Juan is chockablock with shops, open-air cafés, private homes, tree-shaded squares, monuments, plaques, pigeons, and people. The traffic is awful. Get an overview of the inner city on a morning's stroll (bearing in mind that this "stroll" includes some steep climbs). However, if you plan to immerse yourself in history or to shop, you'll need two or three days. You may want to set aside extra time to see El Morro and Fort San Cristóbal, especially if you're an aficionado of military history. UNESCO has designated each fortress a World Heritage Site; each is also a National Historic Site. Both are administered by the National Park Service; you can take one of its tours or wander around on your own.

SIGHTS TO SEE

**6 Casa Blanca.** The original structure on this site, not far from the ramparts of El Morro, was a frame house built in 1521 as a home for Ponce de León. But Ponce de León died in Cuba, never having lived in it, and it was virtually destroyed by a hurricane in 1523, after which his son-in-law had the present masonry home built. His descendants occupied it for 250 years. From the end of the Spanish-American War in 1898 to 1966, it was the home of the U.S. Army commander in Puerto Rico. A museum devoted to archaeology is on the second floor. The lush surrounding gardens, cooled by spraying fountains, are a tranquil spot for a restorative pause. ✉ *1 Calle San Sebastián,* ☎ *787/724–4102.* ▧ *$2.* ☉ *Tues.–Sat. 9–noon and 1–3:45.*

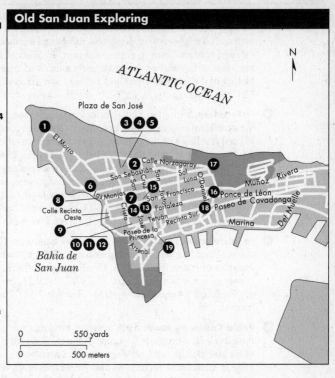

**Old San Juan Exploring**

⓫ **Casa del Libro.** This 18th-century building contains exhibits devoted to books and bookbinding. The museum's 5,000 books include many rare volumes. ⌧ *255 Calle Cristo,* ☎ *787/723–0354.* 🎫 *Free.* ☉ *Tues.–Sat. 11–4:30.*

⓯ **City Hall.** Called the *Alcaldía,* this structure was built between 1604 and 1789. In 1841 extensive renovations were done to make the Alcaldía resemble Madrid's city hall, with arcades, towers, balconies, and a lovely inner courtyard. A tourist information center and an art gallery are on the first floor. ⌧ *North side of Plaza de Armas,* ☎ *787/724–7171, ext. 2391.* ☉ *Weekdays 8–4.*

❿ **Cristo Chapel.** According to legend, in 1753 a young horseman, carried away during festivities in honor of the patron saint, raced down the street and plunged over the steep precipice. A witness to the tragedy promised to build a chapel if the young man's life could be saved. Historical records maintain the man died, though legend contends that he lived. Inside is a small silver altar, dedicated to the Christ of Miracles. ⌧ *Calle Cristo.* ☉ *Tues. and Fri. 10–3:30.*

❺ **Dominican Convent.** Built by Dominican friars in 1523, the convent often served as a shelter during Carib Indian attacks and, more recently, as headquarters for the Antilles command of the U.S. Army. Now home to the Institute of Puerto Rican Culture, the beautifully restored building contains an ornate 18th-century altar, religious manuscripts, artifacts, and art. The institute also maintains a bookshop here, and occasionally classical concerts are held. The convent is the intended future home of the city's museum of fine arts. ⌧ *98 Calle Norzagaray,* ☎ *787/721–6866.* 🎫 *Free.* ☉ *Mon.–Sat. 9–5.*

🖑 ❶ **Fuerte San Felipe del Morro.** On a rocky promontory on the northwestern tip of the old city is El Morro, a fortress built by the Spaniards between

1540 and 1783. Rising 140 ft above the sea, the massive six-level fortress covers enough territory to accommodate a nine-hole golf course. It is a labyrinth of dungeons, ramps and barracks, turrets, towers, and tunnels. Built to protect the port, El Morro has a commanding view of the harbor. Its small, air-conditioned museum traces the history of the fortress. Tours and a video show are available in English. ⊠ *Calle Norzagaray,* ☎ *787/729–6960.* ⊒ *Free.* ☉ *Daily 9–5.*

**❾ La Fortaleza.** Sitting on a hill overlooking the harbor, La Fortaleza, the Western Hemisphere's oldest executive mansion in continuous use and official residence of the present governor of Puerto Rico, was built as a fortress. The original primitive structure, built in 1540, has seen numerous changes over the past four centuries, resulting in the present collection of marble and mahogany, medieval towers, and stained-glass galleries. Guided tours are conducted every hour on the hour in English, on the half hour in Spanish. ⊠ *Calle Recinto Oeste,* ☎ *787/721–7000, ext. 2211 or 2358.* ⊒ *Free.* ☉ *Weekdays 9–4.*

**⓮ La Intendencia.** From 1851 to 1898, this handsome three-story neoclassical building was home to the Spanish Treasury; now it is the headquarters of Puerto Rico's State Department. ⊠ *Calle San José, at the corner of Calle San Francisco,* ☎ *787/722–2121, ext. 230.* ⊒ *Free.* ☉ *Weekdays 8–noon and 1–4:30. Tours at 2 and 3 in Spanish, 4 in English.*

**❹ Pablo Casals Museum.** This museum contains memorabilia of the famed cellist, who made his home in Puerto Rico for the last 16 years of his life. Manuscripts, photographs, and his favorite cellos are on display, in addition to recordings and videotapes of Casals Festival concerts (the latter shown on request). ⊠ *101 Calle San Sebastián, Plaza de San José,* ☎ *787/723–9185.* ⊒ *$1.* ☉ *Tues.–Sat. 9:30–5:30.*

**⓲ Paseo de la Princesa.** This street down at the port is spruced up with flowers, trees, benches, and street lamps. Take a seat and watch the boats zip across the water.

**⓭ Plaza de Armas.** This is the original main square of Old San Juan. The plaza, bordered by Calles San Francisco, Fortaleza, San José, and Cruz, has a lovely fountain with 19th-century statues representing the four seasons.

NEED A BREAK? **La Bombonera** (⊠ 259 Calle San Francisco, ☎ 787/722-0658), established in 1903, is known for its strong Puerto Rican coffee and *Mallorca*— a Spanish pastry made of light dough, toasted, buttered, and sprinkled with powdered sugar. Breakfast, for under $5, is served until 11. It's a favorite Sunday-morning gathering place in Old San Juan.

**⓰ Plaza de Colón.** This bustling square has a statue of Christopher Columbus atop a high pedestal. Originally called St. James Square, it was renamed in honor of Columbus on the 400th anniversary of the discovery of Puerto Rico. Bronze plaques in the base of the statue relate various episodes in the life of the great explorer. On the north side of the plaza is a terminal for buses to and from San Juan. ⊠ *On pedestrian mall of Calle Fortaleza.*

**❽ Plazuela de la Rogativa.** In this little plaza, statues of a bishop and three women commemorate a legend, according to which the British, while laying siege to the city in 1797, mistook the flaming torches of a *rogativa* (religious procession) for Spanish reinforcements and beat a hasty retreat. The monument was donated to the city in 1971 on its 450th anniversary. ⊠ *Caleta de las Monjas.*

⑫ **Popular Arts and Crafts Center.** Run by the Institute of Puerto Rican Culture, the center is in a colonial building next door to the Casa del Libro (☞ *above*) and is a superb repository of island craft work, some of which is for sale. ⊠ *253 Calle Cristo,* ☎ *787/722–0621.* ⊑ *Free.* ☉ *Mon.–Sat. 9–5.*

☝ ⑰ **San Cristóbal.** This 18th-century fortress guarded the city from land attacks. Even larger than El Morro, San Cristóbal, during the 17th and 18th centuries, was known as the Gibraltar of the West Indies. ⊠ *Norzagaray Blvd.,* ☎ *787/729–6960.* ⊑ *Free.* ☉ *Daily 9–5.*

❸ **San José Church.** With its series of vaulted ceilings, this is a splendid example of 16th-century Spanish Gothic architecture. The church, one of the oldest Christian houses of worship in the Western Hemisphere, was built in 1532 under the supervision of the Dominican friars. The body of Ponce de León, the Spanish explorer who came to the New World seeking the Fountain of Youth, was buried here for almost three centuries before being removed in 1913 and placed in the San Juan Cathedral (☞ *below*). ⊠ *Calle San Sebastián, Plaza de San José,* ☎ *787/725–7501.* ⊑ *Free.* ☉ *Mon.–Sat. 8:30–4; mass Sun. at 12:15 PM.*

❼ **San Juan Cathedral.** This great Catholic shrine of Puerto Rico had humble beginnings in the early 1520s as a thatch-topped wood structure. Hurricane winds tore off the thatch and destroyed the church. It was reconstructed in 1540, when the graceful circular staircase and vaulted Gothic ceilings were added, but most of the work on the church was done in the 19th century. The remains of Ponce de León are in a marble tomb near the transept. ⊠ *153 Calle Cristo,* ☎ *787/722–0861.* ☉ *Weekdays 8:30–4; masses Sat. 7 PM, Sun. 9 and 11 AM, weekdays 12:15 PM.*

❷ **San Juan Museum of Art and History.** A bustling marketplace in 1855, this handsome building is now a modern cultural center that houses exhibits of Puerto Rican art. Multi-image audiovisual shows present the history of the island; concerts and other cultural events take place in the huge courtyard. ⊠ *Calle Norzagaray, at the corner of Calle MacArthur,* ☎ *787/724–1875.* ⊑ *Free.* ☉ *Tues.–Sun. 10–4.*

⑱ **Tapia Theater.** This theater was named after the Puerto Rican playwright Alejandro Tapia y Rivera. Built in 1832 and remodeled in 1949 and again in 1987, the municipal theater is the site of ballets, plays, and operettas. Stop by the box office to find out what's showing. ⊠ *Calle Fortaleza at Plaza de Colón,* ☎ *787/722–0407.*

## San Juan

You'll need to resort to taxis, buses, públicos, or a rental car to reach the points of interest in "new" San Juan.

Avenida Muñoz Rivera, Avenida Ponce de León, and Avenida Fernández Juncos are the main thoroughfares that cross Puerta de Tierra, just east of Old San Juan, to the business and tourist districts of Santurce, Condado, and Isla Verde. Dos Hermanos Bridge connects Puerta de Tierra with Miramar, Condado, and Isla Grande. Isla Grande Airport, from which you can take short hops, is on the bay side of the bridge. On the other side of the bridge, the Condado Lagoon is bordered by Avenida Ashford, which threads past the high-rise Condado hotels and El Centro Convention Center, and Avenida Baldorioty de Castro Expreso, which barrels all the way east to the airport and beyond. Due south of the lagoon is Miramar, a primarily residential area with fashionable turn-of-the-century homes and a cluster of hotels and restaurants.

South of Santurce is the "Golden Mile"—Hato Rey, the city's bustling financial hub. Isla Verde, with its glittering beachfront hotels, casinos, discos, and public beach, is to the east, near the airport.

*Numbers in the margin correspond to points of interest on the San Juan Exploring, Dining, and Lodging map.*

SIGHTS TO SEE

❶ **Capitol.** In Puerta de Tierra is Puerto Rico's capitol, a white marble building that dates from the 1920s. The grand rotunda, with mosaics and friezes, was completed a few years ago. The seat of the island's bicameral legislature, the capitol contains Puerto Rico's constitution and is flanked by the modern buildings of the Senate and the House of Representatives. There are spectacular views from the observation plaza on the sea side of the capitol. Pick up a booklet about the building from the House Secretariat on the second floor. Guided tours are by appointment only. ⊠ *Av. Ponce de León, Puerta de Tierra,* ☎ *787/ 721–6040, ext. 2458 or 3548.* 🎫 *Free.* ☉ *Weekdays 8–4.*

❸ **Centro de Bellas Artes.** Internationally acclaimed performers appear at the Fine Arts Center. This completely modern facility, the largest of its kind in the Caribbean, has a full schedule of concerts, plays, and operas. ⊠ *Corner of Av. De Diego and Av. Ponce de León, Box 41287, Minillas Station, Santurce 00940,* ☎ *787/725–7353.*

❷ **Fort San Jeronimo.** At the eastern tip of Puerta de Tierra, behind the splashy Caribe Hilton, this tiny fort is perched over the Atlantic like an afterthought. Added to San Juan's fortifications in the late 18th century, the structure barely survived the British attack of 1797. Restored in 1983 by the Institute of Puerto Rican Culture, it is now a military museum. At press time, however, the museum remained closed for repairs, and no reopening date had been announced, so visitors could only view the fort from the outside. ⊠ *Calle Rosales, Puerta de Tierra,* ☎ *787/724–5477.*

☝ ❻ **Luis Muñoz Marín Park.** This idyllic, 90-acre tree-shaded spot is dotted with gardens, lakes, playgrounds, and picnic areas. An aerial gondola connects the park with the parking area and provides a 6½-minute tour of the park. An outdoor amphitheater is the venue for plays, concerts, and folk performances. ⊠ *Next to Las Américas Expressway, west on Av. Jesús Piñero, Hato Rey,* ☎ *787/751–3353.* 🎫 *Free; parking $1 per vehicle.* ☉ *Tues.–Sun. 9–5.*

❺ **San Juan Central Park.** Southeast of Miramar, Avenida Muñoz Rivera skirts along the northern side of this mangrove-bordered park, a convenient place for jogging and tennis. The park was built for the 1979 Pan-American Games. ⊠ *Cerra St. exit on Rte. 2, Santurce,* ☎ *787/ 722–1646.* 🎫 *Free.* ☉ *Mon. 2–9:45, Tues.–Fri. 6:30 AM–9:45 PM, weekends 6:30 AM–6 PM.*

❹ **Santurce.** The area that lies between Miramar on the west and the Laguna San José on the east is a busy mixture of shops, markets, and offices. The classically designed **Sacred Heart University** is the home of the **Museum of Contemporary Puerto Rican Art** (⊠ *Barat Bldg.,* ☎ *787/ 268–0049*), which showcases the works of such modern masters as Rodon, Campeche, and Oller. The museum is free and is open weekdays from 9 to 5.

NEED A      **Pescadería Atlántica** (⊠ 81 Calle Loiza, ☎ 787/726-6654) is a com-
BREAK?      bination seafood restaurant and retail store. Stop in for a cool drink at
            the bar and a side dish of calamares, lightly breaded squid in a hot,
            spicy sauce.

❼ **University of Puerto Rico.** Río Piedras, a southern suburb of San Juan, is home to the university, between Avenida Ponce de León and Avenida Barbosa. The university's campus is one of two sites for performances of the Puerto Rico Symphony Orchestra. Theatrical productions and other concerts are also scheduled here throughout the year. The **University Museum** has permanent archaeological and historical exhibits and occasionally mounts special art displays. ⊠ *Next to university's main entrance on Av. Ponce de León, Río Piedras,* ☎ *787/764–0000, ext. 2452.* ⊙ *Mon.–Wed. and Fri. 9–4:30, Thurs. 9–9, Sat. 9–3.*

The university's main attraction is the **Botanical Garden,** a lush forest of more than 200 species of tropical and subtropical vegetation. Footpaths lead to a graceful lotus lagoon, a bamboo promenade, an orchid garden, and a palm garden. ⊠ *Intersection of Rtes. 1 and 847 at entrance to Barrio Venezuela, Río Piedras,* ☎ *787/763–4408.* ⊠ *Free.* ⊙ *Daily 9–4:30.*

## San Juan Environs
*Numbers in the margin correspond to points of interest on the Puerto Rico map.*

SIGHTS TO SEE

**❸ Bacardi Rum Plant.** Visitors can take a 45-minute tour of the bottling plant, museum, and distillery (called the Cathedral of Rum), which has the capacity to produce 100,000 gallons of rum a day. There is a gift shop. (Yes, you'll be offered a sample.) ⊠ *Rte. 888, Km 2.6, Cataño,* ☎ *787/788–1500.* ⊠ *Free.* ⊙ *Tours every 30 mins Mon.–Sat. 9–10:30 and noon–4.*

**❷ Barrilito Rum Plant.** On the grounds are a 200-year-old plantation home and a 150-year-old windmill, listed on the National Register of Historic Places. ⊠ *Rte. 5, Km 1.6, Bayamón,* ☎ *787/785–3490.* ⊠ *Free.* ⊙ *Weekdays 8–11:30 and 1–4:30.*

**❹ Bayamón.** In the central park, across from Bayamón's city hall, there are some historical buildings and a 1934 sugarcane train that runs through the park (☎ 787/798–8191), open daily 8 AM–5 PM. On the plaza, in the city's historic district, stands the 18th-century Catholic church of Santa Cruz and the old neoclassical city hall, which now houses the **Francisco Oller Art and History Museum** (⊠ Calle Santiago Veve, ☎ 787/787–8620). The museum is free and is open Tuesday–Saturday 9–4.

**❶ Caparra Ruins.** In 1508 Ponce de León established the island's first settlement here. The ruins are that of an ancient fort. Its small **Museum of the Conquest and Colonization of Puerto Rico** contains historical documents, exhibits, and excavated artifacts. (You can see the museum's contents in less time than it takes to say the name.) ⊠ *Rte. 2, Km 6.6, Guaynabo,* ☎ *787/781–4795.* ⊠ *Free.* ⊙ *Tues.–Sat. 8:30–4:30.*

## Out on the Island
Puerto Rico's 3,500 square mi is a lot of land to explore. While you can get from town to town via público, we don't recommend traveling that way unless your Spanish is good and you know exactly where you're going. The public cars stop in each town's main square, leaving you on your own to reach the beaches, restaurants, paradores, and sightseeing attractions. You'll do much better if you rent a car. Most of the island's roads are excellent. However, there is a tangled web of roads through the mountains, and they are not always well marked. It helps to buy a good road map.

*Numbers in the margin correspond to points of interest on the Puerto Rico map.*

EASTERN PUERTO RICO

**❺ Caribbean National Forest.** To take full advantage of the 28,000-acre El Yunque (as it's commonly known) rain forest, go with a tour. Dozens of trails lead through the thick jungle (it sheltered the Carib Indians for 200 years), and the tour guides take you to the best observation points, bathing spots, and waterfalls. Some of the trails are slippery, and there are occasional washouts.

However, if you'd like to drive there yourself, take Route 3 east from San Juan and turn right (south) on Route 191, about 25 mi from the city. The **El Portal Tropical Forest Center** (☎ 787/888–1810 or 787/888–1880) is on Route 191 at the entrance to the park. Nature talks, programs, and displays at the center are in Spanish and English. The center is open daily 9–5; admission is $3.

El Yunque, named after the good Indian spirit Yuquiyu, is in the Luquillo mountain range. The rain forest is verdant with feathery ferns, thick ropelike vines, white tuberoses and ginger, miniature orchids, and some 240 different species of trees. More than 100 billion gallons of rainwater fall on it annually. Rain-battered, wind-ravaged dwarf vegetation clings to the top peaks. (El Toro, the highest peak in the forest, is 3,532 ft.) El Yunque is also a bird sanctuary and the base of the rare Puerto Rican parrot. Millions of tiny, inch-long coquis can be heard singing (or squawking, depending on your sensibilities). ⊠ *For further information write Caribbean National Forest, Box B, Palmer, PR 00721, or call Catalina Field Office,* ☎ *787/887–2875 or 787/766–5335.*

**9** **Culebra.** This island off the east coast of Puerto Rico has lovely white-sand beaches, coral reefs, and a wildlife refuge. In the sleepy town of Dewey, on Culebra's southwestern side, check at the visitor information center at city hall (☎ 787/742–3291) about boat, bike, or car rentals. Don't miss **Playa Flamenco,** 3 mi north of Dewey, or **Playa Soni** on the eastern end of the island: They are two of the prettiest beaches in the Caribbean.

**8** **Fajardo.** This is a major fishing and sailing center with thousands of boats tied and stacked in tiers at its three large marinas. Boats can be rented or chartered here, and the *East Wind,* a 53-ft catamaran, can take you out for a full day of snorkeling, swimming, and sunning for $55 per person. Fajardo is also the embarkation point for ferries to the islands of Culebra (a $2.25 fare) and Vieques ($2). ⊠ *Rte. 3.*

**7** **Las Cabezas de San Juan Nature Reserve.** Opened in 1991, the reserve contains mangrove swamps, coral reefs, beaches, and a dry forest—most of Puerto Rico's natural habitats rolled into a microcosmic 316 acres. The only habitat missing is a rain forest. Nineteenth-century El Faro, one of the island's oldest lighthouses, is restored and still functioning; its first floor contains a small nature center that has an aquarium and other exhibits. The reserve is open, by reservation only, to the general public Friday–Sunday and to tour groups Wednesday–Thursday. Tours are given on request (in advance, by telephone) four times a day. ⊠ *Rte. 987, Km 5.8,* ☎ *787/722–5882; 787/860–2560 on weekends.* ⊡ *$5.*

**6** **Luquillo Beach.** One of the island's best and most popular beaches, Luquillo was once a flourishing coconut plantation. Coral reefs protect its calm, pristine lagoon, making it an ideal place for a swim. The entrance fee is $1 per car, and there are lockers, showers, and changing rooms, as well as stands selling savory Puerto Rican delicacies. The beach gets crowded on weekends, when it seems as if the whole world heads for Luquillo. ⊠ *Rte. 3, Km 35.4.* ⊡ *$1 per car.*

**10** **Vieques.** On this island off the east coast of Puerto Rico, is **Sun Bay public beach,** a gorgeous stretch of sand with picnic facilities and shade trees. **Red** and **Blue** beaches, on the U.S. Marine/Camp Garcia base (open to the public 6 AM–6 PM), are superb for snorkeling and privacy. **Mosquito Bay** is best experienced on moonless nights, thanks to the millions of bioluminescent organisms that glow when disturbed—it's like swimming in a cloud of fireflies. Seventy percent of Vieques is owned by the U.S. Navy, ensuring it will remain unspoiled. The deserted beaches—Green, Red, Blue, Navia, and Media Luna—are among the Caribbean's loveliest; you might see a wild paso fino horse galloping in the surf. The **visitor information center** (☎ 787/741-5000) is in the fishing village of Esperanza. Both Vieques and Culebra (☞ *above*), parched in contrast to the lush eastern end of Puerto Rico, are havens for colorful "expatriates" escaping the rat race stateside. This is pure old-time Caribbean: fun, funky, and unspoiled—the kind of getaway that is fast disappearing.

WESTERN PUERTO RICO

⓮ **Aguadilla.** In this area, somewhere between Aguadilla and Añasco, south of Rincón, Columbus dropped anchor on his second voyage in 1493. Both Aguadilla and **Aguada**, a few miles to the south, claim to be the spot where his foot first hit ground, and both towns have plaques to commemorate the occasion. ⊠ *Rte. 111.*

⓭ **Arecibo Observatory.** The town of Arecibo is home to one of the world's largest radar/radio telescopes. A 20-acre radar dish, with a 600-ton suspended platform hovering over it, sits in a 565-ft-deep sinkhole (karst fields, an alien landscape of collapsed limestone sinkholes, are the prevalent geology throughout this part of the island). You can take a self-guided tour of the observatory, where groundbreaking work in astronomy, including SETI (the search for extraterrestrial intelligence), continues. ⊠ *Rte. 625,* ☎ *787/878-2612.* ☞ *Free.* ☉ *Tues.–Fri. 2–3, Sun. 1–4:30.*

⓴ **Boquerón.** This tiny, funky, pastel village has sidewalk oyster vendors, bars, restaurants serving fresh seafood, and several of the standard T-shirt shops. There are also diving and snorkeling tours at the Boquerón Dive Shop on Main Street. Boquerón's balneario is one of the best beaches on the island. Parking is $2 per car, and two-room rustic cabins are for rent (☎ 787/724-2500, ext. 130 or 131). ⊠ *Rte. 101.*

⓲ **Cabo Rojo.** Once a pirates' hangout, this town is now a favorite resort area of Puerto Ricans. The area has long stretches of white-sand beaches on the clear, calm Caribbean Sea, as well as many seafood restaurants, bars, and hotels. There are also several paradores in the region. ⊠ *Rte. 102.*

⓫ **Caguana Indian Ceremonial Park.** This area was used 800 years ago by the Taíno tribes for recreation and worship. Mountains surround a 13-acre site planted with royal palms and guava. According to Spanish historians, the Taínos played a game similar to soccer, and in this park there are 10 courts (*bateyes*) bordered by cobbled walkways. There are also stone monoliths, some with colorful petroglyphs; a small museum; and a souvenir shop. ⊠ *Rte. 111, Km 12.3,* ☎ *787/894-7325.* ☞ *Free.* ☉ *Daily 9–4:30.*

⓱ **Mayagüez.** Puerto Rico's fourth-largest city has a population approaching 100,000. Although bypassed by the mania for restoration that saw Ponce and Old San Juan spruced up for the Columbus quincentennial, Mayagüez is graced by some lovely turn-of-the-century architecture, such as the landmark Art Deco Teatro Yagüez and the Plaza de Colón.

☙ North of town visit the **Mayagüez Zoo,** a 45-acre tropical compound that's home to exotic animals from around the world. The zoo's massive three-year renovation plan has just begun, so some exhibits may be sporadically closed. ⊠ *Rte. 108 at Barrio Miradero,* ☎ *787/834–8110.* 🎫 *$3; parking $1.* ☉ *Wed.–Sun. 9–4.*

**16**   **Mona Island.** Fifty miles west of Mayagüez in the turbulent shark-infested Mona Passage, Mona Island is nicknamed the Galápagos of the Caribbean, thanks to the plethora of endangered and unique indigenous species that call it home. The variety of marine and bird life is especially breathtaking. The coastline is rimmed with imposing limestone cliffs up to 200 ft high pocked with caves that are said to contain buried treasure; the many perfectly preserved Taíno hieroglyphs and rock paintings there are of great archaeological value. Access to the island is only via private plane or boat. Very limited camping facilities are available on the pristine beaches. Call the Department of Natural Resources for information and camping reservations (☎ 787/723–1616 or 787/721–5495).

**21**   **Phosphorescent Bay.** The fishing village of **La Parguera,** an area of simple seafood restaurants, mangrove cays, and small islands, lies south of San Germán at the end of Route 304, off Route 116. This is an excellent scuba-diving area, but the main attraction is Phosphorescent Bay. Boats tour the bay, where microscopic dinoflagellates (marine plankton) light up like Christmas trees when disturbed by any kind of movement. The phenomenon can be seen only on moonless nights. Boats leave for the hour-long trip nightly from dusk until midnight, depending on demand, and the trip costs $5 per person. You can also rent or charter a small boat to explore the numerous cays.

**22**   **Ponce.** From San Germán (☞ *below*), Route 2 traverses splendid peaks and valleys; pastel houses cling to the sides of steep green hills. The Cordillera Central mountains run parallel to Route 2 here and provide a stunning backdrop to the drive. East of Yauco, the road dips and sweeps right along the Caribbean and into Ponce.

Puerto Rico's second-largest city (population 300,000) underwent a massive restoration in preparation for its 300th anniversary, celebrated in 1996, of the city's first settlement.

The town's 19th-century style has been recaptured with pink marble-bordered sidewalks, gas lamps, painted trolleys, and horse-drawn carriages. You have not seen a firehouse until you've seen the red-and-black-striped **Parque de Bombas,** a structure built in 1882 for an exposition and converted to a firehouse the following year. The city hired architect Pablo Ojeda O'Neill to restore it, and it is now a museum of Ponce's history, which, not surprisingly, has a display of Fire Brigade memorabilia. ⊠ *Plaza Las Delicias,* ☎ *787/284–4141, ext. 342.* 🎫 *Free.* ☉ *Wed.–Mon. 9:30–6.*

Ponce's charm stems from a combination of neoclassical, Ponce Creole, and art deco styles. The tiny streets lined with wrought-iron balconies are reminiscent of New Orleans's French Quarter. Stop in and pick up information about this seaside city at the columned **Casa Armstrong-Poventud,** the home of the Institute of Puerto Rican Culture and a Tourism Information Office, open weekdays 8–noon and 1–4:30 (use the side entrance). Stroll around the **Plaza Las Delicias,** with its perfectly pruned India-laurel fig trees, graceful fountains, gardens, and park benches. View **Our Lady of Guadelupe Cathedral** (masses are held daily), and walk down Calles Isabel and Christina to see turn-of-the-century wooden houses with wrought-iron balconies.

Two superlative examples of early 20th-century architecture house the **Ponce History Museum** (Museo de la Historia de Ponce), where 10 rooms of exhibits vividly re-create Ponce's golden years, providing especially fascinating glimpses into the worlds of culture, high finance, and journalism during the 19th century. ⊠ *53 Calle Isabel,* ☎ *787/844–7071.* 🖾 *$3.* ☉ *Mon. and Wed.–Fri. 10–5, weekends 10–6.*

Continue as far as Calles Mayor and Christina to the white stucco **La Perla Theater,** with its Corinthian columns. Be sure to allow time to visit the **Ponce Museum of Art** (Museo de Arte de Ponce). The architecture alone is worth seeing: The modern, two-story building designed by Edward Durell Stone (who designed New York's Museum of Modern Art) has seven interconnected hexagons, glass cupolas, and a pair of curved staircases. The collection includes late Renaissance and Baroque works from Italy, France, and Spain, as well as contemporary art by Puerto Ricans. ⊠ *Av. Las Américas,* ☎ *787/848–0505 or 787/ 848–0511.* 🖾 *$4.* ☉ *Daily 10–5.*

Another fine museum is **Castillo Serrallés,** a splendid Spanish Revival mansion perched on El Vigía Hill, with smashing views of Ponce and the Caribbean. This former residence of the Serrallés family, owners of the Don Q rum distillery, has been restored with a mix of original furnishings and antiques that recall the era of the sugar barons, including a baronial dining room with heavy carved mahogany and wrought-iron doors. A short film details the history of the sugar and rum industries. The unusual, rather ugly 100-ft-tall cross (La Cruceta del Vigía) looming behind the museum is being restored; when it is finished (a completion date had not been set at press time), visitors will be able to climb to its observation tower. ⊠ *17 El Vigía Hill,* ☎ *787/259– 1774.* 🖾 *$3.* ☉ *Tues.–Sun. 10–5.*

There are two intriguing historical sights just outside the city. **Hacienda Buena Vista** is a 19th-century coffee plantation, restored by the Conservation Trust of Puerto Rico, with much of the authentic machinery and furnishings intact. Reservations are required for the 90-minute tours; tours in English are given on request (in advance) once a day. ⊠ *Rte. 10, Km 16.8, north of Ponce,* ☎ *787/722–5882 weekdays, 787/848– 7020 weekends.* 🖾 *$5.* ☉ *Wed.–Fri. open to tour groups; Fri.–Sun. open to public.*

The **Tibes Indian Ceremonial Center** is the oldest cemetery in the Caribbean. It is a treasure trove of pre-Taíno ruins and burials, dating from AD 300 to AD 700. Some archaeologists, noting the symmetrical arrangement of stone pillars, surmise the cemetery may have been of great religious significance. The complex includes a detailed re-creation of a Taíno village and a museum. ⊠ *Rte. 503, Km 2.7,* ☎ *787/840– 2255 or 787/840–5685.* 🖾 *$2.* ☉ *Wed.–Sun. 9–4.*

**⓯ Rincón.** Located along Route 115, one of the island's most scenic areas of rolling hills dotted with pastel-colored houses, Rincón is perched on a hill and overlooks its beach, the site of the World Surfing Championship in 1968. Skilled surfers flock to Rincón during the winter, when the water is rough and challenging. The town is also increasingly popular with divers. Locals boast that the best diving and snorkeling in Puerto Rico (and some even say the Caribbean) is off the Rincón coast, particularly around the island of Desecheo, a federal wildlife preserve. Whale-watching is another draw for this town; humpback whales winter off the coast from December through February. ⊠ *Rte. 115.*

**⓬ Río Camuy Cave Park.** This 268-acre reserve contains one of the world's largest cave networks. Guided tours take you on a tram down through dense tropical vegetation to the entrance of the cave, where you continue on foot over underground trails, ramps, and bridges. The caves, sinkholes, and subterranean streams are all spectacular (the world's second-largest underground river runs through here), but this trip is not for the claustrophobic. Be sure to call ahead; the tours allow only a limited number of people, and hours change slightly in the off-season. ⊠ *Rte. 129, Km 18.9,* ☎ *787/898–3100 or 787/756–5555.* 🎫 *$10; parking $2.* ☉ *Tues.–Sun. 8–4. Last tour starts at 3:50.*

**⑲** **San Germán.** This quiet and colorful Old World town is home to the oldest intact church under the U.S. flag. Built in 1606, **Porta Coeli** (Gates of Heaven) overlooks one of the town's two plazas (where the townspeople continue the Spanish tradition of promenading at night). The church is now a museum of religious art, housing 18th- and 19th-century paintings and wooden statues. ⊠ *Rte. 102,* ☎ *787/892–5845.* 🎫 *Free.* ☉ *Tues.–Sun. 9–noon and 1–4.*

# Puerto Rico A to Z

## Arriving and Departing

### BY PLANE

The **Luis Muñoz Marín International Airport** (☎ 787/462–3147), east of downtown San Juan, is one of the easiest and cheapest destinations to reach in the Caribbean. The airport is the Caribbean hub for **American Airlines** (☎ 787/749–1747 or 800/433–7300). American has daily nonstop flights from New York, Newark, Miami, Boston, Philadelphia, Chicago, Nashville, Los Angeles, Dallas, Baltimore, Hartford, Raleigh-Durham, Tampa, and Washington, DC. **Continental** (☎ 800/231–0856) has nonstop service from Newark. **Delta** (☎ 800/221–1212) has nonstop service from Atlanta and Orlando, as well as connecting service from other major cities. **Northwest** (☎ 800/447–4747) has seasonal nonstop flights from Detroit, Minneapolis, Memphis, and Washington, DC, to San Juan. **TWA** (☎ 800/892–4141) flies nonstop from New York and St. Louis. **United** (☎ 800/241–6522) flies nonstop from Chicago. **US Airways** (☎ 800/428–4322) offers nonstop flights from Baltimore, Philadelphia, and Charlotte. Puerto Rico–based **Carnival Airlines** (☎ 800/437–2110) operates nonstop flights from New York and Newark to Aguadilla and Ponce, and from Miami to San Juan. **Tower Air** (☎ 800/221–2500) flies nonstop from New York/JFK. **American Trans Air (ATA)** (☎ 800/382–5892) operates nonstop from Orlando.

Foreign carriers include **Air Canada** (☎ 800/776–3000), **Air France** (☎ 800/237–2747), **British Airways** (☎ 800/247–9297), **BWIA** (☎ 800/327–7401), **Iberia** (☎ 800/772–4642), **LACSA** (☎ 800/225–2272), and **Lufthansa** (☎ 800/645–3880).

Connections between Caribbean islands can be made through **American Eagle** (☎ 800/433–7300), **Air Jamaica** (☎ 800/523–5585), **ANA** (☎ 800/693–0007), **LIAT** (☎ 800/468–0482), and **Sunaire Express** (☎ 800/595–9501).

### FROM THE AIRPORT

**Taxi Turisticos** (☞ Getting Around, *below*) charge set rates depending on the destination. Uniformed and badged officials help you find a cab at the airport (look for the tourism company booth) and hand you a slip with your fare, which you can present to your driver. To Isla Verde, the fare is $8; to Condado, it's $12; to Old San Juan, it's $16. If you don't hail one of these cabs, you're at the mercy of the meter and the cabdriver. Other options are the **Airport Limousine Service** (☎ 787/791–4745), which provides minibus service to hotels in the Isla Verde, Condado, and Old San Juan areas at basic fares of $2.50, $3.50, and $4.50, respectively; the fares do vary, depending on the time of day and number of passengers. Limousines of **Dorado Transport Service** (☎ 787/796–1214) serve hotels and villas in the Dorado area for $15 per person.

## Currency

The U.S. dollar is the official currency of Puerto Rico.

## Emergencies

**Police, fire, and medical emergencies:** ☎ 911. **Hospitals:** Hospitals in the Condado-Santurce area with 24-hour emergency rooms are **Ashford Memorial Community Hospital** (⊠ 1451 Av. Ashford, Condado, ☎ 787/721–2160) and **San Juan Health Centre** (⊠ 200 Av. De Diego, ☎ 787/725–0202). **Pharmacies:** In San Juan, **Walgreens** (⊠ 1130 Av. Ashford, Condado, ☎ 787/725–1510) operates a 24-hour pharmacy; in Old San Juan, try **Puerto Rico Drug Company** (⊠ 157 Calle San Francisco, ☎ 787/725–2202). Walgreens operates more than 30 pharmacies on the island.

## Getting Around

If you are staying in San Juan, you can get around by walking, bus, taxi, or hotel shuttle. However, if you venture out on the island, a rental car is your best transportation option.

Roads in Puerto Rico are generally well marked; however, a good road map is helpful when traveling to more remote areas on the island. Some car-rental agencies distribute free maps of the island when you pick up your car. These maps lack detail and are usually out-of-date due to new construction. The simplest thing to do is head to the nearest gas station—most of them sell better maps. Good maps are also available at the **Book Store** (⊠ 257 Calle San José, Old San Juan, ☎ 787/724–1815). Keep in mind that distances are posted in kilometers while road speed signs are in mph.

### BUSES

The **Metropolitan Bus Authority (AMA)** (☎ 787/250–6064) operates *guaguas* (buses) that thread through San Juan. The fare is 25¢, and the buses run in exclusive lanes, *against the traffic* on major thoroughfares, stopping at magenta, orange, and white signs marked *Parada* or *Parada de Guaguas*. The main terminals are Covadunga parking lot and Plaza de Colón, in Old San Juan, and Capetillo Terminal in Rio Piedras, next to the central business district.

### CAR RENTALS

U.S. driver's licenses are valid in Puerto Rico for three months. All major U.S. car-rental agencies are represented on the island, including **Avis** (☎ 787/721–4499 or 800/874–3556), **Hertz** (☎ 787/791–0840 or 800/654–3131), **Budget** (☎ 787/791–3685 or 800/468–5822), **Thrifty** (☎ 787/253–2525 or 800/367–2277), and **National** (☎ 787/791–1805 or 800/568–3019). Local rental companies, sometimes less expensive, include **Charlie Car Rental** (☎ 787/728–2418 or 800/289–1227), **L & M Car Rental** (☎ 787/725–8416 or 800/666–0807), and **Target** (☎ 787/728–1447 or 800/934–6457). Prices start at about $35 (plus insurance), with unlimited mileage. Discounts are offered for long-term rentals, and insurance can be waived for those who rent with American Express or certain gold credit cards (be sure to check with your credit-card company before renting). Some discounts are offered for AAA or 72-hour advance bookings. Most car rentals have shuttle service to or from the airport and the pickup point. If you plan to drive across the island, arm yourself with a good map and be aware that there are many unmarked roads up in the mountains. Many service stations in the central mountains do not take credit cards. Speed limits are posted in miles, distances in kilometers, and gas prices in liters.

### FERRIES

The ferry between Old San Juan (Pier 2) and Cataño (☎ 787/788–1155) costs a mere 50¢ one-way. The ferry runs every half hour from 6 AM to

10 PM. The 400-passenger ferries of the **Fajardo Port Authority** (☎ 787/863–0852), which carry cargo as well as passengers, make the 90-minute trip between Fajardo and the island of Vieques twice on week-days and three times on weekends ($2 one-way). They make the 90-minute run between Fajardo and the island of Culebra once a day Monday–Thursday and twice a day Friday–Sunday ($2.25 one-way).

### LINÉAS

*Linéas* are private taxis you share with three to five other passengers. There are more than 20 companies, each usually specializing in a cer-tain region. Most will arrange door-to-door service. Check local yel-low-pages listings under Linéas de Carros. They're a cheaper method of transport and a great way to meet people, but be prepared to wait: They usually don't leave until they have a full load.

### PLANES

From the Isla Grande Airport, you can take a **Vieques Air-Link** (☎ 787/722–3736) flight to Vieques ($35 one-way), or a **Flamenco Airways** (☎ 787/725–7707) flight to Culebra for ($30 one-way).

### PÚBLICOS

*Públicos* (literally, "public cars"), with yellow license plates ending in "P" or "PD," scoot to towns throughout the island, stopping in each town's main plaza. These 17-passenger vans operate primarily during the day, with routes and fares fixed by the Public Service Commission. In San Juan, the main terminals are at the airport and at Plaza Colón on the waterfront in Old San Juan.

### TAXIS

The Puerto Rico Tourism Company has recently instituted a much-needed and well-organized taxi program for tourists. Taxis painted white and sporting the *garita* (sentry box) logo and **Taxi Turistico** label charge set rates depending on the destination; they run from the airport or the cruise-ship piers to Isla Verde, Condado/Ocean Park, and Old San Juan, with rates ranging from $6 to $16. Metered cabs authorized by the **Public Service Commission** (☎ 787/751–5050) start at $1 and charge 10¢ for every additional tenth of a mile, 50¢ for every suitcase, and $1 for home or business calls. Waiting time is 10¢ for each 45 seconds. The minimum charge is $3. Be sure the driver starts the meter. You can also call **Major Taxicabs** (☎ 787/723–2460) in San Juan and **Ponce Taxi** (☎ 787/840–0088).

### TROLLEYS

If your feet fail you in Old San Juan, climb aboard the free open-air trolleys that rumble and roller-coast through the narrow streets. De-partures are from La Puntilla and from the marina, but you can board anywhere along the route.

## Guided Tours

Old San Juan can be seen either on the free trolley, on self-guided walk-ing tour, or using an excellent tour guide from **Colonial Adventure** (✉ 201 Recinto Sur, ☎ 787/729–0114) tours. The small tour com-pany offers a variety of informative walking tours of the old city. To explore the rest of the city and the island, consider renting a car. (We do, however, recommend a guided tour of the vast El Yunque rain for-est.) If you'd rather not do your own driving, there are several tour companies you can call. Most San Juan hotels have a tour desk that can make arrangements for you. The three standard half-day tours ($15–$30) are of Old and "new" San Juan; Old San Juan and the Bacardi Rum Plant; and Luquillo Beach and El Yunque rain forest. All-day tours ($25–$45) can include a trip to Ponce, a day at El Comandante Race-track, or a combined tour of the city and El Yunque rain forest.

Leading tour operators include **Gray Line of Puerto Rico** (☎ 787/727–8080), **Normandie Tours, Inc.** (☎ 787/722–6308), **Rico Suntours** (☎ 787/722–2080 or 787/722–6090), **Tropix Wellness Tours** (☎ 787/268–2173), and **United Tour Guides** (☎ 787/725–7605 or 787/723–5578). **Cordero Caribbean Tours** (☎ 787/786–9114 or 787/780–2442 evenings) runs tours in air-conditioned limousines for an hourly rate.

## Language

Puerto Rico's official language is Spanish, and although English is widely spoken, you will probably want to take a Spanish phrase book along if you rent a car to travel around the island.

## Opening and Closing Times

Shops are open from 9 to 6 (from 9 to 9 during Christmas holidays). Banks are open weekdays from 8:30 to 2:30 and Saturday from 9:45 to noon.

## Passports and Visas

Puerto Rico is a commonwealth of the United States, and U.S. citizens do not need passports to visit the island. British citizens must have passports. Canadian citizens need proof of citizenship (preferably a passport).

## Precautions

San Juan, like any other big city and major tourist destination, has its share of crime, so guard your wallet or purse on the city streets. Puerto Rico's beaches are open to the public, and muggings can occur at night even on the beaches of the posh Condado and Isla Verde tourist hotels. While you certainly can and should explore the city and its beaches, using common sense will make your stay more secure and enjoyable. Don't leave anything unattended on the beach. Leave your valuables in the hotel safe, and stick to the fenced-in beach areas of your hotel. Always lock your car and stash valuables and luggage out of sight. Avoid deserted beaches at night.

## Taxes and Service Charges

The government tax on room charges is 7% (9% in hotels with casinos). Some hotels automatically add a 10%–15% service charge to your bill. In restaurants, a 15%–20% tip is expected. There is no departure tax.

## Telephones and Mail

Note that the area code for Puerto Rico changed from 809 to 787 as of March 1, 1996. Puerto Rico uses U.S. postage stamps and has the same mail rates (22¢ for a postcard, 32¢ for a first-class letter). Post offices in major Puerto Rican cities offer Express Mail next-day service to the U.S. mainland and to Puerto Rican destinations.

## Visitor Information

Before you go, contact the **Puerto Rico Tourism Company** (✉ Box 4435, Old San Juan Station, San Juan, PR 00902-4435, ☎ 787/721–2400, FAX 787/722–1093). From the States, you can call toll-free at ☎ 800/223–6530. Other branches: ✉ 575 5th Ave., 23rd floor, New York, NY 10017, ☎ 212/599–6262, FAX 212/818–1866; ✉ 3575 W. Cahuenga Blvd., Suite 560, Los Angeles, CA 90068, ☎ 213/874–5991, FAX 213/874–7257; ✉ 901 Ponce de León Blvd., Suite 604, Coral Gables, FL 33134, ☎ 305/445–9112, FAX 305/445–9450.

On Puerto Rico, the **Puerto Rico Tourism Company** (✉ Paseo de la Princesa, Old San Juan 00901, ☎ 787/721–2400) is an excellent source for maps and printed tourist materials. Be sure to pick up a free copy of *Qué Pasa*, the official visitors' guide.

Government and tourism-company information offices are also found at **Luis Muñoz Marín International Airport** in Isla Verde (☎ 787/791–1014 or 787/791–2551), **La Casita** (☎ 787/722–1709), near Pier 1 in Old San Juan, and at **La Playita la Condado,** the small public beach at the Condado Plaza Hotel. Out on the island, information offices are located in **Ponce** (✉ Fox Delicias Mall, 2nd floor, Plaza Las Delicias, ☎ 787/840–5695), **Aguadilla** (✉ Rafael Hernández Airport, ☎ 787/890–3315), **Cabo Rojo** (✉ Rte. 100, Km 13.7, ☎ 787/851–7070), and in many towns' city halls on the main plaza. Offices are usually open weekdays from 8 to noon and 1 to 4:30.

# 18 Saba

*Tiny Saba, one of the premier diving centers of the world, hosts some of the region's most dramatic scenery in its sweeping, steep mountainsides and sheer cliffs. The breeze is always pleasant, the Sabans more so, and the quiet backdrop and comfortable facilities make this one of the true, and undiscovered, gems of the Caribbean.*

Updated by
Karl Luntta

**T**HIS 5-SQUARE-MILE FAIRY-TALE ISLE is not for everybody. If you're looking for exciting nightlife or lots
of shopping, forget Saba, or make it a one-day excursion from St. Maarten. There are only a handful of shops here, even
fewer inns and eateries, and the island's movie theater closed with the
arrival of cable. Saba has only 1,200 friendly inhabitants, a small
enough population that everyone knows everyone and crime is virtually nonexistent, as is unemployment. Beach lovers should also take
note that Saba is an essentially beachless volcanic island: Steep cliffs
ring the island and plummet sharply to the sea.

So, why Saba? The island is a perfect hideaway, a challenge for hikers
(Mt. Scenery rises to a height of 2,855 ft), a haven for seasoned divers,
and, for Sabans, heaven on water. It's no wonder they call their island
the Unspoiled Queen.

The capital of Saba (pronounced *say*-ba) is the Bottom, which sits in
the bottom of a volcanic crater, hence the name. Meandering goats have
the right of way on the Road (there's only one); chickens cross at their
own risk. In tiny, toylike villages, flower-draped walls and neat picket
fences border narrow paths. Tidy houses with red roofs and gingerbread trim are planted on the mountainside among the bromeliads,
palms, hibiscus, orchids, and Norwegian pines. Saba may be one of
the most picturesque islands in the Caribbean; it's certainly the most
immaculate and has a make-believe air to it. Despite such modern additions as television sets (since 1965) and 24-hour electricity (installed
in 1970), the island's uncomplicated lifestyle has persevered. Saban ladies
still hand-embroider delicate Saba lace—a reminder of Saban gentil-
ity that has flourished since the 1870s—and brew a potent rum-based
liquor, Saba Spice, sweetened with secret herbs and spices. Families still
follow the generations-old tradition of burying their dead in their
neatly tended gardens.

Saba is part of the Netherlands Antilles Windward Islands and is 28
mi—a 15-minute flight with a hair-raising landing—from St. Maarten.
The island is a volcano that has been extinct for 5,000 years. Columbus spotted the little speck in 1493, but somehow Saba, except for the
Carib Indians that may have lived here around AD 800, remained uninhabited until the first Dutch settlers arrived from Statia in 1640. In
the 17th, 18th, and early 19th centuries the French, Dutch, English,
and Spanish vied for control of the island, and Saba changed hands
12 times before permanently raising the Dutch flag in 1816.

Sabans are a hardy lot. To get from Fort Bay to the Bottom, the early
Sabans carved 900 steps out of the mountainside. Everything that arrived on the island, from a pin to a piano, had to be hauled up. Those
rugged steps remained the only way to travel until the Road was built
by Josephus Lambert Hassell (a carpenter who took correspondence
courses in engineering) in the 1940s. An extraordinary feat of engineering,
the handmade road took 25 years to build. If you like roller coasters,
you'll love the 9-mi, white-knuckle route, which begins at sea level in
Fort Bay, zigs up to 1,968 ft, and zags down to 131 ft above sea level
at the airport, constructed on the island's only flat point, called (what
else?) Flat Point.

## Lodging

Like everything else on Saba, the hotel–guest houses are tiny and
tucked into tropical gardens. The selection is limited, and because
most restaurants are in the guest houses, you would do well to take

advantage of meal plans. Accommodations are invariably neat and quite reasonably priced. Saba has experienced a (relative) boom in hotel development of late but is still very low-key compared to other islands. Dive packages are available with almost all accommodations, so be sure to ask.

| CATEGORY | COST* |
|---|---|
| $$$ | over $125 |
| $$ | $75–$125 |
| $ | under $75 |

*All prices are for a standard double room in high season, excluding 5% tax and 10%–15% service charge.*

## Hotels

**$$$ ★ 🏨 Captain's Quarters.** A three-bedroom cottage and four other units center around a small pool on grounds graced with hibiscus, poinsettia, and papaya trees. All rooms are spacious and airy with ocean views and are furnished with Victorian antiques (including canopied four-poster beds in most rooms). Two choice bedrooms are in the small main house, built by a Saban sea captain in 1832. The older rooms in the street-side building can be somewhat noisy due to neighbors' TV sets. The long bungalow has four rooms; Nos. 9 and 10 can easily sleep four. Two cliffside rooms beneath the restaurant, bar, and library have stunning views of the sea. ⊠ *Windwardside,* ☎ *599/4–62201; 212/289–6031 in NY;* 𝔽𝔸𝕏 *599/4–62377; 212/289–1931 in NY. 15 rooms. Restaurant, bar, pool. AE, D, MC, V. BP.*

**$$$ ★ 🏨 Willard's of Saba.** This is the most luxurious and expensive place to stay on the island. Set 2,000 ft up the side of a cliff with stunning panoramic vistas of the Caribbean and the neighboring islands of St. Kitts, Nevis, and St. Barts, Willard's has the largest and nicest pool (and it's heated) on the island and is the only hotel with a tennis court. Spacious rooms and bungalows are individually decorated, but all have tile floors, white walls, ceiling fans, Dominican rattan furniture, and a balcony. The three types of room—bungalow, luxury, and VIP—vary in size, furnishings, and whether the bathrooms have a tub or shower. Willard's does not allow children younger than 14 due to its precarious perch. Some may find its location somewhat isolated and inconvenient to town—although the restaurant is quite good—but others will relish the view and privacy. ⊠ *Box 515, Windwardside,* ☎ *599/4–62498 or 800/613–1511,* 𝔽𝔸𝕏 *599/4–62482. 7 rooms. Restaurant, bar, pool, hot tub, tennis court. AE, D, MC, V. EP, MAP.*

**$$ 🏨 Cottage Club.** Local brothers Dean and Mark Johnson run this property. Ten gingerbread bungalows, nestled amid rainbow-hued tropical gardens, have balconies overlooking either the water or the village of English Quarter. You can even catch a glimpse of the airstrip below. Interiors are large and breezy, with gleaming tile floors and high beamed ceilings. Pastel shell prints are used for drapes and spreads, and local art decorates the walls. Each bungalow has its own fully equipped kitchen, dining area, bath (shower only), balcony, telephone, and cable TV. The stone, colonial-style main house holds the reception area and is a showplace for antiques from the owners' collection, accented with potted plants and Saba-lace curtains. Bungalows 1, 2, and 6 have the best views. A swimming pool was completed in 1997, and a conference room and small gym were under construction. If you give the owners a shopping list, they'll stock your kitchen for you. ⊠ *Windwardside,* ☎ *599/4–62486 or 599/4–62386,* 𝔽𝔸𝕏 *599/4–62476. 10 units. Pool, cable TV. MC, V. EP.*

**$$ 🏨 Gate House.** The secluded location of this six-room inn, between the airport and Windwardside in the tiny village of Lower Hell's Gate, makes this somewhat of a getaway, even for Saba. Spacious rooms have

Saba

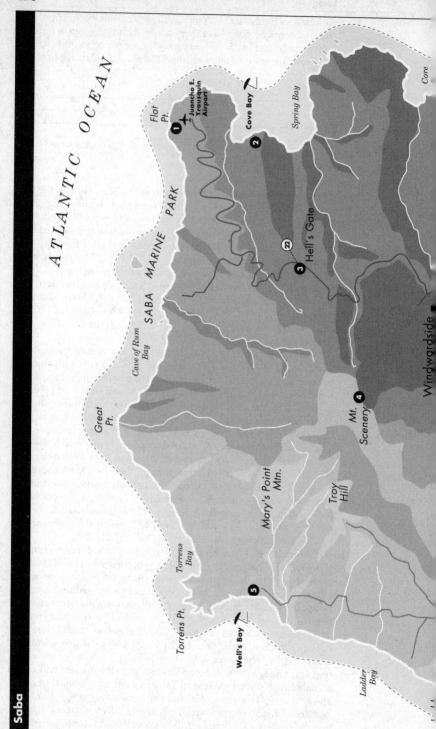

ATLANTIC OCEAN

Flat Pt.

Joancho E. Yrausquin Airport

Cove Bay

Spring Bay

Core

Hell's Gate

Windwardside

SABA MARINE PARK

Cave of Rum Bay

Great Pt.

Mt. Scenery

Mary's Point Mtn.

Troy Hill

Torrens Bay

Torrens Pt.

Well's Bay

Ladder Bay

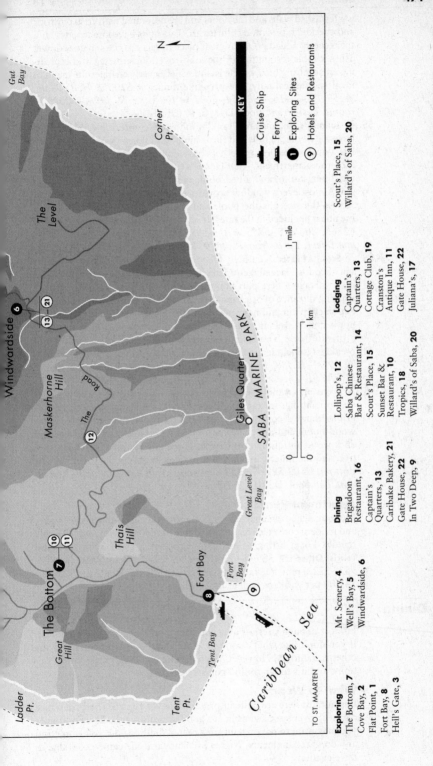

The Bottom

Windwardside  6

The Level

Maskerhorne Hill

13  21

The Road

12

Giles Quarter

SABA MARINE PARK

Great Level Bay

Great Hill

10
11
7

Thais Hill

Fort Bay

Tent Bay

8

9

Ladder Pt.

Tent Pt.

Caribbean Sea

TO ST. MAARTEN

Gut Bay

Corner Pt.

KEY

- Cruise Ship
- Ferry
1 Exploring Sites
9 Hotels and Restaurants

N

1 mile
1 km
0
0

**Exploring**
The Bottom, 7
Cove Bay, 2
Flat Point, 1
Fort Bay, 8
Hell's Gate, 3
Mt. Scenery, 4
Well's Bay, 5
Windwardside, 6

**Dining**
Brigadoon Restaurant, 16
Captain's Quarters, 13
Caribake Bakery, 21
Gate House, 22
In Two Deep, 9
Lollipop's, 12
Saba Chinese Bar & Restaurant, 14
Scout's Place, 15
Sunset Bar & Restaurant, 10
Tropics, 18
Willard's of Saba, 20

**Lodging**
Captain's Quarters, 13
Cottage Club, 19
Cranston's Antique Inn, 11
Gate House, 22
Juliana's, 17
Scout's Place, 15
Willard's of Saba, 20

whitewashed walls and tile floors and are decorated with crisp pinstripe and checked fabrics and colorful art. Two units have kitchenettes, and the recently added pool is a great place to relax as the sun goes down. The six-table restaurant off the lobby overlooks the sea and is creating an admiring buzz on the island. Chef Beverly changes the menu of local specialties daily; the prix-fixe dinner is $20. ⊠ *Hell's Gate,* ☎ *599/4–62416; 708/354–9641 in the U.S.; FAX 599/4–62529. 6 rooms. Restaurant, pool. D, MC, V. CP, MAP.*

**$$**   🏠 **Juliana's.** Juliana and Franklin Johnson's comfortable, tidy studios
**★**  have tile floors, light wood furnishings, and floral-print spreads. One has a queen-size bed; the others have doubles and twins. There's also a 2½-room apartment (Aunt Flossie's Cottage) with a kitchenette, a living-dining room, and a bedroom, as well as a large porch facing the sea. Almost every window provides fabulous views of the Caribbean. Across the street is the pool, and the café, Tropics, where the full breakfast (included in the rates) is served. ⊠ *Windwardside,* ☎ *599/4–62269; 800/328–5285 in the U.S.; FAX 599/4–62389. 9 studios, 1 apartment, 1 2-bedroom cottage. Restaurant, pool. MC, V. BP.*

**$–$$**   🏠 **Scout's Place.** Accurately billed as "Bed 'n Board, Cheap 'n Cheerful," Scout's Place makes up in convenience and value what it lacks in luxury. Staying here puts you in the center of Windwardside, within walking distance of Sea Saba dive center. The four original rooms are extremely plain and have no hot water. Eleven newer rooms do have hot water, as well as four-poster beds and balconies. All rooms have a private bath. The restaurant serves three meals daily, and a full breakfast is included in the rates. ⊠ *Windwardside,* ☎ *599/4–62205, FAX 599/4–62388. 15 rooms. Restaurant, bar, pool, shop, car rental. MC, V. BP.*

**$**   🏠 **Cranston's Antique Inn.** The six rooms of this slightly run-down spot are popular digs for the diving set. The shared baths are far from luxurious (dingy decor à la early '70s), but the rooms have attractive hardwood floors and are neatly decorated with pink or blue fabrics and dark wood antiques; most have four-poster beds. The pool bar is festive, and the Inner Circle disco is practically across the street. ⊠ *The Bottom,* ☎ FAX *599/4–63203. 6 rooms, 1 with private bath. Restaurant, bar, pool. D, MC, V. EP.*

### Apartment Rentals

More than a dozen apartments, cottages, and villas, all with hot water and modern conveniences, are available for daily, weekly, and monthly rentals. For a listing of all rental properties, check with the **Saba Tourist Office** (☎ 599/4–62231 or 800/722–2394). **WIMCO** (☎ 800/ 932–3222) rents the fabulous and palatial Haiku House for $2,000– $4,500 per week, as well as other villas.

## Dining

In most of Saba's restaurants you pretty much have to take potluck. If you don't like what's cooking in one place, you can check out the other restaurants. However, it won't take you long to run out of options, and it's tough to find gourmet cooking.

### What to Wear

Restaurants here are quite informal wherever you go. Shorts or a nice cover-up over your swimsuit is a good idea during the day. For dinner you may want to put on pants or a casual sundress, but you won't find any dress requirements. Nights in Windwardside can be cool due to the elevation.

| CATEGORY | COST* |
|---|---|
| $$$ | over $25 |
| $$ | $15–$25 |
| $ | under $15 |

*per person for a three-course meal, excluding drinks and service*

**$$$** ✕ **Willard's of Saba.** Stunningly set on a cliff high above Windwardside, Saba's most expensive restaurant has views of the sea a dizzying 2,000 ft below. The fusion menu of international and Asian cuisine includes such specialties as chicken adobo, Shanghai rolls, and fresh lobster. A unique touch is the restaurant's hot-lava stone grill, where you grill your seafood or meat as you like it and add the chef's sauces. Order one of the Bava wines from Italy; Willard's is the only restaurant in the Caribbean that offers them. Access to the restaurant is up a steep drive, and only a few taxis will make the climb. Be sure to call the restaurant to arrange transport. ⊠ *Windwardside,* ☎ *599/4–62498. AE, MC, V.*

**$$–$$$** ✕ **Captain's Quarters.** At this newly renovated restaurant you can dine in comfort on a breezy terrace surrounded by flowers and mango trees. The chef artfully blends French and Creole cuisines. The fish (whatever's fresh that day) is prepared with a variety of sauces, including lime butter. On Saturday night the owner takes over the grill and barbecues steaks, chicken, and fish. Service is pleasant but can be slow. ⊠ *Windwardside,* ☎ *599/4–62201. Reservations essential. AE, D, MC, V.*

**$$** ✕ **Tropics.** A black-and-white-checked tile floor, crisp black-and-white napery, and gleaming silver flatware create a chic, if not exactly tropical, atmosphere in this poolside restaurant at Juliana's cottages (☞ Lodging, *above*). The entrées, a mix of Continental and West Indian dishes, can be on the bland side; stick with steak and simply prepared fresh seafood. Try the croquette appetizer: a spicy blend of meat lightly breaded and deep-fried. Tropics serves lunch weekdays and Saturday, and dinner Tuesday through Friday.⊠ *Windwardside,* ☎ *599/4–62469. MC, V. Closed Sun.*

**$–$$** ✕ **Brigadoon Restaurant.** A local favorite, this open-front restaurant
★ on the first floor of a colonial building allows you to take in the passing action on the street—which doesn't mean a whole lot on Saba. Fresh fish grilled and served with a light Creole sauce is the specialty, but there are also chicken and steak dishes, lobster, and flavorful creations such as shrimp encrusted with salt and pepper. Monday night is Mexican night. ⊠ *Windwardside,* ☎ *599/4–62380. AE, D, MC, V. No lunch.*

**$–$$** ✕ **Gate House.** Slightly out of the way, on the road to the airport, this restaurant features Caribbean cuisine. The menu changes daily, making use of the freshest seafood, poultry, and meats, as well as local produce and herbs. ⊠ *Hell's Gate,* ☎ *599/4–62416. MC, V. Closed Wed. No lunch.*

**$–$$** ✕ **Lollipop's.** Owner Carmen Caines was nicknamed Lollipop in honor
★ of her sweet disposition. Lollipop, along with husband Will, prepares land crab, goat, and fresh grilled fish. Meals are served on the tranquil outdoor terrace, with its stonework and charming aqua-and-white trellis. If you make a reservation, Carmen will pick you up and drop you off at your hotel after dinner. ⊠ *St. John's,* ☎ *599/4–63330. MC, V.*

**$–$$** ✕ **Scout's Place.** Chef and manager Diana Medero cooks up braised steak with mushrooms, curried goat, and chicken cordon bleu. You can also opt for a simple sandwich—the crab is best. Tables covered with flowered plastic cloths are arranged on a porch with stunning views of the water. Wednesday breakfast serves as the unofficial town meeting for expatriate locals. ⊠ *Windwardside,* ☎ *599/4–62205. Reservations essential. MC, V.*

**$** ✕ **Caribake Bakery.** This small bakery behind the tourist office serves coffee, cookies, cold drinks, pastries, sandwiches, and the island's freshest bread. There is a small sitting area for those who want to take a load off their feet. It's open from 7 to 7. ⊠ *Windwardside*, ☎ *599/4–62539. No credit cards. Closed Sun.*

$ ✕ **In Two Deep.** The owners of Saba Deep run this delightful harborside spot, with its stained-glass window and mahogany bar. The soups, sandwiches (especially the Reuben), and smoothies (try the lemon pucker) are excellent, and the customers are usually high-spirited—most have just come from a dive. It's open daily 8 AM–4 PM. ⊠ *Fort Bay*, ☎ *599/4–63438. MC, V.*

$ ✕ **Saba Chinese Bar & Restaurant.** In this plain little house with plastic tablecloths you can get, among other things, sweet-and-sour pork or chicken, cashew chicken, and curried dishes. ⊠ *Windwardside*, ☎ *599/4–62268. No credit cards. Closed Mon.*

$ ✕ **Sunset Bar & Restaurant.** Artificial flowers and colorful place mats enliven this humble, homey place. Authentic Creole food—heavenly johnnycakes, bread tart pudding, and lip-smacking ribs—is served. ⊠ *The Bottom*, ☎ *599/4–63332. No credit cards.*

## Outdoor Activities and Sports

### Deep-Sea Fishing

Saba is not a big fishing destination, but a few Sabans will take you out on their boats. Keep in mind that these are not big, fancy vessels. If you want to arrange a fishing trip, contact the tourist office or Saba Deep (☞ *below*), or ask your hotel to arrange it for you.

### Hiking

You can't avoid some hiking, even if you just go to mail a postcard. The big deal, of course, is Mt. Scenery, with 1,064 steps leading up to the top.

Many of the trails, including the Mt. Scenery trail, have interpretive signboards that describe the flora you'll encounter. For information about Saba's 18 recommended botanical hiking trails, check with the tourist office or the **Saba Conservation Foundation** (☎ 599/4–63348), which maintains the trails. The foundation operates the small **Trail Shop** behind the tourist office, which carries gifts and information on the trails. Botanical tours are available upon request. A guided, strenuous full-day hike through the undeveloped back side of Mt. Scenery costs about $50.

### Scuba Diving and Snorkeling

**Saba Deep** (☎ 599/4–63347, FAX 599/4–63397) and **Sea Saba** (☎ 599/4–62246, FAX 599/4–62362) will take you to explore Saba's 26 dive sites. Both offer rental equipment, SSI- (Scuba Schools International) and PADI-certified instructors, and dive packages that include accommodations anywhere on the island. For information on dive packages, call the dive shops directly, or contact **Dive Saba Travel** (☎ 713/789–1396 or 800/883-7222, FAX 713/461–6044) or **Go-Diving** (☎ 612/931–9101 or 800/328–5285, FAX 612/931–0209).

## Shopping

### Gift Ideas

The island's most popular purchases are Saba lace and Saba Spice. The history of Saba lace (also called Spanish lace) goes back more than a century to Saban Gertrude Johnson, who attended a Caracas convent school where she learned the art of drawing and tying threads to adorn fine linens. When she returned home in the 1870s, she taught lace making to other Saban ladies, and the art has endured ever since. Every weekday Saban ladies display and sell their creations at the community center in Hell's Gate. Many also sell their wares from their houses; just follow the signs. Collars, tea towels, napkins, and other small items are relatively inexpensive, but larger items, such as tablecloths, can be pricey. You should also know that the fabric requires some care—it is not drip-dry. Although Saba Spice may *sound* as delicate as Saba lace and the aroma is as sweet as can be, the base for the liqueur is 151-proof rum, and all the rest is window dressing.

## Shops

Saba's famed souvenirs can be found in almost every shop. Most of the shops (with the exception of Around the Bend) are closed Sunday. While you're wandering around Windwardside (the streets here have no names), stop in at **Saba Tropical Arts** (☎ 599/4–62373), which sells silk-screened T-shirts and souvenirs. The **Square Nickel** (☎ 599/4–62477) is Saba's five-and-dime. The **Breadfruit Gallery** (☎ 599/4–62509) is an art gallery featuring local artists' work. **Around the Bend** (☎ 599/4–62519), next to Scout's Place (☞ Dining, *above*), carries island souvenirs and clothing, and "Gifts, Oddments, and Pretties." The **Little Shop** (☎ 599/4–62519) features bags and handmade items by Frieda. **Jobean Designs** (☎ 599/4–62490) features intricate handmade glass-bead jewelry as well as sterling silver and gold pieces by artist and owner Jo Bean. **Sea Saba** (☎ 599/4–62246) carries T-shirts, diving equipment, and beach paraphernalia.

In the Bottom, the **Saba Artisan Foundation** (☎ 599/4–63260) turns out hand-screened fabrics that you can buy by the yard or already made into resort clothing for men, women, and children. It also sells printed T-shirts, spices, and clothing. Look also for the superlative *Saba Cottages: A Book of Watercolors,* sold at the tourist office and several stores.

# Nightlife

Guido's Pizzeria is transformed into the **Mountain High Club disco** (✉ Windwardside, ☎ 599/4–62330)—there's even a mirrored disco ball suspended from the ceiling—on Friday and Saturday nights, and you can dance till 2 AM. Do the nightclub scene at the **Inner Circle** (✉ The Bottom, ☎ 599/4–62240), or just hang out at **Scout's Place** or the **Captain's Quarters** (☞ Dining, *above*). Consult the bulletin board in each village for a listing of the week's events.

# Exploring Saba

Saba is a steep mountain set in the middle of the cobalt-blue Caribbean. Getting around the island means negotiating the narrow, twisting roadway that clings to the mountainside and rises from sea level to almost 2,000 ft. Although driving is not difficult, just be sure to go slowly and cautiously. If in doubt, leave the driving to an experienced taxi driver so you can enjoy the stunning views and verdant scenery that graces this tiny island.

*Numbers in the margin correspond to points of interest on the Saba map.*

SIGHTS TO SEE

❼ **The Bottom.** Sitting in a bowl-shape valley 820 ft above the sea, this town is the seat of government and the home of the lieutenant governor. The gubernatorial mansion, next to Wilhelmina Park, has fancy fretwork, a high-pitched roof, and wraparound double galleries. In 1993 Saba University opened a medical school in the Bottom, at which about 70 students are enrolled.

On the other side of town is the **Wesleyan Holiness Church,** a small stone building with white fretwork, dating from 1919. Stroll by the church, beyond a place called the Gap, to a lookout point where you can see the 400 rough-hewn steps leading down to **Ladder Bay.** Ladder Bay and Fort Bay were the two landing sites from which Saba's first settlers had to haul themselves and their possessions. Sabans sometimes walk down to Ladder Bay to picnic. Think long and hard before you do: It's 400 steps back *up* to the Road.

➋ **Cove Bay.** On the northeastern side of the island, a 20-ft-long strip of rocks and pebbles laced with gray sand is now the only place for sunning (and moonlit dips after a Saturday night out). There's a picnic area there, and a small tidal pool encircled by rocks for children to swim in.

➊ **Flat Point.** It is the only place on the island where planes can land. The runway here is among the world's smallest, measuring only 1,200 ft. Only STOL (Short Takeoff and Landing) prop planes dare land here, as each end of the runway drops off more than 100 ft into the crashing surf below.

➑ **Fort Bay.** The end of the Road is also the jumping-off place for all of the island's dive operations and the location of the St. Maarten ferry dock. The island's only gas station is here, a 277-ft deep-water pier that accommodates the tenders from ships. On the quay is a recompression chamber, one of the few in the Caribbean, and Saba Deep's dive shop; its snack bar, In Two Deep, is a good place to catch your breath while enjoying some refreshments and the view of the water.

➌ **Hell's Gate.** The island's main road makes 20 hairpin turns up over 1,000 vertical ft to Hell's Gate. **Holy Rosary Church,** poised on Hell's Gate's hill, is a stone church that looks medieval but was built in 1962. In the **community center** behind the church, village ladies sell blouses, handkerchiefs, tablecloths, and tea towels embellished with the delicate and unique Saba lace. The same ladies make innocent-sounding Saba Spice, each according to her old family recipe. The rum-based liqueur will knock your socks off. The truly intrepid can venture to Lower Hell's Gate, where the **Old Sulphur Mine Walk** leads to bat caves (with typical sulfuric stench) that can—with caution—be explored.

➍ **Mt. Scenery.** Stone and concrete steps—1,064 of them—rise to the top of Mt. Scenery. The steps lead past giant elephant ears, ferns, begonias, mangoes, palms, and orchids up to a mahogany grove at the summit: six identifiable ecosystems in all. Helpful signs have been posted naming the trees, plants, and shrubs, and the tourist office can provide a field guide describing what you'll see along the way. On a cloudless day the view is spectacular. Have your hotel pack a picnic lunch, wear nonslip shoes, take along a jacket and a canteen of water, and hike away. The round-trip excursion will take about three hours and is best begun in the early morning.

**Saba Bank.** This fertile fishing ground 3 mi southwest of Saba is an excellent diving spot because of its coral gardens and undersea mountains. As other islands become "dived out," Saba is dedicated to preserving its marine life, which attracts more than 3,000 divers each year.

**Saba Marine Park.** Established in 1987 to preserve and manage the island's marine resources, the park circles the entire island, dipping down to 200 ft, and is zoned for diving, swimming, fishing, boating, and anchorage. One of the unique features of Saba's diving is the submerged pinnacles of land (islands that never made it) at about the 70-ft depth mark. Here all forms of sea creatures rendezvous. The information center offers talks and slide shows for divers and snorkelers and provides brochures and literature on marine life. (Divers are requested to contribute $2 a dive to help maintain the park facilities.) Before you go, call first to see if anyone is around. ✉ *Harbor Office, Box 18, Fort Bay,* ☎ *599/4–63295,* FAX *599/4–63435.* ⏰ *Weekdays 8–5.*

**⑤ Well's Bay.** Saba's famous, disappearing black-sand beach, on the northwestern coast, is usually around for a few months in the summer. (The sand is washed in and out by rough winter surf.)

**⑥ Windwardside.** The island's second-largest village, perched at an altitude of 1,968 ft, commands magnificent views of the Caribbean. Here, among the oleander bushes, you'll find rambling lanes and narrow alleyways winding through the hills and a cluster of tiny, neat houses and shops.

At the northern end of the village is the **Church of St. Paul's Conversion,** a colonial building with a red-and-white steeple. Just down the road is the **Saba Tourist Office,** where you can pick up brochures and books about Saba. You may want to spend some time browsing through the shops in town.

The **Saba Museum,** surrounded by lemongrass and clover, lies just behind the Captain's Quarters. There are small signs marking the way to the 150-year-old house, which has been set up to look much as it did when it was a sea captain's home. Period pieces on display include a handsome mahogany four-poster bed with pineapple design, an antique organ, and, in the kitchen, a rock oven. You can also look at old documents, such as a letter a Saban wrote after the hurricane of 1772, in which he sadly says, "We have lost our little all." The first Sunday of each month, the museum holds croquet matches on its grounds; all-white attire is requested at this formal but fun social event. ✉ *Windwardside, no phone.* 🎟 *$1 donation requested.* ⏰ *Weekdays 10–4.*

| | |
|---|---|
| NEED A BREAK? | **Tropics Café** (☎ 599/4–62469) is the place to rest your feet after walking up and down the steep hills of Windwardside. This small, poolside café serves up good burgers and sandwiches, to be enjoyed while taking in the sweeping view of the azure Caribbean, 1,500 ft below. |

# Saba A to Z

## Arriving and Departing

### BY BOAT

*The Edge,* a high-speed ferry, leaves St. Maarten's Pelican Marina in Simpson Bay on Wednesday, Friday, and Sunday at 9 AM and returns by 5 PM. The trip to Saba's Fort Bay takes an hour, and the round-trip fare is $60 (☎ 599/5–42640 in St. Maarten). *The Voyager* (☎ 599/5–24096 in St. Maarten) also makes regularly scheduled trips on Thursday and Saturday from St. Maarten to Saba. If you take the watery way, however, you'll have lost more than an hour of sightseeing time on Saba.

### BY PLANE

Unless you parachute in, you'll arrive from St. Maarten via **Windward Islands Airways** (Winair) (☎ 599/5–54210 or 800/634–4907). The approach to Saba's tiny airstrip is the stuff of which nightmares are made. The strip is only a quarter mile long, but the STOL aircraft are built for it, and the pilot needs only half of it. Try not to panic; remember that the pilot knows what he is doing and wants to live just as much as you do. (If you're nervous, don't sit on the right. The wing just misses grazing the cliffside on the approach.) Once you've touched down on the airstrip, the pilot taxis an inch or two, turns, and deposits you just outside a little shoe box called the Juancho E. Yrausquin Airport.

Taxis meet planes and take you to your destination. They charge a set rate for up to four people per taxi, with additional cost for each person more than four. The fare from the airport to Hell's Gate is $6, to Windwardside is $8, to the Bottom is $12.50. A taxi from Windwardside to the Bottom is $6.50.

## Currency

U.S. dollars are accepted everywhere, but Saba's official currency is the Netherlands Antilles florin (NAf; also called the guilder). The exchange rate fluctuates slightly but was around NAf1.80 to US$1 at press time. Prices quoted here are in U.S. dollars unless noted otherwise. **Barclays Bank** and **Commercial Bank** in Windwardside are the only banks on the island. Barclays is open weekdays 8:30–2; Commercial, 8:30–4.

## Emergencies

**Police:** ☎ 599/4–63237 in the Bottom, 599/4–62221 in Windwardside. **Hospital:** The **A. M. Edwards Medical Center** (⊠ The Bottom, ☎ 599/4–63288) is a 10-bed hospital with a full-time physician. **Pharmacy:** The **Pharmacy** (⊠ The Bottom, ☎ 599/4–63289).

## Getting Around

CAR RENTALS

Saba's one and only road—the Road—is serpentine, with many a hairpin (read hair-raising) curve. However, if you dare to drive, cars can be rented at **Scout's Place** (⊠ Windwardside, ☎ 599/4–62205) and at **Johnson's Rent A Car** (⊠ Juliana's, Windwardside, ☎ 599/4–62469). A car rents for about $40 per day, with a full tank of gas and unlimited mileage. (If you run out of gas, call the island's only gas station, down at Fort Bay, ☎ 599/4–63272. It closes at noon.)

HITCHHIKING

Carless Sabans get around the old-fashioned ways—walking and hitchhiking (very popular and safe). If you choose to get around by thumbing rides, you'll need to know the rules of the Road. To get a ride from the Bottom (which actually is near the top of the island), sit on the wall opposite the Anglican church; to catch a ride in Fort Bay, sit on the wall opposite Saba Deep dive center, where the road begins to twist upward.

## Guided Tours

BY BOAT

**Saba Deep** (☎ 599/4–63347, FAX 599/4–63397) occasionally conducts one-hour, round-island cruises that include cocktails, hors d'oeuvres, and a marvelous view of the sunset.

BY CAR

All 12 of the taxi drivers who meet the planes at Yrausquin Airport also conduct tours of the island. The cost for a full-day tour is $40 for one to four passengers and $10 per person for groups larger than four. If you're just in from St. Maarten for a day trip, have your driver make lunch reservations for you at **Scout's Place** or the **Captain's Quarters** before starting the tour. After a full morning of sightseeing, your driver will drop you off for lunch, complete the tour afterward, and return you to Yrausquin in time to make the last flight back to St. Maarten. Guides are available for hiking; arrangements may be made through the tourist office.

## Language

Saba's official language is Dutch, but everyone on the island speaks English.

## Opening and Closing Times

Businesses and government offices on Saba are open weekdays 8 AM to 5 PM. Most shops are closed Sunday.

## Passports and Visas

U.S. citizens need proof of citizenship. A passport is preferred, but a birth certificate or voter registration card will do (a driver's license will *not*). British citizens must have a British passport. All visitors must have an ongoing or return ticket.

## Precautions

Take along insect repellent, sunscreen, and sturdy, no-nonsense shoes that get a good grip on the ground.

## Taxes and Service Charges

Hotels collect a 5% government tax. Most hotels and restaurants add a 10%–15% service charge to your bill. You must pay a $2 departure tax when leaving Saba for either St. Maarten or St. Eustatius, or $10 when continuing on an international flight.

## Telephones and Mail

To call Saba from the United States, dial 011/599/4 followed by the five-digit number, which always begins with a 6. On the island, it is only necessary to dial the five-digit number. Telephone communications are excellent on the island, and you can dial direct long distance. Public phone booths are located in the Bottom and Windwardside.

Airmailing a letter to the United States costs NAf2.25; a postcard, NAf1.10.

## Visitor Information

For help planning your trip, contact, in the United States, the **Saba Tourist Office** (✉ Box 6322, Boca Raton, FL 33427, ☎ 561/394–8580 or 800/722–2394, FAX 561/488–4294). **Unique Destinations** (✉ 307 Peaceable St., Ridgefield, CT 06877, ☎ 203/431–1571) organizes diving and hiking tours.

On Saba, the amiable Glenn Holm and Wilma Hassell are at the helm of the **Saba Tourist Office** (✉ Box 527, Windwardside, ☎ 599/4–62231, FAX 599/4–62350). It's open weekdays 8–noon and 1–5, Sunday 10–2. The tourist office can help you make guest-house reservations.

Book reservations through a travel agent or over the telephone; mail can take a week or two to reach the island.

# 19 St. Barthélemy

*St. Barts is St. Tropez in the Caribbean—from chic boutiques and gourmet eateries to casual waterfront bars and yachts bobbing in the harbor—only with better beaches and even more beautiful bronzed bodies.*

Updated by
Jordan Simon

**S**T. BARTHÉLEMY'S MAGIC lies in the way this tiny tropical isle blends the essence of the Caribbean with the
essence of France. You can spend the day on a deserted beach lying under a palm tree, then choose from more than 50
excellent restaurants for an elegant evening meal. When you tire of the
sun, you can easily drive all over the island, taking in the vistas and
the soft breezes, and then stop off for an exquisitely prepared gourmet
lunch. Or you can head to one of the three shopping areas for duty-
free French perfumes and the latest in French fashion.

The island itself is a mere 8 square mi, with lots of hills and sheltered
inlets. Gustavia, the only sizable town, wraps itself neatly around a lil-
liputian harbor. Red-roof bungalows dot the hillsides. And beaches that
run the gamut from calm to "surfable," shell to fine white sand, and
crowded to deserted encircle the island. The French cuisine here is tops
in the Caribbean, and gourmet lunches and dinners are rallying points
of island life. A French *savoir vivre* pervades, and the island is definitely for the style conscious—casual but always chic.

Rothschild owns property and Rockefeller built an estate here, and for
a long time the island, 15 mi from St. Martin in the French West Indies, was the haunt of the well heeled and well informed. Although
the island still has cachet for the cash-flow set, the tourist base has expanded in the last decade. Last year, almost 200,000 visitors stopped
by, including day-trippers from nearby islands and passengers from cruise
ships that anchor just outside the harbor.

Longtime visitors speak wistfully of the old, quiet St. Barts. Although
development has quickened the pace, the island has not been overrun
with prefab condos or glitzy resorts, although vacation villas under construction are sprouting up everywhere. The largest hotel has fewer than
100 rooms, and the remaining rooms are scattered in about 40 small
hotels around the island; no high-rises are allowed. The tiny airport
accommodates nothing bigger than 19-passenger planes (and only
during daylight hours), and there aren't any flashy late-night attractions. Moreover, St. Barts is not a destination for the budget-minded:
Development has largely been in luxury lodgings and gourmet restaurants.

Christopher Columbus "discovered" the island in 1493 and named it
after his brother, Bartholomeo. A small group of French colonists arrived from nearby St. Kitts in 1656 but were wiped out by the fierce
Carib Indians who dominated the area. A new group from Normandy
and Brittany arrived in 1694. This time the settlers prospered—with
the help of French buccaneers, who took advantage of the island's strategic location and protected harbor. In 1784 the French traded the island to King Gustav III of Sweden in exchange for port rights in
Göteborg. He dubbed the capital Gustavia, laid out and paved streets,
built three forts, and turned the capital into a prosperous free port.
The island thrived as a major shipping and commercial center until the
19th century, when earthquakes, fire, and hurricanes brought financial ruin. Many residents fled for newer lands of opportunity, and in
1878 France agreed to repurchase its beleaguered former colony.

Today the island is still a free port and, as a dependency of Guadeloupe,
is part of an overseas department of France. Dry, sunny, and rocky, St.
Barts was never one of the Caribbean's "sugar islands" and thus never
developed an industrial slave base. Most natives are descendants of those
tough Norman and Breton settlers of three centuries ago. They are feisty,
industrious, and friendly, but insular. However, you will find many new,

# St. Barthélemy

*Ile Chevreau*

Pte. à
Colombier

TO
ILE FRÉGATE

Anse de
Colombier **1**

*La Petite
Anse*

Anse de
Flamands

**46**
**2**

*Anse à
Galets*

*Anse de
Petit Jean*

○ Colombier

**42** — **45**

Anse de
Cayes
**4** St. Jean

Corossol
**3**

**36** — **41**

Baie de
St. Jean

**47** **48**

**Corossol Beach**

**49**

St. Jean
Airport

**Public Beach**

*Les Islettes
La Baleine*

TO ST. MARTIN

*Caribbean Sea*

*Les Saintes*

Gustavia
**5**

**12** — **20**

**6**

Lurin ○

**Petite Anse
de Galet**

*Mt.*

### KEY

🛳 Ferry

**1** Exploring Sites

**8** Hotels and Restaurants

Anse
du
Gouvern

*Grande Pt.*

**Exploring**
Anse de Colombier, **1**
Anse des Flamands, **2**
Anse du
Gouverneur, **7**
Corossol, **3**
Grand Cul de Sac, **10**
Grande Saline, **8**
Gustavia, **5**

Lorient, **9**
Petite Anse
de Galet, **6**
St. Jean, **4**
Toiny coast, **11**

**Dining**
Adam, **36**
Le Bambou, **27**

Brasserie
La Creole, **37**
Carl Gustaf, **16**
La Crémaillère, **20**
L'Escale, **12**
François
Plantation, **47**
Le Gaiac, **23**
Gloriette, **25**

Ines' Ghetto, **15**
Le Lafayette
Club, **24**
Le Mandala, **21**
Marigot Bay
Club, **30**
La Marine, **19**
Maya's, **49**
New Born, **42**

↑ TO
ILE TOC VERS

ATLANTIC OCEAN

Les Grenadiers

La Tortue

Pte. Milou ③②

③④ ③③  Lorient
Beach

Marigot ③⓪ ②⑨  Marechal
Beach

②④ — ②⑧

Lorient

⑨

③⑤

①⓪  Grand
Marigot  Cul de Sac

③①  Vitet

Petit
Cul de Sac

Mt. du
Grand Fond

Toiny

Toiny
Coast

Morne Vitet ②③  ⑪

②②

⑧

Grande
Saline

Morne de
Grand Fond

Pt. à Toiny

Anse de
Grand Fond

N

urin

Grande
Saline

⑦

Pt. du Gouverneur

0 _____ 1 mile
0 _____ 1 km

L'Orchidée, **32**
Paradiso, **14**
Le Patio, **44**
Le Repaire, **13**
Le Rivage, **28**
Le Sapotillier, **17**
Le Tamarin, **22**
Wall House, **18**

West Indies Café, **31**
**Lodging**
Carl Gustaf, **16**
Club La Banane, **34**
Eden Rock, **38**
El Sereno Beach Hotel
and Villas, **26**
Filao Beach, **39**

François
Plantation, **47**
Guanahani, **29**
Hostellerie des Trois
Forces, **31**
Hotel Christopher, **32**
Hotel Manapany
Cottages, **43**
Hotel Isle de France, **46**

Hotel Yuana, **45**
Les Mouettes, **33**
La Normandie, **35**
Le P'tit Morne, **48**
Le Toiny, **23**
Tropical Hotel, **40**
Village St. Jean, **41**

young French arrivals—predominantly from northwestern France—who also speak English well.

You may hear some old-timers speak the old Norman patois of their ancestors or see the older women dressed in the traditional garb of provincial France. They have prospered with the tourist boom, but some are worried that the upward swing of prices may turn people away, particularly tour groups and families, and threaten business. So far, though, this gem of an island continues to draw an ever-widening circle of fans.

Be aware that timing here is very important. A larger number of hotels and restaurants have seasonal closings than on other islands. There are still some places open in August, but your selections will be more limited; places begin reopening at the end of October. Fortunately, the gorgeous beaches never close. The advantage of traveling in the off-season is enormous savings—sometimes half of the high-season rate.

In the fall of 1995, Hurricane Luis tore through St. Barts, causing major damage to some hotels and restaurants. Some establishments are gone for good, like Castelets and Baie des Flamands; other favorites, like Baie des Anges and the Pelican, are still closed until further notice. Yet others, like the Filao Beach, Taiwana, Eden Rock, Le Tom, Emeraude Plage, and Hotel Isle de France, have been rebuilt or relocated. Almost every business has been newly painted and, in many cases, refurbished, so the upside is that you'll notice a freshness to the island. Many beaches are wider than before, including Flamands and Gouverneur.

## Lodging

Expect to be shocked at the prices of accommodations. You pay for the privilege of staying on the island rather than for the hotel. Even at $500 a night, bedrooms tend to be small, but that does not detract from the lure of St. Barts for those who can afford it. Away from the beaches are a number of small hotels that are surprisingly reasonable, as well as a multitude of rental bungalows that offer less expensive accommodations, or, in the case of more luxurious villas, good value for the money. Those in the know always rent villas, including celebrities, the rich and famous, and those who wish they were.

### Villas

On St. Barthélemy, "villa" is used to describe anything from a small cottage to a truly luxurious house with a cook, a maid, and a pool. You get what you pay for. In-season rates range from $900 to $25,000 a week. For the price of a moderately expensive hotel room, you can get a villa or a small cottage. If you get a group of friends together, you can get a villa with a number of rooms and a private pool for significantly less than it would cost for each person to stay in one of the expensive hotels. How to choose between a villa and a hotel? It may depend on whether you want the full kitchen that comes with a villa or would rather pay the sometimes expensive restaurant tabs to sample the island's exceptional food. Whether you stay in a villa or a hotel, you will almost always want to rent a car, so be sure to figure this as part of your budget, no matter where you stay. *Reserve your villa as far in advance as possible*. Peak periods, like the holiday season, are usually booked solid by the previous summer. Cancellations do occur, so you may luck out, but the best plan is to reserve as soon as you can.

Villas can be rented through **Sibarth** (☎ 590/27–62–38, ℻ 590/27–60–52), where Madame Lecour, the reigning queen of St. Barts's real estate, oversees more than 200 properties. **WIMCO** (☎ 800/932–3222), based in Newport, Rhode Island, is the agency's representative in the United States. Its pleasant reservations agents are very knowledgeable about the properties. Rents range from $1,000 to $2,000 per week for one-bedroom villas, $1,600 to $7,000 for two- and three-bedroom villas. Larger villas rent from $9,000 to $19,000 per week. Another company, **Country Village Rentals–St. Barth's** (☎ 802/253–8777 or 800/320–8777, ℻ 802/253–2144), based in Stowe, Vermont, also rents villas and distinguishes itself with a very friendly staff and a personal touch. Owner Doug Foregger, who represents more than 200 villas on the island, tries to match the customer with the perfect villa. Prices range from $700 to $25,000 per week.

## Hotels

While there are more affordable lodgings found in the hills, most top hotels are concentrated on four northern beaches: Anse de Flamands, Anse des Cayes, Baie de St. Jean, and Grand Cul de Sac. Hotels may have as many as six different rate periods during a year. The highest rates are in effect from mid-December to early January, and hotels are booked far in advance for this holiday period. Rates used for the listings below are for the second highest period, early January through April—still in season, but not the holiday peak. At all other times, rates are usually lower. If you are flexible in your planning, you can save a good deal of money.

| CATEGORY | COST* |
|---|---|
| $$$$ | over $450 |
| $$$ | $325–$450 |
| $$ | $200–$325 |
| $ | under $200 |

*All prices are for a standard double room, excluding 10%–15% service charge; there is no government room tax.*

**$$$$** 🏨 **Carl Gustaf.** Red-tile-roofed buildings spill down the hillside at this
★ very expensive, small luxury resort at the head of Gustavia harbor. Each one- and two-bedroom suite looks out across a deck with a small private plunge pool, to spectacular views of the harbor, the quaint town of Gustavia, and the hilly coastline of the island. Units have spacious, gleaming-white bedrooms and living rooms stylishly highlighted with nautical and tropical prints, plus rough marble floors, high ceilings, tiny but state-of-the-art kitchens, marble baths, and other extras, like a fax machine, two TVs, and two stereos. The glittering nighttime view from the piano-bar lounge and elegant, open-air restaurant (known for its classic French cuisine) is one of the most spectacular on the island. ⊠ *Box 700, rue des Normands, Gustavia 97133,* ☎ *590/27–82–83 or 800/932–3222,* ℻ *590/27–82–37. 14 1- and 2-bedroom suites. Restaurant, air-conditioning, kitchenettes, minibars, refrigerators, in-room VCRs, pool, sauna, health club. AE, DC, MC, V. CP.*

**$$$$** 🏨 **El Sereno Beach Hotel and Villas.** The quiet, casual chic of this small—some would say cramped—resort attracts many repeat guests (although at these prices one may wonder why). The compact, simply furnished rooms, with whitewashed walls and blue beams, have either a sea or garden view and a patio. High walls and plants provide privacy. The beach, with its exceptionally calm waters, is just steps away. There are also nine comfortably furnished one-bedroom, gingerbread-trimmed villas. The West Indies Café has replaced La Tocque Lyonnaise as the hotel's restaurant and is now the locale for the dazzling Parisian-style revue once mounted by the late, lamented Jean-Marie Rivière of Club La Banane. ⊠ *Box 19, Grand Cul de Sac 97133,* ☎ *590/27–64–80,* ℻ *590/27–75–47. 20 rooms, 9 1-bedroom villas. 2 restaurants, bar, air-conditioning, refrigerators, pool, beach, water sports, shop. AE, DC, MC, V. EP.*

**$$$$** 🏨 **Filao Beach.** Its place on one of St. Barts's most popular beaches combined with excellent service win many repeat guests at this casual resort. Rooms are in two-unit bungalows—many completely rebuilt after Hurricane Luis swept them away in 1995—set back from the beach amid gardens. Although simple and smallish, they are brightly decorated with rattan furniture and pastel-print fabrics; all have a patio. Bathrooms are compact but neat. Rooms closer to the beach rise accordingly in price, but the garden rooms are still only steps away from the sand. On the raised wooden deck that surrounds the pool, there's a restaurant, open for breakfast and lunch, with a bartender well known for his killer cocktails. The hotel is a member of the prestigious Relais & Châteaux organization. ⊠ *Box 667, St. Jean 97099,* ☎ *590/ 27–64–84 or 800/742–4276,* ℻ *590/27–62–24. 30 rooms. Restaurant, bar, air-conditioning, refrigerators, pool. AE, MC, V. CP.*

**$$$$** 🏨 **Guanahani.** This elegant 7-acre resort, the island's largest, is set be-
★ tween two beaches, one sheltered and one open to ocean waves. The lobby is a riot of color—deep greens, soothing blues, and rich plaids— and has a terrace where you can relax over a drink. Rooms and one-bedroom suites are in tightly clustered bungalows, expensively decorated with bright tropical fabrics and Georgian-style furniture. Some newer units are done in a stunning contemporary style, with wood floors and dark wood furniture, colorful walls, funky art and sculpture, a sunken seating area, and a partial curved wall between the sleeping and bath areas. Suites have either private pools or Jacuzzis. Units vary tremendously in terms of privacy, views, and distance from activities—there are just six rooms on the beach—so to get exactly what you want, make your preferences known when making your reservation. A poolside restaurant is open for breakfast and lunch. The more formal Bartolomeo is open for dinner and serves classic French cuisine in both an indoor dining room and an outside tropical garden. The impeccable service meets the rigorous standards of the Leading Hotels of the World, of which the Guanahani is a member. ⊠ *Box 609, Grand Cul de Sac 97098,* ☎ *590/27–66–60 or 800/223–6800,* ℻ *590/27–70– 70. 17 double rooms, 39 deluxe rooms, 21 suites. 2 restaurants, 2 pools, beauty salon, hot tubs, 2 tennis courts, windsurfing, water sports. AE, MC, V. CP.*

**$$$$** 🏨 **Hotel Isle de France.** This intimate luxury enclave, on one of the island's prettiest beaches, lost its beachside pool and restaurant to Hurricane Luis (both reopened in late 1996). Everything is in tip-top shape, having been spruced up since the storm. Enormously spacious rooms and suites are either beachfront, in the two-story clubhouse, or across the street in bungalows facing gardens and one of the hotel's two pools. All units are decorated with mahogany furniture (including some magnificent secretaries and free-standing mirrors), authentic 19th-century island prints, and white cotton bedspreads and have a patio or balcony. Some garden bungalows have a kitchenette. The restaurant serves breakfast and lunch, or if you prefer, you can take breakfast in your room. ⊠ *Box 612, Baie des Flamands 97098,* ☎ *590/ 27–61–81,* ℻ *590/27–86–83. 12 rooms, 18 bungalows, 3 beach junior suites. Restaurant, bar, refrigerators, 2 pools, tennis court, exercise room, squash. AE, MC, V. CP.*

**$$$$** 🏨 **Hotel Manapany Cottages.** A ramshackle entry road ends at this luxury enclave of closely spaced units that stretch back from a narrow and not very swimmable beach. Accommodations vary from rather snug St. Barts–style cottages and suites tucked into the hillside to much-in-demand beachfront suites with marble baths and four-poster beds. Bronze bodies ring the pretty but small pool, and outsiders drop in regularly to dine at the hotel's two restaurants. The atmosphere here is sophisticated and cosmopolitan, and there are many repeat guests. Airport transfers are complimentary. ⊠ *Box 114, Anse des Cayes 97133,* ☎ *590/27–66–55 or 800/847–4249,* FAX *590/27–75–28. 32 units. 2 restaurants, 2 bars, pool, hot tub, tennis court, exercise room, water sports, shop. AE, D, DC, MC, V. CP.*

**$$$$** ⊞ **Le Toiny.** Luxury awaits you at this exquisite little hideaway tucked
★ into the hillside at a remote end of the island. Twelve spacious, greenroof villas, each with a private patio and pool (10 by 20 ft), are arranged for maximum privacy. Each is elegantly appointed, with a massive four-poster mahogany bed and armoire, Chinese porcelain vases, Italian fabrics, and fine linens. There's a fax machine, a stereo, and three telephones, and you can request either a stair-stepper or a stationary bike. The bathroom has a walk-in shower as well as a tub. The elegant, alfresco restaurant, Le Gaiac, overlooks the Italian-tiled communal swimming pool and offers sweeping views of the distant ocean. A wonderful beach, Saline, is a 10-minute drive away. ⊠ *Anse de Toiny 97133,* ☎ *590/27–88–88 or 800/932–3222,* FAX *590/27–89–30. 13 villas. Restaurant, bar, air-conditioning, in-room safes, minibars, in-room VCRs, pool, laundry service. AE, DC, MC, V. CP.*

**$$$–$$$$** ⊞ **Club La Banane.** If you're looking for privacy, you may like this intimate hideaway, where guests keep pretty much to themselves. The nine unique units are decorated with plants, antique furniture, and a bit of whimsy. There are four-poster beds, sunken bath areas, all kinds of antiques, Haitian artwork, and unusual pottery. Rooms look out on dense tropical greenery and therefore tend to be dark. There are two small swimming pools (one with a waterfall), and it's a three-minute walk to the beach. The restaurant is open only to hotel guests for breakfast and lunch. Visitors come from around the island for dinner, served alfresco around the lily-filled pool. ⊠ *Quartier Lorient 97133,* ☎ *590/ 27–68–25,* FAX *590/27–68–44. 9 rooms. Restaurant, bar, 2 pools. AE, MC, V. CP.*

**$$$–$$$$** ⊞ **Eden Rock.** Set on a craggy bluff that abruptly splits St. Jean Beach
★ is St. Barts's first hotel, opened in the '50s by Rémy de Haenen and completely restored by the owners from Britain, Jane and David Matthews. It's a fabulous, fun, slightly funky choice. The six original rooms cling to the rock (the other four are on the beach); painted in bold colors, all have four-poster beds, tropical-print fabrics, mosquito netting, sparkling silver fixtures, terra-cotta floors, whimsical old-fashioned touches like steamer trunks, and a stunning view of St. Jean Bay. Marvelous watercolors and gouaches of local scenes rendered by Jane and the couple's two children adorn nearly every room, giving them a homey touch. You can breakfast in the restaurant or in your room. The spectacular open-air bar and French-Creole gourmet restaurant, which stretch along the top of the rock, are great places to enjoy the sea breeze and watch the frigate birds dive-bomb for fish. Construction was ongoing at press time to add some beachfront units and a beachfront bar-restaurant, which David hopes to use as a caviar and cigar bar. Jane anticipates importing more of their family heirlooms and antiques from their Surrey estate to fill the new rooms. ⊠ *St. Jean 97133,* ☎ *590/27–72–94,* FAX *590/27–88–37. 10 rooms. Restaurant, bar, minibars, windsurfing, water sports. AE, MC, V. CP.*

**$$$–$$$$** ⊞ **Hotel Christopher.** All in all, the Christopher, with its oversize rooms
★ and gracious attentive staff, represents one of the island's best buys. Sofitel Resorts manages this full-service hotel. Four two-story colonial-style buildings overlooking the water (but not on the beach) hold beautifully furnished rooms with panoramic views of St. Martin and nearby islets. Each room has a private terrace or balcony with sitting area, colonial reproduction furnishings, delightful island artwork and clever fabrics that depict local scenes, and contemporary marble bath. Some bathrooms have little gardens: If the sight of a small lizard in

here will ruin your vacation, ask for a bath sans greenhouse. There is a giant (4,500-square-ft) swimming pool—by far the largest on the island—with islands and footbridges. L'Orchidée serves French and Creole cuisine. In season, there is a complimentary shuttle to St. Jean Beach twice daily except Sunday. Many packages are available. ⊠ *Pointe Milou 97133,* ☎ *590/27–63–63 or 800/221–4542,* 𝕱𝕬𝕏 *590/27–92–92. 40 suites. 2 restaurants, air-conditioning, room service, pool, exercise room. AE, DC, MC, V. EP, CP, MAP, FAP.*

**$$–$$$$**   🏨 **François Plantation.** A colonial-era graciousness pervades this elegant hillside complex of West Indian–style cottages. It's owned and managed by longtime island habitués Françoise and François Beret. Monsieur Beret is a passionate gardener, and the grounds are an intensely colorful display of tropical flowers and greenery. The smallish rooms (four with garden view, eight with sea view) are dominated by the antique mahogany queen-size four-poster beds and decorated with brightly colored fabrics. Two units are larger and can accommodate an extra bed. The pool is at the top of a very steep hill, with magnificent views of the beach below, the hills of St. Barts, and nearby islets. You'll need a car to get to the beach and to go out for lunch (the restaurant is open only for breakfast and dinner); some packages include a rental car. ⊠ *Colombier 97133,* ☎ *590/27–78–82, 800/932–3222 in the U.S.;* 𝕱𝕬𝕏 *590/27–61–26. 12 rooms. Restaurant, air-conditioning, refrigerators, pool. AE, MC, V. CP.*

**$$–$$$**   🏨 **Hotel Yuana.** Green-roof, West Indian–style cottages are strung along a flowery hillside at this small complex overlooking Anse des Cayes. Appealing rooms have white tile floors, colorful tile baths, blue or peach painted wicker furniture, floral-print fabrics, a kitchenette, and a wide terrace overlooking the ocean. Each unit has both a ceiling fan and air-conditioning. A 30-ft boat is available to rent. Airport transfers are included, package rates are available, and children under 12 stay free. ⊠ *Anse des Cayes 97133,* ☎ *590/27–80–84 or 800/645–6030,* 𝕱𝕬𝕏 *590/27–78–45. 12 rooms. Bar, breakfast room, air-conditioning, kitchenettes, in-room VCRs, pool. AE, MC, V. EP.*

**$–$$**   🏨 **Tropical Hotel.** This complex is straight up the hill from St. Jean Beach. Rooms are in a motel-like, one-story, L-shape building and open onto patios and views of either the ocean (the lower numbers are best) or thick tropical foliage. They are simple but well maintained. White walls, linens, and furnishings are mostly pristine white as well, giving it a light, airy feel. Beamed ceilings, and beds swaddled in mosquito netting add to the airy atmosphere. The main building houses reception, a TV/game room, and an open-air bar and lounge, where the charming owner offers a sensational three-salad lunch special for only 70F. The Tropical is a classic example of what the French affectionately call a hotel bourgeois: simple, stylish, and good value. ⊠ *Box 147, St. Jean 97133,* ☎ *590/27–64–87,* 𝕱𝕬𝕏 *590/27–81–74. 21 rooms. Bar, snack bar, air-conditioning, refrigerators, pool, recreation room. AE, MC, V. CP.*

**$–$$**   🏨 **Village St. Jean.** The second generation of the Charneau family now
★   runs this popular cottage colony, which has acquired a strong following over the years. The accent is on service and affordability, and this is one of the best values on the island. The handsome stone-and-redwood cottages are spacious, although a bit sparsely furnished (except for the two-bedroom cottages), and have open-air kitchenettes and patios. There are also six hotel rooms without kitchenettes but with refrigerators. Rooms have elegant natural fabrics and dark wood furniture, including some teak pieces from Bali; some have beam ceilings and cheerful striped awnings, and most have king-size beds. Units have a variety of views, from full ocean to almost none; note that the units closest to the road are subject to the ongoing noise of minimoke engines struggling with the steep terrain. The open-air restaurant, Le Patio, serves

excellent Italian fare. From the hotel it is an easy five-minute walk down to popular St. Jean Beach and to a variety of stores and restaurants (the walk back up is a bit more strenuous). ⊠ *Box 623, St. Jean 97098,* ☎ *590/27–61–39 or 800/633–7411,* ⨳ *590/27–77–96. 6 rooms, 20 cottages. Restaurant, bar, grocery, air-conditioning, kitchenettes, pool, hot tub, shop, library. AE, MC, V. EP.*

$ ⬚ **Hostellerie des Trois Forces.** This pastoral, fairly isolated mountaintop
★ inn is an idiosyncratic delight, with a string of tiny, gingerbread-trimmed West Indian–style cottages charmingly decorated according to astrological color schemes (Libra is soft blue; Leo, bright red; etc.). All have a terrace with a breathtaking ocean view as well as air-conditioning or a ceiling fan. Most have four-poster beds; all furnishings were specially handcrafted to suit each sign by the owner. The tinkle of chimes floats through the pleasant restaurant. Astrologer Hubert de la Motte (he's a Gemini, by the way) is the very personable owner and talented chef (along with chef Bernard Calci), and he may arrange a reading for you, perhaps a yoga class, or even a past-life regression therapy session. The slogan of the rustic restaurant is "Food is love"; appropriately, Hubert was recently named a Chevalier de la Marmite d'Or, a prestigious culinary academy in France, founded in 1557. ⊠ *Morne Vitet,* ☎ *590/27–61–25,* ⨳ *590/27–81–38. 8 rooms. Restaurant, bar, air-conditioning, minibars, pool. AE, MC, V. EP.*

$ ⬚ **La Normandie.** This small, family-run, cozy hotel offers modestly furnished rooms that are about a five-minute walk from the beach and extremely inexpensive for the island (well under $100 per day)—probably one of the best values in St. Barts. Some rooms have TVs, and there is a small pool. ⊠ *Lorient 97133,* ☎ *590/27–61–66,* ⨳ *590/27–68–64. 8 rooms. Air-conditioning, pool. No credit cards. EP.*

$ ⬚ **Le P'tit Morne.** There is good value in these modestly furnished moun-
★ tainside studios, each with a private balcony and panoramic views of the coastline below. Small kitchenettes are adequate for creating light meals or packing picnic lunches. The snack bar serves breakfast. It's relatively isolated here, and the beach is a 10-minute drive away. ⊠ *Box 14, Colombier 97133,* ☎ *590/27–62–64,* ⨳ *590/27–84–63. 14 rooms. Snack bar, air-conditioning, kitchenettes, pool, library. AE, MC, V. CP.*

$ ⬚ **Les Mouettes.** Six spacious, simply furnished bungalows open onto
★ the island's best surfing beach. Each has a bathroom with shower, a kitchenette, a patio, two double beds, and a twin bed or fold-out sofa, making it a good bet for families. ⊠ *Lorient 97133,* ☎ *590/27–60–74. 6 rooms. Kitchenette, shop, car rental. No credit cards. EP.*

# Dining

The French reverence for food is evident everywhere on St. Barts, from the most expensive classic French restaurant to the simplest beachside café. If you enjoy exquisitely prepared cuisine served at an enjoyable pace (and don't mind paying for it), then you've come to the right island. À la carte prices at the well-known French restaurants are very high, but many offer a prix-fixe menu for a very reasonable price—a nice way to sample the cuisine. Lunch prices are usually cheaper than evening prices (with the infamous exception of Le Lafayette), and Italian, Creole, and French-Creole restaurants tend to be less expensive day and night. Beware that restaurants here typically charge for drinking water (a French custom), which comes by the bottle, both sparkling and flat, and costs about $4. *Accras* (salt cod fritters) with Creole sauce (minced hot peppers in oil), spiced christophine (a kind of squash), *boudin Créole* (a very spicy blood sausage), and a lusty *soupe de poissons* (fish soup) are some of the delicious and ubiquitous Creole dishes.

Reservations are always recommended; on weekend nights in season, they're essential almost everywhere.

## What to Wear

Jackets are rarely required and rarely worn, but this is a tony island and people here are fashionably dressed. Jeans are de rigueur when worn with a hip collared shirt or T-shirt. Shorts at the dinner table will label you *américain*. Think casual chic when planning your wardrobe and you'll be fine.

| CATEGORY | COST* |
|---|---|
| $$$$ | over $60 |
| $$$ | $45–$60 |
| $$ | $30–$45 |
| $ | under $30 |

*per person for a three-course meal, excluding drinks, service, and 4% sales tax*

$$$$ ✕ **Carl Gustaf.** Not even the sweeping views of the harbor can deflect
★ attention from the sublime creations of Patrick Gateau. Monsieur Gateau, who trained at the Crillon in Paris, deftly weaves tropical influences into his classical cuisine. Among his standouts are warm goat-cheese salad, lobster spring rolls, ravioli in shellfish cream sauce, and grilled swordfish steak with stewed aubergines, tomatoes, sweet peppers, and onions. You choose your dessert when you order your meal to allow time for it to be prepared. Look no further than the warm chocolate praline cake—with a center unexpectedly flooded with warm gooey chocolate, it will reduce a chocolate lover to tears. The large, breezy, white dining room has an open-air terrace that overlooks Gustavia harbor, as well as a piano bar. ⊠ *Rue des Normands, Gustavia,* ☎ *590/27–82–83. AE, MC, V. No lunch Sun. in summer.*

$$$$ ✕ **François Plantation.** Follow the lanterns down the flower-draped ar-
★ borway to this elegant restaurant. Inside, mahogany tables and chairs are surrounded by beautiful plants. Chef Philippe Ruiz's cuisine legère, a lighter version of classic French cuisine, draws guests from all over the island; locals consistently rate it in their top three. Try his ravioli of goat cheese and foie gras, and move on to roasted sea bass spiced with vanilla or lamb fillet roasted in a light crust with basil and Gorgonzola cheese and served with sautéed fennel and tomato. You can also order the rare Coutancie beef: The cattle must drink three liters of beer and receive a 20-minute rubdown twice daily, among other strict guidelines, to qualify. Dessert specials include a remarkable warm dark-chocolate tart served with vanilla ice cream. ⊠ *Colombier,* ☎ *590/ 27–78–82. Reservations essential. AE, D, MC, V. Closed Sept.–Oct. No lunch.*

$$$ ✕ **Le Gaiac.** Cool breezes waft through this open-air restaurant at the elegant, out-of-the-way Le Toiny hotel. Pale blue napery and blue canvas chairs beautifully complement the blue bay view. Chef Maxime Des Champs hails from France and combines local ingredients with traditional French cooking techniques. Appetizers at lunch include duck carpaccio with coffee-flavored vinaigrette and a delicious chilled spicy mango soup. Entrées feature club sandwiches, salads, and grilled fish and shellfish. The dinner menu expands with roast rack of lamb in a clay shell with thyme and honey, yellowtail snapper with lightly curried lentils and squash, and pigeon layered with red cabbage and sweet potato, spiced with local herbs. Don't miss the fabulous buffet lunch on Sundays. ⊠ *Le Toiny, Anse de Toiny,* ☎ *590/27–88–88. AE, DC, MC, V. Closed Sept.–mid-Oct. and Tues. in summer.*

$$$ ✕ **Le Lafayette Club.** Despite truly outrageous prices, this lunch-only, beachside bistro is such an in-season in spot that reservations are necessary if you want to eat between noon and 2. Expect to pay about

$18 for a green salad with bacon and croutons or goat cheese and sliced tomatoes, $30 and up for grilled local fish, fillet of duck, and shrimp with fresh pasta. The grilled lobster entrée is a whopping $70. ⊠ *Grand Cul de Sac,* ☎ *590/27–62–51. No credit cards. Closed May–mid-Nov. No dinner.*

$$$ ✕ **Le Sapotillier.** Dining in this cozy boîte or in the courtyard under a
★ grand old sapodilla tree, you may feel like a guest in the owners' house—a loving re-creation of a typical St. Barts case (Creole for cottage), down to the brick walls, hand-painted wooden chairs, exquisite white linen tablecloths, and vivid Creole paintings. Yet the food is anything but down-home. This long-established French-Creole restaurant serves such delicacies as frogs' legs, fillet of baby turbot in potato crust, and snail lasagna with spinach, walnuts, and Roquefort sabayon. The sumptuous black-and-white-chocolate mousse is a house favorite. ⊠ *Rue de Centenaire, Gustavia,* ☎ *590/27–60–28. Reservations essential. MC, V. Closed May–mid-Oct. No lunch.*

$$$ ✕ **L'Orchidée.** This elegant French-Creole restaurant with coral stucco walls and mahogany archways is in the Hotel Christopher. Have a seat in a casual captain's chair on the deck, amid the white napery and gleaming silver, and listen to the waves on the rocky shore. The staff is friendly and solicitous, the atmosphere romantic, and the food beautifully presented. Try roast lobster with mango and ginger, grilled mahimahi with lime, or chicken with curry-and-coconut sauce served with two kinds of mashed potatoes. A prix-fixe menu is available for about $45. ⊠ *Hotel Christopher, Pointe Milou,* ☎ *590/27–63–63. AE, MC, V. No lunch.*

$$$ ✕ **West Indies Café.** On the site of the former La Tocque Lyonnaise, this café is set on a terraced, outdoor pavilion overlooking the bay. Chef Yvan, hailing from St. Tropez and Paris, prepares French cuisine à la Provence; he's best known for his innovative cooking with beer. Try the veal kidneys with basil and beer sauce and the crispy pineapple with caramelized juice. Weekend nights, the staff performs their rather racy Caribbean version of a typical Parisian floor show, in tribute to the great Jean Marie Rivière, the cabaret impresario who ran Club La Banane for years. ⊠ *El Sereno Beach Hotel and Villas, Grand Cul de Sac,* ☎ *590/27–64–80. AE, DC, MC, V. Closed June–Aug.*

$$–$$$ ✕ **Adam.** Vincent Adam, a graduate of the Culinary Academy of France, opened this haute cuisine gem in the hills just off St. Jean Beach. Dinner is served in the Creole-style house or in the garden. While standards have lowered since Bernard Hinault supplanted Vincent as chef, Adam still offers splendid bargains with its more extensive à la carte menu (offered only in season) and a very reasonable prix-fixe menu (about $38). Offerings include lobster tabbouleh, salmon tartare with caviar and oysters, terrine of sweetbreads, and fillet of beef. ⊠ *St. Jean,* ☎ *590/27–93–22. AE, MC, V. No lunch.*

$$–$$$ ✕ **Le Bambou.** In the hills above Grand Cul du Sac is this small restaurant, serving creative Asian fare. A Laotian chef, Monsieur Thao, prepares Vietnamese, Thai, and Chinese food. You can dine inside, where all black lacquer and impeccable floral arrangements, with a changing art gallery on the walls is soothing, but most guests opt for the breezy terrace with a fine view of the countryside and the sea in the distance. Reservations are a good idea if you want to sit outside. ⊠ *Grand Cul de Sac,* ☎ *590/27–75–65. MC, V. Closed Mon. No lunch.*

$$–$$$ ✕ **Le Tamarin.** Always among the favorite restaurants of those who live
★ on St. Barts, this open-air eatery on the way to Saline Beach is famous for its French and Creole fusion cuisine and its resident noisy parrot, Cooky. Relax in a hammock under the tamarind tree with a 'ti punch and then savor some of the house specialties, including carpaccios of salmon, tuna, and beef; fresh grilled lobster; and the renowned lemon

tart and chocolate cake. ✉ *Salines,* ☎ *590/27–72–12. AE, MC, V. Closed Mon. No dinner in summer.*

**$$–$$$  ✕ Marigot Bay Club.** Have a seat at the dark-wood bar or at a table on the beam-ceiling patio, and take in the views of the colorful sailboats moored in the bay. The owner of this casual spot loves to fish and often reels in the catch of the day himself. It might be grouper, tuna, red snapper, or yellowtail and is frequently served with a Creole sauce. Other specials here include lobster ravioli, conch sausages, codfish fritters, and steamed shark in a red pepper and butter sauce. Lunch is served in season, except on Mondays. ✉ *Marigot,* ☎ *590/27–75–45. Reservations essential. AE, MC, V. No lunch Mon.*

**$$–$$$  ✕ Maya's.** Locals, visitors, and celebs keep returning to pack this informal, open-air restaurant, just outside of Gustavia on the north end of Public Beach. Relax in a colorful deck chair and watch the boats in Gustavia's harbor as you contemplate the Creole, Vietnamese, and Thai menu. You choose from five selections for each of three courses. The menu changes nightly, but you might find christophine au gratin, several fresh salads, duck à l'orange, salmon teriyaki, and shrimp curry. ✉ *Public Beach,* ☎ *590/27–75–73. AE, D, MC, V. Closed Sun. and June–Oct. No lunch.*

**$$–$$$  ✕ Wall House.** Consistently excellent French cuisine is the hallmark of this restaurant on the far end of the far side of Gustavia's harbor. The interior is glistening white—shiny white wicker furniture, white tile floors, white tablecloths and walls—with pots of greenery here and there. Owner Gerard Began is unobtrusively on-site most evenings, and the staff is gracious and will make enthusiastic recommendations. Start with marinated salmon with dill, gazpacho, grilled mahimahi over sliced cucumbers, foie gras, or cold eggplant mousse. For your main course, try fillet of shark in lobster sauce, duck in cassis sauce with sautéed potatoes, or beef with pepper sauce. Three prix-fixe menus offer excellent value. The lunch menu features lighter fare. ✉ *Gustavia,* ☎ *590/27–71–83. AE, MC, V.*

**$$  ✕ La Crémaillère.** The setting, a 19th-century Swedish stone-wood-and-brick house, is sublime: several intimate, individually decorated rooms—with beamed wood ceilings, wrought-iron wall sconces, hurricane lamps, and peacock rattan chairs—surround a cool, dark, romantic tiled courtyard. The food is solidly traditional, but rather than having a standard, if fine, veal in mushroom cream sauce or pork dijonnaise, try the best fondues on island—especially more unusual suggestions like forestière (wild mushrooms) or cabrette (goat cheese). The real treat here are "Les Pierrades," items like beef or various kinds of seafood grilled on hot stones. ✉ *Rue de Général de Gaulle, Gustavia,* ☎ *590/ 27–82–95. AE, MC, V. No lunch Sun.*

**$$  ✕ Le Patio.** Some of the best classic Italian food on the island is served à la Creole at this pleasant hillside restaurant. Dine inside by candlelight, where it's romantic and intimate, or on the terrace, with nice views of the bay. Entrées change weekly, but you may find snapper in parchment with fines herbes and peppers, chicken breast in caramelized onions, or grouper medallions rolled in black peppercorns with a light ginger and lime sauce, in addition to six or seven pasta offerings and various pizzas, both traditional and inventive. The antipasto here is renowned. Service is unhurried, despite the remarkably reasonable prices: witness the $36 prix-fixe menu. ✉ *Village St. Jean Hotel,* ☎ *590/27–61–39. MC, V. Closed Wed. and June. No lunch.*

**$$  ✕ New Born.** For authentic Creole cuisine, head down the bumpy road that leads to the Hotel Manapany. The sky-blue restaurant is somewhat devoid of decoration except for a large aquarium in the back; ask for a table near it if you want to watch the sharks, turtles, and tropical fish swim while you eat. The fresh seafood is caught at the beach (just steps away) by owners Franky and David. This is the place to sample such Creole specialties as accras, boudin, curried goat or shrimp, and salt cod salad. For dessert try the coconut custard or bananas flambé. ⊠ *Anse des Cayes,* ☎ *590/27–67–07. AE, MC, V. Closed Sun. in off-season. No lunch.*

**$–$$** ✕ **Gloriette.** This beachside spot serves delicious local Creole dishes, such as crunchy accras and cassoulet of local lobster, as well as light salads. ⊠ *Grand Cul de Sac,* ☎ *590/27–75–66. AE, MC, V.*

**$–$$** ✕ **Ines' Ghetto.** The combination of imaginatively prepared, modestly
★ priced fare—barbecued ribs (a house specialty), crab salad, ragout of beef, crème caramel—wild decor (including a virtual jungle of plants, bamboo furnishings, and metal garbage-can sculpture) and a disarmingly fun-loving atmosphere guarantees things run smoothly even though Edward Stakelborough sold this open-air restaurant to open a tonier competitor down the block. The crowd is lively, and the wine list is impressive (but avoid the house white). ⊠ *Gustavia, just off rue du Général de Gaulle. No phone. No credit cards.*

**$–$$** ✕ **La Marine.** Mussels from France arrive on Thursday, and in-the-know islanders are there to eat them at the very popular dockside picnic tables. The lunch menu always includes fresh fish, hamburgers, and omelets; dinner adds more grilled meat and fish. ⊠ *Rue Jeanne d'Arc, Gustavia,* ☎ *590/27–70–13. AE, MC, V.*

**$–$$** ✕ **Le Mandala.** The decor at this new ultrahip hot spot ranges from fancy (wrought-iron chairs, a mahogany bar) to fanciful (huge painted ceramic frogs, enormous ashtrays shaped like a hand). The owners, Boubou and Christophe, and their food are equally witty. They offer a full restaurant menu (including a three-course buy at 170F) with offerings like chicken breast in coconut milk. But this is the place to sample tapas, that wonderful Spanish tradition of small tasting platters, especially over a potent rum punch whose colors match the setting sun, clearly visible fireballing across the harbor from the sweeping terrace. ⊠ *Rue Thiers, Gustavia,* ☎ *590/27–96–96. AE, MC, V. No lunch June and Sept.*

**$–$$** ✕ **Le Repaire.** This busy brasserie overlooks Gustavia's harbor and is a popular spot from early breakfast until the wee hours of the morning (it's open from 6 AM to 1 AM). Grab a cappuccino, pull a captain's chair up to the front window, and watch cruise-ship passengers come off the boats to descend upon the town. The menu includes everything from cheeseburgers to foie gras and grilled fish and lobster. Stick to the simpler bistro and Creole, favorites like steak frites or crab Creole salad. There is a billiards table and live music on weekends. ⊠ *Quai de la République, Gustavia,* ☎ *590/27–72–48. MC, V. Closed Sun.*

**$–$$** ✕ **Le Rivage.** Bathing suits are acceptable attire at this popular Creole establishment on the beach at Grand Cul de Sac. Delicious lobster salad, sandwiches, and fresh grilled fish are served at indoor and outdoor tables. The relaxed atmosphere and surprisingly low prices can make for an enjoyable meal, but the service gets frantic when the restaurant is busy. ⊠ *St. Barth Beach Hotel, Grand Cul de Sac,* ☎ *590/ 27–82–42. AE, MC, V.*

**$–$$** ✕ **L'Escale.** Great food, ambience, and views draw locals and visitors
★ alike to this open-air restaurant, at the water's edge on the far side of Gustavia's harbor. The varied menu includes a wide range of pasta (lasagna, tortellini, ravioli, and spaghetti with marinara, Bolognese, and other sauces), as well as fresh local fish, veal scallopini in an assortment of sauces, steak tartare, chicken, and 12 kinds of pizza. Many dishes are cooked in a wood-burning oven. ⊠ *Rue Jeanne d'Arc, Gustavia,* ☎ *590/27–81–06. Reservations essential. MC, V. No lunch.*

**$–$$** ✕ **Paradisio.** Five kinds of homemade pasta and carpaccios are served each day at this friendly eatery in a historic apricot-and-white gingerbread Creole building. Specialties include fresh lobster medallions served on a bed of lentils, veal kidneys sautéed and served with a mustard sauce, and lamb filet mignon with rosemary. You can eat in the air-conditioned dining room, festively painted in canary yellow and teal, or on the breezy terrace. ⊠ *Rue du Roi, Gustavia,* ☎ *590/27–80–78. AE, MC, V. No lunch Sun.*

$ ✕ **Brasserie La Creole.** Right in the center of the St. Jean shopping arcade, this casual brasserie has indoor seating, a comfortable bar, and outdoor umbrella tables. Drop by in the morning for freshly baked croissants and great coffee. At lunch try the croque-monsieur. There is a full breakfast menu (the restaurant opens at 7 AM), and from noon until midnight, sandwiches, salads, and various beef, chicken, and fish entrées are served. ⊠ *St. Jean,* ☎ *590/27–68–09. AE.*

## Beaches

There are nearly 20 *plages* (beaches) scattered around the island, each with a distinctive personality and all of them public. Even in season, it is possible to find a nearly empty beach. Topless sunbathing is common, but nudism is forbidden—although both Saline and Gouverneur are de facto nude beaches. Here are the main attractions:

**St. Jean** is like a mini Côte d'Azur—beachside bistros, bungalow hotels, bronze beauties, windsurfing, and lots of day-trippers. The reef-protected strip is divided by Eden Rock promontory, and there's good snorkeling west of the rock. **Lorient** is popular with St. Barts families and surfers, who like its rolling waves. **Marigot** is a tiny, calm beach with good snorkeling along the rocky far end. Around the point from Marigot, next to the Guanahani Hotel, is tiny **Marechal Beach,** which offers some of the best snorkeling on the island. Shallow, reef-protected **Grand Cul de Sac** is especially nice for small children and windsurfers; it has excellent lunch spots and lots of pelicans. Secluded **Grande Saline,** with its sandy ocean bottom, is just about everyone's favorite beach and is great for swimmers. Despite the law, young and old alike go nude. It can get windy here, so go on a calm day. **Anse du Gouverneur** is more secluded than Grande Saline—hence the nude sunbathing—and truly beautiful, with good snorkeling and views of St. Kitts, Saba, and St. Eustatius. A five-minute walk from Gustavia is **Petite Anse de Galet** (Shell Beach), named after the tiny shells on its shore. **Public Beach** is an excellent place to enjoy the sunset and watch the boats. **Corossol Beach** is a top boat- and sunset-watching spot. The beach at **Colombier** is the least accessible but the most private; you'll have to take either a rocky footpath from Petite Anse or brave the 30-minute climb down a cactus-bordered trail from the top of the mountain behind the beach. A lot of boaters favor this beach and cove for its calm anchorage. **Flamands** is the most beautiful of the hotel beaches—a roomy strip of silken sand, now even wider due to Hurricane Luis.

## Outdoor Activities and Sports

### Boating

St. Barts is a popular yachting and sailing center, thanks to its location midway between Antigua and St. Thomas. Gustavia's harbor, 13 to 16 ft deep, has mooring and docking facilities for 40 yachts. There are also good anchorages available at Public, Corossol, and Colombier. **Loulou's Marine** (☎ 590/27–62–74), a ship chandlery, is the place for yachting information and supplies. **Marine Service** (☎ 590/27–70–34) offers full-day outings on a 40-ft catamaran to the uninhabited Ile Fourchue for swimming, snorkeling, cocktails, and lunch; the cost is $96 per person. Marine Service also arranges deep-sea-fishing trips, with a full-day charter of a 30-ft crewed cabin cruiser running $800; an unskippered motor rental runs about $260 a day. You can also take an hour's cruise on the glass-bottom boat *L'Aquascope* by contacting Marine Service. **OcéanMust Marina** (☎ 590/27–62–25), in Gustavia, offers all kinds of boat charters. **St. Barth Caraibes Yachting** (☎ 590/27–52–48), in Gustavia, can charter any type of boat you require. **Nautica** (☎ 590/27–56–50) specializes in day sails and charters.

### Diving and Deep-Sea Fishing

Deep-sea fishing can be arranged through **Marine Service, St. Barth Caraibes Yachting,** or **OcéanMust Marina** (☞ Boating, *above*). Marine Service also operates a PADI-certified diving center, with scuba-diving trips for about $50–$80 per person, gear included. The CMAS-certified **Club La Bulle** (☎ 590/27–62–25), **Odysee Caraibe** (☎ 590/27–55–94), and PADI-certified **St. Barth Plongée** (☎ 590/27–54–44), all in Gustavia, are other scuba options.

### Horseback Riding

Laure Nicolas leads two-hour excursions in the morning and afternoons for $35 per person from **Ranch des Flamands** (✉ Anse des Flamands, ☎ 590/27–80–72).

### Tennis

If you wish to play tennis at a hotel at which you are not a guest, be sure to call ahead to inquire about fees and reservations. There are two lighted tennis courts each at the **Guanahani** (☎ 590/27–66–60), **Le Flamboyant Tennis Club** (☎ 590/27–75–65), and the **Sports Center of Colombier** (☎ 590/27–61–07). There is one lighted court each at **Hotel Manapany Cottages** (☎ 590/27–66–55), **Taiwana** (☎ 590/27–65–01), and **Hotel Isle de France** (☎ 590/27–61–81), which also has the island's only squash court.

### Windsurfing

Windsurfing fever has definitely caught on here. Boards can be rented for about $20 an hour at water-sports centers along St. Jean and Grand Cul de Sac beaches. Lessons are offered for about $40 an hour at **St. Barth Wind School** (✉ St. Jean, ☎ 590/27–71–22), **Le Centre Nautique** (✉ Eden Roc, St. Jean, ☎ 590/27–72–94), and at **Wind Wave Power** (✉ St. Barths Beach Hotel, ☎ 590/27–60–70), which also has parasailing. You can also hang glide at **St. Barth Parasail** (✉ Marigot, ☎ 590/27–61–76).

## Shopping

St. Barts is a duty-free port, and there are especially good bargains in jewelry, porcelain, imported liquors, and French perfumes, cosmetics, and designer resort wear.

### Shopping Areas

Shops are clustered in **Gustavia, La Savane Commercial Center** (across from the airport), and **La Villa Créole,** an appealing shopping complex in St. Jean.

### Good Buys

CLOTHES

A number of boutiques in all three shopping areas carry the latest in French and Italian sportswear and haute couture fashion items. The price tags may astound you (even after you convert the francs to dollars you may still be in high three figures), but these prices are actually well below the Paris price for the same item, and so they are considered bargains by some. Shops to look for include Stéphane & Bernard, Libertine, Hermès, Gucci, Cartier, Gianni Versace, Tommy

Hilfiger, Giorgio Armani, and Black Swan, all of which are in Gustavia and have branches either across from the airport or in St. Jean or both; but there are many other stores and boutiques to be found. At both St. Jean's La Villa Créole and La Savane (across from the airport), it is worth working your way from one end of the shopping complex to the other.

### ISLAND CRAFTS

Stop in Corossol to pick up some of the intricate straw work—wide-brim beach hats, mobiles, handbags—that the ladies of Corossol create by hand. In Gustavia, look for hand-turned pottery at **St. Barts Pottery** (☎ 590/27–62–74). Fabienne Miot displays her utterly unique, stylish gold jewelry at **L'Atelier de Fabienne** (☎ 590/27–63–31) . You'll see coral and exotic shell jewelry at the **Shell Shop** (no phone). **La Boutique Roots** (☎ 590/27–53–53) fashions marvelous sandals, sunbonnets, and handbags from straw. **M'Bolo** (☎ 590/27–90–54) is a fragrant grab bag of local spices, flavored rums, pareus, and hand-painted blouses, T-shirts, bags, and bikinis. Superb local skin-care products are available at **Ligne de St. Barth** (☎ 590/27–82–63) in Lorient. Gustavia also has a market, **Le 'Ti Marché,** dedicated to arts and crafts handmade on the island. Open every day except Sunday, the market is set up in stalls on the corner of rue du Roi Oscar II near the city hall. The much-sought-after Belou's P line of aromatic oils is available here. For details call 590/27–83–72 or the tourist office, which can also provide information on artists' studios around the island, such as Robert Danet, Marion Vinot, Patricia Guyot, Nathalie Daniel, Rose Lemen, Christian Bretoneiche, and Eliane Lefèvre.

### WINE, CIGAR, AND GOURMET SHOPS

Wine lovers will enjoy **La Cave** (✉ Rue Général de Gaulle, Marigot, ☎ 590/27–63–21), where an excellent collection of French vintages is stored in temperature-controlled cellars.

On rue du Général de Gaulle, **Le Comptoir du Cigare** (☎ 590/27–50–62), which includes a walk-in humidor, is one of the finest purveyors of cigars (and accessories) in the Caribbean, with a comprehensive selection from Davidoff to Dunhill, including the oh-so-tempting Cubanos.

## Supermarkets and Gourmet Shops

A gourmet supermarket, **Match,** is across from the airport, as is **Unic Plus,** another supermarket with a good selection of fruits, vegetables, and meats. Two other supermarkets worth checking out are **Sodexa** in La Villa Créole and **MonoShop** in Marigot.

For exotic groceries or picnic fixings, stop by one of St. Barts's fabulous gourmet delis, **La Rotisserie** (☎ 590/27–63–13), on rue du Roi Oscar II (branches in St. Jean and Pointe Milou).

# Nightlife

For an island of its petite size, St. Barts offers a surprising number of things to do at night, notably on weekends. There are many special places to go for cocktail hour, and some of the hotels and restaurants provide late-night fun.

**American Bar** (☎ 590/27–86–07), at **L'Escale** restaurant, is an after-dinner hangout for the retro-hip; there's a 1968 Cadillac Eldorado outside and lots of neon inside. A few steps away from American Bar is **Jungle Cafe** (☎ 590/27–67–29), an upstairs eatery overlooking the harbor that jumps and jives at happy hour, with knockout drink specials and fairly priced Asian snack fare. **Bar de l'Oubli** (☎ 590/27–70–06), where the young French who work on the island gather for drinks, gets hopping late-night. **Carl Gustaf** (☎ 590/27–82–83) lures those in search of quiet conversation and some gentle piano music at the day's end. It's also Gustavia's best sunset-watching spot. **Feeling** (☎ 590/27–88–67) is one of the island's hot spots for dancing. An indoor dance floor and spacious outdoor bar-patio make this a fun place to hang out. The disco is in the hills above Gustavia, just past the Santa Fe Restaurant. **Guanahani** (☎ 590/27–66–60) has a piano bar, as well as *spectacle* (nightclub revue-style) shows and theme evenings (Latin dancing night is particularly wild) a couple of times weekly in season at its poolside L'Indigo restaurant. **La Licorne** (☎ 590/27–83–94), in Lorient, is very hot with a local crowd and open only on Saturday night. **Manapany** (☎ 590/27–66–55) has a piano bar. **Le Petit Club** (☎ 590/27–66–33), in Gustavia, is the place to head for real late-night dancing. **Le Repaire** (☎ 590/27–72–48), in Gustavia, lures a crowd for cocktail hour. **Le Select** (☎ 590/27–86–87), in Gustavia, is St. Barts's original hangout and has a boisterous garden where the barefoot boating set gathers for a brew.

# Exploring St. Barthélemy

Getting around this hilly and very picturesque isle is easy on the excellent and well-marked roads. Since St. Barts is small, you can rent a four-wheel drive or moke at the airport and see the entire island in half a day.

*Numbers in the margin correspond to points of interest on the St. Barthélemy map.*

### SIGHTS TO SEE

❶ **Anse de Colombier.** At the end of Flamands Road, a 25-minute hike around a rocky footpath leads to a pretty beach and cove, popular with boaters.

❷ **Anse des Flamands.** This wide beach has small hotels, including the Hotel Isle de France, and many rental villas. From here you can take a brisk hike to the top of the now-extinct volcano believed to have given birth to St. Barts. From the peak are gorgeous views of the islands.

❼ **Anse du Gouverneur.** Legend has it that pirates' treasure is buried at this, one of St. Barts's most beautiful beaches. The road here from Gustavia supplies some spectacular vistas. If the weather is clear, you will be able to see the islands of Saba, St. Eustatius, and St. Kitts from the beach.

| NEED A BREAK? | The hilltop **Sante Fe Restaurant** (✉ Morne Lorne, at the turnoff to Gouverneur Beach, ☎ 590/27–61–04) is a popular spot for sunsets and American-style hamburgers, not to mention homesick Americans and Brits who remain glued to the sports on the wide-screen TV. |
|---|---|

❸ **Corossol.** The island's French provincial origins are most evident in this two-street fishing village with a little rocky beach. Residents speak an old Norman dialect, and some of the older women still wear traditional garb—ankle-length dresses, bare feet, and starched white sunbonnets called quichenottes (kiss-me-not hats). The women don't like to be photographed. However, they are not shy about selling you some of their handmade straw work—handbags, baskets, broad-brim hats, and delicate strings of birds—made from lantana palms. The palms were introduced to the island 100 years ago by foresighted Father Morvan, who planted a grove in Corossol and Flamands, thus providing the country folk with a living that is still pursued today. Here, too, is the **Inter**

Oceans Museum, which features more than 7,000 seashells from around the world. ☎ 590/27–62–97. ▣ 20F. ☉ Daily 9–5.

**⑩ Grand Cul de Sac.** A winding road passes through the mangroves, ponds, and beach of Grand Cul de Sac, where there are plenty of water-sports concessions and excellent beachside restaurants, including the West Indies Cafe and the ultrachic Le Lafayette Club (☞ Dining, *above*).

**⑧ Grande Saline.** The big salt ponds of Grande Saline are no longer in use, and the place looks desolate, but climb the short hillock behind the ponds for a surprise—the long arc of **Anse de Grande Saline.**

**⑤ Gustavia.** With just a few streets on three sides of its tiny harbor, Gustavia is easily explored in a two-hour stroll. Here you will find excellent shopping, many restaurants and cafés, and a museum. Remember that most shops close from noon to 2, so you might want to combine shopping with an enjoyable lunch at one of the restaurants overlooking the harbor.

A good place to park your car is rue de la République, where flashy catamarans, yachts, and sailboats are moored. If you haven't gotten a map or have some questions, head to the **tourist office** on the pier, where you can pick up an island map and a free copy of *St. Barth Magazine,* a monthly publication on island happenings. If you feel like stopping for a café au lait, a croissant, or a drink, settle in at either **Bar de l'Oubli** or **Le Select,** two cafés just a few steps away. The former tends to attract a more American crowd, the latter a youthful French bunch shrouded in a Gauloise haze. There are also two ultracasual hangouts on the quai that have become equally popular among the young, trendy, and relatively penniless, **L'Entracte** and **Cantina.** On the "unfashionable" side of the harbor, the vibrantly colored **Bistrot des Arts** attracts equally colorful yet tony types who enjoy gazing at the harbor, the powerful, almost disturbing Creole artworks, or each other, usually over a lobster selected from the enormous aquarium.

As you stroll through the little streets, you will notice that plaques sometimes spell out names in both French and Swedish, a reminder of the days when the island was a Swedish colony. Small shops along rue du Roi Oscar II, rue de la France, rue du Bord de Mer, and rue du Général de Gaulle sell French perfumes, the latest in French and Italian designer wear, resort wear, crystal, gold jewelry, and other luxury items.

On the far side of the harbor known as Le Pointe is the charming **Municipal Museum,** where you will find watercolors, portraits, photographs, and historic documents detailing the island's history as well as displays of the island's flowers, plants, and marine life. ☎ 599/27–89–07. ▣ 10F. ☉ Mon.–Thurs. 8:30–12:30 and 2:30–6, Fri. 8:30–12:30 and 3–6, Sat. 9–11.

**⑨ Lorient.** Site of the first French settlement, Lorient is one of the island's two parishes, and a restored church, historic headstones, a school, post office, and gas station mark the spot. Lorient Beach has royal palms and rolling waves.

One of St. Barthélemy's treasured secrets, **Le Manoir,** a 1610 Norman manor, was painstakingly shipped from France and reconstructed here in 1984 by the charming Jeanne Audy Rowland in tribute to the island's Viking forebears. The tranquil surrounding courtyard and garden contain a waterfall and a lily-strewn pool. Madame Rowland is no longer on island, but the Savoyard family, who purchased the property, graciously allow visitors. Cramped cottages surrounding the manor are available at a very reasonable daily or weekly rate (☎ 590/27–79–27). It helps if you speak some French.

❻ **Petite Anse de Galet.** Just south of Gustavia, this quiet little *plage* is also known as Shell Beach because of the tiny shells heaped ankle-deep in some places.

❹ **St. Jean.** Brimming with bungalows, bistros, sunbathers, and windsurfing sails, the half-mile crescent of sand at St. Jean is the island's most popular beach. Informal restaurants are scattered here and there along the shore, and windsurfers skim along the water, catching the strong trade winds. If you walk as far to the west as possible, you can get a close look at the little planes taking off from the airport. For respite from the sun, cross the street near Eden Rock and you will find many branches of Gustavia boutiques and several restaurants.

⓫ **Toiny coast.** Over the hills beyond Grand Cul de Sac is this much-photographed coastline. Drystone fences crisscross the steep slopes of Morne Vitet along a rocky shoreline that resembles the rugged coast of Normandy.

NEED A BREAK? **Chez Pompi** (✉ Petit Cul de Sac, ☎ 590/27-75-67), on the road to Toiny, is a delightful cottage straight from a Cézanne painting. Pompi (a.k.a. Louis Ledee) is an artist of some repute, whose naive, slightly abstract artwork clutters the walls of his tiny studio. You can browse and chat with the amiable Monsieur Pompi while enjoying his fine Creole and country French cuisine. The gallery is open daily (except Sundays) from 9 to 6.

# St. Barthélemy A to Z

## Arriving and Departing

### BY BOAT

Catamarans leave Philipsburg in St. Maarten at 9 AM daily, arriving in Gustavia's harbor around 11 AM. These are one-day, round-trip excursions (about $50, including open bar), with departures from St. Barts at 3:30 PM. If there's room, one-way passengers ($25) are often taken as well. The seas can be choppy, and it is not uncommon for passengers to get seasick. Contact **Bobby's Marina** in Philipsburg (☎ 599/5-23170) for reservations. The **St. Barth Express** (☎ 590/27-77-24) sails from Gustavia at 7:30 AM for the trip to Philipsburg (Bobby's Marina), and Marigot (Port la Royale); it leaves Marigot at 3:30 PM for the return trip (stopping at Philipsburg). **Voyageur** (☎ 590/27-77-24) offers ferry service several times between St. Barts and Marigot on weekends for 310F round-trip, 220F one-way. **White Octopus** (☎ 599/52-40-96) makes the run from Philipsburg to Gustavia at 9 AM Tuesdays and Thursday–Saturday, returning at 4 PM for the same fares as for Voyageur. **St. Barth Yachting Service** (☎ 590/27-64-49), **Marine Service** (☎ 590/27-70-34), and **OcéanMust Marina** (☎ 590/27-62-25) in Gustavia have boats for private charter.

### BY PLANE

The principal gateway from North America is St. Maarten's Juliana International Airport. Although it is only 10 minutes by air to St. Barts, the last two may take your breath away. Don't worry when you see those treetops out your window. You're just clearing a hill before dropping down to the runway. Flights leave at least once an hour between 7:30 AM and 5:30 PM on either **Windward Islands Airways** (☎ 590/27-61-01 or 599/5-54210) or **Air St. Barthélemy** (☎ 590/27-71-90 or 599/5-3150). **Air Guadeloupe** (☎ 590/27-61-90 or 599/5-4212) offers daily service from Espérance Airport in St. Martin. Air Guadeloupe also has direct flights to St. Barts from Guadeloupe and San Juan, while **Air St. Thomas** (☎ 590/27-71-76) operates daily flights between St. Barts and both St. Thomas and San Juan. You must re-confirm your return interisland flight, even during off-peak seasons, or you may very well lose your reservation. Be prepared to fly at a more convenient time for the airlines if they don't have enough passengers to justify a previously scheduled flight.

FROM THE AIRPORT

Airport taxi service costs $5–$20 (to the farthest hotel). Since the cabs are unmetered, you may be charged more if you make stops on the way. Cabs meet some flights, and a taxi dispatcher (☎ 590/27–66–31) is there some of the time, but if you plan to rent a car, which most people do, it's really easiest to do it at the airport. Many hotels offer free pickup and drop-off.

## Currency

The French franc is legal tender. Figure about 5F to the U.S. dollar. U.S. dollars are accepted in most establishments, but you may receive change in francs. Credit cards are accepted at most shops, hotels, and restaurants. Note: Prices quoted here are in U.S. dollars unless indicated otherwise.

## Emergencies

**Hospital: Gustavia Clinic** (☎ 590/27–60–35) is on the corner of rue Jean Bart and rue Sadi Carnot. For the doctor on call, dial 590/27–76–03. **Pharmacies:** There is a pharmacy in Gustavia on quai de la République (☎ 590/27–61–82) and one in St. Jean at the **La Savane Commercial Center** (☎ 590/27–66–61).

## Getting Around

CAR RENTALS

Most people opt to rent cars. There are excellent beaches, restaurants, and vistas all around the island. As you venture farther out on the island, beware the steep, curvy, haphazardly paved roads; get a map; and check the rental car's brakes before you drive away. The most common—and by far the most fun—rental car is the minimoke, a small open-air vehicle with a bumper-car feel. St. Barts drivers seem to be in some kind of unending grand prix and keep their minimokes maxed out at all times. Prepare yourself for cars charging every which way, making sudden changes in direction while honking wildly, and backing up at astonishingly high speeds. They pause for no one.

**Avis** (☎ 590/27–71–43), **Budget** (☎ 590/27–83–94), **Hertz** (☎ 590/27–71–14), and **Europcar** (☎ 590/27–73–33) are represented at the airport, among others. Check with several of the rental counters for the best price. All accept credit cards. You must have a valid driver's license, and in high season there may be a three-day minimum (or no cars available). During peak periods, like Christmas week and February, be sure to arrange for your car rental ahead of time. Your choices will most likely be limited to minimokes, Suzuki Jeeps, and open-sided Gurgels (VW four-wheel-drive vehicles)—all with stick shift only, which rent in season for about $50 a day—with unlimited mileage and limited collision insurance. A few hotels have their own car fleets, and you should rent a car at the time you make your room reservation. The choice of vehicles may be limited, but many hotels offer 24-hour emergency road service, which most rental companies do not. There are only two gas stations on the island, one near the airport and one in Lorient. They are not open after 5 PM or on Sunday, but you can use the one near the airport with a credit card at any time.

HITCHHIKING

Hitching rides is a popular, safe, legal, and interesting way to get around; it is widely practiced in the more heavily trafficked areas on the island.

MOTORBIKES

Motorbike companies rent motorbikes, scooters, mopeds, and mountain bikes. Motorbikes go for about $30 per day and require a $100 deposit. Call **Rent Some Fun** (☎ 590/27–70–59 or 590/27–83–05) and **St. Barth Motobike** (☎ 590/27–67–89).

TAXIS

Taxis are expensive and not particularly easy to arrange, especially in the evening. There are two taxi stations on the island, in Gustavia and at the airport, or call 590/27–66–31 or 590/27–75–81. There is a flat rate of 25F for rides up to five minutes long. Each additional three minutes is 20F. Usually, however, cabbies name a fixed rate—and will not budge. Fares are 50% higher from 8 PM to 6 AM and on Sunday and holidays.

## Guided Tours

Tours are by minibus or taxi. There are three tours offered by the tourist office (approximately 45 minutes, 1 hour, or 1½ hours in length); these are less expensive—about $10 per person for the shortest one—than private tours. A private five-hour island tour costs about $100 per vehicle (three to four people); an hour-long tour costs about $40 for up to three people and $50 for up to eight people. Itineraries are negotiable.

Tours can be arranged at hotel desks, through the tourist office, or through any of the island's taxi operators (☎ 590/27–66–31 in Gustavia; ☎ 590/27–75–81 at the airport). If you don't speak French, be sure to request a driver whose English is good; Stephane Brin (☎ 590/27–75–21) is highly recommended. **St. Barth's Services** (☎ 590/27–56–26, FAX 590/27–56–81) can arrange customized tours as well as take care of virtually any other needs you may have, including airline ticketing, maid service, private parties, etc. Helicopter tours are offered by **Trans Helico Caraibes** (☎ 590/27–40–68) for about $65 per person.

## Language

French is the official language, though a Norman dialect is spoken by some longtime islanders. Most hotel and restaurant employees speak some English—at least enough to help you find what you need.

## Opening and Closing Times

Businesses and offices close from noon to 2 during the week and are closed Saturday and Sunday. Shops are generally open weekdays 8:30–noon and 2–5, and Saturday 8:30–noon. Some of the shops across from the airport and in St. Jean also open on Saturday afternoon and until 7 PM on weekdays. The banks are open weekdays 8–noon and 2–3:30.

## Passports and Visas

U.S. and Canadian citizens need either a passport (one that expired no more than five years ago will suffice) or a notarized birth certificate with a raised seal accompanied by photo identification. A valid passport is required for stays of more than three months. British and other EU citizens need a national identity card. All visitors need a return or ongoing ticket.

## Precautions

Roads are frequently unmarked, so be sure to get a map. Instead of road signs, look for signs pointing to a destination. These will be nailed to posts at all crossroads. Roads are narrow and sometimes very steep, so check the brakes and gears of your rental car before you drive away.

Some hillside restaurants and hotels have steep entranceways and difficult steps that require a bit of climbing or negotiating. If this could be a problem for you, ask about accessibility ahead of time.

## Taxes and Service Charges

A 10F departure tax is charged for departure to other French islands, and a 16F departure tax is charged to all other destinations. Some hotels add a 10%–15% service charge to bills; others include it in their tariffs. Many restaurants include a 15% service charge in their published prices. Be sure to ask if service is included. It is especially important to remember this when your credit-card receipt is presented to be signed with the tip space blank (just draw a line through it), or you could end up paying a 30% service charge. Most taxi drivers own their vehicles and do not expect a tip.

## Telephones and Mail

To phone St. Barts from the United States, dial 011–590 and the local six-digit number. To call the United States from St. Barts, dial 19–1, the area code, and the local number. For St. Martin, dial just the six-digit number; for St. Maarten, dial 3 plus the five-digit number. For local information, dial 12. Public telephones do not accept coins; they accept Télécartes, a type of prepaid credit card that you can purchase from the post offices at Lorient, St. Jean, and Gustavia, as well as at the gas station next to the airport. Making an international call with a Télécarte is less expensive than making the call from your hotel.

Mail is slow. It can take up to three weeks for correspondence between the United States and the island. Post offices are in Gustavia, St. Jean, and Lorient. It costs 3.10F to mail a postcard to the United States, 3.90F to mail a letter.

## Visitor Information

Information can be obtained by writing the **French West Indies Tourist Board** (⊠ 610 5th Ave., New York, NY 10020) or by calling France-on-Call at 900/990–0040 (50¢ per minute). You can also write to or visit the U.S. branches of the **French Government Tourist Office** (⊠ 444 Madison Ave., 16th floor, New York, NY 10022; ⊠ 9454 Wilshire Blvd., Suite 303, Beverly Hills, CA 90212; ⊠ 645 N. Michigan Ave., Suite 3360, Chicago, IL 60611), and write, visit, or call the branches in Canada (⊠ 1981 McGill College Ave., Suite 490, Montréal, Québec H3A 2W9, ☎ 514/288–4264; ⊠ 30 St. Patrick St., Suite 700, Toronto, Ontario M5T 3A3, ☎ 416/593–4723) or the United Kingdom (⊠ 178 Piccadilly, London W1V OAL, ☎ 0171/629–9376).

The **Office du Tourisme** (☎ 590/27–87–27, FAX 590/27–74–47) is in a white-and-blue-trimmed building on the Gustavia pier; the people who work there are most eager to please. Hours are weekdays from 8:30 to 6 and Saturday from 9 to noon.

# 20 St. Eustatius

*Tiny St. Eustatius is ideal for those with a penchant for quiet times and strolls through history. Statia, as the island is called, was once one of the most powerful merchant centers in the Caribbean; today the island is home to remnants of those times in its forts, narrow cobblestone streets, and historic buildings. Of course, Statians themselves, among the most welcoming people in the region, are reason enough to visit.*

Updated by
Karl Luntta

**T**HE FLIGHT APPROACH to the tiny Dutch island of St. Eustatius, commonly known as Statia (pronounced *stay*-sha) in the Netherlands Antilles, is almost worth the visit itself. In the distance looms the Quill, an extinct volcano that encloses a stunning primeval rain forest within its crater. Although Statia is a dry island, the higher elevations are alive with untended greenery and abloom with flowers—bougainvillea, oleander, and hibiscus. Little 12-square-mi Statia, past which Columbus sailed in 1493, prospered almost from the day the Dutch Zeelanders colonized it in 1636. In the 1700s, a double row of warehouses crammed with goods stretched for a mile along the bay, and there were sometimes as many as 200 ships tied up at the duty-free port. The island was called the "Emporium of the Western World" and "Golden Rock." There were almost 8,000 Statians on the island in the 1790s (today, there are about 2,100). Holland, England, and France fought one another for possession of the island, which changed hands 22 times. In 1816 it became a Dutch possession and has remained so to this day.

During the American War of Independence, when the British blockaded the North American coast, food, arms, and other supplies for the American revolutionaries were diverted through the West Indies, notably through neutral Statia. (Benjamin Franklin had his mail routed through Statia to ensure its safe arrival in Europe.) On November 16, 1776, the brig-of-war *Andrew Doria,* commanded by Captain Isaiah Robinson of the Continental Navy, sailed into Statia's port flying the Stars and Stripes and fired a 13-gun salute to the Royal Netherlands standard. Governor Johannes de Graaff ordered the cannons of Fort Oranje to return the salute, and that first official acknowledgment of the new American flag by a foreign power earned Statia the nickname America's Childhood Friend. In retaliation, British admiral George Rodney attacked and destroyed the island in 1781. Statia has yet to recover its prosperity, which, ironically, ended partly because of the success of the American Revolution: The island was no longer needed as a transshipment port, and its bustling economy gradually came to a stop.

Statia is in the Dutch Windward Triangle, 178 mi east of Puerto Rico and 35 mi south of St. Maarten. Oranjestad, the capital and only "city" (note quotes), is on the western side facing the Caribbean. The island is anchored at the north and the south by extinct volcanoes, like the Quill, that are separated by a central, dry plain.

Statia is a playground for hikers and divers. Colorful coral reefs and myriad ancient ships rest on the ocean floor alongside 18th-century warehouses that were slowly buried in the sea by storms. Much of the aboveground activity has to do with archaeology and restoration; students from William and Mary's College of Archaeology converge on the island each summer, the University of Leiden in the Netherlands has a pre-Columbian program, and the island's Historical Foundation is actively engaged in restoring Statian landmarks. Statia is also a way station for oil, with a 16-million-barrel storage bunker encased in the Boven, an extinct volcano on the northern end of the island. On any given day, there will be several oil tankers at anchor waiting to give or receive the liquid gold.

Most visitors will be content with a day visit from nearby St. Maarten, exploring some of the historical sights and enjoying a meal at the Ocean View Terrace Restaurant. Those who stay longer tend to be collectors of unspoiled islands with a need to relax and a taste for history. Perhaps the locals are the best reason to visit this island. Statians are warm, welcoming, and happy to stop and chat. People still say hello to strangers here—when passing drivers beep or wave, return the gesture. This is one of the very few remaining islands where tourists will not feel that locals resent their perceived wealth and luxurious lifestyle. Statia is mindful of the potential gold mine of tourism and is making the necessary investments to restore the many historical buildings and forts, expand pier facilities, and improve the tourism infrastructure.

## Lodging

There are no luxury accommodations on Statia; as a rule, cheerful is the best you can expect. Many of the properties include breakfast, making most of them quite affordable.

| CATEGORY | COST* |
|---|---|
| $$$$ | over $125 |
| $$$ | $100–$125 |
| $$ | $75–$100 |
| $ | under $75 |

*All prices are for a standard double room, excluding 7% tax and 10%–15% service charge.*

### Hotels

$$ 🏨 **Golden Era Hotel.** This harbor-front hotel is in need of some sprucing up. Rooms are air-conditioned and motel-modern, with mini-refrigerators, TVs, phones, and simple, well-worn furniture. All have little terraces, but only half have a full or partial view of the sea; the rest look out over concrete or down onto the roof of the restaurant. There is little that is aesthetically attractive about this hotel, but at least it is central, by the water, and enjoys a cheerful clientele and an accommodating and friendly staff. ⊠ *Bay Rd., Box 109, Lower Town, Oranjestad,* ☎ *599/3–82345 or 800/223–9815,* 📠 *599/3–82445. 19 rooms, 1 suite. Restaurant, bar, air-conditioning, saltwater pool. AE, D, MC, V. EP.*

$$ 🏨 **La Maison sur la Plage.** The main attraction of this isolated area is the Atlantic, whose wild waters slap the 2-mi crescent of gray sand. The undertow for much of the strip here can be dangerous, but there is a safer area a few minutes' walk down the beach. The hotel's cozy lobby has well-worn rattan furnishings, a checkerboard on the coffee table, and shelves filled with weathered books. There's a stone-and-wood bar, and a very French dining room bordered by a trellis and greenery. Owners Therese and Michel Viali are slowly redecorating each of the five peach-color stucco cottages with pastel-print spreads and drapes, natural wood furnishings, and ceiling fans. Rooms do not have phones; some rooms have TV with VCRs. Continental breakfast is served on the porch of the main building, overlooking the water. ⊠ *Zeelandia Rd., Box 157, Zeelandia,* ☎ *599/3–82256,* 📠 *599/3–82831. 10 rooms. Restaurant, bar, fans, pool. MC, V. CP.*

$–$$ 🏨 **King's Well Hotel.** Perched on the cliffs between Upper Town and Lower
★ Town, this small hotel offers nine rooms, two of which are efficiencies. All rooms are pleasant but sparsely furnished, with a balcony, mini-refrigerator, TV, mosquito net, and bath with shower only; there are no phones. The four back rooms, which face the water, are more spacious, offer the best views, have ceiling fans, and feature queen-size waterbeds. The hotel is still in the first stages of renovation; a new dining area, more rooms, and a combination pool and Jacuzzi were under construction at press time. The owners, Win and Laura Piechutzki, an expatriate couple, hope to attract a sailing clientele; they will lease their yacht-charter license to interested parties and arrange sailing lessons. They also plan to open a small health spa, with massage and skin treatments. The

---

---

506

**St. Eustatius**

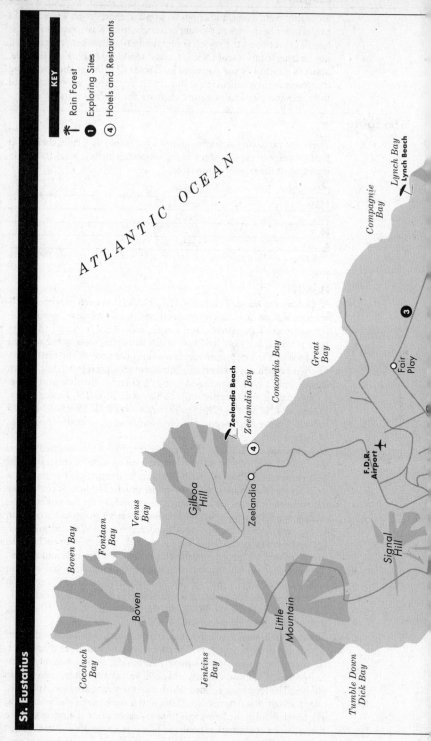

KEY

米 Rain Forest

❶ Exploring Sites

④ Hotels and Restaurants

ATLANTIC OCEAN

Cocoluch Bay

Boven Bay

Fontaan Bay

Venus Bay

Boven

Jenkins Bay

Gilboa Hill

Little Mountain

Tumble Down Dick Bay

Signal Hill

Zeelandia

Zeelandia Bay

Zeelandia Beach

④

F.D.R. Airport

Concordia Bay

Great Bay

Compagnie Bay

Lynch Bay

**Lynch Beach**

Fair Play

❸

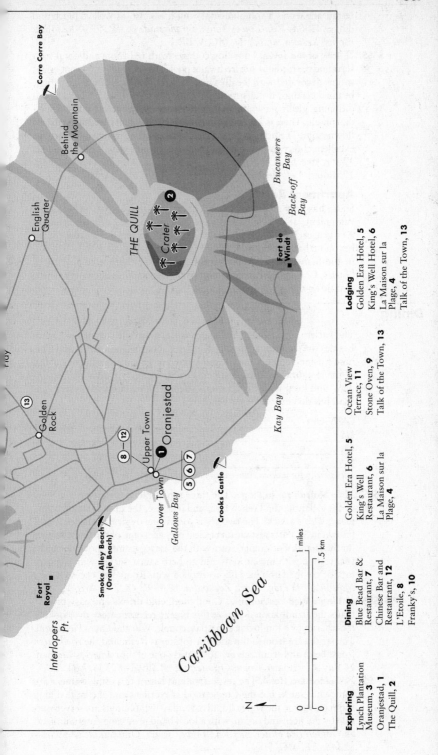

Corre Corre Bay

Behind the Mountain

English Quarter

THE QUILL

*Crater*

2

Bucaneers Bay

Back-off Bay

Fort de Windt ■

Golden Rock

13

Upper Town

Oranjestad

1

8 — 12

5 6 7

Lower Town

Gallows Bay

Kay Bay

Crooks Castle

Fort Royal ■

Smoke Alley Beach
(Oranje Beach)

Interlopers Pt.

Caribbean Sea

N

0        1 miles
0        1.5 km

**Exploring**
Lynch Plantation
Museum, **3**
Oranjestad, **1**
The Quill, **2**

**Dining**
Blue Bead Bar &
Restaurant, **7**
Chinese Bar and
Restaurant, **12**
L'Etoile, **8**
Franky's, **10**

Golden Era Hotel, **5**
King's Well
Restaurant, **6**
La Maison sur la
Plage, **4**

Ocean View
Terrace, **11**
Stone Oven, **9**
Talk of the Town, **13**

**Lodging**
Golden Era Hotel, **5**
King's Well Hotel, **6**
La Maison sur la
Plage, **4**
Talk of the Town, **13**

restaurant serves a complimentary full breakfast, as well as lunch and
dinner. ⊠ *Bay Rd., Lower Town, Oranjestad,* ☎ FAX *599/3–82538. 9
rooms. Restaurant, bar. D, MC, V. BP.*

**$–$$**   🏠 **Talk of the Town.** Four tidy cottages with red roofs and coral trim
★ surround the medium-size freshwater pool. They contain simple but bright
rooms decorated with locally handcrafted furnishings, dark carpeting,
beamed ceilings, floral spreads, and local art. All rooms have air-conditioning, gleaming white baths with shower only, cable TV, and direct-
dial phone. There is a poolside deck with lounge chairs, and a restaurant
downstairs. The hotel is on the road between the airport and town, an
excellent choice for those who don't need a water view. Children under
12 stay free. ⊠ *L. E. Saddlerweg,* ☎ *599/3–82236,* FAX *599/3–82640.
17 rooms, 3 efficiencies. Restaurant, bar, pool. AE, D, MC, V. CP.*

### Apartment Rentals

Statia has only a handful of apartments, though a spate of small developments and guest houses have gone up recently to meet demand.
As a general rule, figure $50 and under per night and don't expect much
beyond a bathroom and kitchenette. **Country Inn** (☎ 599/3–82484),
in Biesheuvelweg near the airport, is one of the newer apartment
houses. Check with the tourist office for information about apartment
rentals on the island.

# Dining

The variety of cuisines here is surprising, given the size of the island.
Besides the traditional West Indian fare, you can find French and Chinese cuisine. Don't come to Statia, however, for the cuisine or quality
of the restaurants. Your best bet is to eat local-style, that is, West Indian, and keep your expectations simple. All restaurants are very casual, but do cover up your beachwear.

| CATEGORY | COST* |
|---|---|
| $$$ | over $25 |
| $$ | $15–$25 |
| $ | under $15 |

*per person for a three-course meal, excluding drinks and service*

**$$$**   ✕ **La Maison sur la Plage.** The three top attractions here are the view
★ of the Atlantic, the French fare, and Therese, the grande dame of the
place, who's a kick. The two chefs (one is the owner; the other is well
known in St. Barts restaurant circles) prepare some of the finest cuisine
on the island. For dinner, start with the escargots and move on to the
veal terrine with mushrooms and an herb sauce, served with a pastry
top, or try the lamb medallions broiled with Roquefort cheese. ⊠ *La
Maison sur la Plage hotel, Zeelandia,* ☎ *599/3–82256. MC, V.*

**$$–$$$**   ✕ **King's Well Restaurant.** "Good food, cold drinks and easy prices"
reads the hand-painted sign at this breezy terrace eatery overlooking
the sea, run by a fun-loving expatriate couple, Win and Laura Piechutzki.
The steaks are from Colorado, the lobster is fresh, and the *rostbraten*
(roast beef) and schnitzels are authentic—one of the owners is German.
⊠ *Bay Rd., Lower Town, Oranjestad,* ☎ *599/3–82538. MC, V.*

**$$**   ✕ **Golden Era Hotel.** The restaurant and bar of this establishment are
somewhat stark, but the Creole food is excellent and the large dining
room is right on the water. Popular Sunday-night buffets are served outside by the pool and ocean, with a local band providing entertainment.
⊠ *Golden Era Hotel, Bay Rd., Lower Town, Oranjestad,* ☎ *599/3–
82345. AE, MC, V.*

**$$**   ✕ **Ocean View Terrace.** This patio spot in the courtyard next to the
★ tourist office serves sandwiches and burgers at lunch and local cuisine,
such as baked snapper with shrimp sauce, spicy chicken, and tender-

loin steak, at dinner. The courtyard is surrounded by the beautiful old stone fort and government buildings. The restaurant serves breakfast as well. ⊠ *Oranjestraat, Upper Town, Oranjestad,* ☏ *599/3–82733. No credit cards. No lunch Sun.*

**$$** ✕ **Talk of the Town.** Breakfast, lunch, and dinner are served at this pleasant restaurant midway between the airport and town. Pink tablecloths, an abundance of hanging plants, and softly seductive calypso music in the background weave a romantic spell. Local, Continental, and American dishes are offered, with seafood (predictably) the standout. Try the curried shrimp or the filet mignon. ⊠ *L. E. Saddlerweg, near Upper Town, Oranjestad,* ☏ *599/3–82236. AE, D, MC, V.*

**$–$$** ✕ **Blue Bead Bar & Restaurant.** A friendly Dutch expatriate couple runs
★ this restaurant with spectacular water views—don't miss a sunset cocktail here. Meals are served on a cheery bright blue- and yellow-trimmed veranda decked with potted plants; the fare runs the gamut of influences: West Indian, Indonesian, Dutch, Mexican, and American. The daily specials are recommended, as is anything made with chef-owner Phil Engeldorp's own *saté* sauce—a spicy, peanutty heaven. A steel band plays here on Saturday night; the bar swings long after the kitchen closes. ⊠ *Bay Rd., Lower Town, Oranjestad,* ☏ *599/3–82873. MC, V.*

**$** ✕ **Chinese Bar and Restaurant.** Owner Kim Cheng serves up tasty Asian and Caribbean dishes—*Bamigoreng* (Indonesian chow mein), pork chops Creole—in hearty portions at his unpretentious establishment. Dining indoors can be slightly claustrophobic, but just ask your waitress if you may tote your Formica-top table out onto the terrace. She'll probably be happy to lend a hand and then serve you under the stars. ⊠ *Prinsesweg, Upper Town, Oranjestad,* ☏ *599/3–82389. No credit cards.*

**$** ✕ **Franky's.** Come here for good local barbecue: ribs, chicken, lobster,
★ and fish served later than at most other places on Statia. Try the bull-foot soup and goat-water stew. The less adventurous can get pizza on the weekend, when there is live music. ⊠ *Ruyterweg, Upper Town, Oranjestad,* ☏ *599/3–82575. No credit cards.*

**$** ✕ **L'Etoile.** West Indian dishes, such as spicy stuffed land crab and goat meat, are served at this simple snack bar–restaurant. You can also order hot dogs, hamburgers, and spareribs. ⊠ *Heiligerweg, Upper Town, Oranjestad,* ☏ *599/3–82299. No credit cards.*

**$** ✕ **Stone Oven.** A Spanish couple runs this cozy little eatery, offering such West Indian specialties as "goat water" (goat stew). You can eat either indoors in the little house or outside on the palm-fringed patio. ⊠ *16A Feaschweg, Upper Town, Oranjestad,* ☏ *599/3–82543. No credit cards.*

## Beaches

Beachcombing is a sport for the intrepid: The beaches are pristine but tiny, unmaintained, and occasionally rocky. Sand is mainly volcanic black (actually varying shades of gray). The nicest strands are on the Atlantic side, but the surf is generally too rough for swimming. It is possible (but not recommended) to hike around the coast at low tide, though a car is advised to reach the more remote Atlantic stretches.

A big deal on the beaches here is searching for Statia's famed blue glass beads. Manufactured in the 17th century by the Dutch West Indies Company, the blue glass beads were traded for rum, slaves, cotton, and tobacco. They were also awarded to faithful slaves or included as a part of the groom's settlement by the bride's father. Although they are found only on Statia, some researchers believe that it was beads like these that were traded for Manhattan. They're best unearthed after a heavy rain, but as the locals chuckle, "If you find one, it's a miracle, man."

**Smoke Alley Beach** (also called **Oranje Beach**) is the nicest and most accessible. The beige-and-black-sand beach is on the Caribbean, off Lower Town, and is relatively deserted until late afternoon, when the locals arrive. A 30-minute hike down an easy, marked trail behind the Mountain Road will bring you to **Corre Corre Bay** and its gold-sand cove. Two bends north of Corre Corre Bay, **Lynch Bay** is somewhat protected from the wild swells. On the Atlantic side, especially around Concordia Bay, the surf is rough and there is sometimes a dangerous undertow, making beaches in this area better for sunning than swimming. **Zeelandia Beach** is a 2-mi strip of black sand on the Atlantic side. A dangerous undertow runs here, but a small section is considered okay for swimming. Plans are being made to construct a breakwater to make the area safer for swimming. As is, it's a lovely and deserted stretch for sunning, walking, and wading.

## Outdoor Activities and Sports

### Fishing
**Golden Rock Dive Center** (☎ FAX 599/3–82964) offers full- and half-day sportfishing trips for $500 and $350, respectively, including gear and bait.

### Hiking
Trails range from the easy to the "Watch out!" The big thrill here is the Quill, the 1,968-ft extinct volcano with its crater full of rain forest. Give yourself two to three hours to make the climb and the return. The tourist office has a list of 12 marked trails and can put you in touch with a guide (whose fee will be about $20). Wear layers: It can be cool on the summit and steamy in the interior. It is rumored that monkeys have taken up residence in the rain forest.

### Scuba Diving
Statia has more than 30 dive sites, including **Barracuda Reef,** where barracudas swim around colorful coral walls, and **Double Wreck,** where coral has taken on the shape of the two disintegrated ships. **Dive Statia** (☎ 599/3–82435 or 800/883–7222, FAX 599/3–82539), a fully equipped and PADI-certified dive shop offering certification courses, is operated by Rudy and Rinda Hees out of a warehouse just down the road from the Old Gin House. Several hotels offer dive packages with Dive Statia, including the Golden Era, King's Well, and Talk of the Town. Courses are also available in underwater photography, night diving, and multilevel diving. Among Statia's other dive shops are the **Golden Rock Dive Center** (☎ FAX 599/3–82964), another PADI facility, and **Blue Nature Water Sports** (☎ 599/3–82725, FAX 599/3–82756), at Cherry Tree.

### Snorkeling
Crooks Castle has several stands of pillar coral, giant yellow sea fans, and sea whips. Jenkins Bay and Venus Bay are other favorites with snorkelers. For equipment rental, contact **Dive Statia** (☎ 599/3–82435). Equipment rentals are about $20 per day.

### Spectator Sports
Cricket and soccer matches are played at the sports complex in Upper Town. Statia hosts teams from other Caribbean islands on weekends; admission is free. Call the office of the sports coordinator (☎ 599/3–82209) for schedules.

### Tennis
There are two lighted tennis courts at the **community center** (☎ 599/3–82249); the center has changing rooms, but you'll have to bring your own rackets and balls. The cost is $2 per hour. Check with the tourist office for more information. (Volleyball and basketball are also played here.)

# Shopping

Though shopping on Statia is duty-free, it is also somewhat limited. A handful of shops do offer unusual items, however. **Mazinga Gift Shop** on Fort Oranjestraat in Upper Town (☎ 599/3–82245) is a small department store of sorts. It has duty-free jewelry, cosmetics, and liquor, in addition to beachwear, sports gear, stationery, film, books, and magazines. The **Paper Corner** (✉ Van Tonningenweg, Upper Town, ☎ 599/3–82208) sells magazines, a few books, and stationery supplies. Check out the **Fun Shop** (✉ Van Tonningenweg, Upper Town, ☎ 599/3–82253) for toys and souvenirs.

# Nightlife

Statia's local bands stay busy on weekends. **Talk of the Town** (☎ 599/3–82236) is the place to be for live music on Sunday night. **Cool Corner** (☎ 599/3–82523), a tiny corner bar in the heart of town, across from the St. Eustatius Historical Foundation Museum, is a lively after-work and weekend hangout. The **Exit Disco** (☎ 599/3–82543), at the Stone Oven restaurant, has dancing on weekends and occasionally hosts live bands. Sometimes the **community center** (☎ 599/3–82249) has a dance. Crowds are found all weekend at **Franky's Place** (☎ 599/3–82575), in the heart of town on the Ruyterweg. Its West Indian fare is very popular. The **Lago Heights Club and Disco** (no phone), at the shopping center in Chapelpiece, is known to all as Gerald's and has dancing and a late-night barbecue.

# Exploring St. Eustatius

Statia is an arid island consisting of a valley between two mountain peaks. Most everything to see lies in the valley, making touring the island easy. From the airport, you can rent a car or take a taxi and be in historic Oranjestad in minutes; those who want to hike the Quill, Statia's highest peak, can drive to the trailhead in under 15 minutes from just about anywhere on the island.

*Numbers in the margin correspond to points of interest on the St. Eustatius map.*

SIGHTS TO SEE

❸ **Lynch Plantation Museum.** Also known as the Berkel Family Plantation, this museum, out in Lynch Bay, is the only domestic museum in the Dutch Caribbean. It consists of two one-room buildings, set up as they were almost 100 years ago. There's a remarkable collection preserving this family's history—family pictures, Bibles, spectacles, a sewing machine, original furniture, and some farming and fishing implements give a detailed perspective of life in Statia. Ismael Berkel guides tours of the houses, and if you ask, he may proudly show you his two medals of honor from the Dutch royal families for his conservation efforts. Be sure to sign the guest register. You'll need either a taxi or a car to visit, and it's well worth the trouble. ✉ *Lynch Bay;* ☎ *599/3–82209 to arrange tour.* 🎫 *Free; donations accepted.*

❶ **Oranjestad.** Statia's capital and only town sits on the western coast facing the Caribbean. It's a split-level town: Upper Town and Lower Town. History buffs will enjoy poking around the ancient Dutch colonial buildings, which are being restored by the historical foundation. Both Upper Town and Lower Town are easily explored on foot. At the **tourist office,** right at the entrance to Fort Oranje, you can pick up maps, brochures, and friendly advice, as well as a listing of 12 marked hiking trails. You can also arrange for guides and guided tours.

With its three bastions, **Fort Oranje** has clutched these cliffs since 1636. In 1976 Statia participated in the U.S. bicentennial celebration by restoring the old fort, and now the black cannons point out over the ramparts. In the parade grounds a plaque, presented in 1939 by Franklin D. Roosevelt, reads, "Here the sovereignty of the United States of America was first formally acknowledged to a national vessel by a foreign official." The post office used to be in the fort but burned in 1991. There are plans under way to rebuild the structure to house boutiques and restaurants.

In the center of Upper Town is the award-winning **St. Eustatius Historical Foundation Museum.** It's set in the Doncker house, a lovely building with slim columns and a high gallery. British admiral Rodney set up his headquarters here during the American Revolution, while he was stealing everything from gunpowder to port in retaliation for Statia's gallant support of the fledgling country. The house, acquired by the foundation in 1983 and completely restored, is Statia's most important intact 18th-century dwelling. Exhibits trace the island's history from the 6th century to the present. The basement exhibit details Statia's pre-Columbian history with the results of archaeological digs on the island. Statia is the only island thus far where ruins and artifacts of the Saladoid, a newly discovered tribe, have been excavated. ⊠ *3 Wilhelminaweg,* ☎ *599/3–82288.* ⌫ *$2.* ☯ *Weekdays 9–5, weekends 9–noon.*

The **Dutch Reformed church,** on Kerkweg (Church Way), was built in 1775. It has been partially restored and has lovely stone arches facing the sea. Ancient tales can be read on the gravestones in the 18th-century cemetery adjacent to the church. On Synagogepad (Synagogue Path) off Kerkweg is **Honen Dalim** ("She Who Is Charitable to the Poor"), one of the Caribbean's oldest synagogues. Dating from 1738, it is now in ruins but is slated for restoration by groups from the United States and Holland.

NEED A BREAK?
> The **Cool Corner** (☎ 599/3–82523), just up from the tourist office, is a cool spot to have a beer and catch up on island gossip. The menu features inexpensive Chinese cuisine. It's open Monday to Saturday 7 AM– 2 AM. For sandwiches, pizzas, or pastries, wander over to the **Sandbox Tree Bakery** (☎ 599/3–82469) just behind the synagogue on Kerkweg. It's open weekdays 5:30 AM–7 PM and Saturday 5:30 AM–1 PM.

**Lower Town** sits below Fort Oranjestraat (Fort Orange St.) and some steep cliffs and is reached from Upper Town on foot via the zigzagging, cobblestone Fort Road or by car via Van Tonningenweg. Warehouses and shops that in the 18th century were piled high with European imports are now either abandoned or simply used to store local fishermen's equipment and house Dive Statia. The **Old Gin House,** a restored 18th-century cotton mill, on the land side of Bay Road, was the best hotel on Statia but is now closed and at press time was slated to reopen under new management in the near future. The palms, flowering shrubs, and park benches along the water's edge are the work of the historical foundation members. All along the beach are the crumbling ruins of 18th-century buildings, dating from Statia's period of prosperity. The sea, which has slowly advanced since then, now surrounds many of the ruins, making for fascinating snorkeling.

➋ **The Quill.** This 1,968-ft-high extinct volcano encloses a primeval rain forest within its crater. Hikers will want to head here to see giant elephant ears, ferns, flowers, wild orchids, fruit trees, wildlife, and birds hiding in the trees. The volcanic cone rises in the southern sector of the island, 3 mi south of Oranjestad on the main road. Local boys go up to the Quill by torchlight to catch delectable sand crabs. You can join them and ask your hotel to prepare your catch for dinner. The tourist board will make arrangements.

## St. Eustatius A to Z

### Arriving and Departing

BY PLANE

**Windward Islands Airways** (✉ Winair, ☎ 599/5–54210 or 800/634–4907) makes the 20-minute flight from St. Maarten five times a day, the 10-minute flight from Saba daily, and the 15-minute flight from St. Kitts twice a week. Be sure to confirm your flight a day or two in advance, as schedules can change abruptly.

FROM THE AIRPORT

Planes put down at the **Franklin Delano Roosevelt Airport,** where taxis meet all flights and charge about $3.50 for the drive into town. There's an Avis outlet at the airport, should you decide to rent a car.

### Currency

U.S. dollars are accepted everywhere, but legal tender is the Netherlands Antilles florin (NAf), also referred to as the guilder, and you shouldn't be surprised to receive change in them. The exchange rate fluctuates slightly but was about NAf1.80 to US$1 at press time. Prices quoted here are in U.S. dollars unless noted otherwise. **Windward Islands Bank** and **Barclays Bank** are the two main banks on the island.

### Emergencies

**Police:** ☎ 599/3–82333. **Hospital: Queen Beatrix Medical Center** (✉ 25 Prinsesweg, ☎ 599/3–82211 or 599/3–82371) has a full-time licensed physician on duty.

### Getting Around

To explore the island (and there isn't very much), car rentals are available through the **Avis** (☎ 599/3–82421 or 800/331–1084) outlet at the airport. **Rainbow Car Rental** (☎ 599/3–82811) has several Hyundais for rent. **Brown's** (☎ 599/3–82266) and **Walter's** (☎ 599/3–82719) rent cars and Jeeps. Statia's roads are pocked with potholes, and the going is slow and bumpy. Goats and cattle have the right of way.

### Guided Tours

All 10 of Statia's taxis are available for island tours. A two- to three-hour outing costs $35 per vehicle of four (extra persons are $5 each), usually including airport transfer. One of the better taxi tour operators is driver/historian **Josser Daniel** (☎ 599/3–82358); ask him to show you his recent citation from President Clinton for rescuing an American tourist from drowning. As well, call **Rainbow Taxis** (☎ 599/3–82811) for pickups or island tours.

The **St. Eustatius Historical Foundation Museum** (☎ 599/3–82288) sells a sightseeing package, which includes a guided walking tour, a booklet detailing the sights on the tour, and museum admission. The tour begins in Lower Town at the Marina and ends at the museum. You can take the tour on your own with the book (there are corresponding numbered blue signs on most of the sights), but a guide may prove more illuminating.

### Language

Statia's official language is Dutch (it's used on government documents), but everyone speaks English. Dutch is taught as the primary language in the schools, and street signs are in both Dutch and English.

## Opening and Closing Times

Most offices are open weekdays 8–noon and 1–4 or 5. Stores are open 8–6, and grocery markets often stay open until 7. **Barclays Bank** is open Thursday 8:30–3:30, Friday 8:30–12:30 and 2–4:30; **Windward Islands Bank** is open weekdays 8–noon with extra hours on Friday 2–4:30. Both banks are in Upper Town.

## Passports and Visas

All visitors must have proof of citizenship. A passport is preferred, but a birth certificate or voter registration card will do. (A driver's license will *not* do.) British citizens need a valid passport. All visitors need a return or ongoing ticket.

## Taxes and Service Charges

Hotels collect a 7% government tax and a 10%–15% service charge. Most restaurants add a 10%–15% service charge. The departure tax is $5 for flights to other islands of the Netherlands Antilles and $10 to foreign destinations. In addition, you'll probably be asked to contribute your leftover guilders to the latest cause.

## Telephones and Mail

Statia has microwave telephone service to all parts of the world. To call Statia from the United States, dial 011–599/3 + the local number, which always begins with 8. When calling interisland, dial only the five-digit number. Direct dial is available. There are two pay phones on the island, one near the airport and one in Landsradio. Airmail letters to the United States are NAf2.25; postcards, NAf.1.10.

## Visitor Information

For help planning your trip, contact the **Statia Tourist Office** (⊠ Box 6322, Boca Raton, FL 33427-6322, ☎ 561/394–8580 or 800/722–2394, FAX 561/488–4294), which is very willing to advise you on any aspect of planning a trip to Statia.

Once on the island, the **tourist board** (⊠ 3 Fort Oranjestraat, ☎ 599/3–82213, ☎ FAX 599/3–82433), at the entrance to Fort Oranje, can provide you with a map and help arrange guided tours. Office hours are weekdays 8–noon and 1–5.

# 21 St. Kitts and Nevis

*These sister islands have developed a sibling rivalry for an increasingly upscale market, thanks to their uncrowded beaches, lush rain forests, historic ruins, and lovingly restored 18th-century plantation inns.*

Updated by
Jordan Simon

**F**OR YEARS, VISITORS TO ST. KITTS AND NEVIS have tended to be self-sufficient types who know how to amuse themselves and appreciate the warmth and character of country inns. The Frigate Bay area of St. Kitts is the only area with a few larger hotels and condominium developments, while the Four Seasons became Nevis's first resort in 1991.

Mountainous St. Kitts, the first English settlement in the Leeward Islands, crams some stunning scenery into its 65 square mi. Vast, brilliant green fields of sugarcane sweep down to the sea. The island is fertile and lush with tropical flora and has some fascinating natural and historical attractions: a rain forest, replete with waterfalls, thick vines, and secret trails; a central mountain range, dominated by the 3,792-ft Mt. Liamuiga, whose crater has long been dormant; and Brimstone Hill, the Caribbean's most impressive fortress, which was known in the 17th century as the Gibraltar of the West Indies.

The island is home to 35,000 people and hosts some 60,000 visitors annually. The shape of St. Kitts has been variously compared to a whale, a cricket bat, and a guitar. It's roughly oval, 19 mi long and 6 mi wide, with a narrow peninsula trailing off toward Nevis, 2 mi southeast across the strait.

The island is known as the mother colony of the West Indies because it was from here that the English settlers sailed to Antigua, Barbuda, Tortola, and Montserrat and that the French dispatched colonizing parties to Martinique, Guadeloupe, St. Martin, St. Barts, La Désirade, and Les Saintes. The French, who inexplicably brought a bunch of African green vervet monkeys with them as pets (which now outnumber residents, according to unofficial census), arrived on St. Kitts a few years after the British. As rich in history as it is fertile and lush with tropical flora, St. Kitts is just beginning to develop its tourism industry, and this quiet member of the Leeward group has that rare combination of natural and historic attractions and fine sailing, island hopping, and water sports.

In 1493, when Columbus spied a cloud-crowned volcanic isle during his second voyage to the New World, he named it *Nieves,* the Spanish word for "snows." It reminded him of the snowcapped peaks of the Pyrenees. Nevis (pronounced *nee*-vis) rises out of the water in an almost perfect cone, the tip of its 3,232-ft central mountain smothered in clouds. It's even less developed than its sister island, St. Kitts.

Nevis is known for its natural beauty—long beaches with white and black sand, lush greenery—for a half dozen mineral-spa baths, and for the restored sugar plantations that now house small, charming inns. In 1628 settlers from St. Kitts sailed across the 2-mi channel that separates the two islands. At first they grew tobacco, cotton, ginger, and indigo, but with the introduction of sugarcane in 1640, Nevis became the island equivalent of a boomtown. As the mineral baths were drawing crowds, the island was producing an abundance of sugar. Slaves were brought from Africa to work on the magnificent estates, many of them nestled high in the mountains amid lavish tropical gardens.

The restored plantation homes that now operate as inns are both islands' most sybaritic lures for the leisurely life. There is plenty of activity for the energetic—mountain climbing, swimming, tennis, horseback riding, snorkeling. But the going is easy here, with hammocks for snoozing, lobster bakes on palm-lined beaches, and candlelit dinners in stately dining rooms and on romantic verandas. Each inn, run by

British or American expatriates, has its own distinct ambience, thanks to the delightful, often eccentric owners.

Nevis is linked with St. Kitts politically. The two islands, together with Anguilla, achieved self-government as an Associated State of Great Britain in 1967. In 1983 St. Kitts and Nevis became a fully independent nation. Nevis papers sometimes run fiery articles advocating independence from St. Kitts, and the sister islands may separate someday. However, it's not likely that a shot will be fired, let alone one that will be heard around the world.

# ST. KITTS

## Lodging

St. Kitts has an appealing variety of places to stay—beautifully restored plantation inns, full-service hotels, simple beachfront cottage colonies, and an all-inclusive hotel. There are also a number of guest houses and self-catering condominiums available.

| CATEGORY | COST* |
|----------|-------|
| $$$$ | over $300 |
| $$$ | $225–$300 |
| $$ | $125–$225 |
| $ | under $125 |

*All prices are for a standard double room, excluding 7% tax and 10% service charge.*

$$$$ ★ **Golden Lemon.** Arthur Leaman, a former decorating editor for *House and Garden,* created and runs this internationally famous, quiet retreat at the isolated north end of the island. The eight rooms in the restored 17th-century great house are each impeccably decorated. There are canopied, wrought-iron, and four-poster beds swaddled in mosquito netting; armoires; chaise longues; rocking chairs; and a variety of stunning fabrics in delectable shades from mango to raspberry. You can also stay in a one- or two-bedroom town house with a wraparound terrace and kitchenette (some have a private pool). These are decorated with an eclectic yet harmonious blend of West Indian crafts, antiques, and artwork culled from Leaman's world travels. The cool, dark, well-appointed bar and lounge offer a peaceful respite from the bright sun, and the restaurant, which serves Continental cuisine with West Indian touches, is one of the best on the island. A gray-sand beach, guarded by rusty cannonballs and shaded by spindly, elegant palms, offers views of St. Martin shimmering in the distance. The hotel allows no children under 18. ✉ *Box 17, Dieppe Bay,* ☎ *869/465–7260 or 800/633–7411,* FAX *869/465–4019. 32 rooms and suites. Restaurant, pool, tennis court, shop. AE, MC, V. MAP.*

$$$$ ★ **Ottley's Plantation Inn.** This former sugar plantation has been transformed into a spectacularly elegant inn. Nestled at the foot of Mt. Liamuiga, on 35 manicured acres that border a rain forest, it has views that sweep out to the wild Atlantic. The beautiful, 18th-century, English colonial–style great house and cut-stone cottages hold 15 spacious guest rooms, many with high ceilings and white wood floors, and decorated with an eclectic mix of white wicker, antiques, and floral-print fabrics. The cottages, with exquisite old tile and stonework and English country house decor, are a honeymoon heaven. The 65-ft spring-fed pool stretches out from the remaining walls of the sugar factory, with an open-air bar at one end and the alfresco Royal Palm restaurant along one side. Take a stroll on the property's rain-forest trail, one of whose forks leads to a magnificent, sprawling banyan tree with

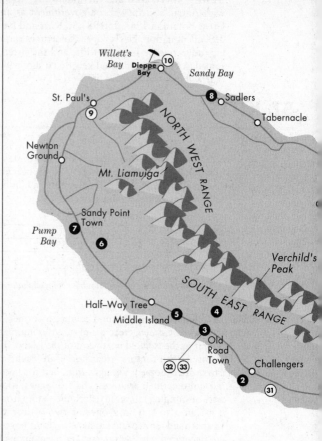

St. Kitts

Willett's Bay
Dieppe Bay — 10
Sandy Bay
St. Paul's
9
8 Sadlers
Tabernacle
Newton Ground
NORTH WEST RANGE
Mt. Liamuiga
Sandy Point Town
7
Pump Bay
6
Verchild's Peak
SOUTH EAST RANGE
Half-Way Tree
Middle Island 5
4
3
Old Road Town
Challengers
32 33
2
31

Caribbean Sea

**KEY**
Ferry
1 Exploring Sites
8 Hotels and Restaurants

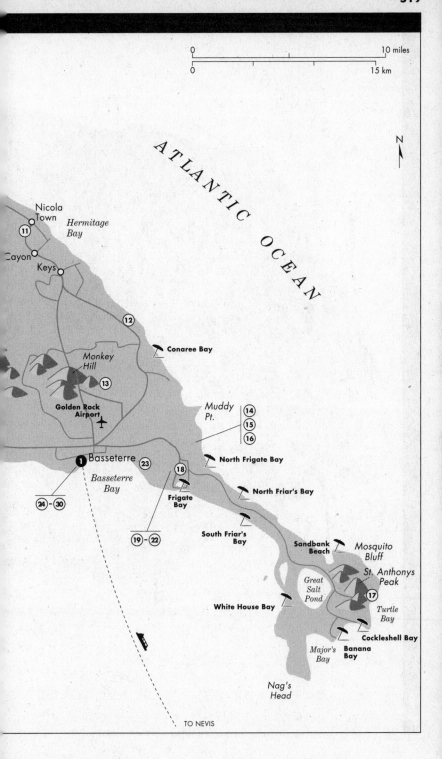

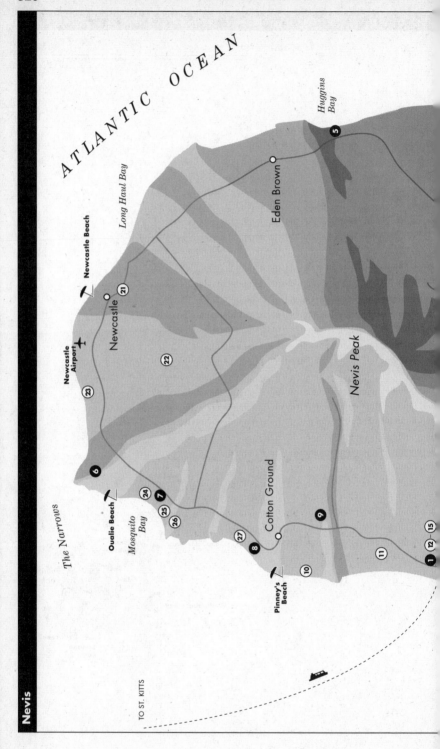

Nevis

ATLANTIC OCEAN

Huggins Bay

Eden Brown

Long Haul Bay

Newcastle Beach

Newcastle Airport

Newcastle

Nevis Peak

The Narrows

Oualie Beach

Mosquito Bay

Cotton Ground

Pinney's Beach

TO ST. KITTS

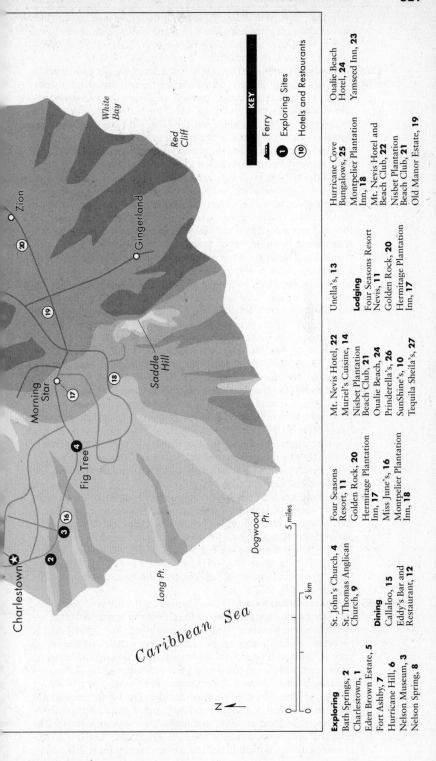

521

**Exploring**
Bath Springs, **2**
Charlestown, **1**
Eden Brown Estate, **5**
Fort Ashby, **7**
Hurricane Hill, **6**
Nelson Museum, **3**
Nelson Spring, **8**

St. John's Church, **4**
St. Thomas Anglican Church, **9**

**Dining**
Callaloo, **15**
Eddy's Bar and Restaurant, **12**

Four Seasons Resort, **11**
Golden Rock, **20**
Hermitage Plantation Inn, **17**
Miss June's, **16**
Montpelier Plantation Inn, **18**

Mt. Nevis Hotel, **22**
Muriel's Cuisine, **14**
Nisbet Plantation Beach Club, **21**
Oualie Beach, **24**
Prinderella's, **26**
SunShine's, **10**
Tequila Sheila's, **27**

Unella's, **13**

**Lodging**
Four Seasons Resort Nevis, **11**
Golden Rock, **20**
Hermitage Plantation Inn, **17**

Hurricane Cove Bungalows, **25**
Montpelier Plantation Inn, **18**
Mt. Nevis Hotel and Beach Club, **22**
Nisbet Plantation Beach Club, **21**
Old Manor Estate, **19**

Oualie Beach Hotel, **24**
Yamseed Inn, **23**

**KEY**
Ferry
Exploring Sites
Hotels and Restaurants

roots like playground slides. The engaging owners or their (grown) kids are always available to help. There's a shuttle to the beach or into town. ⊠ *Box 345, Ottley's,* ☎ *869/465–7234 or 800/772–3039,* FAX *869/465–4760. 15 rooms. Restaurant, bar, pool. AE, MC, V. MAP.*

$$$$      🏨 **Rawlins Plantation.** This lovely inn, a former sugar plantation, is
★        fairly isolated, on 20 acres at the northern end of the island (the no-toriously bumpy, rutted dirt access road emphasizes the wilderness feel). The views are spectacular: on one side of the inn, lush greenery climbs to the peak of Mt. Liamuiga; on the other side, the Caribbean sea stretches out to the island of Statia. Hammocks are slung among the pear and almond trees, and the plantation's original copper syrup vats crop up everywhere you look. Ten rooms, each with bath, are scattered across the lavishly landscaped grounds in various restored buildings of the old estate (including the original sugar mill). You'll find mahogany four-poster beds, wicker chairs, hardwood floors, and fabrics in soft pastel prints. The charming owners, Claire and Paul Rawson, admit they use their annual trips to London as an excuse to redecorate. There is no air-conditioning, but all units have ceiling fans and good cross-ventilation. The restaurant, well known on the island for its Continental Caribbean cuisine, is also decorated with antiques. Claire is so fanatic about food that she is instituting special "A Taste of St. Kitts" weeks, which will include Caribbean cooking classes, trips to the local market, lessons in herbal folklore, and the like. You can also take a stroll to the studio of Kate Spencer (an expat Brit who's become the leading local artist), which sits on the estate. This is a great place to get away from it all. ⊠ *Box 340, Mt. Pleasant,* ☎ *869/465–6221 or 800/346–5358,* FAX *869/465–4954. 10 rooms. Restaurant, pool, fans, 8 tennis courts, croquet, laundry service. AE, MC, V. MAP.*

$$$$      🏨 **White House.** Three radiant acres of flowering gardens and mani-cured lawns surround this small, secluded property in the foothills above Basseterre. There are views of the Caribbean in the distance, but you'll have to take a 10-minute ride in the hotel's shuttle to get to the beach. You'll be greeted by three bounding English boxers (they're actually lambs), then by the gracious owners, Janice and Malcolm Barber. The 18th-century plantation great house has been beautifully restored, and the stable and carriage house have been rebuilt. The tasteful, unclut-tered bedrooms have hardwood floors and are decorated with 19th-century antiques, mahogany beds (many are four-poster), and Laura Ashley fabrics. Janice and Malcolm have worked hard to duplicate an authentic plantation experience (albeit with plumbing and electricity). There is no air-conditioning, but all rooms have ceiling fans. ⊠ *Box 436, St. Peter's,* ☎ *869/465–8162 or 800/223–1108,* FAX *869/465–8275. 10 rooms. Restaurant, bar, fans, pool, tennis court, croquet, laun-dry service. AE, MC, V. MAP.*

$$$–$$$$   🏨 **Horizons Villas Resort.** These gleaming coral-white-and-jade villas, most affording stunning views of the Caribbean and/or Atlantic, are meticulously maintained. The smaller one-bedroom villas have an enormous terrace; the larger three-bedroom units include a private plunge pool. All offer every conceivable amenity, from full kitchen (including dishwasher, and thoughtful touches like beer mugs left in the freezer) and huge bathtubs fit for a Roman emperor to washer-dryer, VCR, and CD player. The individually owned and decorated units favor sooth-ing pink, olive, teal, and taupe tones, with rattan and blond-wood fur-nishings, vivid local artwork, and immaculate white tile floors. The pool-grill area is uncommonly pleasant, Frigate Bay Beach is a two-minute walk down the hill, and the golf course is a short drive away. Twenty-eight more villas, another pool, and a restaurant are scheduled for completion in 1998. ⊠ *Box 1143, Basseterre,* ☎ *869/465–0584*

or 800/830–9069, FAX 869/465–0785. 46 units (only a few in rental pool at any given time). Restaurant, grill, 2 pools. AE, D, MC, V.

**$$–$$$**  🏨 **Jack Tar Village Beach Resorts and Casino.** A lively atmosphere pervades this bargain-basement but appealing all-inclusive resort, whose motto could well be "Moderate prices, but nothing in moderation." Sports of all sorts are available, and each day has a schedule of recreational activities and contests. Two pools are a nice touch: One is for the volleyball and water-aerobics crowd, the other for those who want a quiet, relaxing dip. Nightly live entertainment, a disco, and the island's only casino keep the action going late into the night. Guest rooms are freshly decorated with floral linens, boating prints, and jade carpets; all rooms were thoroughly renovated following Hurricanes Luis and Marilyn in 1996. Each room has a small terrace or balcony, but there are no water views from any of them (unless you count water hazards on the golf course, or a sliver of ocean from some top-floor rooms). The restaurants are noted for their theme buffets, as well as for solid Continental and Creole fare. ⊠ Box 406, Frigate Bay, ☎ 869/465–8651 or 800/999–9182, FAX 869/465–8651. 240 rooms, 2 suites. 2 restaurants, bars, 2 pools, beauty salon, massage, spa, 4 tennis courts, aerobics, basketball, health club, Ping-Pong, shuffleboard, dive shop, water sports, shops, casino, nightclub, baby-sitting. AE, D, DC, MC, V. All-inclusive.

**$$**  🏨 **Bird Rock Beach Resort.** Perched on a bluff overlooking its own poky beach, a few miles from the airport and downtown, this rather plain-looking resort consists of several two-story buildings. The ordinary yet satisfactory tile-floored rooms are furnished with rattan and wicker furniture, floral fabrics, and paintings of birds. Rooms and suites have balcony and ocean views, and the suites also have kitchenettes and sofa beds, making them an excellent family value. An informal, alfresco dining room with views of Basseterre turns out Continental favorites with local ingredients. Golf and the larger Frigate Bay beaches are just five minutes away (there's a shuttle), but there is particularly excellent snorkeling and diving in the waters just off the resort's golden-sand cove. The staff is most hospitable, and the invigorating mix of young Europeans on a budget and divers from around the world gives Bird Rock an international flavor and flair. ⊠ Box 227, Basseterre, ☎ 869/465–8914 or 800/621–1270, FAX 869/465–1675. 38 units. Restaurant, 2 bars, grill, air-conditioning, kitchenettes, 2 pools, tennis court, beach, dive shop, shop. AE, DC, MC, V. EP, MAP.

**$$**  🏨 **Colony's Timothy Beach Resort.** If you don't mind trading a bit of atmosphere for modern comfort at a good price, this could well be the ideal spot for a beach-oriented vacation. The management is attentive and friendly at this casual hotel, set at the end of Frigate Bay beach, overlooking the Caribbean. Simple beige-stucco buildings hold comfortable, adequately furnished rooms and suites. Larger units have kitchens and multiple bedrooms. Opt to stay in one of the original buildings, which sit right on the beach; they have better views than the most recent additions and are larger and airier. You can choose from a wide variety of sports activities. Greens fees for the nearby golf course are included in the room rate. The hotel's Coconut Cafe is a local favorite. ⊠ Box 81, Frigate Bay, ☎ 869/465–8597 or 800/838–5375, FAX 869/465–7723. 60 rooms. Restaurant, air-conditioning, pool, water sports. AE, MC, V. EP.

**$$**  🏨 **Frigate Bay Beach Hotel.** The third fairway of the island's golf course adjoins this property (guests get discounts on greens fees), and the two nearby beaches—Caribbean and Atlantic—are reached by complimentary shuttle buses (the Caribbean beach is also easily reached by following the path from the far end of the pool, along the edge of the golf course). The whitewashed buildings contain standard rooms

as well as condominium units with fully equipped kitchens. There are
hillside and poolside units; the latter have nicer views and fresher ambience but tend to be noisier. Rooms and condos have beige or navy
tile floors and are decorated with floral linens and sailing prints. All
have ceiling fans and sliding glass doors leading to a terrace or balcony. There's an Olympic-size pool with swim-up bar and a terraced
restaurant overlooking the pool, where raucous buffet theme nights
with live music are the rule. ⊠ *Box 137, Basseterre,* ☎ *869/465–8935
or 800/468–3750,* FAX *869/465–7050. 64 rooms. Restaurant, bar,
fans, pool. AE, D, MC, V. EP, MAP.*

**$$**  ⊞ **Ocean Terrace Inn.** Referred to locally as OTI, this is a rarity: a stylish,
★  intimate business hotel. The main building—which houses the fancier
restaurant, reception, a pool with a swim-up bar, and many of the
rooms—is set high on a hill overlooking the ocean, amid lovingly
tended gardens dotted with gazebos. Even the bar areas are distinc-
tive, with African masks, aquariums, screeching birds, and brilliantly
back-lit murals of cavorting dancers and drummers. One- and two-bed-
room condos are farther down the hill but also have water views. All
are handsomely decorated in rattan and bright fabrics. Fisherman's
Wharf, on the waterfront at the bottom of the hill, is a casual seafood
restaurant. The hotel's Pelican Cove Marina has its own fleet of boats
that you can take out or charter. There is a daily shuttle to nearby beaches.
New ownership plans to expand over the next few years but vows to
retain the hotel's cozy appeal. ⊠ *Box 65, Basseterre,* ☎ *869/465–2754
or 800/524–0512,* FAX *869/465–1057. 54 units. 2 restaurants, 2 bars,
air-conditioning, 2 pools, outdoor hot tub, water sports, 2 shops. AE,
MC, V. EP, MAP.*

**$$**  ⊞ **Sun 'n' Sand Beach Village.** American and British families come to
stay at this simple complex is on the beach at North Frigate Bay, on
the Atlantic side of the island. Studios in two-story buildings and two-
bedroom, self-catering units in pretty, Antillean-style wood-and-stucco
cottages stretch back from the beach. Decor is simple and tropical, with
rattan furnishings, island prints and batiks, and beige tile floors. Studios have twin or queen-size beds, bath with shower, and a private terrace. The cottages have a convertible sofa in the living room and a fully
equipped kitchen; there's a window air conditioner in the bedroom and
a ceiling fan in the living room. ⊠ *Box 341, Frigate Bay,* ☎ *869/465–
8037 or 800/223–6510,* FAX *869/465–6745. 32 studios, 18 2-bed-
room cottages. Restaurant, bar, grocery, air-conditioning, pool, wading
pool, 2 tennis courts, beach, shop. AE, D, MC, V. CP, MAP.*

**$–$$**  ⊞ **Fort Thomas Hotel.** The Canadian owners of this hotel, which has
long been popular with business travelers and tour groups, have sunk
a great deal of money into much-needed renovations. The original hotel
is built on the site of an old fort, on a hillside overlooking Basseterre
and the harbor. Unfortunately, the cannons anchoring the driveway and
a few ramparts scattered about the grounds near the pool are the only
reminders of its storied past. The building resembles an antiseptic
stateside motel, but the owners have softened it by adding "colonial"
touches like gingerbread trim and arched picture windows. The rooms
are spacious, with seashell colors and wicker furnishings. The second-
floor rooms have far better views and are worth the minimal surcharge. The pool has great views of Basseterre and the ocean, which
can also be enjoyed from canopied porch swings and gingerbread
gazebos. There's a free shuttle bus to the Frigate Bay beaches, and the
hotel is within walking distance of town and the stores at Pelican
Mall. ⊠ *Box 407, Basseterre,* ☎ *869/465–2695,* FAX *869/465–7518.
64 rooms. Restaurant, bar, pizzeria, pool, putting green, shop, recreation room. AE, D, MC, V. EP, MAP.*

**$–$$** ☷ **Morgan Heights Condominiums.** There's a laid-back atmosphere at this complex along the Atlantic (it's a shuttle to the beach), 10 minutes from Basseterre. The reasonably priced rooms are clean and comfortable, with simple, contemporary white wicker furniture and ceramic tile floors. Five two-bedroom units can be rented as one-bedroom units or individual rooms; all have covered patios that overlook the water. The buildings are along a main highway and can be somewhat noisy during the day. The Atlantic Club serves excellent local cuisine and piña coladas with a punch. ⊠ *Box 536, Basseterre,* ☎ *869/465–8633,* ℻ *869/465–9272. 5 units. Restaurant, air-conditioning, pool. AE, D, MC, V. EP.*

**$** ☷ **Palms Hotel.** This delightful all-suites hotel has a prime location right
★ in Palms Arcade for those wishing to explore Basseterre. Units are decorated mainly in corals and teals, with bright throw rugs, pastel floral linens and art deco–style fixtures, including elaborate chandeliers. Even the smaller junior suites have cable TVs, refrigerators, coffeemakers, and phones. Drawbacks? The nearest beach is a 10-minute drive, and the central location means it can be rather noisy (under no circumstances rent during Carnival or other major festivals if you crave peace). ⊠ *Box 64, The Circus, Basseterre,* ☎ *869/465–0800,* ℻ *869/465–5889. 10 units. Bar, air-conditioning, shops. AE, MC, V. EP.*

**$** ☷ **Rock Haven Bed and Breakfast.** Judith and Keith Blake have converted their stylish gingerbread house in the Frigate Bay area, just 2 minutes' drive from the beaches, into a relaxing, homey B&B. The living and dining rooms are stunning, with carved mahogany doors, crystal chandeliers, English rugs, straw mats, and hardwood floors. There are two units, both with cable TV, ceiling fan, and iron beds draped with mosquito netting. The larger one is more basic, but has a full kitchen, private patio, and separate entrance. The vast, breezy terrace is lovely, with a terra-cotta floor, white wicker chaise longues, and majestic sea views. Judith prepares sumptuous breakfasts with such specialties as banana pancakes and Spanish omelets, along with fresh fruit and local side dishes like fried plantains and pumpkin fritters. She is also beloved on the island for her homemade ice cream, which she purveys to the supermarkets (sneak to the adjoining studio for a taste). ⊠ *Box 821, Frigate Bay,* ☎ ℻ *869/465–5503. 2 units. Fans, laundry service. No credit cards. BP.*

# Dining

St. Kitts restaurants range from funky little beachfront bistros to small, elegant plantation dining rooms; there is an interesting variety of cuisine to sample, most tinged, one way or another, with the flavors of the Caribbean. Many restaurants offer a variety of West Indian specialties that are popular on St. Kitts, such as curried mutton, pepper pot, honey-glazed garlic spareribs, and Arawak chicken (seasoned chicken, rice, and almonds served on breadfruit leaf).

## What to Wear

Dress is casual at lunch (but no bathing suits) throughout the island. Dinner, although not necessarily formal, definitely calls for long pants and sundresses.

| CATEGORY | COST* |
|---|---|
| $$$$ | over $40 |
| $$$ | $30–$40 |
| $$ | $20–$30 |
| $ under | $20 |

*per person for a three-course meal, excluding drinks and service; there is no sales tax on St. Kitts

**$$$$**  ✕ **Golden Lemon.** Owner Arthur Leaman creates the recipes himself
★ for the West Indian, Continental, and American dishes served in his
hotel, and he never repeats them more than once in a two-week period. The evening begins with cocktails and hors d'oeuvres on the patio.
The three-course dinner, with its fixed menu, is served in a tasteful room,
with crystal chandeliers, white rattan furnishings, antiques, and arched
doorways that welcome the island breezes. The longtime Kittitian
chef, Trevor Browne, makes delicious pumpkin soup, chicken with peanut
sauce, and lobster medallions Creole. The patio, lush with bougainvillea and ferns, is a popular spot for Sunday brunch, which can include
banana pancakes, rum beef stew, and curried conch fritters. ⊠ *Dieppe
Bay,* ☎ *869/465–7260. Reservations essential. AE, MC, V.*

**$$$$**  ✕ **Patio Restaurant.** In their flower-filled home, Joan and Peter Mal-
lalieu prepare, with the help of their staff, a full à la carte menu with
complimentary wine and liqueur. Try the flame-broiled mahimahi with
shrimp or rack of lamb with mango glaze, or treat yourself to a sampling of traditional local dishes, including *conki* (a coconut side dish)
and pepper pot. Piña colada gâteau and homemade tropical fruit ice
creams make tempting desserts. ⊠ *Frigate Bay Beach,* ☎ *869/465–
8666. Reservations essential. MC, V. Closed May–Oct.*

**$$$$**  ✕ **Rawlins Plantation.** Make your reservations early for the elegant din-
★ ners served in a lovely room with fieldstone walls and high-vaulted ceilings. The fixed-price, four-course dinner ($45 per person) changes
nightly but always emphasizes local ingredients. Dishes may include
christophine or pumpkin-and-coconut soup, smoked snapper and wa-
tercress salad, shrimp seviche with coriander and sour oranges, or
lobster in puff pastry with tarragon sauce. The guava and lime par-
faits and chocolate terrine with passion-fruit sauce are delicious. The
bountiful lunch buffet ($28) offers such items as breadfruit salad, fly-
ing-fish fritters, and *bobote* (ground beef, eggplant, spices, curry, and
homemade chutney). ⊠ *Mt. Pleasant,* ☎ *869/465–6221. Reservations
essential. AE, MC, V. No dinner Sun.*

**$$$$**  ✕ **Royal Palm.** Set beside the pool at Ottley's Plantation, this is a
★ restaurant to experience at night, under the latticed roof, gazing across
manicured lawns to the lights of the elegantly restored great house. The
menu is an eclectic mix of Californian and Caribbean dishes, with some
classic Italian, French, and Asian items. Start with porcini-apple tart-
let, marinated prawn and chorizo skewers, or Creole pumpkin soup,
and then have grilled sea scallops with Kittitian salsa or lobster bam-
baya (sautéed with ginger, tamarind, key lime juice, shallots, garlic, and
sun-dried tomatoes). For dessert, try banana fritters *l'antillaise* (spiced
and fried in rum) or mango mousse with raspberry sauce. The presentation is just as artful and appetizing. This is the island's merriest
dining spot, in no small part due to co-owners Art and Ruth Keusch,
their daughters Karen and Nancy; and Nancy's husband, Marty. Art
serenades diners with a twinkle in his eye while Ruth comically rolls
her eyes. The combination of superb food and warm bonhomie they
offer is unbeatable. ⊠ *Ottley's Plantation Inn,* ☎ *869/465–7234. Reservations essential. AE, D, MC, V.*

**$$$$**  ✕ **White House.** Enjoy lunch on the garden terrace or a romantic dinner, complete with candlelight and crystal, in the elegant, antiques-filled
dining room or outside under a marquee tent. The chef prepares a four-
course dinner each night, which may include pumpkin or crab soup,
Cornish game hen with banana stuffing, or fresh broiled local seafood.
Many of the ultrafresh ingredients are cultivated in owner Janice Barber's gardens. Afternoon tea is also served. ⊠ *St. Peter's,* ☎ *869/465–
8162. Reservations essential. AE, MC, V.*

**$$$–$$$$**  ✕ **Georgian House.** Janice and Malcolm Barber, owners of the delightful
★ White House (☞ *above*), took over and reinvigorated this once-tired

institution, occupying a magnificent 1750 brick-and-fieldstone town house with gorgeous parquet floors. Enjoy drinks in the courtyard before repairing to the sumptuous dining area. Everything is "just so"— almost to a fault: Bernadaud and Wedgwood china, crisp white tablecloths, candles gleaming in oversized glass vases, vaulting floral arrangements, high-back mahogany chairs. The fare is equally elegant without being pretentious. The main menu changes weekly, but among the signature dishes are conch scallopini, a near perfect rack of lamb, and snapper brilliantly complemented by shrimp and sesame sauce. The prices aren't stratospheric, given the quality and refined atmosphere; even the wine list is carefully considered and reasonably priced. The Georgian House offers an unbeatable combination of classic haute cuisine, classical music, and classy ambience. ⊠ *S. Independence Sq.,* ☎ *869/465–4049. AE, MC, V. Closed Sun. No lunch.*

**$$–$$$** ✕ **Fisherman's Wharf.** Part of the Ocean Terrace Inn (head straight rather than up the hill to the hotel's main building), this extremely casual waterfront eatery is decorated in swaggering nautical style, with rustic wood beams, rusty anchors, cannons, and buoys. Try the excellent conch chowder, followed by fresh grilled lobster or other shipshape seafood, and finish off your meal with a slice of the memorable banana cheesecake. The tables are long, wooden affairs, and it's generally lively, especially on weekend nights. ⊠ *Fortlands, Basseterre,* ☎ *869/465–6623. AE, MC, V. No lunch.*

**$$** ✕ **Arlecchino.** The stark interior defines nondescript, but the shaded courtyard of this breezy trattoria is a pleasant place to while away the afternoon or evening. Enjoy the fantastic minestrone, fresh pastas (try the spaghetti in conch sauce), creative pizzas (the picante—salami and chilies—is as hot as the name promises; the tropical, with pineapples, quite refreshing), excellent veal Parmigiana, or swordfish pizzaiola; then top off the meal with the best cappuccino and cannolis on St. Kitts. ⊠ *Cayon St., Basseterre,* ☎ *869/465–9927. AE, MC, V. Closed Sun.*

**$–$$** ✕ **Fairview Inn.** The main building of this old, quiet, and rather simple inn is an 18th-century great house, with graceful white verandas and Oriental rugs on hardwood floors. Banks of yellow allemanda climb the trellises surrounding the pool, where some tables face the ocean and some have views of Mt. Liamuiga glowering in the distance. The food is as authentic as you'll find on the island, with marvelous baked chicken in Creole sauce, curries, and specials like goat stew or rotis. Regrettably, despite the owner's grandiose ambitions (and insanely grand room prices to reflect them), the inn is definitely not recommended for lodging. ⊠ *Coastal Rd., Basseterre,* ☎ *869/465–2472. AE, D, MC, V.*

**$–$$** ✕ **Turtle Beach Bar and Grill.** Simple but scrumptious cuisine has made this informal restaurant a popular daytime watering hole. Treats include honey-mustard ribs, calypso chicken, coconut-shrimp salad, and grilled lobster. The glorified shack is on an isolated beach at the south end of the South East Peninsula Road; just look for the signs. Business cards and pennants from around the world plaster the bar, and the room is brightly decorated with a small sailboat, colorful crusted bottles dredged from the deep, old ships' lanterns, conch shells, and painted wooden fish, lobsters, and toucans. You can snorkel here, look out for green vervet monkeys and hawksbill turtles, schedule a deep-sea fishing trip, or rent a kayak, Windsurfer, or mountain bike to help you work off your meal. Sunday nights are popular among locals for dinner, dancing, and volleyball. ⊠ *Turtle Beach,* ☎ *869/469–9086. AE, MC, V. No dinner Mon.–Sat.*

**$** ✕ **Ballahoo.** This second-floor terrace restaurant, in the heart of downtown, overlooking the Circus, draws a crowd of locals and tourists for breakfast, lunch, and dinner. Lilting calypso and reggae on the sound system, whirring ceiling fans, potted palms, and colorful island prints create the appropriate tropical ambience. Specialties include conch simmered in garlic butter, madras beef curry, lobster and shrimp in a light creamy sauce, and (it's true) a rum-and-banana toasted sandwich. ⊠ *Fort St., Basseterre,* ☎ *869/465–4197. AE, MC, V. Closed Sun.*

**$** ✕ **Chef's Place.** Inexpensive West Indian meals are the draw here, as well as the best eavesdropping—the clientele runs toward local cops, cabbies, and middle-level government workers. Try the local version of jerk chicken (moister than usual) or the goat stew. The best seats are outside on the wide, white veranda. ⊠ *Upper Church St., Basseterre,* ☎ *869/465–6176. No credit cards. Closed Sun.*

**$** ✕ **Manhattan Gardens.** Even the exterior of this delightful ginger-bread 17th-century Creole house looks appetizing, in tangerine, teal, and peach. Inside is remarkably cozy, like eating in the owner's dining room, with batik hangings, lace tablecloths, and wood carvings. The garden in back overlooks the sea and comes alive every Saturday and Sunday brunch with, respectively, a Caribbean Food Fest and lively barbecue that draw locals from around the island. The regular menu offers savory island fare, including lobster in lemon butter and wahoo in Creole sauce, augmented by specials from around the Caribbean like goat water, souse, jerk, and saltfish. ⊠ *Old Rd.,* ☎ *869/ 465–9121. No credit cards. No dinner Sun.*

**$** ✕ **PJ's Pizza.** "Garbage pizza" may not sound too appetizing, but this pie, topped with everything but the kitchen sink, is a favorite here. You can also choose from 10 other varieties of pizza or create your own. Sandwiches and other Italian standards are available (lasagna is a house specialty). Finish your meal with delicious, moist rum cake. This casual spot, bordering the golf course and open to cooling breezes, is always boisterous. ⊠ *Frigate Bay,* ☎ *869/465–8373. AE, MC, V. Closed Mon. and Sept.*

**$** ✕ **Sprat Net.** This simple cluster of picnic tables, sheltered by a brilliant turquoise, corrugated tin roof and decorated with driftwood and fish nets, sits on a strip of sand that could barely be called a beach. Nonetheless, it has become one of the hottest spots on St. Kitts. There's nothing fancy on the menu: just grilled fish, lobster, chicken, and meats, served with mountains of cole slaw and peas and rice. But locals and knowledgeable visitors know that the fishermen owners heap their amazingly fresh catch on a center table, where you choose your own dinner just as if you were at market and watch it grilled to your specification. ⊠ *Old Rd., no phone. No credit cards. Closed Sun. No lunch.*

## Beaches

The powdery white-sand beaches, free and open to the public (even those occupied by hotels), are all in the Frigate Bay area of the island or on the lower peninsula.

Two of the island's best are the twin beaches of **Banana Bay** and **Cockleshell Bay,** which together cover more than 2 mi at the southeastern tip of the island. Several large hotels, including the Banana Bay and Casablanca, were abandoned in the early stages of development—their skeletal structures marring an otherwise idyllic scene.

**Conaree Bay** on the Atlantic side is a narrow strip of gray-black sand where the water is good for body surfing.

Snorkeling and windsurfing are good at **Dieppe Bay,** a black-sand beach on the north coast, home of the Golden Lemon hotel.

Locals consider the Caribbean side of **Friar's Bay** the island's finest beach. You can haggle with fishermen here to take you out snorkeling off the eastern point. The waters on the Atlantic side are rougher, but the beach itself has a wild, desolate beauty.

**Frigate Bay,** on the Caribbean, has talcum-powder-fine sand, while on the Atlantic side, **North Frigate Bay** is 4 mi wide and a favorite with horseback riders (☞ Outdoor Activities and Sports, *below*).

A tiny dirt road, virtually impassable after heavy rains, leads to **Sandbank Beach,** a long, taupe crescent on the Atlantic. The shallow coves are protected here, making it ideal for families, and it's usually deserted.

**White House Bay** is rocky, but the snorkeling, taking in several reefs surrounding a sunken tugboat, is superb.

## Outdoor Activities and Sports

### Boating
Sunfish and Hobie Cats can be rented at **Tropical Surf** (⊠ Turtle Bay, ☎ 869/469–9086) and **Mr. X Watersports** (⊠ Frigate Bay, ☎ 869/465–4995).

### Deep-Sea Fishing
Angle for yellowtail snapper, wahoo, mackerel, tuna, dolphin, shark, and barracuda with **Tropical Tours** (☎ 869/465–4167), **Turtle Tours** (☎ 869/469–9086), and **Captain Redbeard Boat Charters** (☎ 869/465–0482).

### Golf
The **Royal St. Kitts Golf Club** (☎ 869/465–8339) is an 18-hole championship course in the Frigate Bay area. Greens fees are $30 for 18 holes, $25 for 9.

### Hiking
Trails in the central mountains vary from easy to don't-try-it-by-yourself. Monkey Hill and Verchild's Peak are not difficult, although the Verchild's climb will take the better part of a day. Don't attempt Mt. Liamuiga without a guide. You'll start at Belmont Estates on horseback, then proceed on foot to the lip of the crater, at 2,600 ft. You can go down into the crater, clinging to vines and roots. **Greg Pereira** (☎ 869/465–4121), whose family has lived on St. Kitts for well over a century, takes groups on half-day trips into the rain forest and on full-day hikes up the volcano and through the grounds of a private 250-year-old great house, followed by excursions down canyons and past petroglyphs. He and his staff provide a running, overflowing commentary of fascinating historical, folkloric, and botanical tidbits, as well as refreshing fruit juices (with CSR [Cane Spirit Rothschild], the local firewater). **Kriss Tours** (☎ 869/465–4042) takes small groups into the crater, through the rain forest, and to Dos d'Anse Pond on Verchild's Mountain. Oliver Spencer's **Off the Beaten Track** (☎ 869/465–6314) does just that with hikers, taking them to the ruins of a fragrant, abandoned coffee plantation taken over by sprawling banyan trees.

### Horseback Riding
Frigate Bay and Conaree Beach are great for riding. Guides from **Trinity Stable** (☎ 869/465–3226) will lead you into the hills at a leisurely gait. **Royal Stables** (☎ 869/465–2222) offers sunset beach rides and tours into the rain forest on horseback.

### Scuba Diving and Snorkeling
Kenneth Samuel of **Kenneth's Dive Centre** (☎ 869/465–7043, 869/466–5320 at Bird Rock Hotel) is a PADI-certified dive master who takes small groups of divers with C-cards to nearby reefs. Auston MacLeod, a PADI-certified dive master–instructor and owner of **Pro-Divers** (☎ 869/465–

3223), offers resort and certification courses. He also has Nikonos camera equipment for rent. **Mr. X Watersports** (☎ 869/465–0673) arranges various snorkeling trips, as well as waterskiing and sailing.

There are more than a dozen excellent **dive sites** on St. Kitts, all with a variety of sea life and color. Coconut Tree Reef, one of the largest in the area, includes sea fans, sponges, and anemones. Black Coral Reef features the rare black coral tree. Brassball Wreck is a shallow-water wreck, good for snorkeling and photography. Redonda Bank is an extensive area of reef that's just beginning to be explored. The shallow Tug Boat is a good spot for snorkelers, who will spot everything from gliding rays to darting grunts and jacks. Bloody Bay Reef is noted for its network of underwater grottoes daubed with purple anemones, sienna bristle worms, and canary-yellow sea fans that seem to wave you in.

## Sea Excursions

**Leeward Island Charters** (☎ 869/465–7474) offers day and overnight charters on two catamarans—the 47-ft *Caona* and the 70-ft *Spirit of St. Kitts*. Day sails are from 9:30 to 4:30 and include barbecue, open bar, and snorkeling equipment. **Tropical Tours** (☎ 869/465–4167) offers moonlight cruises on the 52-ft catamaran *Cileca III* and glass-bottom-boat tours. **Jazzie II** (☎ 869/465–3529) is another glass-bottom boat that cruises the southeastern coast, with free snorkeling equipment. **Tropical Dreamer** (☎ 869/465–8224) is another catamaran available for day and sunset cruises. For the ultimate underwater trip, call **Blue Frontier Ltd.** (☎ 869/465–4945); owner Lindsey Beck will take you for a half-hour ride off Frigate Bay in his two-man submarine.

## Spectator Sports

**Cricket** matches are played in Warner Park from January to July, **soccer** from July to December, **softball** from January to August. Contact the tourist board (☞ Visitor Information *in* St. Kitts and Nevis A to Z, *below*) for schedules.

## Tennis

There are four lighted courts at **Jack Tar Village Beach Resorts** (☎ 869/465–8651), two lighted courts at **Sun 'n' Sand Beach Village** (☎ 869/465–8037), as well as one court each (unlighted) at **Bird Rock Beach Resort** (☎ 869/465–8914), the **Golden Lemon** (☎ 869/465–7260), and **Rawlins Plantation** (☎ 869/465–6221).

## Waterskiing and Windsurfing

**Turtle Tours** (☎ 869/469–9086) at Turtle Bay rents Windsurfers, surfboards, kayaks, and boogie boards.

# Shopping

St. Kitts has limited shopping, but there are a few duty-free shops where you can find some good buys in jewelry, watches, perfume, china, and crystal. Excellent paintings and sculptures can be found at several galleries around the island. Among the island crafts, the best known are the batik fabrics, scarves, caftans, and wall hangings of Caribelle Batik. There are also locally produced jams, jellies, herb teas, and handcrafts of local shell, straw, and coconut. And CSR (Cane Spirit Rothschild) is a "new cane spirit drink" that's distilled from fresh sugarcane right on St. Kitts.

## Shopping Districts

Most shopping plazas are in downtown Basseterre near the Circus. Some shops have tiny branches in other areas, particularly in Dieppe Bay. **Palms Arcade** is on Fort Street, near the Circus. The **Pelican Mall** has 26 stores, a restaurant, tourism offices, and a bandstand. This shopping arcade is designed to look like a traditional Caribbean street. **Shore-line Plaza** is next to the Treasury Building, right on the waterfront in Basseterre. **TDC Mall** is just off the Circus in downtown Basseterre.

## Good Buys

**Caribelle Batik** (⊠ Romney Manor, ☎ 869/465–6253) sells batik wraps, T-shirts, dresses, wall hangings, and the like.

**Island Hopper** (⊠ The Circus, ☎ 869/465–2905) is a good place for island crafts, especially wood carvings, pottery, and textiles, as well as humorous T-shirts and trinkets.

**Music World** (⊠ The Circus, ☎ 869/465–1998) offers a vast selection of island rhythms—lilting soca and zouk, pulsating salsa and merengue, wicked hip-hop, and mellow reggae and calypso.

**Palm Crafts** (⊠ Palms Arcade, ☎ 869/465–2599) sells a variety of good-ies, including savory Caribbean jams and jellies, resort wear by noted island designer John Warden, and hand-painted ceramic ware.

**Plantation Picture House** (⊠ Fort St., ☎ 869/465–5265) showcases the enchanting silk pareus, jewelry, prints, papier-mâché works of Kate Spencer (who also has a studio just outside the Rawlins Planta-tion), and the fanciful, striking hats of Dale Isaacs.

**Rosemary Lane Antiques** (⊠ 7 Rosemary La., ☎ 869/465–5450) oc-cupies a beautifully restored 18th-century town house and is crammed with superlative, affordable antiques and objets d'art from through-out the Caribbean. They will gladly ship any purchases.

**Slice of the Lemon** (⊠ Palms Arcade, ☎ 869/465–2889) stocks fine perfumes but is better known for elegant jewelry.

**Spencer Cameron Art Gallery** (⊠ N. Independence Sq., ☎ 869/465–1617) has historical reproductions of Caribbean island charts and prints, in addition to owner Rosey Cameron's popular Carnevale clown prints and a wide selection of exceptional artwork by Caribbean artists. They will mail anywhere, so you don't have to lug home some-thing that catches your eye.

**Splash** (⊠ TDC Plaza, Fort St., ☎ 869/465–9279) carries colorful beach-wear by local designers.

**TDC** (⊠ TDC Plaza, Fort St., ☎ 869/465–2511) sells fine china and crystal, along with cameras and other imports.

# Nightlife

Most of the Kittitian nightlife revolves around the hotels, which host folkloric shows and calypso and steel bands.

## Casinos

The only game in town is at the **Jack Tar Village Beach Resorts and Casino** (☞ Lodging, *above*), where you'll find blackjack tables, roulette wheels, craps tables, and one-armed bandits. Dress is casual, and play continues till the last player leaves. You do not need to purchase Jack Tar passes to play, even though the casino entrance is in the hotel lobby.

## Discos and Live Music

On Saturday night head for the **Turtle Beach Bar and Grill** (⊠ Turtle Bay, ☎ 869/469–9086), where there is a beach dance-disco. Play vol-leyball into the evening, and then dance under the stars into the night. At **J's Place** (⊠ Across from Brimstone Hill, ☎ 869/465–6264), you can dance the night away with locals on Friday and Saturday. **Henry's Night Spot** (⊠ Dunn's Cottage, Lower Cayon St., Basseterre, ☎ 869/

465–3508) is the most popular disco in town for locals. The **Cotton House Club** (⊠ Canada Estate, no phone), open weekends from 10 PM, is considered to have the best sound system and dance mixes. Weekends, **Kool Runnins** (⊠ Morris Paul Dr., Pond Industrial Site, ☎ 869/ 466–5665) serves up jerk chicken, roti (East Indian burrito), and goatwater stew, to the accompaniment of live local bands in an open-air gazebo. The hot spot for happy hour (free eats and occasional live music) is the tropical courtyard bar **Stonewalls** (⊠ Princes St., Basseterre, ☎ 869/465–5248). A favorite happy-hour watering hole is the **Circus Grill** (⊠ Bay Rd., Basseterre, ☎ 869/46–0143), a second-floor eatery whose wraparound veranda offers views of both the harbor and the activity on the Circus. **Bayembi Cultural Entertainment Bar and Cafe** (⊠ Just off the Circus, ☎ 869/466–5280) looks like a United Nations garage sale, and the ambience is definitely Peace Corps hip, with jazz guitar sets Wednesdays, karaoke Saturdays, joyous happy hours daily, and even poetry readings. It also offers light snacks and local artwork for sale.

## Exploring St. Kitts

Main Road traces the perimeter of the large, northwestern part of the island, through seas of sugarcane that encircle the island's mountain range, past breadfruit trees and old stone walls. The drive back to Basseterre around the other side of the island is a pleasant one, through small, neat villages with centuries-old stone churches and pastel-colored cottages, although villages with tiny houses of stone and weathered wood are scattered throughout the island. The most spectacular stretch of scenery is on the splendid Dr. Kennedy Simmonds Highway to the tip of the South East Peninsula. Reminiscent of California's famed Highway 1, this ultrasleek modern road twists and turns through the undeveloped grassy hills that rise between the calm Caribbean sea and the windswept Atlantic, past the shimmering pink Great Salt Pond, a volcanic crater, and the island's most seductive beaches. You can see the main sights of the capital city in a half hour or so; allow three to four hours for an island tour.

*Numbers in the margin correspond to points of interest on the St. Kitts map.*

SIGHTS TO SEE

**❶ Basseterre.** Set in the southern part of the island, the capital city of St. Kitts is an easily walkable town. It is graced with tall palms, and although many of the buildings appear run-down and in need of paint, you will find interesting shopping areas, excellent art galleries, and some beautifully maintained houses.

The octagonal **Circus,** built in the style of London's famous Piccadilly Circus, has duty-free shops along the streets and courtyards leading off from it.

There are lovely gardens on the site of a former slave market at **Independence Square** (⊠ Off Bank St.). The square is surrounded on three sides by 18th-century Georgian buildings.

**St. George's Anglican Church** (⊠ Cayon St.) is a handsome stone building with a crenellated tower originally built by the French in 1670 and called Nôtre Dame. The British burned it down in 1706 and rebuilt it four years later, naming it after the patron saint of England. Since then, it has suffered fire, earthquake, and hurricanes and was once again rebuilt in 1859.

**8** **Black Rocks.** This series of lava deposits was spat into the sea ages ago when the island's volcano erupted. It has since been molded into fanciful shapes by centuries of pounding surf. ⊠ *On Atlantic coast, just outside town of Sadlers, in Sandy Bay.*

**2** **Bloody Point.** French and British soldiers joined forces here in 1629 to repel a mass Carib attack. ⊠ *Outside village of Challengers.*

**6** **Brimstone Hill.** This well-restored 38-acre fortress is the most important historic site on St. Kitts. From the parking area it's quite a steep walk up to the top of the fort, but it's well worth it if military history and/or spectacular views interest you. After routing the French in 1690, the English erected a battery on top of Brimstone Hill, and by 1736 there were 49 guns in the fortress. In 1782 8,000 French troops lay siege to the fortress, which was defended by 350 militia and 600 regular troops of the Royal Scots and East Yorkshires. A plaque in the old stone wall marks the place where the fort was breached. When the English finally surrendered, the French allowed them to march from the fort in full formation out of respect for their bravery. (The English afforded the French the same honor when they surrendered the fort a mere year later.) A hurricane did extensive damage to the fortress in 1834, and in 1852 it was evacuated and dismantled. The beautiful stones were carted away to build houses.

The citadel has been partially reconstructed and its guns remounted. A seven-minute orientation film recounts the fort's history and restoration. You can see what remains of the officers' quarters, the redoubts, barracks, the ordinance store, and the cemetery. Its museums display, among other things, pre-Columbian artifacts, a collection of objects pertaining to the African heritage of the island's slaves (masks, ceremonial tools, etc.), weaponry, uniforms, photographs, and old newspapers. In 1985 Queen Elizabeth visited Brimstone Hill and officially opened it as part of a national park. There's a splendid view from here that includes Montserrat and Nevis to the southeast, Saba and Statia to the northwest, and St. Barts and St. Maarten to the north. Nature trails snake through the tangle of surrounding hardwood forest and savannah (a fine spot to catch the green vervet monkeys skittering about). ⊠ *Main Rd., Brimstone Hill.* 🎫 *$5.* ⊙ *Daily 9:30–5:30.*

NEED A BREAK?    **J's Place** (☎ 869/465–6264), across from the entrance to Brimstone Hill, is ideal for a drink, a sandwich, or a full West Indian meal, including a sensational lobster salad.

**5** **Middle Island.** Thomas Warner, the "gentleman of London" who brought the first settlers to St. Kitts, died here in 1648 and is buried beneath a green gazebo in the churchyard of St. Thomas Church.

**3** **Old Road Town.** This site marks the first permanent English settlement in the West Indies, founded in 1624 by Thomas Warner. Take the side road toward the interior to find some well-preserved **Carib petroglyphs,** testimony of even older habitation. ⊠ *Main Rd., west of Challengers.*

**4** **Romney Manor.** This house is set in 6 acres of gardens, with exotic flowers, an old bell tower, and a 350-year-old saman tree (sometimes called a rain tree). Inside, at **Caribelle Batik** (☞ Shopping, *above*), you can watch artisans hand-printing fabrics by a 2,500-year-old Indonesian process known as batik. Look for signs indicating a turnoff for Romney Manor near Old Road Town.

❼ **Sandy Point Town.** This quaint village contains West Indian–style raised cottages and features a Roman Catholic church with lovely stained-glass windows.

# NEVIS

## Lodging

With the exception of the Four Seasons Resort, most hotels on Nevis are beautifully restored manor or plantation houses. Typically, the owners of the inn live there with their families, and visitors are received warmly and graciously, almost like friends. It is easy to begin thinking you have been personally invited down for a visit. In the evening, before dinner, it is common for the family, inn guests, and those visitors who have come to eat at the restaurant to gather in a drawing room or on a terrace for cocktails and to exchange stories of the day. Most of the inns operate on the Modified American Plan (MAP) and offer a free shuttle to their private stretch on Pinney's Beach.

| CATEGORY | COST* |
|---|---|
| $$$$ | over $325 |
| $$$ | $240–$325 |
| $$ | $150–$240 |
| $ | under $150 |

*All prices are for a standard double room, MAP, excluding 7% tax and 10% service charge.*

$$$$ 🏨 **Four Seasons Resort Nevis.** There's no denying that the 196-room
★ property is run flawlessly and manages to combine world-class elegance with West Indian ambience and hospitality. On a stunning stretch of Pinney's Beach, with a spectacular view of St. Kitts in the distance, the hotel offers a complete range of water activities, along with clay and all-weather tennis courts, a free-form pool, a challenging 18-hole golf course designed by Robert Trent Jones II, and a full-service health club. Spacious guest rooms are richly furnished with mahogany armoires and headboards as well as cushioned rattan sofas and chairs, and have large indoor and veranda seating areas, which can be used for private dining. There are two outstanding restaurants, one of which is fairly formal (although jacket and tie are not required). Special activities for children are scheduled regularly. There are usually good-value sports and romantic packages, even during the high season. Twenty sparkling new villas, Nevis Resort Estates, were added in 1996, with more to come. Most are available in the rental pool; guests enjoy full services of the pampering resort. The villas feature cedar cathedral ceilings, tile floors, open kitchens, masterful master bedrooms, and enormous verandas—all within "Fore!" shouting distance of the golf course. ⊠ *Box 565, Charlestown,* ☎ *869/469–1111; 800/332–3442 in the U.S.; 800/268–6288 in Canada;* ☒ *869/469–1112. 196 rooms. 2 restaurants, pub, air-conditioning, fans, pool, 18-hole golf course, 10 tennis courts, aerobics, fitness center, beach, water sports, boating, 2 shops, baby-sitting, children's program, laundry service and coin laundry, car rental. AE, D, MC, V. EP, MAP, FAP.*

$$$$ 🏨 **Nisbet Plantation Beach Club.** From the manor house of this 18th-
★ century plantation you can see the beach at the end of a long avenue of coconut palms, and from the bar you look out over an old sugar mill covered with hibiscus, cassia, frangipani, and flamboyants. Well-maintained Nisbet offers a range of accommodations, from plantation-style cottages to lanai suites, all simply but tastefully appointed in whitewashed wicker and rattan and tropical prints. They are along an avenue lined with palms that leads to a blinding white-sand beach and

the ocean. ✉ *Newcastle Beach,* ☎ *869/469–9325; 800/344–2049 in the U.S.;* ℻ *869/469–9864. 38 rooms. 2 restaurants, 2 bars, beach, pool, tennis court, croquet, snorkeling, shop, laundry services. AE, MC, V. EP, MAP.*

$$$
★ 🏨 **Hermitage Plantation Inn.** A 250-year-old great house—said to be the oldest wooden house on the island—has a restaurant in it and forms the core of this appealing inn set in the hills. The duplex guest cottages are some of the prettiest accommodations on Nevis, with the Blue Cottage and Yellow Room absolute knockouts. Rooms are furnished with antiques, including four-poster canopy beds (mostly king-size), and have patios or balconies; some also have lovely views of the distant ocean and full kitchens. Also available is a two-bedroom replica of a manor house, with its own pool. The beach is 15 minutes away, and if you haven't got a car, transportation will be arranged. Many guests simply relax in a hammock or spend a peaceful day by the pool. What really makes the Hermitage special is vivacious owners Maureen and Richard Lupinacci, who will quickly introduce you to everyone who's anyone (and then some) on Nevis. ✉ *St. John's, Fig Tree Parish,* ☎ *869/469–3477,* ℻ *869/469–2481. 12 suites. Restaurant, bar, fans, refrigerators, pool, tennis court, horseback riding. AE, MC, V. EP, MAP.*

$$$
🏨 **Montpelier Plantation Inn.** Iron gates provide a majestic entrance to this intimate and charming inn, set on 100 beautifully landscaped hillside acres. Reception, evening cocktails, and dinner take place in and around the great house—an imposing fieldstone structure furnished with antiques. Accommodations are in simple cottages scattered along the hillside. Each cottage contains one or two rooms, has two patios, and is spare but sparkling. Rooms have Italian-ceramic tile floors and large bathrooms; most have marvelous four-poster or rattan beds. A gorgeous mural decorates one of the walls around the large pool, but beach lovers can head (via complimentary transportation) to Pinney's Beach, where the estate has a 3-acre private section of beach and a pavilion. Guests come not for the amenities so much as for the incomparable air of quiet, unpretentious elegance. Owners James and Celia Gaskell downplay their royal connections (Princess Di stays here); James prefers to talk about his extensive organic gardens. Montpelier is the most civilized hostelry on Nevis. ✉ *Box 474, Charlestown,* ☎ *869/469–3462 or 800/243–9420,* ℻ *869/469–2932. 17 rooms. Restaurant, bar, pool, tennis court, beach. AE, MC, V. Closed late Aug.–early Oct. BP, MAP.*

$$
🏨 **Golden Rock.** Co-owner Pam Barry runs this inn, built by her great-great-great-grandfather more than 200 years ago. She has decorated the 16 units with four-poster beds of mahogany or bamboo, native grass rugs, straw and glass-bottle lamps, brilliantly hued wooden fish, rocking chairs, and bright French floral-print fabrics. All rooms have a private bath and a patio. The restored sugar mill is a two-level suite (with a glorious wood-and-bamboo staircase), and the old cistern is now a spring-fed swimming pool. The estate covers 150 mountainous acres and is surrounded by 25 acres of lavish tropical gardens, including a sunken garden. Green vervet monkeys skitter about the premises. Enjoy the Atlantic view and cooling breeze from the bar. The Saturday-night West Indian buffet is very popular December through June. An avid horticulturalist, Barry also organizes historical and nature hikes. ✉ *Box 493, Gingerland,* ☎ *869/469–3346 or 800/223–9815,* ℻ *869/469–2113. 16 rooms, 1 suite. Restaurant, bar, fans, pool, tennis court. AE, MC, V. Closed Sept.–early Oct. EP, MAP.*

$$
🏨 **Mt. Nevis Hotel and Beach Club.** The Mt. Nevis is the perfect choice for those seeking contemporary accommodations with typical Nevisian warmth, yet without the stratospheric prices of the Four Seasons. Deluxe rooms and suites are fitted with handsome white wicker fur-

nishings, southwestern pastel fabrics, glass-top tables, and colorful island prints. Suites have full, modern kitchens and dining areas; all units have a balcony. The main building houses the casual restaurant and bar, which open onto a terrace that overlooks the pool and provides a jaw-dropping view of St. Kitts in the distance. Shuttle service is provided to the outdoor restaurant-bar, which serves grilled items and pizzas at Newcastle Beach. Deep-sea fishing, scuba diving, and other water sports are available at the hotel's other facility farther down Newcastle Beach; horseback riding, tennis, and golf privileges at the Four Seasons can be arranged. The owner is also building six fully equipped houses on the hill (two were completed in 1996). All have two or three bedrooms, handsome individual decor, and spacious patios with amazing sea views. ⊠ *Box 494, Newcastle,* ☎ *869/469–9373 collect,* FAX *869/469–9375. 32 units, 2 houses in rental pool. Restaurant, bar, air-conditioning, refrigerators, pool, water sports. AE, D, MC, V. EP, MAP.*

$$ 🏨 **Old Manor Estate.** Vast tropical gardens surround this sugar plantation in the shadow of Mt. Nevis. The outbuildings, such as the smokehouse and jail, have been imaginatively restored as public spaces used for barbecue nights, music nights, and banqueting; the old cistern is now the pool. The property had been left in sad neglect; new ownership has already brightened the dour exteriors in peach and forest green and is slowly redecorating. Many of the enormous guest rooms have high ceilings, gorgeous stone or tile floors, marble vanities, exposed wood beams, king-size four-poster beds, and colonial reproductions; some units, however, remain a bit gloomy and dark, with old-fashioned dowdy madras settees and soiled carpets. Construction and rebuilding will be ongoing, with ambitious plans to move the respected Cooperage restaurant to the original great house and add several rooms and conference facilities in its place, overlooking the sea. There's transportation to and from the beach. The hotel is not recommended for children under 12. ⊠ *Box 70, Charlestown,* ☎ *869/469–3445; 800/223–9815 or 800/892–7093 in the U.S.;* FAX *869/469–3388. 14 rooms. 2 restaurants, 2 bars, fans, pool. AE, MC, V. EP, MAP.*

$$ 🏨 **Oualie Beach Hotel.** This congenial, cozy resort consists of several
★ charming West Indian–style cottages staggered along a beautiful tawny beach. All rooms look across the water to stunning views of neighboring St. Kitts. The air-conditioned rooms are bright, airy, and tastefully furnished. Deluxe rooms have mahogany four-poster canopy beds and marble vanities. Studio units have a full kitchen. There is a full dive shop here offering NAUI-certified instruction, and dive packages are available. Sunfish and Windsurfers may be rented, and the hotel has introduced Skimmer waterborne rowing machines. Breakfast, lunch, and dinner are served at an informal restaurant and bar. ⊠ *Oualie Beach,* ☎ *869/469–9735,* FAX *869/469–9176. 22 rooms. Restaurant, bar, air-conditioning, in-room safes, refrigerators, beach, dive shop, water sports. AE, D, MC, V. EP, MAP.*

$–$$ 🏨 **Hurricane Cove Bungalows.** Don't be deceived by the ramshackle exterior of these cottages clinging precariously to a hill overlooking lovely Tamarind Bay. The interiors are charmingly rustic, with hand-carved wood furnishings and gleaming tile floors. All have full kitchens and an enclosed patio with breathtaking ocean views (save for one cottage, far in the back). Several have private pools. The postage-stamp-size hotel pool is in the foundation of a 250-year-old fort. The beach is a three-minute walk away. The only drawback is these glorified tree houses can be stifling on still days. ⊠ *Tamarind Bay,* ☎ FAX *869/469–9462. 10 1-, 2-, and 3-bedroom bungalows. Pool. MC, V.*

$ 🏨 **Yamseed Inn.** A very rough access road leads to this pale yellow bed-and-breakfast overlooking St. Kitts, tucked away from resort and plantation hotels on its own private patch of white sand. Friendly innkeeper Sybil Siegfried offers four rooms in her house (with a three-night minimum), nestled amid beautiful grounds (Sybil's an avid gardener). Chirping hummingbirds welcome you into the stylish reception area. Each room has a private bath and is handsomely appointed with a mahogany bed, wood-panel ceiling, throw rugs, white-tile floors, and antiques. Breakfast includes delicious homemade muffins and grated coconut muesli. The only flaw in paradise is Yamseed's location near the airport, which puts it in the flight path (fortunately, air traffic isn't busy). ⊠ *On the beach, Newcastle,* ☎ *869/469–9361. 4 rooms. Beach. No credit cards. BP.*

## Dining

Dinner options on Nevis include the elegance of the dining room at the Four Seasons Resort, intimate dinners at plantation guest houses (where the menu is often set), and a variety of more casual eateries. Seafood is ubiquitous, and there are many places in which to sample excellent West Indian fare.

### What to Wear

As in St. Kitts, dress is casual at lunch, although beach attire is unacceptable. Dress pants or a sundress is apropos for dinner; men may even want to put on a jacket in season at some of the inns and at the Four Seasons Resort.

| CATEGORY | COST* |
|---|---|
| $$$$ | over $40 |
| $$$ | $30–$40 |
| $$ | $20–$30 |
| $ | under $20 |

*per person for a three-course meal, excluding drinks and service*

$$$$  ✕ **Four Seasons Resort.** This elegant dining room, paneled in imported South American hardwood, has tables set with glistening silver and china and graceful, 12-ft-high doors that open to the breezes and sweeping views of Pinney's Beach and the sea beyond. The nouvelle cuisine has a Caribbean flair—Antiguan wahoo baked in a banana leaf with coconut milk; curry and scotch bonnet broth; and pan-seared local red snapper with mango salsa and bitter orange sauce. There is a weekly Caribbean buffet with a full steel band. ⊠ *Pinney's Beach,* ☎ *869/469–1111. Reservations essential. AE, D, MC, V.*

$$$$  ✕ **Miss June's.** Dinner with Miss June Mestier, a lady from Trinidad, ★  could never be called ordinary. While she prepares the fare, her son serves drinks—from Miss June's secret rum punch to a very proper martini—to the guests (limited to 20) on the veranda. Promptly at 8:30 everyone heads to the dining room, where several tables are set with mismatched fine china and crystal. The first course is a soup of Miss June's creation, usually something spicy; the second course, fresh fish prepared in some exotic local style, followed by salad. "Now that you've had your dinner," Miss June announces, "it's time to have fun!" as guests turn to the buffet table laden with at least 18 dishes. Selections change nightly but always include curries; local vegetable dishes; meats like leg of lamb in champagne orange sauce, chicken simmered in coconut milk, or ribs in mauby (a bark distillation) and pineapple; and seafood—all adapted by Miss June from Trinidadian recipes. Wine flows freely throughout (this is truly an all-inclusive meal at $65). At the end, Miss June will join you for coffee and brandy; she won't kick you out, but you may be asked to turn the lights out when you leave—regretfully. No wonder several guests invite Miss June to stay with them when-

ever she's abroad. ⊠ *Jones Bay,* ☎ *869/469–5330. Reservations essential. MC, V.*

**$$$$**   ✕ **Nisbet Plantation Beach Club.** The antiques-filled dining room in the
    ★    great house at Nisbet—an oasis of polished hardwood floors, mahogany and cherrywood furnishings, and stone walls—has long been
a popular place for lunch and dinner. There are also tables on the
screened-in veranda, where there's a view down the palm-tree-lined fairway to the sea. The five-course menu is unusually varied for Nevis. A
combination of Continental and Caribbean cuisines is prepared with
many local ingredients. Sumptuous choices include sautéed scallops on
angel-hair pasta in cinnamon sauce, chilled avocado and apricot soup,
roast quail stuffed with herb duxelles in raspberry sauce, grilled red
grouper in lemongrass sauce, and banana and Tia Maria mousse in a
chocolate shell. Lighter fare (sandwiches, salads, hamburgers) is served
at lunch at the beach restaurant, Coconuts. ⊠ *Nisbet Plantation,*
☎ *869/469–9325. Reservations essential. AE, MC, V.*

**$$$**   ✕ **Golden Rock.** Tables are draped in pink and arranged in a romantic, dimly lit room whose fieldstone walls date back to when this was
a plantation house. Enchanting Eva Wilkin originals grace the walls
(be sure to admire the mural behind the bamboo bar). Local Nevisian
cuisine is the specialty here; velvety pumpkin soup, chicken in a raisin
curry, grilled local snapper with tania (a type of tuber) fritters, and green
papaya pie are house favorites. ⊠ *Golden Rock,* ☎ *869/469–3346.
Reservations essential. AE, MC, V. Closed Sun.*

**$$$**   ✕ **Hermitage Plantation Inn.** After cocktails in the antiques-filled par-
    ★    lor, dinner is served at one long table on the outside veranda. The four-course preset menu might include carrot and tarragon soup, red snapper
in ginger sauce, fried conch steak, and a rum soufflé. The conversation is always lively, thanks to witty, gregarious owners Maureen and
Richard "Loopy" Lupinacci. ⊠ *Hermitage Plantation,* ☎ *869/469–
3477. Reservations essential. AE, MC, V.*

**$$$**   ✕ **Montpelier Plantation Inn.** Genial owners James and Celia Gaskell
    ★    preside over an elegant evening. Cocktails and hors d'oeuvres are
served amid the antiques in the parlor of the great house. Then dinner
is by candlelight on the white terrace. Cream of avocado and coconut
soup, lobster, red snapper, chicken calypso, sirloin steak bordelaise, and
roast beef and Yorkshire pudding are some of the choices on Stuart
Jones's sterling menu. Many of the fresh ingredients are homegrown
in the extensive gardens. ⊠ *Montpelier Plantation,* ☎ *869/469–3462.
Reservations essential. AE, MC, V. Closed late Aug.–early Oct.*

**$$$**   ✕ **Mt. Nevis Hotel.** White wicker tables are set with coral tablecloths,
flickering candles, china, and silver in this airy 60-seat dining room,
which opens onto the terrace and pool. During the day, there is a splendid view of St. Kitts in the distance. The menu is one of the island's
most creative, thanks to head chef Jeff de Barbieri, who apprenticed
at New York's St. Regis Hotel and Tavern on the Green. He deftly blends
local ingredients with classic haute preparations. Starters include grilled
baby blackfin snapper with stewed pumpkin and basil or ginger lobster wontons. Entrées may include yellowtail fragrant with coriander,
mango, and ginger; orecchiette pasta with sautéed duck, spinach, and
wild mushrooms; or tenderloin of pork with kumquat chutney and
mashed breadfruit. ⊠ *Mt. Nevis Hotel and Beach Club, Newcastle,*
☎ *869/469–9373. AE, D, MC, V.*

**$–$$**   ✕ **Oualie Beach.** This low-key bar and restaurant on Oualie Bay is the
perfect stop for authentic Nevisian fare with French flair after a long
day on the beach. Try the delicious homemade soups, including groundnut or breadfruit vichyssoise. Then move on to Creole conch stew, lobster crepes, or chicken breasts stuffed with spinach. The atmosphere

is rollicking on weekends, with live music and local crowds. ⊠ *Oualie Beach,* ☎ *869/469–9735. AE, D, MC, V.*

**$–$$** ✕ **Prinderella's.** This casual open-air restaurant enjoys a stunning setting on Tamarind Bay, with views across the channel to St. Kitts. A lovely mural behind the bamboo bar suffices for decor. Seafood is the obvious specialty, although the English owners, Ian and Charlie Mintrim, do a proper shepherd's pie and roast beef with Yorkshire pudding. Yachties (it has a great anchorage) buzz around the bar; there's wonderful snorkeling right around the point; and Friday brings a boisterous happy hour, with free finger food like salmon mousse, hummus, and chicken wings. Ask Charlie to tell you the story behind the restaurant's name; it features Prinderella, a cince, and a gairy frogmother. You'll want a bouble dourbon when she's finished. ⊠ *Jones Bridge,* ☎ *869/469–1291. AE, MC, V. Closed Mon. June–Sept.; Mon.–Wed. Oct.–Nov.; and Apr. 15–May.*

**$** ✕ **Callaloo.** This simple but stylish eatery, run by genial Abdul Hill who learned to cook with French-Creole flair on St. Martin, is another local standout. Delicious rotis make a quick, cheap lunch. Or opt for the yummy grilled kingfish in lemon butter, conch Creole, curried goat, or ribs, all served with generous side portions of rice, beans, and salad. ⊠ *Government Rd. and Main St.,* ☎ *869/469–5389. AE, D, MC, V. Closed Sun.*

**$** ✕ **Eddy's Bar and Restaurant.** Colorful flags flutter from the veranda
★ of this second-story restaurant overlooking Charlestown's Memorial Square in the center of town. A local artist designed the tablecloths and bright, boldly colored wall hangings. You'll find fine stir-fries and local West Indian specialties, such as cream of cauliflower soup and tender, crispy conch fritters with just the right amount of sass in the sauce. Eddy's mom, Eulalie Williams, makes the terrific hot sauce, which you can buy at the Main Street Supermarket down the street. Stop by here between 5 and 8 on Wednesday for happy hour; drinks are half-price, snacks free. ⊠ *Main St., Charlestown,* ☎ *869/469–5958. AE, MC, V. Closed Thurs., Sun., and Sept.*

**$** ✕ **Muriel's Cuisine.** Hanging plants, local still lifes, and table vases dress
★ up this eatery. Three meals are served daily, except Sunday. Bountiful entrées come with mounds of rice and peas as well as fresh vegetables, a side salad, and garlic bread. The subtly spiced jerk chicken would pass muster in many a Jamaican kitchen, and the goat-water and beef stew are fabulous: full-bodied and fragrant with garlic and coriander. Muriel St. Jean is the gracious hostess. Her restaurant attracts a very local clientele—women in hair curlers and young men who come to flirt shyly with the waitresses. ⊠ *Upper Happy Hill Dr., Charlestown,* ☎ *869/469–5920. AE, D, MC, V. Closed Sun.*

**$** ✕ **SunShine's.** Everything about this palm-thatched beach shack is colorful and larger-than-life, including the Rasta man SunShine himself. Flags from around the world—Bavaria to Brazil—drape the lean-to; the clientele is almost as international, including such celebrities as Woody Allen, Robert Plant, Alan Alda, and Wayne Gretzky (who wandered over unsuspectingly from the adjacent Four Seasons). They found picnic tables splashed with bright Rasta sunup-to-sunset colors; nothing has been left unpainted, including the palm trees. Fishermen literally cruise right up to the grill with their catch; you might savor lobster rolls, conch fritters, curried conch, or snapper Creole. Try the lethal house specialty, the Killer Bee. As SunShine boasts in his take on the rum punch, "One and you're stung, two you're stunned, three it's a knockout." ⊠ *Pinney's Beach, no phone. No credit cards.*

**$** ✕ **Tequila Sheila's.** This rustic, corrugated tin-and-wood shack sits right on a beach with glorious views of St. Kitts (management even provides chaise longues). The hybrid Pacific Rim–California menu is written daily on a blackboard; you might find anything from cheeseburgers with eggplant pepper relish to tequila lime chicken. It's regular events like Sunday Beach Party Brunch and Saturday Night Fever discos, however, that lasso locals and tourists. ⊠ *Cades Bay,* ☎ *869/469–1633. MC, V. Closed Mon. No lunch Tues.*

$ ✕ **Unella's.** The atmosphere is nothing fancy—just tables set on a second-floor porch overlooking the waterfront in Charlestown—but the fare is good West Indian. Stop here for exceptional lobster (more expensive than the rest of the menu), curried lamb, island-style spareribs, and steamed conch, all served with local vegetables, rice, and peas. Unella opens shop around 9 in the morning, when locals and boaters appear waiting for their breakfast, and stays open all day. ⊠ *Waterfront, Charlestown,* ☎ *869/469–5574. No credit cards.*

# Beaches

All the beaches on the island are free to the public and there are no changing facilities, so you'll have to wear a swimsuit under your clothes. If you're doing a cab tour, you may arrange with your driver to drop you off at the beach and pick you up later.

**Newcastle Beach** is by Nisbet Plantation (☞ Lodging, *above*). Popular among snorkelers, it's a broad beach of soft, white sand shaded by coconut palms at the northernmost tip of the island, on the channel between St. Kitts and Nevis.

**Oualie Beach,** at Mosquito Bay, just north of Pinney's, is a black-sand beach where **Oualie Beach Club** (☎ 869/469–9518) can mix you a drink and fix you up with water-sports equipment.

**Pinney's Beach** is the island's showpiece beach. It's almost 4 mi of soft, golden sand, on the calm Caribbean Sea, lined with a magnificent grove of palm trees. The palm-shaded lagoon is a scene right out of *South Pacific.* The Four Seasons Resort is now here, and several of the mountain inns have private cabanas and pavilions on the beach; it is, nevertheless, a public beach.

# Outdoor Activities and Sports
## Boating
Hobie Cats and Sunfish can be rented from **Oualie Beach Club** (☎ 869/469–9518). **Newcastle Bay Marina** (⊠ Newcastle, ☎ 869/469–9395) has Phantom sailboats, a 23-ft KenCraft powerboat, and several inflatables with outboards available for rent.

## Deep-Sea Fishing
The game here is kingfish, wahoo, grouper, tuna, and yellowtail snapper. If you want local expertise, call **Captain Valentine Glasgow** (☎ 869/469–1989), who has a 31-ft Ocean Master, *Lady James,* to take you in search of the big ones. **Jans Travel Agency** (☎ 869/469–5578) and **Mt. Nevis Hotel and Beach Club** (☎ 869/469–9373) arrange deep-sea fishing trips.

## Golf
Duffers doff their hats to the beautiful, impeccably maintained Robert Trent Jones II–designed 18-hole championship course at the **Four Seasons** (☎ 869/469–1111). Greens fees are $75 per person for nine holes; $125 for 18.

## Hiking
The center of the island is Nevis Peak, which soars up to 3,232 ft, flanked by Hurricane Hill on the north and Saddle Hill on the south. If you plan to scale Nevis Peak, a daylong affair, it is highly recommended that you go with a guide. Your hotel can arrange it for you; you can also ask the

hotel to pack a picnic lunch. Both the **Nevis Academy** (☎ 869/469–2091, FAX 869/469–9080), headed by David Rollinson, and **Top to Bottom** (☎ 869/469–5371) offer eco-rambles (slower tours) and hikes. Three-hour rambles or hikes are $20 per person, $30 for the more strenuous climb up Mt. Nevis. **Michael Herbert** (☎ 869/469–2856) offers four-hour nature hikes up to his 1,500-ft-high property, Herbert Heights, where he offers fresh local juices as you drink in the sublime views of Montserrat; his powerful telescope makes you feel as if you're staring right into that unfortunate island's simmering volcano.

## Horseback Riding
You can arrange for mountain-trail and beach rides through **Cane Gardens** (☎ 869/469–5648).

## Scuba Diving and Snorkeling
The village of Jamestown was washed into the sea around Fort Ashby, making the area a popular spot for snorkeling and diving. Reef-protected Pinney's Beach offers especially good snorkeling. Try **Scuba Safaris** (⊠ Oualie Beach, ☎ 869/469–9518), **Dive Nevis** (⊠ Pinney's Beach, ☎ 869/469–9373), or **Nevis Water Sports** (⊠ Oualie Beach, ☎ 869/469–9690) for everything from a resort course to full certification.

## Spectator Sports
Grove Park is the venue for **cricket** (January–July) and **soccer** (July–December). Your hotel or the tourist board can fill you in on dates, times, and grudge matches of particular interest between Kittitians and Nevisians.

One of the Caribbean's most endearing, unusual events is the occasional "Day at the Races," sponsored by the **Nevis Turf and Jockey Club** (☎ 869/469–3477). The races, which attract a "pan-Caribbean field" (as the club likes to boast), are held on a wild, windswept course called Eden Castle overlooking the "white horses" of the Atlantic. Last-minute changes and scratches are common, and a party atmosphere prevails.

## Tennis
There are 10 tennis courts at the **Four Seasons Resort** (☎ 869/469–1111), two at **Pinney's Beach Hotel** (☎ 869/469–5207), and one court each at **Nisbet** (☎ 869/469–9325), **Montpelier Plantation** (☎ 869/469–3462), and **Golden Rock** (☎ 869/469–3346).

## Water Sports
Snorkeling and waterskiing trips can be arranged through **Oualie Beach Club** (☎ 869/469–9518), **Dive Nevis** (☎ 869/369–9373), and **Newcastle Bay Marina** (☎ 869/469–9395). Windsurfers can also be rented at each place. **Ron Liburd** (☎ 869/469–1993) offers a catamaran at Cades Bay for snorkeling and island sunset cruises.

## Windsurfing
For windsurfing, **Winston Crooke** (☎ 869/469–9615) rents equipment and teaches classes. A two-hour beginner's class is $40 per person. If you rent equipment only, it's $12 an hour per person. **Windsurfing Nevis** (⊠ Oualie Beach Hotel, ☎ 869/469–9682) also offers top-notch instructors and equipment for $25 per half hour.

# Shopping

Nevis is certainly not the place for a shopping spree, but there are unique and wonderful surprises here, notably the island's stamps and batik and hand-embroidered clothing.

**Caribco Gifts** (⊠ Main St., ☎ 869/469–1432) is a cheaper alternative for T-shirts, candles, and pottery emblazoned with Nevis logos.

Local items of note are the batik caftans, scarves, and fabrics found in the Nevis branch of **Caribelle Batik** (⊠ In the Arcade of downtown Charlestown, ☏ 869/469–1491).

For more than 50 years Dame Eva Wilkins painted island people, flowers, and landscapes. An Eva Wilkins mural hangs over the bar at the Golden Rock (☞ Dining, *above*). Her originals sell for $100 and up, and prints are available in some of the local shops. The **Eva Wilkin Gallery** (⊠ Clay Ghaut, Gingerland, ☏ 869/469–2673) occupies her former light-filled atelier; the terraces afford understandably inspiring ocean views. If the paintings, drawings, and prints are out of your price range, consider buying the lovely note cards based on her designs.

**Knick Knacks** (⊠ The Courtyard, off Main St., Charlestown, ☏ 869/ 469–5784) showcases top local artisans, including Marvin Chapman (stone and wood carvings) and Jeannie Rigby (exquisite dolls). It also sells whimsical hats, beach wraps, and pottery.

Beekeeping is a buzzing biz on Nevis, and you'll find beeswax candles (which burn longer than the regular wax variety) and the fragrant, tropically flavored honey at many stores. Currently, Quentin Henderson, the affable head of the **Nevis Beekeeping Cooperative,** will even arrange trips (by appointment only) to various hives and his Beehouse to demonstrate the procedures (⊠ Gingerbread, ☏ 869/469–5521, ext. 2086).

The **Nevis Handicraft Co-op Society** (☏ 869/469–5509), next door to the tourist office, offers work by local artisans, including clothing, ceramic ware, woven goods, and homemade jellies.

Stamp collectors should head for the **Philatelic Bureau** (☏ 869/469– 0617), just off Main Street opposite the tourist office. St. Kitts and Nevis are famous for their decorative, and sometimes lucrative, stamps. An early Kittitian stamp recently brought in $7,000.

Kate Spencer's lovely island paintings and silk scarves and pareus are on sale at the **Plantation Picture House** (⊠ Main St., Charlestown, ☏ 869/469–5694).

**Beach Works** (⊠ Pinney's Beach inside the Beachcomber restaurant, ☏ 869/469–0620) has become the island's classiest boutique, with an excellent selection of everything from bathing suits to Balines crafts. The adjoining restaurant also exhibits a rotating gallery of local works on its walls.

For dolls and baskets handcrafted in Nevis, visit the **Sandbox Tree** (⊠ Evelyn's Villa, Charlestown, ☏ 869/469–5662). Among other items available here are hand-painted chests.

## Nightlife

In season, it is usually easy to find a local calypso singer or a steel or string band performing at one of the hotels on weekends. You can count on entertainment at the **Four Seasons Resort** (☏ 869/469–1111) on both Friday and Saturday nights. On Friday night the Shell All-Stars steel band entertains in the gardens at **Old Manor Estate** (☏ 869/469– 3445). The **Golden Rock** (☏ 869/469–3346) brings in David Freeman's Honeybees String Band to jazz things up for the Saturday-night buffet. You can have dinner and a dance on Wednesday night at **Pinney's Beach Hotel** (☏ 869/469–5207). **Oualie Beach Hotel** (☏ 869/469–9735) throws a popular Saturday-night buffet with live string band and masquerade troupe. **Eddy's Bar and Restaurant** (☞ Dining, *above*) holds raucous West Indian nights with theme buffet and live string band Friday and Saturday. **Tequila Sheila's** (☞ Dining, *above*) is already legendary for its wild (for Nevis) Saturday Night Fever Disco, when locals trot out their best polyester, and Sunday Beach Party Brunches, which often continue past dark. A new and improved **Beachcomber** (☎ 869/469–1192), on Pinney's Beach, is starting to rival others in popularity, with huge barbecues in addition to a fine simple menu of burgers and grilled items.

Apart from the hotel scene, there are a few places where young locals go for late-night calypso, reggae, and other island music. **Club Trenim** (✉ Government Rd., Charlestown, no phone) has disco dancing starting at 8:30 every night except Tuesday. **Dick's Bar** (✉ Brickiln, no phone) has live music or a DJ on Friday and Saturday evenings.

# Exploring Nevis

The main road of Nevis makes a 20-mi circuit, with various offshoots bumping and winding into the mountains. You can tour Charlestown, the capital city, in a half hour or so, but you'll need three to four hours to explore the entire island.

*Numbers in the margin correspond to points of interest on the Nevis map.*

SIGHTS TO SEE

❷ **Bath Springs.** The springs and the ruins of **Bath Hotel,** built by John Huggins in 1778, sustained recent hurricane damage, but both were expected to reopen by 1998. The springs, with temperatures of 104–108°F, emanate from the hillside. Huggins's 50-room hotel, the first hotel in the Caribbean, was adjacent to the waters. Eighteenth-century accounts reported that a few days of imbibing and immersing in these waters resulted in miraculous cures. It would take a minor miracle to restore the decayed hotel to anything like grandeur—it closed down in the late 19th century—but the spring house has been partially restored, and some of the springs are still as hot and restorative as ever. ⌧ *Bathing costs $2.* ☉ *Weekdays 8–noon and 1–3:30, Sat. 8–noon.*

❶ **Charlestown.** About 1,200 of the island's 9,300 inhabitants live in the capital of Nevis. The town faces the Caribbean, about 12½ mi south of Basseterre in St. Kitts. If you arrive by ferry, as most people do, you'll walk smack onto Main Street from the pier. Although it is true that tiny Charlestown, founded in 1660, has seen better days, it's easy to imagine how it must have looked in its heyday. The buildings, a bit weathered and worse for wear, still have their fanciful galleries, elaborate gingerbread, wood shutters, and colorful hanging plants. The stonework building with the clock tower houses the **courthouse** and **library,** open Monday through Saturday from 9 to 6. A fire in 1873 severely damaged the building and destroyed valuable records; the current building dates from the turn of the century. You're welcome to poke around the second-floor library, one of the coolest places on the island. The little park opposite the courthouse is **Memorial Square,** dedicated to the fallen of World Wars I and II.

NEED A BREAK?
Drop into the **Courtyard Cafe** (✉ Across the street from tourist office, ☎ 869/469–5685), Caribbean Confections' lush, foliage-filled outdoor restaurant, for coffee and homemade pastries. There are also sandwiches; black bean soup; ginger pumpkin; a special pasta like fettuccine with avocado, garlic, tomatoes, and beans; peanut-butter cookies; and popcorn.

The **Alexander Hamilton Birthplace,** which contains the **Museum of Nevis History,** is on the waterfront, covered in bougainvillea and hi-

biscus. This Georgian-style house is a reconstruction of the states-
man's original home, built in 1680 and thought to have been destroyed during an earthquake in the mid-19th century. Hamilton was
born here in 1755. He left for the American colonies 17 years later to
continue his education; he became secretary to George Washington and
died in a duel with political rival Aaron Burr. The **Nevis House of Assembly** sits on the second floor of this building, and the museum downstairs contains Hamilton memorabilia and documents pertaining to the
island's history, as well as fascinating displays on island geology, politics, and cuisine. ⊠ *Low St.,* ☎ *869/469/5786.* ☞ *$2.* ☉ *Weekdays
8–4, Sat. 10–1.*

**❺ Eden Brown Estate.** This government-owned mansion, built around 1740,
is known as Nevis's haunted house or, rather, haunted ruins. In 1822,
apparently, a Miss Julia Huggins was to marry a fellow named May-
nard. However, on the day of the wedding, the groom and his best man
had a duel and killed each other. The bride-to-be became a recluse, and
the mansion was closed down. Local residents claim they can feel the
presence of "someone" whenever they go near the eerie old house,
shrouded in weeds and wildflowers. You're welcome to drop by; it's
always open and it's free.

**❼ Fort Ashby.** Overgrown with tropical vegetation, this site overlooks the
place where the settlement of Jamestown fell into the sea after a tidal
wave hit the coast in 1680. Needless to say, this is a favored target of
scuba divers. ⊠ *1½ mi southwest of Hurricane Hill, on Main Rd.*

**❻ Hurricane Hill.** Many people take the drive up here to see the splendid
view of St. Kitts. ⊠ *West of Newcastle Airport.*

**❸ Nelson Museum.** This collection merits a visit for the memorabilia of
Lord Nelson, including letters, documents, paintings, and even furniture from his flagship. Nelson was based in Antigua but returned often
to court, and eventually to marry, Frances Nisbet, who lived on a 64-
acre plantation here. ⊠ *Bath Rd.,* ☎ *869/469–0408.* ☞ *$2 ($1 if admission paid to Museum of Nevis History).* ☉ *Weekdays 9–4, Sat. 10–1.*

**❽ Nelson Spring.** The spring's waters have considerably decreased since
the 1780s, when young Captain Horatio Nelson periodically filled his
ships with fresh water here.

**❹ St. John's Church.** Among the records of this church built in 1680 is a
tattered, prominently displayed marriage certificate that reads: "Horatio Nelson, Esquire, to Frances Nisbet, Widow, on March 11, 1787."
⊠ *Fig Tree.*

**❾ St. Thomas Anglican Church.** The island's oldest church was built in
1643 and has been altered many times over the years. The gravestones
in the old churchyard have stories to tell, and the church itself contains memorials to the early settlers of Nevis.

# ST. KITTS AND NEVIS A TO Z

## Arriving and Departing

### BY BOAT

The 150-passenger government-operated ferry M/V *Caribe Queen*
makes the 45-minute crossing from Nevis to St. Kitts twice daily except Thursday and Sunday. The schedule is a bit erratic, so confirm
departure times with the tourist office. Round-trip fare is $8. An air-
conditioned, 110-passenger ferry, M/V *Spirit of Mount Nevis,* makes
the run twice daily Thursday and Sunday. The fare is $12 round-trip.
Call **Nevis Cruise Lines** (☎ 869/469–9373) for information and reser-

vations. Sea-taxi service between the two islands is operated by dive master **Kenneth Samuel** (☎ 869/465–2670) and by Auston MacLeod of **Pro-Divers** (☎ 869/465–3223) for $20 one-way in summer, $25 in winter; discounts can be negotiated for small groups.

BY PLANE
**American** (☎ 869/465–0500 or 800/433–7300) and **Delta** (☎ 800/221–1212) fly from the United States to Antigua, St. Croix, St. Thomas, St. Maarten, and San Juan, Puerto Rico, where connections to St. Kitts (and, to a lesser extent, to Nevis) can be made on regional carriers such as **American Eagle** (☎ 800/433–7300), **LIAT** (☎ 869/465–2511), and **Windward Island Airways** (☎ 869/465–0810). LIAT has two flights daily between St. Kitts and Nevis. **British Airways** (☎ 800/247–9297) flies from London to Antigua, and **Air Canada** (☎ 800/776–3000) flies from Toronto to Antigua. **Air St. Kitts–Nevis** (☎ 869/465–8571), **Nevis Express** (☎ 869/469–9756), and **Carib Aviation** (☎ 869/465–3055 in St. Kitts; 869/469–9295 in Nevis; ℻ 869/469–9185) are reliable air-charter operations providing service between St. Kitts and Nevis and other islands.

FROM THE AIRPORT
Taxis meet every flight at both island's airports. The taxis are unmetered, but fixed rates, in E.C. dollars, are posted at the airport and at the jetty. On St. Kitts the fare from the airport to the closest hotel in Basseterre is EC$16; to the farthest point, EC$56. On Nevis some sample fares are from the ferry slip to Nisbet Plantation, EC$36, and to Golden Rock, EC$30. From the airport, the rates are, respectively, EC$17 and EC$40. Be sure to clarify whether the rate quoted is in E.C. or U.S. dollars. There is a 50% surcharge for trips made between 10 PM and 6 AM.

## Currency
Legal tender is the Eastern Caribbean (E.C.) dollar. At press time, the rate of exchange was EC$2.60 to US$1. U.S. dollars are accepted practically everywhere, but you'll usually get change in E.C. dollars. Prices quoted here are in U.S. dollars unless noted otherwise. Most large hotels, restaurants, and shops accept major credit cards, but small inns and shops often do not. It's always a good idea to check current credit-card policies before you turn up with only plastic in your pocket.

## Emergencies
**Police:** ☎ 911. **Hospital:** There is a 24-hour emergency room at the **Joseph N. France General Hospital** (✉ Basseterre, ☎ 869/465–2551) and at **Alexandra Hospital** (✉ Charlestown, ☎ 869/469–5473). **Pharmacies:** In St. Kitts, **Skerritt's Drug Store** (✉ Fort St., ☎ 869/465–2008) is open Monday–Wednesday 8–5, Thursday 8–1, Friday 8–5:30, and Saturday 8–6; **City Drug** (✉ Fort St., Basseterre, ☎ 869/465–2156) is open Monday–Wednesday and Friday–Saturday 8–7, Thursday 8–5, Sunday 8–10 AM; and **City Drug** (✉ Sun 'n' Sand, Frigate Bay, ☎ 869/465–1803) is open Monday–Saturday 8:30–8, Sunday 8:30–10:30 AM and 4–6 PM. In Nevis, **Evelyn's Drugstore** (✉ Charlestown, ☎ 869/469–5278) is open weekdays 8–5, Saturday 8–7:30, and Sunday 7 AM–8 PM; the **Claxton Medical Centre** (✉ Charlestown, ☎ 869/469–5357) is open Monday–Wednesday and Friday 8–6, Thursday 8–4, Saturday 7:30–7, and Sunday 6–8 PM.

## Getting Around
BUSES
A privately owned minibus circles St. Kitts. Check with the tourist office (☞ Visitor Information, *below*) about schedules.

CAR RENTALS AND SCOOTERS

You'll need a local driver's license, which you can get by presenting yourself, your valid driver's license, and EC$30 (US$12) at the police station on Cayon Street in Basseterre. (In Nevis, the car-rental agency will help you obtain a local license at the police station.) The license is valid for one year.

In St. Kitts, try **Avis** (☎ 869/465–6507), which has the best selection of Suzuki and Daihatsu four-wheel-drive vehicles, **Budget** (☎ 869/466–5585), **Delise Walwyn** (☎ 869/465–8449), and **Sunshine** (☎ 869/465–2193). **TDC Rentals** (☎ 869/465–2991) has a wide selection of vehicles and the best service. Car rentals start at about $35 per day for a compact; expect to pay a few extra bucks for air-conditioning. Most agencies offer substantial discounts when you rent by the week. At press time, the price of gas was $2 per gallon. Remember to drive on the left.

You may not want to drive in Nevis. The island's roads are pocked with crater-size potholes; driving is on the left, and, to make it more difficult, you may be given a right-drive vehicle. Pigs, goats, and cattle crop up out of nowhere to amble along the road, and if you deviate from Main Street, you're likely to have trouble finding your way. But if you can't resist, **TDC Rentals** (⊠ Charlestown, ☎ 869/469–5690), known for its exceptional service, rents a wide range of vehicles, has offices on St. Kitts, and offers a three-day rental that includes a car on both islands. **Avis** (⊠ Stoney Grove, ☎ 869/469–1240) provides Suzuki Jeeps and Nissan cars. **Nisbett Rentals** (⊠ Newcastle Airport, ☎ 869/469–9211) rents cars, minimokes, and Jeeps. None of these companies charge for mileage, and all of them accept major credit cards.

TAXIS

Taxis rates are government-regulated, and the rates are posted at the airport, the dock, and in the free **visitor tourist guide.** There are fixed rates to and from all the hotels and to and from major points of interest. In St. Kitts, you can call the **St. Kitts Taxi Association** (☎ 869/465–8487; 869/465–7818 after hrs). In Nevis, taxi service (☎ 869/469–5621; 869/469–5515 after dark) is available at the airport, by the dock in Charlestown, as well as through arrangement with your hotel.

## Guided Tours

The taxi driver who picks you up will probably offer to act as your guide to the island. Each driver is knowledgeable and does a three-hour tour for $60. He can also make a lunch reservation at one of the plantation restaurants, and you can incorporate this into your tour. In St. Kitts, **Tropical Tours** (☎ 869/465–4167) can run you around the island and take you to the rain forest. **Kriss Tours** (☎ 869/465–4042) and **Greg's Safari** (☎ 869/465–4121) specialize in rain-forest and volcano tours. Also try **Kantours** (☎ 869/465–2098) for general island tours.

In Nevis, **Fitzroy "Teach" Williams** (☎ 869/469–1140) is particularly recommended: He's perennial president of the taxi association—even older cabbies call him "the Dean." **All Seasons Streamline Tours** (☎ 869/469–1138, FAX 869/469–1139) has a fleet of air-conditioned, 14-seat vans and uniformed drivers to take you around the island at a cost of $75 for three hours. **Jan's Travel Agency** (⊠ Arcade, Charlestown, ☎ 869/469–5578) arranges half- and full-day tours of the island. You can also stop by the **Nevis Tourist Office** (☞ Visitor Information, *below*) to pick up a copy of the Nevis Historical Society's self-guided tour of the island.

## Language
English with a strong West Indian lilt is spoken here.

## Opening and Closing Times
Although shops used to close for lunch from noon to 1, more and more establishments are remaining open Monday–Saturday 8–4. Some shops close earlier on Thursday. Hours vary somewhat from bank to bank but are typically Monday–Thursday 8–3 and Friday 8–5. **St. Kitts & Nevis National Bank** is also open Saturday 8:30–11 AM.

## Passports and Visas
Although it is always wiser to travel in the Caribbean with a valid passport, U.S. and Canadian citizens need produce only proof of citizenship in the form of a voter registration card or birth certificate (a driver's license will not suffice). British citizens must have a passport; visas are not required. A return or ongoing ticket is mandatory.

## Precautions
Visitors, especially women, should not jog on long, lonely roads.

## Taxes and Service Charges
Hotels collect a 7% government tax and add a 10% service charge to your bill. In restaurants, a tip of 15% is appropriate. The departure tax is $10. There is no departure tax from St. Kitts to Nevis, or vice versa. Taxi drivers typically receive a 10% tip.

## Telephones and Mail
To call St. Kitts and Nevis from the United States, dial area code 869, then access code 465, 466, 468, or 469 and the local four-digit number. Caribbean Phone Cards, which can be purchased in denominations of $5, $10, and $20, are handy for making local phone calls, calling other islands, and accessing USADirect lines. To make an intraisland call, simply dial the seven-digit number. Warning for both islands: Many private lines and hotels charge access rates if you use your ATT, Sprint, or MCI phonecard; there's no regularity, and it can be frustrating. Avoid using the widely advertised **Skantel** (☎ 800/877–8000), which ostensibly allows you to make credit-card calls; rates are usurious and they usually freeze an outrageous amount for up to a week on your credit card until they finally put through the exact bill.

Airmail letters to the United States and Canada cost EC80¢ per half ounce; postcards require EC50¢. Mail takes at least 7–10 days to reach the United States. St. Kitts and Nevis issue separate stamps, but each honors the other's. The beautiful stamps are collector's items, and you may have a hard time pasting them on postcards.

## Visitor Information
Contact the **St. Kitts & Nevis Tourist Board** (⌧ 414 E. 75th St., New York, NY 10021, ☎ 212/535–1234 or 800/582–6208, FAX 212/734–6511), **St. Kitts & Nevis Tourist Office** (⌧ 11 Yorkville Ave., Suite 508, Toronto, Ontario M4W 1L3, ☎ 416/921–7717, FAX 416/921–7997), and **St. Kitts & Nevis Tourist Office** (⌧ 10 Kensington Ct., London W8 5DL, ☎ 0171/376–0881, FAX 0171/937–3611).

In St. Kitts, contact **St. Kitts/Nevis Department of Tourism** (⌧ Pelican Mall, Bay Rd., Box 132, Basseterre, ☎ 869/465–2620 or 869/465–4040, FAX 869/465–8794) and the **St. Kitts–Nevis Hotel Association** (⌧ Box 438, Basseterre, ☎ 869/465–5304, FAX 869/465–7746).

The **Nevis Tourist Office** (☎ 869/469–1042, FAX 869/469–1066) is on Main Street in Charlestown. The office is open Monday–Tuesday 8–4:30 and Wednesday–Friday 8–4.

# 22 St. Lucia

*An island of breathtaking vistas—its
trademark Pitons, enchanting bays and
sandy coves, sleepy villages, endless
banana plantations, and a corkscrew
road that winds along the coast, cuts
through dense jungle, and dips into
deep mountain ravines—St. Lucia is
self-described as "Simply beautiful!"
That's an understatement.*

Updated by
Jane E. Zarem

**C**ONTRARY TO POPULAR FOLKLORE, Columbus never set foot on St. Lucia; until a few years ago, neither had most Americans. A boom in all-inclusive resort construction has been drawing increasing droves of North Americans—a bit to the dismay of Brits and Europeans who've cherished this lush, tropical paradise for decades. St. Lucia, a 238-square-mi island toward the southern end of the Windwards, has honey-color sand beaches and posh hotels in the north. In the south, striking natural attractions dominate: The Pitons (Petit and Gros), the island's twin peaks, rise from the sea to a height of more than 2,400 ft; a dense rain forest blankets much of the topography; and bubbling sulfur springs gurgle at the mouth of a low-lying volcano that erupted thousands of years ago and now produces highly acclaimed curative waters.

Because of its natural beauty, St. Lucia is often referred to as "the Helen of the West Indies." The coastline is familiar to sailors and divers alike—the reefs near the Pitons are especially sought-after scuba sites. In between the populous north and the gorgeous south a tortuously winding road passes through lush valleys, rain forest, banana plantations, secluded bays, and small villages. Marigot Bay, whose claim to fame is having been the filming location for *Doctor Doolittle,* is on the west coast and is one of the Caribbean's prettiest bays. The village of Choiseul, on the south coast, is an important arts center, maintaining Carib traditions and nurturing local talent.

In its less secluded regions, St. Lucia is noticeably sophisticated, hosting not only Carnival in February but also a world-renowned Jazz Festival in May. Another St. Lucian festival, National Day, celebrates December 13, 1502—even though historians now think the island was sighted in 1499 by Juan de la Cosa, Columbus's navigator. In any case, the island's true first inhabitants, the Arawaks, paddled up from South America sometime before AD 200. The warlike Caribs followed and conquered around AD 800, and they were still here when the first Europeans attempted to set up camp.

In 1605, 67 English settlers bound for Guiana were blown off course and landed near Vieux Fort. Within a few weeks the Caribs had killed all but 19, who escaped in a canoe. Another group of English settlers dropped by 30 years later but were met with a similar lack of hospitality. Finally, the French signed a treaty with the Caribs in 1660 and took control of the island.

Thus began a 150-year period of battles between the French and the English that saw a dizzying 14 changes in power before the British took permanent possession in 1814. During those battle-filled years, Europeans colonized the island. They developed sugar plantations, using slaves from West Africa to work the fields. By 1838, when slaves were emancipated, more than 90% of the island consisted of African descendants. This is still largely true of today's 140,000 St. Lucians.

On February 22, 1979, St. Lucia became an independent state within the British Commonwealth of Nations, with a resident governor-general appointed by the queen. Still, there are many relics of French occupation, notably in the island patois—spoken everywhere—the Creole cuisine, and the names of the places and the people.

St. Lucia's coal industry began on the island in 1883; until about 1920, Castries, the capital, was a leading coal port in the West Indies. Sugarcane became the next major money crop, followed by bananas during the 1960s. Today, the tourism industry is running neck and neck with

**550**

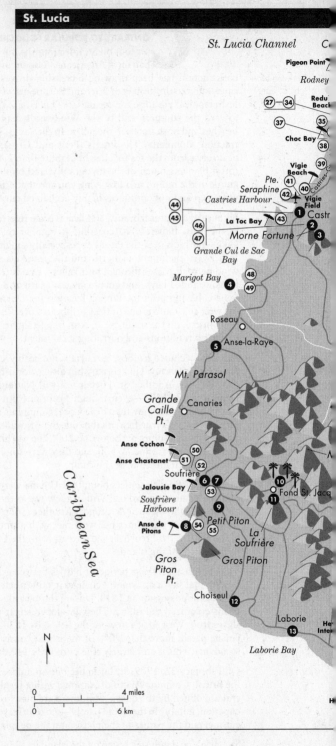

St. Lucia

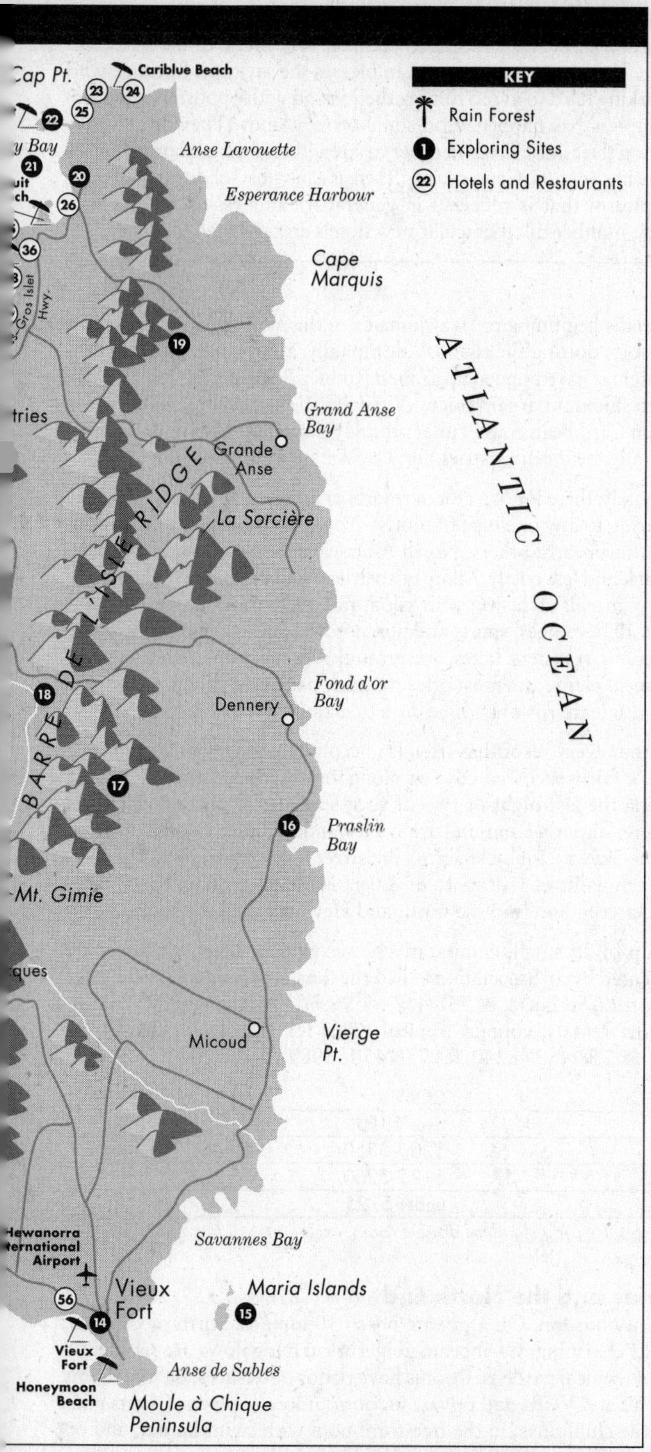
KEY
Rain Forest
Exploring Sites
Hotels and Restaurants
Cariblue Beach
Anse Lavouette
Esperance Harbour
Cape Marquis
ATLANTIC OCEAN
Grand Anse Bay
Grande Anse
La Sorcière
BARRE DE L'ISLE RIDGE
Fond d'or Bay
Dennery
Praslin Bay
Mt. Gimie
Micoud
Vierge Pt.
Savannes Bay
Maria Islands
Vieux Fort
Anse de Sables
Moule à Chique Peninsula
Vieux Fort
Honeymoon Beach
Airport
Gros Islet Hwy.

**Lodging**

Anse Chastanet Hotel, **51**
Auberge Seraphine, **41**
Bay Gardens, **33**
Candyo Inn, **32**
Club St. Lucia, **25**
East Winds Inn, **37**
Green Parrot, **46**
Harmony Marina Suites, **29**
Humming Bird Beach Resort, **52**
Ladera, **55**
LeSPORT, **24**
Marigot Beach Club, **48**
Orange Grove Hotel, **36**
Rendezvous, **40**
Rex Papillon, **34**
Rex St. Lucian, **30**
Royal St. Lucian, **31**
Sandals Halcyon St. Lucia, **39**
Sandals St. Lucia at La Toc, **43**
Skyway Inn, **56**
Still Plantation & Beach Resort, **53**
Tuxedo Villas, **45**
Windjammer Landing Villa Beach Resort, **35**
Wyndham Morgan Bay Resort, **38**

bananas, particularly since the banana-growing countries of the Eastern Caribbean are now having to compete for a share of the European market. The importance of tourism pleases the savvy St. Lucians, who are working hard to avoid ruining their island with opportunistic over-building—as has happened on some other islands. They are also diversifying their agriculture in order to strengthen their economy further by reducing imports. Consequently, there is a tangible solidity to St. Lucia, an optimism that is reflected in general friendliness as well as in a startling number of spectacular new hotels and resorts.

## Lodging

St. Lucia is beginning to rival Jamaica in the number of all-inclusives and resorts dotting the island. Additionally, a few small and inexpensive lodgings have popped up around Rodney Bay, offering bright, clean modern suites at bargain prices. Virtually all the development is along the calm Caribbean coast, either around Soufrière to the south or, more commonly, between Castries and Cap Estate in the north.

Fortunately, there is not a glut of resorts or hotels in any one price range or catering to any one type of tourist. You'll find some that draw principally Europeans; others, North Americans. Some are lavish; others, laid-back and less costly. Many properties listed under the highest price category are all-inclusive; your room rate includes three meals a day, snacks, all beverages, sports and nonmotorized water sports (including instruction), transfers, taxes, and gratuities. Some properties offer MAP or EP meal plans, and most offer wedding packages: St. Lucian law requires residence for only three days to acquire a marriage license.

Just about every resort has friendly, accommodating service and is either in a fairly secluded cove or along an unspoiled beach. Consider spending the last night or two of your stay at one of the lodgings in Soufrière, about 45 minutes from Hewanorra International Airport, or at the Skyway Inn, just across the street from the airport. The foremost complaint of visitors to St. Lucia is the 60-minute, topsy-turvy drive between hotels in the north and Hewanorra in the south.

A group of 29 small, comparatively inexpensive hotels and inns are represented by an association called the **Inns of St. Lucia** (⊠ 20 Bridge St., Castries, St. Lucia, ☎ 758/452–4599, FAX 758/452–5428). For private villa rentals, contact **Tropical Villas** (⊠ Box 189, Castries, St. Lucia, ☎ 758/452–8240, FAX 758/450–8089).

| CATEGORY | COST* |
|---|---|
| $$$$ | over $350 |
| $$$ | $200–$350 |
| $$ | $125–$200 |
| $ | under $125 |

*All prices are for a standard double room, excluding 8% tax and 10% service charge.*

### Castries and the North End

$$$$  🏨 **East Winds Inn.** On a private beach 10 minutes north of Castries, these 13 charming, Caribbean, gingerbread bungalows are set amid 8 acres of tropical gardens. Rooms have patios or terraces; deluxe rooms have TVs and VCRs and private indoor/outdoor showers. Guests mingle at the clubhouse, in the free-form pool with swim-up bar, and on the beach—where kayaks, aqua boards, aqua trikes, and snorkeling equipment are provided. The international and Creole creations of a French chef are served in the inn's open-air, thatched-roof restaurant (vegetarian selections are always included). ⊠ *Box 1477, La Brelotte Bay, Gros Islet,* ☎ *758/452–8212,* FAX *758/452–9941. 26 rooms.*

*Restaurant, bar, fans, minibars, pool, beach, water sports, shop. AE, MC, V. All-inclusive.*

**$$$$** ★ 🏨 **LeSPORT.** Though crowned by the Oasis—a temple to well-being that looks like a sun-bleached Moorish palace—LeSPORT is not entirely a spa. Health nuts will be very happy here, and you can experiment with the spa cuisine; but it is also possible to eat enormous quantities of the chef's excellent meals and lounge on the perfect U-shape beach. Most guests laze around in white robes awaiting thalassotherapy—sea-water beauty treatments—before throwing themselves into one of the 30-something things-to-do (archery, tai chi, fencing, waterskiing, scuba, tennis, volleyball etc., etc.). Rooms have queen-size beds, marble baths, and small balconies with ocean views; costlier versions have cool marble floors and four-poster beds. The only disappointment is the small, low-tech gym. ✉ *Box 437, Cariblue Beach,* ☎ *758/450–8551 or 800/544–2883,* FAX *758/452–0368. 100 rooms, 2 suites, 1 plantation house. Restaurant, 2 bars, air-conditioning, refrigerators, 3 pools, beauty salon, hot tub, sauna, tennis court, aerobics, exercise rooms, beach, water sports, bicycles, shop. AE, DC, MC, V. All-inclusive.*

**$$$$** 🏨 **Wyndham Morgan Bay Resort.** Eight three-story buildings fan out from a central pool-restaurant area at this all-inclusive resort on Choc Bay. Rooms are decorated in the usual Caribbean pale florals and peach wicker and are furnished with comfortable king-size beds. Each has a color television, radio, coffeemaker, and small veranda with either a garden or partial sea view. Drinks and entertainment flow freely—from early morning aerobics to midnight pizza at the beach-side Palm Grill—to the delight of a largely European crowd. ✉ *Box 2167, Gros Islet,* ☎ *758/450–2511,* FAX *758/450–1050. 238 rooms. 2 restaurants, 2 bars, beach grill, air-conditioning, pool, hot tub, sauna, 4 tennis courts, aerobics, archery, exercise room, beach, water sports, shop, recreation room. AE, D, MC, V. All-inclusive.*

**$$$–$$$$** 🏨 **Club St. Lucia.** Set on 50 acres at the northernmost point of St. Lucia, this bustling, friendly resort is the island's largest. It caters mostly to Brits, but tennis enthusiasts come here to be close to the adjacent St. Lucia Racquet Club (☞ Outdoor Activities and Sports, *below*), which is free for guests. Others come here to get hitched; expect to see several weddings each day. Rooms and suites are in bungalows scattered over the hillside, and there are two beaches. Accommodations are spacious, with king-size beds, tile floors, patios, and air-conditioning in all but some standard rooms, which have ceiling fans. Live entertainment is scheduled nightly. Though the food is adequate at best, guests receive a discount and free transportation to the Great House restaurant (☞ Dining, *below*). ✉ *Box 915, Smugglers Village, Castries,* ☎ *758/450–0551 or 800/777–1250,* FAX *758/450–0281. 372 rooms and suites. 2 restaurants, 3 bars, air-conditioning, 3 pools, hot tub, 2 tennis courts, 2 beaches, water sports, shops, dance club, children's program, laundry service. AE, DC, MC, V. All-inclusive.*

**$$$–$$$$** 🏨 **Rendezvous.** This all-inclusive, couples-only resort, under the same ownership as LeSPORT, is set amid 7 acres of tropical gardens on 2-mi-long Malabar Beach. Things tend to be quite active, with volleyball in the pool and on the beach, and aerobics and water exercise classes. The activities desk can arrange anything, including a wedding. Accommodations have pink marble floors, king-size four-poster beds, and a balcony or terrace—but no TVs. There is nightly live music for dancing and a piano bar that's open until the last couple leaves. ✉ *Box 190, Malabar Beach,* ☎ *758/452–4211 or 800/544–2883,* FAX *758/452–7419. 84 rooms, 8 suites, 8 cottages. 2 restaurants, 3 bars, air-conditioning, 2 pools, 2 hot tubs, sauna, 2 tennis courts, exercise room, beach, boating, water sports, dive shop, bicycles. AE, MC, V. All-inclusive.*

$$$–$$$$   ⌂ **Royal St. Lucian.** This classy resort, facing beautiful Reduit Beach,
   ★       caters to your every whim. The colonnaded reception area is stunning—
           an Italian palazzo with vaulted atrium, cool marble walls, a gurgling
           fountain, and a sweeping grand staircase. The russet-roofed white
           buildings form a "U" in the pristine landscaped grounds. The large,
           rambling pool has Japanese-style bridges, a natural rock waterfall, and
           a swim-up bar. The split-level suites are sumptuous (maybe the best
           on the island), with a separate sitting area, luxurious bathroom, large
           patio or balcony, soothing pastel color scheme, cable TV, three phones,
           and jet shower. Food and service are stellar. Guests may use the ten-
           nis and water-sports facilities at the adjacent sister property, the Rex
           St. Lucian. ⊠ *Box 977, Castries,* ☎ *758/452–9999 or 800/225–
           5859,* ℻ *758/452–9639. 96 suites. 3 restaurants, 2 bars, air-condi-
           tioning, minibars, pool, spa, beach, snorkeling, meeting rooms. AE,
           DC, MC, V. EP, MAP.*

$$$–$$$$   ⌂ **Sandals St. Lucia at La Toc.** This secluded 155-acre property, one of
   ★       two Sandals resorts on the island, is a 10-minute drive south of Cas-
           tries and Vigie Airport. The list of facilities and amenities is almost end-
           less: private plunge pools, a ¼-acre swimming pool, a lovely beach, a
           nine-hole golf course, floodlit tennis courts, an outstanding fitness cen-
           ter, nightly entertainment, etc. There's no shortage of restaurants either;
           choose Asian, Continental, French, southwestern, or Caribbean cuisine.
           Guest rooms and suites, with mahogany furniture and king-size four-
           poster beds, all have hair dryers, direct-dial telephones, and cable TV.
           Suites have concierge service. Most important, guests seem to have a
           blast—thanks in part to a young, fun-loving staff. No tipping is allowed.
           ⊠ *La Toc Rd., Castries,* ☎ *758/452–3081,* ℻ *758/453–7089. 213
           rooms, 60 suites. 5 restaurants, 5 bars, air-conditioning, 3 pools, 9-hole
           golf course, 5 tennis courts, health club, beach, water sports. AE, DC,
           MC, V. All-inclusive.*

$$$        ⌂ **Sandals Halcyon St. Lucia.** This second, smaller Sandals couples-only
           resort is at Choc Bay, 10 minutes north of Castries and Vigie Airport.
           More low-key than its sister resort, there's still a lot of activity and en-
           thusiasm on the part of both guests and staff. All rooms are sur-
           rounded by lovely gardens and are attractively decorated with mahogany
           furniture, king-size four-poster beds with bright-print spreads, and
           white tile floors. The sea here is generally calm, and guests enjoy a wide
           range of water sports and other activities—exercise equipment, nightly
           entertainment, and more. A shuttle runs hourly between the two San-
           dals resorts, so guests can "stay at one, play at two." Three restau-
           rants serve Italian, Caribbean, and international cuisine at dinner;
           sumptuous buffet breakfasts and lunches; and light food and snacks
           all day long. Seaside weddings take place often. ⊠ *Box GM 910,
           Choc Bay, Castries,* ☎ *758/453–0222,* ℻ *758/451–8435. 170 rooms.
           3 restaurants, 3 bars, snack bar, air-conditioning, 3 pools, 2 tennis courts,
           basketball, health club, volleyball, Ping-Pong, shuffleboard, beach, water
           sports. AE, DC, MC, V. All-inclusive.*

$$$        ⌂ **Windjammer Landing Villa Beach Resort.** This sun-kissed resort, with
           sweeping views of one of St. Lucia's prettiest bays, fulfills anyone's beach-
           combing fantasies. White stucco villas crowned with tile alternate with
           a porticoed reception area and thatched-hut public rooms. Villas are
           huge and tastefully decorated in the ubiquitous island pastels and rat-
           tan furnishings. You can arrange to have dinner prepared and served
           in your villa. The ambience is rustic simplicity with painted natural wood
           timbers, tile floors, wicker chairs, and straw mats. A people-mover trans-
           ports guests up the steep hill from the main building and shops to their
           villas. A waterfall connects two bi-level pools; two- and three-bedroom
           villas have private plunge pools. ⊠ *Box 1504, La Brelotte Bay, Cas-
           tries,* ☎ *758/452–0913,* ℻ *758/452–9454. 131 1-, 2-, 3-, and 4-bed-*

*room villas. 3 restaurants, 3 bars, air-conditioning, 2 pools, 2 tennis courts, scuba diving, snorkeling, windsurfing, boating, waterskiing, shops, children's program, laundry service. AE, MC, V. EP, MAP.*

**$$** 🏨 **Harmony Marina Suites.** Your suite may have a view of the pool or Rodney Bay Marina, but Reduit Beach is only 200 yards away. The 22 one-bedroom suites each have a large bathroom with hair dryer, a red-tile balcony or terrace, cable TV, kitchenette, and wet bar. Eight VIP suites also have double hot tubs and four-poster beds. The property also has its own waterfront restaurant. This is a nice alternative to the megaresort scene, and the adjacent minimarket—one of the best-stocked on the island—makes the suites ideal for long-term stays. ⊠ *Box 155, Castries,* ☎ *758/452–8756,* 𝖥𝖠𝖷 *758/452–8677. 30 suites. Restaurant, bar, air-conditioning, kitchenettes, pool, beauty salon, windsurfing, boating, fishing, baby-sitting, laundry service. MC, V. EP, MAP.*

**$$** 🏨 **Marigot Beach Club.** On beautiful Marigot Bay, this quiet spot 9 mi south of Castries is not too far from the mountains and sights around Soufrière. Guest quarters climb the steep hillside that forms a backdrop for the resort, and a tram transports guests up and down. Studios and one-bedroom apartments have kitchenettes, pickled-wood furniture, and private patios that overlook the water. Marigot Bay is a favorite of yachtspeople, so the boating activity adds atmosphere. The resort has an excellent water-sports center, where you can arrange diving and snorkeling, windsurfing, kayaking, waterskiing, or sailing. The lovely beach, shaded by coconut palms, looks like one you'd see in the South Seas. Club Paradis, the open-air waterfront bar and restaurant, offers a wide selection of Caribbean and Continental fare. ⊠ *Box 101, Marigot Bay, Castries,* ☎ *758/451–4974,* 𝖥𝖠𝖷 *758/451–4973. 44 units. Restaurant, bar, kitchenettes, pool, beach, water sports, shops. MC, V. EP, MAP.*

**$$** 🏨 **Rex Papillon.** Spun off from neighboring Rex St. Lucian, this property on Reduit Beach has become an all-inclusive resort. A brand-new pool in the shape of a butterfly has been added. Rooms are furnished with one king-size or two twin beds. Deluxe and superior rooms are air-conditioned with full baths; standard rooms have ceiling fans and shower only. Deluxe rooms also have cable TV, sitting area, minibar, and a guaranteed ocean view. Rooms are furnished in rattan and tropical prints (blues and peaches), with tile floors. Some rooms are designed especially for guests with disabilities. Meals are served at Monarch, the main restaurant, or Clipper, the informal beachside snack bar. Evening entertainment is presented at Tropigala lounge. ⊠ *Box 512, Castries,* ☎ *758/727–4556,* 𝖥𝖠𝖷 *758/452–8331. 140 rooms. 2 restaurants, 3 bars, pool, 2 tennis courts, beach, water sports, shop, children's program, baby-sitting. AE, DC, MC, V. All-inclusive.*

**$$** 🏨 **Rex St. Lucian.** The broad, white, informal lobby, with potted plants and upholstered sofas, leads to the gardens, pool area, and beautiful Reduit Beach. Rooms are attractively decorated in rattan and tropical prints and have two double beds, TVs, and patios or terraces. Deluxe rooms have minibars, hair dryers, and a guaranteed ocean view. Guests can enjoy fine dining at either the Oriental or Mariners open-air restaurant—or stroll to several restaurants and nightspots in the Rodney Bay Marina area. ⊠ *Box 512, Reduit Beach, Castries,* ☎ *758/452–8351,* 𝖥𝖠𝖷 *758/452–8331. 120 rooms. 2 restaurants, 2 bars, ice cream parlor, air-conditioning, pool, 2 tennis courts, beach, dive shop, water sports, shops, baby-sitting, children's program. AE, DC, MC, V. EP, MAP.*

**$$** 🏨 **Tuxedo Villas.** This pristine-white apartment complex set around a tiny swimming pool in a peaceful corner of Rodney Bay, close to Reduit Beach, is good value. Each of the small but comfortable villas has a living room, dining room, kitchen, cable TV, and air-conditioning. There are six two-bedroom, two-bath units and four one-bedroom, one-bath units. Larger villas have kitchens equipped with full-size fridge-freezers, glass-topped bamboo tables and breakfast bars, and patios. There's nothing exciting here, but everything works, everything's spotless, and the staff is friendly. ⊠ *Box 419, Castries,* ☎ *758/452–8553,* FAX *758/452–8577. 10 apartments. Restaurant, bar, air-conditioning, pool. AE, MC, V. EP.*

$  🏨 **Auberge Seraphine.** This impressive small inn overlooks Vigie Cove and is minutes from Vigie Airport, Pointe Seraphine, and downtown Castries. Accommodations are spacious, cheerful, and bright, and most have a view of the cove and Vigie Yacht Marina. All have cable TV and direct-dial telephones. A broad clay-tiled sundeck—the center of activity—surrounds a small pool. A shuttle service transports guests to and from a nearby beach. The popular restaurant offers fine Caribbean, French, and Continental cuisine; the management is proud of its well-stocked wine cellar. One child (age 2–12) stays free when sharing a room with two adults. ⊠ *Box 390, Castries,* ☎ *758/453–2073,* FAX *758/451-7001. 22 rooms. Restaurant, bar, pool, shop, meeting rooms. AE, MC, V. EP, MAP.*

$  🏨 **Bay Gardens.** Conveniently located on the south side of Rodney Bay
★  and 7 mi north of Castries, this compact resort is an easy walk from beautiful Reduit Beach, several popular restaurants and nightclubs, and the marina. Shuttle service to the beach is free. Bay Gardens is modern and colorful—the lime-green building is studded with flower gardens. Guest rooms surround a courtyard with a double serpentine pool and Jacuzzi. They're furnished with white wicker furniture and colorful print spreads in tropical colors, and each has a balcony or patio. Executive rooms also have a trouser press and whirlpool bath. Eight self-contained apartments with kitchenettes and separate sitting rooms cater especially to families. Spices restaurant offers a varied menu, along with a weekly barbecue, Caribbean buffet, and Sunday brunch. One child (age 2–12) stays free when sharing a room with two adults. ⊠ *Box 1892, Rodney Bay, Castries,* ☎ *758/452–8060,* FAX *758/452–8059. 45 rooms, 8 apartments. Restaurant, bar, ice cream parlor, air-conditioning, 2 pools, beauty parlor, shops, meeting rooms. AE, MC, V. EP, MAP.*

$  🏨 **Candyo Inn.** This small pink hotel, in the heart of Rodney Bay, is one of the best buys in the Caribbean. It's a five-minute walk to beaches and several good restaurants. The inn has a small pool and lanai area. An outdoor bar near the pool serves drinks and snacks. The two-story building and its lush grounds are carefully looked after and spotless. All rooms have cable TV, veranda, white-tile floors, and white contemporary furniture with floral upholstery. The eight suites have kitchenettes, larger sitting areas, and tubs; they're worth the extra $15 a night. ⊠ *Box 386, Rodney Bay,* ☎ *758/452–0712,* FAX *758/452–0774. 4 rooms, 8 suites. Bar, air-conditioning, pool. AE, MC, V. EP.*

$  🏨 **Green Parrot.** The hillside setting is the draw at this small hotel, set high above Castries and the harbor on Morne Fortune. The motel-like rooms have cable TV and patios. A free bus scoots you to town and the beach; the hotel also arranges excursions to Anse Jambette, a private beach, for swimming and snorkeling. The Green Parrot restaurant (☞ Dining, *below*), open to the public, is internationally acclaimed for its cuisine. ⊠ *Box 648, the Morne, Castries,* ☎ *758/452–3399,* FAX *758/453–2272. 55 rooms. Restaurant, bar, air-conditioning, pool, billiards, cabaret, shop. AE, MC, V. EP, MAP.*

$  🏨 **Orange Grove Hotel.** Up a long hill, off the road to Windjammer Landing, you'll find this small hotel on a French colonial plantation. The rooms—large, light, and clean—are packed with all the conveniences you'd expect at a larger resort. Standard rooms have showers; superior rooms and suites have bath and shower. All have tropical-print decor, tile floors, and Caribbean-style rattan furniture, as well as separate sitting areas and balconies or patios overlooking the hillside. And although you're away from the beach, you are welcome to use the facilities at Club St. Lucia, 15 minutes away; free transportation is available. Its Café Clementine serves West Indian and International cuisine. The hotel is getting to be better known among Americans. ⊠ *Box GM 702, Castries,* ☎ *758/452–9040,* ⅮⱯⅩ *758/452–8094. 51 rooms, 11 suites. Restaurant, bar, air-conditioning, pool, beauty salon, shop. AE, MC, V. EP, MAP.*

## Soufrière Area

$$$–$$$$   ★  ⚕ **Anse Chastanet Hotel.** If you invest in one of the Hillside Premium or Deluxe rooms (Numbers 7 and 14) here, you are in for a slice of heaven. Nick Troubetzkoy, the Canadian owner-architect, designed them to meld into the tropical mountainside, with louvered wooden walls that open to stunning Piton and Caribbean vistas or to the deep green of the forest. Each has a terra-cotta-tiled floor, madras cotton fabrics, chunky handmade wood furniture, baskets for lamp shades, and truly covetable artwork. Rooms are typically 900–1,600 square ft, and most have an irresistible quirk: a tree growing in the bathroom or a shower completely open to the panorama of the Pitons. Standard rooms are mostly octagonal gazebos, with the same decor but far less drama. No rooms have a phone or TV. This is a magical setting, as long as you're fit to climb the 100 steps from the gray-sand beach up to the restaurant and then another steep climb to your room. Great diving is one of the attractions: Divers come from the earth's four corners to peep at the reefs near here. ⊠ *Box 7000, Soufrière,* ☎ *758/459–7000,* ⅮⱯⅩ *758/459–7700. 48 rooms. 2 restaurants, 2 bars, fans, refrigerators, tennis court, 2 beaches, dive shop, water sports, shops. AE, DC, MC, V. EP, MAP.*

$$$–$$$$   ★  ⚕ **Ladera.** This quiet, elegantly rustic hideaway is nestled in lush botanical gardens, high in the mountains, overlooking the Pitons and the Caribbean sea. It is one of the most sophisticated and unusual small resorts in the Caribbean—a home away from home for rock stars, corporate VIPs, and honeymooners. Many people stay here for the last night or two of a vacation spent at a larger resort up north. The villas and suites, stylishly furnished with a harmonious blend of French colonial antiques and local crafts, have a completely open west wall that provides a dazzling, unobstructed view of the Pitons. Most units have small plunge pools, and one has a Jacuzzi. Daily shuttle service to Soufrière and Anse Chastanet Beach is provided. Dasheene Restaurant (☞ Dining, *below*) is considered by many to be the best on the island. Certainly the view is! Transfers to Hewanorra are complimentary for guests staying four nights. ⊠ *Box 225, Soufrière,* ☎ *758/459–7323,* ⅮⱯⅩ *758/459–5156. 6 villas, 13 suites. Restaurant, bar, pool, shop. AE, MC, V. EP, MAP.*

$   ★  ⚕ **Humming Bird Beach Resort.** This charming little resort is on the bay at the northern edge of Soufrière. Rooms are in small seaside cabins adjoined by a maze of wooden decking. Most have breathtaking views of the Pitons. The decor is attractive but simple; a primitive motif is emphasized by African sculptures. Two rooms each have a dark mahogany four-poster bed hung with a sheer mosquito-net drape; the cool breezes of the trade winds will lull you to sleep without any annoying bug bites spoiling the atmosphere. Most rooms have private modern baths; two rooms and a suite have a shared bathroom. The two-bedroom country cottage—with sitting room, kitchenette, and a spectacular Piton view—is suitable for a family or two couples vacationing together. The Lifeline Bar and Restaurant is a favorite hangout of locals and expatriates. ⊠ *Box 280, Soufrière,* ☎ *758/459–7232,* ⅮⱯⅩ *758/459–7033. 9 rooms, 1 suite, 1 2-bedroom cottage. Restaurant, bar, pool, beach, shop. D, MC, V. EP, MAP.*

$ ⊠ **Skyway Inn.** If you're staying in the north but have an early morning flight to catch from Hewanorra, this is an ideal place to stay. It's just 100 yards from the airport and minutes from Vieux Fort, the beach, and the Windsurfing Center. The inn is clean and comfortable. There's an open-air rooftop restaurant and bar and a pool down below. A free shuttle runs to both the beach and the airport. You don't want to spend a week here, but as far as airport hotels go, it's quite impressive. ⊠ *Box 353, Vieux Fort,* ☎ *758/454–7111,* 𝔽𝔸𝕏 *758/454–7116. 44 rooms. Restaurant, bar, air-conditioning, windsurfing, shop, meeting room, airport shuttle. AE, MC, V.*

$ ⊠ **Still Plantation & Beach Resort.** At the Still Plantation, about a five-minute walk inland from Soufrière, there are one- and two-bedroom modern self-catering apartments with sitting rooms and kitchenettes, as well as studios with no kitchens. The restaurant here is well known for its excellent Caribbean cuisine. There's a swimming pool and boutique. The Still Beach Resort, at the northern end of Soufrière Bay, has just three one-bedroom apartments and two studios that are right on the black-sand beach with a commanding view of the Pitons. There's a restaurant at the beach resort, as well, but most units have a kitchenette and all have a beachfront patio, where you can dine alfresco. If hiking and nature walks are more important than a beach, the Plantation is the better choice; it's en route to Diamond Falls, the volcano, and rain forest. If you prefer sand and sea to pool and gardens, choose the Beach Resort. Guests at one can use the facilities of the other. ⊠ *Box 246, Soufrière,* ☎ *758/459–7261,* 𝔽𝔸𝕏 *758/459–7301. 13 apartments, 6 studios. 2 restaurants, 2 bars, pool, beach, shops. MC, V. EP.*

# Dining

If you stop by the Castries market (☞ Exploring St. Lucia, *below*) on a Saturday, you'll see the riches produced in this island's fertile volcanic soil. Mangoes, plantains, breadfruits, limes, pumpkins, cucumbers, papaya (pawpaw), yams, christophines (a green, squashlike vegetable), and coconuts are among the fruits and vegetables that appear on menus throughout the island. Every menu also lists fresh-caught fish (usually snapper, kingfish, or dolphinfish) along with the ever-popular lobster. And you may see the national dish—saltfish and green fig—a concoction of dried, salted white fish and boiled green banana, which is definitely an acquired taste. More usual Eastern Caribbean standards include callaloo, stuffed crab back, curried chicken or goat, and *lambi* (conch). Chicken, pork, and barbecues are also popular here. Most of the meats are imported—beef from Argentina and Iowa, lamb from New Zealand. The French influence is strong in St. Lucian restaurants, and most chefs cook with a Creole flair. With the increase in tourism, a broader mix of cuisines is apparent, particularly in Castries and the Rodney Bay area.

## What to Wear

Dress on St. Lucia is casual but conservative. Shorts are usually fine during the day, but bathing suits and immodest clothing are frowned upon in restaurants and other public places. In the evening, the mood is casually elegant, but even the fanciest places generally expect only a collared shirt for men and a dress for women.

| CATEGORY | COST* |
|---|---|
| $$$$ | over $40 |
| $$$ | $25–$40 |
| $$ | $15–$25 |
| $ | under $15 |

*per person for a three-course meal, excluding drinks, 8% government tax, and 10% service charge

## Castries Area

**$$$$** ✕ **San Antoine.** High on the Morne, with splendid views of Castries
★ below and Martinique in the distance, this historic building was originally the great house of the San Antoine Hotel, built in the late 1800s,
destroyed by fire in 1970, and restored soon after. The hotel once hosted
literary luminary Somerset Maugham. Now San Antoine is one of the
most elegantly appointed restaurants on the island, and the cuisine is
arguably the best. Try the superbly grilled fish, caramelized fillet steak
Robert, or honey-roast rack of lamb; all entrées are served with a selection of fresh vegetables. You may dine à la carte or opt for the five-
course prix-fixe dinner. Complimentary taxi service is available for parties
of four or more. ⊠ *Old Morne Rd., south of Castries,* ☎ *758/452–
4660. AE, MC, V. Closed Sun.*

**$$$** ✕ **Green Parrot.** The Green Parrot comes complete with sommelier and
★ crisp napery. The menu of West Indian, Creole, and international
dishes, prepared by chef Harry Edwards (who was trained at London's
prestigious Claridge's hotel), always includes a lot of seafood. There's
lively entertainment—a belly dancer on Wednesday night and limbo
night on Saturday—but the real reason to dine here is the view over
Castries and the harbor. This is a hot spot for locals and tourists alike.
⊠ *The Morne, Castries,* ☎ *758/452–3399. Reservations essential. Jacket
required. AE, MC, V.*

**$$–$$$** ✕ **Jimmie's.** This popular, open-air mom-and-pop restaurant and bar
perched above the bay makes a relaxing daytime stop and becomes a
romantic dinner spot when the harbor lights twinkle below. Appetiz-
ers on the seafood-dominated menu include a great Creole stuffed
crab, while a wise choice of entrée is the special seafood platter with
samplings from every part of the day's catch. If you want to try the
national dish—saltfish and green fig—it's the lunch special on Fridays
and Saturdays. All entrées come with several local vegetables—pump-
kin, black beans, christophines, greens—plus garlic bread. Dessert
lovers had better be in a banana mood, since the menu lists about 10
options—from warm fritters to ice cream. ⊠ *Vigie Marina, Vigie Cove,
Castries,* ☎ *758/452–5142. Reservations not accepted. AE, MC, V.*

**$$–$$$** ✕ **Naked Virgin.** Tucked away in the quiet Castries suburb of Marchand
(just opposite the local post office—keep asking), this pleasant hangout
offers terrific Creole cuisine and mellow music, and every couple leaves
with a free T-shirt. The owner, Paul John, has worked in many of the is-
land's major hotels; his rum concoction, the Naked Virgin, could be the
best punch you've ever tasted. You can try one, with his compliments,
with your dinner. Shrimp Creole and fried flying fish are highly recom-
mended. You'll also find duck à l'orange, stuffed Cornish game hen, and
T-bone steak on the menu. ⊠ *Marchand Rd., Castries,* ☎ *758/452–5594.
AE, MC, V.*

**$** ✕ **J. J.'s.** Not only are the prices right here, but the food is some of
the best on the island. Superbly grilled fish with fresh vegetables is tops.
The welcome is friendly and the atmosphere is casual; tables are set
on a terrace above the road. On Friday nights the music blares, and
the locals come to hang out and dance in the street. ⊠ *Marigot Bay
Rd. (3 mi before bay), Marigot,* ☎ *758/451–4076. Reservations not
accepted. No credit cards.*

## Rodney Bay and the North End

**$$$$** ✕ **Great House.** From this romantic spot, perched on a hill overlook-
ing Anse Becune Bay, you can enjoy views of the water and of Mar-
tinique in the distance. The restaurant is run by the owners of Club
St. Lucia (☞ *Lodging, above*), and guests there are given a discount
and free transportation. Traditional French dishes have Creole over-
tones, as in the appetizer of pumpkin and potato soup and entrées like

lime-grilled dorado fillet, Antillean shrimp sautéed in a Creole sauce, and broiled sirloin with thyme butter and sweet-potato chips. The menu changes nightly and always includes vegetarian dishes. The Derek Walcott Theatre is next door. ⊠ *Cap Estate,* ☎ *758/450–0450 or 758/450–0211. AE, DC, MC, V. No lunch.*

**$$–$$$**    ✕ **Capone's.** The tropics meet the Jazz Age in this restaurant. In a setting of black-and-white tile floors, a polished wood bar, and a player piano, waiters dressed like gangsters serve rum drinks called "Valentine's Day Massacre" and "Mafia Mai Tai." Your check is delivered in a violin case. The pasta is fresh, and the meat dishes include *osso buco alla Milanese* (veal knuckle) and chicken rotisserie. The **Pizza Parlour,** open 11 AM–midnight, turns out burgers and sandwiches, as well as pizza. ⊠ *Rodney Bay, across from Rex St. Lucian hotel,* ☎ *758/452–0284. AE, MC, V. Closed Mon. No lunch.*

**$$**    ✕ **The Lime.** The Lime is a favorite place for "liming" (hanging out). A
★    casual bistro with lime-colored gingham curtains, straw hats decorating the ceiling, and hanging plants, it offers a businessperson's three-course lunch and a buffet of local dishes, like callaloo and *lambi* (conch). Starters may include homemade pâté or stuffed crab back. Entrée choices may be medallions of pork fillet with the chef's special orange-and-ginger sauce, stewed lamb, or fish fillet poached in white wine and mushroom sauce. The prices are reasonable, which is perhaps why expatriates and locals gather here in the evenings. Next door is Late Lime's, the nightclub where the crowd gathers as evening turns to morning. ⊠ *Rodney Bay,* ☎ *758/452–0761. MC, V. Closed Tues.*

**$–$$**    ✕ **Key Largo.** Brick-oven gourmet pizzas are the specialty at this casual eatery at Rodney Bay Marina, across the lagoon from Rodney Bay's many hotels. You're welcome simply to stop in for an espresso or cappuccino, but the popular Pizza Key Largo—topped with shrimp, artichokes, and what seems like a few pounds of mozzarella—is tough to pass up. ⊠ *Rodney Bay,* ☎ *758/452–0282. MC, V.*

## Soufrière Area

**$$$$**    ✕ **Dasheene Restaurant and Bar.** Part of the striking Ladera resort (☞
★    Lodging, *above*), Dasheene is a small, casual mountaintop retreat with breathtaking views of the Pitons and the clear Caribbean sea between them. This is some of the best food in St. Lucia—Caribbean specialties with new American and Continental accents. Appetizers on a frequently changing menu may include smoked kingfish crepes and spicy seafood gazpacho. Typical entrées are tuna steak with coconut-avocado cream sauce and chicken breast with a mango or a pecan-and-peanut sauce. For dessert, the chocolate crème brûlée flambée takes about five minutes to cool down but is well worth the wait. There's live entertainment many nights, and soft, jazzy background music otherwise. This is a favorite dinnertime spot for those celebrating an anniversary or other special event—try to arrive in time to watch the sunset. ⊠ *Soufrière,* ☎ *758/459–7323. AE, DC, MC, V.*

**$$$**    ✕ **Piton Restaurant and Bar.** Too many cooks spoil the broth? Not here
★    on two terraces—one magically suspended among the trees, the other a spacious rooftop—at the wonderful mountainside Anse Chastanet Hotel (☞ Lodging, *above*), where the French executive chef, Jacky Rioux, works with a St. Lucian maestro to invent sublime variations on local dishes. The menus might include a creamed conch soup *en croute* (with a latticed puff-pastry lid), roast grouper stuffed with lobster mousse, dolphinfish poached in coconut milk with a lime sauce, and—the best local food joke you'll ever taste—"St. Lucian apple pie," made not with apples but with candied, spiced christophines and served with passion-fruit ice cream. Between them, these chefs cater to every culinary fantasy. Be prepared to hike up a couple of dozen steps to get

to the restaurant. ⊠ *Anse Chastanet, 2 mi north of Soufrière,* ☎ *758/459–7000. AE, DC, MC, V.*

**$$** ✕ **Beach Restaurant and Bar.** This open-air lunch spot on the beach at the Anse Chastanet Hotel (☞ Lodging, *above*) is the perfect place to take a break from a day of diving, boating, or sunbathing. The West Indian cuisine is delicious, and many specialties are prepared right before your eyes on a barbecue grill. The *rotis* (Caribbean-style turnovers) here are the best on the island, served with homemade mango chutney you could eat by the jar. Try also the island pepperpot—pork, beef, or lamb simmered for many hours with local veggies and spices; or a good old tuna melt in case you're homesick. Dessert always features an unusual flavor of ice cream. There's a young and lively crowd here, and although the restaurant caters mostly to the resort's guests, everyone is quite welcome. Mainly, lunch is served; but on Tuesday and Friday nights, the beach barbecue–Creole buffet is very popular. ⊠ *Anse Chastanet, Soufrière,* ☎ *758/459–7000. AE, DC, MC, V.*

**$$** ✕ **Still Plantation.** For visitors to Diamond Falls, lunching at the Still is a good option. The two dining rooms in this attractive restaurant seat up to 400 people, so it is a popular stop for tour groups and cruise passengers. The emphasis is on Creole cuisine using local vegetables—christophines, breadfruits, yams, callaloo—and seafood, but there are also pork chops and beef dishes. All fruits and vegetables used in the restaurant are produced organically on the estate. ⊠ *Soufrière,* ☎ *758/459–7224 or 758/459–7060. MC, V.*

**$–$$** ✕ **Bang . . . between the Pitons.** The eccentric Brit Colin Tennant (a.k.a. Lord Glenconner), founder of the glamorous hideaway island of Mustique, came to St. Lucia to open his dream resort between the Pitons, over which he eventually lost control (it's a long story). But Tennant stayed on to open this wickedly cute spoof on a Jamaican jerk joint, with ice-cream-colored paintwork, assorted wooden chairs and cushion-strewn booths, a cerise velvet-draped stage for music, and a buzz like that of the early days of Mustique—when Jagger was young. The best way to arrive is by boat. But beware, the place closes on a whim. ⊠ *On waterfront at Anse des Pitons, south of Soufrière,* ☎ *758/459–7864. DC, MC, V .*

**$** ✕ **Camilla's.** Tiny, second-floor Camilla's is pretty in pink, somewhat underventilated on a hot night (apart from the two balcony tables) but friendly as anything. The menu is admirably simple and all local—you can have today's catch curried, Creole-style, or grilled with lemon sauce; there's barbecue chicken with garlic sauce and fries, or lobster salad. Vegetarian specials are available as well. There's also a list of tropical cocktails bigger than the entire restaurant! ⊠ *7 Bridge St., Soufrière,* ☎ *758/459–5379. AE.*

## Beaches

Beaches are all public, and many are flanked by hotels, where you can rent water-sports equipment and have a rum punch. On the other hand, some are difficult to reach because they abut resort property. There are also secluded beaches, accessible only by water, to which hotels can arrange boat trips. Don't swim along the windward (east) coast; the Atlantic waters are rough and sometimes dangerous.

In front of the resort of the same name, just north of Soufrière, **Anse Chastanet** is a palm-studded, gray-sand beach with a backdrop of green hills, brightly painted fishing skiffs bobbing at anchor, and the island's best reefs for snorkeling and diving. The wooden gazebos of the hotel are nestled among the palms; its dive shop, restaurant, and bar are on the beach (☞ Dining and Lodging, *above*). On an uncrowded cove south of Anse-la-Raye, **Anse Cochon** is a remote, black-sand beach accessible by boat. The waters are superb for both swim-ming and snorkeling. South of Soufrière on Jalousie Bay, **Anse des Pitons** is a black-sand beach directly between the Pitons. It's accessible through Jalousie Plantation or by boat and offers great snorkeling and diving. Just west of Vieux Fort, **Honeymoon Beach** is a sandy escape near the airport. **Pigeon Point** beach is part of the Pigeon Island National His-toric Park. It's a small beach and there's a restaurant; it's also a per-fect spot for picnicking. **Reduit Beach** is a long stretch of beige sand next to Rodney Bay. The Rex St. Lucian Hotel, which faces the beach, has a water-sports center where you can rent equipment. Many feel Reduit (pronounced red-wee) is the finest beach on the island. At the southernmost tip of St. Lucia, **Vieux Fort** has miles of secluded white sand and clear waters protected by reefs.

# Outdoor Activities and Sports

Most hotels offer Sunfish, water skis, snorkeling gear, and other non-motorized water-sports equipment free to guests and for a fee to nonguests. Rodney Bay in the north and Marigot Bay on the west coast are the two boating centers. The waters around Anse-la-Raye and Anse Chastanet are the most popular sites for diving and snorkeling.

## Boating
Bareboat or crewed yachts are available for charter through **Destina-tion St. Lucia Ltd.** (✉ Rodney Bay, ☎ 758/453–8531), **Douglas' Sail-ing Tours** (✉ Manoel St., Castries, ☎ 758/452–7596), **Moorings Yacht Charter** (✉ Marigot Bay, ☎ 758/451–4357 or 800/535–7289), **Sun-sail Stevens** (✉ Rodney Bay, ☎ 758/452–8648), and **Trade Wind Yacht Charters** (✉ Rodney Bay, ☎ 758/452–8424).

## Camping
St. Lucia's first campsite opened in 1997 at the **Environmental Educa-tional Centre** at Anse Liberté on the west coast near Canaries. Rough campsites and platformed tent huts are available, along with commu-nal toilets and showers, a cooking center, a beautiful beach, and hik-ing trails. Outdoor cooking and charcoal production will be part of the experience. The campsite is administered by the St. Lucia National Trust (☎ 758/452–5005).

## Deep-Sea Fishing
Spearfishing and collecting live fish in coastal waters are not permit-ted. Among the deep-sea creatures, you'll find dolphinfish, Spanish mack-erel, barracuda, kingfish, and white marlin. For half- or full-day fishing excursions, contact **Captain Mike's** (✉ Vigie Bay Marina, ☎ 758/452–1216 or 758/452–7044), **Mako Watersports** (✉ Rodney Bay Marina, ☎ 758/452–0412), or **Red Affair Charters** (☎ 758/452–6736).

## Fitness Centers
If your resort lacks the kind of equipment you'd expect for what you're paying—and many do—try the **St. Lucia Racquet Club** (✉ Club St. Lucia, Cap Estate, ☎ 758/450–0551), which has Nautilus equipment, exer-cise machines, and aerobics and step classes. It's the best gym on the island. **Body Inc.** (✉ Gablewoods Mall, ☎ 758/451–9744) is a well-equipped gym and aerobics studio. At **Caribbean Fitness Expressions** (✉ Vide Boutielle, north of Castries, ☎ 758/451–6853), enjoy jazzer-cize step, stretch, and tone sessions. Day passes are also available to **LeSPORT** (✉ Cap Estate, ☎ 758/450–8551), which has complete spa facilities.

## Golf
The golf courses on St. Lucia are scenic and good fun, but they're not quite up to the standards of a first-class facility in the United States.

**Sandals St. Lucia** (✉ La Toc Rd., Castries, ☎ 758/452–3081) has a newly improved nine-hole course for guests. Greens fees for nonguests are $15–$20 for 18 holes, club rental an additional $10, and a caddy ($4) is required. **St. Lucia Golf Club** (✉ Cap Estate, ☎ 758/452–8523) is the island's only golf course (nine holes, soon to become 18) open to the public. A $49.50 package includes 18 holes of golf, cart, and club rental. Reservations are recommended.

## Hiking

The island is laced with trails, but you should not attempt the challenging peaks on your own. Your hotel, the tourist board, or the **Forest and Land Department** (☎ 758/450–2231 or 758/450–2078) can give you information about finding a guide. The **St. Lucia National Trust** (☎ 758/452–5005), established to preserve the island's natural and cultural heritage, offers hiking tours to several areas, including Pigeon Island, the Maria Islands, and Fregate Island. Full-day excursions, including lunch, cost about $40 per person and are available through hotels or ground-tour operators.

## Horseback Riding

For trail rides and excursions, contact **International Riding Stables** (✉ Gros Islet, ☎ 758/452–8139), **North Point Riding Stables** (✉ Cap Estate, ☎ 758/450–8853), or **Trim's Riding School** (✉ Cas-en-Bas, ☎ 758/452–8273). The cost is about $30 per half hour.

## Jogging

Jog on the beach by yourself or team up with the **Roadbusters** (☎ 758/452–5112 and ask for Jimmy James; 758/452–4790 evenings). They meet near Vigie Airport Tuesday and Thursday evenings and Sunday morning.

## Parasailing

Contact the **Rex St. Lucian** hotel (✉ Rodney Bay, ☎ 758/452–8351).

## Scuba Diving

**Scuba St. Lucia** (☎ 758/459–7355 or 800/223–1108 ) is a PADI five-star training facility, with a dive shop at Anse Chastanet (one of the most highly regarded dive sites anywhere) and at the Rex St. Lucian hotel. Daily beach and boat dives, resort courses, underwater photography, and day trips are offered. Dive trips can also be arranged through **Buddies Scuba** (✉ Vigie Marina, Castries, ☎ 758/452–5288), **Dolphin Divers** (✉ Rodney Bay Marina, ☎ 758/452–9485), the **Moorings Scuba Centre** (✉ Marigot Bay, ☎ 758/451–4357), and **Windjammer Diving** (✉ Castries, ☎ 758/452–0913).

## Sea and Snorkeling Excursions

Several yachts take passengers on day sails to Soufrière and the Pitons for about $70 per person. From Vigie Cove, Castries, sail on the 140-ft **Brig Unicorn** (☎ 758/452–6811), used in the filming of the TV miniseries *Roots*; the 56-ft catamarans **Endless Summer I** and **II** (☎ 758/450–8651); **Surf Queen** (☎ 758/452–8232), a trimaran; and **Calypso Queen** (☎ 758/452–8232), a motor yacht. From Pigeon Island, Rodney Bay, sail on a 56-ft luxury cruiser, the **MV Vigie** (☎ 758/452–8232).

Sea and snorkeling excursions can be arranged through **Mako Watersports** (☎ 758/452–0412), **Captain Mike's** (☎ 758/452–0216 or 758/452–7044), or through your hotel.

## Spectator Sports

Cricket and soccer, the two national pastimes, are played at Mindoo Philip Park in Marchand, 2 mi east of Castries. The **St. Lucia Racquet Club** (☎ 758/450–0551), which hosted the Davis Cup in 1994, is the site of regional tennis events, the most important being the St. Lucian

Open in early December. Contact the tourist board (☎ 758/452–4094) for specific information regarding schedules.

## Squash

**St. Lucia Racquet Club** (✉ Adjacent to Club St. Lucia, Cap Estate, ☎ 758/450–0551) has a court and a pro who gives lessons and holds clinics; it is not air-conditioned. **St. Lucia Yacht Club** (✉ Rodney Bay, ☎ 758/452–8350), at the north end of the island, has two air-conditioned courts.

## Tennis

All large resorts have their own tennis facilities, most of which are floodlit for night play. **St. Lucia Racquet Club** (✉ Adjacent to Club St. Lucia, ☎ 758/450–0551) is one of the top tennis facilities in the Caribbean—probably the best in the Lesser Antilles. Apart from hosting many tour events, its nine flood-lit courts are in perfect shape, the pro shop is extensive, and the staff knowledgeable. The **Rex St. Lucian** hotel (✉ Rodney Bay, ☎ 758/452–8351) has two courts available to the public.

## Waterskiing

Contact **Waves** (✉ Choc Beach, ☎ 758/451–3000). Rentals are also available at some hotels.

## Windsurfing

Most of the major resorts have Windsurfers and instruction available and will accommodate nonguests for a fee. Reduit Beach and Vieux Fort have the best wind; in the fall, from August to October, the wind loses strength island-wide. **Island Windsurfing Ltd.** (✉ Anse de Sables Beach, Vieux Fort, ☎ 758/454–7400) and **Sandy Beach Hotel & Windsurfing Center** (✉ Anse de Sables, Vieux Fort, ☎ 758/454–7411) each offer board hire and instruction. The **Rex St. Lucian** hotel (✉ Rodney Bay, ☎ 758/452–8351) is the local agent for Mistral Windsurfers. Also contact **Marigot Bay Resort** (✉ Marigot Bay, ☎ 758/453–4357).

# Shopping

As tourism increases in St. Lucia, so do the options for shopping. The island's best-known products are the unique hand-silk-screened and hand-printed designs of Bagshaw Studios, which are designed, printed, and sold only on St. Lucia. You can also bring home native-made wood carvings, pottery, straw hats and baskets, and locally grown cocoa, coffee, and spices.

## Shopping Areas

In **Castries,** the market and vendor's arcade are well worth a visit. William Peter Boulevard, the capital's main shopping street, is where the locals shop. You can find many of the same items at crafts stands and at gift shops at virtually every resort.

Die-hard shoppers will be happy at the duty-free shops at **Pointe Seraphine,** a Spanish-style complex by the harbor, where 23 shops sell designer perfumes, china and crystal, jewelry, watches, leather goods, liquor, and cigarettes. Native crafts are also sold in the shopping center. Be sure to bring your passport and airline ticket to get duty-free prices.

**Gablewoods Mall** (✉ Gros Islet Hwy., north of Castries) has about 35 shops selling groceries, spirits and wines, jewelry, clothing, local crafts, foreign newspapers, books, music, souvenirs, and household goods.

## Good Buys

### DUTY-FREE

Pointe Seraphine and Hewanorra International Airport are the only places on the island where you can purchase goods duty-free. In Pointe Seraphine, look for the following:

**Images** (☎ 758/452–6883) stocks designer fragrances, watches, cameras, electronics, and gifts. **Little Switzerland** (☎ 758/452–7587) specializes in fine china and crystal. **Meli's Boutique** (☎ 758/452–7587) has leather handbags, jewelry, crystal, and perfumes. **A Touch of Class** (☎ 758/452–7443) is the place for Caribbean literature and local souvenirs.

### FABRICS AND CLOTHING

**Bagshaw Studios** (✉ La Toc Rd., La Toc Bay, ☎ 758/452–2139; ✉ Pointe Seraphine, ☎ 758/452–7570; ✉ Marigot Bay, ☎ 758/451–4378) sells silk-screened fabrics, clothing, and table linens in wildly tropical colors and intricate designs. **Batik Studio** (✉ Humming Bird Beach Resort, Soufrière, ☎ 758/459–7232) offers superb sarongs, scarves, and wall panels created by Joan Alexander, the proprietor of the hotel. **Caribelle Batik** (✉ 37 Old Victoria Rd., the Morne, Castries, ☎ 758/452–3785) creates batik clothing and wall hangings; visitors are welcome to watch the craftspeople at work. **Sea Island Cotton Co.** (✉ Bridge St., Castries, ☎ 758/452–3674; ✉ Gablewoods Mall, ☎ 758/451–6946) sells quality T-shirts, Caribelle Batik clothing, and other resort wear, as well as souvenir items.

### MUSIC

Take home a cassette recording of the band you've been dancing to every night from **Jeremies** (✉ 83 Brazil St., Castries, ☎ 758/452–5079). **Sights 'n Sounds** (✉ 46 Micoud St., Castries, ☎ 758/451–9600; ✉ Gablewoods Mall, ☎ 758/451–7300) also sells island CDs and cassettes—reggae, zouk, soca, steelband.

### NATIVE CRAFTS

**Artsibit Gallery** (✉ Corner of Brazil and Mongiraud Sts., ☎ 758/452–7865) exhibits and sells artwork by top St. Lucian artists. **Choiseul Art & Craft Centre** (✉ La Fargue, ☎ 758/454–3226) stands among the remnants of the last Carib presence in St. Lucia. The center, in the southwest coast village of Choiseul, has a huge selection of handmade Amerindian basketware and pottery, as well as sculpture and bas-reliefs carved from local woods. The quality is excellent, and prices are reasonable. **Eudovic Art Studio** (✉ Morne Fortune, ☎ 758/452–2747) is a workshop and studio where trays, masks, and figures sculpted from local mahogany, red cedar, and eucalyptus wood are created, displayed, and sold. **Made in St. Lucia** (✉ Gablewoods Mall, ☎ 758/453–2788) is a fabulous shop that sells only items that are made on the island of St. Lucia. You'll find sandals, shirts, hot sauces, costume jewelry, carved wooden objects, steel drums, clay cooking pots, original art, and other quality items at fair prices. **Noah's Arkade** (✉ Jeremie St., Castries, ☎ 758/452–2523; ✉ Pointe Seraphine, ☎ 758/452–7488) has hammocks, wood carvings, and straw mats, baskets, and hats. Also for sale are island-inspired books and maps of St. Lucia. **Vendor's Arcade** (✉ Jeremie St., Castries), across from the market, is a maze of stalls and booths where you'll find handmade wood carvings and other handicrafts among the T-shirts and costume jewelry.

### SPICES

At the **Castries Market**, local vendors have gathered for more than a century to sell fruits and vegetables, which, alas, you can't import to the United States. But you can bring home the spices, such as cocoa, turmeric, ginger, peppercorns, cinnamon, nutmeg, mace, and vanilla essence. You can find a variety of bottled hot pepper sauces for sale. Prices are a fraction of what you'd spend in the supermarket back home. The market is especially lively on Saturday.

STAMPS

The **St. Lucia Philatelic Bureau,** at the General Post Office (⊠ Bridge St., Castries, ☎ 758/452–2671), supplies collectors and stamp dealers throughout the world with the beautiful and sought-after commemoratives issued by the St. Lucia government.

# Nightlife and the Arts

## Nightlife

The large, all-inclusive hotels feature nightly entertainment—island music, calypso singers, and steel-band jump-ups, as well as disco, karaoke, and even talent shows and toga parties. Many offer entertainment packages, including dinner, to nonguests.

CASTRIES

**Green Parrot** (⊠ Morne Fortune, ☎ 758/452–3399) is in a class all by itself. On Wednesday and Saturday evenings, chef Harry Edwards hosts the floor show, singing and dancing—and shimmying under the limbo pole—himself. There is also a full complement of musicians and native dancers. Dress semiformally for this evening of fun and frolic.

GROS ISLET

On Friday nights, sleepy Gros Islet becomes carnival city, as the entire village is transformed into a street fair. Mammoth stereos loudly beat out the sounds of reggae and soca, vendors sell barbecued chicken and other foods and beverages, and locals and strangers all let their hair down. It can get rowdy, so it's best to travel in a group and keep your wits about you. But then, Friday night is *the* night to jump.

**Banana Split** (⊠ St. George's St., ☎ 758/450–8125) offers entertainment and special theme nights, with a perpetual spring-break atmosphere. The **Captain's Cellar** (⊠ Pigeon Island, ☎ 758/450–0253) is a cozy pub that features live jazz on weekends. **Golden Apple** (⊠ Grande Rivière, ☎ 758/450–0634), a lively restaurant and bar with a party atmosphere, is probably one of the best spots for meeting locals.

MARIGOT BAY

Another Friday-night street scene and a popular alternate venue for liming can be found just before you enter Marigot Bay. The music is supplied by **J. J.'s** (☎ 758/451–4076), and the popular fare is curried goat. More and more locals are choosing to come here instead of the Gros Islet happening, which is becoming more touristy.

RODNEY BAY

A number of nightspots are at Rodney Bay, and they jump on weekends. Most have a cover charge of EC$15–$20.

**A-Pub** (☎ 758/452–8725) is a lounge in an A-frame building overlooking Rodney Bay. **Bistro** (☎ 758/452–9494) is where young boaters tie up for drinks, chess, darts, and backgammon. **Capone's** (☎ 758/452–0284) is an art deco place right out of the Roaring '20s, with a player piano and rum drinks. **Charthouse** (☎ 758/452–8115) has a popular bar, jazz on stereo, and live music on Saturday. **Indies** (☎ 758/452–0727) is a disco where you can dance to Caribbean and international rhythms Tuesdays through Saturdays from 10 PM on; dress is casual, though smart—no hats or sandals, no shorts or sleeveless shirts for men. The **Late Lime** (☎ 758/452–0761) is a particular favorite of the locals, with dance music and local entertainment every night but Tuesdays.

## The Arts

**Derek Walcott Center for the Arts.** This small, open-air theater in the ruins of an old Cap Estate plantation house seats just 200 people for monthly productions of music, dance, and drama, as well as Sunday brunch programs. The Trinidad Theatre Workshop also presents an annual performance here. For schedule and ticket information, contact the Great House Restaurant (✉ Cap Estate, ☎ 758/450–0551 or 758/450–0450, FAX 758/450–0451).

# Exploring St. Lucia

One road encircles the island, so it's impossible to get lost. The road, however, snakes through mountains with hairpin turns, sheer drops, and dizzying elevations and is often full of potholes. It takes about three hours to drive the whole loop from Castries, down the West Coast Road, back up the East Coast, and across the Barre de l'Isle Ridge. And that's with no stops. Even under ideal conditions, it's a tiring drive, so plan to stop several times along the way.

The West Coast Road from Castries to Soufrière has undergone a widening and major face-lift that began in 1992 and was completed in 1995. It still has steep hills and sharp turns, but it's pothole-free (so far), well marked, and incredibly scenic. South of Castries, the road climbs Morne Fortune, cuts through a huge banana plantation (more than 127 different varieties of bananas, often called "figs," are grown on the island), and passes by small fishing communities. The area just north of Soufrière is the island's breadbasket, where most of the mangoes, breadfruit, tomatoes, limes, and oranges are grown. In the mountainous region, you'll see Mt. Parasol and Mt. Gimie (pronounced "Jimmy"), St. Lucia's highest peak, which rises to 3,117 ft. As you approach Soufrière, you'll have several opportunities for spectacular views of the Pitons.

The landscape changes dramatically between the Pitons in the southwest and Hewanorra International Airport on the southeast tip of the island. The terrain starts as steep mountainside with dense vegetation, progresses to undulating hills that form a backdrop for tiny coastal fishing villages, and finally becomes rather flat. Anyone arriving at Hewanorra and staying at a resort near Soufrière will travel along this South Coast Road, a journey of about an hour.

A road leads up the East Coast from Vieux Fort through the villages of Micoud and Dennery on the Atlantic coast. Don't be fooled by the road's smooth start; it gets bumpier and bumpier as you progress, twisting and turning through villages and up, down, and around mountains. The reward, however, is an opportunity to see absolutely breathtaking scenery. The fierce Atlantic pounds against rocky cliffs, and dense vegetation—mostly acres and acres of bananas and coconut palms—covers the mountainsides. Visitors who arrive at Hewanorra and stay at a resort near Castries get two opportunities—coming and going—to travel along the East Coast Road, a 60-minute, 33-mi, stomach-churning journey each way (although the road has been somewhat improved).

The area north of Castries is the most developed part of the island; the roads are relatively straight and flat and easy to navigate. This area features some of the island's best beaches, numerous resorts, and a major marina. One of the island's important historical sites, Pigeon Island, is at the island's northwestern tip.

*Numbers in the margin correspond to points of interest on the St. Lucia map.*

SIGHTS TO SEE

**❺ Anse-la-Raye.** The beachfront of this small West Coast village is a colorful sight, with fishing nets hanging on poles to dry and brightly painted fishing boats bobbing in the water. The fishermen of Anse-la-Raye still make canoes by the old-fashioned method of burning out the center of a log.

**⑱ Barre de l'Isle Forest Reserve.** Barre de l'Isle Ridge divides the eastern and western halves of St. Lucia. A mile-long trail cuts through the Forest Reserve; four lookout points provide panoramic views of the island. Visible in the distance are Mount Gimie, the Caribbean Sea and the Atlantic coast, immense green valleys, and tiny coastal communities. The reserve is about a half hour from Castries. It takes about an hour to walk the trail and another hour to climb Mt. La Combe ridge. Permission of the Forest and Lands Department (☎ 758/450–2231 or 758/450–2078) is required to access the trail; a naturalist or forest officer guide will accompany you.

**❶ Castries.** On the northwest coast, Castries is a busy commercial city of about 60,000 people that wraps around a sheltered bay. Morne Fortune rises sharply to the south of town, creating a dramatic green backdrop for the capital city. Castries' charm lies entirely in its liveliness, since practically all the colorful old colonial buildings were razed by four great fires between 1796 and 1948. Ships carrying bananas, coconut, cocoa, mace, nutmeg, and citrus fruits for export leave from **Castries Harbour,** one of the busiest ports in the Caribbean.

Cruise ships dock at **Pointe Seraphine,** about a 20-minute walk or short cab ride from the city center—or you can take the boat that shuttles passengers across the harbor when ships are in port. Spanish-style Pointe Seraphine has more than 20 mostly upscale duty-free shops, a tourist information center where you can get island maps, a taxi stand, and car-rental agencies. This is also the starting point for many island tours.

**Derek Walcott Square** is a green oasis bordered by Brazil, Laborie, Micoud, and Bourbon streets. Formerly Columbus Square, it was renamed in 1993 to honor poet Derek Walcott, who won the 1992 Nobel Prize in Literature—one of two Nobel laureates from St. Lucia. (The late Sir W. Arthur Lewis won the 1979 Nobel Prize in Economics.) Some of the 19th-century buildings that managed to survive fire, winds, and rains can be seen on Brazil Street, the southern border of the square. At the corner of Laborie and Micoud streets there is a 400-year-old **samaan tree.** A favorite local story tells of the English botanist who came to St. Lucia many years ago to catalog the flora. Awestruck by this huge old tree, she asked a passerby what it was. "Massav," he replied, and she dutifully jotted that down in her notebook, unaware that "massav" is patois for "I don't know!" Directly across the street is the Roman Catholic **Cathedral of the Immaculate Conception,** which was built in 1897.

☾ At the corner of Jeremie and Peynier streets, spreading beyond its brilliant orange roof, is the open-air **Castries Market.** Full of excitement and bustle, the market is open every day but is most lively on Saturday mornings, when farmers bring their fresh produce to town as they have for more than a century. Across Peynier Street is the **Vendor's Arcade,** where local artisans sell crafts and souvenirs.

Just 2 mi south of downtown, next to Sandals St. Lucia resort at La Toc, **Bagshaw Studios** combines the opportunity to see how Stanley Bagshaw's original tropical prints are processed into colorful silk-screened fabrics and to shop for fashions and household items created on site. ✉ *La Toc*

*Rd., La Toc Bay,* ☎ *758/452–7570.* ☐ *Free.* ☺ *Weekdays 8:30–5, Sat.
8:30–4, Sun. 10–1; weekend hrs extended if cruise ship in port.*

| NEED A BREAK? | Stop for refreshment at **Chez Paul** (⌧ 19 Brazil St., Castries, ☎ 758/452–3022), set in the courtyard of one of the last remaining authentic colonial buildings in Castries. The chef blends Pacific Rim and haute French cuisine at breakfast, lunch, and dinner. |
| --- | --- |

**⓬ Choiseul.** This small village on the southwest coast is the island's wood-carving and pottery center. At the turn of the road past the Anglican Church, built in 1846, a bridge crosses the River Dorée, so named because the riverbed is blanketed with fool's gold. In La Fargue, just to the south, the **Choiseul Art & Craft Centre** (☎ 758/459–3226) displays and sells superb traditional Carib handicrafts, including pottery, wickerwork, and braided khuskhus grass mats and baskets.

**☺ ❼ Diamond Falls and Mineral Baths and Botanical Gardens.** King Louis XIV of France provided funds in 1713 for the construction of these baths, fed by an underground flow of water from the sulfur springs, to fortify his troops against the St. Lucian climate. It is claimed that Josephine Bonaparte bathed here as a young girl while visiting her father's plantation in Soufrière. During the Brigand's War, just after the French Revolution, the baths were destroyed. The site was excavated in 1932, and two of the baths were restored. Today, you walk through beautifully tended botanical gardens to reach the waterfall; then you can slip into your swimsuit for a dip in the steaming, curative baths. ⌧ *Soufrière Estate, Soufrière,* ☎ *758/452–4759 or 758/454–7565.* ☐ *EC$5.* ☺ *Daily 10–5.*

**⓱ Errard Plantation.** Near the village of Dennery, this family-operated cocoa plantation provides an excellent opportunity to see how cocoa beans are processed on a working agricultural estate. Tours end with a Creole lunch, accompanied by fresh fruit juices. For arrangements, call 758/453–1260.

**❷ Fort Charlotte.** Begun in 1764 by the French as the Citadelle du Morne Fortune, Fort Charlotte was completed after 20 years of battling and changing hands. Its old barracks and batteries have now been converted to government buildings and local educational facilities, but you can drive around and look at the remains, including redoubts, a guardroom, stables, and cells. You can also walk up to the Inniskilling Monument, a tribute to the battle fought in 1796, when the 27th Foot Royal Inniskilling Fusiliers wrested the Morne from the French. At the Military Cemetery, which was first used in 1782, faint inscriptions on the tombstones tell the tales of French and English soldiers who died here. Six former governors of the island are buried here, as well. From this vantage point on the top of Morne Fortune, you'll see Martinique to the north and the twin peaks of the Pitons to the south.

**⓰ Fregate Island Nature Reserve.** A mile-long trail encircles the preserve, which you reach from the small fishing village of Praslin. A natural promontory provides a lookout where you can view the two small islets, Fregate Major and Fregate Minor, and—with luck—the migratory frigate birds that nest here in summer. Guided tours, which include a ride in an Amerindian-style canoe to a tiny island for a picnic lunch and swim, are arranged through the St. Lucia National Trust (⌧ Box 595, Castries, ☎ 758/453–7656 or 758/452–8735 , ℻ 758/453–2791). All visitors must be accompanied by a guide.

**⓴ Gros Islet.** North of the lagoon at Rodney Bay, Gros Islet (pronounced "grow zee*lay*") is a quiet little fishing village. But on Friday nights, Gros

Islet springs to life with a wild and raucous street festival ("jump-up") to which everyone is invited (☞ Nightlife, *above*).

**⓭ Laborie.** Located on the south coast, this is the prototypical St. Lucian fishing village, little changed over the centuries. You can stop to buy some local bread and fresh fish. Above the village is Morne Le Blanc, which offers a panoramic view of the entire southern plain of St. Lucia. The crest, with picnic facilities and viewing platform, can be reached by trail (a 45-minute hike) or by road.

**⓫ La Soufrière Drive-in Volcano.** Your nose will pick up the strong scent of the sulphur springs—more than 20 belching pools of smelly, black, boiling water; multicolored sulfur deposits; and assorted other minerals baking and steaming on the surface. Actually, you don't drive in; you walk—behind your guide, whose service is included in admission—around a fault in the substratum rock, which makes for a fascinating 20-minute experience but one that can be stinky on a hot day. ⊠ *Bay St., Soufrière,* ☎ *758/459–5500.* ☒ *EC$3.* ☉ *Daily 9–5.*

**⓯ Maria Islands Nature Reserve.** Two tiny islands in the Atlantic, off the southeast coast, compose the reserve, which has its own interpretive center. The 25-acre Maria Major and 4-acre Maria Minor, its little sister, are inhabited by rare species of lizards and snakes that share their home with frigate birds, terns, doves, and other wildlife. There's a small private beach for swimming and snorkeling; bring a picnic. Boat trips are arranged by the St. Lucia National Trust. ⊠ *Moule à Chique,* ☎ *758/453–7656 or 758/452–8735.* ☒ *EC$3 Wed.–Sat., EC$50¢ Sun.* ☉ *Wed.–Sun. 9:30–5.*

**❹ Marigot Bay.** A few miles south of Castries, this is one of the most beautiful natural harbors in the Caribbean. In 1778 British admiral Samuel Barrington sailed into this secluded bay-within-a-bay and covered his ships with palm fronds to hide them from the French. Today, this resort community—where parts of the movie *Doctor Doolittle* were filmed more than 30 years ago—is a great favorite of yachtspeople. You can charter a yacht, swim, snorkel, or simply mingle with the yachting crowd at one of the bars. A 24-hour ferry connects the two sides of the bay.

NEED A
BREAK?
Stop for a rum punch and lunch and soak up the atmosphere at the open-air **Café Paradis** (⊠ Marigot Beach Club, Hurricane Hole, Marigot, ☎ 758/451–4974), a happy haunt of boaters and landlubbers alike.

**⓱ Marquis Estate.** If you want a close-up view of a working plantation and are willing to get a little wet and muddy in the process, you can tour the island's largest one. The 600-acre Marquis Estate (☎ 758/452–3762) is at Marquis Bay, on the north Atlantic coast. The estate began as a sugar plantation. Now it produces bananas and copra (dried coconut processed for oil) for export, as well as a number of other tropical fruits and vegetables for local consumption. St. Lucia Representative Services Ltd. (☞ Guided Tours, *below*) conducts the tour and will pick you up at your hotel in an air-conditioned bus. You may tour the estate by bus or by horseback, and a river ride to the coast and lunch at the plantation house are included. Self-drive or private taxi tours are not permitted. Wear your most casual clothes, and be prepared to rough it.

**❾ Morne Coubaril Estate.** This 250-acre coconut and cocoa plantation, the first major estate established in St. Lucia, has a rich French history that dates back to 1713, when Crown land was granted to three St. Lucian brothers by King Louis IV. Authentic 18th-century plantation life is explained, as a guide escorts you along an original mule-carriage pathway and through a typical reconstructed "village." You'll see how cocoa, copra, and manioc were processed in the days before mechanization. This is a fascinating 90-minute eco-tour. The foliage is thick and green; the tropical flowers, beautiful. There's a small gift shop where you can purchase freshly made cocoa, straw items, and hand-carved wooden pieces. If you wish to have lunch, a Creole buffet is available at the Pitt for EC$25 per person. ⊠ *Soufrière,* ☎ *758/459–7340.* ☜ *EC$15.* ☉ *Daily 9–5.*

❸ **Morne Fortune.** Just to the south of Castries, Morne Fortune forms a striking backdrop for the capital. With a name that translates to "Hill of Good Luck," this mountain has, ironically, seen more than its share of bad luck over the years—including devastating hurricanes and those four fires that leveled Castries. The drive to Morne Fortune from Castries will take you past the **Government House,** on Government House Road, the official residence of the governor-general of St. Lucia and one of the island's few remaining examples of Victorian architecture.

☙ ㉒ **Pigeon Island.** Jutting out of the northwest coast, Pigeon Island is connected to the mainland by a causeway that was built several years ago. Tales are told of the pirate Jambe de Bois (Wooden Leg), who used to hide out here. This 44-acre hilltop island, a strategic point during the struggles for control of St. Lucia, is now a national landmark, with a small beach with calm waters for swimming and snorkeling, a restaurant, and picnic areas. Scattered around the grounds are ruins of barracks, batteries, and garrisons dating from 18th-century French and English battles. In the Museum and Interpretative Centre, housed in the restored British officers' mess, a multimedia display unfolds the ecological and historical significance of this island. ⊠ *Pigeon Island, St. Lucia National Trust,* ☎ *758/450–8167 or 758/452–5005,* ℻ *758/453–2791.* ☜ *EC$10.* ☉ *Daily 9–5.*

❽ **The Pitons.** These incredible mountains have become the symbol of St. Lucia. The road south out of Soufrière offers a magnificent view of these twin peaks, which rise precipitously out of the azure Caribbean. The two perfectly shaped pyramidal cones, covered with thick tropical vegetation, were formed by lava from a volcanic eruption 30 million to 40 million years ago. They are not identical twins since—confusingly—Petit Piton, at 2,619 ft, is taller than Gros Piton (2,461 ft), though Gros is, as the word translates, broader. Gros Piton is currently the only one recommended for climbing, though the trail up even this shorter Piton is one very tough trek and requires the permission of the Forest and Lands Department (☎ 758/450–2231 or 758/450–2078) and a knowledgeable guide.

㉑ **Rodney Bay.** About 15 minutes north of Castries, the body of water named for Admiral Rodney is an 80-acre, man-made lagoon surrounded by hotels and many popular restaurants. The Rex St. Lucian and Royal St. Lucian hotels are in this area, as is the Rodney Bay Marina—one of the Caribbean's premier water-sports centers. The Rodney Bay Ferry makes the trip between the marina and the shopping complex hourly, 9–4, for $4 round-trip.

❿ **St. Lucia National Rain Forest.** Dense tropical rain forest stretches from one side of the island to the other, sprawling over 19,000 acres of mountains and valleys. The **Edmund Forest Reserve,** on the western side of the island, is most easily accessible from the east of Soufrière on the road to Fond St. Jacques. A trek through the lush landscape, with spectacular views of mountains, valleys, and the sea beyond, can take a full day. It takes an hour or so just to reach the preserve from the north end of the island. You'll also need plenty of stamina and strong hiking shoes. The permission of the Forest and Lands Department (☎ 758/450–

2231 or 758/450–2078) is required to access the trails, and the department provides a naturalist or forest officer guide.

**6** **Soufrière.** The oldest town in St. Lucia, Soufrière was founded by the French in 1746 and named for the nearby volcano. The former French colonial capital currently has a population of about 9,000. Its harbor is the deepest on the island, accommodating smaller cruise ships that tie up at the wharf. On a nearby jetty, there's a small crafts center. The market is decorated with colorful murals and gingerbread trim. The **Soufrière Tourist Information Centre** (⊠ Bay St., ☎ 758/459–7200) provides information about area attractions.

**14** **Vieux Fort.** St. Lucia's second-largest city is the location of Hewanorra International Airport. From the **Moule à Chique Peninsula,** the southernmost tip of the island, you can see all of St. Lucia to the north and the island of St. Vincent 21 mi south. This is also where the clear waters of the Caribbean blend with those of the deeper blue Atlantic Ocean.

NEED A BREAK? **Sandy Beach Restaurant and Bar** (⊠ Vieux Fort, ☎ 758/454–7416) is right on the beach and specializes in light lunches. It's a popular place for families on weekends and holidays.

## St. Lucia A to Z

### Arriving and Departing

BY PLANE

There are two airports on the island. Wide-body planes use modern Hewanorra International Airport, on the southern tip of the island. Vigie Airport, a small airport in Castries, services interisland and charter flights.

**American Airlines** (☎ 758/454–6777 or 800/433–7300) has daily service through San Juan from New York and most major other U.S. cities. **American Eagle** (☎ 758/452–1820) flights from San Juan land at Vigie Airport. **Air Canada** (☎ 758/454–6038 or 800/776–3000; 800/268–7240 in Canada) has direct weekend service from Toronto. **Air Jamaica** (☎ 800/523–5585) flies nonstop to Hewanorra from New York on Tuesday and Thursday. **British Airways** (☎ 758/452–3951 or 0181/897–4000) has direct service from London to St. Lucia. **BWIA** (☎ 758/452–3778 or 800/327–7401) has direct service from Miami, New York, and London. **Helenair** (☎ 758/452–7196) flies into Vigie from Grenada, St. Vincent, and other islands in the eastern Caribbean. **LIAT** (☎ 758/452–3051 or 758/452–2348) services the island with small island-hoppers that fly into Vigie, linking St. Lucia with Barbados, Trinidad, Antigua, Martinique, Dominica, Guadeloupe, and other islands.

FROM THE AIRPORT

Taxis are unmetered, and the government's list of suggested fares is not binding. Negotiate with the driver *before* you get in, and be sure that you both understand whether you've agreed upon E.C. or U.S. dollars. The drive from Hewanorra to Castries takes about 60 minutes and costs about $50. From Vigie Airport, the 10–20 minute ride to most resorts in the north costs $10–$15. Many resorts include airport transfers in their rates.

Some visitors to St. Lucia opt for the expensive but quick means of helicopter transportation. The cost for the 15-minute flight from Hewanorra to Castries is $90 per person, including luggage; for the 10-minute flight to Soufrière, it costs $75 per person. There are helipads at Pointe Seraphine, Windjammer Landing, Jalousie Plantation, and several other locations. Contact **Eastern Caribbean Helicopters** (⊠ Pointe Seraphine,

☎ 758/453–6952 or 758/454–7313) or **St. Lucia Helicopters** (✉ Pointe Seraphine, ☎ 758/453–6950, FAX 758/452–1553).

## Currency

The official currency is the Eastern Caribbean dollar (EC$). Figure about EC$2.70 to US$1. U.S. dollars are readily accepted, but you'll usually get change in E.C. dollars. Major credit cards and traveler's checks are widely accepted. Prices quoted in this chapter are in U.S. dollars unless indicated otherwise.

## Emergencies

**Police:** ☎ 999. **Fire and Hospital:** ☎ 911. Hospitals with 24-hour emergency rooms are **Victoria Hospital** (✉ Hospital Rd., Castries, ☎ 758/452–2421), St. Lucia's largest hospital; **St. Jude's Hospital** (✉ Vieux Fort, ☎ 758/454–7671), a privately endowed hospital run by nuns; **Soufrière Hospital** (☎ 758/459–7258); and **Dennery Hospital** (☎ 758/453–3310). **Pharmacies:** Try **Williams Pharmacy** (✉ Bridge St., Castries, ☎ 758/452–2797) or **M & C Drugstore** (✉ Bridge St., Castries, ☎ 758/452–2811; ✉ Gablewoods Mall, Gros Islet Hwy., north of Castries, ☎ 758/451–7808).

## Getting Around

### BUSES

This is an inexpensive and colorful, though not always dependable, means of transportation. There is no published bus schedule, although they run until approximately 10 PM. The fare from Castries to the north end of the island is EC$1.50; from Castries to the southern end (Vieux Fort), EC$7. Minivans cruise the island and, like taxis, will stop when hailed. You can also catch a minivan in Castries, at the corner of Micoud and Bridge streets.

### CAR RENTALS

Driving in St. Lucia is on the left, British-style, and the roads are often deeply potholed. Almost two-thirds of the island's 500 mi of road are not paved at all; you may wish to think twice about driving.

To rent a car, you must be 25 years or older and hold a valid driver's license and a credit card. If you don't have an International Driver's License, you must buy a temporary St. Lucian license available through car-rental agents. The license costs $12 and is valid for three months. Car-rental rates begin at about $50 per day for a four-wheel-drive vehicle and $75 for a car with standard transmission, with discounts for weekly rentals. Gasoline is expensive: EC$6.10 per gallon.

Car-rental agencies include **Avis** (✉ Pointe Seraphine, ☎ 758/452–2700; ✉ Hewanorra, ☎ 758/454–6325; ✉ Vigie, ☎ 758/452–2046), **Budget** (✉ Castries, ☎ 758/452–0233; ✉ Hewanorra, ☎ 758/454–5311), **Hertz** (✉ Castries, ☎ 758/452–0679; ✉ Hewanorra, ☎ 758/454–9636; ✉ Vigie, ☎ 758/451–7351), and **National** (✉ Castries, ☎ 758/450–8721; ✉ Pointe Seraphine, ☎ 758/453–0085; ✉ Hewanorra, ☎ 758/454–6699; ✉ Vigie, ☎ 758/452–3050). Local agencies are **C.T.L. Rent-a-Car** (✉ Rodney Bay Marina, ☎ 758/452–0732), **Cool Breeze Jeep/Car Rental** (✉ Hewanorra, ☎ 758/454–7898; ✉ Soufrière, ☎ 758/459–7729), and **S.L.Y.S. Car Rentals** (✉ Castries, ☎ 758/452–5057).

### FERRIES

The **Rodney Bay Ferry** (✉ Box 672, Castries, ☎ 758/452–0087, FAX 758/452–8816) has ferry service twice daily from Rodney Bay (right by the Lime restaurant) to Pigeon Island. The round-trip fare is $40 and includes lunch and the entrance fee to Pigeon Island. Snorkel equipment can be rented for $12.

TAXIS

Taxis are always available at the airport, the harbor, and in front of the major hotels, but they are expensive and do not have meters. Determine the fare and the currency being quoted before you get into the cab.

## Guided Tours

BY AIR

**Eastern Caribbean Helicopters** (☎ 758/453–6952) and **St. Lucia Helicopters** (☎ 758/453–6950) provide sightseeing tours of the island. The 10-minute North Island Tour ($45 per person) leaves from Pointe Seraphine, in Castries, and flies up the west coast to Pigeon Island, then along the rugged Atlantic coastline before returning inland over Castries. The 20-minute South Island Tour ($80 per person) starts at Pointe Seraphine and follows the western coastline, circling picturesque Marigot Bay, Soufrière, and the majestic Pitons before returning inland over the volcanic hot springs and tropical rain forest.

BY LAND AND SEA

**Barnards Travel** (✉ Micoud St., Castries, ☎ 758/452–2214) offers a full range of half- and full-day island tours, as well as excursions to Dominica, Martinique, St. Vincent, and the Grenadines. **St. Lucia Representative Services Ltd.** (☎ 758/452–3762) has half- and full-day island tours, as well as excursions to a number of neighboring islands. **Sunlink International** (☎ 758/452–8232) offers a variety of half- and full-day tours, as well as a day trip to the Grenadines aboard a 60-ft catamaran. **Taxi drivers** generally know the island and can give you a full tour—and often an excellent one, since government-sponsored training programs were introduced in 1994. Expect to pay $20 per hour plus tip for up to four people.

## Language

The official language is English, but you'll also hear the local French Creole patois.

## Opening and Closing Times

Most shops are open weekdays 8 or 8:30–4, Saturday 8–noon. Gablewoods Mall shops are open Monday–Saturday 8–6. Banks are open Monday–Thursday 8–3, Friday 8–5, and, at a few branches in Rodney Bay, Saturday 9–noon.

## Passports and Visas

U.S., Canadian, and British citizens whose stay does not exceed six months must produce a valid passport (or a birth certificate or other proof of citizenship along with a photo ID) and a return or ongoing ticket.

## Precautions

Bring along insect repellent to ward off mosquitoes and sand flies. Be aware that sea urchins live among the rocks on the coastline; should one's long black spines lodge under your skin, don't try to pull them out. Apply an ammonia-based liquid and the spine will retreat, allowing you to ease it out. Manchineel trees have poisonous fruit and leaves that can cause skin blisters on contact. Even raindrops falling off the trees can cause blisters; these trees are usually marked when on hotel property. Do not swim on the rough Atlantic side of the island. And, of course, don't take unnecessary risks—lock your door, secure your valuables, and don't carry too much money or wear expensive jewelry on the street. Tap water is perfectly safe to drink throughout the island.

## Taxes and Service Charges

Hotels and restaurants collect an 8% government tax. Hotels and most restaurants add a 10% service charge. Taxi drivers appreciate a

10% tip; porters and bellhops, 75¢ per bag. The airport departure tax is $11 or EC$27.

## Telephones, Electricity, and Mail

The area code for St. Lucia is 758. You can make direct-dial overseas and interisland calls from St. Lucia, and the connections are excellent.

Electric voltage is 220/240 AC, 50 cycles, with a square three-pin plug; American appliances require an adapter and/or transformer. A few hotels have 110 AC voltage capability available to guests.

The General Post Office is on Bridge Street, Castries, open weekdays 8:30–4. All towns and villages have sub-offices. Postage for airmail letters to the United States, Canada, and Great Britain is EC95¢ for up to 1 ounce. Postcards are EC75¢ to the United States and Canada, EC.85¢ to Great Britain.

Courier service is available to and from the island via Federal Express (Box 1255, Castries, ☎ 758/452–1230 or 758/452–1388) and UPS (20 Bridge St., Castries, ☎ 758/452–5898 or 758/452–5428).

## Visitor Information

Contact the **St. Lucia Tourist Board** (✉ 820 2nd Ave., 9th floor, New York, NY 10017, ☎ 212/867–2950 or 800/456–3984, FAX 212/867–2795 in the U.S. or Canada; ✉ 421A Finchley Rd., London NW3 6HJ, ☎ 0171/431–3675, FAX 0171/437–7920 in the U.K.).

In St. Lucia, the **St. Lucia Tourist Board** is based at the Pointe Seraphine duty-free complex on Castries Harbor (✉ Box 221, Castries, ☎ 758/452–4094 or 758/452–5968, FAX 758/453–1121). The office is open weekdays 8–4:30. There are also information offices in downtown Castries (✉ Jeremie St., ☎ 758/452–2479), Soufrière (✉ Bay St., ☎ 758/459–7200), at Vigie Airport (☎ 758/452–2596), and at Hewanorra International Airport (☎ 758/454–6644).

# 23 St. Martin/ St. Maarten

*The dual nature of this small spit of land, with its Dutch side, Saint Maarten, and its French St. Martin, makes it ideal for those hoping to experience lots in little time. The island is thoroughly inhabited by tourism: world-class beaches, elegant restaurants, lively casinos, and some of the best duty-free shopping in the region.*

**T**HERE'S A CRITICAL ADVANTAGE to St. Martin/St. Maarten—planes fly nonstop all the time from the United States, so you don't have to spend half your vacation getting there. The 37-square-mi island is home to two sovereign nations, St. Maarten (Dutch) and St. Martin (French), so you can experience two cultures for the price of one, although the Dutch side has lost most of its European flavor.

Updated by
Karl Luntta

The island is ideal for people who like to have lots of things to do. Whatever can be done in or on the water—snorkeling, windsurfing, waterskiing—is available here; there is golf and tennis as well. Especially on the French side, there are enough good-quality restaurants for serious diners to try a different one each night, even on a two-week stay. The duty-free shopping is as good as anywhere else in the Caribbean. There's an active nightlife, with discos and casinos. Day trips can be taken by ship or plane to the nearby islands of Anguilla, Saba, St. Eustatius, and St. Barthélemy. There are hotels for every taste and budget—from motel-type units for the package tour trade to some of the most exclusive resorts in the Caribbean. The standard of living is one of the highest in the Caribbean, so the islanders can afford to be honest and to treat visitors as welcome guests. If you wander even slightly off the beaten track, you'll find friendly and opinionated locals willing and eager to share their insider knowledge. Corruption and crime, which had been on the rise, have decreased dramatically in the '90s, thanks to an exemplary cooperative effort between the two governments.

On the negative side, St. Martin/St. Maarten has been thoroughly discovered and exploited; unless you stay in an exclusive resort, you will often find yourself sharing beachfronts with tour groups or conventioneers (the exception being some of the beaches in Terres Basses on the French side). Yes, there is gambling, but the table limits are so low that hard-core gamblers will have a better time gamboling on the beach. As is often the case in the Caribbean, the island infrastructure has not kept pace with development. There are plans to expand marina, airport, and road services, but meanwhile, you will probably run into congestion at the airport and seemingly endless traffic on the roads.

## Lodging

Until recently, the Dutch side commanded all the big, splashy resorts. The casinos are still to be found exclusively on the Dutch side—gambling is illegal on the French side. However, St. Martin is having something of a building boom, especially in the area around Nettlé and Orient bays. All hotels on the French side have an English-speaking staff. There are also small inns and Mediterranean-style facilities on both sides of the island. Many hotels offer enticing packages and you'll save substantially if you travel off-season, although many hotels and restaurants are closed to recover from the winter onslaught. In general, the French resorts are more intimate, but what the Dutch properties lack in ambience, they compensate for in clean, functional, comfortable rooms with all the "extras." Most of the larger Dutch resorts feature timeshare annexes; the units are often available for rental for those who prefer the condo lifestyle at comparable rates. Most properties are EP or CP (the latter usually only in season), though meal plans are sometimes available.

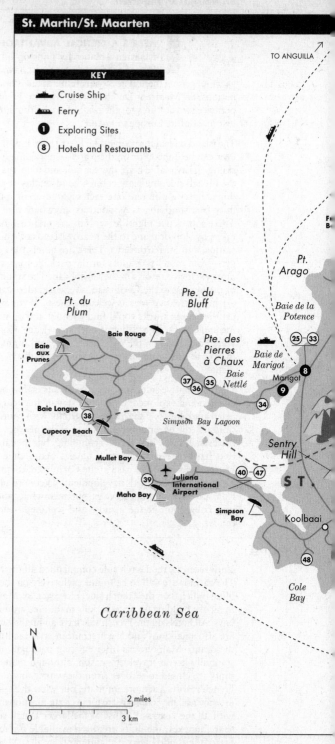

**Exploring**
French Cul de Sac, **5**
Friar's Beach, **7**
Grand Case, **6**
Guana Bay Point, **2**
Marigot, **8**
Orléans, **4**
Oyster Pond, **3**
Philipsburg, **1**
St. Martin
Museum, **9**

**Dining**
Alizéa, **13**
Antoine, **50**
Le Bec Fin, **54**
Bistrot Nu, **25**
Chesterfield's, **51**
Chez Martine, **17**
Don Camillo da
Enzo, **26**
L'Escargot, **53**
Felix, **46**
Harbour Lights, **52**
Maison sur le Port, **30**
Le Marocain, **32**
Oyster Bay Beach
Resort, **60**
Le Perroquet, **41**
La Plaisance, **33**
Le Poisson d'Or, **29**
Le Pressoir, **16**
Rainbow, **19**
La Samanna, **38**
Le Santal, **34**
Saratoga, **47**
Shiv Sagar, **55**
Spartaco, **48**
Le Tastevin, **18**
Turtle Pier Bar &
Restaurant, **42**
La Vie En Rose, **28**
Wajang Doll, **56**
Yvette's, **62**

**Lodging**
Alizéa, **13**
Anse Margot, **37**
Captain Oliver's, **61**
Esmeralda Resort, **12**
Grand Case Beach
Club, **20**
Great Bay Beach Hotel
& Casino, **49**
Green Cay Village, **10**
Hévéa, **21**
Holland House
Beach Hotel, **57**
Horny Toad
Guesthouse, **43**
Hôtel l'Atlantide, **23**

## St. Martin/St. Maarten

**KEY**

⛴ Cruise Ship

🚤 Ferry

❶ Exploring Sites

⑧ Hotels and Restaurants

TO ANGUILLA

Pt.
Arago

Pt. du
Plum

Pte. du
Bluff

Baie de la
Potence

Baie Rouge

Pte. des
Pierres
à Chaux

Baie de
Marigot

Baie
aux
Prunes

Baie
Nettlé

㉕ ㉝

㊳ ㉟
㊱

⑧

Marigot

⑨

㉞

Baie Longue

㊳

Simpson Bay Lagoon

Cupecoy Beach

Sentry
Hill

Mullet Bay

㊴ ㊲

㊴

Juliana
International
Airport

S T.

Maho Bay

Simpson
Bay

Koolbaai

㊸

Cole
Bay

Caribbean Sea

N

0          2 miles
0       3 km

Hôtel L'Esplanade
Caraïbes, **24**
Hôtel Mont
Vernon, **11**
Maho Beach Hotel &
Casino, **39**
Marine Hotel
Simson Beach, **36**
Le Méridien, **15**
Nettlé Bay Beach
Club, **35**
Oyster Bay
Beach Resort, **60**
Passangrahan Royal
Guest House, **58**
Pavillon Beach
Hotel, **22**
Pelican Resort &
Casino, **44**
Le Privilege Resort
& Spa, **14**
La Residence, **27**
Royal Palm Beach
Club, **40**
Le Royale
Louisiana, **31**
La Samanna, **38**
Seaview Hotel &
Casino, **59**
La Vista, **45**

Worth noting on the French side is a coalition of seven small inns called Les Hôtels de Charme. They are dedicated to providing "warmth, individual attention, and homey feeling," with rates in the $–$$ price range; some include breakfast. The participating hotels are Alizéa, Panoramic Privilege, L'Hoste, Blue Beach, Hotel du Golf, Chez Martine, and the Sunrise Hotel. For information on any of these inns, call 800/468–6796 in the United States or 590/87–33–44 in St. Martin.

Both sides of the island offer a wide variety of homes, villas, condominiums, and housekeeping apartments. Information in the United States can be obtained through **WIMCO** (⊠ Box 1461, Newport, RI 02840, ☎ 800/932–3222), **Caribbean Vacation Villas** (⊠ 35 Pleasant St., Concord, NH 03301, ☎ 603/226–3762 or 800/530–2212) or **Villas of Distinction** (⊠ Box 55, Armonk, NY 10504, ☎ 914/273–3331 or 800/289–0900). On the island, contact **Carimo** (⊠ Box 220, rue de Générale de Gaulle, Marigot 97150, ☎ 590/87–57–58), which has some truly fabulous villas for rent in the tony and desirable Terres Basses section of the island, or **St. Martin Rentals** (⊠ 91 South River Rd., Bedford, NH 03110, ☎ 599/5–54330; 800/308–8455 in the U.S.).

| CATEGORY | COST* |
|---|---|
| **$$$$** | over $300 |
| **$$$** | $225–$300 |
| **$$** | $150–$225 |
| **$** | under $150 |

*All prices are for a standard double room in high season, excluding 5% tax (Dutch side), a taxe de séjour (set by individual hotels on the French side), and a 10%–15% service charge.*

## Dutch Side

**$$$$**    🏨 **Royal Palm Beach Club.** A complex of suites and shops sitting on Kimsha Beach, the Royal Palm is in an excellent location for exploring Simpson Bay and the rest of the island. Each room comes with a full kitchen, including a full-size refrigerator. The rooms all face the sea and are decorated in standard floral patterns and lots of rattan furniture. Rooms can accommodate as many as six and come equipped with two full baths and a TV and VCR. The small beachfront restaurant and bar is okay for the daytime, but hit other restaurants at night. The pool has a small swim-up bar. ⊠ *Airport Rd., Simpson Bay,* ☎ *599/5–43732,* FAX *599/5–43727. 140 suites. Restaurant, bar, air-conditioning, in-room VCRs, pool, water sports, shops, baby-sitting, laundry services. AE, D, MC, V. EP.*

**$$$**    🏨 **Maho Beach Hotel & Casino.** This pink-and-white self-contained megaresort is almost an institution on St. Maarten. The spacious rooms have cathedral ceilings and light pastel and deep ocean-color decor, plus sea or garden views from their balconies. The trick is to get a room far enough away from the airport's landing strip (those behind the main lobby are the quietest). Restaurants include excellent Italian dining at Tiberio, burgers and live music at Cheri's Café, and beachside Middle Eastern food at Orient Express. The hotel complex is home to both the island's largest casino, the Casino Royal (☞ Nightlife and the Arts, *below*), and its largest pool. Unfortunately the service can't keep up with the sprawl, and you may be neglected as the staff struggles to meet guest needs. ⊠ *Maho Bay,* ☎ *599/5–52115 or 800/223–0757,* FAX *599/ 5–53180. 600 rooms, 29 suites. 10 restaurants, 3 bars, air-conditioning, 3 pools, hot tub, spa, 3 tennis courts, health club, water sports, 75 shops, casino, dance club, baby-sitting, business services, car rental. AE, D, MC, V. EP, MAP.*

**$$$**    🏨 **Pelican Resort & Casino.** An assortment of white stucco buildings house the resort's apartments, suites, and deluxe studios, all of which

have sweeping views of the Caribbean. This centrally located resort
has 1,400 ft of beach (though it's not great for swimming because of
the seaweed) and its own 60-ft catamaran, *El Tigre,* available for charters. Walk into the reception area and you're greeted by gaming tables.
On the lower level is a sales office enticing you to buy into this hotel-
condo complex. Sadly, the resort has not kept up with the pace of refurbishment that swept most of the island after 1995's Hurricane Luis,
and the staff seems more interested in selling time-share units than attending to guests. ⊠ *Simpson Bay,* ☎ *599/5–42503 or 800/626–
9637,* FAX *599/5–42133. 660 suites and studios. 2 restaurants, 4 bars,
grocery, kitchens, 8 pools, spa, 6 tennis courts, water sports, casino,
playground, car rental. AE, D, DC, MC, V. EP.*

**$$–$$$** 🏨 **Horny Toad Guesthouse.** This is one of the most charming proper-
   ★ ties on the island, thanks to the caring touch of owners Betty and Earle
Vaughan, who keep things immaculate. The eight apartments on the
beach, some with air-conditioning, are individually decorated, and the
blue-and-white sun terrace duplicates the patterns of delft china. There
is a barbecue area for guests, but no restaurant. ⊠ *Box 3029, Simpson Bay,* ☎ *599/5–54323 or 800/417–9361, ext. 3013,* FAX *599/5–
53316. 2 studios, 6 1-bedroom apartments. Barbecue, fans, library. No
credit cards. EP.*

**$$–$$$** 🏨 **La Vista.** On this intimate property, Antillean buildings are connected
by brick walkways lined with riotous hibiscus and bougainvillea. All
accommodations are suites with a small stove, cable TV, mini-refrigerator, and private balcony. Guests have the use of the pool, tennis courts,
and spa facilities at the adjacent Pelican Resort. The views from the
wood-decked pool are fabulous. ⊠ *Box 2086, Pelican Key,* ☎ *599/5–
43005,* FAX *599/5–43010. 32 suites. Restaurant, air-conditioning, refrigerators. AE, MC, V. EP.*

**$$–$$$** 🏨 **Oyster Bay Beach Resort.** The refined elegance of this hotel is quite
   ★ out of character with the rest of St. Maarten. Two towers with Moorish arches and stone walls surround a courtyard. There are split-level
suites and standard rooms, all with terra-cotta floors, a balcony or terrace, and pastel French cottons. A newer building has larger rooms whose
balconies face the sea. The hotel is a one-minute walk from Dawn Beach,
which is excellent for snorkeling, sunbathing, and swimming. The dining room opens onto the Atlantic Ocean, and the pool is perched right
at the water's edge. Breakfast is included. ⊠ *Oyster Pond, Box 239,
Philipsburg,* ☎ *599/5–22206, 599/5–23206, or 800/231–8331;*
FAX *599/5–25695. 40 rooms and suites. Restaurant, bar, air-conditioning, fans, saltwater pool, dive shop, water sports, car rental. AE,
D, MC, V. BP.*

**$$** 🏨 **Great Bay Beach Hotel & Casino.** One of the island's few proper-
ties operating as an all-inclusive as well as a room-only rate, this re-
sort, a 10-minute walk from the center of Philipsburg, has its own stretch
of beach and terrific views of the bay. The bustling open-air lobby, with
striped awnings overlooking the sea, is more striking than the rooms,
furnished in typical muted pastels. You do get a private balcony or ter-
race with an ocean or mountain view. A list of activities is posted each
morning, and the hotel staff can arrange virtually any type of island
excursion or sport. ⊠ *Box 910, Philipsburg,* ☎ *599/5–22446 or
800/223–0757,* FAX *599/5–23859. 285 rooms, 10 1-bedroom suites.
2 restaurants, 3 bars, 2 pools, beauty salon, tennis court, exercise
room, beach, water sports, shop, casino, nightclub, car rental. AE, DC,
MC, V. EP, All-inclusive.*

**$–$$** 🏨 **Holland House Beach Hotel.** This is a centrally situated hotel, with
the shops of Front Street at its doorstep and mile-long Great Bay Beach
as its backyard. Each room has muted-pastel spreads and drapes and
a balcony; most have kitchenettes. Ask for a beach view. The delight-

ful open-air restaurant overlooking the water serves reasonably priced dinners, and the indoor-outdoor patio lounge is a popular spot to watch the sunset. ⊠ *35 Front St., Box 393, Philipsburg,* ☎ *599/5–22572 or 800/223–9815,* 𝔽𝔸𝕏 *599/5–24673. 54 rooms, 6 suites. Restaurant, lounge, air-conditioning, shop, meeting room. AE, D, DC, MC, V. EP.*

$ ▥ **Passangrahan Royal Guest House.** It's entirely appropriate that
★ the bar here is named Sidney Greenstreet. This is the island's oldest inn, and it looks like a set for an old Bogie-Greenstreet film. The green-and-white building was once Queen Wilhelmina's residence and the government guest house. Wicker peacock chairs, balconies shaded by tropical greenery, and a broad tile veranda are some of the hallmarks of this guest house. There are no TVs or phones in the rooms, and you're offered just a sliver of Great Bay Beach. ⊠ *15 Front St., Box 151, Philipsburg,* ☎ *599/5–23588 or 599/5–22743,* 𝔽𝔸𝕏 *599/5–22885. 30 rooms, 1 suite. Restaurant, bar. AE, MC, V. EP.*

$ ▥ **Seaview Hotel & Casino.** This is one of the good buys on Front Street and Great Bay Beach. The air-conditioned, twin-bed rooms are very modest, cheerful, and clean. Ten of the rooms look out on the courtyard, where breakfast is sometimes served; four rooms face the sea. Children under 12 stay free. ⊠ *59 Front St., Box 65, Philipsburg,* ☎ *599/5–22323 or 800/223–9815; 212/545–8469 in NY; 800/468–0023 in Canada;* 𝔽𝔸𝕏 *599/5–24356. 46 rooms. Breakfast room, air-conditioning, casino. AE, D, MC, V. EP.*

## French Side

$$$$ ▥ **La Samanna.** This secluded hotel changed hands in 1996, but the
★ new owners (the Orient Express hotel group) have, thankfully, left well enough alone. The resort, set in a tropical garden on a slope overlooking the ravishing Baie Longue beach, looks as if it were transported to St. Martin from Morocco. Red hibiscus sprawls everywhere. Studios and one- and two-bedroom villas all have a private patio and small luxuries such as potpourri and fresh flowers. The decor is stunning: cool mint, apricot, and teal fabrics; unusual ceramic work; painted tiles; and clever variations on traditional Caribbean wicker and rattan. The beach is right outside your door and the restaurant is one of the island's finest. ⊠ *BP 159, Marigot 97150,* ☎ *590/87–64–00 or 800/854–2252,* 𝔽𝔸𝕏 *590/87–87–86. 80 rooms and suites. Restaurant, lounge, minibars, pool, 3 tennis courts, exercise room, water sports, shop, library. AE, MC, V. CP.*

$$$$ ▥ **Le Méridien.** There are better bargains on the island, yet this bustling resort, comprising two smaller complexes called L'Habitation and Le Domaine, remains wildly popular with tour groups and families. There are 1,600 ft of white-sand beach and a slew of sports facilities, but no matter where you stay on the compound, few units have an ocean view. The service is polite but impersonal, and French Muzak is annoyingly omnipresent. The setting is pleasant—at the end of a white-knuckle road, amid beautifully landscaped gardens on enchanting but windless Marcel Cove. All the rooms, suites, and apartments have balconies, and the one-bedroom apartments on the marina have fully equipped kitchens and private patios. Guests have free access to the facilities of Le Privilege Resort & Spa (☞ *below*). La Belle France is a typically solid and *très cher* gourmet restaurant. ⊠ *BP 581, Anse Marcel 97150,* ☎ *590/87–60–00; 800/543–4300 in the U.S.;* 𝔽𝔸𝕏 *590/87–30–38. 400 rooms, 82 suites. 4 restaurants, 4 bars, air-conditioning, refrigerators, 2 pools, miniature golf, 6 tennis courts, aerobics, racquetball, squash, beach, water sports, marina, shops, dance club, car rental. AE, DC, MC, V. EP.*

**$$$$**  🏨 **Le Privilege Resort & Spa.** So heavy was the damage from Hurricane Luis, that this resort, all of three years old, had to be virtually rebuilt. The result is a sparkling new Le Privilege, perched above Anse Marcel and Le Méridien. Those into the spa life can take advantage of all kinds of treatments available, from massage to lymphatic drainage. Rooms and suites are spacious and very comfortably furnished, with tile floors, marble baths, and such thoughtful touches as CD players and in-room safes. There is a free shuttle service to the beach and the resort's excellent marina. ✉ *Anse Marcel 97150,* ☎ *590/87–38–38 or 800/874–8541,* FAX *590/87–44–12. 16 rooms, 18 suites. 2 restaurants, bar, in-room safes, in-room VCRs, 3 pools, beauty salon, spa, 6 tennis courts, health club, racquetball, squash, marina, scuba diving, windsurfing, boating, fishing, nightclub. AE, MC, V. CP.*

**$$$–$$$$**  🏨 **Esmeralda Resort.** The green roofs and stacked ambience make it look like a Sun Belt housing development, but the interiors of these deluxe villas are tastefully decorated. The 51 rooms and suites in 15 villas can be combined any way you like, from studio to five-bedroom palatial digs. Each villa has a private pool, and all the rooms have a private terrace. L'Astrolabe has a reputation for excellent French cuisine. ✉ *BP 5141, Orient Bay,* ☎ *590/87–36–36 or 800/622–7836,* FAX *590/87–35–18. 18 villas. 6 restaurants, kitchenettes, 18 pools, 2 tennis courts, water sports, shop. AE, MC, V. CP.*

**$$–$$$$**  🏨 **Green Cay Village.** Set high above Orient Beach facing the trade winds,
★  this villa-hotel is a great choice for small groups or families. One of the Orient Bay resorts, Green Cay offers spacious one-, two-, and three-bedroom villas, each with its own private pool, large deck, fully equipped kitchen, and outdoor dining patio. Daily maid service is included. Although all villas have plenty of privacy, those highest on the hill enjoy the most seclusion, as well as the most stunning views. A reasonably priced breakfast is served by the pool, and at Orient Bay Resort, guests have charge privileges at all the restaurants and bars and access to tennis and water-sport facilities. ✉ *BP 3006, Parc Baie Orientale 97064,* ☎ *590/87–38–63 or 800/932–3222,* FAX *590/87–39–27. 16 villas. Kitchens, room service, in-room VCRs, 16 pools. AE, MC, V. EP.*

**$$$**  🏨 **Grand Case Beach Club.** This informal condo complex is on Grand Case's crescent-shape beach, with another "secret" strand of sand a two-minute walk away. Damaged by Hurricane Luis, the club has undergone a complete restoration, including new furnishings and new decor. Studios and one- and two-bedroom apartments all have balconies or patios; the 62 oceanfront units are much in demand. The kitchen at the aptly named Café Panoramique restaurant has been turning out French fare since it spirited chef Alain Billard away from Le Bec Fin. ✉ *BP 339, Grand Case 97150,* ☎ *590/87–51–87 or 800/223–1588,* FAX *590/87–59–93. 71 rooms, 15 suites. Restaurant, lounge, air-conditioning, kitchenettes, tennis court, billiards, car rental. AE, D, MC, V. CP.*

**$$–$$$**  🏨 **Captain Oliver's.** This property straddles the St. Maarten–St. Martin border: Stay in France, and dine in the Netherlands. The bungalows
★  are a good bargain and a good way to avoid the hustle and bustle of St. Maarten. The small hotel faces a beautiful horseshoe-shape bay; bungalows have a view of the bay or garden. The exceptionally clean, fresh rooms have a patio/deck; sail-and-stay packages can be arranged by the friendly and helpful staff. ✉ *Oyster Pond 97150,* ☎ *590/87–40–26 or 800/223–9862,* FAX *590/87–40–84. 50 rooms. Restaurant, snack bar, air-conditioning, kitchenettes, minibars. AE, DC, MC, V. CP.*

**$$–$$$**  🏨 **Nettlé Bay Beach Club.** The 240 units of this large resort, about five minutes from Marigot, are spread across the sands of striking Baie Nettlé. Four sets of villa suites and one set of garden bungalows, each set with its own pool, face the waterfront and, across the bay, Dutch Sint Maarten. The rooms and suites are furnished simply but comfortably and come with kitchens, TVs, and patios or balconies. On the grounds are two restaurants, including the South American–influenced La Parilla and the French La Fayette, as well as the beach bar Le Grand Bleu. This is an excellent location for exploring Marigot and the south side of the island. ✉ *Sandy Ground Rd., BP 4081, Marigot 97064,* ☎ *590/ 87–68–68 or 800/999–3543,* FAX *590/87–21–51. 240 units. 3 restaurants, 5 pools, air-conditioning, kitchens, 3 tennis courts, water sports, shop. AE, MC, V. EP.*

**$$–$$$**  🏨 **Pavillon Beach Hotel.** Every room and suite at this small hotel faces the sea and has a private balcony. The spacious studios and one-bedroom suites are decorated in warm pastel colors and have tile floors and elegant rattan furniture. Bathrooms come with a hair dryer and shower but no tub. From the ground-level rooms, you can walk right onto the beach through sliding wooden shutters. ✉ *Plage de Grand Case, RN 7, Grand Case 97150,* ☎ *590/87–96–46 or 800/223– 9815,* FAX *590/87–71–04. 16 rooms. Kitchenettes. AE, MC, V. EP.*

**$–$$$**  🏨 **Hôtel Mont Vernon.** Gingerbread work decorates this rambling hotel, which sits on a bluff overlooking Orient Bay, but its multicolored veneer makes it a sprawling eyesore when seen from the beach. Looking out is another story: The rooms in the buildings on the crest facing the ocean have the best views and are slightly larger than the others. The other choice rooms are in the buildings by the pools and beach. All rooms have a private balcony. This is a big resort that lures package-tour groups as well as business seminars. ✉ *Baie Orientale, BP 1174, 97062,* ☎ *590/87–62–00 or 800/223–0888,* FAX *590/87– 37–27. 394 suites. 2 restaurants, 2 bars, pool, 2 tennis courts, exercise room, snorkeling, windsurfing, shops, children's program, car rental. AE, DC, MC, V. CP, MAP.*

**$$**  🏨 **Alizéa.** The view of Orient Bay from this Mont Vernon hill setting is stunning. An open-air feeling pervades the hotel, from its terrace restaurant—the food is superb—to the 26 guest apartments done up with contemporary light-wood furnishings. Rooms vary in style and design, but all are tasteful and each has a kitchenette and a large private balcony. There is a path to the beach (a 10-minute walk). ✉ *Mont Vernon 25, 97150,* ☎ *590/87–33–42,* FAX *590/87–41–15. 8 1-bedroom bungalows, 18 studios. Restaurant, bar, kitchenettes, pool. AE, D, MC, V. CP.*

**$$**  🏨 **Anse Margot.** This quiet, thoroughly French property is one of the many hotels that line the stretch of land between the sea and Simpson Bay Lagoon, known as Baie Nettlé. The rooms here are in eight three-story town-house buildings. All units have a private balcony with either a garden or beach view. Upholstery, drapes, and spreads are a brown-and-coral geometric print. There is a stretch of beach along the lagoon that's good for sunbathing but not swimming; you may prefer the Nettlé beach across the street. A complimentary breakfast buffet is served in the open-air Entre Deux Mers, one of the better hotel restaurants. It's about a five-minute drive to Marigot. ✉ *BP 979, Baie Nettlé 97150,* ☎ *590/87–92–01 or 800/742–4276,* FAX *590/87–92–13. 96 rooms and 1-bedroom suites. Restaurant, bar, 2 pools, hot tub, water sports, shop, business services, meeting room. AE, D, DC, MC, V. BP.*

**$–$$**  🏨 **Hôtel l'Atlantide.** This small hotel has 10 sun-drenched units, ranging in size from a studio to a two-bedroom suite. Private balconies overlook Grand Case Bay and the beach. The decor is airy, with gleaming white tile floors and crisp pastel-striped or floral upholstery. There's no restaurant or bar, but the village of Grand Case is known for its lively restaurant scene. ✉ *BP 5140, Grand Case 97150,* ☎ *590/87– 09–80,* FAX *590/87–12–36. 9 apartments, 1 suite. MC, V. EP.*

$–$$  🏨 **Hôtel L'Esplanade Caraïbes.** Opened in 1992, this complex still
★       sparkles as if brand new. It's built on a hillside overlooking Grand Case
Bay, a three-minute walk from the beach. Two curved stone staircases
with inlaid tile and brick lead up from the bougainvillea beds to the
open-air reception area. The standard suites are large, with private balconies and gleaming wood ceilings; some have an office alcove with a
desk (but hopefully you've left your work at home). Duplexes have elegant cathedral ceilings and mahogany staircases, as well as an extra
half bath and an upstairs loft bedroom; upholstery throughout is
striped with muted pinks and corals. There is no restaurant at the hotel,
but Grand Case's roster of gourmet spots is just a short walk away. ✉
*BP 5007, Grand Case 97150,* ☎ *590/87–06–55,* 📠 *590/87–29–15.*
*23 units. Pool, wading pool, boating. AE, MC, V. EP.*

$–$$  🏨 **Marine Hotel Simson Beach.** This sprawling complex may be the best
★       bargain on the Nettlé Bay hotel strip. Rooms and duplex suites are cheer-
fully decorated; most have a view of the water, and all have a kitchenette and balcony. Budget-conscious Europeans love this place because
of the many extras, like a huge breakfast buffet and nightly local entertainment. There are shuttles (not complimentary) to Marigot, Philipsburg, and beaches. ✉ *BP 172, Nettlé Bay 97150,* ☎ *590/87–54–54,*
📠 *590/87–92–11. 120 studios, 45 1-bedroom duplexes. Restaurant,*
*bar, grocery, kitchenettes, pool, tennis court, beach, dive shop, water*
*sports, bicycles, shop, coin laundry, car rental. AE, DC, MC, V. CP.*

$  🏨 **Hévéa.** This small white guest house with smart striped awnings is
★    across the street from the beach in the heart of Grand Case. The rooms
are dollhouse small but will appeal to romantics. There are beam ceilings, washstands, and carved-wood beds with lovely white coverlets
and mosquito nets. The five rooms, studios, and apartment are on the
terrace level; two studios and one apartment are on the garden level.
Hotel guests can get a special "house" dinner at the delightful gourmet
restaurant for $30. ✉ *163 blvd. de Grand Case, Grand Case 97150,*
☎ *590/87–56–85 or 800/423–4433,* 📠 *590/87–83–88. 8 units.*
*Restaurant. MC, V. EP.*

$  🏨 **La Residence.** The downtown location and soundproof rooms of this
★    Marigot hotel make it a popular place for business travelers. All the accommodations have a balcony, dark rattan furniture, and tile floors. You've
a choice among single or double rooms, some with loft beds. The intimate restaurant offers a good $28 three-course menu. You'll have to take
a cab or drive to the beach. ✉ *Rue du Général de Gaulle, Marigot 97150,*
☎ *590/87–70–37 or 800/223–9815,* 📠 *590/87–90–44. 24 rooms.*
*Restaurant, lounge, minibars, shop. AE, D, MC, V. MAP, CP.*

$  🏨 **Le Royale Louisiana.** In downtown Marigot in the boutique shop-
ping area, this upstairs hotel has white and pale green galleries that
overlook the flower-filled courtyard. There's a selection of twin, double, and triple duplexes. You can reach the nearest beach by a 20-minute
walk or by taxi. ✉ *Rue du Général de Gaulle, BP 476, Marigot 97055,*
☎ *590/87–86–51,* 📠 *590/87–96–49. 58 rooms. Restaurant, snack*
*bar, air-conditioning, beauty salon. AE, D, MC, V. CP.*

# Dining

It may seem that this island has no monuments, but they're here—all
dedicated to gastronomy, making St. Martin one of the best Caribbean
islands for gourmets. You'll scarcely find a touch of Dutch; the major
influences are French and Italian. This season's "in" eatery may be next
season's remembrance of things past, as things do have a way of changing rapidly. The generally steep prices reflect both the island's high culinary reputation and the difficulty of obtaining fresh ingredients. Not
surprisingly, the hotel restaurants on the French side are usually more

sophisticated, but sometimes at budget-breaking prices. In high season, *be sure to make reservations,* and call to cancel if you can't make it. Many restaurants close completely or just for lunch during August, September, and into October. We've tried to note all seasonal closings, but since not all restaurants have official policies, it's a good idea to call ahead during the off-season.

## What to Wear

Appropriate dining attire on this island ranges from swimsuits to sport jackets. For men, a jacket and khakis or jeans will take you anywhere; for women, dressy pants, a skirt, or even fancy shorts will be acceptable almost everywhere. Jeans are de rigueur in the less formal and more trendy eateries. In the listings below, dress is casual (and chic, of course) unless otherwise noted, but ask when making reservations if you're unsure.

| CATEGORY | COST* |
| --- | --- |
| $$$$ | over $50 |
| $$$ | $35–$50 |
| $$ | $25–$35 |
| $ | under $25 |

*per person for a three-course meal, excluding drinks and service*

DUTCH SIDE

**$$$$  ✕ Felix.** This classy yet casual little beachside eatery serves dinner by candlelight. At lunchtime, take a dip at Simpson Bay Beach (you can come here in your swimsuit as long as you're not wet) before feasting on salad Felix (an imaginative concoction of bananas, sweet potatoes, and avocado), rack of lamb Provençale, or steak au poivre. The restaurant is on the right on the road to the Pelican Resort. ⊠ *Pelican Key,* ☎ *599/5–42797. AE, D, DC, MC, V. No dinner Wed.*

**$$$  ✕ Le Bec Fin.** You stroll through a flowery courtyard to reach this well-known upstairs restaurant. The rotation of chefs has unfortunately led to inconsistency in the quality of the classical French cuisine, but it's pleasant for its ambience and views of Great Bay. Starters include vol-au-vent (pastry) bursting with escargots in fennel cream sauce and tagliatelle with shrimp in ginger. Fish, such as red snapper fillet in rum butter sauce, is your best bet for a main course. The meringue swan with mint ice cream is delightful to the eye and the palate. The breezy downstairs café annex serves breakfast and lunch with great crepes (try the seafood) and salads. ⊠ *119 Front St., Philipsburg,* ☎ *599/5–24508. AE, MC, V.*

**$$$  ✕ Le Perroquet.** A cool green-and-white West Indian–style house overlooking a lagoon is the peaceful—and romantic—setting for this restaurant. Chef Pierre Castagna prepares exotic specialties, such as grilled breast of ostrich in a bordelaise sauce, as well as savory dishes featuring duck, veal, beef, and more. ⊠ *Airport Rd., Simpson Bay,* ☎ *599/5–54339. AE, MC, V. Closed Mon.*

**$$$  ✕ Oyster Bay Beach Resort.** A more genteel evening on St. Maarten
★ is hard to find. A delightful terrace with wonderful sea views is decked with linens, china, and fresh flowers. Lobster medallions dancing in a truffle, tomato, and basil sauce; fillet of red snapper in sauce piquant; and sweet, billowy dessert soufflés are specialties. The hotel's guests have priority in this romantic dining room, so you should reserve well in advance. ⊠ *Oyster Pond,* ☎ *599/5–22206 or 599/5–23206. Reservations essential. AE, MC, V.*

**$$$  ✕ Saratoga.** The handsome mahogany-outfitted dining room in the
★ Yacht Club's stucco and red-tile building has views of the Simpson Bay Marina. The menu changes daily, borrowing from various influences, including Asian and southwestern. You might start with Malpeque oysters with balsamic-horseradish sauce or seven-seaweed salad with sea

beans, daikon, and sesame, then segue into crispy fried roundhead snapper in fermented black bean sauce or grilled chicken breast in a cumin-Gouda crust. The wine list is admirably balanced and reasonably priced, with 10–12 wines offered by the glass. ⊠ *Simpson Bay Yacht Club, Airport Rd.,* ☎ *599/5–42421. Reservations essential. AE, MC, V. Closed Sun. No lunch.*

**$$$** ✗ **Spartaco.** Every element of the northern Italian cuisine served in this 200-year-old stone plantation house is either homemade or imported from Italy. Some of the specialties are black angel-hair pasta with shrimp and garlic; swordfish baked with pink peppercorns and rosemary, served over linguine; and veal Vesuviana, with mozzarella, oregano, and tomato sauce. ⊠ *Almond Grove, Cole Bay,* ☎ *599/5–45379. AE, MC, V. Closed Mon. No lunch.*

**$$–$$$** ✗ **Antoine.** Enjoy a romantic evening at this elegant, airy Front Street terrace overlooking Great Bay. Candles glow on tables set with crisp blue-and-white tablecloths and gleaming silver, and the sound of the surf drifts up from the beach. You might start your meal with French onion soup or lobster bisque, then move on to steak au poivre, duck in brandy sauce with cherries, or lobster thermidor. Pastas and Creole specials are also available. For dessert, try the sublime Grand Marnier soufflé. ⊠ *49 Front St., Philipsburg,* ☎ *599/5–22964. Reservations essential. AE, MC, V. Closed Sun.*

**$$** ✗ **L'Escargot.** A lovely 19th-century house wrapped in verandas is home to one of St. Maarten's oldest classic French restaurants. Starters include frogs' legs in garlic sauce and crepes filled with caviar and sour cream. There is also, of course, a variety of snail dishes. For an entrée, try grilled red snapper with red wine and shallot sauce or *canard de l'escargot* (crisp duck in pineapple and banana sauce). There's a fun cabaret Wednesday night; you don't have to pay the cover charge if you come for dinner. ⊠ *84 Front St., Philipsburg,* ☎ *599/5–22483. AE, MC, V.*

**$–$$** ✗ **Wajang Doll.** Indonesian dishes are served in the garden of this West Indian–style house. *Nasi goreng* (fried rice) and red snapper in a sweet soy glaze are standouts, but the specialty is rijsttafel, a traditional Indonesian meal of rice accompanied by 15 to 20 different dishes. A wajang doll is used in Indonesian shadow plays, a traditional art form. ⊠ *137 Front St., Philipsburg,* ☎ *599/5–22687. AE, MC, V. Closed Sun. No lunch.*

**$** ✗ **Chesterfield's.** Casual lunches of burgers and salads and more elaborate Continental dinners are served at this informal, nautically themed restaurant at the marina. The dinner menu includes French onion soup, roast duckling with fresh pineapple and banana sauce, and several different preparations of shrimp. The Mermaid Bar is a popular spot with yachties. ⊠ *Great Bay Marina, Philipsburg,* ☎ *599/5–23484. No credit cards.*

**$** ✗ **Harbour Lights.** This modest family-run spot is in a historic building built in 1870. The decor is warm, with peach and coral walls and sea-foam-green tablecloths. Choose among excellent rotis and pilafs and, even better, stewed or curried chicken, meats, and seafood. Try one of the knockout cocktails made with the local guavaberry liqueur. Tables on the second-floor balcony overlook Back Street and make for pleasant alfresco dining. ⊠ *30 Back St., Philipsburg,* ☎ *599/5–23504. AE, MC, V.*

**$** ✗ **Shiv Sagar.** Authentic East Indian cuisine, emphasizing Kashmiri and ★ Mogul specialties, is served in this small mirrored room fragrant with cumin and coriander. Marvelous tandooris and curries are offered, but try one of the less-familiar preparations like *madrasi machi* (red snapper cooked in a blend of hot spices). A large selection of vegetarian dishes is also offered. There's a friendly open-air bar out front. ⊠ *3*

*Front St., Philipsburg,* ☎ *599/5–22299. AE, D, DC, MC, V. Closed Sun.*

$ ✕ **Turtle Pier Bar & Restaurant.** Chattering monkeys and squawking
★ parrots greet you at the entrance to this classic Caribbean hangout, tee-
tering over the lagoon and festooned with creeping vines. There are
200 animals in this informal zoo, but that's nothing compared to the
menagerie hanging out at the bar during happy hour. The genial owner,
Sid Wathey, whose family is one of the island's oldest, and his American wife, Lorraine, have fashioned one of the funkiest, most endearing places in the Caribbean, with cheap beer on draft, huge American
breakfasts, all-you-can-eat rib dinners, and live music several nights a
week. ⊠ *Airport Rd., Simpson Bay,* ☎ *599/5–52230. No credit cards.*

## French Side

$$$$ ✕ **Chez Martine.** A charming, globe-trotting French couple, Eliane
★ and Jean-Pierre Bertheau, have made this small hotel into a personable hostelry with an excellent French restaurant. Dine by the water's
edge in an intimate room with polished silverware, blue glassware, and
white napkins. You might begin with superb velvety seafood con-
sommé, then segue into roast lamb on a bed of eggplant and spinach
in corn sauce or lobster in puff pastry; the homemade duck-liver pâté
also claims a loyal following. The wine list has several very drinkable
wines for under $20. ⊠ *140 blvd. de Grand Case, Grand Case,* ☎ *590/
87–51–59. DC, MC, V. No lunch off-season.*

$$$$ ✕ **La Samanna.** This restaurant has an exquisite setting in the celebrated
hotel; you'll dine by candlelight on a tented terrace surrounded by
bougainvillea. The clientele is chic, international, and often famous.
Innovative chef Mark Ehrler (from Maxim's in Paris and New York)
might seduce the palate with seafood risotto, sautéed snapper over Creole black sausage, or roasted lamb chops with seasonal salad and
chickpeas sprinkled with fruity cold-press olive oil. Three kinds of caviar
are served with blinis and chilled Absolut. Dinner for two (with wine)
can easily set you back $175. The superb wine cellar holds more than
25,000 bottles. ⊠ *Baie Longue, Terres Basses,* ☎ *590/87–64–00. Reservations essential. Jacket required. AE, DC, MC, V.*

$$$$ ✕ **Le Santal.** The approach to this dazzler, through a working-class sub-
★ urb of Marigot, is forbidding. The exterior appears ramshackle, but
the interior is transformed by soft lighting, china, and crystal. Specialties
of the house include lobster soufflé on a bed of spinach and eggplant,
foie gras sautéed in cassis, and lacquered duck. The owners also run
the excellent Jean Dupont and Asia, but this is their showplace. Reservations are not required, but they're highly recommended if you want
to eat at one of the five tables by the water. ⊠ *Sandy Ground,* ☎ *590/87–
53–48. AE, MC, V. No lunch.*

$$$–$$$$ ✕ **La Vie En Rose.** This bustling restaurant is right off the pier, about
a 30-second stroll from the tourist information office. The menu is clas-
sic French with an occasional Caribbean twist—fillet of swordfish
sautéed in a passion-fruit butter sauce, freshwater crayfish in puff pas-
try. Appetizers include a delightful warm smoked salmon with pota-
toes and chives and lobster salad spiced with a touch of ginger. Save
room for chocolate mousse cake topped with vanilla sauce. The ground-
floor tearoom and pastry shop serve an excellent luncheon with wine
for $20. In season, you may make dinner reservations up to one month
in advance. ⊠ *Rue de la République and blvd. de France, Marigot,*
☎ *590/87–54–42. Reservations essential in season. AE, D, DC, MC,
V. No lunch Sun.*

$$$–$$$$ ✕ **Le Poisson d'Or.** Feast in this posh, popular place on a constantly
★ changing menu of dishes such as sautéed foie gras with pear and wal-
nut cream sauce or smoked lobster in champagne sauce. Light piano

classics provide a backdrop for the setting, a restored stone house with a huge veranda holding 20 tables. The space doubles as a gallery exhibiting works of top-notch Caribbean artists. ⊠ *14 rue d'Anguille, Marigot,* ☎ *590/87–72–45. AE, MC, V. Closed Sept.–early Oct. No lunch.*

$$$–$$$$ ✕ **Rainbow.** In a town of splendid seaside boîtes, this is one of the best.
★ The cobalt-blue-and-white decor of the split-level dining room is strikingly simple, and the atmosphere, created by lapping waves and murmuring guests, is highly romantic. Fleur and David are the stylish, energetic hosts, and chef Mario Tardif is from one of the world's gastronomic capitals, Québec City. Try his shrimp and scallop fricassee with Caribbean chutney, duck *maigret* (breast meat served with its skin), grilled swordfish, or sautéed veal scallopini with capers, garlic, and chives. Dishes are dressed with fanciful touches like red cabbage crisps. Finish the meal off with sublime orange, honey, and ginger soufflé. ⊠ *176 blvd. de Grand Case, Grand Case,* ☎ *590/87–55–80. AE, MC, V. Closed Sun. No lunch.*

$$$ ✕ **Alizéa.** Many claim that this elegant terrace restaurant offers the best
★ cuisine on the island. French chef Laurent Guyon trained with Roger Verge from the famous Moulin de Mougins. Sample the homemade foie gras with red wine jelly or roasted sea scallop appetizers. Entrées include mahimahi with fennel and sweet potatoes, and beef tenderloin with stewed shallots in red wine sauce. There are several vegetarian selections. You won't go wrong with the crème brûlée with honey and vanilla for dessert. ⊠ *Hotel Alizéa, Mont Vernon,* ☎ *590/87–41–20. AE, DC, MC, V.*

$$$ ✕ **Le Tastevin.** A chic pavilion, with tropical plants, ceiling fans, and water views, provides an elegant dining setting. Owner Daniel Passeri, a native of Burgundy, also founded the homey Auberge Gourmande across the street. The menu here is more ambitious, including foie gras in Armagnac sauce, duck breast in banana-lime sauce, and red snapper fillet with curry and wild-mushroom sauce. ⊠ *86 blvd. de Grand Case, Grand Case,* ☎ *590/87–55–45. Reservations essential. AE, DC, MC, V. No credit cards at lunch.*

$$–$$$ ✕ **Le Pressoir.** Many say that presentation is everything. Combine that
★ with excellent food in a charming West Indies house, where the bill won't break the bank, and you have a great restaurant. French and Creole fusion cuisine reigns; go for the fresh local fish prepared with tropical fruit glazes and sauces. The crème brûlée is superb. ⊠ *Grand Case,* ☎ *590/87–76–62. AE, MC, V.*

$$–$$$ ✕ **Maison sur le Port.** Watching the sunset from the palm-fringed terrace is not the least of the pleasures in this old West Indian house surrounded by romantically lit garden fountains. Try the sautéed duck fillet in passion-fruit sauce or red snapper with beurre blanc. There are also three-course fixed-price menus at $21.50 and $29. Chef Jean-Paul Fahrner's imaginative salads are lunchtime treats. There is a children's menu with burgers and chicken sandwiches. ⊠ *On the port, Marigot,* ☎ *590/87–56–38. AE, D, MC, V. Closed Sun., June, and Sept.*

$$ ✕ **Le Marocain.** This exotic oasis in the middle of Marigot resembles a pasha's posh digs, with lush potted plants, intricate mosaics, hand-painted tiles, and wood carvings. The food is as colorful and enticing as the decor, with wonderfully perfumed *tajines* (casseroles of chicken or meat) and *pastillas* (fragrant pastries filled with spices, raisins, and meat or chicken) among the standouts. ⊠ *147 rue de Hollande, Marigot,* ☎ *590/87–83–11. AE, MC, V.*

$–$$ ✕ **Bistrot Nu.** For simple, unadorned fare at a reasonable price, this
★ may be the best spot on the islands. Traditional brasserie-style food—coq au vin, fish soup, snails, pizza, and seafood—is served in a friendly atmosphere. The place is enormously popular; its tables are packed until

it closes at 2 AM. ⊠ *Rue de Hollande, Marigot,* ☎ *590/87–97–09. MC, V. Closed Sun.*

**$–$$** ✕ **Don Camillo da Enzo.** Country-style decor and excellent service distinguish this small eatery. Both northern and southern Italian dishes are served. Some favorites are the carpaccio, green gnocchi in Gorgonzola cream sauce, and veal medallions in marsala sauce. ⊠ *La Marina Port la Royale, Marigot,* ☎ *590/87–52–88. AE, MC, V.*

**$–$$** ✕ **La Plaisance.** The cool strains of jazz waft through this lively open-air brasserie as you sample terrific salads (try the Niçoise or *landaine*— duck, smoked ham, croutons, and fried egg), pizzas (wonderful lobster), pastas (garlic and basil pistou), and fresh grilled seafood at unbeatable prices. This is one of several fine, ultracasual eateries at Port La Royale, all offering simple, appetizing food; fixed-price menus; and happy hours. ⊠ *La Marina Port la Royale, Marigot,* ☎ *590/87–85–00. AE, MC, V.*

**$** ✕ **Yvette's.** The attempts at romance couldn't be more endearing:
★ Classical music plays softly, and the tiny, eight-table room is a symphony in Valentine red, from the curtains, tablecloths, and roses to the hot pepper sauce. Yvette herself couldn't be more down-home, nor her food more delicious. Plates are piled high with lip-smacking Creole specialties, such as *accras* (spicy fish fritters), stewed chicken with rice and beans, and conch and dumplings. This is the kind of place that is so good you're surprised to see other tourists—but word gets around. ⊠ *Orleans,* ☎ *590/87–32–03. AE.*

# Beaches

The island's 10 mi of beaches are all open to the public. Beaches occupied by resort properties may charge a small fee (about $3) for changing facilities, and water-sports equipment can be rented in most of the hotels. You cannot, however, enter the beach via the hotel unless you are a paying guest or will be renting equipment there. Some of the 37 beaches are secluded, and some are in the thick of things, but on several you'll find vendors who will rent beach umbrellas and chairs for $5 for the day. Topless bathing is virtually de rigueur on the French side, where the beaches are generally better than on the Dutch side. If you take a cab to a remote beach, be sure to arrange a specific, clearly understood time for your driver to return to pick you up. Don't leave valuables unattended on the beach or in your rental car, even in the trunk.

Hands down, **Baie Longue** (Long Bay) is the best beach on the island. It's a beautiful, mile-long curve of white sand on the westernmost tip of the island. This is a good place for snorkeling and swimming, but beware of a strong undertow when the waters are rough. You can sunbathe in the buff, though only a few do. There are no facilities. Beyond Baie Longue is **Baie aux Prunes** (Plum Bay), where the oft-rocky beach arcs between two headlands and the occasional sunbather discloses all. **Baie Rouge** (Red Bay) is right off the main road past Baie aux Prunes. Some rate it the prettiest beach on the island. The waves here can be rough. You'll find refreshments and beach chair and umbrellas rentals. **Cupecoy Beach** is a small shifting arc of white sand fringed with eroded limestone cliffs, just south of Baie Longue on the western side of the island, near the Dutch-French border. On the eastern part of the beach, swimwear is worn, but farther west, sun worshipers start shedding their attire. This section is also the island's gay beach. On the beach you'll find vendors who sell cold sodas and beers and rent chairs and umbrellas. There are two parking spots for the beach, one near the Cupecoy and Sapphire beach clubs, and the other just a few yards west, where you can park for $2. The advantage here is that your car is safe.

You have to approach the **Dawn Beach–Oyster Pond** area through the grounds of the Dawn Beach Hotel. The long white-sand beach is partly protected by reefs (good for snorkeling), but the water is not always calm. When the waves come rolling in, this is the best spot on the island for bodysurfing. **Ilet Pinel** is a little speck off the northeast coast with about 500 yards of beach where you can have picnics and privacy. There are no facilities. Putt putts (small boats) are available to take you from French Cul de Sac and Orient Beach. Ecru-color sand, palm and sea-grape trees, calm waters, and the roar of jets lowering to nearby Juliana International Airport distinguish the beach at **Maho Bay.** Concession stand, beach chairs, and facilities are available. At **Mullet Bay,** the powdery white-sand beach is crowded with guests of the Mullet Bay Resort (closed at press time). Hurricane Luis made **Orient Beach** much wider and sandier, the silver lining of such a devastating storm. This is the island's best-known "clothes-optional" beach—on the agenda for voyeurs from visiting cruise ships. You can enter from the parking area. The nude section is to the right on the southern end of the beach. Farther down toward the middle of the beach is the Orient Bay Resort, with several restaurants, bars, and chaises (with food and beverage service) for rent. This is windsurfing heaven, with a couple of rental shops on the beach to take advantage of the steady onshore trade winds. **Simpson Bay** is a long half moon of white sand near Simpson Bay Village, one of the last undiscovered hamlets on the island. In this small fishing village you'll find refreshments, a dive shop for water-sports-equipment rentals, and neat little ultra-Caribbean town homes.

## Outdoor Activities and Sports

### Boating

Motorboats, speedboats, sailboats, and Waverunners can be rented at **Caribbean Watersports** (⌧ Nettlé Bay, ☎ 590/87–58–66), and **Caraibes Sport Boats** (⌧ Marina Port la Royale, ☎ 590/87–89–38).

**Sun Yacht-Charters** (☎ 800/772–3500), based in Oyster Pond, has a fleet of 50 Centurion sailboats for hire. The cost of a week's bareboat charter for a 36-ft Centurion with six berths is $2,850 in peak winter season. Also in Oyster Pond, the **Moorings** (☎ 590/87–32–55 or 800/535–7289) has a fleet of Beneteau yachts, and bareboat and crewed catamarans. **Dynasty** (☎ 590/87–85–21), in Marigot's Port la Royale Marina, offers an excellent fleet of Dynamique yachts, ranging in size from 47 to 80 ft. Prices vary depending on the type of yacht and crew requirements. For the best full-service yacht and water-sports rentals on the French side, contact **Marine Time** (☎ 590/87–20–28, FAX 590/87–20–78), behind the tourist office on the port in Marigot.

### Deep-Sea Fishing

Angle for yellowtail, snapper, grouper, marlin, tuna, and wahoo on half- or full-day deep-sea excursions, from $300 (four people) for the half-day to $600 for the full-day trip. Prices usually include bait and tackle, instruction for novices, and an open bar. Contact **Bobby's Marina** (⌧ Philipsburg, ☎ 599/5–22366), **Lee Deepsea Fishing** (⌧ Philipsburg, ☎ 599/5–44233, 599/5–44234, or 599/5–70747), **Rudy's Fishing** (⌧ Simpson Bay, ☎ 599/5–52177), or **Sailfish Caraibes** (⌧ Port Lonvilliers, ☎ 590/87–31–94 or 590/27–40–90).

### Fitness

**L'Aqualigne** (☎ 599/5–42426), on the Dutch side at the Pelican Resort, is a health spa with gym, sauna, and beauty treatments, including manicures, facials, and massages. **Fitness Caraibes** (☎ 590/87–35–81) is a toning center at Nettlé Bay. **Future Fitness Center**

(☎ 590/87–90–27), in Marigot, has decent free-weight equipment as well as machines and aerobics. **Le Privilège** (☎ 590/87–37–37), a sports complex at Anse Marcel above Le Meridien L'Habitation, has a full range of exercise equipment and the island's best spa.

## Golf

**Mullet Bay Resort** (☎ 599/5–52801) has an 18-hole championship course. Surprisingly, this is the only course on the island. Greens fees are $105, and club rental is $25 for 18 holes. The course remains open, even though the resort was closed at press time.

## Horseback Riding

Rides can be arranged through your hotel, or you can contact **Crazy Acres Riding Center** (⊠ Wathey Estate, Cole Bay, ☎ 599/5–42793), **Bayside Riding Club** (⊠ Orient Bay, ☎ 590/87–36–64), **O.K. Corral** (⊠ Oyster Pond, ☎ 590/87–40–72), or **Caid & Isa** (⊠ Anse Marcel, ☎ 590/87–45–70). All the outfits offer beach rides and can accommodate different skill levels; cost is about $45 for a two-hour ride.

## Jet Skiing and Water-Skiing

On the Dutch side, rent equipment through the **Divi Little Bay Resort**'s (closed for refurbishment at press time, due to open 1998) watersports activity center (☎ 599/5–22333). On the French side, try **Orient Bay Watersports** (☎ 590/87–40–75) or **Laguna Watersports** (☎ 590/87–91–75) at Nettlé Bay.

## Parasailing

On the French side, **Orient Bay Watersports** (☎ 590/87–40–75) offers parasailing rides on Orient Bay.

## Running

The **Road Runners Club** meets Wednesday in the parking lot of the Raoul Illidge Sportscomplex for a 5 PM Fun Run and Sunday at 6:45 AM in the parking lot of the Pelican Resort for a 2K–15K run. For more information, contact Dr. Frits Bus (☎ 599/5–22467) or Ron van Sittert (☎ 599/5–22842).

## Scuba Diving

The water temperature here is rarely below 70°F, and visibility is usually excellent. There are many diving attractions, both right around the island and around numerous nearby islands. On the Dutch side is Proselyte Reef, named for the British frigate HMS *Proselyte,* which sank south of Great Bay in 1801. In addition to wreck dives, reef, night, and cave dives are popular. Off the northeast coast of the French side, dive sites include Ilet Pinel, for good shallow diving; Green Key, with its vibrant barrier reef; and Tintamarre, for sheltered coves and underwater geologic faults.

On the Dutch side, SSI- (Scuba Schools International) and PADI-certified dive centers include **Trade Winds Dive Center** (⊠ Bobby's Marina, ☎ 599/5–75176), **St. Maarten Divers** (⊠ Philipsburg, ☎ 599/5–22446), **Leeward Island Divers** (⊠ Simpson Bay, ☎ 599/5–42268), **Ocean Explorers Dive Shop** (⊠ Simpson Bay, ☎ 599/5–45252), and **Pelican Dive Adventures** (⊠ Pelican Resort Marina, ☎ 599/5–42503, ext. 1553). On the French side, **Lou Scuba** (⊠ Marine Hotel Simson Beach, Nettlé Bay, ☎ 590/87–16–61) is a PADI-certified dive center. **Blue Ocean** (⊠ Marigot, ☎ 590/87–89–73) is PADI- and CMAS-certified. **Octoplus** (⊠ Blvd. de Grand Case, ☎ 590/87–20–62) is a complete dive center.

## Sea Excursions

You can take a daylong picnic sail to nearby islands or secluded coves aboard the 45-ft ketch *Gabrielle* (☎ 599/5–23170), or the sleek 76-

ft catamaran *Golden Eagle* (☎ 599/5–30068). The 50-ft catamaran *Bluebeard II* (☎ 599/5–52898), moored in Simpson Bay, sails around Anguilla's south and northwest coasts to Prickly Pear, where there are excellent coral reefs for snorkeling and powdery white sands for sunning. The average range for these excursions is $45–$65 per person. The 85-ft *Lady Mary* (☎ 599/5–53892) sails around the island each evening from La Palapa Center on Simpson Bay; the fare, about $65 per person, includes dinner, open bar, and live calypso music. It's tremendous fun. The *Laura Rose* (☎ 599/5–70710) offers a variety of half- and full-day sails, ranging $25–$65 per person.

The luxurious 75-ft motor catamaran *White Octopus* (☎ 599/5–24096 or 599/5–23170) makes the run to St. Barts, departing at 9 AM from Bobby's Marina or Captain Oliver's Marina and returning at 5 PM. Cost is $50 per person, $25 for children 12 and under, which includes an open bar, snacks, and snorkel equipment.

In St. Martin, sailing, snorkeling, and picnic excursions to nearby islands can be arranged through **Orient Bay Watersports** (✉ Club Orient, ☎ 590/87–40–75), **Le Meridien L'Habitation** (☎ 590/87–33–33), **La Belle Creole** (☎ 590/87–66–00), and **La Samanna** (☎ 590/87–51–22).

## Snorkeling

Coral reefs around the island teem with marine life, and clear water allows visibility of up to 200 ft. Some of the best snorkeling on the Dutch side can be found around the rocks below Fort Amsterdam off Little Bay Beach, in the west end of Maho Bay, off Pelican Key, and around the reefs off Dawn Beach and Oyster Pond. On the French side, the area around Orient Bay, Green Key, Ilet Pinel, and Flat Island (or Tintamarre) is especially lovely and should soon be officially classified a regional underwater nature reserve. Arrange rentals and trips through **Ocean Explorers** (☎ 599/5–45252) and **Orient Bay Watersports** (☎ 590/87–40–75).

## Tennis

If you want to play tennis at a hotel at which you are not a guest, be sure to call ahead to find out whether it allows visitors. You'll probably need to make reservations, and there's usually an hourly fee. There are three lighted courts at the **Pelican Resort** (☎ 599/5–42503); three lighted courts at the **Divi Little Bay Beach Resort** (☎ 599/5–22333), which was closed for refurbishment at press time but due to open 1998; three lighted courts at the **Maho Beach Hotel** (☎ 599/5–52115); six lighted courts at **Le Privilège** (✉ Anse Marcel, ☎ 590/87–38–38), which also has four squash and two racquetball courts; two lighted courts at the **Mont Vernon Hotel** (☎ 590/87–62–00); one lighted court at the **Marine Hotel Simson Beach** (☎ 590/87–54–54); and nine lighted courts each at the **Grand Case Beach Club** (☎ 590/87–51–87) and the **Coralita Beach Hotel** (☎ 590/87–31–81).

## Windsurfing

Rental and instruction are available at **Orient Bay Watersports** (☎ 590/87–40–75). The **Nathalie Simon Windsurfing Club** (☎ 590/87–48–16) offers rentals and lessons in Orient Bay.

# Shopping

About 180 cruise ships call at St. Maarten each year, and they do so for about 500 reasons. That's roughly the number of duty-free shops on the island.

Prices can be 25%–50% below those in the United States and Canada on French perfumes, liquor, cognac and fine liqueurs, cigarettes and cigars, Swedish crystal, Finnish stoneware, Irish linen, Italian leather, German cameras, European designer fashions, Swiss watches, plus thousands of other things you never knew you wanted. But check prices before you leave home, especially if you live in the New York City area—Manhattan's prices (including mail order) for cameras and electronics equipment are hard to beat anywhere. If you're shopping for electronics in Philipsburg, try negotiating for a lower price. Competition is fierce, and some stores will bargain if you pay cash. In general, you will find more fashion on the French side in Marigot, although stalwarts like Polo Ralph Lauren and Benetton have Philipsburg outlets. You will also find Marigot to be a much more pleasant place to shop and stroll.

St. Maarten's best-known "craft" is its guavaberry liqueur, made from rum and the wild local berries (not to be confused with guavas) that grow only on this island's central mountains.

Prices are quoted in florins, francs, and dollars; shops take credit cards and traveler's checks. Most shopkeepers, especially on the Dutch side, speak English. (If more than one cruise ship is in port, avoid Front Street. It's so crowded you won't be able to move.) Although most merchants are reputable, there are occasional reports of inferior or fake merchandise passed off as the real thing. As a rule of thumb, if you can bargain excessively, it's probably not worth it.

## Shopping Areas

**Front Street,** Philipsburg, is one long strip lined with sleek boutiques and colorful shops, including, oddly, a Harley-Davidson outlet. **Old Street,** near the end of Front Street, has 22 stores, boutiques, and open-air cafés. There is a slew of boutiques in the **Mullet** (closed at press time) and **Maho** shopping plazas, as well as at the **Plaza del Lago,** at the Simpson Bay Yacht Club complex.

Wrought-iron balconies, colorful awnings, and gingerbread trim decorate Marigot's smart shops, tiny boutiques, and bistros in the **Marina Port La Royale** complex and on the main streets, **rue de la Liberté** and **rue de la République.**

## Good Buys

**Carat** (⊠ Marigot, ☎ 590/87–73–40; ⊠ Philipsburg, ☎ 599/5–22180) sells china and jewelry. **H. Stern** (⊠ Philipsburg, ☎ 599/5–23328) specializes in colorful jewelry and elegant watches. **Havane** (⊠ Marigot, ☎ 590/87–70–39) sells designer fashions. **La Cave du Savour Club** (⊠ Marigot, ☎ 590/87–58–51) is the place to pick up a bottle of wine for your picnic. **La Romana** (⊠ Front St., Philipsburg, ☎ 599/5–22181) stocks designer fashions. **Lil' Shoppe** (⊠ Philipsburg, ☎ 599/5–22177) carries eel-skin wallets, handbags, perfumes, and a large selection of swimwear. **Lipstick** (⊠ Marina Port la Royale, ☎ 590/87–73–24; ⊠ Marigot, ☎ 590/87–53–92; ⊠ Philipsburg, ☎ 599/5–26051) carries an enormous selection of perfume and cosmetics (including sunscreen). **Little Europe** (⊠ Philipsburg, ☎ 599/5–24371) sells fine jewelry, along with crystal and china. **Little Switzerland** (⊠ Marigot, ☎ 590/87–50–03; ⊠ Philipsburg, ☎ 599/5–23530) sells fine crystal, china, perfume, and jewelry. **New Amsterdam Store** (⊠ Philipsburg, ☎ 599/5–22787) handles designer fashions, fine linens, and porcelain. **Oro de Sol** (⊠ Marigot, ☎ 590/87–56–51) carries jewelry and watches, as well as perfume, cosmetics, and Cuban cigars. **Yellow House** (⊠ Philipsburg, ☎ 599/5–23438) carries perfumes, cosmetics, and gifts.

## Island Specialties

**ABC Art Gallery** (⊠ Marigot, ☎ 590/87–96–00) exhibits the work of local artists. **Galerie Lynn** (⊠ 83 blvd. de Grand Case, ☎ 590/87–77–24) sells stunning paintings and sculptures. **Gingerbread Galerie** (⊠ Port La Royale, ☎ 590/87–73–21) specializes in Haitian art. **Green-with Galleries** (⊠ Front St., Philipsburg, ☎ 599/5–23842) specializes in Caribbean art. **Le Poisson D'Or** (⊠ Marigot, ☎ 590/87–72–45) restaurant houses a gallery featuring the work of local artists. **Minguet** (⊠ Rambaud Hill, ☎ 590/87–76–06) carries pictures by the artist Minguet depicting island life. **Shipwreck Shop** (⊠ Front St., Philipsburg, ☎ 599/5–22962; ⊠ Port La Royale, ☎ 590/87–27–37) stocks Caribelle batik, hammocks, handmade jewelry, the local guavaberry liqueur, and herbs and spices. The **Guavaberry Shop** (⊠ Front St., Philipsburg, ☎ 599/5–22965) is the small factory where the famous guavaberry liqueur is made by the Sint Maarten Guavaberry Company; on sale are myriad versions of the liqueur (including a version made with jalapeño peppers), as well as spices, batiks, and souvenirs.

# Nightlife

To find out what's doing on the island, pick up any of the following publications: *St. Maarten Nights, What to Do in St. Maarten, St. Maarten Events, Focus St. Maarten/St.Martin,* or *St. Maarten Holiday*—all distributed free in the tourist office and hotels. *Discover St. Martin/St. Maarten,* also free, is a glossy magazine that includes articles about the island's history and the latest on shops, discos, restaurants, and even archaeological digs.

Most of the resort hotels have a Caribbean spectacular one night a week, replete with limbo and fire dancers and steel bands.

Casinos are the main focus on the Dutch side, but there are discos that usually start late and keep on till the fat lady sings.

### Bars and Nightclubs

**Bamboo Cocktail Bar** (⊠ Rue de la Liberté, Marigot, ☎ 590/29–01–00) is the place for karaoke fans. **Cheri's Cafe** (⊠ Across from Maho Beach Hotel & Casino, Airport Rd., Simpson Bay, ☎ 599/5–53361) is a local institution, with cheap food and great live bands. **Le Bar de la Mer** (⊠ Market Square, Marigot, ☎ 590/87–81–79) on the harbor is a popular gathering spot in the evening (it's open until 2). **News Cafe** (⊠ Airport Rd., Simpson Bay, ☎ 599/5–42236) is a friendly spot where you can order food into the wee hours. **Peace and Love Disco** (⊠ La Savanne, ☎ 590/87–58–34) features local bands, calypso, and dancing. **Surf Club South** (⊠ Just east of Grand Case Town, ☎ 590/87–50–40) is American-owned and comes complete with road signs from the Garden State Parkway posted at the entrance. **Turtle Pier Bar & Restaurant** (⊠ Airport Rd., Simpson Bay, ☎ 599/5–52230) always hops with a lively crowd.

### Casinos

All the casinos have craps, blackjack, roulette, and slot machines. You must be 18 years old or older to gamble. The casinos are located at the **Great Bay Beach Hotel, Divi Little Bay Beach Resort** (closed for refurbishment at press time, due to open 1998), Pelican Resort, Seaview Hotel, and the **Coliseum** (⊠ Cay Bay Hill, ☎ 599/5–25629) in Philipsburg; and **Casino Royal at Maho Beach** (which produces the splashy Paris Revue Show).

### Discos

**Amnesia** (⊠ Maho Beach Hotel & Casino, ☎ 599/5–22962), formerly La Luna, is Maho's disco, popular with young people. Like the Amnesia in Ibiza, it sometimes features "foam" dancing. **L'Atmo 2000** (✉ Marina Royale, Marigot, no phone), formerly the Copacabana, is where French nationals and locals flock for salsa and soca on Fridays. It's open every night but Monday. **L'Aventure** (✉ Front de Mer, Marigot, ☎ 590/87–01–97) attracts a young crowd of locals, French nationals, and gays who gyrate to the latest house music. It's open every night but Sunday.

## Exploring St. Martin/St. Maarten

St. Martin/St. Maarten's roads are in very good condition and are generally well marked. With the exception of some annoying traffic congestion, especially in and around Philipsburg and Marigot, the island is easily traversed, and there is much to see in its historic forts, museums, beaches, and rich countryside.

*Numbers in the margin correspond to points of interest on the St. Martin/St. Maarten map.*

SIGHTS TO SEE

**❺ French Cul de Sac.** Just north of Orient Beach, you'll find the French colonial mansion of St. Martin's mayor nestled in the hills. Little red-roof houses look like open umbrellas tumbling down the green hillside. The scenery here is glorious, and the area is great for hiking. There is a lot of construction, however, as the surroundings are slowly being developed, including a hideous eyesore of the Mont Vernon Hotel, which looks like a hospital. From the beach here, shuttle boats make the five-minute trip to **Ilet Pinel,** an uninhabited island that's fine for picnicking, sunning, and swimming.

**❼ Friar's Beach.** This small, picturesque cove between Marigot and Grand Case attracts a casual crowd of locals. A small snack bar, **Kali's,** owned by a welcoming gentleman wearing dreadlocks, serves refreshments. A bumpy, tree-canopied road leads inland to **Pic du Paradis,** at 1,278 ft the highest point on the island, affording breathtaking vistas of the Caribbean.

**❻ Grand Case.** The most picturesque town on the island is set in the heart of the French side on the beach at the foot of green hills and pastures. Though it has only one mile-long main street, it's known as the "Restaurant Capital of the Caribbean": More than 20 restaurants serve French, Italian, Indonesian, and Vietnamese fare, as well as fresh seafood. The budget-minded love the "lolos"—kiosks at the far end of town selling savory barbecue (many were destroyed by Hurricane Luis, but several more sturdy versions have been rebuilt). Grand Case Beach Club is at the end of this road and has two beaches where you can take a short dip.

**❷ Guana Bay Point.** North of Philipsburg off Sucker Garden Road, Guana Bay Point offers a splendid view of the island's east coast, tiny deserted islands, and petite St. Barts, which is anything but deserted.

**❽ Marigot.** This town is a wonderful place to tarry awhile if you are a shopper, a gourmet, or just a Francophile. Marina Port La Royale is the shopping complex at the port, but rue de la République and rue de la Liberté, which border the bay, are also filled with duty-free shops, boutiques, and bistros. The harbor area has a new crafts pavilion selling everything from handmade crafts to fish so fresh they're still mad. You are likely to find more creative and fashionable buys in Marigot than in Philipsburg. There is less bustle here, and the open-air cafés are tempting places in which to stop for a rest. Unlike Philipsburg, Marigot does not die at night, so you may wish to stay into the evening.

Across the parking lot, on the pier road leading to the ferries for Anguilla, is the helpful **French tourist office,** where you can pick up the usual assortment of free maps and brochures. Just north of town there is a shopping complex on the inland side of the main road. At the back of it is **Match** (☎ 590/87–92–36), the largest supermarket on the French side, carrying a broad selection of tempting picnic makings—from country pâté to foie gras—and a vast selection of wines.

---

NEED A
BREAK?

With a roguish glint in his eye, owner Roger Drovin proclaims the melt-in-your-mouth croissants at **Cafe Terrasse Mastedana** (✉ Rue de la Liberté, no phone) to be "zee best"—perfect for a light breakfast or snack.

---

**4** **Orléans.** North of Oyster Pond and the Etang aux Poissons (Fish Lake) is the oldest settlement on the island, also known as the French Quarter. Noted local artist Roland Richardson makes his home here. He opens his **studio** to the public on Thursday from 10 to 6, or by appointment (☎ 590/87–32–24). He's a proud islander ready to share his wealth of knowledge about the island's cultural history.

**3** **Oyster Pond.** Just north of Dawn Beach on Sucker Garden Road is the legendary point where two early settlers, a Frenchman and a Dutchman, allegedly began to pace in opposite directions around the island to divide it between their respective countries. Local legend maintains that the obese sweaty Hollander stopped frequently to refresh himself with gin—the reason that the French side is nearly twice the size of the Dutch. (The official boundary marker is on the other side of the island.)

**1** **Philipsburg.** The Dutch capital of St. Maarten stretches about a mile along an isthmus between Great Bay and the Salt Pond and has three more or less parallel streets: Front Street, Back Street, and Pondfill. Front Street has been recobbled, cars are discouraged from using it, and the pedestrian area has been widened. Shops, restaurants, and casinos vie for the hordes coming off the cruise boats. Little lanes called *steegjes* connect Front Street with Back Street, considerably less congested because it has fewer shops.

**Wathey Square** is in the middle of the isthmus on which Philipsburg sits. The square bustles with vendors, souvenir shops, and tourists. Directly across the street from the square is a striking white building with a cupola. It was built in 1793 and has since served as the commander's home, a fire station, and a jail. It now serves as the town hall, courthouse, and the post office and was beautifully restored in 1995. The streets surrounding the square are lined with hotels, duty-free shops, fine restaurants, and cafés, most of them in pastel-colored West Indian cottages gussied up with gingerbread trim. Narrow alleyways lead to arcades and flower-filled courtyards where there are yet more boutiques and eateries. The **Capt. Hodge Pier** just off the square is a good spot to view Great Bay and the beach that stretches alongside it for about a mile.

The **Sint Maarten Museum** hosts rotating cultural exhibits and a permanent historical display entitled "Forts of St. Maarten/St. Martin," featuring artifacts ranging from Arawak pottery shards to articles salvaged from the wreck of HMS *Proselyte.* ✉ 7 Front St., Philipsburg, ☎ 599/5–24917. 🖾 $1. 🕑 Mon.–Sat. 10–4.

**9** **St. Martin Museum.** The Musée de Saint-Martin, subtitled "On the Trail of the Arawaks," is a small and ambitious museum presenting artifacts from the island's pre-Columbian days. Included are pottery displays, rock carvings, and petroglyphs, as well as displays from the colonial

and sugar plantation days. Upstairs is a small art gallery, featuring locally produced art, lithographs, and posters. ⊠ *Sandy Ground Rd.,
Marigot,* ☎ *590/29–22–84.* ⊠ *$5.* ☺ *Mon.–Sat. 9–1 and 3–7.*

**Sucker Garden Road.** This road runs north of Philipsburg through spectacular scenery—soaring mountains, turquoise waters, quaint West Indian houses, and wonderful views of St. Barts. The paved roller-coaster
road eventually leads down to **Dawn Beach,** one of the island's best
snorkeling beaches.

**Terres Basses.** This area of the island incorporates the coastline from
Sandy Ground, just south of Marigot, to Cupecoy Beach, a small but
beautiful beach of sandstone cliffs and coves, on the Dutch side. Some
of the island's nicest beaches are found in this region: **Baie Rouge, Baie
aux Prunes,** and **Baie Longue** cling to its westernmost point. They are
all accessible down bumpy but short dirt roads and are perfect for swimming and picnicking. Also found here is Baie Nettlé, with its many reasonably priced hotels, and the Mediterranean-style village resort of **La
Belle Creole,** commanding Pointe du Bluff.

# St. Martin/St. Maarten A to Z

## Arriving and Departing

### BY BOAT

Motorboats zip several times a day from Anguilla and St. Barts to the
French side at Marigot, and three times a week from St. Barts. Catamaran service is available daily from the Dutch side to St. Barts on the
***White Octopus*** (☎ 599/5–24096 or 599/5–23170). Cost is $50 per
person, $25 for children 12 and under, including an open bar, snacks,
and snorkel equipment. The high-speed ferries ***Edge*** (☎ 599/5–22167)
and ***Voyager*** (☎ 599/5–24096) motor across from Saba three times
a week and twice a week, respectively. The round-trip fare is $60.

### BY PLANE

There are two airports on the island. **L'Espérance** (☎ 590/87–53–03)
on the French side is small and handles only island-hoppers. Jumbo
jets fly into **Princess Juliana International Airport** (☎ 599/5–4211) on
the Dutch side.

The most convenient carrier from the United States is **American Airlines** (☎ 599/5–2040 or 800/433–7300), with daily nonstop flights
from New York and Miami, as well as connections from more than
100 U.S. cities via its San Juan hub. **Continental Airlines** (☎ 599/5–
3444 or 800/231–0856) has several flights a week from Newark. **LIAT**
(☎ 599/5–4203 or 800/468–0482) has daily service from San Juan
and several Caribbean islands including Antigua, the B.V.I., and St. Kitts.
**ALM** (☎ 599/5–4240 or 800/327–7230) has daily service from Aruba,
Bonaire, Curaçao, the Dominican Republic, and from Atlanta and Miami
via Curaçao. **BWIA** (☎ 599/5–4344 or 800/327–7401) offers service
from Trinidad and Barbados. **Air Martinique** (☎ 596/51–08–09 or
599/5–4212) connects the island with Martinique twice a week. **Windward Islands Airways** (Winair, ☎ 599/5–4230 or 800/634–4907),
which is based on St. Maarten, has daily scheduled service to Anguilla,
Saba, St. Barts, St. Eustatius, St. Kitts/Nevis, and St. Thomas. **Air
Guadeloupe** (☎ 599/5–4212 or 590/87–53–74) has several flights daily
to St. Barts and Guadeloupe from both sides of the island. **Air St.
Barthélemy** (☎ 590/87–73–46 or 599/5–3150) has frequent service
between Juliana and St. Barts. Tour and charter services are available
from Winair and **St. Martin Helicopters** (☎ 599/5–4287, Dutch side).

## Currency

Legal tender on the Dutch side is the Netherlands Antilles florin (guilder), written NAf; on the French side, the French franc (F). The exchange rate fluctuates, but in general it is about NAf1.80 to the US$1 and 5F to the US$1. On the Dutch side, prices are usually given in both NAf and U.S. dollars, which are accepted all over the island, as are credit cards. Note: Prices quoted here are in U.S. dollars unless otherwise noted.

## Emergencies

**Police:** Dutch side (☎ 599/5–22222), French side (☎ 590/87–50–06). **Ambulance:** Dutch side (☎ 599/5–22111), French side (☎ 590/87–50–25 ). **Hospital: St. Maarten Medical Center** (✉ Cay Hill, ☎ 599/5–31111) is a fully equipped hospital. **Pharmacies: Central Drug Store** (✉ Philipsburg, ☎ 599/5–22321) and **Pharmacie du Port** (✉ Marigot, ☎ 590/87–50–79) are open Monday–Saturday 7–5.

## Getting Around

Although there are other means of transportation, we recommend renting a car. You'll find it's needed to explore the island fully and visit a variety of beaches and restaurants.

### BUSES

One of the island's best bargains at 80¢ to $2, depending on your destination, buses operate frequently between 7 AM and 7 PM (less often 7–10 PM) and run from Philipsburg through Cole Bay to Marigot. There are no official stops: You just stand by the side of the road and flag the bus down. Exact change is preferred though not required, and drivers don't accept bills over $5.

### CAR RENTALS

You can book a car at Juliana International Airport, where all major rental companies have booths. If you don't have a reservation and aren't exactly sure whom to rent from, be prepared for an onslaught of hawkers, most of whom represent local companies, shouting that they have newer cars with more features and better prices. The upside of this is that prices tend to go down the longer your wait. Depending on demand, you can get a car as low as $25 a day. There are also rentals at every hotel area. Rental cars, in general, are inexpensive—approximately $35–$45 a day for a subcompact car. All foreign driver's licenses are honored, and major credit cards are accepted. If you opt for collision coverage, most policies still require a $500 or more deductible. Check with your credit card company about coverage. **Avis** (☎ 800/331–1084), **Budget** (☎ 800/472–3325), **Dollar** (☎ 800/800–4000), **Hertz** (☎ 800/654–3131), and **National (Eurocar)** (☎ 800/328–4567) all have offices on the island. Scooters rent for $20–$30 a day at **Eugene Moto** (✉ Sandy Ground Rd., ☎ 590/87–13–97).

### TAXIS

Taxi rates are government regulated, and authorized taxis display stickers of the St. Maarten Taxi Association. There is a taxi service at the Marigot port near the Tourist Information Bureau. Fixed fares apply from Juliana International Airport and the Marigot ferry to the various hotels and around the island. Fares are 25% higher between 10 PM and midnight, 50% higher between midnight and 6 AM.

## Guided Tours

A 2½-hour taxi tour of the island costs $30 for one or two people, $10 for each additional person. Your hotel or the tourist office can arrange it for you. Best bets are **St. Maarten Sightseeing Tours** (✉ Philipsburg, ☎ 599/5–22753) and **Calypso Tours** (✉ Philipsburg, ☎ 599/5–42858), which offer, among other options, a three-hour island tour for $17 per person. You can tour in deluxe comfort with **St. Maarten Limousine Service** (☎ 599/5–24698) for $40–$50 per hour; there's a three-hour minimum. Fully equipped Lincoln Continentals accommodate up to six people and are furnished with stereo, fully stocked bar, and air-conditioning. The limo service also offers transportation to and from Juliana Airport at rates ranging from $30 to $65 one-way. (This includes one hour of waiting time free of charge for late arrivals.) On the French side, **R&J Tours** (✉ Colombier, ☎ 590/87–56–20) will show you the island; prices vary with the number of people and the itinerary; a three-hour tour for one person is $15.

A cross between a submarine and a glass-bottom boat, the **Seaworld Explorer** (✉ Grand Case, ☎ 599/5–24978) crawls along the water's surface while passengers in the submerged lower chamber view marine life and coral through large windows. Kids will love it as divers jump off the boat and circle among and feed the fish and eels. The cost is $30, and, for an extra $10, they'll provide transport to and from your hotel.

## Language
Dutch is the official language of St. Maarten, and French is the official language of St. Martin, but almost everyone speaks English. If you hear a language you can't quite place, it's Papiamento, a Spanish-based Creole of the Netherlands Antilles.

## Opening and Closing Times
Shops on the Dutch side are open Monday–Saturday 8–noon and 2–6; on the French side, Monday–Saturday 9–noon or 12:30 and 2–6. Some of the larger shops on both sides of the island open Sunday and holidays when the cruise ships are in port. Some of the small Dutch and French shops set their own capricious hours.

Banks on the Dutch side are open Monday–Thursday 8:30–3:30 and Friday 8:30–4:40. French banks are open weekdays 8:30–1:30 and 2–3 and close afternoons preceding holidays.

## Passports and Visas
U.S. citizens need proof of citizenship. A passport (valid or not expired more than five years) is preferred. An original birth certificate with raised seal (or a photocopy with notary seal) or a voter registration card is also acceptable. All visitors must have a confirmed room reservation and an ongoing or return ticket. British and Canadian citizens need valid passports.

## Taxes and Service Charges
On the Dutch side, a 5% government tax is added to hotel bills. On the French side, a *taxe de séjour* (visitor's tax) is tacked on to hotel bills (the amount differs from hotel to hotel, but the maximum is $3 per day, per person). Departure tax from Juliana Airport is $5 to destinations within the Netherlands Antilles and $12 to all other destinations. It will cost you 15F to depart by plane from l'Espérance Airport or by ferry to Anguilla from Marigot's pier.

In lieu of tipping, service charges are added to hotel and restaurant bills all over the island and, by law, are included in all menu prices on the French side. On the Dutch side, most restaurants add 10%–15% to the bill.

Hotels on the Dutch side add a 15% service/energy charge to the bill. Hotels on the French side add 10%–15% for service.

Taxi drivers expect a 10% tip.

## Telephones and Mail

To call the Dutch side from the United States, dial 011–599 + local number; for the French side, 011–590 + local number. To phone from the Dutch side to the French, dial 06 + local number; from the French side to the Dutch, 00–5995 + local number. Keep in mind that a call from one side to the other is an overseas call, not a local call.

At the Landsradio in Philipsburg, there are facilities for overseas calls and an AT&T USADirect telephone, where you are directly in touch with an AT&T operator who will accept collect or credit-card calls.

On the French side, it is not possible to make collect calls to the United States, and there are no coin phones. If you need to use public phones, go to the special desk at Marigot's post office and buy a Telecarte (it looks like a credit card), which gives you 40 units (it takes 120 units to cover a five-minute call to the United States) for around 31F or 120 units for 93F. There is a public phone on the side of the tourist office in Marigot where you can make credit-card calls: The operator takes your credit-card number (any major card) and assigns you a PIN (Personal Identification Number), which you can then use to charge calls to your card.

Calls from anywhere on the island to the United States cost about $4 per minute.

Letters from the Dutch side to the United States and Canada cost NAf2.25; postcards, NAf1.10. From the French side, letters up to 20 grams and postcards are 3.80F.

## Visitor Information

For information about the Dutch side, contact the **tourist office** on the island directly (☎ 599/5–22337), or, in New York, contact the **St. Maarten Tourist Office** (✉ 675 3rd Ave., Suite 1806, New York, NY 10017, ☎ 212/953–2084, FAX 212/953–2145). In Canada, contact **St. Maarten Tourist Information** (✉ 243 Ellerslie Ave., Willowdale, Toronto, Ontario M2N 1Y5, ☎ 416/223–3501, FAX 416/223–6887). Information about French St. Martin can be obtained by writing the **St. Martin Office of Tourism** (✉ 10 E. 21st St., Suite 600, New York, NY 10010, ☎ 212/529–8484, FAX 212/460–8287) or by calling France-on-Call at 900/990–0040 (95¢ per minute). You can also write to or visit the U.S. branches of the **French Government Tourist Office** (✉ 444 Madison Ave., 16th floor, New York, NY 10022; ✉ 9454 Wilshire Blvd., Suite 715, Beverly Hills, CA 90212; ✉ 676 N. Michigan Ave., Suite 3360, Chicago, IL 60611), and write, visit, or call the Canadian and U.K. offices (✉ 1981 McGill College Ave., Suite 490, Montréal, Québec H3A 2W9, ☎ 514/288–4264; ✉ 30 St. Patrick St., Suite 700, Toronto, Ontario M5T 3A3, ☎ 416/593–6427; ✉ 178 Piccadilly, London W1V OAL, ☎ 0171/629–9376).

On the Dutch side, the **tourist information bureau** is on Cyrus Wathey (pronounced "watty") Square in the heart of Philipsburg, at the pier where the cruise ships send their tenders. The administrative office is at Walter Nisbeth Road 23 (Imperial Building) on the third floor. ☎ 599/5–22337, FAX 599/5–22734. ☉ Weekdays 8–noon and 1–5.

On the French side, there is the very helpful **tourist information office** on the Marigot pier. ☎ 590/87–57–21, FAX 590/87–56–43. ☉ Weekdays 8:30–1 and 2:30–5:30, Sat. 8–noon.

# 24 St. Vincent and the Grenadines

*Point . . . counterpoint. St. Vincent's lush mountains, fertile valleys, and quiet villages are still relatively undiscovered by tourists. Its Grenadines tempt vacationers with exclusive resorts, beautiful secluded beaches, and some of the world's finest sailing waters.*

Updated by
Jane E. Zarem

**T**HE MOUNTAINOUS ISLAND OF ST. VINCENT and a string of 32 lush islands and cays in the Grenadines compose one nation called St. Vincent and the Grenadines—often abbreviated SVG. This group of islands is in the southern Windwards—only Grenada and Trinidad and Tobago are farther south in the chain. St. Vincent, only 18 mi long and 11 mi wide, is just over 13° north of the equator; its Grenadines line up like a tadpole tail for 45 mi to the southwest. Each of the islands is, in a different way, a refuge for the demanding escapist, who will be hard put to find glitzy resorts, discos, or duty-free shopping malls; rather, these islands excel in natural beauty.

St. Vincent's major export is bananas, and these plants, along with coconut palms and breadfruit trees, crowd more of the island than the 107,000-person population. This has obvious charm for the nature lover, who can spend days hiking St. Vincent's well-defined walking and hiking trails, perhaps sighting the rare St. Vincent parrot in the Vermont Valley, or climbing La Soufrière, an active volcano that last erupted in 1979. Below sea level, snorkeling and scuba landscapes are similarly exciting, both off St. Vincent and around the Grenadines.

Despite its beauty, most people don't linger long in St. Vincent; they simply stop off en route to their preferred Grenadine. That has a lot to do with the beaches, which are mostly narrow with dark, coarse sand—in contrast to the Grenadines' picture-postcard expanses of powdery white sand. But St. Vincent deserves more than a passthrough. It has spectacular scenery, cascading waterfalls, a rugged coastline, and a fascinating history.

Although these islands have their share of the poor and unemployed, the superfertile soil allows everyone to grow enough food to eat and trade for necessities. Progress, however, has its price: Hiking alone on forest trails is not recommended, and petty theft is an unfortunate reality.

Historians believe that in 4300 BC, long before King Tut ruled Egypt, the Ciboney Indians inhabited St. Vincent. Unencumbered by the need for passports and political unrest, the Ciboney made their way to Cuba and Haiti, leaving St. Vincent to the Arawaks. Columbus sailed by in 1492, while the Arawaks were involved in intermittent skirmishes with the bellicose Caribs. Though Columbus never actually stopped on St. Vincent, Discovery Day (or St. Vincent and the Grenadines' Day) is commemorated each January 22.

Declared a neutral island by French and British agreement in 1748, St. Vincent became something of a political football in the years that followed. Ceded to the British in 1763, it was captured by the French in 1779 and restored to the British by the Treaty of Versailles in 1783. By the 19th century, St. Vincent had become more British than French; on October 27, 1979, it gained independence from Great Britain.

In contrast to this colorful regional history, the Grenadines seem timeless, as free from politics as the beaches are free from debris and crowds. Just south of St. Vincent is Bequia, the largest of the Grenadine Islands. Its Admiralty Bay is one of the finest anchorages in the Caribbean. With superb views, snorkeling, hiking, and swimming, the island has much to offer the international mix of backpackers and luxury-yacht owners who frequent its shores.

A two-hour sail (or 10-minute flight) south is the private island of Mustique. More arid than Bequia, Mustique does not tout itself to tourists, least of all those hoping for a glimpse of the rich and famous (Princess Margaret, Mick Jagger, David Bowie) who own houses here. The appeal of Mustique is seclusion and privacy.

Just over 3 square mi, Canouan is an unspoiled island that offers travelers an opportunity to relax, snorkel, and hike.

The tiny island of Mayreau has 182 residents and one of the area's most beautiful beaches. The Caribbean is often mirror-calm, yet just yards away, on the southern end of this narrow island, is the rolling Atlantic surf.

John Caldwell has spent 20 years turning Palm Island from a mosquito-infested mangrove swamp into a small island paradise. The Caldwell family also hosts day-tripping cruise passengers who like to lounge on the wide white-sand beaches, which are dotted and fringed with palm trees.

Union Island isn't really a place for landlubbers: The island caters almost exclusively to French sailors, who keep very much to themselves. Surface transport is limited, and to see the island you need a boat. You won't find the laid-back friendliness of the other Grenadines here.

Petit St. Vincent is another private luxury-resort island, reclaimed from the jungle by owner-manager Hazen K. Richardson II. It's actually possible to spend your entire vacation in one of the resort's widely spaced stone houses without ever seeing another human being.

Yachts and catamarans can be chartered for day sails from any of the Grenadines to the tiny, uninhabited Tobago Cays. Avid snorkelers claim that these cays have some of the best hard and soft coral formations found outside the Pacific Ocean. The beaches here are perfect for secluded picnics.

# ST. VINCENT

## Lodging

Luxury resorts may require booking months in advance, but most St. Vincent hotels can squeeze you in with far less notice. There's a bit of a lull in January, between Christmas week and the February rush, when rooms are sometimes available with little notice. Many hotels offer MAP (Modified American Plan, with breakfast and dinner included).

| CATEGORY | COST* |
|---|---|
| **$$$$** | over $200 |
| **$$$** | $130–$200 |
| **$$** | $80–$130 |
| **$** | under $80 |

*All prices are for a standard double room, excluding 7% tax and 10% service charge.*

### Kingstown

**$$**   🏨 **Camelot Inn.** Nestled in the hills of Kingstown Park, just five minutes from downtown and 10 minutes from the airport, this small guest house was the former residence of St. Vincent's first French governor. Built in 1781, it's the oldest guest house on the island. The location offers a magnificent view of the capital, lush green hills, and sparkling blue Caribbean sea. Owners Ken and Audrey Ballantyne renovated the building in 1996 and decorated each guest room in pastel colors, and each has a patio. Bathrooms are playfully decorated with a cobalt-blue and white-rabbit design. The inn has a restaurant (room service, too), a patio for outside dining, and afternoon tea served in the garden. Guests can enjoy day use of the beach and facilities (tennis and water sports) at Young Island Resort; transportation is included. ✉ *Kingstown, St. Vincent,* ☎ *809/456-2100,* FAX *809/456–2233. 20 rooms. Restaurant, bar, air-conditioning, fans, in-room safes, beauty salon, exercise room, shop. AE, MC, V.*

$ ☷ **Cobblestone Inn.** Downtown in the city, as Vincentians call Kingstown, this former sugar warehouse, built in 1814 of local stone, has a delightful, sunny interior courtyard and arched passageways that lead to most rooms. A popular rooftop bar-restaurant serves breakfast and soup-salad-burger lunches. All the rooms have exposed stone walls, rattan furniture, and small, sparkling bathrooms. Many are rather dark, with a faint, not unpleasant smell of dungeon emanating from the stones. Number 5 at the front is lighter and bigger than most of the other rooms but noisier, too. Downstairs you'll find Basil's Restaurant and an array of shops selling local crafts and fashions. ✉ *Box 867, Kingstown, St. Vincent,* ☎ *809/456–1937,* FAX *809/456–1938. 19 rooms. Restaurant, bar, air-conditioning. AE, D, MC, V. CP.*

$ ☷ **Heron Hotel.** Steps away from the Grenadines wharf, on the second floor above a Georgian plantation warehouse that now contains shops but once provided lodgings for the plantation bosses, the Heron caters mostly to stopover island-hoppers. It has managed to retain an old-fashioned atmosphere: Rooms are straight out of a '50s boardinghouse, with thin, wine-red or navy-blue carpets; billowing, faded floral drapes; single beds; bentwood chairs; and tiny cream-color bathrooms. The rooms fan out from a palm-filled central courtyard. Tables on the veranda are set for breakfast, light lunches, and West Indian dinners. A corner TV lounge is rather austere, with its black floorboards, two giant ficus plants, and rows of wooden armchairs. ✉ *Box 226, Kingstown, St. Vincent,* ☎ *809/457–1631,* FAX *809/457–1189. 12 rooms. Dining room, lounge, air-conditioning. MC, V. CP.*

## Villa Beach Area

$$$$ ☷ **Grand View Beach Hotel.** The Sardine family's turn-of-the-century
★  cotton-plantation great house is now Tony and Heather Sardine's beautiful hotel, perched on a lookout point just east of Indian Bay. It manages to have both great facilities and down-home charm. Most of the simple, white-walled rooms with hardwood floors offer guests a sweeping vista toward the Grenadines, and all have air-conditioning or fan, direct-dial phones, and satellite TV. A "Luxury Level" has big ocean-facing terraces and a pair of honeymoon suites with king-size beds and whirlpool tubs. A good restaurant serves West Indian and Continental meals. There's also a congenial bar and a small pool. Sailboats, Windsurfers, and snorkeling equipment are complimentary. ✉ *Box 173, Villa Point, St. Vincent,* ☎ *809/458–4811,* FAX *809/457–4174. U.S. agent: Charms Caribbean Vacations,* ☎ *800/223–6510. 19 rooms. Restaurant, air-conditioning, pool, massage, sauna, tennis court, health club, squash, library. AE, MC, V. CP, MAP.*

$$$$ ☷ **Young Island Resort.** A mere 200 yards from Villa Beach lies a 35-
★  acre island populated by prosperous couples who dream of being shipwrecked on a tropical island but don't want to get their feet wet. You arrive by ferry, are handed a rum punch crowned with a hibiscus blossom, and escorted to one of 29 small cottages with tropical print and rattan decor. Each has its own sitting room or area, patio, and bathroom with a private indoor/outdoor shower. Two luxury beachfront cottages have their own private plunge pools. Phones are nonexistent, but messages are brought promptly. Superior accommodations are lower down the hillside, among tumbling masses of flamboyant nutmeg, almond, mango, ferns, coffee, breadfruit, etc., etc. The more ex-

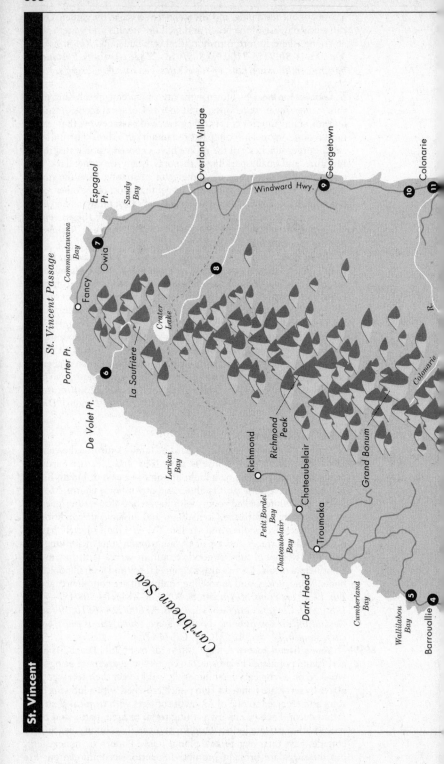

St. Vincent

St. Vincent Passage

Caribbean Sea

Overland Village

Georgetown

Colonarie

Windward Hwy.

Espagnol Pt.

Sandy Bay

Commantawana Bay

Owia

Fancy

Porter Pt.

De Volet Pt.

La Soufrière

Crater Lake

Larikai Bay

Richmond

Richmond Peak

Chateaubelair

Petit Bordel Bay

Chateaubelair Bay

Troumaka

Dark Head

Grand Bonum

Colonarie

Cumberland Bay

Wallilabou Bay

Barrouallie

6 7 8 9 10 11 5 4

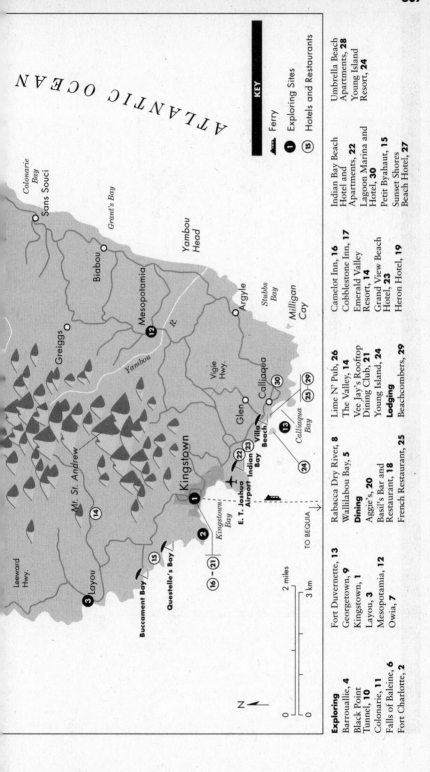

## ATLANTIC OCEAN

**Exploring**
Barrouallie, **4**
Black Point
Tunnel, **10**
Colonarie, **11**
Falls of Baleine, **6**
Fort Charlotte, **2**

Fort Duvernette, **13**
Georgetown, **9**
Kingstown, **1**
Layou, **3**
Mesopotamia, **12**
Owia, **7**

Rabacca Dry River, **8**
Wallilabou Bay, **5**

**Dining**
Aggie's, **20**
Basil's Bar and
Restaurant, **18**
French Restaurant, **25**

Lime N' Pub, **26**
The Valley, **14**
Vee Jay's Rooftop
Dining Club, **21**
Young Island, **24**

**Lodging**
Beachcombers, **29**

Camelot Inn, **16**
Cobblestone Inn, **17**
Emerald Valley
Resort, **14**
Grand View Beach
Hotel, **23**
Heron Hotel, **19**

Indian Bay Beach
Hotel and
Apartments, **22**
Lagoon Marina and
Hotel, **30**
Petit Byahaut, **15**
Sunset Shores
Beach Hotel, **27**

Umbrella Beach
Apartments, **28**
Young Island
Resort, **24**

**KEY**
Ferry
Exploring Sites
Hotels and Restaurants

TO BEQUIA

**The Grenadines**

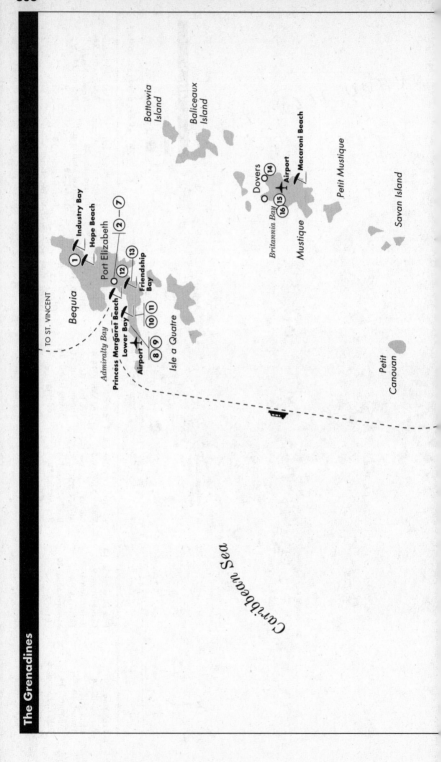

TO ST. VINCENT

Bequia

Admiralty Bay

① Industry Bay
Hope Beach
Port Elizabeth
Princess Margaret Beach
Lower Bay
Airport
Friendship Bay
Isle a Quatre

② — ⑦
⑬
⑫
⑩ ⑪
⑧ ⑨

Battowia Island
Baliceaux Island

Dovers
⑭
Britannia Bay
⑮
⑯
Airport
Macaroni Beach
Mustique

Petit Mustique

Savan Island

Petit Canouan

Caribbean Sea

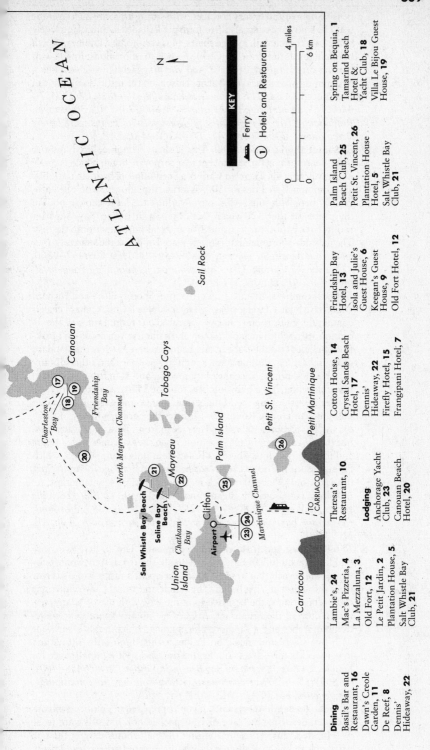

pensive deluxe and luxury cottages, with sitting area, are high over the sea. The landscape conceals a free-form pool, shaded hammocks, a lovely white-sand beach with lounge chairs, plus various bird families. Watch hummingbirds flutter over a Creole French-toast breakfast (made with banana bread) on your terrace, and you may feel like you've taken a five-minute boat to heaven. Yacht charters on the resort's sailboat can be arranged. ⊠ *Box 211, Young Island,* ☎ *809/458–4826,* 𝔽𝔸𝕏 *809/457– 4567. U.S. agent: Ralph Locke Islands,* ☎ *800/223–1108. 30 cottages. Restaurant, 2 bars, in-room safes, refrigerators, pool, tennis court, beach, scuba diving, water sports. AE, D, MC, V. MAP, FAP.*

$$$   🏨 **Sunset Shores Beach Hotel.** This U-shape, lemon-colored low-rise is the nearest thing on St. Vincent to a corporate hotel, which is really not very near at all. There's a Caribbean news-update board in the lobby and conference facilities for 100; as a rule, though, you won't be bothered by people in suits. All rooms overlook the large-enough pool in the center of the "U" which faces the sea at Indian Bay. Superior rooms have patios, carpets, and TVs and really are superior to the rest. The poolside Sunrunner Bar is nicely placed opposite the sunset. ⊠ *Box 849, Villa Beach, St. Vincent,* ☎ *809/458–4411,* 𝔽𝔸𝕏 *809/457–4800. 32 rooms. Restaurant, 2 bars, air-conditioning, pool, Ping-Pong, meeting rooms. AE, D, MC, V. EP, MAP.*

$   🏨 **Beachcombers.** At Villa, next to Sunset Shores, Flora and Richard Gunn have built a darling village on their sloping lawns. A pair of chalets contain the guest rooms, an open-terraced bar-restaurant, and the reception area, which includes a shop and a library. You could eat breakfast (included) off the floor of any bedroom here, such is the standard of housekeeping, though some rooms are prettier than others. Numbers 1–3 are prime, since they face the sea, and 1, in top-to-toe dark-wood paneling, has a baby kitchen, too, for $5 extra; 4–6 are in back of these, overlooking the Mango Tree Lounge and garden. The other building, containing Rooms 7–12, faces the garden's frenzy of flowers and has a communal red-tile terrace in front. Bathrooms lack tubs, but this is an insignificant privation when the welcome is this warm and the rates this low. There's a brand-new, fully equipped spa, which Flora uses for her other career—as beauty and massage therapist. Yes, this is the only Vincentian B&B featuring top-class aromatherapy, reflexology, facials, sauna, steam, and Turkish bath. ⊠ *Box 126, Villa Beach, St Vincent,* ☎ *809/458–4283,* 𝔽𝔸𝕏 *809/458–4385. 14 rooms. Restaurant, bar, fans, sauna, spa, steam room, Turkish bath, shop. AE, MC, V. BP.*

$   🏨 **Indian Bay Beach Hotel and Apartments.** This pretty, two-story building sits on Indian Bay, with its small, sheltered, somewhat rocky white-sand beach that appeals to snorkelers. It's just a stone's throw from the action at Villa Beach. The simple apartments have either one or two bedrooms; the best overlook the bay, with use of a large terrace on top of the restaurant, A La Mer—an airy space with white-trellised arches and a sapphire-blue awning, which holds a barbecue with live steel-band music on Friday nights. Both baby-sitting and lower weekly rates are available, making this spot especially nice for families. ⊠ *Box 538, Indian Bay Beach, St. Vincent,* ☎ *809/458–4001,* 𝔽𝔸𝕏 *809/457–4777. 14 apartments. Restaurant, bar, air-conditioning, kitchenettes, beach, AE, MC, V. EP, CP, MAP.*

$   🏨 **Umbrella Beach Apartments.** If you're prepared to sacrifice gorgeous bedroom decor for the sake of your pocketbook but still want to be well located, this very simple cluster of small rooms may fit the bill. All are clean but have shower-only bathroom and are dark and plain, with white walls, red marble-chip floors with a rush mat, and plastic chairs at a small Formica table. Steps away are Villa Beach, across from Young Island (ask permission to take the ferry over); the Lime N' Pub;

and the French Restaurant, where you could spend the cash you saved on the room. ✉ *Box 530, Villa Beach, St. Vincent,* ☎ *809/458–4651,* FAX *809/457–4930. 9 rooms. Fans, kitchenettes. MC, V. EP.*

## Elsewhere on St. Vincent

$$$ 🏨 **Petit Byahaut.** Sort of a Young Island for those with Swiss Family Robinson fantasies who *do* want to get their feet wet, this 50-acre valley resort accommodates its guests in tents, albeit permanent, wood-floored, 10- by 13-ft tents, complete with private deck, queen-size beds, and solar-heated showers. This adults' camp is accessible only by boat, which collects you from Kingstown (rates include this, as well as all meals), and there is a selection of other boats to play with once you're settled in, along with scuba and snorkeling equipment. On the grounds are a big black-sand beach, hammocks, and some interesting Carib Indian finds. There's a boutique, excursions are easily arranged, and that's about the extent of the facilities, but then, you don't stay here unless you're reasonably adventuresome and interested in seclusion. ✉ *Petit Byahaut Bay, St. Vincent,* ☎ FAX *809/457–7008. 6 tents. Restaurant, bar, scuba diving, snorkeling, beach. MC, V. FAP.*

$$ 🏨 **Lagoon Marina and Hotel.** The only hotel overlooking sheltered Blue
★ Lagoon Bay may well be the friendliest hotel on the island. Thanks to its full-service yacht marina, complete with the best-equipped marine shop in St. Vincent, there are usually seafaring types liming in the terrace bar, and plenty of yacht traffic to watch from your big, comfortable balcony with its two couches. Sliding patio doors lead onto these from the high wood-ceilinged, carpeted rooms; you can practically dive into the sea from numbers 1–9, which hang over the wooden quay and face the sunset; 10–20 overlook the narrow, curved black-sand beach. Basic wooden furniture, twin beds, rather dim lighting, tiled bathrooms, and ceiling fans provide an adequate level of comfort; about half the rooms have air-conditioning (for a few dollars extra), but don't expect luxury. Sloping garden grounds contain a secluded two-level pool and the St. Vincent Dive Experience Headquarters, and there's a pretty, candlelit terrace restaurant. ✉ *Box 133, Blue Lagoon, St. Vincent,* ☎ *809/458–4308,* FAX *809/ 457–4716. U.S. agent: Charms Caribbean Vacations,* ☎ *800/742– 4276. 19 rooms. Restaurant, bar, pool, beach, scuba diving, snorkeling, windsurfing, boating, meeting room. AE, V. EP.*

$–$$ 🏨 **Emerald Valley Resort.** The rural, rain-forested Penniston Valley, a half-hour drive from Kingstown, is the unlikely setting for the Grenadines' only casino, which is, equally improbably, attached to this recently renovated family-friendly 5-acre resort. Two pairs of Brits toiled for two years to bring a run-down property up to very high standards. The 12 chalets have locally made wood-frame king-size or twin beds, stone-floored terraces, and kitchenettes (but no stoves). In the garden grounds are an outdoor bar, a two-level pool bisected by a wooden bridge and diving platform, a stage for local bands on weekends, two tennis courts (pro lessons available), a new golf course, and the pretty Valley restaurant (☞ *Dining, below*). What you don't get, of course, is a beach, and the nearest groceries are in Kingstown, but the Vermont Nature Trail is 2½ mi away, and you can gamble till the small hours if bored. ✉ *Penniston Valley, Box 1081, St. Vincent,* ☎ *809/456–7140,* FAX *809/ 456–7145. 12 chalets. Restaurant, 2 bars, air-conditioning, fans, kitchenettes, in-room VCRs, pool, 2 tennis courts, croquet, volleyball, casino. AE, MC, V. EP.*

# Dining

West Indian food is the way to go in St. Vincent. You'll enjoy interesting local fare that is reasonably priced at all but the most expensive hotels. Dishes include callaloo (spinachlike) soup, curry goat, *rotis* (turnovers filled with curried meat, chicken, or vegetables and potatoes), seasonal seafood (lobster, kingfish, snapper, and dolphinfish), local vegetables (christophines, breadfruit, dasheen, and eddoes), and exotic fruit (from sugar apples and soursop to pineapple and papaya). Fried chicken and burgers are available everywhere, but look for the "imported beef" note on the menu; local beef is not aged, so it tends to be extremely chewy. The local lager, Hairoun, is brewed at Camden Park, on the leeward coast, according to a German recipe.

## What to Wear

Restaurants on St. Vincent are, for the most part, very casual. In Kingstown, you may want to dress up a little—maybe long pants or a sundress—but none of the places listed below require gentlemen to wear a jacket or tie. On the Grenadines, ultracasual is fine everywhere.

| CATEGORY | COST* |
| --- | --- |
| $$$ | over $20 |
| $$ | $10–$20 |
| $ | under $10 |

*per person for a three-course meal, excluding drinks and 7% sales tax*

**$$$**  ✕ **Basil's Bar and Restaurant.** This air-conditioned restaurant, downstairs in the Cobblestone Inn, is owned by the infamous Basil of Mustique but has little else in common with that laid-back Grenadine glitterati hangout. This is the Kingstown power-lunch venue, serving a daily buffet of local fish dishes, plus seafood pasta and chicken poached in fresh ginger and coconut milk, to local businesspeople and yachties for about $12 an entrée. The bar can get lively in the evenings, when dinner tables are candlelit. There's a Chinese buffet on Fridays. ⊠ Bay St., Kingstown, ☎ 809/457–2713. AE, MC, V.

**$$$**  ✕ **French Restaurant.** Referred to as "The French," this Caribbean in★  stitution on Villa Beach, facing Young Island, is where people go when feeling posh—especially when in a lobster mood, since there is a state-of-the-art lobster pool on the terrace. You can watch the staff fish for your supper. As befits a place run by a couple from Orléans, most dishes are the Gallic version of local cuisine. Stuffed crab back, for instance, comes in a shell of pastry, not crab; steak—*au poivre,* with garlic butter, or béarnaise—is imported; onion soup and lemon tart are *comme il faut;* and bread is warm, fresh—a real baguette. At the inside bar, complete with an eccentric, giggling barman, frothy cocktails and Martinique-style 'ti punch are served to yachties who hang out here in the winter season. ⊠ Young Island Channel, Villa Beach, ☎ 809/458–4972. AE, V.

**$$$**  ✕ **The Valley.** This pretty terrace hung with fishing nets is part of the Emerald Valley Resort—which includes the only casino in St. Vincent and the Grenadines. And if it's Saturday (also some Fridays), a local band serenades diners. The pride of the kitchen is river lobster, retrieved from the Vermont River, which runs through this area. Other dishes are a local-international mix: tomato, mozzarella, and basil salad; baked red snapper with coconut stuffing; broiled *poussin* (young chicken) with local herbs. Get directions if you're driving, and call first—the restaurant has an unpredictable tendency to be closed. ⊠ Penniston Valley, ☎ 809/456–7140. AE, MC, V.

**$$$**  ✕ **Young Island.** Five-course chef's-choice dinners of seafood, roast pig, ★  beef, and chicken tend to be heavy and old-fashioned, but fare is lighter at the lavish Tuesday buffets and at the Saturday barbecues, when a steel band makes it an event. Lunch is served buffet- or barbecue-style on the beach daily and features seafood, fresh fruits, salads, and cold cuts, with an assortment of fresh breads. Pink-clothed tables are secreted individually in palm-thatched huts dotted around the beach, with more in the stone-floored terrace dining room; they're romantically candlelit at night. ✉ *Young Island,* ☎ *809/458–4826. Reservations essential. AE, MC, V.*

**$–$$**  ✕ **Lime N' Pub.** Although this sprawling, waterfront, indoor-outdoor restaurant and bar is named after the *pursuit* of liming, its decor happens to feature a great deal of virulent green! An eclectic all-day menu caters to seafood fans. Rotis and coconut shrimp go down well with a bottle of Hairoun, the local brew. The mood is casual and congenial during the day, romantic and candlelit at night. Shop before dinner at the swimwear-and-batik boutique, or stay late and dance on weekends, when the atmosphere resembles that of a singles bar. ✉ *Young Island Channel, Villa Beach,* ☎ *809/458–4227. AE.*

**$–$$**  ✕ **Vee Jay's Rooftop Dining Club.** This local restaurant above Roger's Photo Studios (have your pix developed while you eat), nearly opposite the Cobblestone Hotel, offers downtown Kingstown's best port view from beneath its green corrugated plastic roof. Among "authentic Vincie cuisine" specials chalked on the blackboard are mutton or fish stew, chicken or vegetable rotis, curried goat, or not remotely Vincie sandwiches and burgers, which can be authentically washed down with mauby (a bittersweet drink made from tree bark—an acquired taste), linseed, peanut punch, sorrel cordials, or a cocktail. Lunch is buffet-style. ✉ *Upper Bay St., Kingstown,* ☎ *809/457–2845. Reservations essential for dinner. AE, MC, V. Closed Sun.*

**$**  ✕ **Aggie's.** Opposite the Sardine Bakery on Grenville, the Kingstown shopping street, is this casual bar and restaurant, with a swimming-pool-blue ceiling and trellised arches. It serves local seafood dishes, like conch souse and kingfish steak, delicious pumpkin or callaloo soup, rotis, baked chicken leg, and salads, right up to midnight. They'll even pack it up to take out. There's a Friday happy hour from 4 to 6. ✉ *Grenville St., Kingstown,* ☎ *809/456–2110. No credit cards.*

## Beaches

Most of the white-sand beaches are just south of Kingstown; black-sand beaches ring the rest of the island. No beach has lifeguards, so even experienced swimmers are taking a risk.

**Buccament Bay,** which is good for swimming, is a tiny black-sand beach on the west coast. The exposed Atlantic coast is dramatic, but the water is rough and unpredictable. The windward side of the island has no beachfront facilities. **Indian Bay,** adjacent to Villa Beach, has white sand but is slightly rocky. **Questelle's Bay** (pronounced keet-*ells*), on the westward (leeward) coast north of Kingstown and next to the Camden Park Industrial Site, has a black-sand beach. **Villa Beach,** south of Kingstown, is the island's main beach (although it's hardly big enough to merit such a title). The beach is a narrow strip of golden sand, and the water is safe. Dive shops are on the shore.

## Outdoor Activities and Sports

### Hiking

**Buccament Valley** contains two well-marked trails, including the Vermont Trail, where you may be lucky enough to see the rare St. Vincent parrot, *Amazona guidingii,* for which a 6:30 AM start is recommended. **Dorsetshire Hill,** about 3 mi from Kingstown, rewards you with a sweeping view of city and harbor; picturesque Queen's Drive is nearby. **La Soufrière,** the queen of climbs, is St. Vincent's active volcano (which last erupted, appropriately enough, on Friday the 13th in 1979). Approachable from both windward and leeward coasts, this is *not* a casual excursion for inexperienced walkers. Climbs are all-day affairs. You'll need stamina and sturdy shoes for this climb of just over 4,000 ft. Be sure to check the weather before you leave; hikers have been sorely disappointed when they reached the top and found the view completely obscured by enveloping clouds. A guide (US$25–$30) can be arranged through your hotel, the Department of Tourism (☎ 809/457–1502), or tour operators (☞ Guided Tours *in* St. Vincent and the Grenadines A to Z, *below*). A four-wheel-drive vehicle will take you past Rabacca Dry River and through the Bamboo Forest. From there it's a two-hour hike to the summit. You can arrange in advance to come down the other side of the mountain to the Châteaubelair area. **Mount St. Andrew,** on the outskirts of Kingstown, is a pleasant climb on a well-marked trail through a rain forest.

### Sailing and Charter Yachting

You may wish to charter a sailboat or catamaran (bareboat or complete with captain, crew, and cook) to weave you around the Grenadines for a day or a week. Boats of all sizes and degrees of luxury are available. Hotels can recommend charter yachts. The **Lagoon Marina and Hotel** (☎ 809/458–4308) in the Blue Lagoon area of St. Vincent has 44-ft crewed sloops from $200 per day. **Blue Water Charters** (☎ 809/456–1232, FAX 809/456–2382), wharfside at the Aquatic Club, Villa Beach, will take you on full-day, half-day, or overnight fishing or sightseeing excursions on its modern, 55-ft sportfishing boat.

### Water Sports

The constant trade winds are perfect for windsurfing, and 80-ft visibility on numerous reefs means superior diving. Many experienced divers find St. Vincent and Bequia far less crowded and nearly as rich in marine life as Bonaire and the Caymans; snorkeling in the Tobago Cays is among the world's best. Dive operations are small and often less luxurious than on other islands, but they are competent and professional. Many offer three-hour beginner "resort" courses, full certification courses, and excursions to nearby reefs, walls, and wrecks. Dive shops are on St. Vincent, Bequia, Canouan, Petit St. Vincent, Mustique, Union, and Palm islands. Most dive shops and larger hotels also rent Sunfish, Windsurfers, and snorkel gear. Depending on the weather, Young Island has some of the area's most colorful snorkeling. If you're not a guest at this private island resort, phone for permission to take the ferry and rent equipment from the resort's water-sports center (☞ Lodging, *above*).

**Dive St. Vincent** (⊠ Young Island Dock, Villa Beach, ☎ 809/457–4714, FAX 809/457–4928) is where NAUI instructor Bill Tewes and his staff offer beginner and certification courses and trips to the Falls of Baleine. A single-tank dive is about $50. **St. Vincent Dive Experience** (⊠ Villa Beach, next to Lime 'N Pub, ☎ 809/456–9006 or 809/457–5130, FAX 809/457–5132), run by NAUI instructor Perry Hughes, offers all levels of training and certification, plus night dives, snorkeling, and tours. A single-tank dive is about $40.

## Shopping

### Local Crafts

Best buys are batik and screen-printed clothing, leather goods, baskets, grass mats, and wood carvings. **Artisans Craft Shop** (⊠ Upstairs in Bonadie's Bldg., Bay St., Kingstown, ☎ 809/458–4436) sells local crafts, such as straw art, macrame, and hand-painted and tie-dyed clothing. **Noah's Arkade** (⊠ Bay St., Kingstown, ☎ 809/457–1513) sells appealing local crafts and resort wear. **St. Vincent Craftsmen Center** (⊠ James St., Kingstown, ☎ 809/457–1288), in the northwest end of the city, sells grass floor mats and other woven items, as well as batik cloth, carved wooden dolls, and framed artwork. **Sprott Bros.** (⊠ Bay St., Kingstown, ☎ 809/457–1121) carries colorful screen-printed garments and crafts designed and made by Vincentians.

### Luxury Goods

St. Vincent isn't a duty-free port, although a few shops sell luxury goods at duty-free prices. Price and selection, however, don't come close to the values available on other Caribbean islands. Swiss watches, crystal, china, and jewelry can be found in Kingstown at **Voyager** (⊠ Halifax St., ☎ 809/456–1686) and at **Y De Lima** (⊠ Bay and Egmont Sts., ☎ 809/457–1681).

# Nightlife

Don't look for fire-eaters and limbo demonstrations on St. Vincent. Nightlife here consists mostly of Friday-night hotel barbecue buffets and jump-ups, so called because the lively steel-band and calypso music makes listeners jump up and dance. But there are nightspots in Kingstown and at Villa where you can join the locals for late-night dancing to live or recorded reggae, hip-hop, and soca music.

Popular nightspots with music and dancing are the **Aquatic Club** (☎ 809/458–4205), at Villa Beach; and **Level 3** (⊠ Grenville St., ☎ 809/456–2015) and **Zone** (⊠ Bay St., ☎ 809/456–2515), both in Kingstown. **Touch Entertainment Centre** (⊠ Grenville St., Kingstown, ☎ 809/457–1825) is a dance hall with disco music on Fridays and live music on Saturdays. It attracts a local crowd of mostly young people. Dance clubs generally require a small cover charge (about EC$10), especially if there's a live band.

The **Attic** (⊠ 1 Melville St., above Kentucky Fried Chicken, Kingstown, ☎ 809/457–2558), a jazz club with modern decor, features international artists and steel bands. There is a small cover charge; call ahead for hours and performers.

**Emerald Valley Casino** (⊠ Penniston Valley, ☎ 809/456–7140) has the homey atmosphere of an English pub but offers bar, food, and all the gaming of Vegas—three roulette tables (the only single-zero ones in the Caribbean), three blackjack, one Caribbean stud poker, one craps, five video slots, three slots—and is open Wednesday–Monday 9 PM–3 AM, until 4 AM on Saturday.

**Young Island** (⊠ Young Island, ☎ 809/458–4826) hosts sunset cocktail parties with hors d'oeuvres once a week on Fort Duvernette, the tiny island behind the resort. On that night, 100 steps up the hill are lit by flaming torches, and a string band plays. Reservations are necessary for nonguests.

# Exploring St. Vincent

Kingstown's shopping and business district, cathedrals, and sights can easily be seen in a half day, with another half day for the Botanical Gardens. Outlying areas and the Falls of Baleine each require a full day; trips to La Soufrière and the Vermont Trail are major undertakings, requiring a very early start and a full day's strenuous hiking. Island maps are in the "Discover SVG" booklet, available everywhere. The coastal roads of St. Vincent offer panoramic views and insights into the island way of life. The Leeward Highway follows the scenic Caribbean coastline; the Windward Highway follows the more dramatic Atlantic coast.

*Numbers in the margin correspond to points of interest on the St. Vincent map.*

SIGHTS TO SEE

**④ Barrouallie.** This used to be an important whaling village; the inhabitants of Barrouallie (pronounced *bar*-relly) now earn their livelihoods trawling for blackfish. The drive north from Kingstown, along the Leeward Highway, takes you along steep ridges that drop precipitously to the sea, before winding through small villages and lush valleys and passing several-black sand beaches with safe bathing.

**⑩ Black Point Tunnel.** In 1815, with the help of Carib and African slaves, British colonel Thomas Browne drilled this 300-ft-long tunnel through volcanic rock to facilitate the transportation of sugar from estates in the north to the port in Kingstown. The tunnel links Grand Sable with Byera Bay, just north of Colonarie.

**⑪ Colonarie.** In the hills behind the town about half way up St. Vincent's east coast, are hiking trails. Signs on the trails are limited, but the local people are helpful with directions. To get to Colonarie, you drive from Kingstown through scenic Mesopotamia, then follow the Windward Highway.

**⑥ Falls of Baleine.** They're impossible to get to by car but an absolute must to see on an escorted all-day boat trip or by chartered boat from Villa Beach or the Lagoon Marina (☞ Outdoor Activities and Sports, *above*). The ride to the falls offers scenic island views. When you arrive, be prepared to climb from the boat into shallow water to get to the beach. Local guides help visitors make the easy five-minute trek to the 60-ft falls and its rock-enclosed freshwater pool. At press time, swimming in the pool was temporarily prohibited because of falling rocks.

**② Fort Charlotte.** Built in 1806 to keep Napoléon at bay and named for the wife of King George III, the fort sits on Berkshire Hill, 636 ft above sea level, with cannons and battlements perched on a dramatic promontory overlooking the city and the Grenadines to the south, Lowman's Beach and the calm east coast to the north. The fort saw little military action. Nowadays it is the island's women's prison. Next to it, and visible from the water, is the old leper's colony.

**⑬ Fort Duvernette.** This tiny island juts up like a loaf of pumpernickel bread behind Young Island. Take the tiny, motor ferry for a couple of E.C. dollars from the dock at Villa Beach (call the boatman from the phone on the dock), and set a time for your return (60–90 minutes is plenty for exploring). Views from the 195-ft summit are terrific, but you'll have to climb the 100 or more steps carved into the mountain to get there. Entering the little overgrown house is not for the squeamish; expect to encounter (harmless) bats. Rusting cannons from the early 1800s are still here, aimed not toward seagoing invaders but defending against marauding Caribs.

**⑨ Georgetown.** Halfway up the island's east coast, amid coconut groves and the long-defunct Mount Bentinck sugar factory, this is St. Vincent's second-largest city.

**① Kingstown.** The capital city and port of St. Vincent is on the island's southwestern coast. It is very much a working city, with few concessions made to tourists. The **harbor** is far more likely to be hosting a freighter than a passenger ship, but that should change during 1998 when Kingstown's new cruise-ship facility is expected to be completed. What few gift shops there are can be found near the harbor, on and around Bay Street. Here you will also find the **financial complex,** a tall, cool-looking structure built in 1992. Among other official offices, the tourist office is in this building.

**Grenadines Wharf,** along the Bayfront at the southeast end of town, is busy with schooners loading supplies bound for the Grenadines. Nearby, several 19th-century buildings are built of bricks used as ballast in vessels that returned to Europe with holds filled with sugar and molasses.

The most exciting thing to do in Kingstown is to browse among the infinite varieties of tropical fruits and vegetables at the **Kingstown Market,** in the center of town on Upper Bay Street, just one block from the waterfront. Produce is laid out in the outdoor section; around the square there are dozens of stalls where you can buy inexpensive homemade meals, drinks, ice cream, bread and cookies, clothing, trinkets, and even get a haircut. Though the bustle is greatest on Saturdays before 11 AM, there is usually a crowd all day long. Be sure to visit the indoor **fish market,** too. This was a gift from the Japanese people, who also donated ecological deep-sea-fishing lessons, plus a sister market on Union Island.

St. Vincent is known worldwide for its particularly beautiful and colorful commemorative stamps, which are illustrated with tropical flowers, undersea creatures, and local architecture. Oddly enough, a recent stamp honored Elvis Presley! You can purchase stamps at the **Philatelic Bureau,** on Lower Bay Street, as well as at the **post office,** on Halifax Street, east of Egmont.

**St. George's Cathedral,** a yellow Anglican church built in the early 19th century, is on Grenville Street, west of the Methodist church. The dignified Georgian architecture includes simple wood pews, an ornate chandelier, and stained-glass windows. The markers in the cathedral's graveyard recount the history of the island. Across the street is **St. Mary's Roman Catholic Cathedral,** built in 1823 and renovated in the early 1940s. The renovations resulted in a strangely appealing blend of Moorish, Georgian, and Romanesque styles applied to black brick.

A few minutes away by taxi or bus is St. Vincent's famous **Botanical Gardens.** Founded in 1765, it is the oldest botanical garden in the Western Hemisphere. Captain Bligh—of *Bounty* fame—brought the first breadfruit tree to this island to feed the slaves. You can see a direct descendant of this tree among the mahogany, rubber, and teak trees in the gardens. Several rare St. Vincent parrots live in the small aviary on the well-kept grounds. Local guides offer their services for about US$3 per person per hour. ⊠ *c/o Minister of Agriculture, Kingstown,* ☎ *809/ 457–1003.* ⊒ *Free.* ☉ *Daily 6–6.*

The **National Museum** houses a series of maps tracing the migrations of the Ciboney, the very first Vincentians, who arrived on the island around 4000 BC. The pre-Columbian Indian clay pottery on exhibit was found by Dr. Earle Kirby, St. Vincent's resident archaeologist and the museum's director. Dr. Kirby's historical knowledge is as entertaining as it is extensive, and a visit here is much enhanced by his annotations. ⊠ *Old Public Library Bldg., Halifax St.,* ☎ *809/456–1787.* ⊒ *$1.* ☉ *Wed. 9–noon, Sat. 2–6.*

**3** **Layou.** Just beyond this small fishing village, about 45 minutes north of Kingstown, are petroglyphs (rock carvings) left by the Caribs 13 centuries ago. If you're seriously interested in archaeological mysteries, you'll want to arrange a visit (through the Tourist Board) with Victor Hendrickson, who owns the land. For EC$5, Hendrickson or his wife will meet you and escort you to the site.

**12** **Mesopotamia.** The rugged, ocean-lashed scenery along St. Vincent's windward coast is the perfect counterpoint to the lush, calm west coast. The Mesopotamia Valley offers a breathtaking panoramic view that is unsurpassed in this part of the Caribbean; you'll see dense forests, streams, and endless banana plantations. Blue plastic bags cover the fruit—particularly important for export—to protect it from wind and insect damage. Coconut, breadfruit, sweet corn, peanuts, and arrowroot also grow in the rich soil here, which is why the area is nicknamed the Breadbasket of St. Vincent. The valley is surrounded by mountain ridges, including 3,181-ft Grand Bonhomme Mountain.

**❼ Owia.** The Carib village of Owia, two hours from Kingstown on the island's far northeast coast, is the home of many of the indigenous Carib people of St. Vincent. It is also the location of the Owia Arrowroot Processing Factory. Used for generations to thicken sauces and flavor cookies, arrowroot is now in demand as a finish for computer paper. Close to the village is the Owia Salt Pond, where you can take a dip before the long ride back to Kingstown.

**❽ Rabacca Dry River.** Looking every bit like a moonscape, this rocky gulch just past the village of Georgetown was carved out of the earth by the lava flow from the 1902 eruption of La Soufrière. The trail to the rim of the volcano, a two-hour ascent, begins here.

**❺ Wallilabou Bay.** You can stop to sunbathe, swim, and have a picnic or simple lunch at the yacht services building at Wallilabou (pronounced wally-la-*boo*) Bay. There are no showers, but a small waterfall is a short, lovely stroll away.

# THE GRENADINES

The Grenadines are wonderful islands to visit for fine diving and snorkeling opportunities, good beaches, and unlimited chances to laze on the beach with a picnic, waiting for the sun to set so you can go to dinner. Travelers seeking privacy, peace and quiet, or active water sports and informal socializing will be happy on a Grenadine, though which one may take some trial and error—these islands are by no means interchangeable.

## Bequia

Just 9 mi south of St. Vincent's southwestern shore, Bequia (pronounced *beck*-wee) is the largest of the Grenadine Islands. Sandy beaches surround the island, and picturesque Admiralty Bay is a favorite anchorage for yachtspeople. Boatbuilding, whaling, and fishing have been the industries here for generations. A range of lodging possibilities and some nightlife attracts visitors who want to stay awhile. Having an airport and regular, frequent ferry service from St. Vincent makes the island a favorite for day trips. Port Elizabeth, where the ferry docks, is a quaint town with bars, restaurants, and crafts shops where you can watch artisans build the model boats for which Bequia is famous.

### Lodging

For price information on hotels, *see* the price chart in the Lodging section of St. Vincent, *above*.

$$$$   ▥ **Plantation House Hotel.** You can't help but pass by the pale peach
  ★    Plantation House when strolling to Princess Margaret or Lower Bay beaches. Set in 10 grassy acres of manicured gardens, dotted with palms, hammocks, loungers, and a raised pool, the five-room main house is appended by 17 garden cabanas plus three deluxe beachfront rooms. Since the current Dutch-Austrian husband-and-wife managers took over in 1994, just about everything has been redone and made gorgeous, with rattan and wicker decor in all rooms and also in the cabanas. The

bar may be *the* Bequia social center due to the presence of the French chef (☞ Dining, *below*). ⊠ *Box 16, Admiralty Bay, Bequia, St. Vincent,* ☎ *809/458–3425,* FAX *809/458–3612. U.S. agent: E & M Assoc., 211 E. 43rd St., New York, NY 10017,* ☎ *800/223–9832. 8 rooms, 17 cabanas. 2 restaurants, bar, air-conditioning, minibars, pool, tennis courts, scuba diving, snorkeling, windsurfing, boating, waterskiing, shop. AE, MC, V. MAP.*

$$$ 🏨 **Spring on Bequia.** Spring is nestled in green hills overlooking groves of tall palms and grazing goats. It's about 1 mi above town (a pretty walk, though you may want to take a taxi back uphill), and the nearest beach, lovely but too shallow for serious swimming and occasionally seaweedy, is a 10-minute stroll away. The large wood-and-stone rooms attract upscale travelers who want serenity and seclusion. The airy veranda bar is the site of manager Candy Leslie's deservedly famous Sunday curry lunch (reservations essential). ⊠ *Spring Bay, Bequia, St. Vincent,* ☎ *809/458–3414. U.S. agent: Spring on Bequia,* ⊠ *Box 19251, Minneapolis, MN 55419,* ☎ *612/823–1202. 10 rooms. Restaurant, bar, pool, tennis court. AE, D, MC, V. EP.*

$$–$$$ 🏨 **Friendship Bay Hotel.** This sprawling white house, with large terraces and sweeping views, is on a hill that rises above another group of pretty, coral stone accommodations close to the beach. Friendship offers a beautiful curve of white-sand beach and tropical plant-filled grounds and, on Saturday nights around the Mau Mau Beach Bar, one of the liveliest barbecue and jump-ups in the Caribbean. This is distinguished from the hundreds of other beach bars you have known by its swing seats, cleverly built to keep you upright even after potent rum punches. ⊠ *Box 9, Friendship, Bequia, St. Vincent,* ☎ *809/458–3222,* FAX *809/458–3840. 27 rooms. Restaurant, 2 bars, tennis court, dive shop, water sports, shop. AE, MC, V. CP.*

$$–$$$ 🏨 **Old Fort Hotel.** A stunning setting on a cliff above the Atlantic, in a stone estate house built by the French 200 years ago, singles out this property from the others and endows its rooms with some of the most panoramic Grenadine vistas around, plus cooling trade-wind breezes that obviate the need for air-conditioning. There are only six rooms here, all done up like a cross between Captain Bligh's cabin and a Provençal farmhouse, with chunky hardwoods and exposed stone. This modest size, and the fact that the nearest beach, Ravine, is nearly 500 ft below and a bit too rough for swimming, makes the Old Fort a getaway destination rather than a lazy vacation base. Fortunately, the restaurant (☞ Dining, *below*) is excellent, because it's a trek into town. ⊠ *Mt. Pleasant, Bequia, St. Vincent,* ☎ *809/458–3440,* FAX *809/458–3824. 6 rooms. Restaurant, bar, hiking. MC, V. EP, MAP.*

$–$$ 🏨 **Frangipani Hotel.** The Frangipani has gained the status of venera-
★ ble institution partly because its owner, St. Vincent prime minister James Mitchell, lives here on Bequia. Surrounded by flowering bushes, the garden units are built of stone, with private verandas and baths. Four simple, less-expensive rooms are in the main shingle-sided house, only one with a private bath. A two-bedroom house with a patio and another apartment with a large bedroom and kitchen are nearby. String bands appear on Mondays, with folksingers on Friday nights during tourist season. The Thursday-night steel-band jump-up at the beachfront bar is a must; the bar, with its huge, white-painted wooden armchairs facing the sunset, is probably the nicest around. ⊠ *Box 1, Port Elizabeth, Bequia, St. Vincent,* ☎ *809/458–3255,* FAX *809/458–3824. 13 rooms. Restaurant, bar, water sports, boating, shop. MC, V. EP.*

$ 🏨 **Isola and Julie's Guest House.** Right on the water in Port Elizabeth, these two separate buildings share a small restaurant and bar. Furnishings are spare and simple, but the rooms are airy and light, with private baths (some have hot water!), and the food is great. ⊠ *Box 12, Port*

*Elizabeth, Bequia, St. Vincent,* ☎ *809/458–3304, 809/458–3323, or 809/458–3220;* FAX *809/457–3812. 25 rooms. Restaurant, bar. No credit cards. MAP.*

$   🏠 **Keegan's Guest House.** If you want budget beach accommodations with a quiet, friendly atmosphere, look no further. On Lower Bay, this *very* simple place offers family-style West Indian breakfasts and dinners for its guests. Rooms 3, 4, and 5 have a shared bath and are cheaper, although there is no hot water to be found (you really do get used to it). ☒ *Lower Bay, Bequia, St. Vincent,* ☎ *809/458–3254 or 809/458–3530. 11 rooms. Dining room. No credit cards. MAP.*

## Dining

Dining on Bequia ranges from West Indian to gourmet cuisine, and it's consistently good. Barbecues at Bequia's hotels mean spicy West Indian seafood, chicken, or beef, plus a buffet of side dishes and sweet desserts. Restaurants are occasionally closed Sunday; phone ahead to check.

For price information on restaurants, *see* the price chart in the Dining section of St. Vincent, *above.*

$$$   ✕ **Old Fort.** Otmar and Sonja Schaedle restored this mid-1700s building overlooking the Atlantic to its bougainvillea-shaded, stone-arched, candlelit beauty and continue to serve food good enough to attract non-hotel guests to the castle-like atmosphere with one of the best views—and coolest breezes—on the island. Try a tuna steak or char-grilled whole snapper, accompanied by fresh, homemade bread and a curry of pigeon peas. ☒ *Old Fort Hotel, Mt. Pleasant,* ☎ *809/458–3440. Reservations essential. MC, V.*

$$$   ✕ **Le Petit Jardin.** The chef at this chalet-style restaurant prepares
★ gourmet lobster and fish with West Indian ingredients and according to French recipes. If you're missing your prime rib, the house specialty is steak imported from the United States, which you can wash down with a bottle from the longer-than-average wine list. ☒ *Port Elizabeth,* ☎ *809/458–3318. Reservations essential. No credit cards.*

$$$   ✕ **Plantation House.** This refurbished, fancy hotel has a fancy chef to match, who earned the ultimate French accolade of a Michelin star in a previous job. Dinner is served nightly (except Saturday) at the hotel's Verandah restaurant, where menu selections reflect a Continental theme with local flair. On Saturday evenings, a barbecue buffet is presented at the hotel's other restaurant, the Green Flash. The buffet includes a variety of barbecued meats and fish, salads, vegetable dishes, and an excellent array of pastries prepared by a local pastry chef. A resident pianist plays during dinner hours at the Verandah, and a local band provides entertainment at the Saturday barbecues. ☒ *Plantation House Hotel, Admiralty Bay,* ☎ *809/458–3425. AE, MC, V.*

$–$$$   ✕ **De Reef.** This duo of a restaurant and a café on Lower Bay is the essential feeding station for long, lazy beach days, with the restaurant taking over when the café closes at dusk, as long as you've made reservations. For lunch or dinner, conch, lobster, whelks, and shrimp are treated the West Indian way, and the mutton curry is famous. For breakfast (from 7 AM), or light lunch, the café bakes its own breads, croissants, coconut cake, and cookies and blends fresh juices to accompany them. ☒ *Lower Bay,* ☎ *809/458–3484. Reservations essential for dinner. No credit cards.*

$$   ✕ **La Mezzaluna.** This is an incongruously traditional Italian trattoria, owned by its Roman chef and useful for city dwellers with pasta-withdrawal symptoms. Here, ravioli is more likely to be stuffed with local lobster than spinach and ricotta, but eggplant parmigiana, beef

carpaccio, and *grissini* (Italian bread sticks) they've got. ⊠ *Above Port Elizabeth,* ☎ *809/457–3080. No credit cards. Closed Tues.*

**$–$$** ✕ **Dawn's Creole Garden.** The walk up the hill is worth it for the delicious West Indian lunches and dinners, especially the Saturday-night barbecue buffet and the major five-course, two-entrée dinners, including the fresh christophine and breadfruit accompaniments that Dawn's is known for. There's a wonderful view and live guitar entertainment most Saturday nights. ⊠ *At far end of Lower Bay beach,* ☎ *809/458–3154. Dinner reservations essential. No credit cards.*

**$–$$** ✕ **Mac's Pizzeria.** The island's best lunches and casual dinners are en-
★    joyed amid fuchsia bougainvillea on the covered outdoor terrace overlooking the harbor. Choose from mouthwatering lobster pizza, quiche, pita sandwiches, lasagna, home-baked cookies, and muffins. ⊠ *On the beach, Port Elizabeth,* ☎ *809/458–3474. Reservations essential for dinner. No credit cards.*

**$–$$** ✕ **Theresa's Restaurant.** On Monday nights, Theresa and John Ben-
★    nett offer a rotating selection of enormous and tasty Greek, Indian, Mexican, or Italian buffets. West Indian dishes are served at lunch and dinner the rest of the week. ⊠ *At far end of Lower Bay beach,* ☎ *809/458–3802. Reservations essential for dinner. No credit cards.*

## Beaches

**Friendship Bay** can be reached by land taxi and is well equipped with windsurfing and snorkeling rentals and an outdoor bar. **Hope Beach,** on the Atlantic side, is accessible by a long taxi ride (about EC$20—every driver knows how to get there) and a mile-long walk downhill on a semipaved path. Your reward is a magnificent beach and total seclusion, and—if you prefer—nude bathing. Be sure to ask your taxi driver to return at a prearranged time. Bring your own lunch and drinks; there are no facilities. Swimming can be dangerous because of rough waters. **Industry Bay** boasts towering palm groves, a nearly secluded beach, and a memorable view of several uninhabited islands. The tiny, three-room Crescent Bay Lodge is here; its huge bar offers drinks and late lunches (☎ 809/458–3400). **Lower Bay,** a wide, palm-fringed beach that can be reached by taking a taxi or hiking beyond Princess Margaret Beach, is an excellent location for swimming and snorkeling; wear sneakers, not flip-flops. Facilities for windsurfing and snorkeling are here, as well as the De Reef restaurant. **Princess Margaret Beach,** which is quiet and wide and has a natural stone arch at one end, is a half-hour walk over rocky bluffs from the Plantation House Hotel. Though it has no facilities, this is a popular spot for swimming, snorkeling, or simply relaxing under palms and sea-grape trees.

## Outdoor Activities and Sports

### SCUBA DIVING AND SNORKELING

Of Bequia's two dozen dive sites, the best are Devil's Table, a shallow dive rich in fish and coral; a sailboat wreck nearby at 90 ft; the 90-ft drop at the Wall, off West Cay; the Bullet, off Bequia's north point for rays, barracuda, and the occasional nurse shark; the Boulders for soft corals, tunnel-forming rocks, and thousands of fish; and Moonhole, shallow enough in places for snorkelers to enjoy. For snorkeling on your own, take a water taxi to the bay at Moonhole and arrange a pickup time.

**Dive Bequia** (⊠ At the Plantation House Hotel, Box 16, Bequia, ☎ 809/458–3504, ℻ 809/458–3886) and **Sunsports** (⊠ Gingerbread Complex, Box 1, Bequia, ☎ 809/458–3577, ℻ 809/457–3031) offer one- and two-tank dives, night dives, and certified instruction, plus snorkel excursions and equipment rental.

TENNIS

Tennis courts are located at four island hotels: **Frangipani Hotel** (⊠ Admiralty Bay, ☎ 809/458–3255), **Friendship Bay Hotel** (⊠ Friendship Bay, ☎ 809/458–3222), **Plantation House Hotel** (⊠ Belmont Beach, ☎ 809/458–3425), and **Spring on Bequia** (⊠ Spring Bay, ☎ 809/458–3414).

## Shopping

All Bequia's shops are in the capital, Port Elizabeth, and are open weekdays 10:30–5 or 6, Saturday 10:30–noon.

BEST BUYS

**Bequia Bookshop** (⊠ Opposite dinghy dock, ☎ 809/458–3905) has an exhaustive selection of Caribbean literature, plus cruising guides and charts, beach novels, souvenir maps, and exquisite scrimshaw and hand-carved whalebone penknives. **Crab Hole** (⊠ Admiralty Bay, ☎ 809/458–3290) sells hand-printed and batik fabric, clothing, and household items. You can see the fabrics being created in the workshop out back. **Local Color** (⊠ Port Elizabeth, ☎ 809/458–3202), above the Porthole restaurant, has an excellent and unusual selection of handmade jewelry, wood carvings, and resort clothing. **Mauvin's Model Boat Shop** (⊠ ¼ mi down the road to the left of main dock, no phone) is where you can buy handmade model boats (you can even special-order a replica of your own yacht). Bequia is renowned for its model boat builders. **Melinda's by Hand** (⊠ Port Elizabeth, ☎ 809/458–3409) sells hand-painted cotton and silk clothing and accessories. **Solana's** (⊠ Port Elizabeth, ☎ 809/458–3554) offers attractive beachwear, saronglike pareus, and handy plastic beach shoes.

## Nightlife

Along with the various jump-ups at hotels, the nearest thing to a nightclub is **Harpoon Saloon** (⊠ Port Elizabeth, ☎ 809/458–3272) clearly visible above the bay to port side as you sail into Bequia; it regularly hosts local bands.

## Bequia A to Z

ARRIVING AND DEPARTING

The MV *Admiral I* and the MV *Admiral II* motor ferries leave Kingstown for Bequia weekdays at 9 AM, 10:30 AM, 4:30 PM, and, depending on availability, 7 PM. Saturday departures are at 12:30 PM and 7 PM; Sunday, 9 AM and 7 PM. Schedules are subject to change, so be sure to check times upon your arrival. All scheduled ferries leave from the main dock in Kingstown. The trip takes 60 minutes and costs $4.

The MV *Snapper* mail boat travels south on Saturday, Monday, and Thursday at about 10:30 AM, stopping at Bequia, Canouan, Mayreau, and Union, and returns north on Tuesday and Friday, departing Bequia at 11 AM. The cost is about $4.

Weekday service between St. Vincent and Bequia is also available on the island schooner *Friendship Rose,* which leaves St. Vincent at about 12:30 PM. The *Discover St. Vincent and the Grenadines* booklet, available in hotels and at the airport, includes current interisland schedules.

**Mustique Airways** (☎ 809/458–4380 or 809/458–4818) flies into Bequia's airport daily from Barbados. The **Bequia shuttle** operates four days a week between St. Vincent, Bequia, and Canouan. **LIAT** (☎ 809/458–4841 or 800/253–5011) offers day-trip airfare to any three Grenadines and back to St. Vincent for around $200.

EMERGENCIES

**Police:** ☎ 809/456–1955. **Medical Emergencies:** ☎ 999. **Hospital: Bequia Hospital** (☎ 809/458–3294).

GUIDED TOURS

To see the views, villages, and boatbuilding around the island, hire a taxi (Gideon, ☎ 809/458–3760, is recommended) and negotiate the fare in advance.

Water taxis, available at any dock, will also take you by Moonhole, a private community of stone homes with glassless windows, some decorated with bleached whale bones. The fare is about $11.

For those who prefer sailboats to motorboats, Arne Hansen and his catamaran *Toien* can be booked through the **Frangipani Hotel** (☎ 809/458–3255). Day sails to Mustique run $35–$40 per person, including drinks. An overnight snorkel-sail trip to the Tobago Cays costs about $150 for two people, including breakfast and drinks.

VISITOR INFORMATION

The **Bequia Tourism Board** (☎ 809/458–3286) is on the main dock at Port Elizabeth and is open daily 9–12:30 and 1:30–4 (except for Saturday afternoons).

# Canouan

Goat-herding is still a career possibility here. This tiny island—just 3½ mi long and 1¼ mi wide—does have a modern airstrip, however, with night-landing facilities. Canouan also claims some of the finest white-sand beaches in the Caribbean. Walk, loaf, swim, dive, or snorkel—these are your options.

## Dining and Lodging

For price information, *see* the price charts in the Dining and Lodging sections of St. Vincent, *above.*

**$$$$** ✗🏠 **Canouan Beach Hotel.** This hotel, perched on a tongue of beach poking out from the southwest end of the island, attracts French tourists, who dominate at any time of year. Simple white cottages have patios. Catamaran day sails weekdays and live music twice a week are offered here. ⊠ *Box 520, Canouan, St. Vincent,* ☎ *809/458–8888,* 📠 *809/458–8875. 43 rooms. Restaurant, bar, air-conditioning, driving range, tennis court, scuba diving, snorkeling, windsurfing. AE, MC, V. MAP, All-inclusive.*

**$$$$** ✗🏠 **Tamarind Beach Hotel & Yacht Club.** This attractive hostelry on a sparkling white-sand beach is Canouan's newest. Guest rooms are in three large two-story buildings that face the beach. The rooms have natural wood walls and are decorated with rattan furniture and louvered wooden doors that open onto spacious balconies and a beautiful Caribbean vista. Ceiling fans join with the trade winds to keep you cool. At the Palapa Restaurant, on the beach, the Italian chef prepares fascinating Caribbean cuisine, grilled meats and fish, as well as pizzas and pasta, which you can enjoy alfresco. ⊠ *Charlestown, Canouan, St. Vincent,* ☎ *809/458–8044 or 800/223–1108,* 📠 *809/458–8851. 48 rooms. Restaurant, 2 bars, fans, dive shop, snorkeling, windsurfing, boating, fishing. No credit cards. FAP.*

**$$–$$$** ✗🏠 **Crystal Sands Beach Hotel.** A local family runs this extremely simple place on Charleston Bay. Cottages share a connecting door for larger groups and have private baths and patios. There's a fine beach and a veranda bar and dining area. If you take the mail boat from Kingstown (☞ Arriving and Departing *in* Bequia A to Z, *above*), pack light and be prepared to climb from the large ferry into a small rowboat to get to shore. ⊠ *Canouan, St. Vincent,* ☎ *809/458–8015. 10 rooms. Bar, snorkeling, fishing. No credit cards. EP.*

**$$–$$$** ✗🏠 **Villa Le Bijou Guest House.** This place is up the hill and only a 10-minute walk from Friendship Bay (15 minutes from the airstrip; pack light—taxis are rarely available). Accommodations border on the primitive (e.g., no hot water in shared baths), and the electricity is often on vacation, but the view is stunning. ⊠ *c/o M. de Roche, Villa Le Bijou, Canouan, St. Vincent,* ☎ *809/458–8025. 6 rooms. Boating, snorkeling, windsurfing. No credit cards. MAP.*

### Outdoor Activities and Sports
SCUBA DIVING AND SNORKELING

Tony Alongi, the owner-operator of **Dive Canouan** (⊠ Box 530, Tamarind Beach Hotel, ☎ 809/458–8044 or 809/458–8234, FAX 809/ 458–8851), offers dive and snorkel packages that include tours to the Tobago Cays, south of Canouan. You can also take a resort or certification course.

### Nightlife
Surprise: There's a bar and disco on weekends at **Villa Le Bijou Guest House** (☞ Dining and Lodging, *above*).

---

## Mayreau

Privately owned Mayreau (pronounced my-*row*) is minuscule—just 1½ square mi. Farm animals outnumber residents. Except for water sports and hiking, there's not much to do, and visitors like it that way. This is the perfect place for a meditative or vegetative vacation. To get here, take a boat from Union Island.

### Dining and Lodging
For price information, *see* the price charts in the Dining and Lodging sections of St. Vincent, *above*.

$$$$    ╳▥ **Salt Whistle Bay Club.** Set far back from the water, Mayreau's only hotel is so cleverly hidden that sailors need binoculars to be sure it's there at all. Each roomy stone cottage, with a name like Oleander or Ivora, has a round-stone, hot-water shower that looks like a large, medieval telephone booth. You can dry your hair on the breezy, shared second-story veranda atop each two-room building. The outdoor dining area has stone tables covered by thatched palms where you can enjoy turtle steak, duckling, lobster, and à la carte lunches. There used to be a jump-up, but guests preferred peace and quiet. ⊠ *Management Offices, 1020 Bayridge Dr., Kingston, Ontario, Canada K7P 2S2,* ☎ *800/ 263–2780 in the U.S.; 613/634–1963 outside the U.S. (call collect);* FAX *800/263–2780 in the U.S.; 613/384–6300 outside the U.S.;* ☎ *809/ 458–8444 in the Caribbean; marine radio VHF channel 68; boat phone 493–9609. 10 cottages, 4 suites. Restaurant, bar, snorkeling, windsurfing, boating. No credit cards. FAP.*

$–$$    ╳▥ **Dennis' Hideaway.** Dennis (who plays the guitar two nights a week) is a charmer, the food is great, the drinks are strong, and the view is heaven. The rooms are clean but very simple: a bed, nightstand, chair, and a place to hang some clothes. ⊠ *Saline Bay,* ☎ *809/458–8594. 7 rooms. Restaurant. No credit cards. EP.*

### Beaches
**Saline Bay Beach** is beautiful, but there are no facilities. The mail boat's tender stops at the dock here. **Salt Whistle Bay Beach** takes top honors—it's one of the Caribbean's prettiest. The beach is an exquisite half-moon of powdery white sand, shaded by perfectly spaced palms and flowering bushes, with the rolling Atlantic a stroll away.

### Outdoor Activities and Sports
HIKING

Hike 25 minutes over Mayreau's mountain (wear shoes; bare feet or flip-flops are a big mistake) to a good photo opportunity at the stone church atop the hill and stunning views of the Cays. Then have a drink at Dennis' Hideaway and enjoy a swim at Saline Bay Beach.

SCUBA DIVING AND SNORKELING

**Grenadines Dive** (☎ 809/458–8138 or 809/458–8122, ℻ 809/458–8122) can arrange scuba-diving trips. **Salt Whistle Bay Club** (☎ 809/458–8444 or 800/263–2780 from the U.S.) will arrange day trips with charter yachts to the cays or nearby islands for swimming and snorkeling. The Salt Whistle Bay's snorkel equipment has seen better days; you may want to buy or rent your own before you arrive.

# Mustique

Trendsetter Princess Margaret put this 3- by 1½-mi former copra, cotton, and sugarcane estate on the map after Colin Tennant (now Lord Glenconner) bought it. The Mustique Company, which he formed in 1968 to develop the island into the glamorous hideaway it has become, now has 37 shareholders and a House Rentals Department. Arrangements must be made about a year in advance to rent Balliceaux, the royal holiday home, or another of the 40-odd luxury villas that pepper the northern half of the island. Some owners, including Mustique's two most glittering habitués, Mick Jagger and David Bowie, keep their villas empty in their absence.

Sooner or later, star-gawkers will get to see whoever's "on island" at Basil's Bar, the island's social center. Next to his bar, in a cluster of candy-color houses that don't quite qualify as a town, Basil also runs a boutique crammed with clothes and accessories imported and specially commissioned from all over the world, a cornucopian delicatessen to feed residents fresh Brie and Moët, and an antiques shop stocked with fabulous pieces for those fabulous houses. There's also a fish market, a grocery warehouse, a gas station—and a police station with nothing much to do. To some, this is paradise; others *hate* it—but you pays yer money, you takes yer choice!

## Lodging

For price information on hotels, *see* the price chart in the Lodging section of St. Vincent, *above*.

$$$$  ⊞ **Cotton House.** The island's only resort centers on the stone-and-coral
★      estate warehouse originally converted by Oliver Messel, the late British theater designer–decorator-architect. Under the aegis of manager Warren Francis and his wife Gilly, it has become a world-class hotel. The 18th-century plantation house and its stone mill (now the boutique) are the oldest structures on Mustique. A wraparound veranda functions as lounge, bar, tea terrace, restaurant, and social center. Small cottages off the pool path have breezy layouts, and the deluxe suites are mere steps away from the main house. Costing significantly less are a fantastic quartet of deluxe rooms in high-up Battowia House, with balconies perched over Mustique's northern coast, and two beach rooms. Decor is sophisticated but faithful to Messel's vision of Caribbean simplicity and light, with white walls and ceiling fans, antiques, and rattan furniture. Bathrooms have marble fittings, and rooms have dressing areas, French windows, desks—and perfect peace. In addition to the restaurant, there's a beach bar with a weekly barbecue. Airport transfers and an island tour are included, as are water sports, tennis, and a driver who will chauffeur you to Basil's or the beach. ⊠ *Box 349, Mustique, St. Vincent,* ☎ *809/456–4777 or 800/447–7462,* ℻ *809/456–5887. 10 rooms, 10 suites. Restaurant, bar, fans, minibars, pool, 2 tennis courts, horseback riding, scuba diving, snorkeling, windsurfing, boating, shop, library, airport shuttle. AE, D, MC, V. FAP.*

$$$$  🏠 **Firefly Hotel.** Tiny and charming with just four rooms, this rather exclusive inn is well located above Britannia Bay. Rooms are attractively appointed and have private baths, and for $5 extra you can have air-conditioning. The restaurant serves Caribbean cuisine, along with gourmet pizza and pasta dishes, in an intimate, candlelit atmosphere. Swim in two swimming pools connected by a waterfall or pack a picnic and spend a day at the beach, just down the garden path. Picnic equipment is provided in each room. Arrangements can be made to play tennis or go horseback riding nearby. ⊠ *Mustique, Box 349,* ☎ *809/456–3414,* 🅵🅰🆇 *809/456–3514. 4 rooms. Restaurant, bar, 2 pools, refrigerators, scuba diving, snorkeling, windsurfing, boating. No credit cards. CP.*

VILLA RENTALS

Renting one of Mustique's privately owned villas is not as expensive as it seems at first glance, since rates include a full staff (with cook but no groceries), laundry service, and a vehicle or two; rates are per house, not per person. Houses range from simple rusticity—if you can call en-suite bathrooms for every bedroom, at least one phone line, probably a pool, cable TV, VCR, CD player, and even fax, rustic—to extravagant, expansive, faux-Palladian follies with resident butler; but all are designer-elegant and immaculately maintained. Rates start at $2,800 a week for the two-bedroom Pelican Beach off-season and go way up to $12,000 a week for the palatial five-bedroom, five-person staff, two-Jeep, one-Jacuzzi Blackstone during winter. Princess Margaret's three-bedroom place is surprisingly modest, at a mere $3,300 a week in summer. ⊠ *House Rentals Dept., Mustique Co. Ltd., Box 349, St. Vincent and the Grenadines,* ☎ *809/458–4621,* 🅵🅰🆇 *809/456–4565. 43 villas. AE, DC, MC, V. FAP.*

## Dining

For price information on restaurants, *see* the price chart in the Dining section of St. Vincent, *above.*

$–$$$  ✕ **Basil's Bar and Restaurant.** Basil's is the only place to be on Mus-
★      tique, and only partly because it *is* the only place on Mustique, apart from the more formal, quieter Cotton House. Resembling many a beachside terrace restaurant, with its wooden deck built over the waves, palm-roofed at the edges with a central bar and dance floor open to the stars, there's something about the atmosphere that hints at happenings. You never know whom you may run into. . . . The food is simple and good—mostly fish hauled from the water a hundred yards away, homemade ice cream, burgers and salads, great French toast, usual cocktails, and unusual wines. The Wednesday barbecue is party night, and there's live music Mondays. ⊠ *Britania Bay,* ☎ *809/458–4621. AE, MC, V.*

## Beaches

**Macaroni Beach** is Mustique's most famous stretch of sand, offering surfy swimming (no lifeguards, so be careful), powdery white sand, a few palm huts for shade, and picnic tables on a grassy garden. From the northern coast, working west, **L'Ansecoy, Endeavour,** and **Britannia bays** are also fine and much calmer, the last being the best for day-trippers, with Basil's Bar adjacent for lunch. Farther south, **Gelliceaux Bay,** by the Cotton House, provides the best snorkeling beach.

## Outdoor Activities and Sports

Water-sports facilities are available at the Cotton House, and most villas have equipment of various sorts. There's a communal tennis court for those whose villa lacks its own, a cricket ground for the Brits, and motorbikes for trail-riding around the bumpy roads for rent at $45 per day.

The best sport to indulge in on Mustique is horseback riding, since this is one of the few islands where you can rent a fine horse. Rides leave Monday–Saturday at 8 and 9 AM, 3 and 4 PM from the **Equestrian Centre** (⊠ Macaroni Bay, ☎ 809/458–4316), and rates are $40 per hour.

Scuba is best arranged through **Dive Mustique** (⊠ Basil's Bar, Mustique Island, ☎ 809/458–4621).

# Palm Island

A private speck of land, Palm Island has wide white-sand beaches and one very casual resort. Access is through Union Island, 1 mi to the west; you're picked up by the resort launch for the 10-minute boat ride to Palm Island.

## Lodging

For price information on hotels, *see* the price chart in the Lodging section of St. Vincent, *above*.

$$$$ 🏨 **Palm Island Beach Club.** An intrepid American sailor, his Australian-born wife, and two sons sailed the oceans of the world for 15 years until they settled on Prune Island, then a swamp-ridden, mosquito-infested jungle in the Grenadines. The family toiled for 25 more years, turning the island into Palm Island Beach Club. You can read all about it over tea, delivered at 4 PM to your cabana terrace. Some cabanas offer a private sunset view over Casuarina Beach through room-width patio doors. Bathrooms aren't the greatest, with dribbly yet scenic outdoor showers in the newer cabanas, but balanced against that is a collective and genuine warmth in the staff. The food is important when you're a captive audience; the island buffets and full-service dinners are just fine, and the pastry chef makes breakfast worth getting up for. Adjacent to the hotel is a separate yacht club, the only change of scene apart from a jog on "Highway 90" (1¼ mi around) or a day sail to the Tobago Cays. Windsurfers, Sunfish, and floating mats are complimentary. Leave your fancy clothes at home—this is a really casual place. And plan on busy, active days. Nightlife is practically nil but for Wednesday and Saturday barbecues with calypso music—in season. ⊠ *Palm Island, St. Vincent,* ☎ *809/458–8824,* ℻ *809/458–8804. U.S. agent: CaribCom,* ☎ *800/999–7256. 24 cottages. Restaurant, bar, grocery, tennis court, jogging, scuba diving, snorkeling, windsurfing, boating, fishing, recreation room, baby-sitting. AE, MC, V. FAP.*

# Petit St. Vincent

This is the southernmost of St. Vincent's Grenadines. Like the others, it is ringed with white-sand beaches and covered with beautiful tropical foliage. Guests are treated royally at the island's one classy, secluded resort. To get here, you fly into Union Island, where the PSV motor launch will meet you for the 30-minute trip.

## Lodging

For price information on hotels, *see* the price chart in the Lodging section of St. Vincent, *above*.

$$$$ 🏨 **Petit St. Vincent.** On this very special 113-acre private island, you can indulge shipwreck fantasies without forgoing the frozen mango daiquiri at sunset, room-service breakfast, the skills of a great chef, and so on. Each of PSV's 22 cottages has a bedroom, sitting room, and one

or two bathrooms, all in a U-shape around a big, partly covered wooden deck. Floors are tiled and grass matted, walls are of stone and—on two sides—glass, with patio doors that slide away entirely, giving you trade winds for a lullaby. Despite their rustic appearance, with copra matting vanities and cobblestone shower stalls, bathrooms conceal the Grenadines' best toiletries, robes, beach bags, towels, and an iron, and they have American-style 110-volt, two-prong outlets, so you don't need transformers. No house is more than a five-minute walk from dinner, yet each is completely private, with a sweet system of signal flags to convey whims to the staff (who outnumber guests two to one). Hoist your red flag, and nobody *dreams* of approaching; hoist the yellow, and you can have lunch or dinner, tea or drinks, a ride to the jetty, or a picnic for a day on the "West End" promptly delivered. Some prefer the houses that fringe the windward beach, others like the distant trio high up on the bluff, and still others swear by the three perched above the Atlantic surf, with stone steps to the beach. ⊠ *PSV, Box 12506, Cincinnati, OH 45212,* ☎ *513/242–1333, 800/654–9326, or 809/458–8801;* FAX *809/458–8428. 22 cottages. Dining room, beach, tennis, snorkeling, boating. No credit cards. FAP. Closed Sept.–Oct.*

## Union

Gorgeous from a distance, 2,100-acre Union Island's Mount Parnassus soars 900 ft into the air. Union is a popular stopping-off point for yachtspeople and visitors heading to some of the smaller islands, but it doesn't offer the charm or friendliness of other Grenadines. The main town, Clifton Harbour, is small and commercial. Beachfront inns are generally simple. The airstrip is right behind the Anchorage Yacht Club.

### Lodging

For price information on hotels, *see* the price chart in the Lodging section of St. Vincent, *above.*

**$$–$$$**  🏨 **Anchorage Yacht Club.** Between the airstrip and a small beach are comfortably furnished rooms and bungalows with concealed outdoor showers and terraces facing the water. You'll find water sports and yacht chartering galore. The full-service marina creates a cosmopolitan buzz throughout the resort. Rates include breakfast at Les Pieds dans l'Eau, the adjoining restaurant, which also serves lunch and dinner. There's a pizza and sandwich counter as well, and a jump-up on Monday for those sailors who get stranded here. ⊠ *Union, St. Vincent,* ☎ *809/458–8221,* FAX *809/458–8365. 10 rooms, 6 bungalows. Restaurant, bar, air-conditioning, water sports, boating. AE, MC, V. CP.*

### Dining

For price information, *see* the price chart in the Dining section of St. Vincent, *above.*

**$$**  ✕ **Lambie's.** On the main street in Clifton, Lambie's specialty is its delicious conch Creole. The word lambie means conch in Caribbean patois, and the restaurant's walls are even constructed from conch shells. There's steel-band music every night in season. ⊠ *Clifton,* ☎ *809/458–8549. No credit cards.*

### Beaches

The beach around Clifton Harbour is narrow, unattractive, rocky, and shadeless. Other beaches have no facilities and are virtually inaccessible without a boat; the desolate but lovely Chatham Bay offers good swimming.

## Outdoor Activities and Sports

SCUBA DIVING

**Grenadines Dive** (☎ 809/458–8138 or 809/458–8122, FAX 809/458–8122), run by NAUI instructor Glenroy Adams, offers Tobago Cays trips and wreck dives at the *Purina,* a sunken World War I English gunship.

## Union Visitor Information

The **Union Island Tourist Bureau** (☎ 809/458–8350), at the airstrip behind the Anchorage Yacht Club, is open daily 8–noon and 1–4.

# ST. VINCENT AND THE GRENADINES A TO Z

## Arriving and Departing

BY PLANE

Most U.S. visitors fly via **American Airlines** (☎ 809/456–5000 or 800/433–7300) into Barbados, Grenada, or St. Lucia, then take a small plane to St. Vincent's E.T. Joshua Airport or to Bequia, Mustique, Canouan, or Union. (Other destinations in the Grenadines require a boat ride on either a scheduled ferry, a chartered boat, or your hotel's launch.) **American Eagle** (☎ 809/456–5000 or 800/433–7300) has scheduled service between San Juan, Puerto Rico, and St. Vincent. Other airlines that connect with interisland flights are **BWIA** (☎ 809/627–2942 or 800/538–2942), **British Airways** (☎ 809/952–3124 or 800/247–9297) from Jamaica, **Air Canada** (☎ 246/428–5077 or 800/776–3000) from Barbados, and **Air France** (☎ 05/90–826–000 in Guadeloupe; 05/96–553–333 in Martinique; or 800/237–2747).

**LIAT** (Leeward Islands Air Transport, ☎ 809/462–0700; 212/251–1717 in NY; 800/253–5011 elsewhere in the U.S.), **Air Martinique** (☎ 809/458–4528), **Mustique Airways** (☎ 809/458–4380), and **SVG AIR** (☎ 809/456–5610, FAX 809/458–4697) fly interisland. Delays are common but usually not outrageous.

FROM THE AIRPORT

Taxis and buses are readily available at E.T. Joshua Airport and are available, but rarer, on those Grenadine islands with airstrips. A taxi from the airport to hotels in the Villa Beach area costs about $5.50 (EC$15); to Kingstown, about $7.50 (EC$20); bus fare is less than 50¢. If you have a lot of luggage, it might be best to take a taxi—buses (actually minivans) are short on space, since they are usually full of people.

## Currency

Although U.S. and Canadian dollars are accepted at all but the smallest shops, Eastern Caribbean currency (EC$) is preferred everywhere. The exchange rate at banks is approximately EC$2.70 to US$1; hotels and shops generally give a rate of EC$2.50–EC$2.60 to US$1. Price quotes are normally given in E.C. dollars; however, especially when you negotiate taxi fares, be sure you know which type of dollar you're agreeing on. Note: Prices quoted here are in U.S. dollars unless indicated otherwise.

## Emergencies

**Police:** ☎ 809/457–1211. **Hospital: Kingstown General Hospital** (☎ 809/456–1185). **Pharmacies:** In Kingstown, Davis Drugmart (✉ Corner of Tyrrell and McCory Sts., ☎ 809/456–1174), **Deane's** (✉ Middle St., ☎ 809/456–2877), **Medix Pharmacy** (✉ Grenville St., ☎ 809/456–2989), or **People's Pharmacy** (✉ Bedford St., ☎ 809/456–1170); on Bequia, **People's Pharmacy** (✉ Port Elizabeth, ☎ 809/458–3936).

## Getting Around

BUSES

Public buses are really privately owned, brightly painted minivans with names like "Easy Na," "Irie," and "Who to Blame." Bus fares run EC$1–EC$6 on St. Vincent; for the 10-minute ride from Kingstown to Villa Beach, for example, the fare is EC$1.50. Buses operate all day long until about midnight, and routes are indicated on a sign on the windshield. Just wave from the road, and the driver will stop for you; pay the man by the door on the way out, with the correct change in EC$ coins, if possible. In Kingstown, buses leave from the Terminus in Market Square; they serve the entire island. Smaller islands in the Grenadines also have taxi-vans and pickup trucks with benches in the back and canvas covers for the occasional rain shower.

CAR RENTALS

Rental cars cost about $50 per day with some free miles. Using a credit card avoids a $300 cash deposit. Gasoline costs $2.50 per gallon. About 300 mi of paved road winds way around the perimeter of the island, so it's impossible to get lost. Be sure to drive on the left, and honk your horn before you enter blind curves out in the countryside—you'll encounter plenty of steep hills and hairpin turns. Although major improvements are being made, roads are not always well marked or maintained. Unless you already have an international driver's license, you'll need to purchase a temporary local license for EC$40. You'll also need to present your valid driver's license. Temporary licenses are valid for six months and can be secured at the airport, at the police station on Bay Street, or at the Licensing Authority on Halifax Street.

Among the rental firms are **David's Auto Clinic** (⊠ Sion Hill, just south of Kingstown, ☎ 809/456–4026), **Kim's Rentals** (⊠ Grenville St., Kingstown, ☎ 809/456–1884), **Star Garage** (⊠ Grenville St., Kingstown, ☎ 809/456–1743), and **UNICO Auto Rentals,** (⊠ Airport, ☎ 809/456–5744).

FERRIES

**MV Baracuda** (☎ 809/456–5180) leaves St. Vincent on Monday and Thursday mornings, stopping in Bequia, Canouan, Mayreau, and Union Island. It makes the return trip Tuesdays and Fridays. On Saturdays, it does the round-trip in a day. Including stopover time, the trip takes 3¼ hours to Canouan (EC$13), 4½ hours to Mayreau (EC$15), and 5 hours to Union Island (EC$20).

TAXIS

Taxi fares are set by the government. Between Kingstown and the hotels and restaurants at Villa Beach, the one-way fare is EC$20. To hire a taxi by the hour, the rate is EC$40.

## Guided Tours

Tours can be arranged informally through taxi drivers, who double as knowledgeable guides. Your hotel or the tourism board will recommend a driver, or call Kelvin Harry (☎ 809/457–1316), president of the Taxi Driver's Association. He'll send one of the association's members, identifiable by a round yellow-and-blue decal on the taxi windshield. Always settle the fare first, in either U.S. or E.C. dollars. The average cost is EC$40 per hour.

**Baleine Tours** (⊠ Villa, St. Vincent, ☎ 809/457–4089) offers scenic coastal trips to the Falls of Baleine, as well as charters to Bequia and Mustique, deep-sea fishing trips, and snorkeling excursions. **Dive St. Vincent** (⊠ Young Island Dock, Villa Beach, St. Vincent, ☎ 809/457–4714) offers a day trip to Baleine that includes a scenic voyage along the coast, snorkeling, and swimming at a black-sand beach. **Grenadine**

**Travel Co.** (✉ Arnos Vale, St. Vincent, ☎ 809/458–4818) arranges air, sea, and land excursions throughout the islands. **Sam's Taxi Tours** (✉ Cane Garden, ☎ 809/456–4338) arranges hiking tours to La Soufrière volcano and scenic walks along the Vermont Nature Trails.

## Language
English is spoken throughout St. Vincent and the Grenadines.

## Opening and Closing Times
Stores and shops in Kingstown are open weekdays 8–4. Many close for lunch from noon to 1 or so. Saturday hours are 8–noon. Banks are open weekdays 8 until 1, 2, or 3, Friday until 5. The branch of National Commercial Bank of St. Vincent at the airport is open Monday–Saturday 7–5.

## Passports and Visas
U.S., Canadian, and U.K. travelers need proof of citizenship (e.g., passport, birth certificate, or voter's registration card). Other nationals must have a valid passport. All visitors must hold return or ongoing tickets. Visas are not required.

## Precautions
There's relatively little **crime** here, but don't tempt fate by leaving your valuables lying around or your room or car unlocked. **Insects** can be a minor problem on the beach during the day, but when hiking and sitting outdoors in the evening, you'll be glad you brought industrial-strength mosquito repellent. Beware of the **manchineel tree,** whose little green apples look tempting but are toxic. Even touching the sap of the leaves will cause an uncomfortable rash, and you should not shelter beneath them during rainstorms. Most trees on hotel grounds are marked with signs; on more remote islands, the bark may be painted red. Hikers should watch for brazilwood trees and bushes, which look and act similar to poison ivy. When taking **photos** of market vendors, private citizens, or homes, be polite enough to ask permission first, and expect to give a gratuity for the favor. **Sea urchins** are spiny black sea creatures that sit on the sand in shallow water. If you happen to step on one, you can put away your dancing shoes. It's painful! Rubbing a little lime—or an ammonia-based liquid—on the wound may help. Water is safe to drink in hotels and restaurants.

## Taxes and Service Charges
The departure tax from St. Vincent and the Grenadines is $7.50 (EC$20). Restaurants and hotels charge a 7% government tax; if a 10% service charge is included in your bill, no additional tip is necessary.

## Telephones and Mail
The area code for St. Vincent and the Grenadines is expected to change from 809 to 784 in early 1998, but either area code may be used for one year following the changeover date. Local information is 118; international information, 115. International direct dialing is available throughout St. Vincent and the Grenadines. When you dial a local number from your hotel in the Grenadines, you can drop the 45 prefix. Pay phones are best operated with a prepaid phonecard, available from stores and usable in several Caribbean islands. The General Post Office, on Halifax Street in Kingstown, is open daily from 8:30 to 3 and Saturdays from 8:30 to 11:30. Mail between St. Vincent and the United States may take about two weeks. Airmail postcards cost EC90¢; airmail letters cost EC$1.80 an ounce.

## Visitor Information
Before you go, contact the **St. Vincent and the Grenadines Tourist Office** (✉ 801 2nd Ave., 21st floor, New York, NY 10017, ☎ 212/687–

4981 or 800/729–1726, FAX 212/949–5946; ✉ 6505 Cove Creek Pl., Dallas, TX 75240, ☎ 214/239–6451 or 800/235–3029, FAX 214/239–1002; ✉ 32 Park Rd., Toronto, Ontario N4W 2N4, ☎ 416/924–5796, FAX 416/924–5844; ✉ 10 Kensington Court, London W8 5DL, ☎ 0171/937–6570, FAX 0171/937–3611). Ask for the visitor's guide, which is filled with useful, up-to-date information.

On St. Vincent, the **St. Vincent Board of Tourism** (✉ Box 834, Upper Bay St., Kingstown, ☎ 809/457–1502, FAX 809/456–2610) is in the financial complex, close to the port. It's open weekdays 8–noon and 1–4:30. There's a tourist information desk at St. Vincent's E.T. Joshua Airport (☎ 809/458–4685) and one at the Grantley Adams International Airport on Barbados (☎ 246/428–0961).

# 25 Trinidad and Tobago

*From the crowded urban streets of Port-of-Spain to lush rain forests, where toucans and hummingbirds play, Trinidad offers visitors plenty of diverse cultural and natural landscapes to explore. If your true pursuit is sun and sand, your better bet is little Tobago, where the beaches are more accessible and tourism is more fully developed.*

Updated by
JoAnn
Milivojevic

**T**HE TWO-ISLAND REPUBLIC of Trinidad and Tobago is
the southernmost link in the Antillean island chain,
lying some 9 mi off the coast of Venezuela and safely
outside the path of all those devastating Caribbean hurricanes. Both
Trinidad and Tobago are more geologically akin to continental South
America than they are to the other Caribbean islands: Tobago's Main
Ridge and Trinidad's Northern Range are believed to represent the farthest reaches of the Andes mountain range. But although the two islands are linked geographically and politically, in some ways they
could not be more dissimilar.

Trinidad's growth arose out of oil prosperity—it remains one of the
largest petroleum producers in the Western Hemisphere—which made
it a prime destination for business travelers. They enjoyed the sophisticated shopping, restaurants, and hotels in the nation's lively capital,
Port-of-Spain, partying late into the night to the syncopated steel-
band sounds that originated in Trinidad.

The economy slumped along with oil prices in the mid-1980s, but
Trinidad is now recovering with an influx of small businesses. Port-
of-Spain is still one of the most active commercial cities in the West
Indies, and the cultural scene is as vital as ever, especially during the
country's riotous Carnival. The capital hosts around 51,000 of Trinidad's
1.3 million residents—Africans, Indians, Americans, Europeans, and
Asians, each with their own language and customs (the official language
is English, however). But you have to leave Port-of-Spain to find a good
beach and to enjoy the island's natural attractions, and there are currently few accommodations in a nonurban setting that offer more
than bare-bones comfort.

It is Tobago, 22 mi away, that affords tourists the lazier life and seaside
lodgings that most of them seek. Unspoiled rain forests and coral reefs
and a largely undeveloped coastline have made the smaller island an ideal
getaway for nature-lovers, divers, and privacy seekers. However, tourism
is being promoted heavily and new hotels are being built; without careful control, Tobago could lose the idyllic quality that led Daniel Defoe
to depict it as the quintessential desert island in *Robinson Crusoe*.

Residents of Tobago pride themselves on their friendliness. But petty
theft does occur. Use hotel safes and don't leave cash in your check-in
bags at the airport.

Columbus reached these islands on his third voyage, in 1498. Three prominent peaks around the southern bay of Trinidad prompted him to name
the land La Trinidad, after the Holy Trinity. Trinidad was captured by
British forces in 1797, ending 300 years of Spanish rule. Tobago's history is more complicated. It was "discovered" by the British in 1508.
The Spanish, Dutch, French, and British all fought for it until it was
ceded to England under the Treaty of Paris in 1814. In 1962 both islands—T&T, as they're commonly called—gained their independence
within the British Commonwealth, finally becoming a republic in 1976.

# TRINIDAD

## Lodging

Trinidad accommodations range from charming guest houses to tony
hotels; most of the acceptable establishments, however, are within the
vicinity of Port-of-Spain, far from any beach. Carnival week is one of
two times in the year for which you should book reservations far in

advance (the other is Christmas); expect to pay twice the price charged the rest of the year.

Most places offer breakfast and dinner for an additional flat rate (MAP), but on the whole these plans mean less variety than you'll get if you strike out for meals on your own.

The number of private homes in Trinidad offering bed-and-breakfast accommodations is growing each year. Contact the **Trinidad and To-bago Bed and Breakfast Co-operative Society** (⊠ Box 3231, Diego Martin, ☎ ℻ 809/627–2337).

| CATEGORY | COST* |
|---|---|
| **$$$$** | over $175 |
| **$$$** | $100–$175 |
| **$$** | $60–$100 |
| **$** | under $60 |

*All prices are for a standard double room, excluding 15% tax and 10% service charge.*

**$$$–$$$$** ⬧ **Trinidad Hilton and Conference Center.** Perched above the Gulf of Paria
★ and Queen's Park Savannah, this large hotel is set on landscaped gardens. It stretches out horizontally across the hilltop and gently moves down the hillside; you take the elevator *down* to your room. The design, with its gleaming dark wood and tropical landscaping, is lovely, and each of the rooms has a balcony, which either opens to a fine view of Queen's Park, the city, and the sea beyond or overlooks the inviting Olympic-size swimming pool. The hotel has its shortcomings: Rooms are somewhat generically decorated and the furniture is a bit dated. The route to the pool is labyrinthine, and service is somewhat erratic (you might find your bed unmade when you return from sightseeing in the afternoon). That said, this hotel is the most upscale and has the most amenities in the city. ⊠ *Lady Young Rd., Box 442, Port-of-Spain,* ☎ *809/624–3211; 800/445–8667 in the U.S.;* ℻ *809/624–4485. 394 rooms. 2 restaurants, 3 bars, air-conditioning, pool, 2 tennis courts, shops, meeting rooms, car rental. AE, DC, MC, V. EP.*

**$$$** ⬧ **Holiday Inn.** Proximity to the port and Independence Square is both the draw and the drawback of this hotel. From any upper floor room you'll have a lovely pastel panorama of the old town and of ships idling in the Gulf of Paria, and you're within walking distance of the downtown sights and shops. But with the action comes traffic: Independence Square is clogged with people and cars throughout the day. Rooms are done in standard international mode, complete with hair dryers, a rarity on Trinidad. La Ronde, a revolving rooftop bistro, offers a striking view of the city at night. ⊠ *Wrightson Rd., Box 1017, Port-of-Spain,* ☎ *809/625–3366; 800/465–4329 in the U.S.;* ℻ *809/625–4166. 235 rooms, 2 suites. Restaurant, air-conditioning, pool, beauty salon, exercise room, shops, baby-sitting, laundry service, business services, car rental. AE, DC, MC, V. BP.*

**$$** ⬧ **Hotel Normandie.** Built by French Creoles in the 1930s on the ruins
★ of an old coconut plantation, the Normandie has touches of Spanish and English colonial architecture. It's set back from residential St. Ann's Road, adjoining an artsy mall of crafts shops and galleries. The standard rooms, set around a pretty courtyard with a pool, have wood floorboards and fittings, the furniture is a bit flimsy, and the air conditioner noisy but efficient. Rooms have only one rectangular window and get very little light. The 13 larger loft rooms are far better: For $25 more, you get a duplex with a bigger bathroom (the fact that two children under 12 can stay free makes them perfect for families). Service is friendly and efficient. La Fantasie (☞ Dining, *below*) provides room service until 11 PM. ⊠ *10 Nook Ave., Box 851, St. Ann's, Port-of-Spain,*

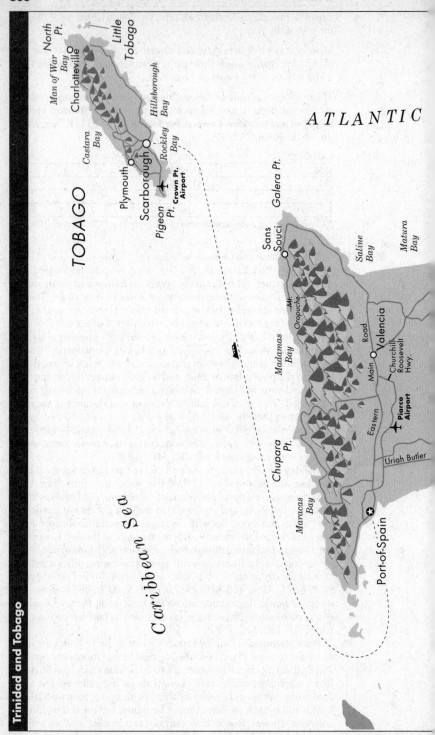

TOBAGO

North Pt.

Man of War Bay

Charlotteville

Little Tobago

Hillsborough Bay

Castara Bay

Rockley Bay

Plymouth

Scarborough

Pigeon Pt. **Crown Pt. Airport**

*Caribbean Sea*

Chupara Pt.

Maracas Bay

Madamas Bay

Mt. Oropuche

Sans Souci

Galera Pt.

Saline Bay

Matura Bay

*ATLANTIC*

Valencia

Main Road

Churchill Roosevelt Hwy.

Eastern

**Piarco Airport**

Uriah Butler

Port-of-Spain

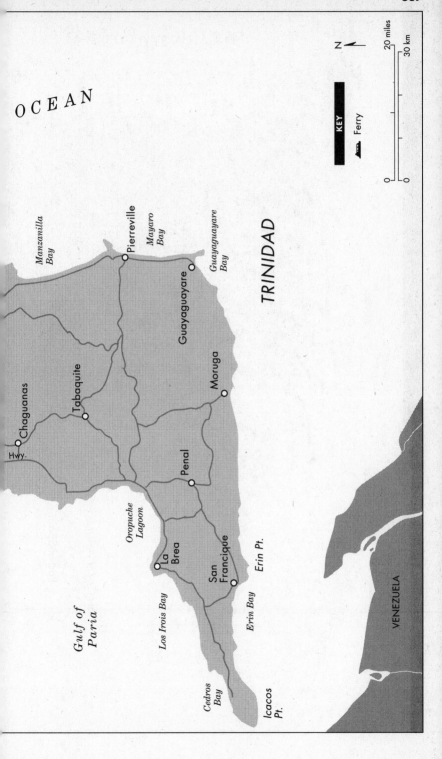

OCEAN

*Manzanilla Bay*

Pierreville

*Mayaro Bay*

Guayaguayare

*Guayaguayare Bay*

TRINIDAD

Tabaquite

Moruga

Chaguanas

Hwy.

Penal

*Oropuche Lagoon*

La Brea

San Francique

Erin Pt.

*Gulf of Paria*

*Los Irois Bay*

*Erin Bay*

*Cedros Bay*

Icacos Pt.

VENEZUELA

N

20 miles

30 km

KEY

Ferry

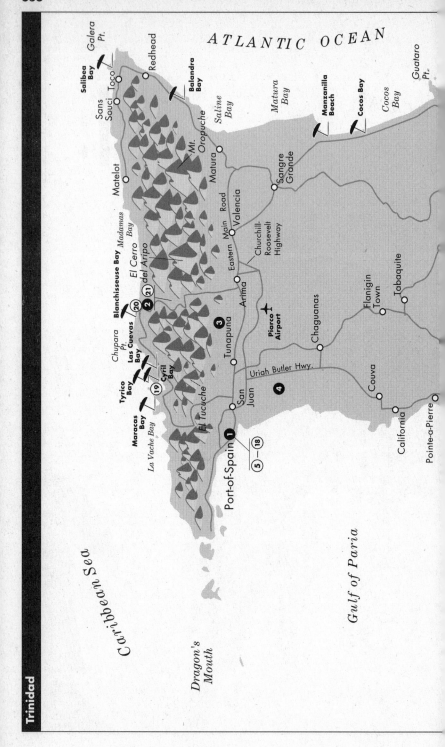

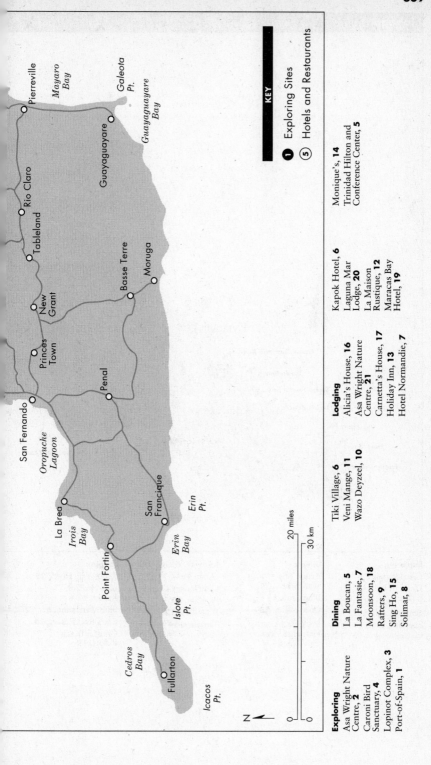

KEY

● Exploring Sites

⑤ Hotels and Restaurants

**Exploring**
Asa Wright Nature
Centre, **2**
Caroni Bird
Sanctuary, **4**
Lopinot Complex, **3**
Port-of-Spain, **1**

**Dining**
La Boucan, **5**
La Fantasie, **7**
Moonsoon, **18**
Rafters, **9**
Sing Ho, **15**
Solimar, **8**

Tiki Village, **6**
Veni Mange, **11**
Wazo Deyzeel, **10**

**Lodging**
Alicia's House, **16**
Asa Wright Nature
Centre, **21**
Carnetta's House, **17**
Holiday Inn, **13**
Hotel Normandie, **7**

Kapok Hotel, **6**
Laguna Mar
Lodge, **20**
La Maison
Rustique, **12**
Maracas Bay
Hotel, **19**

Monique's, **14**
Trinidad Hilton and
Conference Center, **5**

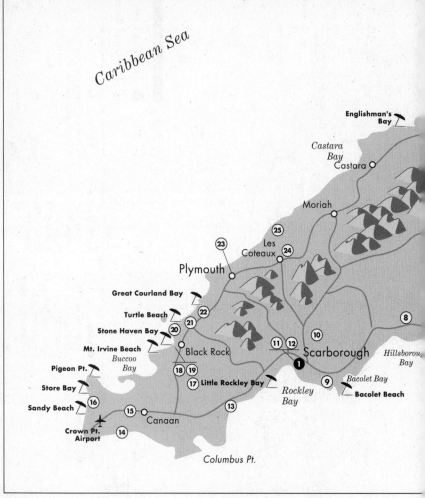

Caribbean Sea

Englishman's Bay

Castara Bay
Castara

Moriah

25
23
Les Coteaux
24

Plymouth

Great Courland Bay

22

Turtle Beach
21

Stone Haven Bay
20

Mt. Irvine Beach
Buccoo Bay
Black Rock
10
11  12
Scarborough

8

Pigeon Pt.
18  19
1
Hillsborough Bay

Store Bay
17
Little Rockley Bay
9
Bacolet Bay
Bacolet Beach

Sandy Beach
16
13
Rockley Bay

15
Canaan

Crown Pt. Airport
14

Columbus Pt.

**Exploring**
Charlotteville, **5**
Flagstaff Hill, **4**
Fort King George, **2**
Scarborough, **1**
Speyside, **3**

**Dining**
Arnos Vale Waterwheel, **24**
Blue Crab, **11**
Cocrico Inn, **23**
Dillon's, **15**
First Historical Cafe/Bar, **8**

Kariwak Village, **14**
Ocean View, **19**
Old Donkey Cart, **9**
Papillon, **20**
Rouselle's, **12**
Tamara's, **14**

**Lodging**
Arnos Vale Hotel, **25**
Blue Horizon Resort, **17**
Blue Waters Inn, **6**
Coco Reef Resort, **16**
Grafton Beach Resort, **19**

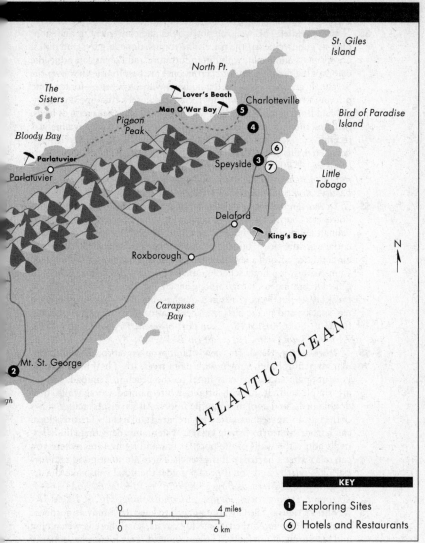

*The Sisters*

*North Pt.*

*St. Giles Island*

**Lover's Beach**

Charlotteville

**Man O'War Bay**

**5**

**4**

*Bird of Paradise Island*

*Pigeon Peak*

**6**

Speyside **3**

**7**

*Little Tobago*

*Bloody Bay*

**Parlatuvier**

Parlatuvier

Delaford

**King's Bay**

Roxborough

*Carapuse Bay*

N

*ATLANTIC OCEAN*

Mt. St. George

**2**

*gh*

0         4 miles

0         6 km

**KEY**

**1** Exploring Sites

**6** Hotels and Restaurants

Kariwak Village, **14**
Manta Lodge, **7**
Mt. Irvine Bay Hotel, **18**
Ocean Point, **13**
Plantation Beach Villas, **22**

Rex Turtle Beach Hotel, **21**
Richmond Great House, **10**

☎ FAX 809/624–1181. *53 rooms. Restaurant, bar, café, air-conditioning, pool, shops, meeting rooms, car rental. AE, DC, MC, V. EP, MAP.*

**$$**    ☎ **Kapok Hotel.** This well-run hotel, quiet and convenient to fine shop-
ping, is good value for the price. The rooms, done in grays and pinks,
are spacious and sunlit, with rattan furniture and Polynesian prints the
colors of highlighting markers. Front ones are best for the view over the
Savannah, and even better are the studios—with kitchenette—for the same
price as a room. Parents will appreciate the hotel's coin-operated laun-
dry and ironing room, and kids will enjoy the lively menagerie of birds,
fish, and monkeys that live by the pool. The hotel's Cafe Savanna was
recently sacrificed to a room expansion, but the Tiki Village (☞ Dining,
*below*) remains popular with locals. ⊠ *16–18 Cotton Hill, St. Clair, Port-
of-Spain,* ☎ *809/622–6441 or 800/344–1212, FAX 809/622–9677. 71
rooms, including 6 suites and 9 studios. Restaurant, air-conditioning, pool,
beauty salon, shops, business services. AE, DC, MC, V. EP.*

**$–$$**   ☎ **La Maison Rustique.** This little bed-and-breakfast in a gingerbread
house is a charmer, and it has a great location, near Queen's Park Sa-
vannah amid other wonderful Victorian homes. Rooms in the garden
cottage are the nicest, but all rooms are clean and serviceable. Some are
air-conditioned, and a few have private baths. The proprietor, Maureen
Chin-Asiong, is a hotel school graduate and lists the Wilton School of
Cake Decorating in Chicago among her credits. She not only serves good
breakfasts—popovers, croissants, quiche—but also whips up afternoon
tea, snacks, and picnic baskets. There's a five-night Carnival package
for $500. ⊠ *16 Rust St., St. Clair, Port-of-Spain,* ☎ FAX *809/622–1512.
7 rooms, 3 with bath. No credit cards. BP.*

**$–$$**   ☎ **Maracas Bay Hotel.** This newly built property sits on a locally pop-
★   ular stretch of beach strewn with palm trees. It's a half hour outside
Port of Spain and is the only hotel on the beach in Trinidad. Rooms
are simple and clean, with bright, white-painted wood walls, firm
double beds, and cool maroon tile floors. All have spectacular views
of the bay. In-house meals are well prepared and usually feature a local
catch from the nearby fishing village. Watercolors depicting Hindu festivals adorn the walls of the popular bar and lounge area where you
can relax after a hard day at the beach. There are some good rain-forest hikes nearby and you'll need a guide; the hotel can make the arrangements. ⊠ *Maracas Bay,* ☎ *809/669–1914, FAX 809/623–1444.
40 rooms. Dining room, lounge, air-conditioning. MC, V. EP, MAP.*

**$**    ☎ **Alicia's House.** The Govias managed to keep the family atmosphere
when they converted their home for guests, so all here is welcoming
and reassuring, if not fancy. The enormous, breezy lounge has squashy
sofas, round tables, cane chairs, a piano, and a tank of fish. Rooms
vary greatly in size and amenities; the large Admiral Rooney offers a
garden-view desk and a giant bathtub, while the little Back Room has
a private spiral staircase to the pool. Some of the furnishings, bed cov-
erings, and curtains have seen better days, but rates are very reasonable and include such extras as a hot tub and a water cooler by the
pool, private bathrooms, and phones in every room. Alicia's House is
a 10-minute walk from the Savannah. ⊠ *7 Coblentz Gardens, St.
Ann's, Port-of-Spain,* ☎ *809/623–2802 or 809/624–8651, FAX 809/622–
8560. 17 rooms. Dining room, lounge, air-conditioning, pool, hot
tub, laundry service. AE, MC, V. EP, CP, MAP.*

**$**    ☎ **Asa Wright Nature Centre.** If swimming in waterfall pools beside
★   vibrantly colored toucans, hawks, and iridescent humming birds is your
idea of a good time, this just might be your heaven. Built in 1908, it's
set in a lush rain forest (about 90 minutes east of Port-of-Spain) populated by nearly 200 species of birds. There are impressive views of
the verdant Arima Valley and the Northern Range from the veranda.
The elegant, comfortable lounge has mahogany floorboards, bookcases,

antiques, and ornithological memorabilia. The two original huge bedrooms are quite romantic, with fans turning slowly on tall ceilings, hardwood closets, and antique beds. All other rooms are in modern lodges near the house, simply outfitted with wood floors, motel-style furniture, and private covered terraces. You'll feel you're miles from anywhere, and, actually, you are, so you'll need the three meals a day and evening rum punch that are included in the rates. (For more information about the center, *see* Exploring, *below*.) ✉ *Box 4710, Arima, Trinidad,* ☎ *809/667–4655,* ℻ *809/273–6370. 24 rooms, 1 bungalow. Dining room, lounge, shop, airport shuttle. No credit cards. FAP.*

**$** ⊞ **Carnetta's House.** When Winston Borrell retired as director of tourism for Trinidad and Tobago, he and his wife, Carnetta, opened up their suburban two-story house to guests. One guest room is on the upper floor, the same level as the lounge and terrace dining room. The other four are on the ground floor, with the choice room, Le Flamboyant, opening onto the garden's patio. All rooms have a private bathroom with shower, telephone, radio, and TV. And, although there is air-conditioning, cool breezes usually do the trick. Unfortunately, the doors need to be shuttered at night for security reasons. Carnetta uses her garden-grown herbs in her cooking and prepares excellent dinners. Carnetta and Winston know what's happening in Trinidad and can make the necessary arrangements to help organize your evenings. ✉ *28 Scotland Terr., Andalusia, Maraval, Port-of-Spain,* ☎ *809/628–2732,* ℻ *809/628–7717. 5 rooms. Dining room, lounge, air-conditioning, laundry service, car rental, airport shuttle. AE, DC, MC, V. EP, BP, MAP.*

**$** ⊞ **Laguna Mar Lodge.** This oceanfront property is an excellent, economical
★ getaway for nature-lovers. With the rain forest all around, you can hike to waterfalls and linger in their inviting natural pools; there's also a friendly fishing village nearby. A wide, golden sandy beach, fringed with coconut palms and wild almond trees, is a two-minute walk away. The rooms are simple and clean, with private tile showers, locally made teak furnishings, nets over the beds (don't forget the bug spray), oscillating table fans, and wide-open balconies. The owner is German and so are many of the visitors to this natural hideaway. Fresh fish is common on a menu that features local cuisine and fruit grown on the property including bananas, oranges, mangos, and breadfruit. ✉ *Mile Marker 65, Paria Main Rd., Blanchisseuse,* ☎ *809/628–3731 or 809/628–8267,* ℻ *809/628–3737. 6 rooms. Bar, dining room. MC, V.*

**$** ⊞ **Monique's.** Mike and Monique Charbonné really *like* having guests,
★ as they have been proving for more than a decade. Rooms are sizable and spotless, and most are bright. Numbers 25 and 26 are enormous and can sleep up to six; they're darker than the other rooms, but each has a little sunken red-stone patio where you can soak up some sun. Breakfast and dinner are available in the parlorlike dining room. The airy, marble-floored lounge (with a TV) is a great place to hang out—with the hosts as often as not. Mike sometimes organizes a picnic to the couple's 100-acre plantation near Blanchisseuse. ✉ *114 Saddle Rd., Maraval, Port-of-Spain,* ☎ *809/628–3334 or 809/628–2351,* ℻ *809/622–3232. 26 rooms. Dining room, air-conditioning. AE. EP, MAP.*

## Dining

There's a distinctively Creole touch to T&T cuisine, but ask what Creole seasoning is and you'll hear a different answer from each person you ask. The herbs and spices used on the islands range from fresh bay leaves (bright green, not dried) to nutmegs from the trees and a variety of peppers. The cooking also uses a lot of guava, plantain, and local fish and meat. Asian, Indian, African, French, and Spanish influences, among others, can be tasted, often in a single meal. Indian food is a favorite: *Rotis* (East Indian sandwiches) are served as a fast food; a mélange of curried meat or fish and vegetables frequently makes an appearance; and a wide selection of *vindaloos* (spicy hot meat, vegetable, and seafood dishes) and poori can be had. Crab lovers will find large blue-backs curried, peppered, and served with tomatoes and used in callaloo soup (a national treasure made of green dasheen leaves mixed with okra, coconut milk, and crabmeat). Shark-and-bake is the sandwich of choice, made of lightly seasoned, fried shark meat.

In addition to excellent Creole fare, good Chinese food and European cuisines can now be had in Trinidad. Hotel restaurants, of course, cater to a less adventuresome market.

No Trinibagan dining experience can be complete, of course, without a rum punch with fresh fruit and the legendary Angostura Bitters, made by the same local company that produces the excellent Old Oak rum, but watch out for the fiendish sugar content. Light, refreshing Carib beer is the local lager; dark-beer aficionados can try Royal Extra Stout (R.E.). Local chocolate, found in supermarkets, is made in squares and often flavored with bay leaf and nutmeg.

## What to Wear

The restaurants of Trinidad and Tobago are informal: You won't find any jacket-and-tie requirements. Beachwear, however, is a little too casual for most places. A nice pair of shorts is apropos for lunch; for dinner, you'll probably feel most comfortable in a pair of slacks or a casual sundress.

| CATEGORY | COST* |
| --- | --- |
| $$$ | over $25 |
| $$ | $15–$25 |
| $ | under $15 |

*per person for a three-course meal, excluding drinks, service, and 15% tax*

$$$   ✕ **La Boucan.** Trinidadian dancer Geoffrey Holder painted the large mural of a social idyll in the Savannah that dominates one wall of this room at the Hilton. A more leisurely Trinidad is also reflected in the old-fashioned charm of silver service, uniformed waiters, soft lighting, pink tablecloths, and the serenade of a grand piano. The menu is international, including steaks, seafood grills, and other simple preparations, but you can also find such local specialties as callaloo soup, shrimp Creole, and West Indian chicken curry (these dishes are served mild unless you assure your waiter you want them spicy). Afternoon tea, served Wednesday through Friday from 4 to 6, is a treat. ⊠ *Trinidad Hilton, Lady Young Rd., Port-of-Spain,* ☎ *809/624–3211. AE, DC, MC, V.*

$$–$$$   ✕ **Solimar.** In a series of dimly lit, plant-filled eating areas, chef Joe Brown offers a menu that tries to travel the world in one meal: You might enjoy shrimp tempura, Irish smoked salmon, Hawaiian barbecued mahimahi, Greek salad, linguine Alfredo, or Zwiebel schnitzel, all the while listening to a live guitarist gently strum 1970s classics. Best bets are the day's specials—seafood mixed grill, perhaps, followed by a light and fluffy hot chocolate soufflé with mango ice cream. Solimar is popular with expat types and tends toward careful casualness. ⊠ *6 Nook Ave., St. Ann's,* ☎ *809/624–6267. AE, DC, MC, V.*

$$   ✕ **La Fantasie.** The Hotel Normandie's restaurant is done up in lovely Caribbean art deco, the clean lines of the design complemented by deep peach, mauve, and other vibrant island colors. La Fantasie pioneered *cuisine nouvelle créole,* and many of the dishes are lighter versions of local fare made with a French flair. Seafood is the best bet—grilled snapper stuffed with shrimp in tart tomato sauce, perhaps. The air-conditioning is blissfully glacial, but on cooler nights it's nice to dine outside

on the terrace, gazing at the moon through the palms. ⊠ *Hotel Normandie, 10 Nook Ave., St. Ann's, Port-of-Spain,* ☎ *809/624–1181. AE, DC, MC, V.*

**$$ ✕ Tiki Village.** Cosmopolitan Port-of-Spainers are as passionate about their Asian food as New Yorkers and San Franciscans are. Everyone touts their favorite, but this capacious eatery, a serious (nonkitsch) version of Trader Vic's, is the most reliable. It's high under the rafters atop the Kapok Hotel, sun-lit during the day and affording good views of an electrified Trinidad at night. Fine Asian food is served, including, on weekends and public holidays, a very popular dim sum, where dishes such as pepper squid and tofu stuffed with fish are ordered in tasting-size portions. ⊠ *Kapok Hotel, 16–18 Cotton Hill, St. Clair,* ☎ *809/622–6441. AE, DC, MC, V.*

**$$ ✕ Veni Mange.** The best lunches in town are served upstairs in a tra-
★ ditional West Indian house that has been renovated for dining. Paintings by local artists hang on the walls. Credit Allyson Hennessy—a Cordon Bleu–trained cook who has become a celebrity of sorts because of a TV talk show she hosts—and her friendly and flamboyant sister-partner, Rosemary Hezekiah. The creative Creole menu changes daily; starters might include callaloo soup, and for a main course you could find stewed oxtail with banana fritters and stewed lentils. There's always a vegetarian entrée option, too. Homemade desserts are divine. It's a popular place; dinner reservations are advised. ⊠ *64A Ariapita Ave., Woodbrook,* ☎ *809/624–4597. AE, MC, V. No dinner Thurs.–Tues.*

**$–$$ ✕ Rafters.** Behind a stone facade with a green tin awning and wooden doors stands a pub that has become an urban institution. Once it was a rum shop; currently it's a bar and a restaurant. The pub is the center of activity, especially Friday night. In late afternoons the place begins to swell with Port-of-Spainers ordering from the tasty selection of burgers, barbecues, and burritos. The Seafood Sampler platter (seasonal fin and shellfish, including shrimp and conch) is served with baked potato and tartar sauce for about $8 (TT$45). In the evening an unexpectedly romantic candlelit restaurant with a mostly Continental menu opens in another part of the delightful old building. ⊠ *6A Warner St., Port-of-Spain,* ☎ *809/628–9258. AE, DC, MC, V.*

**$ ✕ Moonsoon.** If you're looking for Trinidad fast food, this take-out place has some of the best roti in town. Similar to a burrito, this east Indian sandwich contains your choice of fillings, including goat, conch, chicken, and delicious curries made with pumpkin, potato, and beans. It's a perfect snack to take to the beach or on your tour around the island. The price is right, too. ⊠ *Corner of Tragarete Rd. and Picton St., Newtown,* ☎ *809/628–7684. No credit cards.*

**$ ✕ Sing Ho.** Venture away from the main drag and you'll find this authentic Chinese restaurant with good food and prices that will make you smile. The main room's decor has red carpeting, white linen tablecloths, and fish tanks filled with large, lazy goldfish; the walls are adorned with gold-gilded Chinese art. There are several private rooms where a screen separates you from an otherwise noisy atmosphere. Besides the typical selections like egg rolls, wonton soup, sesame chicken, and shrimp foo young, there are also some island-inspired dishes, such as shark-fin soup and shredded seafood with bean cake. ⊠ *Long Circular Mall, Level 3, Port-of-Spain,* ☎ *809/628–2077. MC, V.*

**$ ✕ Wazo Deyzeel.** "Oiseaux des îles" (or, "Island Birds")—get it?—is adored by all for its setting, high up in the hills of St. Ann, with Port-of-Spain spread out below; its live bands and dancing on weekends; its friendliness; and its prizewinning cocktails (the cucumber-lime-rum-syrup Wazo Combo is essential), as well as for its food. The Thursday-night all-you-can-eat Caribbean buffet might include grouper, flying fish, red snapper, macaroni pie, *cou-cou* (cornmeal and coconut dumplings), *bhajia* (East Indian spinach fritters), and savory pumpkin pie, and at about $10 it is probably the best bargain in the city. Friday, Saturday, and Sunday nights you could go for a seafood platter or a beef pot roast, all cooked by three Jamaican ladies. Candy-color director's chairs; white walls; a big, open-air terrace for admiring the view; wining (a naughty dance style); and liming (hanging out) set the tone. ✉ *Carib Way, 23 Sydenham Ave., St. Ann's,* ☎ *809/623–0115. MC, V. Closed Mon.–Wed.*

# Beaches

Although Trinidad is not the beach destination Tobago is, it has its share of fine shoreline, spread out along the North Coast Road within an hour's drive of Port-of-Spain. The drive to the beaches of the east coast takes several hours. To get there you must take the detour road to Arima, but "goin' behind God's back," as the Trinis say, rewards the persistent traveler with gorgeous vistas and secluded beaches.

**Balandra Bay,** sheltered by a rocky outcropping, is popular among bodysurfers.

**Blanchisseuse Bay,** on the North Coast Road, is a narrow, palm-fringed beach. Facilities are nonexistent, but the beach is ideal for a romantic picnic. You can haggle with local fishermen to take you out in their boats to explore the coast.

**Las Cuevas Bay,** on the North Coast Road, is a narrow, picturesque strip of sand named for the series of partially submerged and explorable caves that ring the beach. A food stand offers tasty snacks, and vendors hawk fresh fruit across the road. There are basic changing and toilet facilities. It's less crowded here than at nearby Maracas Bay (☞ *below*), and seemingly serene, although, as at Maracas, the current can be treacherous.

**Manzanilla Beach** has picnic facilities and a postcard-pretty view of the Atlantic, though its water is occasionally muddied by the Orinoco River, which flows in from South America. The road here, nicknamed the Cocal, is lined with stately palms whose fronds vault like the arches at Chartres. This is where many well-heeled Trinis have vacation homes.

**Maracas Bay** is a long stretch of sand with a cove and a fishing village at one end. It's *the* local favorite, so it can get crowded on weekends. Watch out for the *very* strong current. Parking sites are ample, and there are snack bars and rest-room facilities. Try a shark-and-bake (a deep-fried shark sandwich, served in a pita-type bread with hot sauce and cilantro-garlic salsa) from one of the huts ranged along the road at Maracas. Patsy's is considered the best. Wash it down with grenadillo (like a giant passion fruit) juice, if it's available, from the stand on Patsy's right.

**Marianne Beach** is the quietest and prettiest of all, with a natural freshwater lagoon at the east end. Pay Vincent James TT$3 to park on his land; you can also rent the three-room first floor of the house you see for about $13—it's very basic (☎ 809/674–7145 after 1 PM).

**Salibea Bay,** just past Galera Point, which juts toward Tobago, is a gentle beach with shallows and plenty of shade—perfect for swimming. Snack vendors abound in the vicinity.

**Tyrico Bay** is a small beach lively with surfers who flock here to enjoy the excellent surfing. The strong undertow may be too much for some swimmers.

# Carnival

Trinidad always seems to be either anticipating, celebrating, or recovering from a festival. Visitors are welcome to these events, and they're a great way to explore the rich cultural traditions. Carnival is the largest event and occurs each year between February and early March. Trinidad's version of the pre-Lenten bacchanal is reputedly the oldest in the Western Hemisphere; there are festivities all over the country, but the most lavish is in Port-of-Spain. Not as overwhelming as its rival in Rio or as debauched as Mardi Gras in New Orleans, Trinidad's Carnival has the warmth and character of a massive family reunion.

Carnival is about extravagant costumes. Colorfully attired troupes—called *mas*—that sometimes number in the thousands march to the beat set by the steel bands. You can visit the various mas "camps" around the city where these elaborate getups are put together—the addresses are listed in the newspapers—and perhaps join one that strikes your fancy. Fees run anywhere from $35 to $100; you get to keep the costume. Children can also parade in a kiddie carnival that takes place on Saturday morning a few days before the real thing.

Carnival is also a showcase for performers of calypso, music that mixes dance rhythms with social commentary, sung by characters with such evocative names as Shadow, the Mighty Sparrow, and Black Stalin. As Carnival approaches, many of these singers perform nightly in calypso tents scattered around the city. You can also visit the pan yards of Port-of-Spain, where steel orchestras, such as the Renegades, Desperadoes, Catelli All-Stars, Invaders, and Phase II, rehearse their calypso arrangements. Most can be heard during the fall and winter seasons.

Carnival officially lasts only two days, from J'ouvert (sunrise) on Monday to midnight the following day. If you're planning to go, it's a good idea to arrive in Trinidad a week or two early to enjoy the preliminary events. For several nights before Carnival, costume makers display their talents, and the steel bands and calypso singers perform in competitions in the grandstands of the old racetrack in Queen's Park. Here the Calypso Monarch was crowned until 1993, when the Dimanche Gras festivities moved to the National Stadium in the Cruise Ship Complex at the Port. At J'ouvert, the city starts filling with metal-frame carts carrying steel bands, flatbed trucks hauling sound systems, and thousands of revelers who squeeze into the narrow streets. Finally, at the stroke of midnight on "Mas Tuesday," Port-of-Spain's exhausted merrymakers go to bed. The next day everybody's back to business.

# Outdoor Activities and Sports

## Bird-Watching

Trinidad and Tobago ranks among the top 10 countries in the world in terms of the number of species of birds per square mile—more than 600 altogether, many living within pristine rain forests, lowlands and savannahs, and fresh- and saltwater swamps. If you're lucky, you might spot the collared trogon, blue-backed manakin, or rare white-tailed Sabrewing hummingbird. Restaurants often hang feeders outside their porches, as much to keep the birds away from your food as to provide a chance for observation.

Bird-watchers can fill up their books with notes on the variety of species to be found in Trinidad at the **Asa Wright Nature Centre** and the **Caroni Bird Sanctuary** (☞ Exploring, *below*), as well as the **Pointe-à-Pierre Wild Fowl Trust** (✉ 42 Sandown Rd., Point Cumana, ☎ 809/637–5145), located on 26 acres within the unlikely confines of a petrochemical complex; you must call in advance for a reservation at Pointe-à-Pierre. **Winston Nanan** (☎ 809/645–1305) runs highly recommended bird-watching tours to nearby Guayana and Venezuela.

### Deep-Sea Fishing

The islands off the northwest coast of Trinidad offer excellent waters for deep-sea fishing; the ocean here was a favorite angling spot of Franklin D. Roosevelt. Members of the **Trinidad and Tobago Yacht Club** (✉ Bayshore, ☎ 809/637–4260) may be willing to arrange a tour.

### Golf

The best golf course in Trinidad is the 18-hole **St. Andrew's Golf Club** (✉ Moka, Maraval, ☎ 809/629–2314), just outside Port-of-Spain.

### Tennis

The following private tennis courts allow nonmembers or nonresidents to play: the **Trinidad Hilton** (☎ 809/624–3211), the **Trinidad Country Club** (✉ Long Circular Rd., Maraval, ☎ 809/622–3470), and the **Tranquility Square Lawn Tennis Club** (✉ Victoria Ave., Port-of-Spain, ☎ 809/625–4182).

## Shopping

Good buys on the islands include such duty-free items as Angostura Bitters and Old Oak or Vat 19 rum, all widely available throughout the country.

### Duty Free

**Stecher's** (✉ Trinidad Hilton, ☎ 809/624–3322; ✉ Long Circular Mall, St. James, ☎ 809/622–0017) is a familiar name for those seeking to avoid taxes on fine perfumes, electronics, and jewelry; you can arrange to have your purchases delivered to the airport the day of your departure. **Y. de Lima** (✉ High St., ☎ 809/655–8872; ✉ West Mall, Western Main Rd., St. James, ☎ 809/622–7050) sells traditional luxury duty-free items.

### Fabric

Thanks in large part to Carnival costumery, there's no shortage of fabric shops on the islands. The best bargains for Asian and East Indian silks and cottons can be found in downtown Port-of-Spain, on **Frederick Street** and around **Independence Square**.

### Local Crafts

The tourism office can provide an extensive list of local artisans who specialize in everything from straw and cane work to miniature steel pans.

**Bonga!** (✉ Ellerslie Plaza, Cotton Hill, behind Kapok Hotel, ☎ 809/624–8819) stocks smart T-shirts, carryalls, shorts, and bathing suits. **Poui Boutique** (✉ Ellerslie Plaza, Cotton Hill, behind Kapok Hotel, ☎ 809/622–5597) has stylish hand-done wax batik clothing and Ajoupa ware, an attractive local terra-cotta pottery. **Craft Boutique** (✉ Corner of Adam Smith Sq. S and Murray St., Woodbrook, ☎ 809/627–2736) is in Monica Monceaux's house, a delight in gingerbread wood tracery. Almost every inch of the house is utilized by Monica and her craftspeople, who make carnival and folk dolls, Christmas ornaments (even those for the Hilton tree), crocheted picture frames, preserves, and dozens of other items in merry disarray. **The Market** (✉ Nook Ave., adjoining Hotel Normandie, ☎ 809/624–1181) is a collection of shops that specialize in indigenous fashions, crafts, jewelry, basketwork, and ceramics. Among them, the **Craft Shop** (☎ 809/623–0377) carries goods more imaginative than its name, including beautiful metallic wall sconces and mirrors.

### Malls

**Ellerslie Plaza** (✉ Cotton Hill, behind Kapok Hotel, no phone) is an attractive outdoor mall well worth browsing through. You can drop by for a snack at the Patisserie or lunch at the stylish Gourmet Club. A fine design clothing shop, **Meiling** (☎ 809/628–6205), features cottons in ecru or white and smart little girls' dresses with shirred tops. **Long Circular Mall** (✉ Long Circular Rd., St. James, ☎ 809/622–4925) has upscale boutiques that will keep you occupied window-shopping. Check out the handcrafted jewelry at the **Signature Collection** (☎ 809/622–9945), with its pricey but one-of-a-kind pieces. **Excellent City Centre** (✉ Downtown Port-of-Spain, off Brian Lara Promenade) is set in an old-style oasis under the lantern roofs of three of Port-of-Spain's oldest commercial buildings. Look for cleverly designed keepsakes, trendy cotton garments, and original artwork. The upstairs food court overlooks bustling Frederick Street.

### Records

**Rhyner's Record Shop** (✉ 54 Prince St., ☎ 809/623–5673; ✉ Piarco International Airport, ☎ 809/669–3064) is where to go for the best selection of calypso and soca music—and it's duty free.

## Nightlife and the Arts

When Nobel prize–winning poet Derek Walcott returns home to Trinidad, he often gives readings or gets involved in one of the productions of the thriving local theater. There are several excellent theaters in Port-of-Spain. Consult local newspapers for listings.

Trinidadian culture doesn't end with music, but it definitely begins with it. Although both calypso and steel bands are best displayed during Carnival, the steel bands play at clubs, dances, and fêtes throughout the year. There's no lack of nightlife in Port-of-Spain, and spontaneity plays a big role—look for the handwritten signs announcing the "pan yard" where the next informal gathering of steel drum bands is going to be. A type of music that's popular right now is "sweet Parang," a mixture of Spanish patois and calypso sung to tunes played on a string instrument much like a mandolin.

**Blue Iguana** (✉ Main street, Chaguanas, no phone) is the place to go for lively late-night action. It's about 20 minutes west of town in Chaguanas, so get a party together from your hotel and hire a cab. It opens at 10 PM, Wednesday through Sunday. **Cricket Wicket** (✉ 149 Tragarete Rd., ☎ 809/622–1808), a popular watering hole with a cupola-shape bar in the center, is a fine place to hear top bands, dance, or just sit and enjoy the nocturnal scenery. **Mas Camp Pub** (✉ Corner of Ariapata Ave. and French St., Woodbrook, ☎ 809/623–3745) is Port-of-Spain's most comfortable and dependable nightspot. Along with a bar and an ample stage where a DJ or live band reigns, there's also an open-air patio. The kitchen dishes up hearty, reasonably priced Creole lunches, and if one of the live bands strikes your fancy, chances are you can buy a cassette of its music here. **Moon over Bourbon Street** (✉ Southern Landing, Westmall, Westmoorings, ☎ 809/637–3448) has comedy or music most nights, plus long, long happy hours. **Pelican** (✉ 2–4 Coblentz Ave., St. Ann's, ☎ 809/627–7486), an English-style pub, gets increasingly frenetic as the week closes, with a singles-bar atmosphere. **Smokey & Bunty** (✉ Western Main Rd. and Dengue St., St. James, no phone) is where to collect gossip over a beer. It calls itself a sports bar but is really just the essential liming corner. **Wazo Deyzeel** (✉ 23 Sydenham Ave., St. Ann's, ☎ 809/623–0115) is the current fave with a mixed age group for its music, dancing, drinking, views, and great food cooked by three Jamaican ladies. It's closed Monday–Wednesday.

# Exploring Trinidad

The intensely urban atmosphere of Port-of-Spain belies the tropical beauty of the countryside surrounding it. It is truly stunning, but you will need a car, and three to eight hours (if you stop at any of the northern beaches; ☞ Beaches, *above*) to see all there is to see. Begin by circling the Savannah—seemingly obligatory to get almost anywhere around here—to Saddle Road, in the residential district of Maraval. After a few miles the road begins to narrow and curve sharply as it climbs into the Northern Range and its undulating hills of lush, junglelike foliage. Stop at the Lookout on North Coast Road, and have Keith Davis sing you a hilarious calypso, complete with any biographical details you give him. (He's not allowed to ask, but a few T&T dollars are appreciated—and deserved.) From the town of Blanchisseuse en route to the Asa Wright Nature Centre, the road winds through canyons of moist, verdant foliage, towering palms, mossy grottoes, and "big bamboo"—so large that a calypso song was written about it. In this tropical rain forest, keep an eye out for vultures, parakeets, hummingbirds, toucans, and, if you're lucky, maybe red-bellied, yellow-and-blue macaws.

*Numbers in the margin correspond to points of interest on the Trinidad map.*

## Port-of-Spain

❶ Be sure to bring along lots of film—the renewed charms of **Port-of-Spain** are well worth photographing. Most sightseeing tours begin at the port. If you're planning to explore by foot, which will take two to four hours, start early in the day; by mid-afternoon the port area can be hot and as packed as Calcutta. You'll want to end up on a bench in the Queen's Park Savannah, sipping a cool coconut water bought from one of the vendors operating out of a flatbed truck. For about 50¢, he'll lop the top off a green coconut with a deft swing of the machete and, when you've finished drinking, lop again, making a bowl and spoon of coconut shell for you to eat the young pulp—the texture of a boiled egg white. According to Trinis, "It'll cure anyt'ing dat ail ya, mon."

SIGHTS TO SEE

🕓 **Emperor Valley Zoo and the Botanical Gardens.** The cultivated expanse of parkland just north of the Savannah is the site of the president's and prime minister's official residences. A meticulous lattice of walkways and local flora, the parkland was first laid out in 1820 for Governor Woodford and is a model of what a tropical garden should be. In the midst of this serene wonderland is the zoo, leisurely apportioned on 8 acres and largely featuring birds and animals of the region—from the brilliantly plumed scarlet ibis to slithering anacondas and pythons; wild parrots breed in the area and can be seen (and heard) in the surrounding foliage. The zoo draws a quarter of a million visitors a year and more than half of them are children, so admission is priced accordingly—a mere TT$ 2 for under-12s. ✉ *Botanical Gardens, Port-of-Spain,* ☎ *809/622–3530.* ☞ *TT$4.* ☉ *Daily 9:30–6.*

**Frederick Street.** Port-of-Spain's main shopping drag, starting north from the midpoint of Independence Square, is a market street of scents—corn roasting and Indian spices—and crowded shops.

**Independence Square.** Across Wrightson Road from the south side of King's Wharf, this is not a square at all: It's a wide, dusty thoroughfare crammed with pedestrians, car traffic, taxi stands, and peddlers of everything from shoes to coconuts—not a pleasant walk for lone females. Flanked by government buildings and the familiar twin towers of the Financial Complex (familiar because it adorns one side of all T&T dollar bills), the square is gloriously chaotic, loud, and confusing. On the south side of Independence Square, the **Cruise Ship Complex,** full of duty-free shops, forms an enclave of international anonymity with the Holiday Inn. On the eastern end of the square is the **Cathedral of the Immaculate Conception,** built by the sea in 1832, but subsequent land-fill around the port gave it an inland location. The imposing Roman Catholic structure is made out of stone from nearby Laventille.

**King's Wharf.** Though it is no longer as frenetic as it was during the oil boom of the 1970s, the town's main dock entertains a steady pa-rade of cruise and cargo ships, a reminder that the city started from this strategic harbor. It's on Wrightson Road, the main street along the water on the southwest side of town.

**Magnificent Seven.** A series of astonishing buildings constructed in a va-riety of 19th-century styles flanks the western side of the Savannah. No-table among them are **Killarney,** patterned (loosely) after Balmoral Castle in Scotland, with an Italian-marble gallery surrounding the ground floor; **Whitehall,** constructed in the style of a Venetian palace by a cacao-plan-tation magnate and currently the office of the prime minister; **Roomor,** a flamboyantly Baroque colonial-period house with a preponderance of towers, pinnacles, and wrought-iron trim that suggests an elaborate French pastry; and the **Queen's Royal College,** in German Renaissance style, with a prominent tower clock that chimes on the hour.

**National Museum and Art Gallery.** It's worth heading over to the south-east corner of the Savannah, if only to see the Carnival exhibits, the Amerindian collection and historical re-creations, and the fine 19th-cen-tury paintings of Trinidadian artist Cazabon. ⊠ *117 Upper Frederick St.,* ☎ *809/623–5941 or 809/624–6477.* 🎟 *Free.* ⊙ *Tues.–Sat. 10–6.*

**Queen's Park Savannah.** If the downtown port area is the pulse of Port-of-Spain, the great green expanse roughly bounded by Maraval Road, Queen's Park West, Charlotte Street, and Saddle Road is the city's soul. Its 2-mi circumference is a popular jogger's track. On the west side of the Savannah, you'll see a garden of architectural delights: the elegant lantern-roof **George Brown House,** what remains of the **Old Queen's Park Hotel,** and the Magnificent Seven (☞ *above*). The **racetrack** at the southern end of the Savannah is no longer a venue for horse racing, but it is still the setting for music and costume competitions during Carni-val and, when not jammed with calypso performers, tends toward qui-etude. The northern end of the Savannah is devoted to plants. A rock garden, known as the **Hollow,** and a fishpond add to the rusticity.

NEED A BREAK?

Two blocks south of the Savannah, and one block west to Rust Street, stop for tea and pastries (or even an American breakfast) at **La Maison Rustique** (☎ 809/622–1512), a pretty white house set amid tropical gardens. It's also a pleasant bed-and-breakfast.

**Water Park.** The water park at the Valley Vue Hotel is open to nonguests and has the biggest, wettest slides in the West Indies—three 400-ft chutes leading to a shallow pool. ⊠ *Ariapita Rd., St. Ann's,* ☎ *809/624–0940.* 🎟 *TT$20.* ⊙ *Daily 10–6.*

**Woodford Square.** At Prince and Frederick streets, the square has served as the site of political meetings, speeches, public protests, and occasional violence. It's dominated by the magnificent **Red House,** a Renaissance-style building that takes up an entire city block. Trinidad's House of Parliament takes its name from a paint job done in antici-pation of Queen Victoria's Diamond Jubilee in 1897. The original Red House was burned to the ground in a 1903 riot, and the present struc-ture was built four years later. The chambers are open to the public.

The view of the south side of the square is framed by the Gothic spires of **Trinity,** the city's Anglican cathedral, consecrated in 1823; its mahogany-beam roof is modeled after that of Westminster Hall in London. On the north is the impressive **public library** building, the **Hall of Justice** and **City Hall.**

## Out on the Island

**2** **Asa Wright Nature Centre.** Its nearly 500 acres are covered with plants, trees, and multihued flowers, and the surrounding acreage is a-twitter with more than 170 species of birds, from the gorgeous blue-green motmot to the rare, nocturnal oilbird. If you stay for two nights or more (☞ Lodging, *above*), the oilbirds' breeding grounds in Dunston Cave are included among the sights along the center's guided hiking trails. Those who don't want to hike can relax on the veranda of the inn and watch the diversity of birds that swoop about the porch feeders—an armchair bird-watcher's nirvana. This stunning plantation house looks out to the Arima valley, as lush and untouched as the earth offers. Even if you're not staying over, book ahead for lunch (TT$37.50) on Monday through Saturday or for a noontime Sunday buffet (TT$62.50). ⊠ *90 mins from Port-of-Spain; look for fork in road about ½ hr outside town of Blanchisseuse; take the right, signposted to Arima, and drive another ½ hr on this road (and a very sharp right at green hut),* ☎ *809/667–4655.* 🎟 *$6.* ☉ *Daily 9–5. Guided tours at 10:30 and 1:30; reservations essential.*

**4** **Caroni Bird Sanctuary.** This large swamp with mazelike waterways is bordered by mangrove trees, some plumed with huge termite nests. In the middle of the sanctuary are several islets that are home to Trinidad's national bird, the scarlet ibis. Just before sunset the ibis arrive by the thousands, their richly colored feathers brilliant in the gathering dusk, and, as more flocks alight, they turn their little tufts of land into bright Christmas trees. It's not something you see every day. Bring a sweater and insect repellent for your return trip.

Across from the sanctuary's parking lot sits a sleepy canal with several boats and guides for hire; the smaller boats are best. The fee is usually about $6–$15. The only official tour operator is Winston Nanan (☞ Guided Tours *in* Trinidad and Tobago A to Z, *below*); phone or write him in advance for reservations. ⊠ *½ hr from Port-of-Spain; take Churchill Roosevelt Hwy. east to Uriah Butler south; turn right and in about 2 mins, after passing Caroni River Bridge, follow sign for sanctuary,* ☎ *809/645–1305.* 🎟 *Free.*

**3** **Lopinot Complex.** It's said that the ghost of the French count Charles Joseph de Lopinot prowls his former home on stormy nights. Lopinot came to Trinidad in 1800 and chose this magnificent site to plant cocoa. His restored estate house has been turned into a museum; a guide is available from 10 to 6. This is one of the main centers for Parang, a beautiful string-based folk music, which has become Trinidad's equivalent of Christmas carols. ⊠ *Take Eastern Main Rd. from Port-of-Spain to Arouca; look for sign that points north, no phone.* 🎟 *Free.* ☉ *Daily 6–6.*

# TOBAGO

## Lodging

On Tobago, there are a few modest lodgings in the towns, but the trend is toward seaside resorts, many of them appealingly low-key. If you're staying on the east side of Tobago, accommodations with meal plans are almost essential because of the dearth of restaurants.

For bed-and-breakfast accommodations contact the **Trinidad and Tobago Bed and Breakfast Co-operative Society** (✉ Box 3231, Diego Martin, ☎ FAX 809/627–2337) or the **Tobago Bed and Breakfast Association** (✉ c/o Federal Villa, 1-3 Crooks River, Scarborough, ☎ 809/639–3926, FAX 809/639–3566).

For price information on hotels, *see* the price chart *in* the Lodging section of Trinidad, *above*.

**$$$$** 🏨 **Arnos Vale Hotel.** It's always been the most romantic spot on Tobago. The sprawling Mediterranean design encompasses lush Tobagonian horticulture spread across 400 acres on the northeast coast of Tobago. The hotel was renovating the rooms at press time. In any event, they'll remain in their wonderful location, in white stucco cottages set on a hill that descends, through a series of winding paths, to a secluded beach, pool, and bar. The elegant hilltop restaurant, with antique pieces, iron-lattice tables, a chandelier, and a hand-painted piano, has a crescent-shape patio that offers a sweeping view of the sea. The hotel once leased half its room to Italian tour groups. Although that is no longer the case, the cuisine retains its wonderful Italian flare. ✉ *Arnos Vale, Box 208, Scarborough,* ☎ *809/639–2881,* FAX *809/639–4629. 35 rooms, 3 suites. Restaurant, bar, air-conditioning, pool, 2 tennis courts, beach, dive shop, snorkeling, shop, dance club. AE, DC, MC, V. EP.*

**$$$$** 🏨 **Coco Reef Resort.** Service and luxury are the twin pillars of this newer, swank resort. Elements of Caribbean, colonial, and Mediterranean architecture blend in an abundance of arches, tiles, and fretwork flourishes; harsh angles have been eliminated to create a soothing space. The room decor makes use of lots of cool tiles, too, along with pretty wall stencils and hand-crafted wicker furniture. Coco Reef is well placed, near Pigeon Point and Store Bay, and has its own small beach, Coco Bay. With its concierge, social director, water sports, and arcade with tony boutiques, this place attracts an active international set who are used to being pampered. ✉ *Box 434, Scarborough,* ☎ *809/639–8571 or 800/221–1294,* FAX *809/639–8574 or 305/639–2717 for reservations. 96 rooms, 39 suites. 2 restaurants, 2 bars, air-conditioning, pool, beauty salon, spa, 2 tennis courts, health club, baby-sitting, car rental. AE, D, DC, MC, V. CP, MAP.*

**$$$$** 🏨 **Grafton Beach Resort.** If any hotel has the action on Tobago, it's
★ the Grafton. Yet it's stretched out languidly along the shore under the tall palms, and so it's possible, with sea-view rooms, to feel away from it all. This sparkling complex has the most international ambience of any Tobago hotel, from the huge lobby-bar-restaurant-pool area to the top-class in-room facilities. Rooms are furnished with solid teak pieces and have cool terra-cotta-tile floors. The Neptune seafood restaurant and the bar, where local folk shows and bands perform nightly, are perched, cruise-liner-style, above and around the bigger-than-average pool, with the Ocean View restaurant (☞ *Dining, below*) to one side. A walkway leads directly to a fine beach, with a bar. You can learn to scuba, play squash, work out in the fitness room, and go canoeing, sailing, windsurfing, or surfing—all inclusive in the rates. ✉ *Black Rock, Tobago,* ☎ *809/639–0191,* FAX *809/639–0030. 99 rooms, 2 suites. 2 restaurants, 3 bars, air-conditioning, pool, sauna, exercise room, squash, beach, scuba training, windsurfing, boating, dance club, shops. AE, DC, MC, V. EP, MAP.*

**$$$$** 🏨 **Mt. Irvine Bay Hotel.** The advantage of this low-key hotel is golf—on the 18-hole, par-72, 127-acre International Championship course—for which guests get special rates. The main-house bedrooms aren't so special, although all amenities are on tap. If you're looking for romance, one of the 51 cottages, set in an arc around the main building and offering private patios, is worth the extra cost. A 17th-century mill is the focal point of the main restaurant, and there are two more restaurants besides—a dressy French one, Le Beau Rivage, and the Jacaranda. You can swim up to the bar at the largest of the island's hotel pools, play tennis on two floodlit courts, and take the private trail across the road to the beach, where there's another bar. The grounds are lovely and the golf is great—it's too bad the service is not always up to par. ⊠ *Mt. Irvine Bay, Box 222, Tobago,* ☎ *809/639–8871,* FAX *809/639–8800 or 800/742–4276. 107 rooms, 5 suites, 51 cottages. 3 restaurants, 2 bars, air-conditioning, pool, beauty parlor, sauna, spa, 18-hole golf course, 2 tennis courts, shops, convention center. AE, DC, MC, V. EP, CP, MAP.*

$$$$  🏨 **Plantation Beach Villas.** Nestled on a hillside above a palm-fringed beach and right next door to a bird sanctuary, these lovely pink-and-white villas are comfortably furnished in plantation style—four-poster beds, rocking chairs, louvre doors, and lots of West Indian fretwork. If you're traveling with a group or a large family, the price is quite reasonable: Each two-story villa has three bedrooms (one air-conditioned, two with ceiling fans) and three baths, as well as a teak veranda with a view of the sea. Cleaning service and linens are included, a cook can be provided on request, and baby-sitting is available. ⊠ *Stonehaven Bay, Blackrock (write to Box 1020, Port-of-Spain, Trinidad),* ☎ FAX *809/639–0455; 800/742–4276 for reservations. 6 villas. Bar, air-conditioning, kitchens, pool, laundry services. MC, V.*

$$$  🏨 **Blue Waters Inn.** The inn is set amid 46 acres of greenery, including
★  massive gnarled beach trees that seem to hold up the complex. A good 90-minute drive from Scarborough and up a bumpy driveway brings you to this beach hotel and its villas on the northeast Atlantic coast, with Little Tobago and Bird of Paradise island across Bateaux Bay. Rooms are fairly standard, in pleasant beach-motel mode, but you're guaranteed the sounds of waves all night. The bungalows have one or two bedrooms, living room, and kitchen. There are only small stores in the area; if you don't want to shop in Scarborough before you set out, you can fax ahead to request the provisions you'd like your room stocked with. But the freshest fish are to be had daily at the restaurant, and the lively bar will keep you occupied with its array of exotic drinks. This is an ideal spot for divers, bird-watchers, and beach loungers alike. ⊠ *Bateaux Bay, Speyside, Tobago,* ☎ *809/660–4341; 800/742–4276 for reservations;* FAX *809/660–5195. 31 rooms, 4 apartments, 3 bungalows. Restaurant, bar, tennis court, beach, dive instruction, windsurfing, boating, car rental. AE, MC, V. EP, CP, MAP, FAP.*

$$$  🏨 **Rex Turtle Beach Hotel.** If you're taking the kids, this may be your
★  ideal hotel: There's baby-sitting and many planned activities for children (on holidays they go all out to entertain the little ones, with hundreds of little lanterns for a Hindu festival and lights climbing way up the skyscraper palm trees at Christmas). Although it was built in 1971, this sprawling beachfront property is very well maintained. Rooms are attractive, with typical Tobagonian teak ceilings, wooden louvre doors, and brightly colored bedspreads; all have garden and ocean views. The family annex room is an especially good deal, offering a small extra bedroom for $21 more. Turtle Beach's popularity is not hard to understand: The relaxed atmosphere, evening entertainment, array of complimentary water sports, and lovely grounds are all appealing. As the name suggests, turtles use this beach to lay their eggs from February through June; you can request a wake-up call (perhaps at 2 or 3 AM) if you want to watch. ⊠ *Great Courland Bay (write to Box 201, Scarborough, Tobago),* ☎ *809/639–2851; 305/471–6170 for U.S. reservations;* FAX *809/639–1495. 125 rooms. Restaurant, 2 bars, coffee shop, pool, 2 tennis courts, volleyball, water sports, bicycles, shop. AE, DC, MC, V. EP, MAP.*

**$$**   **★**   🏠 **Kariwak Village.** There are many return guests to Allan and Cynthia Clovis's charming and reasonably priced cabana village. There is a peaceful feel to this property, reflected in the chemical-free, all-natural cuisine (vegetarians will love this place) and the weekly yoga classes held in an outdoor conference area that has a large thatched roof and a gleaming teak floor. Room renovations and new cabanas were under way at press time, as was a Jacuzzi. The relaxing lobby and bar area are made of bamboo, raw teak, and coral stone. In a bamboo pavilion is the highly respected restaurant (☞ Kariwak Village *in* Dining, *below*). Lush flora makes a fairly small site seem more spacious, and an herb-and-vegetable garden out back, which furnishes Cynthia's kitchen with ingredients, provides a place for a stroll. Great rum punches and local bands playing on weekends make this a favored liming spot. The beach is only a 10-minute walk, and it's very near the airport, Store Bay, and Pigeon Point. ✉ *Crown Point, Tobago (write to Box 27, Scarborough, Tobago),* ☎ *809/639–8442,* 🖷 *809/639– 8441. 24 rooms. Restaurant, bar, air-conditioning, pool. AE, DC, MC, V. EP, MAP.*

**$$**   🏠 **Richmond Great House.** Dating back to the late 18th century, with panoramic views of the rain forest and sea, this property is a retreat for those keen to experience a quiet Caribbean estate life. The house is owned by a Tobago-born professor of African history; his collection of African art is sprinkled throughout the house as are artifacts of plantation days. The rooms in the great house are all differently furnished with antiques and have fine mahogany floors. The rain-forest suite offers a fabulous sunset view. There are also several newly built rooms just under the Great House; they are more private but lack the ambience of the older rooms. The kitchen serves delicious island food, and meal plans are available and necessary, as you really are off the beaten path here. ✉ *Belle Garden, Tobago,* ☎ 🖷 *809/660–4467. 3 suites, 7 double rooms. Restaurant, bar, pool. MC, V.*

**$–$$**   🏠 **Blue Horizon Resort.** "Resort" is a misnomer for this compact, red-roofed apartment complex set above the Mt. Irvine golf course, since all it offers in the way of facilities are a small pool, which the apartments overlook, a barbecue pit, and an understocked minimart. However, it does offer peace and quiet and sunset views from the deluxe apartments, which are a far better deal than the first-floor, viewless standards. Another advantage is the spaciousness of the rooms, and parents can observe their children in the pool from each unit. Decor is basic—small, straight-backed plaid sofas and chairs around the satellite TV are the only lounge furniture—with kitchens and bathrooms. Deluxe apartments have spiral staircases leading to galleried lofts that children will adore—though little ones could easily fall from them. Balconies overlook each other, except for that of the single "luxurious" apartment, with an extra bedroom and tons of space. This is a good budget pick for families. ✉ *Jacamar Dr., Mt. Irvine, Tobago,* ☎ *809/639–0433,* 🖷 *305/592– 4935. 13 apartments. Grocery, pool, airport shuttle. AE, MC, V. EP.*

**$–$$**   🏠 **Manta Lodge.** Instead of being identified by numbers, rooms in this comfortable lodge are marked by the names of fish and fowl like Green Moray, Tarpon, and Toucan (lest you forget, there's an etching of the creature on the tiled bath). All rooms have a lovely view of the ocean and the beach just across the street, wooden walls are accented with brilliant blues or reds, floors are white tile, and the furniture is of a heavy wicker. Though the island breezes might be enough, you might want the option of air conditioning, available in some rooms. Scuba diving is the main attraction here, and there's a fully equipped dive shop with certification classes and dive packages. ✉ *Box 433, Scarborough, Tobago,* ☎ 🖷 *809/660–5268. 20 rooms, 2 lofts. Restaurant, bar, air-conditioning, pool, dive shop. AE, DC, MC, V. MAP, FAP.*

**$–$$** ⊡ **Ocean Point.** A resort in miniature, this friendly "condo hotel" is complete with tiny kitsch fountain, a quartet of parakeets and Raj the macaw, a barbecue pit, and a palm-thatched bar-restaurant (East Indian food is the specialty) at one end of a child-size, kidney-shape pool. Five studios with five split-level loft apartments above them constitute the living quarters, all sparkly white with pine fittings and terra-cotta floors, big showers in the bathrooms, plus an inviting hammock on the balcony (upstairs) or porch (downstairs). Lofts offer views of the sunrise over the ocean. The studios face the pool, and the noise can be annoying during the day. (Little Rockley beach is a minute's walk away, but it's narrow and rocky—not the best for sunbathing.) A 10-minute drive takes you to Store Bay. A free shuttle to the airport and supermarket is provided. Dive packages are available. ⊠ *Milford Rd., Lowlands, Tobago,* ☏ ℻ *809/639–0973. 5 studios, 5 apartments. Restaurant, bar, air-conditioning, kitchenettes, pool, airport shuttle. AE, DC, MC, V. EP.*

# Dining

Macaroni pie and chicken is Tobago's Sunday dinner favorite, perhaps with fried plantain or potatoes. Oil Down tastes better than it sounds: It's a gently seasoned mixture of boiled breadfruit and salted beef or pork flavored with coconut milk. Mango ice cream or a sweetly sour tamarind ball makes a tasty finish. You may want to take home some hot pepper sauce or chutney to a spice-loving friend or relative.

For price information on restaurants, *see* the price chart *in* the Dining section of Trinidad, *above.*

**$$$** ✕ **Tamara's.** In the elegant Coco Reef Resort, this is possibly the is-
★ land's best gourmet restaurant. Local musicians stroll among the dinners playing upbeat island songs on stringed instruments. The peach decor and white-washed wood ceiling give the place a light feel, and island breezes waft though the palm-tree-lined terrace. You might start with the homemade chicken liver pâté with pear chutney and char-grilled brioche, followed by the grilled barracuda set on a bed of black olive puree and dressed with pepper sauce. If you have room for dessert, the cherry yogurt parfait is very good. Full tropical buffet breakfast is served daily; dinner, nightly. ⊠ *Coco Reef Resort, Scarborough,* ☏ *809/639–8571. AE, MC, V.*

**$$–$$$** ✕ **Arnos Vale Waterwheel.** This popular eatery is set on landscaped grounds in a rain-forest nature park, where gleaming hardwood walkways take you past remnants of an old sugar mill. There's a roof overhead, but otherwise you are completely outdoors, so you may want a bit of bug spray. The decor is naturally elegant with evergreen wrought-iron tables and chairs and lights fashioned in the shape of large pineapples. The menu changes but has an Italian flare with choices like shaved pear and Parmesan salad, focaccia with grilled goat cheese, seviche of kingfish, or caramelized breast of chicken on wet polenta with a callaloo sauce. There's no admission cost to the park if you're dining. ⊠ *Arnos Vale Estate, Franklyn Rd.,* ☏ *809/660–0815. MC, V.*

**$$–$$$** ✕ **Dillon's.** Stanley Dillon's other career as a fishing-charter operator
★ guarantees the freshest catch at his seafood restaurant by the airport. White walls hung with local art, red plaid tablecloths, and a silver-service waitstaff create a soothing atmosphere halfway between homey and posh. The menu mixes traditional favorites, such as shrimp cocktail, French onion soup, lobster thermidor, and surf and turf with callaloo, stuffed kingfish, chunky fish broth, and other Creole dishes. Get here early on weekends, before the line stretches to the runway. ⊠ *Airport Rd. near Crown Point,* ☏ *809/639–8765. AE, MC, V.*

**$$–$$$  ✕ Ocean View.** Grafton Beach Resort's main restaurant is a large open terrace overlooking the Caribbean, but with a clearer view of the hotel pool, bar, and evening's entertainment than of the waves. Four times a week, you can enjoy an all-you-can-eat dinner buffet, which might include char-grilled chicken, steak and pork, Creole dolphinfish, curried blue crab, any number of root vegetables, spaghetti, *pelau* (rice and peas), cauliflower with cheese, a salad bar, and an array of desserts: You'll wish you'd remembered to pack the Tums. ⊠ *Grafton Beach Resort, Black Rock,* ☎ *809/639–0191. AE, DC, MC, V.*

**$$  ✕ Cocrico Inn.** In a simple café and bar, the Cocrico offers delectable home cooking. The three rotating chefs use fresh fruits and vegetables grown in the neighborhood. They zealously guard their recipes, including a marvelous cou-cou and lightly breaded, subtly spiced grouper. There is nothing fancy here, just warm and delicious food and cool air-conditioning. ⊠ *Corner of North and Commissioner Sts., Plymouth,* ☎ *809/639–2661. AE, V.*

**$$  ✕ Kariwak Village.** Recorded steel-band music plays gently in the
**★**  background at this romantic candlelit spot. In a bamboo pavilion created to resemble an Amerindian round hut, Cynthia Clovis orchestrates a very original four-course menu. Changing daily, the choices may include christophine soup, curried green fig, kingfish with shrimp sauce, and coconut cake. Whatever it is, it will be full of herbs and vegetables freshly picked from Cynthia's own organic garden, and home-baked breads. It's a treat for vegetable lovers, because Kariwak knows how to honor the simple squash and green beans. The nonalcoholic drinks are wonderful, even the iced coffee, which is more like a frozen coconut cappuccino. Saturday buffets, with live jazz or calypso, are a Tobagonian highlight. ⊠ *Kariwak Village, Crown Point,* ☎ *809/639–8442. AE, DC, MC, V.*

**$$  ✕ Old Donkey Cart.** Dine in the outdoor tropical palm garden or inside this 100-year-old French Colonial–style home. Friendly cats wind their way around your legs and welcome the occasional pat on the head. The menu has both international and local cuisine; the callaloo soup is wonderful, as are the conch fritters. There is an extensive wine list. Try the specialty drink made fresh from hibiscus (with or without rum), a thirst-quenching way to get your Vitamin C. ⊠ *Bacolet St. 73, Scarborough,* ☎ *809/639–3551. MC, V.*

**$$  ✕ Papillon.** Named after one of the proprietor's favorite books, this seafood restaurant is a homey room with an adjoining patio. Lobster Buccoo Bay is marinated in sherry and broiled with herbs. Seafood casserole au gratin means chunks of lobster, shrimp, fish, and cream, all seasoned in ginger wine. Baby shark is marinated in rum and lime. Or you can just enjoy some good broiled chicken or pork cutlets with pineapple. Papillon is one good reason for staying at the Old Grange Inn next door, owned by the same Trinidadian family. ⊠ *Buccoo Bay Rd., Mt. Irvine,* ☎ *809/639–0275. AE, DC, MC, V.*

**$$  ✕ Rouselle's.** An enchanting terrace high above Scarborough Bay with
**★**  a big, congenial bar, Rouselle's was just a liming spot until friends and regulars demanded proper food. Bet they didn't expect food this good. The small menu dons different accessories rather than changing completely, so you may find grouper, broiled and served with a fresh Creole sauce and several vegetables—garlicky green beans, carrots with ginger, a raw bok choy salad, and potato croquette with spices and celery; dolphinfish with white wine sauce; or lobster, which is very hard to procure, steamed just so. Whatever there is, you can trust that it'll be delicious. A sizable *amuse-gueule* (appetizer), hot garlic bread, plus dessert (save room for pineapple pie or homemade ice cream) are included in the entrée price. Don't forgo the Rouselle's punch: The recipe's a secret, but the lovely, welcoming co-owners, Bobbie and Charlene, will

probably let you in on it. ✉ *Old Windward Rd., Bacolet,* ☎ *809/639–4738. Reservations essential for lunch. AE, MC, V.*

**$-$$** ✕ **Blue Crab.** Alison Sardinha is Tobago's most ebullient and kindly host-
★ ess, and her husband, Ken, one of its best chefs. He cooks "like our mothers cooked," serving the local food with heavy East Indian influence, a
bit of Portuguese, and occasionally Asian, too. There might be kingfish, *katchowrie* (spiced split pea patties, a little like falafel), curry
chicken, or long-cooked suckling pig. There's always a callaloo, differently
flavored on different days, fine rotis and cou-cou, and sometimes a
"cookup"—pelau-type rice, with *everything* in it. The place is officially
open only on Wednesday and Friday nights, but Miss Alison will open
up on other evenings (and for weekend lunches, too) even for one table,
if you call in the morning. The setting, on a wide, shady terrace overlooking the bay, is just about perfect. If you want to see the joy of
Caribbean cooking in one presentation, ask Alison how to make one
of the dishes. The Sardinhas epitomize the joy of living. ✉ *Robinson
St. at Main St., Scarborough,* ☎ *809/639–2737. AE, MC, V.*

**$** ✕ **First Historical Cafe/Bar.** This funky little roadside eatery is housed
in a traditional West Indian building from the 1960s. The back-porch
dining area has a crushed-rock-and-coral floor and brightly painted yellow, green, and red bamboo walls with a thatched roof overhead. The
main attractions are the time-line posters that present historical tidbits
of Tobago. Do you want to know the definition of the Tobago Jig, the
Tobago Reel, or the Tobago Bongo? This is the place to find out. The
food is simple but good, featuring island delights like fruit plates and
delicious fish sandwiches. ✉ *Mile Marker 8, Windward Main Rd. in
Studley Park area en route to Charlotteville, no phone. No credit cards.*

## Beaches

Traveling to Tobago without sampling the beaches is like touring
France's Burgundy region without drinking the wine. You'll not find
manicured, country-club sand here, but those who enjoy feeling as though
they've landed on a private desert island will relish the untouched quality of these shores.

**Bacolet Beach** is a dark-sand beach that was the setting for the films
*Swiss Family Robinson* and *Heaven Knows, Mr. Allison.*

**Englishman's Bay** is a charming beach; what's more, it's completely
deserted.

**Great Courland Bay,** near Fort Bennett, is a long stretch of clear, tranquil water. The sandy beach—one of Tobago's longest—is home to several glitzy hotels. A recently built marina attracts the yachting crowd.

**King's Bay Beach,** surrounded by steep green hills, is the most visually
satisfying of the swimming sites off the road from Scarborough to Speyside—the bay hooks around so severely that you feel as if you're swimming in a lake. The crescent-shape beach is easy to find because it's
marked by a sign about halfway between Roxborough and Speyside.
Just before you reach the bay there is a bridge with an unmarked turnoff
that leads to a gravel parking lot; beyond that, a landscaped path
leads to a waterfall with a rocky pool where you can refresh yourself.
You may meet enterprising locals who'll offer to guide you to the top
of the falls, a climb that you may find not worth the effort.

**Little Rockley Bay** is just west of Scarborough (take Milford Road off
the main highway). The beach is craggy and not much good for swimming, but it is quiet and offers a pleasing view of Tobago's capital across
the water.

**Lover's Beach** is so called because of its pink sand and because of its seclusion: You have to hire a local to take you there by boat.

**Man O' War Bay,** in Charlotteville, is flanked by one of the prettiest fishing villages in the Caribbean. You can lounge on the sand and purchase the day's catch for your dinner.

**Mt. Irvine Beach,** across the street from the Mt. Irvine Bay Hotel, is an unremarkable setting, but it has great surfing in July and August; the snorkeling is excellent too. It's also ideal for windsurfing in January and April. There are picnic tables surrounded by painted concrete pagodas and a snack bar.

**Parlatuvier,** on the north side of the island, is best approached via the road from Roxborough. The beach here is a classic Caribbean crescent, a scene peopled by villagers and local fishermen.

**Pigeon Point** is the stunningly beautiful locale inevitably displayed on Tobago travel brochures. Although the beach is public, it abuts part of what was once a large coconut estate, and you must pay a token admission (about TT$10) to enter the grounds and use the facilities. The beach is lined with towering royal palms, and there's a food stand, a few gift shops, a diving concession, and paddleboats for rent. The waters are calm.

**Sandy Beach,** along Crown Point, is abutted by several hotels. You won't lack for amenities around here.

**Stone Haven Bay** is a gorgeous beach that's across the street from Grafton Beach Resort, a luxury hotel complex.

**Store Bay,** where boats depart for Buccoo Reef, is probably the most socially convivial setting in the area. The beach is little more than a small sandy cove between two rocky breakwaters, but, ah, the food stands here: six shacks licensed by the tourist board to local ladies, featuring roti, pelau, and the world's messiest dish, crab and dumplings. Miss Jean's (☎ 809/639–0563) is the most popular; try Miss Esmie's crab, though.

**Turtle Beach** is named for the turtles that lay their eggs here at night between February and June. (If you're very quiet, you can watch; the turtles don't seem to mind.) It's set on Great Courland Bay (☞ *above*).

# Outdoor Activities and Sports

## Bird-Watching
The naturalist **David Rooks** (☎ 809/639–4276) offers walks inland and trips to offshore bird colonies. Call Pat Turpin (☎ 809/660–4327) or Renson Jack (☎ 809/660–5175) at **Pioneer Journeys** for information about their 6½-hour bird-watching tours of Bloody Bay rain forest.

## Boating
**Bayshore Charters** (✉ Bayshore, ☎ 809/637–8711). Fish for an afternoon or hire the boat for a weekend, the *Melissa Ann* is fully equipped for comfortable cruising, sleeps six, and has an air-conditioned cabin, refrigerator, cooking facilities, and, of course, fishing equipment. Captain Sa Gomes is among the most experienced charter captains on the islands.

**Kalina Kats** (✉ Scarborough, ☎ 809/639–6304). Sail around the Tobago coastline on a 50-ft catamaran with stops for snorkeling and exploring the rain forest. The romantic sunset cruise with cocktails is a great way to end the day.

## Deep-Sea Fishing

**Dillon's Fishing Charter** (⊠ Pigeon Point, ☎ 809/639–8765) is excellent for full- and half-day trips for kingfish, barracuda, wahoo, dolphinfish, blue marlin, etc. Trips start at $165 for four hours, including equipment.

## Golf

The 18-hole course at the **Mt. Irvine Golf Club** (⊠ Mt. Irvine Bay Hotel, ☎ 809/639–8871) has been ranked among the top five in the Caribbean.

## Nature Preserves

Eco-consciousness is strong on both islands and especially on Tobago, where the rain forests of the Main Ridge were set aside for protection in 1764, creating the first such preserve in the Western Hemisphere. Natural areas now include Little Tobago and St. Giles Islands, both major seabird sanctuaries. In addition, the endangered leatherback turtles maintain breeding grounds on some of Tobago's leeward beaches.

**Arnos Vale Waterwheel.** They groomed some of the rain forest here to insert a series of shiny wooden walkways that take you past the remnants of an old sugar factory. The walkways allow you to see much of the ruins without disturbing nature. There's also a small museum, an excellent restaurant (☞ Dining, *above*), and several hiking trails around the property. The remnants of the Buckra Estate house is on a hilltop that has spectacular views of Tobago. There are also two Amerindian sights, a slave village, and a tomb. Guides are available and can make your nature-history walk truly come alive. There's an TT$10 admission charge unless you're dining at the restaurant. ⊠ *Arnos Vale Estate, Franklyn Rd.,* ☎ *809/660–0815. MC, V.*

## Scuba Diving

An abundance of fish and coral thrive on the nutrients of South America's Orinoco River, which are brought to Tobago by the Guayana current. There are many good spots to submerge, including Crown Point, St. Giles Islands, and off the west coast, but it's the waters off Speyside that draw scuba-diving aficionados from around the world. You can get information, supplies, and instruction at **AquaMarine Dive Ltd.** (⊠ Blue Waters Inn, ☎ 809/660–4341), **Dive Tobago** (⊠ Pigeon Point, Box 53, Scarborough, ☎ 809/639–0202), **Man Friday Diving** (⊠ Charlotteville, ☎ 809/660–4676), **Tobago Dive Experience** (⊠ Crown Point, ☎ 809/639–7034), and **Tobago Dive Masters** (⊠ Speyside, ☎ 809/639–4697).

## Snorkeling

Tobago offers many wonderful spots for snorkeling. Although the reefs around Speyside are becoming better known, **Buccoo Reef** is easily still the most popular—perhaps too popular. Over the years the reef has been damaged by the ceaseless boat traffic and by the thoughtless visitors who take pieces of coral for souvenirs. Even so, it's still a trip worth experiencing, particularly if you have children. Daily 2½-hour tours by flat, glass-bottom boats let you snorkel at the reef, swim in a shallow lagoon pool, and take a look at Coral Gardens, where fish and coral are yet untouched. The trip costs about $8, and masks, snorkeling equipment, and reef shoes are provided. Departure is at 11 AM from Pigeon Point. Most of the scuba-diving companies also arrange snorkeling tours. There is also good snorkeling by the beach near the **Arnos Vale Hotel** and the **Mt. Irvine Bay Hotel.**

## Tennis

**Rex Turtle Beach** (☎ 809/639–2851), **Mt. Irvine** (☎ 809/639–8871), and the **Blue Waters Inn** (☎ 809/660–4341) allow nonmembers and nonresidents to play.

# Shopping

The souvenir-bound will do better in Trinidad than they will in Tobago, but determined shoppers should manage to ferret out some things to take home: Scarborough has the largest collection of shops, and Burnett Street, which slopes sharply from the port to St. James Park, is a good place to browse.

### Local Crafts

**Cotton House** (⊠ Bacolet St., Scarborough, ☎ 809/639–2727) is a good bet for jewelry and imaginative batik work. Paula Young runs her shop like an art school. You can visit the upstairs studio; if it's not too busy, you can even make a batik square at no charge. **Forro's** (⊠ Wilson Rd., across from Scarborough market, Scarborough, ☎ 809/639–2979; ⊠ Crown Point Airport, Tobago, no phone) sells its own fine line of homemade tamarind chutney, lemon or lime marmalade, hot sauce, and guava or golden apple jelly. Mrs. Eileen Forrester, wife of the Anglican priest at St. David's in Plymouth, supervises a kitchen full of good cooks who boil and bottle the condiments and pack them in little straw baskets. Most jars are small, easily carried, and very inexpensive. **Souvenir and Gift Shop** (⊠ Port Mall, Scarborough, ☎ 809/639–5632) stocks straw baskets and other crafts.

# Nightlife and the Arts

People will tell you there's no nightlife on Tobago. Don't believe them. Whatever you do the rest of the week, don't miss the huge impromptu party, affectionately dubbed Sunday School, that gears up after midnight on all the street corners of Buccoo and breaks up around dawn. Pick your band, hang out for a while, then move on. In downtown Scarborough on weekend nights, you can also expect to find competing sound systems blaring at informal parties that welcome extra guests. In addition, "Blockos" (spontaneous block parties) spring up all over the island; look for the hand-painted signs. Tobago also has Harvest parties on Sunday, when a particular village opens its doors to visitors for hospitality. These occur throughout the year and are a great way to meet the locals.

**Bonkers** (⊠ Store Bay local road, Crown Point, tel. 809/639–7173), a hot new bar and disco with a castaway theme (watch out—the DJ may make you walk the plank into the pool) draws a younger crowd. The music ranges from jazz and reggae to soca (calypso with a political bite). More sedentary types might consider coming on games night, when chess and domino players take the floor. **Grafton Beach Resort** (⊠ Black Rock, ☎ 809/639–0191) has some kind of organized cabaret-style event every night. Even if you hate that touristy stuff, check out Les Couteaux Cultural Group, who do a high-octane dance version of Tobagonian history. **Kariwak Village** (⊠ Crown Point, ☎ 809/639–8442) has hip hotel entertainment, frequented as much by locals as tourists, on Friday and Saturday nights—almost always one of the better local jazz-calypso bands. **Rex Turtle Beach Hotel** (⊠ Great Courland Bay, ☎ 809/639–2851) hosts Les Couteaux Cultural Group and other similar shows on Wednesday and Sunday. **Starting Gate** (⊠ Shirvan Rd., Mt. Irvine, ☎ 809/639–0225), a casual indoor-outdoor pub, is the venue for frequent party-discos.

# Exploring Tobago

A driving tour of Tobago, from Scarborough to Charlotteville and back, can be done in about four hours, but you'd never want to undertake this spectacular, and very hilly, ride in that time. Plan to spend at least one night at the Speyside end of the island and give yourself a chance to enjoy this largely untouched country and seaside at leisure. The Blue Waters Inn (☞ Lodging, *above*) is open for meals and for overnighting; it's about as close to the sea as you can get without swimming.

*Numbers in the margin correspond to points of interest on the Tobago map.*

SIGHTS TO SEE

**❺ Charlotteville.** This delightful fishing village is enfolded in a series of steep hills. Fishermen here announce the day's catch (usually flying fish, redfish, or bonito) by sounding their conch shells. A view of Man O' War Bay with Pigeon Peak, Tobago's highest mountain, behind it at sunset is an exquisite treat for the eye. The underwater cliffs and canyons at the nearby **St. Giles Islands** draw divers to this spot where the Atlantic meets the Caribbean. ⊠ *Take Windward Rd. inland across mountains from Speyside.*

**❹ Flagstaff Hill.** One of the highest points of the island sits at the northern tip of Tobago. Surrounded by ocean on three sides and with a view of the hills, Charlotteville, and St. Giles Islands, this was the site of an American military lookout and radio tower during World War II. It's an ideal spot for a sunset picnic.

**❷ Fort King George.** On Mt. St. George, a few miles east of the town of Scarborough, Tobago's best-preserved historic monument clings to a cliff high above the ocean. Fort King George was built in the 1770s and operated until 1854. It's hard to imagine that this lovely, tranquil spot commanding sweeping views of the bay and landscaped with lush tropical foliage was ever the site of any military action, but the prison, officer's mess, and several stabilized cannons attest otherwise.

Just to the left of the tall wooden figures dancing a traditional Tobagonian jig is the former barrack guardhouse, now home to the small **Tobago Museum.** Exhibits include a variety of weapons along with pre-Columbian artifacts found in the area; the fertility figures are especially interesting. Upstairs are maps and photographs of Tobago past. Be sure to check out the gift display cases for the perversely fascinating jewelry made from embalmed and painted lizards and sea creatures; you might find it hard to resist a pair of bright yellow shrimp earrings. ⊠ *84 Fort King George, Scarborough,* ☎ *809/639–3970.* 🖾 *TT$5.* ☉ *Weekdays 9–5.*

In addition to the museum, a **Fine Arts Centre** at the foot of the fort complex features the work of local artists.

NEED A
BREAK?

After touring the fort, head for the **Old Donkey Cart House** (⊠ Bacolet St., ☎ 809/639–3551), 2 mi south of Scarborough, a green-and-white colonial house with an outdoor terrace—the perfect spot to relax with a glass of Rhine wine or German beer.

**❶ Scarborough.** Nestled around Rockley Bay on the island's leeward hilly side, this town is near the airport and is a popular cruise ship port, but it conveys the feeling that not much has changed here since the area was settled two centuries ago. It may not be one of the pastel-color, delightful cities of the Caribbean, but Scarborough does have its charms, including an array of interesting little shops. Note the red-and-yellow Methodist church on the hillside, one of Tobago's oldest churches.

**❸ Speyside.** At the far reach of the windward coast of Tobago, this small fishing village has a few lodgings and restaurants. Glass-bottom boats operate between Speyside and **Little Tobago Island,** one of the most

important seabird sanctuaries in the Caribbean. Divers are drawn to
the unspoiled reefs in the area and to the strong possibility of spotting
giant manta rays. The approach to Speyside from the south affords one
of the most spectacular vistas of the island.

NEED A
BREAK?

**Jemma's Sea View Kitchen** (☎ 809/660–4066), along the main road in
Speyside, offers tasty West Indian meals served in a house on stilts by
the ocean. You'll find nothing fancy here, just delicious Tobagonian
home cooking, including a wondrous baked chicken, and great views.

# TRINIDAD AND TOBAGO A TO Z

## Arriving and Departing

### BY BOAT

The Port Authority maintains ferry service every day except Saturday
between Trinidad and Tobago, although flying is preferable, because
the sea can be very rough. The ferry leaves once a day, and the trip
takes about five hours. Round-trip fare is TT$60. Cabins, when avail-
able, run TT$160 (one-way, double occupancy). Tickets are sold at of-
fices in Port-of-Spain (☎ 809/625–3055) and at Scarborough, in
Tobago (☎ 809/639–2417).

### BY PLANE

There are daily direct flights to Trinidad's Piarco Airport, about 30 minutes east of Port-of-Spain, from New York and Miami, and frequent
direct flights from Toronto and London on **BWIA** (☎ 809/625–1010
or 809/664–4268), Trinidad and Tobago's national airline. BWIA
flies direct to Tobago's Crown Point Airport from New York's JFK and
from Miami International. BWIA also offers flights to Port-of-Spain
from other cities in the Caribbean. BWIA flights from Trinidad to Tobago take about 15 minutes and depart six to 10 times a day. **American** (☎ 809/664–4661) offers direct flights from Miami to Trinidad;
as of press time, there are no direct flights from the United States to
Tobago, although **American Eagle** does offer a nonstop flight from San
Juan. **Air Canada** (☎ 809/664–4065) flies nonstop to Trinidad from
Toronto. There are numerous flights to Port-of-Spain from other
Caribbean cities on **LIAT** (☎ 809/627–2942 or 809/623–1838). LIAT
also has service from the eastern Caribbean islands to Tobago. **Air
Caribbean** (☎ 809/623–2500) has 15-minute flights from Trinidad to
Tobago that depart several times a day.

Package tours aren't generally touted as heavily as they are for other
Caribbean islands, but there are bargains to be had, especially around
Carnival. One particularly good tour operator is **Pan Caribe Tours**
(✉ Box 3223, Austin, TX 78764, ☎ 512/266–7995 or 800/525–6896,
FAX 512/266–7986). BWIA also has a variety of Caribbean tours.

### FROM THE AIRPORT

Taxis are readily available at Piarco Airport. The fare to Port-of-Spain
is set at $20 ($30 after 10 PM), to the Hilton at $24. By car, take Golden
Grove Road north to Arouca, and then follow Eastern Main Road west
for about 10 mi to Port-of-Spain. In Tobago, the fare from Crown Point
Airport to Scarborough is fixed at $8, to Speyside at $36.

## Currency

The Trinidadian dollar (TT$) has been devalued twice in recent years.
The current exchange rate is about TT$5.50 to US$1. The major hotels
in Port-of-Spain have exchange facilities whose rates are comparable to
official bank rates. Trinidad's best rate is found at the Hilton. Most busi-

nesses on the island will accept U.S. currency if you're in a pinch. Note: Prices quoted here are in U.S. dollars unless indicated otherwise.

## Emergencies

**Police:** ☎ 999. **Fire and Ambulance:** ☎ 990. **Hospitals: Port-of-Spain General Hospital** (✉ 169 Charlotte St., ☎ 809/623–2951), **Tobago County Hospital** (✉ Fort St., Scarborough, ☎ 809/639–2551). **Late-Night Pharmacies: Bhaggan's** (☎ 809/627–4657) is at Charlotte and Oxford streets near the Port-of-Spain General Hospital; **Ross Drugs** (☎ 809/639–2658) is in Scarborough. For a complete list of other pharmacies, check the T&T Yellow Pages.

## Getting Around

### CAR RENTALS

It's not worth renting a car if you are staying in Port-of-Spain, where the streets are often jammed with traffic and drivers who routinely play chicken with one another; taxis are your best bet. If you're planning to tour Trinidad, however, it's worth your while to get some wheels. As befits one of the world's largest exporters of asphalt, Trinidad's roads are generally good, although you may encounter roadwork in progress as major resurfacing is done. In the outback, roads are often narrow, twisting, and prone to washouts in the rainy season. Inquire about conditions before you take off, particularly if you're heading toward the north coast. Never drive into downtown Port-of-Spain during afternoon rush hour.

In Tobago you might be better off renting a four-wheel drive vehicle than relying on taxi service, which is much more expensive. A four-wheel-drive vehicle is far better and safer than a car, because many roads, particularly in the interior, or on the far coast near Speyside and Charlotteville, are bumpy, pitted, winding, and/or steep (though the main highways are smooth and fast).

Various tours are also offered by rental agencies on both islands, and rates are negotiable. All agencies require a credit-card deposit, and in season you must make reservations well in advance of your arrival. Figure on paying $40–$60 per day. Don't forget to drive on the left.

Trinidad has a **Thrifty** (✉ Piarco International Airport, ☎ 809/669–0602) office. Reliable local companies include **Auto Rentals** (✉ Piarco International Airport, ☎ 809/669–2277), with many other locations; **Econo-Car Rentals** (✉ Piarco International Airport, ☎ 809/669–2342); and **Southern Sales Car Rentals** (✉ Piarco International Airport and other locations, ☎ 809/669–2424, or dial 269 from courtesy phone in baggage area).

In Tobago, **Thrifty** is represented at the Rex Turtle Beach Hotel (☎ 809/639–8507). Other options are **Rattan's Car Rentals** (✉ Crown Point Airport, ☎ 809/639–8271) and **Singh's Auto Rentals** (✉ Grafton Beach Resort, ☎ 809/639–0191, ext. 53).

### TAXIS

Taxis in Trinidad are easily identified by their license plates, which begin with the letter H. Passenger vans, called Maxi Taxis, pick up and drop off passengers as they travel and are color-coded according to which of the six areas they cover (yellow for Port-of-Spain, blue for Tobago). They are easily hailed day or night along most of the main roads near Port-of-Spain. For longer trips you will need to hire a private taxi. Taxis are not metered; many routes have fixed rates, though they are not always observed, particularly at Carnival. Pick up a rate sheet from the tourism office. On the whole, the drivers are honest, friendly, and informative, and the experience of riding in a Maxi Taxi with a souped-up sound system during Carnival is worth whatever fare you pay.

## Guided Tours

Almost any taxi driver in Port-of-Spain will be willing to take you around the town and to the beaches on the north coast. It costs around $70 for up to four people to go Maracas Bay beach, plus $20 per hour extra if you decide to go farther; you may be able to haggle for a cheaper rate. For a complete list of tour operators and sea cruises, contact the tourism office.

**Tobago Travel** (⊠ Box 163, Scarborough, ☎ 809/639−8778, FAX 809/639−8786), the most experienced tour operator on Tobago, offers a wide array of travel services. **Travel Centre** (⊠ 44−58 Edward St., Port-of-Spain, ☎ 809/623−5096, FAX 809/623−5101) is one of Trinidad's best tour operators. Its office is also American Express's card-member service office, for check-cashing and other matters. **Winston Nanan** (⊠ Nanan Bird Sanctuary Tours, 38 Bamboo Grove No. 1, Uriah Butler Hwy., Valsayn, ☎ 809/645−1305) is the only official tour operator at the Caroni Bird Sanctuary (☞ Exploring Trinidad, *above*); phone or write him in advance for reservations. **Rooks Nature Tours** (⊠ Box 348, Scarborough, ☎ 809/639−4276) offers a variety of tours with ornithologist David Rooks; they include rain-forest hikes and bird-watching expeditions.

## Language

The official language is English, although there is no end of idiomatic expressions used by the loquacious Trinis. You will also hear smatterings of French, Spanish, Chinese, and Hindi. (Trinidad's population is about one-quarter Indian.)

## Opening and Closing Times

Most shops open Monday–Friday 8–4:30, Saturday 8–noon; malls stay open later during the week and operate all day Saturday. Banking hours are Monday–Thursday 8–2 and Friday 8–noon and 3–5.

## Passports and Visas

Citizens of the United States, the United Kingdom, and Canada who expect to stay for less than six weeks may enter the country with a valid passport. A visa is required for longer stays.

## Precautions

Insect repellent is a must during the rainy season (June–December) and is worth having around anytime. Trinidad is only 11 degrees north of the equator, and the sun here can be intense; bring a strong sunblock.

Petty theft does occur, so don't leave cash in bags that you check in at the airport. It would also be wise to use hotel safes for valuables.

## Taxes and Service Charges

Restaurants and hotels add a 15% value-added tax (VAT). Many also add a 10% service charge to your bill. If the service charge is not added, you should tip 10%–15% of the bill for a job well done. The airport departure tax is TT$75 plus another TT$5 for security tax.

## Telephones and Mail

The area code for both islands is 809. Starting in 1998 it will change to 868, although both codes can be used for 12 months. For telegraph, telefax, teletype, and telex, contact **Textel** (⊠ 1 Edward St., Port-of-Spain, ☎ 809/625−4431). Faxes can be sent from major hotels.

Postage for first-class letters to the United States is TT$2.25; for postcards, TT$2.

## Visitor Information

For advance information, there's a new **Travel Trade Hotline** (☎ 800/748–4224 in the U.S.). You can also contact offices of the **Tourism and Industrial Development Company of Trinidad and Tobago Ltd. (TIDCO)** (✉ 7000 Blvd. E, Guttenberg, NJ 07093, ☎ 201/662–3403 or 201/662–3408, FAX 201/869–7628; ✉ International House, 47 Chase Side, Enfield, Middlesex, EN2 6NB2, ☎ 0181/367–5175, FAX 0181/367–9949; ✉ Taurus House, 512 Duplex Ave., Toronto, Ontario M4R 2E3, ☎ 416/484–4864, FAX 416/484–8256).

In Trinidad, information is available from **TIDCO** (✉ 10–14 Phillips St., Port-of-Spain, ☎ 809/623–1932, FAX 809/623–3848; ✉ Piarco Airport, ☎ 809/669–5196). For Tobago, contact the **Tobago Division of Tourism** (✉ N.I.B. Mall, Level 3, Scarborough, ☎ 809/639–2125, FAX 809/639–3566), or drop in at its information booth at Crown Point Airport (☎ 809/639–0509).

# 26 Turks and Caicos Islands

*From above, it looks as if someone poured pancake batter on the sea, that is how flat these islands are. Though there may not be pretty hills and valleys to view, the islands are ringed by sugary sand beaches and offer plenty of places to stroll along the clear blue sea. For the more adventurous, there's excellent scuba diving and sportfishing.*

Updated by
JoAnn
Milivojevic

**T**HE TURKS AND CAICOS ISLANDS are relatively unknown except to scuba divers and aficionados of
beautiful beaches, who religiously return to these waters year after year. Miles-long, soft, sparkling white-sand beaches
ring the flat islands, and offshore, pristine reefs overflow with a variety of fish, crustaceans, and coral, making for excellent snorkeling and
scuba diving. The islands' slogan, "Beautiful by Nature," reflects its
tranquillity and natural wonders.

It is claimed that Columbus's first landfall was on Grand Turk. First
settled by the English more than 200 years ago, the British Crown Colony
of Turks and Caicos is renowned in two respects: Its booming banking and insurance institutions lure investors from the United States and
elsewhere, and its offshore reef formations entice divers to the world
of colorful marine life surrounding its more than 40 islands and small
cays, only eight of which are inhabited. The total landmass is 193 square
mi; the population of the eight inhabited islands and cays is some 12,350.

The Turks and Caicos are two groups of islands in an archipelago lying
575 mi southeast of Miami and about 90 mi north of Haiti. The Turks
Islands include Grand Turk, which is the capital and seat of government, and Salt Cay, with a population of about 200. According to local
legend, these islands were named by early settlers who thought the scarlet blossoms on the local cactus resembled the Turkish fez.

Approximately 22 mi west of Grand Turk, across the 7,000-ft-deep
Christopher Columbus Passage, is the Caicos group, which includes
South, East, West, Middle, and North Caicos and Providenciales.
South Caicos, Middle Caicos, North Caicos, and Providenciales (nicknamed Provo) are the only inhabited islands in this group; Pine Cay
and Parrot Cay are the only inhabited cays. "Caicos" is derived from
*cayos,* the Spanish word for cay, and is believed to mean, appropriately, "string of islands."

Around 1678, Bermudians, lured by the wealth of salt in these islands,
began raking salt from the flats and returning to Bermuda to sell their
crop. Despite French and Spanish attacks and pirate raids, the Bermudians persisted and established a trade that became the bedrock of the
Bermudian economy. In 1766 Andrew Symmers settled here to hold
the islands for England. Later, Loyalists from Georgia obtained land
grants in the Caicos Islands, imported slaves, and continued the lifestyle
of the pre–Civil War American South.

Today, the government has devised a long-term development plan to
improve the visibility of the Turks and Caicos in the Caribbean tourism
market. Providenciales, in particular, is well under way as a tourist destination and also as an offshore financial center. Mass tourism on the
scale of that of some other island destinations, however, is not in the
cards; government guidelines promote a "quality, not quantity," policy toward tourism, including conservation awareness and firm restrictions on building heights and casino construction. Without a port
for cruise ships, the islands remain uncrowded and peaceful.

# GRAND TURK

Bermudian colonial architecture abounds on this string bean of an island that is just 6 mi long and 1 mi wide. Buildings have walled-in courtyards to keep wandering donkeys from nibbling on the foliage.

## Lodging

| CATEGORY | COST* |
| --- | --- |
| $$$$ | over $250 |
| $$$ | $170–$250 |
| $$ | $110–$170 |
| $ | under $110 |

*All prices are for a standard double room in winter, excluding 7% tax and 10%–15% service charge. Some hotels are now charging 8% tax.*

**$$–$$$** 🏨 **Guanahani Beach Hotel.** One of the finest stretches of beach on the island belongs to this hotel; the palm-tree-lined property is popular with honeymooners. Fully renovated by new owners in 1994, the rooms have pale ceramic tile floors and bright, primary-color Caribbean-print bedspreads and curtains. Every room has an ocean view, two double beds, and a full bathroom. A crewed 35-ft yacht is available to rent for day trips or romantic moonlight rides. Dive packages are available. ⊠ *Box 178,* ☎ *649/94–62135,* ☏ *649/94–61460. 16 rooms. Restaurant, 2 bars, pool, shop. MC, V.*

**$$** 🏨 **Sitting Pretty Hotel.** Formerly known as Kittina and under new
**★** ownership, the hotel is split in two by the town's main drag. On one side, comfortable, lodge-style rooms and sleek balconied suites with kitchens sit on a gleaming white-sand beach. In 1996 beachfront rooms were completely refurbished with new furniture and updated baths. Across the street, the older main house holds a lively dining room and rooms that ooze island atmosphere. Behind the house are the pool and garden. All rooms and suites are air-conditioned and have tile floors. ⊠ *Duke St., Box 42,* ☎ *649/94–62232,* ☏ *649/94–62877. 40 rooms, 2 suites. 2 restaurants, 2 bars, air-conditioning, room service, pool, dive shop, windsurfing, boating, bicycles, shop, baby-sitting, travel services. AE, MC, V. EP, MAP.*

**$** 🏨 **Coral Reef Beach Club.** One- and two-bedroom units here have complete kitchens, air-conditioning, and contemporary furnishings. The resort is a short drive from town, and the beach is a few steps from your door. ⊠ *Box 10,* ☎ *649/94–62055,* ☏ *649/94–62911. 18 units. Restaurant, bar, air-conditioning, pool, tennis court, health club, shop. AE, MC, V. EP, MAP.*

**$** 🏨 **Salt Raker Inn.** Across the street from the beach, this galleried house was the home of a Bermudian shipwright 180 years ago. The rooms and suites are not elegant but are individually decorated and have a homey atmosphere, and each has air-conditioning and a mini-refrigerator. The three garden rooms are desirable for their screened porches and ocean views. Dive packages are available. ⊠ *Duke St., Box 1,* ☎ *649/94–62260,* ☏ *649/94–62817. U.K. reservations:* ⊠ *44 Birchington Rd., London NW6 4LJ,* ☎ *0171/328–6474. 10 rooms, 2 suites. Restaurant, bar, air-conditioning, bicycles. AE, D, MC, V. EP.*

**$** 🏨 **Turk's Head Inn.** Built in 1850 by a prosperous salt miner, this classic Bermudian building has had incarnations as the American Consulate and as the governor's guest house (the queen reportedly took a room here on her last visit to the island). Now run by a Frenchman known as Mr. X, the inn has acquired a strong European flavor. A plethora of Brits and other expat Europeans make it their stomping ground. The seven distinctive rooms have the owner's own drawings, and detailed maps adorn many of the walls. In the front courtyard, an oversize hammock provides the perfect vantage point from which to admire the well-tended garden. The beach is only a few strides away. The bar and restaurant area bustle at night. Dive packages are available. ⊠ *Duke St., Box 58,* ☎ *649/94–62466,* ☏ *649/94–62825. 7 rooms, 1 apartment. Showers only. Restaurant, bar, air-conditioning. AE, MC, V.*

## Turks and Caicos Islands

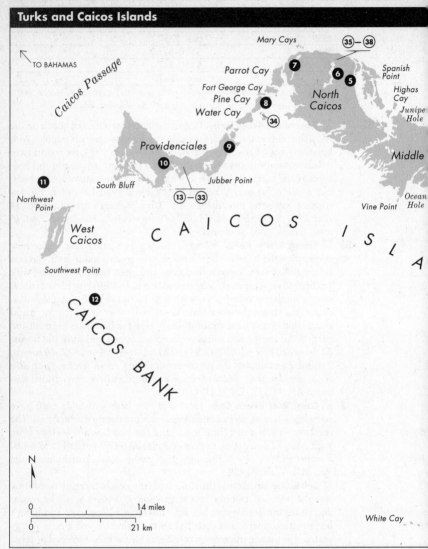

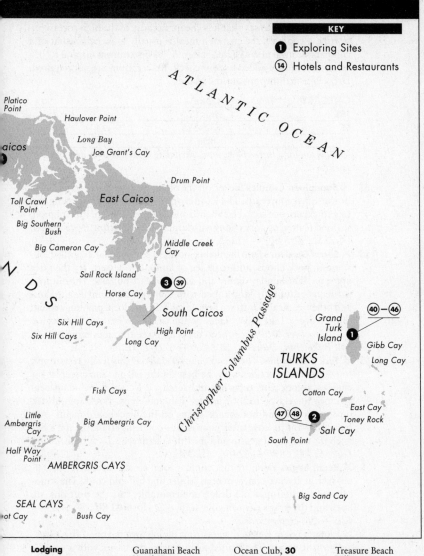

## Dining

Like everything else on these islands, dining out is a very laid-back affair, which is not to say that it is cheap. Because of the high cost of importing all edibles, the cost of a meal is usually higher than that of a comparable meal in the United States. A 7% government tax and a 10% service charge are added to your check. Reservations are not required. Dress is casual throughout the island.

| CATEGORY | COST* |
|---|---|
| $$$ | over $25 |
| $$ | $15–$25 |
| $ | under $15 |

*per person for a three-course meal, excluding drinks, service, and 7% sales tax

$$  ✕ **Sandpiper.** Candles flicker on the Sandpiper's terrace, set beside a flower-filled courtyard. The leisurely pace here creates a relaxing setting to experience such blackboard specialties as lobster, filet mignon, seafood platter, or pork chops with applesauce. ⊠ *Sitting Pretty Hotel, Duke St.,* ☎ *649/94–62232. AE, D, MC, V.*

$$  ✕ **Secret Garden.** Menu highlights include a seafood platter, grilled lobster tail, pork chops, and roast leg of lamb. For dessert, try the tasty apple pie. The Sunday dinner and sing-along are popular. The outdoor garden is beautifully landscaped with hibiscus, bougainvillea, palms, and other tropical plants; sea nets, glass balls and local paintings round out the decor. Like most places on the island, shorts and T-shirts are fine. However, locals are apt to dress up more for an evening out. ⊠ *Salt Raker Inn, Duke St.,* ☎ *649/94–62260. AE, D, MC, V.*

$–$$  ✕ **Turk's Head Inn.** The menu changes daily at this lively restaurant, touted by many residents as the best on the island. Some staples include escargots, pâté, and a handful of other delectables, including local grouper fingers perfectly fried for fish-and-chips. Look for lobster, quiche, steaks, and homemade soups on the blackboard menu. You may not want to leave after your meal—come nightfall, the inn's bar is abuzz with local gossip and mirthful chatter. ⊠ *Turk's Head Inn, Duke St.,* ☎ *649/94–62466. AE, MC, V.*

$  ✕ **Regal Begal.** Drop by this popular local eatery for native specialties such as cracked conch, minced lobster, and fish-and-chips. The atmosphere is casual and the decor unmemorable, but the portions are large and the prices easy on your wallet. ⊠ *Hospital Rd.,* ☎ *649/94–62274. No credit cards.*

$  ✕ **Water's Edge.** Relaxed waterfront dining awaits you at this pleasantly rustic eatery. The limited menu covers the basics with a twist—from barbecued grouper to a fresh seafood crepe. A kids' menu is also available. The food is authentic and filling, and the view at sunset breathtaking, but the irresistible homemade pies are enough to justify a visit. ⊠ *Duke St.,* ☎ *649/94–61680. MC, V. Closed Mon.*

## Beaches

There are more than 230 mi of beaches in the Turks and Caicos Islands, ranging from secluded coves to miles-long stretches. Most beaches are soft coralline sand. Tiny uninhabited cays offer complete isolation for nude sunbathing and skinny-dipping. Many are accessible only by boat. **Governor's Beach,** a long white strip on the west coast of Grand Turk, is one of the nicest beaches on this island.

## Outdoor Activities and Sports

BICYCLING

In Grand Turk on Duke Street, both the **Salt Raker Inn** (☎ 649/94–62260) and the **Sitting Pretty Hotel** (☎ 649/94–62232) rent bikes for $10 per day, $40 per week.

HORSEBACK RIDING

Horses roam lazily around the main roads on Grand Turk. While there is no organized riding program, most hotels will make arrangements for guests, and rates can be negotiated with individual owners.

SCUBA DIVING

Diving is the top attraction here. (All divers must carry and present a valid certificate card before they'll be allowed to dive.) These islands are surrounded by a reef system of more than 200 square mi—much of it unexplored. Grand Turk's famed wall drops more than 7,000 ft and is one side of a 22-mi-wide channel called the Christopher Columbus Passage. From January through March, an estimated 6,000 eastern Atlantic humpback whales swim through this passage en route to their winter breeding grounds. There are undersea cathedrals, coral gardens, and countless tunnels. Operations that provide instruction, equipment rentals, underwater video equipment, and trips are **Sea Eye Divers** (⊠ Duke St., Grand Turk, ☎ 649/94–61407), **Blue Water Divers** (⊠ Front St., Salt Raker Inn, Grand Turk, ☎ 649/94–62432), and **Off the Wall Divers** (⊠ Pond St., Grand Turk, ☎ 649/94–62159).

Note: Divers in need of a hyperbaric/recompression chamber are airlifted to the one on Provo—a 30-minute flight.

SNORKELING

**Blue Water Divers** (⊠ Front St., Salt Raker Inn, Grand Turk, ☎ 649/94–62432) and **Sea Eye Diving** (⊠ Duke St., Grand Turk, ☎ 649/94–61407) both offer equipment and trips, as well as diving packages and instruction.

TENNIS

The **Coral Reef Resort** (⊠ The Ridge, ☎ 649/94–62055) has one lighted court.

## Nightlife

On Grand Turk, Xavier Tonneau (a.k.a. Mr. X) leads sing-alongs in his bar at the **Turk's Head Inn** (⊠ Duke St., ☎ 649/94–62466) almost every night. There's folk and pop music at the **Salt Raker Inn** (⊠ Duke St., ☎ 649/94–62260) on Wednesday and Sunday nights. Weekends and on holidays, head over to the **Nookie Hill Club** (⊠ Nookie Hill, no phone) for dancing.

## Exploring Grand Turk

Pristine beaches with vistas of turquoise waters, small local settlements, historic ruins, and native flora and fauna are among the sights to be seen on these islands. Keep an eye out for fruit-bearing trees like lime, papaya, and custard apple. Birds to look for include the great blue heron, the woodstar hummingbird, and the squawking Cuban crow. It's hard to get lost on any of the islands, as there aren't many roads; given the low amount of traffic, motor scooters can be a fun way to explore.

*Numbers in the margin correspond to points of interest on the Turks and Caicos Islands map.*

Fewer than 4,000 people live on Grand Turk, a 7½-square-mi island. Diving is definitely the big deal here. Grand Turk's Wall, with a sheer drop to 7,000 ft, is well known to divers.

**❶ Cockburn Town.** The buildings in this, the colony's capital and seat of government, reflect the 19th-century Bermudian style of architecture. The narrow streets are lined with low stone walls and old street lamps, now powered by electricity. Horses and cattle wander around as if they own the place, and the occasional donkey cart clatters by, carrying a load of water or freight. In one of the oldest stone buildings in the islands, the **Turks & Caicos National Museum** houses the Molasses Reef wreck of 1513, the earliest shipwreck discovered in the Americas. The natural-history exhibits include artifacts left by African, North American, Bermudian, French, Hispanic, and Taino settlers. An impressive addition to the museum is the coral reef and sea-life exhibit, faithfully modeled on a popular dive site just off the island. ☎ 649/94–62160. ✉ $5. ⊙ Mon.–Tues. and Thurs.–Fri. 9–4, Wed. 9–6, Sat. 10–1.

| NEED A BREAK? | The **Pepper Pot** (no phone) is a little blue shack at the end of Front Street where Peanuts Butterfield makes her famous conch fritters. |
| --- | --- |

# NORTH CAICOS

Thanks to abundant rainfall, this island is the garden center of the Turks and Caicos Islands. Bird-lovers will see a large flock of flamingos here, and fisherman will find the creeks full of bonefish and tarpon. Bring all your own gear, as this quiet island has no water-sports shops.

## Lodging

**$$$** 🏨 **Club Vacanze Prospect of Whitby Hotel.** An Italian resort chain, Club
★ Vacanze, took over this secluded retreat in 1994. Miles of beach are yours for sunbathing, windsurfing, or snorkeling. Spacious guest rooms are simple; in true getaway fashion, they lack TVs and radios. The restaurant here is quite good. ⊠ *Kew Post Office, North Caicos,* ☎ *649/94– 67119,* FAX *649/94–67114. 28 rooms, 4 suites. Restaurant, bar, pool, tennis court, dive shop, windsurfing, baby-sitting, travel services. AE, MC, V. EP, MAP.*

**$$** 🏨 **Ocean Beach Hotel Condominiums.** This unpretentious place provides family-style accommodations on a 10-mi stretch of sheltered beach. The spacious units, each with kitchenette, face the ocean. Constant trade winds, invited in through large sliding glass doors, replace the need for air-conditioning. The hotel offers an intimate lifestyle away from the fray. ⊠ *Whitby, North Caicos,* ☎ *649/94–67113 or 800/710– 5204; 905/336–2876 in Canada;* FAX *649/94–67386. 10 units. Restaurant, bar, fishing, bicycles, car rental. MC, V. MAP.*

**$$** 🏨 **Pelican Beach Hotel.** This hotel has large rooms done in pastels and dark wood trim. Ask to stay on the second floor, where rooms have high wood ceilings and fabulous ocean views. Ceiling fans and constant sea breezes keep you cool. ⊠ *Whitby, North Caicos,* ☎ *649/94– 67112,* FAX *649/94–67139. 14 rooms, 2 suites. Restaurant, bar, fishing. MC, V.*

**$** 🏨 **JoAnne's B&B.** This no-frills, charming bed-and-breakfast on the beach is the perfect spot for those seeking peace and quiet. Rooms are light and airy with cool, white tile floors. Two friendly dogs escort you to the sea and trot along with you as you shell hunt and sun on a very private stretch of beach. The owner, a former Peace Corps worker, also runs Papa Grunts, an excellent restaurant nearby. Her island stories entertain and delight. Faxing is the best way to make reservations. ⊠ *Whitby, North Caicos,* ☎ FAX *649/94–67301. 3 rooms. MC, V.*

## Beaches

The beaches of North Caicos, a 41-square-mi island, are superb for shelling and lolling, and the waters offshore offer excellent snorkeling, bonefishing, and scuba diving (there are no scuba outfitters on the island, so divers will have to make arrangements with dive shops on Provo). **Three Mary's Cays** has excellent snorkeling with a friendly ancient barracuda named Old Man.

### Exploring North Caicos

**6** **Flamingo Pond.** This is a regular nesti  
birds. They tend to wander out in the m  
ulars to see them better.

**5** **Kew.** The ruins of old plantations  
includes a small post office, school, and  
ical trees bearing limes, papayas, and custa  
to gain a better understanding of what life is like  
landers.

**7** **Sandy Point.** Getting to this settlement is half the fun, as you ra  
dirt and stone-filled roads. You'll pass salt flats where you'll very lik  
see flamingos standing around in the shallow waters. They're shy  
birds, so bring binoculars to see them better. A secluded cove here pro-  
vides excellent snorkeling.

# PINE CAY

One of a chain of small cays connecting North Caicos and Provo, 800-  
acre Pine Cay is privately owned and under development as a planned  
community.

### Lodging

**$$$$** **Meridian Club.** High rollers vacation in high style on this privately  
★ owned 800-acre island. Club guests enjoy an unspoiled cay with 2½  
mi of soft white sand and a 500-acre nature reserve with tropical land-  
scaping, freshwater ponds, and nature trails that lure bird-watchers and  
botanists. A stay here is truly getting away from it all, as there are no  
air conditioners, telephones, or TVs. The accommodations range from  
spacious rooms with king-size beds (or twin beds on request) and pat-  
ios to one- to four-bedroom cottage homes that range in decor and ameni-  
ties from rustic to well appointed. There's also a "round room" cottage  
and two ocean-view atrium units that are separated by a lovely inte-  
rior garden. Rooms in the main complex run over $485 a night for  
two in winter and include all meals. Cottage homes start at $3,000 a  
week EP. ⊠ *Pine Cay,* ☎ *800/331–9154,* ℻ *649/94–65128. 12 rooms,  
13 cottage homes. Restaurant, bar, pool, tennis court, windsurfing, boat-  
ing, bicycles. No credit cards. EP, AP.*

### Exploring Pine Cay

**8** It's home to the exclusive **Meridian Club** resort, playground of jet-set-  
ters, and its 2½-mi beach is the most beautiful in the archipelago. The  
island has a 3,800-ft airstrip and electric carts for getting around.

# PROVIDENCIALES

About 6,000 people live on Provo (as everybody calls it), a consider-  
able number of whom are expatriate U.S. and Canadian business-  
people and retirees. Provo's 44 square mi are by far the most developed  
in the Turks and Caicos.

### Lodging

**$$$** **Club Med Turkoise.** This lavish $23 million resort is one of the most  
sumptuous of all Club Med's villages. One-, two-, and three-story  
bungalows line a mile-long beach, and all the usual sybaritic pleasures  
are here. This club is especially geared toward couples, singles aged  
28 and over, and divers. The package includes all the diving, water sports,  
and daytime activities you can handle, plus nightly entertainment. ⊠  
*Providenciales,* ☎ *649/94–65500 or 800/258–2633; 212/750–1684  
or 212/750–1687 in NY;* ℻ *649/94–65501. 298 rooms. 3 restaurants,*

ar, snack bar, pool, 8 tennis courts, exercise room, beach, dive shop,
water sports, fishing, bicycles, shop, dance club, video games, library.
AE, MC, V. All-inclusive (drinks not included).

**$$** ⊞ **Grace Bay Club.** Staying at this Swiss-owned, Mediterranean-style
★ resort is a little like being the guest of honor of a very gracious host
with unbeatable taste. The suites, which all feature a breathtaking view
of Grace Bay's stunning turquoise waters, are furnished with rattan
and pickled wood. Mexican-tile floors are elegantly appointed with throw
rugs from Turkey and India. If you choose to take advantage of the
myriad activities (from diving to golf to individually planned and
catered picnics on surrounding islands), you will be expertly provided
for; but the main attraction here is natural beauty. Relax and enjoy a
getaway that is peaceful, invigorating, and wonderfully pampering. ⊠
Box 128, Providenciales, ☎ 649/94–65757 or 800/946–5757, FAX
649/94–65758. 22 suites. Restaurant, bar, pool, hot tub, 2 tennis
courts, beach, water sports, video games, library. AE, MC, V. EP,
MAP.

**$$$** ⊞ **Sandals, Turks and Caicos.** A row of giant palm trees lines the ap-
proach to this new, elegant pink-and-white resort, a couples-only, all-
inclusive retreat. Stroll among the lush tropical landscaping, take a dip
in the free-form lap pool, and dine in one of the delicious restaurants—there are plenty of sports and activities to work off the extra
calories. You'll be sufficiently pampered with bar service that extends
to the beach. Luxurious accommodations combined with white-glove
service make this all-inclusive resort a truly relaxing experience. ⊠ Grace
Bay, ☎ 649/94–68000 or 800/726–3257, FAX 649/94-68001. 200
rooms. 3 restaurants, pool, hot tub, 2 tennis courts, exercise room, water
sports, dive shop. AE, MC, V. All-inclusive.

**$$$** ⊞ **Turquoise Reef Resort & Casino.** Oversize oceanfront rooms have
★ rattan furniture and a rich Caribbean color scheme. Furnished with a
king or two double beds, all rooms are air-conditioned and have a color
TV and ceiling fan, and either a terrace or a patio. The island's only
casino is here, and there's live nightly entertainment. Guests enjoy a
free daily activities program that includes pool volleyball and children's
treasure hunts. ⊠ Box 205, Provo, ☎ 649/94–65555, FAX 649/94–
65522. 228 rooms. 3 restaurants, 3 bars, air-conditioning, fans, room
service, pool, hot tub, 2 tennis courts, exercise room, beach, dive shop,
water sports, shops, casino, dance club, baby-sitting, travel services.
AE, MC, V. EP, MAP.

**$$** ⊞ **Island Princess.** Wood walkways at this hotel lead up to and around
the rooms, which are in two wings. All rooms have cable TV and a
private balcony. This is a suitable little hotel for families. It's on the
beach, the restaurant serves excellent Italian and Caribbean food, and
there's nightly entertainment. ⊠ The Bight, ☎ 649/94–64260, FAX
649/94–64666. 80 rooms. Restaurant, bar, 2 pools, water sports,
boating, recreation room, playground. AE, D, MC, V. MAP.

**$$** ⊞ **Le Deck Hotel & Beach Club.** This 27-room pink hostelry was built
★ in classic Bermudian style around a tropical courtyard. It offers clean
rooms with a tile floor, color TV, phone, and air-conditioning. Le
Deck is especially popular with divers, and its atmosphere is informal
and lively with a mostly thirty-something-and-over crowd. ⊠ Box 144,
Grace Bay, Provo, ☎ 649/94–65547, FAX 649/94–65770. 25 rooms,
2 suites. Restaurant, bar, air-conditioning, pool, beach, water sports,
shop. AE, D, MC, V. EP, CP, AP, MAP.

**$$** ⊞ **Ocean Club.** "Escape the Stress of Success" is the slogan for this luxury beachfront suite resort. It's on Grace Bay's 12-mi stretch of pris-
tine beach, a short walk away from Provo's only golf course. The all-suite
accommodations range from efficiency studios to deluxe versions
with ocean view, screened balcony, kitchen, dining room, and living

room. Third-floor rooms have striking slanted ceilings, and all but efficiency accommodations include washer and dryer. Efficiency studios fall into our $ category. ✉ *Box 240, Providenciales,* ☎ *649/94–65880 or 800/457–8787,* ℻ *649/94–65845. 86 suites. 2 restaurants, bar, pool, 18-hole golf course, tennis court, exercise room, dive shop, shop. AE, MC, V. EP.*

$$ 🏨 **Treasure Beach Villas.** These one- and two-bedroom modern, self-catering apartments have fully equipped kitchens and ceiling fans. You may want a car or bike (Treasure Beach has rentals) to reach the grocery store or restaurants; bus service is limited. Provo's 12 mi of white sandy beach is just outside your door, and the hotel can organize fishing, snorkeling, and scuba expeditions. ✉ *The Bight,* ☎ *649/94–64325,* ℻ *649/94–64108; or* ✉ *Box 8409, Hialeah, FL 33012. 8 single, 10 double rooms. Pool, tennis court. AE, D, MC, V. EP.*

$$ 🏨 **Turtle Cove Inn.** A marina, a free-form pool, a dive shop with equipment rentals and instruction, and lighted tennis courts attract the sporting crowd to Turtle Cove. There's a free boat shuttle to the nearby beach and snorkeling reef. All rooms have a TV, phone, and air-conditioning, and eight also have mini-refrigerators. A handful of good restaurants are within walking distance. ✉ *Providenciales,* ☎ *649/94–64203 or 800/887–0477,* ℻ *649/94–64141. 30 rooms, 1 suite. 2 restaurants, 2 bars, air-conditioning, 2 tennis courts, pool, dive shop, bicycles. AE, MC, V. EP.*

$–$$ 🏨 **Erebus Inn Resort.** This environmentally sensitive resort sits on a cliff
★ overlooking Turtle Cove and has wonderful panoramic views. All units have two double beds, modern wicker furnishings, and original island artwork, including some lovely and unique Haitian wall hangings. Rooms in the older chalet cost under $110 a night (double occupancy) in winter. For those preferring creature comforts, we recommend the units in the newer section ($$); each has air-conditioning, cable TV, and phone. Frequent bus shuttles take guests to a nearby beach. The restaurant and bar, always one of Provo's liveliest spots, has a menu of French and Caribbean cuisine. Five affordable restaurants are within walking distance, as are snorkeling sites, a shopping center, and several dive operations. ✉ *Turtle Cove, Box 238, Providenciales,* ☎ *649/94–64240,* ℻ *649/94–64704. 30 rooms. Restaurant, bar, air-conditioning, 2 pools (1 saltwater), 2 tennis courts, aerobics, exercise room, baby-sitting. AE, MC, V. EP, MAP.*

## Dining

$$$ ✕ **Gecko Grille.** Gourmet dining can be enjoyed either indoors amid tropical hand-painted murals or out on the garden patio. The menu features creative dishes such as almond-cracked conch with a lime *rémoulade* (a cold, mayonnaise-based sauce), and grilled pork chops marinated in papaya juice. Portions are quite large, so either share or bring a hearty appetite. ✉ *Ocean Club Resort, Grace Bay,* ☎ *649/94–65880. AE, MC, V.*

$$$ ✕ **The Terrace.** The cuisine here has a Euro-Caribbean flair, and the menu changes according to the freshest ingredients available. You can make a meal from such delicious starters as freshly baked tomato-and-goat-cheese tarts, lobster bisque, and simmered mussels. Main courses include roast rack of lamb, and fresh conch encrusted with pecans. Top it all off with a classic crème brûlée. ✉ *Turtle Cove,* ☎ *649/94–64763. AE, MC, V. Closed Sun.*

$$–$$$ ✕ **Alfred's Place.** Austrian owner Alfred Holzfeind caters to an Amer-
★ ican palate with an extensive menu featuring everything from prime rib to chicken salad. The alfresco lounge is a popular watering hole for locals and tourists alike ✉ *Turtle Cove,* ☎ *649/94–64679. AE, D, MC, V. Closed Mon. July–Oct. No lunch weekends.*

**$$–$$$** ✕ **Anacaona.** At the impressive Grace Bay Club, this exquisitely de-
★ signed restaurant offers a true gourmet dining experience minus the
tie, the air-conditioning, and the attitude. Start with a bottle of fine
wine from the extensive cellar, and then enjoy a three- or four-course
meal of the chef's light but flavorful cooking, which combines traditional French recipes with fresh seafood and Caribbean fruits, vegetables,
and spices. Oil lamps on the tables, gently circulating ceiling fans, and
the natural sounds of the breeze, ocean, birds, and tree frogs all add
to the Eden-like environment. ⊠ *Grace Bay Club, Providenciales,* ☎
*649/94–65050. AE, MC, V.*

**$–$$** ✕ **Dora's.** This popular local eatery serves island fare—turtle, shred-
ded lobster, spicy conch chowder—seven days a week, from 7 AM until
the last person leaves the bar. Plastic print and lace tablecloths, hanging plants, and Haitian art add to the island ambience. Soups come
with homemade bread, and entrées such as fish-and-chips, conch Creole, and grilled pork chops come with a choice of vegetable. Be sure
to come early for the packed Monday- and Thursday-night all-you-
can-eat $20 seafood buffet. The price includes round-trip transporta-
tion to your hotel. ⊠ *Leeward Hwy.,* ☎ *649/94–64558. No credit cards.*

**$–$$** ✕ **Fast Eddie's.** Plants festoon this cheerful restaurant, which is across
from the airport. Broiled turtle steak, fried grouper fingers, and other
island specialties are joined on the menu by old American standbys such
as cheeseburgers and cherry pie. Wednesday evening there's a $20
($10 for children) all-you-can-eat seafood buffet. Friday is prime rib
and live music night. Free transportation to and from your hotel is provided. ⊠ *Airport Rd.,* ☎ *649/94–13175. MC, V.*

**$–$$** ✕ **Hong Kong Restaurant.** A no-frills place with plain wood tables and
chairs, the Hong Kong offers dine-in, delivery, and take-out. The menu
includes lobster with ginger and green onions, chicken with black-bean
sauce, sliced duck with salted mustard greens, and sweet-and-sour
chicken. ⊠ *Leeward Hwy.,* ☎ *649/94–65678. V. No lunch Sun.*

**$** ✕ **Banana Boat.** Buoys and other sea relics deck the walls of this
brightly painted casual restaurant on the wharf. Grilled grouper, lob-
ster-salad sandwiches, conch fritters, and a refreshing conch salad are
among the menu options. Excellent tropical drinks include the house
specialty, the rum-filled Banana Breeze. ⊠ *Turtle Cove,* ☎ *649/94–
15706. AE, MC, V.*

**$** ✕ **Caicos Cafe.** There's a pervasive air of celebration in the uncovered
outdoor dining area of this popular eatery. Choose from a selection of
local and American cuisine, including lobster sandwiches, hamburgers, and a variety of excellent salads. ⊠ *Across from Turquoise Reef,*
☎ *649/94–65278. AE. No lunch Sun.*

**$** ✕ **Hey, José.** Frequented by locals, this restaurant claims to serve the
★ island's best margaritas. Customers also return for the tasty Tex-Mex
treats: tacos, tostados, nachos, burritos, fajitas, and José's special-
recipe hot chicken wings. Creative types can build their own pizzas.
⊠ *Central Square,* ☎ *649/94–64812. AE, MC, V. Closed Sun.*

**$** ✕ **Pub on the Bay.** If beachfront dining is what you're after, it doesn't
get much better than this. Located in the Blue Hill residential district,
a five-minute drive from downtown Provo, this restaurant serves fried
or steamed fish, oxtail stew, barbecue ribs, chicken, various sandwiches, and even turtle steak. There is no air-conditioning inside the
restaurant, so you may as well cross the street to one of three thatched
roof "huts," which stand on the beach. ⊠ *Blue Hill Rd.,* ☎ *649/94–
15309. AE, MC, V.*

**$** ✕ **Top O' the Cove Gourmet Delicatessen.** You can easily walk to this
tiny café on Leeward Highway from the Turtle Cove and Erebus Inns.
Don't be put off by the location in the Napa Auto Parts plaza. Order
breakfast, deli subs, sandwiches, salads, and cool soft-swirl frozen yo-

gurt. It's open every day but Christmas and New Year's from 7 AM to 3:30 PM. ✉ *Leeward Hwy.,* ☎ *649/94–64694. No credit cards.*

## Beaches

A fine white-sand beach stretches 12 mi along the northeast coast of **Providenciales.** There are good beaches at **Sapodilla Bay**; for excellent close-to-shore snorkeling there's a reef near the White House off Penn's Road.

## Outdoor Activities and Sports

### BICYCLING

Provo has a few steep grades to conquer, but they're short, and there's little traffic. Bikes can be rented at the **Island Princess** hotel (☎ 649/94–64260) at the Bight for $10 a day, through **Turtle Inn Divers** (✉ Turtle Cove Inn, ☎ 649/94–15389) for $12 a day and $60 a week, or at the **Turquoise Reef Resort & Casino** (✉ Grace Bay, ☎ 649/94–65555) for $14 a day.

### BOAT RENTALS

You can rent a boat with a private captain for a half or full day of sport-fishing through **J&B Tours** (✉ Leward Marina, Provo, ☎ 649/94–65047) for about $300 a day. **Dive Provo** (✉ Turquoise Reef Resort, Grace Bay, Provo, ☎ 649/94–65040) rents small sailboats for $20 per hour and provides beginning instruction for $40 for up to two hours. Sailing not your bent? Try open-cockpit ocean kayaking, available at Dive Provo for $10 per hour for one and $15 per hour for two.

### FISHING

**Silver Deep** (✉ Turtle Cove Marina, Provo, ☎ 649/94–15595) will take you out for half- or full-day bonefishing or bottom-fishing expeditions, bait and tackle included. The same outfit will arrange half- or full-day deep-sea fishing trips in search of shark, marlin, kingfish, sawfish, wahoo, and tuna, with all equipment furnished. Deep-sea, bone-, and bottom fishing are also available aboard the *Sakitumi* (☎ 649/94–64065).

### GOLF

**Provo Golf Club** (☎ 649/94–65991) has a par-72, 18-hole championship course, designed by Karl Litten, that is sustained by a desalination plant producing 250,000 gallons of water a day. The turf is sprinkled in green islands over 12 acres of natural limestone outcroppings, creating a desert-style design of narrow "target areas" and sandy waste areas—a formidable challenge to anyone playing from the championship tees. Fees are $90, which includes a shared electric cart. A pro shop, driving ranges, and a restaurant and bar round out the club's facilities.

### PARASAILING

A 15-minute flight is available for $45 at either **Dive Provo** (✉ Turquoise Reef Resort, Provo, ☎ 649/94–65040 or 800/234–7768) or **J&B Tours** (✉ Leward Marina, ☎ 649/94–65047).

### SCUBA DIVING

As diving is the number one tourist activity on the island, there are lots of dive operators to choose from: **Art Pickering's Provo Turtle Divers** (✉ Turtle Cove Marina, Provo, ☎ 649/94–64232), **Aquanaut** (✉ Turtle Cove, Provo, ☎ 649/94–64048), **Caicos Adventures** (✉ Turtle Cove Marina, Provo, ☎ 649/94–63346), **Dive Provo** (✉ Turquoise Reef Resort, Provo, ☎ 649/94–65040 or 800/234–7768), **Flamingo Divers** (✉ Turtle Cove, Provo, ☎ 649/94–64193), **J&B Tours** (✉ Leward Marina, ☎ 649/94–65047).

Note: A modern hyperbaric/recompression chamber is located on Provo in the **Menzies Medical Centre** (☎ 649/94–64242) on Leeward Highway.

SEA EXCURSIONS

The **Ocean Outback** (☎ 649/94–64080), a 70-ft motor cruiser, has barbecue-and-snorkel cruises to uninhabited islands. Both the 37-ft catamaran **Beluga** (☎ 649/94–15196), $39 per half day, and the 56-ft trimaran **Tao** (☎ 649/94–65040) run sunset cruises, as well as sailing and snorkeling outings. A full-day outing on the *Tao* is $59 per person, including snorkel rental and lunch. For $20 per person, **Dive Provo** (✉ Turquoise Reef Resort, ☎ 649/94–65040 or 800/234–7768) gives two-hour glass-bottom-boat tours of the spectacular reefs. **Turtle Inn Divers** (✉ Turtle Cove Inn, ☎ 649/94–15389) offers full-day Sunday excursions for divers for $64.50 per person ($25 per person for nondivers and snorkelers). The **Turks and Caicos Aggressor** (✉ Turtle Cove Marina, ☎ 504/385–2416, FAX 504/384–0817) offers luxury six-day dive cruises with full accommodations.

SNORKELING

**Dive Provo** (✉ Turtle Cove Marina, Provo, ☎ 649/94–65040 or 800/234–7768) and **Provo Turtle Divers** (✉ Turtle Cove Marina, Provo, ☎ 649/94–64232) provide rentals for about $10 and trips for $20.

SPECTATOR SPORTS

Cricket is the most popular game in town. The season runs from July through August. Tennis, basketball, softball, and darts are other local favorites. You're welcome to join in. Inquire at the tourist board (☎ 800/241–0824) for a list of events.

TENNIS

There are two lighted courts at **Turtle Cove Inn** (☎ 649/94–64203), eight courts (four lighted) at **Club Med Turkoise** (☎ 649/94–65500), two lighted courts at the **Turquoise Reef Resort** (☎ 649/94–65555), two lighted courts at the **Erebus Inn** (☎ 649/94–64240), one unlighted court at **Treasure Beach Villas** (☎ 649/94–64211), and two lighted courts at **Grace Bay Club** (☎ 649/94–65050).

WATERSKIING

Water-skiers will find the calm turquoise water ideal for long-distance runs. **Dive Provo** (✉ Turquoise Reef Resort, Provo, ☎ 649/94–65040 or 800/234–7768) charges $35 for a 15-minute run.

WINDSURFING

Rental and instruction are available at **Dive Provo** (✉ Turquoise Reef Resort, Provo, ☎ 649/94–65040 or 800/234–7768).

## Shopping

Shopping is limited to hotel gift shops, airports, and occasional street vendors, except on Provo, where new shops and franchises open every month. Most of these stores can be found in five main shopping complexes: Market Place, Central Square, Caribbean Place, all on Leeward Highway; Turtle Cove Landing, in Turtle Cove; and the newest complex, Ports of Call, in Grace Bay. Delicate baskets woven from the local top grasses and small metalworks are the only crafts native to the Turks and Caicos, and they are sold in many shops.

The **Bamboo Gallery** (✉ Market Place, Provo, ☎ 649/94–064748) sells all types of Caribbean art, from vivid Haitian paintings to wood carvings and local metal sculptures. **Greensleeves** (✉ Central Square, Provo, ☎ 649/94–64147) is the place to go for paintings by local artists, island-made rag rugs, baskets, jewelry, and sisal mats and bags. **Mama's Gifts** (✉ Ports of Call, Provo, ☎ 649/94–13338) sells hand-woven and embroidered straw baskets, handbags, hats, and shell and wood jewelry. **Maison Creole** (⊠ Grace Bay, Provo, no phone) sells unique Caribbean arts and crafts, including painted metal sculptures, furniture, carved wood masks, canes, and bowls. **Pelican's Pouch/Designer I** (⊠ Turtle Cove Landing, Provo, ☎ 649/94–64343) displays resort wear, sandals, Provo T-shirts, perfumes, and gold jewelry on the ground floor; head upstairs for basketry, sculpture, and watercolors. **Paradise Gifts/Arts** (⊠ Central Square, Provo, ☎ 649/94–64637) has a ceramics studio on the premises; in addition to ceramics, jewelry, T-shirts, and paintings by local artists are sold here. **Royal Jewels** (⊠ Leeward Hwy., Provo, ☎ 649/94–64885; ⊠ Turquoise Reef Resort, Provo, ☎ 649/94–65311; ⊠ Airport, Provo, ☎ 649/94–65311) sells gold and jewelry, designer watches, and perfumes—all duty-free.

## Nightlife

On Provo, the newest hot spot is **Casablanca** (⊠ Next to Club Med, ☎ 649/94–65449), a Monte Carlo–style nightclub complete with mirrors and a decked-out crowd. **Disco Elite** (⊠ Airport Rd., ☎ 649/94–64592) has strobe lights and an elevated dance floor. A full band plays native, reggae, and contemporary music on Thursday night at the **Erebus Inn** (⊠ Turtle Cove, ☎ 649/94–64240). **Le Deck** (⊠ Grace Bay, ☎ 649/94–65547) offers one-armed bandits every night. A lively lounge can be found at the **Turquoise Reef Resort** (⊠ Grace Bay, ☎ 649/94–65555), where a musician plays to the mostly tourist crowd. **Port Royale** (⊠ Turquoise Reef Resort, ☎ 649/94–65508) is the island's only gambling casino.

## Exploring Providenciales

In the mid-18th century, so the story goes, a French ship was wrecked near here and the survivors were washed ashore on an island they gratefully christened La Providentielle. Under the Spanish, the name was changed to Providenciales.

With its rolling ridges and 12-mi beach, the island is a prime target for developers. More than two decades ago a group of U.S. investors, including the DuPonts, Ludingtons, and Roosevelts, opened up this island for visitors and those seeking homesites in the Caribbean. In 1990 the island's first luxury resort, the Turquoise Reef Resort & Casino, opened, and with it, the island's first gourmet Italian restaurant. The luxurious Ocean Club, a condominium resort at Grace Bay, was also completed in 1990 and was followed by the upscale Grace Bay Club resort in 1992. The newest luxury resort is the Royal Bay, which opened in 1995. Competition created by the new resorts spurred many of the older hotels to undertake much-needed renovations.

🔟 **Downtown Provo.** Near Providenciales International Airport, the downtown is really a strip mall that houses car-rental agencies, law offices, boutiques, banks, and other businesses.

❾ **Island Sea Center.** On the northeast coast, this is the place to learn about the sea and its inhabitants. Here you'll find the **Caicos Conch Farm**, a major mariculture operation where the mollusks are farmed commercially. The farm's tourist facilities include a video show, boutique, and a hands-on tank with conchs in various stages of growth. There are more than 2.5 million conchs in their inventory. Established by the PRIDE Foundation (Protection of Reefs and Islands from Degradation and Exploitation), the **JoJo Dolphin Project**, named after a 7-ft-long male bottlenose dolphin who cruises these waters and enjoys playing with local divers, is also here. You can watch a video on JoJo and learn how to interact with him safely if you see him on one of your dives.

✉ *Island Sea Center,* ☎ *649/94–65330;* ✉ *Caicos Conch Farm,* ☎ *649/94–65849.* 🖼 *$6.* ☉ *Mon.–Sat. 9–5.*

# SALT CAY

Only 200 people live on this tiny 2½-square-mi dot of land. There's not much in the way of development, but there are splendid beaches on the north coast.

## Lodging

**$$$$** 🏨 **Windmills Plantation.** The attraction here is the lack of distraction:
★ no nightlife, no cruise ships, no crowds, and no shopping. Owner-manager-architect Guy Lovelace and his interior designer wife, Patricia, built the hotel as their version of a colonial-era plantation. The great house has four suites, each with a sitting area, four-poster bed, ceiling fans, and a veranda or balcony with a view of the sea. All are furnished in a mix of antique English and wicker furniture. Four other rooms are housed in two adjacent buildings. Room rates, which during the height of winter run from $415 a night and up for two people, include snorkeling equipment, three meals, and unlimited bar drinks, wine, and beer. ✉ *Salt Cay,* ☎ *649/94–66962 or 800/822–7715,* 🆋 *649/94–66930. 4 rooms, 4 suites. Restaurant, bar, pool, hiking, horseback riding, beach, snorkeling, fishing, library. AE, MC, V. AP.*

**$–$$** 🏨 **Mount Pleasant Guest House.** This simple, somewhat rustic hotel offers guests inexpensive lodging at a remote location. Not all rooms have private baths. ✉ *Salt Cay,* ☎ *649/94–66927 or 800/821-6670. 7 rooms, 1 with bath. Restaurant, bar, horseback riding, scuba diving, bicycles, library. MC, V.*

## Beaches

There are superb beaches on the north coast of **Salt Cay. Big Sand Cay,** 7 mi to the south of Salt Cay, is also known for its excellent beaches.

## Outdoor Activities and Sports

SCUBA DIVING
**Porpoise Divers** (✉ Salt Cay, ☎ 649/94–66927) rents all the necessary equipment.

## Exploring Salt Cay

Salt sheds and salt ponds are silent reminders of the days when the island was a leading producer of salt. February through March, whales pass by on the way to their winter breeding grounds. Scuba divers can dive the *Endymion,* a recently discovered 140-ft wooden-hull British warship that sank in 1790.

**❷ Balfour Town.** What little development there is on Salt Cay is found in this town. It's home to the Windmills Plantation hotel, the Mount Pleasant Guest House, and a few stores.

# SOUTH CAICOS

This 8½-square-mi island was once an important salt producer; today it's the heart of the fishing industry. The beaches here are small and unremarkable, but the vibrant reef makes it a popular destination for divers.

## Lodging

**$–$$** 🏨 **Club Caribe Beach & Harbour Hotel.** Cockburn Harbour, the only natural harbor in the Turks and Caicos Islands, is the perfect setting for this hotel. The 16 beachfront villas, which can be rented as studios or as one-, two-, or three-bedroom apartments, have cool tile floors and kitchenettes equipped with mini-refrigerator and microwave. Half of the rooms don't have air-conditioning, but they get a nice breeze around the clock. The 22 harbor rooms are smaller than the others but have air-conditioning. There's a dive shop with a full-time instructor. ⊠ *Box 1, South Caicos,* ☎ *649/94–63444 or 800/722–2582,* FAX *649/94–63446. 38 rooms. Restaurant, bar, dive shop, windsurfing, bicycles. AE, D, MC, V. EP, MAP.*

### Beaches

Due south is **Big Ambergris Cay,** an uninhabited cay about 14 mi beyond the Fish Cays, with a magnificent beach at Long Bay. To the north is **East Caicos,** an uninhabited island has a beautiful 17-mi-long beach along its north coast. The island was once a cattle range and the site of a major sisal-growing industry. Both these cays are accessible only by boat.

### Exploring South Caicos

Spiny lobster and queen conch are found in the shallow Caicos bank to the west and are harvested for export by local processing plants. The bonefishing here is some of the best in the West Indies. At the northern end of the island are fine, white-sand beaches; the south coast is great for scuba diving along the drop-off; and there's excellent snorkeling off the windward (east) coast, where large stands of elkhorn and staghorn coral shelter a variety of small tropical fish.

❸ **Cockburn Harbour.** The best natural harbor in the Caicos chain is home to the South Caicos Regatta, held each year in May.

# MIDDLE CAICOS

This is the largest (48 square mi) and least developed of the inhabited Turks and Caicos Islands. Since telephones are a rare commodity, the boats that dock here and the planes that land on the little airstrip provide the island's 275 residents with their main connection to the outside world. **J&B Tours** offers boat tours from Provo to the mysterious Conch Bar Caves (☞ *below*).

### Exploring Middle Caicos

❹ **Conch Bar Caves.** These limestone caves have eerie underground lakes and milky-white stalactites and stalagmites. Archaeologists have discovered Arawak and Lucayan Indian artifacts in the caves and the surrounding area.

# WEST CAICOS

Accessible only by boat, this island is uninhabited and untamed, and there are no facilities whatsoever. A glorious white beach stretches for a mile along the northwest point, and offshore diving is among the most exotic in the islands. A wall inhabited by countless species of large marine life begins ¼ mi offshore. If you do tour West Caicos, take along several vats of insect repellent. It won't help much with the sharks, but it should fend off the mosquitoes and sand flies. Be advised, too, that the interior is overgrown with dense shrubs, including manchineel, whose green fruit is poisonous. Sap and even raindrops falling from the trees onto your skin can be painful.

### Exploring West Caicos

⓬ **Molasses Reef.** It is rumored to be the final resting place of the *Pinta,* which is thought to have been wrecked here in the early 1500s. Over the past few centuries numerous wrecks have occurred in the area between West Caicos and Provo, and author Peter Benchley is among the treasure seekers who have been lured to this island.

**⑪** **Northwest Reef.** The site offers great stands of elkhorn coral and acres of staghorn brambles. But this area is only for experienced divers. The wall starts deep, the currents are strong—and there are sharks in the waters.

# TURKS AND CAICOS ISLANDS A TO Z

## Arriving and Departing

### BY BOAT

Because of the superb diving, three live-aboard dive boats call regularly. Contact the **Aquanaut** (✉ c/o See & Sea, ☎ 800/348–9778), the **Sea Dancer** (✉ c/o Peter Hughes Diving, ☎ 800/932–6237), or the **Turks and Caicos Aggressor** (✉ c/o Aggressor Fleet, ☎ 504/385–2628 or 800/348–2628, FAX 504/384–0817).

### BY PLANE

**American Airlines** (☎ 800/433–7300) flies daily between Miami and Provo. **Turks & Caicos Islands Airlines** (☎ 649/94–64255) is the only regularly scheduled carrier that flies between Provo, Grand Turk, and other outer Turks and Caicos islands. Many air charter services also connect the islands (☞ Guided Tours, *below*).

### FROM THE AIRPORT

Taxis are available at the airports; expect to share a ride. Rates are fixed. A trip between Provo's airport and most major hotels runs about $15. On Grand Turk, a trip from the airport to town is about $5; from the airport to hotels outside town, $6–$11.

## Currency

The unit of currency is U.S. dollars.

## Emergencies

**Police:** Grand Turk, ☎ 649/94–62299; Providenciales, ☎ 649/94–64259; North Caicos, ☎ 649/94–67116; South Caicos, ☎ 649/94–63299. **Hospitals:** There is a 24-hour emergency room at **Grand Turk Hospital** (✉ Hospital Rd., ☎ 649/94–62333) and at **Providenciales Health-Medical Center** (✉ Leeward Hwy., ☎ 649/94–64201). **Pharmacies:** Prescriptions can be filled at the **Government Clinic** (✉ Grand Turk Hospital, ☎ 649/94–62040) and at the **Providenciales Health-Medical Center** in Provo (✉ Leeward Hwy., ☎ 649/94–64201).

## Getting Around

### BUSES

On Provo, shuttle buses operated by **Executive Tours** (☎ 649/94–64524) run from the hotels into town every hour, Monday through Saturday 9–6. Fares are $2 each way. A new public bus system on Grand Turk charges 50¢ one-way to any scheduled stop.

### CAR RENTALS

Local rental agencies on Provo are **Turks & Caicos National** (☎ 649/94–64701), **Provo Rent-a-Car** (☎ 649/94–64404), **Rent a Buggy** (☎ 649/94–64158), and **Turquoise Jeep Rentals** (☎ 649/94–64910); on Grand Turk, try **Dutchie's Car Rental** (☎ 649/94–62244). Rates average $40 to $65 per day, plus a $10-per-rental-agreement government tax. To rent cars on South Caicos, check with your hotel manager for rates and information.

### FERRIES

Ferries are available between some islands; check with local marinas. The only government ferry (no phone) runs between Grand Turk and Salt Cay.

You can scoot around Provo by contacting **Scooter Bob's** (☎ 649/94–64684) or the **Honda Shop** (☎ 649/94–64397). On North Caicos, contact **North Caicos Scooter Rentals** (☎ 649/94–67301). Rates generally start at $25 per day for a one-seater and $40 a day for a two-seater, plus a onetime $5 government tax and gas.

Taxis are unmetered, and rates, posted in the taxis, are regulated by the government. In Provo, call the Provo taxi association (☎ 649/94–65481).

## Guided Tours

A **taxi** tour of the islands costs between $25 and $30 for the first hour and $25 for each additional hour. On Provo, contact **Paradise Taxi Company** (☎ 649/94–13555). **Turtle Tours** (☎ 649/94–65585) offers a variety of bus and small-plane tours. You can also fly to Middle Caicos, the largest of the islands, for a visit to its mysterious caves or to North Caicos to see the ruins of a former slave plantation. If you want to island-hop on your own schedule, air charters are available through **Blue Hills Aviation** (☎ 649/94–15290), **Flamingo Air Services** (☎ 649/94–62109 or 649/94–64933), and **SkyKing** (☎ 649/94–15464).

## Language

The official language of the Turks and Caicos is English.

## Lodging

Hotel accommodations are available on Grand Turk, North Caicos, South Caicos, Pine Cay, and Provo. There are also some small, non-air-conditioned guest houses on Salt Cay and Middle Caicos. Accommodations range from small island inns to the splashy Club Med Turkoise to the luxury Grace Bay Club in Providenciales. Because of the popularity of scuba diving here, virtually all the hotels have dive shops and offer dive packages. Dive packagers offering air-hotel-dive packages include **Dive Provo** (☎ 800/234–7768) and **Undersea Adventures** (☎ 800/234–7768). Most of the medium and large hotels offer a choice of EP and MAP. People who don't rent a car or scooter tend to eat at their hotels, so MAP may be the better option. Another option favored by many visitors, particularly families, is renting a self-contained villa or private home; contact the **Ministry of Tourism** (☎ 649/94–62321) three to six months in advance for more information. Please note that the government hotel tax does not apply to guest houses with fewer than four rooms.

## Opening and Closing Times

Most offices are open weekdays from 8 or 8:30 till 4 or 4:30. Banks are open Monday–Thursday 8:30–2:30, Friday 8:30–12:30 and 2:30–4:30.

## Passports and Visas

U.S. citizens need some proof of citizenship, such as a birth certificate (original or certified copy), plus a photo ID or a current passport. British subjects must have a current passport. All visitors must have an ongoing or return ticket.

## Precautions

Petty crime does occur here, and you're advised to leave your valuables in the hotel safe-deposit box. Bring along a can of insect repellent: The mosquitoes and no-see-ums can be vicious.

If you plan to explore the uninhabited island of West Caicos, be advised that the interior is overgrown with dense shrubs that include manchineel, which has a milky, poisonous sap that can cause painful, scarring blisters.

In some hotels on Grand Turk, Salt Cay, and South Caicos, there are signs that read PLEASE HELP US CONSERVE OUR PRECIOUS WATER. These islands have no freshwater supply other than rainwater collected in cisterns, and rainfall is scant. Drink only from the decanter of fresh water your hotel provides; tap water is safe for brushing your teeth or other hygiene uses.

## Taxes and Service Charges
Most hotels collect a 7%–8% government tax; all add a 10%–15% service charge to your bill. Restaurants collect a 7% government tax and add a 10% service charge to your bill. Taxi drivers expect a token tip. The departure tax is $15.

## Telephones and Mail
You can call the islands direct from the United States by dialing 809 and the number. To call home from Turks and Caicos, dial direct from most hotels, from some pay phones, and from **Cable and Wireless,** which has offices in Provo (☎ 649/94–64499) and Grand Turk (☎ 649/94–62200), open Monday–Thursday 8–4:30 and Friday 8–4. You must dial 0, followed by the country code (1 for U.S. and Canada; 44 for U.K.), area code, and local number.

Postal rates for letters to the United States, Bahamas, and Caribbean are 50¢ per half ounce; postcards, 35¢. Letters to the United Kingdom and Europe, run 65¢ per half ounce; postcards, 45¢. Letters to Canada, Puerto Rico, and South America cost 65¢; postcards, 45¢.

## Visitor Information
For tourist information contact the **Turks and Caicos Islands Tourist Board** (☎ 800/241–0824). The **Caribbean Tourism Organization** (✉ 20 E. 46th St., New York, NY 10017, ☎ 212/682–0435) is another source of information. In the United Kingdom, contact **Morris-Kevan International Ltd.** (✉ International House, 47 Chase Side, Enfield Middlesex EN2 6NB, ☎ 0181/367–5175).

On Grand Turk, the **Government Tourist Office** (✉ Front St., Cockburn Town, Grand Turk, ☎ 649/94–62321; ✉ Turtle Cove Landing, Provo, ☎ 649/94–64970) is open Monday–Thursday 8–4:30 and Friday 8–5.

# 27 The U.S. Virgin Islands

*St. Thomas, St. Croix, St. John*

*Palms sway, boats anchor tranquilly on a turquoise bay, and the sun warms bright white beaches with its golden rays—it's another day in America's paradise.*

Updated by
Carol
Bareuther and
Lynda Lohr

**I** **T IS THE COMBINATION** of the familiar and the exotic in the U.S. Virgin Islands that defines this "American paradise" and explains much of its appeal. The effort to be all things to all people—while remaining true to the best of itself—has created a sometimes paradoxical blend of island serenity and American practicality in this U.S. territory 1,000 mi from the southern tip of the mainland.

The postcard images you'd expect from a tropical paradise are here: Stretches of beach arc into the distance and white sails skim across water so blue and clear it stuns the senses; red-roof houses add their spot of color to the green hillsides' mosaic, along with the orange of the flamboyant tree, the red of the hibiscus, the magenta of the bougainvillea, and the blue stone ruins of old sugar mills; and towns of pastel-tone European-style villas, decorated by filigree wrought-iron terraces, line narrow streets climbing up from a harbor.

The other part of the picture are all those things that make it so easy and appealing for Americans to visit this cluster of islands. The official language is English, the money is the dollar, and the U.S. government runs things. There's cable TV, Pizza Hut, and McDonald's. There's unfettered immigration to and from the mainland, and investments are protected by the U.S. flag. Visitors to the U.S.V.I. have the opportunity to delve into a "foreign" culture while anchored by familiar language and landmarks.

Your destination here will be St. Thomas (13 mi long); its neighbor St. John (9 mi long); or, 40 mi to the south, St. Croix (23 mi long). A pro/con thumbnail sketch of these three might have it that St. Thomas is bustling (hustling), the place for shopping and nightlife (commercial glitz and overdevelopment); St. Croix is more Danish, picturesque, and rural (more provincial and dull, particularly after dark); and St. John is matchless in the beauty of its National Park Service–protected land and beaches (a one-town island mostly for villa vacationers or campers). Surely not everything will suit your fancy, but chances are that among the three islands you'll find your own idea of paradise.

## Lodging

The U.S.V.I. has lodging options to suit any style. Each island has luxury retreats of understated elegance that offer rest and relaxation of a high—and pricey—order. On St. Thomas, there are also guest houses and smaller hotels, typically not on the beach but with pools and shuttle service to nearby beaches (St. Thomas is not a walking island), and the several historic inns above town have a pleasing island ambience. In keeping with its small-town atmosphere and more relaxed pace, St. Croix has a good variety of moderately priced small hotels and guest houses, which are either on the beach or in a rural setting where a walk to the beach is easy. Accommodations on St. John defy easy categorization. There's a collection of small inns and vacation villas, and the national-park and private campgrounds have a range of sites, from bare campsites to tents to small cottages.

The prices below reflect rates during high season, which generally runs from December 15 to April 15. Rates are 25% to 50% lower the rest of the year.

| CATEGORY | COST* |
|----------|-------|
| $$$$ | over $200 |
| $$$ | $150–$200 |
| $$ | $100–$150 |
| $ | under $100 |

*All prices are for a standard double room, excluding 8% accommodations tax.*

## St. Thomas

$$$$ 🏨 **Bolongo Bay Beach Club & Villas.** This 75-room beachfront resort also includes the 20-room Bolongo Villas next door and the six-room Bolongo Bayside Inn across the street. All resort rooms have efficiency kitchens and balconies and are just steps from a strand of white beach. The oceanfront villas feature minisuites, and one-, two-, and three-bedroom units with full kitchens and large balconies overlooking the ocean. The inn's rooms are air-conditioned and have private baths. The resort offers a choice of all-inclusive or semi-inclusive plans, which means you'll pay less if you want fewer activities. ⊠ *50 Estate Bolongo, 00802,* ☎ *809/775–1800 or 800/524–4746,* FAX *809/775–3208. 101 units. 2 restaurants, 3 pools, 2 tennis courts, health club, volleyball, beach. AE, D, DC, MC, V.*

$$$$ 🏨 **Marriott's Frenchman's Reef and Morning Star Beach Resorts.** Like
★ a permanently anchored cruise ship on the prime harbor promontory east of Charlotte Amalie, these two sprawling, luxurious resorts are full-service American superhotels. All rooms are spacious and furnished with contemporary furniture in soft pastels. Many Frenchman's Reef rooms have glorious ocean and harbor views, but a few look out over the parking lot. Morning Star rooms are more luxurious, in buildings tucked among the foliage that stretches along the fine white sand of Morning Star Beach; the sound of the surf can lull you to sleep. In addition to enjoying various snack and sandwich stops and a raw bar, you can dine alfresco on American or gourmet Caribbean fare, or oceanfront at the Tavern on the Beach. There's also a lavish buffet served overlooking the sparkling lights of Charlotte Amalie and the harbor. Live entertainment and disco, scheduled activities for all ages, and a shuttle boat to town make having fun easy. This is a property you don't have to leave. ⊠ *Box 7100, 00801,* ☎ *809/776–8500 or 800/524–2000,* FAX *809/776–3054. 517 rooms, 18 suites. 6 restaurants, 6 bars, 2 snack bars, 2 pools, 4 tennis courts, beach. AE, D, DC, MC, V.*

$$$$ 🏨 **Renaissance Grand Beach Resort.** This resort's zigzag architectural
★ angles spell luxury, from the marble atrium lobby to the one-bedroom suites with private whirlpool baths. The beach is excellent, and there's a fitness center with Nautilus machines. The lobby is often populated by those lucky business types whose companies favor the resort as a convention-and-conference center. Daily organized activities for children include iguana hunts, T-shirt painting, and sand-castle building. This tends to be a very busy hotel, with lots of people in the restaurants and on the beach. ⊠ *Smith Bay Rd., Box 8267, 00801,* ☎ *809/ 775–1510 or 800/468–3571,* FAX *809/775–2185. 290 rooms. 2 restaurants, snack bar, 2 pools, 6 tennis courts, health club, beach. AE, D, DC, MC, V.*

$$$$ 🏨 **Ritz-Carlton St. Thomas.** Formerly named the Grand Palazzo, this
★ premier luxury resort, which opened in December 1996, resembles a villa in Venice and offers stunning ocean views through the lobby's glass doors. Guest rooms, in six buildings that fan out from the main villa, are spacious and tropically furnished—they just might tempt you to stay inside. When you do venture out, you'll find elegance everywhere, from the beautiful pool to the gourmet restaurant and the casual al-

**The U.S. Virgin Islands**

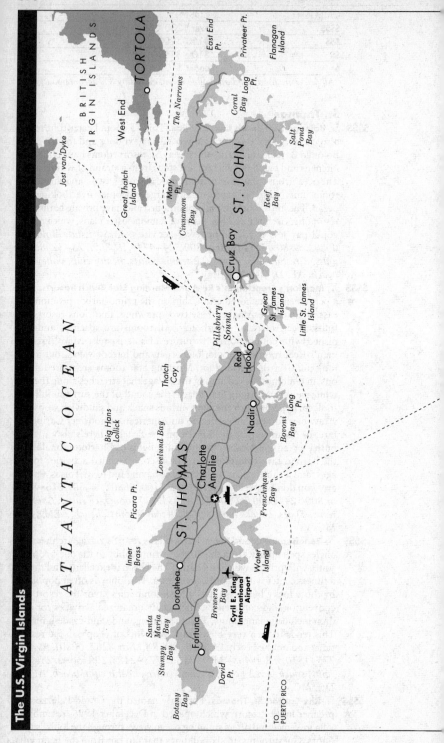

ATLANTIC OCEAN

BRITISH VIRGIN ISLANDS

TORTOLA

West End

The Narrows

East End Pt.

Privateer Pt.

Flanagan Island

Jost van Dyke

Great Thatch Island

Coral Bay

Long Bay

Salt Pond Bay

Mary Pt.

Cinnamon Bay

ST. JOHN

Reef Bay

Cruz Bay

Pillsbury Sound

Great St. James Island

Little St. James Island

Red Hook

Thatch Cay

Nadir

Bovoni Bay

Long Pt.

Big Hans Lollick

Lovelund Bay

Charlotte Amalie

ST. THOMAS

Frenchman Bay

Picara Pt.

Inner Brass

Water Island

Dorothea

Santa Maria Bay

Cyril E. King International Airport

Brewers Bay

Fortuna

Stumpy Bay

Botany Bay

David Pt.

TO PUERTO RICO

## St. Thomas

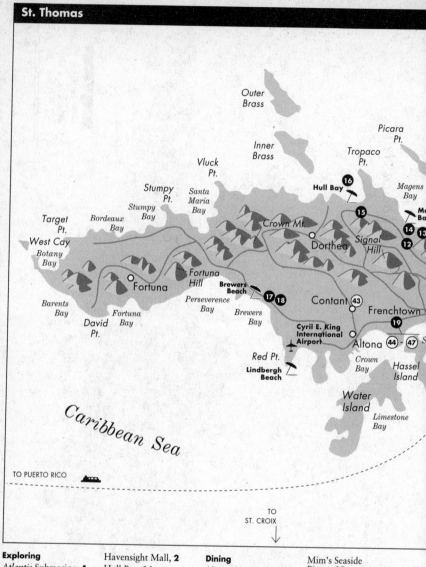

**Exploring**

*Atlantis* Submarine, **4**
Brewers Beach, **17**
Charlotte Amalie, **1**
Clinton Phipps Racetrack, **5**
Coki Point, **10**
Compass Point, **6**
Coral World, **9**
Drake's Seat, **13**
Estate St. Peter Greathouse Botanical Gardens, **15**
Frenchtown, **19**

Havensight Mall, **2**
Hull Bay, **16**
Magens Bay Beach, **14**
Mountain Top, **12**
Paradise Point Tramway, **3**
Red Hook, **8**
Reichhold Center for the Arts, **18**
Tillett Gardens, **11**
Virgin Islands National Park Headquarters, **7**

**Dining**

Alexander's Cafe, **44**
Blue Marlin, **35**
Chart House, **45**
Craig & Sally's, **47**
Entre Nous, **23**
Eunice's Terrace, **39**
Gladys' Cafe, **24**
Hard Rock Cafe, **28**
Hotel 1829, **21**

Mim's Seaside Bistro, **29**
Raffles, **31**
Romanos, **42**
Tickles Dockside Pub, **34**
Virgilio's, **22**
Zorba's Cafe, **26**

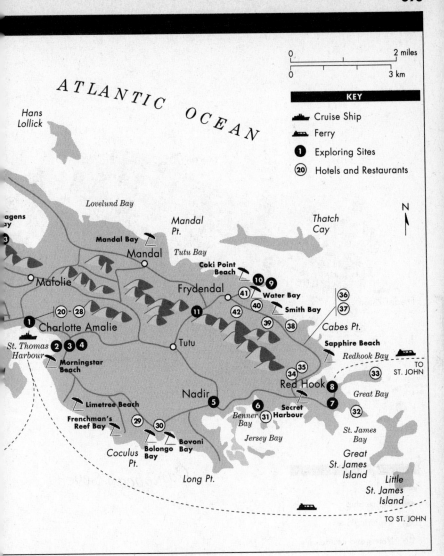

# St. Croix

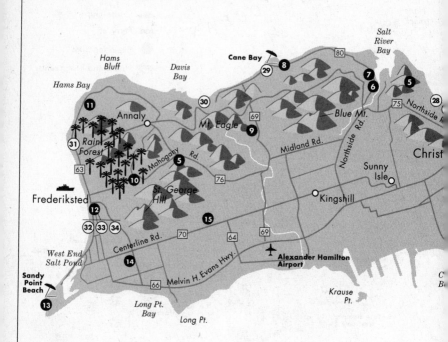

TO
ST. THOMAS

Salt
River
Bay

Hams
Bluff

Davis
Bay

Cane Bay

Hams Bay

Annaly

Mt. Eagle

Blue Mt.

Salt River Rd.

Northside Rd.

Christ

Rain
Forest

Mahogany Rd.

Midland Rd.

Northside Rd.

Sunny
Isle

Kingshill

Frederiksted

St. George
Hill

Centerline Rd.

West End
Salt Pond

Alexander Hamilton
Airport

Melvin H. Evans Hwy.

Sandy
Point
Beach

Long Pt.
Bay

Long Pt.

Krause
Pt.

C
B

## Caribbean Sea

**KEY**

🚗 Ferry

🚢 Cruise Ship

❶ Exploring Sites

⑯ Hotels and Restaurants

**Exploring**

Buck Island Reef
National
Monument, **2**

Cane Bay, **8**

Christiansted, **1**

Cramer's Park, **3**

Estate Mount
Washington
Plantation, **11**

Estate Whim
Plantation
Museum, **14**

Frederiksted, **12**

Judith's Fancy, **5**

Mount Eagle, **9**

Mt. Pellier Domino
Club, **5**

Point Udall, **4**

St. Croix Leap, **10**

St. George Village
Botanical
Gardens, **15**

Salt River Bay
National Historic
Park and Ecological
Preserve, **7**

Salt River Marina, **6**

Sandy Point
Beach, **13**

**Dining**

Blue Moon, **32**

Camille's, **17**

Great House at Villa
Madeleine, **25**

Harvey's, **21**

Kendricks, **20**

Le St. Tropez, **34**

Top Hat, **18**

**Lodging**

The Buccaneer, **23**

Club St. Croix, **26**

Cormorant Beach
Club and Villas, **27**

The Frederiksted, **33**

Hibiscus Beach
Hotel, **28**

Hotel Caravelle, **16**

King's Alley
Hotel, **22**

Pink Fancy, **19**

Sprat Hall, **31**

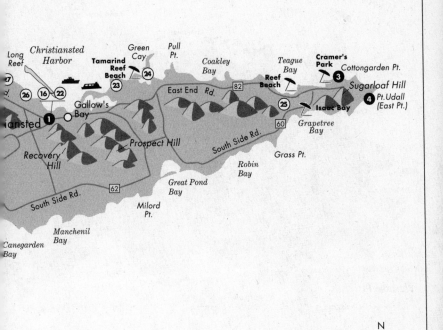

Buck Island

Buck Island Beach
2

Long
Reef

*Christiansted
Harbor*

Green
Cay

Pull
Pt.

**Tamarind
Reef
Beach** 24

*Coakley
Bay*

*Teague
Bay*

**Cramer's
Park** 3

Cottongarden Pt.

**Reef
Beach**

*Sugarloaf Hill*

27

26 16 22

23

*East End Rd.* 82

25

4 Pt.Udall
(East Pt.)

iansted 1 Gallow's
Bay

*Isaac Bay*

60

*Grapetree
Bay*

*Prospect Hill*

*South Side Rd.*

*Grass Pt.*

*Recovery
Hill*

*Robin
Bay*

62

*Great Pond
Bay*

*South Side Rd.*

*Milord
Pt.*

*Manchenil
Bay*

*Canegarden
Bay*

N

0                    2 miles
0                    3 km

Tamarind Reef
Hotel, **24**
Villa Madeleine, **16**
Waves at Cane
Bay, **29**
Westin Carambola
Beach Resort, **30**

# St. John

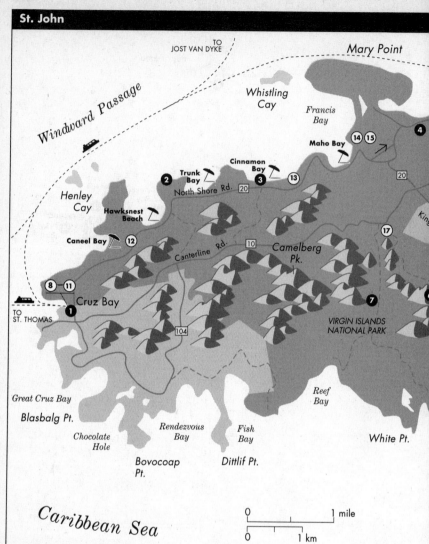

**Exploring**

Annaberg Plantation, **4**

Bordeaux Mountain, **6**

Cinnamon Bay, **3**

Coral Bay, **5**

Cruz Bay, **1**

Peace Hill, **2**

Reef Bay Trail **7**

**Dining**

Asolare, **11**

Le Chateau de Bordeaux, **17**

Ellington's, **8**

Fish Trap, **10**

Paradiso, **9**

Shipwreck Landing, **18**

**Lodging**

Caneel Bay Resort, **12**

Cinnamon Bay Campground, **13**

Estate Concordia, **16**

Gallows Point Suite Resort, **8**

Harmony, **15**

Maho Bay Camp, **14**

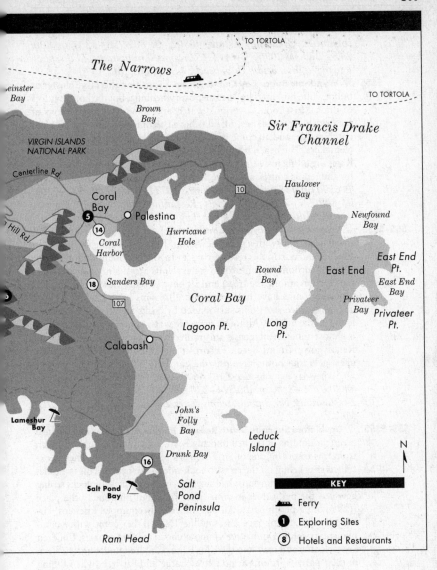

To Tortola

The Narrows

einster Bay

Brown Bay

VIRGIN ISLANDS NATIONAL PARK

Centerline Rd

Coral Bay

5

14 Palestina

Hill Rd

Coral Harbor

18 Sanders Bay

107

Calabash

Lameshur Bay

Drunk Bay

16

Salt Pond Bay

Salt Pond Peninsula

Ram Head

To Tortola

Sir Francis Drake Channel

10

Haulover Bay

Newfound Bay

Hurricane Hole

Round Bay

Coral Bay

Lagoon Pt.

Long Pt.

East End

East End Pt.

East End Bay

Privateer Bay

Privateer Pt.

John's Folly Bay

Leduck Island

N

KEY

Ferry

1 Exploring Sites

8 Hotels and Restaurants

fresco lunch area. A multilingual staff, a variety of music from classical to calypso, and 24-hour room service enhance the sophisticated atmosphere. ⊠ *Great Bay Estate, 00802,* ☎ *809/775–3333 or 800/ 241–3333,* ℻ *809/775–4444. 152 rooms. 3 restaurants, 3 bars, pool, 3 tennis courts, health club, beach. AE, D, DC, MC, V.*

$$$$  🏨 **Wyndham Sugar Bay Club & Resort.** From afar, this large cluster of bulky white buildings looks rather overwhelming, but the hotel has lots to offer. Most rooms overlook water, and some have great views of the British Virgin Islands. All units have balconies and are spacious and comfortable, and all come with such amenities as hair dryers and coffeemakers. The beach is small, but there's a giant pool with waterfalls. Rates are all-inclusive, covering meals, beverages, use of the fitness center and tennis courts, a daily activity program, and many water sports. ⊠ *6500 Estate Smith Bay, 00802,* ☎ *809/777–7100 or 800/927–7100,* ℻ *809/777–7200. 300 rooms. Restaurant, bar, 3 pools, 2 tennis courts, health club, beach, snorkeling. AE, D, DC, MC, V.*

$$$–$$$$  🏨 **Colony Point Pleasant Resort.** Stretching up a steep, tree-filled hill
★  from Smith Bay, with a great view of St. John and Drake's Channel to the east and north, this resort offers a range of accommodations, from simple bedrooms to multiroom suites. Units are in a number of buildings hidden among the trees, and all have striking views. The air-conditioned rooms have balconies, and all rooms have kitchens. Three appealing, nice-size pools surrounded by decks are placed at different levels on the hillside. Although there are water sports here, the "beach" is almost nonexistent; guests are granted beach privileges at next door's Renaissance Grand Beach Resort, a one-minute walk away. Every guest gets four hours' free use of a car daily. (You need only pay the $9.50 per-day insurance cost.) ⊠ *6600 Estate Smith Bay, No. 4, 00802,* ☎ *809/775–7200 or 800/524–2300,* ℻ *809/776–5694. 134 rooms. 2 restaurants, bar, 3 pools, tennis court, exercise room, beach. AE, D, MC, V.*

$$$–$$$$  🏨 **Doubletree Sapphire Beach Resort & Marina.** On a clear day the lush
★  green mountains of the neighboring B.V.I. seem close enough to touch from this resort on one of St. Thomas's prettiest beaches. There's excellent snorkeling on the reefs to each side of the beach. This is a quiet retreat where you can nap while swinging in one of the hammocks strung between the palm trees in your front yard, but on Sunday the place rocks with a beach party. All units have fully equipped kitchens, air-conditioning, telephones, and satellite TV, and they come with a complimentary can of Doubletree's famous chocolate chip cookies. Children are welcome and may join the Kids Klub. Children under age 12 sleep in their parents' rooms at no extra charge and eat free (when dining with their parents) at the Seagrape Restaurant. ⊠ *Box 8088, 00801,* ☎ *809/775–6100 or 800/524–2090,* ℻ *809/775–2403. 171 rooms. 3 restaurants, 2 bars, 4 tennis courts, beach. AE, MC, V.*

$$$–$$$$  🏨 **Pavilions & Pools.** You'll find simple, tropical-cool decor and privacy at this small hotel, where each island-style room has its own very private 22- by 14-ft or 18- by 16-ft pool and a small sunning deck. The unpretentious accommodations include air-conditioning, telephones, full kitchens, and VCRs. Water sports are available at Sapphire Beach on the adjacent property. Snorkel gear is provided. ⊠ *6400 Estate Smith Bay, 00802,* ☎ *809/775–6110 or 800/524–2001,* ℻ *809/ 775–6110. 25 rooms. Restaurant, pools. AE, MC, V.*

$$$  🏨 **Blackbeard's Castle.** This small and very popular hillside inn is laid out around a tower from which, it's said, Blackbeard kept watch for invaders on the horizon. It's an elegantly informal kind of place, where guests while away Sunday morning with the *New York Times.* Stunning views (especially at sunset) of the harbor and Charlotte Amalie can be had from the gourmet restaurant, the large freshwater pool, and

the outdoor terraces, where locals come for cocktails. Charlotte Amalie is a short walk down the hill, and beaches are a short taxi ride away. Rates include Continental breakfast. ⊠ *Box 6041, 00804,* ☎ *809/776–1234 or 800/344–5771,* 𝖥𝖠𝖷 *809/776–4321. 24 rooms. Restaurant, bar, pool. AE, D, DC, MC, V.*

**$$** ⌘ **Villa Blanca Hotel.** Above Charlotte Amalie on Raphune Hill is this secluded hotel, surrounded by an attractive garden and with modern, balconied rooms with rattan furniture, kitchenettes, cable TVs, and ceiling fans (six have air-conditioning). All the rooms have views of Charlotte Amalie's harbor as well as partial views of Drake's Channel and the B.V.I. ⊠ *Box 7505, 00801,* ☎ *809/776–0749 or 800/231–0034,* 𝖥𝖠𝖷 *809/779–2661. 14 rooms. Pool. AE, D, DC, MC, V.*

**$–$$** ⌘ **Hotel 1829.** This historic Spanish-style inn is popular with visiting
★ government officials and people with business at Government House down the street. It's on Government Hill, just at the edge of Charlotte Amalie's shopping area. Rooms, on several levels (no elevator), range from elegant and roomy to quite small but are priced accordingly, so there's one for every budget. Author Graham Greene is said to have stayed here, and it's easy to imagine him musing over a drink in the small, dark bar. The gourmet terrace restaurant is a romantic spot for dinner. The rooms have refrigerators, TVs, and air-conditioning. There's a tiny, tiny pool for cooling off. ⊠ *Box 1567, 00801,* ☎ *809/776–1829 or 800/524–2002,* 𝖥𝖠𝖷 *809/776–4313. 15 rooms. Restaurant, bar, pool. AE, D, MC, V.*

**$–$$** ⌘ **Villa Santana.** Built by General Santa Anna of Mexico circa 1857,
★ the villa still provides a panoramic view of the Charlotte Amalie harbor along with plenty of age-old West Indian charm. This St. Thomas landmark, close to town, has villa-style rooms. Dark wicker furniture, white plaster and stone walls, shuttered windows, cathedral ceilings, and interesting nooks contribute to the feeling of romance and history. Villas La Torre and La Mansion are split-level with spiral staircases, and all units have full kitchens and either four-poster or cradle beds. Rooms are kept cool by ceiling fans and natural trade winds and do not have telephones. ⊠ *Denmark Hill, 00802,* ☎ *809/776–1311,* 𝖥𝖠𝖷 *809/776–1311. 5 rooms. Pool. AE.*

**$** ⌘ **Admiral's Inn.** This charming inn stretches down a hillside on the
★ point of land known as Frenchtown, just west of Charlotte Amalie. All rooms have wonderful views of either the town and the harbor or the ocean; the four ocean-view rooms have private balconies and refrigerators. All units have rattan furniture; cream- or teal-color bedspreads; vertical blinds; coral, teal, and cream carpeting; and large, tiled vanity areas. The rocky shoreline is perfect for snorkeling. The inn's freshwater pool is surrounded by a large wooden deck ideal for sunning. There's bar service at the pool, and a Continental breakfast is included in the room rate. ⊠ *Villa Olga, 00802,* ☎ *809/774–1376 or 800/544–0493,* 𝖥𝖠𝖷 *809/774–8010. 14 rooms. Restaurant, bar, pool. AE, D, MC, V.*

**$** ⌘ **Island View Guest House.** This clean, simply furnished guest house rests amid tropical foliage on the south face of 1,500-ft Crown Mountain, the highest point on St. Thomas. As a result, it has one of the most sweeping views of Charlotte Amalie harbor available from its pool and shaded terrace, where complimentary breakfast is served. All rooms have some view of the water, but on the balconies of the six newer rooms (all with air-conditioning and a ceiling fan), perched on the very edge of the hill, you feel suspended in midair. ⊠ *Box 1903, 00801,* ☎ *809/774–4270 or 800/524–2023,* 𝖥𝖠𝖷 *809/774–6167. 13 rooms with bath, 2 rooms share bath. Pool. AE, MC, V.*

## St. Croix

$$$$  ⬚ **The Buccaneer.** This self-contained hotel on the grounds of an old 300-acre sugar plantation has it all. Look for palm-fringed sandy beaches, swimming pools, golf, all water sports, tennis, a nature and jogging trail, shopping arcade, health spa, and four restaurants. A palm-tree-lined main drive leads to the large pink hotel at the top of a hill, and a number of smaller guest cottages, shops, and restaurants are scattered throughout the property's rolling, manicured lawns. The ambience is Mediterranean rather than tropical, with marble or colorful tile floors, four-poster beds and massive wardrobes of pale wood, pastel fabrics, and locally produced artwork. All rooms have such modern conveniences as hair dryers, refrigerators, and cable TV. Spacious bathrooms are noteworthy for their marble bench showers and double sinks. ⬚ *Box 25200, Gallows Bay 00824,* ☎ *809/773–2100 or 800/225–3881,* ⬚ *809/778–8215. 150 rooms. 4 restaurants, in-room safes, 2 pools, spa, 8 tennis courts, jogging, 3 beaches. AE, D, DC, MC, V.*

$$$$  ⬚ **Cormorant Beach Club and Villas.** Breeze-bent palm trees, hammocks, the thrum of north-shore waves, and respected privacy rule here. The open-air public spaces are filled with tropical plants and comfy wicker furniture. Ceiling fans and tile floors add to the atmosphere at this resort, which resembles a series of connected Moorish villas. The beachfront rooms are lovely, with dark wicker furniture, pale-peach walls, white-tile floors, and floral-print fabrics; all rooms have a patio or balcony and telephone, and cable TV. Bathrooms stand out for their coral rock–wall showers, marble-top double sinks, and brass fixtures. Morning coffee and afternoon tea are set out daily in the building breezeways; the airy, high-ceiling restaurant is one of St. Croix's best. The hotel offers partial and all-inclusive meal plans that include all drinks. ⬚ *4126 La Grande Princesse, Christiansted 00820,* ☎ *809/778–8920 or 800/548–4460,* ⬚ *809/778–9218. 34 rooms, 4 suites, 14 2- and 3-bedroom villas. Restaurant, bar, pool, in-room safes, 2 tennis courts, croquet, beach, snorkeling. AE, DC, MC, V.*

$$$$  ⬚ **Villa Madeleine.** A West Indian plantation great house is the cen-
★  terpiece of this exquisite hotel, one of St. Croix's most attractive. Richly upholstered furniture, Oriental rugs, teal walls, and whimsically painted driftwood set the mood in the billiards room, the austere library, and the sitting room. The great house sits atop a hill, and private guest villas are scattered in both directions, with a spectacular view of both the north and south shores. The villa decor is modern tropical: rattan and plush cushions, rocking chairs, and, in many villas, bamboo four-poster beds. Each villa has a full kitchen and a private swimming pool. Special touches in the rooms include pink-marble showers and, in many cottages, hand-painted floral borders along the walls, done in splashy tropical colors. Enjoy fine dining on the terrace at Cafe Madeleine or steak at the Turf Club. ⬚ *Box 26160, Teague Bay 00824,* ☎ *809/778–8782 or 800/496–7379,* ⬚ *809/773–2150. 43 villas. 2 restaurants, bar, tennis court, billiards, library, concierge. AE, D, DC, MC, V.*

$$$$  ⬚ **Westin Carambola Beach Resort.** The 26 quaint, two-story red-
★  roofed villas, including one that's wheelchair-accessible, are connected by lovely arcades that seem hacked from the luxuriant undergrowth. The rooms are identical; the only difference is the view—ocean or garden. Decor is Laura Ashley–style English country house, with rocking chairs and sofas upholstered in soothing floral patterns, terra-cotta floors, rough-textured ceramic lamps, and mahogany ceilings and furnishings. All have private patios and huge baths (showers only). The two-bedroom suite, with its 3-ft-thick plantation walls and large patio, is the *perfect* Caribbean family dwelling. There are two fine restaurants (the

Sunday buffet brunch is legendary for its munificent table), an exquisite ecru beach, and lots of quiet nooks for a secluded drink. ⊠ *Box 3031, Kingshill 00851,* ☎ *809/778–3800 or 800/228–3000,* ℻ *809/778–1682. 150 rooms, 1 2-bedroom cottage. 2 restaurants, deli, pool, 2 hot tubs, 4 tennis courts, library. AE, D, DC, MC, V.*

$$$-$$$$ ⊡ **Hibiscus Beach Hotel.** This affordable, appealing property is on the same stretch of palm-tree-lined beach as its sister hotel, the Cormorant. Guest rooms are divided among five two-story pink buildings, each named for a tropical flower. Most have views of the oceanfront, thanks to the staggered placement of the buildings, but request a room in the Hibiscus building—it's closest to the water. Rooms have welcome amenities, such as cable TV, safe, and minibar, and are tastefully furnished: White tile floors and white walls are brightened with pink-striped curtains; bright, flowered bedspreads; and fresh-cut hibiscus blossoms. Bathrooms are clean but nondescript—both the shower stalls and the vanity mirrors are on the small side. Every unit has a roomy balcony that faces the sea. The staff is friendly and helpful, and the manager's party in the open-air bar-restaurant is a pleasant gathering. ⊠ *4131 Estate La Grande Princesse, Christiansted 00820-4441,* ☎ *809/773–4042 or 800/442–0121,* ℻ *809/773–7668. 37 rooms. Restaurant, in-room safes, minibars, pool, snorkeling. AE, D, MC, V.*

$$$ ⊡ **Tamarind Reef Hotel.** A casual, seaside place, this small motel-like property provides good snorkeling as well as excellent sunning at its large pool and sandy beach. Serious swimmers won't be happy because the reef comes right to the shore, making it hard to even get in the water and too shallow for swimming. The spacious, modern rooms have rattan furniture and tropical-print drapes and bedspreads, and all have either a terrace or deck with views of the sea and St. Croix's sister islands to the north. Many of the rooms come with basic kitchenettes. Three rooms have handicapped facilities. There's a bar and snack bar just off the beach and a restaurant at the adjacent Green Cay Marina. ⊠ *5001 Tamarind Reef 00820,* ☎ *809/773–4455,* ℻ *809/773–3989 or 800/619–0014. 46 rooms. Snack bar, pool. AE, MC, V.*

$$-$$$ ⊡ **King's Alley Hotel.** In the center of Christiansted's hustle and bus-
★ tle, this small hotel provides convenience plus charm. It puts you within walking distance of many of the island's best restaurants and finest shops. The 12 premium rooms in the just-completed section across the courtyard feature mahogany four-poster beds, Mexican tile floors, and Indonesian print fabrics. French doors open onto balconies with a view of the waterfront and the shopping arcade. The 23 standard rooms in the older section are a tad less interesting but still attractive. The staff can arrange all water sports, tours, golf, and tennis. The hotel is part of the recently reconstructed Kings Alley Complex. ⊠ *57 King St., Box 4120, Christiansted 00822,* ☎ *809/773–0103 or 800/843–3574,* ℻ *809/773–4431. 35 rooms. Pool. AE, D, DC, MC, V.*

$$-$$$ ⊡ **Sprat Hall.** This 20-acre seaside property about 1 mi north of Frederiksted appeals to a special sort of guest, one who enjoys the vagaries of a visit to someone's home. Joyce Hurd presides over the slightly ramshackle 17th-century plantation where she was born. Some of the guest rooms in the rather cluttered antiques-filled great house have four-poster beds and planter's chairs. More modern rooms and cottages spread out all over the estate. Only one of the great-house rooms has air-conditioning. The glorious strand of beach that runs north from Frederiksted sits a good hike down a gentle hill. Hurd conjures up dinner for guests and visitors, but you'll have to order your choice when she delivers your complimentary Continental breakfast. A rental car will give you more flexibility. The Hurd family also operates extensive horseback-riding facilities here. ⊠ *Box 695, Frederiksted 00841,* ☎ *809/772–*

*0305 or 800/843–3584. 9 rooms, 8 suites, 1 1-bedroom cottage, 2 2-bedroom cottages. Restaurant, horseback riding, beach. AE.*

**$$–$$$** 🏨 **Waves at Cane Bay.** The sound of crashing waves will lull you to sleep at this 12-room inn perched at the water's edge. It caters to couples as well as divers who take advantage of the world-famous Cane Bay Wall just 100 yards offshore. The hotel is rather isolated and its beachfront is rocky, but Cane Bay Beach is right next door and there is a small patch of sand poolside for sunbathing. The unusual pool was carved from the coral along the shore. The floor and one wall are concrete, but the seaside wall is made of natural coral, and the pool water is circulated as the waves crash dramatically over the side, creating a foamy whirlpool on blustery days. The two peach and mint-green buildings house enormous, balconied guest rooms done in cream and soft pastel prints, all with kitchens or kitchenettes. ⊠ *Box 1749, Kingshill 00851,* ☎ *809/778–1805 or 800/545–0603. 12 rooms, 8 with air-conditioning, 1 suite. Restaurant, bar, in-room safes, pool, snorkeling. AE, MC, V.*

**$$** 🏨 **Hotel Caravelle.** The charming three-story Caravelle is an excellent moderately priced hotel in Christiansted. All rooms have refrigerators, television with free HBO, and telephones. They're decorated in tasteful dusky blues and whites, with floral-print fabrics, and have vaulted ceilings. Baths are clean and new, though the unique tile in the showers is a holdover from when the hotel was built in 1968. Superior rooms overlook the harbor, but most rooms have some sort of ocean view. Owners Sid and Amy Kalmans are friendly and helpful. The Seaport Grille, a casual terrace eatery, serves seafood and Continental cuisine. ⊠ *44 A Queen Cross St., Christiansted 00820,* ☎ *809/773–0687 or 800/524–0410,* FAX *809/778–7004. 43 rooms, 1 2-bedroom suite. Restaurant, bar, pool, meeting room. AE, D, DC, MC, V.*

**$–$$** 🏨 **The Frederiksted.** Don't be put off by the neat but unprepossessing exterior. This modern four-story inn is your best bet for lodging in Frederiksted. In the inviting, outdoor tile courtyard, the glass tables and yellow chairs of the hotel's bar and restaurant crowd around a small freshwater swimming pool. Yellow-striped awnings and tropical greenery create a sunny, welcoming atmosphere. Steps at one side of the courtyard lead to the second floor's main desk and sundeck. The bright, pleasant guest rooms have bar refrigerators and microwaves and are decorated with light-color rattan furniture and print bedspreads. Bathrooms are on the small side but are bright and clean. The nicest rooms are those with an ocean view; these are also the only rooms that have a bathtub in addition to a shower. ⊠ *20 Strand St., Frederiksted 00840,* ☎ *809/772–0500 or 800/595–9519,* FAX *809/772–0500, ext. 399. 40 rooms. Restaurant, bar, pool. AE, D, DC, MC, V.*

## St. John

**$$$$** 🏨 **Caneel Bay Resort.** This incredibly lush 170-acre peninsula resort ★ was originally part of the Durloo plantation owned by the Danish West India Company. It opened as a resort in 1936, was bought by Laurance S. Rockefeller in 1952, and joined Rosewood Resorts in 1991. While there are no crowds and no glitz, the grand dame of the island's tourism industry has begun to shake out her skirts with the development of a children's program. There are still no room phones, but management will loan you a cellular at no charge except for the phone bill. You'll find tasteful tropical furnishing in spacious, airy rooms sans air-conditioning. There are seven beaches, one more gorgeous than the next, peace and quiet, and a luxurious air. Guests come here to enjoy the ambience and the pampering. Jackets are requested for men (during winter season) in two of the restaurants after 6 PM. Peter Burwash International runs the tennis program here. ⊠ *Box 720, Cruz Bay 00830,*

☎ *809/776–6111 or 800/223–7637. 166 rooms. 3 restaurants, 11 tennis courts, 7 beaches, meeting rooms. AE, MC, V.*

**$$$$** ⊞ **Gallows Point Suite Resort.** These soft-gray buildings with peaked roofs and shuttered windows are clustered on the peninsula south of the Cruz Bay ferry dock. The garden apartments have kitchens and skylighted, plant-filled showers big enough to frolic in. The upper-level apartments have loft bedrooms and better views. There's no air-conditioning; the harborside villas get better trade winds, but they're also noisier. Daily maid service is included. The entranceway is bridged by Ellington's restaurant. ⊠ *Box 58, Cruz Bay 00831,* ☎ *809/776–6434 or 800/323–7229,* ℻ *809/776–6520. 60 rooms. Pool, beach, snorkeling. AE, DC, MC, V.*

**$–$$$** ⊞ **Estate Concordia.** The latest brainchild of Stanley Selengut, the developer of Maho Bay Camp, these environmentally correct studios and duplexes are on 51 oceanfront acres on remote Salt Pond Bay. The spacious units are constructed from recycled materials, and energy is wind- and solar-generated (even the ice maker is solar-powered). Next door are the resort's five eco-tents—upscale camping structures made of environmentally friendly materials and with solar power and composting toilets. ⊠ *Box 310, Cruz Bay 00830,* ☎ *800/392–9004 or 212/472–9453,* ℻ *212/861–6210. 14 units. Pool, beach. MC, V.*

**$$** ⊞ **Harmony.** Nestled in the tree-covered hills adjacent to the Maho Bay Camp is a Stanley Selengut eco-tourism resort. The spacious two-story units here have your Caribbean basics—decks, sliding glass doors, living-dining areas, and great views—but staying here is definitely a learning experience. As at Estate Concordia, buildings, including walls and floors, are made from recycled materials. You'd never know the carpeting came from milk cartons and ketchup bottles, the doormat from recycled tires, and the pristine white walls from old newspapers. Energy for the low-wattage appliances comes entirely from wind and sun. Use your unit's laptop computer to explore environmental preservation and monitor your unit's energy consumption. Tile floors, undyed organic cotton linens, and South American handicrafts create a look to match the ideals. ⊠ *Box 310, Cruz Bay 00830,* ☎ *212/472–9453 or 800/392–9004,* ℻ *212/861–6210. 12 units. Restaurant, beach, scuba diving, snorkeling, windsurfing, boating. MC, V.*

**$** ⚠ **Cinnamon Bay Campground.** Very basic cottages, tents, and bare sites are available at this National Park Service location surrounded by jungle and at the edge of big, beautiful Cinnamon Bay Beach. The tents and cottages both come with outdoor propane camping stoves, coolers, cooking gear, and sheets and towels. You'll read by electric lights in the cottages and propane lanterns in the tents. There are no locks on cottage doors. Bring your own tent and supplies for the bare sites. All have grills and picnic tables. You'll have to trek down the path for cool showers and flush toilets. Hiking, snorkeling, swimming, and evening environmental or history programs are free and at your doorstep. Reserve a space for the winter months far in advance (a maximum of one year ahead). If you're willing to schlep your tent and all your gear, the $17 a night bare sites are St. John's biggest bargain. The T'Ree Lizards Restaurant serves very good dinners that attract more than just campers. ⊠ *Box 720, Cruz Bay 00830-0720,* ☎ *809/776–6330 or 800/539–9998,* ℻ *809/776–6458. 44 tents, 38 cottages, 26 bare sites. Restaurant, beach, snorkeling, windsurfing, boating. AE, MC, V.*

**$** ⚠ **Maho Bay Camp.** Eight miles from Cruz Bay, this private eco-campground is a lush hillside community of rustic tent cottages made of canvas and screen linked by environmentally protective elevated wooden walkways, boardwalks, stairs, and ramps, which also lead down to the beach. The 16- by 16-ft shelters have beds, dining table and chairs, electric lamps with outlets, propane stove, ice cooler, kitchenware, and cutlery. All units are nestled among the trees, some hidden in the tropical greenery and others with spectacular views of the Caribbean. The camp has the chummy feel of a retreat and is very popular, so book well in advance. ⊠ *Box 310, Cruz Bay 00830,* ☎ *212/472–9453 or 800/392–9004,* FAX *212/861–6210. 113 tent cottages. Restaurant, beach, scuba diving, snorkeling, windsurfing, boating. MC, V.*

### Villa and Condominium Rentals

The island has about 350 villas, condominiums, and cottages tucked here and there between Cruz Bay and Coral Bay. Many villas come with pools; most have hot tubs; a few have private beaches. The condominiums are located in complexes with pools and modern amenities. Cottages tend to be more modest. While most of the condominiums are located within walking distance of Cruz Bay, you'll need a rental car to get from your home to the beach, dinner out, and shopping if you rent a villa or cottage. Many on-island managers pick you up at the ferry dock, answer all your questions, and are available during your stay to solve problems and provide advice.

For luxury villas, try **Caribbean Villas and Resorts** (⊠ Box 48, 00830, ☎ 809/776–6152 or 800/338–0987, FAX 809/779–4044), **Catered To, Inc.** (⊠ Box 704, 00830, ☎ 809/776–6641, FAX 809/693–8191), **Destination St. John** (⊠ Box 8306, 00831, ☎ FAX 809/776–6969 or 800/562–1901), **Private Homes for Private Vacations** (⊠ Mamey Peak, 00830, ☎ 809/776–6876), **Vacation Homes** (⊠ Box 272, 00830, ☎ 809/776–6094, FAX 809/693–8455), **Vacation Vistas** (⊠ Box 476, 00831, ☎ FAX 809/776–6462), **Windspree** (⊠ 6-2-1A Estate Carolina, 00830, ☎ FAX 809/693–5423).

For condominiums, call **Caribbean Villas and Resorts** (⊠ Box 48, 00830, ☎ 809/776–6152 or 800/338–0987, FAX 809/779–4044). It manages Cruz Views, Cruz Bay Villas, and Pastory Estates. **Coconut Coast** (⊠ Box 618, 00831, ☎ FAX 809/693–9100 or ☎ 800/858–7989) has on-the-water condominiums. **Destination St. John** (⊠ Box 8306, 00831, ☎ 809/776–6969 or 800/562–1901) handles Lavender Hill. **Park Isle Villas** (⊠ Box 1263, 00831, ☎ FAX 809/693–8261 or ☎ 800/416–1205) manages Battery Hill and Villa Caribe. **Star Villa** (⊠ Box 999, 00830, ☎ 809/776–6704, FAX 809/776–6183) has 11 lovely units. The **Virgin Grand Villas** (⊠ Great Cruz Bay, 00830, ☎ 809/693–8856, FAX 809/693–8878) sits across the road from what was the Hyatt Regency St. John Hotel. At press time, that hotel was slated to reopen as the Westin Resort St. John in late 1997, at which time the villas will become Westin Vacation Club Resort at St. John. Until then, villa guests can use the pool, public beach, and tennis courts, but no other hotel facilities. When the hotel reopens, all facilities will be available.

## Dining

Just about every kind of cuisine you can imagine is available in the U.S.V.I. The beauty and freedom of the islands have attracted a cadre of professionally trained chefs who know their way around fresh fish and local fruits. If you are staying in a large hotel, you will pay big city prices—in other words, dining out is usually expensive.

St. Thomas is the most cosmopolitan of the islands and has the most visitors, so it is not surprising that the island also has the largest number and greatest variety of restaurants. St. Croix restaurants are both more relaxed and, in some ways, more elegant. Dining in St. John ranges from casual open-air eateries to a handful of sophisticated spots with upscale fine dining.

## What to Wear

Restaurants in the U.S.V.I. are relaxed and informal. During the day, many people eat in beach attire, although a shirt and shoes are usually requested. In the evening, however, shorts and T-shirts are inappropriate for the nicer restaurants and luxury resorts. Pants and collared shirts, for men and women, are usually appropriate.

| CATEGORY | COST* |
|---|---|
| $$$$ | over $35 |
| $$$ | $25–$35 |
| $$ | $15–$25 |
| $ | under $15 |

*per person for a three-course meal, excluding drinks and service; there is no sales tax in the U.S.V.I.*

## St. Thomas

**$$$$** ✕ **Entre Nous.** The view here, from high over Charlotte Amalie's harbor, is as exhilarating as the dining is elegant. In the evening, you can watch the light-bedecked cruise ships pull slowly out of the harbor while you decide among such main courses as rack of lamb, Caribbean lobster, veal, and Chateaubriand. ⊠ *Bluebeard's Castle, Charlotte Amalie,* ☎ *809/774–4050. AE, MC, V. No lunch.*

**$$$$** ✕ **Hotel 1829.** You'll dine by candlelight flickering over stone walls
★ and pink table linens at this restaurant on the terrace of the hotel. The menu and wine list are extensive, from Caribbean rock lobster to rack of lamb. Many items, including a warm spinach salad, are prepared tableside, and the restaurant is justly famous for its dessert soufflés, made of chocolate, Grand Marnier, raspberry, or coconut, to name a few. ⊠ *Government Hill, near Main St., Charlotte Amalie,* ☎ *809/776–1829. Reservations essential. AE, D, MC, V. No lunch.*

**$$$$** ✕ **Romanos.** Inside this huge old stucco house in Smith Bay is a de-
★ lightful surprise: a spare, elegant setting and superb northern Italian cuisine. Owner Tony hasn't advertised since the restaurant opened in 1988, and it is always packed. Try the pastas, either with a classic sauce or one of Tony's unique creations, such as a cream sauce with mushrooms, prosciutto, pine nuts, and Parmesan. ⊠ *97 Smith Bay,* ☎ *809/775–0045. MC, V. Closed Sun. No lunch.*

**$$$$** ✕ **Virgilio's.** This intimate, elegant hideaway serves the best northern
★ Italian cuisine on the island. Eclectic groupings of paintings and prints cover the two-story-high brick walls. Come here for more than 40 homemade pastas complemented by superb sauces, including capellini with fresh tomatoes and garlic and spaghetti peasant-style (in a rich tomato sauce with mushrooms and prosciutto). Try Virgilio's own mango flambé with crepes or a steaming cup of cappuccino for dessert. Maître d' Regis is on hand day and night, welcoming customers and helping the very gracious staff. ⊠ *18 Main St., Charlotte Amalie,* ☎ *809/776–4920. AE, MC, V. Closed Sun.*

**$$$–$$$$** ✕ **Craig & Sally's.** In the heart of Frenchtown, Sally Darash whips up
★ such eclectic starters as grilled shrimp and melon kebabs and entrées such as polenta-crusted yellowtail snapper with artichoke and olive sauce. Save room for homemade desserts—the white chocolate cheesecake is truly special. Sally's husband, Craig, makes sure more than a dozen wines are available by the glass and many more by the bottle. ⊠ *22 Honduras, Frenchtown,* ☎ *809/777–9949. AE, MC, V.*

**$$$** ✕ **Blue Marlin.** Dockside dining at its friendliest is the trademark of this open-air restaurant close to the St. John ferry dock at Red Hook. The fish is so fresh you may see it coming in from one of the boats docked just steps away. For starters, try the medallion of yellowfin tuna seviche marinated in lime, onion, and white wine. Entrées include a grilled fillet of wahoo with pineapple and cucumber sauce and sea bass poached in spiced carrot essence and topped with caviar. Steak, poultry, and pasta lovers will find something to please on the menu, too. ⊠ *Red Hook,* ☎ *809/775–6350. AE, MC, V.*

**$$$**  ✕ **Chart House.** In an old great house on the tip of the Frenchtown peninsula, this restaurant has a superb view. The menu includes fresh fish and teriyaki dishes, lobster, and Hawaiian chicken; there's also a large salad bar. ⊠ *Villa Olga, Frenchtown,* ☎ *809/774–4262. AE, D, DC, MC, V.*

**$$–$$$**  ✕ **Alexander's Cafe.** This charming restaurant is a favorite with the
  ★  people in the restaurant business on St. Thomas—always a sign of quality. Alexander is Austrian, and the schnitzels are delicious and reasonably priced; pasta specials are fresh and tasty. Save room for strudel. Next door is Alexander's Bar & Grill, serving food from the same kitchen but in a more casual setting and at slightly lower prices. ⊠ *24A Honduras, Frenchtown,* ☎ *809/776–4211. AE, D, MC, V. Closed Sun.*

**$$–$$$**  ✕ **Mim's Seaside Bistro.** Walk from the beach onto the patio of this open-air eatery, where you can sip a Beach Bar Bomber while listening to lapping waves. Try a ham and baked Brie sandwich for lunch; for dinner, indulge in fish—served grilled, sautéed, blackened, broiled, or island-style. Thursday is all-you-can-eat shrimp night. ⊠ *Watergate Villas, East End,* ☎ *809/775–2081. AE, MC, V.*

**$$–$$$**  ✕ **Raffles.** In the cozy comfort of a homelike dining room, owner-chef
  ★  Sandra Englesburger puts on a one-woman culinary show. Her all-from-scratch creations include an English shepherd's pie, mahimahi in a rich lobster sauce, and a two-day Peking duck. The dessert special is Peter's Paradise—a dark chocolate sphere filled with white chocolate mousse and tropical fruit. Raffles is definitely a find. ⊠ *Compass Point Marina,* ☎ *809/775–6004. AE, MC, V.*

**$$**  ✕ **Tickles Dockside Pub.** The Crown Bay location has been a locals' choice for years, and this second branch of the casual, alfresco pub, just off the docks, is a welcome addition to East End. Enjoy sandwiches, ribs, and chicken (served with sweet-potato french fries) while you watch the iguanas beg for table scraps—and bring your camera! ⊠ *American Yacht Harbor, Bldg. D, Red Hook,* ☎ *809/775–9425. MC, V.*

**$$**  ✕ **Zorba's Cafe.** Tired of shopping? Summon up one last ounce of en-
  ★  ergy and head up Government Hill to Zorba's. Sit and have a cold beer or bracing iced tea in the 19th-century stone-paved courtyard surrounded by banana trees. Greek salads and appetizers, moussaka, and an excellent vegetarian plate top the menu. ⊠ *Government Hill, Charlotte Amalie,* ☎ *809/776–0444. AE, MC, V. No lunch Sun.*

**$–$$**  ✕ **Eunice's Terrace.** This excellent West Indian cook is justly famous. Her roomy, two-story restaurant has a bar and a menu of native dishes, including callaloo (a West Indian soup made with spinach and seafood), conch fritters, fried fish, local sweet potato, fungi, and green banana. ⊠ *Rte. 38, near Renaissance Grand Beach Resort and Coral World, Smith Bay,* ☎ *809/775–3975. AE, MC, V.*

**$–$$**  ✕ **Hard Rock Cafe.** A hot spot from the day it opened, this waterfront restaurant is pretty much like its namesakes around the world. Rock-and-roll memorabilia dominates the decor, and the menu is full of hamburgers, sandwiches, salads, and great desserts. Doors open at 11 AM and stay open until 2 AM, and there's always a wait during prime mealtimes. ⊠ *International Plaza on the Waterfront, Charlotte Amalie,* ☎ *809/777–5555. AE, MC, V.*

**$**  ✕ **Gladys' Cafe.** Even if the great local specialties such as conch in but-
  ★  ter sauce, saltfish and dumplings, and hearty red-bean soup didn't make this a recommended café, it would be worth going to for Gladys's smile. While you're there, pick up her special hot sauce for $6 a bottle. There are burgers and a hot chicken salad for less adventurous palates. ⊠ *Royal Dane Mall, Charlotte Amalie,* ☎ *809/774–6604. AE. No dinner.*

## St. Croix

**$$$$**  ✕ **Great House at Villa Madeleine.** This elegant restaurant, part of the Villa Madeleine resort nestled in the hills on St. Croix's East End, serves such diverse cuisine as chicken alla Bolognese, swordfish medallions sautéed with green tomato and asparagus, and a number of fine beef dishes. The wine list is extensive. ✉ *19A Teague Bay (take Rte. 82 out of Christiansted and turn right at Reef Condominiums),* ☎ *809/778–7377. AE, D, DC, MC, V.*

**$$$$**  ✕ **Top Hat.** Owned by a delightful Danish couple, this restaurant has
★ been in business since 1970, serving international cuisine with an emphasis on Danish specialties—roast duck stuffed with apples and prunes, *frikadeller* (savory meatballs in a tangy cocktail sauce), fried Camembert with lingonberries, and smoked eel. The old West Indian structure, complete with gingerbread trim, is nicely accented in gray, white, and pink. The salad bar features such Danish delights as herring in sour cream and duck liver pâté. ✉ *52 Company St., Christiansted,* ☎ *809/773–2346. AE, D, MC, V. Closed May–Aug. No lunch.*

**$$$**  ✕ **Blue Moon.** This terrific little bistro, popular for its live jazz on Friday nights, has an eclectic, often-changing menu that draws heavily on Asian, Cajun, and French influences. Try the delicious seafood chowder or luna pie (veggies and cheese baked in phyllo dough) as an appetizer and the sweet-potato ravioli in mushroom sauce as an entrée; for dessert, the chocolate mint napoleon is heavenly. ✉ *17 Strand St., Frederiksted,* ☎ *809/772–2222. AE. Closed Mon. and July–Sept.*

**$$$**  ✕ **Kendricks.** This restaurant, a longtime favorite with locals, moved
★ its great food and tranquil ambience to Gallows Bay and didn't miss a beat. At the upstairs restaurant, waiters in bow ties dote on customers seated at tables laid with crisp linens and fine china. The menu is stylish Continental, and dishes are lovingly presented. Try the lobster spring rolls with warm ginger and soy butter to start, or the silken cream of shiitake soup. Move on to the house specialty, roasted pecan-crusted pork loin with ginger mayonnaise. At the downstairs café, enjoy the nightly jazz band while you dine on lighter fare, such as fettuccine with grilled Portobello mushrooms. ✉ *12 Chandlers Wharf, Gallows Bay, Christiansted,* ☎ *809/773–9199. AE, MC, V. Closed Sun.*

**$$$**  ✕ **Le St. Tropez.** A ceramic-tiled bar and soft lighting add to the Mediterranean atmosphere at this pleasant bistro, tucked into a courtyard off Frederiksted's main thoroughfare. Diners, seated either inside or on the adjoining patio, enjoy French fare such as salads, brochettes, and grilled meats in delicate sauces. The menu changes daily, often taking advantage of fresh local seafood. The fresh basil, tomato, and mozzarella salad is heavenly. ✉ *67 King St., Frederiksted,* ☎ *809/772–3000. AE, MC, V. Closed Sun.*

**$$**  ✕ **Camille's.** This tiny, lively spot, whose exposed brick walls are splashed with colorful prints, is perfect for lunch or a light supper. Sandwiches and burgers are the big draw, though the daily seafood special, often wahoo or mahimahi, is also popular. ✉ *Corner of Company and Queen Cross Sts., Christiansted,* ☎ *809/773–2985. MC, V. Closed Sun.*

**$$**  ✕ **Harvey's.** The plain, even dowdy room contains just 12 tables, and plastic, flowered tablecloths constitute the sole attempt at decor. But who cares? The delicious local food ranks among the island's best. Daily specials, such as mouthwatering goat stew and melting whelks in butter, served with heaping helpings of rice, fungi, and vegetables, are listed on the blackboard. Genial owner Sarah Harvey takes great pride in her kitchen, bustling out from behind the stove to chat and urge you to eat up. ✉ *11B Company St., Christiansted,* ☎ *809/773–3433. No credit cards. Closed Sun. No dinner Mon.–Wed.*

## St. John

**$$$$  ✕ Asolare.** Eclectic Asian dining dominates the menu at this elegant open-air eatery in an old St. John house. Come early and relax over drinks while you enjoy the sunset over the harbor. Start with a crayfish summer roll, a new twist on the usual spring roll, with tamarind peanut sauce. Dinners include such delights as rice noodles with shrimp, chicken, and chilies. If you still have room for dessert, try the chocolate pyramid, a luscious chocolate cake with homemade ice cream. ⊠ *Caneel Hill, Cruz Bay,* ☎ *809/779–4747. AE, MC, V. No lunch.*

**$$$$  ✕ Le Chateau de Bordeaux.** One of the best views you'll dine by anywhere is on the terrace here or in the air-conditioned dining room. The ★ rustic cabin is practically a glorified tree house, magically transformed into an elegant, ultraromantic aerie by wrought-iron chandeliers, lace tablecloths, and antiques. The innovative preparations appeal equally to the eye and the palate. You might start with velvety carrot soup, perfectly contrasted with roasted chilies. Segue into the rosemary-perfumed rack of lamb with a honey-Dijon-nut crust, or the salmon with mustard and maple glaze served on a bed of pasta. Don't miss the whelks, done to perfection. The comprehensive, moderately priced wine list is predictably strong on Bordeaux reds. ⊠ *Rte. 10, just east of Centerline Rd.,* ☎ *809/776–6611. AE, MC, V.*

**$$$$  ✕ Paradiso.** This popular spot is on the upper level of Mongoose ★ Junction, the island's largest shopping area. The menu is an eclectic mix, including everything from the slightly Italian wahoo putanesca (a local fish with a black olive sauce) to grilled New York strip steak to roasted rack of lamb. One can dine indoors in the comfort of air-conditioning or outdoors on a small terrace overlooking the street.⊠ *Mongoose Junction,* ☎ *809/693–8899. AE, MC, V. No lunch.*

**$$$  ✕ Ellington's.** This peaceful, appealing spot extends out onto the second-story veranda of the Gallows Point Suite Resort's central building. The outside tables are particularly quiet and romantic. The menu is Continental, with dishes of chicken, fish, and steak. You might start with the jumbo shrimp cooked in sweet coconut and served with mango sauce, or the seafood chowder. Entrées include sea scallops and pesto, swordfish scampi, filet mignon, and fresh lobster. Save room for dessert, though, perhaps the banana–chocolate-chip cake or the white-chocolate brownie. ⊠ *Gallows Point Suite Resort, Cruz Bay,* ☎ *809/ 693–8490. AE, MC, V. No lunch.*

**$$$  ✕ Fish Trap.** The rooms and terraces here all open to the breezes and buzzing with truly happy diners. Chef Aaron Willis conjures up tasty appetizers such as conch fritters and Fish Trap Chowder. The menu also includes an interesting pasta of the day, steak, chicken, and hamburgers. ⊠ *Cruz Bay,* ☎ *809/693–9994. AE, D, MC, V. Closed Mon.*

**$$  ✕ Shipwreck Landing.** Start with one of the house drinks, perhaps a fresh-squeezed concoction of lime, coconut, and rum, and then move on to hearty taco salads, fried shrimp, teriyaki chicken, and conch fritters. The birds keep up a lively chatter in the bougainvillea that surrounds the open-air restaurant, and there's live music on Sunday night in season. ⊠ *Coral Bay,* ☎ *809/693–5640. MC, V.*

# Beaches

All beaches on these islands are open to the public, but often you will have to walk through a resort to reach them. Once there, you'll find that resort guests may have access to lounge chairs and beach bars that are off limits to you; for this reason, you may feel more comfortable at one of the beaches not associated with a resort. Whichever one you choose, remember to remove your valuables from the car.

## St. Thomas

**Coki Point Beach,** next to Coral World, is a popular snorkeling spot for cruise-ship passengers; it's common to find them among the reefs on the east and west ends of the beach. If Coral World has reopened by the end of 1997, you can use its lockers and changing rooms. **Magens Bay's** spectacular ½-mi arc of white sand is usually lively. Two peninsulas protect its calm waters. The bottom is flat and sandy, so this is a place for sunning and swimming rather than snorkeling. At **Morning Star Beach,** close to Charlotte Amalie, many young residents show up for bodysurfing or volleyball. This pretty curve of beach fronts the Morning Star section of the Marriott's Frenchman's Reef Hotel. Snorkeling is good near the rocks. From **Sapphire Beach** there is a fine view of St. John and other islands. Snorkeling is excellent at the reef to the right or east, near Pettyklip Point. All kinds of water-sports gear is for rent. If you're on St. Thomas at full moon, grab the champagne (and the bug spray) and head here for the moonrise. The moon rises out of the sea, illuminating the beach in a most romantic light. The condo resort at **Secret Harbour** doesn't detract from the attractiveness of this covelike East End beach. Not only is it pretty, it is also superb for snorkeling—go out to the left, near the rocks. **Hull Bay,** on the north shore, faces Inner and Outer Brass cays and attracts fishermen and beachcombers. It is open to rough Atlantic waves and is the only place to surf on the island.

## St. Croix

**Buck Island** and its reef, controlled by the National Park Service, can be reached only by boat; nonetheless, a visit here is a must on any trip to St. Croix. Buck Island beach is beautiful, but its finest treasures are those you see when you plop off the boat and adjust your face mask, snorkel, and flippers. The waters are not always gentle at **Cane Bay,** a breezy north-shore beach, but the scuba diving and snorkeling are wondrous, and there are never many people around. Just swim straight out to see elkhorn and brain corals. Less than 200 yards out is the drop-off or so-called Cane Bay Wall. South of Frederiksted, try the beach at **On the Beach Resort**; palm trees provide plenty of shade for those who need it, and there is a fine restaurant for a casual lunch on weekends. **Rainbow Beach,** at the West End Beach Club, has a bar, water sports, and volleyball. **Tamarind Reef Beach** is a small but attractive beach east of Christiansted. Both Green Cay and Buck Island seem smack in front of you and make the view arresting. Snorkeling is good. There are several popular West beaches along the coast north of Frederiksted.

## St. John

**Caneel Bay** is actually seven white-sand beaches on the north shore, six of which can be reached only by water if you do not care to traipse across the hotel's lush grounds. The main beach (ask for directions at the gatehouse) provides easy access to the public. **Cinnamon Bay,** a long, sandy beach facing beautiful cays, serves the adjoining national-park campground. Facilities (showers, toilets, commissary, restaurant, beach shop, gift shop, small museum, kayak and windsurfing rentals) are open to all. There's good snorkeling off the point to the right, and rental equipment is available. **Hawksnest Beach** is becoming more popular every day; it's narrow and lined with sea-grape trees. There are rest rooms, cooking grills, and a covered shed for picnicking. It's popular for group outings and is the closest beach to town, so it is often fairly crowded. The gorgeous bay here may look familiar; you've seen it in Alan Alda's film *Four Seasons*. **Salt Pond Bay,** on the southeastern coast of St. John, is a scenic area to explore, next to Coral Bay and rugged Drunk Bay. This beach is for the adventurous. It's a short hike down a hill from the parking lot, and the only facility is an outhouse. The beach is a little rockier here, but there are interesting tidal pools and the snorkeling is good. Take care to leave nothing valuable in the car, because reports of thefts are numerous here. It's well worth hiking the trail south to the spectacular cliffs of Ram Head. Be sure at least to get a view of **Lameshur Bay,** one of the best snorkeling places on St. John and an area once used for underwater training by the U.S. Navy. **Trunk Bay** is probably St. John's most-photographed beach and the most popular spot for beginning snorkelers because of its underwater trail. It's the St. John stop for cruise-ship snorkelers, so if you're looking for seclusion, check cruise-ship listings in *St. Thomas This Week* to find out what days the lowest number are in port. There are changing rooms, a snack bar, picnic tables, a gift shop, telephones, small lockers, and snorkeling equipment for rent.

## Outdoor Activities and Sports

### Fishing

In the past quarter-century, some 20 world records, many for blue marlin, have been set in the waters surrounding the Virgin Islands, most notably at St. Thomas's famed North Drop. To book a boat from St. Thomas or St. John, call the **Charter Boat Center** (☎ 809/775–7990 or 800/866–5714), **American Yacht Harbor** (☎ 809/775–6454), or **Sapphire Beach Marina** (☎ 809/777–6100). On St. Croix, contact **Cruzan Divers** (☎ 809/772–3701), **Captain Bunny's** (☎ 809/778–6987), or **Ruffian Enterprises** (✉ St. Croix Marina, ☎ 809/773–6011 day, 809/773–0917 night).

### Golf

On St. Thomas, scenic **Mahogany Run** (☎ 809/775–5000), with a par-70, 18-hole course and a view of the B.V.I., lies to the north of Charlotte Amalie and has the especially tricky "Devil's Triangle" trio of holes. On St. Croix, the **Buccaneer**'s (☎ 809/773–2100) 18-hole course is conveniently close to (east of) Christiansted. More spectacular is the course at **Westin Carambola Beach Resort** (☎ 809/778–5638), in the valleyed northwestern part of the island, designed by Robert Trent Jones. The **Reef Club** (☎ 809/773–8844), at the northeastern part of the island, has nine holes.

### Horseback Riding

At Sprat Hall on St. Croix, near Frederiksted, Jill Hurd runs **Paul and Jill's Equestrian Stables** (☎ 809/772–2880 or 809/772–2627) and will take you clip-clopping through the rain forest, along the coast, or on moonlit rides. Costs range from $50 to $75 for the three-hour rides.

### Mountain Biking

**St. Thomas Mountain Bike Adventure** (✉ Box 7037, 00801, ☎ 809/776–1727) will take you on a 1½-hour cycle out past Magens Bay to Peterborg Point on Trek 830 21-speed mountain bikes. Photo opportunities abound for flora, fauna, and a lesser-seen side of Magens' picturesque half-moon bay. Helmets, water, and guide are provided.

### Sailing and Boating

The U.S.V.I. constitutes one of the biggest charter-boat fleet bases in the Western Hemisphere. You can go through a broker to book a private sailing vessel with crew or contact a charter-boat company directly. Among brokers for the U.S.V.I., **Blue Water Cruises** (✉ Box 1345, Camden, ME 04843, ☎ 800/524–2020) has an excellent worldwide reputation. Charter-boat companies on St. Thomas include **Regency Yacht Vacations** (✉ 5200 Long Bay Rd., 00802, ☎ 809/776–5950 or 800/524–7676) at the Yacht Haven Marina; **VIP Yacht Charters** (✉ 6118 Estate Frydenhoj 58, 00802-1402, ☎ 809/776–1510 or 800/524–

2015) near Red Hook, and **Island Yachts** (⊠ 6100 Red Hook Quarter, Suite 4, 00802, ☎ 809/775–6666 or 800/524–2019), in Red Hook. On St. Croix, the **Annapolis Sailing School** (⊠ Box 3334, 601 6th St., Annapolis, MD 21403, ☎ 410/267–7205 or 800/638–9192) offers one-week live-aboard cruises leaving from Christiansted.

### SMALL POWERBOAT RENTALS

This is an interesting—and surprisingly affordable—way to see the islands. **Club Nautico** (⊠ American Yacht Harbor, St. Thomas, 00802, ☎ 809/779–2555) and **Nauti Nymph** (⊠ American Yacht Harbor, St. Thomas 00802, ☎ 809/775–5066) both have a variety of 21- to 29-ft boats.

### DAY-SAIL CHARTER COMPANIES

The following businesses can effortlessly book you on a submarine ride, a parasail boat, a kayak trip, a Jet Ski ride, a Hobie Cat sail, a half-day inshore light-tackle fishing trip, or an excursion over to the neighboring British Virgin Islands. They get customer feedback on a daily basis and know exactly what type of boats and crew they are booking. They will be happy to answer any questions.

On St. Thomas, call the **Charter Boat Center** (⊠ 6300 Smith Bay 16-3, 00802-1304, ☎ 809/775–7990), the **Adventure Center** (⊠ Marriott Frenchman's Reef Hotel, Box 7100, 00801, ☎ 809/774–2990), **VI Eco-tours** (⊠ Box 11612, 00802, ☎ 809/779–2155), or **Limnos Charters** (⊠ )Limnos Marina, 00802, ☎ 809/775–3203).

On St. Croix, try **Mile-Mark Charters** (⊠ Box 3045, 59 Kings Wharf, Christiansted 00822, ☎ 809/773–2628 or 800/523–3483, ℻ 809/773–7400). **Big Beard's Adventure Tours** (⊠ Box 4534, Pan Am Pavilion, Christiansted 00822, ☎ 809/773–4482) runs trips to Buck Island and beach barbecues using two catamarans, one with a glass bottom. **Buck Island Charters** (⊠ Box 25273, Gallows Bay 00824, ☎ 809/773–3161) with Captain Heinz's trimaran, the *Teroro II,* departs for full- or half-day Buck Island trips from Green Cay Marina.

On St. John, **Connections** (⊠ Box 37, 00831, ☎ 809/776–6922) represents a dozen of the finest local boats; many of its employees have actually worked on the boats they book. **Proper Yachts** (⊠ Box 1570, 00831, ☎ 809/776–6256) has a fleet of luxury day-sail boats.

## Scuba Diving and Snorkeling

There are numerous dive operators on the three islands, and some of the hotels offer dive packages. Many of the operators listed below also offer snorkeling trips; call individual operators for details.

### ST. THOMAS

**Aqua Action Watersports** (⊠ 6501 Red Hook Plaza, Suite 15, 00802, ☎ 809/775–6285). This full-service, PADI five-star shop offers all levels of instruction. It also rents sea kayaks and Windsurfers.

**Chris Sawyer Diving Center** (⊠ 6300 Estate Frydenhoj, 00802-1411, Suite 29, ☎ 809/775–7320 or 800/882–2965; locations at Compass Point, American Yacht Harbor, and the Renaissance Grand Beach Resort). Vice president Al Gore took a dive trip with this PADI five-star outfit, which specializes in dives to the 310-ft RMS *Rhone*. There's also a NAUI certification center offering instruction up to dive master.

**Seahorse Dive Boats** (⊠ Crown Bay Marina, Suite 505, 00802, ☎ 809/774–2001). This PADI five-star operation does both day and night dives on local wrecks and reefs.

**Underwater Safaris** (⊠ Box 8469, 00801, ☎ 809/774–1350). Conveniently located in Long Bay at the Yacht Haven Marina—which is also home to the U.S.V.I. charter-boat fleet—this PADI five-star dive operation specializes in Buck Island dives to the wreck of the World War I cargo ship *Cartenser Sr.*

### ST. CROIX

**Anchor Dive** (⊠ Salt River Marina, Box 5588, Sunny Isle 00823, ☎ 809/778–1522) has wall and boat dives.

**Dive Experience, Inc.** (⊠ Box 4254, 1 Strand St., Christiansted 00822-4254, ☎ 809/773–3307 or 800/235–9047) is a PADI five-star training facility providing the range from certification to introductory dives.

**Dive St. Croix** (⊠ 59 Kings Wharf, Box 3045, Christiansted 00820, ☎ 809/773–3434 or 800/523–3483, FAX 809/773–7400) takes divers to walls and wrecks—more than 50 sites—and offers introductory, certification, and PADI, NAUI, and SSI C-card completion courses. It has custom packages with five hotels. Dive St. Croix is the only dive operation on the island allowed to run dives to Buck Island.

**V.I. Divers, Ltd.** (⊠ Pan Am Pavilion, Christiansted 00820, ☎ 809/773–6045 or 800/544–5911) is a PADI five-star training facility with a 32-ft dive boat and hotel packages.

### ST. JOHN

**Cruz Bay Watersports Co., Inc.** (⊠ Box 252, 00830, ☎ 809/776–6234 or 800/835–7730, FAX 809/693–8720) is a PADI five-star diving center with two locations in Cruz Bay. Owner-operators Patty and Marcus Johnston offer regular reef, wreck, and night dives aboard three custom dive vessels.

**Low Key Water Sports** (⊠ Box 716, 00830, ☎ FAX 809/693–8999), at the Wharfside Village, offers PADI certification and resort courses, one- and two-tank dives, wreck dives, and specialty courses.

**St. John Watersports** (⊠ Box 1570, 00830, ☎ 809/776–6256) is a PADI five-star center in the Mongoose Junction shopping mall.

## Stargazing

**Star Charters Astronomy Adventures** (⊠ Nisky Mail Center, No. 693, St. Thomas 00802, ☎ 809/774–9211) will let you scan the heavens with the Caribbean's largest optical telescope, an 18-inch Newtonian reflector, and learn both the science and lore of the stars.

## Tennis

### ST. THOMAS

Most hotels rent time to nonguests. For reservations call **Bluebeard's Castle Hotel** (☎ 809/774–1600, ext. 196), **Mahogany Run Tennis Club** (☎ 809/775–5000), **Marriott Frenchman's Reef Tennis Courts** (☎ 809/776–8500, ext. 444), **Sapphire Beach Resort** (☎ 809/775–6100, ext. 2131), **Renaissance Grand Beach Resort** (☎ 809/775–1510), **Ritz-Carlton** (☎ 809/775–3333), or **Wyndham Sugar Bay** (☎ 809/777–7100). All of the above courts have lights and are open into the evening. There are two public courts at **Sub Base** (next to the Water and Power Authority), open on a first-come, first-served basis. The lights are on here until 8 PM.

### ST. CROIX

The public courts found in Frederiksted and out east at Cramer Park are in pretty questionable shape: It's better to pay the fees to play at the many hotel courts around the island.

There is a pro, a full tennis pro shop, and eight courts (two lighted) at the **Buccaneer Hotel** (☎ 809/773–2100); four courts (two lighted) at the **Westin Carambola Beach Resort** (☎ 809/778–3800); three lighted courts at **Club St. Croix** (☎ 809/773–4800); and two unlighted courts at the **Chenay Bay Beach Resort** (☎ 809/773–2918).

**Caneel Bay Resort** (☎ 809/776–6111) has 11 courts (none lighted) for guests only and a pro shop. The **public courts** near the fire station are lighted until 10 PM and are available on a first-come, first-served basis.

# Shopping

## St. Thomas
Most people would agree that St. Thomas lives up to its self-described billing as a shopper's paradise. Even if shopping isn't your idea of paradise, you still may want to slip in on a quiet day (check the cruise-ship listings—Monday and Saturday are usually the least crowded) to check out the prices. Among the best buys are liquor, linens, imported china, crystal (most stores ship), and jewelry. The sheer volume of jewelry available makes this one of the few items for which comparison shopping is worth the effort.

Most stores take major credit cards. There is no sales tax in the U.S.V.I., and shoppers can take advantage of the $1,200 duty-free allowance per family member. Shoppers also get an additional 5% discount on the duty on the next $1,000 worth of goods, but remember to save your receipts.

### SHOPPING DISTRICTS
The prime shopping area in Charlotte Amalie is between Post Office and Market squares and consists of three parallel streets running east to west (Waterfront Highway, Main Street, and Back Street) and the alleyways connecting them. **Vendors Plaza,** on the Waterfront at Emancipation Gardens, is a centralized location for all the vendors who used to clog the sidewalks with their merchandise.

**Havensight Mall,** next to the cruise-ship dock, has parking and many of the same stores as Charlotte Amalie, though it's not as charming. Next door, the dozen-plus **Port of Sale** shops offer brand-name factory-outlet bargains.

West of town, the pink-stucco **Nisky Center** is more of a hometown shopping center than a tourist area, but there's a pharmacy and convenience store, fast-food sub shop, bank, clothing stores, and electronics shop.

Out east, there are grocery stores galore, a Kmart, discount warehouse store, clothing and gift shops at the **Four Winds Shopping Center,** and the 47-store **Tutu Park Mall.** Across the street at **Tillett Gardens,** artists and craftspeople produce silk-screen fabrics, pottery, watercolors, and other handicrafts.

In Red Hook, **American Yacht Harbor** is a waterfront shopping arcade with branches of some of the Charlotte Amalie stores as well as a deli, a candy store, and a few restaurants.

### ART GALLERIES
**A. H. Riise Caribbean Print Gallery** (✉ Riise's Alley off Main St., ☎ 809/776–2303). Haitian and Virgin Islands art are displayed and sold here, along with art books, exquisite botanical prints, and historical note cards from MAPes MONDe.

**The Gallery** (✉ Waterfront Hwy. at Post Office Alley, ☎ 809/776–4641). Inside the waterfront branch of Down Island Traders (and owned by the same people), the Gallery carries Haitian art along with works by a number of Virgin Islands artists. Items on display include oil paint-

ings, metal sculpture, wood carvings, painted screens and boxes, figures carved from stone, and oversize papier-mâché figures. Prices range
from $50 to $5,000.

**Mango Tango** (⊠ Al Cohen Plaza at Raphune Hill, ☎ 809/777–3995).
Here you'll find the work of a variety of U.S.V.I. artists and some from
neighboring islands as well. A framing service is available.

**Van Rensselaer Art Gallery** (⊠ Al Cohen Mall, Rte. 30, ☎ 809/774–
4598). Owner Corrine Van Rensselaer exhibits her own artwork plus
the best from the island's many artists. Look for watercolors, batik,
paintings, ceramics, and oils.

### BOOKS AND MAGAZINES
**Dockside Bookshop** (⊠ Havensight Mall, Bldg. IV, ☎ 809/774–4937).
This place is packed with books for children, travelers, cooks, and historians, as well as a good selection of paperback mysteries, best-sell-
ers, art books, calendars, and art prints. It carries a selection of books
written in and about the Caribbean and the Virgin Islands, from literature to chartering guides to books on seashells and tropical flowers. There's no markup here.

**Education Station Books** (⊠ Wheatley Center, ☎ 809/776–3008).
There is no markup at this full-service bookstore, which concentrates
on Caribbean literature and black American and African history.
There's also a large cookbook selection, a music section featuring jazz
and "world beat" tapes from Africa, and prints by local artists. In addition, you can buy and sell used books of all types here. Visit **Education Station Ltd.**, just next door, for children's books.

**Island Newsstand** (⊠ Grand Hotel in Charlotte Amalie) and **Magazines** (⊠ Fort Mylner Shopping Center near Tillett Gardens). These
two shops have the largest selection of magazines and newspapers on
St. Thomas. Expect to pay about 20% above stateside prices.

### CAMERAS AND ELECTRONICS
**Boolchand's** (⊠ 31 Main St., ☎ 809/776–0794; ⊠ Havensight Mall,
☎ 809/776–0302). Choose from a variety of brand-name cameras as
well as audio and video equipment.

**Royal Caribbean** (⊠ Main St., ☎ 809/776–4110; ⊠ Havensight Mall,
☎ 809/776–8890). Prices are attractive on some cameras and accessories here. Portable cassette players are usually good buys.

### CHINA AND CRYSTAL
**A. H. Riise Gift Shops** (⊠ 37 Main St., at Riise's Alley, ☎ 809/776–
2303; ⊠ Havensight Mall, ☎ 809/776–2303). Look for Waterford,
Wedgwood, Royal Crown, and Royal Doulton at good prices.

**English Shop** (⊠ Waterfront Hwy., ☎ 809/776–5399; ⊠ Havensight
Mall, ☎ 809/776–3776). China and crystal come from major European and Japanese manufacturers.

**Little Switzerland** (⊠ Emancipation Garden, 5 Main St., Havensight
Mall, and American Yacht Harbor, ☎ 809/776–2010). Shops carry
crystal from Baccarat, Waterford, and Riedel, as well as china from
Wedgwood and others.

### CLOTHING
**G'Day** (⊠ Waterfront Hwy. at Royal Dane Mall, ☎ 809/774–8855).
Everything in this tiny shop is drenched in the bright colors of Aus-
tralian artist Ken Done, Scandinavian artist Sigrid Olsen, and items by
Cotton Fields—swimwear, resort wear, accessories, and umbrellas.

**Janine's Boutique** (⊠ A-2 Palm Passage, ☎ 809/774–8243). Women's and men's dressy and casual apparel are from European designers and manufacturers, including the Louis Feraud collection. Look for select finds from Valentino, Christian Dior, YSL, and Pierre Cardin.

**Java Wraps** (⊠ Waterfront Hwy. at Royal Dane Mall, ☎ 809/774–3700). Wear the snazzy Indonesian batik creations the U.S. Virgin Islands' athletes modeled at the opening ceremonies of the 1996 Summer Olympic Games in Atlanta. There is a complete line of beach coverups, swimwear, and leisure wear for women, men, and children.

**Local Color** (⊠ Hibiscus Alley, ☎ 809/774–3727). St. John artist Sloop Jones exhibits colorful hand-painted dresses, T-shirts, and sweaters. There are also brightly printed sundresses, shorts, and shirts by Jam's World; big-brim straw hats dipped in fuchsia, turquoise, and other tropical colors; and unique jewelry for sale here.

CRAFTS AND GIFTS

The **Caribbean Marketplace** (⊠ Havensight Mall, ☎ 809/776–5400). This is the place to look for Caribbean handicrafts, including Caribelle batiks from St. Lucia; bikinis from the Cayman Islands; Sunny Caribee spices, soaps, and teas from Tortola; and coffees from Trinidad.

The **Cloth Horse** (⊠ Fort Mylner Shopping Center, ☎ 809/779–2222). Find signed pottery from the Dominican Republic; wicker furniture and household goods from the island of Hispaniola; and pottery, rugs, and bedspreads from all over the world.

**Down Island Traders** (⊠ Waterfront Hwy. at Post Office Alley, ☎ 809/776–4641). Look for hand-painted calabash bowls; finely printed Caribbean note cards; jams, jellies, spices, and herbs; herbal teas made of rum, passion fruit, and mango; high-mountain coffee from Jamaica; and a variety of handicrafts from throughout the Caribbean.

**Pampered Pirate** (⊠ 4 Norre Gade, ☎ 809/775–5450). Island-made dolls, Christmas ornaments, prints and paintings along with other gift items seem to cover the walls in this always busy store.

FOOD

**Gourmet Gallery** (⊠ Crown Bay Marina, ☎ 809/776–8555) and **Havensight Market** (⊠ Havensight Mall, ☎ 809/777–6738) have an excellent and reasonably priced wine selection, as well as condiments, cheeses, and specialty ingredients for everything from tacos to curries to chow mein. Both groceries have in-store bakeries and delis, too. For fruits and vegetables, go to the **Fruit Bowl** (⊠ Wheatley Center, ☎ 809/774–8565). **Marina Market** (⊠ Across from Red Hook ferry, ☎ 809/779–2411) offers the islands' freshest meats and seafoods as well as various sundries. There are also **supermarkets** at Sub Base, Four Winds, Tutu Park Mall, and the Havensight area.

JEWELRY

**A. H. Riise Gift Shop** (⊠ 37 Main St., at Riise's Alley, ☎ 809/776–2303; ⊠ Havensight Mall, ☎ 809/776–2303). Shop in St. Thomas's oldest and largest store for such luxury items as jewelry, pearls, ceramics, china, crystal, flatware, perfumes, and watches.

**Amsterdam Sauer** (⊠ 14 Main St., ☎ 809/774–2222). Find many one-of-a-kind designs.

**Blue Carib Gems** (⊠ 2–3 Back St., ☎ 809/774–8525). Watch Alan O'Hara Sr. polish Caribbean amber, black coral, agate, and other gems and fashion them into gold and silver settings.

**Cardow's** (⊠ 3 stores on Main St., ☎ 809/776–1140; 2 at Havensight Mall, ☎ 809/774–0530 or 809/774–5905). Take your pick from an enormous "chain bar" more than 100 ft long, where you're guaranteed 30%–50% savings off U.S. retail prices or your money will be refunded within 30 days of purchase.

**Cartier** (⊠ 30 Trompeter Gade, ☎ 809/774–1590). There are lots of beautiful items at fantastic prices here, as well as a surprising number of affordable ones.

**Colombian Emeralds** (⊠ 30 Main St., Waterfront Hwy., and Havensight Mall, ☎ 809/774–3400). Here you'll find set and unset gems of every description, including high-quality emeralds.

**H. Stern** (⊠ 12 Main St., ☎ 809/776–1939; ⊠ 32AB Main St., ☎ 809/776–1146; ⊠ Havensight Mall, ☎ 809/776–1223). This is one of the most respected names in gems; you're sure to find your heart's desire.

**Irmela's Jewel Studio** (⊠ Grand Hotel Court, Toldbod Gade entrance, ☎ 809/774–5875). See some of the Caribbean's most exquisite gems in the historic stone walls of the Grand Hotel.

**Little Switzerland** (⊠ Main St., Emancipation Gardens, Havensight Mall, ☎ 809/776–2010; ⊠ American Yacht Harbor, ☎ 809/777–3100). This is the U.S.V.I.'s sole distributor of Rolex watches. The store also does a booming mail-order business.

**Opals of Australia** (⊠ Drakes Passage, ☎ 809/774–8244). Look for a wide variety of these iridescent wonders.

### LEATHER GOODS

**Gucci** (⊠ Riise's Alley off Main St., ☎ 809/774–7841; ⊠ Havensight Mall, ☎ 809/774–4090). Find the traditional insignia-designed items for men and women.

**Leather Shop** (⊠ Main St., ☎ 809/776–3995; ⊠ Havensight Mall, ☎ 809/776–0040). Fendi and Bottega Veneta are big names at big prices. However, there are also reasonably priced purses, wallets, and briefcases.

**Traveler's Haven** (⊠ Havensight Mall, ☎ 809/775–1798). Leather bags, backpacks, vests, and money belts for the adventurer on the go can be found here.

**Zora's** (⊠ Norre Gade across from Roosevelt Park, ☎ 809/774–2559). Fine leather sandals made to order are the specialty here, as well as made-only-in-the-Virgin-Islands backpacks, briefcases, and "fish" purses in durable, brightly colored canvas.

### LINENS

**Mr. Tablecloth** (⊠ Main St., ☎ 809/774–4343). Choose from a floor-to-ceiling array of linens while being assisted by an ever-smiling staff.

**Shanghai Linen** (⊠ Waterfront Hwy., ☎ 809/776–2828). Business is brisk and you can usually find a deal.

### LIQUOR AND WINE

**A. H. Riise Liquors** (⊠ Main St. and Riise's Alley, ☎ 809/776–2303; ⊠ Havensight Mall, ☎ 809/776–7713). Browse among a large selection of liquors, cordials, wines, and tobacco, including rare vintage cognacs, Armagnacs, ports, and Madeiras. They also stock imported cigars, fruits in brandy, and barware from England.

**Al Cohen's Discount Liquor** (⊠ Across from Havensight Mall, Long Bay Rd., ☎ 809/774–3690). This warehouse-style store has a large wine department.

**Modern Music** (✉ Across from Havensight Mall, ☎ 809/774–3100; ✉ Nisky Center, ☎ 809/777–8787). Look for the latest stateside and Caribbean CD and cassette releases, plus oldies, classical, and new-age music.

**Parrot Fish Records and Tapes** (✉ Back St., ☎ 809/776–4514). Stateside tapes and compact discs sit side-by-side with a good selection of music by Caribbean artists, including local groups. For a catalog of calypso, soca, steel band, and reggae music, write to Parrot Fish, Box 9206, St. Thomas 00801.

PERFUMES
**Sparky's** (✉ Main St., ☎ 809/776–7510). Impeccably turned-out salesclerks can give you a facial and makeup lesson.

**Tropicana Perfume Shoppes** (✉ 2 Main St., ☎ 809/774–0010 or 809/774–1834). This is the largest selection of fragrances for men and women in all of the Virgin Islands.

SUNGLASSES
**Fashion Eyewear** (✉ 20A Garden St., ☎ 809/776–9075). Tucked into a tiny building is an even tinier shop that sells sunglasses priced from $40 to $450. They'll also copy the prescription from your glasses and make new clear-lens glasses or sunglasses in a few hours.

**Sun Glass Hut** (✉ Main St., ☎ 809/777–5585). Take your pick from among brand-name eyewear—Biagiotti, Serengetti, Carrera, and others.

TOYS
**Mini Mouse House** (✉ 3A Trompeter Gade, ☎ 809/776–4242). Birds sing, dogs bark, and fish swim in this animated toyland. Adults have as much fun trying out the wares as do the kids.

## St. Croix
Although St. Croix doesn't offer as many shopping opportunities as St. Thomas, it does have an array of smaller stores with unique merchandise. In Christiansted, the best areas are the **Pan Am Pavilion** and **Caravelle Arcade** off Strand Street and along **King and Company streets.**

BOOKS
**The Bookie** (✉ 1111 Strand St., Christiansted, ☎ 809/773–2592) carries paperback novels, stationery, newspapers, and greeting cards. Stop in for the latest local gossip and events.

**Trader Bob's Dockside Book Store** (✉ 5030 Anchor Way, Gallows Bay, ☎ 809/773–6001). If you're looking for Caribbean books or the latest good read, try this bookstore located across from the post office in the Gallows Bay shopping area.

CHINA AND CRYSTAL
**Little Switzerland** (✉ Hamilton House, 1108 King St., Christiansted, ☎ 809/773–1976). The St. Croix branch of this Virgin Islands institution features a variety of Rosenthal flatware, Lladro figurines, Waterford and Baccarat crystal, Lalique figurines, and Wedgwood and Royal Doulton china.

CLOTHING
**Caribbean Clothing Company** (✉ 41 Queen Cross St., Christiansted, ☎ 809/773–5012) features contemporary sportswear by top American designers as well as Bally shoes for men.

**From the Gecko** (✉ 1233 Queen Cross St., ☎ 809/778–9433) offers the hippest buys on St. Croix, from superb batik sarongs to hand-painted scarves.

**Java Wraps** (✉ 51 Company St., Christiansted, ☎ 809/773–2920; ✉ Pan Am Pavilion, ☎ 809/773–3770) sells Indonesian batik cover-ups and resort wear for men, women, and children as well as fine home furnishings from around the world.

**Skirt Tails** (✉ Pan Am Pavilion, Christiansted, ☎ 809/773–1991) has hand-painted batik and washable silk clothing in a rainbow of colors, perfect for vacations in the tropics. The store carries swimwear, sarongs, pant and short sets, and flowing dresses.

**Urban Threadz** (✉ 52 C Company St., Christiansted, ☎ 809/773–2883). Urban island wear by Karl Kani, No Fear, and many other popular lines for contemporary men and women is available here. Check the **Urban Kidz** store three doors down for Guess, Calvin Klein, Boss, Nautica, and Fila children's clothes.

**The White House** (✉ Kings Alley Walk, Christiansted, ☎ 809/773-9222). This contemporary store features clothes in all-white or natural colors. Look for exquisite lingerie, elegant evening wear, and unusual casual clothes.

CRAFTS AND GIFTS

**Folk Art Traders** (✉ 1B Queen Cross St., at Strand St., Christiansted, ☎ 809/773–1900) has energetic owners who travel to Haiti, Jamaica, Guayama, and elsewhere in the Caribbean to find the treasures sold in their shop, including baskets, masks, pottery, and ceramics.

**Green Papaya** (✉ Caravelle Arcade No. 15, Christiansted, ☎ 809/773–8848) sells handcrafted furniture and accessories for the home with attention to the unusual. Asian baskets and lovely wrought-iron lamps and hurricanes with handblown teardrop lanterns are among its selection of goods from all over the world.

JEWELRY

**Colombian Emeralds** (✉ 43 Queen Cross St., Christiansted, ☎ 809/773–1928 or 809/773–9189) specializes—of course—in emeralds, including some that are under $100, and also carries diamonds, rubies, sapphires, and gold. A branch store, **Jewelers' Warehouse** (☎ 809/773–5590), is across the street. The chain, the Caribbean's largest jeweler, offers certified appraisals and international guarantees.

**Crucian Gold** (✉ 59 King St., Christiansted, ☎ 809/773–5241). This store, in a small courtyard in a West Indian–style cottage, carries the unique gold creations of St. Croix native Brian Bishop. His trademark piece is the Turk's Head ring, made of an interwoven gold strand.

**Sonya's** (✉ 1 Company St., Christiansted, ☎ 809/778–8605) is the home of the island's signature hook bracelet, which was designed by owner Sonya Hough.

LIQUOR

**Harborside Market and Spirits** (✉ 59 Kings Wharf, Christiansted, ☎ 809/773–8899) has a good selection of liquor at duty-free prices in its conveniently located shop.

**Woolworth's** (✉ Sunny Isle Shopping Center, Centerline Rd., ☎ 809/778–5466) carries a huge line of discount, duty-free liquor.

PERFUMES

**St. Croix Perfume Center** (⊠ 1114 King St., Christiansted, ☎ 809/773–7604) offers an extensive array of fragrances, including all the major brands.

**Violette Boutique** (⊠ Caravelle Arcade, 38 Strand St., Christiansted, ☎ 809/773–2148). Perfume, skin-care, and makeup products are the draw here.

## St. John

Because of the island's many natural wonders, travel literature about St. John often all but overlooks the pleasures of shopping here. But the blend of luxury items and handicrafts found in the shops on St. John makes for potentially excellent shopping opportunities. With several levels of cool, stone-wall shops, set off by colorfully planted terraces and courtyards, **Mongoose Junction** is one of the prettiest malls in the Caribbean. **Wharfside Village,** on the other side of Cruz Bay, is a painted-clapboard village with shops and restaurants.

# Nightlife

Nightlife in the U.S.V.I. is a spontaneous affair. Although there are many tourist-oriented cultural shows that can make for a fun night out—including broken-bottle dancing at various hotels—socializing is what the evenings are about. Most of the music scene is in small clubs with dance floors.

## St. Thomas

NIGHTSPOTS

**Barnacle Bill's** (⊠ 8136 Sub Base, ☎ 809/774–7444). Bill Grogan's Crown Bay landmark is a musicians' home away from home; it has hosted such greats as David Bromberg, Bonnie Raitt, and Maria Muldaur.

**The Greenhouse** (⊠ Waterfront Hwy. at Storetvaer Gade, ☎ 809/774–7998). This place is something like a T.G.I. Friday's in the United States. It caters to all tastes, with eggs-and-bacon breakfasts, burger and taco lunches, and Maine lobster specials for dinner. After 10 PM, the restaurant turns into a rock-and-roll club with a DJ or live reggae bands rousting the weary to their feet six days a week.

**Old Mill Complex** (⊠ 193 Contant, ☎ 809/776–3004). Located in—you guessed it—an old mill, this rock-till-you-drop late-night spot hops Thursday through Sunday. There's a small dance floor, as well as a good sound system.

**Stixx on the Water** (⊠ Ramada Yacht Haven Marina, ☎ 809/774–4480). Old salts and yuppie yachties rendezvous at this Yacht Haven Marina watering hole for lively libations. Nightly rock, country, and reggae tunes keep the dance floor full.

JAZZ AND PIANO BARS

You'll find piano bars at **Entre Nous** at Bluebeard's Castle Hotel (☎ 809/776–4050) and **Randy's Bistro** at Al Cohen Mall on Raphune Hill (☎ 809/777–3199). "Gray, Gray, Gray" plays piano at both. An island favorite, he's been around for years and shouldn't be missed.

## St. Croix

Christiansted has a lively and casual club scene near the waterfront. At **Mango Grove** (⊠ 53 King St., ☎ 809/773–0200) on weekends you'll hear live guitar and vocals in an open-air courtyard with a bar and Cinzano umbrella–covered tables. Easy jazz can be heard in the courtyard bar at **Indies** (⊠ 55–56 Company St., ☎ 809/692–9440) Saturday evenings. To party under the stars in a very, very informal setting, head to the **Wreck Bar** (☎ 809/773–6092), on Christiansted's Hospital Street, for crab races as well as rock and roll. **Hotel on the Cay** (⊠ Protestant Cay, ☎ 809/773–2035) has a West Indian buffet on Tuesday night that features a broken-bottle dancer and Mocko Jumbie. On Thursday night, the **Cormorant** (⊠ 4126 La Grande Princesse, ☎ 809/778–8920) throws a similar event. The **2 Plus 2 Disco** (⊠ 17 La Grande Princesse, ☎ 809/773–3710) spins a great mix of calypso, soul, disco, and reggae, with live music on weekends.

### Frederiksted

Although less hopping than those in Christiansted, Frederiksted restaurants and clubs have a variety of weekend entertainment. **Blue Moon** (⊠ 17 Strand St., ☎ 809/772–2222), a waterfront restaurant, is the place to be for live jazz on Friday 9 PM–1 AM.

### St. John

Some friendly hubbub can be found at the rough-and-ready **Backyard** (☎ 809/693–8886), *the* place for sports watching as well as grooving to Bonnie Raitt et al. There's calypso and reggae on Wednesday and Friday at **Fred's** (☎ 809/776–6363). The **Inn at Tamarind Court** (☎ 809/776–6378) serves up a blend of jazz and rock on Friday.

Notices on the bulletin board across from the U.S. post office and on telephone poles will keep you posted on special events: comedy nights, movies, and the like.

## Exploring St. Thomas

St. Thomas is only 13 mi long and less than 4 mi wide, but it's an extremely hilly island, and even an 8- or 10-mi trip could take several hours. Don't let that discourage you, though, because the ridge of mountains that runs from east to west through the middle, and separates the Caribbean and Atlantic sides of the island, offers spectacular vistas and is a lot of fun to explore—especially in a four-wheel drive and with lots of time. The best views come on the north side, but the others are all something to write home about. Look for glimpses of St. Croix some 40 mi to the south. Watch out for wandering cows and goats when you get into the hills. Don't hesitate to take an unexpected turn off the main road—after all, discovery is what trips are all about.

You'll find plenty of restaurants and watering holes spread around the island, so food and drink won't ever be too far away.

*Numbers in the margin correspond to points of interest on the St. Thomas map.*

### Charlotte Amalie

① Tour historic (and sometimes hilly) **Charlotte Amalie** with comfortable shoes, start early, and stop often to refresh. A note about the street names: In deference to the island's heritage, the streets downtown are labeled by their Danish names. Locals will use both the Danish name and the English name (such as Dronningen's Gade and Main Street).

SIGHTS TO SEE

**All Saints Anglican Church.** Built in 1848 from stone quarried on the island, the church has thick, arched window frames lined with the yellow brick that came to the islands as ballast aboard merchant ships. The merchants left the brick on the waterfront when they filled their boats with molasses, sugar, mahogany, and rum for the return voyage. The church was built to celebrate the end of slavery in the Virgin Islands in 1848. ⊠ *Domini Gade,* ☎ *809/774–0217.* ☉ *Mon.–Sat. 6 AM–3 PM.*

**Cathedral of St. Peter and St. Paul.** This building was consecrated as a parish church in 1848 and is the seat of the territory's Roman Catholic diocese. The soft tones of murals covering the ceiling and walls of the church were painted in 1899 by two Belgian artists, Father Leo Servais and Brother Ildephonsus. The San Juan–marble altar and side walls were added in the 1960s. ⊠ *Lower Main St.,* ☎ *809/774–0201.* ⊙ *Mon.–Sat. 8–5.*

**Danish Consulate Building.** Built in 1830, it housed the Danish Consulate until the Danish West Indian Company sold its properties to the local government in 1992. It now serves as home to the territory's governor. ⊠ *Take stairs north at corner of Bjerge Gade and Crystal Gade to Denmark Hill.*

**Dutch Reformed Church.** Founded in 1744, burned down in 1804 and rebuilt in 1844, then blown down by 1995's Hurricane Marilyn and again reconstructed in 1996, this structure has an austere loveliness. The unembellished cream-color hall exudes peace—albeit monochromatically. The only touches of another color are the forest-green shutters and carpet. ⊠ *Corner of Nye Gade and Crystal Gade,* ☎ *809/ 776–8255.* ⊙ *Weekdays 9–5. Call ahead; doors are sometimes locked.*

**Educators Park.** A peaceful place amid the town's hustle and bustle, this park has memorials to three famous Virgin Islanders: educator Edith Williams; J. Antonio Jarvis, a founder of the V.I. *Daily News*; and educator and author Rothchild Francis, for whom Market Square is named. The last gave many speeches from this location. ⊠ *Main St. across from U.S. Post Office.*

**Emancipation Garden.** Across from Fort Christian, this garden honors the freeing of slaves in 1848 and features a smaller version of the Liberty Bell. Today the gazebo's smooth floor is used for official ceremonies. The many benches are a preferred picnic location for clerks from nearby shops and offices as well as visitors. ⊠ *Between Tolbod Gade and Fort Christian.*

**Enid M. Baa Public Library.** The library is a large pink building typical of the 18th-century town houses common to the north side of Main Street. The merchants' homes were built across from the brick warehouses, with their stores downstairs and living quarters upstairs. The library was the home of St. Thomas merchant and landowner Baron von Bretton. It's the first recorded fireproof building. Its high-ceiling, cool, stone-floor interior is perfect for an afternoon of browsing through the historic-papers collection or just sitting in the breeze by an open window reading the daily paper. ⊠ *Main St.,* ☎ *809/774– 0630.* ⊙ *Weekdays 9–5, Sat. 9–3.*

↺ **Fort Christian.** St. Thomas's oldest standing structure anchors the shopping district. It was built in 1672–80 and carries a U.S. national landmark status. The clock tower was added in the 19th century. This formidable fortress has, over time, been used as a jail, governor's residence, town hall, courthouse, and church. It houses a museum featuring artifacts of U.S.V.I. history, natural history, and turn-of-the-century furnishings. There is a spectacular view from the roof. ⊠ *Waterfront Hwy. just east of shopping district,* ☎ *809/776–4566.* ⊙ *Weekdays 9–4.*

**Frederick Lutheran Church.** This historic church features a massive mahogany altar. The pews, each with its own door, were once rented to families of the congregation. Lutheranism is the state religion of Denmark, and, when the territory was without a minister, the governor— who had his own elevated pew—would fill in. ⊠ *Norre Gade,* ☎ *809/ 776–1315.* ⊙ *Mon.–Sat. 9–4.*

**Government House.** Built as an elegant home in 1867, this building now serves as the governor's office. The first floor is open to the public. The staircases are of native mahogany, as are the plaques hand-lettered in gold with the names of the governors appointed and, since 1970, elected. Brochures detailing the history of Government House are available, but you may have to search for them. Look behind or under the guest book to the left of the entrance.

The three murals at the back of the lobby were painted by Pepino Mangravatti in the 1930s as part of the U.S. government's Works Projects Administration (WPA). The murals depict Columbus's landing on St. Croix during his second voyage in 1493; the transfer of the islands from Denmark to the United States in 1917; and a sugar plantation on St. John.

To tour the second floor you will have to be accompanied by the deputy administrator. Call ahead to make an appointment for a tour, or take a chance that the officials will be in. It's worth the extra effort it takes to visit the second floor if for no reason other than the view from the terrace. Imagine the affairs of state of a colonial time being conducted in the hush of the high-ceiling, chandeliered ballroom. In the reception room are four small paintings by Camille Pissarro, but unfortunately they are hard to appreciate because they are enclosed in frosted-glass cases. More interesting, and visible, is the large painting by an unknown artist that was found in Denmark and depicts a romanticized version of St. Croix; the painting was purchased by former governor Ralph M. Paiewonsky, who then gave it to Government House. ⊠ *Government Hill,* ☎ *809/774–0001.* ⊙ *Weekdays 8–5.*

**Grand Hotel.** This imposing building stands at the head of Main Street. Once the island's premier hotel, it now houses offices and shops. ⊠ *Tolbod Gade at Norre Gade.*

**Hassel Island.** East of Water Island in Charlotte Amalie harbor, this island is part of the Virgin Islands National Park and houses the ruins of the British military garrison (built during a brief British occupation of the U.S.V.I. during the 1800s) and the remains of a marine railway (where ships were hoisted onto land to the ship repair yard). Also on Hassel Island is the shell of the hotel that writer Herman Wouk's fictitious character Norman Paperman tried to turn into his own paradise in the book *Don't Stop the Carnival.* Presently there is no transportation to the island and nothing to service visitors once they arrive.

**Hotel 1829.** Dating from the same year, this building was originally the residence of a prominent merchant named Lavalette. The hotel's bright coral-color walls are accented with fancy black wrought iron and the interior is darkly cool. From the dining terrace where gourmet food is served, see an exquisite view of the harbor framed by tangerine-color bougainvillea. ⊠ *Government Hill.*

**Legislature Building.** Its pastoral-looking lime-green exterior conceals the vociferous political wrangling of the Virgin Islands Senate going on inside. Built originally by the Danish as a police barracks, the building was later used to billet U.S. Marines, and much later it housed a public school. Visitors are welcome to sit in on sessions in the upstairs chambers. ⊠ *Waterfront Hwy. across from Fort Christian,* ☎ *809/774–0880.* ⊙ *Daily 8–5.*

**Market Square.** Formally called Rothchild Francis Square, it's a good place to stop for fresh fruit snacks. A cadre of old-timers sell papaya, tannia roots, and herbs. Sidewalk vendors offer a variety of African fabrics and artifacts, tie-dyed cotton clothes at good prices, and fresh-squeezed fruit juices. ⊠ *Turn north off Main St. at Strand Gade.*

**Memorial Moravian Church.** Built in 1884, it was named to commemorate the 150th anniversary of the Moravian Church in the Virgin Islands. ⊠ *17 Norre Gade,* ☎ *809/776–0066.* ☉ *Weekdays 8–5.*

**99 Steps.** A staircase "street" built by the Danes in the 1700s leads to the residential area above Charlotte Amalie and Blackbeard's Castle. The castle tower, built in 1679, was used by the notorious pirate Edward Teach and today houses a small hotel. If you count the stairs as you go up, you'll discover, as have thousands before you, that there are more than 99. ⊠ *Look for steps heading north from Government Hill.*

**Pissarro Building.** Home to several shops, this was the birthplace of French Impressionist painter Camille Pissarro. ⊠ *Main St.*

**Roosevelt Park.** This is a good spot to people-watch; you'll see members of the local legal community head to the nearby court buildings while you rest on the park benches. The small monument on the south side of the park is dedicated to U.S.V.I. war veterans. There's a wood-and-tire playground that's popular with children. ⊠ *Norre Gade.*

**Savan.** A neighborhood of small streets and small houses, Savan was first laid out in the 1700s as the residential area for a growing class of "free coloreds," a middle class of artisans, clerks, and shopkeepers. You'll find a row of Rastafarian shops along the first block and a restaurant that sells pâté, a delicious turnover-type pastry stuffed with meat or vegetables. ⊠ *Turn north off lower Main St. onto General Gade.*

NEED A BREAK?

Stop for a refreshing glass of *bush* (the local lingo for "herb") tea in the charming courtyard of the **Seven Arches Museum.** Located in a restored West Indian home built about 1800 are historic furnishings, cannonballs, and gas lamps. Behind the house is a quaint West Indian cottage. ☎ *809/774-9295.* ☞ *$5 (suggested contribution).* ☉ *Tues.–Sun. 10-3 or by appointment.*

**Synagogue of Beracha Veshalom Vegmiluth Hasidim.** The synagogue's Hebrew name translates as the Congregation of Blessing, Peace, and Loving Deeds. The small building's white pillars contrast with rough stone walls, as does the rich mahogany of the pews and altar. The sand on the floor symbolizes the exodus from Egypt. Since the synagogue first opened its doors in 1833, it has held a weekly Sabbath service, making it the oldest synagogue building in continuous use under the American flag and the second oldest (after the one on Curaçao) in the Western Hemisphere. Its **Weibel Museum** covers the 300-year history of the Jews on St. Thomas. ⊠ *15 Crystal Gade,* ☎ *809/774-4312.* ☉ *Weekdays 9–4.*

**Tortola Wharf.** Catch the *Native Son* and other ferries to the B.V.I. There's an upstairs restaurant where you can watch the Charlotte Amalie harbor traffic as you enjoy a glass of iced tea. ⊠ *Waterfront Hwy.*

**U.S. Post Office.** While you buy your postcard stamps, contemplate the murals of waterfront scenes by *Saturday Evening Post* artist Stephen Dohanos. His art was commissioned as part of the WPA in the 1930s. ⊠ *Tolbod Gade and Main St.*

**Vendors Plaza.** Merchants sell everything from T-shirts to African attire to leather goods that may carry name brands but aren't. Look for local art among the ever-changing selections at this busy market. ⊠ *West of Fort Christian at the Waterfront.*

**Visitors Bureau and Tourist Information Center.** Tucked away in the block between the U.S. Post Office and Waterfront Highway is a hospitality lounge complete with bathrooms and a place to stash your luggage if you want to shop on your way to the airport. ⊠ *Tolbod Gade across from Emancipation Garden,* ☎ *809/774–8784 or 800/372–8784,* FAX *809/777–9695.* ☾ *Weekdays 8–6, Sat. 9–1.*

**Water Island.** Look about a quarter of a mile out in the Charlotte Amalie harbor for a view of this island. It was once a peninsula of St. Thomas, but a channel was cut through so U.S. submarines could get to their base in a bay just to the west, known today as Sub Base. In 1996 the U.S. Department of the Interior transferred 50 acres of the island to the territorial government, making Water Island the fourth largest of the U.S. Virgin Islands.

## Around the Island

The rest of St. Thomas is best visited by car or taxi tour. Your rental car should come with a good map; if not, ask for one. The roads are marked with route numbers, but they're confusing and seem to switch numbers suddenly. If you stop to ask for directions, it's best to have your map in hand because the locals probably know the road you're looking for by another name. And remember, driving is on the left.

SIGHTS TO SEE

**Atlantis Submarine.** Probably the only way any of us are going to go 150 ft underwater, this submarine carries 46 passengers on a two-hour ride; it's air-conditioned and there's a surface vessel that maintains constant radio contact. While submerged, you may see stingrays, turtles, colorful coral, and more fish than any aquarium ever imagined. Watch for the remains of the *Michelle* and an occasional lemon shark. ⊠ *Havensight Mall,* ☎ *800/253–0493.* ▱ *$72.*

**Brewer's Beach.** Popular with the students at the nearby University of the Virgin Islands, this is a long strand of powdery beach. If you're hungry, trucks selling lunch, snacks, and drinks often park along the road. ⊠ *Rte. 30 across runway from airport.*

**Clinton Phipps Racetrack.** Try your luck at the scheduled races held here, especially on local holidays. Be prepared for large crowds; it's a popular sport. ⊠ *Rte. 30 at Nadir,* ☎ *809/775–4555.*

**Coki Point.** Snorkel the reefs at its eastern and western ends. You may want to dash in for a swim or just do some people-watching while nibbling on a meat pâté, which you can buy from one of the vendors. Don't leave valuables unattended in your car or on the beach at Coki Point. After leaving the beach, stop by one of the tropical fruit stands in Smith Bay and pick up a juicy mango, tender ripe papaya, or supersweet bunch of midget finger bananas. ⊠ *Turn north off Rte. 38.*

**Compass Point.** Home to a fair-size marina and several shops and restaurants that cater to boaters, the colorful area is a good spot to while away an afternoon walking around. And it's easy to engage the boaters—many sailed here from points around the globe—in conversation. You'll find everything from burgers to Continental fare at the area's restaurants. ⊠ *Turn south off Red Hook Rd. at well-marked entrance road just east of Independent Boat Yard.*

**Coral World.** Coral World, at Coki Point, is home to a three-level underwater observatory (call ahead for shark-feeding times), the world's largest reef tank, and an aquarium with more than 20 TV-size tanks providing capsulated views of life in the waters of the Virgin Islands and around the world. Coral World's staff will answer your questions about the turtles, iguanas, parrots, and flamingos that inhabit the park, and there's a restaurant, souvenir shop, and the world's only underwater mailbox, from which you can send postcards. ⊠ *Turn north off Smith Bay Rd. at sign,* ☎ *809/775–1555.*

🖐 ⑬ **Drake's Seat.** Sir Francis Drake was supposed to have kept watch over his fleet and looked for enemy ships of the Spanish fleet from this vantage point. Magens Bay and Mahogany Run are to the north, with the B.V.I. and Drake's Channel to the east. Off to the west are Fairchild Park, Mountain Top, Hull Bay, and smaller islands such as the Inner and Outer Brass islands. The panoramic vista is especially breathtaking (and romantic) at dusk, and if you arrive late in the day you'll miss the hordes of day-trippers on taxi tours who stop at Drake's Seat to take a picture and buy a T-shirt from one of the many vendors. By afternoon the crowd thins and most of the vendors are gone. ⊠ *Rte. 40.*

⑮ **Estate St. Peter Greathouse Botanical Gardens.** This unusual spot is perched on a mountainside 1,000 ft above sea level, with views of more than 20 other islands and islets. You can wander through a gallery displaying local art, sip a complimentary rum or virgin punch while looking out at the view, or follow a nature trail that leads through nearly 200 varieties of tropical trees and plants, including an orchid jungle. ⊠ *Rte. 40, St. Peter Mountain Rd.,* ☎ *809/774–4999.* 🖃 *$8.* ⊙ *Mon.–Sat. 9–4:30.*

⑲ **Frenchtown.** Popular with tourists for its several bars and restaurants, Frenchtown also serves as home to the descendants of immigrants from St. Barthélemy (St. Barts). You can watch them pull up their boats and display their catch of the day along the waterfront. Frenchtown's harbor has an abundance of yellowtail, parrot fish, and oldwife nearly as colorful as the fishermen's small boats. You may see a number of people cleaning fish on the jetty or rubbing elbows at Betsy's Bar. If you want to get a feel for the residential district, walk west to some of the town's winding streets, where the tiny wood houses have been passed down from generation to generation. ⊠ *Turn south off Waterfront Hwy. at U.S. Post Office.*

❷ **Havensight Mall.** If you're not up for the crowds on Main Street, do your shopping here, a 15-minute walk from Charlotte Amalie. Just about all the major stores have branches here to cater to cruise-ship passengers who disembark nearby. It is also where you'll find the offices for *Atlantis* submarine (☞ *above*), and the Dockside Book Shop, a bookstore with stateside prices instead of hotel markups. ⊠ *Rte. 30 at Havensight.*

⑯ **Hull Bay.** You may come across the fishing boats and homes of the descendants of settlers from the French West Indies who fled to St. Thomas more than 200 years ago. If you have the opportunity to engage them in conversation, you will hear speech patterns slightly different from those of other St. Thomians. Hull Bay, with its rougher Atlantic surf and relative isolation, is one of the best surfing spots on St. Thomas. Take a break from the rigors of sightseeing at the **Hull Bay Hideaway,** a rustic beach bar that features live rock and roll played by a local band on Sunday afternoons. ⊠ *Rte. 37.*

🖐 ⑭ **Magens Bay Beach.** Popular with tourists and locals, this is the island's busiest beach. It's often listed among the world's most beautiful beaches, and on weekends and holidays it hops with groups partying under the sheds. There's also an outdoor bar, bathhouses, a nature trail, and a snack bar. ⊠ *Take Rte. 35 till it ends at admission booth.* 🖃 *$1.*

NEED A BREAK? After a vigorous swim at Magens Bay, do like the locals and stop for an afternoon delight at the **Udder Delight.** This one-room shop next to St.

Thomas Dairies serves up a Virgin Islands tradition—a milk shake enlivened by a splash of Cruzan rum. The kids can get their shakes virgin-style with a touch of soursop, mango, or banana flavoring.

**Mountain Top.** Don't forget to stop for a banana daiquiri and spectacular views from the observation deck more than 1,500 ft above sea level. There are also a number of shops selling everything from Caribbean art to nautical antiques, ship models, and T-shirts. Kids will like talking to the tropical parrots—and hearing the birds answer back. ⊠ *Head north off Rte. 33.*

**Paradise Point Tramway.** Fly skyward in a gondola straight up the hill to Paradise Point, a scenic overlook with breathtaking views of Charlotte Amalie and the harbor. There's a bar, restaurant, and several shops. You can also drive to the point. ⊠ *Rte. 30 at Havensight,* ☎ *809/774–9809.* ⊠ *$10.* ☉ *Daily 9–4:30.*

**Red Hook.** A busy shopping area, it has grown from a sleepy little town connected to the rest of the island only by dirt roads (or by boat) to an increasingly self-sustaining village. There are several small branches of some Charlotte Amalie shops, including Little Switzerland, at the newly expanded American Yacht Harbor. There is also a deli and candy store. Tickles Dockside Pub and Mackenzie's Restaurant both serve burgers, salads, and sandwiches. There are more restaurants, two small grocery stores, and a few shops spread up and down the busy road. Visit with the fishing and sailing charter crews tending their boats along the docks.

**Reichhold Center for the Arts.** This open-air amphitheater has its more expensive seats covered by a roof. It offers an eclectic selection of events ranging from local beauty pageants to traveling theater groups. Schedules vary, so check the local paper to see what's on when you're in town. ⊠ *Rte. 30 across from Brewers Beach,* ☎ *809/693–1559.*

**Tillett Gardens.** Clustered in this complex in a booming local shopping area, many local artisans craft stained glass, pottery, gold jewelry, and ceramics. Tillett's paintings and silk-screened fabrics are also on display and for sale. The gardens encircle a shaded courtyard with fountains and Polli's, an outdoor Mexican restaurant. ⊠ *Rte. 38 across from Four Winds Shopping Center.*

**Virgin Islands National Park Headquarters.** This park facility consists of a dock, a small grassy area with picnic tables, and a visitor center where maps and brochures are available. Iguanas are common here. If you see one, hold out a red hibiscus flower, this prehistoric-looking creature's favorite food. ⊠ *Turn east off Rte. 32 at sign,* ☎ *809/775–6238.*

## Exploring St. Croix

St. Croix is a big island, as the Virgin Islands go, and a study in contrasting beauty. The island is not as hilly as St. Thomas or St. John; a lush rain forest envelops the northwest, the East End is dry and barren, and palm-lined beaches with startlingly clear aquamarine water ring the island. The island's capital, Christiansted, and its other major town, Frederiksted, are both named after Danish kings, and both have tin-roofed, 18th-century buildings in pale yellow, pink, and ocher. There are lots of interesting spots spread out between the towns and to the east of Christiansted.

*Numbers in the margin correspond to points of interest on the St. Croix map.*

## Christiansted

❶ A historic, Danish-style town, **Christiansted** always served as St. Croix's commercial center. Trade here in the 1700s and 1800s was in sugar, rum, and molasses. Today the town is home to law offices, tourist shops, and restaurants, but many of the buildings, built from the harbor up into the gentle hillsides, date from the 18th century.

SIGHTS TO SEE

**D. Hamilton Jackson Park.** When you're tired of sightseeing, stop here for a rest. It's named for a famed labor leader, judge, and journalist who started the first newspaper not under the thumb of the Danish crown. ⊠ *Between Fort Christiansvaern and Danish Customs House.*

**Danish Customs House.** Built in 1830 on foundations that date to 1734, this building served as a customhouse, where officers collected duties on arriving merchandise. The post office was on the second floor. In 1926 it became the Christiansted Library. It has been the National Park Service headquarters since 1972. ⊠ *King St.* ☉ *Weekdays 8–5.*

**Fort Christiansvaern.** This large yellow structure dominates the harbor front. In 1749 the Danish built the fort to protect the harbor, but the structure was repeatedly damaged by hurricane-force winds and was partially rebuilt in 1771. It is now a National Historic Site and the best preserved of the five remaining Danish-built forts in the Virgin Islands. ⊠ *Hospital St., Christiansted,* ☎ *809/773–1460.* 🎟 *$2, includes admission to Steeple Bldg. (☞ below).* ☉ *Weekdays 8–5, weekends 9–5.*

**Government House.** One of the town's most elegant buildings, it was built as a home for a Danish merchant in 1747. The building today houses U.S.V.I. government offices. Slip into the peaceful inner courtyard to admire the still pools and gardens. A sweeping staircase leads visitors to a second-story ballroom, still the site of official government functions. ⊠ *King St.,* ☎ *809/773–1404.* ☉ *Weekdays 8–5.*

**The Market.** Built in 1735 as a slave market, this wood-and-galvanized-aluminum structure is where today's farmers and others sell their goods every Wednesday and Saturday from 8 to 5. ⊠ *Company St.*

**Post Office.** Built in 1749, it once housed the Danish West India & Guinea Company warehouse. The Danish Customs House and the post office building were once one structure. ⊠ *Church St.*

🔆 **St. Croix Aquarium.** The tanks are home to an ever-changing variety of local sea creatures. Children are invited to explore the discovery room with its microscopes, interactive displays, and educational videos. ⊠ *Caravelle Arcade,* ☎ *809/773–8995.* 🎟 *$4.50.* ☉ *Tues.–Sat. 11–4.*

**Scale House.** Closed for renovation at press time, the Scale House should open under National Park Service authority by 1998. The building was constructed in 1856 and once served as a scale house, where goods passing through the port were weighed and inspected. ⊠ *King St.*

**Steeple Building.** Built by the Danes in 1753, this was the first Danish Lutheran church on St. Croix. It is now a national-park museum and contains exhibits documenting the island's Indian habitation. There is also an extensive array of archaeological artifacts; a handful of displays concerning the plantation experience; and exhibits on the architectural development of Christiansted, the early history of the church, and Alexander Hamilton, the first secretary of the U.S. Treasury, who grew up in St. Croix. ⊠ *Church St., Christiansted,* ☎ *809/773–1460.* 🎟 *$2, includes admission to fort (☞ above).* ☉ *Open when staffing permits. Check at Fort Christiansvaern.*

**Visitor's Center.** You'll find maps, brochures, and friendly advice at this local government-operated location. ⊠ *41A–B Queen Cross St., Box 4538, Christiansted 00822,* ☎ *809/773–0495.* ⊙ *Weekdays 8–5.*

## Outside Christiansted and Points East

An easy drive to the East End takes you through some of the island's choicest real estate. The roads are flat and well marked. Ruins of old sugar estates dot the landscape. You can make the entire loop in about an hour, a good way to end the day.

SIGHTS TO SEE

🖑 ❷ **Buck Island Reef National Monument.** Off the northeast coast and reached only by boat, this is a must-see on any visit to St. Croix. Charter-boat trips leave daily from the Christiansted waterfront or from Green Cay Marina, about 2 mi east of Christiansted. Check with your hotel for recommendations. The island's pristine beaches are just right for sunbathing, but there's enough shade for those who don't want to fry. The spectacular snorkeling trail set in the reef allows visitors the opportunity for a close-up study of coral formations and tropical fish. The crew members give special attention to novice snorkelers and children. A hiking trail to Buck Island's highest point offers spectacular views of the reef below and St. John to the north. ⊠ *Northshore,* ☎ *809/773–1460.*

❸ **Cramer's Park.** This territorial beach on the northeast coast is very popular with locals. It's a spot for beach picnics and camping on long weekends. ⊠ *Rte. 82.*

❹ **Point Udall.** This rocky promontory, the easternmost point in the United States, juts into the Caribbean Sea. The climb to this point, by a rutted dirt road, may be slow, but it's worth the effort. On the way back, look for "the Castle," an enormous mansion atop the cliffs that resembles a cross between a Moorish mosque and the Taj Mahal. It was built by an extravagant recluse known only as the Contessa. ⊠ *Rte. 82.*

## Between Christiansted and Frederiksted

A drive through St. Croix's countryside is a trip back in time. Ruins of old plantations, many bearing whimsical names bestowed by early owners, dot the landscape. When you get to Slob, you may think you're passing by a spot where some messy soul lived. Not so. Long ago it was a low-lying area, or "slob."

The roads west are fairly flat, making for an easy drive. While the traffic moves quickly—by island standards—on the main roads, don't hesitate to poke around down some side lanes to see what there is to see.

SIGHTS TO SEE

❽ **Cane Bay.** This is one of St. Croix's best launches for scuba diving, and you may see a few wet-suited, tank-backed figures near the small stone jetty making their way out to the drop-off (a bit farther out there is a steeper drop-off to 12,000 ft). ⊠ *Rte. 80.*

NEED A
BREAK?

Just past Cane Bay, on the sea side of the road, is the popular **Picnic in Paradise,** a gourmet delicatessen, restaurant, and beach club. Pick up quiche, pasta, or salad to take to the beach for lunch, or dine alfresco at one of the outdoor tables. ⊠ *Rte. 80,* ☎ *809/778-1212.*

⓫ **Estate Mount Washington Plantation.** Several years ago, while surveying the property, the owners discovered the ruins of a historic sugar plantation buried beneath the rain-forest brush. The grounds have since been cleared and opened to the public. A free, self-guided walking tour of the animal-powered mill, rum factory, and other ruins is available daily, and the antiques shop in the old stables is open on Saturdays from 10 to 4. ⊠ *Rte. 63 (watch for antiques shop sign),* ☎ *809/772–1026.* ⊙ *Ruins open daily.*

🖑 ⑭ **Estate Whim Plantation Museum.** The lovingly restored estate, with a windmill, cookhouse, and other buildings, will give you a true sense of what life was like on St. Croix's sugar plantations in the 1800s. The oval-shape great house has high ceilings, antique furniture, decor, and utensils well worth seeing. Notice its fresh and airy atmosphere—the waterless stone moat around the great house was used not for defense but for gathering cooling air. The apothecary exhibit is the largest in all the West Indies. You will also find a museum gift shop. This is a great place for your kids to stretch their legs on the spacious grounds. ⊠ *Rte. 70, Box 2855, Frederiksted 00841,* ☎ *809/772–0598.* 🖘 *$5.* ⊙ *Mon.–Sat. 10–4.*

❺ **Judith's Fancy.** This upscale neighborhood is home to the ruins of an old great house and tower of the same name left from a 17th-century château that was once home to the governor of the Knights of Malta. The "Judith" comes from the first name of a woman buried on the property. From the guardhouse at the neighborhood entrance, follow Hamilton Drive past some of St. Croix's loveliest homes. At the end of Hamilton Drive, the road overlooks Salt River Bay, where Christopher Columbus anchored in 1493. A skirmish between members of Columbus's crew and a group of Arawak-speaking Indians resulted in the first bloody encounter between Europeans and West Indians. The peninsula on the east side of the bay is named for the event: Cabo de las Flechas (Cape of the Arrows). On the way back, make a detour left off Hamilton Drive onto Caribe Road, for a close look at the ruins. ⊠ *Turn north onto Rte. 751 off Rte. 75.*

❾ **Mount Eagle.** This is St. Croix's highest peak, at 1,165 ft. Leaving Cane Bay and passing North Star beach, follow the beautiful coastal road that dips briefly into the forest, and then turn left onto Route 69. Just after you make the turn, the pavement is marked with the words THE BEAST and a set of giant paw prints. The hill you're about to climb is the location of the infamous Beast of the America's Paradise Triathlon, an annual St. Croix event in which participants must bike up this intimidating slope. ⊠ *Rte. 69.*

❿ **St. Croix Leap.** Located in the heart of the rain forest, this is a workshop where you can purchase a wide range of articles, including mirrors, tables, bread boards, and jewelry boxes made of mahogany, saman, or thibet wood crafted by local artisans. ⊠ *Rte. 76,* ☎ *809/772–0421.*

⓯ **St. George Village Botanical Gardens.** At this 17-acre estate, you'll find lush and fragrant flora amid the ruins of a 19th-century sugarcane plantation village. You'll see miniature versions of each ecosystem on St. Croix, from a semiarid cactus grove to a verdant rain forest. Turn north off Route 70 at the sign for the gardens. ⊠ *Box 3011, Kingshill 00851-3011,* ☎ *809/692–2874.* 🖘 *$5.* ⊙ *Daily 9–4.*

❼ **Salt River Bay National Historical Park and Ecological Preserve.** This joint national and local park was dedicated in November 1993. In addition to such sites of cultural significance as a prehistoric ceremonial ball court and burial site, it encompasses a biodiverse coastal estuary that hosts the largest remaining mangrove forest in the U.S.V.I., a submarine canyon, and several endangered species, including the hawksbill turtle and roseate tern. At present, few sites are of more than archaeological interest to laypeople, but plans call for a museum, interpretive walking trails, and a replica of a Carib village. ⊠ *Rte. 75 to Rte. 80.*

**❻ Salt River Marina.** This lush lagoon is home to the Anchor Dive Shop, a shipbuilding company, and a couple of casual eateries catering to yachties. The road that veers to the left behind the marina leads to the beach where Columbus landed. ⊠ *Tradewinds Rd. at Rte. 80,* ☏ *809/ 778–1522.*

**⓭ Sandy Point Beach.** A ritual that began millions of years ago is played out annually in spring. That's when the majestic **leatherback turtles** come ashore to lay their eggs. These creatures, which can weigh up to 800 pounds and are of an older species than the dinosaurs, are oblivious to onlookers when they lay their eggs in the sand. With only the moonlight to guide them, Earthwatch volunteers patrol the beach nightly during the turtles' nesting season to protect the eggs from predators and poachers. The beach is a federal wildlife preserve. ⊠ *Rte. 66, west on unpaved road,* ☏ *809/773–1989.* ☉ *Spring turtle-watching days and hrs vary.*

## Frederiksted

**⓬** St. Croix's other town, **Frederiksted,** was founded in 1751. It's noted less for its Danish than for its Victorian architecture, which dates from after the uprising of former slaves and the great fire of 1878. A single long cruise-ship pier juts into the sparkling sea. A stroll around will take you no more than an hour. There are several restaurants and bars, so you won't go hungry.

SIGHTS TO SEE

**Apothecary Hall.** Built in 1839, this is a good example of 19th-century architecture. ⊠ *King Cross St.*

**Fort Frederik.** In 1848 the slaves of the Danish West Indies were freed by Governor General Peter van Scholten as he stood on the fort's ramparts. The fort, completed in 1760, houses a number of interesting historical exhibits as well as an art gallery. ⊠ *Waterfront,* ☏ *809/772–2021.* 🎟 *Free.* ☉ *Weekdays 8:30–4:30.*

**Market Place.** Stop here for fresh fruits and vegetables sold early in the morning, just as they have been for more than 200 years. ⊠ *Queen St.*

**St. Patrick's Church.** This Roman Catholic church was built in 1843 of coral. ⊠ *Prince St.*

**St. Paul's Episcopal Church.** This church is a mixture of classic and Gothic Revival architecture, built in 1812. ⊠ *Prince St.*

**Visitor's Center.** Right on the pier, it once served as a Customs House. Built at the end of the 1700s, the two-story gallery was added in the 1800s. ⊠ *Waterfront,* ☏ *809/772–0357.* ☉ *Weekdays 8–5.*

NEED A        If you're hungry as you head out of town, stop about ½ mi north at the
BREAK?        seaside **La Grange Beach Club** for a yummy salad or sandwich and then
              enjoy a swim at the beach. ⊠ *Rte. 63,* ☏ *809/772-5566.*

# Exploring St. John

St. John may be small, but the roads are narrow and wind up and down steep hills, so don't expect to get anywhere in a hurry. Bring along your swimsuit for stops at some of the most beautiful beaches in the world.

*Numbers in the margin correspond to points of interest on the St. John map.*

SIGHTS TO SEE

**4** **Annaberg Plantation.** In the 18th century, sugar plantations dotted the steep hills of the U.S.V.I., and slaves, Danes, and Dutchmen toiled to harvest the sugarcane that produced sugar, molasses, and rum for export. Built in the 1780s, the partially restored plantation at Leinster Bay was once an important sugar mill. There are no official visiting hours and no charge for entry. The National Park Service has regular tours, and some well-informed taxi drivers will show you around. Occasionally you'll find what the park calls a living-history demonstration—someone making johnnycake or weaving baskets. For information on tours and cultural demonstrations, call the St. John National Park Service Visitor's Center (☎ 809/776–6201). ⊠ *Leinster Bay Rd.*

**6** **Bordeaux Mountain.** St. John's highest peak rises to 1,277 ft. Centerline Road passes near enough to the top to offer breathtaking views before the road plunges down to Coral Bay. Drive nearly to the end of the dirt road for spectacular views at Picture Point and the trailhead for the hike downhill to Lameshur. Get a trail map available from the National Park Service before you start. ⊠ *Centerline Rd.*

**3** **Cinnamon Bay.** There are more than 20 mi of hiking trails in the St. John National Park. Two good trails begin at Cinnamon Bay, just across the road from the beach. The ruins of a sugar mill mark the trailhead to an easy nature trail. It takes you on a flat circle through the woods, past an old Danish cemetery and signs that identify the flora. The other trail, which starts where the road bends past the ruins, heads all the way up to Centerline Road. The national-park campground is here, and history buffs will enjoy the little, self-guided **Cinnamon Bay Museum.** Snorkelers will find good snorkeling around the point to the right, although watch out if the waves are up. Look for the big angelfish and the schools of blue tangs that live here. ⊠ *North Shore Rd.*

**5** **Coral Bay.** This laid-back community at the dry, eastern end of the island is named for its shape rather than for its underwater life—the word *coral* comes from *krawl,* Danish for *corral.* It's a quiet, neighborhoody, local, and quite small settlement; a place to get away from it all. You'll need a four-wheel drive if you plan to stay at this end of the island, as some of the roads are on the rough side. ⊠ *Rte. 10.*

**1** **Cruz Bay.** Start at the town dock for a leisurely stroll through the streets of this colorful, compact town: There are plenty of shops through which to browse, along with a number of watering holes where you can stop to take a breather.

To pick up a handy guide to St. John's hiking trails, see various large maps of the island, and check out current park-service programs and program schedules, including guided walks and cultural demonstrations, stop by the **V.I. National Park Visitor's Center.** There's also an 18-minute video tour you can watch and a 90-gallon aquarium. ⊠ *North Shore Rd./Rte. 20 in Cruz Bay,* ☎ *809/776–6201.* 🎟 *Free.* ☉ *Daily 8–4:30.*

**2** **Peace Hill.** It's worth a stop at this unmarked spot just past the Hawksnest Bay overlook for breathtaking views of St. John, St. Thomas, and the nearby British Virgin Islands. The flat promontory features an old sugar mill. The pile of white stones you'll see is what remains of *Christ of the Caribbean,* a statue honoring world peace erected in 1953 by Col. Julius Wadsworth. The statue fell to Hurricane Marilyn's winds in 1995, and the National Park Service decided not to rebuild it. From the parking lot, the statue is about 100 yards up a rocky path. ⊠ *Peace Hill, off North Shore Rd.*

❼ **Reef Bay Trail.** Hike down to Reef Bay by yourself or on a hike led by a National Park Service ranger. The rangers identify the trees and plants on the hike down, fill you in on the history of the Reef Bay Plantation, and tell you about the carvings you'll find in the rocks at the bottom of the trail. The National Park Service provides a boat ($10) to take you back to Cruz Bay, saving you the uphill return climb (☞ Guided Tours *in* U.S. Virgin Islands A to Z, *below*). ⊠ *Centerline Rd./Rte. 10.*

---

# U.S. Virgin Islands A to Z

## Arriving and Departing

BY BOAT

Some 20 cruise lines, ranging from floating budget hotels to small luxury yachts taking only 100 passengers stop at St. Thomas, St. John, or St. Croix.

Virtually every type of ship and major cruise line calls at St. Thomas; only a few call at St. Croix and St. John. One of these ports is usually included as part of a ship's eastern Caribbean itinerary. Many of the ships that call at St. Thomas also call at St. John or offer an excursion to that island. For a cruise aboard an ocean liner, contact **Cunard Line** (⊠ 555 5th Ave., New York, NY 10017, ☏ 800/528–6273), **Dolphin Cruise Lines** (⊠ 901 South America Way, Miami, FL 33132, ☏ 800/ 222–1003), **Holland America Line** (⊠ 300 Elliot Ave. W, Seattle, WA 98119, ☏ 800/426–0327), **Norwegian Cruise Lines** (⊠ Box 025403, Miami, FL 33102, ☏ 800/327–7030), **Princess Cruises** (⊠ 10100 Santa Monica Blvd., Los Angeles, CA 90067, ☏ 800/421–0522), **Royal Caribbean Cruise Line** (⊠ 1050 Caribbean Way, Miami, FL 33132, ☏ 800/327–6700), or **Royal Cruise Lines** (⊠ 1 Maritime Plaza, San Francisco, CA 94111, ☏ 800/622–0538). For a cruise aboard a luxury yacht, contact **Renaissance Cruises** (⊠ 1800 Eller Dr., Suite 300, Box 350307, Fort Lauderdale, FL 33335-0307, ☏ 800/525–2450) or **Seabourn Cruise Line** (⊠ 55 Francisco St., San Francisco, CA 94133, ☏ 800/929–9595).

Increasingly popular are cruises aboard oversize sailboats. Although the sails on these rather odd-looking ships are more often cosmetic than functional, the ships usually offer a more relaxed itinerary and stop at less-traveled anchorages. Itineraries and ship deployments change frequently, so contact your cruise line or travel agent for the latest scheduled sailings. **Windstar Cruises** (⊠ 300 Elliot Ave. W, Seattle, WA 98119, ☏ 800/258–7245) stops in St. John. You can experience a **Club Med** (☏ 800/258–2633) all-inclusive vacation on the sea aboard *Club Med I,* a 617-ft ship with seven computerized sails that Club Med bills as the largest sailing ship in the world. The ship sails out of Martinique on seven-day winter cruises (it's in St. Thomas for one day) and spends summers in the Mediterranean. **Windjammer Barefoot Cruises** (⊠ Box 190120, Miami Beach, FL 33119-0120, ☏ 800/327–2601) sails from the nearby British Virgin Islands to neighboring islands on cruises of 6- to 13-day durations.

BY PLANE

One advantage of visiting the U.S.V.I. is the abundance of nonstop and connecting flights that can have you at the beach in three to four hours from most East Coast departures. You may fly into the U.S.V.I. direct on **Delta** (☏ 800/221–1212) from Atlanta and on **US Airways** (☏ 800/ 622–2025) from Baltimore. **American** (☏ 800/474–4884) flies direct from Miami, New York, and San Juan and **Prestige Airways** (☏ 800/

229–8784) comes in direct from Washington, DC, via Miami as well. Another option is to pick up a local flight from San Juan on **American Eagle** (☎ 800/474–4884).

## Currency
The U.S. dollar is the medium of exchange here.

## Emergencies
**Police** and **Ambulance:** Dial ☎ 911.

**Hospitals:** The emergency room of the **Roy L. Schneider Community Hospital & Health Center** (☎ 809/776–8311) in Sugar Estate, Charlotte Amalie, is open 24 hours a day. On St. Croix, there is the **Governor Juan F. Luis Hospital and Health Center** (✉ 6 Diamond Ruby, north of Sunny Isle Shopping Center, on Rte. 79, Christiansted, ☎ 809/778–6311) and the **Frederiksted Health Center** (✉ 516 Strand St., ☎ 809/772–1992). On St. John contact the **Myrah Keating Smith Community Health Center** on Centerline Road (✉ Susanaberg, ☎ 809/693–8900).

**Air Ambulance: Bohlke International Airways** (☎ 809/778–9177) operates out of the St. Croix airport. **Medical Air Services** (☎ 809/777–8580 or 800/966–6272) has its Caribbean headquarters in St. Thomas. **Air Ambulance Network** (☎ 800/327–1966) also serves the area from Florida.

**Coast Guard:** For emergencies on St. Thomas or St. John, call the **Marine Safety Detachment** (☎ 809/776–3497) from 7 to 3:30 weekdays; on St. Croix, call 809/778–8185. If there is no answer, call the **Rescue Coordination Center** (☎ 809/729–6770 in San Juan), open 24 hours a day.

**Pharmacies: Sunrise Pharmacy** is open at Red Hook (☎ 809/775–6600). **Kmart** operates a pharmacy inside its Tutu Park Mall (☎ 809/777–3854). **Havensight Pharmacy** is in the Havensight Mall (☎ 809/776–1235). On St. Croix, try **People's Drug Store, Inc.** in Christiansted (☎ 809/778–7355), and **Sunny Isle Shopping Center** (☎ 809/778–5537) or **D & D Apothecary Hall** (☎ 809/772–1890) in Frederiksted. On St. John, the **St. John Drug Center** (☎ 809/776–6353) is in Cruz Bay.

## Getting Around
### BY BUS
Public buses are not the quickest way to get around on the islands, because service is minimal, but the deluxe mainland-size buses on St. Thomas and St. Croix make public transportation a very reasonable and comfortable way to get from east and west to town and back (on St. Thomas there is no service north). Fares are $1 between outlying areas and town and 75¢ in town. St. John has no public bus system, and residents rely on the kindness of taxi vans and safari buses for mass transportation.

### CAR RENTALS
Any U.S. driver's license is good for 90 days here; the minimum age for drivers is 18, although many agencies won't rent to anyone under the age of 25. A seat-belt law is strictly enforced. Driving is on the left side of the road (although your steering wheel will be on the left side of the car). Many of the roads are narrow and the islands are dotted with hills, so there is ample reason to drive carefully. Four-wheel-drive vehicles are particularly useful on St. John, which has well-paved main roads but many dirt side roads.

On St. Thomas, you can rent a car from **ABC Rentals** (☎ 809/776–1222 or 800/524–2080), **Anchorage E-Z Car** (☎ 809/775–6255 or 800/524–2027), **Avis** (☎ 809/774–1468 or 800/331–1084), **Budget**

(☎ 809/776–5774 or 800/527–0700), **Cowpet Car Rental** (☎ 809/775–7376 or 800/524–2072), **Dependable** (☎ 809/774–2253 or 800/522–3076), **Discount** (☎ 809/776–4858), **Hertz** (☎ 809/774–1879 or 800/654–3131), **Sea Breeze** (☎ 809/774–7200), or **Thrifty** (☎ 809/776–7282).

On St. Croix, call **Atlas** (☎ 809/773–2886 or 800/426–6009), **Avis** (☎ 809/778–9355), **Budget** (☎ 809/778–9636), **Caribbean Jeep & Car** (☎ 809/773–4399), **Fair Auto Rental** (☎ 809/773–5031), **Midwest** (☎ 809/772–0438), **Olympic** (☎ 809/773–2208 or 800/344–5776), or **Thrifty** (☎ 809/773–7200).

On St. John, call **Avis** (☎ 809/776–6374), **Cool Breeze** (☎ 809/776–6588), **O'Connor Jeep** (☎ 809/776–6343), **St. John Car Rental** (☎ 809/776–6103), or **Spencer's Jeep** (☎ 809/776–6628).

### BY FERRY

Ferries ply two routes between St. Thomas and St. John—either between the Charlotte Amalie waterfront and Cruz Bay or between Red Hook and Cruz Bay. Ferries from Charlotte Amalie leave every few hours starting at 9 AM. The last one runs at 5:30 PM. From Cruz Bay, the first one goes at 7:15 AM and the last one at 3:45 PM. The trip costs $7 each way. Ferries leave Red Hook at 6:30 AM and 7:30 AM, and hourly from 8 AM to midnight. They leave Cruz Bay for Red Hook hourly 6 AM to 10 PM and at 11:15 PM. The 15- to 20-minute ferry ride is $3 one-way.

A ferry from Charlotte Amalie, St. Thomas, makes a two-hour trip to san Juan, Puerto Rico, two Fridays a month. The fare is $60 one-way; $80 round-trip. You must make reservations—call the ferry office for more informaion at 809/776–6282.

A hydrofoil, the *Katrun II,* runs between St. Thomas and St. Croix daily. The boat leaves from the Charlotte Amalie waterfront on St. Thomas at 7:15 AM and 3:15 PM and departs from Gallows Bay outside of Christiansted, St. Croix, at 9:15 AM and 5:00 PM. The 1-hr, 15-minute trip costs $37 one-way and $70 round-trip.

### BY TAXI

Taxis of all shapes and sizes are available at various ferry, shopping, resort, and airport areas on St. Thomas and respond quickly to a call.

In Charlotte Amalie, taxi stands are across from Emancipation Gardens (in front of Little Switzerland behind the post office) and along Waterfront Highway. Away from Charlotte Amalie, you'll find taxis available at all major hotels and at such public beaches as Magens Bay and Coki Point, as well as at the Red Hook ferry dock. Calling taxis will work, too, but allow plenty of time.

Taxis on St. Croix, generally station wagons or minivans, are a phone call away from most hotels and are available in downtown Christiansted, at the Alexander Hamilton Airport, and at the Frederiksted pier during cruise-ship arrivals. Rates, set by law, are prominently displayed at the airport, and drivers are required to show a rate sheet if passengers request it. Try the **St. Croix Taxi Association** (☎ 809/778–1088) at the airport and **Antilles Taxi Service** (☎ 809/773–5020) or **Cruzan Taxi and Tours** (☎ 809/773–6388) in Christiansted.

On St. John buses and taxis are the same thing: open-air safari buses. Technically the safari buses are private taxis, but everyone uses them as an informal bus system. They congregate at the Cruz Bay Dock, ready to take you to any of the beaches or other island destinations; you can also pick them up anywhere on the road by signaling.

## Guided Tours

On St. Thomas, the **V.I. Taxi Association City-Island Tour** (☎ 809/774–4550) gives a two-hour tour aimed at cruise-ship passengers that includes stops at Drake's Seat and Mountain Top. **Tropic Tours** (☎ 809/774–1855 or 800/524–4334) offers half-day shopping and sightseeing tours of St. Thomas by bus six days a week for $20 per person, and full-day snorkeling tours to St. John every day for $60 per person (including lunch). It picks up at all the major hotels. Bird-watching, whale-watching, and a chance to wait hidden on a beach while the magnificent turtles come ashore to lay their eggs are all open to visitors. Write the **St. Croix Environmental Association** (✉ Arawak Bldg. No. 3, Gallows Bay, St. Croix 00820, ☎ 809/773–1989) or **EAST** (Environmental Association of St. Thomas–St. John) (✉ Box 12379, St. Thomas 00801, ☎ 809/776–1976) for more information on hikes and special programs, or check the community calendar in the *Daily News* for up-to-date information.

Van tours of St. Croix are offered by **St. Croix Safari Tours** (☎ 809/773–6700) and **St. Croix Transit** (☎ 809/772–3333). The tours, which depart from Christiansted and last about three hours, start at $25 per person. One of the best ways to see the rain forest and hills of the West End may be a tour by horseback with **Paul and Jill's Equestrian Stable** (☎ 809/772–2880 or 809/772–2627).

On St. John, stop at the taxi stand in the Cruz Bay Park for tours of the island. The park service also gives a variety of guided tours on- and offshore. For more information, or to arrange a tour, contact the **V.I. National Park Visitor's Center** (✉ Cruz Bay, ☎ 809/776–6201).

## Language

English, often with a Creole or West Indian lilt, is what's spoken on these islands.

## Opening and Closing Times

On St. Thomas, Charlotte Amalie's Main Street–area shops are open weekdays and Saturday 9–5. Havensight Mall shops (next to the cruise-ship dock) hours are the same, though some shops sometimes stay open until 9 on Friday, depending on how many cruise ships are staying late at the dock. You may also find some shops open on Sunday if a lot of cruise ships are in port. American Yacht Harbor stores are open weekdays and Saturday 9–6. St. Croix store hours are usually weekdays 9–5, but you will definitely find some shops in Christiansted open in the evening. On St. John, store hours are reliably similar to those on the other two islands, and Mongoose Junction and Wharfside Village shops in Cruz Bay are often open into the evening.

## Passports and Visas

No proof of citizenship is required for U.S. citizens entering the U.S.V.I. However, you may need proof of citizenship to return to the U.S. mainland. Canadian citizens are required to present some proof of citizenship—if not a passport, then a birth certificate—to enter. If you are arriving from the U.S. mainland or Puerto Rico, you need no inoculation or health certificate.

Britons need a valid passport to enter the U.S.V.I. Passport fees are £15 for a standard 32-page passport, £30 for a 94-page passport. You do not need a visa for the U.S.V.I. if you are visiting either on business or pleasure, are staying fewer than 90 days, have a return ticket or ongoing ticket, are traveling with a major airline (in effect, any airline that flies from the United Kingdom to the United States), and complete visa waiver I-94W, which is supplied either at the airport of departure or on the plane.

## Precautions

Crime exists here, but not to the same degree that it does in larger cities on the U.S. mainland. Still, it's best to stick to well-lit streets at night and use the same kind of street sense (don't wander the back alleys of Charlotte Amalie after five rum punches, for example) that you would in any unfamiliar territory. If you plan on carrying things around, rent a car, not an open vehicle such as a Jeep, and lock possessions in the trunk. Keep your rental car locked wherever you park. Don't leave cameras, purses, and other valuables lying on the beach while you're off on an hour-long snorkel, whether at the deserted beaches of St. John or the more crowded Magens and Coki beaches on St. Thomas.

## Taxes and Service Charges

An 8% tax is added to hotel rates. Departure tax for the U.S.V.I. is included in the cost of your airplane ticket. Some hotels and restaurants add a 10% or 15% service charge to your bill, generally only if you are part of a group of 15 or more. There is no sales tax in the U.S.V.I.

## Telephones and Mail

The area code for all the U.S.V.I. is set to change from 809 to 340. Either area code will work until June 30, 1998, after which the transition will be complete. There is direct dial to the mainland. Local calls from a public phone cost 25¢ for each five minutes. On St. John the place to go for any telephone or message needs is **Connections** (☎ 809/776–6922). On St. Thomas, it's **Islander Services** (☎ 809/774–5302), behind the Greenhouse Restaurant in Charlotte Amalie, or **East End Secretarial Services** (☎ 809/775–5262, FAX 809/775–3590), upstairs at the Red Hook Plaza. **AT&T** has a state-of-the-art telecommunications center complete with 15 desk booths, fax and copy services, video phone, and TDD (hearing impaired) equipment, located across from the Havensight Mall on St. Thomas. On St. Croix, visit **AnswerPLUS** (✉ 5005B Chandlers Wharf, Gallows Bay, ☎ 809/773–4444) or **Worldwide Calling** (head of the pier in Frederiksted, ☎ 809/772–2490).

The main U.S. post office on St. Thomas is near the hospital, with branches in Charlotte Amalie, the Tutu Mall, and Frenchtown; there's a post office at Christiansted, Gallows Bay, Sunny Isle, and Frederiksted on St. Croix, and at Cruz Bay on St. John. Postal rates are the same as elsewhere in the United States: 32¢ for a letter, 20¢ for a postcard to anywhere in the United States, 50¢ for a ½-ounce letter mailed to a foreign country.

## Visitor Information

Information about the United States Virgin Islands is available through the **U.S.V.I. Government Tourist Offices** (✉ 225 Peachtree St., Suite 760, Atlanta, GA 30303, ☎ 404/688–0906, FAX 404/525–1102; ✉ 500 N. Michigan Ave., Suite 2030, Chicago, IL 60611, ☎ 312/670–8784, FAX 312/670–8789; ✉ 3460 Wilshire Blvd., Suite 412, Los Angeles, CA 90010, ☎ 213/739–0138, FAX 213/739–2005; ✉ 2655 Le Jeune Rd., Suite 907, Coral Gables, FL 33134, ☎ 305/442–7200, FAX 305/445–9044; ✉ 1270 Avenue of the Americas, Room 2108, New York, NY 10020, ☎ 212/332–2222, FAX 212/332–2223; ✉ 900 17th Ave. NW, Suite 500, Washington, DC 20006, ☎ 202/293–3707, FAX 202/785–2542; ✉ 1300 Ashford Ave., Condado, Santurce, Puerto Rico 00907, ☎ 809/724–3816, FAX 809/724–7223; ✉ 3300 Bloor St., Suite 3120, Center Tower, Toronto, Ontario, Canada M8X 2X3, ☎ 416/233–1414, FAX 416/233–9367; ✉ 2 Cinnamon Row, Plantation Wharf, York Pl., London SW11 3TW, ☎ 0171/978–5262, FAX 0171/924–3171). You can also call the **Division of Tourism**'s toll-free number (☎ 800/878–4463).

The **U.S. Virgin Islands Division of Tourism** has an office in St. Thomas (✉ Box 6400, Charlotte Amalie 00804, ☎ 809/774–8784 or 800/372–8784, FAX 809/774–4390). The **visitor center** in Charlotte Amalie across from Emancipation Garden (☞ Exploring St. Thomas, *above*) has longer hours, a lounge, and luggage storage. There's also a **visitor information** kiosk at Havensight Mall. In St. Croix, you'll find visitor centers on Queen Cross Street in Christiansted (✉ Box 4538, Christiansted, U.S.V.I. 00822, ☎ 809/773–0495) and on the Frederiksted pier (✉ Strand St., Frederiksted, U.S.V.I. 00840, ☎ 809/772–0357). In St. John, there is one in the compound between Sparky's and the U.S. Post Office (✉ Box 200, Cruz Bay, U.S.V.I. 00830, ☎ 809/776–6450).

# INDEX

# NOTES

# Fodor's Travel Publications

*Available at bookstores everywhere, or call 1–800–533–6478, 24 hours a day.*

## Gold Guides

### U.S.

| | | | |
|---|---|---|---|
| Alaska | Florida | New Orleans | Seattle & Vancouver |
| Arizona | Hawai'i | New York City | The South |
| Boston | Las Vegas, Reno, Tahoe | Pacific North Coast | U.S. & British Virgin Islands |
| California | | Philadelphia & the Pennsylvania Dutch Country | |
| Cape Cod, Martha's Vineyard, Nantucket | Los Angeles | | USA |
| | Maine, Vermont, New Hampshire | The Rockies | Virginia & Maryland |
| The Carolinas & Georgia | Maui & Lāna'i | San Diego | Walt Disney World, Universal Studios and Orlando |
| Chicago | Miami & the Keys | San Francisco | |
| Colorado | New England | Santa Fe, Taos, Albuquerque | Washington, D.C. |

### Foreign

| | | | |
|---|---|---|---|
| Australia | Europe | Montréal & Québec City | Scotland |
| Austria | Florence, Tuscany & Umbria | Moscow, St. Petersburg, Kiev | Singapore |
| The Bahamas | | | South Africa |
| Belize & Guatemala | France | The Netherlands, Belgium & Luxembourg | South America |
| Bermuda | Germany | | Southeast Asia |
| Canada | Great Britain | New Zealand | Spain |
| Cancún, Cozumel, Yucatán Peninsula | Greece | Norway | Sweden |
| | Hong Kong | Nova Scotia, New Brunswick, Prince Edward Island | Switzerland |
| Caribbean | India | | Thailand |
| China | Ireland | | Toronto |
| Costa Rica | Israel | Paris | Turkey |
| Cuba | Italy | Portugal | Vienna & the Danube |
| The Czech Republic & Slovakia | Japan | Provence & the Riviera | |
| Eastern & Central Europe | London | Scandinavia | |
| | Madrid & Barcelona | | |
| | Mexico | | |

## Special-Interest Guides

| | | | |
|---|---|---|---|
| Adventures to Imagine | Fodor's Gay Guide to the USA | Halliday's New Orleans Food Explorer | Rock & Roll Traveler USA |
| Alaska Ports of Call | Fodor's How to Pack | Healthy Escapes | Sunday in San Francisco |
| Ballpark Vacations | Great American Learning Vacations | Kodak Guide to Shooting Great Travel Pictures | Walt Disney World for Adults |
| Caribbean Ports of Call | | | |
| The Official Guide to America's National Parks | Great American Sports & Adventure Vacations | National Parks and Seashores of the East | Weekends in New York |
| Disney Like a Pro | Great American Vacations | National Parks of the West | Wendy Perrin's Secrets Every Smart Traveler Should Know |
| Europe Ports of Call | Great American Vacations for Travelers with Disabilities | Nights to Imagine | |
| Family Adventures | | Rock & Roll Traveler Great Britain and Ireland | |

# Fodor's Special Series

## Fodor's Best Bed & Breakfasts

America

California

The Mid-Atlantic

New England

The Pacific Northwest

The South

The Southwest

The Upper Great Lakes

## Compass American Guides

Alaska

Arizona

Boston

Chicago

Colorado

Hawaii

Idaho

Hollywood

Las Vegas

Maine

Manhattan

Minnesota

Montana

New Mexico

New Orleans

Oregon

Pacific Northwest

San Francisco

Santa Fe

South Carolina

South Dakota

Southwest

Texas

Utah

Virginia

Washington

Wine Country

Wisconsin

Wyoming

## Citypacks

Amsterdam

Atlanta

Berlin

Chicago

Florence

Hong Kong

London

Los Angeles

Montréal

New York City

Paris

Prague

Rome

San Francisco

Tokyo

Venice

Washington, D.C.

## Exploring Guides

Australia

Boston & New England

Britain

California

Canada

Caribbean

China

Costa Rica

Egypt

Florence & Tuscany

Florida

France

Germany

Greek Islands

Hawaii

Ireland

Israel

Italy

Japan

London

Mexico

Moscow & St. Petersburg

New York City

Paris

Prague

Provence

Rome

San Francisco

Scotland

Singapore & Malaysia

South Africa

Spain

Thailand

Turkey

Venice

## Flashmaps

Boston

New York

San Francisco

Washington, D.C.

## Fodor's Gay Guides

Los Angeles & Southern California

New York City

Pacific Northwest

San Francisco and the Bay Area

South Florida

USA

## Pocket Guides

Acapulco

Aruba

Atlanta

Barbados

Budapest

Jamaica

London

New York City

Paris

Prague

Puerto Rico

Rome

San Francisco

Washington, D.C.

## Languages for Travelers (Cassette & Phrasebook)

French

German

Italian

Spanish

## Mobil Travel Guides

America's Best Hotels & Restaurants

California and the West

Major Cities

Great Lakes

Mid-Atlantic

Northeast

Northwest and Great Plains

Southeast

Southwest and South Central

## Rivages Guides

Bed and Breakfasts of Character and Charm in France

Hotels and Country Inns of Character and Charm in France

Hotels and Country Inns of Character and Charm in Italy

Hotels and Country Inns of Character and Charm in Paris

Hotels and Country Inns of Character and Charm in Portugal

Hotels and Country Inns of Character and Charm in Spain

## Short Escapes

Britain

France

New England

Near New York City

## Fodor's Sports

Golf Digest's Places to Play

Skiing USA

USA Today The Complete Four Sport Stadium Guide

# CNN ✈
## Airport Network

## Your
### Window
### To The
## World
### While You're
### On The
## Road

Keep in touch when you're traveling. Before you take off, tune in to CNN Airport Network. Now available in major airports across America, CNN Airport Network provides nonstop news, sports, business, weather and lifestyle programming. Both domestic and international. All piloted by the top-flight global resources of CNN. All up-to-the-minute reporting. And just for travelers, CNN Airport Network features intriguing segments such as "Travel Facts." With an information source like Fodor's this series of fascinating travel trivia will definitely make time fly while you're waiting to board. SO KEEP YOUR WINDOW TO THE WORLD WIDE OPEN. ESPECIALLY WHEN YOU'RE ON THE ROAD. TUNE IN TO CNN AIRPORT NETWORK TODAY.

# WHEREVER YOU TRAVEL, *H*ELP IS NEVER FAR AWAY.

From planning your trip to providing travel assistance along the way, American Express® Travel Service Offices are always there to help.

## Caribbean

**ANTIGUA**
St. John's

**ARUBA**
Oranjestad

**BAHAMAS**
Freeport
Nassau

**BARBADOS**
Bridgetown

**BRITISH VIRGIN ISLANDS**
Tortola
Virgin Gorda

**CAYMAN ISLANDS**
Grand Cayman

**CURAÇAO**
Willemstad

**DOMINICA**
Roseau

**DOMINICAN REPUBLIC**
Santo Domingo

**FRENCH WEST INDIES**
St. Barthelemy

**GRENADA**
St. George's

**GUADELOUPE**
Pointe-à-Pitre

**HAITI**
Port-au-Prince

**JAMAICA**
Kingston
Montego Bay
Negril
Ocho Rios
Port Antonio

**MARTINIQUE**
Fort de France

**MONTSERRAT**
Plymouth

**PUERTO RICO**
Mayagüez
San Juan

**ST. KITTS**
Basseterre

**ST. LUCIA**
Castries

**ST. MAARTEN**
Philipsburg

**ST. VINCENT**
Kingstown

**TURKS & CAICOS**
Providenciale

**U.S. VIRGIN ISLANDS**
St. Croix
St. Thomas

## Travel

http://www.americanexpress.com/travel

**American Express Travel Service Offices are found in central locations throughout the Caribbean.**